Adriana Rodgers —

Pocket
Dictionary
& Thesaurus

Collins

An Imprint of HarperCollins*Publishers*

third edition 2003

©HarperCollins Publishers 1993, 1998, 2003

www.collinsdictionaries.com

Collins® and Bank of English® are registered trademarks
of HarperCollins Publishers Limited.

ISBN 0-00-714305-2

Acknowledgments
We would like to thank those authors and publishers who
kindly gave permission for copyright material to be used
in the Bank of English. We would also like to thank
Times Newspapers Ltd for providing valuable data.

Note
Entered words that we have reason to believe constitute trademarks
have been designated as such. However, neither the presence nor
absence of such designation should be regarded as affecting the
legal status of any trademark.

A catalogue record for this book is available from the British Library

Typeset by Morton Word Processing Ltd, Scarborough

Printed and bound in Italy by Amadeus, S.p.A.

CONTENTS

EDITORIAL STAFF

v

FEATURES OF THE DICTIONARY & THESAURUS

Short, clear definitions

Headwords in colour for ease of use

❶ symbol directs you to the thesaurus entry

Word tips give helpful advice

mistletoe *n* evergreen plant with white berries growing as a parasite on trees.
mistress ❶ *n* 1 woman who has a continuing sexual relationship with a married man. 2 woman in control of people or animals. 3 female teacher.
mistrust ❶ *v* 1 have doubts or suspicions about. ♦ *n* 2 lack of trust. **mistrustful** *adj*
misunderstand ❶ *v* fail to understand properly. **misunderstanding** *n*
misuse ❶ *n* 1 incorrect, improper, or careless use. ♦ *v* 2 use wrongly. 3 treat badly.
mite *n* 1 very small spider-like animal. 2 very small thing or amount.
mitigate ❶ *v* make less severe. **mitigation** *n*

> ✓ **WORD TIP**
> *Mitigate* is often confused with *militate* 'have an influence on'.

mitre [**my**-ter] *n* 1 bishop's pointed headdress. 2 joint between two pieces of wood bevelled to meet at right angles. ♦ *v* 3 join with a mitre joint.
mitt *n* 1 short for MITTEN. baseball catcher's glove.

─────────────────── THESA

Key opposites highlighted

Key synonyms highlighted

misread 3 = **confuse with**, mix up with, take for
mistress *n* 1 = **lover**, concubine, girlfriend, kept woman, paramour
mistrust *v* 1 = **doubt**, be wary of, distrust, fear, suspect ♦ *n* 2 = **suspicion**, distrust, doubt, misgiving, scepticism, uncertainty, wariness ≠ **faith**
misunderstand *v* = **misinterpret**, be at cross-purposes, get the wrong end of the stick, misapprehend, misconstrue, misjudge, misread, mistake
misuse *n* 1 = **waste**, abuse, desecration, misapplication, squandering ♦ *v* 3 = **waste**, abuse, desecrate, misapply, prostitute, squander
mitigate *v* = **ease**, extenuate, lessen, lighten, moderate, soften, subdue, temper
mix *v* 1, 2 = **combine**, blend, cross, fuse,

vi

FEATURES OF THE DICTIONARY & THESAURUS

mitten *n* glove with one section for the thumb and one for the four fingers together. ⟶ **Parts of speech**

mix ❶ *v* 1 combine or blend into one mass. 2 form (something) by mixing. 3 be sociable. ◆ *n* 4 mixture. **mixed** *adj* **mix up** *v* 1 confuse. 2 make into a mixture. **mixed up** *adj* **mix-up** *n* **mixer** *n* **mixture** *n* 1 something mixed. 2 combination. ⟶ **Pronunciation help**

mm millimetre(s).

mnemonic [nim–on–ik] *n, adj* (something, such as a rhyme) intended to help the memory.

moan ❶ *n* 1 low cry of pain. 2 *Informal* grumble. ◆ *v* 3 make or utter with a moan. 4 *Informal* grumble. ⟶ **Usage labels**

moat *n* deep wide ditch, esp. round a castle.

mob ❶ *n* 1 disorderly crowd. 2 *Slang* gang. ◆ *v* **mobbing, mobbed** 3 surround in a mob to acclaim or attack.

mobile ❶ *adj* 1 able to move. ◆ *n* 2 same as MOBILE PHONE. 3 hanging structure designed to move in air currents. **mobile phone** cordless phone powered by batteries. **mobility** *n*

mobilize ❶ *v* 1 (of the armed services) prepare for active service. 2 organize for a ⟶ **Numbers link thesaurus and dictionary meanings**

URUS

intermingle, interweave, join, jumble, merge, mingle 3 = **socialize**, associate, consort, fraternize, hang out (*inf*), hobnob, mingle ◆ *n* 4 = **mixture**, alloy, amalgam, assortment, blend, combination, compound, fusion, medley

moan *n* 1 = **groan**, lament, sigh, sob, wail, whine 2 *Inf* = **grumble**, complaint, gripe (*inf*), grouch (*inf*), grouse, protest, whine ◆ *v* 3 = **groan**, lament, sigh, sob, whine 4 *Inf* = **grumble**, bleat, carp, complain, groan, grouse, whine, whinge (*inf*) ⟶ **Generous choice of synonyms**

mob *n* 1 = **crowd**, drove, flock, horde, host, mass, multitude, pack, swarm, throng 2 *Sl* = **gang**, crew (*inf*), group, lot, set ◆ *v* 3 = **surround**, crowd around, jostle, set upon, swarm around ⟶ **Restrictive labels show the context of use**

mobile *adj* 1 = **movable**, itinerant, moving, peripatetic, portable, travelling, wandering

ABBREVIATIONS USED IN THE TEXT

abbrev	abbreviation	lb(s)	pound(s)
adj	adjective	Lit	Literary
adv	adverb		
Afr	African	masc	masculine
Amer	American	Maths	Mathematics
Anat	Anatomy	Med	Medicine
Arch	Archaic	Mil	Military
Aust	Australian	Mus	Music
		Myth	Mythology
Bot	Botany		
Brit	Britain, British	n	noun
		N	North(ern)
Canad	Canadian	Naut	Nautical
cap.	capital	NZ	New Zealand
Chem	Chemistry		
comb.	combining	Obs	Obsolete
conj	conjuction	Offens	Offensive
		oft.	often
Dial	Dialect	orig.	originally
E	East(ern)		
Eng	England, English	Pathol	Pathology
e.g.	for example	pert.	pertaining
esp.	especially	Photog	Photography
etc.	et cetera	pl	plural
		Poet	Poetic
fem	feminine	prep	preposition
Fig	Figurative	pron	pronoun
Fr	French		
		S	South(ern)
Geog	Geography	Scot	Scottish
		sing.	singular
Hist	History	Sl	Slang
		US(A)	United States
Inf	Informal		(of America)
interj	interjection	usu.	usually
kg	kilogram(s)	v	verb
km	kilometre(s)	Vulg	Vulgar
Lat	Latin	W	West(ern)

A a

a *adj* indefinite article, used before a noun being mentioned for the first time.

AA 1 Alcoholics Anonymous. **2** Automobile Association.

aardvark *n* S African anteater with long ears and snout.

aback *adv* **taken aback** startled or disconcerted.

abandon ❶ *v* **1** desert or leave (one's wife, children, etc.). **2** give up (hope etc.) altogether. ♦ *n* **3** lack of inhibition. **abandoned** *adj* **1** deserted. **2** uninhibited. **abandonment** *n*

abase *v* humiliate or degrade (oneself). **abasement** *n*

abashed ❶ *adj* embarrassed and ashamed.

abate ❶ *v* make or become less strong. **abatement** *n*

abattoir [ab–a–twahr] *n* slaughterhouse.

abbey ❶ *n* dwelling place of, or a church belonging to, a community of monks or nuns.

abbreviate ❶ *v* shorten (a word) by leaving out some letters. **abbreviation** *n* shortened form of a word or words.

abdicate ❶ *v* give up (the throne or a responsibility). **abdication** *n*

abdomen *n* part of the body containing the stomach and intestines. **abdominal** *adj*

abduct ❶ *v* carry off, kidnap. **abduction** *n* **abductor** *n*

aberration ❶ *n* **1** sudden change from what is normal, accurate, or correct. **2** brief lapse in control of one's thoughts or feelings. **aberrant** *adj*

abet ❶ *v* **abetting, abetted** help or encourage in wrongdoing. **abettor** *n*

abeyance ❶ *n* in abeyance not in use.

abhor ❶ *v* **–horring, –horred** detest utterly. **abhorrent** *adj* hateful, loathsome. **abhorrence** *n*

abide ❶ *v* **1** endure, put up with. **2** *Obs* stay or dwell, e.g. *abide with me.* **abide by** *v* obey (the law, rules, etc.). **abiding** *adj*

THESAURUS

abandon *v* **1** = **leave**, desert, forsake, strand ≠ **maintain 2** = **give up**, relinquish, surrender, yield ≠ **take** ♦ *n* **3** = **wildness**, recklessness ≠ **control**

abashed *adj* = **embarrassed**, ashamed, chagrined, disconcerted, dismayed, humiliated, mortified, shamefaced, taken aback

abate *v* = **decrease**, decline, diminish, dwindle, fade, lessen, let up, moderate, outspan (*S Afr*) relax, slacken, subside, weaken ≠ **increase**

abbey *n* = **monastery**, convent, friary, nunnery, priory

abbreviate *v* = **shorten**, abridge, compress, condense, contract, cut, reduce, summarize

abdicate *v* = **give up**, abandon, quit, relinquish, renounce, resign, step down (*inf*)

abduct *v* = **kidnap**, carry off, seize, snatch (*sl*)

aberration *n* **1** = **oddity**, abnormality, anomaly, defect, irregularity, peculiarity, quirk **2** = **lapse**

abet *v* = **help**, aid, assist, connive at, support

abeyance *n* in abeyance = **shelved**, hanging fire, on ice (*inf*), pending, suspended

abhor *v* = **hate**, abominate, detest, loathe, shrink from, shudder at lasting.

ability ⊕ *n, pl* **–ties 1** competence, power. **2** talent.

abject ⊕ *adj* **1** utterly miserable. **2** lacking all self–respect.

ablaze ⊕ *adj* burning fiercely.

able ⊕ *adj* capable, competent. **ably** *adv* **able–bodied** *adj* strong and healthy.

abnormal ⊕ *adj* not normal or usual. **abnormally** *adv* **abnormality** *n*

aboard *adv, prep* on, in, onto, or into (a ship, train, or plane).

abolish ⊕ *v* do away with. **abolition** *n*

abort ⊕ *v* **1** have an abortion or perform an abortion on. **2** have a miscarriage. **3** end a plan or process before completion. **abortion** *n* **1** operation to end a pregnancy. **2** *Informal* something grotesque. **abortionist** *n* person who performs abortions, esp. illegally. **abortive** *adj* unsuccessful.

abound ⊕ *v* be plentiful. **abounding** *adj*

about ⊕ *prep* **1** concerning, on the subject of. **2** in or near (a place). ◆ *adv* **3** nearly, approximately. **4** nearby. **about to** shortly going to. **about–turn** *n* complete change of attitude.

above ⊕ *adv, prep* **1** over or higher (than). **2** greater (than). **3** superior (to). **above board** in the open, without dishonesty.

abrasion ⊕ *n* scraped area on the skin. **abrasive** *adj* harsh and unpleasant in manner.

abreast ⊕ *adv, adj* side by side. **abreast of** up to date with.

abridge ⊕ *v* shorten by using fewer words. **abridgment, abridgement** *n*

abroad ⊕ *adv* **1** to or in a foreign country. **2** at large.

abrupt ⊕ *adj* **1** sudden, unexpected. **2** blunt and rude. **abruptly** *adv* **abruptness** *n*

abscess *n* inflamed swelling containing pus.

——————— THESAURUS ———————

abide *v* **1 = tolerate**, accept, bear, endure, put up with, stand, suffer

ability *n* **1 = skill**, aptitude, capability, competence, expertise, proficiency ≠ **inability 2 = talent**

abject *adj* **1 = miserable**, deplorable, forlorn, hopeless, pitiable, wretched **2 = servile**, cringing, degraded, fawning, grovelling, submissive ≠ **dignified**

ablaze *adj* **= on fire**, aflame, alight, blazing, burning, fiery, flaming, ignited, lighted

able *adj* **= capable**, accomplished, competent, efficient, proficient, qualified, skilful ≠ **incapable**

abnormal *adj* **= unusual**, atypical, exceptional, extraordinary, irregular, munted (*NZ sl*), odd, peculiar, strange, uncommon ≠ **common**

abolish *v* **= do away with**, annul, cancel, destroy, eliminate, end, eradicate, put an end to, quash, rescind, revoke, stamp out ≠ **continue**

abort *v* **1 = terminate** (*a pregnancy*) **2 = miscarry 3 = stop**, arrest, axe (*inf*), call

off, check, end, fail, halt, terminate

abound *v* **= be plentiful**, flourish, proliferate, swarm, teem, thrive

about *prep* **1 = regarding**, as regards, concerning, dealing with, on, referring to, relating to **2 = near**, adjacent to, beside, circa (*used with dates*), close to, nearby ◆ *adv* **3 = nearly**, almost, approaching, approximately, around, close to, more or less, roughly

above *prep* **1 = over**, higher than, on top of, upon ≠ **under 2 = greater than**, beyond, exceeding ≠ **less than**

abrasion *n* **= graze**, chafe, scrape, scratch, scuff, surface injury

abreast *adv, adj* **= alongside**, beside, side by side

abridge *v* **= shorten**, abbreviate, condense, cut, decrease, reduce, summarize

abroad *adv* **1 = overseas**, in foreign lands, out of the country

abrupt *adj* **1 = sudden**, precipitate, quick, surprising, unexpected ≠ **slow 2 = curt**, brusque, gruff, impatient, rude, short, terse ≠ **polite**

abscond ❶ v leave secretly.

absent ❶ adj 1 not present. 2 lacking. 3 inattentive. ◆ v 4 stay away. **absently** adv **absence** n 1 being away. 2 lack. **absentee** n person who should be present but Is not. **absenteeism** n persistent absence from work or school. **absent–minded** adj inattentive or forgetful.

absolute ❶ adj 1 complete, perfect. 2 not limited, unconditional. 3 pure, e.g. absolute alcohol. **absolutely** adv 1 completely. ◆ interj 2 certainly, yes. **absolutism** n government by a ruler with unrestricted power.

absolve ❶ v declare to be free from blame or sin. **absolution** n

absorb ❶ v 1 soak up (a liquid). 2 take in. 3 engage the interest of (someone). **absorption** n **absorbent** adj able to absorb liquid. **absorbency** n

abstain ❶ v 1 choose not to do something. 2 choose not to vote. **abstainer** n **abstention** n abstaining, esp. from voting. **abstinence** n abstaining, esp. from drinking alcohol. **abstinent** adj

abstemious ❶ adj taking very little alcohol or food.

abstract ❶ adj 1 existing as a quality or idea rather than a material object. 2 theoretical. 3 (of art) using patterns of shapes and colours rather than realistic likenesses. ◆ n 4 summary. 5 abstract work of art. 6 abstract word or idea. ◆ v 7 summarize. 8 remove. **abstracted** adj lost in thought. **abstraction** n

abstruse ❶ adj not easy to understand.

absurd ❶ adj incongruous or ridiculous. **absurdity** n

abundant ❶ adj plentiful. **abundantly** adv **abundance** n

abuse ❶ v 1 use wrongly. 2 ill-treat violently. 3 speak harshly and rudely to. ◆ n 4 prolonged ill-treatment. 5 harsh and vulgar comments. 6 wrong use. **abuser** n **abusive** adj **abusively** adv **abusiveness** n

abut v **abutting**, **abutted** be next to or

---

abscond v = **flee**, clear out, disappear, escape, make off, run off, steal away

absent adj 1 = **missing**, away, elsewhere, gone, nonexistent, out ≠ **present** 2 = **lacking**, unavailable ≠ **present** 3 = **absent–minded**, blank, distracted, inattentive, oblivious, preoccupied, vacant, vague ≠ **aware** ◆ v 4 absent oneself = **stay away**, keep away, play truant, withdraw

absolute adj 1 = **total**, complete, outright, perfect, pure, sheer, thorough, utter 2 = **supreme**, full, sovereign, unbounded, unconditional, unlimited, unrestricted

absolve v = **forgive**, deliver, exculpate, excuse, let off, pardon, release, set free

absorb v 1 = **soak up**, suck up 2 = **take in**, consume, digest, imbibe, incorporate, receive 3 = **preoccupy**, captivate, engage, engross, fascinate, rivet

abstain v 1 = **refrain**, avoid, decline, deny (oneself), desist, fast, forbear, forgo, give up, keep from

abstemious adj = **self–denying**, ascetic, austere, frugal, moderate, sober, temperate

abstract adj 1 = **indefinite**, general ≠ **specific** 2 = **theoretical**, hypothetical, notional ≠ **real** ◆ n 4 = **summary**, abridgment, digest, epitome, outline, précis, résumé, synopsis ≠ **expansion** ◆ v 7 = **summarize**, abbreviate, abridge, condense, digest, epitomize, outline, précis, shorten 8 = **remove**, detach, extract, isolate, separate, take away, take out, withdraw ≠ **add**

abstruse adj = **obscure**, arcane, complex, deep, enigmatic, esoteric, recondite, unfathomable, vague

absurd adj = **ridiculous**, crazy (inf), farcical, foolish, idiotic, illogical, inane, incongruous, irrational, ludicrous, nonsensical, preposterous, senseless, silly, stupid, unreasonable

abundant adj = **plentiful**, ample, bountiful, copious, exuberant, filled, full, luxuriant, profuse, rich, teeming

abuse v 1 = **misuse** 2 = **ill-treat**, damage,

touching.

abysmal ⓘ *adj Informal* extremely bad, awful. **abysmally** *adv*

abyss ⓘ *n* very deep hole or chasm.

AC alternating current.

acacia [a–**kay**–sha] *n* tree or shrub with yellow or white flowers.

academy *n, pl* **–mies 1** society to advance arts or sciences. **2** institution for training in a particular skill. **3** *Scot* secondary school. **academic** *adj* **1** of an academy or university. **2** of theoretical interest only. ◆ *n* **3** lecturer or researcher at a university. **academically** *adv* **academician** *n* member of an academy.

accede ⓘ *v* **1** consent or agree (to). **2** take up (an office or position).

accelerate ⓘ *v* (cause to) move faster. **acceleration** *n* **accelerator** *n* pedal in a motor vehicle to increase speed.

accent ⓘ *n* **1** distinctive style of pronunciation of a local, national, or social group. **2** mark over a letter to show how it is pronounced. **3** stress on a syllable or musical note. ◆ *v* **4** place emphasis on.

accentuate ⓘ *v* stress, emphasize. **accentuation** *n*

accept ⓘ *v* **1** receive willingly. **2** agree to. **3** consider to be true. **acceptance** *n* **acceptable** *adj* **1** tolerable. **2** satisfactory. **acceptably** *adv* **acceptability** *n*

access ⓘ *n* **1** means of or right to approach or enter. ◆ *v* **2** obtain (data) from a computer. **accessible** *adj* easy to reach. **accessibility** *n*

accession *n* taking up of an office or position.

accessory ⓘ *n, pl* **–ries 1** supplementary part or object. **2** person involved in a crime although not present when it is committed.

accident ⓘ *n* **1** mishap, usu. one causing injury or death. **2** event happening by chance. **accidental** *adj* happening by chance or unintentionally. **accidentally** *adv*

———————— THESAURUS ————————

exploit, harm, hurt, injure, maltreat, take advantage of ≠ **protect 3 = insult**, castigate, curse, defame, disparage, malign, rouse on (*Aust*), scold, vilify ≠ **respect** ◆ *n* **4 = ill–treatment**, damage, exploitation, harm, hurt, injury, maltreatment, manhandling **5 = insults**, blame, castigation, censure, defamation, derision, disparagement, invective, reproach, scolding, vilification **6 = misuse**, misapplication

abysmal *adj Inf* = **terrible**, appalling, awful, bad, dire, dreadful

abyss *n* = **pit**, chasm, crevasse, fissure, gorge, gulf, void

accede *v* **1 = agree**, accept, acquiesce, admit, assent, comply, concede, concur, consent, endorse, grant **2 = inherit**, assume, attain, come to, enter upon, succeed, succeed to (*as heir*)

accelerate *v* = **speed up**, advance, expedite, further, hasten, hurry, quicken ≠ **slow down**

accent *n* **1 = pronunciation**, articulation,

brogue, enunciation, inflection, intonation, modulation, tone **3 = emphasis**, beat, cadence, force, pitch, rhythm, stress, timbre ◆ *v* **4 = emphasize**, accentuate, stress, underline, underscore

accentuate *v* = **emphasize**, accent, draw attention to, foreground, highlight, stress, underline, underscore

accept *v* **1 = receive**, acquire, gain, get, obtain, secure, take **2 = agree to**, approve, concur with, consent to, cooperate with **3 = believe**, admit, recognize

access *n* **1 = entrance**, admission, admittance, approach, entry, passage, path, road

accessory *n* **1 = addition**, accompaniment, adjunct, adornment, appendage, attachment, decoration, extra, supplement, trimming **2 = accomplice**, abettor, assistant, associate (*in crime*), colleague, confederate, helper, partner

accident *n* **1 = misfortune**, calamity, collision, crash, disaster, misadventure,

acclaim ❶ v 1 applaud, praise. ◆ n 2 enthusiastic approval. **acclamation** n

acclimatize ❶ v adapt to a new climate or environment. **acclimatization** n

accolade ❶ n 1 award, honour, or praise. 2 award of knighthood.

accommodate ❶ v 1 provide with lodgings. 2 have room for. 3 oblige, do a favour for. 4 adapt or adjust (to something). **accommodation** n house or room for living in. **accommodating** adj obliging.

> ✓ **WORD TIP**
> Note the double 'c' and double 'm'. This word is very commonly misspelled.

accompany ❶ v –nying, –nied 1 go along with. 2 occur with. 3 provide a musical accompaniment for. **accompaniment** n 1 something that accompanies. 2 *Music* supporting part that goes with a solo. **accompanist** n

accomplice ❶ n person who helps another to commit a crime.

accomplish ❶ v 1 manage to do. 2 finish. **accomplishment** n 1 completion.

2 personal ability or skill. **accomplished** adj expert, proficient.

> ✓ **WORD TIP**
> The usual pronunciation of the syllable 'com' in British English sounds like 'kum', but the sound 'kom' is increasingly used.

accord ❶ n 1 agreement, harmony. ◆ v 2 fit in with.

> ✓ **WORD TIP**
> Do not confuse *of one's own accord* with *on one's own account* 'for one's own benefit'.

accordion n portable musical instrument played by moving the two sides apart and together, and pressing a keyboard or buttons to produce the notes. **accordionist** n

accost ❶ v approach and speak to.

account ❶ n 1 report, description. 2 business arrangement making credit available. 3 record of money received and paid out with the resulting balance. 4 importance, value. ◆ v 5 judge to be. **on**

THESAURUS

mishap 2 = **chance**, fate, fluke, fortuity, fortune, hazard, luck

acclaim v 1 = **praise**, applaud, approve, celebrate, cheer, clap, commend, exalt, hail, honour, salute ◆ n 2 = **praise**, acclamation, applause, approval, celebration, commendation, honour, kudos ≠ **criticism**

acclimatize v = **adapt**, accommodate, accustom, adjust, get used to, habituate, inure, naturalize

accolade n 1 = **praise**, acclaim, applause, approval, commendation, compliment, ovation, recognition, tribute

accommodate v 1 = **house**, cater for, entertain, lodge, put up, shelter 3 = **help**, aid, assist, oblige, serve 4 = **adapt**, adjust, comply, conform, fit, harmonize, modify, reconcile, settle

accompany v 1 = **go with**, attend, chaperon, conduct, convoy, escort, hold (someone's) hand 2 = **occur with**, belong to, come with, follow, go together with, supplement

accomplice n = **helper**, abettor, accessory, ally, assistant, associate, collaborator, colleague, henchman, partner

accomplish v 1 = **do**, achieve, attain, bring about, carry out, effect, execute, fulfil, manage, perform, produce 2 = **finish**, complete

accord n 1 = **agreement**, conformity, correspondence, harmony, rapport, sympathy, unison ≠ **conflict** ◆ v 2 = **agree**, conform, correspond, fit, harmonize, match, suit, tally

accost v = **approach**, buttonhole, confront, greet, hail

account of because of. **accountable** adj responsible to someone or for something. **accountability** n

accoutrements pl n clothing and equipment for a particular activity.

accredited ❶ adj authorized, officially recognized.

accrue ❶ v **–cruing, –crued** increase gradually. **accrual** n

accumulate ❶ v gather together in increasing quantity. **accumulation** n **accumulator** n rechargeable electric battery.

accurate ❶ adj exact, correct. **accurately** adv **accuracy** n

accursed ❶ adj 1 under a curse. 2 detestable.

accuse ❶ v charge with wrongdoing. **accused** n **accuser** n **accusation** n **accusatory** adj

accustom ❶ v make used to. **accustomed** adj 1 usual. 2 used (to). 3 in the habit (of).

ace ❶ n 1 playing card with one symbol on

it. 2 Informal expert. 3 Tennis unreturnable serve. ◆ adj 4 Informal excellent.

acetylene [ass–**set**–ill–een] n colourless flammable gas used in welding metals.

ache ❶ n 1 dull continuous pain. ◆ v 2 be in or cause continuous dull pain.

achieve ❶ v gain by hard work or ability. **achievement** n something accomplished.

✔ **WORD TIP**
Note the 'ie'. This word is very commonly misspelled.

---

acid ❶ n 1 Chem one of a class of compounds, corrosive and sour when dissolved in water, that combine with a base to form a salt. 2 Slang LSD. ◆ adj 3 containing acid. 4 sour–tasting. 5 sharp or sour in manner. **acidic** adj **acidity** n **acid rain** rain containing acid from atmospheric pollution. **acid test** conclusive test of value.

acknowledge ❶ v 1 admit, recognize.

─────| T H E S A U R U S |─────

account n 1 = **description**, explanation, narrative, report, statement, story, tale, version 3 = **statement**, balance, bill, books, charge, invoice, reckoning, register, score, tally 4 = **importance**, consequence, honour, note, significance, standing, value, worth ◆ v 5 = **consider**, count, estimate, judge, rate, reckon, regard, think, value

accredited adj = **authorized**, appointed, certified, empowered, endorsed, guaranteed, licensed, official, recognized

accrue v = **increase**, accumulate, amass, arise, be added, build up, collect, enlarge, flow, follow, grow

accumulate v = **collect**, accrue, amass, build up, gather, hoard, increase, pile up, store

accurate adj = **exact**, authentic, careful, close, correct, faithful, precise, scrupulous, spot–on (Brit inf), strict, true, unerring ≠ **wrong**

accursed adj 1 = **cursed**, bewitched, condemned, damned, doomed, hopeless,

ill–fated, ill–omened, jinxed, unfortunate, unlucky, wretched ≠ **favoured** 2 = **hateful**, abominable, despicable, detestable, execrable, hellish, horrible ≠ **wonderful**

accuse v = **charge**, blame, censure, denounce, impeach, impute, incriminate, indict

accustom v = **adapt**, acclimatize, acquaint, discipline, exercise, familiarize, train

ace n 1 = **one**, single point 2 Inf = **expert**, champion, dab hand (Brit inf), fundi (S Afr), master, star, virtuoso, wizard (inf) ◆ adj 4 Inf = **excellent**, awesome (sl), brilliant, fine, great, outstanding, superb

ache n 1 = **pain**, hurt, pang, pounding, soreness, suffering, throbbing ◆ v 2 = **hurt**, pain, pound, smart, suffer, throb, twinge

achieve v = **attain**, accomplish, acquire, bring about, carry out, complete, do, execute, fulfil, gain, get, obtain, perform

acid adj 4 = **sour**, acerbic, acrid, pungent, tart, vinegary ≠ **sweet** 5 = **sharp**, biting, bitter, caustic, cutting, harsh, trenchant,

2 indicate recognition of (a person). 3 say one has received. **acknowledgment**, **acknowledgement** n

> ✓ **WORD TIP**
> The alternative spellings with or without an 'e' between 'g' and 'm' are equally acceptable.

acme [ak–mee] n highest point of achievement or excellence.

acne [ak–nee] n pimply skin disease.

acorn n nut of the oak tree.

acoustic adj 1 of sound and hearing. 2 (of a musical instrument) not electronically amplified. **acoustics** n 1 science of sounds. ◆ pl 2 features of a room or building determining how sound is heard within it.

acquaint ⊕ v make familiar, inform. **acquainted** adj **acquaintance** n 1 person

acquiesce ⊕ [ak–wee–**ess**] v agree to what someone wants. **acquiescence** n **acquiescent** adj

> ✓ **WORD TIP**
> The use of to after acquiesce was formerly regarded as incorrect, but is now acceptable.

acquire ⊕ v gain, get. **acquisition** n 1 thing acquired. 2 act of getting.

acquisitive adj eager to gain material possessions.

acquit ⊕ v –quitting, –quitted 1 pronounce (someone) innocent. 2 behave in a particular way. **acquittal** n

acre n measure of land, 4840 square yards. **acreage** [ake er–rij] n land area in acres.

acrid ⊕ [ak–rid] adj pungent, bitter. **acridity** n

acrobat n person skilled in gymnastic feats requiring agility and balance. **acrobatic** adj **acrobatics** pl n acrobatic feats.

acronym n word formed from the initial letters of other words, such as NASA.

across adv, prep 1 from side to side (of). 2 on or to the other side (of). **across the board** applying equally to all.

acrylic n, adj (synthetic fibre, paint, etc.) made from acrylic acid.

act ⊕ n 1 thing done. 2 law or decree. 3 section of a play or opera. 4 one of several short performances in a show. 5 pretended attitude. ◆ v 6 do something. 7 behave in a particular way. 8 perform in a play, film, etc. **act of God** unpredictable natural event. **acting** n 1 art of an actor. ◆ adj 2 temporarily performing the duties of. **action** n process of doing something. **active** adj moving, working. **actor**, **actress** n person who acts in a play, film, etc.

ACT Australian Capital Territory.

vitriolic ≠ **kindly**

acknowledge v 1 = **accept**, admit, allow, concede, confess, declare, grant, own, profess, recognize, yield ≠ **deny** 2 = **greet**, address, hail, notice, recognize, salute ≠ **ignore** 3 = **reply to**, answer, notice, react to, recognize, respond to, return ≠ **deny**

known. 2 personal knowledge.

acquaint v = **tell**, disclose, divulge, enlighten, familiarize, inform, let (someone) know, notify, reveal

acquiesce v = **agree**, accede, accept, allow, approve, assent, comply, concur, conform, consent, give in,

go along with, play ball (inf), submit, yield

acquire v = **get**, amass, attain, buy, collect, earn, gain, gather, obtain, receive, secure, win ≠ **lose**

acquit v 1 = **clear**, discharge, free, liberate, release, vindicate ≠ **sentence** 2 = **behave**, bear, comport, conduct, perform

acrid adj = **pungent**, bitter, caustic, harsh, sharp, vitriolic

act n 1 = **deed**, accomplishment, achievement, action, exploit, feat, performance, undertaking 2 = **law**, bill, decree, edict, enactment, measure, ordinance, resolution, statute

actual ❶ *adj* existing in reality. **actually** *adv* really, indeed. **actuality** *n*

> ✓ **WORD TIP**
>
> Avoid using *actual* or *actually* when it adds nothing to the sense of the sentence. Compare: *It's an actual fact: It's a fact.*

actuary *n, pl* **–aries** statistician who calculates insurance risks. **actuarial** *adj*

actuate *v* start up (a device).

acumen ❶ [ak–yew–men] *n* ability to make good judgments.

acupuncture *n* medical treatment involving the insertion of needles at various points on the body. **acupuncturist** *n*

acute ❶ *adj* **1** severe. **2** keen, shrewd. **3** sharp, sensitive. **4** (of an angle) less than 90°. ♦ *n* **5** accent (ˊ) over a letter to indicate the quality or length of its sound, as in café. **acutely** *adv*

ad *n Informal* advertisement.

AD anno Domini.

adage *n* wise saying, proverb.

adagio *n, pl* **–gios,** *adv Music* (piece to be played) slowly and gracefully.

adamant ❶ *adj* unshakable in determination or purpose.

Adam's apple *n* projecting lump of thyroid cartilage at the front of the throat.

adapt ❶ *v* alter for new use or new conditions. **adaptable** *adj* **adaptability** *n* **adaptation** *n* **1** thing produced by adapting something. **2** adapting. **adaptor, adapter** *n* device for connecting several electrical appliances to a single socket.

add ❶ *v* **1** combine (numbers or quantities). **2** join (to something). **3** say or write further. **addition** *n* thing added.

addendum ❶ *n, pl* **–da 1** an addition. **2** appendix to a book etc.

adder *n* small poisonous snake.

addict ❶ *n* **1** person who is unable to stop taking drugs. **2** *Informal* person devoted to something. **addicted** *adj* **addiction** *n* **addictive** *adj* causing addiction.

address ❶ *n* **1** place where a person lives. **2** direction on a letter. **3** location. **4** formal public speech. ♦ *v* **5** mark the destination, as on an envelope. **6** speak to. **7** give attention to (a problem, task, etc.). **addressee** *n* person addressed.

——— THESAURUS ———

4 = **performance**, routine, show, sketch, turn **5** = **pretence**, affectation, attitude, front, performance, pose, posture, show ♦ *v* **6** = **do**, carry out, enact, execute, function, operate, perform, take effect, work **8** = **perform**, act out, impersonate, mimic, play, play or take the part of, portray, represent

actual *adj* = **definite**, concrete, factual, physical, positive, real, substantial, tangible ≠ **supposed**

acumen *n* = **judgment**, astuteness, cleverness, ingenuity, insight, intelligence, perspicacity, shrewdness

acute *adj* **1** = **sharp**, excruciating, fierce, intense, piercing, powerful, severe, shooting, violent **2** = **perceptive**, astute, clever, insightful, keen, observant, sensitive, sharp, smart ≠ **slow**

adamant *adj* = **determined**, firm, fixed,

obdurate, resolute, stubborn, unbending, uncompromising

adapt *v* = **adjust**, acclimatize, accommodate, alter, change, conform, convert, modify, remodel, tailor

add *v* **1** = **count up**, add up, compute, reckon, total, tot up ≠ **remove 2** = **include**, adjoin, affix, append, attach, augment, supplement

addendum *n* **1** = **addition**, appendage, attachment, extension, extra **2** = **appendix**, postscript, supplement

addict *n* **1** = **junkie** (*inf*), fiend (*inf*), freak (*inf*) **2** *Inf* = **fan**, adherent, buff (*inf*), devotee, enthusiast, follower, nut (*sl*)

address *n* **3** = **location**, abode, dwelling, home, house, residence, situation, whereabouts **4** = **speech**, discourse, dissertation, lecture, oration, sermon, talk ♦ *v* **6** = **speak to**, approach, greet, hail,

adenoids [ad–in–oidz] *pl n* mass of tissue at the back of the throat. **adenoidal** *adj* having a nasal voice caused by swollen adenoids.

adept ❶ *adj, n* very skilful (person).

adequate ❶ *adj* 1 sufficient, enough. 2 not outstanding. **adequately** *adv* **adequacy** *n*

adhere ❶ *v* 1 stick (to). 2 be devoted (to). **adherence** *n* **adherent** *n* devotee, follower. **adhesion** *n* 1 sticking (to). 2 joining together of parts of the body that are normally separate, as after surgery.

ad hoc *adj, adv Latin* for a particular purpose only.

adieu ❶ [a–dew] *interj* farewell, goodbye.

adjacent ❶ *adj* 1 near or next (to). 2 having a common boundary. 3 *Geom* (of a side in a right–angled triangle) lying between a specified angle and the right angle.

adjective *n* word that adds information about a noun or pronoun. **adjectival** *adj*

adjoin ❶ *v* be next to. **adjoining** *adj*

adjourn ❶ *v* 1 close (a court) at the end of a session. 2 postpone temporarily. 3 *Informal* go elsewhere. **adjournment** *n*

adjudge *v* declare (to be).

adjudicate ❶ *v* 1 give a formal decision on (a dispute). 2 judge (a competition).

adjudication *n* **adjudicator** *n*

adjunct *n* subordinate or additional person or thing.

adjure *v* 1 command (to do). 2 appeal earnestly.

adjust ❶ *v* 1 adapt to new conditions. 2 alter slightly so as to be suitable. **adjustable** *adj* **adjuster** *n* **adjustment** *n*

adjutant [aj–oo–tant] *n* army officer in charge of routine administration.

ad–lib ❶ *v* –libbing, –libbed 1 improvise a speech etc. without preparation. ♦ *n* 2 improvised remark.

administer ❶ *v* 1 manage (business affairs). 2 organize and put into practice. 3 give (medicine or treatment).

administrate *v* manage (an organization). **administration** *n* **administrative** *adj* **administrator** *n*

admiral *n* highest naval rank. **Admiralty** *n* former government department in charge of the Royal Navy.

admire ❶ *v* regard with esteem and approval. **admirable** *adj* **admirably** *adv* **admiration** *n* **admirer** *n* **admiring** *adj*

admit ❶ *v* –mitting, –mitted 1 confess, acknowledge. 2 concede the truth of. 3 allow in. **admission** *n* permission to enter. **admittance** *n* permission to enter.

——————— THESAURUS ———————

talk to 7 = **concentrate on**, apply (oneself) to, attend to, devote (oneself) to, engage in, focus on, take care of

① **adept** *adj* = **skilful**, able, accomplished, adroit, expert, practised, proficient, skilled, versed ≠ **inept**

② **adept** *n* = **expert**, dab hand (*Brit inf*), fundi (*S Afr*), genius, hotshot (*inf*), master

adequate *adj* 1 = **enough**, satisfactory, sufficient ≠ **lacking** 2 = **fair**, competent, satisfactory, tolerable, up to scratch (*inf*) ≠ **inadequate**

adhere *v* 1 = **stick**, attach, cleave, cling, fasten, fix, glue, hold fast, paste

adieu *interj* = **goodbye**, farewell

adjacent *adj* 1 = **next**, adjoining, beside, bordering, close, near, neighbouring, next door, touching ≠ **separated**

adjoin *v* = **connect**, border, join, link, touch

adjourn *v* 2 = **postpone**, defer, delay, discontinue, interrupt, put off, suspend

adjudicate *v* 1 = **judge**, adjudge, arbitrate, decide, determine, mediate, referee, settle, umpire

adjust *v* 1 = **adapt**, accustom 2 = **alter**, make conform, modify

ad–lib *v* 1 = **improvise**, busk, extemporize, make up, speak off the cuff, wing it (*inf*)

administer *v* 1, 2 = **manage**, conduct, control, direct, govern, handle, oversee, run, supervise 3 = **give**, apply, dispense, impose, mete out, perform, provide

admire *v* = **respect**, appreciate, approve, esteem, look up to, praise, prize, think highly of, value

admittedly adv it must be agreed.
admonish ❶ v reprove sternly.
  admonition n
ad nauseam [ad naw–zee–am] adv Latin
  to a boring or sickening extent.
ado n fuss, trouble.
adolescence ❶ n period between puberty
  and adulthood. **adolescent** n, adj (person)
  between puberty and adulthood.
adopt ❶ v 1 take (someone else's child) as
  one's own. 2 take up (a plan or principle).
  adoption n **adoptive** adj related by
  adoption.
adore ❶ v 1 love intensely. 2 worship.
  adorable adj **adoration** n **adoring** adj
adorn ❶ v decorate, embellish.
  adornment n
adrenal [ad–reen–al] adj near the kidneys.
  adrenal glands glands covering the top of
  the kidneys.
adrift ❶ adj, adv 1 drifting. 2 without a
  clear purpose.

adroit ❶ adj quick and skilful. **adroitly** adv
adulation ❶ n uncritical admiration.
adult ❶ adj 1 fully grown, mature. ◆ n 2
  adult person or animal. **adulthood** n
adulterate v spoil something by adding
  inferior material. **adulteration** n
adultery n, pl -teries sexual unfaithfulness
  of a husband or wife. **adulterer,**
  adulteress n **adulterous** adj
advance ❶ v 1 go or bring forward. 2
  further (a cause). 3 propose (an idea). 4
  lend (a sum of money). ◆ n 5 forward
  movement. 6 improvement. 7 loan. ◆ pl 8
  approaches to a person with the hope of
  starting a romantic or sexual relationship.
  ◆ adj 9 done or happening before an
  event. **in advance** ahead. **advanced** adj 1
  at a late stage in development. 2 not
  elementary. **advancement** n promotion.
advantage ❶ n 1 more favourable
  position or state. 2 benefit or profit. 3
  Tennis point scored after deuce. **take**

admit v 1 = **confess**, acknowledge, declare,
  disclose, divulge, own, reveal 2 = **allow,**
  agree, grant, let, permit, recognize ≠ **deny**
  3 = **let in**, accept, allow, give access,
  initiate, introduce, receive, take in
  ≠ **exclude**
admonish v = **reprimand**, berate, chide,
  rebuke, rouse on (Aust), scold, slap on the
  wrist, tell off (inf) ≠ **praise**
adolescence n = **youth**, boyhood,
  childishness, girlhood, immaturity,
  minority, teens, youthfulness
adopt v 1 = **foster**, take in ≠ **give up**
  2 = **choose**, assume, espouse, follow,
  maintain, take up ≠ **reject**
adore v 1 = **love**, admire, cherish, dote on,
  esteem, honour ≠ **hate** 2 = **worship**, exalt,
  glorify, idolize, revere
adorn v = **decorate**, array, embellish,
  festoon
adrift adj 1 = **drifting**, afloat, unanchored,
  unmoored 2 = **aimless**, directionless,
  goalless, purposeless
adroit adj = **skilful**, adept, clever, deft,
  dexterous, expert, masterful, neat,

  proficient, skilled
adulation n = **worship**, fawning, fulsome
  praise, servile flattery, sycophancy
adult adj 1 = **fully grown**, full grown, fully
  developed, grown–up, mature, of age,
  ripe ◆ n 2 = **grown–up**, grown or grown–
  up person (man or woman), person of
  mature age
advance v 1 = **progress**, accelerate, bring
  forward, come forward, go on, hasten,
  make inroads, proceed, speed ≠ **retreat**
  2 = **benefit**, further, improve, prosper
  3 = **suggest**, offer, present, proffer, put
  forward, submit ≠ **withhold** 4 = **lend**, pay
  beforehand, supply on credit ≠ **defer**
  payment ◆ n 5 = **progress**, advancement,
  development, forward movement,
  headway, inroads, onward movement
  6 = **improvement**, breakthrough, gain,
  growth, progress, promotion, step
  7 = **loan**, credit, deposit, down payment,
  prepayment, retainer ◆ pl 8 = **overtures**,
  approach, approaches, moves, proposals,
  proposition ◆ adj 9 = **prior**, beforehand,
  early, forward, in front **in advance**

advantage of 1 use (a person) unfairly. **2** use (an opportunity). **advantageous** adj

advent n **1** arrival. **2** (A–) season of four weeks before Christmas.

adventure ⊙ n exciting and risky undertaking or exploit. **adventurer, adventuress** n **1** person who unscrupulously seeks money or power. **2** person who seeks adventures. **adventurous** adj

adverb n word that adds information about a verb, adjective, or other adverb. **adverbial** adj

adverse ⊙ adj **1** unfavourable. **2** antagonistic or hostile. **adversely** adv **adversity** n very difficult or hard circumstances.

advert ⊙ n Informal advertisement.

advertise ⊙ v **1** present or praise (goods or services) to the public in order to encourage sales. **2** make (a vacancy, event, etc.) known publicly. **advertisement** n public announcement to sell goods or publicize an event. **advertiser** n **advertising** adj, n

---

✔ **WORD TIP**
Note that the standard pronunciation of *advertisement* differs from *advertise*. The main stress is on 'ver', while 'tise' is pronounced 'tiz'.

---

advice ⊙ n recommendation as to what to do. **advise** v **1** offer advice to. **2** notify (someone). **adviser, advisor** n **advisable** adj prudent, sensible. **advisability** n

advisory adj giving advice. **advised** adj considered, thought–out, e.g. *ill–advised*. **advisedly** adv deliberately.

advocate ⊙ v **1** propose or recommend. ♦ n **2** person who publicly supports a cause. **3** *Scot* barrister. **advocacy** n

aeon [ee on] n immeasurably long period of time.

aerate v put gas into (a liquid), as when making a fizzy drink. **aeration** n

aerial adj **1** in, from, or operating in the air. **2** relating to aircraft. ♦ n **3** metal pole, wire, etc., for receiving or transmitting radio or TV signals.

aerobatics pl n stunt flying. **aerobatic** adj

aerobics n exercises designed to increase the amount of oxygen in the blood. **aerobic** adj

aerodrome n small airport.

aerodynamics n study of how air flows around moving solid objects. **aerodynamic** adj

aeronautics n study or practice of aircraft flight. **aeronautical** adj

aeroplane n powered flying vehicle with fixed wings.

aerosol n pressurized can from which a substance can be dispensed as a fine spray.

✔ **WORD TIP**
Be careful not to confuse the spelling 'aer–' with 'air–'.

---

aerospace n earth's atmosphere and

———————————— THESAURUS ————————————

= **beforehand**, ahead, earlier, previously

advantage n **1** = **superiority**, ascendancy, dominance, lead, precedence, sway **2** = **benefit**, good, help, profit

adventure n = **escapade**, enterprise, experience, exploit, incident, occurrence, undertaking, venture

adverse adj **1** = **unfavourable**, contrary, detrimental, inopportune, negative ≠ **favourable 2** = **hostile**, antagonistic, opposing

advert n Inf = **advertisement**, ad (inf), announcement, blurb, commercial, notice, plug (inf), poster

advertise v **1** = **publicize**, plug (inf), promote, tout **2** = **announce**, make known

advice n = **guidance**, counsel, help, opinion, recommendation, suggestion

advocate v **1** = **recommend**, advise, argue for, campaign for, champion, commend, encourage, promote, propose, support, uphold ≠ **oppose** ♦ n **2** = **supporter**, space beyond.

aesthetic [iss–**thet**–ik] *adj* relating to the appreciation of art and beauty. **aesthetics** *n* study of art, beauty, and good taste. **aesthetically** *adv* **aesthete** [**eess**–theet] *n* person who has or affects an extravagant love of art. **aestheticism** *n*

afar *adv* from or at a great distance.

affable ❶ *adj* friendly and easy to talk to. **affability** *n*

affair ❶ *n* **1** event or happening. **2** sexual relationship outside marriage. **3** thing to be done or attended to. ◆ *pl* **4** personal or business interests. **5** matters of public interest.

affect[1] ❶ *v* **1** act on, influence. **2** move (someone) emotionally.

> ✓ **WORD TIP**
> Note the difference between the verbs *affect* meaning 'influence' and *effect* meaning 'accomplish'.

affect[2] ❶ *v* **1** put on a show of. **2** wear or use by preference. **affectation** *n* attitude or manner put on to impress. **affected** *adj* **1** displaying affectation. **2** pretended.

affection *n* fondness or love.

affidavit [af–fid–**dave**–it] *n* written statement made on oath.

affiliate ❶ *v* (of a group) link up with a larger group. **affiliation** *n*

affinity ❶ *n, pl* –**ties 1** close connection or liking. **2** close resemblance. **3** chemical attraction.

affirm ❶ *v* **1** declare to be true. **2** uphold or confirm (an idea or belief). **affirmation** *n* **affirmative** *n, adj* (word or phrase) indicating agreement.

affix *v* **1** attach or fasten. ◆ *n* **2** word or syllable added to a word to change its meaning.

afflict ❶ *v* give pain or grief to. **affliction** *n*

affluent ❶ *adj* having plenty of money. **affluence** *n* wealth.

afford ❶ *v* **1** have enough money to buy. **2** be able to spare (the time etc.). **3** give or supply. **affordable** *adj*

affront ❶ *v, n* insult.

> ✓ **WORD TIP**
> *Affront* is often followed by 'to': *An affront to my feelings.*

——————— THESAURUS ———————

campaigner, champion, counsellor, defender, promoter, proponent, spokesman, upholder **3** *Scot* = **lawyer**, attorney, barrister, counsel, solicitor

affable *adj* = **friendly**, amiable, amicable, approachable, congenial, cordial, courteous, genial, pleasant, sociable, urbane

affair *n* **1** = **event**, activity, business, episode, happening, incident, matter, occurrence **2** = **relationship**, amour, intrigue, liaison, romance

affect[1] *v* **1** = **influence**, act on, alter, bear upon, change, concern, impinge upon, relate to **2** = **move**, disturb, overcome, perturb, stir, touch, upset

affect[2] *v* **1** = **put on**, adopt, aspire to, assume, contrive, feign, imitate, pretend, simulate

affiliate *v* = **join**, ally, amalgamate,

associate, band together, combine, incorporate, link, unite

affinity *n* **1** = **attraction**, fondness, inclination, leaning, liking, partiality, rapport, sympathy ≠ **hostility** **2** = **similarity**, analogy, closeness, connection, correspondence, kinship, likeness, relationship, resemblance ≠ **difference**

affirm *v* **1** = **declare**, assert, maintain, state, swear ≠ **reject** **2** = **confirm**, certify, pronounce, testify ≠ **deny**

afflict *v* = **torment**, distress, grieve, harass, hurt, oppress, pain, plague, trouble

affluent *adj* = **wealthy**, loaded (*sl*), moneyed, opulent, prosperous, rich, well–heeled (*inf*), well–off, well–to–do

afford *v* **2** = **spare**, bear, manage, stand, sustain **3** = **give**, offer, produce, provide, render, supply, yield

afield *adv* **far afield** far away.

aflame ❶ *adj* burning.

afloat *adv, adj* **1** floating. **2** at sea.

afoot ❶ *adv, adj* happening, in operation.

aforesaid, aforementioned *adj* referred to previously.

afraid ❶ *adj* **1** frightened. **2** regretful.

afresh ❶ *adv* again, anew.

African *adj* **1** of Africa. ♦ *n* **2** person from Africa.

aft *adv* at or towards the rear of a ship or aircraft.

after *prep* **1** following in time or place. **2** in pursuit of. **3** in imitation of. ♦ *conj* **4** at a later time than. ♦ *adv* **5** at a later time. **afters** *pl n Informal* dessert.

afterbirth *n* material expelled from the womb after childbirth.

aftermath ❶ *n* results of an event considered together.

afternoon *n* time between noon and evening.

aftershave *n* lotion applied to the face after shaving.

afterwards, afterward *adv* later.

again ❶ *adv* **1** once more. **2** in addition.

against ❶ *prep* **1** in opposition or contrast to. **2** in contact with. **3** as a protection from.

agape *adj* **1** (of the mouth) wide open. **2** (of a person) very surprised.

agate [**ag**–git] *n* semiprecious form of quartz with striped colouring.

age ❶ *n* **1** length of time a person or thing has existed. **2** time of life. **3** latter part of human life. **4** period of history. **5** long time. ♦ *v* **ageing** *or* **aging, aged 6** make or grow old. **aged** *adj* **1** [**ay**–jid] old. **2** [rhymes with **raged**] being at the age of. **ageing, aging** *n, adj* **ageless** *adj* **1** apparently never growing old. **2** seeming to have existed for ever. **age–old** *adj* very old.

✔ **WORD TIP**

Both spellings of *ageing*, with or without an 'e', are equally acceptable.

---

agenda ❶ *n* list of things to be dealt with, esp. at a meeting.

agent ❶ *n* **1** person acting on behalf of another. **2** person or thing producing an effect. **agency** *n* organization providing a service.

THESAURUS

① **affront** *v* = **offend**, anger, annoy, displease, insult, outrage, provoke, slight
② **affront** *n* = **insult**, offence, outrage, provocation, slap in the face (*inf*), slight, slur

aflame *adj* = **burning**, ablaze, alight, blazing, fiery, flaming, lit, on fire

afoot *adj* = **going on**, abroad, brewing, current, happening, in preparation, in progress, on the go (*inf*), up (*inf*)

afraid *adj* **1** = **scared**, apprehensive, cowardly, faint–hearted, fearful, frightened, nervous ≠ **bold 2** = **sorry**, regretful, unhappy ≠ **happy**

afresh *adv* = **again**, anew, newly, once again, once more, over again

after *adv* **5** = **following**, afterwards, behind, below, later, subsequently, succeeding, thereafter ≠ **before**

aftermath *n* = **effects**, aftereffects, consequences, end result, outcome, results, sequel, upshot, wake

again *adv* **1** = **once more**, afresh, anew, another time **2** = **also**, besides, furthermore, in addition, moreover

against *prep* **1** = **opposed to**, anti (*inf*), averse to, hostile to, in defiance of, in opposition to, resisting, versus **2** = **beside**, abutting, facing, in contact with, on, opposite to, touching, upon **3** = **in preparation for**, in anticipation of, in expectation of, in provision for

age *n* **1** = **lifetime**, generation *n* **3** = **old age**, advancing years, decline (*of life*), majority, maturity, senescence, senility, seniority ≠ **youth 4** = **time**, date, day(s), duration, epoch, era, period, span

agenda *n* = **list**, calendar, diary, plan, programme, schedule, timetable

agent *n* **1** = **representative**, envoy, go–

aggrandize v make greater in size, power, or rank. **aggrandizement** n

aggravate 🟊 v 1 make worse. 2 *Informal* annoy. **aggravating** adj **aggravation** n

aggregate 🟊 n 1 total. 2 rock consisting of a mixture of minerals. 3 sand or gravel used to make concrete. ◆ adj 4 gathered into a mass. 5 total or final. ◆ v 6 combine into a whole. **aggregation** n

aggression 🟊 n 1 hostile behaviour. 2 unprovoked attack. **aggressive** adj 1 showing aggression. 2 forceful. **aggressively** adv **aggressiveness** n **aggressor** n

aggrieved 🟊 adj upset and angry.

aghast 🟊 adj overcome with amazement or horror.

agile 🟊 adj 1 nimble, quick–moving. 2 mentally quick. **agilely** adv **agility** n

agitate 🟊 v 1 disturb or excite. 2 stir or shake (a liquid). 3 stir up public opinion for or against something. **agitation** n **agitator** n

aglow adj glowing.

AGM annual general meeting.

agnostic n 1 person who believes that it is impossible to know whether God exists.

◆ adj 2 of agnostics. **agnosticism** n

ago adv in the past.

agog 🟊 adj eager or curious.

agony 🟊 n, pl –nies extreme physical or mental pain. **agonize** v 1 worry greatly. 2 (cause to) suffer agony. **agonizing** adj **agony aunt** journalist who gives advice in an agony column. **agony column** newspaper or magazine feature offering advice on personal problems.

agoraphobia n fear of open spaces. **agoraphobic** n, adj

agree 🟊 v **agreeing, agreed** 1 be of the same opinion. 2 consent. 3 reach a joint decision. 4 be consistent. 5 (foll. by *with*) be suitable to (one's health or digestion). **agreeable** adj 1 pleasant and enjoyable. 2 prepared to consent. **agreeably** adv **agreement** n 1 agreeing. 2 contract.

> ✔️ **WORD TIP**
> *Agree* is usually followed by a preposition. Use agree *on* something; agree *with* someone; agree *to* do something.

agriculture 🟊 n raising of crops and

between, negotiator, rep (*inf*), surrogate 2 = **force**, agency, cause, instrument, means, power, vehicle

aggravate v 1 = **make worse**, exacerbate, exaggerate, increase, inflame, intensify, magnify, worsen ≠ **ease** 2 *Inf* = **annoy**, bother, get on one's nerves (*inf*), irritate, nettle, provoke ≠ **please**

aggregate n 1 = **total**, accumulation, amount, body, bulk, collection, combination, mass, pile, sum, whole ◆ adj 4 = **accumulated**, collected, combined, composite, mixed 5 = **total**, cumulative ◆ v 6 = **combine**, accumulate, amass, assemble, collect, heap, mix, pile

aggression n 1 = **hostility**, antagonism, belligerence, destructiveness, pugnacity 2 = **attack**, assault, injury, invasion, offensive, onslaught, raid

aggrieved adj = **hurt**, afflicted, distressed,

disturbed, harmed, injured, unhappy, wronged

aghast adj = **horrified**, amazed, appalled, astonished, astounded, awestruck, confounded, shocked, startled, stunned

agile adj 1 = **nimble**, active, brisk, lithe, quick, sprightly, spry, supple, swift 2 = **acute**, alert, bright (*inf*), clever, lively, quick–witted, sharp

agitate v 1 = **upset**, disconcert, distract, excite, fluster, perturb, trouble, unnerve, worry ≠ **calm** 2 = **stir**, beat, convulse, disturb, rouse, shake, toss

agog adj = **eager**, avid, curious, enthralled, enthusiastic, excited, expectant, impatient, in suspense

agony n = **suffering**, anguish, distress, misery, pain, throes, torment, torture

agree v 1 = **concur**, assent, be of the same opinion, comply, consent, see eye to eye

livestock. **agricultural** adj **agriculturalist** n
aground ❶ adv onto the bottom of
shallow water.
ahead ❶ adv 1 in front. 2 forwards.
ahoy interj shout used at sea to attract
attention.
aid ❶ v, n (give) assistance or support.
aide ❶ n assistant.
AIDS acquired immunodeficiency
syndrome, a viral disease that destroys the
body's ability to fight infection.
ail v 1 trouble, afflict. 2 be ill. **ailing** adj
sickly. **ailment** n illness.
aim ❶ v 1 point (a weapon or missile) or
direct (a blow or remark) at a target. 2
propose or intend. ◆ n 3 aiming. 4
intention, purpose. **aimless** adj having no
purpose. **aimlessly** adv

✓ **WORD TIP**
The idiom is *aim at* something or *aim
to do* something.

ain't Not standard 1 am not. 2 is not. 3 are
not. 4 has not. 5 have not.
air ❶ n 1 mixture of gases forming the
earth's atmosphere. 2 space above the
ground, sky. 3 breeze. 4 quality or
manner. 5 tune. ◆ pl 6 affected manners.
◆ v 7 make known publicly. 8 expose to

air to dry or ventilate. **on the air** in the act
of broadcasting on radio or television.
airless adj stuffy. **airborne** adj 1 carried by
air. 2 (of aircraft) flying. **airbrush** n
atomizer spraying paint by compressed
air. **airfield** n place where aircraft can land
and take off. **air force** branch of the
armed forces responsible for air warfare.
air gun gun fired by compressed air. **airlift**
n 1 transport of troops or cargo by aircraft
when other routes are blocked. ◆ v 2
transport by airlift. **airlock** n air bubble
blocking the flow of liquid in a pipe.
airmail n 1 system of sending mail by
aircraft. 2 mail sent in this way. **airman** n
member of the air force. **airplay** n
broadcast performances of a record on
radio. **airport** n airfield for civilian aircraft,
with facilities for aircraft maintenance and
passengers. **air raid** attack by aircraft.
airship n lighter-than-air self-propelled
aircraft. **airspace** n atmosphere above a
country, regarded as its territory. **airstrip** n
cleared area where aircraft can take off
and land. **airtight** adj sealed so that air
cannot enter.
aisle ❶ [rhymes with mile] n passageway
separating seating areas in a church,
theatre, etc., or row of shelves in a
supermarket.

THESAURUS

≠ **deny** 4 = **match**, coincide, conform,
correspond, tally
agriculture n = **farming**, cultivation,
culture, husbandry, tillage
aground adv = **beached**, ashore,
foundered, grounded, high and dry, on
the rocks, stranded, stuck
ahead adv 1 = **in front**, at an advantage, at
the head, before, in advance, in the lead,
leading, to the fore
① **aid** v = **help**, assist, encourage, favour,
promote, serve, subsidize, support, sustain
≠ **obstruct**
② **aid** n = **help**, assistance, benefit,
encouragement, favour, promotion, relief,
service, support ≠ **hindrance**
aide n = **assistant**, attendant, helper,

right-hand man, second, supporter
aim v 2 = **intend**, attempt, endeavour,
mean, plan, point, propose, seek, set one's
sights on, strive, try ◆ n 4 = **intention**,
ambition, aspiration, desire, goal,
objective, plan, purpose, target
air n 1, 2 = **atmosphere**, heavens, sky
3 = **wind**, breeze, draught, zephyr
4 = **manner**, appearance, atmosphere,
aura, demeanour, impression, look, mood
5 = **tune**, aria, lay, melody, song ◆ pl
6 = **affectation**, arrogance, haughtiness,
hauteur, pomposity, pretensions,
superciliousness, swank (inf) ◆ v
7 = **publicize**, circulate, display, exhibit,
express, give vent to, make known, make
public, reveal, voice 8 = **ventilate**, aerate,

ajar adj, adv (of a door) partly open.

AK Alaska.

akimbo adv **with arms akimbo** with hands on hips and elbows outwards.

akin adj **akin to** similar, related.

AL Alabama.

alabaster n soft white translucent stone.

à la carte adj, adv (of a menu) having dishes individually priced.

alacrity ⊕ n speed, eagerness.

alarm ⊕ n 1 sudden fear caused by awareness of danger. 2 warning sound. 3 device that gives this. 4 alarm clock. ◆ v 5 fill with fear. **alarming** adj **alarmist** n person who alarms others needlessly. **alarm clock** clock which sounds at a set time to wake someone up.

alas adv unfortunately, regrettably.

albatross n large sea bird with very long wings.

albino n, pl **–nos** person or animal with white skin and hair and pink eyes.

album n 1 book with blank pages for keeping photographs or stamps in. 2 long-playing record.

alchemy n medieval form of chemistry concerned with trying to turn base metals into gold and to find the elixir of life. **alchemist** n

alcohol n 1 colourless flammable liquid present in intoxicating drinks. 2

intoxicating drinks generally. **alcoholic** adj 1 of alcohol. ◆ n 2 person addicted to alcohol. **alcoholism** n addiction to alcohol.

alcove ⊕ n recess in the wall of a room.

alder n tree related to the birch.

alderman n formerly, senior member of a local council.

ale n kind of beer.

alert ⊕ adj 1 watchful, attentive. ◆ n 2 warning of danger. ◆ v 3 warn of danger. 4 make (someone) aware of (a fact). **on the alert** watchful. **alertness** n

alfresco adv, adj in the open air.

algae [al–jee] pl n plants which live in or near water and have no true stems, leaves, or roots.

algebra n branch of mathematics using symbols to represent numbers. **algebraic** adj

alias ⊕ adv 1 also known as. ◆ n 2 false name.

alibi ⊕ n 1 plea of being somewhere else when a crime was committed. 2 Informal excuse.

alien ⊕ adj 1 foreign. 2 repugnant (to). 3 from another world. ◆ n 4 foreigner. 5 being from another world. **alienate** v cause to become hostile. **alienation** n

alight¹ ⊕ v 1 step out of (a vehicle). 2 land.

alight² ⊕ adj 1 on fire. 2 lit up.

align ⊕ [a–line] v 1 bring (a person or

——————| THESAURUS |——————

expose, freshen

aisle n = **passageway**, alley, corridor, gangway, lane, passage, path

alacrity n = **eagerness**, alertness, enthusiasm, promptness, quickness, readiness, speed, willingness, zeal

alarm n 1 = **fear**, anxiety, apprehension, consternation, fright, nervousness, panic, scare, trepidation ≠ **calm** 2, 3 = **danger signal**, alarm bell, alert, bell, distress signal, hooter, siren, warning ◆ v 5 = **frighten**, daunt, dismay, distress, give (someone) a turn (inf), panic, scare, startle, unnerve ≠ **comfort**

alcove n = **recess**, bay, compartment, corner, cubbyhole, cubicle, niche, nook

alert adj 1 = **watchful**, attentive, awake, circumspect, heedful, observant, on guard, on one's toes, on the lookout, vigilant, wide–awake ≠ **slow** ◆ n 2 = **warning**, alarm, signal, siren ≠ **all clear** ◆ v 3 = **warn**, alarm, forewarn, signal ≠ **lull** 4 = **inform**, notify ≠ **lull**

alias adv 1 = **also known as**, also called, otherwise, otherwise known as ◆ n 2 = **pseudonym**, assumed name, nom de guerre, nom de plume, pen name, stage name

alibi n 2 Inf = **excuse**, defence, explanation, justification, plea, pretext, reason

alien adj 1 = **strange**, exotic, foreign, unfamiliar ≠ **like** ◆ n 4 = **foreigner**, group) into agreement with the policy of another. **2** place in a line. **alignment** n

alike ❶ adj **1** like, similar. ♦ adv **2** in the same way.

alimony n allowance paid under a court order to a separated or divorced spouse.

alive ❶ adj **1** living, in existence. **2** lively. **alive to** aware of. **alive with** swarming with.

alkali [alk-a-lie] n substance which combines with acid and neutralizes it to form a salt. **alkaline** adj **alkalinity** n **alkaloid** n any of a group of organic compounds containing nitrogen.

all ❶ adj **1** whole quantity or number (of). ♦ adv **2** wholly, entirely. **3** (in the score of games) each. **give one's all** make the greatest possible effort. **all in** adj **1** exhausted. **2** (of wrestling) with no style forbidden. ♦ adv **3** with all expenses included. **all right** adj **1** adequate, satisfactory. **2** unharmed. ♦ interj **3** expression of approval or agreement. **all-rounder** n person with ability in many

fields.

allay v reduce (fear or anger).

allege ❶ v state without proof. **allegedly** adv **allegation** n unproved accusation.

allegiance ❶ n loyalty to a person, country, or cause.

allegory ❶ n, pl -ries story with an underlying meaning as well as the literal one. **allegorical** adj

allegro n, pl -gros, adv Music (piece to be played) in a brisk lively manner.

allergy ❶ n, pl -gies extreme sensitivity to a substance, which causes the body to react to it. **allergic** adj having or caused by an allergy. **allergen** n substance capable of causing an allergic reaction.

alleviate ❶ v lessen (pain or suffering). **alleviation** n

alley ❶ n **1** narrow street or path. **2** long narrow enclosure in which tenpin bowling or skittles is played.

alliance ❶ n **1** state of being allied. **2** formal relationship between countries or groups for a shared purpose.

──── THESAURUS ────

newcomer, outsider, stranger

alight¹ v **1** = **get off**, descend, disembark, dismount, get down **2** = **land**, come down, come to rest, descend, light, perch, settle, touch down ≠ **rise**

alight² adj **1** = **on fire**, ablaze, aflame, blazing, burning, fiery, flaming, lighted, lit **2** = **lit up**, bright, brilliant, illuminated, shining

align v **1** = **ally**, affiliate, agree, associate, cooperate, join, side, sympathize **2** = **line up**, even up, order, range, regulate, straighten

alike adj **1** = **similar**, akin, analogous, corresponding, identical, of a piece, parallel, resembling, the same ≠ **different** ♦ adv **2** = **similarly**, analogously, correspondingly, equally, evenly, identically, uniformly ≠ **differently**

alive adj **1** = **living**, animate, breathing, existing, extant, in existence, in the land of the living (inf), subsisting ≠ **dead** **2** = **lively**, active, alert, animated,

energetic, full of life, vital, vivacious ≠ **lifeless**

all adj **1** = **entire**, complete, each, each and every, every, every bit of, every one of, every single, full, the whole of, total ♦ adv **2** = **completely**, altogether, entirely, fully, totally, utterly, wholly

allege v = **claim**, affirm, assert, charge, declare, maintain, state

allegiance n = **loyalty**, constancy, devotion, faithfulness, fidelity, obedience

allegory n = **symbol**, fable, myth, parable, story, symbolism, tale

allergy n = **sensitivity**, antipathy, hypersensitivity, susceptibility

alleviate v = **ease**, allay, lessen, lighten, moderate, reduce, relieve, soothe

alley n **1** = **passage**, alleyway, backstreet, lane, passageway, pathway, walk

alliance n **1** = **connection**, affiliation, agreement, association, combination, marriage, partnership ≠ **break 2** = **union**, coalition, confederation, federation,

alligator *n* reptile of the crocodile family, found in the southern US and China.

alliteration *n* use of the same sound at the start of words occurring together. **alliterative** *adj*

allocate ⓣ *v* assign to someone or for a particular purpose. **allocation** *n*

allot ⓣ *v* **–lotting, –lotted** assign as a share or for a particular purpose. **allotment** *n* 1 distribution. 2 portion allotted. 3 small piece of public land rented to grow vegetables on.

allow ⓣ *v* 1 permit. 2 set aside. 3 acknowledge (a point or claim). **allow for** *v* take into account. **allowable** *adj* **allowance** *n* 1 amount of money given at regular intervals. 2 amount permitted. **make allowances for** 1 treat or judge (someone) less severely because he or she has special problems. 2 take into account.

alloy ⓣ *n* 1 mixture of two or more metals. ◆ *v* 2 mix (metals).

allspice *n* spice made from the berries of a tropical American tree.

allude ⓣ *v* (foll. by *to*) refer indirectly to. **allusion** *n* indirect reference. **allusive** *adj*

✓ **WORD TIP**

Allude is followed by *to*. Be careful not to confuse this word with *elude* meaning 'escape'. Also be careful not to confuse *allusion* with *illusion* meaning 'fallacy' or 'fantasy'.

---

allure ⓣ *n* 1 attractiveness. ◆ *v* 2 entice or attract. **alluring** *adj*

ally ⓣ *n, pl* **–lies** 1 country, person, or group with an agreement to support another. ◆ *v* **–lying, –lied** 2 **ally oneself with** join as an ally. **allied** *adj*

almanac *n* yearly calendar with detailed information on anniversaries, phases of the moon, etc.

almighty ⓣ *adj* 1 having absolute power. 2 *Informal* very great. ◆ *n* 3 **the Almighty** God.

almond *n* edible oval–shaped nut which grows on a small tree.

almost ⓣ *adv* very nearly.

aloft *adv* 1 in the air. 2 in a ship's rigging.

alone ⓣ *adj, adv* without anyone or anything else.

══════ THESAURUS ══════

league, pact, treaty

allocate *v* = **assign**, allot, allow, apportion, budget, designate, earmark, mete, set aside, share out

allot *v* = **assign**, allocate, apportion, budget, designate, earmark, mete, set aside, share out

allow *v* 1 = **permit**, approve, authorize, enable, endure, let, sanction, stand, suffer, tolerate 2 = **set aside**, allocate, allot, assign, give, grant, provide, spare 3 = **acknowledge**, admit, concede, confess, grant, own

alloy *n* 1 = **mixture**, admixture, amalgam, blend, combination, composite, compound, hybrid ◆ *v* 2 = **mix**, amalgamate, blend, combine, compound, fuse

allude *v* (foll. by *to*) = **refer**, hint, imply, intimate, mention, suggest, touch upon

allure *n* 1 = **attractiveness**, appeal,

attraction, charm, enchantment, enticement, glamour, lure, persuasion, seductiveness, temptation ◆ *v* 2 = **attract**, captivate, charm, enchant, entice, lure, persuade, seduce, tempt, win over

ally *n* 1 = **partner**, accomplice, associate, cobber (*Aust or old–fashioned NZ inf*), collaborator, colleague, friend, helper ≠ **rival** ◆ *v* 2 **ally oneself with** = **unite with**, associate with, collaborate with, combine with, join forces with, join with

almighty *adj* 1 = **all–powerful**, absolute, invincible, omnipotent, supreme, unlimited ≠ **weak** 2 *Inf* = **great**, enormous, excessive, intense, loud, severe, terrible ≠ **poor**

almost *adv* = **nearly**, about, approximately, close to, just about, not quite, on the brink of, practically, virtually

alone *adj* = **by oneself**, apart, detached, isolated, lonely, only, on one's tod (*sl*),

along prep 1 over part or all the length of.
♦ adv 2 forward. 3 in company with
others. **alongside** prep, adv beside
(something).

aloof ❶ adj distant or haughty in manner.
aloofness n
aloud ❶ adv in an audible voice.
alphabet n set of letters used in writing a
language. **alphabetical** adj in the
conventional order of the letters of an
alphabet. **alphabetically** adv **alphabetize** v
put in alphabetical order.
already ❶ adv 1 before the present time. 2
sooner than expected.
Alsatian n large wolflike dog.
also ❶ adv in addition, too. **also-ran** n
loser in a race, competition, or election.
altar n 1 table used for Communion in
Christian churches. 2 raised structure on
which sacrifices are offered and religious
rites are performed. **altarpiece** n work of
art above and behind the altar in some
Christian churches.

alter ❶ v make or become different.
alteration n
altercation n heated argument.
alternate ❶ v 1 (cause to) occur by turns.
♦ adj 2 occurring by turns. 3 every second
(one) of a series. **alternately** adv
alternative n one of two choices.
alternator n electric generator for
producing alternating current. **alternating
current** electric current that reverses
direction at frequent regular intervals.
although ❶ conj despite the fact that.
altitude n height above sea level.
alto n, pl –tos Music 1 short for CONTRALTO. 2
(singer with) the highest adult male voice.
3 instrument with the second-highest
pitch in its group.
altogether ❶ adv 1 entirely. 2 on the
whole. 3 in total.
altruism n unselfish concern for the
welfare of others. **altruistic** adj
aluminium n Chem light silvery-white
metal that does not rust.
always ❶ adv 1 at all times. 2 for ever.
am v see BE.
a.m. ante meridiem: before noon.
amalgamate ❶ v combine or unite.
amalgamation n

———————————— THESAURUS ————————

separate, single, solitary, unaccompanied
≠ **accompanied**
aloof adj = **distant**, detached, haughty,
remote, standoffish, supercilious,
unapproachable, unfriendly
aloud adv = **out loud**, audibly, clearly,
distinctly, intelligibly, plainly
already adv 1 = **before now**, at present,
before, by now, by then, even now,
heretofore, just now, previously
also adv = **too**, additionally, and, as well,
besides, further, furthermore, in addition,
into the bargain, moreover, to boot
alter v = **change**, adapt, adjust, amend,
convert, modify, reform, revise, transform,
turn, vary
alternate v 1 = **change**, act reciprocally,
fluctuate, interchange, oscillate, rotate,
substitute, take turns ♦ adj 3 = **every**

other, alternating, every second
although conj = **though**, albeit, despite the
fact that, even if, even though,
notwithstanding, while
altogether adv 1 = **completely**, absolutely,
fully, perfectly, quite, thoroughly, totally,
utterly, wholly ≠ **relatively** 2 = **on the
whole**, all in all, all things considered, as a
whole, collectively, generally, in general
3 = **in total**, all told, everything included,
in all, in sum, taken together
always adv 1 = **continually**, consistently,
constantly, every time, invariably,
perpetually, repeatedly, twenty-four-
seven (inf), without exception ≠ **hardly**
2 = **forever**, eternally, evermore
amalgamate v = **combine**, ally, blend,
fuse, incorporate, integrate, merge,
mingle, unite

amass ❶ *v* collect or accumulate.

amateur ❶ *n* 1 person who engages in a sport or activity as a pastime rather than as a profession. 2 person unskilled in something. ◆ *adj* 3 not professional. **amateurish** *adj* lacking skill.

amaze ❶ *v* surprise greatly, astound. **amazing** *adj* **amazement** *n*

ambassador ❶ *n* senior diplomat who represents his or her country in another country. **ambassadorial** *adj*

amber *n* 1 clear yellowish fossil resin. ◆ *adj* 2 brownish–yellow.

ambidextrous *adj* able to use both hands with equal ease.

ambience *n* atmosphere of a place.

ambiguous ❶ *adj* having more than one possible meaning. **ambiguity** *n*

ambition ❶ *n* 1 desire for success. 2 something so desired, goal. **ambitious** *adj*

ambivalence *n* state of feeling two conflicting emotions at the same time. **ambivalent** *adj*

amble ❶ *v* 1 walk at a leisurely pace. ◆ *n* 2 leisurely walk or pace.

ambulance *n* motor vehicle designed to carry sick or injured people.

ambush ❶ *n* 1 act of waiting in a concealed position to make a surprise attack. 2 attack from a concealed position. ◆ *v* 3 attack from a concealed position.

ameliorate [am–**meal**–yor–rate] *v* make (something) better. **amelioration** *n*

amen *interj* so be it: used at the end of a prayer.

amenable ❶ *adj* likely or willing to cooperate.

amend ❶ *v* make small changes to correct or improve (something). **amendment** *n*

amenity ❶ *n, pl* **–ties** useful or enjoyable feature.

amiable ❶ *adj* friendly, pleasant–natured. **amiably** *adv*

amicable ❶ *adj* friendly. **amicably** *adv*

amid ❶ **amidst** *prep* in the middle of, among. **amidships** *adv* at or towards the middle of a ship.

> ✓ **WORD TIP**
> The meaning of *amid* overlaps with that of *among*, but the form *amidst* is old-fashioned. Nowadays use *amid* or *among*.

——————————| THESAURUS |——————————

amass *v* = **collect**, accumulate, assemble, compile, gather, hoard, pile up

amateur *n* 1 = **nonprofessional**, dabbler, dilettante, layman

amaze *v* = **astonish**, alarm, astound, bewilder, dumbfound, shock, stagger, startle, stun, surprise

ambassador *n* = **representative**, agent, consul, deputy, diplomat, envoy, legate, minister

ambiguous *adj* = **unclear**, dubious, enigmatic, equivocal, inconclusive, indefinite, indeterminate, obscure, vague

ambition *n* 1 = **enterprise**, aspiration, desire, drive, eagerness, longing, striving, yearning, zeal 2 = **goal**, aim, aspiration, desire, dream, hope, intent, objective, purpose, wish

amble *v* 1 = **stroll**, dawdle, meander, mosey (*inf*), ramble, saunter, walk, wander

ambush *n* 1 = **trap**, lying in wait, waylaying ◆ *v* 3 = **trap**, attack, bushwhack (*US*), ensnare, surprise, waylay

amenable *adj* = **receptive**, able to be influenced, acquiescent, agreeable, compliant, open, persuadable, responsive, susceptible

amend *v* = **change**, alter, correct, fix, improve, mend, modify, reform, remedy, repair, revise

amenity *n* = **facility**, advantage, comfort, convenience, service

amiable *adj* = **pleasant**, affable, agreeable, charming, congenial, engaging, friendly, genial, likable *or* likeable, lovable

amicable *adj* = **friendly**, amiable, civil, cordial, courteous, harmonious, neighbourly, peaceful, sociable

amid, amidst *prep* = **in the middle of**, among, amongst, in the midst of, in the

amiss ⊕ *adv* 1 wrongly, badly. ♦ *adj* 2 wrong, faulty. **take something amiss** be offended by something.

ammonia *n* 1 strong–smelling alkaline gas containing hydrogen and nitrogen. 2 solution of this in water.

ammunition ⊕ *n* 1 bullets, bombs, and shells that can be fired from or as a weapon. 2 facts that can be used in an argument.

amnesia *n* loss of memory. **amnesiac** *adj, n*

amnesty ⊕ *n, pl* **–ties** general pardon for offences against a government.

amniotic fluid *n* fluid surrounding a fetus in the womb.

amoeba [am–**mee**–ba] *n, pl* **–hae, –bas** microscopic single–celled animal able to change its shape.

amok ⊕ *adv* **run amok** run about in a violent frenzy.

among ⊕ **amongst** *prep* 1 in the midst of. 2 in the group or number of. 3 to each of, e.g. *divide it among yourselves*.

> ✓ **WORD TIP**
> *Among* is generally used when more than two things are mentioned: *It's hard to choose among friends.* The form *amongst* is rather old–fashioned.

amoral [aim–**mor**–ral] *adj* without moral standards.

> ✓ **WORD TIP**
> *Amoral* should not be confused with *immoral*, 'acting contrary to moral standards'.

amorous ⊕ *adj* feeling, showing, or relating to sexual love.

amorphous *adj* without distinct shape.

amount ⊕ *n* 1 extent or quantity. ♦ *v* 2 (foll. by *to*) be equal or add up to.

amp *n* 1 ampere. 2 *Informal* amplifier.

ampere [**am**–pair] *n* basic unit of electric current.

ampersand *n* the character (&), meaning *and*.

> ✓ **WORD TIP**
> It is best to avoid using an *ampersand* (&) to replace the word *and* in formal writing.

amphibian *n* 1 animal that lives on land but breeds in water. 2 vehicle that can travel on both land and water. **amphibious** *adj* living or operating both on land and in water.

amphitheatre *n* open oval or circular building with tiers of seats rising round an arena.

ample ⊕ *adj* 1 more than sufficient. 2 large. **amply** *adv*

amplify ⊕ *v* **–fying, –fied** 1 increase the

—————————— THESAURUS ——————————

thick of, surrounded by

amiss *adv* 1 = **wrongly**, erroneously, improperly, inappropriately, incorrectly, mistakenly, unsuitably ♦ *adj* 2 = **wrong**, awry, faulty, incorrect, mistaken, untoward ≠ **right**

ammunition *n* 1 = **munitions**, armaments, explosives, powder, rounds, shells, shot

amnesty *n* = **general pardon**, absolution, dispensation, forgiveness, immunity, remission (*of penalty*), reprieve

amok *adv* **run amok** = **madly**, berserk, destructively, ferociously, in a frenzy,

murderously, savagely, uncontrollably, violently, wildly

among, amongst *prep* 1 = **in the midst of**, amid, amidst, in the middle of, in the thick of, surrounded by, together with, with 2 = **in the group of**, in the class of, in the company of, in the number of, out of 3 = **to each of**, between

amorous *adj* = **loving**, erotic, impassioned, in love, lustful, passionate, tender

amount *n* 1 = **quantity**, expanse, extent, magnitude, mass, measure, number, supply, volume ♦ *v* 2 (foll. by *to*) = **add up to**, become, come to, develop into, equal, strength of (a current or sound signal). **2** explain in more detail. **3** increase the size or effect of. **amplification** *n* **amplifier** *n* device used to amplify a current or sound signal.

amplitude *n* greatness of extent.

amputate ❶ *v* cut off (a limb or part of a limb) for medical reasons. **amputation** *n*

amulet *n* something carried or worn as a protection against evil.

amuse ❶ *v* **1** cause to laugh or smile. **2** entertain or divert. **amusing** *adj* **amusement** *n* **1** state of being amused. **2** something that amuses.

an *adj* form of **a** used before vowels, and sometimes before *h*.

> ✓ **WORD TIP**
>
> This form of the indefinite article is also used with abbreviations which have a vowel sound when read aloud: *an MA*. It is old–fashioned to use *an* before words like *hotel* or *historic*.

---

anachronism [an–**nak**–kron–iz–zum] *n* person or thing placed in the wrong historical period or seeming to belong to another time. **anachronistic** *adj*

anaconda *n* large S American snake which kills by constriction.

anaemia [an–**neem**–ee–a] *n* deficiency in the number of red blood cells. **anaemic** *adj* **1** having anaemia. **2** pale and sickly. **3** lacking vitality.

anaesthetic ❶ [an–niss–**thet**–ik] *n, adj* (substance) causing loss of bodily feeling. **anaesthesia** [an–niss–**theez**–ee–a] *n* loss of bodily feeling. **anaesthetist** [an–**neess**–thet–ist] *n* doctor trained to administer anaesthetics. **anaesthetize** *v*

anagram *n* word or phrase made by rearranging the letters of another word or phrase.

anal [**ain**–al] *adj* of the anus.

analgesic [an–nal–**jeez**–ik] *n, adj* (drug) relieving pain. **analgesia** *n* absence of pain.

analogy ❶ *n, pl* **–gies 1** similarity in some respects. **2** comparison made to show such a similarity. **analogical** *adj*

analysis ❶ *n, pl* **–ses 1** separation of a whole into its parts for study and interpretation. **2** psychoanalysis. **analyse** *v* **1** make an analysis of (something). **2** psychoanalyse. **analyst** *n* person skilled in analysis. **analytical, analytic** *adj* **analytically** *adv*

anarchy ❶ [**an**–ark–ee] *n* **1** lawlessness and disorder. **2** lack of government in a state. **anarchic** *adj*

anathema [an–**nath**–im–a] *n* detested person or thing.

anatomy ❶ *n, pl* **–mies 1** science of the structure of the body. **2** physical structure. **3** person's body. **4** detailed analysis. **anatomical** *adj* **anatomically** *adv*

————————| THESAURUS |————————

mean, total

ample *adj* **1** = **plenty**, abundant, bountiful, copious, expansive, extensive, full, generous, lavish, plentiful, profuse ≠ **little**

amplify *v* **2** = **go into detail**, develop, elaborate, enlarge, expand, explain, flesh out ≠ **simplify 3** = **expand**, enlarge, extend, heighten, increase, intensify, magnify, strengthen, widen ≠ **reduce**

amputate *v* = **cut off**, curtail, lop, remove, separate, sever, truncate

amuse *v* **2** = **entertain**, charm, cheer, delight, interest, please ≠ **bore**

① **anaesthetic** *n* = **painkiller**, analgesic,

anodyne, narcotic, opiate, sedative, soporific

② **anaesthetic** *adj* = **pain–killing**, analgesic, anodyne, deadening, dulling, numbing, sedative, soporific

analogy *n* **1** = **similarity**, correlation, correspondence, likeness, parallel, relation, resemblance **2** = **comparison**

analysis *n* **1** = **examination**, breakdown, dissection, inquiry, investigation, scrutiny, sifting, test

anarchy *n* **1** = **lawlessness**, chaos, confusion, disorder, disorganization, revolution, riot anatomist *n* expert in anatomy.

ancestor ❶ *n* 1 person from whom one is descended. 2 forerunner. ancestral *adj* ancestry *n* lineage or descent.

anchor *n* 1 heavy hooked device attached to a boat by a cable and dropped overboard to fasten the ship to the sea bottom. ◆ *v* 2 fasten with or as if with an anchor. anchorage *n* place where boats can be anchored. anchorman, anchorwoman *n* 1 broadcaster in a central studio who presents items from outside cameras and other studios. 2 last person to compete in a relay team.

anchovy [an-chov-ee] *n, pl* -vies small strong-tasting fish.

ancient *adj* 1 dating from very long ago. 2 very old.

ancillary ❶ *adj* 1 supporting the main work of an organization. 2 used as an extra or supplement.

and ❶ *conj* 1 in addition to. 2 as a consequence. 3 then, afterwards.

✔ **WORD TIP**

Avoid using *and/or* where *or* alone will do. Its use generally suggests commercial and official correspondence.

---

andante [an-dan-tay] *n, adv Music* (piece to be played) moderately slowly.

androgynous *adj* having both male and female characteristics.

android *n* robot resembling a human.

anecdote ❶ *n* short amusing account of an incident. anecdotal *adj*

anemia *n US* anaemia

anemone [an-nem-on-ee] *n* plant with white, purple, or red flowers.

anew *adv* 1 once more. 2 in a different way.

angel ❶ *n* 1 spiritual being believed to be an attendant or messenger of God. 2 person who is kind, pure, or beautiful. angelic *adj* angelically *adv*

anger ❶ *n* 1 fierce displeasure or extreme annoyance. ◆ *v* 2 make (someone) angry.

angina [an-jine-a] *n* heart disorder causing sudden severe chest pains (also angina pectoris).

angle¹ ❶ *n* 1 space between or shape formed by two lines or surfaces that meet. 2 divergence between these, measured in degrees. 3 corner. 4 point of view. ◆ *v* 5 bend or place (something) at an angle.

angle² ❶ *v* 1 fish with a hook and line. 2 (foll. by *for*) try to get by hinting. angler *n* angling *n*

Anglican *n, adj* (member) of the Church of

---

anatomy *n* 2 = **structure**, build, composition, frame, framework, make-up 4 = **examination**, analysis, dissection, division, inquiry, investigation, study

ancestor *n* = **forefather**, forebear, forerunner, precursor, predecessor ≠ **successor**

ancient *adj* = **old**, aged, antique, archaic, old-fashioned, primeval, primordial, timeworn ≠ **new**

ancillary *adj* 1 = **supporting**, auxiliary, secondary, subordinate, subsidiary 2 = **supplementary**, additional, extra

and *conj* 1 = **also**, along with, as well as, furthermore, in addition to, including, moreover, plus, together with

anecdote *n* = **story**, reminiscence, short

story, sketch, tale, urban legend, urban myth, yarn

angel *n* 1 = **divine messenger**, archangel, cherub, seraph 2 = **dear**, beauty, darling, gem, jewel, paragon, saint, treasure

anger *n* 1 = **rage**, annoyance, displeasure, exasperation, fury, ire, outrage, resentment, temper, wrath ≠ **liking** ◆ *v* 2 = **enrage**, annoy, displease, exasperate, gall, incense, infuriate, madden, outrage, rile, vex ≠ **please**

angle¹ *n* 1 = **intersection**, bend, crook, elbow, nook 2 = **corner**, edge, point 4 = **point of view**, approach, aspect, outlook, perspective, position, side, slant, standpoint, viewpoint

angle² *v* 1 = **fish**, cast

England.

Anglo– *combining form* 1 English, e.g. *Anglo–Scottish.* 2 British, e.g. *Anglo–American.*

angora *n* 1 variety of goat, cat, or rabbit with long silky hair. 2 hair of the angora goat or rabbit. 3 cloth made from this hair.

anguish ⊕ *n* great mental pain. **anguished** *adj*

angular *adj* 1 (of a person) lean and bony. 2 having angles. 3 measured by an angle. **angularity** *n*

animal ⊕ *n* 1 living creature with specialized sense organs and capable of voluntary motion, esp. one other than a human being. 2 quadruped. ◆ *adj* 3 of animals. 4 sensual, physical.

animate ⊕ *v* 1 give life to. 2 make lively. 3 make a cartoon film of. ◆ *adj* 4 having life. **animated** *adj* **animation** *n* 1 technique of making cartoon films. 2 liveliness and enthusiasm. **animator** *n*

animosity ⊕ *n, pl* –ties hostility, hatred.

animus *n* hatred, animosity.

aniseed *n* liquorice–flavoured seeds of the anise plant.

ankle *n* joint between the foot and leg. **anklet** *n* ornamental chain worn round the ankle.

annals ⊕ *pl n* yearly records of events.

annex ⊕ *v* 1 seize (territory). 2 take (something) without permission. 3 join or add (something) to something larger. **annexation** *n*

annexe *n* 1 extension to a building. 2 nearby building used as an extension.

annihilate ⊕ *v* destroy utterly. **annihilation** *n*

anniversary *n, pl* –ries 1 date on which something occurred in a previous year. 2 celebration of this.

anno Domini *adv Latin* (indicating years numbered from the supposed year of the birth of Christ) in the year of our Lord.

annotate *v* add notes to (a written work). **annotation** *n*

announce ⊕ *v* 1 make known publicly. 2 proclaim. **announcement** *n* **announcer** *n* person who introduces radio or television programmes.

annoy ⊕ *v* irritate or displease. **annoyance** *n*

annual ⊕ *adj* 1 happening once a year. 2 lasting for a year. ◆ *n* 3 plant that completes its life cycle in a year. 4 book published once every year. **annually** *adv*

annul ⊕ *v* –nulling, –nulled declare (something, esp. a marriage) invalid. **annulment** *n*

──────┤ T H E S A U R U S ├──────

anguish *n* = **suffering**, agony, distress, grief, heartache, misery, pain, sorrow, torment, woe

animal *n* 2 = **creature**, beast, brute ◆ *adj* 4 = **physical**, bestial, bodily, brutish, carnal, gross, sensual

animate *v* 2 = **enliven**, energize, excite, fire, inspire, invigorate, kindle, move, stimulate ◆ *adj* 4 = **living**, alive, alive and kicking, breathing, live, moving

animosity *n* = **hostility**, acrimony, antipathy, bitterness, enmity, hatred, ill will, malevolence, malice, rancour, resentment

annals *pl n* = **records**, accounts, archives, chronicles, history

annex *v* 1 = **seize**, acquire, appropriate,

conquer, occupy, take over 3 = **join**, add, adjoin, attach, connect, fasten ≠ **remove**

annihilate *v* = **destroy**, abolish, eradicate, exterminate, extinguish, obliterate, wipe out

announce *v* = **make known**, advertise, broadcast, declare, disclose, proclaim, report, reveal, tell ≠ **hide**

annoy *v* = **irritate**, anger, displease, disturb, exasperate, get on one's nerves (*inf*), hassle (*inf*), madden, molest, pester, plague, trouble, vex

annual *adj* 1 = **yearly**, once a year 2 = **yearlong**

annul *v* = **invalidate**, abolish, cancel, declare *or* render null and void, negate, nullify, repeal, retract

anodyne n 1 something that relieves pain or distress. ♦ adj 2 relieving pain or distress.

anoint ❶ v smear with oil as a sign of consecration.

anomaly ❶ [an-**nom** a-lee] n, pl –lies something that deviates from the normal, irregularity. **anomalous** adj

anon. anonymous.

anonymous ❶ adj 1 by someone whose name is unknown or withheld. 2 having no known name. **anonymously** adv **anonymity** n

anorak n waterproof hooded jacket.

anorexia n psychological disorder characterized by fear of becoming fat and refusal to eat (also **anorexia nervosa**). **anorexic** adj, n

another adj, pron 1 one more. 2 a different (one).

answer ❶ n 1 reply to a question, request, letter, etc. 2 solution to a problem. 3 reaction or response. ♦ v 4 give an answer (to). 5 be responsible to (a person). 6 respond or react. **answerable** adj (foll. by for or to) responsible for or accountable to. **answering machine** device for answering a telephone automatically and recording messages.

ant n small insect living in highly organized colonies. **anteater** n mammal which feeds on ants by means of a long snout.

antagonist ❶ n opponent or adversary. **antagonism** n open opposition or hostility. **antagonistic** adj **antagonize** v arouse hostility in, annoy.

Antarctic n 1 the Antarctic area around the South Pole. ♦ adj 2 of this region.

ante– prefix before in time or position, e.g. antedate, antechamber.

antecedent n 1 event or circumstance happening or existing before another. ♦ adj 2 preceding, prior.

antelope n deerlike mammal with long legs and horns.

antenatal adj during pregnancy, before birth.

antenna n 1 (pl –nae) insect's feeler. 2 (pl –nas) aerial.

anterior adj 1 to the front. 2 earlier.

anthem ❶ n 1 song of loyalty, esp. to a country. 2 piece of music for a choir, usu. set to words from the Bible.

anther n part of a flower's stamen containing pollen.

anthology ❶ n, pl –gies collection of poems or other literary pieces by various authors.

anthracite n hard coal burning slowly with little smoke or flame but intense heat.

anthrax n dangerous disease of cattle and sheep, communicable to humans.

anthropoid adj 1 like a human. ♦ n 2 ape, such as a chimpanzee, that resembles a human.

anthropology n study of human origins, institutions, and beliefs. **anthropological** adj **anthropologist** n

anti– prefix 1 against, opposed to, e.g. anti–war. 2 opposite to, e.g. anticlimax 3 counteracting, e.g. antifreeze.

antibiotic n 1 chemical substance capable

——— THESAURUS ———

anoint v = **consecrate**, bless, hallow, sanctify

anomaly n = **irregularity**, abnormality, eccentricity, exception, incongruity, inconsistency, oddity, peculiarity

anonymous adj 1 = **uncredited**, unacknowledged, unknown, unsigned ≠ **signed** 2 = **unnamed**, incognito, nameless, unidentified ≠ **known**

answer n 1 = **reply**, comeback, defence, rejoinder, response, retort, return, riposte

≠ **question** 2 = **solution**, explanation 3 = **reaction**, response ♦ v 4 = **reply**, respond, retort, return ≠ **ask** 6 = **react**, respond

antagonist n = **opponent**, adversary, competitor, contender, enemy, foe, rival

anthem n 1 = **song of praise**, paean 2 = **hymn**, canticle, carol, chant, chorale, psalm

anthology n = **collection**, compendium, compilation, miscellany, selection, treasury of destroying bacteria. ◆ adj 2 of antibiotics.

antibody n, pl **–bodies** protein produced in the blood, which destroys bacteria.

anticipate ❶ v 1 foresee and act in advance of. 2 look forward to. **anticipation** n

anticlimax ❶ n disappointing conclusion to a series of events.

anticlockwise adv, adj in the opposite direction to the rotation of the hands of a clock.

antics ❶ pl n absurd acts or postures.

anticyclone n area of moving air of high pressure in which the winds rotate outwards.

antidote ❶ n substance that counteracts a poison.

antifreeze n liquid added to water to lower its freezing point, used in car radiators.

antihistamine n drug used to treat allergies.

antimony n Chem brittle silvery–white metallic element.

antipathy ❶ [an–**tip**–a–thee] n dislike, hostility. **antipathetic** adj

antiperspirant n substance used to reduce or prevent sweating.

antipodes [an–**tip**–pod–deez] pl n any two places diametrically opposite one another

on the earth's surface. **the Antipodes** Australia and New Zealand. **antipodean** adj

antique ❶ n 1 object of an earlier period, valued for its beauty, workmanship, or age. ◆ adj 2 made in an earlier period. 3 old–fashioned.

antiseptic ❶ adj 1 preventing infection by killing germs. ◆ n 2 antiseptic substance.

antisocial ❶ adj 1 avoiding the company of other people. 2 (of behaviour) harmful to society.

antithesis ❶ [an–**tith**–iss–iss] n, pl **–ses** [–seez] 1 exact opposite. 2 placing together of contrasting ideas or words to produce an effect of balance. **antithetical** adj

antitrust adj Aust, S Afr & US (of laws) opposing business monopolies.

antler n branched horn of male deer.

antonym n word that means the opposite of another.

anus [**ain**–uss] n opening at the end of the alimentary canal, through which faeces are discharged.

anvil n heavy iron block on which metals are hammered into particular shapes.

anxious ❶ adj 1 worried and tense. 2 intensely desiring. **anxiety** n **anxiously** adv

any adj, pron 1 one or some, no matter which. ◆ adv 2 at all, e.g. it isn't any worse. **anybody** pron anyone. **anyhow** adv

───────┤ THESAURUS ├───────

anticipate v 1 = **expect**, await, foresee, foretell, predict, prepare for 2 = **look forward to**, hope for

anticlimax n = **disappointment**, bathos, comedown (inf), letdown

antics pl n = **clowning**, escapades, horseplay, mischief, playfulness, pranks, tomfoolery, tricks

antidote n = **cure**, countermeasure, remedy

antipathy n = **hostility**, aversion, bad blood, dislike, enmity, hatred, ill will

antique n 1 = **period piece**, bygone, heirloom, relic ◆ adj 2 = **vintage**, antiquarian, classic, olden 3 = **old–fashioned**, archaic, obsolete, outdated

antiseptic adj 1 = **hygienic**, clean, germ–free, pure, sanitary, sterile, uncontaminated ≠ **dirty** ◆ n 2 = **disinfectant**, germicide, purifier

antisocial adj 1 = **unsociable**, alienated, misanthropic, reserved, retiring, uncommunicative, unfriendly, withdrawn ≠ **social** 2 = **disruptive**, antagonistic, belligerent, disorderly, hostile, menacing, rebellious, uncooperative

antithesis n 1 = **opposite**, contrary, contrast, converse, inverse, reverse

anxious adj 1 = **uneasy**, apprehensive, concerned, fearful, in suspense, nervous, on tenterhooks, tense, troubled, worried ≠ **certain** 2 = **eager**, desirous, impatient, anyway. **anyone** *pron* **1** any person. **2** person of any importance. **anything** *pron* **anyway** *adv* **1** at any rate, nevertheless. **2** in any manner. **anywhere** *adv* in, at, or to any place.

✓ WORD TIP

It is acceptable to use *anyone* with a following plural form as in *Has anyone lost their purse?*.

---

aorta [eh–**or**-ta] *n* main artery of the body, carrying oxygen–rich blood from the heart.

apace *adv Lit* swiftly.

apart ❶ *adv* **1** to or in pieces. **2** to or at a distance. **3** individual, distinct.

apartheid *n* former official government policy of racial segregation in S Africa.

apartment ❶ *n* **1** room in a building. **2** flat.

apathy ❶ *n* lack of interest or enthusiasm. **apathetic** *adj*

ape *n* **1** tailless monkey such as the chimpanzee or gorilla. **2** stupid, clumsy, or ugly man. ◆ *v* **3** imitate.

aperitif [ap–per–rit–**teef**] *n* alcoholic drink taken before a meal.

aperture *n* opening or hole.

apex ❶ *n* highest point.

aphid [**eh**–fid], **aphis** [**eh**–fiss] *n* small insect which sucks the sap from plants.

aphorism *n* short clever saying expressing a general truth.

aphrodisiac [af–roh–**diz**–zee–ak] *n* **1** substance that arouses sexual desire. ◆ *adj* **2** arousing sexual desire.

apiece ❶ *adv* each.

aplomb ❶ *n* calm self-possession.

apocalypse *n* **1** end of the world. **2** event of great destruction. **the Apocalypse** book of Revelation, the last book of the New Testament. **apocalyptic** *adj*

apocryphal ❶ *adj* (of a story) of questionable authenticity.

apology ❶ *n*, *pl* –**gies 1** expression of regret for wrongdoing. **2** (foll. by *for*) poor example (of). **3** **apologetic** *adj* showing or expressing regret. **apologetically** *adv* **apologist** *n* person who formally defends a cause. **apologize** *v* make an apology.

apoplexy *n Med* stroke. **apoplectic** *adj* **1** of apoplexy. **2** *Informal* furious.

Apostle ❶ *n* **1** one of the twelve disciples chosen by Christ to preach his gospel. **2** (a–) ardent supporter of a cause or movement. **apostolic** *adj*

apostrophe [ap–**poss**–trof–fee] *n* **1** punctuation mark (') showing the omission of a letter or letters in a word, e.g. *don't*, or forming the possessive, e.g. *Jill's car*. **2** digression from a speech to

---

intent, itching, keen, yearning ≠ **reluctant**

apart *adv* **1** = **to pieces**, asunder, in bits, in pieces, to bits **2** = **separate**, alone, aside, away, by oneself, isolated, to one side

apartment *n* **1** = **room**, accommodation, living quarters, quarters, rooms, suite **2** = **flat**, penthouse

apathy *n* = **lack of interest**, coolness, indifference, inertia, nonchalance, passivity, torpor, unconcern

apex *n* = **highest point**, crest, crown, culmination, peak, pinnacle, point, summit, top ≠ **base**

apiece *adv* = **each**, for each, from each, individually, respectively, separately, to each

aplomb *n* = **self-possession**, calmness, composure, confidence, level–headedness, poise, sang–froid, self–assurance, self–confidence

apocryphal *adj* = **dubious**, doubtful, legendary, mythical, questionable, unauthenticated, unsubstantiated

apology *n* **1** = **defence**, acknowledgment, confession, excuse, explanation, justification, plea **2** (foll. by *for*) = **mockery**, caricature, excuse, imitation, travesty

Apostle *n* **1** = **evangelist**, herald, messenger, missionary, preacher **2** (not cap.) = **supporter**, advocate, champion, pioneer, propagandist, proponent address an imaginary or absent person or thing. **apostrophize** *v* address an apostrophe to.

appal ❶ *v* **–palling, –palled** dismay, terrify. **appalling** *adj* dreadful, terrible.

apparatus ❶ *n* equipment for a particular purpose.

apparel *n Old–fashioned* clothing.

apparent ❶ *adj* **1** readily seen, obvious. **2** seeming as opposed to real. **apparently** *adv*

apparition ❶ *n* ghost or ghostlike figure.

appeal ❶ *v* **1** make an earnest request. **2** attract, please, or interest. **3** request a review of a lower court's decision by a higher court. ♦ *n* **4** earnest request. **5** attractiveness. **6** request for a review of a lower court's decision by a higher court. **appealing** *adj*

appear ❶ *v* **1** become visible or present. **2** seem. **3** be seen in public. **appearance** *n* **1** an appearing. **2** outward aspect.

appease ❶ *v* **1** pacify (a person) by yielding to his or her demands. **2** satisfy or relieve (a feeling). **appeasement** *n*

append *v* join on, add. **appendage** *n* thing joined on or added.

appendicitis *n* inflammation of the appendix.

appendix ❶ *n, pl* **–dices, –dixes 1** separate additional material at the end of a book. **2** *Anat* short closed tube attached to the large intestine.

✓ **WORD TIP**

Extra sections at the end of a book are *appendices*. The plural *appendixes* is used in medicine.

---

appertain *v* (foll. by *to*) **1** belong to. **2** be connected with.

appetite ❶ *n* **1** desire for food or drink. **2** liking or willingness. **appetizer** *n* thing eaten or drunk to stimulate the appetite. **appetizing** *adj* stimulating the appetite.

applaud ❶ *v* **1** show approval of by clapping one's hands. **2** approve strongly. **applause** *n* approval shown by clapping one's hands.

apple *n* round firm fleshy fruit that grows on trees. **in apple–pie order** *Informal* very tidy.

appliance ❶ *n* device with a specific function.

THESAURUS

---

appal *v* = **horrify**, alarm, daunt, dishearten, dismay, frighten, outrage, shock, unnerve

apparatus *n* = **equipment**, appliance, contraption (*inf*), device, gear, machinery, mechanism, tackle, tools

apparent *adj* **1** = **obvious**, discernible, distinct, evident, manifest, marked, unmistakable, visible ≠ **uncertain 2** = **seeming**, ostensible, outward, superficial ≠ **real**

apparition *n* = **ghost**, chimera, phantom, spectre, spirit, wraith

appeal *v* **1** = **plead**, ask, beg, call upon, entreat, pray, request ≠ **refuse 2** = **attract**, allure, charm, entice, fascinate, interest, please, tempt ♦ *n* **4** = **plea**, application, entreaty, petition, prayer, request, supplication ≠ **refusal 5** = **attraction**, allure, beauty, charm, fascination ≠ **repulsiveness**

appear *v* **1** = **come into view**, be present, come out, come to light, crop up (*inf*), emerge, occur, show up (*inf*), surface, turn up ≠ **disappear 2** = **look (like** or **as if)**, occur, seem, strike one as

appease *v* **1** = **pacify**, calm, conciliate, mollify, placate, quiet, satisfy, soothe ≠ **upset 2** = **ease**, allay, alleviate, calm, relieve, soothe

appendix *n* **1** = **supplement**, addendum, addition, adjunct, appendage, postscript

appetite *n* **1** = **desire**, craving, demand, hunger, relish, stomach, taste ≠ **disgust 2** = **liking**, longing, passion, yearning

applaud *v* **1** = **clap**, cheer ≠ **pan** (*inf*) **2** = **approve**, acclaim, commend, compliment, encourage, extol, praise ≠ **blast**

appliance *n* = **device**, apparatus, gadget, implement, instrument, machine,

apply ⓥ v **–plying, –plied 1** make a formal request. **2** put to practical use. **3** put onto a surface. **4** be relevant or appropriate. **apply oneself** concentrate one's efforts. **applicant** n **application** n formal request. **applied** adj (of a skill, science, etc.) put to practical use.

appoint ⓥ v **1** assign to a job or position. **2** fix or decide, e.g. *appoint a time*. **3** equip or furnish. **appointment** n **1** arrangement to meet a person. **2** act of placing someone in a job. **3** the job itself. ◆ pl **4** fixtures or fittings.

apportion ⓥ v divide out in shares.

apposite ⓥ adj suitable, apt. **apposition** n grammatical construction in which two nouns or phrases referring to the same thing are placed one after another without a conjunction, e.g. *my son the doctor*.

appraise ⓥ v estimate the value or quality of. **appraisal** n

appreciate ⓥ v **1** value highly. **2** be aware of and understand. **3** be grateful for. **4** rise in value. **appreciable** adj enough to be noticed. **appreciably** adv **appreciation** n **appreciative** adj feeling or showing appreciation.

apprehend ⓥ v **1** arrest and take into custody. **2** grasp (something) mentally. **apprehension** n **1** dread, anxiety. **2** arrest. **3** understanding. **apprehensive** adj fearful or anxious.

apprentice ⓥ n **1** someone working for a skilled person for a fixed period in order to learn his or her trade. ◆ v **2** take or place (someone) as an apprentice. **apprenticeship** n

apprise v make aware (of).

approach ⓥ v **1** come near or nearer (to). **2** make a proposal or suggestion to. **3** begin to deal with (a matter). ◆ n **4** approaching or means of approaching. **5** approximation. **approachable** adj

approbation n approval.

mechanism, tool

apply v **1** = **request**, appeal, claim, inquire, petition, put in, requisition **2** = **use**, bring to bear, carry out, employ, exercise, exert, implement, practise, utilize **3** = **put on**, cover with, lay on, paint, place, smear, spread on **4** = **be relevant**, be applicable, be appropriate, bear upon, be fitting, fit, pertain, refer, relate

appoint v **1** = **assign**, choose, commission, delegate, elect, name, nominate, select ≠ **fire 2** = **decide**, allot, arrange, assign, choose, designate, establish, fix, set ≠ **cancel 3** = **equip**, fit out, furnish, provide, supply

apportion v = **divide**, allocate, allot, assign, dispense, distribute, dole out, give out, ration out, share

apposite adj = **appropriate**, applicable, apt, fitting, pertinent, relevant, suitable, to the point

appraise v = **assess**, estimate, evaluate, gauge, judge, rate, review, value

appreciate v **1** = **value**, admire, enjoy, like, prize, rate highly, respect, treasure **2** = **be aware of**, perceive, realize, recognize, sympathize with, take account of, understand ≠ **misunderstand 3** = **be grateful for**, be appreciative, be indebted, be obliged, be thankful for, give thanks for ≠ **be ungrateful for 4** = **increase**, enhance, gain, grow, improve, rise ≠ **fall**

apprehend v **1** = **arrest**, capture, catch, nick (sl, chiefly Brit), seize, take prisoner ≠ **free 2** = **understand**, comprehend, conceive, get the picture, grasp, perceive, realize, recognize ≠ **miss**

apprentice n **1** = **trainee**, beginner, learner, novice, probationer, pupil, student

approach v **1** = **move towards**, come close, come near, draw near, near, reach **2** = **make a proposal to**, appeal to, apply to, make overtures to, sound out **3** = **set about**, begin work on, commence, embark on, enter upon, make a start, undertake ◆ n **4** = **coming**, advance, arrival, drawing near, nearing **5** = **proposal**, advance, appeal, application, invitation, offer, overture, proposition

appropriate ⊕ *adj* 1 suitable, fitting. ♦ *v* 2 take for oneself. 3 put aside for a particular purpose. **appropriately** *adv* **appropriateness** *n* **appropriation** *n*

approve ⊕ *v* 1 consider good or right. 2 authorize, agree to. **approval** *n* 1 consent. 2 favourable opinion. **on approval** (of goods) with an option to be returned without payment if unsatisfactory.

approx. approximate(ly).

approximate ⊕ *adj* 1 almost but not quite exact. ♦ *v* (foll. by *to*) 2 come close to. 3 be almost the same as. **approximately** *adv* **approximation** *n*

Apr. April.

après–ski [ap–ray–**skee**] *n* social activities after a day's skiing.

apricot *n* 1 yellowish–orange juicy fruit like a small peach. ♦ *adj* 2 yellowish–orange.

April *n* fourth month of the year. **April fool** victim of a practical joke played on April 1 (**April Fools' Day**).

apron ⊕ *n* 1 garment worn over the front of the body to protect the clothes. 2 area at an airport or hangar for manoeuvring and loading aircraft. 3 part of a stage in front of the curtain.

apropos [ap–prop–**poh**] *adj, adv* appropriate(ly). **apropos of** with regard to.

apt ⊕ *adj* 1 having a specified tendency. 2 suitable. 3 quick to learn. **aptly** *adv* **aptness** *n* aptitude = natural ability.

aqualung *n* mouthpiece attached to air cylinders, worn for underwater swimming.

aquamarine *n* 1 greenish–blue gemstone. ♦ *adj* 2 greenish–blue.

aquarium *n*, *pl* **aquariums**, **aquaria** 1 tank in which fish and other underwater creatures are kept. 2 building containing such tanks.

aquatic *adj* 1 living in or near water. 2 done in or on water. **aquatics** *pl n* water sports.

aqueduct *n* structure carrying water across a valley or river.

aquiline *adj* 1 (of a nose) curved like an eagle's beak. 2 of or like an eagle.

arable ⊕ *adj* suitable for growing crops on.

arbiter ⊕ *n* 1 person empowered to judge in a dispute. 2 person with influential opinions about something.

arboreal *adj* of or living in trees.

arc ⊕ *n* 1 part of a circle or other curve. 2 luminous discharge of electricity across a small gap between two electrodes. ♦ *v* 3 form an arc.

arcade ⊕ *n* 1 covered passageway lined with shops. 2 set of arches and their supporting columns.

THESAURUS

appropriate *adj* 1 = **suitable**, apt, befitting, fitting, pertinent, relevant, to the point, well–suited ≠ **irrelevant** ♦ *v* 2 = **seize**, commandeer, confiscate, embezzle, filch, impound, misappropriate, pilfer, pocket, steal, take possession of, usurp ≠ **give** 3 = **allocate**, allot, apportion, assign, devote, earmark, set aside ≠ **withhold**

approve *v* 1 = **favour**, admire, commend, have a good opinion of, like, praise, regard highly, respect 2 = **agree to**, allow, assent to, authorize, consent to, endorse, pass, permit, recommend, sanction

approximate *adj* 1 = **close**, estimated, inexact, loose, near, rough ≠ **specific** ♦ *v* (foll. by *to*) 2 = **come close**, approach,

border on, come near, reach, touch, verge on 3 = **resemble**

apron *n* 1 = **pinny** (*inf*), pinafore

apt *adj* 1 = **inclined**, disposed, given, liable, likely, of a mind, prone, ready 2 = **appropriate**, fitting, pertinent, relevant, suitable, to the point ≠ **irrelevant** 3 = **gifted**, clever, quick, sharp, smart, talented ≠ **slow**

arable *adj* = **productive**, farmable, fertile, fruitful

arbiter *n* 1 = **judge**, adjudicator, arbitrator, referee, umpire 2 = **authority**, controller, dictator, expert, governor, lord, mana (*NZ*), master, pundit, ruler

arc *n* 1 = **curve**, arch, bend, bow, crescent, half–moon

arcane ● *adj* mysterious and secret.

arch¹ ● *n* **1** curved structure supporting a bridge or roof. **2** something curved. **3** curved lower part of the foot. ♦ *v* **4** (cause to) form an arch. **archway** *n* passageway under an arch.

arch² ● *adj* **1** superior, knowing. **2** coyly playful.

arch– *combining form* chief, principal, e.g. *archenemy*.

archaeology *n* study of ancient cultures from their physical remains. **archaeological** *adj* **archaeologist** *n*

archaic ● [ark–**kay**–ik] *adj* **1** ancient. **2** out–of–date. **archaism** [ark–kay–iz–zum] *n* archaic word or phrase.

archbishop *n* chief bishop.

archetype ● [**ark**–ee–type] *n* **1** perfect specimen. **2** original model. **archetypal** *adj*

archipelago [ark–ee–**pel**–a–go] *n, pl* **–gos** **1** group of islands. **2** sea full of small islands.

architect ● *n* person qualified to design and supervise the construction of buildings. **architecture** *n* **1** style in which a building is designed and built. **2** designing and construction of buildings. **architectural** *adj*

Arctic ● *n* **1** the **Arctic** area around the North Pole. ♦ *adj* **2** of this region. **3** (a–) *Informal* very cold.

ardent ● *adj* **1** passionate. **2** eager, zealous. **ardently** *adv* **ardour** *n* **1** passion. **2** enthusiasm, zeal.

arduous ● *adj* hard to accomplish, strenuous.

are *v* see BE.

area ● *n* **1** part or region. **2** size of a two–dimensional surface. **3** subject field. **4** small sunken yard giving access to a basement.

arena ● *n* **1** seated enclosure for sports events. **2** area of a Roman amphitheatre where gladiators fought. **3** sphere of intense activity.

argon *n* Chem inert gas found in the air.

argue ● *v* **–guing, –gued 1** try to prove by giving reasons. **2** debate. **3** quarrel, dispute. **arguable** *adj* **arguably** *adv* **argument** *n* **1** quarrel. **2** discussion. **3** point presented for or against something. **argumentative** *adj* given to arguing.

————— THESAURUS —————

arcade *n* = **gallery**, cloister, colonnade, portico

arcane *adj* = **mysterious**, esoteric, hidden, occult, recondite, secret

arch¹ *n* **1** = **archway**, curve, dome, span, vault **2** = **curve**, arc, bend, bow, hump, semicircle ♦ *v* **4** = **curve**, arc, bend, bow, bridge, span

arch² *adj* **2** = **playful**, frolicsome, mischievous, pert, roguish, saucy, sly, waggish

archaic *adj* **1** = **old**, ancient, antique, bygone, olden (*arch*), primitive ≠ **new 2** = **old–fashioned**, antiquated, behind the times, obsolete, outmoded, out of date, passé ≠ **new**

archetype *n* **1** = **standard**, model, paradigm, pattern, prime example **2** = **original**, prototype

architect *n* = **designer**, master builder, planner

Arctic *adj* **2** = **polar**, far–northern, hyperborean **3** (not cap.) *Inf* = **freezing**, chilly, cold, frigid, frozen, glacial, icy

ardent *adj* **1** = **passionate**, amorous, hot–blooded, impassioned, intense, lusty ≠ **cold 2** = **enthusiastic**, avid, eager, keen, zealous ≠ **indifferent**

arduous *adj* = **difficult**, exhausting, fatiguing, gruelling, laborious, onerous, punishing, rigorous, strenuous, taxing, tiring

area *n* **1** = **region**, district, locality, neighbourhood, part, portion, section, sector, zone **3** = **field**, department, domain, province, realm, sphere, territory

arena *n* **1** = **ring**, bowl, enclosure, field, ground, stadium **2** = **amphitheatre 3** = **sphere**, area, domain, field, province, realm, sector, territory

argue *v* **1** = **maintain**, assert, claim, dispute, remonstrate **2** = **debate**, discuss,

aria [ah–ree–a] n elaborate song for solo voice, esp. one from an opera.
arid 🛈 adj 1 parched, dry. 2 uninteresting. **aridity** n
arise 🛈 v **arising, arose, arisen 1** come about. 2 come into notice. 3 get up.
aristocracy 🛈 n, pl **–cies 1** highest social class. 2 **aristocrat** n member of the aristocracy. **aristocratic** adj
arithmetic n 1 calculation by or of numbers. ◆ adj 2 of arithmetic. **arithmetical** adj **arithmetician** n
ark n 1 Old Testament boat built by Noah, which survived the Flood. 2 (**A–**) Judaism chest containing the writings of Jewish Law.
arm¹ 🛈 n 1 upper limb from the shoulder to the wrist. 2 sleeve of a garment. 3 side of a chair. **armful** n as much as can be held in the arms. **armchair** n upholstered chair with side supports for the arms. **armhole** n opening in a garment through which the arm passes. **armpit** n hollow under the arm at the shoulder.
arm² 🛈 v 1 supply with weapons. 2 prepare (a bomb etc.) for use. **arms** pl n 1

weapons. 2 military exploits. 3 heraldic emblem.
armada 🛈 n large number of warships.
armadillo n, pl **–los** small S American mammal covered in strong bony plates.
armistice 🛈 [arm–miss–stiss] n agreed suspension of fighting.
armour 🛈 n 1 metal clothing formerly worn to protect the body in battle. 2 metal plating of tanks, warships, etc. **armourer** n maker, repairer, or keeper of arms or armour. **armoury** n place where weapons are stored.
army 🛈 n, pl **armies 1** military land forces of a nation. 2 great number.
aroma 🛈 n pleasant smell. **aromatic** adj **aromatherapy** n massage with fragrant oils to relieve tension.
around 🛈 prep, adv 1 on all sides (of). 2 from place to place (in). 3 somewhere in or near. 4 approximately.
arouse 🛈 v 1 stimulate, make active. 2 awaken.
arraign [ar–rain] v 1 bring (a prisoner) before a court to answer a charge. 2 accuse. **arraignment** n

——————— THESAURUS ———————

reason 3 = **quarrel**, bicker, disagree, dispute, fall out (inf), fight, squabble
arid adj 1 = **dry**, barren, desert, parched, sterile, torrid, waterless ≠ **rich** 2 = **boring**, dreary, dry, dull, tedious, tiresome, uninspired, uninteresting ≠ **interesting**
arise v 1 = **happen**, begin, emerge, ensue, follow, occur, result, start, stem 3 = **get up**, get to one's feet, go up, rise, stand up, wake up
aristocracy n 1 = **upper class**, elite, gentry, nobility, patricians, peerage, ruling class
arm¹ n 1 = **upper limb**, appendage, limb
arm² v 1 = **equip**, accoutre, array, deck out, furnish, issue with, provide, supply 2 = **prime**
armada n = **fleet**, flotilla, navy, squadron
armistice n = **truce**, ceasefire, peace, suspension of hostilities
armour n = **protection**, armour plate,

covering, sheathing, shield
army n 1 = **soldiers**, armed force, legions, military, military force, soldiery, troops 2 = **vast number**, array, horde, host, multitude, pack, swarm, throng
aroma n = **scent**, bouquet, fragrance, odour, perfume, redolence, savour, smell
① **around** prep 1 = **surrounding**, about, encircling, enclosing, encompassing, on all sides of, on every side of 4 = **approximately**, about, circa (used with dates), roughly
② **around** adv 1 = **everywhere**, about, all over, here and there, in all directions, on all sides, throughout 3 = **near**, at hand, close, close at hand, nearby, nigh (arch or dial)
arouse v 1 = **stimulate**, excite, incite, instigate, provoke, spur, stir up, summon up, whip up ≠ **still** 2 = **awaken**, rouse, waken, wake up

arrange ❶ *v* **1** plan. **2** agree. **3** put in order. **4** adapt (music) for performance in a certain way. **arrangement** *n*

array ❶ *n* **1** impressive display or collection. **2** orderly arrangement, esp. of troops. **3** *Poetic* rich clothing. ♦ *v* **4** arrange in order. **5** dress in rich clothing.

arrears *pl n* money owed. **in arrears** late in paying a debt.

arrest ❶ *v* **1** take (a person) into custody. **2** stop the movement or development of. **3** catch and hold (the attention). ♦ *n* **4** act of taking a person into custody. **5** slowing or stopping. **arresting** *adj* attracting attention, striking.

arrive ❶ *v* **1** reach a place or destination. **2** happen, come. **3** *Informal* be born. **4** *Informal* attain success. **arrival** *n* **1** arriving. **2** person or thing that has just arrived.

arrow ❶ *n* **1** pointed shaft shot from a bow. **2** arrow–shaped sign or symbol used to show direction. **arrowhead** *n* pointed tip of an arrow.

arsenal ❶ *n* place where arms and ammunition are made or stored.

arsenic *n* **1** toxic grey element. **2** highly poisonous compound of this.

arson *n* crime of intentionally setting property on fire. **arsonist** *n*

art ❶ *n* **1** creation of works of beauty, esp. paintings or sculpture. **2** works of art collectively. **3** skill. ♦ *pl* **4** nonscientific branches of knowledge. **artist** *n* **1** person who produces works of art, esp. paintings or sculpture. **2** person skilled at something. **3** artiste. **artiste** *n* professional entertainer such as a singer or dancer. **artistic** *adj* **artistically** *adv* **artistry** *n* artistic skill. **arty** *adj* **artier, artiest** *Informal* having an affected interest in art.

artefact *n* something made by human beings.

artery *n, pl* **–teries** **1** one of the tubes carrying blood from the heart. **2** major road or means of communication. **arterial** *adj* **1** of an artery. **2** (of a route) major.

arthritis *n* painful inflammation of a joint or joints. **arthritic** *adj, n*

artichoke *n* flower head of a thistle–like plant, cooked as a vegetable.

article ❶ *n* **1** written piece in a magazine or newspaper. **2** item or object. **3** clause in a document. **4** *Grammar* any of the words *the, a,* or *an.*

——————— THESAURUS ———————

arrange *v* **1** = **plan**, construct, contrive, devise, fix up, organize, prepare **2** = **agree**, adjust, come to terms, compromise, determine, settle **3** = **put in order**, classify, group, line up, order, organize, position, sort ≠ **disturb** **4** = **adapt**, instrument, orchestrate, score

array *n* **1, 2** = **arrangement**, collection, display, exhibition, formation, line–up, parade, show, supply **3** *Poet* = **clothing**, apparel, attire, clothes, dress, finery, garments, regalia ♦ *v* **4** = **arrange**, display, exhibit, group, parade, range, show **5** = **dress**, adorn, attire, clothe, deck, decorate, festoon

arrest *v* **1** = **capture**, apprehend, catch, detain, nick (*sl, chiefly Brit*), seize, take prisoner ≠ **release** **2** = **stop**, block, delay, end, inhibit, interrupt, obstruct, slow, suppress ≠ **encourage** **3** = **grip**, absorb,

engage, engross, fascinate, hold, intrigue, occupy ♦ *n* **4** = **capture**, bust (*inf*), cop (*sl*), detention, seizure **5** = **stopping**, blockage, delay, end, hindrance, interruption, obstruction, suppression ≠ **promotion**

arrive *v* **1** = **come**, appear, enter, get to, reach, show up (*inf*), turn up ≠ **go 4** *Inf* = **succeed**, become famous, make good, make it (*inf*), make the grade (*inf*)

arrow *n* **1** = **dart**, bolt, flight, quarrel, shaft (*arch*) **2** = **pointer**, indicator

arsenal *n* = **armoury**, ammunition dump, arms depot, ordnance depot, stockpile, store, storehouse, supply

art *n* **3** = **skill**, craft, expertise, ingenuity, mastery, virtuosity

article *n* **1** = **piece**, composition, discourse, essay, feature, item, paper, story, treatise **2** = **thing**, commodity, item, object, piece,

articulate ● *adj* 1 able to express oneself clearly and coherently. 2 (of speech) clear, distinct. 3 *Zool* having joints. ◆ *v* 4 speak or say clearly and coherently. **articulately** *adv* **articulated** *adj* jointed. **articulated lorry** large lorry in two separate sections joined by a pivoted bar. **articulation** *n*

artifice ● *n* 1 clever trick. 2 cleverness, skill. **artificial** *adj* man–made, not occurring naturally.

artillery ● *n* 1 large–calibre guns. 2 branch of the army who use these.

artisan ● *n* skilled worker, craftsman.

as ● *conj* 1 while, when. 2 in the way that. 3 that which, e.g. *do as you are told.* 4 since, seeing that. 5 for instance. ◆ *adv, conj* 6 used to indicate amount or extent in comparisons, e.g. *he is as tall as you.* ◆ *prep* 7 in the role of, being, e.g. *as a mother, I am concerned.*

asbestos *n* fibrous mineral which does not burn. **asbestosis** *n* lung disease caused by inhalation of asbestos fibre.

ascend ● *v* go or move up. **ascent** *n* 1 ascending. 2 upward slope. **ascendant** *adj* 1 dominant or influential. ◆ *n* 2 in the

ascendant increasing in power or influence. **ascendancy** *n* condition of being dominant.

ascertain ● *v* find out definitely. **ascertainable** *adj* **ascertainment** *n*

ascetic ● [ass–**set**–tik] *n, adj* (person) abstaining from worldly pleasures and comforts. **asceticism** *n*

ascribe ● *v* attribute, as to a particular origin. **ascription** *n*

asexual [eh–**sex**–yew–al] *adj* without sex. **asexually** *adv*

ash¹ *n* 1 powdery substance left when something is burnt. ◆ *pl* 2 remains after burning, esp. of a human body after cremation. **ashen** *adj* pale with shock. **ashtray** *n* receptacle for tobacco ash and cigarette butts.

ash² *n* tree with grey bark.

ashamed ● *adj* feeling shame.

ashore ● *adv* towards or on land.

aside ● *adv* 1 to one side. 2 out of other people's hearing, e.g. *he took me aside to tell me his plans.* ◆ *n* 3 remark not meant to be heard by everyone present.

asinine ● *adj* stupid, idiotic.

substance, unit 3 = **clause**, item, paragraph, part, passage, point, portion, section

articulate *adj* 1, 2 = **expressive**, clear, coherent, eloquent, fluent, lucid, well–spoken ≠ **halting** ◆ *v* 4 = **express**, enunciate, pronounce, say, speak, state, talk, utter, voice

artifice *n* 1 = **trick**, contrivance, device, machination, manoeuvre, stratagem, subterfuge, tactic 2 = **cleverness**, ingenuity, inventiveness, skill

artillery *n* 1 = **big guns**, battery, cannon, cannonry, gunnery, ordnance

artisan *n* = **craftsman**, journeyman, mechanic, skilled workman, technician

as *conj* 1 = **when**, at the time that, during the time that, just as, while 2 = **in the way that**, in the manner that, like 3 = **what**, that which 4 = **since**, because, considering that, seeing that 5 = **for instance**, like,

such as ◆ *prep* 7 = **being**, in the character of, in the role of, under the name of

ascend *v* = **move up**, climb, go up, mount, scale ≠ **fall**

ascertain *v* = **find out**, confirm, determine, discover, establish, learn

① **ascetic** *n* = **monk**, abstainer, hermit, nun, recluse ≠ **hedonist**

② **ascetic** *adj* = **self–denying**, abstinent, austere, celibate, frugal, puritanical, self–disciplined ≠ **abandoned**

ascribe *v* = **attribute**, assign, charge, credit, impute, put down, refer, set down

ashamed *adj* = **embarrassed**, distressed, guilty, humiliated, mortified, remorseful, shamefaced, sheepish, sorry ≠ **pleased**

ashore *adv* = **on land**, aground, landwards, on dry land, on the beach, on the shore, shorewards, to the shore

aside *adv* 1 = **to one side**, apart, beside, on one side, out of the way, privately,

ask ⊕ *v* **1** say or write (something) in a form that requires an answer. **2** make a request or demand. **3** invite.

askance [ass-**kanss**] *adv* **look askance at 1** look at with an oblique glance. **2** regard with suspicion.

askew ⊕ *adv, adj* to one side, crooked.

asleep ⊕ *adj* **1** sleeping. **2** (of limbs) numb.

asp *n* small poisonous snake.

asparagus *n* plant whose shoots are cooked as a vegetable.

aspect ⊕ *n* **1** feature or element. **2** position facing a particular direction. **3** appearance or look.

aspen *n* kind of poplar tree.

aspersion *n* **cast aspersions on** make derogatory remarks about.

asphalt *n* **1** black hard tarlike substance used for road surfaces etc.

aspic *n* savoury jelly used to coat meat, eggs, fish, etc.

aspidistra *n* plant with long tapered leaves.

aspire ⊕ *v* (foll. by *to*) yearn (for), hope (to do or be). **aspiration** *n* strong desire or aim.

aspirin *n* **1** drug used to relieve pain and fever. **2** tablet of this.

ass ⊕ *n* **1** donkey. **2** stupid person.

assail ⊕ *v* attack violently. **assailant** *n*

assassin ⊕ *n* person who murders a prominent person. **assassinate** *v* murder (a prominent person). **assassination** *n*

assault ⊕ *n* **1** violent attack. ♦ *v* **2** attack violently. **assault course** series of obstacles used in military training.

assemble ⊕ *v* **1** collect or congregate. **2** put together the parts of (a machine). **assemblage** *n* **1** collection or group. **2** assembling. **assembly** *n* (*pl* -blies) **1** assembled group. **2** assembling. **assembly line** sequence of machines and workers in a factory assembling a product.

assent ⊕ *n* **1** agreement or consent. ♦ *v* **2** agree or consent.

——————————— THESAURUS ———————————

separately, to the side ♦ *n*
3 = **interpolation**, parenthesis

asinine *adj* = **stupid**, fatuous, foolish, idiotic, imbecilic, moronic, senseless

ask *v* **1** = **inquire**, interrogate, query, question, quiz ≠ **answer 2** = **request**, appeal, beg, demand, plead, seek
3 = **invite**, bid, summon

① **askew** *adv* = **crookedly**, aslant, awry, obliquely, off-centre, to one side

② **askew** *adj* = **crooked**, awry, cockeyed (*inf*), lopsided, oblique, off-centre, skewwhiff (*Brit inf*) ≠ **even**

asleep *adj* **1** = **sleeping**, dormant, dozing, fast asleep, napping, slumbering, snoozing (*inf*), sound asleep

aspect *n* **1** = **feature**, angle, facet, side
2 = **position**, outlook, point of view, prospect, scene, situation, view
3 = **appearance**, air, attitude, bearing, condition, demeanour, expression, look, manner

aspire *v* (foll. by *to*) = **aim**, desire, dream, hope, long, seek, set one's heart on, wish

ass *n* **1** = **donkey**, moke (*sl*) **2** = **fool**, blockhead, halfwit, idiot, jackass, numbskull or numskull, oaf, twit (*inf, chiefly Brit*)

assail *v* = **attack**, assault, fall upon, lay into (*inf*), set upon

assassin *n* = **murderer**, executioner, hatchet man (*sl*), hit man (*sl*), killer, liquidator, slayer

assault *n* **1** = **attack**, charge, invasion, offensive, onslaught ≠ **defence** ♦ *v*
2 = **attack**, beset, fall upon, lay into (*inf*), set about, set upon, strike at ≠ **protect**

assemble *v* **1** = **gather**, amass, bring together, call together, collect, come together, congregate, meet, muster, rally
≠ **dismiss 2** = **put together**, build up, connect, construct, fabricate, fit together, join, piece together, set up ≠ **divide**

assent *n* **1** = **agreement**, acceptance, approval, compliance, concurrence, consent, permission, sanction ≠ **refusal** ♦
v **2** = **agree**, allow, approve, consent, grant, permit

assert ❶ v **1** declare forcefully. **2** insist upon (one's rights etc.). **assert oneself** put oneself forward forcefully. **assertion** n **assertive** adj **assertively** adv

assess ❶ v **1** judge the worth or importance of. **2** estimate the value of (income or property) for taxation purposes. **assessment** n **assessor** n

asset ❶ n **1** valuable or useful person or thing. ◆ pl **2** property that a person or firm can sell, esp. to pay debts.

assiduous ❶ adj hard–working. **assiduously** adv **assiduity** n

assign ❶ v **1** appoint (someone) to a job or task. **2** allot (a task). **3** attribute. **assignation** n **1** secret arrangement to meet. **assignment** n **1** task assigned. **2** assigning.

assimilate ❶ v **1** learn and understand (information). **2** absorb or be absorbed or incorporated. **assimilation** n

assist ❶ v give help or support. **assistance** n **assistant** n **1** helper. ◆ adj **2** junior or deputy.

associate ❶ v **1** connect in the mind. **2** mix socially. ◆ n **3** partner in business. **4** friend or companion. ◆ adj **5** having partial rights or subordinate status, e.g. associate member. **association** n **1** society or club. **2** associating.

assonance n rhyming of vowel sounds but not consonants, as in time and light.

assorted ❶ adj consisting of various types mixed together. **assortment** n assorted mixture.

assume ❶ v **1** take to be true without proof. **2** take upon oneself, e.g. he assumed command. **3** pretend, e.g. I assumed indifference. **assumption** n **1** thing assumed. **2** assuming.

assure ❶ v **1** promise or guarantee. **2** convince. **3** make (something) certain. **4** insure against loss of life. **assured** adj **1** confident. **2** certain to happen. **assuredly** adv definitely. **assurance** n assuring or being assured.

—————————— THESAURUS ——————————

assert v **1** = **state**, affirm, declare, maintain, profess, pronounce, swear ≠ **deny 2** = **insist upon**, claim, defend, press, put forward, stand up for, stress, uphold ≠ **retract assert oneself** = **be forceful**, exert one's influence, make one's presence felt, put oneself forward, put one's foot down (inf)

assess v **1** = **judge**, appraise, estimate, evaluate, rate, size up (inf), value, weigh **2** = **evaluate**, fix, impose, levy, rate, tax, value

asset n **1** = **benefit**, advantage, aid, blessing, boon, feather in one's cap, help, resource, service ≠ **burden** ◆ pl **2** = **property**, capital, estate, funds, goods, money, possessions, resources, wealth

assiduous adj = **diligent**, hard–working, indefatigable, industrious, persevering, persistent, unflagging

assign v **1** = **select**, appoint, choose, delegate, designate, name, nominate **2** = **give**, allocate, allot, apportion, consign, distribute, give out, grant

3 = **attribute**, accredit, ascribe, put down

assimilate v **1** = **learn**, absorb, digest, take in **2** = **adjust**, adapt, blend in, digest, incorporate, mingle, take in

assist v = **help**, abet, aid, cooperate, lend a helping hand, serve, support ≠ **resist**

associate v **1** = **connect**, ally, combine, identify, join, link, lump together ≠ **separate 2** = **mix**, accompany, consort, hobnob, mingle, socialize ≠ **avoid** ◆ n **3** = **partner**, collaborator, colleague, confederate, co–worker **4** = **friend**, ally, cobber (Aust or old–fashioned NZ inf), companion, comrade, mate (inf)

assorted adj = **various**, different, diverse, miscellaneous, mixed, motley, sundry, varied

assume v **1** = **take for granted**, believe, expect, fancy, imagine, infer, presume, suppose, surmise, think ≠ **know 2** = **take on**, accept, enter upon, put on, shoulder, take, take over **3** = **put on**, adopt, affect, feign, imitate, impersonate, mimic, pretend to, simulate

☑ **WORD TIP**
When used in the context of business, *assurance* and *insurance* have the same meaning.

aster *n* plant with daisy–like flowers.
asterisk *n* **1** star–shaped symbol (*) used in printing or writing to indicate a footnote etc. ♦ *v* **2** mark with an asterisk.
astern *adv* **1** at or towards the stern of a ship. **2** backwards.
asteroid *n* any of the small planets that orbit the sun between Mars and Jupiter.
asthma [ass–ma] *n* illness causing difficulty in breathing. **asthmatic** *adj, n*
astigmatism [eh–**stig**–mat–tiz–zum] *n* inability of a lens, esp. of the eye, to focus properly. **astigmatic** *adj*
astir *adj* **1** out of bed. **2** in motion.
astonish ❶ *v* surprise greatly. **astonishment** *n*
astound *v* overwhelm with amazement. **astounding** *adj*
astral *adj* **1** of stars. **2** of the spirit world.
astray ❶ *adv* off the right path.
astride *adv, prep* with a leg on either side (of).
astringent *adj* **1** causing contraction of body tissue. **2** checking the flow of blood from a cut. **3** severe or harsh. ♦ *n* **4** astringent substance. **astringency** *n*
astrology *n* study of the alleged influence

of the stars, planets, and moon on human affairs. **astrologer** *n* **astrological** *adj*
astronaut *n* person trained for travelling in space.
astronomy *n* scientific study of heavenly bodies. **astronomer** *n* **astronomical** *adj* **1** very large. **2** of astronomy. **astronomically** *adv*
astute ❶ *adj* perceptive or shrewd. **astutely** *adv* **astuteness** *n*
asunder *adv* into parts or pieces.
asylum ❶ *n* **1** refuge or sanctuary. **2** old name for a mental hospital.
asymmetry *n* lack of symmetry. **asymmetrical, asymmetric** *adj*
at *prep* indicating position in space or time, movement towards an object, etc., e.g. *at midnight; throwing stones at windows.*
atheism ❶ [aith–ee–iz–zum] *n* belief that there is no God. **atheist** *n* **atheistic** *adj*
atlas *n* book of maps.
atmosphere ❶ *n* **1** mass of gases surrounding a heavenly body, esp. the earth. **2** prevailing tone or mood (of a place etc.). **3** unit of pressure. **atmospheric** *adj* **atmospherics** *pl n* radio interference due to electrical disturbance in the atmosphere.
atoll *n* ring–shaped coral reef enclosing a lagoon.
atom ❶ *n* **1** smallest unit of matter which can take part in a chemical reaction. **2** very small amount. **atom bomb** same as

—————— THESAURUS ——————

assure *v* **1** = **promise**, certify, confirm, declare confidently, give one's word to, guarantee, pledge, swear, vow
2 = **convince**, comfort, embolden, encourage, hearten, persuade, reassure
3 = **make certain**, clinch, complete, confirm, ensure, guarantee, make sure, seal, secure
astonish *v* = **amaze**, astound, bewilder, confound, daze, dumbfound, stagger, stun, surprise
astray *adv* = **off the right track**, adrift, amiss, lost, off, off course, off the mark
astute *adj* = **intelligent**, canny, clever,

crafty, cunning, perceptive, sagacious, sharp, shrewd, subtle
asylum *n* **1** = **refuge**, harbour, haven, preserve, retreat, safety, sanctuary, shelter
2 *Old–fashioned* = **mental hospital**, hospital, institution, madhouse (*inf*), psychiatric hospital
atheism *n* = **nonbelief**, disbelief, godlessness, heathenism, infidelity, irreligion, paganism, scepticism, unbelief
atmosphere *n* **1** = **air**, aerosphere, heavens, sky **2** = **feeling**, ambience, character, climate, environment, mood, spirit, surroundings, tone

ATOMIC BOMB.

atonal [eh–**tone**–al] *adj* (of music) not written in an established key.

atone ❶ *v* make amends (for sin or wrongdoing). **atonement** *n*

atop *prep* on top of.

atrocious ❶ *adj* 1 extremely cruel or wicked. 2 horrifying or shocking. 3 *Informal* very bad. **atrociously** *adv* **atrocity** *n* 1 wickedness. 2 (*pl* –**ties**) act of cruelty.

atrophy [**at**–trof–fee] *n, pl* –**phies** 1 wasting away of an organ or part. ◆ *v* –**phying,** –**phied** 2 (cause to) waste away.

attach ❶ *v* 1 join, fasten, or connect. 2 attribute or ascribe. **attached** *adj* (foll. by *to*) fond of. **attachment** *n*

attaché [at–**tash**–shay] *n* specialist attached to a diplomatic mission. **attaché case** flat rectangular briefcase for papers.

attack ❶ *v* 1 launch a physical assault (against). 2 criticize. 3 set about (a job or problem) with vigour. 4 affect adversely. ◆ *n* 5 act of attacking. 6 sudden bout of illness. **attacker** *n*

attain ❶ *v* 1 achieve or accomplish (a task or aim). 2 reach. **attainable** *adj* **attainment** *n* accomplishment.

attempt ❶ *v* 1 try, make an effort. ◆ *n* 2 effort or endeavour.

attend ❶ *v* 1 be present at. 2 go regularly to a school, college, etc. 3 look after. 4 pay attention. 5 apply oneself (to). **attendance** *n* 1 attending. 2 number attending. **attendant** *n* 1 person who assists, guides, or provides a service. ◆ *adj* 2 accompanying. **attention** *n* 1 concentrated direction of the mind. 2 consideration. 3 care. 4 alert position in military drill. **attentive** *adj* 1 giving attention. 2 considerately helpful. **attentively** *adv* **attentiveness** *n*

attest *v* affirm the truth of, be proof of.

attic ❶ *n* space or room within the roof of a house.

attire ❶ *n* fine or formal clothes.

attitude ❶ *n* 1 way of thinking and behaving. 2 posture of the body.

attorney *n* 1 person legally appointed to

—————— THESAURUS ——————

atom *n* 2 = **particle**, bit, dot, speck, spot, trace

atone *v* = **make amends**, compensate, do penance, make redress, make reparation, make up for, pay for, recompense, redress

atrocious *adj* 1 = **cruel**, barbaric, brutal, fiendish, infernal, monstrous, savage, vicious, wicked ≠ **good** 2 = **shocking**, appalling, detestable, grievous, horrible, horrifying, terrible ≠ **fine**

attach *v* 1 = **connect**, add, couple, fasten, fix, join, link, secure, stick, tie ≠ **remove** 2 = **put**, ascribe, assign, associate, attribute, connect

attack *v* 1 = **assault**, invade, lay into (*inf*), raid, set upon, storm, strike (at) ≠ **support** 2 = **criticize**, abuse, blame, censure, have a go (at) (*inf*), put down, vilify ◆ *n* 5 a = **assault**, campaign, charge, foray, incursion, invasion, offensive, onslaught, raid, strike ≠ **support** b = **criticism**, abuse, blame, censure, denigration, stick (*sl*), vilification 6 = **bout**, convulsion, fit,

paroxysm, seizure, spasm, stroke

attain *v* 1 = **achieve**, accomplish, acquire, complete, fulfil, gain, get, obtain

attempt *v* 1 = **try**, endeavour, seek, strive, undertake, venture ◆ *n* 2 = **try**, bid, crack (*inf*), effort, go (*inf*), shot (*inf*), stab (*inf*), trial

attend *v* 1 = **be present**, appear, frequent, go to, haunt, put in an appearance, show oneself, turn up, visit ≠ **miss** 3 = **look after**, care for, mind, minister to, nurse, take care of, tend 4 = **pay attention**, hear, heed, listen, mark, note, observe, pay heed ≠ **ignore** 5 **attend to** = **apply oneself to**, concentrate on, devote oneself to, get to work on, look after, occupy oneself with, see to, take care of

attic *n* = **loft**, garret

attire *n* = **clothes**, apparel, costume, dress, garb, garments, outfit, robes, wear

attitude *n* 1 = **disposition**, approach, frame of mind, mood, opinion, outlook, perspective, point of view, position, stance act for another. **2** *US* lawyer.

attract ❶ *v* **1** arouse the interest or admiration of. **2** draw (something) closer by exerting a force on it. **attraction** *n* **1** power to attract. **2** something that attracts. **attractive** *adj* **attractively** *adv* **attractiveness** *n*

attribute ❶ *v* **1** (usu. foll. by *to*) regard as belonging to or produced by. ◆ *n* **2** quality or feature representative of a person or thing. **attributable** *adj* **attribution** *n* **attributive** *adj Grammar* (of an adjective) preceding the noun modified.

attrition *n* constant wearing down to weaken or destroy.

attune ❶ *v* adjust or accustom (a person or thing).

atypical [eh-**tip**-ik-al] *adj* not typical.

aubergine [**oh**-bur-zheen] *n* dark purple tropical fruit, cooked and eaten as a vegetable.

auburn *adj* (of hair) reddish-brown.

auction *n* **1** public sale in which articles are sold to the highest bidder. ◆ *v* **2** sell by auction. **auctioneer** *n* person who conducts an auction.

audacious ❶ *adj* **1** recklessly bold or daring. **2** impudent. **audaciously** *adv* **audacity** *n*

audible ❶ *adj* loud enough to be heard. **audibly** *adv* **audibility** *n*

audience ❶ *n* **1** group of spectators or listeners. **2** formal interview.

audio *adj* **1** of sound or hearing. **2** of or for the transmission or reproduction of sound.

audit *n* **1** official examination of business accounts. ◆ *v* **auditing, audited 2** examine (business accounts) officially. **auditor** *n*

audition *n* **1** test of a performer's ability for a particular role or job. ◆ *v* **2** test or be tested in an audition.

Aug. August.

augment *v* increase or enlarge. **augmentation** *n*

augur *v* be a sign of (future events). **augury** *n* **1** foretelling of the future. **2** (*pl* **-ries**) omen.

August *n* eighth month of the year.

auk *n* northern sea bird with short wings and black-and-white plumage.

aunt *n* **1** father's or mother's sister. **2** uncle's wife. **auntie, aunty** *n*, *pl* **aunties** *Informal* aunt. **Aunt Sally 1** figure used in fairgrounds as a target. **2** target of abuse or criticism.

au pair *n* young foreign woman who does housework in return for board and lodging.

aura ❶ *n* distinctive air or quality of a person or thing.

aural *adj* of or using the ears or hearing.

auricle *n* **1** upper chamber of the heart. **2** outer part of the ear. **auricular** *adj*

aurora *n*, *pl* **-ras, -rae** bands of light sometimes seen in the sky in polar regions. **aurora australis** aurora seen near the South Pole. **aurora borealis** aurora seen near the North Pole.

auspices [**aw**-spiss-siz] *pl n* under the

2 = **position**, pose, posture, stance

attract *v* **1** = **appeal to**, charm, enchant **2** = **draw**, allure, entice, lure, pull (*inf*), tempt ≠ **disgust**

attribute *v* **1** (usu. foll. by *to*) = **ascribe**, charge, credit, put down to, set down to ◆ *n* **2** = **quality**, aspect, character, characteristic, facet, feature, peculiarity, property, trait

attune *v* = **accustom**, adapt, adjust, familiarize, harmonize, regulate

audacious *adj* **1** = **daring**, bold, brave, courageous, fearless, intrepid, rash, reckless ≠ **guarded 2** = **cheeky**, brazen, defiant, impertinent, impudent, insolent, presumptuous, shameless ≠ **gracious**

audible *adj* = **clear**, detectable, discernible, distinct, hearable, perceptible

audience *n* **1** = **spectators**, assembly, crowd, gallery, gathering, listeners, onlookers, turnout, viewers **2** = **interview**, consultation, hearing, meeting, reception

aura *n* = **air**, ambience, atmosphere, feeling, mood, quality, tone

auspices of with the support and approval of.

austere 🌐 *adj* 1 stern or severe. 2 ascetic or self–disciplined. 3 severely simple or plain. **austerely** *adv* **austerity** *n*

authentic 🌐 *adj* known to be real, genuine. **authentically** *adv* **authenticity** *n* **authenticate** *v* establish as genuine. **authentication** *n*

author 🌐 *n* 1 writer of a book etc. 2 originator or creator. **authorship** *n*

authority 🌐 *n, pl* **–ties** 1 power to command or control others. 2 (often *pl*) person or group having this power. 3 expert in a particular field. **authoritarian** *n, adj* (person) insisting on strict obedience to authority. **authoritative** *adj* 1 recognized as being reliable. 2 possessing authority. **authoritatively** *adv* **authorize** *v* 1 give authority to. 2 give permission for. **authorization** *n*

autism *n Psychiatry* disorder, usu. of children, characterized by lack of response to people and limited ability to communicate. **autistic** *adj*

auto– *combining form* self–, e.g. *autobiography.*

autobiography *n, pl* **–phies** account of a person's life written by that person. **autobiographical** *adj*

autocrat 🌐 *n* 1 ruler with absolute authority. 2 dictatorial person. **autocratic** *adj* **autocratically** *adv* **autocracy** *n* government by an autocrat.

Autocue *n* ® electronic television prompting device displaying a speaker's script, unseen by the audience.

autogiro, autogyro *n, pl* **–ros** self–propelled aircraft resembling a helicopter but with an unpowered rotor.

autograph *n* 1 handwritten signature of a (famous) person. ♦ *v* 2 write one's signature on or in.

automatic 🌐 *adj* 1 (of a device) operating mechanically by itself. 2 (of a process) performed by automatic equipment. 3 done without conscious thought. 4 (of a firearm) self–loading. ♦ *n* 5 self–loading firearm. 6 vehicle with automatic transmission. **automatically** *adv*

automobile *n US* motor car.

autonomy 🌐 *n* self–government. **autonomous** *adj*

autopsy *n, pl* **–sies** examination of a corpse to determine the cause of death.

autumn *n* season between summer and winter. **autumnal** *adj*

auxiliary 🌐 *adj* 1 secondary or supplementary. 2 supporting. ♦ *n, pl* **–ries** 3 person or thing that supplements or supports. **auxiliary verb** verb used to form the tense, voice, or mood of another, such

─────┤ THESAURUS ├─────

austere *adj* 1 = **stern**, forbidding, formal, serious, severe, solemn, strict ≠ **kindly** 2 = **ascetic**, abstemious, puritanical, self–disciplined, sober, solemn, strait–laced, strict ≠ **abandoned** 3 = **plain**, bleak, harsh, simple, spare, Spartan, stark ≠ **comfortable**

authentic *adj* = **genuine**, actual, authoritative, bona fide, legitimate, pure, real, true–to–life, valid ≠ **supposed**

author *n* 1 = **writer**, composer, creator 2 = **creator**, architect, designer, father, founder, inventor, originator, producer

authority *n* 1 = **power**, command, control, direction, influence, mana (*NZ*), supremacy, sway, weight 2 (often *pl*)

= **powers that be**, administration, government, management, officialdom, police, the Establishment 3 = **expert**, connoisseur, guru, judge, master, professional, specialist

autocrat *n* 1 = **dictator**, absolutist, despot, tyrant

automatic *adj* 1, 2 = **mechanical**, automated, mechanized, push–button, self–propelling ≠ **human** 3 = **involuntary**, instinctive, mechanical, natural, reflex, spontaneous, unconscious, unwilled ≠ **conscious**

autonomy *n* = **independence**, freedom, home rule, self–determination, self–government, self–rule, sovereignty as *will* in *I will go.*

avail ⊕ *v* 1 be of use or advantage (to). ♦ *n* 2 use or advantage, esp. in *to no avail.* **avail oneself of** make use of. **available** obtainable or accessible.

avalanche ⊕ *n* 1 mass of snow or ice falling down a mountain. 2 sudden overwhelming quantity of anything.

avant–garde ⊕ [av–ong–**gard**] *n* 1 group of innovators, esp. in the arts. ♦ *adj* 2 innovative and progressive.

avarice ⊕ [**av**–a–riss] *n* greed for wealth. **avaricious** *adj*

avenge ⊕ *v* take revenge in retaliation for (harm done) or on behalf of (a person harmed). **avenger** *n*

avenue ⊕ *n* 1 wide street. 2 road between two rows of trees. 3 way of approach.

aver [av–**vur**] *v* **averring, averred** state to be true.

average ⊕ *n* 1 typical or normal amount or quality. 2 result obtained by adding quantities together and dividing the total

by the number of quantities. ♦ *adj* 3 usual or typical. 4 calculated as an average. ♦ *v* 5 calculate the average of. 6 amount to as an average.

averse ⊕ *adj* (usu. foll. by *to*) disinclined or unwilling. **aversion** *n* 1 strong dislike. 2 person or thing disliked.

avert ⊕ *v* 1 turn away. 2 ward off.

aviary *n, pl* **aviaries** large cage or enclosure for birds.

aviation *n* art of flying aircraft. **aviator** *n*

avid ⊕ *adj* 1 keen or enthusiastic. 2 greedy (for). **avidly** *adv* **avidity** *n*

avocado *n, pl* **–dos** pear–shaped tropical fruit with a leathery green skin and yellowish–green flesh.

avoid ⊕ *v* 1 prevent from happening. 2 refrain from. 3 keep away from. **avoidable** *adj* **avoidance** *n*

avow *v* 1 state or affirm. 2 admit openly. **avowal** *n* **avowed** *adj*

await ⊕ *v* 1 wait for. 2 be in store for.

awake ⊕ *v* **awaking, awoke, awoken** 1

———————————— THESAURUS ————————————

auxiliary *adj* 1 = **supplementary**, back–up, emergency, fall–back, reserve, secondary, subsidiary, substitute 2 = **supporting**, accessory, aiding, ancillary, assisting, helping ≠ **first** ♦ *n* 3 = **helper**, assistant, associate, backup, companion, reserve, subordinate, supporter

avail *v* 1 = **benefit**, aid, assist, be of advantage, be useful, help, profit ♦ *n* 2 = **benefit**, advantage, aid, good, help, profit, use

avalanche *n* 1 = **snow–slide**, landslide, landslip 2 = **flood**, barrage, deluge, inundation, torrent

avant–garde *adj* 2 = **progressive**, experimental, ground–breaking, innovative, pioneering, unconventional

avarice *n* = **greed**, covetousness, meanness, miserliness, niggardliness, parsimony, stinginess

avenge *v* = **get revenge for**, get even for (*inf*), get one's own back, hit back, punish, repay, retaliate

avenue *n* 1 = **street**, boulevard, course,

drive, passage, path, road, route, way

average *n* 1 = **usual**, norm, normal, par, standard 2 = **mean**, medium, midpoint ♦ *adj* 3 = **usual**, commonplace, fair, general, normal, ordinary, regular, standard, typical ≠ **great** 4 = **mean**, intermediate, median, medium, middle ≠ **minimum** ♦ *v* 6 = **make on average**, balance out to, be on average, do on average, even out to

averse *adj* (usu. foll. by *to*) = **opposed**, disinclined, hostile, ill–disposed, loath, reluctant, unwilling

avert *v* 1 = **turn away**, turn aside 2 = **ward off**, avoid, fend off, forestall, frustrate, preclude, prevent, stave off

avid *adj* 1 = **enthusiastic**, ardent, devoted, eager, fanatical, intense, keen, passionate, zealous ≠ **indifferent** 2 = **insatiable**, grasping, greedy, hungry, rapacious, ravenous, thirsty, voracious

avoid *v* 1 = **prevent**, avert 2 = **refrain from**, dodge, duck (out of) (*inf*), eschew, fight shy of, shirk 3 = **keep away from**, bypass, dodge, elude, escape, evade, shun, steer

emerge or rouse from sleep. **2** (cause to) become alert. ◆ *adj* **3** not sleeping. **4** alert.
award ⊕ *v* **1** give (something, such as a prize) formally. ◆ *n* **2** something awarded, such as a prize.
aware ⊕ *adj* having knowledge, informed. **awareness** *n*
awash *adv* washed over by water.
away ⊕ *adv* **1** from a place, e.g. *go away.* **2** to another place, e.g. *put that gun away.* **3** out of existence, e.g. *fade away.* **4** continuously, e.g. *laughing away.* ◆ *adj* **5** not present. **6** distant, e.g. *two miles away.* **7** *Sport* played on an opponent's ground.
awe ⊕ *n* **1** wonder and respect mixed with dread. ◆ *v* **2** fill with awe. **awesome** *adj* **1** inspiring awe. **2** *Slang* excellent or outstanding. **awestruck** *adj* filled with awe.
awful ⊕ *adj* **1** very bad or unpleasant. **2** *Informal* very great. **3** *Obs* inspiring awe.

awfully *adv* **1** in an unpleasant way. **2** *Informal* very.
awhile *adv* for a brief time.
awkward ⊕ *adj* **1** clumsy or ungainly. **2** embarrassed. **3** difficult to use or handle. **4** inconvenient. **awkwardly** *adv* **awkwardness** *n*
awl *n* pointed tool for piercing wood, leather, etc.
awning *n* canvas roof supported by a frame to give protection against the weather.
AWOL *adj Mil* absent without leave.
awry [a-**rye**] *adv, adj* **1** with a twist to one side, askew. **2** amiss.
axe ⊕ *n* **1** tool with a sharp blade for felling trees or chopping wood. **2** *Informal* dismissal from employment etc. ◆ *v* **3** *Informal* dismiss (employees), restrict (expenditure), or terminate (a project).
axiom ⊕ *n* **1** generally accepted principle.

──────| THESAURUS |──────

clear of ≠ seek out
await *v* **1** = **wait for**, abide, anticipate, expect, look for, look forward to, stay for **2** = **be in store for**, attend, be in readiness for, be prepared for, be ready for, wait for
awake *v* **1** = **wake up**, awaken, rouse, wake **2** = **alert**, arouse, kindle, provoke, revive, stimulate, stir up ◆ *adj* **3** = **not sleeping**, aroused, awakened, aware, conscious, wakeful, wide-awake ≠ **sleeping 4** = **alert**, alive, attentive, aware, heedful, observant, on the lookout, vigilant, watchful
award *v* **1** = **give**, bestow, confer, endow, grant, hand out, present ◆ *n* **2** = **prize**, decoration, gift, grant, trophy
aware *adj* = **knowing**, acquainted with, conscious of, conversant with, enlightened, familiar with, informed, in the loop, in the picture, knowledgeable, mindful of
away *adv* **1** = **from here**, abroad, apart, at a distance, elsewhere, far, from home, hence, off, remote **2** = **aside**, out of the way, to one side **4** = **continuously**, incessantly, interminably, relentlessly,

repeatedly, uninterruptedly, unremittingly ◆ *adj* **5** = **not present**, abroad, absent, elsewhere, gone, not at home, not here, out
awe *n* **1** = **wonder**, admiration, amazement, astonishment, dread, fear, horror, respect, reverence, terror ≠ **contempt** ◆ *v* **2** = **impress**, amaze, astonish, frighten, horrify, intimidate, stun, terrify
awful *adj* **1** = **terrible**, abysmal, appalling, deplorable, dreadful, frightful, ghastly, horrendous ≠ **great 3** *Obs* = **awe-inspiring**, awesome, fearsome, majestic, solemn
awkward *adj* **1** = **clumsy**, gauche, gawky, inelegant, lumbering, uncoordinated, ungainly ≠ **graceful 2** = **embarrassed**, ill at ease, uncomfortable ≠ **comfortable 3** = **difficult**, cumbersome, troublesome, unmanageable, unwieldy **4** = **inconvenient** ≠ **convenient**
axe *n* **1** = **hatchet**, adze, chopper **2** *Inf* = **the sack** (*inf*), dismissal, termination, the boot (*sl*), the chop (*sl*) ◆ *v* **3** *Inf* = **cut back**, cancel, dismiss, dispense with,

2 self–evident statement. **axiomatic** *adj* **1** self–evident.

axis ❶ *n, pl* **axes 1** (imaginary) line round which a body can rotate or about which an object or geometrical figure is symmetrical. **2** one of two fixed lines on a graph, against which quantities or positions are measured. **axial** *adj*

axle ❶ *n* shaft on which a wheel or pair of wheels turns.

aye, ay *interj* **1** yes. ◆ *n* **2** affirmative vote or voter.

azalea [az–**zale**–ya] *n* garden shrub grown for its showy flowers.

azure *adj, n* (of) the colour of a clear blue sky.

THESAURUS

eliminate, fire (*inf*), get rid of, remove, sack (*inf*)

axiom *n* **1** = **principle**, adage, aphorism, dictum, maxim, precept **2** = **truism**

axis *n* **1** = **pivot**, axle, centre line, shaft, spindle

axle *n* = **shaft**, axis, pin, pivot, rod, spindle

B b

BA Bachelor of Arts.

baas *n S Afr* boss.

babble ❶ *v* 1 talk excitedly or foolishly. 2 (of streams) make a low murmuring sound. ◆ *n* 3 muddled or foolish speech.

babe *n* baby.

baboon *n* large monkey with a pointed face and a long tail.

baby ❶ *n, pl* **–bies** 1 very young child or animal. 2 *Slang* sweetheart. ◆ *adj* 3 comparatively small of its type. **babyish** *adj* **baby–sit** *v* take care of a child while the parents are out. **baby–sitter** *n*

bach *n NZ* small holiday cottage.

bachelor *n* 1 unmarried man. 2 person who holds the lowest university or college degree.

bacillus [bass–**ill**–luss] *n, pl* **–li** [–lie] rod–shaped bacterium.

back ❶ *n* 1 rear part of the human body, from the neck to the pelvis. 2 part or side of an object opposite the front. 3 part of anything less often seen or used. 4 *Ball games* defensive player or position. ◆ *v* 5 (cause to) move backwards. 6 provide money for (a person or enterprise). 7 bet on the success of. 8 (foll. by *onto*) have the back facing towards. ◆ *adj* 9 situated behind. 10 owing from an earlier date. ◆ *adv* 11 at, to, or towards the rear. 12 to or towards the original starting point or condition. **backer** *n* person who gives financial support. **backfire** *v* fail to have the desired effect. **background** *n* space behind chief figures of a picture, etc. **backing** *n* 1 support. 2 musical accompaniment for a pop singer. **backlash** *n* sudden and adverse reaction. **backward** *adj* 1 directed towards the rear. 2 retarded in physical, material, or intellectual development. **backwardness** *n* **backwards** *adv* 1 towards the rear. 2 with the back foremost. 3 in the reverse of the usual direction. **back up** *v* support. **backup** *n* 1 support or reinforcement. 2 reserve or substitute.

bacon *n* salted or smoked pig meat.

bacteria ❶ *pl n, sing* **–rium** large group of microorganisms, many of which cause disease. **bacterial** *adj* **bacteriology** *n* study of bacteria.

> ✓ **WORD TIP**
> Note that the word *bacteria* is already plural and does not need an '–s'.

bad ❶ *adj* **worse, worst** 1 of poor quality. 2 lacking skill or talent. 3 harmful. 4

THESAURUS

babble *v* 1 = **gabble**, burble, chatter, gibber, jabber, prattle, waffle (*inf, chiefly Brit*) 2 = **gurgle** ◆ *n* 3 = **gabble**, burble, drivel, gibberish, waffle (*inf, chiefly Brit*)

baby *n* 1 = **infant**, babe, babe in arms, bairn (*Scot*), child, newborn child ◆ *adj* 3 = **small**, little, mini, miniature, minute, teeny–weeny, tiny, wee

back *n* 1 = **rear**, end, hindquarters ≠ **head**

3 = **end**, far end, hind part, rear, reverse, stern, tail end ◆ *v* 6 = **support**, advocate, assist, champion, endorse, promote, sponsor ◆ *adj* 9 = **rear**, end, hind, hindmost, posterior, tail ≠ **front** 10 = **previous**, delayed, earlier, elapsed, former, overdue, past ≠ **later**

bacteria *pl n* = **microorganisms**, bacilli, bugs (*sl*), germs, microbes, pathogens, immoral or evil. **5** naughty or mischievous. **6** rotten or decayed. **7** unpleasant. **badly** *adv* **badness** *n*

badge ⊕ *n* emblem worn to show membership, rank, etc.

badger ⊕ *n* **1** nocturnal burrowing mammal with a black and white head. ◆ *v* **2** pester or harass.

badminton *n* game played with rackets and a shuttlecock, which is hit back and forth over a high net.

baffle ⊕ *v* **1** perplex or puzzle. ◆ *n* **2** device to limit or regulate the flow of fluid, light, or sound. **bafflement** *n*

bag ⊕ *n* **1** flexible container with an opening at one end. **2** handbag or piece of luggage. **3** *Offens* ugly or bad-tempered woman. ◆ *v* **bagging, bagged** **4** put into a bag. **5** succeed in capturing, killing or scoring. **baggy** *adj* (of clothes) hanging loosely.

bagatelle *n* **1** something of little value. **2** board game in which balls are struck into holes.

baggage ⊕ *n* suitcases packed for a journey.

bagpipes *pl n* musical wind instrument with reed pipes and an inflatable bag.

bail[1] ⊕ *n* **1** *Law* money deposited with a court as security for a person's reappearance in court. ◆ *v* **2** pay bail for (a person).

bail[2] ⊕ , **bale** *v* (foll. by *out*) **1** remove (water) from (a boat). **2** *Informal* help (a person or organization) out of a predicament. **3** make an emergency parachute jump from an aircraft.

bail[3] *n* *Cricket* either of two wooden bars across the tops of the stumps.

bailiff *n* **1** sheriff's officer who serves writs and summonses. **2** landlord's agent.

bait ⊕ *n* **1** piece of food on a hook or in a trap to attract fish or animals. ◆ *v* **2** put a piece of food on or in (a hook or trap). **3** persecute or tease.

> ✓ **WORD TIP**
> The phrase *with bated breath* is sometimes wrongly spelled *with baited breath*.

baize *n* woollen fabric used to cover billiard and card tables.

bake *v* **1** cook by dry heat as in an oven. **2** make or become hardened by heat. **baker** *n* person whose business is to make or sell

—————— THESAURUS ——————

viruses

bad *adj* **1** = **inferior**, defective, faulty, imperfect, inadequate, poor, substandard, unsatisfactory **3** = **harmful**, damaging, dangerous, deleterious, detrimental, hurtful, ruinous, unhealthy ≠ **good** **4** = **wicked**, corrupt, criminal, evil, immoral, mean, sinful, wrong ≠ **good** **5** = **naughty**, disobedient, mischievous, unruly **6** = **rotten**, decayed, mouldy, off, putrid, rancid, sour, spoiled **7** = **unfavourable**, adverse, distressing, gloomy, grim, troubled, unfortunate, unpleasant

badge *n* = **mark**, brand, device, emblem, identification, insignia, sign, stamp, token

badger *v* **2** = **pester**, bully, goad, harass, hound, importune, nag, plague, torment

baffle *v* **1** = **puzzle**, bewilder, confound,

confuse, flummox, mystify, nonplus, perplex, stump ≠ **explain**

bag *n* **1** = **container**, receptacle, sac, sack ◆ *v* **5** = **catch**, acquire, capture, kill, land, shoot, trap

baggage *n* = **luggage**, accoutrements, bags, belongings, equipment, gear, paraphernalia, suitcases, things

bail[1] *n* **1** *Law* = **security**, bond, guarantee, pledge, surety, warranty

bail[2] , **bale** *v* (foll. by *out*) **2** *Inf* = **help**, aid, relieve, rescue, save (someone's) bacon (*inf, chiefly Brit*) **3** = **escape**, quit, retreat, withdraw

bait *n* **1** = **lure**, allurement, attraction, decoy, enticement, incentive, inducement, snare, temptation ◆ *v* **3** = **tease**, annoy, bother, harass, hassle (*inf*), hound, irritate, persecute, torment, wind up (*Brit sl*)

bread, cakes, etc. **baker's dozen** thirteen.
bakery *n, pl* **–eries** place where bread,
cakes, etc. are baked or sold. **baking
powder** powdered mixture containing
sodium bicarbonate, used as a raising
agent in baking.

bakkie *n S Afr* small truck.

balaclava, balaclava helmet *n* close–
fitting woollen hood that covers the ears
and neck.

balalaika *n* guitar–like musical instrument
with a triangular body.

balance ➊ *n* 1 state in which a weight or
amount is evenly distributed. 3 amount
that remains, e.g. *the balance of what you
owe*. 4 weighing device. 5 difference
between the credits and debits of an
account. ◆ *v* 6 weigh in a balance. 7 make
or remain steady. 8 consider or compare.
9 compare or equalize the money going
into or coming out of an account.

balcony ➊ *n, pl* **–nies** 1 platform on the
outside of a building with a rail along the
outer edge. 2 upper tier of seats in a
theatre or cinema.

bald ➊ *adj* 1 having little or no hair on the
scalp. 2 plain or blunt. 3 (of a tyre) having
a worn tread. **balding** *adj* becoming bald.
baldness *n*

bale *n* 1 large bundle of hay or goods
tightly bound together. ◆ *v* 2 make or put
into bales.

baleful *adj* vindictive or menacing.

balk ➊ **baulk** *v* 1 be reluctant to (do
something). 2 thwart or hinder.

ball¹ ➊ *n* 1 round or nearly round object,
esp. one used in games. 2 single delivery
of the ball in a game. ◆ *pl Taboo slang* 3
testicles. 4 nonsense. ◆ *v* 5 form into a
ball. **ball bearings** steel balls between
moving parts of a machine to reduce
friction. **ballpoint, ballpoint pen** *n* pen
with a tiny ball bearing as a writing point.

ball² *n* formal social function for dancing.
ballroom *n*

ballad *n* 1 narrative poem or song. 2 slow
sentimental song.

ballast ➊ *n* substance, such as sand, used
to stabilize a ship when it is not carrying
cargo.

ballet *n* 1 classical style of expressive
dancing based on conventional steps. 2
theatrical performance of this. **ballerina** *n*
female ballet dancer.

ballistics *n* study of the flight of
projectiles, such as bullets. **ballistic
missile** missile guided automatically in
flight but which falls freely at its target.

balloon ➊ *n* 1 inflatable rubber bag used
as a plaything or decoration. 2 large bag
inflated with air or gas, designed to float
in the atmosphere with passengers in a
basket underneath. ◆ *v* 3 fly in a balloon. 4
swell or increase rapidly in size. **balloonist**
n

ballot ➊ *n* 1 method of voting secretly. 2

━━━━━━ THESAURUS ━━━━━━

balance *n* 1 = **stability**, composure,
equanimity, poise, self–control, self–
possession, steadiness 2 = **equilibrium**,
correspondence, equity, equivalence,
evenness, parity, symmetry ≠ **instability**
3 = **remainder**, difference, residue, rest,
surplus ◆ *v* 6 = **weigh** 7 = **stabilize**, level,
match, parallel, steady ≠ **upset**
8 = **compare**, assess, consider, deliberate,
estimate, evaluate 9 = **calculate**, compute,
settle, square, tally, total

balcony *n* 1 = **terrace**, veranda 2 = **upper
circle**, gallery, gods

bald *adj* 1 = **hairless**, baldheaded,

depilated 2 = **plain**, blunt, direct,
forthright, straightforward, unadorned,
unvarnished

balk, baulk *v* 1 = **recoil**, evade, flinch,
hesitate, jib, refuse, resist, shirk, shrink
from ≠ **accept** 2 = **foil**, check, counteract,
defeat, frustrate, hinder, obstruct, prevent,
thwart

ball¹ *n* 1 = **sphere**, drop, globe, globule,
orb, pellet, spheroid

ballast *n* = **counterbalance**, balance,
counterweight, equilibrium, sandbag,
stability, stabilizer, weight

balloon *v* 4 = **swell**, billow, blow up,

actual vote or paper indicating a person's choice. ◆ v **–loting, –loted** 3 vote or ask for a vote from.

balm ❶ n 1 aromatic substance used for healing and soothing. 2 anything that comforts or soothes.

balmy ❶ adj **balmier, balmiest** (of weather) mild and pleasant.

balsa [bawl–sa] n very light wood from a tropical American tree.

balsam n soothing ointment.

bamboo n tall treelike tropical grass with hollow stems.

bamboozle ❶ v Informal 1 cheat or mislead. 2 confuse, puzzle.

ban ❶ v **banning, banned** 1 prohibit or forbid officially. ◆ n 2 official prohibition.

banal ❶ [ban–nahl] adj ordinary and unoriginal. **banality** n

banana n yellow crescent–shaped fruit.

band¹ ❶ n 1 group of musicians playing together. 2 group of people having a common purpose. **bandstand** n roofed outdoor platform for a band. **band together** v unite.

band² ❶ n 1 strip of some material, used to hold objects. 2 Physics range of frequencies or wavelengths between two limits.

bandanna, bandana n large brightly coloured handkerchief or neckerchief.

bandit ❶ n robber, esp. a member of an armed gang. **banditry** n

bandwagon n **jump, climb on the bandwagon** join a party or movement that seems assured of success.

bandy adj **–dier, –diest** 1 (also **bandy–legged**) having legs curved outwards at the knees. ◆ v **–dying, –died** 2 exchange (words) in a heated manner. 3 use (a name, term, etc.) frequently.

bane ❶ n person or thing that causes misery or distress. **baneful** adj

bang ❶ n 1 short loud explosive noise. 2 hard blow or loud knock. ◆ v 3 hit or knock, esp. with a loud noise. 4 close (a door) noisily. ◆ adv 5 precisely. 6 with a sudden impact.

banger n 1 Informal old decrepit car. 2 Slang sausage. 3 firework that explodes loudly.

bangle n bracelet worn round the arm or the ankle.

banish ❶ v 1 send (someone) into exile. 2 drive away. **banishment** n

———— THESAURUS ————

dilate, distend, expand, grow rapidly, inflate, puff out

ballot n 1 = **vote**, election, poll, polling, voting

balm n 1 = **ointment**, balsam, cream, embrocation, emollient, lotion, salve, unguent 2 = **comfort**, anodyne, consolation, curative, palliative, restorative, solace

balmy adj = **mild**, clement, pleasant, summery, temperate

bamboozle v Inf 1 = **cheat**, con (inf), deceive, dupe, fool, hoodwink, swindle, trick 2 = **puzzle**, baffle, befuddle, confound, confuse, mystify, perplex, stump

ban v 1 = **prohibit**, banish, bar, block, boycott, disallow, disqualify, exclude, forbid, outlaw ≠ **let** ◆ n 2 = **prohibition**, boycott, disqualification, embargo,

restriction, taboo ≠ **sanction**

banal adj = **unoriginal**, hackneyed, humdrum, mundane, pedestrian, stale, stereotyped, trite, unimaginative

band¹ n 1 = **ensemble**, combo, group, orchestra 2 = **gang**, body, company, group, party, posse (inf)

band² n 1 = **strip**, belt, bond, chain, cord, ribbon, strap

bandit n = **robber**, brigand, desperado, highwayman, marauder, outlaw, thief

bane n = **plague**, bête noire, curse, nuisance, pest, ruin, scourge, torment

bang n 1 = **explosion**, clang, clap, clash, pop, slam, thud, thump 2 = **blow**, bump, cuff, knock, punch, smack, stroke, whack ◆ v 3 = **hit**, belt (inf), clatter, knock, slam, strike, thump ◆ adv 5 = **straight**, precisely, slap, smack 6 = **hard**, abruptly, headlong, noisily, suddenly

banisters ❶ *pl n* railing supported by posts on a staircase.

banjo *n, pl* –jos, –joes guitar–like musical instrument with a circular body.

bank¹ ❶ *n* 1 institution offering services such as the safekeeping and lending of money. 2 any supply, store, or reserve. ◆ *v* 3 deposit (cash or cheques) in a bank. 4 transact business with a bank. **banking** *n* **bank holiday** public holiday when banks are closed by law. **banknote** *n* piece of paper money. **bank on** *v* rely on.

bank² ❶ *n* 1 raised mass, esp. of earth. 2 slope, as of a hill. 3 sloping ground at the side of a river. ◆ *v* 4 form into a bank. 5 cover (a fire) with ashes and fuel so that it will burn slowly. 6 cause (an aircraft) or (of an aircraft) to tip to one side on turning.

bankrupt ❶ *n* 1 person declared by a court to be unable to pay his or her debts. ◆ *adj* 2 financially ruined. ◆ *v* 3 make bankrupt. **bankruptcy** *n*

banner ❶ *n* 1 long strip of cloth displaying a slogan, advertisement, etc. 2 placard carried in a demonstration or procession.

banns *pl n* public declaration, esp. in a church, of an intended marriage.

banquet ❶ *n* elaborate formal dinner.

banshee *n* (in Irish folklore) female spirit whose wailing warns of a coming death.

bantam *n* small breed of chicken. **bantamweight** *n* boxer weighing up to 118lb (professional) or 54kg (amateur).

banter ❶ *v* 1 tease jokingly. ◆ *n* 2 teasing or joking conversation.

bar ❶ *n* 1 rigid length of metal, wood, etc. 2 solid, usu. rectangular block, of any material. 3 anything that obstructs or prevents. 4 counter or room where drinks are served. 5 heating element in an electric fire. 6 place in court where the accused stands during trial. 7 *Music* group of beats repeated throughout a piece of music. ◆ *v* barring, barred 8 secure with a bar. 9 obstruct. 10 ban or forbid. ◆ *prep* 11 (also **barring**) except for. **the Bar** barristers collectively. **barman, barmaid, bartender** *n*

barb ❶ *n* 1 cutting remark. 2 point facing in the opposite direction to the main point of a fish–hook etc. **barbed wire** strong wire with protruding sharp points.

banish *v* 1 = **expel**, deport, eject, evict, exile, outlaw ≠ **receive** 2 = **get rid of**, ban, cast out, discard, dismiss, oust, remove

banisters *pl n* = **railing**, balusters, balustrade, handrail, rail

bank¹ *n* 1 = **storehouse**, depository, repository 2 = **store**, accumulation, fund, hoard, reserve, reservoir, savings, stock, stockpile ◆ *v* 3 = **save**, deposit, keep

bank² *n* 1 = **mound**, banking, embankment, heap, mass, pile, ridge 3 = **side**, brink, edge, margin, shore ◆ *v* 4 = **pile**, amass, heap, mass, mound, stack 6 = **tilt**, camber, cant, heel, incline, pitch, slant, slope, tip

bankrupt *adj* 2 = **insolvent**, broke (*inf*), destitute, impoverished, in queer street, in the red, munted (*NZ sl*), ruined, wiped out (*inf*) ≠ **sound**

banner *n* 1 = **flag**, colours, ensign, pennant, standard, streamer 2 = **placard**

banquet *n* = **feast**, dinner, meal, repast, revel, treat

banter *v* 1 = **joke**, jest, kid (*inf*), rib (*inf*), taunt, tease ◆ *n* 2 = **joking**, badinage, jesting, kidding (*inf*), repartee, teasing, wordplay

bar *n* 1 = **rod**, paling, palisade, pole, rail, shaft, stake, stick 3 = **obstacle**, barricade, barrier, block, deterrent, hindrance, impediment, obstruction, stop ≠ **help** 4 = **public house**, boozer (*Brit, Aust & NZ inf*), canteen, counter, inn, pub (*inf, chiefly Brit*), saloon, tavern, watering hole (*facetious sl*) ◆ *v* 8 = **fasten**, barricade, bolt, latch, lock, secure 9 = **obstruct**, hinder, prevent, restrain 10 = **exclude**, ban, black, blackball, forbid, keep out, prohibit ≠ **let in the Bar** = **barristers**, body of lawyers, counsel, court, judgment, tribunal

barb *n* 1 = **dig**, affront, cut, gibe, insult,

barbecue n 1 grill on which food is cooked over hot charcoal, usu. outdoors. ◆ v 2 cook (food) on a barbecue.

barber n person who cuts men's hair and shaves beards.

barbiturate n drug used as a sedative.

bard n Lit poet.

bare ⊕ adj 1 unclothed, naked. 2 without the natural or usual covering. 3 unembellished, simple. 4 just sufficient. ◆ v 5 uncover. **barely** adv only just. **bareness** n

---

✓ **WORD TIP**

As *barely* already has a negative meaning, it should never be used with *not* or other negatives.

---

bargain ⊕ n 1 agreement establishing what each party will give, receive, or perform in a transaction. 2 something bought or offered at a low price. ◆ v 3 negotiate the terms of an agreement. **bargain for** v anticipate or take into account.

barge ⊕ n 1 flat–bottomed boat used to transport freight. ◆ v 2 Informal push violently. **barge in, into** v interrupt rudely.

baritone n (singer with) the second lowest adult male voice.

barium n Chem soft white metallic element.

bark¹ ⊕ n 1 loud harsh cry of a dog. ◆ v 2 (of a dog) make its typical cry. 3 shout in an angry tone.

bark² ⊕ n tough outer layer of a tree.

barley n tall grasslike plant cultivated for grain.

barmy ⊕ adj –mler, –mlest Slang Insane.

barn n large building on a farm used for storing grain.

barnacle n shellfish that lives attached to rocks, ship bottoms, etc.

barometer n instrument for measuring atmospheric pressure. **barometric** adj

baron n 1 member of the lowest rank of nobility. 2 powerful businessman. **baroness** n **baronial** adj

baronet n commoner who holds the lowest hereditary British title.

baroque [bar–**rock**] n 1 highly ornate style of art, architecture, or music from the late 16th to the early 18th century. ◆ adj 2 ornate in style.

barque [**bark**] n sailing ship, esp. one with three masts.

barracks ⊕ pl n building used to accommodate military personnel.

barrage ⊕ [**bar**–rahzh] n 1 continuous delivery of questions, complaints, etc. 2 continuous artillery fire. 3 artificial barrier across a river to control the water level.

barrel n 1 cylindrical container with rounded sides and flat ends. 2 tube in a

=== THESAURUS ===

sarcasm, scoff, sneer 2 = **point**, bristle, prickle, prong, quill, spike, spur, thorn

bare adj 1 = **naked**, nude, stripped, unclad, unclothed, uncovered, undressed, without a stitch on (inf) ≠ **covered** 3 = **plain**, austere, basic, sheer, simple, spare, spartan, stark, unadorned, unembellished ≠ **adorned**

bargain n 1 = **agreement**, arrangement, contract, pact, pledge, promise 2 = **good buy**, (cheap) purchase, discount, giveaway, good deal, reduction, snip (inf), steal (inf) ◆ v 3 = **negotiate**, agree, contract, covenant, cut a deal, promise, stipulate, transact

barge n 1 = **canal boat**, flatboat, lighter, narrow boat

bark¹ n 1 = **yap**, bay, howl, woof, yelp ◆ v 2 = **yap**, bay, howl, woof, yelp

bark² n = **covering**, casing, cortex (Anat, bot), crust, husk, rind, skin

barmy adj Sl = **insane**, crazy, daft (inf), foolish, idiotic, nuts (sl), out of one's mind, stupid ≠ **reasonable**

barracks pl n = **camp**, billet, encampment, garrison, quarters

barrage n 1 = **torrent**, burst, deluge, hail, mass, onslaught, plethora, stream 2 = **bombardment**, battery, cannonade, fusillade, gunfire, salvo, shelling, volley

firearm through which the bullet is fired.
barrel organ musical instrument played by
turning a handle.
barren ⦿ adj 1 (of a woman or female
animal) incapable of producing offspring.
2 (of land) unable to support the growth
of crops, fruit, etc. **barrenness** n
barricade ⦿ n 1 barrier, esp. one erected
hastily for defence. ◆ v 2 erect a barricade
across (an entrance).
barrier ⦿ n anything that prevents access,
progress, or union.
barrister n lawyer qualified to plead in a
higher court.
barrow n 1 wheelbarrow. 2 movable stall
used by street traders.
barter ⦿ v 1 trade (goods) in exchange for
other goods. ◆ n 2 trade by the exchange
of goods.
base¹ ⦿ n 1 bottom or supporting part of
anything. 2 fundamental part. 3 centre of
operations, organization, or supply. 4
starting point. ◆ v 5 (foll. by on or upon)
use as a basis (for). 6 (foll. by at or in)
station or place. **baseless** adj **basement** n
partly or wholly underground storey of a
building.

base² ⦿ adj 1 dishonourable or immoral. 2
of inferior quality or value. **basely** adv
baseness n
baseball n 1 team game in which runs are
scored by hitting a ball with a bat then
running round four bases. 2 ball used for
this.
bash ⦿ Informal ◆ v 1 hit violently or
forcefully. ◆ n 2 heavy blow.
bashful ⦿ adj shy or modest.
basic ⦿ adj 1 of or forming a base or basis.
2 elementary or simple. **basics** pl n
fundamental principles, facts, etc.
basically adv
basil n aromatic herb used in cooking.
basin n 1 round open container. 2 sink for
washing the hands and face. 3 sheltered
area of water where boats may be
moored. 4 catchment area of a particular
river.
basis ⦿ n, pl **–ses** fundamental principles
etc. from which something is started or
developed.
bask ⦿ v lie in or be exposed to
something, esp. pleasant warmth.
basket n container made of interwoven
strips of wood or cane.

——————[THESAURUS]——————

barren adj 1 = **infertile**, childless, sterile
2 = **unproductive**, arid, desert, desolate,
dry, empty, unfruitful, waste ≠ **rich**
barricade n 1 = **barrier**, blockade, bulwark,
fence, obstruction, palisade, rampart,
stockade ◆ v 2 = **bar**, block, blockade,
defend, fortify, obstruct, protect, shut in
barrier n a = **barricade**, bar, blockade,
boundary, fence, obstacle, obstruction,
wall b = **hindrance**, difficulty, drawback,
handicap, hurdle, obstacle, restriction,
stumbling block
barter v 1 = **trade**, bargain, drive a hard
bargain, exchange, haggle, sell, swap,
traffic
base¹ n 1 = **bottom**, bed, foot, foundation,
pedestal, rest, stand, support ≠ **top**
2 = **basis**, core, essence, heart, key, origin,
root, source 3 = **centre**, camp,
headquarters, home, post, settlement,

starting point, station ◆ v 5 (foll. by on or
upon) = **found**, build, construct, depend,
derive, establish, ground, hinge 6 (foll. by
at or in) = **place**, locate, post, station
base² adj 1 = **dishonourable**, contemptible,
despicable, disreputable, evil, immoral,
scungy (Aust & NZ inf), shameful, sordid,
wicked 2 = **bad**, deficient, dire, mean,
poor, rotten
bash Inf v 1 = **hit**, belt (inf), smash, sock
(sl), strike, wallop (inf)
bashful adj = **shy**, blushing, coy, diffident,
reserved, reticent, retiring, timid
basic adj 1 = **essential**, fundamental, key,
necessary, primary, vital ≠ **secondary**
2 = **elementary**, simple
basis n = **foundation**, base, bottom,
footing, ground, groundwork, support
bask v = **lie in**, laze, loll, lounge, outspan (S
Afr), relax, sunbathe

bass¹ ⊕ **[base]** n 1 (singer with) the lowest adult male voice. ♦ adj 2 of the lowest range of musical notes.

bass² n edible sea fish.

bassoon n low-pitched woodwind instrument.

bastard ⊕ n 1 Offens obnoxious or despicable person. 2 person born of parents not married to each other. **bastardize** v debase or corrupt.

baste v moisten (meat) during cooking with hot fat.

bastion ⊕ n 1 projecting part of a fortification. 2 thing or person regarded as defending a principle.

bat¹ ⊕ n 1 any of various types of club used to hit the ball in certain sports. ♦ v **batting, batted** 2 strike with or as if with a bat. **batsman** n Cricket person who bats or specializes in batting.

bat² n nocturnal mouselike flying animal.

batch ⊕ n group of people or things dealt with at the same time.

bated adj **with bated breath** in suspense or fear.

bath ⊕ n 1 large container in which to wash the body. 2 act of washing in such a container. ♦ pl 3 public swimming pool. ♦ v 4 wash in a bath. **bathroom** n room with a bath, sink, and usu. a toilet.

bathe ⊕ v 1 swim in open water for

pleasure. 2 apply liquid to (the skin or a wound) in order to cleanse or soothe. 3 (foll. by in) fill (with), e.g. bathed in sunlight. **bather** n

baton ⊕ n 1 thin stick used by the conductor of an orchestra. 2 short bar transferred in a relay race. 3 police officer's truncheon.

battalion n army unit consisting of three or more companies.

batten ⊕ n strip of wood fixed to something, esp. to hold it in place. **batten down** v secure with battens.

batter¹ ⊕ v 1 hit repeatedly. 2 damage or injure, as by blows, heavy wear, etc., e.g. battered by gales. **battering ram** large beam used to break down fortifications.

batter² n mixture of flour, eggs, and milk, used in cooking.

battery ⊕ n, pl **-teries** 1 device that produces electricity in a torch, radio, etc. 2 group of heavy guns operating as a single unit. ♦ adj 3 kept in series of cages for intensive rearing.

battle ⊕ n 1 fight between large armed forces. 2 conflict or struggle. ♦ v 3 struggle.

battlement n wall with gaps along the top for firing through.

battleship ⊕ n large heavily armoured warship.

bass¹ adj 3 = **deep**, deep-toned, low, low-pitched, resonant, sonorous

bastard n 1 Offens = **rogue**, blackguard, miscreant, reprobate, scoundrel, villain, wretch 2 = **illegitimate child**, love child, natural child

bastion n 1 = **stronghold**, bulwark, citadel, defence, fortress 2 = **tower of strength**, mainstay, prop, rock, support

bat¹ v 2 = **hit**, bang, smack, strike, swat, thump, wallop (inf), whack

batch n = **group**, amount, assemblage, bunch, collection, crowd, lot, pack, quantity, set

bath n 2 = **wash**, cleansing, douche, scrubbing, shower, soak, tub ♦ v

4 = **wash**, bathe, clean, douse, scrub down, shower, soak

bathe v 1 = **swim** 2 = **wash**, cleanse, rinse 3 (foll. by in) = **cover**, flood, immerse, steep, suffuse

baton n 1 = **stick**, wand 3 = **truncheon**, club, rod

batter¹ v 1 = **beat**, buffet, clobber (sl), pelt, pound, pummel, thrash, wallop (inf)

battery n 2 = **artillery**, cannon, cannonry, gun emplacements, guns

battle n 1 = **fight**, action, attack, combat, encounter, engagement, hostilities, skirmish ≠ accord 2 = **conflict**, campaign, contest, crusade, dispute, struggle ♦ v 3 = **struggle**, argue, clamour, dispute,

batty ❶ *adj* **–tier, –tiest** *Slang* eccentric or crazy.

bauble ❶ *n* trinket of little value.

bawdy ❶ *adj* **bawdier, bawdiest** (of writing etc.) containing humorous references to sex. **bawdiness** *n*

bawl ❶ *v* shout or weep noisily.

bay¹ ❶ *n* stretch of coastline that curves inwards.

bay² ❶ *n* 1 recess in a wall. 2 area set aside for a particular purpose, e.g. *loading bay*. 3 compartment in an aircraft, e.g. *bomb bay*. **bay window** window projecting from a wall.

bay³ ❶ *n* 1 deep howl of a hound or wolf. ◆ *v* 2 howl in deep prolonged tones. **at bay** 1 forced to turn and face attackers. 2 at a safe distance.

bayonet *n* 1 sharp blade that can be fixed to the end of a rifle. ◆ *v* **–neting, –neted** 2 stab with a bayonet.

bazaar ❶ *n* 1 sale in aid of charity. 2 market area, esp. in Eastern countries.

bazooka *n* portable rocket launcher that fires an armour–piercing projectile.

B & B bed and breakfast.

BBC British Broadcasting Corporation.

BC 1 before Christ. 2 British Columbia.

be ❶ *v*, *present sing 1st person* **am**. *2nd person* **are**. *3rd person* **is**. *present pl* **are**. *past sing 1st person* **was**. *2nd person* **were**.

3rd person **was**. *past pl* **were**. *present participle* **being**. *past participle* **been** 1 exist or live. 2 used as a linking between the subject of a sentence and its complement, e.g. *John is a musician*. 3 forms the progressive present tense, e.g. *the man is running*. 4 forms the passive voice of all transitive verbs, e.g. *a good film is being shown on television tonight*.

beach ❶ *n* 1 area of sand or pebbles on a shore. ◆ *v* 2 run or haul (a boat) onto a beach.

beacon ❶ *n* fire or light on a hill or tower, used as a warning.

bead ❶ *n* 1 small piece of plastic, wood, etc., pierced for threading on a string to form a necklace etc. 2 small drop of moisture. **beaded** *adj* **beading** *n* strip of moulding used for edging furniture. **beady** *adj* small, round, and glittering, e.g. *beady eyes*.

beagle *n* small hound with short legs and drooping ears.

beak ❶ *n* 1 projecting horny jaws of a bird. 2 *Slang* nose. **beaky** *adj* **beakier, beakiest**

beaker *n* 1 large drinking cup. 2 lipped glass container used in laboratories.

beam ❶ *n* 1 broad smile. 2 ray of light. 3 narrow flow of electromagnetic radiation or particles. 4 long thick piece of wood, metal, etc., used in building. ◆ *v* 5 smile

────────┤ T H E S A U R U S ├────────

fight, lock horns, strive, war

battleship *n* **= warship**, gunboat, man–of–war

batty *adj* *Sl* **= crazy**, daft (*inf*), dotty (*sl, chiefly Brit*), eccentric, mad, munted (*NZ sl*), odd, peculiar, potty (*Brit inf*), touched

bauble *n* **= trinket**, bagatelle, gewgaw, gimcrack, knick–knack, plaything, toy, trifle

bawdy *adj* **= rude**, coarse, dirty, indecent, lascivious, lecherous, lewd, ribald, salacious, scungy (*Aust & NZ inf*), smutty

bawl *v* **a = shout**, bellow, call, clamour, howl, roar, yell **b = cry**, blubber, sob, wail, weep

bay¹ *n* **= inlet**, bight, cove, gulf, natural

harbour, sound

bay² *n* 2 **= recess**, alcove, compartment, niche, nook, opening

bay³ *n* 1 **= howl**, bark, clamour, cry, yelp ◆ *v* 2 **= howl**, bark, clamour, cry, yelp

bazaar *n* 1 **= fair**, bring–and–buy, fete, sale of work 2 **= market**, exchange, marketplace

be *v* 1 **= exist**, be alive, breathe, inhabit, live

beach *n* 1 **= shore**, coast, sands, seashore, seaside, water's edge

beacon *n* **= signal**, beam, bonfire, flare, sign

bead *n* 2 **= drop**, bubble, droplet, globule

beak *n* 1 **= bill**, mandible, neb (*arch or*

broadly. **6** divert or aim (a radio signal, light, etc.) in a certain direction.

bean n seed or pod of various plants, eaten as a vegetable or used to make coffee etc.

beanie n Brit, Aust & NZ close–fitting woollen hat.

bear¹ ⊕ v **bearing, bore, borne 1** support or hold up. **2** bring, e.g. to bear gifts. **3** (passive **born**) give birth to. **4** produce as by natural growth. **5** tolerate or endure. **6** hold in the mind. **7** show or be marked with. **8** move in a specified direction. **bearable** adj **bear out** v show to be truthful.

bear² n large heavy mammal with a shaggy coat. **bearskin** n tall fur helmet worn by some British soldiers.

beard n hair growing on the lower parts of a man's face.

bearing ⊕ n **1** relevance (to). **2** person's general social conduct. **3** part of a machine that supports another part, esp. one that reduces friction. ♦ pl **4** sense of one's own relative position.

beast ⊕ n **1** large wild animal. **2** brutal or uncivilized person. **beastly** adj unpleasant or disagreeable.

beat ⊕ v **beating, beat, beaten** or **beat 1** hit hard and repeatedly. **2** move (wings) up and down. **3** throb rhythmically. **4** stir or mix vigorously. **5** overcome or defeat. ♦ n **6** regular throb. **7** assigned route, as of a policeman. **8** basic rhythmic unit in a piece of music. **beat up** v injure (someone) by repeated blows or kicks.

beau ⊕ [boh] n, pl **beaux, beaus 1** boyfriend or admirer. **2** man greatly concerned with his appearance.

beauty ⊕ n, pl **–ties 1** combination of all the qualities of a person or thing that delight the senses and mind. **2** very attractive woman. **3** Informal something outstanding of its kind. **beautiful** adj very attractive to look at.

beaver n amphibious rodent with a big flat tail. **beaver away** v work industriously.

becalmed ⊕ adj (of a sailing ship) motionless through lack of wind.

because ⊕ conj on account of the fact that. **because of** on account of.

──────── THESAURUS ────────

dial), nib **2** Sl = **nose**, proboscis, snout

beam n **1** = **smile**, grin **2** = **ray**, gleam, glimmer, glint, glow, shaft, streak, stream **4** = **rafter**, girder, joist, plank, spar, support, timber ♦ v **5** = **smile**, grin **6** = **send out**, broadcast, emit, transmit

bear¹ v **1** = **support**, have, hold, maintain, possess, shoulder, sustain, uphold ≠ **drop 2** = **carry**, bring, convey, hump (Brit sl), move, take, transport ≠ **drop 3**, **4** = **produce**, beget, breed, bring forth, engender, generate, give birth to, yield **5** = **tolerate**, abide, allow, brook, endure, permit, put up with (inf), stomach, suffer

bearing n **1** = **relevance**, application, connection, import, pertinence, reference, relation, significance ≠ **irrelevance 2** = **manner**, air, aspect, attitude, behaviour, demeanour, deportment, posture ♦ pl **4** = **position**, aim, course, direction, location, orientation, situation, track, way, whereabouts

beast n **1** = **animal**, brute, creature **2** = **brute**, barbarian, fiend, monster, ogre, sadist, savage, swine

beat v **1** = **hit**, bang, batter, buffet, knock, pound, strike, thrash **2** = **flap**, flutter **3** = **throb**, palpitate, pound, pulsate, quake, thump, vibrate **5** = **defeat**, conquer, outdo, overcome, overwhelm, surpass, vanquish ♦ n **6** = **throb**, palpitation, pulsation, pulse **7** = **route**, circuit, course, path, rounds, way **8** = **rhythm**, accent, cadence, metre, stress, time

beau n **1** = **boyfriend**, admirer, fiancé, lover, suitor, sweetheart **2** = **dandy**, coxcomb, fop, gallant, ladies' man

beauty n **1** = **attractiveness**, charm, comeliness, elegance, exquisiteness, glamour, grace, handsomeness, loveliness ≠ **ugliness 2** = **belle**, good–looker, lovely (sl), stunner (inf)

becalmed adj = **still**, motionless, settled,

✓ **WORD TIP**

It is unnecessary to follow *because* with
*the reason is/was: He was cold because
the window was open* or *The reason he
was cold was that the window was open.*

beck *n* **at someone's beck and call** having
to be constantly available to do as
someone asks.

beckon ● *v* summon with a gesture.

become ● *v* –coming, –came, –come 1
come to be. 2 (foll. by *of*) happen to. 3
suit. **becoming** *adj* 1 attractive or pleasing.
2 appropriate or proper.

bed ● *n* 1 piece of furniture on which to
sleep. 2 garden plot. 3 bottom of a river,
lake, or sea. 4 layer of rock. **bed down** *v*
go to or put into a place to sleep or rest.
bedpan *n* shallow bowl used as a toilet by
bedridden people. **bedridden** *adj* confined
to bed because of illness or old age.
bedrock *n* 1 solid rock beneath the surface
soil. 2 basic facts or principles. **bedroom** *n*
bedsit, bedsitter *n* furnished sitting room
with a bed.

bedevil ● *v* –illing, –illed harass, confuse,
or torment.

bedlam ● *n* noisy confused situation.

bedraggled ● *adj* untidy, wet, or dirty.

bee *n* insect that makes wax and honey.
beehive *n* structure in which bees live.
beeswax *n* wax secreted by bees, used in
polishes etc.

beech *n* European tree with a smooth
greyish bark.

beef *n* flesh of a cow, bull, or ox. **beefy** *adj*
1 like beef. 2 *Informal* strong and
muscular. **beefburger** *n* flat grilled or fried
cake of minced beef.

beer *n* alcoholic drink brewed from malt
and hops.

beet *n* plant with an edible root and leaves.
beetroot *n* type of beet plant with a dark
red root.

beetle *n* insect with a hard wing cover on
its back.

befall ● *v* *Old–fashioned* happen to
(someone).

befit *v* be appropriate or suitable for.
befitting *adj*

before ● *conj, prep, adv* indicating
something earlier in time, in front of, or
preferred to, e.g. *before the war; brought
before a judge; death before dishonour.*
beforehand *adv* in advance.

befriend ● *v* become friends with.

beg ● *v* begging, begged 1 solicit (for
money or food), esp. in the street. 2 ask
formally or humbly.

stranded, stuck

because *conj* = **since**, as, by reason of, in
that, on account of, owing to, thanks to

beckon *v* = **gesture**, bid, gesticulate,
motion, nod, signal, summon, wave at

become *v* 1 = **come to be**, alter to, be
transformed into, change into, develop
into, grow into, mature into, ripen into
3 = **suit**, embellish, enhance, fit, flatter, set
off

bed *n* 1 = **bedstead**, berth, bunk, cot,
couch, divan 2 = **plot**, area, border,
garden, patch, row, strip 3 = **bottom**, base

bedevil *v* = **torment**, afflict, confound,
confuse, distress, harass, plague, trouble,
vex, worry

bedlam *n* = **pandemonium**, chaos,

commotion, confusion, furore, tumult,
turmoil, uproar

bedraggled *adj* = **messy**, dirty,
dishevelled, disordered, muddied,
unkempt, untidy

befall *v* *Old–fashioned* = **happen**, chance,
come to pass, fall, occur, take place,
transpire (*inf*)

① **before** *prep* a = **earlier than**, in advance
of, prior to b = **ahead of**, in advance of, in
front of

② **before** *adv* a = **previously**, ahead,
earlier, formerly, in advance, sooner b = **in
front**, ahead

befriend *v* = **help**, aid, assist, back,
encourage, side with, stand by, support,
welcome

begin ⊕ *v* **–ginning, –gan, –gun 1** start. **2** bring or come into being. **beginner** *n* person who has just started learning to do something. **beginning** *n*

begonia *n* tropical plant with waxy flowers.

begrudge ⊕ *v* **1** envy (someone) the possession of something. **2** give or allow unwillingly.

beguile ⊕ [big–gile] *v* **1** cheat or mislead. **2** charm or amuse. **beguiling** *adj*

behalf *n* **on behalf of** in the interest of or for the benefit of.

behave ⊕ *v* **1** act or function in a particular way. **2** conduct (oneself) properly. **behaviour** *n* manner of behaving.

behead *v* remove the head from.

behest *n* order or earnest request.

behind ⊕ *prep, adv* **1** indicating position to the rear, lateness, responsibility, etc., e.g. *behind the wall; behind schedule; the reasons behind her departure.* ◆ *n* **2** *Informal* buttocks.

behold ⊕ *v* **–holding, –held** *Old–fashioned* look (at). **beholder** *n*

beholden ⊕ *adj* indebted or obliged.

beige *adj* pale brown.

being ⊕ *n* **1** state or fact of existing. **2** something that exists or is thought to exist. **3** human being. ◆ *v* **4** present participle of BE.

belated ⊕ *adj* late or too late. **belatedly** *adv*

belch ⊕ *v* **1** expel wind from the stomach noisily through the mouth. **2** expel or be expelled forcefully, e.g. *smoke belched from the factory.* ◆ *n* **3** act of belching.

beleaguered ⊕ *adj* **1** struggling against difficulties or criticism. **2** besieged by an enemy.

belfry *n, pl* **–fries** part of a tower where bells are hung.

belie *v* show to be untrue.

belief ⊕ *n* **1** faith or confidence. **2** opinion. **3** principle accepted as true, often without

——————— THESAURUS ———————

beg *v* **1** = **scrounge**, bludge (*Aust & NZ*), cadge, seek charity, solicit charity, sponge on, touch (someone) for (*sl*) ≠ **give 2** = **implore**, beseech, entreat, petition, plead, request, solicit

begin *v* **1** = **start**, commence, embark on, initiate, instigate, institute, prepare, set about ≠ **end 2** = **happen**, appear, arise, come into being, emerge, originate, start ≠ **cease**

begrudge *v* **1** = **resent**, be jealous, envy, grudge

beguile *v* **1** = **fool**, cheat, deceive, delude, dupe, hoodwink, mislead, take for a ride (*inf*), trick ≠ **alert 2** = **charm**, amuse, distract, divert, engross, entertain, occupy

behave *v* **1** = **act**, function, operate, perform, run, work **2** = **conduct oneself properly**, act correctly, keep one's nose clean, mind one's manners ≠ **carry on** (*inf*)

① **behind** *prep* **a** = **after**, at the back of, at the heels of, at the rear of, following, later than ≠ **in front of b** = **causing**, at the bottom of, initiating, instigating, responsible for

② **behind** *adv* **a** = **after**, afterwards, following, in the wake (of), next, subsequently **b** = **overdue**, behindhand, in arrears, in debt

behold *v Old–fashioned* = **look at**, observe, perceive, regard, survey, view, watch, witness

beholden *adj* = **indebted**, bound, grateful, obliged, owing, under obligation

being *n* **1** = **existence**, life, reality ≠ **oblivion 2** = **nature**, entity, essence, soul, spirit, substance **3** = **human being**, creature, individual

belated *adj* = **late**, behindhand, behind time, delayed, late in the day, overdue, tardy

belch *v* **1** = **burp** (*inf*), hiccup **2** = **emit**, discharge, disgorge, erupt, give off, spew forth, vent

beleaguered *adj* **1** = **harassed**, badgered, hassled (*inf*), persecuted, pestered, plagued, put upon, vexed **2** = **besieged**, assailed, beset, blockaded, hemmed in, proof. **believe** v **1** accept as true or real. **2** think, assume, or suppose. **3** accept (someone's) statement or opinion as true, e.g. *I don't believe you!* **believe in** be convinced of the truth or existence of. **believable** adj

belittle ⊕ v treat as having little value or importance.

bell n **1** hollow, usu. metal, cup–shaped instrument that emits a ringing sound when struck. **2** device that rings or buzzes as a signal.

belle n beautiful woman, esp. the most attractive woman at a function.

bellicose adj warlike and aggressive.

belligerent ⊕ adj **1** hostile and aggressive. **2** engaged in war. ◆ n **3** person or country engaged in war. **belligerence** n

bellow ⊕ v **1** make a low deep cry like that of a bull. **2** shout in anger. ◆ n **3** loud deep roar.

bellows pl n instrument for pumping a stream of air into something.

belly ⊕ n, pl –**lies 1** part of the body of a vertebrate which contains the intestines. **2** stomach. **3** front, lower, or inner part of something. ◆ v –**lying, –lied 4** (cause to) swell out.

belong ⊕ v **1** (foll. by *to*) be the property of. **2** (foll. by *to*) be a part or member of. **belongings** pl n personal possessions.

beloved ⊕ adj **1** dearly loved. ◆ n **2** person dearly loved.

below ⊕ prep, adv at or to a position lower than, under.

belt ⊕ n **1** band of cloth, leather, etc., worn usu. around the waist. **2** long narrow area, e.g. *a belt of trees.* **3** circular strip of rubber that drives moving parts in a machine. ◆ v **4** fasten with a belt. **5** *Slang* hit very hard. **6** *Slang* move very fast.

bemoan v express sorrow or dissatisfaction about.

bench ⊕ n **1** long seat. **2** long narrow work table. **the bench** judge or magistrate sitting in court, or judges and magistrates collectively. **benchmark** n criterion by which to measure something.

bend ⊕ v **bending, bent 1** (cause to) form a curve. **2** (often foll. by *down*) etc. incline the body. ◆ n **3** curved part. ◆ pl **4** *Informal* decompression sickness. **bendy** adj

beneath ⊕ adv, prep **1** below. **2** not

surrounded

belief n **1** = **faith**, assurance, confidence, conviction, trust ≠ **doubt 2** = **opinion**, feeling, impression, judgment, notion **3** = **faith**, credo, creed, doctrine, dogma, ideology, principles, tenet

belittle v = **disparage**, decry, denigrate, deprecate, deride, scoff at, scorn, sneer at

belligerent adj **1** = **aggressive**, bellicose, combative, hostile, pugnacious, unfriendly, warlike, warring ≠ **friendly** ◆ n **3** = **fighter**, combatant, warring nation

bellow v **2** = **shout**, bawl, cry, howl, roar, scream, shriek, yell ◆ n **3** = **shout**, bawl, cry, howl, roar, scream, shriek, yell

belly n **1, 2** = **stomach**, abdomen, corporation (*inf*), gut, insides (*inf*), paunch, potbelly, tummy ◆ v **4** = **swell out**, billow, bulge, fill, spread, swell

belong v **1** (foll. by *to*) = **be the property**

of, be at the disposal of, be held by, be owned by **2** (foll. by *to*) = **be a member of**, be affiliated to, be allied to, be associated with, be included in

beloved adj **1** = **dear**, admired, adored, darling, loved, pet, precious, prized, treasured, valued, worshipped

① **below** prep = **lower than**, inferior, lesser, less than, subject, subordinate

② **below** adv = **lower**, beneath, down, under, underneath

belt n **1** = **waistband**, band, cummerbund, girdle, girth, sash **2** = **zone**, area, district, layer, region, stretch, strip, tract

bemoan v = **lament**, bewail, deplore, grieve for, mourn, regret, rue, weep for

bench n **1** = **seat**, form, pew, settle, stall **2** = **worktable**, board, counter, table, trestle table, workbench **the bench 1** = **court**, courtroom, judges, judiciary, worthy of.

benefit ⊕ n 1 something that improves or promotes. 2 advantage or sake, e.g. *I'm doing this for your benefit.* 3 payment made by a government to a poor, ill, or unemployed person. ♦ v –**fiting**, –**fited** 4 do or receive good. **beneficial** *adj*

benign ⊕ [bi–**nine**] *adj* 1 showing kindliness. 2 (of a tumour) not threatening to life.

bent ⊕ v 1 past of BEND. ♦ *adj* 2 curved. 3 *Slang* dishonest or corrupt. ♦ n 4 personal inclination or aptitude. **bent on** determined to pursue (a course of action).

benzene n flammable poisonous liquid used as a solvent, insecticide, etc.

bequeath ⊕ v dispose of (property) as in a will. **bequest** n legal gift of money or property by someone who has died.

berate ⊕ v scold harshly.

beret [**ber**–ray] n round flat close–fitting brimless cap.

berg n S Afr mountain.

berm n NZ narrow grass strip between the road and the footpath in a residential area.

berry n, pl –**ries** small soft stoneless fruit.

berserk ⊕ *adj* **go berserk** become violent or destructive.

berth ⊕ n 1 bunk in a ship or train. 2 place assigned to a ship at a mooring. ♦ v 3 dock (a ship).

beryl n hard transparent mineral.

beseech ⊕ v –**seeching**, –**sought** or –**seeched** ask earnestly; beg.

beset ⊕ v trouble or harass constantly.

beside ⊕ prep 1 at, by, or to the side of. 2 as compared with. **beside oneself** overwhelmed or overwrought. **besides** *adv, prep* in addition.

besiege ⊕ v 1 surround with military forces. 2 overwhelm, as with requests.

besotted ⊕ *adj* infatuated.

bespoke *adj* (esp. of a suit) made to the customer's specifications.

best ⊕ *adj* 1 most excellent of a particular group etc. ♦ *adv* 2 in a manner surpassing

magistrates, tribunal

bend v 1 = **curve**, arc, arch, bow, turn, twist, veer 2 = **lean**, bow ♦ n 3 = **curve**, angle, arc, arch, bow, corner, loop, turn, twist

① **beneath** *adv* 1 = **underneath**, below, in a lower place

② **beneath** *prep* 1 = **under**, below, lower than, underneath ≠ **over** 2 = **unworthy of**, below, inferior to, less than, unbefitting

benefit n 1 = **help**, advantage, aid, asset, assistance, favour, good, profit ≠ **loss** ♦ v 4 = **help**, aid, assist, avail, enhance, further, improve, profit ≠ **damage**

benign *adj* 1 = **kindly**, amiable, friendly, genial, kind, obliging, sympathetic ≠ **bad** 2 = **harmless**, curable, remediable ≠ **malignant**

bent *adj* 2 = **curved**, angled, arched, bowed, crooked, hunched, stooped, twisted ≠ **even** ♦ n 4 = **inclination**, ability, aptitude, leaning, penchant, preference, propensity, tendency

bequeath v = **leave**, bestow, endow,

entrust, give, grant, hand down, impart, pass on, will

berate v = **scold**, castigate, censure, chide, criticize, harangue, rebuke, reprimand, reprove, rouse on (*Aust*), tell off (*inf*), upbraid

berserk *adj* **go berserk** = **go crazy**, go mad, go wild, raging, rampage, run amok

berth n 1 = **bunk**, bed, billet, hammock 2 = **anchorage**, dock, harbour, haven, pier, port, quay, wharf ♦ v 3 = **anchor**, dock, drop anchor, land, moor, tie up

beseech v = **beg**, ask, call upon, entreat, implore, plead, pray, solicit

beset v = **plague**, bedevil, harass, pester, trouble

beside prep 1 = **next to**, abreast of, adjacent to, alongside, at the side of, close to, near, nearby, neighbouring

besiege v 1 = **surround**, blockade, encircle, hem in, lay siege to, shut in 2 = **harass**, badger, harry, hassle (*inf*), hound, nag, pester, plague

besotted *adj* = **infatuated**, doting,

all others. ◆ *n* **3** most outstanding or excellent person, thing, or group in a category. **best man** groom's attendant at a wedding. **bestseller** *n* book or other product that has sold in great numbers.

bestial ● *adj* **1** brutal or savage. **2** of or like a beast. **bestiality** *n*

bestir *v* cause (oneself) to become active.

bestow ● *v* present (a gift) or confer (an honour).

bet ● *n* **1** the act of staking a sum of money or other stake on the outcome of an event. **2** stake risked. ◆ *v* **betting, bet** or **betted 3** make or place (a bet). **4** *Informal* predict.

betray ● *v* **1** hand over or expose (one's nation, friend, etc.) treacherously to an enemy. **2** disclose (a secret or confidence) treacherously. **3** reveal unintentionally. **betrayal** *n* **betrayer** *n*

better ● *adj* **1** more excellent than others. **2** improved or fully recovered in health. ◆

adv **3** in a more excellent manner. **4** in or to a greater degree. ◆ *pl n* **5** one's superiors. ◆ *v* **6** improve upon.

between ● *prep, adv* indicating position in the middle, alternatives, etc.

✔ **WORD TIP**

Between is used when two people or things are mentioned: *the trade war between Europe and America.* Otherwise use *among*.

bevel *n* **1** slanting edge. ◆ *v* **–elling, –elled 2** cut a bevel on (a piece of timber etc.).

beverage ● *n* drink.

bevy ● *n, pl* **bevies** flock or group.

bewail ● *v* express great sorrow over.

beware ● *v* be on one's guard (against).

bewilder ● *v* confuse utterly. **bewildering** *adj* **bewilderment** *n*

bewitch ● *v* **1** attract and fascinate. **2** cast a spell over. **bewitching** *adj*

──────── THESAURUS ────────

hypnotized, smitten, spellbound

best *adj* **1** = **finest**, foremost, leading, most excellent, outstanding, pre–eminent, principal, supreme, unsurpassed ◆ *adv* **2** = **most highly**, extremely, greatly, most deeply, most fully ◆ *n* **3** = **finest**, cream, elite, flower, pick, prime, top

bestial *adj* **1** = **brutal**, barbaric, beastly, brutish, inhuman, savage

bestow *v* = **present**, award, commit, give, grant, hand out, impart, lavish

bet *n* **1** = **gamble**, long shot, risk, speculation, venture, wager **2** = **stake** ◆ *v* **4** = **gamble**, chance, hazard, risk, speculate, stake, venture, wager

betray *v* **1** = **be disloyal**, be treacherous, be unfaithful, break one's promise, double–cross (*inf*), inform on *or* against, sell out (*inf*), stab in the back **2, 3** = **give away**, disclose, divulge, let slip, reveal

better *adj* **1** = **superior**, excelling, finer, greater, higher–quality, more desirable, preferable, surpassing ≠ **worse 2** = **well**, cured, fully recovered, on the mend (*inf*), recovering, stronger ≠ **worse** ◆ *adv* **3** = **in**

a more excellent manner, in a superior way, more advantageously, more attractively, more competently, more effectively ≠ **worse 4** = **to a greater degree**, more completely, more thoroughly ◆ *v* **6** = **improve**, enhance, further, raise ≠ **lower**

between *prep* = **amidst**, among, betwixt, in the middle of, mid

beverage *n* = **drink**, liquid, liquor, refreshment

bevy *n* = **group**, band, bunch (*inf*), collection, company, crowd, gathering, pack, troupe

bewail *v* = **lament**, bemoan, cry over, deplore, grieve for, moan, mourn, regret

beware *v* = **be careful**, be cautious, be wary, guard against, heed, look out, mind, take heed, watch out

bewilder *v* = **confound**, baffle, bemuse, confuse, flummox, mystify, nonplus, perplex, puzzle

bewitch *v* = **enchant**, beguile, captivate, charm, enrapture, entrance, fascinate, hypnotize

beyond *prep* 1 at or to a point on the other side of. 2 outside the limits or scope of. ♦ *adv* 3 at or to the far side of something.

bias *n* 1 mental tendency, esp. prejudice. 2 diagonal cut across the weave of a fabric. 3 *Bowls* bulge or weight on one side of a bowl that causes it to roll in a curve. ♦ *v* –asing, –ased *or* –assing, –assed 4 cause to have a bias. **biased, biassed** *adj*

bib *n* 1 piece of cloth or plastic worn to protect a young child's clothes when eating. 2 upper front part of dungarees etc.

Bible *n* 1 sacred writings of the Christian religion. 2 (b–) book regarded as authoritative. **biblical** *adj*

bibliography *n, pl* –phies 1 list of books on a subject. 2 list of sources used in a book etc.

bicentenary *n, pl* –naries 200th anniversary.

biceps *n* muscle with two origins, esp. the muscle that flexes the forearm.

bicker *v* argue over petty matters.

bicycle *n* vehicle with two wheels, one behind the other, pedalled by the rider.

bid *v* bidding, bade, bidden 1 say (a greeting). 2 command. 3 (*past* bid) offer (an amount) in an attempt to buy something. ♦ *n* 4 offer of a specified amount. 5 attempt. **bidder** *n* **biddable** *adj* obedient. **bidding** *n* command.

bide *v* bide one's time wait patiently for an opportunity.

bier *n* stand on which a corpse or coffin rests before burial.

big *adj* bigger, biggest 1 of considerable size, height, number, or capacity. 2 important through having power, wealth, etc. 3 elder. 4 generous. ♦ *adv* 5 on a grand scale. **bighead** *n* Informal conceited person. **big-headed** *adj* **big shot, bigwig** *n* Informal important person.

bigamy *n* crime of marrying a person while still legally married to someone else. **bigamist** *n* **bigamous** *adj*

bigot *n* person who is intolerant, esp. regarding religion or race. **bigoted** *adj* **bigotry** *n*

bike *n* Informal bicycle or motorcycle.

bikini *n* woman's brief two-piece swimming costume.

bilberry *n* bluish-black edible berry.

bile *n* bitter yellow fluid secreted by the liver.

bilge *n* 1 Informal nonsense. 2 ship's bottom.

bilingual *adj* involving or using two languages.

bill¹ *n* 1 statement of money owed for goods or services supplied. 2 draft of a proposed new law. 3 poster. 4 Chiefly US & Canadian piece of paper money. 5 list of events, such as a theatre programme. ♦ *v* 6 send or present a bill to. 7 advertise by posters.

——————————— THESAURUS ———————————

beyond *prep* 1 = past, above, apart from, at a distance, away from, over 2 = exceeding, out of reach of, superior to, surpassing

bias *n* 1 = prejudice, favouritism, inclination, leaning, partiality, tendency ≠ equity ♦ *v* 4 = prejudice, distort, influence, mana (NZ), predispose, slant, sway, twist, warp, weight

bicker *v* = quarrel, argue, disagree, dispute, fight, row (inf), squabble, wrangle

bid *v* 1 = say, call, greet, tell, wish 2 = tell, ask, command, direct, instruct, order,

require 3 = offer, proffer, propose, submit, tender ♦ *n* 4 = offer, advance, amount, price, proposal, sum, tender 5 = attempt, crack (*inf*), effort, go (*inf*), stab (*inf*), try

big *adj* 1 = large, enormous, extensive, great, huge, immense, massive, substantial, vast ≠ little 2 = important, eminent, influential, leading, main, powerful, prominent, significant ≠ ordinary 3 = grown-up, adult, elder, grown, mature ≠ young 4 = generous, altruistic, benevolent, gracious, magnanimous, noble, unselfish

bill² ● n bird's beak.

billet ● v –leting, –leted 1 assign a lodging to (a soldier). ◆ n 2 accommodation for a soldier in civil lodgings.

billiards n game played on a table with balls and a cue.

billion n 1 one thousand million. 2 formerly, one million million. **billionth** adj

billow ● n 1 large sea wave. ◆ v 2 rise up or swell out.

biltong n S Afr strips of dried meat.

bin n container for rubbish or for storing grain, coal, etc.

binary adj 1 composed of two parts. 2 Maths, computers of or in a counting system with only two digits, 0 and 1.

bind ● v binding, bound 1 make secure with or as if with a rope. 2 place (someone) under obligation. 3 enclose and fasten (the pages of a book) between covers. ◆ n 4 Informal annoying situation. **binder** n firm cover for holding loose sheets of paper together. **binding** n 1 anything that binds or fastens. 2 book cover.

binge ● n Informal bout of excessive indulgence, esp. in drink.

bingo n gambling game in which numbers are called out and covered by the players on their individual cards.

binoculars pl n optical instrument consisting of two small telescopes joined together.

bio– combining form life or living organisms, e.g. biology.

biodegradable adj capable of being decomposed by natural means.

biography ● n, pl –phies account of a person's life by another person. **biographical** adj **biographer** n

biology n study of living organisms. **biologist** n

bionic adj having a part of the body that is operated electronically.

biopsy n, pl –sies examination of tissue from a living body.

biped [bye–ped] n animal with two feet.

birch n 1 tree with thin peeling bark. 2 birch rod or twigs used, esp. formerly, for flogging offenders.

bird n 1 creature with feathers and wings, most types of which can fly. 2 Slang young woman.

birdie n Golf score of one stroke under par for a hole.

Biro n ® ballpoint pen.

birth ● n 1 process of bearing young; childbirth. 2 act of being born. 3 ancestry. **give birth to** bear (offspring). **birth control** any method of contraception. **birthday** n anniversary of the day of one's birth. **birthmark** n blemish on the skin formed before birth. **birthright** n privileges or possessions that someone is entitled to

bigot n = fanatic, racist, sectarian, zealot

bill¹ n 1 = charges, account, invoice, reckoning, score, statement, tally 2 = proposal, measure, piece of legislation, projected law 3 = advertisement, bulletin, circular, handbill, hand–out, leaflet, notice, placard, poster 5 = list, agenda, card, catalogue, inventory, listing, programme, roster, schedule ◆ v 6 = charge, debit, invoice 7 = advertise, announce, give advance notice of, post

bill² n = beak, mandible, neb (arch or dial), nib

billet v 1 = quarter, accommodate, berth, station ◆ n 2 = quarters, accommodation, barracks, lodging

billow n 1 = wave, breaker, crest, roller, surge, swell, tide ◆ v 2 = surge, balloon, belly, puff up, rise up, roll, swell

bind v 1 = tie, fasten, hitch, lash, secure, stick, strap, wrap ≠ free 2 = oblige, compel, constrain, engage, force, necessitate, require ◆ n 4 Inf = nuisance, bore, difficulty, dilemma, drag (inf), pain in the neck (inf), quandary, spot (inf)

binge n Inf = bout, bender (inf), feast, fling, orgy, spree

biography n = life story, account, curriculum vitae, CV, life, memoir, profile, as soon as he or she is born.

biscuit n small flat dry sweet or plain cake.

bisect ⊕ v divide into two equal parts.

bisexual adj sexually attracted to both men and women.

bishop n 1 clergyman who governs a diocese. 2 chessman which is moved diagonally. **bishopric** n diocese or office of a bishop.

bison n, pl **–son** large hairy animal of the cattle family.

bistro n, pl **–tros** small restaurant.

bit¹ ⊕ n 1 small piece, portion, or quantity. 2 short time or distance. **a bit** rather, somewhat. **bit by bit** gradually.

bit² ⊕ n 1 metal mouthpiece on a bridle. 2 cutting or drilling part of a tool.

bit³ v past tense of BITE.

bit⁴ n Maths, computers 1 single digit of binary notation, either 0 or 1. 2 smallest unit of information.

bitch n 1 female dog, fox, or wolf. 2 Offens spiteful woman. ◆ v 3 Informal complain or grumble. **bitchy** adj **bitchiness** n

bite ⊕ v **biting**, **bit**, **bitten** 1 grip, tear, or puncture the skin, as with the teeth or jaws. 2 take firm hold of or act effectively upon. ◆ n 3 act of biting. 4 wound or sting inflicted by biting. 5 snack. **biting** adj 1 piercing or keen. 2 sarcastic.

bitter ⊕ adj 1 having a sharp unpleasant taste. 2 showing or caused by hostility or resentment. 3 extremely cold. ◆ n 4 beer with a slightly bitter taste. ◆ pl 5 bitter-tasting alcoholic drink. **bitterly** adv **bitterness** n

bittern n wading marsh bird with a booming call.

bitty adj lacking unity, disjointed. **bittiness** n

bitumen n black sticky substance obtained from tar or petrol.

bivouac n 1 temporary camp in the open air. ◆ v **–acking**, **–acked** 2 camp in a bivouac.

bizarre ⊕ adj odd or unusual.

blab ⊕ v **blabbing**, **blabbed** reveal (secrets) indiscreetly.

black ⊕ adj 1 of the darkest colour, like coal. 2 (B–) dark-skinned. 3 without hope. 4 angry or resentful, e.g. black looks. 5 unpleasant in a macabre manner, e.g. black comedy. ◆ n 6 darkest colour. 7 (B–) member of a dark-skinned race. 8 complete darkness. ◆ v 9 make black. 10 (of trade unionists) boycott (goods or people). **blackness** n **blacken** v 1 make or become black. 2 defame or slander. **black magic** magic used for evil purposes. **black market** illegal trade in goods or currencies. **black sheep** person who is regarded as a disgrace by his or her family. **black spot** place on a road where accidents frequently occur.

———————————————————————— THESAURUS ————————————————————————

record

birth n 1 = **childbirth**, delivery, parturition ≠ **end** 2 = **nativity** 3 = **ancestry**, background, blood, breeding, lineage, parentage, pedigree, stock

bisect v = **cut in two**, cross, cut across, divide in two, halve, intersect, separate, split

bit¹ n 1 = **piece**, crumb, fragment, grain, morsel, part, scrap, speck

bit² n 1 = **curb**, brake, check, restraint, snaffle

bite v 1 = **cut**, chew, gnaw, nip, pierce, pinch, snap, tear, wound ◆ n 4 = **wound**, nip, pinch, prick, smarting, sting, tooth

marks 5 = **snack**, food, light meal, morsel, mouthful, piece, refreshment, taste, tucker (Aust & NZ inf)

bitter adj 1 = **sour**, acid, acrid, astringent, harsh, sharp, tart, unsweetened, vinegary ≠ **sweet** 2 = **resentful**, acrimonious, begrudging, hostile, sore, sour, sullen ≠ **happy** 3 = **freezing**, biting, fierce, intense, severe, stinging ≠ **gentle**

bizarre adj = **strange**, eccentric, extraordinary, fantastic, freakish, ludicrous, munted (NZ sl), outlandish, peculiar, unusual, zany

blab v = **tell**, blurt out, disclose, divulge, give away, let slip, let the cat out of the

✅ **WORD TIP**

When *black* is used as a political or racial term it has a capital letter.

blackguard ❶ [**blag**–gard] *n* unprincipled person.

blackmail ❶ *n* **1** act of attempting to extort money by threats. ♦ *v* **2** (attempt to) obtain money by blackmail.

blackout ❶ *n* **1** extinguishing of all light as a precaution against an air attack. **2** momentary loss of consciousness or memory. **black out** *v* **1** extinguish (lights). **2** lose consciousness or memory temporarily.

blacksmith *n* person who works iron with a furnace, anvil, etc.

bladder *n* **1** sac in the body where urine is held. **2** hollow bag which may be filled with air or liquid.

blade *n* **1** cutting edge of a weapon or tool. **2** thin flattish part of a propeller, oar, etc. **3** leaf of grass.

blame ❶ *v* **1** consider (someone) responsible for. ♦ *n* **2** responsibility for something that is wrong. **blameless** *adj* **blameworthy** *adj* deserving blame.

blanch *v* **1** become white or pale. **2** prepare (vegetables etc.) by plunging them in boiling water.

bland ❶ *adj* dull and uninteresting. **blandly** *adv*

blank ❶ *adj* **1** not written on. **2** showing no interest or expression. **3** *n* **4** empty space. **5** cartridge containing no bullet. **blankly** *adv* **1** **blank verse** unrhymed verse.

blanket ❶ *n* **1** large thick cloth used as covering for a bed. **2** concealing cover, as of snow. ♦ *v* **3** cover as with a blanket.

blare ❶ *v* **1** sound loudly and harshly. ♦ *n* **2** loud harsh noise.

blarney ❶ *n* flattering talk.

blasé ❶ [**blah**–zay] *adj* indifferent or bored through familiarity.

———— THESAURUS ————

bag, reveal, spill the beans (*inf*)

black *adj* **1** = **dark**, dusky, ebony, jet, pitch–black, raven, sable, swarthy ≠ **light 4** = **gloomy**, depressing, dismal, foreboding, hopeless, ominous, sad, sombre ≠ **happy 5** = **angry**, furious, hostile, menacing, resentful, sullen, threatening ≠ **happy** ♦ *v* **10** = **boycott**, ban, bar, blacklist

blackguard *n* = **scoundrel**, bastard (*offens*), bounder (*old–fashioned Brit sl*), rascal, rogue, swine, villain

blackmail *n* **1** = **threat**, extortion, hush money (*sl*), intimidation, ransom ♦ *v* **2** = **threaten**, coerce, compel, demand, extort, hold to ransom, intimidate, squeeze

blackout *n* **2** = **unconsciousness**, coma, faint, loss of consciousness, oblivion, swoon

blame *v* **1** = **hold responsible**, accuse, censure, chide, condemn, criticize, find fault with, reproach ≠ **clear** ♦ *n* **2** = **responsibility**, accountability,

accusation, culpability, fault, guilt, liability, onus ≠ **credit**

bland *adj* = **dull**, boring, flat, humdrum, insipid, tasteless, unexciting, uninspiring, vapid ≠ **interesting**

blank *adj* **1** = **unmarked**, bare, clean, clear, empty, void, white ≠ **full 2** = **expressionless**, deadpan, empty, impassive, poker–faced (*inf*), vacant, vague ≠ **interested** ♦ *n* **4** = **empty space**, emptiness, gap, nothingness, space, vacancy, vacuum, void

blanket *n* **1** = **cover**, coverlet, rug **2** = **covering**, carpet, cloak, coat, layer, mantle, sheet ♦ *v* **3** = **cover**, cloak, coat, conceal, hide, mask, obscure, suppress

blare *v* **1** = **sound out**, blast, clamour, clang, resound, roar, scream, trumpet

blarney *n* = **flattery**, blandishments, cajolery, coaxing, soft soap (*inf*), spiel, sweet talk (*inf*), wheedling

blasé *adj* = **indifferent**, apathetic, lukewarm, nonchalant, offhand, unconcerned

blaspheme ❶ v speak disrespectfully of (God or sacred things). **blasphemy** n **blasphemous** adj

blast ❶ n 1 explosion. 2 sudden strong gust of air or wind. 3 sudden loud sound, as of a trumpet. ◆ v 4 blow up (a rock etc.) with explosives. **blastoff** n launching of a rocket.

blatant ❶ adj glaringly obvious. **blatantly** adv

blaze¹ ❶ n 1 strong fire or flame. 2 very bright light. ◆ v 3 burn or shine brightly.

blaze² n mark made on a tree to indicate a route.

blazer n lightweight jacket, often in the colours of a school etc.

bleach ❶ v 1 make or become white or colourless. ◆ n 2 bleaching agent.

bleak ❶ adj 1 exposed and barren. 2 offering little hope.

bleary ❶ adj **–rier, –riest** with eyes dimmed, as by tears or tiredness. **blearily** adv

bleat v 1 (of a sheep, goat, or calf) utter its plaintive cry. ◆ n 2 cry of sheep, goats, and calves.

bleed ❶ v **bleeding, bled** 1 lose or emit blood. 2 draw blood from (a person or animal). 3 Informal obtain money by extortion.

bleep n 1 short high-pitched sound made by an electrical device. ◆ v 2 make a bleeping sound. **bleeper** n small portable radio receiver that makes a bleeping signal.

blemish ❶ n 1 defect or stain. ◆ v 2 spoil or tarnish.

blend ❶ v 1 mix or mingle (components or ingredients). 2 look good together. ◆ n 3 mixture. **blender** n electrical appliance for puréeing vegetables etc.

bless ❶ v 1 make holy by means of a religious rite. 2 call upon God to protect. 3 endow with health, talent, etc. **blessed** adj holy. **blessing** n 1 invoking of divine aid. 2 happy event.

—————————— THESAURUS ——————————

blaspheme v = **profane**, abuse, curse, damn, desecrate, execrate, revile, swear

blast n 1 = **explosion**, bang, burst, crash, detonation, discharge, eruption, outburst, salvo, volley 2 = **gust**, gale, squall, storm, strong breeze, tempest 3 = **blare**, blow, clang, honk, peal, scream, toot, wail ◆ v 4 = **blow up**, break up, burst, demolish, destroy, explode, put paid to, ruin, shatter

blatant adj = **obvious**, brazen, conspicuous, flagrant, glaring, obtrusive, ostentatious, overt

blaze¹ n 1 = **fire**, bonfire, conflagration, flames 2 = **glare**, beam, brilliance, flare, flash, gleam, glitter, glow, light, radiance ◆ v 3 = **burn**, beam, fire, flame, flare, flash, glare, gleam, glow, shine

bleach v 1 = **whiten**, blanch, fade, grow pale, lighten, wash out

bleak adj 1 = **exposed**, bare, barren, desolate, unsheltered, weather-beaten, windswept ≠ **protected** 2 = **dismal**, cheerless, depressing, discouraging,

dreary, gloomy, grim, hopeless, joyless, sombre ≠ **promising**

bleary adj = **dim**, blurred, blurry, foggy, fuzzy, hazy, indistinct, misty, murky

bleed v 1 = **lose blood**, flow, gush, ooze, run, shed blood, spurt 2 = **draw** or **take blood**, extract, leech 3 Inf = **extort**, drain, exhaust, fleece, milk, squeeze

blemish n 1 = **mark**, blot, defect, disfigurement, fault, flaw, imperfection, smudge, stain, taint ≠ **improvement** ◆ v 2 = **mark**, damage, disfigure, impair, injure, mar, spoil, stain, sully, taint, tarnish ≠ **improve**

blend v 1 = **mix**, amalgamate, combine, compound, merge, mingle, unite 2 = **go well**, complement, fit, go with, harmonize, suit ◆ n 3 = **mixture**, alloy, amalgamation, combination, compound, concoction, mix, synthesis, union

bless v 1 = **sanctify**, anoint, consecrate, dedicate, exalt, hallow, ordain ≠ **damn** 3 = **endow**, bestow, favour, give, grace, grant, provide ≠ **trouble**

blether *Scot* ◆ *v* talk, esp. foolishly or at length.

blight ❶ *n* 1 person or thing that spoils or prevents growth. 2 withering plant disease. ◆ *v* 3 frustrate or disappoint.

blighter *n Informal* irritating person.

blind ❶ *adj* 1 unable to see. 2 unable or unwilling to understand. 3 not determined by reason, e.g. *blind hatred*. ◆ *v* 4 deprive of sight. 5 deprive of good sense, reason, or judgment. ◆ *n* 6 covering for a window. 7 something that serves to conceal the truth. **blindly** *adv* **blindness** *n*

> ### ✓ WORD TIP
> The use of *the blind, the disabled,* etc. can be offensive and should be avoided. Instead you should talk about *blind people, disabled people,* etc.

blink ❶ *v* 1 close and immediately reopen (the eyes). 2 shine intermittently. ◆ *n* 3 act of blinking. **on the blink** *Slang* not working properly.

blip *n* spot of light on a radar screen indicating the position of an object.

bliss ❶ *n* perfect happiness. **blissful** *adj* **blissfully** *adv*

blister ❶ *n* 1 small bubble on the skin. 2 swelling, as on a painted surface. ◆ *v* 3 (cause to) have blisters. **blistering** *adj* 1 (of weather) very hot. 2 (of criticism) extremely harsh.

blithe ❶ *adj* casual and indifferent. **blithely** *adv*

blitz ❶ *n* 1 violent and sustained attack by aircraft. 2 intensive attack or concerted effort. ◆ *v* 3 attack suddenly and intensively.

blizzard ❶ *n* blinding storm of wind and snow.

blob ❶ *n* 1 soft mass or drop. 2 indistinct or shapeless form.

block ❶ *n* 1 large solid piece of wood, stone, etc. 2 large building of offices, flats, etc. 3 group of buildings enclosed by intersecting streets. 4 obstruction or hindrance. 5 *Slang* person's head. ◆ *v* 6 obstruct or impede by introducing an obstacle. **blockage** *n* **blockhead** *n* stupid person.

blockade ❶ *n* 1 sealing off of a place to

blight *n* 1 = **curse**, affliction, bane, contamination, corruption, evil, plague, pollution, scourge, woe ≠ **help**
2 = **disease**, canker, decay, fungus, infestation, mildew, pest, pestilence, rot ◆
v 3 = **frustrate**, crush, dash, disappoint, mar, ruin, spoil, undo, wreck

blind *adj* 1 = **sightless**, eyeless, unseeing, unsighted, visionless ≠ **seeing**
2 = **unaware of**, careless, heedless, ignorant, inattentive, inconsiderate, indifferent, insensitive, oblivious, unconscious of ≠ **concerned**
3 = **unreasoning**, indiscriminate, prejudiced ◆ *n* 7 = **cover**, camouflage, cloak, facade, feint, front, mask, masquerade, screen, smoke screen

blink *v* 1 = **wink**, bat, flutter 2 = **flicker**, flash, gleam, glimmer, shine, twinkle, wink
on the blink *Sl* = **not working (properly)**, faulty, malfunctioning, out of action, out

of order, playing up

bliss *n* = **joy**, beatitude, blessedness, blissfulness, ecstasy, euphoria, felicity, gladness, happiness, heaven, nirvana, paradise, rapture ≠ **distress**

blister *n* 1 = **sore**, abscess, boil, carbuncle, cyst, pimple, pustule, swelling

blithe *adj* = **heedless**, careless, casual, indifferent, nonchalant, thoughtless, unconcerned, untroubled ≠ **concerned**

blitz *n* 1 = **attack**, assault, blitzkrieg, bombardment, offensive, onslaught, raid, strike

blizzard *n* = **snowstorm**, blast, gale, squall, storm, tempest

blob *n* 1 = **drop**, ball, bead, bubble, dab, droplet, globule, lump, mass

block *n* 1 = **piece**, bar, brick, chunk, hunk, ingot, lump, mass 4 = **obstruction**, bar, barrier, hindrance, impediment, jam, obstacle ◆ *v* 6 = **obstruct**, bung up (*inf*), prevent the passage of goods. ◆ v 2 impose a blockade on.

bloke ❶ n Informal man.

blood ❶ n 1 red fluid that flows around the body. 2 race or kinship. **in cold blood** done deliberately. **bloodless** adj **blood bath** massacre. **bloodhound** n large dog formerly used for tracking. **bloodshed** n slaughter or killing. **bloodshot** adj (of an eye) inflamed. **blood sport** sport involving the killing of animals. **bloodstream** n flow of blood round the body. **bloodsucker** n 1 animal that sucks blood. 2 Informal person who extorts money from other people. **bloodthirsty** adj taking pleasure in violence.

bloom ❶ n 1 blossom on a flowering plant. 2 youthful or healthy glow. ◆ v 3 bear flowers. 4 be in a healthy, glowing condition.

bloomer n Informal stupid mistake.

bloomers pl n woman's baggy knickers.

blossom ❶ n 1 flowers of a plant. ◆ v 2 (of plants) flower. 3 come to a promising stage.

blot ❶ n 1 spot or stain. 2 something that spoils. ◆ v **blotting, blotted** 3 cause a blemish in or on. 4 soak up (ink) by using

blotting paper. **blotter** n **blot out** v darken or hide completely. **blotting paper** soft absorbent paper for soaking up ink.

blotch n discoloured area or stain. **blotchy** adj

blouse n woman's shirtlike garment.

blow¹ ❶ v **blowing, blew, blown 1** (of air, the wind, etc.) move. 2 move or be carried as if by the wind. 3 expel (air etc.) through the mouth or nose. 4 cause (a musical instrument) to sound by forcing air into it. 5 burn out (a fuse etc.). 6 Slang spend (money) freely. **blower** n **blowy** adj windy. **blow-dry** v style (the hair) with a hand-held dryer. **blowout** n 1 sudden loss of air in a tyre. 2 escape of oil or gas from a well. **blow up** v 1 explode. 2 fill with air. 3 Informal lose one's temper. 4 Informal enlarge (a photograph).

blow² ❶ n 1 hard hit. 2 sudden setback. 3 attacking action.

blubber n 1 fat of whales, seals, etc. ◆ v 2 sob without restraint.

bludge v 1 Aust & NZ informal evade work. 2 scrounge. **bludger** n person who scrounges.

bludgeon ❶ n 1 short thick club. ◆ v 2 hit with a bludgeon. 3 force or bully.

━━━━━ THESAURUS ━━━━━

choke, clog, close, impede, plug, stem the flow, stop up ≠ **open**

blockade n 1 = **stoppage**, barricade, barrier, block, hindrance, impediment, obstacle, obstruction, restriction, siege

bloke n Inf = **man**, chap, character (inf), fellow, guy (inf), individual, person

blood n 1 = **lifeblood**, gore, vital fluid 2 = **family**, ancestry, birth, descent, extraction, kinship, lineage, relations

bloom n 1 = **flower**, blossom, blossoming, bud, efflorescence, opening 2 = **prime**, beauty, flourishing, freshness, glow, health, heyday, lustre, radiance, vigour ≠ **whiteness** ◆ v 3 = **blossom**, blow, bud, burgeon, open, sprout 4 = **flourish**, develop, fare well, grow, prosper, succeed, thrive, wax ≠ **fail**

blossom n 1 = **flower**, bloom, bud, floret,

flowers ◆ v 2 = **flower**, bloom, burgeon 3 = **grow**, bloom, develop, flourish, mature, progress, prosper, thrive

blot n 1 = **spot**, blotch, mark, patch, smear, smudge, speck, splodge 2 = **stain**, blemish, defect, fault, flaw, scar, spot, taint ◆ v 3 = **stain**, disgrace, mark, smirch, smudge, spoil, spot, sully, tarnish 4 = **soak up**, absorb, dry, take up

blow¹ v 2 = **carry**, drive, fling, flutter, move, sweep, waft 3 = **exhale**, breathe, pant, puff 4 = **play**, blare, mouth, pipe, sound, toot, trumpet, vibrate

blow² n 1 = **knock**, bang, clout (inf), punch, smack, sock (sl), stroke, thump, wallop (inf), whack 2 = **setback**, bombshell, calamity, catastrophe, disappointment, disaster, misfortune, reverse, shock

blue ❶ *n* **1** colour of a clear unclouded sky. ♦ *pl* **2** feeling of depression. **3** type of folk music of Black American origin. ♦ *adj* **bluer, bluest 4** of the colour blue. **5** depressed. **6** pornographic. **out of the blue** unexpectedly. **bluish** *adj* **bluebell** *n* flower with blue bell–shaped flowers. **bluebottle** *n* large fly with a dark–blue body. **blue–collar** *adj* denoting manual industrial workers. **blueprint** *n* **1** photographic print of a plan. **2** description of how a plan is expected to work.

bluff[1] ❶ *v* **1** pretend to be confident in order to influence (someone). ♦ *n* **2** act of bluffing.

bluff[2] ❶ *n* **1** steep cliff or bank. ♦ *adj* **2** good–naturedly frank and hearty.

blunder ❶ *n* **1** clumsy mistake. ♦ *v* **2** make a blunder. **3** act clumsily.

blunt ❶ *adj* **1** not having a sharp edge or point. **2** (of people, speech, etc.) straightforward or uncomplicated. ♦ *v* **3** make less sharp. **bluntly** *adv*

blur ❶ *v* **blurring, blurred 1** make or become vague or less distinct. ♦ *n* **2** something vague, hazy, or indistinct. **blurry** *adj*

blurb *n* promotional description, as on the jacket of a book.

blurt ❶ *v* (foll. by *out*) utter suddenly and involuntarily.

blush ❶ *v* **1** become red in the face, esp. from embarrassment or shame. ♦ *n* **2** reddening of the face.

bluster ❶ *v* **1** speak loudly or in a bullying way. ♦ *n* **2** empty threats or protests. **blustery** *adj* (of weather) rough and windy.

BO *Informal* body odour.

boa *n* **1** large nonvenomous snake. **2** long

———————— THESAURUS ————————

bludgeon *n* **1** = **club**, cosh (*Brit*), cudgel, truncheon ♦ *v* **2** = **club**, beat up, cosh (*Brit*), cudgel, knock down, strike **3** = **bully**, bulldoze (*inf*), coerce, force, railroad (*inf*), steamroller

blue *n* **1** = **azure**, cobalt, cyan, navy, sapphire, ultramarine ♦ *pl* **2** = **depression**, doldrums, dumps (*inf*), gloom, low spirits, melancholy, unhappiness ♦ *adj* **4** = **azure**, cerulean, cobalt, cyan, navy, sapphire, sky–coloured, ultramarine **5** = **depressed**, dejected, despondent, downcast, low, melancholy, sad, unhappy **6** = **smutty**, indecent, lewd, obscene, risqué, X–rated (*inf*) ≠ **decent**

bluff[1] *v* **1** = **deceive**, con, delude, fake, feign, mislead, pretend, pull the wool over someone's eyes ♦ *n* **2** = **deception**, bluster, bravado, deceit, fraud, humbug, pretence, sham, subterfuge

bluff[2] *n* **1** = **precipice**, bank, cliff, crag, escarpment, headland, peak, promontory, ridge ♦ *adj* **2** = **hearty**, blunt, blustering, genial, good–natured, open, outspoken, plain–spoken ≠ **sensitive**

blunder *n* **1** = **mistake**, bloomer (*Brit inf*), clanger (*inf*), error, fault, faux pas, gaffe,

howler (*inf*), inaccuracy, indiscretion, oversight, slip, slip–up (*inf*) ≠ **accuracy** ♦ *v* **2** = **make a mistake**, botch, bungle, err, put one's foot in it (*inf*), slip up (*inf*) ≠ **be correct 3** = **stumble**, bumble, flounder

blunt *adj* **1** = **dull**, dulled, edgeless, pointless, rounded, unsharpened ≠ **pointed 2** = **forthright**, bluff, brusque, frank, outspoken, plain–spoken, rude, straightforward, tactless ≠ **sensitive** ♦ *v* **3** = **dull**, dampen, deaden, numb, soften, take the edge off, water down, weaken ≠ **stimulate**

blur *v* **1** = **make indistinct**, cloud, darken, make hazy, make vague, mask, obscure ♦ *n* **2** = **indistinctness**, confusion, fog, haze, obscurity

blurt *v* (foll. by *out*) = **exclaim**, disclose, let the cat out of the bag, reveal, spill the beans (*inf*), tell all, utter suddenly

blush *v* **1** = **turn red**, colour, flush, go red (as a beetroot), redden, turn scarlet ≠ **pale** ♦ *n* **2** = **reddening**, colour, flush, glow, pink tinge, rosiness, rosy tint, ruddiness

bluster *v* **1** = **roar**, bully, domineer, hector, rant, storm ♦ *n* **2** = **hot air** (*inf*), bluff, bombast, bravado scarf of fur or feathers. **boa constrictor** large snake that kills its prey by crushing.

boar n **1** uncastrated male pig. **2** wild pig.

board ❶ n **1** long flat piece of sawn timber. **2** smaller flat piece of rigid material for a specific purpose, e.g. *ironing board; chess board*. **3** group of people who administer a company, trust, etc. **4** meals provided for money. ◆ v **5** go aboard (a train, aeroplane, etc.). **6** cover with boards. **7** receive meals and lodgings in return for money. **on board** on or in a ship, aeroplane, etc. **boarder** n pupil who lives at school during the school term. **boarding house** private house that provides meals and accommodation for paying guests. **boardroom** n room where the board of a company meets.

boast ❶ v **1** speak too proudly about one's talents etc. **2** possess (something to be proud of). ◆ n **3** bragging statement. **boastful** adj

boat n small vehicle for travelling across water. **boater** n flat straw hat.

bob¹ ❶ v **bobbing, bobbed 1** move up and down repeatedly. ◆ n **2** short abrupt movement.

bob² n **1** hairstyle in which the hair is cut short evenly all round the head. **2** weight on a pendulum or plumb line. ◆ v **bobbing, bobbed 3** cut (the hair) in a bob.

bobbin n reel on which thread is wound.

bobble n small ball of material, usu. for decoration.

bobby n, pl **-bies** *Informal* policeman.

bobotie n *S Afr* dish of curried mince.

bobsleigh n **1** sledge for racing down an icy track. ◆ v **2** ride on a bobsleigh.

bode ❶ v be an omen of (good or ill).

bodice n upper part of a dress.

bodkin n blunt large-eyed needle.

body ❶ n, pl **bodies 1** entire physical structure of an animal or human. **2** trunk or torso. **3** corpse. **4** group regarded as a single entity. **5** main part of anything. **6** woman's one-piece undergarment. **bodily** adj **1** relating to the body. ◆ adv **2** by taking hold of the body. **body-board** n *Aust, NZ, S Afr & US* small polystyrene surfboard. **bodyguard** n person or group of people employed to protect someone. **bodywork** n outer shell of a motor vehicle.

boffin ❶ n *Brit informal* scientist or expert.

bog ❶ n **1** wet spongy ground. **2** *Slang* toilet. **boggy** adj **bog down** v **bogging, bogged** impede physically or mentally.

bogan n *Aust dated & NZ slang* youth who dresses and behaves rebelliously.

bogey ❶ bogy n **1** something that worries or annoys. **2** *Golf* score of one stroke over par on a hole.

boggle v be surprised, confused, or

board n **1** = **plank**, panel, piece of timber, slat, timber **3** = **directors**, advisers, committee, conclave, council, panel, trustees **4** = **meals**, daily meals, provisions, victuals ◆ v **5** = **get on**, embark, enter, mount ≠ **land 7** = **lodge**, put up, quarter, room

boast v **1** = **brag**, blow one's own trumpet, crow, skite (*Aust & NZ*), strut, swagger, talk big (*sl*), vaunt ≠ **cover up 2** = **possess**, be proud of, congratulate oneself on, exhibit, flatter oneself, pride oneself on, show off ◆ n **3** = **brag**, avowal

bob¹ v **1** = **duck**, bounce, hop, nod, oscillate, waggle, wobble

bode v = **portend**, augur, be an omen of, forebode, foretell, predict, signify, threaten

body n **1** = **physique**, build, figure, form, frame, shape **2** = **torso**, trunk **3** = **corpse**, cadaver, carcass, dead body, remains, stiff (*sl*) **4** = **organization**, association, band, bloc, collection, company, confederation, congress, corporation, society **5** = **main part**, bulk, essence, mass, material, matter, substance

boffin n *Brit inf* = **expert**, brainbox, egghead, fundi (*S Afr*), genius, intellectual, inventor, mastermind

bog n **1** = **marsh**, fen, mire, morass,

alarmed.

bogus 🐱 *adj* not genuine.

bohemian *n, adj* (person) leading an unconventional life.

boil¹ 🐱 *v* 1 (cause to) change from a liquid to a vapour so quickly that bubbles are formed. 2 bubble like something boiling. ◆ *n* 3 state or action of boiling. **boiler** *n* piece of equipment which provides hot water.

boil² 🐱 *n* red pus–filled swelling on the skin.

boisterous 🐱 *adj* noisy and lively.

bold 🐱 *adj* 1 confident and fearless. 2 immodest or impudent. **boldly** *adv* **boldness** *n*

bole *n* tree trunk.

bolero *n, pl* **–ros** 1 (music for) traditional Spanish dance. 2 short open jacket.

bollard *n* short thick post used to prevent the passage of motor vehicles.

bolshie, bolshy *adj Informal* difficult or rebellious.

bolster 🐱 *v* 1 support or strengthen. ◆ *n* 2 long narrow pillow.

bolt 🐱 *n* 1 sliding metal bar for fastening a door etc. 2 metal pin which screws into a nut. 3 flash (of lightning). ◆ *v* 4 run away suddenly. 5 fasten with a bolt. 6 eat hurriedly. **bolt upright** stiff and rigid. **bolt hole** place of escape.

bomb 🐱 *n* 1 container fitted with explosive material. 2 *Slang* large amount of money. ◆ *v* 3 attack with bombs. 4 move very quickly. **bomber** *n* 1 aircraft that drops bombs. 2 person who throws or puts a bomb in a particular place. **bombshell** *n* shocking or unwelcome surprise.

bona fide 🐱 [**bone**–a **fide**–ee] *adj* genuine.

bonanza *n* sudden good luck or wealth.

bond 🐱 *n* 1 something that binds, fastens or holds together. 2 something that unites people. 3 written or spoken agreement. 4 *Finance* certificate of debt issued to raise funds. 5 *S Afr* conditional pledging of property, esp. a house, as security for the repayment of a loan. ◆ *pl* 6 something that restrains or imprisons. ◆ *v* 7 bind.

———————————| THESAURUS |———————————

quagmire, slough, swamp, wetlands

bogey *n* 1 = **bugbear**, bête noire, bugaboo, nightmare

bogus *adj* = **fake**, artificial, counterfeit, false, forged, fraudulent, imitation, phoney *or* phony (*inf*), sham

① **bohemian** *n* = **nonconformist**, beatnik, dropout, hippy, iconoclast

② **bohemian** *adj* = **unconventional**, alternative, artistic, arty (*inf*), left bank, nonconformist, offbeat, unorthodox ≠ **conservative**

boil¹ *v* 1 = **bubble** 2 = **froth**, bubble, effervesce, fizz, foam, seethe

boil² *n* = **pustule**, blister, carbuncle, gathering, swelling, tumour, ulcer

boisterous *adj* = **unruly**, disorderly, loud, noisy, riotous, rollicking, rowdy, unrestrained, vociferous, wild ≠ **controlled**

bold *adj* 1 = **fearless**, adventurous, audacious, brave, courageous, daring, enterprising, heroic, intrepid, valiant ≠ **fearful** 2 = **impudent**, barefaced, brazen,

cheeky, confident, forward, insolent, rude, shameless ≠ **conservative**

bolster *v* = **support**, augment, boost, help, reinforce, shore up, strengthen

bolt *n* 1 = **bar**, catch, fastener, latch, lock, sliding bar 2 = **pin**, peg, rivet, rod ◆ *v* 4 = **run away**, abscond, dash, escape, flee, fly, make a break (for it), run for it 5 = **lock**, bar, fasten, latch, secure 6 = **gobble**, cram, devour, gorge, gulp, guzzle, stuff, swallow whole, wolf

bomb *n* 1 = **explosive**, device, grenade, mine, missile, projectile, rocket, shell, torpedo ◆ *v* 3 = **blow up**, attack, blow sky–high, bombard, destroy, shell, strafe, torpedo

bona fide *adj* = **genuine**, actual, authentic, honest, kosher (*inf*), legitimate, real, true

bond *n* 1 = **fastening**, chain, cord, fetter, ligature, manacle, shackle, tie 2 = **tie**, affiliation, affinity, attachment, connection, link, relation, union 3 = **agreement**, contract, covenant,

bondage ❶ *n* slavery.
bone *n* **1** any of the hard parts in the body that form the skeleton. ♦ *v* **2** remove the bones from (meat for cooking etc.). **bony** *adj* **1** having many bones. **2** thin or emaciated. **bone–dry** *adj* completely dry. **bone–idle** *adj* extremely lazy.
bonfire *n* large outdoor fire.
bongo *n, pl* **-gos, –goes** small drum played with the fingers.
bonk *v Informal* **1** have sex with. **2** hit.
bonnet *n* **1** metal cover over a vehicle's engine. **2** hat which ties under the chin.
bonny *adj* **–nier, –niest** *Scot* beautiful.
bonsai *n, pl* **–sai** ornamental miniature tree or shrub.
bonus ❶ *n* something given, paid, or received above what is due or expected.
boo *interj* **1** shout of disapproval. ♦ *v* **booing, booed 2** shout 'boo' to show disapproval.
boob *Slang* ♦ *n* **1** foolish mistake. **2** female breast.
boogie *v Informal* dance to fast pop music.
book ❶ *n* **1** number of pages bound together between covers. **2** long written work. **3** number of tickets, stamps, etc. fastened together. ♦ *pl* **4** record of

transactions of a business or society. ♦ *v* **5** reserve (a place, passage, etc.) in advance. **6** record the name of (a person) who has committed an offence. **booklet** *n* thin book with paper covers.
boom¹ ❶ *v* **1** make a loud deep echoing sound. **2** prosper vigorously and rapidly. ♦ *n* **3** loud deep echoing sound. **4** period of high economic growth.
boom² *n* **1** pole to which the foot of a sail is attached. **2** pole carrying an overhead microphone. **3** barrier across a waterway.
boomerang *n* **1** curved wooden missile which can be made to return to the thrower. ♦ *v* **2** (of a plan) recoil unexpectedly.
boon ❶ *n* something helpful or beneficial.
boor *n* rude or insensitive person. **boorish** *adj*
boost ❶ *n* **1** encouragement or help. **2** increase. ♦ *v* **3** improve. **4** increase. **booster** *n* small additional injection of a vaccine.
boot ❶ *n* **1** outer covering for the foot that extends above the ankle. **2** space in a car for luggage. **3** *Informal* kick. **4** *Slang* dismissal from employment. ♦ *v* **5** *Informal* kick. **6** start up (a computer). **bootee** *n*

———————— THESAURUS ————————

guarantee, obligation, pledge, promise, word ♦ *v* **7 = hold together,** bind, connect, fasten, fix together, glue, paste
bondage *n* **= slavery,** captivity, confinement, enslavement, imprisonment, subjugation
bonus *n* **= extra,** dividend, gift, icing on the cake, plus, premium, prize, reward
book *n* **1 = notebook,** album, diary, exercise book, jotter, pad **2 = work,** publication, title, tome, tract, volume ♦ *v* **5 = reserve,** arrange for, charter, engage, make reservations, organize, programme, schedule **6 = note,** enter, list, log, mark down, put down, record, register, write down
boom¹ *v* **1 = bang,** blast, crash, explode, resound, reverberate, roar, roll, rumble, thunder **2 = flourish,** develop, expand,

grow, increase, intensify, prosper, strengthen, swell, thrive ≠ **fall** ♦ *n* **3 = bang,** blast, burst, clap, crash, explosion, roar, rumble, thunder
4 = expansion, boost, development, growth, improvement, increase, jump, upsurge ≠ **decline** upswing, upturn
boon *n* **= benefit,** advantage, aid, assistance, blessing, favour, gain, gift, godsend, hand-out, interest, manna from heaven, windfall
boost *n* **1 = help,** encouragement, gee-up, praise, promotion ≠ **knock 2 = rise,** addition, expansion, improvement, increase, increment, jump ≠ **fall** ♦ *v* **3 = promote,** advertise, encourage, foster, further, gee up, hype, improve, plug (*inf*), praise **4 = increase,** add to, amplify, develop, enlarge, expand, heighten, raise,

baby's soft shoe.

booth *n* **1** small partly enclosed cubicle. **2** stall at a fair or market.

bootleg *adj* **1** produced, distributed, or sold illicitly. ♦ *v* **–legging, –legged 2** make, carry, or sell (illicit goods). **bootlegger** *n*

booty ⊕ *n, pl* **–ties** valuable articles obtained as plunder.

booze *v, n Informal* (consume) alcoholic drink. **boozy** *adj* **boozer** *n Informal* **1** person who is fond of drinking. **2** pub. **booze–up** *n Informal* drinking spree.

border ⊕ *n* **1** dividing line between political or geographical regions. **2** band around or along the edge of something. ♦ *v* **3** provide with a border. **4** be nearly the same as, e.g. *resentment that borders on hatred.*

bore¹ ⊕ *v* **1** make (a hole) with a drill etc. ♦ *n* **2** hole or tunnel drilled in search of oil, minerals, etc. **3** (diameter of) the hollow of a gun barrel.

bore² ⊕ *v* **1** make weary by being dull or repetitive. ♦ *n* **2** dull or repetitive person or thing. **bored** *adj* **boredom** *n*

> ✔ **WORD TIP**
>
> *Bored* is followed by *with* or *by*: ...*bored by his conversation*; ...*bored with reading*. The usage *bored of* is not fully accepted.

boron *n Chem* element used in hardening steel.

borough *n* town or district with its own council.

borrow ⊕ *v* **1** obtain (something) temporarily. **2** adopt (ideas etc.) from another source. **borrower** *n*

> ✔ **WORD TIP**
>
> *Borrow* is followed by *from*: *Borrow a pound from Frank*. The use of *borrow* followed by *off of* is nonstandard. Avoid confusing the meanings of *borrow* and *lend*.

borscht or **borsch** *n* a Russian soup based on beetroot.

borstal *n* (formerly) prison for young criminals.

borzoi *n* tall dog with a long silky coat.

bosom ⊕ *n* **1** chest of a person, esp. the female breasts. ♦ *adj* **2** very dear, e.g. *a bosom friend.*

boss ⊕ *n* **1** person in charge of or employing others. ♦ *v* **2 boss around, about** be domineering towards. **bossy** *adj* **bossier, bossiest**

botany *n* study of plants. **botanical, botanic** *adj* **botanist** *n*

botch ⊕ *v* **1** spoil through clumsiness. ♦ *n* **2** (also **botch–up**) badly done piece of work or repair.

widen ≠ **cut**

boot *v Inf* **5** = **kick**, drive, drop–kick, knock, punt, put the boot in(to) (*sl*), shove

booty *n* = **plunder**, gains, haul, loot, prey, spoils, swag (*sl*), takings, winnings

border *n* **1** = **frontier**, borderline, boundary, line, march **2** = **edge**, bounds, brink, limits, margin, rim, verge ♦ *v* **3** = **edge**, bind, decorate, fringe, hem, rim, trim

bore¹ *v* **1** = **drill**, burrow, gouge out, mine, penetrate, perforate, pierce, sink, tunnel

bore² *v* **1** = **tire**, be tedious, fatigue, jade, pall on, send to sleep, wear out, weary ≠ **interest** ♦ *n* **2** = **nuisance**, anorak (*inf*),

pain (*inf*), yawn (*inf*)

borrow *v* **1** = **take on loan**, bludge (*Aust & NZ*), cadge, scrounge (*inf*), touch (someone) for (*sl*), use temporarily ≠ **lend 2** = **steal**, adopt, copy, obtain, plagiarize, take, usurp

bosom *n* **1** = **breast**, bust, chest ♦ *adj* **2** = **intimate**, boon, cherished, close, confidential, dear, very dear

boss *n* **1** = **head**, chief, director, employer, gaffer (*inf, chiefly Brit*), leader, manager, master, supervisor

botch *v* **1** = **spoil**, blunder, bungle, cock up (*Brit sl*), make a pig's ear of (*inf*), mar, mess up, screw up (*inf*) ♦ *n* **2** = **mess**,

both *adj, pron* two considered together.

> ✓ **WORD TIP**
>
> After *both* the use of *of* is optional: *both of the boys* or *both (the) boys*.

bother ⊕ *v* **1** take the time or trouble. **2** give annoyance or trouble to. **3** pester. ◆ *n* **4** trouble, fuss, or difficulty. **bothersome** *adj*

bottle *n* **1** container for holding liquids. **2** *Slang* courage. ◆ *v* **3** put in a bottle. **bottleneck** *n* narrow stretch of road where traffic is held up. **bottle up** *v* restrain (powerful emotion).

bottom ⊕ *n* **1** lowest, deepest, or farthest removed part of a thing. **2** buttocks. ◆ *adj* **3** lowest or last. **bottomless** *adj*

bough *n* large branch of a tree.

boulder *n* large rounded rock.

boulevard *n* wide, usu. tree-lined, street.

bounce ⊕ *v* **1** (of a ball etc.) rebound from an impact. **2** *Slang* (of a cheque) be returned uncashed owing to a lack of funds in the account. ◆ *n* **3** act of rebounding. **4** springiness. **5** *Informal* vitality or vigour. **bouncer** *n* person employed at a disco etc. to remove unwanted people. **bouncing** *adj* vigorous and robust.

bound¹ ⊕ *v* **1** past of BIND. ◆ *adj* **2** destined or certain. **3** compelled or obliged.

bound² ⊕ *v* **1** move forwards by jumps. ◆ *n* **2** jump upwards or forwards.

bound³ ⊕ *v* **1** form a boundary of. ◆ *pl n* **2** limit. **boundary** *n* dividing line that indicates the farthest limit.

bound⁴ *adj* going or intending to go towards, e.g. *homeward bound*.

bounty ⊕ *n, pl* **–ties 1** generosity. **2** generous gift or reward. **bountiful, bounteous** *adj*

bouquet ⊕ *n* **1** bunch of flowers. **2** aroma of wine.

bourbon [**bur**–bn] *n* whiskey made from maize.

bourgeois ⊕ [**boor**–zhwah] *adj, n Offens* middle–class (person).

bout ⊕ *n* **1** period of activity or illness. **2** boxing or wrestling match.

———————— THESAURUS ————————

blunder, bungle, cock–up (*Brit sl*), failure, hash, pig's ear (*inf*)

bother *v* **3 = trouble**, disturb, harass, hassle (*inf*), inconvenience, pester, plague, worry ≠ **help** ◆ *n* **4 = trouble**, difficulty, fuss, hassle (*inf*), inconvenience, irritation, nuisance, problem, worry

bottom *n* **1 = lowest part**, base, bed, depths, floor, foot, foundation, lower side, sole, underneath, underside ≠ **top** **2 = buttocks**, backside, behind (*inf*), posterior, rear, rump, seat ◆ *adj* **3 = lowest**, last ≠ **higher**

bounce *v* **1 = rebound**, bob, bound, jump, leap, recoil, ricochet, spring ◆ *n* **4 = springiness**, elasticity, give, recoil, resilience, spring **5** *Inf* **= life**, dynamism, energy, go (*inf*), liveliness, vigour, vivacity, zip (*inf*)

bound¹ *adj* **1 = tied**, cased, fastened, fixed, pinioned, secured, tied up **2 = certain**, destined, doomed, fated, sure **3 = obliged**, beholden, committed, compelled, constrained, duty–bound, forced, pledged, required

bound² *v* **1 = leap**, bob, bounce, gambol, hurdle, jump, skip, spring, vault ◆ *n* **2 = leap**, bob, bounce, gambol, hurdle, jump, skip, spring, vault

bound³ *v* **1 = limit**, confine, demarcate, encircle, enclose, hem in, restrain, restrict, surround ◆ *pl n* **2 = boundary**, border, confine, edge, extremity, limit, rim, verge

bounty *n* **1 = generosity**, benevolence, charity, kindness, largesse or largess, liberality, philanthropy **2 = reward**, bonus, gift, present

bouquet *n* **1 = bunch of flowers**, buttonhole, corsage, garland, nosegay, posy, spray, wreath **2 = aroma**, fragrance, perfume, redolence, savour, scent

bourgeois *adj Offens* **= middle–class**, conventional, hidebound, materialistic, traditional

boutique *n* small clothes shop.
bow¹ ❶ [rhymes with **now**] *v* **1** lower (one's head) or bend (one's knee or body) as a sign of respect or shame. **2** comply or accept. ♦ *n* **3** movement made when bowing.
bow² [rhymes with **go**] *n* **1** knot with two loops and loose ends. **2** weapon for shooting arrows. **3** long stick stretched with horsehair for playing stringed instruments. **bow–legged** *adj* having legs that curve outwards at the knees.
bow³ ❶ [rhymes with **now**] *n* front end of a ship.
bowel *n* **1** intestine, esp. the large intestine. ♦ *pl* **2** innermost part.
bowl¹ ❶ *n* **1** round container with an open top. **2** hollow part of an object.
bowl² ❶ *n* **1** large heavy ball. ♦ *pl* **2** game played on smooth grass with wooden bowls. ♦ *v* **3** *Cricket* send (a ball) towards the batsman. **bowler** *n* **bowling** *n* game in which bowls are rolled at a group of pins.
bowler *n* stiff felt hat with a rounded crown.
box¹ ❶ *n* **1** container with a firm flat base and sides. **2** separate compartment in a theatre, stable, etc. ♦ *v* **3** put into a box. **the box** *Informal* television. **box office** place where theatre or cinema tickets are sold.
box² ❶ *v* fight (an opponent) in a boxing match. **boxer** *n* **1** person who participates in the sport of boxing. **2** medium–sized

dog with smooth hair and a short nose. **boxer shorts, boxers** *pl n* men's underpants shaped like shorts but with a front opening. **boxing** *n* sport of fighting with the fists.
box³ *n* evergreen tree with shiny leaves.
boy ❶ *n* male child. **boyish** *adj* **boyhood** *n* **boyfriend** *n* male friend with whom a person is romantically or sexually involved.
boycott ❶ *v* **1** refuse to deal with (an organization or country). ♦ *n* **2** instance of boycotting.
bra *n* woman's undergarment for supporting the breasts.
braaivlies, braai *S Afr* ♦ *n* **1** grill on which food is cooked over hot charcoal, usu. outdoors. ♦ *v* **2** cook (food) in this way.
brace ❶ *n* **1** object fastened to something to straighten or support it. **2** pair, esp. of game birds. ♦ *pl* **3** straps worn over the shoulders to hold up trousers. ♦ *v* **4** steady or prepare (oneself) for something unpleasant. **5** strengthen or fit with a brace. **bracing** *adj* refreshing and invigorating.
bracken *n* large fern.
bracket *n* **1** pair of characters used to enclose a section of writing. **2** group falling within certain defined limits. **3** support fixed to a wall. ♦ *v* **–eting, –eted 4** put in brackets. **5** class together.
brackish *adj* (of water) slightly salty.
brag ❶ *v* **bragging, bragged** speak arrogantly and boastfully. **braggart** *n*

bout *n* **1** = **period**, fit, spell, stint, term, turn **2** = **fight**, boxing match, competition, contest, encounter, engagement, match, set–to, struggle
bow¹ *v* **1** = **bend**, bob, droop, genuflect, nod, stoop **2** = **give in**, acquiesce, comply, concede, defer, kowtow, relent, submit, succumb, surrender, yield ♦ *n* **3** = **bending**, bob, genuflexion, kowtow, nod, obeisance
bow³ *n* = **prow**, beak, fore, head, stem
bowl¹ *n* **1** = **basin**, dish, vessel
bowl² *v* **3** *Cricket* = **throw**, fling, hurl, pitch

box¹ *n* **1** = **container**, carton, case, casket, chest, pack, package, receptacle, trunk ♦ *v* **3** = **pack**, package, wrap
box² *v* = **fight**, exchange blows, spar
boy *n* = **lad**, fellow, junior, schoolboy, stripling, youngster, youth
boycott *v* **1** = **embargo**, ban, bar, black, exclude, outlaw, prohibit, refuse, reject
brace *n* **1** = **support**, bolster, bracket, buttress, prop, reinforcement, stay, strut, truss ♦ *v* **5** = **support**, bolster, buttress, fortify, reinforce, steady, strengthen
brag *v* = **boast**, blow one's own trumpet,

braid ⊕ v 1 interweave (hair, thread, etc.).
♦ n 2 length of hair etc. that has been
braided. 3 narrow ornamental tape of
woven silk etc.

Braille n system of writing for the blind,
consisting of raised dots interpreted by
touch.

brain ⊕ n 1 soft mass of nervous tissue in
the head. 2 intellectual ability. ♦ v 3 hit
(someone) hard on the head. **brainless** adj
stupid. **brainy** adj Informal clever.
brainchild n idea produced by creative
thought. 1 **brainwash** v cause (a person)
to alter his or her beliefs, esp. by methods
based on isolation, sleeplessness, etc.
brainwave n sudden idea.

braise v cook slowly in a covered pan with
a little liquid.

brake ⊕ n 1 device for slowing or stopping
a vehicle. ♦ v 2 slow down or stop by
using a brake.

bramble n prickly shrub that produces
blackberries.

bran n husks of cereal grain.

branch ⊕ n 1 secondary stem of a tree. 2
offshoot or subsidiary part of something
larger or more complex. ♦ v 3 (of stems,
roots, etc.) divide, then develop in

different directions. **branch out** v expand
one's interests.

brand ⊕ n 1 particular product. 2
particular kind or variety. 3 identifying
mark burnt onto the skin of an animal. ♦
v 4 mark with a brand. 5 denounce as
being. **brand–new** adj absolutely new.

brandish ⊕ v wave (a weapon etc.) in a
threatening way.

brandy n, pl –**dies** alcoholic spirit distilled
from wine.

brash ⊕ adj offensively loud, showy, or
self–confident. **brashness** n

brass n 1 alloy of copper and zinc. 2 family
of wind instruments made of brass. **brassy**
adj 1 brazen or flashy. 2 like brass, esp. in
colour.

brassiere n bra.

brat n unruly child.

bravado ⊕ n showy display of self–
confidence.

brave ⊕ adj 1 having or showing courage,
resolution, and daring. ♦ n 2 Native
American warrior. ♦ v 3 confront with
resolution or courage. **bravery** n

bravo interj well done!

brawl ⊕ n 1 noisy fight. ♦ v 2 fight noisily.

brawn ⊕ n 1 physical strength. 2 pressed

── THESAURUS ──

bluster, crow, skite (Aust & NZ), swagger,
talk big (sl), vaunt

braid v 1 = **interweave**, entwine, interlace,
intertwine, lace, plait, twine, weave

brain n 2 = **intelligence**, intellect, sense,
understanding

brake n 1 = **control**, check, constraint,
curb, rein, restraint ♦ v 2 = **slow**, check,
decelerate, halt, moderate, reduce speed,
slacken, stop

branch n 1 = **bough**, arm, limb, offshoot,
shoot, spray, sprig 2 = **division**, chapter,
department, office, part, section,
subdivision, subsection, wing

brand n 1 = **label**, emblem, hallmark, logo,
mark, marker, sign, stamp, symbol,
trademark 2 = **kind**, cast, class, grade,
make, quality, sort, species, type, variety ♦
v 4 = **mark**, burn, burn in, label, scar,

stamp 5 = **stigmatize**, censure, denounce,
discredit, disgrace, expose, mark

brandish v = **wave**, display, exhibit, flaunt,
flourish, parade, raise, shake, swing, wield

brash adj = **bold**, brazen, cocky,
impertinent, impudent, insolent, pushy
(inf)

bravado n = **swagger**, bluster,
boastfulness, boasting, bombast,
swashbuckling, vaunting

brave adj 1 = **courageous**, bold, daring,
fearless, heroic, intrepid, plucky, resolute,
valiant ≠ **afraid** ♦ v 3 = **confront**, defy,
endure, face, stand up to, suffer, tackle,
withstand ≠ **give in to**

brawl n 1 = **fight**, affray, altercation, clash,
dispute, fracas, fray, mêlée, punch–up
(inf), rumpus, scuffle, skirmish ♦ v
2 = **fight**, scrap (inf), scuffle, tussle, wrestle

meat from the head of a pig or calf. **brawny** adj

bray v 1 (of a donkey) utter its loud harsh sound. ♦ n 2 donkey's loud harsh sound.

brazen ❶ adj shameless and bold.

brazier [bray-zee-er] n portable container for burning charcoal or coal.

breach ❶ n 1 breaking of a promise, obligation, etc. 2 gap or break. ♦ v 3 break (a promise, law, etc.). 4 make a gap in.

bread ❶ n 1 food made by baking a mixture of flour and water or milk. 2 Slang money. **breadwinner** n person whose earnings support a family.

breadth ❶ n 1 extent of something from side to side. 2 lack of restriction.

break ❶ v breaking, broke, broken 1 separate or become separated into two or more pieces. 2 damage or become damaged so as to be inoperative. 3 fail to observe (an agreement etc.). 4 disclose or be disclosed, e.g. he broke the news. 5 bring or come to an end, e.g. the good weather broke at last. 6 weaken or be weakened, as in spirit. 7 cut through or penetrate. 8 improve on or surpass, e.g. break a record. 9 (of the male voice) become permanently deeper at puberty. ♦ n 10 act or result of breaking. 11 gap or

interruption in continuity. 12 Informal fortunate opportunity. **break even** make neither a profit nor a loss. **breakable** adj **breakage** n **breaker** n large wave. **break down** v 1 cease to function. 2 yield to strong emotion. 3 **breakdown** n 1 act or instance of breaking down. 2 nervous breakdown. **breakfast** v, n (eat) the first meal of the day. **break-in** n illegal entering of a building, esp. by thieves. **breakneck** adj fast and dangerous. **break off** v 1 sever or detach. 2 end (a relationship etc.). **break out** v begin or arise suddenly. **breakthrough** n important development or discovery. **break up** v 1 (cause to) separate. 2 come to an end. 3 (of a school) close for the holidays. **breakwater** n wall that extends into the sea to protect a harbour or beach from the force of waves.

bream n freshwater silvery fish.

breast ❶ n 1 either of the two soft fleshy milk-secreting glands on a woman's chest. 2 chest. **breastbone** n long flat bone in the front of the body, to which most of the ribs are attached. **breaststroke** n swimming stroke in which the arms are extended in front of the head and swept back on either side.

———————————————| THESAURUS |———————————————

brawn n 1 = **muscle**, beef (inf), might, muscles, power, strength, vigour

brazen adj = **bold**, audacious, barefaced, brash, defiant, impudent, insolent, shameless, unabashed, unashamed ≠ **modest**

breach n 1 = **nonobservance**, contravention, infraction, infringement, noncompliance, transgression, trespass, violation ≠ **performance** 3 = **crack**, cleft, fissure, gap, opening, rift, rupture, split

bread n 2 Sl = **money**, cash, dough (sl), lolly (Aust & NZ sl)

breadth n 1 = **width**, broadness, latitude, span, spread, wideness 2 = **extent**, compass, expanse, range, scale, scope

break v 1 = **separate**, burst, crack, destroy, disintegrate, fracture, fragment, shatter,

smash, snap, split, tear ≠ **unite**
3 = **disobey**, breach, contravene, disregard, infringe, renege on, transgress, violate ≠ **follow** 4 = **reveal**, announce, disclose, divulge, impart, inform, let out, make public, proclaim, tell 5 = **stop**, abandon, cut, discontinue, give up, interrupt, pause, rest, suspend
6 = **weaken**, demoralize, dispirit, subdue, tame, undermine 8 = **beat**, better, exceed, excel, go beyond, outdo, outstrip, surpass, top ♦ n 10 = **division**, crack, fissure, fracture, gap, hole, opening, split, tear
11 = **rest**, breather (inf), hiatus, interlude, intermission, interruption, interval, let-up (inf), lull, pause, respite 12 Inf = **stroke of luck**, advantage, chance, fortune, opening, opportunity

breath ⊕ *n* **1** taking in and letting out of air during breathing. **2** air taken in and let out during breathing. **breathless** *adj* **breathtaking** *adj* causing awe or excitement. **breathe** *v* **1** take in oxygen and give out carbon dioxide. **2** whisper. **breather** *n Informal* short rest. **breathing** *n*

Breathalyser *n* ® device for estimating the amount of alcohol in the breath. **breathalyse** *v*

breech *n* **1** buttocks. **2** part of a firearm behind the barrel.

breed ⊕ *v* **breeding, bred 1** produce new or improved strains of (domestic animals or plants). **2** bear (offspring). **3** produce or be produced, e.g. *breed trouble.* ◆ *n* **4** group of animals etc. within a species that have certain clearly defined characteristics. **5** kind or sort. **breeder** *n* **breeding** *n* result of good upbringing or training.

breeze ⊕ *n* **1** gentle wind. ◆ *v* **2** move quickly or casually. **breezy** *adj* **1** windy. **2** casual or carefree.

brethren *pl n Old-fashioned* (used in religious contexts) brothers.

brevity ⊕ *n* shortness.

brew ⊕ *v* **1** make (beer etc.) by steeping, boiling, and fermentation. **2** prepare (a drink) by infusing. **3** be about to happen or forming. ◆ *n* **4** beverage produced by

brewing. **brewer** *n* **brewery** *n, pl* **-eries** place where beer etc. is brewed.

briar, brier *n* **1** European shrub with a hard woody root. **2** tobacco pipe made from this root.

bribe ⊕ *v* **1** offer or give something to someone to gain favour, influence, etc. ◆ *n* **2** something given or offered as a bribe. **bribery** *n*

bric-a-brac ⊕ *n* miscellaneous small ornamental objects.

brick *n* **1** (rectangular block of) baked clay used in building. ◆ *v* **2** (foll. by *up* or *over*) build, enclose, or fill with bricks. **bricklayer** *n* person who builds with bricks.

bride *n* woman who has just been or is about to be married. **bridal** *adj* **bridegroom** *n* man who has just been or is about to be married. **bridesmaid** *n* girl who attends a bride at her wedding.

bridge¹ ⊕ *n* **1** structure for crossing a river etc. **2** platform from which a ship is steered or controlled. **3** upper part of the nose. **4** piece of wood supporting the strings of a violin etc. ◆ *v* **5** build a bridge over (something). **bridgehead** *n* fortified position at the end of a bridge nearest the enemy.

bridge² *n* card game based on whist,

THESAURUS

breast *n* **1** = **bosom**, bust, chest, front, teat, udder

breath *n* **1** = **respiration**, breathing, exhalation, gasp, gulp, inhalation, pant, wheeze

breed *v* **1** = **cultivate**, develop **2** = **reproduce**, bear young, bring forth young, develop, generate offspring, hatch, multiply, procreate, produce, propagate **3** = **produce**, arouse, bring about, cause, create, generate, give rise to, stir up ◆ *n* **4** = **variety**, pedigree, race, species, stock, strain, type **5** = **kind**, brand, sort, stamp, type, variety

breeze *n* **1** = **light wind**, air, breath of wind, current of air, draught, gust, waft, zephyr ◆ *v* **2** = **move briskly**, flit, glide,

hurry, pass, sail, sweep

brevity *n* = **shortness**, briefness, conciseness, crispness, curtness, economy, impermanence, pithiness, succinctness, terseness, transience, transitoriness ≠ **rambling**

brew *v* **1, 2** = **make** (*beer*), boil, ferment, infuse (*tea*), soak, steep, stew **3** = **develop**, foment, form, gather, start, stir up ◆ *n* **4** = **drink**, beverage, blend, concoction, infusion, liquor, mixture, preparation

bribe *v* **1** = **buy off**, corrupt, grease the palm *or* hand of (*sl*), pay off (*inf*), reward, suborn ◆ *n* **2** = **inducement**, allurement, backhander (*sl*), enticement, kickback (*US*), pay-off (*inf*), sweetener (*sl*)

bric-a-brac *n* = **knick-knacks**, baubles,

played between two pairs.

bridle ❶ n 1 headgear for controlling a horse. ◆ v 2 show anger or indignation. 3 **bridle path** path suitable for riding horses.

brief ❶ adj 1 short in duration. ◆ n 2 condensed statement or written synopsis. 3 (also **briefing**) set of instructions. ◆ pl 4 men's or women's underpants. ◆ v 5 give information and instructions to (a person). **briefly** adv **briefcase** n small flat case for carrying papers, books, etc.

brier, briar n wild rose with long thorny stems.

brigade ❶ n 1 army unit smaller than a division. 2 group of people organized for a certain task. **brigadier** n high–ranking army officer.

brigand ❶ n bandit.

bright ❶ adj 1 emitting or reflecting much light. 2 (of colours) intense. 3 clever. **brightly** adv **brightness** n **brighten** v

brilliant ❶ adj 1 shining with light. 2 splendid. 3 extremely clever. **brilliance, brilliancy** n

brim ❶ n 1 upper rim of a cup etc. 2 projecting edge of a hat. ◆ v **brimming, brimmed** 3 be full to the brim.

brine n salt water. **briny** adj very salty.

bring ❶ v **bringing, brought** 1 carry, convey, or take to a designated place or person. 2 cause to happen. 3 *Law* put forward (charges) officially. **bring about** v cause to happen. **bring off** v succeed in achieving. **bring out** v 1 publish or have (a book) published. 2 reveal or cause to be seen. **bring up** v 1 rear (a child). 2 mention. 3 vomit (food).

brinjal n S Afr dark purple tropical fruit, cooked and eaten as a vegetable.

brink ❶ n edge of a steep place.

brisk ❶ adj lively and quick. **briskly** adv

brisket n beef from the breast of a cow.

————— THESAURUS —————

curios, ornaments, trinkets

bridge¹ n 1 = **arch**, flyover, overpass, span, viaduct ◆ v 5 = **connect**, join, link, span ≠ **separate**

bridle n 1 = **curb**, check, control, rein, restraint ◆ v 2 = **get angry**, be indignant, bristle, draw (oneself) up, get one's back up, raise one's hackles, rear up

brief adj 1 = **short**, ephemeral, fleeting, momentary, quick, short–lived, swift, transitory ≠ **long** ◆ n 2 = **summary**, abridgment, abstract, digest, epitome, outline, précis, sketch, synopsis 3 = **instructions**, conference, directions, guidance, information, preparation, priming, rundown ◆ v 5 = **inform**, advise, explain, fill in (*inf*), instruct, keep posted, prepare, prime, put (someone) in the picture (*inf*)

brigade n 2 = **group**, band, company, corps, force, outfit, squad, team, troop, unit

brigand n = **bandit**, desperado, freebooter, gangster, highwayman, marauder, outlaw, plunderer, robber

bright adj 1, 2 = **shining**, brilliant, dazzling,

gleaming, glowing, luminous, lustrous, radiant, shimmering, vivid ≠ **dark** 3 = **intelligent**, astute, aware, clever, inventive, quick–witted, sharp, smart, wide–awake ≠ **simple**

brilliant adj 1 = **shining**, bright, dazzling, glittering, intense, luminous, radiant, sparkling, vivid ≠ **dark** 2 = **splendid**, celebrated, famous, glorious, illustrious, magnificent, notable, outstanding, superb 3 = **intelligent**, clever, expert, gifted, intellectual, inventive, masterly, penetrating, profound, talented ≠ **simple**

brim n 1 = **rim**, border, brink, edge, lip, margin, skirt, verge ◆ v 3 = **be full**, fill, fill up, hold no more, overflow, run over, spill, well over

bring v 1 = **take**, bear, carry, conduct, convey, deliver, escort, fetch, guide, lead, transfer, transport 2 = **cause**, contribute to, create, effect, inflict, occasion, produce, result in, wreak

brink n = **edge**, border, boundary, brim, fringe, frontier, limit, lip, margin, rim, skirt, threshold, verge

bristle ❼ n 1 short stiff hair. ◆ v 2 (cause to) stand up like bristles. 3 show anger. **bristly** adj

brittle ❼ adj hard but easily broken. **brittleness** n

broach ❼ v 1 introduce (a topic) for discussion. 2 open (a bottle or barrel).

broad ❼ adj 1 having great breadth or width. 2 not detailed. 3 extensive, e.g. broad support. 4 strongly marked, e.g. a broad Bristol accent. **broadly** adv **broaden** v **broad bean** thick flat edible bean. **broadcast** n programme or announcement on radio or television. **broad-minded** adj tolerant. **broadside** n 1 strong verbal or written attack. 2 Naval firing of all the guns on one side of a ship at once.

brocade n rich fabric woven with a raised design.

broccoli n type of cabbage with greenish flower heads.

brochure ❼ n booklet that contains information about a product or service.

broekies [brook-eez] pl n S Afr informal underpants.

brogue¹ n sturdy walking shoe.

brogue² n strong accent, esp. Irish.

broil v Aust, NZ, US & Canadian same as GRILL.

broke ❼ v 1 past tense of BREAK. ◆ adj 2 Informal having no money.

broker ❼ n agent who sells or sells goods, securities, etc.

bromide n chemical compound used in medicine and photography.

bromine n Chem dark red liquid element that gives off a pungent vapour.

bronco n, pl –cos (in the US) wild or partially tamed pony.

brontosaurus n very large plant-eating four-footed dinosaur.

bronze ❼ n 1 alloy of copper and tin. 2 statue, medal, etc. made of bronze. ◆ adj 3 made of, or coloured like, bronze. ◆ v 4 (esp. of the skin) make or become brown.

brooch n ornament with a pin, worn fastened to clothes.

brood ❼ n 1 number of birds produced at one hatching. 2 all the children of a family. ◆ v 3 think long and unhappily. **broody** adj 1 moody and sullen. 2 Informal (of a woman) wishing to have a baby.

brook¹ ❼ n small stream.

brook² ❼ v bear or tolerate.

broom n 1 long-handled sweeping brush.

THESAURUS

brisk adj = **lively**, active, bustling, busy, energetic, quick, sprightly, spry, vigorous ≠ **heavy**

bristle n 1 = **hair**, barb, prickle, spine, stubble, thorn, whisker ◆ v 2 = **stand up**, rise, stand on end 3 = **be angry**, bridle, flare up, rage, see red, seethe

brittle adj = **fragile**, breakable, crisp, crumbling, crumbly, delicate, frail, frangible, friable ≠ **strong**

broach v 1 = **bring up**, introduce, mention, open up, propose, raise the subject, speak of, suggest, talk of, touch on 2 = **open**, crack, draw off, pierce, puncture, start, tap, uncork

broad adj 1 = **wide**, ample, expansive, extensive, generous, large, roomy, spacious, vast, voluminous, widespread ≠ **close** 3 = **general**, all-embracing,

comprehensive, encyclopedic, inclusive, overarching, sweeping, wide, wide-ranging

brochure n = **booklet**, advertisement, circular, folder, handbill, hand-out, leaflet, mailshot, pamphlet

broke adj 2 Inf = **penniless**, bankrupt, bust (inf), down and out, impoverished, insolvent, in the red, munted (NZ sl), ruined, short, skint (Brit sl)

broker n = **dealer**, agent, factor, go-between, intermediary, middleman, negotiator

bronze adj 3 = **reddish-brown**, brownish, chestnut, copper, rust, tan

brood n 1 = **offspring**, clutch, family, issue, litter, progeny ◆ v 3 = **think upon**, agonize, dwell upon, mope, mull over, muse, obsess, ponder, ruminate

2 yellow–flowered shrub. **broomstick** *n* handle of a broom.

broth *n* soup, usu. containing vegetables.

brothel *n* house where men pay to have sex with prostitutes.

brother ● *n* **1** boy or man with the same parents as another person. **2** member of a male religious order. **brotherly** *adj* **brotherhood** *n* **1** fellowship. **2** association, such as a trade union. **brother–in–law** *n*, *pl* **brothers–in–law 1** brother of one's husband or wife. **2** husband of one's sister.

brow *n* **1** part of the face from the eyes to the hairline. **2** eyebrow. **3** top of a hill.

brown ● *n* **1** colour of earth or wood. ◆ *adj* **2** of the colour brown. ◆ *v* **3** make or become brown. **browned–off** *adj Informal* bored and depressed.

browse ● *v* **1** look through (a book or articles for sale) in a casual manner. **2** nibble on young shoots or leaves. ◆ *n* **3** instance of browsing.

bruise ● *n* **1** discoloured area on the skin caused by an injury. ◆ *v* **2** cause a bruise on. **bruiser** *n* strong tough person.

brumby *n Aust* **1** wild horse. **2** unruly person.

brunch *n Informal* breakfast and lunch combined.

brunette *n* girl or woman with dark brown hair.

brunt ● *n* main force or shock of a blow, attack, etc.

brush¹ ● *n* **1** device made of bristles, wires, etc. used for cleaning, painting, etc. **2** brief unpleasant encounter. **3** fox's tail. ◆ *v* **4** clean, scrub, or paint with a brush. **5** touch lightly and briefly. **brush off** *v Slang* dismiss or ignore (someone). **brush up** *v* refresh one's knowledge of (a subject).

brush² ● *n* thick growth of shrubs.

brusque ● *adj* blunt or curt in manner or speech. **brusquely** *adv* **brusqueness** *n*

Brussels sprout *n* vegetable like a tiny cabbage.

brute ● *n* **1** brutal person. **2** animal other than man. ◆ *adj* **3** wholly instinctive or physical, like an animal. **4** without reason. **brutish** *adj* of or like an animal. **brutal** *adj* **1** cruel and vicious. **2** extremely honest in speech or manner. **brutally** *adv* **brutality** *n* **brutalize** *v*

—————————— THESAURUS ——————————

brook¹ *n* = **stream**, beck, burn, rill, rivulet, watercourse

brook² *v* = **tolerate**, abide, accept, allow, bear, countenance, endure, hack (*sl*), put up with (*inf*), stand, stomach, suffer, support, swallow, thole (*dial*), withstand

brother *n* **1** = **sibling**, blood brother, kin, kinsman, relation, relative **2** = **monk**, cleric, friar

brown *adj* **2** = **brunette**, auburn, bay, bronze, chestnut, chocolate, coffee, dun, hazel, sunburnt, tan, tanned, tawny, umber ◆ *v* **3** = **fry**, cook, grill, sauté, seal, sear

browse *v* **1** = **skim**, dip into, examine cursorily, flip through, glance at, leaf through, look round, look through, peruse, scan, survey **2** = **graze**, eat, feed, nibble

bruise *n* **1** = **discoloration**, black mark, blemish, contusion, injury, mark, swelling

◆ *v* **2** = **discolour**, damage, injure, mar, mark, pound

brunt *n* = **full force**, burden, force, impact, pressure, shock, strain, stress, thrust, violence

brush¹ *n* **1** = **broom**, besom, sweeper **2** = **encounter**, clash, conflict, confrontation, skirmish, tussle ◆ *v* **4** = **clean**, buff, paint, polish, sweep, wash **5** = **touch**, flick, glance, graze, kiss, scrape, stroke, sweep

brush² *n* = **shrubs**, brushwood, bushes, copse, scrub, thicket, undergrowth

brusque *adj* = **curt**, abrupt, discourteous, gruff, impolite, sharp, short, surly, terse

brute *n* **1** = **savage**, barbarian, beast, devil, fiend, monster, sadist, swine **2** = **animal**, beast, creature, wild animal ◆ *adj* **3** = **physical**, bodily, carnal, fleshly **4** = **mindless**, instinctive, senseless, unthinking

BSc Bachelor of Science.

BST British Summer Time.

bubble ⊕ n 1 ball of air in a liquid or solid. ◆ v 2 form bubbles. 3 move or flow with a gurgling sound. **bubbly** adj 1 excited and lively. 2 full of bubbles.

bubonic plague [bew–**bonn**–ik] n acute infectious disease characterized by swellings.

buccaneer ⊕ n pirate.

buck¹ n 1 male of the goat, hare, kangaroo, rabbit, and reindeer. ◆ v 2 (of a horse etc.) jump with legs stiff and back arched. 3 Informal resist or oppose obstinately, e.g. to buck a trend. **buckshot** n large lead pellets used for shooting game. **buck up** v make or become more cheerful.

buck² n US, Canadian & Aust slang dollar.

bucket n 1 open–topped round container with a handle. ◆ v **–eting, –eted** 2 rain heavily. **bucketful** n

buckle ⊕ n 1 clasp for fastening a belt or strap. ◆ v 2 fasten or be fastened with a buckle. 3 (cause to) bend out of shape through pressure or heat. **buckle down** v Informal apply oneself with determination.

bud ⊕ n 1 swelling on a tree or plant that develops into a leaf or flower. ◆ v **budding, budded** 2 produce buds.

budding adj beginning to develop or grow.

budge ⊕ v move slightly

budgerigar n small cage bird bred in many different–coloured varieties.

budget ⊕ n 1 financial plan for a period of time. 2 money allocated for a specific purpose. ◆ v **–eting, –eted** 3 plan the expenditure of (money or time). ◆ adj 4 cheap. **budgetary** adj

buff¹ ⊕ adj 1 dull yellowish–brown. ◆ v 2 clean or polish with soft material.

buff² ⊕ n Informal expert on or devotee of a given subject.

buffalo n 1 type of cattle. 2 US bison.

buffer ⊕ n something that lessens shock or protects from damaging impact, circumstances, etc.

buffet¹ ⊕ [**boof**–ay] n counter where drinks and snacks are served.

buffet² ⊕ [**buff**–it] v **–feting, –feted** knock against or about.

buffoon ⊕ n clown or fool. **buffoonery** n

bug ⊕ n 1 small insect. 2 Informal minor illness. 3 small mistake in a computer program. 4 concealed microphone. ◆ v **bugging, bugged** 5 Informal irritate (someone). 6 conceal a microphone in (a room or phone).

THESAURUS

bubble n 1 = **air ball**, bead, blister, blob, drop, droplet, globule ◆ v 2 = **foam**, boil, effervesce, fizz, froth, percolate, seethe, sparkle 3 = **gurgle**, babble, burble, murmur, ripple, trickle

buccaneer n = **pirate**, corsair, freebooter, privateer, sea–rover

buckle n 1 = **fastener**, catch, clasp, clip, hasp ◆ v 2 = **fasten**, clasp, close, hook, secure 3 = **distort**, bend, bulge, cave in, collapse, contort, crumple, fold, twist, warp

bud n 1 = **shoot**, embryo, germ, sprout ◆ v 2 = **develop**, burgeon, burst forth, grow, shoot, sprout

budge v = **move**, dislodge, push, shift, stir

budget n 2 = **allowance**, allocation, cost, finances, funds, means, resources ◆ v 3 = **plan**, allocate, apportion, cost, estimate, ration

buff¹ adj 1 = **yellowish–brown**, sandy, straw, tan, yellowish ◆ v 2 = **polish**, brush, burnish, rub, shine, smooth

buff² n Inf = **expert**, addict, admirer, aficionado, connoisseur, devotee, enthusiast, fan, fundi (S Afr)

buffer n = **safeguard**, bulwark, bumper, cushion, fender, intermediary, screen, shield, shock absorber

buffet¹ n = **snack bar**, brasserie, café, cafeteria, refreshment counter, sideboard

buffet² v = **batter**, beat, bump, knock, pound, pummel, strike, thump, wallop (inf)

buffoon n = **clown**, comedian, comic, fool,

bugbear ⊕ *n* thing that causes obsessive anxiety.

bugger *n* 1 *Taboo slang* unpleasant or difficult person or thing. 2 *v* 3 *Slang* tire. 4 practise buggery with. **buggery** *n* anal intercourse.

bugle *n* instrument like a small trumpet. **bugler** *n*

build ⊕ *v* **building**, **built** 1 make, construct, or form by joining parts or materials. ◆ *n* 2 shape of the body. **builder** *n* building *n* structure with walls and a roof. **building society** organization where money can be borrowed or invested. **build-up** *n* gradual increase.

bulb *n* 1 same as LIGHT BULB. 2 onion-shaped root which grows into a flower or plant. **bulbous** *adj* round and fat.

bulge ⊕ *n* 1 swelling on a normally flat surface. 2 sudden increase in number. ◆ *v* 3 swell outwards.

bulk ⊕ *n* 1 size or volume, esp. when great. 2 main part. **in bulk** in large quantities. **bulky** *adj*

bull *n* male of some animals, such as cattle, elephants, and whales. **bullock** *n* castrated bull. **bulldog** *n* thickset dog with a broad

head and a muscular body. **bulldozer** *n* powerful tractor for moving earth. **bulldoze** *v* 1 demolish or flatten with a bulldozer. 2 *Informal* achieve (something) or persuade (someone) by intimidation, e.g. *the new law was bulldozed through parliament.* **bullfight** *n* public show in which a matador kills a bull. **bullfinch** *n* common European songbird. **bullfrog** *n* large American frog with a deep croak. **bull's-eye** *n* central disc of a target. **bull terrier** terrier with a short smooth coat.

bullet ⊕ *n* small piece of metal fired from a gun.

bulletin ⊕ *n* short official report or announcement.

bullion *n* gold or silver in the form of bars.

bully ⊕ *n, pl* **-lies** 1 person who hurts, persecutes, or intimidates a weaker person. ◆ *v* **-lying, -lied** 2 hurt, intimidate, or persecute (a weaker person).

bulrush *n* tall stiff reed.

bulwark ⊕ *n* 1 wall used as a fortification. 2 person or thing acting as a defence.

bum *n Slang* buttocks or anus. **bumbag** *n* small bag attached to a belt and worn

───| THESAURUS |───

harlequin, jester, joker, wag

bug *n* 2 *Inf* = **illness**, disease, infection, virus 3 = **fault**, defect, error, flaw, glitch, gremlin 4 *v* 5 *Inf* = **annoy**, bother, disturb, get on one's nerves (*inf*), hassle (*inf*), irritate, pester, vex 6 = **tap**, eavesdrop, listen in, spy

bugbear *n* = **pet hate**, bane, bête noire, bogey, dread, horror, nightmare

build *v* 1 = **construct**, assemble, erect, fabricate, form, make, put up, raise ≠ **dismantle** ◆ *n* 2 = **physique**, body, figure, form, frame, shape, structure

bulge *n* 1 = **swelling**, bump, hump, lump, projection, protrusion, protuberance ≠ **hole** 2 = **increase**, boost, intensification, rise, surge ◆ *v* 3 = **swell out**, dilate, distend, expand, project, protrude, puff out, stick out

bulk *n* 1 = **size**, dimensions, immensity,

largeness, magnitude, substance, volume, weight 2 = **main part**, better part, body, lion's share, majority, mass, most, nearly all, preponderance

bullet *n* = **projectile**, ball, missile, pellet, shot, slug

bulletin *n* = **announcement**, account, communication, communiqué, dispatch, message, news flash, notification, report, statement

bully *n* 1 = **persecutor**, browbeater, bully boy, coercer, intimidator, oppressor, ruffian, tormentor, tough ◆ *v* 2 = **persecute**, browbeat, coerce, domineer, hector, intimidate, oppress, push around (*sl*), terrorize, tyrannize

bulwark *n* 1 = **fortification**, bastion, buttress, defence, embankment, partition, rampart 2 = **defence**, buffer, guard, mainstay, safeguard, security, support round the waist.

bumble v speak, do, or move in a clumsy way. **bumbling** adj, n

bumblebee n large hairy bee.

bumf, bumph n Informal official documents or forms.

bump ❶ v 1 knock or strike with a jolt. 2 travel in jerks and jolts. ◆ n 3 dull thud from an impact or collision. 4 raised uneven part. **bumpy** adj **bump off** v Informal murder.

bumper n bar on the front and back of a vehicle to protect against damage.

bumpkin ❶ n awkward simple country person.

bumptious ❶ adj offensively self–assertive.

bun n 1 small sweet bread roll or cake. 2 hair gathered into a bun shape at the back of the head.

bunch ❶ n 1 number of things growing or grouped together. 2 group. ◆ v 3 group or be grouped together in a bunch.

bundle ❶ n 1 number of things gathered loosely together. ◆ v 2 cause to go roughly or unceremoniously.

bung n 1 stopper for a cask etc. ◆ v 2 (foll. by up) Informal close with a bung. 3 Slang throw (something) somewhere in a

careless manner.

bungalow n one–storey house.

bungle ❶ v spoil through incompetence. **bungler** n **bungling** adj, n

bunion n inflamed swelling on the big toe.

bunk n narrow shelflike bed. **bunk bed** one of a pair of beds constructed one above the other.

bunker n 1 sand–filled hollow forming an obstacle on a golf course. 2 underground shelter. 3 large storage container for coal etc.

bunny n, pl –nies child's word for a rabbit.

bunting n decorative flags.

bunyip n Aust legendary monster said to live in swamps and lakes.

buoy ❶ n 1 floating marker anchored in the sea. ◆ v 2 prevent from sinking. 3 encourage or hearten. **buoyant** adj 1 able to float. 2 cheerful or resilient. **buoyancy** n

burden ❶ n 1 heavy load. 2 something difficult to cope with. ◆ v 3 put a burden on. 4 oppress. **burdensome** adj

bureau ❶ n, pl –reaus, –reaux 1 office that provides a service. 2 writing desk with shelves and drawers. **bureaucracy** n administrative system based on complex rules and procedures.

————— THESAURUS —————

bump v 1 = **knock**, bang, collide (with), crash, hit, slam, smash into, strike 2 = **jerk**, bounce, jolt, rattle, shake ◆ n 3 = **knock**, bang, blow, collision, crash, impact, jolt, thud, thump 4 = **lump**, bulge, contusion, hump, nodule, protuberance, swelling

bumpkin n = **yokel**, country bumpkin, hick (inf, chiefly US & Canad), hillbilly, peasant, rustic

bumptious adj = **cocky**, arrogant, brash, conceited, forward, full of oneself, overconfident, pushy (inf), self–assertive

bunch n 1 = **number**, assortment, batch, bundle, clump, cluster, collection, heap, lot, mass, pile 2 = **group**, band, crowd, flock, gang, gathering, party, team ◆ v 3 = **group**, assemble, bundle, cluster, collect, huddle, mass, pack

bundle n 1 = **bunch**, assortment, batch,

collection, group, heap, mass, pile, stack ◆ v 2 = **push**, hurry, hustle, rush, shove, thrust

bungle v = **mess up**, blow (sl), blunder, botch, foul up, make a mess of, muff, ruin, spoil

buoy n 1 = **marker**, beacon, float, guide, signal ◆ v 3 = **encourage**, boost, cheer, cheer up, hearten, lift, raise, support, sustain

burden n 1 = **load**, encumbrance, weight 2 = **trouble**, affliction, millstone, onus, responsibility, strain, weight, worry ◆ v 3 = **weigh down**, bother, encumber, handicap, load, oppress, saddle with, tax, worry

bureau n 1 = **office**, agency, branch, department, division, service 2 = **desk**, writing desk

burgeon v develop or grow rapidly.

burglar ❶ n person who enters a building to commit a crime, esp. theft. **burglary** n **burgle** v

burgundy adj dark–purplish red.

burlesque ❶ n artistic work which satirizes a subject by caricature.

burly ❶ adj –lier, –liest (of a person) broad and strong.

burn ❶ v **burning, burnt** or **burned** 1 be or set on fire. 2 destroy or be destroyed by fire. 3 damage, injure, or mark by heat. 4 feel strong emotion. ♦ n 5 injury or mark caused by fire or exposure to heat. **burner** n part of a stove or lamp that produces the flame. **burning** adj 1 intense. 2 urgent or crucial.

✔ **WORD TIP**

Either *burnt* or *burned* may be used as a past form.

burnish ❶ v make smooth and shiny by rubbing.

burp v, n Informal belch.

burrow ❶ n 1 hole dug in the ground by a rabbit etc. ♦ v 2 dig holes in the ground.

bursar n treasurer of a school, college, or university. **bursary** n scholarship.

burst ❶ v **bursting, burst** 1 (cause to) break open or apart noisily and suddenly. 2 come or go suddenly and forcibly. 3 be full to the point of breaking open. ♦ n 4 instance of breaking open suddenly. 5 sudden outbreak or occurrence.

bury ❶ v **burying, buried** 1 place in a grave. 2 place in the earth and cover with soil. 3 conceal or hide.

bus n 1 large motor vehicle for carrying passengers. ♦ v **bussing, bussed** 2 travel or transport by bus.

bush ❶ n 1 dense woody plant, smaller than a tree. 2 wild uncultivated part of a country. **bushy** adj (of hair) thick and shaggy. **bushbaby** n small African tree–living mammal with large eyes.

bushel n obsolete unit of measure equal to 8 gallons.

business ❶ n 1 purchase and sale of goods and services. 2 commercial establishment. 3 trade or profession. 4 proper concern or responsibility. 5 affair, e.g. *it's a dreadful business*. **businesslike** adj efficient and methodical. **businessman, businesswoman** n

busker n street entertainer. **busk** v act as a

——————— THESAURUS ———————

burglar n = **housebreaker**, cat burglar, filcher, pilferer, robber, sneak thief, thief

burlesque n = **parody**, caricature, mockery, satire, send–up (*Brit inf*), spoof (*inf*), takeoff (*inf*), travesty

burly adj = **brawny**, beefy (*inf*), bulky, hefty, stocky, stout, sturdy, thickset, well–built

burn v 1 = **be on fire**, be ablaze, blaze, flame, flare, glow, go up in flames, smoke 3 = **set on fire**, char, ignite, incinerate, kindle, light, parch, scorch, sear, singe, toast 4 = **be passionate**, be angry, be aroused, be inflamed, fume, seethe, simmer, smoulder

burnish v = **polish**, brighten, buff, furbish, glaze, rub up, shine, smooth ≠ **scratch**

burrow n 1 = **hole**, den, lair, retreat, shelter, tunnel ♦ v 2 = **dig**, delve,

excavate, hollow out, scoop out, tunnel

burst v 1 = **explode**, blow up, break, crack, puncture, rupture, shatter, split, tear apart 2 = **rush**, barge, break, break out, erupt, gush forth, run, spout ♦ n 4 = **explosion**, bang, blast, blowout, break, crack, discharge, rupture, split 5 = **rush**, gush, gust, outbreak, outburst, outpouring, spate, spurt, surge, torrent

bury v 1 = **inter**, consign to the grave, entomb, inhume, lay to rest ≠ **unearth** 2 = **embed**, engulf, submerge 3 = **hide**, conceal, cover, enshroud, secrete, stow away ≠ **find**

bush n 1 = **shrub**, hedge, plant, shrubbery, thicket 2 = **the wild**, backwoods, brush, scrub, scrubland, woodland

business n 1 = **trade**, bargaining, commerce, dealings, industry, busker.

bust[1] **➊** n 1 woman's bosom. 2 sculpture of the head and shoulders.

bust[2] **➊** *Informal* ◆ v **busting, bust** or **busted 1** burst or break. **2** (of the police) raid (a place) or arrest (someone). ◆ *adj* **3** broken. **go bust** become bankrupt.

bustle **➊** v **1** hurry with a show of activity or energy. ◆ n **2** energetic and noisy activity. **bustling** *adj*

busy **➊** *adj* **busier, busiest 1** actively employed. **2** crowded or full of activity. ◆ v **busying, busied 3** keep (someone, esp. oneself) busy. **busily** *adv* **busybody** n meddlesome or nosy person.

but **➊** *conj* **1** contrary to expectation. **2** in contrast. **3** other than. **4** without it happening. ◆ *prep* **5** except. ◆ *adv* **6** only. **but for** were it not for.

butane n gas used for fuel.

butch *adj Slang* markedly or aggressively masculine.

butcher **➊** n **1** person who slaughters animals or sells their meat. **2** brutal

murderer. ◆ v **3** kill and prepare (animals) for meat. **4** kill (people) brutally or indiscriminately. **butchery** n

butler n chief male servant.

butt[1] **➊** n **1** thicker end of something. **2** unused end of a cigar or cigarette. **3** *Chiefly US & Canadian slang* buttocks.

butt[2] **➊** n **1** person or thing that is the target of ridicule. **2** mound of earth behind a target. ◆ *pl* **3** target range.

butt[3] **➊** v **1** strike with the head or horns. ◆ n **2** blow with the head or horns. **butt in** v interrupt a conversation.

butter n **1** edible fatty solid made by churning cream. ◆ v **2** put butter on. **buttery** *adj* **butter up** v flatter.

buttercup n small yellow flower.

butterfly n **1** insect with brightly coloured wings. **2** swimming stroke in which both arms move together in a forward circular action.

butterscotch n kind of hard brittle toffee.

buttock n either of the two fleshy masses that form the human rump.

━━━━━━━━━━ THESAURUS ━━━━━━━━━━

manufacturing, selling, transaction **2** = **establishment**, company, concern, corporation, enterprise, firm, organization, venture **3** = **profession**, career, employment, function, job, line, occupation, trade, vocation, work, yakka (*Aust & NZ inf*) **4** = **concern**, affair, assignment, duty, pigeon (*inf*), problem, responsibility, task

bust[1] n = **bosom**, breast, chest, front, torso

bust[2] *inf* v **1** = **break**, burst, fracture, rupture **2** = **arrest**, catch, fossick (*Aust & NZ*), raid, search **go bust** = **go bankrupt**, become insolvent, be ruined, fail

bustle v **1** = **hurry**, fuss, hasten, rush, scamper, scurry, scuttle ≠ **rest** ◆ n **2** = **activity**, ado, commotion, excitement, flurry, fuss, hurly-burly, stir, to-do ≠ **inactivity**

busy *adj* **1** = **occupied**, active, employed, engaged, hard at work, industrious, on duty, rushed off one's feet, working ≠ **relaxed 2** = **lively**, energetic, exacting,

full, hectic, hustling ◆ v **3** = **occupy**, absorb, employ, engage, engross, immerse, interest ≠ **off duty**

but *conj* **1** = **however**, further, moreover, nevertheless, on the contrary, on the other hand, still, yet ◆ *prep* **5** = **except**, bar, barring, excepting, excluding, notwithstanding, save, with the exception of ◆ *adv* **6** = **only**, just, merely, simply, singly, solely

butcher n **2** = **murderer**, destroyer, killer, slaughterer, slayer ◆ v **3** = **slaughter**, carve, clean, cut, cut up, dress, joint, prepare **4** = **kill**, assassinate, cut down, destroy, exterminate, liquidate, massacre, put to the sword, slaughter, slay

butt[1] n **1** = **end**, haft, handle, hilt, shaft, shank, stock **2** = **stub**, fag end (*inf*), leftover, tip

butt[2] n **1** = **target**, Aunt Sally, dupe, laughing stock, victim

butt[3] v **1** = **knock**, bump, poke, prod, push, ram, shove, thrust ◆ n **2** = **knock**, bump,

button *n* **1** small disc or knob sewn to clothing, which can be passed through a slit in another piece of fabric to fasten them. **2** knob that operates a piece of equipment when pressed. ◆ *v* **3** fasten with buttons. **buttonhole** *n* **1** slit in a garment through which a button is passed. **2** flower worn on a lapel. ◆ *v* **3** detain (someone) in conversation.

buttress *n* **1** structure to support a wall. ◆ *v* **2** support with, or as if with, a buttress.

buxom *adj* (of a woman) healthily plump and full–bosomed.

buy *v* **buying, bought 1** acquire by paying money for. **2** *Slang* accept as true. ◆ *n* **3** thing acquired through payment. **buyer** *n* **1** customer. **2** person employed to buy merchandise.

✓ **WORD TIP**

Be careful not to confuse the past forms *bought* (from *buy*) with *brought* (from *bring*).

---

buzz *n* **1** rapidly vibrating humming sound. **2** *Informal* sense of excitement. ◆ *v* **3** make a humming sound. **4** be filled with an air of excitement. **buzzer** *n* **buzz word** jargon word which becomes fashionably popular.

buzzard *n* bird of prey of the hawk family.

by *prep* **1** indicating the doer of an action, nearness, movement past, time before or during which, etc., e.g. *bitten by a dog; down by the river; driving by the school; in bed by midnight.* ◆ *adv* **2** near. **3** past. **by and by** eventually. **by and large** in general.

bye, bye–bye *interj Informal* goodbye.

by–election *n* election held during parliament to fill a vacant seat.

bygone *adj* past or former.

bylaw, bye–law *n* rule made by a local authority.

bypass *n* **1** main road built to avoid a city. **2** operation to divert blood flow away from a damaged part of the heart. ◆ *v* **3** go round or avoid.

byre *n* shelter for cows.

byte *n Computers* group of bits processed as one unit of data.

byway *n* minor road.

byword *n* person or thing regarded as a perfect example of something.

————————————| THESAURUS |————————————

poke, prod, push, ram, shove, thrust

buttress *n* **1** = **support**, brace, mainstay, prop, reinforcement, stanchion, strut ◆ *v* **2** = **support**, back up, bolster, prop up, reinforce, shore up, strengthen, sustain, uphold

buxom *adj* = **plump**, ample, bosomy, busty, curvaceous, healthy, voluptuous, well–rounded

buy *v* **1** = **purchase**, acquire, get, invest in, obtain, pay for, procure, shop for ≠ **sell** ◆ *n* **3** = **purchase**, acquisition, bargain, deal

by *prep* **1 a** = **via**, by way of, over **b**

= **through**, through the agency of **c** = **near**, along, beside, close to, next to, past ◆ *adv* **2** = **near**, at hand, close, handy, in reach

bygone *adj* = **past**, antiquated, extinct, forgotten, former, lost, of old, olden

bypass *v* **3** = **go round**, avoid, circumvent, depart from, detour round, deviate from, get round, give a wide berth to, pass round ≠ **meet**

byword *n* = **saying**, adage, maxim, motto, precept, proverb, slogan

C c

C 1 *Chem* carbon. 2 Celsius. 3 centigrade.
4 century. 5 the Roman numeral for 100.

c. circa.

CA California.

cab ❶ *n* 1 taxi. 2 enclosed driver's
compartment on a train, lorry, etc. **cabbie,
cabby** *n, pl* **-bies** *Informal* taxi driver.

cabal ❶ [kab-**bal**] *n* 1 small group of
political plotters. 2 secret plot.

cabaret [**kab**-a-ray] *n* dancing and singing
show in a nightclub.

cabbage *n* vegetable with a large head of
green leaves.

cabin ❶ *n* 1 compartment in a ship or
aircraft. 2 small hut.

cabinet ❶ *n* 1 piece of furniture with
drawers or shelves. 2 (**C-**) committee of
senior government ministers. **cabinet-
maker** *n* person who makes fine furniture.

cable *n* 1 strong thick rope. 2 bundle of
wires that carries electricity or electronic
signals. 3 telegram sent abroad. ◆ *v* 4 send
(someone) a message by cable. **cable car**
vehicle pulled up a steep slope by a
moving cable. **cable television** television
service conveyed by cable to subscribers.

cache [kash] *n* hidden store of weapons or
treasure.

cackle *v* 1 laugh shrilly. 2 (of a hen)
squawk with shrill broken notes. ◆ *n*
3 cackling noise.

cacophony [kak-**koff**-on-ee] *n* harsh
discordant sound. **cacophonous** *adj*

cactus *n, pl* **-tuses, -ti** fleshy desert plant
with spines but no leaves.

cad ❶ *n Old-fashioned* dishonourable man.
caddish *adj*

cadaver [kad-**dav**-ver] *n* corpse.
cadaverous *adj* pale, thin, and haggard.

caddie, caddy *n, pl* **-dies** 1 person who
carries a golfer's clubs. ◆ *v* **-dying, -died**
2 act as a caddie.

caddy *n, pl* **-dies** small container for tea.

cadence [**kade**-enss] *n* 1 rise and fall in the
pitch of the voice. 2 close of a musical
phrase.

cadenza *n* complex solo passage in a piece
of music.

cadet *n* young person training for the
armed forces or police.

cadge *v Informal* get (something) by taking
advantage of someone's generosity.

cadmium *n Chem* bluish-white metallic
element used in alloys.

caecum [**seek**-um] *n, pl* **-ca** [-ka] pouch at
the beginning of the large intestine.

Caesarean section [see-**zair**-ee-an] *n*
surgical incision into the womb to deliver
a baby.

caesium *n Chem* silvery-white metallic

THESAURUS

cab *n* 1 = **taxi**, hackney carriage, minicab,
taxicab

cabal *n* 1 = **clique**, caucus, conclave,
faction, league, party, set 2 = **plot**,
conspiracy, intrigue, machination, scheme

cabin *n* 1 = **room**, berth, compartment,
quarters 2 = **hut**, chalet, cottage, lodge,
shack, shanty, shed

cabinet *n* 1 = **cupboard**, case, chiffonier,
closet, commode, dresser, escritoire,
locker 2 (usu. cap.) = **council**,
administration, assembly, counsellors,
ministry

cad *n Old-fashioned* = **scoundrel**, bounder
(*old-fashioned Brit sl*), heel (*sl*), rat (*inf*),
rotter (*sl, chiefly Brit*)

element used in photocells.

café ❶ n **1** small or inexpensive restaurant serving light refreshments. **2** S Afr corner shop or grocer. **cafeteria** n self–service restaurant.

caffeine n stimulant found in tea and coffee.

caftan n same as KAFTAN.

cage ❶ n **1** enclosure of bars or wires, for keeping animals or birds. **2** enclosed platform of a lift in a mine.

cagoule n lightweight hooded waterproof jacket.

cairn n mound of stones erected as a memorial or marker.

cajole ❶ v persuade by flattery.

cake ❶ n **1** sweet food baked from a mixture of flour, eggs, etc. **2** flat compact mass of something, such as soap. ◆ v **3** form into a hardened mass or crust.

calamine n pink powder consisting chiefly of zinc oxide, used in skin lotions and ointments.

calamity ❶ n, pl **–ties** disaster. **calamitous** adj

calcium n Chem silvery–white metallic element found in bones, teeth, limestone, and chalk.

calculate ❶ v **1** solve or find out by a mathematical procedure or by reasoning. **2** aim to have a particular effect. **calculable** adj **calculating** adj selfishly

scheming. **calculation** n **calculator** n small electronic device for making calculations.

calendar n **1** chart showing a year divided up into months, weeks, and days. **2** system for determining the beginning, length, and division of years. **3** schedule of events or appointments.

calf[1] n, pl **calves 1** young cow, bull, elephant, whale, or seal. **2** leather made from calf skin. **calve** v give birth to a calf. **calf love** adolescent infatuation.

calf[2] n, pl **calves** back of the leg between the ankle and knee.

calibre ❶ n **1** person's ability or worth. **2** diameter of the bore of a gun or of a shell or bullet. **calibrate** v mark the scale or check the accuracy of (a measuring instrument). **calibration** n

calico n, pl **–coes** white cotton fabric.

call ❶ v **1** name. **2** shout to attract attention. **3** telephone. **4** summon. **5** (often foll. by on) visit. **6** arrange (a meeting, strike, etc.). ◆ n **7** cry, shout. **8** animal's or bird's cry. **9** telephone communication. **10** short visit. **11** summons, invitation. **12** need, demand. **caller** n **calling** n vocation, profession. **call box** kiosk for a public telephone. **call for** v require. **call off** v cancel. **call up** v **1** summon to serve in the armed forces. **2** cause one to remember.

calligraphy n (art of) beautiful

café n **1** = **snack bar**, brasserie, cafeteria, coffee bar, coffee shop, lunchroom, restaurant, tearoom

cage n **1** = **enclosure**, pen, pound

cajole v = **persuade**, coax, flatter, seduce, sweet–talk (inf), wheedle

cake n **2** = **block**, bar, cube, loaf, lump, mass, slab ◆ v **3** = **encrust**, bake, coagulate, congeal, solidify

calamity n = **disaster**, cataclysm, catastrophe, misadventure, misfortune, mishap, ruin, tragedy, tribulation

calculate v **1** = **work out**, compute, count, determine, enumerate, estimate, figure, reckon **2** = **plan**, aim, design, intend

calibre n **1** = **worth**, ability, capacity, distinction, merit, quality, stature, talent **2** = **diameter**, bore, gauge, measure

call v **1** = **name**, christen, describe as, designate, dub, entitle, label, style, term **2** = **cry**, arouse, hail, rouse, shout, yell **3** = **phone**, ring up (inf, chiefly Brit), telephone **4** = **summon**, assemble, convene, gather, muster, rally ≠ **dismiss** **5** (often foll. by on) = **visit**, drop in on, look in on, look up, see ◆ n **7** = **cry**, hail, scream, shout, signal, whoop, yell **11** = **summons**, appeal, command, demand, invitation, notice, order, plea, request **12** = **need**, cause, excuse, handwriting.

callous ⊕ *adj* showing no concern for other people's feelings.

callow ⊕ *adj* young and inexperienced.

callus *n, pl* **–luses** area of thick hardened skin.

calm ⊕ *adj* **1** not agitated or excited. **2** not ruffled by the wind. **3** windless. ◆ *n* **4** peaceful state. ◆ *v* **5** (often foll. by *down*) make or become calm. **calmly** *adv* **calmness** *n*

calorie *n* **1** unit of measurement for the energy value of food. **2** unit of heat. **calorific** *adj* of calories or heat.

calypso *n, pl* **–sos** West Indian song with improvised topical lyrics.

cam *n* device that converts a circular motion to a to-and-fro motion. **camshaft** *n* part of an engine consisting of a rod to which cams are fixed.

camaraderie *n* comradeship.

camber *n* slight upward curve to the centre of a surface.

cambric *n* fine white linen fabric.

camcorder *n* combined portable video camera and recorder.

camel *n* humped mammal that can survive long periods without food or water in desert regions.

camellia [kam–**meel** ya] *n* evergreen ornamental shrub with white, pink, or red flowers.

cameo *n, pl* **cameos 1** brooch or ring with a profile head carved in relief. **2** small part in a film or play performed by a well-known actor or actress.

camera *n* apparatus used for taking photographs or pictures for television or cinema. **in camera** in private session.

camisole *n* woman's bodice–like garment.

camouflage ⊕ [kam–moo–flahzh] *n* **1** use of natural surroundings or artificial aids to conceal or disguise something. ◆ *v* **2** conceal by camouflage.

camp¹ ⊕ *n* **1** (place for) temporary lodgings consisting of tents, huts, or cabins. **2** group supporting a particular doctrine. ◆ *v* **3** stay in a camp. **camper** *n*

camp² ⊕ *adj Informal* **1** effeminate or homosexual. **2** consciously artificial or affected.

campaign ⊕ *n* **1** series of coordinated activities designed to achieve a goal. ◆ *v* **2** take part in a campaign.

camphor *n* aromatic crystalline substance used medicinally and in mothballs.

campus *n, pl* **–puses** grounds of a university or college.

can¹ *v, past* **could 1** be able to. **2** be allowed to.

can² *n* **1** metal container for food or liquids. ◆ *v* **canning, canned 2** put (something) into a can. **canned** *adj* **1** preserved in a can. **2** (of music) prerecorded. **cannery** *n,*

grounds, justification, occasion, reason

callous *adj* = **heartless**, cold, hard–bitten, hardened, hardhearted, insensitive, uncaring, unfeeling

callow *adj* = **inexperienced**, green, guileless, immature, naive, raw, unsophisticated

calm *adj* **1** = **cool**, collected, composed, dispassionate, relaxed, sedate, self-possessed, unemotional ≠ **worried 2**, **3** = **still**, balmy, mild, quiet, serene, smooth, tranquil, windless ≠ **wild** ◆ *n* **4** = **peacefulness**, hush, peace, quiet, repose, serenity, stillness ≠ **disturbance** ◆ *v* **5** (often foll. by *down*) = **quieten**, hush,

mollify, outspan (*S Afr*), placate, relax, soothe ≠ **stir**

camouflage *n* **1** = **disguise**, blind, cloak, concealment, cover, mask, masquerade, screen, subterfuge ≠ **display** ◆ *v* **2** = **disguise**, cloak, conceal, cover, hide, mask, obfuscate, obscure, screen, veil

camp¹ *n* **1** = **camp site**, bivouac, camping ground, encampment, tents

camp² *adj Inf* **1** = **effeminate 2** = **affected**, artificial, mannered, ostentatious, posturing

campaign *n* **1** = **operation**, crusade, drive, movement, push **2** = **attack**, expedition, offensive *pl* factory where food is canned.

canal ❶ *n* **1** artificial waterway. **2** passage in the body.

canary *n, pl* **–ries** small yellow songbird often kept as a pet.

canasta *n* card game like rummy, played with two packs.

cancan *n* lively high–kicking dance performed by a female group.

cancel ❶ *v* **–celling, –celled 1** stop (something that has been arranged) from taking place. **2** mark (a cheque or stamp) with an official stamp to prevent further use. **cancellation** *n* **cancel out** *v* counterbalance, neutralize.

cancer ❶ *n* **1** serious disease resulting from a malignant growth or tumour. **2** malignant growth or tumour. **3** evil, spreading influence. **cancerous** *adj*

candid ❶ *adj* honest and straightforward.

candidate ❶ *n* **1** person seeking a job or position. **2** person taking an examination. **candidacy, candidature** *n*

candle *n* stick of wax enclosing a wick, which is burned to produce light. **candlestick** *n* holder for a candle.

candy *n, pl* **–dies** *US* a sweet or sweets. **candied** *adj* coated with sugar. **candyfloss** *n* light fluffy mass of spun sugar on a stick. **candy–striped** *adj* having coloured stripes on a white background.

cane *n* **1** stem of the bamboo or similar plant. **2** flexible rod used to beat someone. **3** slender walking stick. ◆ *v* **4** beat with a cane.

canine *adj* **1** of or like a dog. ◆ *n* **2** sharp pointed tooth between the incisors and the molars.

canister *n* metal container.

canker ❶ *n* **1** ulceration, ulcerous disease. **2** something evil that spreads and corrupts.

cannabis *n* **1** Asian plant with tough fibres. **2** drug obtained from the dried leaves and flowers of this plant, which can be smoked or chewed.

cannelloni *pl n* tubular pieces of pasta filled with meat etc.

cannibal *n* **1** person who eats human flesh. **2** animal that eats others of its own kind. **cannibalism** *n* **cannibalize** *v* use parts from (one machine) to repair another.

cannon ❶ *n* **1** large gun on wheels. **2** billiard stroke in which the cue ball hits two balls successively. **cannonade** *n* continuous heavy gunfire. **cannonball** *n* heavy metal ball fired from a cannon.

cannot can not.

canny ❶ *adj* **–nier, –niest** shrewd, cautious. **cannily** *adv*

canoe *n* light narrow open boat propelled by a paddle or paddles. **canoeing** *n* sport of rowing in a canoe. **canoeist** *n*

canon ❶ *n* **1** Church decree regulating morals or religious practices. **2** general rule or standard. **3** list of the works of an author that are accepted as authentic. **4** piece of music in which the same melody is taken up in different parts. **canonical** *adj* **canonize** *v* declare (a person) officially to be a saint. **canonization** *n*

canopy ❶ *n, pl* **–pies 1** covering above a

————————— THESAURUS —————————

canal *n* **1 = waterway**, channel, conduit, duct, passage, watercourse

cancel *v* **1 = call off**, abolish, abort, annul, delete, do away with, eliminate, erase, expunge, obliterate, repeal, revoke

cancer *n* **1 = sickness**, pestilence **2 = growth**, malignancy, tumour **3 = corruption**

candid *adj* **= honest**, blunt, forthright, frank, open, outspoken, plain, straightforward, truthful ≠ **diplomatic**

candidate *n* **1 = contender**, applicant, claimant, competitor, contestant, entrant, nominee, runner

canker *n* **1 = disease**, cancer, infection, rot, sore, ulcer **2 = corruption**, blight, rot, scourge

cannon *n* **1 = gun**, big gun, field gun, mortar

canny *adj* **= shrewd**, astute, careful, cautious, clever, judicious, prudent, wise

canon *n* **2 = rule**, criterion, dictate,

bed, door, etc. **2** any large or wide covering.

cant ❶ n **1** insincere talk. **2** specialized vocabulary of a particular group. ◆ v **3** use cant.

cantankerous ❶ adj quarrelsome, bad–tempered.

cantata n musical work consisting of arias, duets, and choruses.

canteen n **1** restaurant attached to a workplace or school. **2** box containing a set of cutlery.

canter ❶ n **1** horse's gait between a trot and a gallop. ◆ v **2** move at a canter.

cantilever n beam or girder fixed at one end only.

canvas n **1** heavy coarse cloth used for sails and tents, and for oil painting. **2** an oil painting on canvas.

canvass ❶ v **1** try to get votes or support (from). **2** find out the opinions of (people) by conducting a survey. ◆ n **3** canvassing.

canyon n deep narrow valley.

cap ❶ n **1** soft close–fitting covering for the head. **2** small lid. **3** small explosive device used in a toy gun. ◆ v **capping, capped 4** cover or top with something. **5** select (a player) for a national team. **6** impose an upper limit on (a tax). **7** outdo, excel.

capable ❶ adj **1** (foll. by of) having the ability (for). **2** competent and efficient. **capably** adv **capability** n, pl **–ties**

capacity ❶ n, pl **–ties 1** ability to contain, absorb, or hold. **2** maximum amount that can be contained or produced. **3** physical or mental ability. **4** position, function. **capacious** adj roomy. **capacitor** n device for storing electrical charge.

cape[1] n short cloak.

cape[2] **❶** n large piece of land that juts out into the sea.

caper ❶ n **1** high–spirited prank. ◆ v **2** skip about.

capillary n, pl **–laries** very fine blood vessel.

capital ❶ n **1** chief city of a country. **2** accumulated wealth. **3** wealth used to produce more wealth. **4** large letter, as used at the beginning of a name or sentence. ◆ adj **5** involving or punishable by death. **6** Old–fashioned excellent. **capitalize** v **1** write or print (words) in capitals. **2** convert into or provide with capital. **capitalize on** v take advantage of (a situation). **capital gain** profit from the sale of an asset. **capitalism** n economic

formula, precept, principle, regulation, standard, statute, yardstick **3 = list**, catalogue, roll

canopy n **1 = awning**, covering, shade, sunshade

cant n **1 = hypocrisy**, humbug, insincerity, lip service, pretence, pretentiousness, sanctimoniousness **2 = jargon**, argot, lingo, patter, slang, vernacular

cantankerous adj **= bad–tempered**, choleric, contrary, disagreeable, grumpy, irascible, irritable, testy, waspish

canter n **1 = jog**, amble, dogtrot, lope ◆ v **2 = jog**, amble, lope

canvass v **1 = campaign**, electioneer, solicit, solicit votes **2 = poll**, examine, inspect, investigate, scrutinize, study ◆ n **3 = poll**, examination, investigation, scrutiny, survey, tally

cap v **7 = beat**, better, crown, eclipse, exceed, outdo, outstrip, surpass, top, transcend

capable adj **1 = able**, accomplished, gifted, qualified, talented ≠ **incapable**
2 = competent, efficient, proficient ≠ **incompetent**

capacity n **1 = size**, amplitude, compass, dimensions, extent, magnitude, range, room, scope, space, volume **3 = ability**, aptitude, aptness, capability, competence, facility, genius, gift **4 = function**, office, position, post, province, role, sphere

cape[2] n **= headland**, head, peninsula, point, promontory

caper n **1 = escapade**, antic, high jinks, jape, lark (inf), mischief, practical joke, prank, stunt ◆ v **2 = dance**, bound, cavort, frolic, gambol, jump, skip, spring, trip system based on the private ownership of industry.

capitulate ⓘ v surrender on agreed terms.

capon n castrated cock fowl fattened for eating.

cappuccino [kap–poo–**cheen**–oh] n, pl –**nos** coffee with steamed milk, sprinkled with powdered chocolate.

caprice ⓘ [kap–**reess**] n sudden change of attitude. **capricious** adj tending to have sudden changes of attitude.

capsize v overturn accidentally.

capstan n rotating cylinder round which a ship's rope is wound.

capsule ⓘ n 1 soluble gelatine case containing a dose of medicine. 2 plant's seed case. 3 detachable crew compartment of a spacecraft.

captain ⓘ n 1 commander of a ship or civil aircraft. 2 middle–ranking naval officer. 3 junior officer in the army. 4 leader of a team or group. ◆ v 5 be captain of. **captaincy** n

caption n 1 title or explanation accompanying an illustration. ◆ v 2 provide with a caption.

captive ⓘ n 1 person kept in confinement. ◆ adj 2 kept in confinement. 3 (of an audience) unable to leave. **captivity** n

capture ⓘ v 1 take by force. 2 succeed in representing (something elusive) artistically. ◆ n 3 capturing.

car ⓘ n 1 motor vehicle designed to carry a small number of people. 2 passenger compartment of a cable car, lift, etc. 3 US railway carriage. **car park** area or building reserved for parking cars.

carafe [kar–**raff**] n glass bottle for serving water or wine.

caramel n 1 chewy sweet made from sugar and milk. 2 burnt sugar, used for colouring and flavouring food. **caramelize** v turn into caramel.

carat n 1 unit of weight of precious stones. 2 measure of the purity of gold in an alloy.

caravan n 1 large enclosed vehicle for living in, designed to be towed by a car or horse. 2 group travelling together in Eastern countries.

caraway n plant whose seeds are used as a spice.

carbohydrate n any of a large group of energy–producing compounds in food, such as sugars and starches.

carbon n nonmetallic element occurring as charcoal, graphite, and diamond, found in all organic matter. **carbonate** n salt or ester of carbonic acid. **carbonated** adj (of a drink) containing carbon dioxide. **carbonize** v 1 turn into carbon as a result of heating. 2 coat with carbon. **carbon copy 1** copy made with carbon paper.

——————— THESAURUS ———————

capital n 2 = **money**, assets, cash, finances, funds, investment(s), lolly (Aust & NZ sl), means, principal, resources, wealth, wherewithal ◆ adj 6 Old–fashioned = **first–rate**, excellent, fine, splendid, sterling, superb

capitulate v = **give in**, cave in (inf), come to terms, give up, relent, submit, succumb, surrender, yield

caprice n = **whim**, fad, fancy, fickleness, impulse, inconstancy, notion, whimsy

capsize v = **overturn**, invert, keel over, tip over, turn over, turn turtle, upset

capsule n 1 = **pill**, lozenge, tablet 2 = **pod**, case, receptacle, seed case, sheath, shell, vessel

captain n = **leader**, boss, chief, commander, head, master, skipper

captive n 1 = **prisoner**, convict, detainee, hostage, internee, prisoner of war, slave ◆ adj 2 = **confined**, caged, enslaved, ensnared, imprisoned, incarcerated, locked up, penned, restricted, subjugated

capture v 1 = **catch**, apprehend, arrest, bag, collar (inf), secure, seize, take, take prisoner ≠ free ◆ n 3 = **catching**, apprehension, arrest, imprisonment, seizure, taking, taking captive, trapping

car n 1 = **vehicle**, auto (US), automobile, jalopy (inf), machine, motor, motorcar, wheels (inf) 3 US = **(railway) carriage**, buffet car, cable car, coach, dining car,

2 very similar person or thing. **carbon dioxide** colourless gas exhaled by people and animals. **carbon paper** paper coated on one side with a dark waxy pigment, used to make a copy of something as it is typed or written.

carbuncle *n* inflamed boil.

carburettor *n* device which mixes petrol and air in an internal–combustion engine.

carcass 🟦 **carcase** *n* dead body of an animal.

card *n* **1** piece of thick stiff paper or cardboard used for identification, reference, or sending greetings or messages. **2** one of a set of cards with a printed pattern, used for playing games. **3** small rectangle of stiff plastic with identifying numbers for use as a credit card, cheque card, or charge card. **4** *Old–fashioned* witty or eccentric person. ◆ *pl* **5** any card game, or card games in general. **cardboard** *n* thin stiff board made from paper pulp. **cardsharp** *n* professional card player who cheats.

cardiac *adj* of the heart. **cardiograph** *n* electrocardiograph. **cardiology** *n* study of the heart and its diseases. **cardiologist** *n* **cardiovascular** *adj* of the heart and the blood vessels.

cardigan *n* knitted jacket.

cardinal 🟦 *n* **1** any of the high–ranking clergymen of the RC Church who elect the Pope and act as his counsellors. ◆ *adj* **2** fundamentally important. **cardinal number** number denoting quantity but not order in a group, for example four as distinct from fourth. **cardinal points** the four main points of the compass.

care 🟦 *v* **1** be concerned. **2** like (to do something). **3** (foll. by *for*) like, be fond of. **4** (foll. by *for*) look after. ◆ *n* **5** careful attention, caution. **6** protection, charge. **7** trouble, worry. **carefree** *adj* **careful** *adj* **carefully** *adv* **carefulness** *n* **careless** *adj* **carelessly** *adv* **carelessness** *n*

career 🟦 *n* **1** series of jobs in a profession or occupation that a person has through their life. **2** part of a person's life spent in a particular occupation. ◆ *v* **3** rush in an uncontrolled way.

> ✓ **WORD TIP**
> Do not confuse *career* 'rush' with *careen* 'tilt'.

caress 🟦 *n* **1** gentle affectionate touch or embrace. ◆ *v* **2** touch gently and affectionately.

caret [kar–rett] *n* symbol (⋀) indicating a place in written or printed matter where something is to be inserted.

cargo 🟦 *n, pl* –**goes** goods carried by a ship, aircraft, etc.

caribou *n, pl* –**bou** or –**bous** large N

━━━━━━━━━━━━ THESAURUS ━━━━━━━━━━━━

sleeping car, van

carcass *n* = **body**, cadaver (*Med*), corpse, dead body, framework, hulk, remains, shell, skeleton

cardinal *adj* **2** = **principal**, capital, central, chief, essential, first, fundamental, key, leading, main, paramount, primary

care *v* **1** = **be concerned**, be bothered, be interested, mind **4** (foll. by *for*) = **look after**, attend, foster, mind, minister to, nurse, protect, provide for, tend, watch over ◆ *n* **5** = **caution**, attention, carefulness, consideration, forethought, heed, management, pains, prudence, vigilance, watchfulness ≠ **abandon**

6 = **protection**, charge, control, custody, guardianship, keeping, management, supervision **7** = **worry**, anxiety, concern, disquiet, perplexity, pressure, responsibility, stress, trouble ≠ **pleasure**

career *n* **1** = **occupation**, calling, employment, life's work, livelihood, pursuit, vocation ◆ *v* **3** = **rush**, barrel (along) (*inf, chiefly US & Canad*), bolt, dash, hurtle, race, speed, tear

caress *n* **1** = **stroke**, cuddle, embrace, fondling, hug, kiss, pat ◆ *v* **2** = **stroke**, cuddle, embrace, fondle, hug, kiss, neck (*inf*), nuzzle, pet

cargo *n* = **load**, baggage, consignment,

American reindeer.

caricature ⊕ *n* 1 drawing or description of a person that exaggerates features for comic effect. ◆ *v* 2 make a caricature of.

cark *v Aust & NZ slang* die.

carnage ⊕ *n* extensive slaughter of people.

carnal ⊕ *adj* of a sexual or sensual nature. **carnal knowledge** sexual intercourse.

carnation *n* cultivated plant with fragrant white, pink, or red flowers.

carnival ⊕ *n* festive period with processions, music, and dancing in the street.

carol ⊕ *n* joyful Christmas hymn.

carouse *v* have a merry drinking party. **carousal** *n* merry drinking party.

carousel [kar–roo–**sell**] *n* 1 revolving conveyor belt for luggage or photographic slides. 2 *US* merry–go–round.

carp[1] *n* large freshwater fish.

carp[2] *v* complain, find fault.

carpenter ⊕ *n* person who makes or repairs wooden structures. **carpentry** *n*

carpet *n* heavy fabric for covering floors. ◆ *v* **carpeting, carpeted** 2 cover with a carpet. **on the carpet** *Informal* being reprimanded.

carriage ⊕ *n* 1 one of the sections of a train for passengers. 2 way a person holds his or her head and body. 3 four–wheeled horse–drawn vehicle. 4 moving part of *a* machine that supports and shifts another

part. 5 charge made for conveying goods. **carriageway** *n* part of a road along which traffic passes in one direction.

carrion *n* dead and rotting flesh.

carrot *n* 1 long tapering orange root vegetable. 2 something offered as an incentive.

carry ⊕ *v* **–rying, –ried** 1 take from one place to another. 2 have with one habitually, in one's pocket etc. 3 transmit (a disease). 4 have as a factor or result. 5 hold (one's head or body) in a specified manner. 6 secure the adoption of (a bill or motion). 7 (of sound) travel a certain distance. **carry on** *v* 1 continue. 2 *Informal* cause a fuss. **carry out** *v* follow, accomplish.

cart *n* 1 open two–wheeled horse–drawn vehicle for carrying goods or passengers. ◆ *v* 2 carry, usu. with some effort. **carthorse** *n* large heavily built horse. **cartwheel** *n* sideways somersault supported by the hands with legs outstretched.

carte blanche *n French* complete authority.

cartel *n* association of competing firms formed to fix prices.

cartilage *n* strong flexible tissue forming part of the skeleton. **cartilaginous** *adj*

cartography *n* map making. **cartographic** *adj*

carton ⊕ *n* container made of cardboard

contents, freight, goods, merchandise, shipment

caricature *n* 1 = **parody**, burlesque, cartoon, distortion, farce, lampoon, satire, send–up (*Brit inf*), takeoff (*inf*), travesty ◆ *v* 2 = **parody**, burlesque, distort, lampoon, mimic, mock, ridicule, satirize, send up (*Brit inf*), take off (*inf*)

carnage *n* = **slaughter**, blood bath, bloodshed, butchery, havoc, holocaust, massacre, mass murder, murder, shambles

carnal *adj* = **sexual**, erotic, fleshly, lascivious, lewd, libidinous, lustful, sensual

carnival *n* = **festival**, celebration, fair, fete,

fiesta, gala, holiday, jamboree, jubilee, merrymaking, revelry

carol *n* = **song**, chorus, ditty, hymn, lay

carp[2] *v* = **find fault**, cavil, complain, criticize, pick holes, quibble, reproach

carpenter *n* = **joiner**, cabinet–maker, woodworker

carriage *n* 1 = **vehicle**, cab, coach, conveyance 2 = **bearing**, air, behaviour, comportment, conduct, demeanour, deportment, gait, manner, posture

carry *v* 1 = **transport**, bear, bring, conduct, convey, fetch, haul, lug, move, relay, take, transfer 6 = **win**, accomplish, capture, or waxed paper.

cartoon ⊕ n 1 humorous or satirical drawing. 2 sequence of these telling a story. 3 film made by photographing a series of drawings which give the illusion of movement when projected. **cartoonist** n

cartridge ⊕ n 1 casing containing an explosive charge and bullet for a gun. 2 part of the pick–up of a record player that converts the movements of the stylus into electrical signals. 3 sealed container of film, tape, etc. **cartridge paper** strong thick drawing paper.

carve ⊕ v 1 cut to form an object. 2 form (an object or design) by cutting. 3 slice (cooked meat). **carving** n

cascade ⊕ n 1 waterfall. 2 something flowing or falling like a waterfall. ◆ v 3 flow or fall in a cascade.

case¹ ⊕ n 1 instance, example. 2 matter for discussion. 3 condition, state of affairs. 4 set of arguments supporting an action or cause. 5 person or problem dealt with by a doctor, social worker, or solicitor. 6 action, lawsuit. 7 Grammar form of a noun, pronoun, or adjective showing its relation to other words in the sentence. **in case** so as to allow for the possibility that.

case² ⊕ n 1 container, protective covering. ◆ v 2 Slang inspect (a building) with the intention of burgling it. **case–hardened** adj having been made callous by experience.

cash ⊕ n 1 banknotes and coins. ◆ v 2 obtain cash for. **cash in on** v Informal gain profit or advantage from. **cash register** till that displays and adds the prices of the goods sold.

cashier¹ ⊕ n person responsible for handling cash in a bank, shop, etc.

cashier² ⊕ v dismiss with dishonour from the armed forces.

cashmere n fine soft wool obtained from goats.

casino n, pl **–nos** public building or room where gambling games are played.

cask n barrel used to hold alcoholic drink.

casket ⊕ n 1 small box for valuables. 2 US coffin.

casserole n 1 covered dish in which food is cooked slowly, usu. in an oven. 2 dish cooked in this way. ◆ v 3 cook in a casserole.

cassette n plastic case containing a reel of film or magnetic tape.

cassock n long tunic, usu. black, worn by priests.

THESAURUS

effect, gain, secure

carton n = **box**, case, container, pack, package, packet

cartoon n 1 = **drawing**, caricature, lampoon, parody, satire, sketch 2 = **comic strip** 3 = **animation**, animated cartoon, animated film

cartridge n 1 = **shell**, charge, round 3 = **container**, capsule, case, cassette, cylinder, magazine

carve v 1, 2 = **cut**, chip, chisel, engrave, etch, hew, mould, sculpt, whittle 3 = **slice**

cascade n 1 = **waterfall**, avalanche, cataract, deluge, downpour, falls, flood, fountain, outpouring, shower, torrent ◆ v 3 = **flow**, descend, fall, flood, gush, overflow, pitch, plunge, pour, spill, surge, teem, tumble

case¹ n 1 = **instance**, example, illustration, occasion, occurrence, specimen 3 = **situation**, circumstance(s), condition, context, contingency, event, position, state 6 = **lawsuit**, action, dispute, proceedings, suit, trial

case² n 1 = **container**, box, canister, capsule, carton, casing, chest, covering, crate, envelope, holder, jacket, receptacle, sheath, shell, wrapper

cash n 1 = **money**, brass (N Eng dial), coinage, currency, dough (sl), funds, lolly (Aust & NZ sl), notes, ready money, silver

cashier¹ n = **teller**, bank clerk, banker, bursar, clerk, purser, treasurer

cashier² v = **dismiss**, discard, discharge, drum out, expel, give the boot to (sl)

casket n 1 = **box**, case, chest, coffer, jewel

cast ❶ *n* **1** actors in a play or film collectively. **2** object shaped by a mould while molten. **3** mould used to shape such an object. **4** rigid plaster–of–Paris casing for immobilizing broken bones while they heal. **5** sort, kind. **6** slight squint in the eye. ◆ *v* **casting, cast 7** select (an actor) to play a part in a play or film. **8** give (a vote). **9** let fall, shed. **10** shape (molten material) in a mould. **11** throw with force. **12** direct (a glance). **castaway** *n* shipwrecked person. **casting vote** *n* deciding vote used by the chairman of a meeting when the votes on each side are equal. **cast–iron** *adj* **1** made of a hard but brittle type of iron. **2** definite, unchallengeable. **cast–off** *adj, n* discarded (person or thing).

castanets *pl n* musical instrument, used by Spanish dancers, consisting of curved pieces of hollow wood clicked together in the hand.

caste ❶ *n* **1** any of the hereditary classes into which Hindu society is divided. **2** social rank.

caster sugar *n* finely ground white sugar.

castigate ❶ *v* reprimand severely.

castle ❶ *n* **1** large fortified building, often built as a ruler's residence. **2** rook in chess.

castor *n* small swivelling wheel fixed to the bottom of a piece of furniture for easy moving.

castor oil *n* oil obtained from an Indian plant, used as a lubricant and purgative.

castrate ❶ *v* **1** remove the testicles of. **2** deprive of vigour or masculinity. **castration** *n*

casual ❶ *adj* **1** careless, nonchalant. **2** (of work or workers) occasional. **3** for informal wear. **4** happening by chance. **casually** *adv* **casualty** *n* person killed or injured in an accident or war.

cat ❶ *n* **1** small domesticated furry mammal. **2** related wild mammal, such as the lion or tiger. **catty** *adj Informal* spiteful. **catkin** *n* drooping flower spike of certain trees. **catcall** *n* derisive whistle or cry. **catgut** *n* strong cord used to string musical instruments and sports rackets. **catnap** *n, v* doze. **Catseyes** *pl n* ® glass reflectors set in the road to indicate traffic lanes. **cat's paw** person used by another to do unpleasant things for him or her. **catwalk** *n* narrow pathway or platform.

cataclysm [kat–a–kliz–zum] *n* **1** violent upheaval. **2** disaster, such as an earthquake. **cataclysmic** *adj*

catalogue ❶ *n* **1** book containing details of items for sale. **2** systematic list of items. ◆ *v* **3** make a systematic list of.

catalyst *n* substance that speeds up a chemical reaction without itself changing. **catalyse** *v* speed up (a chemical reaction) by a catalyst. **catalytic** *adj*

———————— THESAURUS ————————

box

cast *n* **1** = **actors**, characters, company, dramatis personae, players, troupe **5** = **type**, complexion, manner, stamp, style ◆ *v* **7, 8** = **choose**, allot, appoint, assign, name, pick, select **9** = **give out**, deposit, diffuse, distribute, emit, radiate, scatter, shed, spread **10** = **form**, found, model, mould, set, shape **11** = **throw**, fling, hurl, launch, pitch, sling, thrust, toss

caste *n* **2** = **class**, estate, grade, order, rank, social order, status, stratum

castigate *v* = **reprimand**, berate, censure, chastise, criticize, lambast(e), rebuke, rouse on (*Aust*), scold

castle *n* **1** = **fortress**, chateau, citadel, keep, palace, stronghold, tower

castrate *v* **1** = **neuter**, emasculate, geld

casual *adj* **1** = **careless**, blasé, cursory, lackadaisical, nonchalant, offhand, relaxed, unconcerned ≠ **concerned 2** = **occasional**, irregular **3** = **informal**, non–dressy, sporty ≠ **formal 4** = **chance**, accidental, incidental, random, unexpected ≠ **planned**

cat *n* **1** = **feline**, kitty (*inf*), moggy (*sl*), puss (*inf*), pussy (*inf*), tabby

catalogue *n* **1** = **directory**, gazetteer **2** = **list**, index, inventory, record, register, roll ◆ *v* **3** = **list**, alphabetize, classify, file,

catamaran *n* boat with twin parallel hulls.

catapult ⊕ *n* **1** Y–shaped device with a loop of elastic, used by children for firing stones. ◆ *v* **2** shoot forwards or upwards violently.

cataract *n* **1** eye disease in which the lens becomes opaque. **2** opaque area of an eye. **3** large waterfall.

catarrh [kat–**tar**] *n* excessive mucus in the nose and throat, during or following a cold. **catarrhal** *adj*

catastrophe ⊕ [kat–**ass**–trof–fee] *n* great and sudden disaster. **catastrophic** *adj*

catch ⊕ *v* **catching, caught 1** seize, capture. **2** surprise in an act, e.g. *two boys were caught stealing.* **3** hit unexpectedly. **4** be in time for (a bus, train, etc.). **5** see or hear. **6** be infected with (an illness). **7** entangle. **8** understand, make out. **9** start burning. ◆ *n* **10** device for fastening a door, window, etc. **11** total number of fish caught. **12** concealed or unforeseen drawback. **13** *Informal* person considered worth having as a husband or wife. **catch it** *Informal* be punished. **catching** *adj* infectious. **catchy** *adj* (of a tune) pleasant and easily remembered. **catchment area** area served by a particular school or hospital. **catch on** *v Informal* **1** become popular. **2** understand. **catch out** *v Informal* trap (someone) in an error or lie. **catch phrase** well–known phrase associated with a particular entertainer. **catch 22** inescapable dilemma. **catchword** *n* well–known and frequently used phrase.

catechism [**kat**–ti–kiz–zum] *n* instruction on the doctrine of a Christian Church in a series of questions and answers. **catechize** *v* **1** instruct by using a catechism. **2** question (someone) thoroughly.

category ⊕ *n, pl* **–ries** class, group. **categorical** *adj* absolutely clear and certain. **categorically** *adv* **categorize** *v* put in a category. **categorization** *n*

cater ⊕ *v* provide what is needed or wanted, esp. food or services. **caterer** *n*

caterpillar *n* **1** wormlike larva of a moth or butterfly. **2** ® endless track, driven by cogged wheels, used to propel a heavy vehicle.

catharsis [kath–**thar**–siss] *n, pl* **–ses** relief of strong suppressed emotions. **cathartic** *adj*

cathedral *n* principal church of a diocese.

Catherine wheel *n* rotating firework.

catholic *adj* **1** (of tastes or interests) covering a wide range. ◆ *n, adj* **2** (C–) (member) of the Roman Catholic Church. **Catholicism** *n*

> ✓ **WORD TIP**
>
> Note that the meaning of *catholic* can change depending on whether it begins with a capital letter or not.

cattle ⊕ *pl n* domesticated cows and bulls.

cauldron *n* large pot used for boiling.

index, inventory, register, tabulate

catapult *n* **1** = **sling**, slingshot (*US*) ◆ *v* **2** = **shoot**, heave, hurl, pitch, plunge, propel

catastrophe *n* = **disaster**, adversity, calamity, cataclysm, fiasco, misfortune, tragedy, trouble

catch *v* **1** = **seize**, apprehend, arrest, capture, clutch, ensnare, entrap, get, grab, grasp, grip, lay hold of, snare, snatch, take, trap ≠ **release 2** = **discover**, catch in the act, detect, expose, find out, surprise, take unawares, unmask

6 = **contract**, develop, get, go down with, incur, succumb to, suffer from ≠ **avoid**
8 = **make out**, comprehend, discern, get, grasp, hear, perceive, recognize, sense, take in ◆ *n* **10** = **fastener**, bolt, clasp, clip, latch **12** *Inf* = **drawback**, disadvantage, fly in the ointment, hitch, snag, stumbling block, trap, trick ≠ **benefit**

category *n* = **class**, classification, department, division, grade, grouping, heading, section, sort, type

cater *v* = **provide**, furnish, outfit, purvey, supply

cauliflower *n* vegetable with a large head of white flower buds surrounded by green leaves.

cause ⊕ *n* 1 something that produces a particular effect. 2 (foll. by *for*) reason, motive. 3 aim or principle supported by a person or group. ◆ *v* 4 be the cause of.

causeway *n* raised path or road across water or marshland.

caustic ⊕ *adj* 1 capable of burning by chemical action. 2 bitter and sarcastic.

cauterize *v* burn (a wound) with heat or a caustic agent to prevent infection.

caution ⊕ *n* 1 care, esp. in the face of danger. 2 warning. ◆ *v* 3 warn, advise. **cautionary** *adj* warning. **cautious** *adj* showing caution.

cavalcade ⊕ *n* procession of people on horseback or in cars.

cavalier ⊕ *adj* showing haughty disregard.

cavalry ⊕ *n, pl* **–ries** part of the army orig. on horseback, but now often using fast armoured vehicles.

cave ⊕ *n* hollow in the side of a hill or cliff. **caving** *n* sport of exploring caves. **cave in** *v* 1 collapse inwards. 2 *Informal* yield under pressure. **caveman** *n* prehistoric cave dweller.

caviar, caviare *n* salted sturgeon roe, regarded as a delicacy.

cavil *v* **–illing, –illed** 1 make petty objections. ◆ *n* 2 petty objection.

cavort *v* skip about.

CBE Commander of the Order of the British Empire.

cc cubic centimetre.

CD compact disc.

cease ⊕ *v* bring or come to an end. **ceaseless** *adj* **ceasefire** *n* temporary truce.

cedar *n* 1 evergreen coniferous tree. 2 its wood.

cede ⊕ *v* surrender (territory or legal rights).

cedilla *n* character (ˌ) placed under a c in some languages, to show that it is pronounced s, not k.

ceilidh [**kay**–lee] *n* informal social gathering for singing and dancing, esp. in Scotland.

ceiling *n* 1 inner upper surface of a room. 2 upper limit set on something.

celebrate ⊕ *v* 1 hold festivities to mark (a happy event, anniversary, etc.). 2 perform (a religious ceremony). **celebrated** *adj* well known. **celebration** *n* **celebrant** *n* person who performs a religious ceremony.

cattle *pl n* = **cows**, beasts, bovines, livestock, stock

cause *n* 1 = **origin**, agent, beginning, creator, genesis, mainspring, maker, producer, root, source, spring 2 (foll. by *for*) = **reason**, basis, grounds, incentive, inducement, justification, motivation, motive, purpose 3 = **aim**, belief, conviction, enterprise, ideal, movement, principle ◆ *v* 4 = **produce**, bring about, create, generate, give rise to, incite, induce, lead to, result in ≠ **stop**

caustic *adj* 1 = **burning**, acrid, astringent, biting, corroding, corrosive, mordant, vitriolic 2 = **sarcastic**, acrimonious, cutting, pungent, scathing, stinging, trenchant, virulent, vitriolic ≠ **loving**

caution *n* 1 = **care**, alertness, carefulness, circumspection, deliberation, discretion, forethought, heed, prudence, vigilance, watchfulness ≠ **daring** 2 = **warning**, admonition, advice, counsel, injunction ◆ *v* 3 = **warn**, admonish, advise, tip off, urge

cavalcade *n* = **parade**, array, march–past, procession, spectacle, train

cavalier *adj* = **haughty**, arrogant, disdainful, lofty, lordly, offhand, scornful, supercilious

cavalry *n* = **horsemen**, horse, mounted troops

cave *n* = **hollow**, cavern, cavity, den, grotto

cease *v* = **stop**, break off, conclude, discontinue, end, finish, halt, leave off, refrain, terminate ≠ **start**

cede *v* = **surrender**, concede, hand over, make over, relinquish, renounce, resign, transfer, yield

celebrity *n, pl* **–rities** 1 famous person. 2 state of being famous.

celery *n* vegetable with long green crisp edible stalks.

celestial ❶ *adj* 1 heavenly, divine. 2 of the sky.

cell ❶ *n* 1 smallest unit of an organism that is able to function independently. 2 small room for a prisoner, monk, or nun. 3 small compartment of a honeycomb etc. 4 small group operating as the core of a larger organization. **cellular** *adj* 1 of or consisting of cells.

cellar *n* 1 underground room for storage. 2 stock of wine.

cello [**chell**–oh] *n, pl* **–los** large low–pitched instrument of the violin family. **cellist** *n*

Cellophane *n* ® thin transparent cellulose sheeting used as wrapping.

cellulose *n* main constituent of plant cell walls, used in making paper, plastics, etc.

Celsius *adj* of the temperature scale in which water freezes at 0° and boils at 100°.

cement ❶ *n* 1 fine grey powder mixed with water and sand to make mortar or concrete. 2 something that unites, binds, or joins. 3 material used to fill teeth. ♦ *v* 4 join, bind, or cover with cement. 5 make (a relationship) stronger.

cemetery ❶ *n, pl* **–teries** place where dead people are buried.

cenotaph *n* monument honouring soldiers who died in a war.

censor ❶ *n* 1 person authorized to examine films, books, etc., to ban or cut anything considered obscene or objectionable. ♦ *v* 2 ban or cut parts of (a film, book, etc.). **censorship** *n* **censorious** *adj* harshly critical.

censure ❶ *n* 1 severe disapproval. ♦ *v* 2 criticize severely.

census *n, pl* **–suses** official count of a population.

cent *n* hundredth part of a monetary unit such as the dollar or euro.

centaur *n* mythical creature with the head, arms, and torso of a man, and the lower body and legs of a horse.

centenary [sen–**teen**–a–ree] *n, pl* **–naries** 100th anniversary or its celebration. **centenarian** *n* person at least 100 years old. **centennial** *n US* centenary.

centigrade *adj* same as CELSIUS.

> ✓ **WORD TIP**
> Scientists now use *Celsius* in preference to *centigrade*.

centimetre *n* one hundredth of a metre.

centipede *n* small wormlike creature with many legs.

centre ❶ *n* 1 middle point or part. 2 place for a specified activity. 3 person or thing that is a focus of interest. 4 *Sport* player who plays in the middle of the field. ♦ *v* 5 put in the centre of something. **central** *adj* **centrist** *n* person favouring political

celebrate *v* 1 = **rejoice**, commemorate, drink to, keep, kill the fatted calf, observe, put the flags out, toast 2 = **perform**, bless, honour, solemnize

celestial *adj* 1 = **heavenly**, angelic, astral, divine, ethereal, spiritual, sublime, supernatural

cell *n* 2 = **room**, chamber, compartment, cubicle, dungeon, stall 3 = **compartment**, cavity 4 = **unit**, caucus, core, coterie, group, nucleus

cement 1 *n* = **mortar**, plaster 2 = **glue**, adhesive, gum, paste, sealant ♦ *v* 4 = **stick**

together, attach, bind, bond, combine, glue, join, plaster, seal, unite, weld

cemetery *n* = **graveyard**, burial ground, churchyard, God's acre, necropolis

censor *v* 2 = **cut**, blue–pencil, bowdlerize, expurgate

censure *n* 1 = **disapproval**, blame, condemnation, criticism, obloquy, rebuke, reprimand, reproach, reproof, stick (*sl*) ≠ **approval** ♦ *v* 2 = **criticize**, blame, castigate, condemn, denounce, rap over the knuckles, rebuke, reprimand, reproach, rouse on (*Aust*), scold, slap on moderation. **centre on** v have as a centre or main theme.

centurion n (in ancient Rome) officer commanding 100 men.

century n, pl **–ries** 1 period of 100 years. 2 cricket score of 100 runs.

cereal n 1 grass plant with edible grain, such as oat or wheat. 2 this grain. 3 breakfast food made from this grain, eaten mixed with milk.

cerebral [ser–rib–ral] adj 1 of the brain. 2 intellectual.

ceremony ❶ n, pl **–nies** 1 formal act or ritual. 2 formally polite behaviour. **ceremonial** adj, n **ceremonious** adj excessively polite or formal.

certain ❶ adj 1 positive and confident. 2 definite. 3 some but not much. **certainly** adv **certainty** n 1 state of being sure. 2 (pl **–ties**) something that is inevitable.

certify ❶ v **–fying, –fied** 1 confirm, attest to. 2 guarantee. 3 declare legally insane. **certifiable** adj considered legally insane. **certification** n

cervix n, pl **cervixes, cervices** 1 narrow entrance of the womb. 2 neck. **cervical** adj

cessation n ceasing.

chafe ❶ v 1 make sore or worn by rubbing. 2 be annoyed or impatient.

chaff[1] ❶ n 1 grain husks. 2 something of little worth.

chaff[2] ❶ v tease good–naturedly.

chaffinch n small European songbird.

chagrin [shag–grin] n annoyance and disappointment.

chain ❶ n 1 flexible length of connected metal links. 2 series of connected facts or events. 3 group of shops, hotels, etc. owned by one firm. ◆ v 4 restrict or fasten with or as if with a chain. **chain reaction** series of events, each of which causes the next. **chain–smoke** v smoke (cigarettes) continuously.

chair n 1 seat with a back, for one person. 2 official position of authority. 3 person holding this. 4 professorship. ◆ v 5 preside over (a meeting). **chairlift** series of chairs suspended from a moving cable for carrying people up a slope. **chairman, chairwoman** n person in charge of a company's board of directors or a meeting (also **chairperson**)

✓ **WORD TIP**

Chairman can seem inappropriate when applied to a woman, while *chairwoman* can be offensive. *Chair* and *chairperson* can be applied to either a man or a woman; *chair* is generally preferred to *chairperson*.

---

chalet n 1 kind of Swiss wooden house

the wrist ≠ **applaud**

centre n 1 = **middle**, core, heart, hub, kernel, midpoint, nucleus, pivot ≠ **edge** 3 = **focus** ◆ v 6 = **focus**, cluster, concentrate, converge, revolve

ceremony n 1 = **ritual**, commemoration, function, observance, parade, rite, service, show, solemnities 2 = **formality**, ceremonial, decorum, etiquette, niceties, pomp, propriety, protocol

certain adj 1 = **sure**, assured, confident, convinced, positive, satisfied ≠ **uncertain** 2 = **definite**, conclusive, decided, established, fixed, incontrovertible, inevitable, irrefutable, known, settled, sure, true, undeniable, unequivocal

≠ **unsettled**

certify v 1 = **confirm**, attest, authenticate, declare, testify, validate, verify 2 = **guarantee**, assure

chafe v 1 = **rub**, abrade, rasp, scrape, scratch 2 = **be annoyed**, be impatient, fret, fume, rage, worry

chaff[1] n 1 = **husks** 2 = **rubbish**, dregs, refuse, remains, trash, waste

chaff[2] v = **tease**, mock, rib (inf), ridicule, scoff, taunt

chain n 1 = **link**, bond, coupling, fetter, manacle, shackle 2 = **series**, progression, sequence, set, string, succession, train ◆ v 4 = **bind**, confine, enslave, fetter, handcuff, manacle, restrain, shackle, tether with a steeply sloping roof. **2** similar house, used as a holiday home.

chalice n large goblet.

chalk n **1** soft white rock consisting of calcium carbonate. **2** piece of chalk, often coloured, used for drawing and writing on blackboards. ◆ v **3** draw or mark with chalk. **chalky** adj

challenge ❶ n **1** demanding or stimulating situation. **2** call to take part in a contest or fight. **3** questioning of a statement of fact. **4** demand by a sentry for identification or a password. ◆ v **5** issue a challenge to. **challenger** n

chamber ❶ n **1** hall used for formal meetings. **2** legislative or judicial assembly. **3** Old-fashioned bedroom. **4** compartment, cavity. ◆ pl **5** set of rooms used as offices by a barrister. **chambermaid** n woman employed to clean bedrooms in a hotel. **chamber music** classical music to be performed by a small group of musicians. **chamber pot** bowl for urine, formerly used in bedrooms.

chameleon [kam–meal–yon] n small lizard that changes colour to blend in with its surroundings.

chamois [sham–wah] n, pl –ois **1** small mountain antelope. **2** [sham–ee] soft suede leather. **3** piece of this, used for cleaning or polishing.

champ v chew noisily. **champ at the bit** Informal be impatient to do something.

champagne n sparkling white French wine.

champion ❶ n **1** overall winner of a competition. **2** (foll. by of) someone who defends a person or cause. ◆ v **3** support. ◆ adj **4** Dialect excellent. **championship** n

chance ❶ n **1** likelihood, probability. **2** opportunity to do something. **3** risk, gamble. **4** unpredictable element that causes things to happen one way rather than another. ◆ v **5** risk, hazard. **chancy** adj uncertain, risky.

chancel n part of a church containing the altar and choir.

chancellor n **1** head of government in some European countries. **2** honorary head of a university. **chancellorship** n

chandelier [shan–dill–**eer**] n ornamental light with branches and holders for several candles or bulbs.

change ❶ n **1** becoming different. **2** variety or novelty. **3** different set, esp. of clothes. **4** balance received when the amount paid is more than the cost of a purchase. **5** coins of low value. ◆ v **6** make or become different. **7** give and receive (something) in return. **8** exchange (money) for its equivalent in a smaller denomination or different currency. **9** put on other clothes. **10** leave one vehicle and board another. **changeable** adj changing often. **changeling** n child believed to have been exchanged by fairies for another.

challenge n **1** = **trial**, test **2** = **confrontation**, provocation, ultimatum **3** = **question** ◆ v **5** = **test**, confront, defy, dispute, object to, question, tackle, throw down the gauntlet

chamber n **1** = **hall**, room **2** = **council**, assembly, legislative body, legislature **3** Old-fashioned = **bedroom**, apartment, room **4** = **compartment**, cubicle, enclosure

champion n **1** = **winner**, conqueror, hero, title holder, victor **2** (foll. by of) = **defender**, backer, guardian, patron, protector, upholder ◆ v **3** = **support**,

advocate, back, commend, defend, encourage, espouse, fight for, promote, uphold

chance n **1** = **probability**, likelihood, odds, possibility, prospect ≠ **certainty** **2** = **opportunity**, occasion, opening, time **3** = **risk**, gamble, hazard, jeopardy, speculation, uncertainty **4** = **luck**, accident, coincidence, destiny, fate, fortune, providence ≠ **planned** ◆ v **5** = **risk**, endanger, gamble, hazard, jeopardize, stake, try, venture, wager

change n **1** = **alteration**, difference, innovation, metamorphosis, modification,

channel ⊕ *n* 1 band of broadcasting frequencies. 2 means of access or communication. 3 broad strait connecting two areas of sea. 4 bed or course of a river, stream, or canal. 5 groove. ◆ *v* –nelling, –nelled 6 direct or convey through a channel.

chant ⊕ *v* 1 utter or sing (a slogan or psalm). ◆ *n* 2 rhythmic or repetitious slogan. 3 psalm that has a short simple melody with several words sung on one note.

chaos ⊕ *n* complete disorder or confusion. **chaotic** *adj*

chap ⊕ *n* Informal man or boy.

chapati, chapatti *n* (in Indian cookery) flat thin unleavened bread.

chapel *n* 1 place of worship with its own altar, within a church. 2 similar place of worship in a large house or institution. 3 Nonconformist place of worship.

chaplain *n* clergyman attached to a chapel, military body, or institution. **chaplaincy** *n*, *pl* –cies

chapter ⊕ *n* 1 division of a book. 2 period in a life or history. 3 branch of a society or club.

char *v* **charring, charred** blacken by partial burning.

character ⊕ *n* 1 combination of qualities distinguishing a person, group, or place. 2 reputation, esp. good reputation. 3 person represented in a play, film, or story. 4 unusual or amusing person. 5 letter, numeral, or symbol used in writing or printing. **characteristic** *n* 1 distinguishing feature or quality. ◆ *adj* 2 typical. **characteristically** *adv* **characterize** *v* 1 be a characteristic of. 2 (foll. by *as*) describe. **characterization** *n*

charade ⊕ [shar–**rahd**] *n* 1 absurd pretence. ◆ *pl* 2 game in which one team acts out a word or phrase, which the other team has to guess.

charcoal *n* black substance formed by partially burning wood.

charge ⊕ *v* 1 ask as a price. 2 enter a debit against a person's account for (a purchase). 3 accuse formally. 4 make a rush at or sudden attack upon. 5 fill (a glass). 6 fill (a battery) with electricity. 7 command, assign. ◆ *n* 8 price charged. 9 formal accusation. 10 attack. 11 command, exhortation. 12 custody, guardianship. 13 person or thing entrusted to someone's care. 14 amount of electricity stored in a battery. **in charge of** in control of. **chargeable** *adj* **charger** *n*

——————————| THESAURUS |——————————

mutation, revolution, transformation, transition 2 = **variety**, break (*inf*), departure, diversion, novelty, variation ≠ **stability** ◆ *v* 6 = **alter**, convert, modify, mutate, reform, reorganize, restyle, shift, transform, vary ≠ **keep** 7 = **exchange**, barter, convert, interchange, replace, substitute, swap, trade

channel *n* 2 = **route**, approach, artery, avenue, canal, conduit, course, duct, means, medium, passage, path, way 3 = **strait** 5 = **groove**, furrow, gutter ◆ *v* 6 = **direct**, conduct, convey, guide, transmit

chant *v* 1 = **sing**, carol, chorus, descant, intone, recite, warble ◆ *n* 3 = **song**, carol, chorus, melody, psalm

chaos *n* = **disorder**, anarchy, bedlam,

confusion, disorganization, lawlessness, mayhem, pandemonium, tumult

chap *n Inf* = **fellow**, bloke (*Brit inf*), character, guy (*inf*), individual, man, person

chapter *n* 1 = **section**, clause, division, episode, part, topic 2 = **period**, part, phase, stage

character *n* 1 = **nature**, attributes, calibre, complexion, disposition, personality, quality, temperament, type 2 = **reputation**, honour, integrity, rectitude, strength, uprightness 3 = **role**, part, persona, portrayal 4 = **eccentric**, card (*inf*), oddball (*inf*), original 5 = **symbol**, device, figure, hieroglyph, letter, mark, rune, sign

charade *n* 1 = **pretence**, fake, farce,

1 device for charging an accumulator. **2** (in the Middle Ages) warhorse.

chargé d'affaires [shar–zhay daf–**fair**] *n*, *pl* **chargés d'affaires** head of a diplomatic mission in the absence of an ambassador or in a small mission.

chariot *n* two–wheeled horse–drawn vehicle used in ancient times in wars and races. **charioteer** *n* chariot driver.

charisma ① [kar–**rizz**–ma] *n* person's power to attract or influence people. **charismatic** [kar–rizz–**mat**–ik] *adj*

charity ① *n*, *pl* –**ties** **1** organization that gives help, such as money or food, to those in need. **2** giving of help to those in need. **3** help given to those in need. **4** kindly attitude towards people. **charitable** *adj* **charitably** *adv*

charlatan ① [**shar**–lat–tan] *n* person who claims expertise that he or she does not have.

charm ① *n* **1** attractive quality. **2** trinket worn on a bracelet. **3** magic spell. ◆ *v* **4** attract, delight. **5** influence by personal charm. **6** protect or influence as if by magic. **charmer** *n* **charming** *adj* attractive.

chart ① *n* **1** graph, table, or diagram showing information. **2** map of the sea or stars. ◆ *v* **3** plot the course of. **4** make a chart of. **the charts** *Informal* weekly lists of the bestselling pop records.

charter ① *n* **1** document granting or demanding certain rights. **2** fundamental principles of an organization. **3** hire of transport for private use. ◆ *v* **4** hire by charter. **5** grant a charter to. **chartered** *adj* officially qualified to practise a profession.

charwoman *n* woman whose job is to clean other people's homes.

chary [**chair**–ee] *adj* –**rier**, –**riest** wary, careful. **charily** *adv*

chase ① *v* **1** run after quickly in order to catch or drive away. **2** *Informal* rush, run. **3** *Informal* try energetically to obtain. ◆ *n* **4** chasing, pursuit. **chaser** *n* milder drink drunk after another stronger one.

pantomime, parody, travesty

charge *v* **3** = **accuse**, arraign, blame, impeach, incriminate, indict **4** = **attack**, assail, assault, rush, stampede, storm ≠ **withdrawal** **5** = **fill**, load **7** = **command**, bid, commit, demand, entrust, instruct, order, require ◆ *n* **8** = **price**, amount, cost, expenditure, expense, outlay, payment, rate, toll **9** = **accusation**, allegation, imputation, indictment ≠ **clearance** **10** = **attack**, assault, onset, onslaught, rush, sortie, stampede **11** = **instruction**, command, demand, direction, injunction, mandate, order, precept **12** = **care**, custody, duty, office, responsibility, safekeeping, trust **13** = **ward**

charisma *n* = **charm**, allure, attraction, lure, magnetism, personality

charity *n* **2** = **help**, assistance, benefaction, philanthropy, relief **3** = **donations**, contributions, endowment, fund, gift, hand–out, largesse *or* largess ≠ **selfishness** **4** = **kindness**, altruism, benevolence, compassion, fellow feeling, generosity, goodwill, humanity, indulgence ≠ **hatred**

charlatan *n* = **fraud**, cheat, con man (*inf*), fake, impostor, phoney *or* phony (*inf*), pretender, quack, sham, swindler

charm *n* **1** = **attraction**, allure, appeal, fascination, magnetism ≠ **unattractiveness** **2** = **trinket**, amulet, fetish, talisman **3** = **spell**, enchantment, magic, sorcery ◆ *v* **4** = **attract**, allure, beguile, bewitch, captivate, delight, enchant, enrapture, entrance, fascinate, mesmerize ≠ **alienate** **5** = **win over**

chart *n* **1** = **table**, blueprint, diagram, graph, plan **2** = **map** ◆ *v* **3** = **plot**, map out **4** = **outline**, delineate, draft, shape, sketch

charter *n* **1** = **document**, contract, deed, licence, permit ◆ *v* **4** = **hire**, commission, employ, lease, rent **5** = **authorize**, sanction

chase *v* **1** = **pursue**, course, drive, drive away, expel, follow, hound, hunt, put to flight, run after, track ◆ *n* **4** = **pursuit**, hunt, hunting, race

chasm ❶ [kaz–zum] n deep crack in the earth.

chassis [shass–ee] n, pl –sis frame, wheels, and mechanical parts of a vehicle.

chaste ❶ adj 1 abstaining from sex outside marriage or altogether. 2 (of style) simple. **chastely** adv **chastity** n

chasten ❶ [chase–en] v subdue by criticism.

chat ❶ n 1 informal conversation. ◆ v **chatting, chatted** 2 have an informal conversation. **chatty** adj **chatroom** n site on the Internet where users have group discussions by e–mail.

chateau [shat–toe] n, pl –teaux, –teaus French castle.

chauffeur n person employed to drive a car for someone. **chauffeuse** n fem

chauvinism [show–vin–iz–zum] n irrational belief that one's own country, race, group, or sex is superior. **chauvinist** n, adj **chauvinistic** adj

cheap ❶ adj 1 costing relatively little. 2 of poor quality. 3 not valued highly. 4 mean, despicable. **cheaply** adv **cheapen** v 1 lower the reputation of. 2 reduce the price of. **cheapskate** n Informal miserly person.

cheat ❶ v 1 act dishonestly to gain profit or advantage. ◆ n 2 person who cheats. 3 fraud, deception.

check ❶ v 1 examine, investigate. 2 slow the growth or progress of. 3 correspond, agree. ◆ n 4 test to ensure accuracy or progress. 5 break in progress. 6 US cheque. 7 pattern of squares or crossed lines. 8 Chess position of a king under attack. **check in** v register one's arrival. **checkmate** n 1 Chess winning position in which an opponent's king is under attack and unable to escape. 2 utter defeat. ◆ v 3 Chess place the king of (one's opponent) in checkmate. 4 thwart, defeat. **check out** v 1 pay the bill and leave a hotel. 2 examine, investigate. **checkout** n counter in a supermarket, where customers pay. **checkup** n thorough medical examination.

Cheddar n firm orange or yellowy–white cheese.

cheek ❶ n 1 either side of the face below the eye. 2 Informal impudence, boldness. ◆ v 3 Informal speak impudently to. **cheeky** adj impudent, disrespectful. **cheekily** adv **cheekiness** n

cheep n 1 young bird's high–pitched cry. ◆ v 2 utter a cheep.

cheer ❶ v 1 applaud or encourage with

————————— THESAURUS —————————

chasm n = **gulf**, abyss, crater, crevasse, fissure, gap, gorge, ravine

chaste adj 1 = **pure**, immaculate, innocent, modest, unaffected, undefiled, virtuous ≠ **dirty** 2 = **simple**

chasten v = **subdue**, chastise, correct, discipline, humble, humiliate, put in one's place, tame

chat n 1 = **talk**, chatter, chinwag (Brit inf), conversation, gossip, heart–to–heart, natter, tête–à–tête ◆ v 2 = **talk**, chatter, gossip, jaw (sl), natter

cheap adj 1 = **inexpensive**, bargain, cut-price, economical, keen, low–cost, low–priced, reasonable, reduced ≠ **dear** 2 = **inferior**, common, poor, second–rate, shoddy, tatty, tawdry, two a penny, worthless ≠ **good** 4 = **despicable**, contemptible, mean

cheat v 1 = **deceive**, beguile, con (inf), defraud, double–cross (inf), dupe, fleece, fool, mislead, rip off (sl), swindle, trick ◆ n 2 = **deceiver**, charlatan, con man (inf), double–crosser (inf), shark, sharper, swindler, trickster 3 = **deception**, deceit, fraud, rip–off (sl), scam (sl), swindle, trickery

check v 1 = **examine**, inquire into, inspect, investigate, look at, make sure, monitor, research, scrutinize, study, test, vet ≠ **ignore** 2 = **stop**, delay, halt, hinder, impede, inhibit, limit, obstruct, restrain, retard ≠ **start** ◆ n 4 = **examination**, inspection, investigation, once–over (inf), research, scrutiny, test

cheek n 2 Inf = **impudence**, audacity, chutzpah (US & Canad inf), disrespect, effrontery, impertinence, insolence, lip shouts. **2** make or become happy. ◆ *n* **3** shout of applause or encouragement. **cheerful** *adj* **cheerfully** *adv* **cheerfulness** *n* **cheerless** *adj* dreary, gloomy. **cheery** *adj* **cheerily** *adv*

cheerio *interj Informal* goodbye.

cheese *n* **1** food made from coagulated milk curd. **2** block of this. **cheesy** *adj* **cheeseburger** *n* hamburger topped with melted cheese. **cheesecake** *n* **1** dessert with a biscuit–crumb base covered with a sweet cream–cheese mixture. **2** *Slang* photographs of naked or near–naked women. **cheesecloth** *n* light cotton cloth. **cheesed off** bored, annoyed. **cheeseparing** *adj* mean, miserly.

cheetah *n* large fast–running spotted African wild cat.

chef *n* cook in a restaurant.

chemistry *n* science of the composition, properties, and reactions of substances. **chemical** *n* substance used in or resulting from a reaction involving changes to atoms or molecules. **chemist** *n* **1** shop selling medicines and cosmetics. **2** qualified dispenser of prescribed medicines. **3** specialist in chemistry.

chemotherapy *n* treatment of disease, often cancer, using chemicals.

chenille [shen–**neel**] *n* (fabric of) thick tufty yarn.

cheque *n* written order to one's bank to pay money from one's account. **cheque card** plastic card issued by a bank guaranteeing payment of a customer's cheques.

chequer *n* **1** piece used in Chinese chequers. ◆ *pl* **2** game of draughts. **chequered** *adj* **1** marked by varied

fortunes. **2** having a pattern of squares.

cherish ⊕ *v* **1** cling to (an idea or feeling). **2** care for.

cherry *n, pl* **–ries 1** small red or black fruit with a stone. **2** tree on which it grows. ◆ *adj* **3** deep red.

cherub *n, pl* **–ubs, –ubim 1** angel, often represented as a winged child. **2** sweet child. **cherubic** [cher–**rew**–bik] *adj*

chess *n* game for two players with 16 pieces each, played on a chequered board of 64 squares. **chessman** *n* piece used in chess.

chest ⊕ *n* **1** front of the body, from neck to waist. **2** large strong box. **chest of drawers** piece of furniture consisting of drawers in a frame.

chestnut *n* **1** reddish–brown edible nut. **2** tree on which it grows. **3** reddish brown horse. **4** *Informal* old joke. ◆ *adj* **5** (of hair or a horse) reddish–brown.

chevron [**shev**–ron] *n* V–shaped pattern, esp. on the sleeve of a military uniform to indicate rank.

chew ⊕ *v* grind (food) between the teeth. **chewy** *adj* requiring a lot of chewing. **chewing gum** flavoured gum to be chewed but not swallowed.

chianti [kee–**ant**–ee] *n* dry red Italian wine

chic ⊕ [**sheek**] *adj* **1** stylish, elegant. ◆ *n* **2** stylishness, elegance.

chicane [shik–**kane**] *n* obstacle in a motor–racing circuit.

chick *n* baby bird. **chickpea** *n* edible yellow pealike seed. **chickweed** *n* weed with small white flowers.

chicken *n* **1** domestic fowl. **2** its flesh, used as food. **3** *Slang* coward. ◆ *adj* **4** *Slang* cowardly. **chicken feed** *Slang* trifling

(*sl*), nerve, temerity

cheer *v* **1** = **applaud**, acclaim, clap, hail ≠ **boo 2** = **cheer up**, brighten, buoy up, comfort, encourage, gladden, hearten, uplift ≠ **depress** ◆ *n* **3** = **applause**, acclamation, ovation, plaudits

cherish *v* **1** = **cling to**, cleave to, encourage, entertain, foster, harbour, hold

dear, nurture, prize, sustain, treasure ≠ **hate 2** = **care for**, comfort, hold dear, love, nurse, shelter, support ≠ **hate**

chest *n* **2** = **box**, case, casket, coffer, crate, strongbox, trunk

chew *v* = **bite**, champ, chomp, crunch, gnaw, grind, masticate, munch

chic *adj* **1** = **stylish**, elegant, fashionable,

amount of money. **chicken out** v *Informal* fail to do something through cowardice. **chickenpox** n infectious disease with an itchy rash.

chicory n, pl **–ries 1** plant whose leaves are used in salads. **2** root of this plant, used as a coffee substitute.

chide 𝗢 v **chiding, chided** or **chid, chid** or **chidden** rebuke, scold.

chief 𝗢 n **1** head of a group of people. ◆ adj **2** most important. **chiefly** adv **1** especially. **2** mainly. **chieftain** n leader of a tribe.

chiffon [shif–fon] n fine see–through fabric.

chilblain n inflammation of the fingers or toes, caused by exposure to cold.

child 𝗢 n, pl **children 1** young human being, boy or girl. **2** son or daughter. **childhood** n **childish** adj **1** immature, silly. **2** of or like a child. **childless** adj **childlike** adj innocent, trustful. **childbirth** n giving birth to a child. **child's play** very easy task.

✓ **WORD TIP**
Note that *childish* has overtones of *foolish* while *childlike* suggests an *innocent* quality.

chill 𝗢 n **1** a feverish cold. **2** moderate coldness. ◆ v **3** make (something) cool or cold. **4** cause (someone) to feel cold or frightened. ◆ adj **5** unpleasantly cold.

chilly adj **1** moderately cold. **2** unfriendly. **chilly–bin** n NZ informal insulated container for carrying food and drink. **chilliness** n

chilli, chili n **1** small red or green hot–tasting capsicum pod, used in cooking. **2** (also **chilli con carne**) hot–tasting Mexican dish of meat, onions, beans, and chilli powder.

chime 𝗢 n **1** musical ringing sound of a bell or clock. ◆ v **2** make a musical ringing sound. **3** indicate (the time) by chiming. **4** (foll. by *with*) be consistent with.

chimney n hollow vertical structure for carrying away smoke from a fire.

chimpanzee n intelligent black African ape.

chin n part of the face below the mouth. **chinwag** n Informal chat.

china 𝗢 n **1** fine earthenware or porcelain. **2** dishes or ornaments made of this.

chinchilla n **1** S American rodent bred for its soft grey fur. **2** its fur.

chink 𝗢 n small narrow opening, e.g. *a chink of light.*

chintz n printed cotton fabric with a glazed finish.

chip 𝗢 n **1** strip of potato, fried in deep fat. **2** tiny wafer of semiconductor material forming an integrated circuit. **3** counter used to represent money in gambling games. **4** small piece removed by chopping, breaking, etc. ◆ v **chipping,**

THESAURUS

smart, trendy (*Brit inf*)

chide v = **scold**, admonish, berate, censure, criticize, lecture, reprove, rebuke, reprimand, reproach, reprove, rouse on (*Aust*), tell off (*inf*), tick off (*inf*)

chief n **1** = **head**, boss (*inf*), captain, commander, director, governor, leader, manager, master, principal, ruler ≠ **subject** ◆ adj **2** = **primary**, foremost, highest, key, leading, main, predominant, pre–eminent, premier, prime, principal, supreme, uppermost ≠ **least**

child n **1** = **youngster**, babe, baby, bairn (*Scot*), infant, juvenile, kid (*inf*), offspring,

toddler, tot

chill n **2** = **cold**, bite, coldness, coolness, crispness, frigidity, nip, rawness, sharpness ◆ v **3** = **cool**, freeze, refrigerate **4** = **dishearten**, dampen, deject, depress, discourage, dismay ◆ adj **5** = **cold**, biting, bleak, chilly, freezing, frigid, raw, sharp, wintry

chime n **1** = **ring**, clang, jingle, peal, sound, tinkle, toll ◆ v **2** = **ring**, clang, jingle, peal, sound, tinkle, toll

china n **1** = **pottery**, ceramics, porcelain **2** = **crockery**, service, tableware, ware

chink n = **opening**, aperture, cleft, crack,

chipped 5 break small pieces from. **have a chip on one's shoulder** *Informal* bear a grudge. **chip in** *v Informal* 1 contribute (money). 2 interrupt with a remark.

chippie *n Brit, Aust & NZ informal* carpenter.

chipmunk *n* small squirrel–like N American rodent with a striped back.

chiropodist [kir–**rop**–pod–ist] *n* person who treats minor foot complaints. **chiropody** *n*

chirp ❶ *v* 1 (of a bird or insect) make a short high–pitched sound. ♦ *n* 2 chirping sound. **chirpy** *adj Informal* lively and cheerful.

chisel *n* 1 metal tool with a sharp end for shaping wood or stone. ♦ *v* **–elling, –elled** 2 carve or form with a chisel.

chit *n* short official note, such as a receipt.

chitchat *n* chat, gossip.

chivalry ❶ *n* 1 courteous behaviour, esp. by men towards women. 2 medieval system and principles of knighthood. **chivalrous** *adj*

chlorine *n* strong–smelling greenish yellow gaseous element, used to disinfect water. **chlorinate** *v* disinfect (water) with chlorine. **chlorination** *n* **chloride** *n* compound of chlorine and another substance.

chloroform *n* strong–smelling liquid formerly used as an anaesthetic.

chlorophyll *n* green colouring matter of plants, which enables them to convert sunlight into energy.

chock *n* block or wedge used to prevent a heavy object from moving. **chock–full, chock–a–block** *adj* completely full.

chocolate *n* 1 sweet food made from cacao seeds. 2 sweet or drink made from this. ♦ *adj* 3 dark brown.

choice ❶ *n* 1 choosing. 2 opportunity or power of choosing. 3 person or thing chosen or that may be chosen. 4 alternative action or possibility. ♦ *adj* 5 of high quality.

choir *n* 1 organized group of singers, esp. in church. 2 part of a church occupied by the choir.

choke ❶ *v* 1 hinder or stop the breathing of (a person) by strangling or smothering. 2 have trouble in breathing. 3 block, clog up. ♦ *n* 4 device controlling the amount of air that is mixed with the fuel in a petrol engine. **choker** *n* tight–fitting necklace. **choke back** *v* suppress (tears or anger).

cholera [**kol**–ler–a] *n* serious infectious disease causing severe vomiting and diarrhoea.

choleric [**kol**–ler–ik] *adj* bad–tempered.

cholesterol [kol–**lest**–er–oll] *n* fatty substance found in animal tissue, an excess of which can cause heart disease.

chook *n Aust & NZ* hen or chicken.

choose ❶ *v* **choosing, chose, chosen** 1 select from a number of alternatives. 2 decide (to do something) because one wants to. **choosy** *adj Informal* fussy, hard to please.

chop ❶ *v* **chopping, chopped** 1 cut with a blow from an axe or knife. 2 cut into pieces. 3 *Boxing, karate* hit (an opponent) with a short sharp blow. ♦ *n* 4 cutting or sharp blow. 5 slice of lamb or pork, usu. with a rib. **chopper** *n* 1 *Informal* helicopter. 2 small axe. 3 butcher's cleaver. 4 cycle

————— THESAURUS —————

cranny, crevice, fissure, gap

chip *n* 4 = **scratch**, fragment, nick, notch, shard, shaving, sliver, wafer ♦ *v* 5 = **nick**, chisel, damage, gash, whittle

chirp, chirrup *v* 1 = **tweet**, cheep, peep, pipe, twitter, warble

chivalry *n* 1 = **courtesy**, gallantry, gentlemanliness, politeness
2 = **knighthood**, courage, knight–errantry

choice *n* 2 = **option**, alternative, pick, preference, say 3 = **selection**, range, variety ♦ *adj* 5 = **best**, elite, excellent, exclusive, premier, rare, select

choke *v* 1 = **strangle**, asphyxiate, gag, overpower, smother, stifle, suffocate, suppress, throttle 3 = **block**, bar, bung, clog, congest, constrict, obstruct, stop

choose *v* = **pick**, adopt, designate, elect,

with very high handlebars. **choppy** *adj*
–**pier**, –**piest** (of the sea) fairly rough.

chopsticks *pl n* pair of thin sticks used to
eat Chinese food.

choral *adj* of a choir.

chorale [kor–**rahl**] *n* slow stately hymn
tune.

chord *n* simultaneous sounding of three or
more musical notes.

chore ⊕ *n* 1 routine task. 2 unpleasant task.

choreography *n* composition of steps and
movements for dancing. **choreographer** *n*

chorister *n* singer in a choir.

chortle ⊕ *v* 1 chuckle in amusement. ♦ *n*
2 amused chuckle.

chorus ⊕ *n, pl* –**ruses** 1 large choir. 2 part
of a song repeated after each verse. 3
something expressed by many people at
once. 4 group of singers or dancers who
perform together in a show. ♦ *v*
chorusing, chorused 5 sing or say
together. **in chorus** in unison.

chow *n* thick–coated dog with a curled tail,
orig. from China.

Christian *n* 1 person who believes in and
follows Christ. ♦ *adj* 2 of Christ or
Christianity. 3 kind, good. **Christianity** *n*
religion based on the life and teachings of
Christ. **Christian name** person's first
name.

Christmas ⊕ *n* 1 annual festival on Dec.
25 commemorating the birth of Christ. 2

period around this time. **Christmassy** *adj*

chromosome *n* microscopic gene–
carrying body in the nucleus of a cell.

chronic *adj* 1 (of an illness) lasting a long
time. 2 habitual, e.g. *chronic drinking*. 3
Informal of poor quality. **chronically** *adv*

chronicle ⊕ *n* 1 record of events in order
of occurrence. ♦ *v* 2 record in or as if in a
chronicle. **chronicler** *n*

chrysalis [**kriss**–a–liss] *n* insect in the stage
between larva and adult, when it is in a
cocoon.

chrysanthemum *n* garden flower with a
large head made up of thin petals.

chub *n* freshwater fish of the carp family.

chubby ⊕ *adj* –**bier**, –**biest** plump and
round. **chubbiness** *n*

chuck ⊕ *v* 1 *Informal* throw. 2 *Informal* give
up, reject. 3 touch (someone)
affectionately under the chin.

chuckle ⊕ *v* 1 laugh softly. ♦ *n* 2 soft
laugh.

chuffed *adj Informal* very pleased.

chum ⊕ *Informal* ♦ *n* 1 close friend. ♦ *v*
chumming, chummed 2 **chum up with**
form a close friendship with. **chummy** *adj*

chunk ⊕ *n* 1 thick solid piece. 2
considerable amount. **chunky** *adj* 1 (of a
person) broad and heavy. 2 (of an object)
large and thick.

church *n* 1 building for public Christian
worship. 2 particular Christian

————— THESAURUS —————

opt for, prefer, select, settle upon ≠ **leave**

chop *v* 1 = **cut**, cleave, fell, hack, hew, lop,
sever

chore *n* 1 = **task**, duty, errand, job
2 = **burden**

chortle *v* 1 = **chuckle**, cackle, crow, guffaw
♦ *n* 2 = **chuckle**, cackle, crow, guffaw

chorus *n* 1 = **choir**, choristers, ensemble,
singers, vocalists 2 = **refrain**, burden,
response, strain 3 = **unison**, accord,
concert, harmony

Christmas *n* = **festive season**, Noel, Xmas
(*inf*), Yule (*arch*)

chronicle *n* 1 = **record**, account, annals,
diary, history, journal, narrative, register,

story ♦ *v* 2 = **record**, enter, narrate, put on
record, recount, register, relate, report, set
down, tell

chubby *adj* = **plump**, buxom, flabby,
podgy, portly, roly–poly, rotund, round,
stout, tubby

chuck *v* 1 *Inf* = **throw**, cast, fling, heave,
hurl, pitch, sling, toss

chuckle *v* 1 = **laugh**, chortle, crow, exult,
giggle, snigger, titter

chum *Inf n* 1 = **friend**, cobber (*Aust or old–
fashioned NZ inf*), companion, comrade,
crony, mate (*inf*), pal (*inf*)

chunk *n* 1 = **piece**, block, dollop (*inf*),
hunk, lump, mass, nugget, portion, slab

denomination. **3** clergy. **churchgoer** n person who attends church regularly. **churchyard** n grounds round a church, used as a graveyard.

churlish ❶ adj surly and rude.

churn ❶ n **1** machine in which cream is shaken to make butter. **2** large container for milk. ♦ v **3** stir (cream) vigorously to make butter. **4** move about violently. **churn out** v Informal produce (things) rapidly in large numbers.

chute [shoot] n steep slope down which things may be slid.

chutney n pickle made from fruit, vinegar, spices, and sugar.

CIA (in the US) Central Intelligence Agency.

CID Criminal Investigation Department.

cider n alcoholic drink made from fermented apple juice.

cigar n roll of cured tobacco leaves for smoking.

cigarette n thin roll of shredded tobacco in thin paper, for smoking.

cinch [sinch] n Informal easy task.

cinder n piece of material that will not burn, left after burning coal.

cinema ❶ n **1** place for showing films. **2** films collectively. **cinematic** adj **cinematography** n technique of making films. **cinematographer** n

cinnamon n spice obtained from the bark of an Asian tree.

cipher ❶ [sife–er] n **1** system of secret writing. **2** unimportant person.

circa [sir–ka] prep Latin approximately, about.

circle ❶ n **1** perfectly round geometric figure, line, or shape. **2** group of people sharing an interest or activity. **3** Theatre section of seats above the main level of the auditorium. ♦ v **4** move in a circle (round). **5** enclose in a circle. **circular** adj round. **circulate** v move round.

circuit ❶ n **1** complete route or course, esp. a circular one. **2** complete path through which an electric current can flow. **3** periodical journey round a district, as made by judges. **4** motor–racing track. **circuitous** [sir–kew–it–uss] adj indirect and lengthy. **circuitry** [sir–kit–tree] n electrical circuit(s).

circumcise v remove the foreskin of. **circumcision** n

circumference ❶ n **1** boundary of a specified area or shape, esp. of a circle. **2** distance round this.

circumflex n mark (ˆ) over a vowel to show that it is pronounced in a particular way.

circumnavigate v sail right round. **circumnavigation** n

circumscribe v **1** limit, restrict. **2** draw a line round.

circumspect adj cautious and careful not to take risks. **circumspection** n

circumstance ❶ n (usu. pl) occurrence or condition that accompanies or influences a person or event. **circumstantial** adj **1** (of evidence) strongly suggesting something but not proving it. **2** very detailed.

——————— THESAURUS ———————

churlish adj = **rude**, brusque, harsh, ill–tempered, impolite, sullen, surly, uncivil

churn v **4** = **stir up**, agitate, beat, convulse, swirl, toss

cinema n **1** = **pictures**, flicks (sl), movies **2** = **films**, big screen (inf), flicks (sl), motion pictures, movies, pictures

cipher n **1** = **code**, cryptograph **2** = **nobody**, nonentity

circle n **1** = **ring**, disc, globe, orb, sphere **2** = **group**, clique, club, company, coterie, set, society ♦ v **4** = **go round**,

circumnavigate, circumscribe, wheel **5** = **enclose**, circumscribe, encircle, envelop, ring, surround

circuit n **1** = **course**, journey, lap, orbit, revolution, route, tour **4** = **track**

circumference n **1** = **boundary**, border, edge, extremity, limits, outline, perimeter, periphery, rim

circumstance n (usu. pl) = **situation**, condition, contingency, event, happening, incident, occurrence, position, state, state of affairs, status

circumvent v avoid or get round (a rule etc.). **circumvention** n

circus n, pl **-cuses** (performance given by) a travelling company of acrobats, clowns, performing animals, etc.

cirrhosis [sir–roh–siss] n serious liver disease, often caused by drinking too much alcohol.

cirrus n, pl **-ri** high wispy cloud.

cistern ⊕ n water tank, esp. one that holds water for flushing a toilet.

citadel ⊕ n fortress in a city.

cite ⊕ v 1 quote, refer to. 2 bring forward as proof. **citation** n

citizen ⊕ n 1 native or naturalized member of a state or nation. 2 inhabitant of a city or town. **citizenship** n

citrus fruit n juicy sharp–tasting fruit such as an orange or lemon.

city ⊕ n, pl **-ties** large or important town.

civic ⊕ adj of a city or citizens. **civics** n study of the rights and responsibilities of citizenship.

civil ⊕ adj 1 relating to the citizens of a state as opposed to the armed services or the Church. 2 polite, courteous. **civilly** adv **civility** n polite or courteous behaviour. **civilian** n, adj (person) not belonging to the armed forces. **civil service** service responsible for the administration of the government. **civil servant** member of the

civil service. **civil war** war between people of the same country.

civilize ⊕ v 1 refine or educate (a person). 2 make (a place) more pleasant or more acceptable. **civilization** n 1 high level of human cultural and social development. 2 particular society which has reached this level.

claim ⊕ v 1 assert as a fact. 2 demand as a right. 3 need, require. ♦ n 4 assertion that something is true. 5 assertion of a right. 6 something claimed as a right. **claimant** n

clairvoyance n power of perceiving things beyond the natural range of the senses. **clairvoyant** n, adj

clam n 1 edible shellfish with a hinged shell. ♦ v **clamming, clammed** 2 **clam up** Informal stop talking, esp. through nervousness.

clamber ⊕ v climb awkwardly.

clammy ⊕ adj **-mier, -miest** unpleasantly moist and sticky.

clamour ⊕ n 1 loud protest. 2 loud persistent noise or outcry. ♦ v 3 make a loud noise or outcry. **clamorous** adj **clamour for** v demand noisily.

clamp ⊕ n 1 tool with movable jaws for holding things together tightly. ♦ v 2 fasten with a clamp. **clamp down on** v 1 become stricter about. 2 suppress.

clan ⊕ n 1 group of families with a

———— THESAURUS ————

cistern n = **tank**, basin, reservoir, sink, vat

citadel n = **fortress**, bastion, fortification, keep, stronghold, tower

cite v 1 = **quote**, adduce, advance, allude to, enumerate, extract, mention, name, specify

citizen n = **inhabitant**, denizen, dweller, resident, subject, townsman

city n = **town**, conurbation, metropolis, municipality

civic adj = **public**, communal, local, municipal

civil adj 1 = **civic**, domestic, municipal, political ≠ state 2 = **polite**, affable, courteous, obliging, refined, urbane, well–mannered

civilize v 1 = **cultivate**, educate, enlighten, refine, sophisticate, tame

claim v 1 = **assert**, allege, challenge, insist, maintain, profess, uphold 2 = **demand**, ask, call for, insist, need, require ♦ n 4 = **assertion**, affirmation, allegation, pretension 6 = **demand**, application, call, petition, request, requirement

clamber v = **climb**, claw, scale, scrabble, scramble, shin

clammy adj = **moist**, close, damp, dank, sticky, sweaty

clamour n 2 = **noise**, commotion, din, hubbub, outcry, racket, shouting, uproar

clamp n 1 = **vice**, bracket, fastener, grip, press ♦ v 2 = **fasten**, brace, fix, make fast, common ancestor, esp. among Scottish Highlanders. 2 close group. **clannish** *adj* (of a group) tending to exclude outsiders.

clandestine ❶ *adj* secret and concealed.

clang *v* 1 make a loud ringing metallic sound. ♦ *n* 2 ringing metallic sound. **clanger** *n Informal* obvious mistake.

clap ❶ *v* **clapping, clapped** 1 applaud by hitting the palms of one's hands sharply together. 2 put quickly or forcibly. 3 strike (someone) lightly with an open hand, for example in greeting. ♦ *n* 4 act or sound of clapping. 5 sudden loud noise, e.g. *a clap of thunder*. **clapped out** *Slang* worn out, dilapidated.

claret [**klar**–rit] *n* dry red wine from Bordeaux.

clarify ❶ *v* **-fying, -fied** make (a matter) clear and unambiguous. **clarification** *n*

clarinet *n* keyed woodwind instrument with a single reed. **clarinettist** *n*

clash ❶ *v* 1 come into conflict. 2 (of events) happen at the same time. 3 (of colours) look unattractive together. 4 (of objects) make a loud harsh sound by being hit together. ♦ *n* 5 fight, argument. 6 fact of two events happening at the same time.

clasp ❶ *n* 1 device for fastening things. 2 firm grasp or embrace. ♦ *v* 3 grasp or embrace firmly. 4 fasten with a clasp.

class ❶ *n* 1 group of people sharing a similar social position. 2 system of dividing society into such groups. 3 group of people or things sharing a common characteristic. 4 group of pupils or students taught together. 5 standard of quality. 6 *Informal* elegance or excellence, e.g. *a touch of class*. ♦ *v* 7 place in a class.

classic ❶ *adj* 1 being a typical example of something. 2 of lasting interest because of excellence. 3 attractive because of simplicity of form. ♦ *n* 4 author, artist, or work of art of recognized excellence. ♦ *pl* 5 study of ancient Greek and Roman literature and culture. **classical** *adj* 1 of or in a restrained conservative style. 2 denoting serious art music. 3 of or influenced by ancient Greek and Roman culture. **classically** *adv* **classicism** *n* artistic style showing emotional restraint and regularity of form. **classicist** *n*

> ✓ **WORD TIP**
>
> *Classic* and *classical* are synonyms except in the context of Greek and Roman culture, which is called *classical*, or highly rated art and literature, which is called *classic*.

THESAURUS

secure

clan *n* 1 = **family**, tribe 2 = **group**, brotherhood, faction, fraternity, society

clandestine *adj* = **secret**, cloak-and-dagger, concealed, covert, furtive, private, stealthy, surreptitious, underground

clap *v* 1 = **applaud**, acclaim, cheer ≠ **boo**

clarify *v* = **explain**, clear up, elucidate, illuminate, interpret, make plain, simplify, throw *or* shed light on

clash *v* 1 = **conflict**, cross swords, feud, grapple, lock horns, quarrel, war, wrangle 4 = **crash**, bang, clang, clank, clatter, jangle, jar, rattle ♦ *n* 5 = **conflict**, brush, collision, confrontation, difference of opinion, disagreement, fight, showdown (*inf*)

clasp *n* 1 = **fastening**, brooch, buckle, catch, clip, fastener, grip, hook, pin 2 = **grasp**, embrace, grip, hold, hug ♦ *v* 3 = **grasp**, clutch, embrace, grip, hold, hug, press, seize, squeeze 4 = **fasten**, connect

class *n* 3 = **group**, category, division, genre, kind, set, sort, type ♦ *v* 7 = **classify**, brand, categorize, designate, grade, group, label, rank, rate

classic *adj* 1 = **typical**, archetypal, characteristic, definitive, exemplary, ideal, model, quintessential, standard 2 = **best**, consummate, finest, first–rate, masterly, world–class ≠ **poor** ♦ *n* 4 = **standard**, exemplar, masterpiece, model, paradigm, prototype

clatter v, n (make) a rattling noise.

clause ❶ n 1 section of a legal document. 2 part of a sentence, containing a verb.

claustrophobia n abnormal fear of confined spaces. **claustrophobic** adj

clavicle n same as COLLARBONE.

claw ❶ n 1 sharp hooked nail of a bird or beast. 2 similar part, such as a crab's pincer. ◆ v 3 tear with claws or nails.

clay n fine–grained earth, soft when moist and hardening when baked, used to make bricks and pottery. **clayey** adj **clay pigeon** baked clay disc hurled into the air as a target for shooting.

clean ❶ adj 1 free from dirt or impurities. 2 not yet used. 3 morally acceptable, inoffensive. 4 (of a reputation or record) free from dishonesty or corruption. 5 complete, e.g. a clean break. 6 smooth and regular. ◆ v 7 make (something) free from dirt. ◆ adv 8 Not standard completely, e.g. I clean forgot. **come clean** Informal reveal or admit something. **cleaner** n **cleanly** adv **cleanliness** n

clear ❶ adj 1 free from doubt or confusion. 2 easy to see or hear. 3 able to be seen through. 4 free from darkness or obscurity. 5 free of obstruction. 6 (of weather) free from clouds. 7 (of skin) without blemish. 8

(of money) without deduction. ◆ adv 9 in a clear or distinct manner. 10 out of the way. ◆ v 11 make or become clear. 12 pass by or over (something) without contact. 13 prove (someone) innocent of a crime or mistake. 14 make as profit. **clearly** adv **clearance** n 1 clearing. 2 official permission. **clearing** n treeless area in a wood. **clear off** v Informal go away. **clear out** v 1 remove and sort the contents of. 2 Informal go away. **clearway** n stretch of road on which motorists may stop in an emergency.

cleave¹ v **cleaving, cleft, cleaved** or **clove, cleft, cleaved** or **cloven** split apart. **cleavage** n 1 space between a woman's breasts, as revealed by a low–cut dress. 2 division, split. **cleaver** n butcher's heavy knife with a square blade.

cleave² v cling or stick.

clef n Music symbol at the beginning of a stave to show the pitch.

cleft n 1 narrow opening or crack. ◆ v 2 a past of CLEAVE¹. **in a cleft stick** in a very difficult position.

clematis n climbing plant with large colourful flowers.

clement adj (of weather) mild. **clemency** n kind or lenient treatment.

──────── THESAURUS ────────

clause n 1 = **section**, article, chapter, condition, paragraph, part, passage

claw n 1 = **nail**, talon 2 = **pincer** ◆ v 3 = **scratch**, dig, lacerate, maul, rip, scrape, tear

clean adj 1 = **pure**, antiseptic, decontaminated, flawless, hygienic, immaculate, impeccable, purified, spotless, sterile, sterilized, unblemished, uncontaminated, unpolluted ≠ **soiled** 3 = **moral**, chaste, decent, good, honourable, innocent, pure, respectable, upright, virtuous ≠ **indecent** 5 = **complete**, conclusive, decisive, entire, final, perfect, thorough, total, unimpaired, whole ◆ v 7 = **cleanse**, disinfect, launder, purge, purify, rinse, sanitize, scour, scrub, wash ≠ **soil**

clear adj 1 = **certain**, convinced, decided, definite, positive, resolved, satisfied, sure ≠ **confused** 2 = **obvious**, apparent, blatant, comprehensible, conspicuous, distinct, evident, manifest, palpable, plain, pronounced, recognizable, unmistakable ≠ **hidden** 3 = **transparent**, crystalline, glassy, limpid, pellucid, see–through, translucent ≠ **muddy** 5 = **unobstructed**, empty, free, open, smooth, unhindered, unimpeded ≠ **closed** 6 = **bright**, cloudless, fair, fine, light, luminous, shining, sunny, unclouded ≠ **dark** 7 = **unblemished**, clean, immaculate ◆ v 11 = **unblock**, disentangle, extricate, free, open, rid 12 = **pass over**, jump, leap, miss, vault 13 = **absolve**, acquit, excuse, exonerate, justify, vindicate ≠ **charge** 14 = **gain**,

clench v 1 close or squeeze (one's teeth or fist) tightly. 2 grasp firmly.

clergy ① n priests and ministers as a group. **clergyman** n

clerical adj 1 of clerks or office work. 2 of the clergy.

clerk n employee in an office, bank, or court who keeps records and files.

clever ① adj 1 intelligent, quick at learning. 2 showing skill. **cleverly** adv **cleverness** n

cliché [klee-shay] n expression or idea that is no longer effective because of overuse.

click n 1 short sharp sound. ♦ v 2 make this sound. 3 Informal (of two people) get on well together. 4 Informal become suddenly clear. 5 Slang be a success.

client ① n person who uses the services of a professional person or company. **clientele** n clients collectively.

cliff ① n steep rock face, esp. along the sea shore. **cliffhanger** n film, game, etc., that is exciting because its outcome is uncertain.

climate ① n typical weather conditions of an area. **climatic** adj

> ### ✓ WORD TIP
> Climatic is sometimes wrongly used where climactic is meant. Climatic should be used to talk about things relating to climate; climactic is used to describe something which forms a climax.

climax ① n 1 most intense point of an experience, series of events, or story. 2 same as ORGASM. **climactic** adj

climb ① v 1 go up, ascend. 2 rise to a higher point or intensity. ♦ n 3 climbing. 4 place to be climbed. **climber** n **climb down** v retreat from an opinion or position.

clinch ① v settle (an argument or agreement) decisively.

clincher n Inf something decisive, such as a fact, argument or point scored.

cling ① v **clinging**, **clung** hold tightly or stick closely. **clingfilm** n thin polythene material for wrapping food.

clinic n 1 building where outpatients receive medical treatment or advice. 2 private or specialized hospital. **clinical** adj 1 of a clinic. 2 logical and unemotional. **clinically** adv

clink v, n (make) a light sharp metallic sound.

clip¹ ① v **clipping**, **clipped** 1 cut with shears or scissors. 2 Informal hit sharply. ♦ n 3 short extract of a film. 4 Informal sharp blow. **clippers** pl n tool for clipping. **clipping** n something cut out, esp. an article from a newspaper.

clip² ① n 1 device for attaching or holding things together. ♦ v **clipping**, **clipped** 2 attach or hold together with a clip.

clipped adj (of speech) abrupt.

THESAURUS

acquire, earn, make, reap, secure

clergy n = **priesthood**, churchmen, clergymen, clerics, holy orders, ministry, the cloth

clever adj 1 = **intelligent**, bright, ingenious, knowledgeable, quick-witted, resourceful, shrewd, smart ≠ **slow** 2 = **talented**, gifted ≠ **awkward**

cliché n = **platitude**, banality, commonplace, hackneyed phrase, stereotype, truism

client n = **customer**, applicant, buyer, consumer, patient, patron, shopper

cliff n = **rock face**, bluff, crag, escarpment, overhang, precipice, scar, scarp

climate n 2 = **weather**, temperature

climax n 1 = **culmination**, height, highlight, high point, peak, summit, top, zenith

climb v 1 = **ascend**, clamber, mount, rise, scale, shin up, soar, top

clinch v 1 = **settle**, conclude, confirm, decide, determine, seal, secure, set the seal on, sew up (inf)

cling v = **stick**, adhere, clasp, clutch, embrace, grasp, grip, hug

clipper n fast commercial sailing ship.
clique ❶ [kleek] n small exclusive group.
clitoris [klit–or–iss] n small sexually sensitive organ at the front of the vulva. **clitoral** adj
cloak ❶ n 1 loose sleeveless outer garment. ◆ v 2 cover or conceal. **cloakroom** n room where coats may be left temporarily.
clobber v Informal 1 hit. 2 defeat utterly.
clock n 1 instrument for showing the time. 2 device with a dial for recording or measuring. **clockwise** adv, adj in the direction in which the hands of a clock rotate. **clock in** or **on**, **out** or **off** v register arrival at or departure from work on an automatic time recorder. **clock up** v reach (a total). **clockwork** n mechanism similar to the kind in a clock, used in wind–up toys.
clod n 1 lump of earth. 2 stupid person.
clog ❶ v **clogging**, **clogged** 1 obstruct. ◆ n 2 wooden or wooden–soled shoe.
cloister n covered pillared arcade, usu. in a monastery. **cloistered** adj sheltered.
clone n 1 animal or plant produced artificially from the cells of another animal or plant, and identical to the original. 2 Informal person who closely resembles another. ◆ v 3 produce as a clone.
close¹ ❶ v [rhymes with **nose**] 1 shut.

2 prevent access to. 3 end, terminate. 4 bring or come nearer together. ◆ n 5 end, conclusion. 6 [rhymes with **dose**] street closed at one end. 7 [rhymes with **dose**] courtyard, quadrangle. **closed shop** place of work in which all workers must belong to a particular trade union.
close² ❶ adj [rhymes with **dose**] 1 near. 2 intimate. 3 careful, thorough. 4 compact, dense. 5 oppressive, stifling. 6 secretive. ◆ adv 7 closely, tightly. **closely** adv **closeness** n **close season** period when it is illegal to kill certain game or fish. **close shave** Informal narrow escape. **close–up** n photograph or film taken at close range.
closet n 1 US cupboard. 2 small private room. ◆ adj 3 private, secret. ◆ v **closeting**, **closeted** 4 shut (oneself) away in private.
clot n 1 soft thick lump formed from liquid. 2 Informal stupid person. ◆ v **clotting**, **clotted** 3 form soft thick lumps.
cloth ❶ n (piece of) woven fabric.
cloud ❶ n 1 mass of condensed water vapour floating in the sky. 2 floating mass of smoke, dust, etc. ◆ v 3 (foll. by over) become cloudy. 4 confuse. 5 make gloomy or depressed. **cloudy** adj 1 having a lot of clouds. 2 (of liquid) not clear.

———————[THESAURUS]———————

clip¹ v 1 = **trim**, crop, curtail, cut, pare, prune, shear, shorten, snip 2 Inf = **smack**, clout (inf), cuff, knock, punch, strike, thump, wallop (inf), whack ◆ n 4 Inf = **smack**, clout (inf), cuff, knock, punch, strike, thump, wallop (inf), whack
clip² v 2 = **attach**, fasten, fix, hold, pin, staple
clique n = **group**, cabal, circle, coterie, faction, gang, set
cloak n 1 = **cape**, coat, mantle, wrap ◆ v 2 = **cover**, camouflage, conceal, disguise, hide, mask, obscure, screen, veil
clog v 1 = **obstruct**, block, congest, hinder, impede, jam
close¹ v 1 = **shut**, bar, block, lock, plug, seal, secure, stop up ≠ **open** 2 = **end**, cease, complete, conclude, finish, shut

down, terminate, wind up 4 = **connect**, come together, couple, fuse, join, unite ≠ **part** ◆ n 5 = **end**, completion, conclusion, culmination, denouement, ending, finale, finish
close² adj 1 = **near**, adjacent, adjoining, at hand, cheek by jowl, handy, impending, nearby, neighbouring, nigh ≠ **far** 2 = **intimate**, attached, confidential, dear, devoted, familiar, inseparable, loving ≠ **cold** 3 = **careful**, detailed, intense, minute, painstaking, rigorous, thorough 4 = **compact**, congested, crowded, dense, impenetrable, jam–packed, packed, tight 5 = **stifling**, airless, heavy, humid, muggy, oppressive, stuffy, suffocating, sweltering ≠ **fresh** 6 = **secretive**, private, reticent, secret, taciturn, uncommunicative

cloudburst n heavy fall of rain.

clout ① Informal ♦ n 1 hard blow. 2 power, influence. ♦ v 3 hit hard.

clove[1] n dried flower bud of a tropical tree, used as a spice.

clove[2] n segment of a bulb of garlic.

clover n plant with three–lobed leaves. **in clover** in luxury.

clown ① n 1 comic entertainer in a circus. 2 amusing person. 3 stupid person. ♦ v 4 behave foolishly. 5 perform as a clown.

club ① n 1 association of people with common interests. 2 building used by such a group. 3 thick stick used as a weapon. 4 stick with a curved end used to hit the ball in golf. 5 playing card with black three–leaved symbols. ♦ v **clubbing, clubbed** 6 hit with a club. **club together** v combine resources for a common purpose.

cluck n 1 low clicking noise made by a hen. ♦ v 2 make this noise.

clue ① n something that helps to solve a mystery or puzzle. **not have a clue** be completely baffled. **clueless** adj stupid.

clump ① n 1 small group of things or people. 2 dull heavy tread. ♦ v 3 walk heavily. 4 form into clumps.

clumsy ① adj –sier, –siest 1 lacking skill or physical coordination. 2 badly made or done. **clumsily** adv **clumsiness** n

cluster ① n 1 small close group. ♦ v 2 gather in clusters.

clutch ① v 1 grasp tightly. 2 (foll. by at) try to get hold of. ♦ n 3 device enabling two revolving shafts to be connected and disconnected, esp. in a motor vehicle. 4 tight grasp.

clutter ① v 1 scatter objects about (a place) untidily. ♦ n 2 untidy mess.

cm centimetre.

Co. 1 Company. 2 County.

co– prefix together, joint, or jointly, e.g. coproduction.

c/o 1 care of. 2 Book–keeping carried over.

coach ① n 1 long–distance bus. 2 railway carriage. 3 large four–wheeled horse–drawn carriage. 4 trainer, instructor. ♦ v 5 train, teach.

coagulate [koh–**ag**–yew–late] v change

cloth n = **fabric**, material, textiles

cloud n 1, 2 = **mist**, gloom, haze, murk, vapour ♦ v 3 (foll. by over) = **obscure**, becloud, darken, dim, eclipse, obfuscate, overshadow, shade, shadow, veil 4 = **confuse**, disorient, distort, impair, muddle, muddy the waters

clout Inf n 2 = **influence**, authority, mana (NZ), power, prestige, pull, weight ♦ v 3 = **hit**, clobber (sl), punch, sock (sl), strike, thump, wallop (inf)

clown n 1 = **comedian**, buffoon, comic, fool, harlequin, jester 2 = **joker**, prankster ♦ v 4 = **play the fool**, act the fool, jest, mess about

club n 1 = **association**, fraternity, group, guild, lodge, set, society, union 3 = **stick**, bat, bludgeon, cosh (Brit), cudgel, truncheon ♦ v 6 = **beat**, bash, batter, bludgeon, cosh (Brit), hammer, pummel, strike

clue n = **indication**, evidence, hint, lead,

pointer, sign, suggestion, suspicion, trace

clump n 1 = **cluster**, bunch, bundle, group, mass ♦ v 3 = **stomp**, lumber, plod, thud, thump, tramp

clumsy adj 1 = **awkward**, bumbling, gauche, gawky, ham–fisted (inf), lumbering, maladroit, ponderous, uncoordinated, ungainly, unwieldy ≠ **expert**

cluster n 1 = **gathering**, assemblage, batch, bunch, clump, collection, group, knot ♦ v 2 = **gather**, assemble, bunch, collect, flock, group

clutch v 1 = **seize**, catch, clasp, cling to, embrace, grab, grasp, grip, snatch

clutter v 1 = **litter**, scatter, strew ≠ **arrange** ♦ n 2 = **untidiness**, confusion, disarray, disorder, hotchpotch, jumble, litter, mess, muddle ≠ **order**

coach n 1 = **bus**, car, charabanc, vehicle 3 = **carriage** 4 = **instructor**, handler, teacher, trainer, tutor ♦ v 5 = **instruct**,

from a liquid to a semisolid mass.
coagulation n

coal n black rock consisting mainly of carbon, used as fuel. **coalfield** n area with coal under the ground.

coalesce ⊕ [koh–a–**less**] v come together, merge. **coalescence** n

coalition ⊕ [koh–a–**lish**–un] n temporary alliance, esp. between political parties.

coarse ⊕ adj 1 rough in texture. 2 unrefined, indecent. 3 of inferior quality. **coarseness** n

coast ⊕ n 1 place where the land meets the sea. ◆ v 2 move by momentum, without the use of power. **coastal** adj **coaster** n small mat placed under a glass. **coastguard** n 1 organization that aids ships and swimmers in trouble and prevents smuggling. 2 member of this. **coastline** n

coat ⊕ n 1 outer garment with long sleeves. 2 animal's fur or hair. 3 covering layer, e.g. *a coat of paint*. ◆ v 4 cover with a layer. **coating** n covering layer. **coat of arms** heraldic emblem of a family or institution.

coax ⊕ v 1 persuade gently. 2 obtain by persistent coaxing.

cob n 1 stalk of an ear of maize. 2 thickset type of horse. 3 round loaf of bread. 4 male swan.

cobalt n Chem brittle sllvery–white metallic element.

cobber n Aust or NZ informal friend.

cobble n cobblestone. **cobbler** n shoe mender. **cobblestone** n rounded stone used for paving. **cobble together** v put together clumsily.

cobra n venomous hooded snake of Asia and Africa.

cobweb n spider's web.

cocaine n addictive drug used as a narcotic and as an anaesthetic.

cochineal n red dye obtained from a Mexican insect, used for food colouring.

cock n 1 male bird, esp. of domestic fowl. 2 stopcock. ◆ v 3 draw back (the hammer of a gun) to firing position. 4 lift and turn (part of the body). **cockerel** n young domestic cock. **cock–a–hoop** adj in high spirits. **cock–and–bull story** improbable story.

cockatoo n crested parrot of Australia or the East Indies.

cockie, cocky n, pl **–kies** Aust & NZ informal farmer.

cockle n edible shellfish.

cockpit n 1 pilot's compartment in an aircraft. 2 driver's compartment in a racing car.

cockroach n beetle–like insect which is a household pest.

cocktail n 1 mixed alcoholic drink. 2 appetizer of seafood or mixed fruits.

cocky ⊕ adj **cockier**, **cockiest** conceited and overconfident. **cockily** adv **cockiness** n

cocoa n 1 powder made from the seed of

——————— THESAURUS ———————

drill, exercise, prepare, train, tutor

coalesce v = **blend**, amalgamate, combine, fuse, incorporate, integrate, merge, mix, unite

coalition n = **alliance**, amalgamation, association, bloc, combination, confederation, conjunction, fusion, merger, union

coarse adj 1 = **rough** ≠ **soft** 2 = **vulgar**, earthy, improper, indecent, indelicate, ribald, rude, smutty ≠ **fine** 3 = **crude**, homespun, impure, unfinished, unpolished, unprocessed, unpurified,

unrefined ≠ **smooth**

coast n 1 = **shore**, beach, border, coastline, seaboard, seaside ◆ v 2 = **cruise**, drift, freewheel, glide, sail, taxi

coat n 2 = **fur**, fleece, hair, hide, pelt, skin, wool 3 = **layer**, coating, covering, overlay ◆ v 4 = **cover**, apply, plaster, smear, spread

coax v 1 = **persuade**, allure, cajole, entice, prevail upon, sweet–talk (*inf*), talk into, wheedle

cocky adj = **overconfident**, arrogant, brash, cocksure, conceited, egotistical, full the cacao tree. **2** drink made from this powder.

coconut *n* **1** large hard fruit of a type of palm tree. **2** edible flesh of this fruit.

cocoon *n* **1** silky protective covering of a silkworm. **2** protective covering. ♦ *v* **3** wrap up tightly for protection.

cod *n* large food fish of the North Atlantic.

COD cash on delivery.

coda *n* final part of a musical composition.

code ❶ *n* **1** system of letters, symbols, or prearranged signals by which messages can be communicated secretly or briefly. **2** set of principles or rules. ♦ *v* **3** put into code. **codify** *v* **-fying, -fied** organize (rules or procedures) systematically. **codification** *n*

codeine [kode–een] *n* drug used as a painkiller.

coerce [koh–**urss**] *v* compel, force. **coercion** *n* **coercive** *adj*

coexist *v* exist together, esp. peacefully despite differences. **coexistence** *n*

C of E Church of England.

coffee *n* **1** drink made from the roasted and ground seeds of a tropical shrub. **2** beanlike seeds of this shrub. ♦ *adj* **3** medium brown.

coffer *n* **1** chest for valuables. ♦ *pl* **2** store of money.

coffin *n* box in which a corpse is buried or cremated.

cog *n* **1** one of the teeth on the rim of a gearwheel. **2** unimportant person in a big organization.

cogent ❶ [koh–jent] *adj* forcefully convincing. **cogency** *n*

cogitate ❶ [koj–it–tate] *v* think deeply about. **cogitation** *n*

cognac [kon–yak] *n* French brandy.

cognizance *n* knowledge, understanding. **cognizant** *adj*

cohabit *v* live together as husband and wife without being married. **cohabitation** *n*

cohere *v* **1** hold or stick together. **2** be logically connected or consistent. **coherence** *n* **coherent** *adj* **1** logical and consistent. **2** capable of intelligible speech. **coherently** *adv* **cohesion** *n* sticking together. **cohesive** *adj*

cohort *n* **1** band of associates. **2** tenth part of an ancient Roman legion.

coiffure *n* hairstyle. **coiffeur, coiffeuse** *n* hairdresser.

coil ❶ *v* **1** wind in loops. **2** move in a winding course. ♦ *n* **3** something coiled. **4** single loop of this. **5** coil-shaped contraceptive device inserted in the womb.

coin ❶ *n* **1** piece of metal money. **2** metal currency collectively. ♦ *v* **3** invent (a word or phrase). **4** make or stamp coins. **coinage** *n* coins collectively.

coincide ❶ *v* **1** happen at the same time. **2** agree or correspond exactly. **coincidence** *n* **1** occurrence of simultaneous or apparently connected events. **2** coinciding. **coincident** *adj* in agreement. **coincidental** *adj* resulting from coincidence. **coincidentally** *adv*

coke[1] *n* solid fuel left after gas has been distilled from coal.

coke[2] *n* Slang cocaine.

THESAURUS

of oneself, swaggering, vain

code *n* **1** = **cipher**, cryptograph **2** = **principles**, canon, convention, custom, ethics, etiquette, manners, maxim, regulations, rules, system

cogent *adj* = **convincing**, compelling, effective, forceful, influential, potent, powerful, strong, weighty

cogitate *v* = **think**, consider, contemplate, deliberate, meditate, mull over, muse,

ponder, reflect, ruminate

coil *v* **1** = **wind**, curl, loop, snake, spiral, twine, twist, wreathe, writhe

coin *n* **1, 2** = **money**, cash, change, copper, silver, specie ♦ *v* **3** = **invent**, create, fabricate, make up, originate **4** = **mint**, forge, mould

coincide *v* **1** = **occur simultaneously**, be concurrent, coexist, synchronize **2** = **agree**, accord, concur, correspond,

cola n dark brown fizzy soft drink.

colander n perforated bowl for straining or rinsing foods.

cold ⊕ adj 1 lacking heat. 2 lacking affection or enthusiasm. 3 (of a colour) giving an impression of coldness. 4 Slang unconscious, e.g. out cold. ◆ n 5 lack of heat. 6 mild illness causing a runny nose, sneezing, and coughing. **coldly** adv **coldness** n **cold–blooded** adj 1 cruel, unfeeling. 2 having a body temperature that varies according to the surrounding temperature. **cold feet** Slang nervousness, fear. **cold–shoulder** v treat with indifference. **cold war** political hostility between countries without actual warfare.

coleslaw n salad dish of shredded raw cabbage in a dressing.

colic n severe pains in the stomach and bowels. **colicky** adj

collaborate ⊕ v 1 work with another on a project. 2 cooperate with an enemy invader. **collaboration** n **collaborative** adj **collaborator** n

collage [kol–lahzh] n 1 art form in which various materials or objects are glued onto a surface. 2 picture made in this way.

collapse ⊕ v 1 fall down suddenly. 2 fail completely. 3 fold compactly. ◆ n 4 collapsing. 5 sudden failure or breakdown. **collapsible** adj

collar ⊕ n 1 part of a garment round the neck. 2 band put round an animal's neck. 3 cut of meat from an animal's neck. ◆ v 4 Informal seize, arrest. 5 catch in order to speak to. **collarbone** n bone joining the shoulder blade to the breastbone.

collate v gather together, examine, and put in order. **collation** n 1 collating. 2 light meal.

collateral n security pledged for the repayment of a loan.

colleague ⊕ n fellow worker, esp. in a profession.

collect ⊕ v 1 gather together. 2 accumulate (stamps etc.) as a hobby. 3 fetch. 4 receive payments of (taxes etc.). 5 regain control of (oneself). **collected** adj calm and controlled. **collection** n 1 things collected. 2 collecting. 3 sum of money collected. **collective** adj of or done by a group. **collector** n

college n 1 place of higher education. 2 group of people of the same profession or with special duties. **collegiate** adj

collide ⊕ v 1 crash together violently. 2 have an argument. **collision** n

collie n silky–haired sheepdog.

colliery n, pl –lieries coal mine. **collier** n 1 coal miner. 2 coal ship.

colloquial ⊕ adj suitable for informal speech or writing. **colloquialism** n colloquial word or phrase.

collusion n secret or illegal cooperation.

———————————[THESAURUS]———————————

harmonize, match, square, tally ≠ **part**

cold adj 1 = **chilly**, arctic, bleak, cool, freezing, frigid, frosty, frozen, icy, wintry ≠ **hot** 2 = **unfriendly**, aloof, distant, frigid, indifferent, reserved, standoffish ≠ **open** ◆ n 5 = **coldness**, chill, frigidity, frostiness, iciness

collaborate v 1 = **work together**, cooperate, join forces, participate, play ball (inf), team up 2 = **conspire**, collude, cooperate, fraternize

collapse v 1 = **fall down**, cave in, crumple, fall, fall apart at the seams, give way, subside 2 = **fail**, come to nothing, fold, founder, go belly–up (inf) ◆ n 4 = **falling down**, cave–in, disintegration, falling apart, ruin, subsidence 5 = **failure**, downfall, flop, slump

collar v 4 Inf = **seize**, apprehend, arrest, capture, catch, grab, nab (inf), nail (inf)

colleague n = **fellow worker**, ally, assistant, associate, collaborator, comrade, helper, partner, team–mate, workmate

collect v 1 = **assemble**, cluster, congregate, convene, flock together, rally ≠ **scatter** 2 = **gather**, accumulate, amass, assemble, heap, hoard, save, stockpile ≠ **spread**

collide v 1 = **crash**, clash, come into collision, meet head–on 2 = **conflict**, clash

collude v act in collusion.
cologne n mild perfume.
colon[1] n punctuation mark (:).
colon[2] n part of the large intestine connected to the rectum.
colonel n senior commissioned army or air-force officer.
colonnade n row of columns.
colony ⊕ n, pl **-nies** 1 group of people who settle in a new country but remain under the rule of their homeland. 2 territory occupied by a colony. 3 group of people or animals of the same kind living together. **colonial** adj, n (inhabitant) of a colony. **colonialism** n policy of acquiring and maintaining colonies. **colonist** n settler in a colony. **colonize** v make into a colony. **colonization** n
colossal ⊕ adj very large.
colour ⊕ n 1 appearance of things as a result of reflecting light. 2 substance that gives colour. 3 complexion. 4 flag of a country or regiment. 5 Sport badge or symbol denoting membership of a team. ◆ v 6 apply colour to. 7 influence (someone's judgment). 8 blush. **colourful** adj 1 with bright or varied colours. 2 vivid, distinctive. **colourfully** adv 1 **colourless** adj **colour-blind** adj unable to distinguish between certain colours.
colt n young male horse.
columbine n garden flower with five petals.

column ⊕ n 1 pillar. 2 vertical division of a newspaper page. 3 regular feature in a newspaper. 4 vertical arrangement of numbers. 5 narrow formation of troops. **columnist** n journalist who writes a regular feature in a newspaper.
coma ⊕ n state of deep unconsciousness. **comatose** adj 1 in a coma. 2 sound asleep.
comb ⊕ n 1 toothed implement for arranging the hair. 2 cock's crest. 3 honeycomb. ◆ v 4 use a comb on. 5 search with great care.
combat ⊕ n, v **-bating, -bated** fight, struggle. **combatant** n **combative** adj
combine ⊕ v 1 join together. ◆ n 2 association of people or firms for a common purpose. **combination** n 1 combining. 2 people or things combined. 3 set of numbers that opens a special lock. ◆ pl 4 old-fashioned undergarment with long sleeves and long legs. **combine harvester** machine that reaps and threshes grain in one process.
combustion n process of burning. **combustible** adj burning easily.
come ⊕ v **coming, came, come** 1 move towards a place, arrive. 2 occur. 3 reach a specified point or condition. 4 be produced. 5 (foll. by *from*) be born in. 6 become, e.g. *a dream come true.* **come**

colloquial adj = **informal**, conversational, demotic, everyday, familiar, idiomatic, vernacular
colony n 1 = **settlement**, community, dependency, dominion, outpost, possession, province, satellite state 2 = **territory**
colossal adj = **huge**, enormous, gigantic, immense, mammoth, massive, monumental, prodigious, vast
colour n 1 = **hue**, shade, tint 2 = **pigment**, colorant, dye, paint, tint ◆ v 6 = **paint**, dye, stain, tinge, tint 8 = **blush**, flush, redden
column n 1 = **pillar**, obelisk, post, shaft,

support, upright 5 = **line**, file, procession, rank, row
coma n = **unconsciousness**, oblivion, stupor, trance
comb v 4 = **untangle**, arrange, dress, groom 5 = **search**, forage, fossick, hunt (*Aust & NZ*), rake, ransack, rummage, scour, sift
① **combat** n = **fight**, action, battle, conflict, contest, encounter, engagement, skirmish, struggle, war, warfare ≠ **peace**
② **combat** v = **fight**, defy, do battle with, oppose, resist, withstand ≠ **support**
combine v 1 = **join together**, amalgamate, blend, connect, integrate, link, merge,

across v 1 meet or find by accident. 2 (often foll. by *as*) give an impression of (being). **comeback** n *Informal* 1 return to a former position. 2 retort. **comedown** n 1 decline in status. 2 disappointment. **comeuppance** n *Informal* deserved punishment.

comedy n, pl **–dies** 1 humorous play, film, or programme. 2 humorous aspect of events. **comedian, comedienne** n entertainer who tells jokes.

comely adj **–lier, –liest** *Old–fashioned* nice–looking.

comet n heavenly body with a long luminous tail.

comfort ⊕ n 1 physical ease or wellbeing. 2 consolation. 3 means of consolation. ◆ v 4 soothe, console. **comfortable** adj 1 giving comfort. 2 free from pain. 3 *Informal* well–off financially. **comfortably** adv **comforter** n

comic ⊕ adj 1 humorous, funny. 2 of comedy. ◆ n 3 comedian. 4 magazine containing strip cartoons. **comical** adj amusing. **comically** adv

comma n punctuation mark (,).

command ⊕ v 1 order. 2 have authority

over. 3 deserve and get. 4 look down over. ◆ n 5 authoritative instruction that something must be done. 6 authority to command. 7 knowledge. 8 military or naval unit with a specific function. **commandant** n officer commanding a military group. **commandeer** v seize for military use. **commander** n 1 military officer in command of a group or operation. 2 middle–ranking naval officer. **commandment** n command from God.

commando n, pl **–dos, –does** (member of) a military unit trained for swift raids in enemy territory.

commemorate ⊕ v honour the memory of. **commemoration** n **commemorative** adj

commence ⊕ v begin. **commencement** n

commend ⊕ v 1 praise. 2 recommend. **commendable** adj **commendably** adv **commendation** n

commensurate adj corresponding in degree, size, or value.

comment ⊕ n 1 remark. 2 talk, gossip. 3 explanatory note. ◆ v 4 make a comment. **commentary** n, pl **–taries** 1 spoken accompaniment to a broadcast or film. 2

───── THESAURUS ─────

mix, pool, unite ≠ **separate**

come v 1 = **arrive**, advance, appear, approach, draw near, materialize, move towards, near, reach, show up (*inf*), turn up (*inf*) 2 = **happen**, fall, occur, take place 4 = **result**, arise, be produced, emanate, emerge, flow, issue, originate

comedy n 1 = **light entertainment**, farce ≠ **opera** 2 = **humour**, fun, hilarity, jesting, joking ≠ **sadness**

comfort ⊕ n 1 = **luxury**, cosiness, ease, opulence, snugness, wellbeing 2 = **relief**, compensation, consolation, help, succour, support ≠ **discomfort** ◆ v 4 = **console**, commiserate with, hearten, reassure, soothe ≠ **trouble**

comic adj 1 = **funny**, amusing, comical, droll, farcical, humorous, jocular, witty ≠ **serious** ◆ n 3 = **comedian**, buffoon, clown, funny man, humorist, jester, wag,

wit

command v 1 = **order**, bid, charge, compel, demand, direct, require ≠ **ask** 2 = **have authority over**, control, dominate, govern, handle, head, lead, manage, rule, supervise ≠ **follow** ◆ n 5 = **order**, commandment, decree, demand, directive, instruction, requirement, ultimatum 6 = **authority**, charge, control, government, mana (*NZ*), management, mastery, power, rule, supervision

commemorate v = **remember**, celebrate, honour, immortalize, pay tribute to, recognize, salute

commence v = **begin**, embark on, enter upon, initiate, open, originate, start ≠ **end**

commend v 1 = **praise**, acclaim, applaud, approve, compliment, extol, speak highly of ≠ **attack** 2 = **recommend**

explanatory notes. **commentate** v provide a commentary. **commentator** n

commerce ❶ n buying and selling, trade. **commercial** adj 1 of commerce. 2 (of television or radio) paid for by advertisers. 3 having profit as the main aim. ◆ n 4 television or radio advertisement. **commercialization** n

commiserate ❶ v (foll. by with) express sympathy (for). **commiseration** n

commission ❶ n 1 piece of work that an artist is asked to do. 2 duty, task. 3 percentage paid to a salesperson for each sale made. 4 group of people appointed to perform certain duties. 5 committing of a crime. 6 Mil rank or authority officially given to an officer. ◆ v 7 place an order for. 8 Mil give a commission to. 9 grant authority to. **out of commission** not in working order. **commissioner** n 1 appointed official in a government department. 2 member of a commission.

commissionaire n uniformed doorman at a hotel, theatre, etc.

commit ❶ v -mitting, -mitted 1 perform (a crime or error). 2 pledge (oneself) to a course of action. 3 send (someone) to prison or hospital. **committal** n sending someone to prison or hospital. **commitment** n 1 dedication to a cause. 2 responsibility that restricts freedom of action.

committee n group of people appointed to perform a specified service or function.

commode n 1 seat with a hinged flap concealing a chamber pot. 2 chest of drawers.

commodity n, pl -ities article of trade.

commodore n senior commissioned officer in the navy.

common ❶ adj 1 occurring often. 2 belonging to two or more people. 3 public, general. 4 lacking in taste or manners. ◆ n 5 area of grassy land belonging to a community. **commonly** adv **commoner** n person who does not belong to the nobility. **common-law** adj (of a relationship) regarded as a marriage through being long-standing. **commonplace** adj 1 ordinary, everyday. ◆ n 2 trite remark. **common sense** good practical understanding.

commotion ❶ n noisy disturbance.

commune¹ ❶ n group of people who live together and share everything. **communal** adj shared. **communally** adv

commune² ❶ v (foll. by with) feel very close (to), e.g. communing with nature. **communion** n 1 sharing of thoughts or feelings. 2 (C–) Christian ritual of sharing consecrated bread and wine. 3 religious group with shared beliefs and practices.

THESAURUS

comment n 1 = **remark**, observation, statement 3 = **note**, annotation, commentary, explanation, exposition, illustration ◆ v 4 = **remark**, mention, note, observe, point out, say, utter

commerce n 1 = **trade**, business, dealing, exchange, traffic

commiserate v (foll. by with) = **sympathize**, console, feel for, pity

commission n 2 = **duty**, errand, mandate, mission, task 3 = **fee**, cut, percentage, rake-off (sl), royalties 4 = **committee**, board, commissioners, delegation, deputation, representatives ◆ v 7 = **appoint**, contract, engage, nominate, order, select 9 = **authorize**, delegate,

depute, empower

commit v 1 = **do**, carry out, enact, execute, perform, perpetrate 3 = **put in custody**, confine, imprison ≠ **free**

common adj 1 = **average**, commonplace, conventional, customary, everyday, familiar, frequent, habitual, ordinary, regular, routine, standard, stock, usual ≠ **strange** 2 = **collective**, communal, public ≠ **private** 3 = **popular**, accepted, general, prevailing, prevalent, universal, widespread ≠ **vulgar**, coarse, inferior, plebeian ≠ **cultured**

commotion n = **disturbance**, disorder, excitement, furore, fuss, hue and cry, rumpus, tumult, turmoil, upheaval, uproar

communicate ❶ v make known or share (information, thoughts, or feelings). **communicable** adj (of a disease) able to be passed on. **communicant** n person who receives Communion. **communicating** adj (of a door) joining two rooms. **communication** n 1 communicating. 2 thing communicated. ◆ pl 3 means of travelling or sending messages. **communicative** adj talking freely.

communiqué [kom–**mune**–ik–kay] n official announcement.

communism ❶ n 1 belief that all property and means of production should be shared by the community. 2 (**C–**) system of state control of the economy and society in some countries. **communist** n, adj

community ❶ n, pl –**ties** 1 all the people living in one district. 2 group with shared origins or interests. 3 the public, society.

commute v 1 travel daily to and from work. 2 reduce (a sentence) to a less severe one. **commuter** n person who commutes to and from work.

compact[1] ❶ adj 1 closely packed. 2 neatly arranged. 3 concise, brief. ◆ n 4 small flat case containing a mirror and face powder. ◆ v 5 pack closely together. **compact disc** small digital audio disc on which the sound is read by an optical laser system.

compact[2] ❶ n contract, agreement.

companion ❶ n 1 person who associates with or accompanies someone. 2 woman paid to live with another woman.

company ❶ n, pl –**nies** 1 business organization. 2 group of actors. 3 small unit of troops. 4 crew of a ship. 5 fact of being with someone. 6 gathering of people. 7 guest or guests. 8 person's associates.

compare ❶ v 1 examine (things) and point out the resemblances or differences. 2 (foll. by to) declare to be (like). 3 (foll. by with) be worthy of comparison. **comparable** adj **comparability** n **comparative** adj 1 relative. 2 involving comparison. 3 Grammar denoting the form of an adjective or adverb indicating more. ◆ n 4 Grammar comparative form of a word. **comparatively** adv **comparison** n 1 comparing. 2 similarity or equivalence.

——— THESAURUS ———

commune[1] n = **community**, collective, cooperative, kibbutz

commune[2] v (foll. by with) = **contemplate**, meditate on, muse on, ponder, reflect on

communicate v = **make known**, convey, declare, disclose, impart, inform, pass on, proclaim, transmit ≠ **sit on** (inf)

communism n (also cap.) = **socialism**, Bolshevism, collectivism, Marxism, state socialism

community n 1 = **populace**, commonwealth, residents, society, state 2 = **public**, general public, people 3 = **group**, brotherhood, company, society

compact[1] adj 1 = **closely packed**, compressed, condensed, dense, pressed together, solid, thick ≠ **loose** 3 = **brief**, compendious, concise, succinct, terse, to the point ≠ **lengthy** ◆ v 5 = **pack closely**,

compress, condense, cram, stuff, tamp ≠ **separate**

compact[2] n = **agreement**, arrangement, bargain, bond, contract, covenant, deal, pact, treaty, understanding

companion n 1 = **friend**, accomplice, ally, associate, cobber (Aust or old-fashioned NZ inf), colleague, comrade, consort, mate (inf), partner 2 = **escort**, aide, assistant, attendant, chaperon, squire

company n 1 = **business**, association, concern, corporation, establishment, firm, house, partnership, syndicate 5 = **companionship**, fellowship, presence, society 6 = **group**, assembly, band, collection, community, crowd, gathering, party, set 7 = **guests**, callers, party, visitors

compare v 1 = **weigh**, balance, contrast, juxtapose, set against 2 (foll. by to) = **liken to**, correlate to, equate to, identify with,

compartment ⊕ *n* **1** section of a railway carriage. **2** separate section.

compass ⊕ *n* **1** instrument for showing direction, with a needle that points north. **2** limits, range. ◆ *pl* **3** hinged instrument for drawing circles.

> ### ✓ WORD TIP
> The drawing instrument is technically *a pair of compasses* and some people insist on this usage.

compassion ⊕ *n* pity, sympathy. **compassionate** *adj*

compatible ⊕ *adj* able to exist, work, or be used together. **compatibility** *n*

compatriot *n* fellow countryman or countrywoman.

compel ⊕ *v* **–pelling, –pelled** force (to be or do).

compendium *n, pl* **–diums, –dia** selection of board games in one box. **compendious** *adj* brief but comprehensive.

compensate ⊕ *v* **1** make amends to (someone), esp. for injury or loss. **2** (foll. by *for*) cancel out (a bad effect).

compensation *n* payment to make up for loss or injury. **compensatory** *adj*

compere *n* **1** person who presents a stage, radio, or television show. ◆ *v* **2** be the compere of.

compete ⊕ *v* try to win or achieve (a prize, profit, etc.). **competition** *n* **1** competing. **2** event in which people compete. **3** people against whom one competes. **competitive** *adj* **competitor** *n*

competent ⊕ *adj* having the skill or knowledge to do something well. **competently** *adv* **competence** *n*

compile ⊕ *v* collect and arrange (information), esp. to make a book. **compilation** *n* **compiler** *n*

complacent ⊕ *adj* self-satisfied. **complacency** *n*

complain ⊕ *v* **1** express resentment or displeasure. **2** (foll. by *of*) say that one is suffering from (an illness). **complaint** *n* **1** complaining. **2** mild illness. **complainant** *n* *Law* plaintiff.

complement ⊕ *n* **1** thing that completes something. **2** complete amount or number. **3** *Grammar* word or words added

mention in the same breath as, parallel, resemble **3** (foll. by *with*) **= be on a par with**, approach, bear comparison, be in the same class as, be the equal of, compete with, equal, hold a candle to, match

compartment *n* **1 = carriage 2 = section**, alcove, bay, berth, booth, cubbyhole, cubicle, locker, niche, pigeonhole

compass *n* **2 = range**, area, boundary, circumference, extent, field, limit, reach, realm, scope

compassion *n* **= sympathy**, condolence, fellow feeling, humanity, kindness, mercy, pity, sorrow, tenderness, understanding

compatible *adj* **= harmonious**, adaptable, congruous, consistent, in harmony, in keeping, suitable ≠ **inappropriate**

compel *v* **= force**, coerce, constrain, dragoon, impel, make, oblige, railroad (*inf*)

compensate *v* **1 = recompense**, atone, make amends, make good, refund, reimburse, remunerate, repay **2** (foll. by *for*) **= cancel (out)**, balance, counteract, counterbalance, make up for, offset, redress

compete *v* **= contend**, be in the running, challenge, contest, fight, strive, struggle, vie

competent *adj* **= able**, adequate, capable, fit, proficient, qualified, suitable ≠ **inadequate**

compile *v* **= put together**, accumulate, amass, collect, cull, garner, gather, marshal, organize

complacent *adj* **= self-satisfied**, contented, pleased with oneself, resting on one's laurels, satisfied, serene, smug, unconcerned

complain *v* **1 = find fault**, bemoan, bewail, carp, deplore, groan, grouse, grumble, to a verb to complete the meaning. ◆ v 4 make complete. **complementary** adj

> **WORD TIP**
> Avoid confusion with *compliment*.

complete ❶ adj 1 thorough, absolute. 2 finished. 3 having all the necessary parts. ◆ v 4 finish. 5 make whole or perfect. **completely** adv **completeness** n **completion** n finishing.
complex ❶ adj 1 made up of parts. 2 complicated. ◆ n 3 whole made up of parts. 4 group of unconscious feelings that influences behaviour. **complexity** n
complexion ❶ n 1 skin of the face. 2 character, nature.
complicate ❶ v make or become complex or difficult to deal with. **complication** n
complicity n fact of being an accomplice in a crime.
compliment ❶ n 1 expression of praise. ◆

pl 2 formal greetings. ◆ v 3 praise. **complimentary** adj 1 expressing praise. 2 free of charge.

> **WORD TIP**
> Avoid confusion with *complement*.

comply ❶ v –plying, –plied (foll. by *with*) act in accordance (with).
component ❶ n, adj (being) part of a whole.
compose ❶ v 1 put together. 2 be the component parts of. 3 create (a piece of music or writing). 4 calm (oneself). 5 arrange artistically. **composer** n **composition** n way that something is put together or arranged.

> **WORD TIP**
> For sense 2 the usual idiom is: *it is/was composed of.*

lament, moan, whine, whinge (*inf*)
complement n 1 = **completion**, companion, consummation, counterpart, finishing touch, rounding–off, supplement 2 = **total**, aggregate, capacity, entirety, quota, totality, wholeness ◆ v 4 = **complete**, cap (*inf*), crown, round off, set off
complete adj 1 = **total**, absolute, consummate, outright, perfect, thorough, thoroughgoing, utter ≠ **mar** 2 = **finished**, accomplished, achieved, concluded, ended ≠ **unsettled** 3 = **entire**, all, faultless, full, intact, plenary, unbroken, whole ≠ **spoilt** ◆ v 4 = **finish**, close, conclude, crown, end, finalize, round off, settle, wrap up (*inf*) ≠ **start**
complex adj 1 = **compound**, composite, heterogeneous, manifold, multifarious, multiple 2 = **complicated**, convoluted, elaborate, intricate, involved, labyrinthine, tangled, tortuous ◆ n 3 = **structure**, aggregate, composite, network, organization, scheme, system ≠ **clear** 4 = **obsession**, fixation, fixed idea,

phobia, preoccupation
complexion n 1 = **skin**, colour, colouring, hue, pigmentation, skin tone 2 = **nature**, appearance, aspect, character, guise, light, look, make–up
complicate v = **make difficult**, confuse, entangle, involve, muddle, ravel
compliment n 1 = **praise**, bouquet, commendation, congratulations, eulogy, flattery, honour, tribute ≠ **blast** 2 ◆ pl = **greetings**, good wishes, regards, remembrances, respects, salutation ≠ **insult** ◆ v 3 = **praise**, commend, congratulate, extol, flatter, pay tribute to, salute, speak highly of
comply v (foll. by *with*) = **obey**, abide by, acquiesce, adhere to, conform to, follow, observe, submit, toe the line
① **component** n = **part**, constituent, element, ingredient, item, piece, unit
② **component** adj = **constituent**, inherent, intrinsic
compose v 1 = **put together**, build, comprise, constitute, construct, fashion, form, make, make up ≠ **destroy**

compos mentis ⓣ *adj Latin* sane.

compost *n* decayed plants used as a fertilizer.

compound¹ ⓣ *n, adj* 1 (thing, esp. chemical) made up of two or more combined parts or elements. ◆ *v* 2 combine or make by combining. 3 intensify, make worse.

compound² *n* fenced enclosure containing buildings.

comprehend ⓣ *v* understand. **comprehensible** *adj* **comprehension** *n* **comprehensive** *adj* 1 of broad scope, fully inclusive. ◆ *n* 2 comprehensive school. **comprehensive school** secondary school for children of all abilities.

compress ⓣ *v* [kum–**press**] 1 squeeze together. 2 make shorter. ◆ *n* [**kom**–press] 3 pad applied to stop bleeding or cool inflammation. **compression** *n* **compressor** *n* machine that compresses gas or air.

comprise ⓣ *v* be made up of or make up.

> ✓ **WORD TIP**
> *Comprise* is not followed by *of* but directly by its object.

compromise ⓣ [**kom**–prom–mize] *n* 1 settlement reached by concessions on each side. ◆ *v* 2 settle a dispute by making concessions. 3 put in a dishonourable position.

comptroller *n* financial controller.

compulsion ⓣ *n* 1 irresistible urge. 2 forcing by threats or violence. **compulsive** *adj* **compulsively** *adv* **compulsory** *adj* required by rules or laws.

compunction *n* feeling of guilt or shame.

compute ⓣ *v* calculate, esp. using a computer. **computation** *n* **computer** *n* electronic machine that stores and processes data. **computerize** *v* 1 adapt (a system) to be handled by computer. 2 store or process in a computer.

comrade ⓣ *n* 1 fellow member of a union or socialist political party. 2 companion. **comradeship** *n*

con¹ ⓣ *Informal* ◆ *n* 1 short for CONFIDENCE TRICK. ◆ *v* **conning, conned** 2 deceive, swindle.

con² *n* an argument against **pros and cons** see PRO¹.

concave ⓣ *adj* curving inwards.

— THESAURUS —

3 = **create**, contrive, devise, invent, produce, write 4 = **calm**, collect, control, pacify, placate, quiet, soothe 5 = **arrange**, adjust

compound¹ *n* 1 = **combination**, alloy, amalgam, blend, composite, fusion, medley, mixture, synthesis ≠ **element** ◆ *v* 2 = **combine**, amalgamate, blend, intermingle, mix, synthesize, unite ≠ **part** 3 = **intensify**, add to, aggravate, augment, complicate, exacerbate, heighten, magnify, worsen ≠ **moderate**

comprehend *v* = **understand**, apprehend, conceive, fathom, grasp, know, make out, perceive, see, take in ≠ **mistake**

compress *v* 1 = **squeeze**, concentrate, condense, contract, crush, press, squash 2 = **shorten**, abbreviate, contract

comprise *v* = **be composed of**, compose, consist of, constitute, contain, embrace, encompass, form, include, make up, take

in

compromise *n* 1 = **give–and–take**, accommodation, adjustment, agreement, concession, settlement, trade–off ≠ **difference** ◆ *v* 2 = **meet halfway**, adjust, agree, concede, give and take, go fifty–fifty (*inf*), settle, strike a balance ≠ **argue** 3 = **weaken**, discredit, dishonour, embarrass, expose, jeopardize, prejudice ≠ **support**

compulsion *n* 1 = **urge**, drive, necessity, need, obsession, preoccupation 2 = **force**, coercion, constraint, demand, duress, obligation, pressure, urgency

compute *v* = **calculate**, add up, count, enumerate, figure out, reckon, tally, total

comrade *n* 2 = **companion**, ally, associate, cobber (*Aust or old–fashioned NZ inf*), colleague, co–worker, fellow, friend, partner

con¹ *Inf n* 1 = **swindle**, deception, fraud,

conceal ⊕ v 1 cover and hide. 2 keep secret. **concealment** n

concede ⊕ v 1 admit to be true. 2 acknowledge defeat in (a contest or argument). 3 grant as a right.

conceit ⊕ n 1 too high an opinion of oneself. 2 far-fetched or clever comparison. **conceited** adj

conceive ⊕ v 1 imagine, think. 2 form in the mind. 3 become pregnant. **conceivable** adj imaginable, possible.

concentrate ⊕ v 1 fix one's attention or efforts on something. 2 bring or come together in large numbers in one place. 3 make (a liquid) stronger by removing water from it. ♦ n 4 concentrated liquid. **concentration** n 1 concentrating. 2 proportion of a substance in a mixture or solution. **concentration camp** prison camp for civilian prisoners, esp. in Nazi Germany.

concentric adj having the same centre.

concept ⊕ n abstract or general idea.

conceptual adj of or based on concepts. **conceptualize** v form a concept of.

conception ⊕ n 1 general idea. 2 becoming pregnant.

concern ⊕ n 1 anxiety, worry. 2 something that is of importance to someone. 3 business, firm. ♦ v 4 worry (someone). 5 involve (oneself). 6 be relevant or important to. **concerned** adj 1 interested, involved. 2 anxious, worried. **concerning** prep about, regarding.

concert n musical entertainment. **in concert** 1 working together. 2 (of musicians) performing live. **concerted** adj done together.

concession ⊕ n 1 grant of rights, land, or property. 2 reduction in price for a specified category of people. 3 conceding. 4 thing conceded. **concessionary** adj

conch n 1 shellfish with a large spiral shell. 2 its shell.

conciliate ⊕ v try to end a disagreement (with). **conciliation** n **conciliatory** adj

———————— THESAURUS ————————

scam (sl), sting (inf), trick ♦ v 2 = **swindle**, cheat, deceive, defraud, double-cross (inf), dupe, hoodwink, rip off (sl), trick

concave adj = **hollow**, indented

conceal v 1 = **hide**, bury, camouflage, cover, disguise, mask, obscure, screen ≠ **show**

concede v 1 = **admit**, accept, acknowledge, allow, confess, grant, own ≠ **deny** 2 = **give up**, cede, hand over, relinquish, surrender, yield

conceit n 1 = **self-importance**, arrogance, egotism, narcissism, pride, swagger, vanity 2 = **fancy**, fantasy, image, whim, whimsy

conceive v 1 = **imagine**, believe, comprehend, envisage, fancy, suppose, think, understand 2 = **think up**, contrive, create, design, devise, formulate 3 = **become pregnant**, become impregnated

concentrate v 1 = **focus one's attention on**, be engrossed in, put one's mind to, rack one's brains ≠ **disregard** 2 = **gather**, accumulate, centre, cluster, collect,

congregate, converge, focus, huddle ≠ **scatter**

concept n = **idea**, abstraction, conception, conceptualization, hypothesis, image, notion, theory, view

conception n 1 = **idea**, concept, design, image, notion, plan 2 = **impregnation**, fertilization, germination, insemination

concern n 1 = **worry**, anxiety, apprehension, burden, care, disquiet, distress 2 = **business**, affair, interest, job, responsibility, task 3 = **business**, company, corporation, enterprise, establishment, firm, organization ♦ v 4 = **worry**, bother, disquiet, distress, disturb, make anxious, perturb, trouble 6 = **be relevant to**, affect, apply to, bear on, interest, involve, pertain to, regard, touch

concession n 1, 2 = **grant**, adjustment, allowance, boon, compromise, indulgence, permit, privilege 3 = **conceding**, acknowledgment, admission, assent, confession, surrender,

concise ❶ *adj* brief and to the point.
concisely *adv* **concision, conciseness** *n*

conclave *n* 1 secret meeting. 2 private meeting of cardinals to elect a new pope.

conclude ❶ *v* 1 decide by reasoning. 2 end, finish. 3 arrange or settle finally. **conclusion** *n* 1 decision based on reasoning. 2 ending. 3 final arrangement or settlement. **conclusive** *adj* ending doubt, convincing. **conclusively** *adv*

concoct ❶ *v* 1 make up (a story or plan). 2 make by combining ingredients. **concoction** *n*

concord *n* state of peaceful agreement, harmony. **concordance** *n* 1 similarity or consistency. 2 index of words in a book. **concordant** *adj* agreeing.

concourse *n* 1 large open public place where people can gather. 2 large crowd.

concrete ❶ *n* 1 mixture of cement, sand, stone, and water, used in building. ◆ *adj* 2 made of concrete. 3 particular, specific. 4 real or solid, not abstract.

concubine [kon-kew-bine] *n* woman living with a man as his wife, but not married to him.

concur ❶ *v* –curring, –curred agree. **concurrence** *n* **concurrent** *adj* happening at the same time or place. **concurrently**

adv at the same time.

concussion *n* period of unconsciousness caused by a blow to the head.

condemn ❶ *v* 1 express disapproval of. 2 sentence, e.g. *he was condemned to death.* 3 force into an unpleasant situation. 4 declare unfit for use. **condemnation** *n* **condemnatory** *adj*

condense ❶ *v* 1 make shorter. 2 turn from gas into liquid. **condensation** *n* **condenser** *n Electricity* capacitor.

condescend ❶ *v* 1 behave patronizingly towards someone. 2 agree to do something, but as if doing someone a favour. **condescension** *n*

condiment *n* seasoning for food, such as salt or pepper.

condition ❶ *n* 1 particular state of being. 2 necessary requirement for something else to happen. 3 restriction, qualification. 4 state of health, physical fitness. 5 medical problem. ◆ *pl* 6 circumstances. ◆ *v* 7 train or influence to behave in a particular way. 8 treat with conditioner. **on condition that** only if. **conditional** *adj* depending on circumstances. **conditioner** *n* thick liquid used when washing to make hair or clothes feel softer

condolence *n* 1 sympathy. ◆ *pl* 2

——————— THESAURUS ———————

yielding

conciliate *v* = **pacify**, appease, clear the air, mediate, mollify, placate, reconcile, soothe, win over

concise *adj* = **brief**, compendious, condensed, laconic, pithy, short, succinct, terse

conclude *v* 1 = **decide**, assume, deduce, gather, infer, judge, surmise, work out
2 = **end**, cease, close, complete, finish, round off, terminate, wind up ≠ **start**
3 = **accomplish**, bring about, carry out, effect, pull off

concoct *v* 1 = **make up**, contrive, devise, formulate, hatch, invent, think up
2 = **prepare**, brew

concrete *adj* 3 = **specific**, definite, explicit ≠ **vague** 4 = **real**, actual, factual, material,

sensible, substantial, tangible ≠ **abstract**

concur *v* = **agree**, acquiesce, assent, consent

condemn *v* 1 = **disapprove**, blame, censure, criticize, damn, denounce, reproach, reprove, upbraid ≠ **approve**
2 = **sentence**, convict, damn, doom, pass sentence on ≠ **free**

condense *v* 1 = **abridge**, abbreviate, compress, concentrate, epitomize, shorten, summarize ≠ **increase**
2 = **concentrate**, boil down, reduce, thicken ≠ **thin (out)**

condescend *v* 1 = **patronize**, talk down to
2 = **lower oneself**, bend, deign, humble *or* demean oneself, see fit, stoop

condition *n* 1 = **state**, circumstances, lie of the land, position, shape, situation, state expression of sympathy.

condom n rubber sheath worn on the penis or in the vagina during sexual intercourse to prevent conception or infection.

condone ❶ v overlook or forgive (wrongdoing).

conducive adj (foll. by to) likely to lead (to).

conduct ❶ n 1 management of an activity. 2 behaviour. ♦ v 3 carry out (a task). 4 behave (oneself). 5 direct (musicians) by moving the hands or a baton. 6 lead, guide. 7 transmit (heat or electricity). **conduction** n transmission of heat or electricity. **conductivity** n ability to transmit heat or electricity. **conductive** adj **conductor** n 1 person who conducts musicians. 2 (fem **conductress**) official on a bus who collects fares. 3 something that conducts heat or electricity.

conduit [kon–dew–it] n channel or tube for fluid or cables.

cone n 1 object with a circular base, tapering to a point. 2 cone–shaped ice–cream wafer. 3 plastic cone used as a traffic marker on the roads. 4 scaly fruit of a conifer tree.

confederate n 1 member of a confederacy. 2 accomplice. ♦ adj 3 united, allied. ♦ v 4 unite in a confederacy. **confederacy** n, pl –cies union of states or people for a common purpose. **confederation** n alliance of political units.

confer ❶ v –ferring, –ferred 1 discuss together. 2 grant, give. **conference** n meeting for discussion. **conferment** n

confess ❶ v 1 admit (a fault or crime). 2 admit to be true. 3 declare (one's sins) to God or a priest, in hope of forgiveness. **confession** n 1 something confessed. 2 confessing. **confessional** n small stall in which a priest hears confessions. **confessor** n priest who hears confessions.

confetti n small pieces of coloured paper thrown at weddings.

confide ❶ v 1 tell someone (a secret). 2 entrust. **confidence** n 1 trust. 2 self–assurance. 3 something confided. **in confidence** as a secret. **confidence trick** swindle involving gaining a person's trust in order to cheat him or her. **confident** adj sure, esp. of oneself. **confidential** adj 1 private, secret. 2 entrusted with someone's secret affairs. **confidentiality** n

configuration n arrangement of parts.

confine ❶ v 1 keep within bounds. 2 restrict the free movement of. **confines** pl

of affairs 2, 3 = **requirement**, limitation, prerequisite, proviso, qualification, restriction, rider, stipulation, terms 4 = **health**, fettle, fitness, kilter, order, shape, state of health, trim 5 = **ailment**, complaint, infirmity, malady, problem, weakness ♦ pl 6 = **circumstances**, environment, milieu, situation, surroundings, way of life ♦ v 7 = **accustom**, adapt, equip, prepare, ready, tone up, train, work out

condone v = **overlook**, excuse, forgive, let pass, look the other way, make allowance for, pardon, turn a blind eye to

conduct n 1 = **management**, administration, control, direction, guidance, handling, organization, running, supervision 2 = **behaviour**, attitude, bearing, demeanour, deportment, manners, ways ♦ v 3 = **carry out**, administer, control, direct, handle, manage, organize, preside over, run, supervise 4 = **behave**, acquit, act, carry, comport, deport 6 = **accompany**, convey, escort, guide, lead, steer, usher

confer v 1 = **discuss**, consult, converse, deliberate, discourse, talk 2 = **grant**, accord, award, bestow, give, hand out, present

confess v 1 = **admit**, acknowledge, come clean (inf), concede, confide, disclose, divulge, own up ≠ **cover up** 2 = **declare**, affirm, assert, confirm, profess, reveal

confide v 1 = **tell**, admit, confess, disclose, divulge, impart, reveal, whisper 2 = **entrust**, commend, commit, consign *n* boundaries, limits. **confinement** *n* 1 being confined. 2 period of childbirth.

confirm ❶ *v* 1 prove to be true. 2 reaffirm, strengthen. 3 administer the rite of confirmation to. **confirmation** *n* 1 confirming. 2 something that confirms. 3 *Christianity* rite that admits a baptized person to full church membership. **confirmed** *adj* firmly established in a habit or condition.

confiscate ❶ *v* seize (property) by authority. **confiscation** *n*

conflict ❶ *n* 1 disagreement. 2 struggle or fight. ◆ *v* 3 be incompatible.

conform ❶ *v* 1 comply with accepted standards or customs. 2 (foll. by *to* or *with*) be like or in accordance with. **conformist** *n, adj* (person) complying with accepted standards or customs. **conformity** *n* compliance with accepted standards or customs.

confound ❶ *v* 1 astound, bewilder. 2 confuse. **confounded** *adj Informal* damned.

confront ❶ *v* come face to face with. **confrontation** *n* serious argument.

confuse ❶ *v* 1 mix up. 2 perplex, disconcert. 3 make unclear. **confusion** *n*

conga *n* 1 dance performed by a number of people in single file. 2 large single-headed drum played with the hands.

congeal *v* (of a liquid) become thick and sticky.

congenial ❶ *adj* 1 pleasant, agreeable. 2 having similar interests and attitudes. **congeniality** *n*

congenital ❶ *adj* (of a condition) existing from birth. **congenitally** *adv*

conger *n* large sea eel.

conglomerate *n* 1 large corporation made up of many companies. 2 thing made up of several different elements. ◆ *v* 3 form into a mass. ◆ *adj* 4 made up of several different elements. **conglomeration** *n*

congratulate ❶ *v* express one's pleasure to (someone) at his or her good fortune or success. **congratulations** *pl n, interj* **congratulatory** *adj*

congregate ❶ *v* gather together in a crowd. **congregation** *n* people who attend a church. **congregational** *adj*

congress ❶ *n* 1 formal meeting for

confine *v* 1 = **imprison**, cage, enclose, incarcerate, intern, shut up 2 = **restrict**, hem in, hold back, keep, limit

confirm *v* 1 = **prove**, authenticate, bear out, corroborate, endorse, ratify, substantiate, validate, verify 2 = **strengthen**, buttress, establish, fix, fortify, reinforce

confiscate *v* = **seize**, appropriate, commandeer, impound, sequester, sequestrate

conflict *n* 1 = **opposition**, antagonism, difference, disagreement, discord, dissension, friction, hostility, strife ≠ **accord** 2 = **battle**, clash, combat, contest, encounter, fight, strife, war ≠ **peace** ◆ *v* 3 = **be incompatible**, be at variance, clash, collide, differ, disagree, interfere ≠ **agree**

conform *v* 1 = **comply**, adapt, adjust, fall in with, follow, obey, toe the line 2 (foll.

by *to* or *with*) = **agree**, accord, correspond, harmonize, match, suit, tally

confound *v* 1 = **bewilder**, astound, baffle, dumbfound, flummox, mystify, nonplus, perplex

confront *v* = **face**, accost, challenge, defy, encounter, oppose, stand up to, tackle

confuse *v* 1 = **mix up**, disarrange, disorder, jumble, mingle, muddle, ravel 2 = **bewilder**, baffle, bemuse, faze, flummox, mystify, nonplus, perplex, puzzle

congenial *adj* 1 = **pleasant**, affable, agreeable, companionable, favourable, friendly, genial, kindly 2 = **compatible**, kindred, like-minded, sympathetic, well-suited

congenital *adj* = **inborn**, immanent, inbred, inherent, innate, natural

congratulate *v* = **compliment**, pat on the back, wish joy to discussion. 2 (**C–**) federal parliament of the US. **congressional** *adj*

conifer *n* cone–bearing tree, such as the fir or pine. **coniferous** *adj*

conjecture ⊕ *n, v* guess. **conjectural** *adj*

conjugal ⊕ *adj* of marriage.

conjugate *v* give the inflections of (a verb). **conjugation** *n* complete set of inflections of a verb.

conjunction *n* 1 combination. 2 simultaneous occurrence of events. 3 part of speech joining words, phrases, or clauses.

conjunctivitis *n* inflammation of the membrane covering the eyeball and inner eyelid. **conjunctiva** *n* this membrane.

conjure ⊕ *v* perform tricks that appear to be magic. **conjuror** *n* **conjure up** *v* produce as if by magic.

conker *n* Informal nut of the horse chestnut.

connect ⊕ *v* 1 join together. 2 associate in the mind. **connection, connexion** *n* 1 relationship, association. 2 link or bond. 3 opportunity to transfer from one public

vehicle to another. 4 influential acquaintance. **connective** *adj*

connive ⊕ *v* 1 (foll. by *at*) allow (wrongdoing) by ignoring it. 2 conspire. **connivance** *n*

connoisseur ⊕ [kon–noss–**sir**] *n* person with special knowledge of the arts, food, or drink.

conquer ⊕ *v* 1 defeat. 2 overcome (a difficulty). 3 take (a place) by force. **conqueror** *n* **conquest** *n* 1 conquering. 2 person or thing conquered.

conscience ⊕ *n* sense of right or wrong as regards thoughts and actions.

conscious ⊕ *adj* 1 alert and awake. 2 aware. 3 deliberate, intentional. **consciousness** *n*

conscript *n* 1 person enrolled for compulsory military service. ◆ *v* 2 enrol (someone) for compulsory military service. **conscription** *n*

consecrate ⊕ *v* 1 make sacred. 2 dedicate to a specific purpose. **consecration** *n*

consecutive ⊕ *adj* in unbroken succession. **consecutively** *adv*

——————— THESAURUS ———————

congregate *v* = **come together**, assemble, collect, convene, converge, flock, gather, mass, meet

congress *n* 1 = **meeting**, assembly, conclave, conference, convention, council, legislature, parliament

① **conjecture** *n* = **guess**, hypothesis, shot in the dark, speculation, supposition, surmise, theory

② **conjecture** *v* = **guess**, hypothesize, imagine, speculate, suppose, surmise, theorize

conjugal *adj* = **marital**, bridal, connubial, married, matrimonial, nuptial, wedded

conjure *v* = **perform tricks**, juggle

connect *v* 1 = **join**, affix, attach, couple, fasten, link, unite ≠ **part**

connive *v* 1 (foll. by *at*) = **turn a blind eye to**, abet, disregard, let pass, look the other way, overlook, wink at 2 = **conspire**, collude, cook up (*inf*), intrigue, plot, scheme

connoisseur *n* = **expert**, aficionado, appreciator, authority, buff (*inf*), devotee, fundi (*S Afr*), judge, mana (*NZ*)

conquer *v* 1 = **defeat**, beat, crush, get the better of, master, overcome, overpower, overthrow, quell, subjugate, vanquish ≠ **lose** 3 = **seize**, acquire, annex, obtain, occupy, overrun, win

conscience *n* = **principles**, moral sense, scruples, sense of right and wrong, still small voice

conscious *adj* 1 = **alert**, awake, responsive ≠ **unconscious** 2 = **aware**, alive to, sensible, sentient ≠ **asleep** 3 = **deliberate**, calculated, intentional, knowing, premeditated, self–conscious, studied, wilful ≠ **unconscious**

consecrate *v* 1 = **sanctify**, hallow, ordain, venerate 2 = **dedicate**, devote, set apart

consecutive *adj* = **successive**, in sequence, in turn, running, sequential, succeeding, uninterrupted

consensus 🜚 *n* general agreement.

> ✓ **WORD TIP**
> Note the spelling of this word, often confused with that of *census*. In view of its meaning, It is redundant to say 'a consensus of opinion'.

consent 🜚 *n* 1 agreement, permission. ♦ *v* 2 (foll. by *to*) permit, agree to.

consequence 🜚 *n* 1 result, effect. 2 importance. **consequent** *adj* resulting. **consequently** *adv* as a result, therefore. **consequential** *adj* important.

conserve 🜚 *v* 1 protect from harm, decay, or loss. 2 preserve (fruit) with sugar. ♦ *n* 3 jam containing large pieces of fruit. **conservancy** *n* environmental conservation. **conservation** *n* 1 protection of natural resources and the environment. 2 conserving. **conservationist** *n* **conservative** *adj* opposing change.

consider 🜚 *v* 1 regard as. 2 think about. 3 be considerate of. 4 discuss. 5 look at. **considerable** *adj* large in amount or degree. **considerably** *adv* **considerate** *adj* thoughtful towards others. **considerately** *adv* **consideration** *n* 1 careful thought. 2 fact that should be considered. 3 thoughtfulness. 4 payment for a service. **considering** *prep* taking (a specified fact) into account.

consign *v* 1 put somewhere. 2 send (goods). **consignment** *n* shipment of goods.

consist 🜚 *v* 1 **consist of** be made up of. 2 **consist in** have as its main or only feature. **consistent** *adj* unchanging, constant.

console[1] 🜚 *v* comfort in distress. **consolation** *n* 1 consoling. 2 person or thing that consoles.

console[2] *n* 1 panel of controls for electronic equipment. 2 cabinet for a television or audio equipment. 3 ornamental wall bracket. 4 part of an organ containing the pedals, stops, and keys.

consolidate 🜚 *v* 1 make or become stronger or more stable. 2 combine into a whole. **consolidation** *n*

consommé [kon-**som**–may] *n* thin clear meat soup.

consonant *n* 1 speech sound made by partially or completely blocking the breath stream, such as *b* or *f*. 2 letter representing this. ♦ *adj* 3 (foll. by *with*) agreeing (with). **consonance** *n* agreement, harmony.

consort 🜚 *v* 1 (foll. by *with*) keep company

consensus *n* = **agreement**, assent, common consent, concord, general agreement, harmony, unanimity, unity

consent *n* 1 = **agreement**, acquiescence, approval, assent, compliance, go–ahead (*inf*), O.K. or okay (*inf*), permission, sanction ≠ **refusal** ♦ *v* 2 = **agree**, acquiesce, allow, approve, assent, concur, permit ≠ **refuse**

consequence *n* 1 = **result**, effect, end result, issue, outcome, repercussion, sequel, upshot 2 = **importance**, account, concern, import, moment, significance, value, weight

conserve *v* 1 = **protect**, hoard, husband, keep, nurse, preserve, save, store up, take care of, use sparingly ≠ **spend**

consider *v* 1 = **think**, believe, deem, hold

to be, judge, rate, regard as 2 = **think about**, cogitate, contemplate, deliberate, meditate, ponder, reflect, ruminate, turn over in one's mind, weigh 3 = **bear in mind**, keep in view, make allowance for, reckon with, remember, respect, take into account

consist *v* 1 **consist of** = **be made up of**, amount to, be composed of, comprise, contain, embody, include, incorporate, involve 2 **consist in** = **lie in**, be expressed by, be found *or* contained in, inhere in, reside in

console[1] *v* = **comfort**, calm, cheer, encourage, express sympathy for, soothe

consolidate *v* 1 = **strengthen**, fortify, reinforce, secure, stabilize 2 = **combine**, amalgamate, federate, fuse, join, unite (with). ◆ *n* 2 husband or wife of a monarch.

conspicuous ❶ *adj* 1 clearly visible. 2 noteworthy, striking.

conspire ❶ *v* 1 plan a crime together in secret. 2 act together as if by design. **conspiracy** *n* 1 conspiring. 2 (*pl* **–cies**) plan made by conspiring. **conspirator** *n* **conspiratorial** *adj*

constable *n* police officer of the lowest rank. **constabulary** *n, pl* **–laries** police force of an area.

constant ❶ *adj* 1 continuous. 2 unchanging. 3 faithful. ◆ *n* 4 unvarying quantity. 5 something that stays the same. **constantly** *adv* **constancy** *n*

constellation *n* group of stars.

consternation ❶ *n* anxiety or dismay.

constipation *n* difficulty in defecating.

constituent ❶ *n* 1 member of a constituency. 2 component part. ◆ *adj* 3 forming part of a whole. **constituency** *n, pl* **–cies** 1 area represented by a Member of Parliament. 2 voters in such an area.

constitute ❶ *v* form, make up. **constitution** *n* 1 principles on which a state is governed. 2 physical condition.

3 structure. **constitutional** *adj* 1 of a constitution. 2 in accordance with a political constitution. ◆ *n* 3 walk taken for exercise. **constitutionally** *adv*

constrain ❶ *v* 1 compel, force. 2 limit, restrict. **constraint** *n*

construct ❶ *v* build or put together. **construction** *n* 1 constructing. 2 thing constructed. 3 interpretation. 4 *Grammar* way in which words are arranged in a sentence, clause, or phrase. **constructive** *adj* (of advice, criticism, etc.) useful and helpful. **constructively** *adv*

construe *v* **–struing, –strued** interpret.

consul *n* 1 official representing a state in a foreign country. 2 one of the two chief magistrates in ancient Rome. **consular** *adj* **consulate** *n* workplace or position of a consul.

consult ❶ *v* go to for advice or information. **consultant** *n* 1 specialist doctor with a senior position in a hospital. 2 specialist who gives professional advice. **consultancy** *n, pl* **–cies** work or position of a consultant. **consultation** *n* (meeting for) consulting. **consultative** *adj* giving advice.

consume ❶ *v* 1 eat or drink. 2 use up. 3

———————— THESAURUS ————————

consort *v* 1 (foll. by *with*) = **associate**, fraternize, go around with, hang about, around *or* out with, keep company, mix ◆ *n* 2 = **spouse**, companion, husband, partner, wife

conspicuous *adj* 1 = **obvious**, blatant, clear, evident, noticeable, patent, salient ≠ **hidden** 2 = **noteworthy**, illustrious, notable, outstanding, prominent, remarkable, salient, signal, striking

conspire *v* 1 = **plot**, contrive, intrigue, machinate, manoeuvre, plan, scheme 2 = **work together**, combine, concur, contribute, cooperate, tend

constant *adj* 1 = **continuous**, ceaseless, incessant, interminable, nonstop, perpetual, sustained, unrelenting ≠ **occasional** 2 = **unchanging**, even, fixed, invariable, permanent, stable, steady, uniform, unvarying ≠ **changing**

3 = **faithful**, devoted, loyal, stalwart, staunch, true, trustworthy, trusty ≠ **fickle**

consternation *n* = **dismay**, alarm, anxiety, distress, dread, fear, trepidation

constituent *n* 1 = **voter**, elector 2 = **component**, element, factor, ingredient, part, unit ◆ *adj* 3 = **component**, basic, elemental, essential, integral

constitute *v* = **make up**, compose, comprise, establish, form, found, set up

constrain *v* 1 = **force**, bind, coerce, compel, impel, necessitate, oblige, pressurize 2 = **restrict**, check, confine, constrict, curb, restrain, straiten

construct *v* = **build**, assemble, compose, create, fashion, form, make, manufacture, put together, shape ≠ **level**

consult *v* = **ask**, compare notes, confer, pick (someone's) brains, question, refer to, destroy. **4** obsess. **consumer** *n* person who buys goods or uses services. **consumption** *n* **1** amount consumed. **2** consuming. **3** *Old–fashioned* tuberculosis. **consumptive** *n, adj Old–fashioned* (person) having tuberculosis.

consummate ⊕ [kon–**sum**–mate] *v* **1** make (a marriage) legal by sexual intercourse. **2** complete or fulfil. ◆ *adj* [kon–**sum**–mit] **3** supremely skilled. **4** complete, extreme. **consummation** *n*

cont. continued.

contact ⊕ *n* **1** communicating. **2** touching. **3** useful acquaintance. **4** connection between two electrical conductors in a circuit. ◆ *v* **5** get in touch with. **contact lens** lens placed on the eyeball to correct defective vision.

contain ⊕ *v* **1** hold or be capable of holding. **2** consist of. **3** control, restrain. **container** *n* **1** object used to hold or store things in. **2** large standard–sized box for transporting cargo by lorry or ship.

containment *n* prevention of the spread of something harmful.

contaminate ⊕ *v* **1** make impure, pollute. **2** make radioactive. **contaminant** *n* contaminating substance. **contamination** *n*

contemplate ⊕ *v* **1** think deeply. **2** consider as a possibility. **3** gaze at. **contemplation** *n* **contemplative** *adj*

contemporary ⊕ *adj* **1** present–day, modern. **2** living or occurring at the same time. ◆ *n, pl* **–raries 3** person or thing living or occurring at the same time as another. **contemporaneous** *adj* happening at the same time.

contempt ⊕ *n* **1** dislike and disregard. **2** open disrespect for the authority of a court. **contemptible** *adj* deserving contempt. **contemptuous** *adj* showing contempt.

contend ⊕ *v* **1** (foll. by *with*) deal with. **2** state, assert. **3** compete. **contender** *n*

content[1] **⊕** *n* **1** meaning or substance of a

take counsel, turn to

consume *v* **1** = **eat**, devour, eat up, gobble (up), put away, swallow **2** = **use up**, absorb, dissipate, exhaust, expend, spend, squander, waste **3** = **destroy**, annihilate, demolish, devastate, lay waste, ravage **4** = **obsess**, absorb, dominate, eat up, engross, monopolize, preoccupy

consummate *v* **2** = **complete**, accomplish, conclude, crown, end, finish, fulfil ≠ **start** ◆ *adj* **3** = **skilled**, accomplished, matchless, perfect, polished, practised, superb, supreme **4** = **complete**, absolute, conspicuous, extreme, supreme, total, utter

contact *n* **1** = **communication**, association, connection **2** = **touch**, contiguity **3** = **acquaintance**, connection ◆ *v* **5** = **get** or **be in touch with**, approach, call, communicate with, reach, speak to, write to

contain *v* **1** = **hold**, accommodate, enclose, have capacity for, incorporate, seat **2** = **include**, comprehend, comprise,

consist of, embody, embrace, involve **3** = **restrain**, control, curb, hold back, hold in, keep a tight rein on, repress, stifle

contaminate *v* **1** = **pollute**, adulterate, befoul, corrupt, defile, infect, stain, taint, tarnish

contemplate *v* **1** = **think about**, consider, deliberate, meditate, muse over, ponder, reflect upon, ruminate (upon) **2** = **consider**, envisage, expect, foresee, intend, plan, think of **3** = **look at**, examine, eye up, gaze at, inspect, regard, stare at, study, survey, view

contemporary *adj* **1** = **modern**, à la mode, current, newfangled, present, present–day, recent, up–to–date ≠ **old 2** = **coexisting**, concurrent, contemporaneous ◆ *n* **3** = **peer**, fellow

contempt *n* **1** = **scorn**, derision, disdain, disregard, disrespect, mockery, slight

contend *v* **1** (foll. by *with*) = **compete**, clash, contest, fight, jostle, strive, struggle, vie **2** = **argue**, affirm, allege, assert, dispute, hold, maintain piece of writing. **2** amount of a substance in a mixture. ◆ *pl* **3** what something contains. **4** list of chapters at the front of a book.

content² 🅣 *adj* **1** satisfied with things as they are. ◆ *v* **2** make (someone) content. ◆ *n* **3** happiness and satisfaction. **contented** *adj* **contentment** *n*

contest 🅣 *n* **1** competition or struggle. ◆ *v* **2** dispute, object to. **3** fight or compete for. **contestant** *n*

context 🅣 *n* **1** circumstances of an event or fact. **2** words before and after a word or sentence that help make its meaning clear. **contextual** *adj*

continent¹ *n* one of the earth's large masses of land. **continental** *adj*

continent² *adj* **1** able to control one's bladder and bowels. **2** sexually restrained. **continence** *n*

contingent *n* **1** group of people that represents or is part of a larger group. ◆ *adj* **2** (foll. by *on*) dependent on (something uncertain). **contingency** *n, pl* **–cies** something that may happen.

continue 🅣 *v* **–tinuing, –tinued 1** (cause to) remain in a condition or place. **2** carry

on (doing something). **3** resume. **continual** *adj* **1** constant. **2** recurring frequently. **continually** *adv* **continuance** *n* continuing. **continuation** *n* **1** continuing. **2** part added. **continuity** *n, pl* smooth development or sequence. **continuous** *adj* continuing uninterrupted.

contort *v* twist out of shape. **contortion** *n* **contortionist** *n* performer who contorts his or her body to entertain.

contour *n* **1** outline. **2** (also **contour line**) line on a map joining places of the same height.

contra– *prefix* against or contrasting, e.g. *contraflow*.

contraband 🅣 *n, adj* smuggled (goods).

contraception *n* prevention of pregnancy by artificial means. **contraceptive** *n* **1** device used or pill taken to prevent pregnancy. ◆ *adj* **2** preventing pregnancy.

contract 🅣 *n* **1** (document setting out) a formal agreement. ◆ *v* **2** make a formal agreement (to do something). **3** make or become smaller or shorter. **4** catch (an illness). **contraction** *n* **contractor** *n* firm that supplies materials or labour, esp. for building. **contractual** *adj*

——————— THESAURUS ———————

content¹ *n* **1** = **meaning**, essence, gist, significance, substance **2** = **amount**, capacity, load, measure, size, volume ◆ *pl* **3** = **constituents**, elements, ingredients, load

content² *adj* **1** = **satisfied**, agreeable, at ease, comfortable, contented, fulfilled **2** = **willing to accept** ◆ *v* **2** = **satisfy**, appease, humour, indulge, mollify, placate, please ◆ *n* **3** = **satisfaction**, comfort, contentment, ease, gratification, peace of mind, pleasure

contest *n* **1** = **competition**, game, match, tournament, trial ◆ *v* **2** = **dispute**, argue, call in *or* into question, challenge, debate, doubt, object to, oppose, question **3** = **compete**, contend, fight, strive, vie

context *n* **1** = **circumstances**, ambience, background, conditions, frame of reference, situation

continue *v* **1** = **remain**, abide, carry on, endure, last, live on, persist, stay, survive ≠ **leave 2** = **keep on**, carry on, go on, maintain, persevere, persist in, stick at, sustain ≠ **stop 3** = **resume**, carry on, pick up where one left off, proceed, recommence, return to, take up ≠ **stop**

① **contraband** *n* = **smuggling**, black–marketing, bootlegging, trafficking

② **contraband** *adj* = **smuggled**, banned, bootleg, forbidden, hot (*inf*), illegal, illicit, prohibited, unlawful

contract *n* **1** = **agreement**, arrangement, bargain, commitment, covenant, pact, settlement ◆ *v* **2** = **agree**, bargain, come to terms, commit oneself, covenant, negotiate, pledge ≠ **refuse 3** = **shorten**, abbreviate, curtail, diminish, dwindle, lessen, narrow, reduce, shrink, shrivel ≠ **increase 4** = **catch**, acquire, be afflicted

contradict ⊕ v 1 declare the opposite of (a statement) to be true. 2 be at variance with. **contradiction** n **contradictory** adj

contraflow n flow of traffic going alongside but in an opposite direction to the usual flow.

contralto n, pl **-tos** (singer with) the lowest female voice.

contraption ⊕ n strange-looking device.

contrary ⊕ n 1 complete opposite. ◆ adj 2 opposed, completely different. 3 perverse, obstinate. ◆ adv 4 in opposition. **contrarily** adv **contrariness** n

contrast ⊕ n 1 obvious difference. 2 person or thing very different from another. ◆ v 3 compare in order to show differences. 4 (foll. by with) be very different (from).

contravene v break (a rule or law). **contravention** n

contribute ⊕ v 1 give for a common purpose or fund. 2 (foll. by to) be partly responsible (for). **contribution** n

contributor n **contributory** adj

contrite ⊕ adj sorry and apologetic. **contritely** adv **contrition** n

contrive ⊕ v 1 make happen. 2 devise or construct. **contrivance** n 1 device. 2 plan. 3 contriving. **contrived** adj planned or artificial.

control ⊕ n 1 power to direct something. 2 curb or check. ◆ pl 3 instruments used to operate a machine. ◆ v **-trolling**, **-trolled** 4 have power over. 5 limit, restrain. 6 regulate, operate. **controllable** adj **controller** n

controversy ⊕ n, pl **-sies** fierce argument or debate. **controversial** adj causing controversy.

> ✓ **WORD TIP**
> Note that the stress used always to be on the first syllable, 'kon', but is now more often on the second syllable, 'trov'.

━━━ THESAURUS ━━━

with, develop, get, go down with, incur ≠ **avoid**

contradict v 1 = **deny**, challenge, rebut 2 = **be at variance with**, belie, controvert, fly in the face of, negate

contraption n Inf = **device**, apparatus, contrivance, gadget, instrument, mechanism

contrary n 1 = **opposite**, antithesis, converse, reverse ◆ adj 2 = **opposed**, adverse, clashing, contradictory, counter, discordant, hostile, inconsistent, opposite, paradoxical ≠ **consistent** 3 = **perverse**, awkward, cantankerous, difficult, disobliging, intractable, obstinate, stroppy (Brit sl), unaccommodating ≠ **willing**

contrast n 1 = **difference**, comparison, disparity, dissimilarity, distinction, divergence, opposition ◆ v 3 = **compare**, differentiate, distinguish, set in opposition, set off 4 (foll. by with) = **differ**, oppose

contribute v 1 = **give**, add, bestow, chip in (inf), donate, provide, subscribe, supply 2 (foll. by to) = **be partly responsible for**,

be conducive to, be instrumental in, help, lead to, tend to

contrite adj = **sorry**, chastened, conscience-stricken, humble, penitent, regretful, remorseful, repentant, sorrowful

contrive v 1 = **bring about**, arrange, effect, manage, manoeuvre, plan, plot, scheme, succeed 2 = **devise**, concoct, construct, create, design, fabricate, improvise, invent, manufacture

control n 1 = **power**, authority, charge, command, guidance, mana (NZ), management, oversight, supervision, supremacy 2 = **restraint**, brake, check, curb, limitation, regulation ◆ pl 3 = **instruments**, console, control panel, dash, dashboard, dials ◆ v 4 = **have power over**, administer, command, direct, govern, handle, have charge of, manage, manipulate, supervise 5 = **restrain**, check, constrain, contain, curb, hold back, limit, repress, subdue

controversy n = **argument**, altercation, debate, dispute, quarrel, row, squabble,

contusion n Formal bruise.

conundrum n riddle.

conurbation n large urban area formed by the growth and merging of towns.

convalesce v recover after an illness or operation. **convalescence** n **convalescent** n, adj

convection n transmission of heat in liquids or gases by the circulation of currents. **convector** n heater that gives out hot air.

convene ❶ v gather or summon for a formal meeting. **convener, convenor** n person who calls a meeting.

convenient ❶ adj 1 suitable or opportune. 2 easy to use. 3 nearby. **conveniently** adv **convenience** n 1 quality of being convenient. 2 useful object. 3 Euphemistic public toilet.

convent n 1 building where nuns live. 2 school run by nuns.

convention ❶ n 1 widely accepted view of proper behaviour. 2 assembly or meeting. 3 formal agreement. **conventional** adj 1 (unthinkingly) following the accepted customs. 2 customary. 3 (of weapons or warfare) not nuclear. **conventionally** adv **conventionality** n

converge ❶ v meet or join. **convergence** n

conversant adj **conversant with** having knowledge or experience of.

converse¹ ❶ v have a conversation. **conversation** n informal talk. **conversational** adj **conversationalist** n person with a specified ability at conversation.

converse² ❶ adj, n opposite or contrary. **conversely** adv

convert ❶ v 1 change in form, character, or function. 2 cause to change in opinion or belief. ♦ n 3 person who has converted to a different belief or religion. **conversion** n 1 (thing resulting from) converting. 2 Rugby score made after a try by kicking the ball over the crossbar. **convertible** adj 1 capable of being converted. ♦ n 2 car with a folding or removable roof.

convex ❶ adj curving outwards.

convey ❶ v 1 communicate (information). 2 carry, transport. **conveyance** n 1 Old–fashioned vehicle. 2 transfer of the legal title to property. **conveyancing** n branch of law dealing with the transfer of ownership of property. **conveyor belt** continuous moving belt for transporting things, esp. in a factory.

─┤ THESAURUS ├─

wrangling

convene v = **gather**, assemble, bring together, call, come together, congregate, convoke, meet, summon

convenient adj 1 = **suitable**, appropriate, fit, timely 2 = **useful**, handy, helpful, labour–saving, serviceable ≠ **awkward** 3 = **nearby**, accessible, at hand, available, close at hand, handy, just round the corner, within reach ≠ **distant**

convention n 1 = **custom**, code, etiquette, practice, propriety, protocol, tradition, usage 2 = **assembly**, conference, congress, convocation, council, meeting 3 = **agreement**, bargain, contract, pact, protocol, treaty

converge v = **come together**, coincide, combine, gather, join, meet, merge

converse¹ v = **talk**, chat, commune, confer, discourse, exchange views

① **converse²** adj = **opposite**, contrary, counter, reverse, reversed, transposed

② **converse²** n = **opposite**, antithesis, contrary, obverse, other side of the coin, reverse

convert v 1 = **change**, adapt, alter, customize, modify, remodel, reorganize, restyle, revise, transform, transpose, turn 2 = **reform**, convince, proselytize ♦ n 3 = **neophyte**, disciple, proselyte

convex adj = **rounded**, bulging, gibbous, protuberant

convey v 1 = **communicate**, disclose, impart, make known, relate, reveal, tell 2 = **carry**, bear, bring, conduct, fetch, guide, move, send, transport

convict ● v 1 declare guilty. ◆ n 2 person serving a prison sentence. **conviction** n 1 firm belief. 2 instance of being convicted.
convince ● v persuade by argument or evidence. **convincing** adj
convivial adj sociable, lively. **conviviality** n
convoluted adj 1 coiled, twisted. 2 (of an argument or sentence) complex and hard to understand. **convolution** n
convoy n group of vehicles or ships travelling together.
convulse v 1 (of part of the body) undergo violent spasms. 2 Informal (be) overcome with laughter. **convulsion** n 1 violent muscular spasm. ◆ pl 2 uncontrollable laughter. **convulsive** adj
coo v cooing, cooed (of a dove or pigeon) make a soft murmuring sound.
cook v 1 prepare (food) by heating. 2 (of food) be cooked. ◆ n 3 person who cooks food. **cook the books** falsify accounts. **cooker** n apparatus for cooking heated by gas or electricity. **cookery** n art of cooking. **cookie** n US biscuit. **cook up** v Informal devise (a story or scheme).
cool ● adj 1 moderately cold. 2 calm and unemotional. 3 indifferent or unfriendly. 4 Informal sophisticated or excellent. 5 Informal (of a large sum of money) without exaggeration, e.g. a cool million. ◆ v 6 make or become cool. ◆ n 7 coolness. 8

Slang calmness, composure. **coolly** adv
coolant n fluid used to cool machinery while it is working. **cool drink** n S Afr nonalcoholic drink. **cooler** n container for making or keeping things cool.
coop[1] n cage or pen for poultry. **coop up** v confine in a restricted place.
coop[2] [koh-op] n (shop run by) a cooperative society.
cooperate ● v work or act together. **cooperation** n **cooperative** adj 1 willing to cooperate. 2 (of an enterprise) owned and managed collectively. ◆ n 3 cooperative organization.
coordinate ● v 1 bring together and cause to act together efficiently. ◆ n 2 Maths any of a set of numbers defining the location of a point. ◆ pl 3 clothes designed to be worn together. **coordination** n **coordinator** n
coot n small black water bird.
cop Slang ◆ n 1 policeman. ◆ v copping, copped 2 take or seize. **cop it** get into trouble or be punished. **cop out** v avoid taking responsibility or committing oneself.
cope ● v (often foll. by with) 1 deal successfully (with). 2 tolerate, endure.
coping n sloping top row of a wall.
copious ● [kope-ee-uss] adj abundant, plentiful.

THESAURUS

convict v 1 = **find guilty**, condemn, imprison, pronounce guilty, sentence ◆ n 2 = **prisoner**, criminal, culprit, felon, jailbird, con (sl)
convince v = **persuade**, assure, bring round, prevail upon, satisfy, sway, win over
cool adj 1 = **cold**, chilled, chilly, nippy, refreshing ≠ **warm** 2 = **calm**, collected, composed, relaxed, sedate, self–controlled, self–possessed, unemotional, unruffled ≠ **troubled** 3 = **unfriendly**, aloof, distant, indifferent, lukewarm, offhand, standoffish, unenthusiastic, unwelcoming ≠ **warm** ◆ v 6 = **chill**, cool off, freeze, lose heat, refrigerate ≠ **heat (up)** ◆ n 8 Sl

= **calmness**, composure, control, poise, self–control, self–discipline, self–possession, temper
cooperate v = **work together**, collaborate, combine, conspire, coordinate, join forces, pool resources, pull together ≠ **fight**
coordinate v 1 = **bring together**, harmonize, integrate, match, organize, synchronize, systematize
cope v (often foll. by with) 1 = **manage**, carry on, get by (inf), hold one's own, make the grade, struggle through, survive 2 = **deal with**, contend with, grapple with, handle, struggle with, weather, wrestle with
copious adj = **abundant**, ample, bountiful,

copper[1] n **1** soft reddish–brown metal. **2** copper or bronze coin. **3 copper–bottomed** adj financially reliable. **copperplate** n fine handwriting style.

copper[2] n Slang policeman.

coppice, copse n small group of trees growing close together.

copulate v have sexual intercourse. **copulation** n

copy ❶ n, pl **copies 1** thing made to look exactly like another. **2** single specimen of a book etc. **3** material for printing. ◆ v **copying, copied 4** make a copy of. **5** act or try to be like. **copyright** n **1** exclusive legal right to reproduce and control a book, work of art, etc. ◆ v **2** take out a copyright on. ◆ adj **3** protected by copyright. **copywriter** n person who writes advertising copy.

coquette n woman who flirts. **coquettish** adj

coracle n small round boat of wicker covered with skins.

coral n **1** hard substance formed from the skeletons of very small sea animals. ◆ adj **2** orange–pink.

cord ❶ n **1** thin rope or thick string. **2** cordlike structure in the body. **3** corduroy. ◆ pl **4** corduroy trousers.

cordial ❶ adj **1** warm and friendly. ◆ n **2** drink with a fruit base. **cordially** adv **cordiality** n

cordon ❶ n chain of police, soldiers, etc., guarding an area. **cordon off** v form a cordon round.

cordon bleu [**bluh**] adj (of cookery or cooks) of the highest standard.

corduroy n cotton fabric with a velvety ribbed surface.

core ❶ n **1** central part of certain fruits, containing the seeds. **2** central or essential part. ◆ v **3** remove the core from.

corgi n short–legged sturdy dog.

coriander n plant grown for its aromatic seeds and leaves.

cork n **1** thick light bark of a Mediterranean oak. **2** piece of this used as a stopper. ◆ v **3** seal with a cork. **corkscrew** n spiral metal tool for pulling corks from bottles.

corm n bulblike underground stem of certain plants.

cormorant n large dark–coloured long–necked sea bird.

corn[1] n **1** cereal plant such as wheat or oats. **2** grain of such plants. **3** US maize. **4** Slang something unoriginal or oversentimental. **corny** adj Slang unoriginal or oversentimental. **cornflakes** pl n breakfast cereal made from toasted maize. **cornflour** n fine maize flour NZ fine wheat flour. **cornflower** n plant with blue flowers.

corn[2] n painful hard skin on the toe.

cornea [**korn**–ee–a] n, pl **–neas, –neae** transparent membrane covering the eyeball.

corner ❶ n **1** area or angle where two converging lines or surfaces meet. **2** place where two streets meet. **3** remote place. **4** Sport free kick or shot from the corner of the field. ◆ v **5** force into a difficult or inescapable position. **6** (of a vehicle) turn a corner. **7** obtain a monopoly of. **cornerstone** n indispensable part or basis.

———————— THESAURUS ————————

extensive, full, lavish, plentiful, profuse

copy ❶ n **1 = reproduction**, counterfeit, duplicate, facsimile, forgery, imitation, likeness, model, replica ≠ **create** ◆ v **4 = reproduce**, counterfeit, duplicate, replicate, transcribe **5 = imitate**, act like, ape, behave like, emulate, follow, mimic, mirror, repeat

cord ❶ n **1 = rope**, line, string, twine

cordial adj **1 = warm**, affable, agreeable,

cheerful, congenial, friendly, genial, hearty, sociable ≠ **cold**

cordon n **= chain**, barrier, line, ring

core n **1 = kernel**, pith **2 = centre**, crux, essence, gist, heart, nub, nucleus

corner n **1 = angle**, bend, crook, joint **3 = space**, hideaway, hide–out, nook, retreat ◆ v **5 = trap**, run to earth **7** As in **corner the market = monopolize**, dominate, engross, hog (sl)

cornet *n* **1** brass instrument similar to the trumpet. **2** cone–shaped ice–cream wafer.

cornice *n* decorative moulding round the top of a wall.

cornucopia [korn–yew–**kope**–ee–a] *n* **1** great abundance. **2** symbol of plenty, consisting of a horn overflowing with fruit and flowers.

corollary *n, pl* **–laries** idea, fact, or proposition which is the natural result of something else.

coronary [**kor**–ron–a–ree] *adj* **1** of the arteries surrounding the heart. ◆ *n, pl* **–naries 2** coronary thrombosis. **coronary thrombosis** condition in which the flow of blood to the heart is blocked by a blood clot.

coronation *n* ceremony of crowning a monarch.

coroner *n* official responsible for the investigation of violent, sudden, or suspicious deaths.

coronet *n* small crown.

corporal[1] *n* noncommissioned officer in an army.

corporal[2] *adj* of the body. **corporal punishment** physical punishment, such as caning.

corporation ⊕ *n* **1** large business or company. **2** city or town council. **3** *Informal* large paunch. **corporate** *adj* **1** of business corporations. **2** shared by a group.

corps ⊕ [kore] *n, pl* **corps 1** military unit

with a specific function. **2** organized body of people.

corpse ⊕ *n* dead body.

corpulent *adj* fat or plump. **corpulence** *n*

corpus *n, pl* **corpora** collection of writings, esp. by a single author.

corpuscle *n* red or white blood cell.

corral *US* ◆ *n* **1** enclosure for cattle or horses. ◆ *v* **–ralling, –ralled 2** put in a corral.

correct ⊕ *adj* **1** free from error, true. **2** in accordance with accepted standards. ◆ *v* **3** put right. **4** indicate the errors in. **5** rebuke or punish. **correctly** *adv* **correctness** *n* **correction** *n* **1** correcting. **2** alteration correcting something. **corrective** *adj* intended to put right something wrong

correlate *v* place or be placed in a mutual relationship. **correlation** *n*

correspond ⊕ *v* **1** be consistent or compatible (with). **2** be the same or similar. **3** communicate by letter. **corresponding** *adj* **correspondence** *n* **1** communication by letters. **2** letters so exchanged. **3** relationship or similarity. **correspondent** *n* **1** person employed by a newspaper etc. to report on a special subject or from a foreign country. **2** letter writer.

corridor ⊕ *n* **1** passage in a building or train. **2** strip of land or airspace providing access through foreign territory.

corroborate ⊕ *v* support (a fact or opinion) by giving proof. **corroboration** *n*

THESAURUS

corporation *n* **1** = **business**, association, corporate body, society **2** = **town council**, civic authorities, council, municipal authorities **3** *Inf* = **paunch**, beer belly (*inf*), middle–age spread (*inf*), potbelly, spare tyre (*Brit sl*), spread (*inf*)

corps *n* **1** = **team**, band, company, detachment, division, regiment, squadron, troop, unit

corpse *n* = **body**, cadaver, carcass, remains, stiff (*sl*)

correct *adj* **1** = **true**, accurate, exact, faultless, flawless, O.K. or okay (*inf*),

precise, right ≠ **false 2** = **proper**, acceptable, appropriate, fitting, kosher (*inf*), O.K. or okay (*inf*), seemly, standard ◆ *v* **3** = **rectify**, adjust, amend, cure, emend, redress, reform, remedy, right ≠ **damage 5** = **punish**, admonish, chasten, chastise, chide, discipline, rebuke, reprimand, reprove, rouse on (*Aust*) ≠ **praise**

correspond *v* **1** = **be consistent**, accord, agree, conform, fit, harmonize, match, square, tally ≠ **vary 3** = **communicate**, exchange letters, keep in touch, write

corridor *n* **1** = **passage**, aisle, alley,

corroborative *adj*

corroboree *n Aust* Aboriginal gathering or dance.

corrode ❶ *v* eat or be eaten away by chemical action or rust. **corrosion** *n* **corrosive** *adj*

corrupt ❶ *adj* 1 open to or involving bribery. 2 morally depraved. 3 (of a text or data) unreliable through errors or alterations. ◆ *v* 4 make corrupt. **corruption** *n* **corruptible** *adj*

corsage [kor-**sahzh**] *n* small bouquet worn on the bodice of a dress.

corset ❶ *n* women's close-fitting undergarment worn to shape the torso.

cortege [kor-**tayzh**] *n* funeral procession.

cortex *n, pl* **-tices** *Anat* outer layer of the brain or other internal organ. **cortical** *adj*

cortisone *n* steroid hormone used to treat various diseases.

cosh *n* 1 heavy blunt weapon. ◆ *v* 2 hit with a cosh.

cosine [**koh**-sine] *n* (in trigonometry) ratio of the length of the adjacent side to that of the hypotenuse in a right-angled triangle.

cosmetic ❶ *n* 1 preparation used to improve the appearance of a person's skin. ◆ *adj* 2 improving the appearance only.

cosmic ❶ *adj* of the whole universe. **cosmic rays** electromagnetic radiation from outer space.

cosmopolitan ❶ *adj* 1 composed of people or elements from many countries. 2 having lived and travelled in many countries. ◆ *n* 3 cosmopolitan person. **cosmopolitanism** *n*

cosmos *n* the universe. **cosmology** *n* study of the origin and nature of the universe. **cosmological** *adj*

cosset *v* **cosseting, cosseted** pamper.

cost ❶ *n* 1 amount of money, time, labour, etc., required for something. ◆ *pl* 2 expenses of a lawsuit. ◆ *v* **costing, cost** 3 have as its cost. 4 involve the loss or sacrifice of. 5 (*past* costed) estimate the cost of. **costly** *adj* 1 expensive. 2 involving great loss or sacrifice.

costume ❶ *n* 1 style of dress of a particular place or time, or for a particular activity. 2 clothes worn by an actor or performer. **costumier** *n* maker or seller of costumes. **costume jewellery** inexpensive artificial jewellery.

cosy ❶ *adj* **-sier, -siest** 1 warm and snug. 2 intimate, friendly. ◆ *n* 3 cover for keeping things warm, e.g. *a tea cosy.* **cosily** *adv* **cosiness** *n*

—————| THESAURUS |—————

hallway, passageway

corroborate *v* = **support**, authenticate, back up, bear out, confirm, endorse, ratify, substantiate, validate

corrode *v* = **eat away**, consume, corrupt, erode, gnaw, oxidize, rust, wear away

corrupt *adj* 1 = **dishonest**, bent (*sl*), bribable, crooked (*inf*), fraudulent, unprincipled, unscrupulous, venal ≠ **straight** 2 = **depraved**, debased, degenerate, dissolute, profligate, vicious ≠ **reform** 3 = **distorted**, altered, doctored, falsified ◆ *v* 4 a = **bribe**, buy off, entice, fix (*inf*), grease (someone's) palm (*sl*), lure, suborn b = **deprave**, debauch, pervert, subvert

corset *n* = **girdle**, belt, bodice

cosmetic *adj* 2 = **beautifying**,

nonessential, superficial, surface

cosmic *adj* = **universal**, stellar

cosmopolitan *adj* 2 = **sophisticated**, broad-minded, catholic, open-minded, universal, urbane, well-travelled, worldly-wise ≠ **limited** ◆ *n* 3 = **man** or **woman of the world**, jet-setter, sophisticate

cost *n* 1 = **price**, amount, charge, damage (*inf*), expense, outlay, payment, worth ◆ *v* 3 = **sell at**, come to, command a price of, set (someone) back (*inf*) 4 = **lose**, do disservice to, harm, hurt, injure

costume *n* 1 = **outfit**, apparel, attire, clothing, dress, ensemble, garb, livery, uniform

cosy *adj* 1 = **snug**, comfortable, comfy (*inf*), homely, sheltered, tucked up, warm 2 = **intimate**, friendly

cot n 1 baby's bed with high sides. 2 small portable bed. **cot death** unexplained death of a baby while asleep.

cote n shelter for birds or animals.

coterie [kote-er-ee] n exclusive group, clique.

cottage ⊕ n small house in the country. **cottage cheese** soft mild white cheese. **cottage industry** craft industry in which employees work at home. **cottage pie** dish of minced meat topped with mashed potato.

cotton n 1 white downy fibre covering the seeds of a tropical plant. 2 cloth or thread made from this. **cotton on (to)** v Informal understand. **cotton wool** fluffy cotton used for surgical dressings etc.

couch n 1 piece of upholstered furniture for seating more than one person. ♦ v 2 express in a particular way. **couch potato** Slang lazy person whose only hobby is watching television.

cougar n puma.

cough ⊕ v 1 expel air from the lungs abruptly and noisily. ♦ n 2 act or sound of coughing. 3 illness which causes coughing.

could v past tense of CAN¹.

coulomb [koo–lom] n SI unit of electric charge.

council ⊕ n 1 group meeting for discussion or consultation. 2 local governing body of a town or region. ♦ adj 3 of or by a council. **councillor** n member of a council. **council tax** tax based on the value of property, to fund local services.

counsel ⊕ n 1 advice or guidance. 2 barrister or barristers. ♦ v –selling, –selled 3 give guidance to. 4 urge, recommend. **counsellor** n

count¹ ⊕ v 1 say numbers in order. 2 find the total of. 3 be important. 4 regard as. 5 take into account. ♦ n 6 counting. 7 number reached by counting. 8 Law one of a number of charges. **countless** adj too many to count. **count on** v rely or depend on.

count² n European nobleman.

countenance n 1 (expression of) the face. ♦ v 2 allow or tolerate.

counter¹ n 1 long flat surface in a bank or shop, on which business is transacted. 2 small flat disc used in board games.

counter² ⊕ v 1 oppose, retaliate against. ♦ adv 2 in the opposite direction. 3 in direct contrast. ♦ n 4 opposing or retaliatory action.

counter– prefix 1 opposite, against, e.g. counterattack. 2 complementary, corresponding, e.g. counterpart.

counteract ⊕ v act against or neutralize.

counterattack n, v attack in response to

THESAURUS

cottage n = **cabin**, chalet, hut, lodge, shack

cough v 1 = **clear one's throat**, bark, hack ♦ n 2 = **frog** or **tickle in one's throat**, bark, hack

council n 1, 2 = **governing body**, assembly, board, cabinet, committee, conference, congress, convention, panel, parliament

counsel n 1 = **advice**, direction, guidance, information, recommendation, suggestion, warning 2 = **legal adviser**, advocate, attorney, barrister, lawyer, solicitor ♦ v 3 = **advise**, instruct, warn 4 = **urge**, advocate, exhort, recommend

count¹ v 1 = **enumerate** 2 = **add (up)**, calculate, compute, number, reckon, tally, tot up 3 = **matter**, be important, carry weight, rate, signify, tell, weigh 4 = **consider**, deem, judge, look upon, rate, regard, think 5 = **take into account** or **consideration**, include, number among ♦ n 6 = **calculation**, computation, enumeration, numbering, poll 7 = **sum**, reckoning, tally

counter² v 1 = **retaliate**, answer, hit back, meet, oppose, parry, resist, respond, ward off ≠ **accept** ♦ adv 3 = **opposite to**, against, at variance with, contrariwise, conversely, in defiance of, versus ≠ **parallel to**

counteract v = **act against**, foil, frustrate,

an attack.

counterbalance ❶ *n* 1 weight or force balancing or neutralizing another. ◆ *v* 2 act as a counterbalance to.

counterfeit ❶ *adj* 1 fake, forged. ◆ *n* 2 fake, forgery. ◆ *v* 3 fake, forge.

counterfoil *n* part of a cheque or receipt kept as a record.

countermand ❶ *v* cancel (a previous order).

counterpane *n* bed covering.

counterpart ❶ *n* person or thing complementary to or corresponding to another.

counterpoint *n Music* technique of combining melodies.

countersign *v* sign (a document already signed by someone) as confirmation.

countersink *v* drive (a screw) into a shaped hole so that its head is below the surface.

countertenor *n* male alto.

country ❶ *n, pl* –tries 1 nation. 2 nation's territory. 3 nation's people. 4 part of the land away from cities. **countrified** *adj* rustic in manner or appearance. **country and western, country music** popular music based on American White folk music. **countryman, countrywoman** *n* 1 person from one's native land. 2 person who lives in the country. **countryside** *n* land away from cities.

county ❶ *n, pl* –ties division of a country.

coup ❶ [koo] *n* 1 successful action. 2 coup d'état.

coupé [koo–pay] *n* sports car with two doors and a sloping fixed roof.

couple ❶ *n* 1 two people who are married or romantically involved. 2 two partners in a dance or game. ◆ *v* 3 connect, associate. 4 **a couple** 1 a pair. 2 *Informal* a few.

couplet *n* two consecutive lines of verse, usu. rhyming and of the same metre.

coupling *n* device for connecting things, such as railway carriages.

coupon ❶ *n* 1 piece of paper entitling the holder to a discount or gift. 2 detachable order form. 3 football pools entry form.

courage ❶ *n* ability to face danger or pain without fear. **courageous** *adj* **courageously** *adv*

courgette *n* type of small vegetable marrow.

courier ❶ *n* 1 person employed to look after holiday–makers. 2 person employed to deliver urgent messages.

negate, neutralize, offset, resist, thwart

counterbalance *v* 2 = **offset**, balance, compensate, make up for, set off

counterfeit *adj* 1 = **fake**, bogus, false, forged, imitation, phoney *or* phony (*inf*), sham, simulated ≠ **real** ◆ *n* 2 = **fake**, copy, forgery, fraud, imitation, phoney *or* phony (*inf*), reproduction, sham ≠ **the real thing** ◆ *v* 3 = **fake**, copy, fabricate, feign, forge, imitate, impersonate, pretend, sham, simulate

countermand *v* = **cancel**, annul, override, repeal, rescind, retract, reverse, revoke

counterpart *n* = **opposite number**, complement, equal, fellow, match, mate, supplement, tally, twin

country *n* 1 = **nation**, commonwealth, kingdom, people, realm, state 2 = **territory**, land, region, terrain

3 = **people**, citizens, community, inhabitants, nation, populace, public, society 4 = **countryside**, backwoods, farmland, green belt, outback (*Aust & NZ*), provinces, sticks (*inf*) ≠ **city**

county *n* = **province**, shire

coup *n* 1 = **masterstroke**, accomplishment, action, deed, exploit, feat, manoeuvre, stunt

couple *n* 1 = **pair**, two, twosome ◆ *v* 3 = **link**, connect, hitch, join, marry, pair, unite, wed, yoke

coupon *n* 1 = **slip**, card, certificate, ticket, token, voucher

courage *n* = **bravery**, daring, fearlessness, gallantry, heroism, mettle, nerve, pluck, resolution, valour

courier *n* 1 = **guide**, representative 2 = **messenger**, bearer, carrier, envoy,

course ⓣ *n* 1 series of lessons or medical treatment. 2 onward movement in space or time. 3 route or direction taken. 4 area where golf is played or a race is run. 5 any of the successive parts of a meal. 6 continuous layer of masonry at one level in a building. 7 mode of conduct or action 8 natural development of events. ♦ *v* 9 (of liquid) run swiftly. 10 hunt with hounds that follow the quarry by sight and not scent. **of course** as expected, naturally.

court ⓣ *n* 1 body which decides legal cases. 2 place where it meets. 3 marked area for playing a racket game. 4 courtyard. 5 residence, household, or retinue of a sovereign. ♦ *v* 6 *Old-fashioned* try to gain the love of. 7 try to win the favour of. 8 invite, e.g. *to court disaster*. **courtier** *n* attendant at a royal court. **courtly** *adj* ceremoniously polite. **courtship** *n* courting of an intended spouse or mate. **court martial** *n*, *pl* **courts**

martial court for trying naval or military offences. **courtyard** *n* paved space enclosed by buildings or walls.

courtesy ⓣ *n* 1 politeness, good manners. 2 (*pl* **-sies**) courteous act. **(by) courtesy of** by permission of. **courteous** *adj* polite.

cousin *n* child of one's uncle or aunt.

cove ⓣ *n* small bay or inlet.

coven [kuv-ven] *n* meeting of witches.

covenant [kuv-ven-ant] *n* 1 formal agreement to make an annual (charitable) payment. ♦ *v* 2 agree by a covenant.

cover ⓣ *v* 1 place something over, to protect or conceal. 2 extend over or lie on the surface of. 3 travel over. 4 keep a gun aimed at. 5 insure against loss or risk. 6 include. 7 report (an event) for a newspaper. 8 be enough to pay for. ♦ *n* 9 anything that covers. 10 outside of a book or magazine. 11 pretext or disguise. 12 insurance. 13 shelter or protection. **coverage** *n* amount or extent covered. **coverlet** *n* bed cover.

━━━ THESAURUS ━━━

runner

course *n* 1 = **classes**, curriculum, lectures, programme, schedule 2 = **progression**, development, flow, movement, order, progress, sequence, unfolding 3 = **route**, direction, line, passage, path, road, track, trajectory, way 4 = **racecourse**, cinder track, circuit 7 = **procedure**, behaviour, conduct, manner, method, mode, plan, policy, programme 8 = **period**, duration, lapse, passage, passing, sweep, term, time ♦ *v* 9 = **run**, flow, gush, race, speed, stream, surge 10 = **hunt**, chase, follow, pursue **of course** = **naturally**, certainly, definitely, indubitably, needless to say, obviously, undoubtedly, without a doubt

court *n* 1 = **law court**, bar, bench, tribunal 4 = **courtyard**, cloister, piazza, plaza, quad (*inf*), quadrangle, square, yard 5 a = **palace**, hall, manor, royal household b = **retinue**, attendants, cortege, entourage, suite, train ♦ *v* 6 *Old-fashioned* = **woo**, date, go (out) with, run after, serenade, set one's cap at, take out, walk out with

7 = **cultivate**, curry favour with, fawn upon, flatter, pander to, seek, solicit 8 = **invite**, attract, bring about, incite, prompt, provoke, seek

courtesy *n* 1 = **politeness**, affability, civility, courteousness, gallantry, good manners, graciousness, urbanity 2 = **favour**, indulgence, kindness

cove *n* = **bay**, anchorage, inlet, sound

covenant *n* 1 = **promise**, agreement, arrangement, commitment, contract, pact, pledge ♦ *v* 2 = **promise**, agree, contract, pledge, stipulate, undertake

cover *v* 1 = **envelop**, cloak, coat, conceal, encase, enshroud, hide, mask, obscure, overlay, put on, shroud, veil, wrap ≠ **show** 2 = **submerge**, engulf, flood, overrun, wash over 3 = **travel over**, cross, pass through *or* over, traverse 7 = **report**, describe, investigate, narrate, relate, tell of, write up ♦ *n* 9 = **covering**, canopy, case, coating, envelope, jacket, lid, top, wrapper 11 = **disguise**, camouflage, concealment, facade, front, mask, pretext,

covert adj 1 concealed, secret. ◆ n 2 thicket giving shelter to game birds or animals.

covet ⓓ v coveting, coveted long to possess (what belongs to someone else). **covetous** adj

cow[1] n 1 mature female of cattle and of certain other mammals, such as the elephant or seal. 2 Informal, offens a disagreeable woman. **cowboy** n 1 (in the US) ranch worker who herds and tends cattle, usu. on horseback. 2 Informal irresponsible or unscrupulous worker.

cow[2] v intimidate, subdue.

coward ⓓ n person who lacks courage. **cowardly** adj **cowardice** n lack of courage.

cower ⓓ v cringe in fear.

cowl n 1 loose hood. 2 monk's hooded robe. 3 cover on a chimney to increase ventilation.

cowslip n small yellow wild flower.

coxswain [kok–sn] n person who steers a rowing boat.

coy ⓓ adj affectedly shy or modest. **coyly** adv **coyness** n

coyote [koy–ote–ee] n prairie wolf of N America.

coypu n beaver–like aquatic rodent, bred for its fur.

crab n edible shellfish with ten legs, the first pair modified into pincers.

crab apple n small sour apple.

crack ⓓ v 1 break or split partially. 2 break with a sharp noise. 3 (cause to) make a sharp noise. 4 (of the voice) become harsh or change pitch suddenly. 5 break down or yield under strain. 6 hit suddenly. 7 solve (a code or problem). 8 tell (a joke). ◆ n 9 sudden sharp noise. 10 narrow gap. 11 sharp blow. 12 Informal gibe, joke. 13 Slang highly addictive form of cocaine. ◆ adj 14 Informal first–rate, excellent, e.g. a crack shot. **cracking** adj very good. **crackdown** n severe disciplinary measures. **crack down on** v take severe measures against.

cradle ⓓ n 1 baby's bed on rockers. 2 place where something originates. 3 supporting structure. ◆ v 4 hold gently as if in a cradle.

craft ⓓ n 1 occupation requiring skill with the hands. 2 skill or ability. 3 (pl craft) boat, ship, aircraft, or spaceship. **crafty** adj skilled in deception. **craftsman**, **craftswoman** n skilled worker. **craftsmanship** n

THESAURUS

screen, smoke screen, veil 12 = **insurance**, compensation, indemnity, protection, reimbursement 13 = **protection**, defence, guard, shelter, shield

covet v = **long for**, aspire to, crave, desire, envy, lust after, set one's heart on, yearn for

coward n = **wimp** (inf), chicken (sl), scaredy–cat (inf), yellow–belly (sl)

cower v = **cringe**, draw back, flinch, grovel, quail, shrink, tremble

coy adj = **shy**, bashful, demure, modest, reserved, retiring, shrinking, timid

crack v 1 = **break**, burst, cleave, fracture, snap, splinter, split 2, 3 = **snap**, burst, crash, detonate, explode, pop 5 = **give in**, break down, collapse, give way, go to pieces, lose control, succumb, yield 6 = **hit**, clip (inf), clout (inf), cuff, slap,

smack, whack 7 = **solve**, decipher, fathom, get the answer to, work out ◆ n 9 = **snap**, burst, clap, crash, explosion, pop, report 10 = **break**, chink, cleft, cranny, crevice, fissure, fracture, gap, rift 11 = **blow**, clip (inf), clout (inf), cuff, slap, smack, whack 12 Inf = **joke**, dig, funny remark, gag (inf), jibe, quip, wisecrack, witticism ◆ adj 14 Inf = **first–class**, ace, choice, elite, excellent, first–rate, hand–picked, superior, world–class

cradle n 1 = **crib**, bassinet, cot, Moses basket 2 = **birthplace**, beginning, fount, fountainhead, origin, source, spring, wellspring ◆ v 4 = **hold**, lull, nestle, nurse, rock, support

craft n 1 = **occupation**, business, employment, handicraft, pursuit, trade, vocation, work, yakka (Aust & NZ inf)

crag ⊕ n steep rugged rock. **craggy** adj

cram ⊕ v **cramming, crammed 1** force into too small a space. **2** fill too full. **3** study hard just before an examination.

cramp¹ ⊕ n **1** painful muscular contraction. **2** clamp for holding masonry or timber together.

cramp² ⊕ v confine, restrict.

cranberry n sour edible red berry.

crane n **1** machine for lifting and moving heavy weights. **2** large wading bird with a long neck and legs. ♦ v **3** stretch (one's neck) to see something.

cranium n, pl **–niums, –nia** skull. **cranial** adj

crank n **1** arm projecting at right angles from a shaft, for transmitting or converting motion. **2** Informal eccentric person. ♦ v **3** start (an engine) with a crank. **cranky** adj Informal **1** eccentric. **2** bad-tempered. **crankshaft** n shaft driven by a crank.

cranny ⊕ n, pl **–nies** narrow opening.

crash ⊕ n **1** collision involving a vehicle or vehicles. **2** sudden loud smashing noise. **3** financial collapse. ♦ v **4** (cause to) collide violently with a vehicle, a stationary object, or the ground. **5** (cause to) make a loud smashing noise. **6** (cause to) fall with a crash. **7** collapse or fail financially. **crash course** short, very intensive course in a particular subject. **crash helmet** protective helmet worn by a motorcyclist. **crash–land** v (of an aircraft) land in an emergency, causing damage. **crash–landing** n

crass ⊕ adj stupid and insensitive.

crate ⊕ n large wooden container for packing goods.

crater ⊕ n very large hole in the ground or in the surface of the moon.

cravat n man's scarf worn like a tie.

crave ⊕ v **1** desire intensely. **2** beg or plead for. **craving** n

craven adj cowardly.

crawl ⊕ v **1** move on one's hands and knees. **2** move very slowly. **3** (foll. by to) flatter in order to gain some advantage. **4** feel as if covered with crawling creatures. ♦ n **5** crawling motion or pace. **6** overarm swimming stroke.

crayfish n edible freshwater shellfish like a

THESAURUS

2 = **skill**, ability, aptitude, art, artistry, expertise, ingenuity, know-how (inf), technique, workmanship **3** = **vessel**, aircraft, boat, plane, ship, spacecraft

crag n = **rock**, bluff, peak, pinnacle, tor

cram v **1** = **stuff**, compress, force, jam, pack in, press, shove, squeeze **3** = **study**, bone up (inf), mug up (sl), revise, swot

cramp¹ n **1** = **spasm**, ache, contraction, convulsion, pain, pang, stitch, twinge

cramp² v = **restrict**, constrain, hamper, handicap, hinder, impede, inhibit, obstruct

cranny n = **crevice**, chink, cleft, crack, fissure, gap, hole, opening

crash n **1** = **collision**, accident, bump, pile–up (inf), prang (inf), smash, wreck **2** = **smash**, bang, boom, clang, clash, clatter, din, racket, thunder **3** = **collapse**, debacle, depression, downfall, failure, ruin ♦ v **4** = **collide**, bump (into), crash–land (an aircraft), drive into, have an accident, hit, plough into, wreck **6** = **hurtle**, fall headlong, give way, lurch, overbalance, plunge, topple **7** = **collapse**, be ruined, fail, fold, fold up, go belly up (inf), go bust (inf), go to the wall, go under

crass adj = **insensitive**, boorish, gross, indelicate, oafish, stupid, unrefined, witless

crate n = **container**, box, case, packing case, tea chest

crater n = **hollow**, depression, dip

crave v **1** = **long for**, desire, hanker after, hope for, lust after, want, yearn for **2** = **beg**, ask, beseech, entreat, implore, petition, plead for, pray for, seek, solicit, supplicate

crawl v **1, 2** = **creep**, advance slowly, inch, slither, worm one's way, wriggle, writhe ≠ **run 3** (foll. by to) = **grovel**, creep, fawn, humble oneself, toady **4** = **be full of**, be alive, be overrun (sl), swarm, teem lobster.

crayon *v, n* (draw or colour with) a stick or pencil of coloured wax or clay.

craze ❶ *n* short–lived fashion or enthusiasm. **crazed** *adj* 1 wild and uncontrolled. 2 (of porcelain) having fine cracks. **crazy** *adj* 1 ridiculous. 2 (foll. by *about*) very fond (of). 3 insane. **craziness** *n*

creak ❶ *v, n* (make) a harsh squeaking sound. **creaky** *adj*

cream ❶ *n* 1 fatty part of milk. 2 food or cosmetic resembling cream in consistency. 3 best part (of something). ◆ *adj* 4 yellowish–white. ◆ *v* 5 beat to a creamy consistency. **creamy** *adj* **cream cheese** rich soft white cheese. **cream off** *v* take the best part from.

crease ❶ *n* 1 line made by folding or pressing. 2 *Cricket* line marking the bowler's and batsman's positions. ◆ *v* 3 crush or line.

create ❶ *v* 1 make, cause to exist. 2 appoint to a new rank or position. 3 *Slang* make an angry fuss. **creation** *n* **creative** *adj* 1 imaginative or inventive. 2 **creativity** *n* **creator** *n*

creature ❶ *n* animal, person, or other

being.

crèche *n* place where small children are looked after while their parents are working, shopping, etc.

credentials ❶ *pl n* document giving evidence of a person's identity or qualifications.

credible ❶ *adj* 1 believable. 2 trustworthy. **credibly** *adv* **credibility** *n*

credit ❶ *n* 1 system of allowing customers to receive goods and pay later. 2 reputation for trustworthiness in paying debts. 3 money at one's disposal in a bank account. 4 side of an account book on which such sums are entered. 5 (source or cause of) praise or approval. 6 influence or reputation based on the good opinion of others. 7 belief or trust. ◆ *pl* 8 list of people responsible for the production of a film, programme, or record. ◆ *v* **crediting, credited** 9 enter as a credit in an account. 10 (foll. by *with*) attribute (to). 11 believe. **creditable** *adj* praiseworthy. **creditably** *adv* **creditor** *n* person to whom money is owed. **credit card** card allowing a person to buy on credit.

credulous *adj* too willing to believe.

——————| THESAURUS |——————

craze *n* = **fad**, enthusiasm, fashion, infatuation, mania, rage, trend, vogue
creak *v, n* = **squeak**, grate, grind, groan, scrape, scratch, screech
cream *n* 2 = **lotion**, cosmetic, emulsion, essence, liniment, oil, ointment, paste, salve, unguent 3 = **best**, elite, flower, pick, prime ◆ *adj* 4 = **off–white**, yellowish–white
crease *n* 1 = **line**, corrugation, fold, groove, ridge, wrinkle ◆ *v* 3 = **wrinkle**, corrugate, crumple, double up, fold, rumple, screw up
create *v* 1 = **make**, bring about, cause, compose, devise, formulate, invent, lead to, occasion, originate, produce, spawn ≠ **destroy** 2 = **appoint**, constitute, establish, install, invest, make, set up
creature *n* = **living thing**, animal, beast, being, brute, human being, individual, man, mortal, person, soul, woman

credentials *pl n* = **certification**, authorization, document, licence, papers, passport, reference(s), testimonial
credible *adj* 1 = **believable**, conceivable, imaginable, likely, plausible, possible, probable, reasonable, thinkable ≠ **unlikely** 2 = **reliable**, dependable, honest, sincere, trustworthy, trusty ≠ **unreliable**
credit *n* 1 = **deferred payment**, hire–purchase, (the) H.P., the slate (*inf*), tick (*inf*) 5 = **praise**, acclaim, acknowledgment, approval, commendation, honour, kudos, recognition, tribute 6 = **prestige**, esteem, good name, influence, mana (*NZ*), position, regard, reputation, repute, standing, status 7 = **belief**, confidence, credence, faith, reliance, trust ◆ *v* 10 (foll. by *with*) = **attribute to**, ascribe to, assign to, impute to 11 = **believe**, accept, have faith in, rely on, trust

credulity n

creed ⊕ n statement or system of (Christian) beliefs or principles.

creek ⊕ n 1 narrow inlet or bay. 2 *Aust, NZ, US & Canadian* small stream.

creep ⊕ v **creeping, crept** 1 move quietly and cautiously. 2 crawl with the body near to the ground. 3 (of a plant) grow along the ground or over rocks. ◆ n 4 *Slang* obnoxious or servile person. **give one the creeps** *Informal* make one feel fear or disgust. **creeper** n creeping plant. **creepy** *adj Informal* causing a feeling of fear or disgust.

creole n language developed from a mixture of languages.

creosote n 1 dark oily liquid made from coal tar and used for preserving wood. ◆ v 2 treat with creosote.

crepe [krayp] n 1 fabric or rubber with a crinkled texture. 2 very thin pancake.

crescendo [krish–**end**–oh] n, pl **–dos** gradual increase in loudness, esp. in music.

crescent ⊕ n 1 (curved shape of) the moon as seen in its first or last quarter. 2 crescent–shaped street.

cress n plant with strong–tasting leaves, used in salads.

crest ⊕ n 1 top of a mountain, hill, or wave. 2 tuft or growth on a bird's or animal's head. 3 heraldic design used on a coat of arms and elsewhere. **crested** *adj* **crestfallen** *adj* disheartened.

cretin n 1 *Informal* stupid person. 2 *Obs* person afflicted with physical and mental retardation caused by a thyroid deficiency. **cretinous** *adj*

crevasse n deep open crack in a glacier.

crevice ⊕ n narrow crack or gap in rock.

crew ⊕ n 1 people who work on a ship or aircraft. 2 group of people working together. 3 *Informal* any group of people. ◆ v 4 serve as a crew member (on). **crew cut** man's closely cropped haircut.

crib ⊕ n 1 piece of writing stolen from elsewhere. 2 translation or list of answers used by students, often illicitly. 3 baby's cradle. 4 rack for fodder. 5 short for CRIBBAGE. ◆ v **cribbing, cribbed** 6 copy (someone's work) dishonestly.

cribbage n card game for two to four players.

crick n 1 muscle spasm or cramp in the back or neck. ◆ v 2 cause a crick in.

cricket[1] n outdoor game played with bats, a ball, and wickets by two teams of eleven. **cricketer** n

cricket[2] n chirping insect like a grasshopper.

crime ⊕ n 1 unlawful act. 2 unlawful acts collectively. **criminal** n 1 person guilty of a crime. ◆ *adj* 2 of crime. 3 *Informal* deplorable. **criminality** n **criminology** n

THESAURUS

creed n = **belief**, articles of faith, catechism, credo, doctrine, dogma, principles

creek n 1 = **inlet**, bay, bight, cove, firth *or* frith (*Scot*) 2 *Aust & NZ, US, & Canadian* = **stream**, bayou, brook, rivulet, runnel, tributary, watercourse

creep v 1 = **sneak**, approach unnoticed, skulk, slink, steal, tiptoe 2 = **crawl**, glide, slither, squirm, wriggle, writhe ◆ n 4 *Sl* = **bootlicker** (*inf*), crawler (*sl*), sneak, sycophant, toady ◆ *pl* **give one the creeps** *Inf* = **disgust**, frighten, make one's hair stand on end, make one squirm, repel, repulse, scare

crescent n 1 = **meniscus**, new moon, sickle

crest n 1 = **top**, apex, crown, highest point, peak, pinnacle, ridge, summit 2 = **tuft**, comb, crown, mane, plume 3 = **emblem**, badge, bearings, device, insignia, symbol

crevice n = **gap**, chink, cleft, crack, cranny, fissure, hole, opening, slit

crew n 1 = **(ship's) company**, hands, (ship's) complement 2 = **team**, corps, gang, posse, squad 3 *Inf* = **crowd**, band, bunch (*inf*), gang, horde, mob, pack, set

crib n 2 = **translation**, key 3 = **cradle**, bassinet, bed, cot 4 = **manger**, rack, stall ◆ v 6 = **copy**, cheat, pirate, plagiarize, purloin, steal study of crime.

crimson adj deep purplish–red.

cringe ① v 1 flinch in fear. 2 behave in a submissive or timid way.

crinkle v, n wrinkle, crease, or fold.

crinoline n hooped petticoat.

cripple ① n 1 person who is lame or disabled. ♦ v 2 make lame or disabled. 3 damage (something).

crisis ① n, pl –ses 1 crucial stage, turning point. 2 time of extreme trouble.

crisp ① adj 1 fresh and firm. 2 dry and brittle. 3 clean and neat. 4 (of weather) cold but invigorating. 5 lively or brisk. ♦ n 6 very thin slice of potato fried till crunchy. **crispy** adj hard and crunchy. **crispbread** n thin dry biscuit.

crisscross v 1 move in or mark with a crosswise pattern. ♦ adj 2 (of lines) crossing in different directions.

criterion ① n, pl –ria standard of judgment.

> ✓ **WORD TIP**
> It is incorrect to use *criteria* as a singular, though this use is often found.

critic ① n 1 professional judge of any of the arts. 2 person who finds fault. **critical** adj 1 very important or dangerous. 2 very seriously ill or injured. 3 fault–finding. 4 able to examine and judge carefully. **criticism** n 1 fault–finding. 2 analysis of a work of art.

croak ① v 1 (of a frog or crow) give a low hoarse cry. 2 utter or speak with a croak. ♦ n 3 low hoarse sound.

crochet [kroh–shay] v –cheting, –cheted 1 make by looping and intertwining yarn with a hooked needle. ♦ n 2 work made in this way.

crock n earthenware pot or jar. **crockery** n dishes.

crocodile n 1 large amphibious tropical reptile. 2 a line of people, esp. schoolchildren, walking two by two. **crocodile tears** insincere show of grief.

crocus n, pl –cuses small plant with yellow, white, or purple flowers in spring.

croft n small farm worked by one family in Scotland. **crofter** n

croissant [krwah–son] n rich flaky crescent–shaped roll.

crone n witchlike old woman.

crony n, pl –nies close friend.

crook ① n 1 Informal criminal. 2 bent or curved part. 3 hooked pole. ♦ adj 4 Aust & NZ slang unwell, injured **go crook** Aust & NZ slang become angry. **crooked** adj 1

─────── THESAURUS ───────

crime n 1 = **offence**, felony, misdeed, misdemeanour, transgression, trespass, unlawful act, violation 2 = **lawbreaking**, corruption, illegality, misconduct, vice, wrongdoing

cringe v 1 = **shrink**, cower, draw back, flinch, recoil, shy, wince 2 = **grovel**, bootlick (inf), crawl, creep, fawn, kowtow, pander to, toady

cripple v 2 = **disable**, hamstring, incapacitate, lame, maim, paralyse, weaken 3 = **damage**, destroy, impair, put out of action, put paid to, ruin, spoil ≠ **help**

crisis n 1 = **critical point**, climax, crunch (inf), crux, culmination, height, moment of truth, turning point 2 = **emergency**, deep water, dire straits, meltdown (inf), panic stations (inf), plight, predicament, trouble

crisp adj 1 = **firm**, crispy, crunchy, fresh ≠ **soft** 2 = **brittle**, crumbly 3 = **clean**, neat, smart, spruce, tidy, trim, well–groomed, well–pressed 4 = **bracing**, brisk, fresh, invigorating, refreshing ≠ **warm**

criterion n = **standard**, bench mark, gauge, measure, principle, rule, test, touchstone, yardstick

critic n 1 = **judge**, analyst, authority, commentator, connoisseur, expert, mana (NZ), pundit, reviewer 2 = **fault–finder**, attacker, detractor, knocker (inf)

croak v 1, 2 = **squawk**, caw, grunt, utter or speak huskily, wheeze bent or twisted. **2** set at an angle. **3** *Informal* dishonest.

croon ⓥ *v* sing, hum, or speak in a soft low tone. **crooner** *n* male singer of sentimental ballads.

crop ⓝ *n* **1** cultivated plant. **2** season's total yield of produce. **3** group of things appearing at one time. **4** (handle of) a whip. **5** pouch in a bird's gullet. **6** very short haircut. ◆ *v* **cropping, cropped 7** cut very short. **8** produce or harvest as a crop. **9** (of animals) feed on (grass). **cropper** *n* **come a cropper** *Informal* have a disastrous failure or heavy fall. **crop up** *v Informal* happen unexpectedly.

croquet [**kroh**–kay] *n* game played on a lawn in which balls are hit through hoops.

croquette [kroh–**kett**] *n* fried cake of potato, meat, or fish.

cross ⓥ *v* **1** move or go across (something). **2** meet and pass. **3** mark with a cross. **4** (with *out*) delete with a cross or lines. **5** place (one's arms or legs) crosswise. **6** make the sign of the cross on (oneself). **7** challenge or oppose. **8** cross–fertilize. ◆ *n* **9** structure, symbol, or mark of two intersecting lines. **10** such a structure of wood as a means of execution. **11** representation of the Cross as an emblem of Christianity. **12** mixture of two things. **13** hindrance or misfortune, e.g. *that's my cross to bear.* ◆ *adj* **14** angry, annoyed. **15** lying or placed across. **crossing** *n* **1** place where a street may be crossed safely. **2** place where one thing

crosses another. **3** journey across water. **crossbar** *n* horizontal bar across goalposts or on a bicycle. **crossbow** *n* weapon consisting of a bow fixed across a wooden stock. **crossbred** *adj* bred from two different types of animal or plant. **crossbreed** *n* crossbred animal or plant. **crosscheck** *v* check using a different method. **cross–country** *adj, adv* by way of open country or fields. **cross–examine** *v Law* question (a witness for the opposing side) to check his or her testimony. **cross–examination** *n* **cross–eyed** *adj* with eyes looking towards each other. **cross–fertilize** *v* fertilize (an animal or plant) from one of a different kind. **crossfire** *n* gunfire crossing another line of fire. **cross–ply** *adj* (of a tyre) having the fabric cords in the outer casing running diagonally. **cross–reference** *n* reference within a text to another part. **crossroads** *n* place where roads intersect. **cross section 1** (diagram of) a surface made by cutting across something. **2** representative sample. **crosswise** *adj, adv* **1** across. **2** in the shape of a cross. **crossword puzzle, crossword** *n* puzzle in which words suggested by clues are written into a grid of squares.

crotch *n* part of the body between the tops of the legs.

crotchet *n* musical note half the length of a minim.

crotchety *adj Informal* bad–tempered.

crouch ⓥ *v* **1** bend low with the legs and body close. ◆ *n* **2** this position.

crook *n* **1** *Inf* = **criminal**, cheat, racketeer, robber, rogue, shark, swindler, thief, villain

croon *v* = **sing**, hum, purr, warble

crop *n* **2** = **produce**, fruits, gathering, harvest, reaping, vintage, yield ◆ *v* **7** = **cut**, clip, lop, pare, prune, shear, snip, trim **9** = **graze**, browse, nibble

cross *v* **1** = **go across**, bridge, cut across, extend over, move across, pass over, span, traverse **2** = **intersect**, crisscross, intertwine **4** (with *out*) = **strike off** *or* **out**, blue–pencil, cancel, delete, eliminate,

score off *or* out **7** = **oppose**, block, impede, interfere, obstruct, resist **8** = **interbreed**, blend, crossbreed, cross–fertilize, cross–pollinate, hybridize, intercross, mix, mongrelize ◆ *n* **11** = **crucifix**, rood **12** = **mixture**, amalgam, blend, combination **13** = **trouble**, affliction, burden, grief, load, misfortune, trial, tribulation, woe, worry ◆ *adj* **14** = **angry**, annoyed, grumpy, ill–tempered, in a bad mood, irascible, put out, short **15** = **transverse**, crosswise,

croupier [kroop–ee–ay] *n* person who collects bets and pays out winnings at a gambling table in a casino.

crouton *n* small piece of fried or toasted bread served in soup.

crow¹ *n* large black bird with a harsh call. **as the crow flies** in a straight line. **crow's feet** wrinkles at the corners of the eyes. **crow's nest** lookout platform at the top of a ship's mast.

crow² ⊕ *v* **1** (of a cock) make a shrill squawking sound. **2** boast or gloat.

crowbar *n* iron bar used as a lever.

crowd ⊕ *n* **1** large group of people or things. **2** particular group of people. ◆ *v* **3** gather together in large numbers. **4** press together in a confined space. **5** fill or occupy fully.

crown ⊕ *n* **1** monarch's headdress of gold and jewels. **2** wreath for the head, given as an honour. **3** top of the head or of a hill. **4** artificial cover for a broken or decayed tooth. ◆ *v* **5** put a crown on the head of (someone) to proclaim him or her

monarch. **6** put on or form the top of. **7** put the finishing touch to (a series of events). **8** *Informal* hit on the head. **the Crown** power of the monarchy.

crucial ⊕ *adj* very important. **crucially** *adv*

crucible *n* pot in which metals are melted.

crude ⊕ *adj* **1** rough and simple. **2** tasteless, vulgar. **3** in a natural or unrefined state. **crudely** *adv* **crudity** *n*

cruel ⊕ *adj* **1** delighting in others' pain. **2** causing pain or suffering. **cruelly** *adv* **cruelty** *n*

cruet *n* small container for salt, pepper, etc., at table.

cruise ⊕ *n* **1** sail for pleasure. ◆ *v* **2** sail from place to place for pleasure. **3** (of a vehicle) travel at a moderate and economical speed. **cruiser** *n* **1** fast warship. **2** motorboat with a cabin.

crumb ⊕ *n* **1** small fragment of bread or other dry food. **2** small amount.

crumble ⊕ *v* **1** break into fragments. **2** fall apart or decay. ◆ *n* **3** pudding of stewed fruit with a crumbly topping. **crumbly** *adj*

———————| THESAURUS |———————

diagonal, intersecting, oblique

crouch *v* **1** = **bend down**, bow, duck, hunch, kneel, squat, stoop

crow² *v* **2** = **gloat**, blow one's own trumpet, boast, brag, exult, skite (*Aust & NZ*), strut, swagger, triumph

crowd *n* **1** = **multitude**, army, horde, host, mass, mob, pack, swarm, throng **2** = **group**, bunch (*inf*), circle, clique, lot, set ◆ *v* **3** = **flock**, congregate, gather, mass, stream, surge, swarm, throng **4** = **squeeze**, bundle, congest, cram, pack, pile

crown *n* **1** = **coronet**, circlet, diadem, tiara **2** = **laurel wreath**, garland, honour, laurels, prize, trophy, wreath **3** = **high point**, apex, crest, pinnacle, summit, tip, top ◆ *v* **5** = **honour**, adorn, dignify, festoon **7** = **cap**, be the climax *or* culmination of, complete, finish, perfect, put the finishing touch to, round off, top **8** *Inf* = **strike**, belt (*inf*), biff (*sl*), box, cuff, hit over the head, punch

crucial *adj* = **vital**, central, critical, decisive, essential, high–priority, important, momentous, pivotal, pressing, urgent

crude *adj* **1** = **primitive**, clumsy, makeshift, rough, rough–and–ready, rudimentary, unpolished **2** = **vulgar**, coarse, dirty, gross, indecent, obscene, scungy (*Aust & NZ inf*), smutty, tasteless, uncouth ≠ **polished 3** = **unrefined**, natural, raw, unprocessed ≠ **processed**

cruel *adj* **1** = **brutal**, barbarous, callous, hard–hearted, heartless, inhumane, malevolent, sadistic, spiteful, unkind, vicious ≠ **kind**

cruise *n* **1** = **sail**, boat trip, sea trip, voyage ◆ *v* **2** = **sail**, coast, voyage **3** = **travel along**, coast, drift, keep a steady pace

crumb *n* = **bit**, fragment, grain, morsel, scrap, shred, *soupçon*

crumble *v* **1** = **crush**, fragment, granulate, grind, pound, powder, pulverize **2** = **disintegrate**, collapse, decay,

crumpet n 1 round soft yeast cake, eaten buttered. 2 *Slang* sexually attractive women collectively.

crumple ⊕ v 1 crush, crease. 2 collapse, esp. from shock.

crunch ⊕ v 1 bite or chew with a noisy crushing sound. 2 make a crisp or brittle sound. ◆ n 3 crunching sound. 4 *Informal* critical moment. **crunchy** adj

crusade ⊕ n 1 medieval Christian war to recover the Holy Land from the Muslims. 2 vigorous campaign in favour of a cause. ◆ v 3 take part in a crusade. **crusader** n

crush ⊕ v 1 compress so as to injure, break, or crumple. 2 break into small pieces. 3 defeat or humiliate utterly. ◆ n 4 dense crowd. 5 *Informal* infatuation. 6 drink made by crushing fruit.

crust ⊕ n 1 hard outer part of something, esp. bread. ◆ v 2 cover with or form a crust. **crusty** adj 1 having a crust. 2 irritable.

crustacean n hard-shelled, usu. aquatic animal with several pairs of legs, such as the crab or lobster.

crutch n 1 long sticklike support with a rest for the armpit, used by a lame person. 2 person or thing that gives support. 3 crotch.

crux n, pl **cruxes** crucial or decisive point.

cry ⊕ v **crying, cried** 1 shed tears. 2 call or utter loudly. ◆ n, pl **cries** 3 fit of weeping.

4 loud utterance. 5 urgent appeal, e.g. *a cry for help.* **crybaby** n person, esp. a child, who cries too readily. **cry off** v *Informal* withdraw from an arrangement. **cry out for** v need urgently.

crypt n vault under a church, esp. one used as a burial place.

crystal n 1 (single grain of) a symmetrically shaped solid formed naturally by some substances. 2 very clear and brilliant glass, usu. with the surface cut in many planes. 3 tumblers, vases, etc., made of crystal. ◆ adj 4 bright and clear. **crystalline** adj 1 of or like crystal or crystals. 2 clear. **crystallize** v 1 make or become definite. 2 form into crystals. **crystallization** n

cu. cubic.

cub ⊕ n 1 young wild animal such as a bear or fox. ◆ v **cubbing, cubbed** 2 give birth to cubs.

cubbyhole n small enclosed space or room.

cube n 1 object with six equal square sides. 2 number resulting from multiplying a number by itself twice. ◆ v 3 cut into cubes. 4 find the cube of (a number). **cubic** adj 1 having three dimensions. 2 cube-shaped. **cubism** n style of art in which objects are represented by geometrical shapes. **cubist** adj, n **cube root** number whose cube is a given number.

━━━━━━━━━━━━━ THESAURUS ━━━━━━━━━━━━━

degenerate, deteriorate, fall apart, go to pieces, go to wrack and ruin, tumble down

crumple v 1 = **crush**, crease, rumple, screw up, wrinkle 2 = **collapse**, break down, cave in, fall, give way, go to pieces

crunch v 1 = **chomp**, champ, chew noisily, grind, munch ◆ n 4 *Inf* = **critical point**, crisis, crux, emergency, moment of truth, test

crusade n 2 = **campaign**, cause, drive, movement, push

crush v 1 = **squash**, break, compress, press, pulverize, squeeze 3 a = **overcome**, conquer, overpower, overwhelm, put

down, quell, stamp out, subdue **b** = **humiliate**, abash, mortify, put down (*sl*), quash, shame ◆ n 4 = **crowd**, huddle, jam

crust n 1 = **layer**, coating, covering, shell, skin, surface

cry v 1 = **weep**, blubber, shed tears, snivel, sob ≠ **laugh** 2 = **shout**, bawl, bellow, call out, exclaim, howl, roar, scream, shriek, yell ≠ **whisper** ◆ n 3 = **weeping**, blubbering, snivelling, sob, sobbing, weep 4 = **shout**, bellow, call, exclamation, howl, roar, scream, screech, shriek, yell 5 = **appeal**, plea

cub n 1 = **young**, offspring, whelp

cubicle *n* enclosed part of a large room, screened for privacy.

cuckoo *n* 1 migratory bird with a characteristic two–note call, which lays its eggs in the nests of other birds. ◆ *adj* 2 *Informal* insane or foolish.

cucumber *n* long green–skinned fleshy fruit used in salads.

cud *n* partially digested food which a ruminant brings back into its mouth to chew again. **chew the cud** think deeply.

cuddle ❶ *v, n* hug. **cuddly** *adj*

cudgel ❶ *n* short thick stick used as a weapon.

cue[1] ❶ *n* 1 signal to an actor or musician to begin speaking or playing. 2 signal or reminder. ◆ *v* **cueing, cued** 3 give a cue to.

cue[2] *n* 1 long tapering stick used in billiards, snooker, or pool. ◆ *v* **cueing, cued** 2 hit (a ball) with a cue.

cuff[1] *n* end of a sleeve. **off the cuff** *Informal* without preparation. **cuff link** one of a pair of decorative fastenings for shirt cuffs.

cuff[2] *v* 1 hit with an open hand. ◆ *n* 2 blow with an open hand.

cuisine [quiz–**zeen**] *n* style of cooking.

cul–de–sac ❶ *n* road with one end blocked off.

culinary *adj* of kitchens or cookery.

cull *v* 1 choose, gather. 2 remove or kill (inferior or surplus animals) from a herd. ◆ *n* 3 culling.

culminate ❶ *v* reach the highest point or climax. **culmination** *n*

culottes *pl n* women's knee–length trousers cut to look like a skirt.

culpable ❶ *adj* deserving blame. **culpability** *n*

culprit ❶ *n* person guilty of an offence or misdeed.

cult ❶ *n* 1 specific system of worship. 2 devotion to a person, idea, or activity. 3 popular fashion.

cultivate ❶ *v* 1 prepare (land) to grow crops. 2 grow (plants). 3 develop or improve (something). 4 try to develop a friendship with (someone). **cultivated** *adj* well–educated. **cultivation** *n*

culture ❶ *n* 1 ideas, customs, and art of a particular society. 2 particular society. 3 developed understanding of the arts. 4 cultivation of plants or rearing of animals. 5 growth of bacteria for study. **cultural** *adj* **cultured** *adj* showing good taste or manners.

culvert ❶ *n* drain under a road or railway.

cumbersome ❶ *adj* awkward because of size or shape.

cummerbund *n* wide sash worn round the waist.

cumulative *adj* increasing steadily.

———————— THESAURUS ————————

cuddle *v* = **hug**, bill and coo, cosset, embrace, fondle, pet, snuggle

cudgel *n* = **club**, baton, bludgeon, cosh (*Brit*), stick, truncheon

cue[1] *n* 1 = **prompt**, catchword 2 = **signal**, hint, reminder, sign, suggestion

cul–de–sac *n* = **dead end**, blind alley

culminate *v* = **end up**, climax, close, come to a climax, come to a head, conclude, finish, wind up

culpable *adj* = **blameworthy**, at fault, found wanting, guilty, in the wrong, to blame, wrong

culprit *n* = **offender**, criminal, evildoer, felon, guilty party, miscreant, transgressor, wrongdoer

cult *n* 1 = **sect**, clique, faction, religion, school 2 = **devotion**, idolization, worship

cultivate *v* 1 = **farm**, plant, plough, tend, till, work 3 = **develop**, foster, improve, promote, refine 4 = **court**, dance attendance upon, run after, seek out

culture *n* 1 = **civilization**, customs, lifestyle, mores, society, way of life 3 = **refinement**, education, enlightenment, good taste, sophistication, urbanity 4 = **farming**, cultivation, husbandry

culvert *n* = **drain**, channel, conduit, gutter, watercourse

cumbersome *adj* = **awkward**, bulky, burdensome, heavy, unmanageable,

cumulus [**kew**–myew–luss] *n, pl* –**li** thick white or dark grey cloud.

cunning ❶ *adj* 1 clever at deceiving. 2 ingenious. ♦ *n* 3 cleverness at deceiving. 4 ingenuity.

cup ❶ *n* 1 small bowl–shaped drinking container with a handle. 2 contents of a cup. 3 (competition with) a cup–shaped trophy given as a prize. 4 hollow rounded shape. ♦ *v* **cupping, cupped** 5 form (one's hands) into the shape of a cup. 6 hold in cupped hands. **cupful** *n*

cur *n Lit* 1 mongrel dog. 2 contemptible person.

curate *n* clergyman who assists a parish priest. **curacy** [**kew**–rah–see] *n, pl* –**cies** work or position of a curate.

curator *n* person in charge of a museum or art gallery.

curb ❶ *n* 1 something that restrains. ♦ *v* 2 control, restrain.

curd *n* coagulated milk, used to make cheese. **curdle** *v* turn into curd, coagulate.

cure ❶ *v* 1 get rid of (an illness or problem). 2 make (someone) well again. 3 preserve by salting, smoking, or drying. ♦ *n* 4 (treatment causing) curing of an illness or person. 5 remedy or solution. **curable** *adj*

curfew *n* 1 law ordering people to stay inside their homes after a specific time at night. 2 time set as a deadline by such a law.

curio *n, pl* –**rios** rare or unusual object valued as a collector's item.

curious ❶ *adj* 1 eager to learn or know. 2 eager to find out private details. 3 unusual or peculiar. **curiously** *adv* **curiosity** *n* 1 eagerness to know or find out. 2 (*pl* –**ties**) rare or unusual object.

curl ❶ *n* 1 curved piece of hair. 2 curved spiral shape. ♦ *v* 3 make (hair) into curls or (of hair) grow in curls. 4 make into a curved spiral shape. **curly** *adj* **curling** *n* game like bowls, played with heavy stones on ice.

curlew *n* long–billed wading bird.

curmudgeon *n* bad–tempered person.

currant *n* 1 small dried grape. 2 small round berry, such as a redcurrant.

current ❶ *adj* 1 of the immediate present. 2 most recent, up–to–date. 3 commonly accepted. ♦ *n* 4 flow of water or air in one direction. 5 flow of electricity. 6 general trend. **currently** *adv* **currency** *n, pl* –**cies** 1 money in use in a particular country. 2 general acceptance or use.

curriculum *n, pl* –**la**, –**lums** all the courses

—————— THESAURUS ——————

unwieldy, weighty ≠ **practical**

cunning *adj* 1 = **crafty**, artful, devious, Machiavellian, sharp, shifty, sly, wily ≠ **frank** 2 = **skilful**, imaginative, ingenious ≠ **clumsy** ♦ *n* 3 = **craftiness**, artfulness, deviousness, guile, slyness, trickery ≠ **sincerity** 4 = **skill**, artifice, cleverness, ingenuity, subtlety ≠ **clumsiness**

cup *n* 1 = **mug**, beaker, bowl, chalice, goblet, teacup 3 = **trophy**

curb *n* 1 = **restraint**, brake, check, control, deterrent, limitation ♦ *v* 2 = **restrain**, check, control, hinder, impede, inhibit, restrict, retard, suppress

cure *v* 1, 2 = **make better**, correct, ease, heal, mend, relieve, remedy, restore 3 = **preserve**, dry, pickle, salt, smoke ♦ *n* 4 = **remedy**, antidote, medicine, nostrum,

panacea, treatment

curious *adj* 1 = **inquiring**, inquisitive, interested, questioning, searching ≠ **indifferent** 2 = **inquisitive**, meddling, nosy (*inf*), prying 3 = **unusual**, bizarre, extraordinary, munted (*NZ sl*), mysterious, novel, odd, peculiar, rare, strange, unexpected

curl *n* 2 = **twist**, coil, kink, ringlet, spiral, whorl ♦ *v* 4 = **twirl**, bend, coil, curve, loop, spiral, turn, twist, wind

current *adj* 1 = **present**, contemporary, present–day ≠ **past** 2 = **up–to–date**, fashionable, in fashion, in vogue, trendy (*Brit inf*) 3 = **prevalent**, accepted, common, customary, in circulation, popular, topical, widespread ♦ *n* 4 = **flow**, course, draught, jet, progression, river,

of study offered by a school or college.
curriculum vitae [**vee**–tie] outline of
someone's educational and professional
history, prepared for job applications.

curry n, pl **–ries 1** Indian dish of meat or
vegetables in a hot spicy sauce. ◆ v –
rying, –ried 2 prepare (food) with mixture
of hot spices. **curry powder** mixture of
spices for making curry.

curse ❶ v **1** swear (at). **2** ask a supernatural
power to cause harm to. ◆ n **3** swearword.
4 (result of) a call to a supernatural
power to cause harm to someone. **5** something
causing trouble or harm. **cursed** adj

cursor n movable point of light that shows
a specific position on a visual display unit.

cursory adj quick and superficial. **cursorily**
adv

curt ❶ adj brief and rather rude.

curtail ❶ v **1** cut short. **2** restrict.
curtailment n

curtain ❶ n **1** piece of cloth hung at a
window or opening as a screen. **2** hanging
cloth separating the audience and the
stage in a theatre. **3** fall or closing of the
curtain at the end, or the rise or opening
of the curtain at the start of a theatrical
performance. **4** something forming a
barrier or screen. ◆ v **5** provide with
curtains. **6** (foll. by off) separate by a
curtain.

curtsy, curtsey n, pl **–sies, –seys 1**

woman's gesture of respect made by
bending the knees and bowing the head.
◆ v **–sying, –sied** or **–seying, –seyed 2**
make a curtsy.

curve ❶ n **1** continuously bending line
with no straight parts. ◆ v **2** form or move
in a curve. **curvy** adj **curvaceous** adj
Informal (of a woman) having a shapely
body. **curvature** n curved shape.
curvilinear adj consisting of or bounded
by a curve.

cushion ❶ n **1** bag filled with soft material,
to make a seat more comfortable. **2**
something that provides comfort or
absorbs shock. ◆ v **3** lessen the effects of.
4 protect from injury or shock.

cushy ❶ adj **cushier, cushiest** Informal
easy.

custard n sweet yellow sauce made from
milk and eggs.

custody ❶ n **1** keeping safe. **2**
imprisonment prior to being tried.
custodial adj **custodian** n person in
charge of a public building.

custom ❶ n **1** long–established activity or
action. **2** usual habit. **3** regular use of a
shop or business. ◆ pl **4** duty charged on
imports or exports. **5** government
department which collects these. **6** area at
a port, airport, or border where baggage
and freight are examined for dutiable
goods. **customary** adj **1** usual.

stream, tide, undertow **6 = mood**,
atmosphere, feeling, tendency, trend,
undercurrent

curse v **1 = swear**, blaspheme, cuss (inf),
take the Lord's name in vain **2 = damn**,
anathematize, excommunicate ◆ n
3 = oath, blasphemy, expletive, obscenity,
swearing, swearword **4 = denunciation**,
anathema, ban, excommunication,
hoodoo (inf), jinx **5 = affliction**, bane,
hardship, plague, scourge, torment,
trouble

curt adj **= short**, abrupt, blunt, brief,
brusque, gruff, monosyllabic, succinct,
terse

curtail v **1 = cut short**, cut back, decrease,
diminish, dock, lessen, reduce, shorten,
truncate

curtain n **1 = hanging**, drape (chiefly US)

curve n **1 = bend**, arc, curvature, loop,
trajectory, turn ◆ v **2 = bend**, arc, arch,
coil, hook, spiral, swerve, turn, twist, wind

cushion n **1 = pillow**, beanbag, bolster,
hassock, headrest, pad ◆ v **3 = soften**,
dampen, deaden, muffle, stifle, suppress

cushy adj Inf **= easy**, comfortable, soft,
undemanding

custody n **1 = safekeeping**, care, charge,
keeping, protection, supervision
2 = imprisonment, confinement,

2 established by custom. **customarily** adv
customer n person who buys goods or services. **custom–built, custom–made** adj made to the specifications of an individual customer.

cut ⊕ v **cutting, cut 1** open up, penetrate, wound, or divide with a sharp instrument. **2** divide. **3** trim or shape by cutting. **4** abridge, shorten. **5** reduce, restrict. **6** Informal hurt the feelings of. **7** pretend not to recognize. **8** Informal n not allowed. **9** stroke or incision made by cutting. **10** piece cut off. **11** reduction. **12** deletion in a text, film, or play. **13** Informal share, of profits. **14** style in which hair or a garment is cut. **cut in** v **1** interrupt. **2** obstruct another vehicle in overtaking it.

cute ⊕ adj **1** appealing or attractive. **2** Informal clever or shrewd. **cutely** adv **cuteness** n

cuticle n skin at the base of a fingernail or toenail.

cutlass n curved one–edged sword formerly used by sailors.

cutlery n knives, forks, and spoons. **cutler** n maker of cutlery.

cutlet n **1** small piece of meat like a chop. **2** flat croquette of chopped meat or fish.

cuttlefish n squidlike sea mollusc.

CV curriculum vitae.

cyanide n extremely poisonous chemical compound.

cybercafé n a café equipped with

computer terminals which customers can use to access the Internet.

cybernetics n branch of science in which electronic and mechanical systems are studied and compared to biological systems.

cyberspace n place said to contain all the data stored on computers.

cybersquatting n registering an Internet domain name belonging to another person in the hope of selling it to them for a profit. **cybersquatter** n

cyclamen [sik–la–men] n plant with red, pink, or white flowers.

cycle ⊕ v **1** ride a bicycle. ♦ n **2** bicycle. **3** US motorcycle. **4** complete series of recurring events. **5** time taken for one such series. **cyclical, cyclic** adj occurring in cycles. **cyclist** n person who rides a bicycle.

cyclometer n a device that records the number of revolutions made by a wheel and the distance travelled.

cyclone n violent wind moving clockwise round a central area.

cygnet n young swan.

cylinder n **1** solid or hollow body with straight sides and circular ends. **2** chamber within which the piston moves in an internal–combustion engine. **cylindrical** adj

cymbal n percussion instrument consisting of a brass plate which is struck against

detention, incarceration
custom n **1** = **tradition**, convention, policy, practice, ritual, rule, usage **2** = **habit**, practice, procedure, routine, way, wont **3** = **customers**, patronage, trade ♦ pl **4** = **duty**, import charges, tariff, tax, toll
cut v **1** = **penetrate**, chop, pierce, score, sever, slash, slice, slit, wound **2** = **divide**, bisect, dissect, slice, split **3** = **shape**, carve, chisel, clip, fashion, form, hew, lop, mow, pare, prune, sculpt, shave, snip, trim, whittle **4** = **abridge**, abbreviate, condense, curtail, delete, shorten ≠ **extend**
5 = **reduce**, contract, cut back, decrease,

diminish, lower, slash, slim (down) ≠ **increase 6** Inf = **hurt**, insult, put down, snub, sting, wound **7** = **ignore**, avoid, cold–shoulder, slight, spurn, turn one's back on ≠ **receive** ♦ n **9** = **incision**, gash, laceration, nick, slash, slit, stroke, wound **11** = **reduction**, cutback, decrease, fall, lowering, saving **13** Inf = **share**, percentage, piece, portion, section, slice **14** = **style**, fashion, look, shape
cute adj **1** = **appealing**, attractive, charming, delightful, engaging, lekker (S Afr sl), lovable
cycle n **4, 5** = **era**, circle, period, phase,

another or hit with a stick.

cynic ➊ [**sin**–ik] n person who believes that people always act selfishly. **cynical** adj **cynically** adv **cynicism** n

cypress n evergreen tree with dark green leaves.

cyst [**sist**] n (abnormal) sac in the body containing fluid or soft matter. **cystic** adj

cystitis [siss–**tite**–iss] n inflammation of the bladder.

cytology [site-**ol**-a-jee] n study of plant and animal cells. **cytological** adj **cytologist** n

cytoplasm n protoplasm of a cell excluding the nucleus.

czar [**zahr**] n same as TSAR.

revolution, rotation

cynic n = **sceptic**, doubter, misanthrope, misanthropist, pessimist, scoffer

cynical = **sceptical**, contemptuous, derisive, ironic, mocking, pessimistic, scoffing, scornful.

D d

dab ❶ *v* **dabbing, dabbed 1** pat lightly. **2** apply with short tapping strokes. ◆ *n* **3** small amount of something soft or moist. **4** light stroke or tap. **dab hand** *Informal* person who is particularly good at something.

dabble ❶ *v* **1** be involved in something superficially. **2** splash about. **dabbler** *n*

dachshund *n* dog with a long body and short legs.

dad *n Informal* father.

daffodil *n* yellow trumpet–shaped flower that blooms in spring.

daft ❶ *adj Informal* foolish or crazy.

dagga *n S Afr informal* cannabis.

dagger ❶ *n* short knifelike weapon with a pointed blade.

dahlia [**day**–lya] *n* brightly coloured garden flower.

daily ❶ *adj* **1** occurring every day or every weekday. ◆ *adv* **2** every day. ◆ *n, pl* **–lies 3** daily newspaper. **4** *Brit informal* person who cleans other people's houses.

dainty ❶ *adj* **–tier, –tiest** delicate or elegant. **daintily** *adv*

dairy *n, pl* **dairies 1** place for the processing or sale of milk and its products. **2** *NZ* small shop selling groceries and milk often outside normal trading hours. ◆ *adj* **3** of milk or its products.

dais [**day**–iss] *n* raised platform in a hall, used by a speaker.

daisy *n, pl* **–sies** small wild flower with a yellow centre and white petals.

dale *n* (esp. in N England) valley.

dally *v* **–lying, –lied 1** waste time. **2** (foll. by *with*) deal frivolously (with). **dalliance** *n* flirtation.

Dalmatian *n* large dog with a white coat and black spots.

dam ❶ *n* **1** barrier built across a river to create a lake. **2** lake created by this. ◆ *v* **damming, dammed 3** build a dam across (a river).

damage ❶ *v* **1** harm, spoil. ◆ *n* **2** harm to a person or thing. **3** *Informal* cost, e.g. *what's the damage?* ◆ *pl* **4** money awarded as compensation for injury or loss.

damask *n* fabric with a pattern woven into it, used for tablecloths etc.

dame ❶ *n* **1** *Slang* woman. **2** (**D–**) title of a woman who has been awarded the OBE

THESAURUS

dab *v* **1** = **pat**, tap, touch **2** = **daub**, stipple ◆ *n* **3** = **spot**, bit, drop, pat, smudge, speck **4** = **pat**, flick, stroke, tap, touch

dabble *v* **1** = **play at**, dip into, potter, tinker, trifle (with) **2** = **splash**, dip

daft *adj Inf* = **foolish**, absurd, asinine, crackpot (*inf*), crazy, idiotic, insane, silly, stupid, witless

dagger *n* = **knife**, bayonet, dirk, stiletto

daily *adj* **1** = **everyday**, diurnal, quotidian ◆ *adv* **2** = **every day**, day by day, once a day

dainty *adj* **1** = **delicate**, charming, elegant, exquisite, fine, graceful, neat, petite, pretty ≠ **awkward**

dam *n* **1** = **barrier**, barrage, embankment, obstruction, wall ◆ *v* **3** = **block up**, barricade, hold back, obstruct, restrict

damage *v* **1** = **harm**, hurt, impair, injure, ruin, spoil, weaken, wreck ◆ *n* **2** = **harm**, destruction, detriment, devastation, hurt, injury, loss, suffering ≠ **gain 3** *Inf* = **cost**, bill, charge, expense ◆ *pl* **4** = **compensation**, fine, reimbursement, reparation, satisfaction or another order of chivalry.

damn ① *interj* 1 *Slang* exclamation of annoyance. ◆ *adv, adj* 2 (also **damned**) *Slang* extreme(ly). ◆ *v* 3 condemn as bad or worthless. 4 (of God) condemn to hell. **damnable** *adj* annoying. **damnably** *adv* **damnation** *interj, n* **damning** *adj* proving or suggesting guilt, e.g. *a damning report.*

damp ① *adj* 1 slightly wet. ◆ *n* 2 slight wetness, moisture. ◆ *v* (also **dampen**) 3 make damp. 4 (foll. by *down*) reduce the intensity of (feelings or actions). **damper** *n* 1 movable plate to regulate the draught in a fire. 2 pad in a piano that deadens the vibration of each string. **put a damper on** have a depressing or inhibiting effect on.

damson *n* small blue–black plumlike fruit.

dance ① *v* 1 move the feet and body rhythmically in time to music. 2 perform (a particular dance). 3 skip or leap. 4 move rhythmically. ◆ *n* 5 series of steps and movements in time to music. 6 social meeting arranged for dancing. **dancer** *n*

dandelion *n* yellow–flowered wild plant.

dandruff *n* loose scales of dry dead skin shed from the scalp.

dandy *n, pl* –**dies** 1 man who is overconcerned with the elegance of his appearance. ◆ *adj* –**dier**, –**diest** 2 *Informal* very good. **dandified** *adj*

danger ① *n* 1 possibility of being injured or killed. 2 person or thing that may cause injury or harm. 3 likelihood that

something unpleasant will happen. **dangerous** *adj* **dangerously** *adv*

dangle ① *v* 1 hang loosely. 2 display as an enticement.

dank *adj* unpleasantly damp and chilly.

dapper ① *adj* (of a man) neat in appearance and slight in build.

dappled *adj* marked with spots of a different colour. **dapple–grey** *n* horse with a grey coat and darker coloured spots.

dare ① *v* 1 be courageous enough to try (to do something). 2 challenge to do something risky. 3 challenge to do something risky. **daring** *adj* 1 willing to take risks. ◆ *n* 2 courage to do dangerous things. **daredevil** *adj, n* recklessly bold (person).

> ✓ **WORD TIP**
> When *dare* is used in a question or as a negative, it does not take an –*s*: *He dare not come.*

dark ① *adj* 1 having little or no light. 2 (of a colour) reflecting little light. 3 (of hair or skin) brown or black. 4 gloomy, sad. 5 sinister, evil. 6 secret, unknown, e.g. *keep it dark.* ◆ *n* 7 absence of light. 8 night. **darkly** *adv* **darkness** *n* **darken** *v* **dark horse** person about whom little is known. **darkroom** *n* darkened room for processing photographic film.

darling ① *n* 1 much–loved person. 2

dame *n* 2 (with cap.) = **noblewoman**, baroness, dowager, *grande dame*, lady, peeress

damn *v* 3 = **criticize**, blast, censure, condemn, denounce, put down ≠ **approve** ◆ *v* = **sentence**, condemn, doom

damp *adj* 1 = **moist**, clammy, dank, dewy, drizzly, humid, soggy, sopping, wet ≠ **dry** ◆ *n* 2 = **moisture**, dampness, dankness, drizzle ≠ **dryness** ◆ *v* 3 = **moisten**, dampen, wet 4 (foll. by *down*) = **curb**, allay, check, diminish, dull, inhibit, lessen, moderate, pour cold water on, reduce, restrain, stifle

dance *v* 1 = **prance**, jig, trip, whirl 3 = **skip**, hop ◆ *n* 6 = **ball**, disco, discotheque, hop (*inf*), knees–up (*Brit inf*), social

danger *n* 1, 2 = **peril**, hazard, jeopardy, menace, pitfall, risk, threat

dangle *v* 1 = **hang**, flap, hang down, sway, swing, trail

dapper *adj* = **neat**, natty (*inf*), smart, soigné, spruce, spry, trim, well–groomed, well turned out

dare *v* 1 = **risk**, hazard, make bold, presume, venture 2 = **challenge**, defy, goad, provoke, taunt, throw down the gauntlet ◆ *n* 3 = **challenge**, provocation, favourite. ♦ *adj* **3** much–loved.

darn ❶ *v* **1** mend (a garment) with a series of interwoven stitches. ♦ *n* **2** patch of darned work.

dart ❶ *n* **1** small narrow pointed missile that is thrown or shot, esp. in the game of darts. **2** sudden quick movement. **3** tapered tuck made in dressmaking. ♦ *pl* **4** game in which darts are thrown at a circular numbered board. ♦ *v* **5** move or direct quickly and suddenly.

dash ❶ *v* **1** move quickly. **2** hurl or crash. **3** frustrate (someone's hopes). ♦ *n* **4** sudden quick movement. **5** small amount. **6** mixture of style and courage. **7** punctuation mark (-) indicating a change of subject. **8** longer symbol used in Morse code. **dashing** *adj* stylish and attractive. **dashboard** *n* instrument panel in a vehicle.

dastardly *adj* wicked and cowardly.

data ❶ *n* **1** information consisting of observations, measurements, or facts. **2** numbers, digits, etc., stored by a computer. **data base** store of information that can be easily handled by a computer. **data processing** series of operations performed on data, esp. by a computer, to extract or interpret information.

✓ **WORD TIP**

Data is a Latin plural word but it is generally used as a singular word in English.

date¹ ❶ *n* **1** specified day of the month. **2** particular day or year when an event happened. **3** *Informal* appointment, esp. with a person of the opposite sex. **4** *Informal* person with whom one has a date. ♦ *v* **5** mark with the date. **6** assign a date of occurrence to. **7** become old–fashioned. **8** (foll. by *from*) originate from. **dated** *adj* old–fashioned.

date² *n* dark–brown sweet–tasting fruit of the date palm.

daub ❶ *v* smear or spread quickly or clumsily.

daughter *n* **1** female child. **2** woman who comes from a certain place or is connected with a certain thing. **daughter–in–law** *n*, *pl* **daughters–in–law** son's wife.

dawdle ❶ *v* walk slowly, lag behind.

———————— T H E S A U R U S ————————

taunt

dark *adj* **1** = **dim**, dingy, murky, shadowy, shady, sunless, unlit **3** = **brunette**, black, dark–skinned, dusky, ebony, sable, swarthy **4** = **gloomy**, bleak, dismal, grim, morose, mournful, sad, sombre ≠ **clear** **5** = **evil**, foul, infernal, sinister, vile, wicked **6** = **secret**, concealed, hidden, mysterious ♦ *n* **7** = **darkness**, dimness, dusk, gloom, murk, obscurity, semi–darkness **8** = **night**, evening, nightfall, night–time, twilight

darling *n* **1** = **beloved**, dear, dearest, love, sweetheart, truelove ♦ *adj* **3** = **beloved**, adored, cherished, dear, precious, treasured

darn *v* **1** = **mend**, cobble up, patch, repair, sew up, stitch ♦ *n* **2** = **mend**, invisible repair, patch, reinforcement

dart *v* **5** = **dash**, fly, race, run, rush, shoot, spring, sprint, tear

dash *v* **1** = **rush**, bolt, fly, hurry, race, run, speed, sprint, tear ≠ **throw** **2** = **throw**, cast, fling, hurl, slam, sling **3** = **frustrate**, blight, foil, ruin, spoil, thwart, undo ♦ *n* **4** = **rush**, dart, race, run, sortie, sprint, spurt **5** = **little**, bit, drop, hint, pinch, *soupçon*, sprinkling, tinge, touch ≠ **much** **6** = **style**, brio, élan, flair, flourish, panache, spirit, verve

data *n* **1** = **information**, details, facts, figures, statistics

date¹ *n* **3** *Inf* = **appointment**, assignation, engagement, meeting, rendezvous, tryst **4** *Inf* = **partner**, escort, friend ♦ *v* **6** = **put a date on**, assign a date to, fix the period of **7** = **become old–fashioned**, be dated, show one's age **8** (foll. by *from*) = **come from**, bear a date of, belong to, exist from, originate in

daub *v* = **smear**, coat, cover, paint, plaster,

dawdler *n*

dawn ❶ *n* 1 daybreak. 2 beginning (of something). ◆ *v* 3 begin to grow light. 4 begin to develop or appear. 5 (foll. by *on*) become apparent (to).

day ❶ *n* 1 period of 24 hours. 2 period of light between sunrise and sunset. 3 part of a day occupied with regular activity, esp. work. 4 period or point in time. 5 time of success. **daybreak** *n* time in the morning when light first appears. **daydream** *n* 1 pleasant fantasy indulged in while awake. ◆ *v* 2 indulge in idle fantasy. **daydreamer** *n* **daylight** *n* light from the sun. **day release** system in which workers go to college one day a week. **day-to-day** *adj* routine.

daze ❶ *v* 1 stun, by a blow or shock. ◆ *n* 2 state of confusion or shock.

dazzle ❶ *v* 1 impress greatly. 2 blind temporarily by sudden excessive light. ◆ *n* 3 bright light that dazzles. **dazzling** *adj*

DC 1 direct current. 2 District of Columbia.

DE Delaware.

de- *prefix* indicating: 1 removal, e.g. *dethrone*. 2 reversal, e.g. *declassify*. 3 departure, e.g. *decamp*.

deacon *n Christianity* 1 ordained minister

ranking immediately below a priest. 2 (in some Protestant churches) lay official who assists the minister.

dead ❶ *adj* 1 no longer alive. 2 no longer in use. 3 numb, e.g. *my leg has gone dead*. 4 complete, absolute, e.g. *dead silence*. 5 *Informal* very tired. 6 (of a place) lacking activity. ◆ *n* 7 period during which coldness or darkness is most intense, e.g. *in the dead of night*. ◆ *adv* 8 extremely. 9 suddenly, e.g. *I stopped dead*. **dead set** firmly decided. **deadbeat** *n Informal* lazy useless person. **dead beat** *Informal* exhausted. **dead end** 1 road with one end blocked off. 2 situation in which further progress is impossible. **dead heat** tie for first place between two participants in a contest. **deadline** *n* time limit. **deadlock** *n* point in a dispute at which no agreement can be reached. **deadlocked** *adj* **deadly** *adj* likely to cause death. **deadpan** *adj, adv* showing no emotion or expression. **dead reckoning** method of establishing one's position using the distance and direction travelled. **dead weight** heavy weight.

deaf ❶ *adj* unable to hear. **deaf to** refusing to listen to or take notice of. **deafen** *v* make deaf, esp. temporarily. **deafness** *n*

———————— | THESAURUS | ————————

slap on (*inf*)

dawdle *v* = **waste time**, dally, delay, drag one's feet *or* heels, hang about, idle, loaf, loiter, trail

dawn *n* 1 = **daybreak**, cockcrow, crack of dawn, daylight, morning, sunrise, sunup 2 = **beginning**, advent, birth, emergence, genesis, origin, rise, start ◆ *v* 3 = **grow light**, break, brighten, lighten 4 = **begin**, appear, develop, emerge, originate, rise, unfold 5 (foll. by *on*) = **hit**, become apparent, come into one's head, come to mind, occur, register (*inf*), strike

day *n* 1 = **twenty-four hours** 2 daylight, daytime 4 = **point in time**, date, time 5 = **time**, age, epoch, era, heyday, period, zenith

daze *v* 1 = **stun**, benumb, numb, paralyse, shock, stupefy ◆ *n* 2 = **shock**,

bewilderment, confusion, distraction, stupor, trance, trancelike state

dazzle *v* 1 = **impress**, amaze, astonish, bowl over (*inf*), overpower, overwhelm, take one's breath away 2 = **blind**, bedazzle, blur, confuse, daze ◆ *n* 3 = **splendour**, brilliance, glitter, magnificence, razzmatazz (*sl*), sparkle

dead *adj* 1 = **deceased**, defunct, departed, extinct, late, passed away, perished ≠ **living** 2 = **not working**, inactive, inoperative, stagnant, unemployed, useless ≠ **working** 3 = **numb**, inert, paralysed 4 = **total**, absolute, complete, outright, thorough, unqualified, utter 5 *Inf* = **exhausted**, dead beat (*inf*), spent, tired, worn out 6 = **boring**, dull, flat, uninteresting ◆ *n* 7 = **middle**, depth, midst ◆ *adv* 8 = **exactly**, absolutely, completely,

✓ **WORD TIP**

The use of *the deaf, the disabled,* etc. can be offensive and should be avoided. Instead you should talk about *deaf people, disabled people,* etc.

deal¹ ⊕ *n* 1 agreement or transaction. 2 kind of treatment, e.g. *a fair deal.* 3 large amount. ♦ *v* dealing, dealt [**delt**] 4 inflict (a blow) on. 5 *Cards* give out (cards) to the players. **dealer** *n* **dealings** *pl n* transactions or business relations. **deal out** *v* distribute. **deal with** *v* 1 take action on. 2 be concerned with.

deal² *n* plank of fir or pine wood.

dean *n* 1 chief administrative official of a college or university faculty. 2 chief administrator of a cathedral. **deanery** *n, pl* –**eries** 1 office or residence of a dean. 2 parishes of a dean.

dear ⊕ *n* 1 someone regarded with affection. ♦ *adj* 2 much–loved. 3 costly. **dearly** *adv*

dearth ⊕ [**dirth**] *n* inadequate amount, scarcity.

death ⊕ *n* 1 permanent end of life in a person or animal. 2 instance of this. 3 ending, destruction. **deathly** *adj, adv* like death, e.g. *a deathly silence; deathly pale.* **death duty** former name for INHERITANCE TAX. **deathtrap** *n* place or vehicle considered very unsafe.

debacle ⊕ [day–**bah**–kl] *n* disastrous failure.

debase ⊕ *v* lower in value, quality, or character. **debasement** *n*

debate ⊕ *n* 1 discussion. ♦ *v* 2 discuss formally. 3 consider (a course of action). **debatable** *adj* not absolutely certain.

debilitate *v* weaken, make feeble. **debilitation** *n* **debility** *n* weakness, infirmity.

debit *n* 1 acknowledgment of a sum owing by entry on the left side of an account. ♦ *v* debiting, debited 2 charge (an account) with a debt.

debonair ⊕ *adj* (of a man) charming and refined.

debrief ⊕ *v* receive a report from (a soldier, diplomat, etc.) after an event. **debriefing** *n*

debris ⊕ [**deb**–ree] *n* fragments of something destroyed.

debt ⊕ *n* something owed, esp. money. **in debt** owing money. **debtor** *n*

━━━━━━━━━ THESAURUS ━━━━━━━━━

directly, entirely, totally

deaf *adj* = **hard of hearing**, stone deaf, without hearing **deaf to** = **oblivious**, indifferent, unconcerned, unhearing, unmoved

deal¹ *n* 1 = **agreement**, arrangement, bargain, contract, pact, transaction, understanding 3 = **amount**, degree, extent, portion, quantity, share

dear *n* 1 = **beloved**, angel, darling, loved one, precious, treasure ♦ *adj* 2 = **beloved**, cherished, close, favourite, intimate, precious, prized, treasured ≠ **hated** 3 = **expensive**, at a premium, costly, high–priced, overpriced, pricey (*inf*) ≠ **cheap**

dearth *n* = **scarcity**, deficiency, inadequacy, insufficiency, lack, paucity, poverty, shortage, want

death *n* 1, 2 = **dying**, demise, departure, end, exit, passing ≠ **birth** 3 = **destruction**, downfall, extinction, finish, ruin, undoing ≠ **beginning**

debacle *n* = **disaster**, catastrophe, collapse, defeat, fiasco, reversal, rout

debase *v* = **degrade**, cheapen, devalue, lower, reduce ≠ **elevate**

debate *n* 1 = **discussion**, argument, contention, controversy, dispute ♦ *v* 3 = **discuss**, argue, dispute, question 4 = **consider**, deliberate, ponder, reflect, ruminate, weigh

debonair *adj* = **elegant**, charming, courteous, dashing, refined, smooth, suave, urbane, well–bred

debrief *v* = **interrogate**, cross–examine, examine, probe, question, quiz

debris *n* = **remains**, bits, detritus,

with a base of ten, in which numbers are expressed by combinations of the digits 0 to 9.

decimate ❶ v destroy or kill a large proportion of. **decimation** n

decipher ❶ v work out the meaning of (something illegible or in code).

deck n 1 area of a ship that forms a floor. 2 similar area in a bus. 3 platform that supports the turntable and pick-up of a record player. **deck chair** folding chair made of canvas over a wooden frame. **deck out** v decorate.

declaim ❶ v 1 speak loudly and dramatically. 2 protest loudly. **declamatory** adj

declare ❶ v 1 state firmly and forcefully. 2 announce officially. 3 acknowledge for tax purposes. **declaration** n

decline ❶ v 1 become smaller, weaker, or less important. 2 refuse politely to accept or do. 3 Grammar list the inflections of (a noun, pronoun, or adjective). ♦ n 4 gradual weakening or loss.

decode ❶ v convert from code into ordinary language. **decoder** n

decompose ❶ v be broken down through chemical or bacterial action. **decomposition** n

decongestant n medicine that relieves nasal congestion.

decontaminate v make safe by removing poisons, radioactivity, etc. **decontamination** n

decor ❶ [day-core] n style in which a room or house is decorated.

decorate ❶ v 1 make more attractive by adding something ornamental. 2 paint or wallpaper. 3 award a (military) medal to. **decoration** n **decorative** adj **decorator** n

decorum ❶ [dik-core-um] n polite and socially correct behaviour.

decoy ❶ n 1 person or thing used to lure someone into danger. 2 dummy bird or animal, used to lure game within shooting range. ♦ v 3 lure away by means of a trick.

decrease ❶ v 1 make or become less. ♦ n 2 lessening, reduction. 3 amount by which something has decreased.

decree ❶ n 1 law made by someone in

2 = **adjudge**, adjudicate

decimate v = **devastate**, ravage, wreak havoc on

decipher v = **figure out** (inf), crack, decode, deduce, interpret, make out, read, solve

declaim v 1 = **orate**, harangue, hold forth, lecture, proclaim, rant, recite, speak
2 = **protest against**, attack, decry, denounce, inveigh, rail

declare v 1 = **state**, affirm, announce, assert, claim, maintain, proclaim, profess, pronounce, swear, utter

decline v 1 a = **lessen**, decrease, diminish, dwindle, ebb, fade, fall off, shrink, wane, weaken b = **deteriorate**, decay, degenerate, sink, worsen ≠ improve
2 = **refuse**, abstain, avoid, reject, say 'no', turn down ≠ agree to ♦ n
4 = **deterioration**, decay, degeneration, downturn, drop, dwindling, failing, falling off, lessening, recession, slump,

weakening, worsening ≠ **improvement**

decode v = **decipher**, crack, decrypt, interpret, solve, unscramble, work out ≠ **scramble**

decompose v = **rot**, break up, crumble, decay, fall apart, fester, putrefy

decor n = **decoration**, colour scheme, furnishing style, ornamentation

decorate v 1 = **adorn**, beautify, embellish, festoon, grace, ornament, trim 2 = **do up** (inf), colour, furbish, paint, paper, renovate, wallpaper 3 = **pin a medal on**, cite, confer an honour on or upon

decorum n = **propriety**, decency, dignity, etiquette, good manners, politeness, protocol, respectability

decoy n 1 = **lure**, bait, enticement, inducement, pretence, trap ♦ v 3 = **lure**, deceive, ensnare, entice, entrap, seduce, tempt

decrease v 1 = **lessen**, cut down, decline, diminish, drop, dwindle, lower, reduce, authority. 2 court judgment. ♦ v 3 order by decree.

decrepit ❶ *adj* weakened or worn out by age or long use. **decrepitude** *n*

decry ❶ *v* –**crying**, –**cried** express disapproval of.

dedicate ❶ *v* 1 commit (oneself or one's time) wholly to a special purpose or cause. 2 inscribe or address (a book etc.) to someone as a tribute. **dedicated** *adj* devoted to a particular purpose or cause. **dedication** *n*

deduce ❶ *v* reach (a conclusion) by reasoning from evidence. **deducible** *adj*

deduct ❶ *v* subtract.

deed ❶ *n* 1 something that is done. 2 legal document.

deem *v* consider, judge.

deep ❶ *adj* 1 extending or situated far down, inwards, backwards, or sideways. 2 of a specified dimension downwards, inwards, or backwards. 3 difficult to

understand. 4 of great intensity. 5 (foll. by *in*) absorbed in (an activity). 6 (of a colour) strong or dark. 7 low in pitch. **the deep** *Poetic* the sea. **deeply** *adv* profoundly or intensely (also **deep down**). **deepen** *v* **deep-freeze** *n* same as FREEZER.

deer *n*, *pl* **deer** large wild animal, the male of which has antlers.

deface ❶ *v* deliberately spoil the appearance of.

defame ❶ *v* attack the good reputation of. **defamation** *n* **defamatory** [dif-**fam**-a-tree] *adj*

default ❶ *n* 1 failure to do something. 2 *Computers* instruction to a computer to select a particular option unless the user specifies otherwise. ♦ *v* 3 fail to fulfil an obligation. **in default of** in the absence of.

defeat ❶ *v* 1 win a victory over. 2 thwart, frustrate. ♦ *n* 3 defeating. **defeatism** *n* ready acceptance or expectation of defeat. **defeatist** *adj*, *n*

────── THESAURUS ──────

shrink, subside ≠ **extend** ♦ *n* 2 = **lessening**, contraction, cutback, decline, dwindling, falling off, loss, reduction, subsidence ≠ **growth**

decree *n* 1 = **law**, act, command, edict, order, proclamation, ruling, statute ♦ *v* 3 = **order**, command, demand, ordain, prescribe, proclaim, pronounce, rule

decrepit *adj* a = **weak**, aged, doddering, feeble, frail, infirm b = **worn-out**, battered, beat–up (*inf*), broken–down, dilapidated, ramshackle, rickety, run–down, tumbledown, weather–beaten

decry *v* = **condemn**, belittle, criticize, denigrate, denounce, discredit, disparage, put down, run down

dedicate *v* 1 = **devote**, commit, give over to, pledge, surrender 2 = **inscribe**, address

deduce *v* = **conclude**, draw, gather, glean, infer, reason, take to mean, understand

deduct *v* = **subtract**, decrease by, knock off (*inf*), reduce by, remove, take away, take off

deed *n* 1 = **action**, achievement, act, exploit, fact, feat, performance

2 = **document**, contract, title

deep *adj* 1 = **wide**, bottomless, broad, far, profound, unfathomable, yawning ≠ **shallow** 3 = **mysterious**, abstract, abstruse, arcane, esoteric, hidden, obscure, recondite, secret 4 = **intense**, extreme, grave, great, profound, serious (*inf*), unqualified ≠ **shallow** 5 (foll. by *in*) = **absorbed**, engrossed, immersed, lost, preoccupied, rapt 6 = **dark**, intense, rich, strong, vivid ≠ **light** 7 = **low**, bass, booming, low–pitched, resonant, sonorous ≠ **high** ♦ *n* **the deep** *Poet* = **ocean**, briny (*inf*), high seas, main, sea

deface *v* = **vandalize**, damage, deform, disfigure, mar, mutilate, spoil, tarnish

defame *v* = **slander**, bad–mouth (*sl, chiefly US & Canad*), cast aspersions on, denigrate, discredit, disparage, knock (*inf*), libel, malign, smear

default *n* 1 = **failure**, deficiency, dereliction, evasion, lapse, neglect, nonpayment, omission ♦ *v* 3 = **fail**, dodge, evade, neglect

defeat *v* 1 = **beat**, conquer, crush, master,

defecate v discharge waste from the body through the anus.

defect ⊕ n 1 imperfection, blemish. ◆ v 2 desert one's cause or country to join the opposing forces. **defective** adj imperfect, faulty. **defection** n **defector** n

defend ⊕ v 1 protect from harm or danger. 2 support in the face of criticism. 3 represent (a defendant) in court. **defendant** n person accused of a crime. **defender** n **defensible** adj capable of being defended because believed to be right. **defensive** adj 1 intended for defence. 2 overanxious to protect oneself against (threatened) criticism. **defensively** adv

defer¹ ⊕ v –ferring, –ferred delay (something) until a future time. **deferment, deferral** n

defer² ⊕ v –ferring, –ferred (foll. by to) comply with the wishes (of). **deference** n polite and respectful behaviour. **deferential** adj

deficient ⊕ adj 1 lacking some essential thing or quality. 2 inadequate in quality or quantity. **deficiency** n 1 state of being deficient. 2 lack, shortage. **deficit** n

amount by which a sum of money is too small.

defile v treat (something sacred or important) without respect. **defilement** n

define ⊕ v 1 state precisely the meaning of. 2 show clearly the outline of. **definable** adj **definite** adj 1 firm, clear, and precise. 2 having precise limits. 3 known for certain. **definitely** adv **definition** n 1 statement of the meaning of a word or phrase. 2 quality of being clear and distinct. **definitive** adj 1 providing an unquestionable conclusion. 2 being the best example of something.

deflate ⊕ v 1 (cause to) collapse through the release of air. 2 take away the self–esteem or conceit of. 3 Economics cause deflation of (an economy). **deflation** n 1 Economics reduction in economic activity resulting in lower output and investment. 2 feeling of sadness following excitement. **deflationary** adj

deflect ⊕ v (cause to) turn aside from a course. **deflection** n

deform ⊕ v put out of shape or spoil the appearance of. **deformation** n **deformity** n

defraud ⊕ v cheat out of money, property,

———————[THESAURUS]———————

overwhelm, rout, trounce, vanquish, wipe the floor with (inf) ≠ **lose** 2 = **frustrate**, baffle, balk, confound, foil, get the better of, ruin, thwart ◆ n 3 = **conquest**, beating, overthrow, pasting (sl), rout ≠ **success**

defect n 1 = **imperfection**, blemish, blotch, error, failing, fault, flaw, spot, taint ◆ v 2 = **desert**, abandon, change sides, go over, rebel, revolt, walk out on (inf)

defend v 1 = **protect**, cover, guard, keep safe, preserve, safeguard, screen, shelter, shield 2 = **support**, champion, endorse, justify, speak up for, stand up for, stick up for (inf), uphold, vindicate

defer¹ v = **postpone**, delay, hold over, procrastinate, put off, put on ice (inf), shelve, suspend

defer² v (foll. by to) = **comply**, accede, bow, capitulate, give in, give way to, submit, yield

deficient adj 1 = **lacking**, inadequate, insufficient, meagre, scant, scarce, short, skimpy, wanting 2 = **unsatisfactory**, defective, faulty, flawed, impaired, imperfect, incomplete, inferior, weak

define v 1 = **describe**, characterize, designate, explain, expound, interpret, specify, spell out 2 = **mark out**, bound, circumscribe, delineate, demarcate, limit, outline

deflate v 1 = **collapse**, empty, exhaust, flatten, puncture, shrink ≠ **expand** 2 = **humiliate**, chasten, disconcert, dispirit, humble, mortify, put down (sl), squash 3 Economics = **reduce**, depress, devalue, diminish

deflect v = **turn aside**, bend, deviate, diverge, glance off, ricochet, swerve, veer

deform v = **distort**, buckle, contort, deface, disfigure, gnarl, maim, mangle, etc.

defrost v 1 make or become free of ice. 2 thaw (frozen food) by removing it from a freezer.

deft ⊕ adj quick and skilful in movement.

defunct ⊕ adj no longer existing or operative.

defuse v 1 remove the fuse of (an explosive device). 2 remove the tension from (a situation).

defy ⊕ v –fying, –fied 1 resist openly and boldly. 2 make impossible, e.g. *the condition of the refugees defied description*. **defiance** n open resistance or disobedience. **defiant** adj

degenerate ⊕ adj 1 having deteriorated to a lower mental, moral, or physical level. ◆ n 2 degenerate person. ◆ v 3 become degenerate. **degeneracy** n degenerate behaviour. **degeneration** n

degrade ⊕ v 1 reduce to dishonour or disgrace. 2 reduce in status or quality. 3 *Chem* decompose into smaller molecules. **degradation** n

degree ⊕ n 1 stage in a scale of relative amount or intensity. 2 academic award

given by a university or college on successful completion of a course. 3 unit of measurement for temperature, angles, or latitude and longitude.

dehydrate v remove water from (food) to preserve it. **be dehydrated** become weak through losing too much water from the body. **dehydration** n

deify [day–if–fie] v –fying, –fied treat or worship as a god. **deification** n

deign [dane] v agree (to do something), but as if doing someone a favour.

dejected ⊕ adj unhappy. **dejection** n

delay ⊕ v 1 put off to a later time. 2 slow up or cause to be late. ◆ n 3 act of delaying. 4 interval of time between events.

delectable adj delightful, very attractive. **delectation** n *Formal* great pleasure.

delegate ⊕ n 1 person chosen to represent others, esp. at a meeting. ◆ v 2 entrust (duties or powers) to someone. 3 appoint as a delegate. **delegation** n 1 group chosen to represent others. 2 delegating.

delete ⊕ v remove (something written or

THESAURUS

mar, misshape, mutilate, ruin, spoil, twist, warp

defraud v = **cheat**, con (*inf*), diddle (*inf*), embezzle, fleece, pilfer, rip off (*sl*), swindle, trick

deft adj = **skilful**, adept, adroit, agile, dexterous, expert, neat, nimble, proficient

defunct adj = **dead**, bygone, deceased, departed, expired, extinct, gone, inoperative, invalid, nonexistent, obsolete, out of commission

defy v 1 = **resist**, brave, confront, disregard, flout, scorn, slight, spurn

degenerate adj 1 = **depraved**, corrupt, debauched, decadent, dissolute, immoral, low, perverted ◆ v 3 = **worsen**, decay, decline, decrease, deteriorate, fall off, lapse, sink, slip

degrade v 1 = **demean**, debase, discredit, disgrace, dishonour, humble, humiliate, shame ≠ **honour** 2 = **demote**, downgrade,

lower ≠ **raise**

degree n 1 = **stage**, grade, notch, point, rung, step, unit

dejected adj = **downhearted**, crestfallen, depressed, despondent, disconsolate, disheartened, downcast, glum, miserable, sad

delay v 1 = **put off**, defer, hold over, postpone, procrastinate, shelve, suspend 2 = **hold up**, bog down, detain, hinder, hold back, impede, obstruct, set back, slow down ≠ **speed (up)** ◆ n 3 = **putting off**, deferment, postponement, procrastination, suspension 4 = **hold–up**, hindrance, impediment, interruption, interval, setback, stoppage, wait

delegate n 1 = **representative**, agent, ambassador, commissioner, deputy, envoy, legate ◆ v 2 = **entrust**, assign, consign, devolve, give, hand over, pass on, transfer 3 = **appoint**, accredit, printed). **deletion** n

deliberate 🛈 adj 1 planned in advance, intentional. 2 careful and unhurried. ◆ v 3 think something over. **deliberately** adv **deliberation** n **deliberative** adj

delicate 🛈 adj 1 fine or subtle in quality or workmanship. 2 having a fragile beauty. 3 (of a taste etc.) pleasantly subtle. 4 easily damaged. 5 requiring tact. **delicately** adv **delicacy** n 1 being delicate. 2 (pl –cies) something particularly good to eat.

delicatessen n shop selling imported or unusual foods, often already cooked or prepared.

delicious 🛈 adj very appealing to taste or smell. **deliciously** adv

delight 🛈 n 1 (source of) great pleasure. ◆ v 2 please greatly. 3 (foll. by in) take great pleasure (in). **delightful** adj **delightfully** adv

delinquent 🛈 n 1 someone, esp. a young person, who repeatedly breaks the law. ◆ adj 2 repeatedly breaking the law.

delinquency n

delirium 🛈 n 1 state of excitement and mental confusion, often with hallucinations. 2 great excitement. **delirious** adj **deliriously** adv

deliver 🛈 v 1 carry (goods etc.) to a destination. 2 hand over. 3 aid in the birth of. 4 present (a lecture or speech). 5 release or rescue. 6 strike (a blow). **deliverance** n rescue from captivity or evil. **delivery** n, pl –eries 1 delivering. 2 something that is delivered. 3 act of giving birth to a baby. 4 style in public speaking.

dell n small wooded hollow.

delta n 1 fourth letter in the Greek alphabet. 2 flat area at the mouth of some rivers where the main stream splits up into several branches.

delude 🛈 v deceive.

deluge 🛈 [del–lyooj] n 1 great flood. 2 torrential rain. 3 overwhelming number. ◆ v 4 flood. 5 overwhelm.

de luxe 🛈 adj rich or sumptuous, superior

——— THESAURUS ———

authorize, commission, depute, designate, empower, mandate

delete v = **remove**, cancel, cross out, efface, erase, expunge, obliterate, rub out, strike out

deliberate adj 1 = **intentional**, calculated, conscious, planned, prearranged, premeditated, purposeful, wilful ≠ **unconscious** 2 = **unhurried**, careful, cautious, circumspect, measured, methodical, ponderous, slow, thoughtful ≠ **fast** ◆ v 3 = **consider**, cogitate, consult, debate, discuss, meditate, ponder, reflect, think, weigh

delicate adj 1 = **fine**, deft, elegant, exquisite, graceful, precise, skilled, subtle 3 = **subtle**, choice, dainty, delicious, fine, savoury, tender ≠ **strong** 4 = **fragile**, flimsy, frail, slender, slight, tender, weak 5 = **considerate**, diplomatic, discreet, sensitive, tactful ≠ **rough**

delicious adj = **delectable**, appetizing, choice, dainty, lekker (S Afr sl), mouthwatering, savoury, scrumptious

(inf), tasty, toothsome ≠ **unpleasant**

delight n 1 = **pleasure**, ecstasy, enjoyment, gladness, glee, happiness, joy, rapture ◆ v 2 = **please**, amuse, charm, cheer, enchant, gratify, thrill ≠ **displease** 3 (foll. by in) = **take pleasure in**, appreciate, enjoy, feast on, like, love, relish, revel in, savour

delinquent n 1 = **criminal**, culprit, lawbreaker, miscreant, offender, villain, wrongdoer

delirium n 1 = **madness**, derangement, hallucination, insanity, raving 2 = **frenzy**, ecstasy, fever, hysteria, passion

deliver v 1 = **carry**, bear, bring, cart, convey, distribute, transport 2 = **hand over**, commit, give up, grant, make over, relinquish, surrender, transfer, turn over, yield 4 = **give**, announce, declare, present, read, utter 5 = **release**, emancipate, free, liberate, loose, ransom, rescue, save 6 = **strike**, administer, aim, deal, direct, give, inflict, launch

delude v = **deceive**, beguile, dupe, fool, hoodwink, kid (inf), mislead, take in (inf), in quality.

delve ❶ v research deeply (for information).

demagogue ❶ n political agitator who appeals to the prejudice and passions of the mob. **demagogic** adj **demagogy** n

demand ❶ v 1 request forcefully. 2 require as just, urgent, etc. 3 claim as a right. ♦ n 4 forceful request. 5 Economics willingness and ability to purchase goods and services. 6 something that requires special effort or sacrifice. **demanding** adj requiring a lot of time or effort.

> ✓ **WORD TIP**
> The verb demand is followed by either of or from: demand too much of them; demand an explanation from you.

demean ❶ v **demean oneself** do something unworthy of one's status or character.

demeanour ❶ n way a person behaves.

demented ❶ adj mad. **dementia** [dim–men–sha] n state of serious mental deterioration.

demerit n fault, disadvantage.

demi– combining form half.

demijohn n large bottle with a short neck, often encased in wicker.

demilitarize v remove the military forces from. **demilitarization** n

demise ❶ n 1 eventual failure (of something successful). 2 Formal death.

demobilize v release from the armed forces. **demobilization** n

democracy ❶ n, pl –cies 1 government by the people or their elected representatives. 2 state governed in this way. **democrat** n 1 advocate of democracy. 2 (D–) member or supporter of the Democratic Party in the US. **democratic** adj 1 of democracy. 2 upholding democracy. 3 (D–) of the Democratic Party, the more liberal of the two main political parties in the US. **democratically** adv

demolish ❶ v 1 knock down or destroy (a building). 2 disprove (an argument). **demolition** n

demon ❶ n 1 evil spirit. 2 person who does something with great energy or skill. **demonic** adj evil. **demoniac, demoniacal** adj 1 appearing to be possessed by a devil. 2 frenzied. **demonology** n study of

——————| THESAURUS |——————

trick

deluge n 1 = **flood**, cataclysm, downpour, inundation, overflowing, spate, torrent 3 = **rush**, avalanche, barrage, flood, spate, torrent ♦ v 4 = **flood**, douse, drench, drown, inundate, soak, submerge, swamp 5 = **overwhelm**, engulf, inundate, overload, overrun, swamp

de luxe adj = **luxurious**, costly, exclusive, expensive, grand, opulent, select, special, splendid, superior

delve v 1 = **research**, burrow, explore, ferret out, forage, investigate, look into, probe, rummage, search

demagogue n = **agitator**, firebrand, rabble–rouser

demand v 1 = **request**, ask, challenge, inquire, interrogate, question 2 = **require**, call for, cry out for, entail, involve, necessitate, need, want ≠ **give** 3 = **claim**,

exact, expect, insist on, order ♦ n 4 = **request**, inquiry, order, question, requisition 5 Economics = **need**, call, claim, market, requirement, want

demean v = **lower**, abase, debase, degrade, descend, humble, stoop

demeanour n = **behaviour**, air, bearing, carriage, comportment, conduct, deportment, manner

demented adj = **mad**, crazed, crazy, deranged, frenzied, insane, maniacal, unbalanced, unhinged

demise n 1 = **failure**, collapse, downfall, end, fall, ruin 2 Formal = **death**, decease, departure

democracy n 1 = **self–government** 2 = **republic**, commonwealth

demolish v 1 = **knock down**, bulldoze, destroy, dismantle, flatten, level, raze, tear down ≠ **build**

demons.

demonstrate ❶ v 1 show or prove by reasoning or evidence. 2 display and explain the workings of. 3 reveal the existence of. 4 show support or opposition by public parades or rallies. **demonstrable** *adj* able to be proved. **demonstrably** *adv* **demonstration** *n* 1 organized expression of public opinion. 2 explanation or display of how something works. 3 proof. **demonstrative** *adj* tending to show one's feelings unreservedly. **demonstrator** *n* 1 person who demonstrates how a device or machine works. 2 person who takes part in a public demonstration.

demoralize ❶ v undermine the morale of. **demoralization** *n*

demote ❶ v reduce in status or rank. **demotion** *n*

demur ❶ v **–murring, –murred** 1 show reluctance. ♦ *n* 2 **without demur** without objecting.

demure ❶ *adj* quiet, reserved, and rather shy. **demurely** *adv*

den ❶ *n* 1 home of a wild animal. 2 small secluded room in a home. 3 place where

people indulge in criminal or immoral activities.

denigrate ❶ v criticize unfairly. **denigration** *n*

denim *n* 1 hard–wearing cotton fabric, usu. blue. ♦ *pl* 2 jeans made of denim.

denizen *n* inhabitant.

denote ❶ v 1 be a sign of. 2 have as a literal meaning.

denouement [day–**noo**–mon] *n* final outcome or solution in a play or book.

denounce ❶ v 1 speak vehemently against. 2 give information against. **denunciation** *n* open condemnation.

dense ❶ *adj* 1 closely packed. 2 difficult to see through. 3 stupid. **densely** *adv* **density** *n, pl* **–ties** 1 degree to which something is filled or occupied. 2 measure of the compactness of a substance, expressed as its mass per unit volume.

dent ❶ *n* 1 hollow in the surface of something, made by hitting it. ♦ v 2 make a dent in.

dental *adj* of teeth or dentistry. **dental floss** waxed thread used to remove food particles from between the teeth.

━━━━━━━━━━━━━━━ THESAURUS ━━━━━━━━━━━━━━━

demon *n* 1 = **evil spirit**, devil, fiend, ghoul, goblin, malignant spirit 2 = **wizard**, ace (*inf*), fiend, master

demonstrate v 1 = **prove**, display, exhibit, indicate, manifest, show, testify to 2 = **show how**, describe, explain, illustrate, make clear, teach 4 = **march**, parade, picket, protest, rally

demoralize v = **dishearten**, deject, depress, discourage, dispirit, undermine, unnerve, weaken

demote v = **downgrade**, degrade, kick downstairs (*sl*), lower in rank, relegate

demur v 1 = **object**, balk, dispute, hesitate, protest, refuse, take exception, waver ♦ *n* 2 **without demur** = **without objection**, without a qualm, without compunction, without hesitation, without misgivings, without protest

demure *adj* = **shy**, diffident, modest, reserved, reticent, retiring, sedate,

unassuming ≠ **forward**

den *n* 1 = **lair**, cave, cavern, haunt, hide–out, hole, shelter 2 = **study**, cubbyhole, hideaway, retreat, sanctuary, sanctum

denigrate v = **disparage**, bad–mouth (*sl, chiefly US & Canad*), belittle, knock (*inf*), malign, rubbish (*inf*), run down, slander, vilify

denote v 1 = **indicate**, betoken, designate, express, imply, mark, mean, show, signify

denounce v 1 = **condemn**, attack, censure, revile, stigmatize, vilify 2 = **accuse**, denunciate

dense *adj* 1 = **thick**, close–knit, compact, condensed, heavy, impenetrable, solid ≠ **light** 2 = **opaque** 3 = **stupid**, dozy (*Brit inf*), dull, dumb (*inf*), obtuse, slow–witted, stolid, thick ≠ **quick**

dent *n* 1 = **hollow**, chip, crater, depression, dimple, dip, impression, indentation, pit ♦ *v* 2 = **make a dent in**, gouge, hollow,

dentifrice [**den**–tif–riss] *n* paste or powder for cleaning the teeth. **dentine** [**den**–teen] *n* hard dense tissue forming the bulk of a tooth. **dentist** *n* person qualified to practise dentistry. **denture** *n* false tooth.

denude *v* remove the covering or protection from.

deny ❶ *v* –nying, –nied **1** declare to be untrue. **2** refuse to give or allow. **3** refuse to acknowledge. **denial** *n* **1** statement that something is not true. **2** rejection of a request.

depart ❶ *v* **1** leave. **2** differ, deviate. **departed** *adj Euphemistic* dead. **departure** *n*

department ❶ *n* **1** specialized division of a large organization. **2** major subdivision of the administration of a government. **departmental** *adj* **department store** large shop selling many kinds of goods.

depend ❶ *v* (foll. by *on*) **1** put trust (in). **2** be influenced or determined (by). **3** rely (on) for income or support. **dependable** *adj* **dependably** *adv* **dependability** *n* **dependant** *n* person who depends on another for financial support. **dependence** *n* state of being dependent. **dependency** *n, pl* –cies **1** country controlled by another country. **2** overreliance on another person or on a drug. **dependent** *adj* depending on someone or something.

depict ❶ *v* **1** produce a picture of. **2** describe in words. **depiction** *n*

deplete ❶ *v* **1** use up. **2** reduce in number. **depletion** *n*

deplore ❶ *v* condemn strongly. **deplorable** *adj* very bad or unpleasant.

deploy ❶ *v* organize (troops or resources) into a position ready for immediate action. **deployment** *n*

depopulate *v* reduce the population of. **depopulation** *n*

deport ❶ *v* remove forcibly from a country. **deportation** *n* **deportee** *n*

deportment *n* way in which a person moves or stands.

depose ❶ *v* **1** remove from an office or position of power. **2** *Law* testify on oath.

deposit ❶ *v* **1** put down. **2** entrust for safekeeping, esp. to a bank. **3** lay down naturally. ◆ *n* **4** sum of money paid into a bank account. **5** money given in part

——————— THESAURUS ———————

press in, push in

deny *v* **1** = **contradict**, disagree with, disprove, rebuff, rebut, refute ≠ **agree 2** = **refuse**, begrudge, disallow, forbid, reject, turn down, withhold ≠ **let 3** = **renounce**, disclaim, disown, recant, repudiate, retract

depart *v* **1** = **leave**, absent (oneself), disappear, exit, go, go away, quit, retire, retreat, withdraw ≠ **remain 2** = **change**, deviate, differ, digress, diverge, stray, swerve, turn aside, vary, veer

department *n* **1** = **section**, branch, bureau, division, office, station, subdivision, unit

depend *v* (foll. by *on*) **1** = **trust in**, bank on, count on, lean on, reckon on, rely upon, turn to **2** = **be determined by**, be based on, be contingent on, be subject to, be subordinate to, hang on, hinge on, rest on, revolve around

depict *v* **1** = **draw**, delineate, illustrate, outline, paint, picture, portray, sketch **2** = **describe**, characterize, narrate, outline, represent

deplete *v* **1** = **use up**, consume, drain, empty, exhaust, expend, impoverish **2** = **reduce**, lessen

deplore *v* = **disapprove of**, abhor, censure, condemn, denounce, object to, take a dim view of

deploy *v* = **position**, arrange, set out, station, use, utilize

deport *v* = **expel**, banish, exile, expatriate, extradite, oust **deport oneself** = **behave**, acquit oneself, act, bear oneself, carry oneself, comport oneself, conduct oneself, hold oneself

depose *v* **1** = **remove from office**, demote, dethrone, dismiss, displace, oust **2** *Law* = **testify**, avouch, declare, make a deposition payment for goods or services. **6** accumulation of sediments, minerals, etc. **depositary** n person to whom something is entrusted for safety. **depositor** n **depository** n store for furniture etc.

depot ❶ [dep–oh] n **1** building where goods or vehicles are kept when not in use. **2** *Chiefly US* bus or railway station.

deprecate v express disapproval of. **deprecation** n **deprecatory** adj

depreciate ❶ v **1** decline in value or price. **2** criticize. **depreciation** n

depress ❶ v **1** make sad. **2** lower (prices or wages). **3** push down. **depressing** adj **depression** n **1** mental state in which a person has feelings of gloom and inadequacy. **2** economic condition in which there is high unemployment and low output and investment. **3** area of low air pressure. **4** sunken place. **depressive** adj **1** tending to cause depression. ✦ n **2** person who suffers from depression.

deprive ❶ v (foll. by *of*) prevent from (having or enjoying). **deprivation** n **deprived** adj lacking adequate living conditions, education, etc.

depth ❶ n **1** distance downwards, backwards, or inwards. **2** intensity of emotion. **3** profundity of character or thought. **4 depth charge** bomb used to attack submarines by exploding at a preset depth of water.

deregulate v remove regulations or controls from. **deregulation** n

derelict ❶ adj **1** unused and falling into ruins. ✦ n **2** social outcast, vagrant. **dereliction** n state of being abandoned.

deride ❶ v treat with contempt or ridicule. **derision** n **derisive** adj mocking, scornful. **derisory** adj too small or inadequate to be considered seriously.

derive ❶ v (foll. by *from*) take or develop (from). **derivation** n **derivative** adj word, idea, etc., derived from another.

dermatitis n inflammation of the skin.

derogatory ❶ [dir–**rog**–a–tree] adj intentionally offensive.

derv n diesel oil, when used for road transport.

descant n tune played or sung above a basic melody.

descend ❶ v **1** move down (a slope etc.). **2** move to a lower level, pitch, etc. **3** (foll. by *to*) stoop to (unworthy behaviour).

———————— THESAURUS ————————

deposit v **1 = put**, drop, lay, locate, place **2 = store**, bank, consign, entrust, lodge ✦ n **5 = down payment**, instalment, part payment, pledge, retainer, security, stake **6 = sediment**, accumulation, dregs, lees, precipitate, silt

depot n **1 = storehouse**, depository, repository, warehouse **2** *Chiefly US* **= bus station**, garage, terminus

depreciate v **1 = decrease**, deflate, devalue, lessen, lose value, lower, reduce ≠ **expand 2 = disparage**, belittle, denigrate, deride, detract, run down, scorn, sneer at

depress v **1 = sadden**, deject, discourage, dishearten, dispirit, make despondent, oppress, weigh down ≠ **cheer 2 = lower**, cheapen, depreciate, devalue, diminish, downgrade, lessen, reduce ≠ **increase 3 = press down**, flatten, level, lower, push down

deprive v (foll. by *of*) **= withhold**, bereave, despoil, dispossess, rob, strip

depth n **1 = deepness**, drop, extent, measure **3 = profoundness**, astuteness, discernment, insight, penetration, profundity, sagacity, wisdom ≠ **emptiness**

derelict adj **1 = abandoned**, deserted, dilapidated, discarded, forsaken, munted (*NZ sl*), neglected, ruined ✦ n **2 = tramp**, bag lady, down–and–out, outcast, vagrant

deride v **= mock**, disdain, disparage, insult, jeer, ridicule, scoff, scorn, sneer, taunt

derive v (foll. by *from*) **= come from**, arise from, emanate from, flow from, issue from, originate from, proceed from, spring from, stem from

derogatory adj **= disparaging**, belittling, defamatory, offensive, slighting, uncomplimentary, unfavourable,

4 (foll. by *on*) visit unexpectedly. **be descended from** be connected by a blood relationship to. **descendant** *n* person or animal descended from an individual, race, or species. **descendent** *adj* descending. **descent** *n* 1 descending. 2 downward slope. 3 derivation from an ancestor.

describe ❶ *v* 1 give an account of (something or someone) in words. 2 trace the outline of (a circle etc.). **description** *n* 1 statement that describes something or someone. 2 sort, e.g. *flowers of every description*. **descriptive** *adj* **descriptively** *adv*

desecrate *v* damage or insult (something sacred). **desecration** *n*

desert[1] ❶ *n* region with little or no vegetation because of low rainfall.

desert[2] ❶ *v* 1 abandon (a person or place) without intending to return. 2 *Mil* leave (a post or duty) with no intention of returning. **deserter** *n* **desertion** *n*

deserve ❶ *v* be entitled to or worthy of. **deserved** *adj* rightfully earned. **deservedly** *adv* **deserving** *adj* worthy of help, praise,

or reward.

design ❶ *v* 1 work out the structure or form of (something), by making a sketch or plans. 2 plan and make artistically. 3 intend for a specific purpose. ◆ *n* 4 preliminary drawing. 5 arrangement or features of an artistic or decorative work. 6 art of designing. 7 intention, e.g. *by design*. **designer** *n* 1 person who draws up original sketches or plans from which things are made. ◆ *adj* 2 designed by a well–known designer. **designing** *adj* cunning and scheming.

designate ❶ [**dez**–zig–nate] *v* 1 give a name to. 2 select (someone) for an office or duty. ◆ *adj* 3 appointed but not yet in office. **designation** *n* name.

desire ❶ *v* 1 want very much. ◆ *n* 2 wish, longing. 3 sexual appetite. 4 person or thing desired. **desirable** *adj* 1 worth having. 2 arousing sexual desire. **desirability** *n* **desirous of** having a desire for.

desist ❶ *v* (foll. by *from*) stop (doing something).

desk *n* 1 piece of furniture with a writing

unflattering

descend *v* 1 = **move down**, drop, fall, go down, plummet, plunge, sink, subside, tumble ≠ **rise** 2 = **slope**, dip, incline, slant 3 = **lower oneself**, degenerate, deteriorate, stoop 4 (foll. by *on*) = **attack**, arrive, invade, raid, swoop **be descended from** = **originate from**, be handed down from, be passed down from, derive from, issue from, proceed from, spring from

describe *v* 1 = **relate**, depict, explain, express, narrate, portray, recount, report, tell 2 = **trace**, delineate, draw, mark out, outline

desert[1] *n* = **wilderness**, solitude, waste, wasteland, wilds

desert[2] *v* 1 = **abandon**, abscond, forsake, jilt, leave, leave stranded, maroon, quit, strand, walk out on (*inf*) ≠ **maintain**

deserve *v* = **merit**, be entitled to, be worthy of, earn, justify, rate, warrant

design *v* 1 = **plan**, draft, draw, outline, sketch, trace 2 = **create**, conceive, fabricate, fashion, invent, originate, think up 3 = **intend**, aim, mean, plan, propose, purpose ◆ *n* 4 = **plan**, blueprint, draft, drawing, model, outline, scheme, sketch 5 = **arrangement**, construction, form, organization, pattern, shape, style 7 = **intention**, aim, end, goal, object, objective, purpose, target

designate *v* 1 = **name**, call, dub, entitle, label, style, term 2 = **appoint**, assign, choose, delegate, depute, nominate, select

desire *v* 1 = **want**, crave, hanker after, hope for, long for, set one's heart on, thirst for, wish for, yearn for ◆ *n* 2 = **wish**, aspiration, craving, hankering, hope, longing, thirst, want 3 = **lust**, appetite, libido, passion

desist *v* (foll. by *from*) = **stop**, break off,

surface and drawers. **2** service counter in a
public building. **3** section of a newspaper
covering a specific subject, e.g. *the sports
desk*. **desktop** *adj* (of a computer) small
enough to use at a desk.

desolate ❶ *adj* **1** uninhabited and bleak. **2**
very sad. ♦ *v* **3** deprive of inhabitants. **4**
make (someone) very sad. **desolation** *n*

despair ❶ *n* **1** total loss of hope. ♦ *v* **2** lose
hope.

desperate ❶ *adj* **1** in despair and reckless.
2 (of an action) undertaken as a last resort.
3 having a strong need or desire.
desperately *adv* **desperation** *n*

despise ❶ *v* regard with contempt.
despicable *adj* deserving contempt.

despite ❶ *prep* in spite of.

despoil *v Formal* plunder.

despondent ❶ *adj* unhappy.
despondency *n*

despot ❶ *n* person in power who acts
unfairly or cruelly. **despotic** *adj* **despotism**
n unfair or cruel government or behaviour.

dessert *n* sweet course served at the end
of a meal. **dessertspoon** *n* spoon between

a tablespoon and a teaspoon in size.

destination ❶ *n* place to which someone
or something is going.

destitute ❶ *adj* having no money or
possessions. **destitution** *n*

destroy ❶ *v* **1** ruin, demolish. **2** put an end
to. **3** kill (an animal). **destroyer** *n* **1** small
heavily armed warship. **2** person or thing
that destroys. **destruction** *n* ruin.

desultory [dez–zl–tree] *adj* **1** jumping
from one thing to another, disconnected.
2 random.

detach ❶ *v* disengage and separate.
detachable *adj* **detached** *adj* **1** (of a
house) not joined to another house. **2**
showing no emotional involvement.
detachment *n* **1** lack of emotional
involvement. **2** small group of soldiers.

detail ❶ *n* **1** individual piece of
information. **2** unimportant item. **3** small
individual features of something,
considered collectively. **4** *Chiefly mil*
(personnel assigned) a specific duty. ♦ *v* **5**
list fully.

detain ❶ *v* **1** delay (someone). **2** hold

———————— THESAURUS ————————

cease, discontinue, end, forbear, leave off,
pause, refrain from

desolate *adj* **1** = **uninhabited**, bare,
barren, bleak, dreary, godforsaken,
solitary, wild ≠ **inhabited 2** = **miserable**,
dejected, despondent, disconsolate,
downcast, forlorn, gloomy, wretched
≠ **happy** ♦ *v* **3** = **lay waste**, depopulate,
despoil, destroy, devastate, lay low,
pillage, plunder, ravage, ruin **4** = **deject**,
depress, discourage, dishearten, dismay,
distress, grieve ≠ **encourage**

despair *n* **1** = **despondency**, anguish,
dejection, depression, desperation, gloom,
hopelessness, misery, wretchedness ♦ *v*
2 = **lose hope**, give up, lose heart

desperate *adj* **1** = **reckless**, audacious,
daring, frantic, furious, risky **2** = **grave**,
drastic, extreme, urgent

despise *v* = **look down on**, abhor, detest,
loathe, revile, scorn

despite *prep* = **in spite of**, against, even

with, in the face of, in the teeth of,
notwithstanding, regardless of, undeterred
by

despondent *adj* = **dejected**, depressed,
disconsolate, disheartened, dispirited,
downhearted, glum, in despair, sad,
sorrowful

despot *n* = **tyrant**, autocrat, dictator,
oppressor

destination *n* = **journey's end**, haven,
resting–place, station, stop, terminus

destitute *adj* = **penniless**, down and out,
impoverished, indigent, insolvent,
moneyless, penurious, poor, poverty–
stricken

destroy *v* **1, 2** = **ruin**, annihilate, crush,
demolish, devastate, eradicate, shatter,
wipe out, wreck

detach *v* = **separate**, cut off, disconnect,
disengage, divide, remove, sever, tear off,
unfasten ≠ **bind**

detail *n* **2** = **fine point**, nicety, particular,

(someone) in custody. **detainee** n
detect ❶ v **1** notice. **2** discover, find.
detectable adj **detection** n **detective** n
policeman or private agent who
investigates crime. **detector** n instrument
used to find something.
deter ❶ v **–terring, –terred** discourage
(someone) from doing something by
instilling fear or doubt. **deterrent** n **1**
something that deters. **2** weapon, esp.
nuclear, intended to deter attack. ◆ adj **3**
tending to deter.
detergent ❶ n chemical substance for
washing clothes or dishes.
deteriorate ❶ v become worse.
deterioration n
determine ❶ v **1** settle (an argument or a
question) conclusively. **2** find out the facts
about. **3** make a firm decision (to do
something). **determinant** n factor that
determines. **determinate** adj definitely
limited or fixed. **determination** n **1** being
determined or resolute. **2** determined adj
firmly decided, unable to be dissuaded.
determinedly adv **determiner** n Grammar
word that determines the object to which

a noun phrase refers, e.g. all. **determinism**
n theory that human choice is not free,
but decided by past events.
detest ❶ v dislike intensely. **detestable** adj
detestation n
dethrone v remove from a throne or
position of power.
detonate ❶ v explode. **detonation** n
detonator n small amount of explosive, or
a device, used to set off an explosion.
detour ❶ n route that is not the most
direct one.
detract ❶ v (foll. by from) make
(something) seem less good. **detractor** n
detriment ❶ n disadvantage or damage.
detrimental adj **detrimentally** adv
deuce [dyewss] n **1** Tennis score of forty
all. **2** playing card with two symbols or
dice with two spots.
devalue v **–valuing, –valued 1** reduce the
exchange value of (a currency). **2** reduce
the value of (something or someone).
devaluation n
devastate ❶ v destroy. **devastated** adj
shocked and extremely upset. **devastation**
n

——————— THESAURUS ———————

triviality **3 = point**, aspect, component,
element, fact, factor, feature, particular,
respect **4** Chiefly mil **= party**, assignment,
body, detachment, duty, fatigue, force,
squad ◆ v **5 = list**, catalogue, enumerate,
itemize, recite, recount, rehearse, relate,
tabulate **6** Chiefly mil **= appoint**, allocate,
assign, charge, commission, delegate,
send
detain v **1 = delay**, check, hinder, hold up,
impede, keep back, retard, slow up (or
down) **2 = hold**, arrest, confine, intern,
restrain
detect v **1 = notice**, ascertain, identify,
note, observe, perceive, recognize, spot
2 = discover, find, track down, uncover,
unmask
deter v **= discourage**, dissuade, frighten,
inhibit from, intimidate, prevent, put off,
stop, talk out of
detergent n **= cleaner**, cleanser

deteriorate v **= decline**, degenerate, go
downhill (inf), lower, slump, worsen
≠ improve
determine v **1 = settle**, conclude, decide,
end, finish, ordain, regulate **2 = find out**,
ascertain, detect, discover, establish, learn,
verify, work out **3 = decide**, choose, elect,
make up one's mind, resolve
detest v **= hate**, abhor, abominate,
despise, dislike intensely, loathe, recoil
from
detonate v **= explode**, blast, blow up,
discharge, set off, trigger
detour n **= diversion**, bypass, indirect
course, roundabout way
detract v (foll. by from) **= lessen**,
devaluate, diminish, lower, reduce, take
away from **≠ improve**
detriment n **= damage**, disadvantage,
disservice, harm, hurt, impairment, injury,
loss

develop ❶ *v* **1** grow or bring to a later, more elaborate, or more advanced stage. **2** come or bring into existence. **3** build houses or factories on (an area of land). **4** produce (photographs) by making negatives or prints from a film. **developer** *n* **1** person who develops property. **2** chemical used to develop photographs or films. **development** *n* **developing country** poor or nonindustrial country that is trying to develop its resources by industrialization.

deviate ❶ *v* **1** differ from others in belief or thought. **2** depart from one's previous behaviour. **deviation** *n* **deviant** *n, adj* (person) deviating from what is considered acceptable behaviour. **deviance** *n*

device ❶ *n* **1** machine or tool used for a specific task. **2** scheme or plan.

devil ❶ *n* **1** evil spirit. **2** evil person. **3** person, e.g. *poor devil*. **4** daring person, e.g. *be a devil!* **5** *Informal* something difficult or annoying, e.g. *a devil of a long time.* ◆ *v* **-illing, -illed 6** prepare (food) with a highly flavoured spiced mixture. **the Devil** *Theology* chief spirit of evil and enemy of God. **devilish** *adj* **1** cruel or unpleasant. ◆ *adv* **2** (also **devilishly**)

Informal extremely. **devilment** *n* mischievous conduct. **devilry** *n* mischievousness. **devil-may-care** *adj* carefree and cheerful. **devil's advocate** person who takes an opposing or unpopular point of view for the sake of argument.

devise ❶ *v* work out (something) in one's mind.

devoid ❶ *adj* (foll. by *of*) completely lacking (in).

devolve *v* (foll. by *on* or *to*) pass (power or duties) or (of power or duties) be passed to a successor or substitute. **devolution** *n* transfer of authority from a central government to regional governments.

devote ❶ *v* apply or dedicate to a particular purpose. **devoted** *adj* showing loyalty or devotion. **devotee** *n* **1** person who is very enthusiastic about something. **2** zealous follower of a religion. **devotion** *n* **1** strong affection for or loyalty to someone or something. **2** religious zeal. ◆ *pl* **3** prayers. **devotional** *adj*

devour ❶ *v* **1** eat greedily. **2** (of an emotion) engulf and destroy. **3** read eagerly.

devout ❶ *adj* deeply religious.

dew *n* drops of water that form on the

═══════════ THESAURUS ═══════════

devastate *v* = **destroy**, demolish, lay waste, level, ravage, raze, ruin, sack, wreck

develop *v* **1** = **advance**, amplify, augment, broaden, elaborate, enlarge, evolve, expand, flourish, grow, mature, progress, prosper, ripen **2** = **form**, breed, establish, generate, invent, originate

deviate *v* = **differ**, depart, diverge, stray, swerve, veer, wander

device *n* **1** = **gadget**, apparatus, appliance, contraption, implement, instrument, machine, tool **2** = **ploy**, gambit, manoeuvre, plan, scheme, stratagem, trick, wile

devil *n* **1** = **brute**, beast, demon, fiend, monster, ogre, terror **2** = **scamp**, rascal, rogue, scoundrel **3** = **person**, beggar, creature, thing, wretch **the Devil** *Theology*

= **Satan**, Beelzebub, Evil One, Lucifer, Mephistopheles, Old Nick (*inf*), Prince of Darkness

devise *v* = **work out**, conceive, construct, contrive, design, dream up, formulate, invent, think up

devoid *adj* (foll. by *of*) = **lacking**, bereft, deficient, destitute, empty, free from, wanting, without

devote *v* = **dedicate**, allot, apply, assign, commit, give, pledge, reserve, set apart

devour *v* **1** = **eat**, consume, gobble, gulp, guzzle, polish off (*inf*), swallow, wolf **2** = **destroy**, annihilate, consume, ravage, waste, wipe out **3** = **enjoy**, read compulsively *or* voraciously, take in

devout *adj* = **religious**, godly, holy, orthodox, pious, prayerful, pure, reverent,

ground at night from vapour in the air.
dewy adj

dexterity ❶ n 1 skill in using one's hands.
2 mental quickness. **dexterous** adj

diabetes [die–a–**beet**–eez] n disorder in
which an abnormal amount of urine
containing an excess of sugar is excreted.
diabetic n, adj

diabolic adj of the Devil. **diabolical** adj
Informal extremely bad.

diadem n Old–fashioned crown.

diagnosis ❶ [die–ag–**no**–siss] n, pl –ses [–
seez] discovery and identification of
diseases from the examination of
symptoms. **diagnose** v **diagnostic** adj

diagonal ❶ adj 1 from corner to corner. 2
slanting. ◆ n 3 diagonal line. **diagonally**
adv

diagram ❶ n sketch showing the form or
workings of something. **diagrammatic** adj

dial n 1 face of a clock or watch. 2
graduated disc on a measuring
instrument. 3 control on a radio or
television set used to change the station. 4
numbered disc on the front of some
telephones. ◆ v **dialling, dialled** 5 operate
the dial or buttons on a telephone in
order to contact (a number).

dialect ❶ n form of a language spoken in a
particular area. **dialectal** adj

dialogue ❶ n 1 conversation between two
people, esp. in a book, film, or play. 2
discussion between representatives of two
nations or groups.

dialysis [die–**al**–iss–iss] n Med filtering of

blood through a membrane to remove
waste products.

diameter n (length of) a straight line
through the centre of a circle or sphere.
diametric, diametrical adj 1 of a diameter.
2 completely opposed, e.g. the diametric
opposite. **diametrically** adv

diamond n 1 exceptionally hard, usu.
colourless, precious stone. 2 Geom figure
with four sides of equal length forming
two acute and two obtuse angles. 3
playing card marked with red diamond–
shaped symbols. 4 **diamond wedding**
sixtieth anniversary of a wedding.

diaphragm [**die**–a–fram] n 1 muscular
partition that separates the abdominal
cavity and chest cavity. 2 contraceptive
device placed over the neck of the womb.

diarrhoea [die–a–**ree**–a] n frequent
discharge of abnormally liquid faeces.

diary ❶ n, pl –ries (book for) a record of
daily events, appointments, or
observations. **diarist** n

diatribe n bitter critical attack.

dice n, pl dice 1 small cube each of whose
sides has a different number of spots (1 to
6), used in games of chance. ◆ v 2 cut
(food) into small cubes. **dice with death**
take a risk. **dicey** adj Informal dangerous or
risky.

dichotomy [die–**kot**–a–mee] n, pl –mies
division into two opposed groups or parts.

dicky ❶ adj dickier, dickiest Informal shaky
or weak, e.g. a dicky heart.

dictate ❶ v 1 say aloud for someone else

—————— THESAURUS ——————

saintly ≠ **irreverent**

dexterity n 1 = **skill**, adroitness, deftness,
expertise, finesse, nimbleness, proficiency,
touch ≠ **inability** 2 = **cleverness**, ability,
aptitude, ingenuity

diagnosis n = **analysis**, conclusion,
examination, investigation, opinion,
scrutiny

diagonal adj 1 = **crossways**, cross,
crosswise 2 = **slanting**, angled, oblique

diagram n = **plan**, chart, drawing, figure,
graph, representation, sketch

dialect n = **language**, brogue, idiom,
jargon, patois, provincialism, speech,
vernacular

dialogue n 1 = **conversation**,
communication, discourse, exchange
2 = **discussion**, conference

diary n = **journal**, appointment book,
chronicle, daily record, engagement book,
Filofax (Trademark)

dicky adj Inf = **weak**, fluttery, shaky, shonky
(Aust & NZ inf), unreliable, unsound,
unsteady

to write down. 2 (foll. by *to*) seek to impose one's will on (other people). ◆ *n* 3 authoritative command. 4 guiding principle. **dictation** *n* **dictator** *n* 1 ruler who has complete power. 2 person in power who acts unfairly or cruelly. **dictatorship** *n* **dictatorial** *adj* like a dictator.

diction ❶ *n* manner of pronouncing words and sounds.

dictionary ❶ *n, pl -aries* 1 book consisting of an alphabetical list of words with their meanings. 2 alphabetically ordered reference book of terms relating to a particular subject.

did *v* past tense of DO.

die¹ ❶ *v* **dying, died** 1 (of a person, animal, or plant) cease all biological activity permanently. 2 (of something inanimate) cease to exist or function. **be dying for, to do something** *Informal* be eager for *or* to do something. **die-hard** *n* person who resists change.

die² *n* 1 shaped block used to cut or form metal.

diesel *n* 1 diesel engine. 2 vehicle driven by a diesel engine. 3 diesel oil. **diesel engine** internal–combustion engine in which oil is ignited by compression. **diesel oil** fuel obtained from petroleum distillation.

diet ❶ *n* 1 food that a person or animal regularly eats. 2 specific range of foods, to control weight or for health reasons. ◆ *v* 3 follow a special diet so as to lose weight. ◆ *adj* 4 (of food) suitable for a weight–reduction diet. **dietary** *adj* **dietary fibre** fibrous substances in fruit and vegetables that aid digestion. **dieter** *n* **dietetic** *adj* prepared for special dietary requirements. **dietetics** *n* study of diet and nutrition. **dietician** *n* person who specializes in dietetics.

differ ❶ *v* 1 be unlike. 2 disagree. **difference** *n* 1 state of being unlike. 2 disagreement. 3 remainder left after subtraction. **different** *adj* 1 unlike. 2 unusual. **differently** *adv*

> ✓ **WORD TIP**
> The accepted idiom is *different from* but *different to* is also used. *Different than* is an Americanism.

differential *adj* 1 of or using a difference. 2 *Maths* involving differentials. ◆ *n* 3 factor that differentiates between two comparable things. 4 *Maths* tiny difference between values in a scale. 5 difference between rates of pay for different types of work. **differential calculus** branch of calculus concerned with derivatives and differentials.

—————— THESAURUS ——————

dictate *v* 1 = **speak**, read out, say, utter 2 (foll. by *to*) = **order**, command, decree, demand, direct, impose, lay down the law, pronounce ◆ *n* 3 = **command**, decree, demand, direction, edict, fiat, injunction, order 4 = **principle**, code, law, rule

diction *n* = **pronunciation**, articulation, delivery, elocution, enunciation, fluency, inflection, intonation, speech

dictionary *n* = **wordbook**, glossary, lexicon, vocabulary

die¹ *v* 1 breathe one's last, cark *Aust & NZ sl* = **pass away**, croak (*sl*), expire, give up the ghost, kick the bucket (*sl*), peg out (*inf*), perish, snuff it (*sl*) ≠ **live** 2 = **stop**,

break down, fade out *or* away, fail, fizzle out, halt, lose power, peter out, run down **be dying for, to do something** *Inf* = **long for**, ache for, be eager for, desire, hunger for, pine for, yearn for

diet *n* 1 = **food**, fare, nourishment, nutriment, provisions, rations, sustenance, tucker (*Aust & NZ inf*), victuals 2 = **regime**, abstinence, fast, regimen ◆ *v* 3 = **slim**, abstain, eat sparingly, fast, lose weight ≠ **indulge**

differ *v* 1 = **be dissimilar**, contradict, contrast, depart from, diverge, run counter to, stand apart, vary ≠ **accord** 2 = **disagree**, clash, contend, debate, demur, dispute, dissent, oppose, take

differentiate v 1 perceive or show the difference (between). 2 make (one thing) distinct from other such things. **differentiation** n

difficult ❶ adj 1 requiring effort or skill to do or understand. 2 not easily pleased. **difficulty** n

diffident ❶ adj lacking self–confidence. **diffidence** n

diffuse v 1 spread over a wide area. ◆ adj 2 widely spread. 3 lacking concision. **diffusion** n

dig ❶ v **digging, dug** 1 cut into, break up, and turn over or remove (earth), esp. with a spade. 2 (foll. by out or up) find by effort or searching. 3 (foll. by in or into) thrust or jab. ◆ n 4 digging. 5 archaeological excavation. 6 thrust or poke. 7 spiteful remark. ◆ pl 8 Informal lodgings. **digger** n machine used for digging.

digest v 1 subject to a process of digestion. 2 absorb mentally. ◆ n 3 shortened version of a book, report, or article. **digestible** adj **digestion** n (body's system for) breaking down food into easily

absorbed substances. **digestive** adj **digestive biscuit** biscuit made from wholemeal flour.

digit [**dij**–it] n 1 finger or toe. 2 numeral from 0 to 9. **digital** adj displaying information as numbers rather than with hands and a dial, e.g. a digital clock. **digital recording** sound–recording process that converts audio or analogue signals into a series of pulses. **digital television** television in which the picture is transmitted in digital form and then decoded. **digitally** adv

dignity ❶ n, pl **–ties** 1 serious, calm, and controlled behaviour or manner. 2 quality of being worthy of respect. 3 sense of self–importance. **dignify** v add distinction to. **dignitary** n person of high official position.

digress ❶ v depart from the main subject in speech or writing. **digression** n

dike n same as DYKE.

dilapidated ❶ adj (of a building) having fallen into ruin. **dilapidation** n

dilate ❶ v make or become wider or

——————— THESAURUS ———————

exception, take issue ≠ **agree**

difficult adj 1 a = **hard**, arduous, demanding, formidable, laborious, onerous, strenuous, uphill ≠ **light** b = **problematical**, abstruse, baffling, complex, complicated, intricate, involved, knotty, obscure ≠ **simple** 2 = **troublesome**, demanding, fastidious, fussy, hard to please, perverse, refractory, unaccommodating ≠ **pleasant**

diffident adj = **shy**, bashful, doubtful, hesitant, insecure, modest, reserved, self–conscious, timid, unassertive, unassuming

dig v 1 = **excavate**, burrow, delve, hollow out, mine, quarry, scoop, tunnel 2 (foll. by out or up) = **find**, delve, dig down, discover, expose, fossick (Aust & NZ), go into, investigate, probe, research, search, uncover, unearth, uproot 3 (foll. by in or into) = **poke**, drive, jab, prod, punch, thrust ◆ n 6 = **poke**, jab, prod, punch, thrust 7 = **cutting remark**, barb, crack (sl),

gibe, insult, jeer, sneer, taunt, wisecrack (inf)

digest v 1 = **ingest**, absorb, assimilate, dissolve, incorporate 2 = **take in**, absorb, consider, contemplate, grasp, study, understand ◆ n 3 = **summary**, abridgment, abstract, epitome, précis, résumé, synopsis

dignity n 1 = **decorum**, courtliness, grandeur, gravity, loftiness, majesty, nobility, solemnity, stateliness 2 = **honour**, eminence, importance, rank, respectability, standing, status 3 = **self–importance**, pride, self–esteem, self–respect

digress v = **wander**, depart, deviate, diverge, drift, get off the point or subject, go off at a tangent, ramble, stray

dilapidated adj = **ruined**, broken–down, crumbling, decrepit, in ruins, munted (NZ sl), ramshackle, rickety, run–down, tumbledown

larger. **dilation, dilatation** n
dilemma ❶ n situation offering a choice between two equally undesirable alternatives.

> ✓ **WORD TIP**
> If a difficult choice involves more than two courses of action, it is preferable to speak of a *problem* or *difficulty*.

dilettante ❶ [dill–it–**tan**–tee] n, pl **–tantes, –tanti** person whose interest in a subject is superficial rather than serious.
dilettantism n
diligent ❶ adj 1 careful and persevering in carrying out duties. 2 carried out with care and perseverance. **diligently** adv **diligence** n
dill n sweet-smelling herb.
dilute ❶ v 1 make (a liquid) less concentrated, esp. by adding water. 2 make (a quality etc.) weaker in force. **dilution** n
dim ❶ adj dimmer, dimmest 1 badly lit. 2 not clearly seen. 3 unintelligent. ◆ v dimming, dimmed 4 make or become dim. **take a dim view of** disapprove of.

dimly adv **dimness** n **dimmer** n device for dimming an electric light.
dime n coin of the US and Canada, worth ten cents.
dimension ❶ n 1 measurement of the size of something in a particular direction. 2 aspect, factor.
diminish ❶ v make or become smaller, fewer, or less. **diminution** n **diminutive** adj 1 very small. ◆ n 2 word or affix which implies smallness or unimportance.
diminuendo n Music gradual decrease in loudness.
dimple n 1 small natural dent, esp. in the cheeks or chin. ◆ v 2 produce dimples by smiling.
din ❶ n 1 loud unpleasant confused noise. ◆ v dinning, dinned 2 (foll. by *into*) instil (something) into someone by constant repetition.
dine ❶ v eat dinner. **diner** n 1 person eating a meal. 2 Chiefly US small cheap restaurant. **dining room** room where meals are eaten.
dinghy [**ding**–ee] n, pl **–ghies** small boat, powered by sails, oars, or a motor.
dingo n, pl **–goes** Australian wild dog.

——— THESAURUS ———

dilate v = **enlarge**, broaden, expand, puff out, stretch, swell, widen
dilemma n = **predicament**, difficulty, mess, plight, problem, puzzle, quandary, spot (inf)
dilettante n = **amateur**, aesthete, dabbler, trifler
diligent adj = **hard–working**, assiduous, attentive, careful, conscientious, industrious, painstaking, persistent, studious, tireless
dilute v 1 = **water down**, adulterate, cut, make thinner, thin (out), weaken ≠ **concentrate** 2 = **reduce**, attenuate, decrease, diffuse, diminish, lessen, mitigate, temper, weaken ≠ **strengthen**
dim adj 1 = **poorly lit**, cloudy, dark, grey, overcast, shadowy, tenebrous ≠ **clear** 2 = **unclear**, bleary, blurred, faint, fuzzy, ill–defined, indistinct, obscured, shadowy

≠ **clear 3 = stupid**, dense, dozy (Brit inf), dull, dumb (inf), obtuse, slow on the uptake (inf), thick ≠ **bright** ◆ v 4 = **dull**, blur, cloud, darken, fade, obscure **take a dim view of = disapprove of**, be displeased with, be sceptical of, look askance at, reject, suspect, take exception to, view with disfavour
dimension n 1 = **measurement**, amplitude, bulk, capacity, extent, proportions, size, volume
diminish v = **decrease**, curtail, cut, decline, die out, dwindle, lessen, lower, recede, reduce, shrink, subside, wane ≠ **increase**
din n 1 = **noise**, clamour, clatter, commotion, crash, pandemonium, racket, row, uproar ≠ **peace** ◆ v 2 (foll. by *into*) = **instil**, drum into, go on at, hammer into, inculcate, instruct, teach

dingy ❶ [**din**–jee] *adj* **–gier, –giest** dull and drab. **dinginess** *n*

dinner ❶ *n* main meal of the day, eaten either in the evening or at midday. **dinner jacket** man's semiformal black evening jacket.

dinosaur *n* extinct gigantic prehistoric reptile.

dint *n* **by dint of** by means of.

diocese [**die**–a–siss] *n* district over which a bishop has control. **diocesan** *adj*

diode *n* semiconductor device for converting alternating current to direct current.

dip ❶ *v* **dipping, dipped 1** plunge quickly or briefly into a liquid. **2** slope downwards. **3** switch (car headlights) from the main to the lower beam. **4** lower briefly. ◆ *n* **5** dipping. **6** brief swim. **7** liquid chemical in which farm animals are dipped to rid them of insects. **8** depression in a landscape. **9** creamy mixture into which pieces of food are dipped before being eaten. **dip into** *v* read passages at random from (a book or journal).

diphtheria [dif–**theer**–ya] *n* contagious disease producing fever and difficulty in breathing and swallowing.

diphthong *n* union of two vowel sounds in a single compound sound.

diploma *n* qualification awarded by a college on successful completion of a course.

diplomacy ❶ *n* **1** conduct of the relations between nations by peaceful means. **2** tact or skill in dealing with people. **diplomat** *n* official engaged in diplomacy. **diplomatic** *adj* **1** of diplomacy. **2** tactful in dealing with people. **diplomatically** *adv*

dipper *n* **1** ladle used for dipping. **2** (also **ousel, ouzel**) songbird that lives by a river.

dipsomania *n* compulsive craving for alcohol. **dipsomaniac** *n, adj*

dire ❶ *adj* disastrous, urgent, or terrible.

direct ❶ *adj* **1** (of a route) shortest, straight. **2** without anyone or anything intervening. **3** likely to have an immediate effect. **4** honest, frank. ◆ *adv* **5** in a direct manner. ◆ *v* **6** lead and organize. **7** tell (someone) to do something. **8** tell (someone) the way to a place. **9** address (a letter, package, remark, etc.). **10** provide guidance to (actors, cameramen, etc.) in (a play or film). **directly** *adv* **1** in a direct manner. **2** at once. ◆ *conj* **3** as soon as. **directness** *n* **direct current** electric current that flows in one direction only. **director** *n* person or thing that directs or controls. **directory** *n* book listing names, addresses, and telephone numbers.

————— THESAURUS —————

dine *v* = **eat**, banquet, feast, lunch, sup

dingy *adj* = **dull**, dark, dim, drab, dreary, gloomy, murky, obscure, sombre

dinner *n* = **meal**, banquet, feast, main meal, repast, spread (*inf*)

dip *v* **1** = **plunge**, bathe, douse, duck, dunk, immerse **2** = **slope**, decline, descend, drop (down), fall, lower, sink, subside ◆ *n* **5** = **plunge**, douche, drenching, ducking, immersion, soaking **6** = **bathe**, dive, plunge, swim **8** = **hollow**, basin, concavity, depression, hole, incline, slope

diplomacy *n* **1** = **statesmanship**, international negotiation, statecraft **2** = **tact**, artfulness, craft, delicacy, discretion, finesse, savoir–faire, skill, subtlety ≠ **awkwardness**

dire *adj* **a** = **disastrous**, awful, calamitous, catastrophic, horrible, ruinous, terrible, woeful **b** = **desperate**, critical, crucial, drastic, extreme, now or never, pressing, urgent

direct *adj* **1** = **straight**, nonstop, not crooked, shortest, through, unbroken, uninterrupted ≠ **subtle 2** = **first–hand**, face–to–face, head–on, immediate, personal ≠ **indirect 4** = **straightforward**, blunt, candid, downright, explicit, frank, honest, open, plain, plain–spoken, point–blank, straight, unambiguous, unequivocal, upfront (*inf*) ≠ **indirect** ◆ *v* **6** = **control**, conduct, guide, handle, lead, manage, oversee, run, supervise **7** = **order**, bid, charge, command, demand, dictate,

direction ❶ n 1 course or line along which a person or thing moves, points, or lies. 2 management or guidance. ◆ pl 3 instructions for doing something or for reaching a place.

dirge ❶ n slow sad song of mourning.

dirt ❶ n 1 unclean substance, filth. 2 earth, soil. 3 obscene speech or writing. 4 Informal harmful gossip. **dirt track** racetrack made of packed earth or cinders.

dis– prefix indicating: 1 reversal, e.g. disconnect. 2 negation or lack, e.g. dissimilar; disgrace. 3 removal or release, e.g. disembowel.

disable ❶ v make ineffective, unfit, or incapable. **disabled** adj lacking a physical power, such as the ability to walk. **disablement** n **disability** n, pl –ties 1 condition of being disabled. 2 something that disables someone.

✓ **WORD TIP**

The use of the disabled, the blind etc. can be offensive and should be avoided. Instead you should talk about disabled people, blind people, etc.

---

disabuse v (foll. by of) rid (someone) of a mistaken idea.

disadvantage ❶ n unfavourable or harmful circumstance. **disadvantageous** adj **disadvantaged** adj socially or economically deprived.

disaffected adj having lost loyalty to or affection for someone or something. **disaffection** n

disagree ❶ v –greeing, –greed 1 argue or have different opinions. 2 be different, conflict. 3 (foll. by with) cause physical discomfort (to), e.g. curry disagrees with me. **disagreement** n **disagreeable** adj 1 unpleasant. 2 (of a person) unfriendly or unhelpful.

disallow ❶ v reject as untrue or invalid.

disappear ❶ v 1 cease to be visible. 2 cease to exist. **disappearance** n

disappoint ❶ v fail to meet the expectations or hopes of. **disappointment** n 1 feeling of being disappointed. 2 person or thing that disappoints.

disapprove v (foll. by of) consider wrong or bad. **disapproval** n

disarm ❶ v 1 deprive of weapons. 2 win the confidence or affection of. 3 (of a

---

——————— THESAURUS ———————

instruct 8 = **guide**, indicate, lead, point in the direction of, point the way, show 9 = **address**, label, mail, route, send

direction n 1 = **way**, aim, bearing, course, line, path, road, route, track 2 = **management**, administration, charge, command, control, guidance, leadership, order, supervision ◆ pl 3 = **instructions**, briefing, guidance, guidelines, plan, recommendation, regulations

dirge n = **lament**, dead march, elegy, funeral song, requiem, threnody

dirt n 1 = **filth**, dust, grime, impurity, muck, mud 2 = **soil**, clay, earth, loam 3 = **obscenity**, indecency, pornography, sleaze, smut

disable v = **handicap**, cripple, damage, enfeeble, immobilize, impair, incapacitate, paralyse, render or declare incapable

disadvantage n = **drawback**, damage, detriment, disservice, downside, handicap, harm, hurt, inconvenience, injury, loss, nuisance, snag, trouble ≠ **benefit**

disagree v 1 = **differ (in opinion)**, argue, clash, cross swords, dispute, dissent, object, quarrel, take issue with ≠ **agree** 2 = **conflict**, be dissimilar, contradict, counter, differ, diverge, run counter to, vary 3 (foll. by with) = **make ill**, bother, discomfort, distress, hurt, nauseate, sicken, trouble, upset

disallow v = **reject**, disavow, dismiss, disown, rebuff, refuse, repudiate

disappear v 1 = **vanish**, evanesce, fade away, pass, recede ≠ **appear** 2 = **cease**, die out, dissolve, evaporate, leave no trace, melt away, pass away, perish

disappoint v = **let down**, disenchant, disgruntle, dishearten, disillusion, dismay, dissatisfy, fail country) decrease the size of one's armed forces. **disarmament** n **disarming** adj removing hostility or suspicion.

disarray ⊕ n **1** confusion and lack of discipline. **2** extreme untidiness.

disaster ⊕ n **1** occurrence that causes great distress or destruction. **2** project etc. that fails. **disastrous** adj

disband v (cause to) cease to function as a group.

disbelieve v **1** reject as false. **2** (foll. by in) have no faith (in). **disbelief** n

disburse v pay out. **disbursement** n

disc n **1** flat circular object. **2** gramophone record. **3** Anat circular flat structure in the body, esp. between the vertebrae. **4** Computers same as DISK. **disc jockey** person who introduces and plays pop records on a radio programme or at a disco.

discard ⊕ v get rid of (something or someone) as useless or undesirable.

discern v see or be aware of (something) clearly. **discernible** adj **discerning** adj

having good judgment. **discernment** n

discharge ⊕ v **1** release, allow to go. **2** dismiss (someone) from duty or employment. **3** fire (a gun). **4** pour forth, send out. **5** meet the demands of (a duty or responsibility). **6** relieve oneself of (a debt). ◆ n **7** substance that comes out from a place. **8** discharging.

disciple ⊕ [diss–**sipe**–pl] n follower of the doctrines of a teacher, esp. Jesus Christ.

discipline ⊕ n **1** practice of imposing strict rules of behaviour. **2** area of academic study. ◆ v **3** attempt to improve the behaviour of (oneself or another) by training or rules. **4** punish. **disciplined** adj able to behave and work in a controlled way. **disciplinarian** n person who practises strict discipline. **disciplinary** adj

disclaim v deny (responsibility for or knowledge of something). **disclaimer** n statement denying responsibility.

disclose ⊕ v **1** make known. **2** allow to be seen. **disclosure** n

disarm v **1** = **render defenceless**, disable **2** = **win over**, persuade, set at ease **3** = **demilitarize**, deactivate, demobilize, disband

disarray n **1** = **confusion**, disorder, disorganization, disunity, indiscipline, unruliness ≠ **plan 2** = **untidiness**, chaos, clutter, hotchpotch, jumble, mess, muddle, shambles ≠ **order**

disaster n **1** = **catastrophe**, adversity, calamity, cataclysm, misfortune, ruin, tragedy, trouble

discard v = **get rid of**, abandon, cast aside, dispense with, dispose of, drop, dump (inf), jettison, reject, throw away or out

discharge v **1** = **release**, allow to go, clear, free, liberate, pardon, set free **2** = **dismiss**, cashier, discard, expel, fire (inf), oust, remove, sack (inf) **3** = **fire**, detonate, explode, let loose (inf), let off, set off, shoot **4** = **pour forth**, dispense, emit, exude, give off, leak, ooze, release **5** = **carry out**, accomplish, do, execute, fulfil, observe, perform **6** = **pay**, clear,

honour, meet, relieve, satisfy, settle, square up ◆ n **7** = **emission**, excretion, ooze, pus, secretion, seepage, suppuration **8 a** = **release**, acquittal, clearance, liberation, pardon **b** = **dismissal**, demobilization, ejection **c** = **firing**, blast, burst, detonation, explosion, report, salvo, shot, volley

disciple n = **follower**, adherent, apostle, devotee, pupil, student, supporter ≠ **leader**

discipline n **1** = **training**, conduct, control, orderliness, practice, regimen, regulation, restraint, self–control, strictness **2** = **field of study**, area, branch of knowledge, course, curriculum, speciality, subject ◆ v **3** = **train**, bring up, drill, educate, exercise, prepare **4** = **punish**, bring to book, castigate, chasten, chastise, correct, penalize, reprimand, reprove

disclose v **1** = **make known**, broadcast, communicate, confess, divulge, let slip, publish, relate, reveal ≠ **keep secret 2** = **show**, bring to light, expose, lay bare,

disco n, pl **-cos 1** nightclub where people dance to amplified pop records. **2** occasion at which people dance to amplified pop records. **3** mobile equipment for providing music for a disco.

discolour ❶ v change in colour, fade. **discoloration** n

discomfit v make uneasy or confused. **discomfiture** n

discomfort ❶ n inconvenience, distress, or mild pain.

disconcert ❶ v embarrass or upset.

disconnect ❶ v **1** undo or break the connection between (two things). **2** stop the supply of electricity or gas of. **disconnected** adj (of speech or ideas) not logically connected. **disconnection** n

disconsolate ❶ adj sad beyond comfort. **disconsolately** adv

discontent ❶ n lack of contentment. **discontented** adj

discontinue ❶ v come or bring to an end.

discord ❶ n **1** lack of agreement or

harmony between people. **2** harsh confused sounds. **discordant** adj **discordance** n

discount ❶ v **1** take no account of (something) because it is considered to be unreliable, prejudiced, or irrelevant. **2** deduct (an amount) from the price of something. ◆ n **3** deduction from the full price of something.

discourse ❶ n **1** conversation. **2** formal treatment of a subject in speech or writing. ◆ v **3** (foll. by on) speak or write (about) at length.

discourteous ❶ adj showing bad manners. **discourtesy** n

discover v **1** be the first to find or to find out about. **2** learn about for the first time. **3** find after study or search. **discoverer** n **discovery** n, pl **-eries 1** discovering. **2** person, place, or thing that has been discovered.

discredit ❶ v **1** damage the reputation of. **2** cause (an idea) to be disbelieved or

——————————— THESAURUS ———————————

reveal, uncover, unveil ≠ **cover**

discolour v = **stain**, fade, mark, soil, streak, tarnish, tinge

discomfort n a = **uneasiness**, annoyance, distress, hardship, irritation, nuisance, trouble ≠ **ease** b = **pain**, ache, hurt, irritation, malaise, soreness ≠ **ease**

disconcert v = **disturb**, faze, fluster, perturb, rattle (inf), take aback, unsettle, upset, worry

disconnect v **1** = **cut off**, detach, disengage, divide, part, separate, sever, take apart, uncouple

disconsolate adj = **inconsolable**, crushed, dejected, desolate, forlorn, grief-stricken, heartbroken, miserable, wretched

discontent n = **dissatisfaction**, displeasure, envy, regret, restlessness, uneasiness, unhappiness

discontinue v = **stop**, abandon, break off, cease, drop, end, give up, quit, suspend, terminate

discord n **1** = **disagreement**, conflict, dissension, disunity, division, friction,

incompatibility, strife ≠ **understanding** **2** = **disharmony**, cacophony, din, dissonance, harshness, jarring, racket, tumult

discount v **1** = **leave out**, brush off (sl), disbelieve, disregard, ignore, overlook, pass over **2** = **deduct**, lower, mark down, reduce, take off ◆ n **3** = **deduction**, concession, cut, rebate, reduction

discourse n **1** = **conversation**, chat, communication, dialogue, discussion, seminar, speech, talk **2** = **speech**, dissertation, essay, homily, lecture, oration, sermon, treatise ◆ v **3** (foll. by on) = **hold forth**, expatiate, speak, talk

discourteous adj = **rude**, bad-mannered, boorish, disrespectful, ill-mannered, impolite, insolent, offhand, ungentlemanly, ungracious

discover v **1** = **find**, come across, come upon, dig up, locate, turn up, uncover, unearth **2, 3** = **find out**, ascertain, detect, learn, notice, perceive, realize, recognize, uncover distrusted. ◆ *n* **3** damage to someone's reputation. **discreditable** *adj* bringing shame.

discreet ⊕ *adj* **1** careful to avoid embarrassment, esp. by keeping confidences secret. **2** unobtrusive.

discrepancy ⊕ *n*, *pl* **–cies** conflict or variation between facts, figures, or claims.

discrete *adj* separate, distinct.

discretion ⊕ *n* **1** quality of behaving in a discreet way. **2** freedom or authority to make judgments and decide what to do. **discretionary** *adj*

discriminate ⊕ *v* **1** (foll. by *against* or *in favour of*) single out (a particular person or group) for worse or better treatment than others. **2** (foll. by *between*) recognize or understand the difference (between). **discriminating** *adj* showing good taste and judgment. **discrimination** *n* **discriminatory** *adj* based on prejudice.

discursive *adj* passing from one topic to another.

discus *n* heavy disc–shaped object thrown in sports competitions.

discuss ⊕ *v* **1** consider (something) by talking it over. **2** treat (a subject) in speech or writing. **discussion** *n*

disdain ⊕ *n* **1** feeling of superiority and dislike. ◆ *v* **2** refuse with disdain. **disdainful** *adj* **disdainfully** *adv*

disease ⊕ *n* illness, sickness. **diseased** *adj*

disembark ⊕ *v* get off a ship, aircraft, or bus. **disembarkation** *n*

disembodied *adj* **1** lacking a body. **2** seeming not to be attached to or coming from anyone.

disembowel *v* **–elling**, **–elled** remove the entrails of.

disenchanted ⊕ *adj* disappointed and disillusioned. **disenchantment** *n*

disengage ⊕ *v* release from a connection. **disengagement** *n*

disfavour ⊕ *n* disapproval or dislike.

disfigure ⊕ *v* spoil the appearance of. **disfigurement** *n*

——————— THESAURUS ———————

discredit *v* **1** = **disgrace**, bring into disrepute, defame, dishonour, disparage, slander, smear, vilify ≠ **credit 2** = **doubt**, challenge, deny, disbelieve, discount, dispute, distrust, mistrust, question ◆ *n* **3** = **disgrace**, dishonour, disrepute, ignominy, ill–repute, scandal, shame, stigma

discreet *adj* **1** = **tactful**, careful, cautious, circumspect, considerate, diplomatic, guarded, judicious, prudent, wary ≠ **rash**

discrepancy *n* = **disagreement**, conflict, contradiction, difference, disparity, divergence, incongruity, inconsistency, variation

discretion *n* **1** = **tact**, carefulness, caution, consideration, diplomacy, judiciousness, prudence, wariness ≠ **indiscretion 2** = **choice**, inclination, pleasure, preference, volition, will

discriminate *v* **1** (foll. by *against* or *in favour of*) = **show prejudice**, favour, show bias, single out, treat as inferior, treat as superior, treat differently, victimize **2** (foll.

by *between*) = **differentiate**, distinguish, draw a distinction, segregate, separate, tell the difference

discuss *v* = **talk about**, argue, confer, consider, converse, debate, deliberate, examine

disdain *n* **1** = **contempt**, arrogance, derision, haughtiness, scorn, superciliousness ◆ *v* **2** = **scorn**, deride, disregard, look down on, reject, slight, sneer at, spurn

disease *n* = **illness**, affliction, ailment, complaint, condition, disorder, infection, infirmity, malady, sickness

disembark *v* = **land**, alight, arrive, get off, go ashore, step out of

disenchanted *adj* = **disillusioned**, cynical, disappointed, indifferent, jaundiced, let down, sick of, soured

disengage *v* = **release**, disentangle, extricate, free, loosen, set free, unloose, untie

disfavour *n* = **disapproval**, disapprobation, dislike, displeasure

disgrace ❶ *n* 1 condition of shame, loss of reputation, or dishonour. 2 shameful person or thing. ◆ *v* 3 bring shame upon (oneself or others). **disgraceful** *adj* **disgracefully** *adv*

disgruntled ❶ *adj* sulky or discontented. **disgruntlement** *n*

disguise ❶ *v* 1 change the appearance or manner in order to conceal the identity of (someone or something). 2 misrepresent (something) in order to obscure its actual nature or meaning. ◆ *n* 3 mask, costume, or manner that disguises. 4 state of being disguised.

disgust ❶ *n* 1 great loathing or distaste. ◆ *v* 2 sicken, fill with loathing.

dish ❶ *n* 1 shallow container used for holding or serving food. 2 particular kind of food. 3 short for DISH AERIAL. 4 *Informal* attractive person. **dishcloth** *n* cloth for washing dishes. **dish out** *Informal* distribute. **dish up** *Informal* serve (food).

dishearten ❶ *v* weaken or destroy the hope, courage, or enthusiasm of.

dishevelled ❶ *adj* (of a person's hair, clothes, or general appearance) disordered and untidy.

dishonest ❶ *adj* not honest or fair. **dishonesty** *n*

dishonour ❶ *v* 1 treat with disrespect. ◆ *n* 2 lack of respect. 3 state of shame or disgrace. 4 something that causes a loss of honour. **dishonourable** *adj* **dishonourably** *adv*

disillusion *v* 1 destroy the illusions or false ideas of. ◆ *n* 2 (also **disillusionment**) state of being disillusioned.

disinformation *n* false information intended to mislead.

disingenuous *adj* not sincere.

disinherit ❶ *v Law* deprive (an heir) of inheritance. **disinheritance** *n*

disintegrate ❶ *v* break up. **disintegration** *n*

disinterested ❶ *adj* free from bias or involvement. **disinterest** *n*

THESAURUS

disfigure *v* = **damage**, blemish, deface, deform, distort, mar, mutilate, scar

disgrace *n* 1 = **shame**, degradation, dishonour, disrepute, ignominy, infamy, odium, opprobrium ≠ **credit** 2 = **stain**, blemish, blot, reproach, scandal, slur, stigma ◆ *v* 3 = **bring shame upon**, degrade, discredit, dishonour, humiliate, shame, sully, taint ≠ **credit**

disgruntled *adj* = **discontented**, annoyed, displeased, dissatisfied, grumpy, irritated, peeved, put out, vexed

disguise *v* 1 = **hide**, camouflage, cloak, conceal, cover, mask, screen, shroud, veil 2 = **misrepresent**, fake, falsify ◆ *n* 3 = **costume**, camouflage, cover, mask, screen, veil 4 = **facade**, deception, dissimulation, front, pretence, semblance, trickery, veneer

disgust *n* 1 = **loathing**, abhorrence, aversion, dislike, distaste, hatred, nausea, repugnance, repulsion, revulsion ≠ **liking** ◆ *v* 2 = **sicken**, displease, nauseate, offend, put off, repel, revolt ≠ **please**

dish *n* 1 = **bowl**, plate, platter, salver 2 = **food**, fare, recipe

dishearten *v* = **discourage**, cast down, deject, depress, deter, dismay, dispirit, put a damper on

dishevelled *adj* = **untidy**, bedraggled, disordered, messy, ruffled, rumpled, tousled, uncombed, unkempt

dishonest *adj* = **deceitful**, bent (*sl*), cheating, corrupt, crooked (*inf*), disreputable, double-dealing, false, lying, treacherous

dishonour *v* 1 = **disgrace**, debase, debauch, defame, degrade, discredit, shame, sully ≠ **respect** ◆ *n* 3 = **disgrace**, discredit, disrepute, ignominy, infamy, obloquy, reproach, scandal, shame ≠ **honour** 4 = **insult**, abuse, affront, discourtesy, indignity, offence, outrage, sacrilege, slight

disinherit *v Law* = **cut off**, disown, dispossess, oust, repudiate

disintegrate *v* = **break up**, break apart, crumble, fall apart, go to pieces, separate,

> ✓ **WORD TIP**
>
> Distinguish *disinterested* from
> *uninterested*, meaning 'apathetic, not
> caring': *We asked him to decide because
> he was a disinterested observer.*

disk n *Computers* storage device, consisting
of a stack of plates coated with a magnetic
layer, which rotates rapidly as a single
unit.

dislike ❶ v 1 consider unpleasant or
disagreeable. ◆ n 2 feeling of not liking
something or someone.

dislocate v 1 displace (a bone or joint)
from its normal position. 2 disrupt or shift
out of place. **dislocation** n

dislodge ❶ v remove (something) from a
previously fixed position.

disloyal ❶ adj not loyal, deserting one's
allegiance. **disloyalty** n

dismal ❶ adj 1 gloomy and depressing. 2
Informal of poor quality. **dismally** adv

dismantle ❶ v take apart piece by piece.

dismay ❶ v 1 fill with alarm or depression.
◆ n 2 alarm mixed with sadness.

dismember ❶ v 1 remove the limbs of. 2
cut to pieces. **dismemberment** n

dismiss ❶ v 1 remove (an employee) from
a job. 2 allow (someone) to leave. 3 put
out of one's mind. 4 (of a judge) state that
(a case) will not be brought to trial.
dismissal n **dismissive** adj scornful,
contemptuous.

dismount v get off a horse or bicycle.

disobey ❶ v neglect or refuse to obey.
disobedient adj **disobedience** n

disorder ❶ n 1 state of untidiness and
disorganization. 2 public violence or
rioting. 3 an illness. **disordered** adj untidy.
disorderly adj 1 untidy and disorganized.
2 uncontrolled, unruly.

disorientate, disorient v cause
(someone) to lose his or her bearings.
disorientation n

disown ❶ v deny any connection with

─────── THESAURUS ───────

shatter, splinter

disinterested adj = **impartial**, detached,
dispassionate, even-handed, impersonal,
neutral, objective, unbiased, unprejudiced
≠ **involved**

dislike v 1 = **be averse to**, despise, detest,
disapprove, hate, loathe, not be able to
bear *or* abide *or* stand, object to, take a
dim view of ≠ **like** ◆ n 2 = **aversion**,
animosity, antipathy, disapproval,
disinclination, displeasure, distaste,
enmity, hostility, repugnance ≠ **liking**

dislodge v = **displace**, disturb, extricate,
force out, knock loose, oust, remove,
uproot

disloyal adj = **treacherous**, faithless, false,
subversive, traitorous, two-faced,
unfaithful, untrustworthy

dismal adj 1 = **gloomy**, bleak, cheerless,
dark, depressing, discouraging, dreary,
forlorn, sombre, wretched ≠ **bright**

dismantle v = **take apart**, demolish,
disassemble, strip, take to pieces

dismay v 1 = **alarm**, appal, daunt,

discourage, dishearten, dispirit, distress,
frighten, horrify, paralyse, put off, scare,
terrify, unnerve ◆ n 2 = **alarm**, anxiety,
apprehension, consternation,
discouragement, dread, fear, horror,
trepidation

dismember v 1 = **amputate** 2 = **cut into
pieces**, dissect, sever

dismiss v 1 = **sack** (*inf*), axe (*inf*), cashier,
discharge, fire (*inf*), give notice to, give
(someone) their marching orders, lay off,
remove 2 = **let go**, disperse, dissolve, free,
release, send away 3 = **put out of one's
mind**, banish, discard, dispel, disregard,
lay aside, reject, set aside

disobey v = **refuse to obey**, contravene,
defy, disregard, flout, ignore, infringe,
rebel, violate

disorder n 1 = **untidiness**, chaos, clutter,
confusion, disarray, jumble, mess, muddle,
shambles 2 = **disturbance**, commotion,
riot, turmoil, unrest, unruliness, uproar
3 = **illness**, affliction, ailment, complaint,
disease, malady, sickness

(someone).

disparage ❶ v speak contemptuously of. **disparagement** n

dispassionate ❶ adj not influenced by emotion. **dispassionately** adv

dispatch ❶ v 1 send off to a destination or to perform a task. 2 carry out (a duty or a task) with speed. 3 Old–fashioned kill. ◆ n 4 official communication or report, sent in haste. 5 report sent to a newspaper by a correspondent. **dispatch rider** motorcyclist who carries dispatches.

dispel ❶ v –pelling, –pelled destroy or remove.

dispense ❶ v 1 distribute in portions. 2 prepare and distribute (medicine). 3 administer (the law etc.). **dispensable** adj not essential. **dispensation** n 1 dispensing. 2 exemption from an obligation. **dispenser** n **dispensary** n, pl –saries place where medicine is dispensed. **dispense with** v do away with, manage without.

disperse ❶ v 1 scatter over a wide area. 2 (cause to) leave a gathering. **dispersal, dispersion** n

displace ❶ v 1 move from the usual location. 2 remove from office. **displacement** n **displaced person** person forced from his or her home or country, esp. by war.

display ❶ v 1 make visible or noticeable. ◆ n 2 displaying. 3 something displayed. 4 exhibition.

displease ❶ v annoy or upset. **displeasure** n

dispose ❶ v place in a certain order. **disposed** adj 1 willing or eager. 2 having an attitude as specified, e.g. he felt well disposed towards her. **disposable** adj 1 designed to be thrown away after use. 2 available for use, e.g. disposable income. **disposal** n getting rid of something. **at one's disposal** available for use. **disposition** n 1 person's usual temperament. 2 desire or tendency to do something. 3 arrangement. **dispose of** v 1 throw away, get rid of. 2 deal with (a problem etc.). 3 kill.

disprove ❶ v show (an assertion or claim) to be incorrect.

———————— THESAURUS ————————

disown v = **deny**, cast off, disavow, disclaim, reject, renounce, repudiate

disparage v = **run down**, belittle, denigrate, deprecate, deride, malign, put down, ridicule, slander, vilify

dispassionate adj = **unemotional**, calm, collected, composed, cool, detached, disinterested, impersonal, imperturbable, serene, unruffled ≠ **excited**

dispatch v 1 = **send**, consign, dismiss, hasten 2 = **carry out**, discharge, dispose of, finish, perform, settle 3 Old–fashioned = **murder**, assassinate, execute, kill, slaughter, slay ◆ n 5 = **message**, account, bulletin, communication, communiqué, news, report, story

dispel v = **drive away**, banish, chase away, dismiss, dissipate, eliminate, expel

dispense v 1 = **distribute**, allocate, allot, apportion, assign, deal out, dole out, share 2 = **prepare**, measure, mix, supply 3 = **administer**, apply, carry out,

discharge, enforce, execute, implement, operate **dispense with** = **do without**, abolish, abstain from, brush aside, cancel, dispose of, do away with, forgo, get rid of, give up

disperse v 1 = **scatter**, broadcast, diffuse, disseminate, distribute, spread, strew 2 = **break up**, disband, dissolve, scatter, separate ≠ **collect**

displace v 1 = **move**, disturb, misplace, shift, transpose 2 = **replace**, oust, succeed, supersede, supplant, take the place of

display v 1 = **show**, demonstrate, disclose, exhibit, expose, flaunt, flourish, manifest, parade, present, reveal, show off, vaunt ≠ **cover** ◆ n 2, 3 = **exhibition**, array, demonstration, presentation, show 4 = **show**, pageant, parade, spectacle

displease v = **annoy**, anger, irk, irritate, offend, pique, put out, upset, vex

dispose v = **arrange**, array, distribute, group, marshal, order, place, put

dispute ⊕ *n* 1 disagreement, argument. ◆ *v* 2 argue about (something). 3 doubt the validity of. 4 fight over possession of.

disqualify ⊕ *v* stop (someone) officially from taking part in something for wrongdoing. **disqualification** *n*

disquiet ⊕ *n* 1 feeling of anxiety. ◆ *v* 2 make (someone) anxious. **disquietude** *n*

disregard ⊕ *v* 1 give little or no attention to. ◆ *n* 2 lack of attention or respect.

disrepair ⊕ *n* condition of being worn out or in poor working order.

disrepute ⊕ *n* loss or lack of good reputation. **disreputable** *adj* having or causing a bad reputation.

disrespect ⊕ *n* lack of respect. **disrespectful** *adj*

disrupt ⊕ *v* interrupt the progress of. **disruption** *n* **disruptive** *adj*

dissatisfied ⊕ *adj* not pleased or contented. **dissatisfaction** *n*

dissect ⊕ *v* 1 cut open (a corpse) to examine it. 2 examine critically and minutely. **dissection** *n*

dissemble *v* conceal one's real motives or emotions by pretence.

disseminate ⊕ *v* spread (information). **dissemination** *n*

dissent ⊕ *v* 1 disagree. 2 *Christianity* reject the doctrines of an established church. ◆ *n* 3 disagreement. 4 *Christianity* separation from an established church. **dissension** *n* **dissenter** *n*

dissertation ⊕ *n* 1 written thesis, usu. required for a higher university degree. 2 long formal speech.

disservice ⊕ *n* harmful action.

dissident ⊕ *n* 1 person who disagrees

──────── THESAURUS ────────

disprove *v* = **prove false**, contradict, discredit, expose, give the lie to, invalidate, negate, rebut, refute

dispute *n* 1 = **disagreement**, altercation, argument, conflict, contention, controversy, debate, dissension, feud, quarrel ◆ *v* 2 = **argue**, clash, cross swords, debate, quarrel, squabble 3 = **doubt**, challenge, contest, contradict, deny, impugn, question, rebut

disqualify *v* = **ban**, debar, declare ineligible, preclude, prohibit, rule out

disquiet *n* 1 = **uneasiness**, alarm, anxiety, concern, disturbance, foreboding, nervousness, trepidation, worry ◆ *v* 2 = **make uneasy**, bother, concern, disturb, perturb, trouble, unsettle, upset, worry

disregard *v* 1 = **ignore**, brush aside *or* away, discount, make light of, neglect, overlook, pass over, pay no heed to, turn a blind eye to ≠ **listen to** ◆ *n* 2 = **inattention**, contempt, disdain, disrespect, indifference, neglect, negligence, oversight

disrepair *n* = **dilapidation**, collapse, decay, deterioration, ruination

disrepute *n* = **discredit**, disgrace,

dishonour, ignominy, ill repute, infamy, obloquy, shame, unpopularity

disrespect *n* = **contempt**, cheek, impertinence, impoliteness, impudence, insolence, irreverence, lack of respect, rudeness, sauce

disrupt *v* = **disturb**, break up *or* into, confuse, disorder, disorganize, interfere with, interrupt, intrude, spoil, unsettle, upset

dissatisfied *adj* = **discontented**, disappointed, disgruntled, displeased, fed up, frustrated, unhappy, unsatisfied

dissect *v* 1 = **cut up** *or* **apart**, anatomize, dismember, lay open 2 = **analyse**, break down, explore, inspect, investigate, research, scrutinize, study

disseminate *v* = **spread**, broadcast, circulate, disperse, distribute, publicize, scatter

dissent *v* 1 = **disagree**, differ, object, protest, refuse, withhold assent *or* approval ◆ *n* 3 = **disagreement**, discord, dissension, objection, opposition, refusal, resistance ≠ **accord**

dissertation *n* 1 = **thesis**, critique, discourse, disquisition, essay, exposition, treatise

with and criticizes the government. ♦ *adj*
2 disagreeing with the government.
dissidence *n*
dissimilar ❶ *adj* not alike, different.
dissimilarity *n*
dissipate ❶ *v* 1 waste or squander. 2
scatter, disappear. **dissipated** *adj* showing
signs of overindulgence in alcohol and
other physical pleasures. **dissipation** *n*
dissociate ❶ *v* regard or treat as separate.
dissociate oneself from deny or break an
association with. **dissociation** *n*
dissolute ❶ *adj* leading an immoral life.
dissolution ❶ *n* 1 official breaking up of
an organization or institution, such as
Parliament. 2 official ending of a formal
agreement, such as a marriage.
dissolve ❶ *v* 1 (cause to) become liquid. 2
break up or end officially. 3 break down
emotionally, e.g. *she dissolved into tears.*
dissuade ❶ *v* deter (someone) by
persuasion from doing something.
dissuasion *n*
distance ❶ *n* 1 space between two points.
2 state of being apart. 3 remoteness in
manner. **the distance** most distant part of

the visible scene. **distance oneself from**
separate oneself mentally from. **distant** *adj*
1 far apart. 2 separated by a specified
distance. 3 remote in manner. **distantly**
adv
distaste ❶ *n* dislike, disgust. **distasteful**
adj unpleasant, offensive.
distemper[1] *n* highly contagious viral
disease of dogs.
distemper[2] *n* paint mixed with water,
glue, etc., used for painting walls.
distend *v* (of part of the body) swell.
distension *n*
distil ❶ *v* –tilling, –tilled 1 subject to or
obtain by distillation. 2 give off (a
substance) in drops. 3 extract the essence
of. **distillation** *n* 1 process of evaporating
a liquid and condensing its vapour. 2 (also
distillate) concentrated essence. **distiller** *n*
person or company that makes strong
alcoholic drink, esp. whisky. **distillery** *n, pl*
–leries place where a strong alcoholic
drink, esp. whisky, is made.
distinct ❶ *adj* 1 not the same. 2 easily
sensed or understood. 3 clear and definite.
distinctly *adv* **distinction** *n* 1 act of

───── THESAURUS ─────

disservice *n* = **bad turn**, harm, injury,
injustice, unkindness, wrong
dissident *n* 1 = **protester**, agitator,
dissenter, rebel ♦ *adj* 2 = **dissenting**,
disagreeing, discordant, heterodox,
nonconformist
dissimilar *adj* = **different**, disparate,
divergent, diverse, heterogeneous, unlike,
unrelated, various
dissipate *v* 1 = **squander**, consume,
deplete, expend, fritter away, run
through, spend, waste 2 = **disperse**,
disappear, dispel, dissolve, drive away,
evaporate, scatter, vanish
dissociate *v* = **separate**, detach,
disconnect, distance, divorce, isolate,
segregate, set apart **dissociate oneself
from** = **break away from**, break off from,
part company from, quit
dissolute *adj* = **immoral**, debauched,
degenerate, depraved, dissipated,

profligate, rakish, wanton, wild
dissolution *n* 1 = **breaking up**,
disintegration, division, parting, separation
2 = **adjournment**, discontinuation, end,
finish, suspension, termination ≠ **union**
dissolve *v* 1 = **melt**, deliquesce, fuse,
liquefy, soften, thaw 2 = **end**, break up,
discontinue, suspend, terminate, wind up
dissuade *v* = **deter**, advise against,
discourage, put off, remonstrate, talk out
of, warn
distance *n* 1 = **space**, extent, gap, interval,
length, range, span, stretch 3 = **reserve**,
aloofness, coldness, coolness, remoteness,
restraint, stiffness ♦ *v* **distance oneself
from** = **separate oneself from**, be
distanced from, dissociate oneself from
distaste *n* = **dislike**, aversion, disgust,
horror, loathing, odium, repugnance,
revulsion
distil *v* 1, 3 = **extract**, condense, purify,

distinguishing. **2** distinguishing feature. **3** state of being different. **4** special honour, recognition, or fame. **distinctive** *adj* easily recognizable. **distinctively** *adv* **distinctiveness** *n*

distinguish ⊕ *v* **1** (usu. foll. by *between*) make, show, or recognize a difference (between). **2** be a distinctive feature of. **3** make out by hearing, seeing, etc. **distinguishable** *adj* **distinguished** *adj* **1** dignified in appearance. **2** highly respected.

distort ⊕ *v* **1** misrepresent (the truth or facts). **2** twist out of shape. **distortion** *n*

distract ⊕ *v* **1** draw the attention of (a person) away from something. **2** entertain. **distracted** *adj* unable to concentrate, preoccupied. **distraction** *n*

distraught ⊕ [diss–trawt] *adj* extremely anxious or agitated.

distress ⊕ *n* **1** extreme unhappiness. **2** great physical pain. **3** poverty. ◆ *v* **4** upset

badly. **distressed** *adj* **1** extremely upset. **2** in financial difficulties. **distressing** *adj* **distressingly** *adv*

distribute ⊕ *v* **1** hand out or deliver. **2** share out. **distribution** *n* **1** distributing. **2** arrangement or spread. **distributor** *n* **1** wholesaler who distributes goods to retailers in a specific area. **2** device in a petrol engine that sends the electric current to the spark plugs. **distributive** *adj*

district ⊕ *n* area of land regarded as an administrative or geographical unit.

distrust ⊕ *v* **1** regard as untrustworthy. ◆ *n* **2** feeling of suspicion or doubt. **distrustful** *adj*

disturb ⊕ *v* **1** intrude on. **2** worry, make anxious. **3** change the position or shape of. **disturbance** *n* **disturbing** *adj* **disturbingly** *adv* **disturbed** *adj* *Psychiatry* emotionally upset or maladjusted.

disuse ⊕ *n* state of being no longer used. **disused** *adj*

refine

distinct *adj* **1** = **different**, detached, discrete, individual, separate, unconnected ≠ **similar 3** = **definite**, clear, decided, evident, marked, noticeable, obvious, palpable, unmistakable, well–defined ≠ **obscure**

distinguish *v* **1** (usu. foll. by *between*) = **differentiate**, ascertain, decide, determine, discriminate, judge, tell apart, tell the difference **2** = **characterize**, categorize, classify, mark, separate, set apart, single out **3** = **make out**, discern, know, perceive, pick out, recognize, see, tell

distort *v* **1** = **misrepresent**, bias, colour, falsify, pervert, slant, twist **2** = **deform**, bend, buckle, contort, disfigure, misshape, twist, warp

distract *v* **1** = **divert**, draw away, sidetrack, turn aside **2** = **amuse**, beguile, engross, entertain, occupy

distraught *adj* = **frantic**, agitated, beside oneself, desperate, distracted, distressed, out of one's mind, overwrought, worked–

up

distress *n* **1** = **worry**, grief, heartache, misery, pain, sorrow, suffering, torment, wretchedness **2** = **pain**, suffering, torment **3** = **need**, adversity, difficulties, hardship, misfortune, poverty, privation, trouble ◆ *v* **4** = **upset**, disturb, grieve, harass, sadden, torment, trouble, worry

distribute *v* **1** = **hand out**, circulate, convey, deliver, pass round **2** = **share**, allocate, allot, apportion, deal, dispense, dole out

district *n* = **area**, locale, locality, neighbourhood, parish, quarter, region, sector, vicinity

distrust *v* **1** = **suspect**, be suspicious of, be wary of, disbelieve, doubt, mistrust, question, smell a rat (*inf*) ◆ *n* **2** = **suspicion**, disbelief, doubt, misgiving, mistrust, question, scepticism, wariness ≠ **trust**

disturb *v* **1** = **interrupt**, bother, butt in on, disrupt, interfere with, intrude on, pester **2** = **upset**, alarm, distress, fluster, harass, perturb, trouble, unnerve, unsettle, worry

ditch ⓣ *n* 1 narrow channel dug in the earth for drainage or irrigation. ♦ *v* 2 *Slang* abandon.

dither ⓣ *v* 1 be uncertain or indecisive. ♦ *n* 2 state of indecision or agitation. **ditherer** *n* **dithery** *adj*

ditto *n, pl* –tos 1 the same. ♦ *adv* 2 in the same way.

ditty *n, pl* –ties short simple poem or song.

divan *n* 1 low backless bed. 2 backless sofa or couch.

dive ⓣ *v* diving, dived 1 plunge headfirst into water. 2 (of a submarine or diver) submerge under water. 3 fly in a steep nose–down descending path. 4 move quickly in a specified direction. 5 (foll. by *in* or *into*) start doing (something) enthusiastically. ♦ *n* 6 diving. 7 steep nose–down descent. 8 *Slang* disreputable bar or club. **diver** *n* 1 person who works or explores underwater. 2 person who dives for sport.

diverge ⓣ *v* 1 separate and go in different directions. 2 deviate (from a prescribed course). **divergence** *n* **divergent** *adj*

diverse ⓣ *adj* 1 having variety, assorted. 2 different in kind. **diversity** *n, pl* –ties 1 quality of being different or varied. 2 range of difference. **diversify** *v* –fying, –fied. **diversification** *n*

divert ⓣ *v* 1 change the direction of. 2 entertain, distract the attention of. **diversion** *n* 1 official detour used by traffic when a main route is closed. 2 something that distracts someone's attention. 3 diverting. 4 amusing pastime. **diversionary** *adj*

divide ⓣ *v* 1 separate into parts. 2 share or be shared out in parts. 3 (cause to) disagree. 4 keep apart, be a boundary between. 5 calculate how many times (one number) can be contained in (another). ♦ *n* 6 division, split. **dividend** *n* 1 sum of money representing part of the profit made, paid by a company to its shareholders. 2 extra benefit. **divider** *n* 1 screen used to divide a room into separate areas. ♦ *pl* 2 compasses with two pointed arms, used for measuring or dividing lines.

divine ⓣ *adj* 1 of God or a god. 2 godlike. 3 *Informal* splendid. ♦ *v* 4 discover (something) by intuition or guessing. **divinely** *adv* **divination** *n* art of discovering future events, as though by supernatural powers. **divinity** *n* 1 study of religion. 2 (*pl* –ties) god. 3 state of being divine. **divining rod** forked twig said to move when held over ground in which water or metal is to be found.

division ⓣ *n* 1 dividing, sharing out. 2 one

THESAURUS

≠ **calm** 3 = **muddle**, disarrange, disorder

disuse *n* = **neglect**, abandonment, decay, idleness

ditch *n* 1 = **channel**, drain, dyke, furrow, gully, moat, trench, watercourse ♦ *v* 2 *Sl* = **get rid of**, abandon, discard, dispose of, drop, dump (*inf*), jettison, scrap, throw out *or* overboard

dither *v* 1 = **vacillate**, faff about (*Brit inf*), hesitate, hum and haw, shillyshally (*inf*), teeter, waver ≠ **decide** ♦ *n* 2 = **flutter**, flap (*inf*), fluster, tizzy (*inf*)

dive *v* 1–3 = **plunge**, descend, dip, drop, duck, nose–dive, plummet, swoop ♦ *n* 6 = **plunge**, jump, leap 7 = **nose dive**, descent, drop, plummet, plunge, swoop

diverge *v* 1 = **separate**, branch, divide,

fork, part, split, spread 2 = **deviate**, depart, digress, meander, stray, turn aside, wander

diverse *adj* 1 = **various**, assorted, manifold, miscellaneous, of every description, several, sundry, varied 2 = **different**, discrete, disparate, dissimilar, distinct, divergent, separate, unlike, varying

divert *v* 1 = **redirect**, avert, deflect, switch, turn aside 2 a = **entertain**, amuse, beguile, delight, gratify, regale b = **distract**, draw *or* lead away from, lead astray, sidetrack

divide *v* 1 = **separate**, bisect, cut (up), part, partition, segregate, split ≠ **unite** 2 = **share**, allocate, allot, deal out, dispense, distribute 3 = **cause to disagree**,

of the parts into which something is
divided. **3** mathematical operation of
dividing. **4** difference of opinion.
divisional *adj* of a division in an
organization. **divisible** *adj* **divisibility** *n*
divisive *adj* tending to cause
disagreement. **divisor** *n* number to be
divided into another number.
divorce ❶ *n* **1** legal ending of a marriage.
2 any separation, esp. a permanent one. ◆
v **3** legally end one's marriage (to). **4**
separate, consider separately. **divorcée**,
(*masc*) **divorcé** *n* person who is divorced.
divulge ❶ *v* make known, disclose.
divulgence *n*
DIY *Brit, Aust & NZ* do–it–yourself.
dizzy ❶ *adj* **–zier, –ziest 1** having or
causing a whirling sensation. **2** mentally
confused. ◆ *v* **–zying, –zied 3** make dizzy.
dizzily *adv* **dizziness** *n*
DJ 1 disc jockey. **2** dinner jacket.
DNA *n* deoxyribonucleic acid, the main
constituent of the chromosomes of all
living things.
do ❶ *v* **does, doing, did, done 1** perform
or complete (a deed or action). **2** be
adequate, e.g. *that one will do*. **3** provide,
serve. **4** make (hair) neat or attractive.

suit or improve, e.g. *that style does nothing
for you.* **6** find the answer to (a problem or
puzzle). **7** cause, produce, e.g. *it does no
harm to think ahead.* **8** give, grant, e.g. *do
me a favour.* **9** work at, as a course of study
or a job. **10** *Informal* cheat or rob. **11** used
to form questions, e.g. *how do you know?*
12 used to intensify positive statements
and commands, e.g. *I do like port; do go
on.* **13** used to form negative statements
and commands, e.g. *I do not know her well;
do not get up.* **14** used to replace an earlier
verb, e.g. *he gets paid more than I do.* ◆ *n*,
pl **dos, do's 15** *Informal* party, celebration.
do away with *v* get rid of. **1 do–it–
yourself** *n* constructing and repairing
things oneself. **do up** *v* **1** fasten. **2**
decorate and repair. **do with** *v* find useful
or benefit from, e.g. *I could do with a rest.*
do without *v* manage without.
Doberman pinscher, Doberman *n*
large dog with a black–and–tan coat.
dob in *v* **dobbing, dobbed** *Aust & NZ
informal* **1** inform against. **2** contribute to a
fund.
docile ❶ *adj* (of a person or animal) easily
controlled. **docilely** *adv* **docility** *n*
dock[1] ❶ *n* **1** enclosed area of water where

break up, come between, estrange, split
divine *adj* **1, 2 = heavenly,** angelic,
celestial, godlike, holy, spiritual,
superhuman, supernatural **3** *Inf*
= wonderful, beautiful, excellent, glorious,
marvellous, perfect, splendid, superlative ◆
v **4 = infer,** apprehend, deduce, discern,
guess, perceive, suppose, surmise
division *n* **1 = separation,** cutting up,
dividing, partition, splitting up **2 = share,**
allotment, apportionment
4 = disagreement, difference of opinion,
discord, rupture, split, variance ≠ **union**
5 = part, branch, category, class,
department, group, section
divorce *n* **1 = separation,** annulment,
dissolution, split–up ◆ *v* **3 = separate,**
disconnect, dissociate, dissolve (*marriage*),
divide, part, sever, split up

divulge *v* **= make known,** confess, declare,
disclose, let slip, proclaim, reveal, tell
dizzy *adj* **1 = giddy,** faint, light–headed, off
balance, reeling, shaky, swimming,
wobbly, woozy (*inf*) **2 = confused,** at sea,
befuddled, bemused, bewildered, dazed,
dazzled, muddled
do[1] *v* **1 = perform,** accomplish, achieve,
carry out, complete, execute **2 = be
adequate,** be sufficient, cut the mustard,
pass muster, satisfy, suffice **4 = get ready,**
arrange, fix, look after, prepare, see to
6 = solve, decipher, decode, figure out,
puzzle out, resolve, work out **7 = cause,**
bring about, create, effect, produce ◆ *n*
15 *Inf* **= event,** affair, function, gathering,
occasion, party **do without = manage
without,** abstain from, dispense with,
forgo, get along without, give up, kick

ships are loaded, unloaded, or repaired. ◆
v 2 bring or be brought into dock. 3 link
(two spacecraft) or (of two spacecraft) be
linked together in space. **docker** n person
employed to load and unload ships.
dockyard n place where ships are built or
repaired.

dock² ⓣ v 1 deduct money from (a
person's wages). 2 remove part of (an
animal's tail) by cutting through the bone.

dock³ n enclosed space in a court of law
where the accused person sits or stands.

dock⁴ n weed with broad leaves.

docket n label on a package or other
delivery, stating contents, delivery
instructions, etc.

doctor ⓣ n 1 person licensed to practise
medicine. 2 person who has been
awarded a doctorate. ◆ v 3 alter in order
to deceive. 4 poison or drug (food or
drink). 5 Informal castrate (an animal).
doctoral adj **doctorate** n highest academic
degree in any field of knowledge.

doctrine ⓣ n 1 body of teachings of a
religious, political, or philosophical group.
2 principle or body of principles that is
taught or advocated. **doctrinal** adj of
doctrines. **doctrinaire** adj stubbornly
insistent on the application of a theory
without regard to practicality.

document ⓣ n 1 piece of paper providing
an official record of something. ◆ v 2

record or report (something) in detail. 3
support (a claim) with evidence.
documentation n

documentary n, pl –ries 1 film or
television programme presenting the facts
about a particular subject. ◆ adj 2 (of
evidence) based on documents.

dodder v move unsteadily. **doddery** adj

dodge ⓣ v 1 avoid (a blow, being seen,
etc.) by moving suddenly. 2 evade by
cleverness or trickery. ◆ n 3 cunning or
deceitful trick. **dodger** n **dodgy** adj
dodgier, dodgiest Informal 1 dangerous,
risky. 2 untrustworthy.

Dodgem n ® small electric car driven and
bumped against similar cars in a rink at a
funfair.

dodo n, pl **dodos, dodoes** large flightless
extinct bird.

doe n female deer, hare, or rabbit.

does v third person singular of the present
tense of DO.

doff v take off or lift (one's hat) in polite
greeting.

dog ⓣ n 1 domesticated four–legged
mammal of many different breeds. 2
related wild mammal, such as the dingo
or coyote. 3 male animal of the dog
family. 4 Informal person, e.g. you lucky
dog! ◆ v **dogging, dogged** 5 follow
(someone) closely. 6 trouble, plague. **go
to the dogs** Informal go to ruin physically

————————— THESAURUS —————————

(inf)

docile adj = **submissive**, amenable,
biddable, compliant, manageable,
obedient, pliant

dock¹ n 1 = **wharf**, harbour, pier, quay,
waterfront ◆ v 2 = **moor**, anchor, berth,
drop anchor, land, put in, tie up 3 Of
spacecraft = **link up**, couple, hook up, join,
rendezvous, unite

dock² v 1 = **deduct**, decrease, diminish,
lessen, reduce, subtract, withhold
≠ **increase** 2 = **cut off**, clip, crop, curtail,
cut short 2 = **shorten**

doctor n 1 = **G.P.**, general practitioner,
medic (inf), medical practitioner, physician

◆ v 3 = **change**, alter, disguise, falsify,
misrepresent, pervert, tamper with
4 = **add to**, adulterate, cut, dilute, mix
with, spike, water down

doctrine n = **teaching**, article of faith,
belief, conviction, creed, dogma, opinion,
precept, principle, tenet

document n 1 = **paper**, certificate, record,
report ◆ v 3 = **support**, authenticate,
certify, corroborate, detail, substantiate,
validate, verify

dodge v 1 = **duck**, dart, sidestep, swerve,
turn aside 2 = **evade**, avoid, elude, get out
of, shirk ◆ n 3 = **trick**, device, ploy, ruse,
scheme, stratagem, subterfuge, wheeze

or morally. **let sleeping dogs lie** leave things undisturbed. **doggy, doggie** n, pl –**gies** child's word for a dog. **dogcart** n light horse–drawn two–wheeled cart. **dog collar 1** collar for a dog. **2** Informal white collar fastened at the back, worn by members of the clergy. **dog–eared** adj **1** (of a book) having pages folded down at the corner. **2** shabby, worn. **dogfight** n close–quarters combat between fighter aircraft. **dogfish** n small shark. **doghouse** n US kennel. **in the doghouse** Informal in disgrace. **dogleg** n sharp bend. **dog–tired** adj Informal exhausted.

doggerel n poorly written poetry, usu. comic.

dogma ❶ n doctrine or system of doctrines proclaimed by authority as true. **dogmatic** adj habitually stating one's opinions forcefully or arrogantly. **dogmatism** n

doily n, pl –**lies** decorative lacy paper mat, laid on a plate.

doldrums ❶ pl n **1** depressed state of mind. **2** state of inactivity.

dole ❶ n **1** Informal money received from the state while unemployed. ◆ v **2** (foll. by out) distribute in small quantities.

doleful adj dreary, unhappy. **dolefully** adv **dolefulness** n

doll n **1** small model of a human being, used as a toy. **2** Slang pretty girl or young woman.

dollar n standard monetary unit of the US, Canada, and various other countries.

dollop ❶ n Informal lump (of food).

dolly n, pl –**lies** child's word for a doll. **2** wheeled support on which a camera may be moved.

dolphin n sea mammal of the whale family, with a beaklike snout.

domain n **1** field of knowledge or activity. **2** land under one ruler or government. **3** Computers group of computers with the same name on the Internet. **4** NZ public park.

dome n **1** rounded roof built on a circular base. **2** something shaped like this. **domed** adj

domestic ❶ adj **1** of one's own country or a specific country. **2** of the home or family. **3** enjoying running a home. **4** (of an animal) kept as a pet or to produce food. ◆ n **5** person whose job is to do housework in someone else's house. **domestically** adv **domesticity** n

domesticate v **1** bring or keep (a wild animal or plant) under control or cultivation. **2** accustom (someone) to home life. **domestication** n **domestic science** study of household skills.

domicile [**dom**–miss–ile] n place where one lives.

dominate ❶ v **1** control or govern. **2** tower above (surroundings). **3** be very significant in. **domination** n

——————| T H E S A U R U S |——————

(Brit sl)
dog n **1 = hound**, canine, cur, man's best friend, pooch (sl) ◆ v **6 = trouble**, follow, haunt, hound, plague, pursue, track, trail **go to the dogs** Inf **= go to ruin**, degenerate, deteriorate, go down the drain, go to pot

dogma n **= doctrine**, belief, credo, creed, opinion, teachings

doldrums n **1 = depression**, dumps (inf), gloom, malaise **2 = inactivity**, listlessness

dole n **1** Inf **= benefit**, allowance, gift, grant, hand–out ◆ v **2** (foll. by out) **= give out**, allocate, allot, apportion, assign,

dispense, distribute, hand out

dollop n Inf **= lump**, helping, portion, scoop, serving

domestic adj **1 = native**, indigenous, internal **2 = home**, family, household, private **3 = home–loving**, domesticated, homely, housewifely, stay–at–home **4 = domesticated**, house–trained, pet, tame, trained ◆ n **5 = servant**, char (inf), charwoman, daily, help, maid

dominate v **1 = control**, direct, govern, have the whip hand over, monopolize, rule, tyrannize **2 = tower above**, loom over, overlook, stand head and shoulders

dominion ⊕ n 1 control or authority. 2 land governed by one ruler or government. 3 (formerly) self–governing division of the British Empire.

don[1] ⊕ v **donning, donned** put on (clothing).

don[2] n 1 Brit member of the teaching staff at a university or college. 2 Spanish gentleman or nobleman. **donnish** adj serious and academic.

donate ⊕ v give, esp. to a charity or organization. **donation** n 1 donating. 2 thing donated. **donor** n 1 Med person who gives blood or organs for use in the treatment of another person. 2 person who makes a donation.

done v past participle of DO.

donkey n long–eared member of the horse family. **donkey jacket** man's long thick jacket with a waterproof panel across the shoulders. **donkey's years** Informal a long time. **donkey–work** n tedious hard work.

doodle v 1 scribble or draw aimlessly. ◆ n 2 shape or picture drawn aimlessly.

doom ⊕ n 1 death or a terrible fate. ◆ v 2 destine or condemn to death or a terrible fate. **doomsday** n 1 Christianity day on which the Last Judgment will occur. 2 any dreaded day.

door ⊕ n 1 hinged or sliding panel for closing the entrance to a building, room, etc. 2 entrance. **doormat** n 1 mat for wiping dirt from shoes before going indoors. 2 Informal person who offers resistance to ill–treatment. 3 **doorway** opening into a building or room.

dope ⊕ n 1 Slang illegal drug, usu. cannabis. 2 medicine, drug. 3 Informal stupid person. ◆ v 4 give a drug to, esp. order to improve performance in a race. **dopey, dopy** adj 1 half–asleep, drowsy. 2 Slang silly.

dormant ⊕ adj temporarily quiet, inactive, or not being used. **dormancy** n

dormitory n, pl **–ries** large room, esp. at a school, containing several beds.

dormouse n, pl **–mice** small mouselike rodent with a furry tail.

dorp n S Afr small town.

dorsal adj of or on the back.

dose ⊕ n 1 specific quantity of a medicine taken at one time. 2 Informal something unpleasant to experience. ◆ v 3 give a dose to. **dosage** n size of a dose.

dossier [**doss**–ee–ay] n collection of documents about a subject or person.

dot ⊕ n 1 small round mark. 2 shorter symbol used in Morse code. ◆ v **dotting, dotted** 3 mark with a dot. 4 scatter, spread around. **on the dot** at exactly the arranged time. **dotty** adj Slang rather eccentric. **dotcom, dot.com** n company that does most of its business on the Internet.

———— THESAURUS ————

above, stand over, survey

dominion n 1 = **control**, authority, command, jurisdiction, mana (NZ), power, rule, sovereignty, supremacy 2 = **kingdom**, country, domain, empire, realm, territory

don[1] v = **put on**, clothe oneself in, dress in, get into, pull on, slip on or into

donate v = **give**, contribute, make a gift of, present, subscribe

doom n 1 = **destruction**, catastrophe, downfall, fate, fortune, ruin ◆ v 2 = **condemn**, consign, damn, destine, sentence

door n = **opening**, doorway, entrance, entry, exit

dope n 1 Sl = **drug**, narcotic, opiate 3 Inf = **idiot**, dimwit (inf), dunce, fool, nitwit (inf), numbskull or numskull, simpleton, twit (inf, chiefly Brit) ◆ v 4 = **drug**, anaesthetize, knock out, narcotize, sedate, stupefy

dormant adj = **inactive**, asleep, hibernating, inert, inoperative, latent, sleeping, slumbering, suspended ≠ active

dose n 1 = **quantity**, dosage, draught, measure, portion, potion, prescription

dot n 1 = **spot**, fleck, jot, mark, point, speck, speckle ◆ v 3 = **spot**, dab, dabble, fleck, speckle, sprinkle, stipple, stud **on the dot** = **on time**, exactly, on the button

dote ❶ v **dote on** love to an excessive degree. **dotage** n weakness as a result of old age.

double ❶ adj 1 as much again in number, amount, size, etc. 2 composed of two equal or similar parts. 3 designed for two users, e.g. *double room*. 4 folded in two. ◆ adv 5 twice over. ◆ n 6 twice the number, amount, size, etc. 7 person who looks almost exactly like another. ◆ pl 8 game between two pairs of players. ◆ v 9 make or become twice as much or as many. 10 bend or fold (material etc.). 11 play two parts. 12 turn sharply. **at, on the double** quickly or immediately. **doubly** adv **double agent** spy employed by two enemy countries at the same time. 1 **double bass** stringed instrument, largest and lowest member of the violin family. **double chin** fold of fat under the chin. **double cream** thick cream with a high fat content. **double–cross** v 1 cheat or betray. ◆ n 2 double–crossing. **double–dealing** n treacherous or deceitful behaviour. **double–decker** n 1 bus with two passenger decks one on top of the other. 2 **double Dutch** *Informal* incomprehensible talk, gibberish. 1 **double glazing** two panes of glass in a window, fitted to reduce heat loss. **double talk** deceptive or ambiguous talk. **double whammy** *Informal* devastating setback made up of two elements.

doubt ❶ n 1 uncertainty about the truth, facts, or existence of something. 2 unresolved difficulty or point. ◆ v 3 question the truth of. 4 distrust or be suspicious of (someone). **doubtful** adj 1 unlikely. 2 feeling doubt. **doubtfully** adv **doubtless** adv probably or certainly.

> ✓ **WORD TIP**
> If *doubt* is followed by a clause it is connected by *whether: I doubt whether she means it.* If it is used with a negative it is followed by *that: I don't doubt that he is sincere.*

dough n 1 thick mixture of flour and water or milk, used for making bread etc. 2 *Slang* money. **doughnut** n small cake of sweetened dough fried in deep fat.

doughty [dowt–ee] adj –tier, –tiest *Old–fashioned* brave and determined.

dour ❶ [doo–er] adj sullen and unfriendly.

douse [rhymes with **mouse**] v 1 drench with water or other liquid. 2 put out (a light).

dove n 1 bird with a heavy body, small head, and short legs. 2 *Politics* person opposed to war. **dovecote, dovecot** n structure for housing pigeons. **dovetail** n 1 joint containing wedge–shaped tenons. ◆ v 2 fit together neatly.

dowager n widow possessing property or a title obtained from her husband.

dowdy ❶ adj –dier, –diest dull and old–fashioned. **dowdily** adv **dowdiness** n

———————————— THESAURUS ————————————

(*inf*), precisely, promptly, punctually, to the minute

dote v **dote on = adore**, admire, hold dear, idolize, lavish affection on, prize, treasure

double adj 1 = **twice**, duplicate, twofold 2 = **dual**, coupled, in pairs, paired, twin ◆ n 7 = **twin**, clone, dead ringer (*sl*), doppelgänger, duplicate, lookalike, replica, spitting image (*inf*) ◆ v 9 = **multiply**, duplicate, enlarge, grow, increase, magnify **at** or **on the double = quickly**, at full speed, briskly, immediately, posthaste, without delay

doubt n 1 = **uncertainty**, apprehension, distrust, hesitancy, hesitation, indecision, irresolution, lack of conviction, misgiving, mistrust, qualm, scepticism, suspense, suspicion ≠ **certainty** ◆ v 3 = **be uncertain**, be dubious, demur 4 = **suspect**, discredit, distrust, fear, lack confidence in, mistrust, query, question ≠ **believe**

dour adj = **gloomy**, dismal, dreary, forbidding, grim, morose, sour, sullen, unfriendly

dowdy adj = **frumpy**, dingy, drab, frowzy,

dowel n wooden or metal peg that fits into two corresponding holes to join two adjacent parts.

down¹ ⊕ prep, adv 1 indicating movement to or position in a lower place. ◆ adv 2 indicating completion of an action, lessening of intensity, etc., e.g. calm down. ◆ adj 3 depressed, unhappy. ◆ v 4 Informal drink quickly. **have a down on** Informal feel hostile towards. **down under** Informal (in or to) Australia or New Zealand. **downward** adj, adv (descending) from a higher to a lower level, condition, or position. **downwards** adv from a higher to a lower level, condition, or position. **down-and-out** n person who is homeless and destitute. ◆ adj without any means of support. **down-to-earth** adj sensible or practical.

down² n soft fine feathers. **downy** adj

downs pl n low grassy hills, esp. in S England.

dowry n, pl –ries property brought by a woman to her husband at marriage.

doyen [doy–en] n senior member of a group, profession, or society. **doyenne** [doy–en] n fem

doze ⊕ v 1 sleep lightly or briefly. ◆ n 2 short sleep. **dozy** adj **dozier, doziest** 1 feeling sleepy. 2 Informal stupid. **doze off** v fall into a light sleep.

dozen adj, n twelve.

drab ⊕ adj **drabber, drabbest** dull and dreary. **drabness** n

draconian adj severe, harsh.

draft ⊕ n 1 plan, sketch, or drawing of something. 2 preliminary outline of a book, speech, etc. 3 written order for payment of money by a bank. 4 US & Aust selection for compulsory military service. ◆ v 5 draw up an outline or plan of. 6 send (people) from one place to another to do a specific job. 7 US & Aust select for compulsory military service.

drag ⊕ v **dragging, dragged** 1 pull with force, esp. along the ground. 2 trail on the ground. 3 persuade or force (oneself or someone else) to go somewhere. 4 (foll. by on or out) last or be prolonged tediously. 5 search (a river) with a dragnet or hook. 6 Computers move (an image) on the screen by use of the mouse. ◆ n 7 person or thing that slows up progress. 8 Informal tedious thing or person. 9 Slang women's clothes worn by a man. **dragnet** n net used to scour the bottom of a pond or river to search for something. **drag race** race in which specially built cars or motorcycles are timed over a measured course.

dragon n 1 mythical fire-breathing monster like a huge lizard. 2 Informal fierce woman. **dragonfly** n brightly coloured insect with a long slender body and two pairs of wings.

dragoon ⊕ n 1 heavily armed cavalryman. ◆ v 2 coerce, force.

drain ⊕ n 1 pipe or channel that carries off

——————— THESAURUS ———————

old-fashioned, shabby, unfashionable

down¹ adj 3 = **depressed**, dejected, disheartened, downcast, low, miserable, sad, unhappy ◆ v 4 Inf = **swallow**, drain, drink (down), gulp, put away, toss off **have a down on** Inf = **be antagonistic or hostile to**, bear a grudge towards, be prejudiced against, be set against, have it in for (sl)

doze v 1 = **nap**, kip (Brit sl), nod off (inf), sleep, slumber, snooze (inf) ◆ n 2 = **nap**, catnap, forty winks (inf), kip (Brit sl), shuteye (sl), siesta, snooze (inf)

drab adj 1 = **dull**, dingy, dismal, dreary, flat, gloomy, shabby, sombre

draft n 1 = **outline**, abstract, plan, rough, sketch, version 3 = **order**, bill (of exchange), cheque, postal order ◆ v 5 = **outline**, compose, design, draw, draw up, formulate, plan, sketch

drag v 1 = **pull**, draw, haul, lug, tow, trail, tug 4 (foll. by on or out) = **last**, draw out, extend, keep going, lengthen, persist, prolong, protract, spin out, stretch out ◆ n 8 Inf = **nuisance**, annoyance, bore, bother, pain (inf), pest water or sewage. **2** cause of a continuous reduction in energy or resources. ♦ *v* **3** draw off or remove liquid from. **4** flow away or filter off. **5** drink the entire contents of (a glass or cup). **6** make constant demands on (energy or resources), exhaust. **drainage** *n* **1** system of drains. **2** process or method of draining.

drake ❶ *n* male duck.

dram *n* **1** small amount of a strong alcoholic drink, esp. whisky. **2** one sixteenth of an ounce.

drama ❶ *n* **1** serious play for theatre, television, or radio. **2** writing, producing, or acting in plays. **3** situation that is exciting or highly emotional. **dramatic** *adj* **1** of or like drama. **2** behaving flamboyantly. **dramatically** *adv* **dramatist** *n* person who writes plays. **dramatize** *v* **1** rewrite (a book) in the form of a play. **2** express (something) in a dramatic or exaggerated way. **dramatization** *n*

drape ❶ *v* **1** cover with material, usu. in folds. **2** place casually. ♦ *n* **3** *Aust, US & Canadian* curtain. **draper** *n* *Brit, Aust & NZ* person who sells fabrics and sewing materials. **drapery** *n, pl* **–peries 1** fabric or clothing arranged and draped. **2** fabrics and cloth collectively.

drastic ❶ *adj* strong and severe.

draught ❶ *n* **1** current of cold air, esp. in an enclosed space. **2** portion of liquid to be drunk, esp. medicine. **3** gulp or swallow. **4** one of the flat discs used in the game of draughts. ♦ *pl* **5** game for two

players using a chessboard and twelve draughts each. ♦ *adj* **6** (of an animal) used for pulling heavy loads. **draughty** *adj* exposed to draughts of air. **draughtsman** *n* person employed to prepare detailed scale drawings of machinery, buildings, etc. **draughtsmanship** *n* **draught beer** beer stored in a cask.

draw ❶ *v* **drawing, drew, drawn 1** sketch (a figure, picture, etc.) with a pencil or pen. **2** pull (a person or thing) closer to or further away from a place. **3** move in a specified direction, e.g. *the car drew near.* **4** take from a source, e.g. *draw money from bank accounts.* **5** attract, interest. **6** formulate or decide, e.g. *to draw conclusions.* **7** (of two teams or contestants) finish a game with an equal number of points. ♦ *n* **8** raffle or lottery. **9** contest or game ending in a tie. **10** event, act, etc., that attracts a large audience. **drawing** *n* **1** picture or plan made by means of lines on a surface. **2** art of making drawings. **drawing pin** short tack with a broad smooth head. **drawing room** *Old–fashioned* room where visitors are received and entertained. **drawback** *n* disadvantage. **drawbridge** *n* bridge that may be raised to prevent access or to enable vessels to pass. **draw out** *v* **1** encourage (someone) to talk freely. **2** make longer. **drawstring** *n* cord run through a hem around an opening, so that when it is pulled tighter, the opening closes. **draw up** *v* **1** prepare and write out

———————— THESAURUS ————————

dragoon *v* **2** = **force**, browbeat, bully, coerce, compel, constrain, drive, impel, intimidate, railroad (*inf*)

drain *n* **1** = **pipe**, channel, conduit, culvert, ditch, duct, sewer, sink, trench **2** = **reduction**, depletion, drag, exhaustion, sap, strain, withdrawal ♦ *v* **3** = **remove**, bleed, draw off, dry, empty, pump off *or* out, tap, withdraw **4** = **flow out**, effuse, exude, leak, ooze, seep, trickle, well out **5** = **drink up**, finish, gulp down, quaff, swallow **6** = **exhaust**,

consume, deplete, dissipate, empty, sap, strain, use up

drama *n* **1** = **play**, dramatization, show, stage show **2** = **theatre**, acting, dramaturgy, stagecraft **3** = **excitement**, crisis, histrionics, scene, spectacle, turmoil

drape *v* **1** = **cover**, cloak, fold, swathe, wrap

drastic *adj* = **extreme**, desperate, dire, forceful, harsh, radical, severe, strong

draught *n* **1** = **breeze**, current, flow, movement, puff **2** = **drink**, cup, dose, (a contract). 2 (of a vehicle) come to a stop.

drawl v 1 speak slowly, with long vowel sounds. ♦ n 2 drawling manner of speech.

drawn ❶ v 1 past participle of DRAW. ♦ adj 2 haggard, tired, or tense in appearance.

dread ❶ v 1 anticipate with apprehension or fear. ♦ n 2 great fear. **dreadful** adj 1 very disagreeable or shocking. 2 extreme. **dreadfully** adv

dream ❶ n 1 imagined series of events experienced in the mind while asleep. 2 cherished hope. 3 Informal wonderful person or thing. ♦ v **dreaming, dreamed** or **dreamt** 4 see imaginary pictures in the mind while asleep. 5 (often foll. by of or about) have an image (of) or fantasy (about). 6 (foll. by of) consider the possibility (of). ♦ adj 7 ideal, e.g. a dream house. **dreamer** n **dreamy** adj 1 vague or impractical. 2 Informal wonderful. **dreamily** adv

dreary ❶ adj **drearier, dreariest** dull, boring. **drearily** adv **dreariness** n

dredge v clear or search (a river bed or harbour) by removing silt or mud.

dredger n boat fitted with machinery for dredging. **dredge up** v Informal remember (something) obscure or half-forgotten.

dregs ❶ pl n 1 solid particles that settle at the bottom of some liquids. 2 most despised elements.

drench ❶ v make completely wet.

dress ❶ n 1 one-piece garment for a woman or girl, consisting of a skirt and bodice and sometimes sleeves. 2 complete style of clothing. ♦ v 3 put clothes on. 4 put on formal clothes. 5 apply a protective covering to (a wound). 6 arrange or prepare. **dressing** n 1 sauce for salad. 2 covering for a wound. **dressing-down** n Informal severe scolding. **dressing gown** coat-shaped garment worn over pyjamas or nightdress. **dressing room** room used for changing clothes, esp. backstage in a theatre. **dressy** adj (of clothes) elegant. **dress circle** first gallery in a theatre. **dressmaker** n person who makes women's clothes. **dressmaking** n **dress rehearsal** last rehearsal of a play or show, using costumes, lighting, etc.

dressage [**dress**-ahzh] n training of a

———— THESAURUS ————

potion, quantity

draw v 1 = **sketch**, depict, design, map out, mark out, outline, paint, portray, trace 2 = **pull**, drag, haul, tow, tug 4 = **take out**, extract, pull out 5 = **attract**, allure, elicit, entice, evoke, induce, influence, invite, persuade 6 = **deduce**, derive, infer, make, take ♦ n 9 = **tie**, dead heat, deadlock, impasse, stalemate 10 = **attraction**, enticement, lure, pull (inf)

drawn adj 2 = **tense**, haggard, pinched, stressed, strained, tired, worn

dread v 1 = **fear**, cringe at, have cold feet (inf), quail, shrink from, shudder, tremble ♦ n 2 = **fear**, alarm, apprehension, dismay, fright, horror, terror, trepidation

dream n 1 = **vision**, delusion, hallucination, illusion, imagination, trance 3 = **ambition**, aim, aspiration, design, desire, fantasy, goal, hope, pipe dream, plan, wish 4 Inf

= **delight**, beauty, gem, joy, marvel, pleasure, treasure ♦ v 5 (often foll. by of or about) = **daydream**, build castles in the air or in Spain, conjure up, envisage, fantasize, imagine, stargaze, visualize

dreary adj = **dull**, boring, drab, humdrum, monotonous, tedious, tiresome, uneventful, wearisome ≠ **interesting**

dregs pl n 1 = **sediment**, deposit, dross, grounds, lees, resi, residuum, scum, waste 2 = **scum**, good-for-nothings, rabble, ragtag and bobtail, riffraff

drench v = **soak**, drown, flood, inundate, saturate, souse, steep, swamp, wet

dress n 1 = **frock**, gown, outfit, robe 2 = **clothing**, apparel, attire, clothes, costume, garb, garments, togs ♦ v 3 = **put on**, attire, change, clothe, don, garb, robe, slip on or into ≠ **undress** 5 = **bandage**, bind up, plaster, treat 6 = **arrange**, adjust, align, get ready,

horse to perform manoeuvres in response
to the rider's body signals.
dresser *n* piece of furniture with shelves
and with cupboards, for storing or
displaying dishes.
drey *n* squirrel's nest.
dribble ❶ *v* 1 (allow) to flow in drops. 2
allow saliva to trickle from the mouth. 3
Sport propel (a ball) by repeatedly tapping
it with the foot, hand, or a stick. ◆ *n* 4
small quantity of liquid falling in drops.
drift ❶ *v* 1 be carried along by currents of
air or water. 2 move aimlessly from one
place or activity to another. ◆ *n* 3
something piled up by the wind or
current, such as a snowdrift. 4 general
movement or development. 5 point,
meaning, e.g. *catch my drift?* **drifter** *n*
person who moves aimlessly from place to
place or job to job. **driftwood** *n* wood
floating on or washed ashore by the sea.
drill¹ ❶ *n* 1 tool or machine for boring
holes. 2 strict and often repetitious
training. 3 *Informal* correct procedure. ◆ *v*
4 bore a hole in (something) with or as if
with a drill. 5 teach by rigorous exercises
or training.
drill² *n* 1 machine for sowing seed in rows.
2 small furrow for seed. ◆ *v* 3 sow (seed)
in drills or furrows.
drink ❶ *v* **drinking, drank, drunk** 1

swallow (a liquid). 2 consume alcohol,
esp. to excess. ◆ *n* 3 (portion of) a liquid
suitable for drinking. 4 alcohol, or its
habitual or excessive consumption.
drinkable *adj* **drinker** *n* **drink in** *v* pay
close attention to. **drink to** *v* drink a toast
to.
drip ❶ *v* **dripping, dripped** 1 (let) fall in
drops. ◆ *n* 2 falling of drops of liquid. 3
sound made by falling drops. 4 *Informal*
weak dull person. 5 *Med* device by which a
solution is passed in small drops through a
tube into a vein. **drip–dry** *adj* denoting
clothing that will dry free of creases if
hung up when wet.
drive ❶ *v* **driving, drove, driven** 1 guide
the movement of (a vehicle). 2 transport
in a vehicle. 3 goad into a specified state.
4 push or propel. 5 *Sport* hit (a ball) very
hard and straight. ◆ *n* 6 journey by car,
van, etc. 7 (also **driveway**) path for
vehicles connecting a building to a public
road. 8 united effort towards a common
goal. 9 energy and ambition. 10 *Psychol*
motive or interest, e.g. *sex drive.* 11 means
by which power is transmitted in a
mechanism. **driver** *n* **drive at** *v Informal*
intend or mean, e.g. *what was he driving
at?* **drive–in** *adj, n* (denoting) a cinema,
restaurant, etc., used by people in their
cars.

───── THESAURUS ─────

prepare, straighten
dribble *v* 1 = **run**, drip, drop, fall in drops,
leak, ooze, seep, trickle 2 = **drool**, drivel,
slaver, slobber
drift *v* 1 = **float**, be carried along, coast, go
(aimlessly), meander, stray, waft, wander
drive, gather ◆ *n* 3 = **pile**, accumulation,
bank, heap, mass, mound 5 = **meaning**,
direction, gist, import, intention, purport,
significance, tendency, thrust
drill¹ *n* 1 = **boring tool**, bit, borer, gimlet
2 = **training**, discipline, exercise,
instruction, practice, preparation,
repetition ◆ *v* 4 = **bore**, penetrate,
perforate, pierce, puncture, sink in
5 = **train**, coach, discipline, exercise,

instruct, practise, rehearse, teach
drink *v* 1 = **swallow**, gulp, guzzle, imbibe,
quaff, sip, suck, sup 2 = **booze** (*inf*), hit the
bottle (*inf*), tipple, tope ◆ *n* 3 = **beverage**,
cup, draught, glass, liquid, potion,
refreshment 4 = **alcohol**, alcoholic drink,
booze (*inf*), Dutch courage, hooch *or*
hootch (*inf, chiefly US & Canad*), liquor,
spirits, the bottle (*inf*)
drip *v* 1 = **drop**, dribble, exude, plop,
splash, sprinkle, trickle ◆ *n* 2 = **drop**,
dribble, leak, trickle 4 *Inf* = **weakling**,
mummy's boy (*inf*), namby–pamby, softie
(*inf*), weed (*inf*), wet (*Brit inf*)
drive *v* 1 = **operate**, direct, guide, handle,
manage, motor, ride, steer, travel

drivel ❶ n 1 foolish talk. ◆ v –**elling**, –**elled** 2 speak foolishly.

drizzle ❶ n 1 very light rain. ◆ v 2 rain lightly. **drizzly** adj

droll ❶ adj quaintly amusing.

dromedary [**drom**–mid–er–ee] n, pl – **daries** camel with a single hump.

drone¹ n male bee.

drone² v, n (make) a monotonous low dull sound. **drone on** v talk for a long time in a monotonous tone.

drool ❶ v 1 (foll. by over) show excessive enthusiasm (for). 2 allow saliva to flow from the mouth.

droop ❶ v hang downwards loosely. **droopy** adj

drop ❶ v **dropping**, **dropped** 1 (allow to) fall vertically. 2 decrease in amount, strength, or value. 3 mention (a hint or name) casually. 4 discontinue. ◆ n 5 small quantity of liquid forming a round shape. 6 any small quantity of liquid. 7 decrease in amount, strength, or value. 8 vertical distance that something may fall. ◆ pl 9

liquid medication applied in small drops. **droplet** n **droppings** pl n faeces of certain animals, such as rabbits or birds. **drop in, by** v pay someone a casual visit. **drop off** v 1 Informal fall asleep. 2 grow smaller or less. **dropout** n 1 person who rejects conventional society. 2 person who does not complete a course of study. **drop out (of)** v abandon or withdraw from (a school, job, etc.).

dropsy n illness in which watery fluid collects in the body.

dross n 1 scum formed on the surfaces of molten metals. 2 anything worthless.

drought ❶ n prolonged shortage of rainfall.

drove ❶ n very large group, esp. of people. **drover** n person who drives sheep or cattle.

drown ❶ v 1 die or kill by immersion in liquid. 2 forget (one's sorrows) temporarily by drinking alcohol. 3 drench thoroughly. 4 make (a sound) inaudible by being louder.

▭ THESAURUS ▭

3 = **goad**, coerce, constrain, force, press, prod, prompt, spur 4 = **push**, hurl, impel, propel, ram, send, thrust. ◆ n 6 = **run**, excursion, jaunt, journey, outing, ride, spin (inf), trip 8 = **campaign**, action, appeal, crusade, effort, push (inf) 9 = **initiative**, ambition, energy, enterprise, get–up–and–go (inf), motivation, vigour, zip (inf)

drivel n 1 = **nonsense**, garbage (inf), gibberish, hogwash, hot air (inf), kak (S Afr sl), poppycock (inf), rubbish, trash, twaddle, waffle (inf, chiefly Brit) ◆ v 2 = **babble**, blether, gab (inf), prate, ramble, waffle (inf, chiefly Brit)

drizzle n 1 = **fine rain**, Scotch mist ◆ v 2 = **rain**, shower, spot or spit with rain, spray, sprinkle

droll adj = **amusing**, comical, entertaining, funny, humorous, jocular, waggish, whimsical

① **drone²** v = **hum**, buzz, purr, thrum, vibrate, whirr

② **drone²** n = **hum**, buzz, murmuring, purr, thrum, vibration, whirring

drool v 1 (foll. by over) = **gloat over**, dote on, gush, make much of, rave about (inf) 2 = **dribble**, drivel, salivate, slaver, slobber, water at the mouth

droop v = **sag**, bend, dangle, drop, fall down, hang (down), sink

drop v 1 = **fall**, descend, plummet, plunge, sink, tumble 2 = **diminish**, decline, fall, plummet, sink 4 = **discontinue**, axe (inf), give up, kick (inf), quit, relinquish ◆ n 5 = **droplet**, bead, bubble, drip, globule, pearl, tear 6 = **dash**, mouthful, shot (inf), sip, spot, tot, trace, trickle 7 = **decrease**, cut, decline, deterioration, downturn, fall–off, lowering, reduction, slump 8 = **fall**, descent, plunge

drought n = **dry spell**, aridity, dehydration, dryness ≠ **flood**

drove n = **herd**, collection, company, crowd, flock, horde, mob, multitude, swarm, throng

drudge ❶ n 1 person who works hard at uninteresting tasks. 2 **drudgery** n

drug ❶ n 1 substance used in the treatment or prevention of disease. 2 chemical substance, esp. a narcotic, taken for the effects it produces. ◆ v **drugging, drugged** 3 give a drug to (a person or animal) to cause sleepiness or unconsciousness. 4 mix a drug with (food or drink). **drugstore** n US pharmacy where a wide range of goods are available.

drum ❶ n 1 percussion instrument sounded by striking a membrane stretched across the opening of a hollow cylinder. 2 cylindrical object or container. ◆ v **drumming, drummed** 3 play (music) on a drum. 4 tap rhythmically or regularly. **drummer** n **drum into** v instil into (someone) by constant repetition. **drumstick** n 1 stick used for playing a drum. 2 lower joint of the leg of a cooked chicken etc. **drum up** v obtain (support or business) by making requests or canvassing.

drunk ❶ v 1 past participle of DRINK. ◆ adj 2 intoxicated with alcohol to the extent of losing control over normal functions. 3 overwhelmed by a strong influence or emotion. ◆ n 4 person who is drunk or who frequently gets drunk. **drunkard** n

person who frequently gets drunk. **drunken** adj 1 drunk or frequently drunk. 2 caused by or relating to alcoholic intoxication. **drunkenness** n

dry ❶ adj **drier, driest** or **dryer, dryest** 1 lacking moisture. 2 having little or no rainfall. 3 Informal thirsty. 4 (of wine) not sweet. 5 uninteresting. 6 (of humour) subtle and sarcastic. 7 prohibiting the sale of alcohol, e.g. a dry town. ◆ v **drying, dried** 8 make or become dry. 9 preserve (food) by removing the moisture. **drily, dryly** adv **dryness** n **dryer** n apparatus for removing moisture. **dry–clean** v clean (clothes etc.) with chemicals rather than water. **dry–cleaner** n **dry–cleaning** n **dry out** v 1 make or become dry. 2 (cause to) undergo treatment for alcoholism. **dry rot** crumbling and drying of timber, caused by certain fungi. **dry run** Informal rehearsal.

dual ❶ adj having two parts, functions, or aspects. **duality** n **dual carriageway** Brit, Aust & NZ road on which traffic travelling in opposite directions is separated by a central strip of grass or concrete.

dub¹ v **dubbing, dubbed** give (a person or place) a name or nickname.

dub² v **dubbing, dubbed** 1 provide (a film) with a new soundtrack, esp. in a different

——————— THESAURUS ———————

drown v 3 = **drench**, deluge, engulf, flood, go under, immerse, inundate, sink, submerge, swamp 4 = **overpower**, deaden, muffle, obliterate, overcome, overwhelm, stifle, swallow up, wipe out

drudge n = **menial**, dogsbody (inf), factotum, servant, skivvy (chiefly Brit), slave, toiler, worker

drug n 1 = **medication**, medicament, medicine, physic, poison, remedy 2 = **dope** (sl), narcotic, opiate, stimulant ◆ v 3 = **dose**, administer a drug, anaesthetize, deaden, dope (sl), knock out, medicate, numb, poison, stupefy, treat

drum v 4 = **beat**, pulsate, rap, reverberate, tap, tattoo, throb **drum into** = **drive**

home, din into, hammer away, harp on, instil into, reiterate

drunk adj 2 = **intoxicated**, drunken, inebriated, legless (inf), merry (Brit inf), plastered (sl), tipsy, under the influence (inf) ◆ n 4 = **drunkard**, alcoholic, boozer (inf), inebriate, lush (sl), wino (inf)

dry adj 1 = **dehydrated**, arid, barren, desiccated, dried up, parched, thirsty ≠ **wet** 5 = **dull**, boring, dreary, monotonous, plain, tedious, tiresome, uninteresting ≠ **interesting** 6 = **sarcastic**, deadpan, droll, low–key, sly ◆ v 8 = **dehydrate**, dehumidify, desiccate, drain, make dry, parch, sear ≠ **wet**

dual adj = **twofold**, binary, double, duplex, duplicate, matched, paired, twin language. 2 provide (a film or tape) with a soundtrack. ♦ n 3 style of reggae record production involving exaggeration of instrumental parts, echo, etc.

dubious ❶ [dew–bee–uss] *adj* feeling or causing doubt. **dubiety** [dew–**by**–it–ee] *n*

duchess *n* 1 woman who holds the rank of duke. 2 wife or widow of a duke.

duck[1] *n* 1 water bird with short legs, webbed feet, and a broad blunt bill. 2 its flesh, used as food. 3 female of this bird. 4 *Cricket* score of nothing. **duckling** *n* baby duck. **duck–billed platypus** see PLATYPUS.

duck[2] ❶ *v* 1 move (the head or body) quickly downwards, to avoid being seen or to dodge a blow. 2 plunge suddenly under water. 3 *Informal* dodge (a duty or responsibility).

duct *n* 1 tube, pipe, or channel through which liquid or gas is conveyed. 2 bodily passage conveying secretions or excretions.

dud ❶ *Informal* ♦ *n* 1 ineffectual person or thing. ♦ *adj* 2 bad or useless.

dude *n US informal* 1 man. 2 *Old-fashioned* dandy. 3 any person.

due ❶ *adj* 1 expected or scheduled to be present or arrive. 2 owed as a debt. 3 fitting, proper. ♦ *n* 4 something that is owed or required. ♦ *pl* 5 charges for membership of a club or organization. ♦ *adv* 6 directly or exactly, e.g. *due south*. **due to** attributable to or caused by.

✓ **WORD TIP**
The use of *due to* as a compound preposition as in *the performance has been cancelled due to bad weather* was formerly considered incorrect, but is now acceptable.

duel ❶ *n* 1 formal fight with deadly weapons between two people, to settle a quarrel. ♦ *v* **duelling, duelled** 2 fight in a duel. **duellist** *n*

duet *n* piece of music for two performers.

duffel, duffle *n* short for DUFFEL COAT. **duffel bag** cylindrical canvas bag fastened with a drawstring. **duffel coat** wool coat with toggle fastenings, usu. with a hood.

duffer *n Informal* dull or incompetent person.

dugout *n* 1 (at a sports ground) covered bench where managers and substitutes sit. 2 canoe made by hollowing out a log. 3 *Mil* covered excavation to provide shelter.

duke *n* 1 nobleman of the highest rank. 2 prince or ruler of a small principality or duchy. **dukedom** *n*

dulcimer *n* tuned percussion instrument consisting of a set of strings stretched over a sounding board and struck with hammers.

dull ❶ *adj* 1 not interesting. 2 (of an ache) not acute. 3 (of weather) not bright or clear. 4 lacking in spirit. 5 not very

———————— THESAURUS ————————

dubious *adj* **a** = **unsure**, doubtful, hesitant, sceptical, uncertain, unconvinced, undecided, wavering ≠ **sure b** = **suspect**, fishy (*inf*), questionable, suspicious, unreliable, untrustworthy ≠ **reliable**

duck[2] *v* 1 = **bob**, bend, bow, crouch, dodge, drop, lower, stoop 2 = **plunge**, dip, dive, douse, dunk, immerse, souse, submerge, wet 3 *Inf* = **dodge**, avoid, escape, evade, shirk, shun, sidestep

dud *Inf n* 1 = **failure**, flop (*inf*), washout (*inf*) ♦ *adj* 2 = **useless**, broken, duff (*Brit inf*), failed, inoperative, worthless

due *adj* 1 = **expected**, scheduled

2 = **payable**, in arrears, outstanding, owed, owing, unpaid 3 = **fitting**, appropriate, deserved, justified, merited, proper, rightful, suitable, well–earned ♦ *n* 4 = **right(s)**, comeuppance (*sl*), deserts, merits, privilege ♦ *pl* 5 = **membership fee**, charge, charges, contribution, fee, levy ♦ *adv* 6 = **directly**, dead, exactly, straight, undeviatingly

duel *n* 1 = **fight**, affair of honour, clash, competition, contest, encounter, engagement, head–to–head, single combat ♦ *v* 2 = **fight**, clash, compete, contend, contest, lock horns, rival, intelligent. **6** (of a blade) not sharp. ◆ v **7** make or become dull. **dullness** n **dully** adv **dullard** n dull or stupid person.

dumb ❶ adj **1** lacking the power to speak. **2** silent. **3** Informal stupid. **dumbly** adv **dumbness** n **dumbbell** n short bar with a heavy ball or disc at each end, used for physical exercise. **dumbfounded** adj speechless with astonishment. **dumb show** meaningful gestures without speech.

dummy ❶ n, pl **-mies 1** figure representing the human form, used for displaying clothes etc. **2** copy of an object, often lacking some essential feature of the original. **3** rubber teat for a baby to suck. **4** Slang stupid person. ◆ adj **5** imitation, substitute. **dummy run** rehearsal.

dump ❶ v **1** drop or let fall in a careless manner. **2** Informal get rid of (someone or something no longer wanted). **3** n **4** place where waste materials are left. **5** Informal dirty unattractive place. **6** Mil place where weapons or supplies are stored. **down in the dumps** Informal depressed and

miserable.

dunce ❶ n person who is stupid or slow to learn.

dune n mound or ridge of drifted sand.

dung n faeces from animals such as cattle.

dungarees pl n trousers with a bib attached.

dungeon ❶ n underground prison cell.

dunk v **1** dip (a biscuit or bread) in a drink or soup before eating it. **2** put (something) in liquid.

duo n, pl **duos 1** pair of performers. **2** Informal pair of closely connected people.

duodenum [dew–oh–**deen**–um] n, pl **-na**, **-nums** first part of the small intestine, just below the stomach. **duodenal** adj

dupe v **1** deceive or cheat. ◆ n **2** person who is easily deceived.

duplicate ❶ adj **1** copied exactly from an original. ◆ n **2** exact copy. ◆ v **3** make an exact copy of. **4** do again (something that has already been done). **duplication** n **duplicator** n

durable ❶ adj long–lasting. **durability** n

duration ❶ n length of time that

──────── THESAURUS ────────

struggle, vie with

dull adj **1** = **boring**, dreary, flat, humdrum, monotonous, plain, run–of–the–mill, tedious, uninteresting ≠ **interesting 3** = **cloudy**, dim, dismal, gloomy, leaden, overcast ≠ **bright 4** = **lifeless**, apathetic, blank, indifferent, listless, passionless, unresponsive ≠ **active 5** = **stupid**, dense, dim–witted (inf), dozy (Brit inf), slow, thick, unintelligent **6** = **blunt**, blunted, unsharpened ≠ **sharp** ◆ v **7** = **relieve**, allay, alleviate, blunt, lessen, moderate, soften, take the edge off

dumb adj **1, 2** = **mute**, mum, silent, soundless, speechless, tongue–tied, voiceless, wordless ≠ **articulate 3** Inf = **stupid**, asinine, dense, dim–witted (inf), dull, foolish, thick, unintelligent ≠ **bright**

dummy n **1** = **model**, figure, form, manikin, mannequin **2** = **copy**, counterfeit, duplicate, imitation, sham, substitute **4** Sl = **fool**, blockhead, dunce, idiot, nitwit

(inf), numbskull or numskull, oaf, simpleton ◆ adj **5** = **imitation**, artificial, bogus, fake, false, mock, phoney or phony (inf), sham, simulated

dump v **1** = **drop**, deposit, fling down, let fall, throw down **2** Inf = **get rid of**, dispose of, ditch (sl), empty out, jettison, scrap, throw away or out, tip, unload ◆ n **5** = **rubbish tip**, junkyard, refuse heap, rubbish heap, tip **6** Inf = **pigsty**, hole (inf), hovel, mess, slum

dunce n = **simpleton**, blockhead, duffer (inf), dunderhead, ignoramus, moron, nincompoop, numbskull or numskull, thickhead

dungeon n = **prison**, cage, cell, oubliette, vault

duplicate adj **1** = **identical**, corresponding, matched, matching, twin, twofold ◆ n **2** = **copy**, carbon copy, clone, double, facsimile, photocopy, replica, reproduction ◆ v **3** = **copy**, clone, double, replicate, something lasts.

duress 🔟 *n* compulsion by use of force or threats.

during *prep* throughout or within the limit of (a period of time).

dusk 🔟 *n* time just before nightfall, when it is almost dark. **dusky** *adj* **1** dark in colour. **2** shadowy.

dust 🔟 *n* **1** small dry particles of earth, sand, or dirt. ◆ *v* **2** remove dust from (furniture) by wiping. **3** sprinkle (something) with a powdery substance. **duster** *n* cloth used for dusting. **dusty** *adj* covered with dust. **dustbin** *n* large container for household rubbish. **dust bowl** dry area in which the surface soil is exposed to wind erosion. **dust jacket** removable paper cover used to protect a book. **dustman** *n Brit* man whose job is to collect household rubbish. **dustpan** *n* short-handled shovel into which dust is swept from floors.

Dutch *adj* of the Netherlands. **go Dutch** *Informal* share the expenses on an outing. **Dutch courage** false courage gained from drinking alcohol.

duty 🔟 *n, pl* **–ties 1** work or a task performed as part of one's job. **2** task that a person feels morally bound to do. **3**

government tax on imports. **on duty** at work. **dutiful** *adj* doing what is expected. **dutifully** *adv*

duvet [**doo**–vay] *n* kind of quilt used in bed instead of a top sheet and blankets.

dwarf 🔟 *n, pl* **dwarfs, dwarves 1** person who is smaller than average. **2** (in folklore) small ugly manlike creature, often possessing magical powers. ◆ *adj* **3** (of an animal or plant) much smaller than the usual size for the species. ◆ *v* **4** cause (someone or something) to seem small by being much larger.

dwell 🔟 *v* **dwelling, dwelt** *or* **dwelled** live, reside. **dwelling** *n* place of residence. **dwell on, upon** *v* think, speak, or write at length about.

dwindle 🔟 *v* grow less in size, strength, or number.

dye 🔟 *n* **1** colouring substance. **2** colour produced by dyeing. ◆ *v* **dyeing, dyed 3** colour (hair or fabric) by applying a dye. **dyer** *n* **dyed–in–the–wool** *adj* uncompromising or unchanging in opinion.

dyke *n* wall built to prevent flooding.

dynamic 🔟 *adj* full of energy, ambition, and new ideas.

dynamics *n* **1** branch of mechanics

---

reproduce **4** = **repeat**

durable *adj* – **long–lasting**, dependable, enduring, hard–wearing, persistent, reliable, resistant, strong, sturdy, tough ≠ **weak**

duration *n* = **length**, extent, period, span, spell, stretch, term, time

duress *n* = **pressure**, coercion, compulsion, constraint, threat

dusk *n* = **twilight**, dark, evening, eventide, gloaming (*Scot or poet*), nightfall, sundown, sunset ≠ **morning**

dust *n* **1** = **grime**, grit, particles, powder ◆ *v* **3** = **sprinkle**, cover, dredge, powder, scatter, sift, spray, spread

duty *n* **1** = **responsibility**, assignment, function, job, obligation, role, task, work, yakka (*Aust & NZ inf*) **2** = **loyalty**,

allegiance, deference, obedience, respect, reverence **3** = **tax**, excise, levy, tariff, toll **on duty** = **at work**, busy, engaged, on active service

dwarf *n* **1** = **midget**, Lilliputian, pygmy *or* pigmy, Tom Thumb ◆ *adj* **3** = **miniature**, baby, bonsai, diminutive, small, tiny, undersized ◆ *v* **4** = **tower above** *or* **over**, diminish, dominate, overshadow

dwell *v* = **live**, abide, inhabit, lodge, reside

dwindle *v* = **lessen**, decline, decrease, die away, diminish, fade, peter out, shrink, subside, taper off, wane

dye *n* **1** = **colouring**, colorant, colour, pigment, stain, tinge, tint ◆ *v* **3** = **colour**, pigment, stain, tinge, tint

dynamic *adj* **1** = **energetic**, forceful, go–ahead, go–getting (*inf*), high–powered, concerned with the forces that change or produce the motions of bodies. ◆ *pl* **2** forces that produce change in a system.

dynamite *n* **1** explosive made of nitroglycerine. **2** *Informal* dangerous or exciting person or thing. ◆ *v* **3** blow (something) up with dynamite.

dynamo *n, pl* **–mos** device for converting mechanical energy into electrical energy.

dynasty ❶ *n, pl* **–ties** sequence of hereditary rulers. **dynastic** *adj*

dysentery *n* infection of the intestine causing severe diarrhoea.

dysfunction *n Med* disturbance or abnormality in the function of an organ or part. **dysfunctional** *adj*

dyslexia *n* disorder causing impaired ability to read. **dyslexic** *adj*

dyspepsia *n* indigestion. **dyspeptic** *adj*

dystrophy [**diss**–trof–fee] *n* see MUSCULAR DYSTROPHY.

———┤THESAURUS├———

lively, powerful, storming (*inf*), vital

dynasty *n* = **empire**, government, house, regime, rule, sovereignty

E e

E East(ern).

each ⊕ *adj, pron* every (one) taken separately.

> ✓ **WORD TIP**
> The expressions *each other* and *one another* are interchangeable.

eager ⊕ *adj* showing or feeling great desire, keen. **eagerly** *adv* **eagerness** *n*

eagle *n* 1 large bird of prey with keen eyesight. 2 Golf score of two strokes under par for a hole.

ear¹ ⊕ *n* 1 organ of hearing, esp. the external part of it. 2 sensitivity to musical or other sounds. **earache** *n* pain in the ear. **earbash** *v Aust & NZ informal* talk incessantly. **eardrum** *n* thin piece of skin inside the ear which enables one to hear sounds. **earmark** *v* 1 set (something) aside for a specific purpose. 2 **earphone** *n* receiver for a radio etc., held to or put in the ear. **earring** *n* ornament for the lobe of the ear. **earshot** *n* hearing range.

ear² *n* head of corn.

earl *n* British nobleman ranking next below a marquess. **earldom** *n*

early ⊕ *adj, adv* **–lier, –liest** 1 before the expected or usual time. 2 in the first part of a period. 3 in a period far back in time.

earn ⊕ *v* 1 obtain by work or merit. 2 (of investments etc.) gain (interest). **earnings** *pl n* money earned.

earnest ⊕ *adj* serious and sincere. **in earnest** seriously. **earnestly** *adv*

earth ⊕ *n* 1 planet that we live on. 2 land, the ground. 3 soil. 4 fox's hole. 5 wire connecting an electrical apparatus with the earth. ♦ *v* 6 connect (a circuit) to earth. **earthen** *adj* made of baked clay or earth. **earthenware** *n* pottery made of baked clay. **earthly** *adj* conceivable or possible. **earthy** *adj* 1 coarse or crude. 2 of or like earth. **earthquake** *n* violent vibration of the earth's surface. **earthwork** *n* fortification made of earth. **earthworm** *n* worm which burrows in the soil.

ease ⊕ *n* 1 freedom from difficulty, discomfort, or worry. 2 rest or leisure. ♦ *v* 3 give bodily or mental ease to. 4 lessen

THESAURUS

① **each** *adj* = **every**
② **each** *pron* = **every one**, each and every one, each one, one and all

eager *adj* = **keen**, agog, anxious, athirst, avid, enthusiastic, fervent, hungry, impatient, longing ≠ **opposed**

ear¹ *n* 2 = **sensitivity**, appreciation, discrimination, taste

① **early** *adj* 1 = **premature**, advanced, forward, untimely ≠ **overdue**
3 = **primitive**, primeval, primordial, undeveloped, young ≠ **seasoned**
② **early** *adv* 1 = **too soon**, ahead of time,

beforehand, in advance, in good time, prematurely ≠ **late**

earn *v* 1 = **deserve**, acquire, attain, be entitled to, be worthy of, merit, rate, warrant, win 2 = **make**, bring in, collect, gain, get, gross, net, receive

earnest *adj* = **serious**, grave, intent, resolute, resolved, sincere, solemn, thoughtful ≠ **trifling in earnest** = **in seriousness**, in sincerity, in truth

earth *n* 1 = **world**, globe, orb, planet, sphere 2, 3 = **soil**, clay, dirt, ground, land, turf (severity, tension, pain, etc.). 5 move carefully or gradually.

easel n frame to support an artist's canvas or a blackboard.

east n 1 (direction towards) the part of the horizon where the sun rises. 2 region lying in this direction. ◆ adj 3 to or in the east. 4 (of a wind) from the east. ◆ adv 5 in, to, or towards the east. **easterly** adj **eastern** adj **eastward** adj, adv **eastwards** adv

Easter n Christian spring festival commemorating the Resurrection of Jesus Christ. **Easter egg** chocolate egg given at Easter.

easy ❶ adj **easier, easiest** 1 not needing much work or effort. 2 free from pain, care, or anxiety. 3 easy–going. **easily** adv **easiness** n **easy chair** comfortable armchair. **easy–going** adj relaxed in attitude, tolerant.

✓ **WORD TIP**

Easy may be used as an adverb in set phrases like *take it easy*.

---

eat ❶ v **eating, ate, eaten** 1 take (food) into the mouth and swallow it. 2 have a meal. 3 (foll. by *away* or *up*) destroy. **eatable** adj fit or suitable for eating.

eau de Cologne [oh de kol–**lone**] n French light perfume.

eaves pl n overhanging edges of a roof.

ebb ❶ v 1 (of tide water) flow back. 2 fall away or decline. ◆ n 3 flowing back of the tide. **at a low ebb** in a state of weakness.

ebony n, pl **–onies** 1 hard black wood. ◆ adj 2 deep black.

ebullient adj full of enthusiasm or excitement. **ebullience** n

eccentric ❶ adj 1 odd or unconventional. 2 (of circles) not having the same centre. ◆ n 3 eccentric person. **eccentricity** n

echo ❶ n, pl **–oes** 1 repetition of sounds by reflection of sound waves off a surface. 2 close imitation. ◆ v **–oing, –oed** 3 repeat or be repeated as an echo. 4 imitate (what someone else has said). **echo sounder** sonar.

éclair n finger–shaped pastry filled with cream and covered with chocolate.

---

ease n 1 a = **effortlessness**, easiness, facility, readiness, simplicity b = **peace of mind**, comfort, content, happiness, peace, quiet, serenity, tranquillity ≠ **tension** 2 = **leisure**, relaxation, repose, rest, restfulness ≠ **pain** ◆ v 3 = **comfort**, calm, outspan (*S Afr*), relax, soothe 4 = **relieve**, alleviate, lessen, lighten, soothe ≠ **irritate** 5 = **move carefully**, edge, inch, manoeuvre, slide, slip

easy adj 1 = **not difficult**, a piece of cake (*inf*), child's play (*inf*), effortless, no trouble, painless, plain sailing, simple, straightforward, uncomplicated, undemanding ≠ **hard** 2 = **carefree**, comfortable, cushy (*inf*), leisurely, peaceful, quiet, relaxed, serene, tranquil, untroubled ≠ **difficult** 3 = **tolerant**, easy–going, indulgent, lenient, mild, permissive, unoppressive ≠ **hard**

eat v 1 = **consume**, chew, devour, gobble, ingest, munch, scoff (*sl*), swallow 2 = **have**

a meal, dine, feed, take nourishment 3 (foll. by *away* or *up*) = **destroy**, corrode, decay, dissolve, erode, rot, waste away, wear away

ebb v 1 = **flow back**, go out, recede, retire, retreat, subside, wane, withdraw 2 = **decline**, decrease, diminish, dwindle, fade away, fall away, flag, lessen, peter out ◆ n 3 = **flowing back**, going out, low tide, low water, retreat, subsidence, wane, withdrawal

eccentric adj 1 = **odd**, freakish, idiosyncratic, irregular, munted (*NZ sl*), outlandish, peculiar, quirky, strange, unconventional ≠ **average** ◆ n 3 = **crank** (*inf*), character (*inf*), nonconformist, oddball (*inf*), weirdo *or* weirdie (*inf*)

echo n 1 = **repetition**, answer, reverberation 2 = **copy**, imitation, mirror image, parallel, reflection, reiteration, reproduction ◆ v 3 = **repeat**, resound, reverberate 4 = **copy**, ape, imitate, mirror,

eclectic adj selecting from various styles, ideas, or sources. **eclecticism** n

eclipse ⊕ n 1 temporary obscuring of one star or planet by another. ◆ v 2 surpass or outclass. **ecliptic** n apparent path of the sun.

economy ⊕ n, pl –mies 1 system of interrelationship of money, industry, and employment in a country. 2 careful use of money or resources to avoid waste. **economic** adj 1 of economics. 2 profitable. 3 Informal inexpensive or cheap. **economics** n 1 social science concerned with the production and consumption of goods and services. ◆ pl 2 financial aspects. **economical** adj not wasteful, thrifty. **economist** n specialist in economics. **economize** v reduce expense or waste.

ecstasy ⊕ n state of intense delight. **ecstatic** adj

eczema [ek-sim-a] n skin disease causing intense itching.

eddy ⊕ n, pl eddies 1 circular movement of air, water, etc. ◆ v eddying, eddied 2 move with a circular motion.

edge ⊕ n 1 border or line where something ends or begins. 2 cutting side of a blade. 3 sharpness of tone. ◆ v 4 provide an edge or border for. 5 push (one's way) gradually. **have the edge on** have an advantage over. **on edge** nervous or irritable. **edgeways** adv with the edge forwards or uppermost. **edging** n anything placed along an edge to finish it. **edgy** adj nervous or irritable.

edible ⊕ adj fit to be eaten.

edict ⊕ [ee-dikt] n order issued by an authority.

edifice ⊕ [ed-if-iss] n large building.

edify ⊕ [ed-if-fie] v –fying, –fied improve morally by instruction. **edification** n

edit ⊕ v prepare (a book, film, etc.) for publication or broadcast. **edition** n number of copies of a new publication printed at one time. **editor** n 1 person who edits. 2 person in charge of one section of a newspaper or magazine. **editorial** n 1 newspaper article stating the opinion of the editor. ◆ adj 2 of editing or editors.

educate ⊕ v 1 teach. 2 provide schooling for. **education** n **educational** adj **educationalist** n expert in the theory of education. **educative** adj educating.

eel n snakelike fish.

eerie ⊕ adj eerier, eeriest uncannily frightening or disturbing. **eerily** adv

---

THESAURUS

---

parallel, recall, reflect, resemble

eclipse n 1 = **obscuring**, darkening, dimming, extinction, shading ◆ v 2 = **surpass**, exceed, excel, outdo, outshine, put in the shade (inf), transcend

economy n 2 = **thrift**, frugality, husbandry, parsimony, prudence, restraint

ecstasy n = **rapture**, bliss, delight, elation, euphoria, fervour, joy, seventh heaven

eddy n 1 = **swirl**, counter–current, undertow, vortex, whirlpool ◆ v 2 = **swirl**, whirl

edge n 1 = **border**, boundary, brink, fringe, limit, outline, perimeter, rim, side, verge ◆ v 4 = **border**, fringe, hem 5 = **inch**, creep, ease, sidle, steal **have the edge on** = **have the advantage over**, have ascendancy over, have dominance over, have

superiority over, have the upper hand over **on edge** = **nervous**, apprehensive, edgy, ill at ease, impatient, irritable, keyed up, on tenterhooks, tense, wired (sl)

edible adj = **eatable**, digestible, fit to eat, good, harmless, palatable, wholesome

edict n = **decree**, act, command, injunction, law, order, proclamation, ruling

edifice n = **building**, construction, erection, house, structure

edify v = **instruct**, educate, enlighten, guide, improve, inform, nurture, school, teach

edit v = **revise**, adapt, condense, correct, emend, polish, rewrite

educate v 1 = **teach**, discipline, enlighten, improve, inform, instruct, school, train,

efface ⊙ *v* 1 remove by rubbing. 2 make (oneself) inconspicuous. **effacement** *n*

effect ⊙ *n* 1 change or result caused by someone or something. 2 condition of being operative, e.g. *the law comes into effect next month.* 3 overall impression. ♦ *pl* 4 personal belongings. 5 lighting, sounds, etc. to accompany a film or a broadcast. ♦ *v* 6 cause to happen, accomplish. **effective** *adj* 1 producing a desired result. 2 operative. **effectively** *adv* **effectual** *adj* producing the intended result. **effectually** *adv*

> ✓ **WORD TIP**
> Note the difference between *effect* meaning 'accomplish' and *affect* meaning 'influence'.

effeminate ⊙ *adj* (of a man) displaying characteristics thought to be typical of a woman. **effeminacy** *n*

efficient ⊙ *adj* functioning effectively with little waste of effort. **efficiently** *adv* **efficiency** *n*

effigy ⊙ [ef–fij–ee] *n, pl* –gies image or likeness of a person.

effluent ⊙ *n* liquid discharged as waste.

effort ⊙ *n* 1 physical or mental exertion. 2 attempt. **effortless** *adj*

effrontery ⊙ *n* brazen impudence.

e.g. for example.

egalitarian *adj* 1 upholding the equality of all people. ♦ *n* 2 person who holds egalitarian beliefs. **egalitarianism** *n*

egg[1] *n* 1 oval or round object laid by the females of birds and other creatures, containing a developing embryo. 2 hen's egg used as food. 3 (also **egg cell**) ovum. **egghead** *n Informal* intellectual person. **eggplant** *n US, Canadian, & Aust* aubergine.

egg[2] ⊙ *v* **egg on** encourage or incite, esp. to do wrong.

ego *n, pl* **egos** 1 the conscious mind of an individual. 2 self–esteem. **egoism, egotism** *n* 1 excessive concern for one's own interests. 2 excessively high opinion of oneself. **egotist, egoist** *n* **egotistic, egoistic** *adj* **egocentric** *adj* self–centred.

egregious [ig–**greej**–uss] *adj* outstandingly bad.

eider *n* Arctic duck. **eiderdown** *n* quilt (orig. stuffed with eider feathers).

———————— THESAURUS ————————

tutor

eerie *adj* = **frightening**, creepy (*inf*), ghostly, mysterious, scary (*inf*), spooky (*inf*), strange, uncanny, unearthly, weird

efface *v* 1 = **obliterate**, blot out, cancel, delete, destroy, eradicate, erase, rub out, wipe out

effect *n* 1 = **result**, conclusion, consequence, end result, event, outcome, upshot 2 = **operation**, action, enforcement, execution, force, implementation 3 = **impression**, essence, impact, sense, significance, tenor ♦ *pl* 4 = **belongings**, gear, goods, paraphernalia, possessions, property, things ♦ *v* 6 = **bring about**, accomplish, achieve, complete, execute, fulfil, perform, produce

effeminate *adj* = **womanly**, camp (*inf*), feminine, sissy, soft, tender, unmanly,

weak, womanish

efficient *adj* = **competent**, businesslike, capable, economic, effective, organized, productive, proficient, well–organized, workmanlike ≠ **inefficient**

effigy *n* = **likeness**, dummy, figure, guy, icon, idol, image, picture, portrait, representation, statue

effluent *n* = **waste**, effluvium, pollutant, sewage

effort *n* 1 = **exertion**, application, elbow grease (*facetious*), endeavour, energy, pains, struggle, toil, trouble, work, yakka (*Aust & NZ inf*) 2 = **attempt**, endeavour, essay, go (*inf*), shot (*inf*), stab (*inf*), try

effrontery *n* = **insolence**, arrogance, audacity, brazenness, cheek (*inf*), impertinence, impudence, nerve, presumption, temerity

egg[2] *v* **egg on** = **encourage**, exhort, goad,

eight *adj, n* **1** one more than seven. ♦ *n* **2** eight–oared boat. **3** its crew. **eighth** *adj, n* (of) number eight in a series. **eighteen** *adj, n* eight and ten. **eighteenth** *adj, n* **eighty** *adj, n* eight times ten. **eightieth** *adj, n*

either *adj, pron* **1** one or the other (of two). **2** each of two. ♦ *conj* **3** used preceding two or more possibilities joined by *or.* ♦ *adv* **4** likewise, e.g. *I don't eat meat and he doesn't either.*

> ✓ **WORD TIP**
> When *either* is followed by a plural noun, it is acceptable to make the verb plural too: *Either of these books are useful.*

ejaculate *v* **1** eject (semen). **2** utter abruptly. **ejaculation** *n*
eject ① *v* force out, expel. **ejection** *n* **ejector** *n*
eke out ① *v* **1** make (a supply) last by frugal use. **2** make (a living) with difficulty.
elaborate ① *adj* **1** with a lot of fine detail. ♦ *v* **2** expand upon. **elaboration** *n*
élan [ale–*an*] *n* style and vigour.
elapse ① *v* (of time) pass by.
elastic ① *adj* **1** resuming normal shape after distortion. **2** adapting easily to change. ♦ *n* **3** tape or fabric containing interwoven strands of flexible rubber. **elasticity** *n*
elbow ① *n* **1** joint between the upper arm and the forearm. ♦ *v* **2** shove or strike with the elbow. **elbow grease** vigorous

physical labour. **elbow room** sufficient room to move freely.
elder[1] ① *adj* **1** older. ♦ *n* **2** older person. **3** (in certain Protestant Churches) lay officer. **elderly** *adj* (fairly) old. **eldest** *adj* oldest.

> ✓ **WORD TIP**
> *Elder* (*eldest*) is used for age comparison in families, *older* for other age comparisons.

elder[2] *n* small tree with white flowers and black berries.
elect ① *v* **1** choose by voting. **2** decide (to do something). ♦ *adj* **3** appointed but not yet in office, e.g. *president elect.* **election** *n* **1** choosing of representatives by voting. **2** act of choosing. **electioneering** *n* active participation in a political campaign. **elective** *adj* **1** chosen by election. **2** optional. **elector** *n* someone who has the right to vote in an election. **electoral** *adj* **electorate** *n* people who have the right to vote.
electricity *n* **1** form of energy associated with stationary or moving electrons or other charged particles. **2** electric current or charge. **electric** *adj* **1** produced by, transmitting, or powered by electricity. **2** exciting or tense. **electrical** *adj* using or concerning electricity. **electrician** *n* person trained to install and repair electrical equipment. **electrics** *pl n* electric appliances. **electric chair** *US* chair in which criminals who have been sentenced

incite, prod, prompt, push, spur, urge
eject *v* = **throw out**, banish, drive out, evict, expel, oust, remove, turn out
eke out *v* **1** = **be sparing with**, economize on, husband, stretch out
elaborate *adj* **1** = **detailed**, complex, complicated, intricate, involved ≠ **simple** ♦ *v* **2** = **expand (upon)**, add detail, amplify, develop, embellish, enlarge, flesh out ≠ **simplify**
elapse *v* = **pass**, glide by, go by, lapse, roll by, slip away

elastic *adj* **1** = **flexible**, plastic, pliable, pliant, resilient, rubbery, springy, stretchy, supple, tensile ≠ **set 2** = **adaptable**, accommodating, adjustable, compliant, flexible, supple, tolerant, variable, yielding ≠ **set**
elbow *n* **1** = **joint**, angle ♦ *v* **2** = **push**, jostle, knock, nudge, shove
elder[1] *adj* **1** = **older**, first–born, senior ♦ *n* **2** = **older person**, senior
elect *v* **1** = **choose**, appoint, determine, opt for, pick, prefer, select, settle on, vote

to death are electrocuted.

> ✔ **WORD TIP**
> Note that *electric* is an adjective. Avoid
> its use as a noun: *The electricity* (not *the
> electric*) *has failed.*

electro– *combining form* operated by or
caused by electricity.

electrocute *v* kill or injure by electricity.
electrocution *n*

electrode *n* conductor through which an
electric current enters or leaves a battery,
vacuum tube, etc.

electron *n* elementary particle in all atoms
that has a negative electrical charge.
electron microscope microscope that uses
electrons, rather than light, to produce a
magnified image.

electronic *adj* 1 (of a device) dependent
on the action of electrons. 2 (of a process)
using electronic devices.

elegant ❶ *adj* pleasing or graceful in dress,
style, or design. **elegance** *n*

elegy [el–lij–ee] *n, pl* **–egies** mournful
poem, esp. a lament for the dead. **elegiac**
adj mournful or plaintive.

element ❶ *n* 1 component part. 2
substance which cannot be separated into
other substances by ordinary chemical
techniques. 3 section of people within a
larger group, e.g. *the rowdy element.* 4
heating wire in an electric kettle, stove,
etc. ♦ *pl* 5 basic principles of something. 6

weather conditions, esp. wind, rain, and
cold. **in one's element** in a situation
where one is happiest. **elemental** *adj* of
primitive natural forces or passions.
elementary *adj* simple and
straightforward.

elephant *n* huge four–footed thick–
skinned animal with ivory tusks and a long
trunk. **elephantine** *adj* unwieldy, clumsy.

elevate ❶ *v* 1 raise in rank or status. 2 lift
up. **elevation** *n* 1 raising. 2 height above
sea level. 3 scale drawing of one side of a
building. **elevator** *n Aust, US & Canadian*
lift for carrying people.

eleven *adj, n* 1 one more than ten. ♦ *n* 2
Sport team of eleven people. **eleventh** *adj,
n* (of) number eleven in a series.
elevenses *n Informal* mid–morning snack.

elf *n, pl* **elves** (in folklore) small mischievous
fairy. **elfin** *adj* small and delicate.

elicit ❶ *v* 1 bring about (a response or
reaction). 2 find out (information) by
careful questioning.

eligible ❶ *adj* 1 meeting the requirements
or qualifications needed. 2 desirable as a
spouse. **eligibility** *n*

eliminate ❶ *v* get rid of. **elimination** *n*

elite ❶ [ill–**eet**] *n* most powerful, rich, or
gifted members of a group. **elitism** *n*
belief that society should be governed by
a small group of superior people. **elitist** *n,
adj*

elixir ❶ [ill–**ix**–er] *n* imaginary liquid that
can prolong life or turn base metals into

──────── THESAURUS ────────

elegant *adj* = **stylish**, chic, delicate,
exquisite, fine, section, graceful, handsome,
polished, refined, tasteful ≠ **plain**
element *n* 1 = **component**, constituent,
factor, ingredient, part, section,
subdivision, unit ♦ *pl* 5 = **basics**, essentials,
foundations, fundamentals, nuts and bolts
(*inf*), principles, rudiments 6 = **weather
conditions**, atmospheric conditions,
powers of nature
elevate *v* 1 = **promote**, advance,
aggrandize, exalt, prefer, upgrade
2 = **raise**, heighten, hoist, lift, lift up, uplift

elicit *v* 1 = **bring about**, bring forth, bring
out, bring to light, call forth, cause,
derive, evolve, give rise to 2 = **obtain**,
draw out, evoke, exact, extort, extract,
wrest
eligible *adj* 1 = **qualified**, acceptable,
appropriate, desirable, fit, preferable,
proper, suitable, worthy ≠ **unsuitable**
eliminate *v* = **get rid of**, cut out, dispose
of, do away with, eradicate, exterminate,
remove, stamp out, take out
elite *n* = **best**, aristocracy, cream, flower,
nobility, pick, upper class

gold.

elk *n* large deer of N Europe and Asia.

ellipse *n* oval shape. **elliptical** *adj* 1 oval–shaped. 2 (of speech or writing) obscure or ambiguous.

elm *n* tree with serrated leaves.

elocution ❶ *n* art of speaking clearly in public.

elongate ❶ [eel–long–gate] *v* make or become longer. **elongation** *n*

elope ❶ *v* (of two people) run away secretly to get married. **elopement** *n*

eloquence ❶ *n* fluent powerful use of language. **eloquent** *adj* **eloquently** *adv*

else *adv* 1 in addition or more, e.g. *what else can I do?* 2 other or different, e.g. *it was unlike anything else that had happened.* **elsewhere** *adv* in or to another place.

elucidate ❶ *v* make (something difficult) clear. **elucidation** *n*

elude ❶ *v* 1 escape from by cleverness or quickness. 2 baffle. **elusive** *adj* difficult to catch or remember.

emaciated ❶ [im–mace–ee–ate–id] *adj* abnormally thin. **emaciation** *n*

emanate ❶ [em–a–nate] *v* issue, proceed

from a source. **emanation** *n*

emancipate ❶ *v* free from social, political, or legal restraints. **emancipation** *n*

emasculate *v* deprive of power. **emasculation** *n*

embalm ❶ *v* preserve (a corpse) from decay by the use of chemicals etc.

embankment *n* man–made ridge that carries a road or railway or holds back water.

embargo ❶ *n, pl* –goes 1 order by a government prohibiting trade with a country. ◆ *v* –going, –goed 2 put an embargo on.

embark ❶ *v* 1 board a ship or aircraft. 2 (foll. by *on*) begin (a new project). **embarkation** *n*

embarrass ❶ *v* cause to feel self–conscious or ashamed. **embarrassed** *adj* **embarrassing** *adj* **embarrassment** *n*

embassy *n, pl* –sies 1 offices or official residence of an ambassador. 2 ambassador and his staff.

embattled *adj* having a lot of difficulties.

embed *v* –bedding, –bedded fix firmly in something solid.

———— THESAURUS ————

elixir *n* = **panacea**, nostrum

elocution *n* = **diction**, articulation, declamation, delivery, enunciation, oratory, pronunciation, speech, speechmaking

elongate *v* = **make longer**, draw out, extend, lengthen, prolong, protract, stretch

elope *v* = **run away**, abscond, bolt, decamp, disappear, escape, leave, run off, slip away, steal away

eloquence *n* = **expressiveness**, expression, fluency, forcefulness, oratory, persuasiveness, rhetoric, way with words

elucidate *v* = **clarify**, clear up, explain, explicate, expound, illuminate, illustrate, make plain, shed *or* throw light upon, spell out

elude *v* 1 = **escape**, avoid, dodge, duck (*inf*), evade, flee, get away from, outrun 2 = **baffle**, be beyond (someone),

confound, escape, foil, frustrate, puzzle, stump, thwart

emaciated *adj* = **skeletal**, cadaverous, gaunt, haggard, lean, pinched, scrawny, thin, undernourished, wasted

emanate *v* = **flow**, arise, come forth, derive, emerge, issue, originate, proceed, spring, stem

emancipate *v* = **free**, deliver, liberate, release, set free, unchain, unfetter

embalm *v* = **preserve**, mummify

embargo *n* 1 = **ban**, bar, boycott, interdiction, prohibition, restraint, restriction, stoppage ◆ *v* 2 = **ban**, bar, block, boycott, prohibit, restrict, stop

embark *v* 1 = **go aboard**, board ship, take ship ≠ land 2 (foll. by *on*) = **begin**, commence, enter, launch, plunge into, set about, set out, start, take up

embarrass *v* = **shame**, discomfit, disconcert, distress, fluster, humiliate,

embellish ⊕ v 1 decorate. 2 embroider (a story). **embellishment** n

ember n glowing piece of wood or coal in a dying fire.

embezzle ⊕ v steal money that has been entrusted to one. **embezzlement** n **embezzler** n

emblem ⊕ n object or design that symbolizes a quality, type, or group. **emblematic** adj

embody ⊕ v –bodying, –bodied 1 be an example or expression of. 2 comprise, include. **embodiment** n

embolism n blocking of a blood vessel by a blood clot or air bubble.

embrace ⊕ v 1 clasp in the arms, hug. 2 accept (an idea) eagerly. 3 comprise. ◆ n 4 act of embracing.

embrocation n lotion for rubbing into the skin to relieve pain.

embroider v 1 decorate with needlework. 2 make (a story) more interesting with fictitious detail. **embroidery** n

embroil ⊕ v involve (a person) in problems.

embryo ⊕ [em–bree–oh] n, pl –bryos 1 unborn creature in the early stages of development. 2 something at an undeveloped stage. **embryonic** adj at an early stage. **embryology** n

emend ⊕ v remove errors from. **emendation** n

emerald n 1 bright green precious stone. ◆ adj 2 bright green.

emerge ⊕ v 1 come into view. 2 (foll. by from) come out of. 3 become known. **emergence** n **emergent** adj

emergency ⊕ n, pl –cies sudden unforeseen occurrence needing immediate action.

emery n hard mineral used for smoothing and polishing.

emigrate ⊕ v go and settle in another country. **emigrant** n **emigration** n

eminent ⊕ adj distinguished, well-known. **eminently** adv **eminence** n 1 position of superiority or fame. 2 (E–) title of a cardinal.

emissary n, pl –saries agent sent on a mission by a government.

emit ⊕ v emitting, emitted 1 give out (heat, light, or a smell). 2 utter. **emission**

——————[THESAURUS]——————

mortify, show up (inf)

embellish v 1 = **decorate**, adorn, beautify, enhance, enrich, festoon, ornament 2 = **elaborate**, embroider

embezzle v = **misappropriate**, appropriate, filch, misuse, peculate, pilfer, purloin, rip off (sl), steal

emblem n = **symbol**, badge, crest, image, insignia, mark, sign, token

embody v 1 = **personify**, exemplify, manifest, represent, stand for, symbolize, typify 2 = **incorporate**, collect, combine, comprise, contain, include

embrace v 1 = **hug**, clasp, cuddle, envelop, hold, seize, squeeze, take or hold in one's arms 2 = **accept**, adopt, espouse, seize, take on board, take up, welcome 3 = **include**, comprehend, comprise, contain, cover, encompass, involve, take in ◆ n 4 = **hug**, clasp, clinch (sl), cuddle, squeeze

embroil v = **involve**, enmesh, ensnare, entangle, implicate, incriminate, mire, mix up

embryo n 2 = **germ**, beginning, nucleus, root, rudiment

emend v = **revise**, amend, correct, edit, improve, rectify

emerge v 1 = **come into view**, appear, arise, come forth, surface 2 (foll. by from) = **issue**, emanate, rise, spring up 3 = **become apparent**, become known, come out, come out in the wash, come to light, crop up, transpire

emergency n = **crisis**, danger, difficulty, extremity, necessity, plight, predicament, quandary, scrape (inf)

emigrate v = **move abroad**, migrate, move

eminent adj = **prominent**, celebrated, distinguished, esteemed, famous, high–ranking, illustrious, noted, renowned, *n*

emollient *adj* **1** softening, soothing. ♦ *n* **2** substance which softens or soothes the skin.

emotion ❶ *n* strong feeling. **emotional** *adj* readily affected by or appealing to the emotions. **emotionally** *adv* **emotive** *adj* tending to arouse emotion.

empathy *n* ability to understand someone else's feelings as if they were one's own.

emperor *n* ruler of an empire. **empress** *n fem*

emphasis ❶ *n, pl* **-ses** **1** special importance or significance. **2** stress on a word or phrase in speech. **emphasize** *v* **emphatic** *adj* showing emphasis. **emphatically** *adv*

emphysema [em-fiss-**see**-ma] *n* condition in which the air sacs of the lungs are grossly enlarged, causing breathlessness.

empire ❶ *n* **1** group of territories under the rule of one state or person. **2** large organization that is directed by one person or group.

empirical ❶ *adj* relying on experiment or experience, not on theory. **empirically** *adv* **empiricism** *n* doctrine that all knowledge derives from experience.

emplacement *n* prepared position for a gun.

employ ❶ *v* **1** hire (a person). **2** provide work or occupation for. **3** use. ♦ *n* **4** in the employ of doing regular paid work for. **employee** *n* **employer** *n* **employment** *n* **1** state of being employed. **2** work done by a person to earn money.

empower ❶ *v* enable, authorize.

empty ❶ *adj* **-tier, -tiest** **1** containing nothing. **2** unoccupied. **3** without purpose or value. **4** (of words) insincere. ♦ *v* **-tying, -tied** **5** make or become empty. **empties** *pl n* empty boxes, bottles, etc. **emptiness** *n*

emu *n* large Australian flightless bird with long legs.

emulate ❶ *v* attempt to equal or surpass by imitating. **emulation** *n*

emulsion *n* **1** light-sensitive coating on photographic film. **2** type of water-based paint. ♦ *v* **3** paint with emulsion paint. **emulsify** *v* (of two liquids) join together or join (two liquids) together. **emulsifier** *n*

enable ❶ *v* provide (a person) with the means, opportunity, or authority (to do something)

THESAURUS

well-known

emit *v* **1** = **give off**, cast out, discharge, eject, emanate, exude, radiate, send out, transmit ≠ **receive**

emotion *n* = **feeling**, ardour, excitement, fervour, passion, sensation, sentiment, vehemence, warmth

emphasis *n* **1** = **importance**, accent, attention, force, priority, prominence, significance, stress, weight **2** = **stress**, accent

empire *n* **1** = **kingdom**, commonwealth, domain, realm

empirical *adj* = **first-hand**, experiential, experimental, observed, practical, pragmatic

employ *v* **1** = **hire**, commission, engage, enlist, retain, take on **2** = **keep busy**, engage, fill, make use of, occupy, take up,

use up **3** = **use**, apply, bring to bear, exercise, exert, make use of, ply, put to use, utilize

empower *v* = **enable**, allow, authorize, commission, delegate, entitle, license, permit, qualify, sanction, warrant

empty *adj* **1, 2** = **bare**, blank, clear, deserted, desolate, hollow, unfurnished, uninhabited, unoccupied, vacant, void ≠ **full** **3** = **purposeless**, banal, fruitless, futile, hollow, inane, meaningless, senseless, vain, worthless **4** = **insincere**, cheap, hollow, idle ♦ *v* **5** = **evacuate**, clear, drain, exhaust, pour out, unload, vacate, void

emulate *v* = **imitate**, compete with, copy, echo, follow, mimic, rival

enable *v* = **allow**, authorize, empower, entitle, license, permit, qualify, sanction,

enact ⓣ v 1 establish by law. 2 perform (a story or play) by acting. **enactment** n

enamel n 1 glasslike coating applied to metal etc. to preserve the surface. 2 hard white coating on a tooth. ◆ v **–elling, –elled** 3 cover with enamel.

encapsulate ⓣ v 1 summarize. 2 enclose as in a capsule.

enchant ⓣ v delight and fascinate. **enchantment** n **enchantress** n fem

encircle v form a circle around. **encirclement** n

enclave n part of a country entirely surrounded by foreign territory.

enclose ⓣ v 1 surround completely. 2 include along with something else. **enclosure** n

encompass ⓣ v 1 surround. 2 include comprehensively.

encore interj 1 again, once more. ◆ n 2 extra performance due to enthusiastic demand.

encounter ⓣ v 1 meet unexpectedly. 2 be faced with. ◆ n 3 unexpected meeting. 4 game or battle.

encourage ⓣ v 1 inspire with confidence. 2 spur on. **encouragement** n

encroach ⓣ v intrude gradually on a person's rights or land. **encroachment** n

encrust v cover with a layer of something.

encumber ⓣ v hinder or impede. **encumbrance** n something that impedes or is burdensome.

encyclopedia, encyclopaedia n book or set of books containing facts about many subjects, usu. in alphabetical order. **encyclopedic, encyclopaedic** adj

end ⓣ n 1 furthest point or part. 2 limit. 3 last part of something. 4 fragment. 5 death or destruction. 6 purpose. 7 Sport either of the two defended areas of a playing field. ◆ v 8 bring or come to a finish. **make ends meet** have just enough money for one's needs. **ending** n **endless** adj endways

endanger ⓣ v put in danger.

———————— THESAURUS ————————

warrant ≠ **stop**

enact v 1 = **establish**, authorize, command, decree, legislate, ordain, order, proclaim, sanction 2 = **perform**, act out, depict, play, play the part of, portray, represent

encapsulate v 1 = **sum up**, abridge, compress, condense, digest, epitomize, précis, summarize

enchant v = **fascinate**, beguile, bewitch, captivate, charm, delight, enrapture, enthral, ravish

enclose v 1 = **surround**, bound, encase, encircle, fence, hem in, shut in, wall in 2 = **send with**, include, insert, put in

encompass v 1 = **surround**, circle, encircle, enclose, envelop, ring 2 = **include**, admit, comprise, contain, cover, embrace, hold, incorporate, take in

encounter v 1 = **meet**, bump into (inf), chance upon, come upon, run across 2 = **face**, confront, experience ◆ n 3 = **meeting**, brush, confrontation, rendezvous 4 = **battle**, clash, conflict,

contest, head–to–head, run–in (inf)

encourage v 1 = **inspire**, buoy up, cheer, comfort, console, embolden, hearten, reassure, support ≠ **depress** 2 = **spur**, advocate, egg on, foster, incite, promote, prompt, urge ≠ **prevent**

encroach v = **intrude**, impinge, infringe, invade, make inroads, overstep, trespass, usurp

encumber v = **burden**, hamper, handicap, hinder, impede, inconvenience, obstruct, saddle, weigh down

end n 1, 2 = **extremity**, boundary, edge, extent, extreme, limit, point, terminus, tip 3 = **finish**, cessation, close, closure, conclusion, culmination, denouement, ending, expiration, expiry, finale, resolution, stop, termination ≠ **start** 4 = **remnant**, butt, fragment, leftover, oddment, remainder, scrap, stub 5 = **destruction**, death, demise, doom, extermination, extinction, ruin 6 = **purpose**, aim, goal, intention, object, objective, point, reason ◆ v 8 = **finish**,

endear v cause to be liked. **endearing** adj **endearment** n affectionate word or phrase.

endeavour ❶ v 1 try. ♦ n 2 effort.

endorse ❶ v 1 give approval to. 2 sign the back of (a cheque). 3 record a conviction on (a driving licence). **endorsement** n

endow ❶ v provide permanent income for. **endowed with** provided with. **endowment** n

endure ❶ v 1 bear (hardship) patiently. 2 last for a long time. **endurable** adj **endurance** n act or power of enduring.

enema [**en**–im–a] n medicine injected into the rectum to empty the bowels.

enemy ❶ n, pl **–mies** hostile person or nation, opponent.

energy ❶ n, pl **–gies** 1 capacity for intense activity. 2 capacity to do work and overcome resistance. 3 source of power, such as electricity. **energetic** adj **energetically** adv **energize** v give vigour to.

enervate v deprive of strength or vitality.

enervation n

enfeeble v weaken.

enfold v 1 cover by wrapping something around. 2 embrace.

enforce ❶ v 1 impose obedience (to a law etc.). 2 impose (a condition). **enforceable** adj **enforcement** n

enfranchise v grant (a person) the right to vote. **enfranchisement** n

engage ❶ v 1 take part, participate. 2 involve (a person or his or her attention) intensely. 3 employ (a person). 4 begin a battle with. 5 bring (a mechanism) into operation. **engaged** adj 1 pledged to be married. 2 in use. **engagement** n **engaging** adj charming.

engender ❶ v produce, cause to occur.

engine ❶ n 1 any machine which converts energy into mechanical work. 2 railway locomotive.

engineer ❶ n 1 person trained in any branch of engineering. ♦ v 2 plan in a clever manner. 3 design or construct as an engineer.

THESAURUS

cease, close, conclude, culminate, stop, terminate, wind up ≠ **start**

endanger v = **put at risk**, compromise, imperil, jeopardize, put in danger, risk, threaten

endeavour v 1 = **try**, aim, aspire, attempt, labour, make an effort, strive, struggle, take pains ♦ n 2 = **effort**, attempt, enterprise, trial, try, undertaking, venture

endorse v 1 = **approve**, advocate, authorize, back, champion, promote, ratify, recommend, support 2 = **sign**, countersign

endow v = **provide**, award, bequeath, bestow, confer, donate, finance, fund, give

endure v 1 = **bear**, cope with, experience, stand, suffer, sustain, undergo, withstand 2 = **last**, continue, live on, persist, remain, stand, stay, survive

enemy n = **foe**, adversary, antagonist, competitor, opponent, rival, the opposition, the other side

energy n 1, 2 = **vigour**, drive, forcefulness, get-up-and-go (inf), liveliness, pep, stamina, verve, vitality

enforce v = **impose**, administer, apply, carry out, execute, implement, insist on, prosecute, put into effect

engage v 1 = **participate**, embark on, enter into, join, set about, take part, undertake 2 = **preoccupy**, absorb, captivate, engross, fix, grip, involve, occupy 3 = **employ**, appoint, enlist, enrol, hire, retain, take on ≠ **remove** 4 = **begin battle with**, assail, attack, encounter, fall on, join battle with, meet, take on 5 = **set going**, activate, apply, bring into operation, energize, switch on

engender v = **produce**, breed, cause, create, generate, give rise to, induce, instigate, lead to

engine n 1 = **machine**, mechanism, motor

engineer v 2 = **bring about**, contrive, create, devise, effect, mastermind, plan, plot, scheme

engineering *n* profession of applying scientific principles to the design and construction of engines, cars, buildings, or machines.

engrave ⏀ *v* 1 carve (a design) onto a hard surface. 2 fix deeply in the mind. **engraver** *n* **engraving** *n* print made from an engraved plate.

engross ⏀ [en–**groce**] *v* occupy the attention of (a person) completely.

engulf ⏀ *v* cover or surround completely.

enhance ⏀ *v* increase in quality, value, or attractiveness. **enhancement** *n*

enigma ⏀ *n* puzzling thing or person. **enigmatic** *adj*

enjoy ⏀ *v* 1 take joy in. 2 have the benefit of. 3 experience. **enjoyable** *adj* **enjoyment** *n*

enlarge ⏀ *v* 1 make or grow larger. 2 (foll. by *on*) speak or write about in greater detail. **enlargement** *n*

enlighten ⏀ *v* give information to. 1 **enlightenment** *n*

enlist ⏀ *v* 1 enter the armed forces. 2 obtain the support of. **enlistment** *n*

enliven ⏀ *v* make lively or cheerful.

enmity ⏀ *n, pl* –**ties** ill will, hatred.

enormous ⏀ *adj* very big, vast. **enormity** *n, pl* –**ties** 1 great wickedness. 2 gross offence. 3 *Informal* great size.

enough ⏀ *adj* 1 as much or as many as necessary. ♦ *n* 2 sufficient quantity. ♦ *adv* 3 sufficiently. 4 fairly or quite, e.g. *that's a common enough experience.*

enquire ⏀ *v* same as INQUIRE. **enquiry** *n*

enrich ⏀ *v* 1 improve in quality. 2 make wealthy or wealthier.

enrol ⏀ *v* –**rolling**, –**rolled** (cause to) become a member. **enrolment** *n*

en route ⏀ *adv French* on the way.

——————— THESAURUS ———————

engrave *v* 1 = **carve**, chisel, cut, etch, inscribe 2 = **fix**, embed, impress, imprint, ingrain, lodge

engross *v* = **absorb**, engage, immerse, involve, occupy, preoccupy

engulf *v* = **immerse**, envelop, inundate, overrun, overwhelm, submerge, swallow up, swamp

enhance *v* = **improve**, add to, boost, heighten, increase, lift, reinforce, strengthen, swell

enigma *n* = **mystery**, conundrum, problem, puzzle, riddle, teaser

enjoy *v* 1 = **take pleasure in** or **from**, appreciate, be entertained by, be pleased with, delight in, like, relish 2 = **have**, be blessed or favoured with, experience, have the benefit of, own, possess, reap the benefits of, use

enlarge *v* 1 = **increase**, add to, amplify, broaden, expand, extend, grow, magnify, swell, widen ≠ **reduce** 2 (foll. by *on*) = **expand on**, descant on, develop, elaborate on, expatiate on, give further details about

enlighten *v* = **inform**, advise, cause to understand, counsel, edify, educate, instruct, make aware, teach

enlist *v* 1 = **join up**, enrol, enter (into), join, muster, register, sign up, volunteer 2 = **obtain**, engage, procure, recruit

enliven *v* = **cheer up**, animate, excite, inspire, invigorate, pep up, rouse, spark, stimulate, vitalize

enmity *n* = **hostility**, acrimony, animosity, bad blood, bitterness, hatred, ill will, malice

enormous *adj* = **huge**, colossal, gigantic, gross, immense, mammoth, massive, mountainous, tremendous, vast ≠ **little**

enough *adj* 1 = **sufficient**, abundant, adequate, ample, plenty ♦ *n* 2 = **sufficiency**, abundance, adequacy, ample supply, plenty, right amount ♦ *adv* 3 = **sufficiently**, abundantly, adequately, amply, reasonably, satisfactorily, tolerably

enquire see INQUIRE

enrich *v* 1 = **enhance**, augment, develop, improve, refine, supplement 2 = **make rich**, make wealthy

enrol *v* = **enlist**, accept, admit, join up, recruit, register, sign up or on, take on

en route *adv French* = **on** or **along the way**, in transit, on the road

ensemble ⊕ [on–**som**–bl] n 1 all the parts of something taken together. 2 complete outfit of clothes. 3 company of actors or musicians. 4 *Music* group of musicians playing together.

enshrine v cherish or treasure.

ensign ⊕ n 1 naval flag. 2 banner. 3 *US* naval officer.

enslave v make a slave of (someone). **enslavement** n

ensnare v catch in or as if in a snare.

ensue ⊕ v come next, result.

ensure ⊕ v 1 make certain or sure. 2 make safe or protect.

entail ⊕ v bring about or impose inevitably.

entangle ⊕ v catch or involve in or as if in a tangle. **entanglement** n

entente [on–**tont**] n friendly understanding between nations.

enter ⊕ v 1 come or go in. 2 join. 3 become involved in, take part in. 4 record (an item) in a journal etc. 5 begin. **entrance** n 1 way into a place. 2 act of entering. 3 right of entering. **entrant** n person who enters a university, contest, etc. **entry** n, pl –**tries** 1 entrance. 2 entering. 3 item entered in a journal etc.

enterprise ⊕ n 1 company or firm. 2 bold or difficult undertaking. 3 boldness and energy. **enterprising** adj full of boldness and initiative.

entertain ⊕ v 1 amuse. 2 receive as a guest. 3 consider (an idea). **entertainer** n **entertainment** n

enthral ⊕ [en–**thrawl**] v –thralling, –thralled hold the attention of. **enthralling** adj

enthusiasm ⊕ n ardent interest, eagerness. **enthuse** v (cause to) show enthusiasm. **enthusiast** n ardent supporter of something. **enthusiastic** adj **enthusiastically** adv

entice ⊕ v attract by exciting hope or desire, tempt. **enticement** n

entire ⊕ adj including every detail, part, or aspect of something. **entirely** adv **entirety** n

ensemble n 1 = **whole**, aggregate, collection, entirety, set, sum, total, totality 2 = **outfit**, costume, get-up (*inf*), suit 3 = **group**, band, cast, chorus, company, troupe

ensign n 1, 2 = **flag**, banner, colours, jack, pennant, pennon, standard, streamer

ensue v = **follow**, arise, come next, derive, flow, issue, proceed, result, stem

ensure v 1 = **make certain**, certify, confirm, effect, guarantee, make sure, secure, warrant 2 = **protect**, guard, make safe, safeguard, secure

entail v = **involve**, bring about, call for, demand, give rise to, necessitate, occasion, require

entangle v = **tangle**, catch, embroil, enmesh, ensnare, entrap, implicate, snag, snare, trap ≠ **free**

enter v 1 = **come** or **go in** or **into**, arrive, make an, pass into, penetrate, pierce 2 = **join**, enlist, enrol ≠ **resign** 3 = **start**, commence, embark upon, set out on, take up 4 = **record**, inscribe, list, log, note, register, set down, take down

enterprise n 1 = **firm**, business, company, concern, establishment, operation 2 = **undertaking**, adventure, effort, endeavour, operation, plan, programme, project, venture 3 = **initiative**, adventurousness, boldness, daring, drive, energy, enthusiasm, resourcefulness

entertain v 1 = **amuse**, charm, cheer, delight, please, regale 2 = **show hospitality to**, accommodate, be host to, harbour, have company, lodge, put up, treat 3 = **consider**, conceive, contemplate, imagine, keep in mind, think about

enthral v = **fascinate**, captivate, charm, enchant, enrapture, entrance, grip, mesmerize

enthusiasm n = **keenness**, eagerness, fervour, interest, passion, relish, zeal, zest

entice v = **attract**, allure, cajole, coax, lead on, lure, persuade, seduce, tempt

entire adj = **whole**, complete, full, gross,

entitle ⊕ v 1 give a right to. 2 give a title to. **entitlement** n

entity ⊕ n, pl **-ties** separate distinct thing.

entomology n study of insects. **entomologist** n

entourage ⊕ [on–toor–ahzh] n group of people who assist an important person.

entrails ⊕ pl n 1 intestines. 2 innermost parts of something.

entrance¹ ⊕ n see ENTER.

entrance² ⊕ v 1 delight. 2 put into a trance.

entreat v ask earnestly. **entreaty** n, pl **-ties** earnest request.

entrench v 1 establish firmly. 2 establish in a fortified position with trenches. **entrenchment** n

entrepreneur ⊕ n business person who attempts to make a profit by risk and initiative.

entrust ⊕ v put into the care or protection of.

entwine ⊕ v twist together or around.

enumerate ⊕ v name one by one.

enunciate ⊕ v 1 pronounce clearly. 2 state precisely or formally.

envelop ⊕ v **enveloping, enveloped** wrap up, enclose.

envelope ⊕ n folded gummed paper cover for a letter.

environment ⊕ [en–**vire**–on–ment] n external conditions and surroundings in which people, animals, or plants live. **environmental** adj **environmentalist** n person concerned with the protection of the natural environment.

> ✓ **WORD TIP**
> Note the 'n' before the 'm' in the spelling of *environment*.

envisage ⊕ v conceive of as a possibility.

envoy ⊕ n 1 messenger. 2 diplomat ranking below an ambassador.

——————| THESAURUS |——————

total

entitle v 1 = **give the right to**, allow, authorize, empower, enable, license, permit 2 = **call**, christen, dub, label, name, term, title

entity n = **thing**, being, creature, individual, object, organism, substance

entourage n = **retinue**, associates, attendants, company, court, escort, followers, staff, train

entrails pl n 1 = **intestines**, bowels, guts, innards (*inf*), insides (*inf*), offal, viscera

entrance¹ n 1 = **way in**, access, door, doorway, entry, gate, opening, passage ≠ **exit** 2 = **appearance**, arrival, coming in, entry, introduction ≠ **departure** 3 = **admission**, access, admittance, entrée, entry, permission to enter

entrance² v 1 = **enchant**, bewitch, captivate, charm, delight, enrapture, enthral, fascinate ≠ **bore** 2 = **mesmerize**, hypnotize, put in a trance

entrepreneur n = **businessman** or **businesswoman**, impresario, industrialist, magnate, tycoon

entrust v = **give custody of**, assign, commit, confide, delegate, deliver, hand over, turn over

entwine v = **twist**, interlace, interweave, knit, plait, twine, weave, wind

enumerate v = **list**, cite, itemize, mention, name, quote, recite, recount, relate, spell out

enunciate v 1 = **pronounce**, articulate, enounce, say, sound, speak, utter, vocalize, voice 2 = **state**, declare, proclaim, promulgate, pronounce, propound, publish

envelop v = **enclose**, cloak, cover, encase, encircle, engulf, shroud, surround, wrap

envelope n = **wrapping**, case, casing, cover, covering, jacket, wrapper

environment n = **surroundings**, atmosphere, background, conditions, habitat, medium, setting, situation

envisage v = **imagine**, conceive (of), conceptualize, contemplate, envision, fancy, foresee, picture, see, think up, visualize

envoy n 1 = **messenger**, agent, courier,

envy ❶ n 1 feeling of discontent aroused by another's good fortune. ◆ v **–vying, –vied** 2 grudge (another's good fortune, success, or qualities). **enviable** adj arousing envy, fortunate. **envious** adj full of envy.

enzyme n any of a group of complex proteins that act as catalysts in specific biochemical reactions.

epaulette n shoulder ornament on a uniform.

ephemeral ❶ adj short-lived.

epic n 1 long poem, book, or film about heroic events or actions. ◆ adj 2 very impressive or ambitious.

epicentre n point on the earth's surface immediately above the origin of an earthquake.

epicure n person who enjoys good food and drink. **epicurean** adj 1 devoted to sensual pleasures, esp. food and drink. ◆ n 2 epicure.

epidemic ❶ n 1 widespread occurrence of a disease. 2 rapid spread of something.

epidermis n outer layer of the skin.

epidural [ep–pid–**dure**–al] adj, n (of) spinal anaesthetic injected to relieve pain during childbirth.

epigram ❶ n short witty remark or poem. **epigrammatic** adj

epigraph n 1 quotation at the start of a book. 2 inscription.

epilepsy n disorder of the nervous system causing loss of consciousness and sometimes convulsions. **epileptic** adj 1 of or having epilepsy. ◆ n 2 person who has epilepsy.

epilogue ❶ n short speech or poem at the end of a literary work, esp. a play.

episcopal [ip–**piss**–kop–al] adj of or governed by bishops. **episcopalian** adj 1 advocating Church government by bishops. ◆ n 2 advocate of such Church government.

episode ❶ n 1 incident in a series of incidents. 2 section of a serialized book, television programme, etc. **episodic** adj occurring at irregular intervals.

epistle ❶ n letter, esp. of an apostle. **epistolary** adj

epitaph ❶ n 1 commemorative inscription on a tomb. 2 commemorative speech or passage.

epithet ❶ n descriptive word or name.

epitome ❶ [ip–**pit**–a–mee] n typical example. **epitomize** v be the epitome of.

> ✅ **WORD TIP**
> Avoid the use of *epitome* to mean 'the peak' of something.

epoch ❶ [**ee**–pok] n period of notable events.

equable ❶ [**ek**–wab–bl] adj even-

———————————— THESAURUS ————————————

delegate, emissary, intermediary, representative 2 = **diplomat**, ambassador

envy n 1 = **covetousness**, enviousness, jealousy, resentfulness, resentment ◆ v 2 = **covet**, be envious (of), begrudge, be jealous (of), grudge, resent

ephemeral adj = **brief**, fleeting, momentary, passing, short–lived, temporary, transient, transitory

epidemic n 1 = **plague**, contagion, outbreak 2 = **spread**, growth, upsurge, wave

epigram n = **witticism**, aphorism, bon mot, quip

epilogue n = **conclusion**, coda, concluding speech, postscript

episode n 1 = **event**, adventure, affair, escapade, experience, happening, incident, matter, occurrence 2 = **part**, chapter, instalment, passage, scene, section

epistle n = **letter**, communication, message, missive, note

epitaph n 1 = **monument**, inscription

epithet n = **name**, appellation, description, designation (sl), nickname, sobriquet, tag, title

epitome n = **personification**, archetype, embodiment, essence, quintessence, representation, type, typical example tempered. **equably** adv

equal ❶ adj 1 identical in size, quantity, degree, etc. 2 having identical rights or status. 3 evenly balanced. 4 (foll. by to) having the necessary ability (for). ◆ n 5 person or thing equal to another. ◆ v **equalling, equalled** 6 be equal to. **equally** adv **equality** n state of being equal. **equalize** v 1 make or become equal. 2 reach the same score as one's opponent. **equalization** n **equal opportunity** nondiscrimination as to sex, race, etc. in employment.

equanimity n calmness of mind.

equate ❶ v make or regard as equivalent. **equation** n 1 mathematical statement that two expressions are equal. 2 act of equating.

equator n imaginary circle round the earth, equidistant from the poles. **equatorial** adj

equestrian adj of horses and riding.

equilateral adj having equal sides.

equilibrium ❶ n, pl **–ria** steadiness or stability.

equinox n time of year when day and night are of equal length.

equip ❶ v **equipping, equipped** provide with supplies, components, etc. **equipment** n 1 set of tools or devices used for a particular purpose. 2 act of equipping.

equivalent ❶ adj 1 equal in value. 2 having the same meaning or result. ◆ n 3 something that is equivalent. **equivalence** n

equivocal ❶ adj 1 ambiguous. 2 deliberately misleading. 3 of doubtful character or sincerity. **equivocate** v use vague or ambiguous language to mislead people. **equivocation** n

era ❶ n period of time considered as distinctive.

eradicate ❶ v destroy completely. **eradication** n

erase ❶ v 1 rub out. 2 remove sound or information from (a magnetic tape or disk). **eraser** n object for erasing something written. **erasure** n 1 erasing. 2 place or mark where something has been erased.

ere prep, conj Poetic before.

——————— THESAURUS ———————

epoch n = **era**, age, date, period, time

equable adj = **even–tempered**, calm, composed, easy–going, imperturbable, level–headed, placid, serene, unflappable (inf) ≠ **nervous**

equal adj 1 = **identical**, alike, corresponding, equivalent, regular, symmetrical, the same, uniform ≠ **different** 3 = **even**, balanced, evenly matched, fifty–fifty (inf), level pegging (Brit inf) ≠ **uneven** 4 (foll. by to) = **capable of**, competent to, fit for, good enough for, ready for, strong enough, suitable for, up to ≠ **inadequate** ◆ n 5 = **match**, counterpart, equivalent, rival, twin ◆ v 6 = **match**, amount to, be tantamount to, correspond to, equate, level, parallel, tie with ≠ **be different**

equate v = **make** or **be equal**, be commensurate, compare, correspond with or to, liken, mention in the same breath,

parallel

equilibrium n = **stability**, balance, equipoise, evenness, rest, steadiness, symmetry

equip v = **supply**, arm, array, fit out, furnish, kit out, provide, stock

equivalent adj 1, 2 = **equal**, alike, commensurate, comparable, corresponding, interchangeable, of a piece, same, similar, tantamount ≠ **different** ◆ n 3 = **equal**, counterpart, match, opposite number, parallel, twin

equivocal adj 1 = **ambiguous**, indefinite, indeterminate, oblique, obscure, uncertain, vague 2 = **misleading**, evasive

era n = **age**, date, day or days, epoch, generation, period, time

eradicate v = **wipe out**, annihilate, destroy, eliminate, erase, exterminate, extinguish, get rid of, obliterate, remove, root out

erect ⊙ v 1 build. 2 found or form. ◆ adj 3 upright. 4 (of the penis, clitoris, or nipples) rigid as a result of sexual excitement. **erectile** adj capable of becoming erect from sexual excitement. **erection** n

ermine n 1 stoat in northern regions. 2 its white winter fur.

erode ⊙ v wear away. **erosion** n

erotic ⊙ adj relating to sexual pleasure or desire. **eroticism** n **erotica** n sexual literature or art.

err ⊙ v make a mistake. **erratum** n, pl -ta error in writing or printing. **erroneous** adj incorrect, mistaken. **error** n mistake, inaccuracy, or misjudgment.

errand ⊙ n short trip to do something for someone.

errant adj behaving in a manner considered to be unacceptable.

erstwhile ⊙ adj former.

erudite ⊙ adj having great academic knowledge. **erudition** n

erupt ⊙ v 1 eject (steam, water, or volcanic material) violently. 2 burst forth suddenly and violently. 3 (of a blemish) appear on the skin. **eruption** n

escalate ⊙ v increase in extent or intensity. **escalation** n

escalator n moving staircase.

escape ⊙ v 1 get free (of). 2 avoid, e.g. escape attention. 3 (of a gas, liquid, etc.) leak gradually. 4 n 5 act of escaping. 6 means of relaxation. **escapee** n person who has escaped. **escapism** n taking refuge in fantasy to avoid unpleasant reality. **escapologist** n entertainer who specializes in freeing himself from confinement.

escarpment n steep face of a ridge or mountain.

eschew [iss–**chew**] v abstain from, avoid.

escort ⊙ n 1 people or vehicles accompanying another person for protection or as an honour. 2 person who accompanies a person of the opposite sex to a social event. ◆ v 3 act as an escort to.

esoteric [ee–so–**ter**–rik] adj understood by only a small number of people with special knowledge.

ESP extrasensory perception.

———— THESAURUS ————

erase v 1 = **remove**, blot, cancel, delete, expunge, obliterate 2 = **wipe out**, rub out

erect v 1 = **build**, construct, put up, raise, set up ≠ **destroy** 2 = **found**, create, establish, form, initiate, institute, organize, set up ◆ adj 3 = **upright**, elevated, perpendicular, straight, vertical ≠ **relaxed** 4 = **stiff**

erode v = **wear down** or **away**, abrade, consume, corrode, destroy, deteriorate, disintegrate, eat away, grind down

erotic adj = **sexual**, amatory, carnal, lustful, seductive, sensual, sexy (inf), voluptuous

err v = **make a mistake**, blunder, go wrong, miscalculate, misjudge, mistake, slip up (inf)

errand n = **job**, charge, commission, message, mission, task

erstwhile adj = **former**, bygone, late, old, once, one–time, past, previous, sometime

erudite adj = **learned**, cultivated, cultured, educated, knowledgeable, scholarly, well–

educated, well–read

erupt v 1, 2 = **explode**, belch forth, blow up, burst out, gush, pour forth, spew forth or out, spout, throw off 3 = **break out**, appear

escalate v = **increase**, expand, extend, grow, heighten, intensify, mount, rise ≠ **contract**

escape v 1 = **get away**, abscond, bolt, break free or out, flee, fly, make one's getaway, run away or off, slip away 2 = **avoid**, dodge, duck, elude, evade, pass, shun, slip 3 = **leak**, emanate, exude, flow, gush, issue, pour forth, seep ◆ n 5 = **getaway**, break, break–out, flight 6 = **relaxation**, distraction, diversion, pastime, recreation

escort n 1 = **guard**, bodyguard, convoy, cortege, entourage, retinue, train 2 = **companion**, attendant, beau, chaperon, guide, partner ◆ v 3 = **accompany**, chaperon, conduct,

especial ⊕ *adj Formal* special. **especially**
adv particularly.

> ✓ **WORD TIP**
> *Special(ly)* is more common than
> *especial(ly)* and is always used in
> preference to *especial* when the sense
> is 'out of the ordinary'.

espionage ⊕ [ess–pyon–ahzh] *n* spying.
esplanade *n* wide open road used as a
public promenade.
espouse *v* adopt or give support to (a
cause etc.). **espousal** *n*
espy *v* **espying, espied** catch sight of.
Esq. esquire.
essay ⊕ *n* 1 short literary composition. 2
short piece of writing on a subject done as
an exercise by a student. ◆ *v* 3 attempt.
essayist *n*
essence ⊕ *n* 1 most important feature of a
thing which determines its identity. 2
concentrated liquid used to flavour food.
essential *adj* 1 vitally important. 2 basic or
fundamental. ◆ *n* 3 something
fundamental or indispensable.

essentially *adv*
establish ⊕ *v* 1 set up on a permanent
basis. 2 make secure or permanent in a
certain place, job, etc. 3 prove. 4 cause to
be accepted. **establishment** *n* 1 act of
establishing. 2 commercial or other
institution. **the Establishment** group of
people having authority within a society.
estate ⊕ *n* 1 landed property. 2 large area
of property development, esp. of new
houses or factories. 3 property of a
deceased person. **estate agent** agent
concerned with the valuation, lease, and
sale of property. **estate car** car with a rear
door and luggage space behind the rear
seats.
esteem ⊕ *n* 1 high regard. ◆ *v* 2 think
highly of. 3 judge or consider.
ester *n Chem* compound produced by the
reaction between an acid and an alcohol.
estimate ⊕ *v* 1 calculate roughly. 2 form
an opinion about. ◆ *n* 3 approximate
calculation. 4 statement from a workman
etc. of the likely charge for a job. 5
opinion. **estimable** *adj* worthy of respect.
estimation *n* considered opinion.

——————— THESAURUS ———————

guide, lead, partner, shepherd, usher
especial *adj Formal* = **exceptional**,
noteworthy, outstanding, principal,
special, uncommon, unusual
espionage *n* = **spying**, counter–
intelligence, intelligence, surveillance,
undercover work
espouse *v* = **support**, adopt, advocate,
back, champion, embrace, promote, stand
up for, take up, uphold
essay *n* 1 = **composition**, article, discourse,
dissertation, paper, piece, tract, treatise ◆
v 3 = **attempt**, aim, endeavour, try,
undertake
essence *n* 1 = **fundamental nature**, being,
core, heart, nature, quintessence, soul,
spirit, substance 2 = **concentrate**,
distillate, extract, spirits, tincture
establish *v* 1 = **create**, constitute, form,
found, ground, inaugurate, institute,
settle, set up 3 = **prove**, authenticate,

certify, confirm, corroborate, demonstrate,
substantiate, verify
estate *n* 1 = **lands**, area, domain, holdings,
manor, property 3 = **property**, assets,
belongings, effects, fortune, goods,
possessions, wealth
esteem *n* 1 = **respect**, admiration, credit,
estimation, good opinion, honour, regard,
reverence, veneration ◆ *v* 2 = **respect**,
admire, love, prize, regard highly, revere,
think highly of, treasure, value
3 = **consider**, believe, deem, estimate,
judge, reckon, regard, think, view
estimate *v* 1 = **calculate roughly**, assess,
evaluate, gauge, guess, judge, number,
reckon, value 2 = **form an opinion**,
believe, conjecture, consider, judge, rank,
rate, reckon, surmise ◆ *n* 3 = **approximate
calculation**, assessment, ballpark figure
(*inf*), guess, guesstimate (*inf*), judgment,
valuation 5 = **opinion**, appraisal,

estranged adj no longer living with one's spouse. **estrangement** n

estuary ❶ n, pl **–aries** mouth of a river.

etc. ❶ et cetera.

> ### ✓ WORD TIP
> *Etc.* means 'and the rest' so it is redundant to write *and etc.* Note the spelling; it comes from the Latin *et cetera*.

et cetera ❶ [et **set**–ra] *Latin* 1 and the rest, and others. 2 or the like. **etceteras** pl n miscellaneous extra things or people.

etch ❶ v 1 wear away or cut the surface of (metal, glass, etc.) with acid. 2 imprint vividly (on someone's mind). **etching** n

eternal ❶ adj 1 without beginning or end. 2 unchanging. **eternally** adv **eternity** n 1 infinite time. 2 timeless existence after death.

ether n 1 colourless sweet–smelling liquid used as an anaesthetic. 2 region above the clouds. **ethereal** [eth–**eer**–ee–al] adj extremely delicate.

ethnic ❶ adj 1 relating to a people or group that shares a culture, religion, or language. 2 belonging or relating to such a group, esp. one that is a minority group in a particular place. **ethnology** n study of human races. **ethnological** adj

ethos [**eeth**–oss] n distinctive spirit and attitudes of a people, culture, etc.

etiquette ❶ n conventional code of conduct.

étude [ay–tewd] n short musical composition for a solo instrument, esp. intended as a technical exercise.

etymology n, pl **–gies** study of the sources and development of words. **etymological** adj

eucalyptus, eucalypt n tree, mainly grown in Australia, that provides timber, gum, and medicinal oil from the leaves.

Eucharist [**yew**–kar–ist] n 1 Christian sacrament commemorating Christ's Last Supper. 2 consecrated elements of bread and wine.

eugenics [yew–**jen**–iks] n study of methods of improving the human race.

eulogy n, pl **–gies** speech or writing in praise of a person. **eulogize** v praise (a person or thing) highly in speech or writing. **eulogistic** adj

eunuch n castrated man, esp. (formerly) a guard in a harem.

euphemism n inoffensive word or phrase substituted for one considered offensive or upsetting. **euphemistic** adj

euphoria ❶ n sense of elation. **euphoric** adj

eureka [yew–**reek**–a] interj exclamation of triumph at finding something.

euthanasia n act of killing someone painlessly, esp. to relieve his or her suffering.

evacuate ❶ v 1 send (someone) away from a place of danger. 2 empty. **evacuation** n **evacuee** n

evade ❶ v 1 get away from or avoid. 2

—————————————— THESAURUS ——————————————

assessment, belief, estimation, judgment

estuary n = **inlet**, creek, firth, fjord, mouth

et cetera *Latin* = **and so on**, and others, and so forth, and the like, and the rest, et al.

etch v 1 = **cut**, carve, eat into, engrave, impress, imprint, inscribe, stamp

eternal adj 1 = **everlasting**, endless, immortal, infinite, never–ending, perpetual, timeless, unceasing, unending ≠ **changing** 2 = **permanent**, deathless, enduring, immutable, imperishable, indestructible, lasting, unchanging

ethnic adj = **cultural**, folk, indigenous, national, native, racial, traditional

etiquette n = **good** or **proper behaviour**, civility, courtesy, decorum, formalities, manners, politeness, propriety, protocol

euphoria n = **elation**, ecstasy, exaltation, exhilaration, intoxication, joy, jubilation, rapture

evacuate v 1 = **clear**, abandon, desert, forsake, leave, move out, pull out, quit, vacate, withdraw

elude. **evasion** n **evasive** adj not
straightforward. **evasively** adv

evaluate ⊕ v find or judge the value of.
evaluation n

evangelical adj 1 of or according to
gospel teaching. 2 of certain Protestant
sects which maintain the doctrine of
salvation by faith. ◆ n 3 member of an
evangelical sect.

evaporate ⊕ v 1 change from a liquid or
solid to a vapour. 2 disappear.
evaporation n **evaporated milk** thick
unsweetened tinned milk.

eve ⊕ n 1 evening or day before some
special event. 2 period immediately before
an event. **evensong** n evening prayer.

even ⊕ adj 1 flat or smooth. 2 (foll. by
with) on the same level (as). 3 constant. 4
calm. 5 equally balanced. 6 divisible by
two. ◆ adv 7 equally. 8 simply. 9
nevertheless. ◆ v 10 make even.

evening ⊕ n 1 end of the day or early part
of the night. ◆ adj 2 of or in the evening.

event ⊕ n 1 anything that takes place. 2
planned and organized occasion. 3
contest in a sporting programme. **eventful**
adj full of exciting incidents.

ever ⊕ adv 1 at any time. 2 always.
evergreen n, adj (tree or shrub) having
leaves throughout the year. **everlasting**
adj **evermore** adv for all time to come.

every ⊕ adj 1 each without exception. 2 all
possible. **everybody** pron every person.
everyday adj usual or ordinary. **everyone**
pron every person. **everything** pron
everywhere adv in all places.

> ✔ **WORD TIP**
>
> *Everybody* and *everyone* are
> interchangeable. Although strict usage
> treats these pronouns as singular,
> modern practice is to use a plural after
> them: *Everyone nodded their head.*

evict ⊕ v legally expel (someone) from his
or her home. **eviction** n

evidence ⊕ n 1 ground for belief. 2 matter
produced before a lawcourt to prove or
disprove a fact. 3 sign, indication. ◆ v 4
demonstrate, prove. **in evidence**
conspicuous. **evident** adj easily seen or
understood. **evidently** adv **evidential** adj
of, serving as, or based on evidence.

evil ⊕ n 1 wickedness. 2 wicked deed. ◆ adj

——————— THESAURUS ———————

evade v 1 = **avoid**, dodge, duck, elude,
escape, get away from, sidestep, steer
clear of ≠ **meet** 2 = **avoid answering**,
equivocate, fend off, fudge, hedge, parry

evaluate v = **assess**, appraise, calculate,
estimate, gauge, judge, rate, reckon, size
up (*inf*), weigh

evaporate v 1 = **dry up**, dry, vaporize
2 = **disappear**, dematerialize, dissolve,
fade away, melt away, vanish

eve n 1 = **night before**, day before, vigil
2 = **brink**, edge, point, threshold, verge

even adj 1 = **level**, flat, horizontal, parallel,
smooth, steady, straight, true, uniform
≠ **rough** 2 (foll. by with) = **equal**,
comparable, fifty–fifty (*inf*), identical, level,
like, matching, neck and neck, on a par,
similar, tied ≠ **irregular** 3 = **regular**,
constant, smooth, steady, unbroken,
uniform, uninterrupted, unvarying,

unwavering ≠ **changing** 4 = **calm**,
composed, cool, even–tempered,
imperturbable, placid, unruffled, well–
balanced ≠ **emotional**

evening n 1 = **dusk**, gloaming (*Scot or
poet*), twilight

event n 1 = **incident**, affair, business,
circumstance, episode, experience,
happening, occasion, occurrence
3 = **competition**, bout, contest, game,
tournament

ever adv 1 = **at any time**, at all, at any
period, at any point, by any chance, in
any case, on any occasion 2 = **always**, at
all times, constantly, continually,
evermore, for ever, perpetually, twenty–
four–seven (*inf*)

every adj = **each**, all, each one

evict v = **expel**, boot out (*inf*), eject, kick
out (*inf*), oust, remove, throw out, turf out

3 harmful. 4 morally bad. 5 very unpleasant. **evilly** adv **evildoer** n wicked person.

evoke ❶ v call or summon up (a memory, feeling, etc.). **evocation** n **evocative** adj

evolve ❶ v 1 develop gradually. 2 (of an animal or plant species) undergo evolution. **evolution** n gradual change in the characteristics of living things over successive generations, esp. to a more complex form. **evolutionary** adj

ewe n female sheep.

ex– prefix 1 out of, outside, from, e.g. exodus. 2 former, e.g. ex–wife.

exacerbate [ig–**zass**–er–bate] v make (pain, emotion, or a situation) worse. **exacerbation** n

exact ❶ adj 1 correct and complete in every detail. 2 precise, as opposed to approximate. ◆ v 3 demand (payment or obedience). **exactly** adv precisely, in every respect. **exactness, exactitude** n **exacting** adj making rigorous or excessive demands.

exaggerate ❶ v 1 regard or represent as greater than is true. 2 make greater or more noticeable. **exaggeration** n

exalt ❶ v 1 praise highly. 2 raise to a higher rank. **exalted** adj **exaltation** n

exam n short for EXAMINATION.

examine ❶ v 1 look at closely. 2 test the knowledge of. 3 ask questions of. **examination** n 1 examining. 2 test of a candidate's knowledge or skill. **examinee** n **examiner** n

example ❶ n 1 specimen typical of its group. 2 person or thing worthy of imitation. 4 punishment regarded as a warning to others.

exasperate ❶ v cause great irritation to. **exasperation** n

excavate ❶ v 1 unearth buried objects from (a piece of land) methodically to learn about the past. 2 make (a hole) in solid matter by digging. **excavation** n **excavator** n large machine used for digging.

THESAURUS

(inf), turn out

evidence n 1, 2 = **proof**, confirmation, corroboration, demonstration, grounds, substantiation, testimony 3 = **sign**, indication ◆ v 4 = **show**, demonstrate, display, exhibit, indicate, prove, reveal, signify, witness

evil n 1 = **wickedness**, badness, depravity, malignity, sin, vice, villainy, wrongdoing 2 = **harm**, affliction, disaster, hurt, ill, injury, mischief, misfortune, suffering, woe ◆ adj 3 = **harmful**, calamitous, catastrophic, destructive, dire, disastrous, pernicious, ruinous 4 = **wicked**, bad, depraved, immoral, malevolent, malicious, sinful, villainous 5 = **offensive**, foul, noxious, pestilential, unpleasant, vile

evoke v = **arouse**, awaken, call, give rise to, induce, recall, rekindle, stir up, summon up ≠ **contain**

evolve v 1 = **develop**, expand, grow, increase, mature, progress, unfold, work out

exact adj 1 = **correct**, faultless, right, true,

unerring 2 = **accurate**, definite, precise, specific ≠ **rough** ◆ v 3 = **demand**, claim, command, compel, extort, extract, force

exaggerate v = **overstate**, amplify, embellish, embroider, enlarge, overemphasize, overestimate

exalt v 1 = **praise**, acclaim, extol, glorify, idolize, set on a pedestal, worship 2 = **raise**, advance, elevate, ennoble, honour, promote, upgrade

examine v 1 = **inspect**, analyse, explore, investigate, peruse, scrutinize, study, survey 2 = **test**, question, quiz 3 = **question**, cross–examine, grill (inf), inquire, interrogate

example n 2 = **specimen**, case, illustration, instance, sample 3 = **model**, archetype, ideal, paradigm, paragon, prototype, standard 4 = **warning**, caution, lesson

exasperate v = **irritate**, anger, annoy, enrage, incense, inflame, infuriate, madden, pique

excavate v 1 = **unearth**, dig out, dig up, mine, quarry, uncover 2 = **dig**, burrow,

exceed ❶ v 1 be greater than. 2 go beyond (a limit). **exceedingly** adv very.

excel ❶ v –celling, –celled 1 be superior to. 2 be outstandingly good at something. **excellent** adj exceptionally good. **excellence** n

except ❶ prep 1 (sometimes foll. by for) other than, not including. ◆ v 2 not include. **except that** but for the fact that. **excepting** prep except. **exception** n 1 excepting. 2 thing that is excluded from or does not conform to the general rule. **exceptionable** adj causing offence. **exceptional** adj 1 not ordinary. 2 much above the average.

excerpt ❶ n passage taken from a book, speech, etc.

excess ❶ n 1 state or act of exceeding the permitted limits. 2 immoderate amount. 3 amount by which a thing exceeds the permitted limits. **excessive** adj **excessively** adv

exchange ❶ v 1 give or receive (something) in return for something else. ◆ n 2 act of exchanging. 3 thing given or received in place of another. 4 centre in which telephone lines are interconnected.

5 *Finance* place where securities or commodities are traded. 6 transfer of sums of money of equal value between different currencies. **exchangeable** adj

excise¹ n tax on goods produced for the home market.

excise² v cut out or away. **excision** n

excite ❶ v 1 arouse to strong emotion. 2 arouse or evoke (an emotion). 3 arouse sexually. **excitement** n **excitable** adj easily excited.

exclaim ❶ v speak suddenly, cry out. **exclamation** n **exclamation mark** punctuation mark (!) used after exclamations. **exclamatory** adj

exclude ❶ v 1 keep out, leave out. 2 leave out of consideration. **exclusion** n **exclusive** adj 1 excluding everything else. 2 not shared. 3 catering for a privileged minority. ◆ n 4 story reported in only one newspaper. **exclusively** adv **exclusivity**, **exclusiveness** n

excommunicate ❶ v exclude from membership and the sacraments of the Church. **excommunication** n

excrement n waste matter discharged from the body.

———————— THESAURUS ————————

delve, tunnel

exceed v 1 = **surpass**, beat, better, cap (inf), eclipse, outdo, outstrip, overtake, pass, top 2 = **go over the limit of**, go over the top, overstep

excel v 1 = **be superior**, beat, eclipse, outdo, outshine, surpass, transcend 2 = **be good**, be proficient, be skilful, be talented, shine, show talent

except prep 1 (sometimes foll. by for) = **apart from**, barring, besides, but, excepting, excluding, omitting, other than, saving, with the exception of ◆ v 2 = **exclude**, leave out, omit, pass over

excerpt n = **extract**, fragment, part, passage, piece, quotation, section, selection

excess n 1 = **overindulgence**, debauchery, dissipation, dissoluteness, extravagance, intemperance, prodigality ≠ **restraint**

2 = **surfeit**, glut, overload, superabundance, superfluity, surplus, too much ≠ **want**

exchange v 1 = **interchange**, barter, change, convert into, swap, switch, trade ◆ n 2 = **interchange**, barter, quid pro quo, reciprocity, substitution, swap, switch, tit for tat, trade

excite v 1, 2 = **arouse**, animate, galvanize, inflame, inspire, provoke, rouse, stir up 3 = **thrill**, electrify, titillate

exclaim v = **cry out**, call out, declare, proclaim, shout, utter, yell

exclude v 1 = **keep out**, ban, bar, boycott, disallow, forbid, prohibit, refuse, shut out ≠ **allow** 2 = **leave out**, count out, eliminate, ignore, omit, pass over, reject, rule out, set aside ≠ **include**

excommunicate v = **expel**, anathematize, ban, banish, cast out, denounce, exclude,

excruciating ❶ *adj* 1 agonizing. 2 hard to bear.

excursion ❶ *n* short journey, esp. for pleasure.

excuse ❶ *n* 1 explanation offered to justify (a fault etc.). ◆ *v* 2 put forward a reason or justification for (a fault etc.). 3 forgive (a person) or overlook (a fault etc.). 4 make allowances for. 5 exempt. 6 allow to leave. **excusable** *adj*

execrable [eks–sik–rab–bl] *adj* of very poor quality.

execute ❶ *v* 1 put (a condemned person) to death. 2 carry out or accomplish. 3 produce (a work of art). 4 render (a legal document) effective, as by signing. **execution** *n* **executioner** *n* **executive** *n* person or group in an administrative position.

exemplify ❶ *v* –fying, –fied 1 show an example of. 2 be an example of. **exemplification** *n*

exempt ❶ *adj* 1 not subject to an obligation etc. ◆ *v* 2 release from an obligation etc. **exemption** *n*

exercise ❶ *n* 1 activity to train the body or mind. 2 set of movements or tasks designed to improve or test a person's ability. 3 performance of a function. ◆ *v* 4 make use of, e.g. *to exercise one's rights.* 5 take exercise or perform exercises.

exert ❶ *v* use (influence, authority, etc.) forcefully or effectively. **exert oneself** make a special effort. **exertion** *n*

exhale *v* breathe out. **exhalation** *n*

exhaust ❶ *v* 1 tire out. 2 use up. 3 discuss (a subject) thoroughly. 4 gases ejected from an engine as waste products. 5 pipe through which an engine's exhaust fumes pass. **exhaustible** *adj* **exhaustion** *n* 1 extreme tiredness. 2 exhausting. **exhaustive** *adj* comprehensive. **exhaustively** *adv*

exhibit ❶ *v* 1 display to the public. 2 show (a quality or feeling). ◆ *n* 3 object exhibited to the public. 4 *Law* document

──── THESAURUS ────

repudiate

excruciating *adj* 1 = **agonizing**, harrowing, intense, piercing, severe, violent 2 = **unbearable**, insufferable

excursion *n* = **trip**, day trip, expedition, jaunt, journey, outing, pleasure trip, ramble, tour

excuse *n* 1 = **justification**, apology, defence, reason, explanation, grounds, mitigation, plea, reason, vindication ≠ **charge** ◆ *v* 2 = **justify**, apologize for, defend, explain, mitigate, vindicate 3, 4 = **forgive**, acquit, exculpate, exonerate, make allowances for, overlook, pardon, tolerate, turn a blind eye to ≠ **accuse** 5 = **free**, absolve, discharge, exempt, let off, release, relieve, spare ≠ **charge**

execute *v* 1 = **put to death**, behead, electrocute, guillotine, hang, kill, shoot 2 = **carry out**, accomplish, administer, discharge, effect, enact, implement, perform, prosecute

exemplify *v* = **show**, demonstrate, display, embody, exhibit, illustrate, represent, serve as an example of

exempt *adj* 1 = **immune**, excepted, excused, free, not liable, released, spared ◆ *v* 2 = **grant immunity**, absolve, discharge, excuse, free, let off, release, relieve, spare

exercise *n* 1 = **exertion**, activity, effort, labour, toil, training, work, work–out 2 = **task**, drill, lesson, practice, problem 3 = **use**, application, discharge, fulfilment, implementation, practice, utilization ◆ *v* 4 = **put to use**, apply, bring to bear, employ, exert, use, utilize 5 = **train**, practise, work out

exert *v* = **use**, apply, bring to bear, employ, exercise, make use of, utilize, wield **exert oneself** = **make an effort**, apply oneself, do one's best, endeavour, labour, strain, strive, struggle, toil, work

exhaust *v* 1 = **tire out**, debilitate, drain, enervate, enfeeble, fatigue, sap, weaken, wear out 2 = **use up**, consume, deplete, dissipate, expend, run through, spend, squander, waste

or object produced in court as evidence.
exhibitor *n* **exhibition** *n* **1** public display
of art, skills, etc. **2** exhibiting.
exhibitionism *n* **1** compulsive desire to
draw attention to oneself. **2** compulsive
desire to display one's genitals in public.
exhibitionist *n*
exhilarate *v* make lively and cheerful.
exhilaration *n*
exhort 𝕧 *v* urge earnestly. **exhortation** *n*
exhume 𝕧 [ig-**zyume**] *v* dig up
(something buried, esp. a corpse).
exigency 𝕧 *n, pl* **-cies** urgent demand or
need. **exigent** *adj*
exile 𝕧 *n* **1** prolonged, usu. enforced,
absence from one's country. **2** person
banished or living away from his or her
country. ◆ *v* **3** expel from one's country.
exist 𝕧 *v* **1** have being or reality. **2** eke out
a living. **3** live. **existence** *n* **existent** *adj*
exit 𝕧 *n* **1** way out. **2** going out. **3** actor's
going off stage. ◆ *v* **4** go out. **5** go
offstage: used as a stage direction.

exodus 𝕧 [**eks**–so–duss] *n* departure of a
large number of people.
exonerate 𝕧 *v* free from blame or a
criminal charge. **exoneration** *n*
exorbitant 𝕧 *adj* (of prices, demands,
etc.) excessive. **exorbitance** *n*
exorcize 𝕧 *v* expel (evil spirits) by prayers
and religious rites. **exorcism** *n* **exorcist** *n*
exotic 𝕧 *adj* **1** having a strange allure or
beauty. **2** originating in a foreign country.
◆ *n* **3** non-native plant. **exotica** *pl n*
(collection of) exotic objects.
expand 𝕧 *v* **1** make or become larger. **2**
spread out. **3** (foll. by *on*) enlarge (on). **4**
become more relaxed, friendly, and
talkative. **expansion** *n* **expanse** *n*
uninterrupted wide area. **expansive** *adj* **1**
wide or extensive. **2** friendly and talkative.
expatiate [iks–**pay**–shee–ate] *v* (foll. by *on*)
speak or write at great length (on).
expatriate 𝕧 [eks–**pat**–ree–it] *adj* **1** living
outside one's native country. ◆ *n* **2** person
living outside his or her native country.

—————— THESAURUS ——————

exhibit *v* **1** = **display**, parade, put on view,
show **2** = **show**, demonstrate, express,
indicate, manifest, reveal
exhort *v* = **urge**, advise, beseech, call
upon, entreat, persuade, press, spur
exhume *v* = **dig up**, disentomb, disinter,
unearth
exigency *n* = **need**, constraint, demand,
necessity, requirement
exile *n* **1** = **banishment**, deportation,
expatriation, expulsion **2** = **expatriate**,
deportee, émigré, outcast, refugee ◆ *v*
3 = **banish**, deport, drive out, eject,
expatriate, expel
exist *v* **1** = **be**, be present, occur
2 = **survive**, eke out a living, get along *or*
by, keep one's head above water, stay
alive, subsist **3** = **live**, endure
exit *n* **1** = **way out**, door, gate, outlet
≠ **entry 2** = **departure**, exodus, farewell,
going, goodbye, leave–taking, retreat,
withdrawal ◆ *v* **4** = **depart**, go away, go
out, leave, make tracks, retire, retreat, take
one's leave, withdraw ≠ **arrive 5** = **go**

offstage (*Theatre*)
exodus *n* = **departure**, evacuation, exit,
flight, going out, leaving, migration,
retreat, withdrawal
exonerate *v* = **clear**, absolve, acquit,
discharge, exculpate, excuse, justify,
pardon, vindicate
exorbitant *adj* = **excessive**, extortionate,
extravagant, immoderate, inordinate,
outrageous, preposterous, unreasonable
exorcize *v* = **drive out**, cast out, deliver
(from), expel, purify
exotic *adj* **1** = **unusual**, colourful,
fascinating, glamorous, mysterious,
strange, striking, unfamiliar ≠ **ordinary**
2 = **foreign**, alien, external, imported,
naturalized
expand *v* **1** = **increase**, amplify, broaden,
develop, enlarge, extend, grow, magnify,
swell, widen ≠ **reduce 2** = **spread (out)**,
diffuse, stretch (out), unfold, unfurl,
unravel, unroll **3** (foll. by *on*) = **go into
detail about**, amplify, develop, elaborate
on, embellish, enlarge on, expatiate on,

expect ⓿ *v* 1 regard as probable. 2 look forward to, await. 3 require as an obligation. **expectancy** *n* 1 something expected on the basis of an average, e.g. *life expectancy*. 2 feeling of anticipation. **expectant** *adj* 1 expecting or hopeful. 2 pregnant. **expectation** *n* 1 act or state of expecting. 2 something looked forward to. 3 attitude of anticipation or hope.

expedient ⓿ *n* 1 something that achieves a particular purpose. ◆ *adj* 2 suitable to the circumstances, appropriate. **expediency** *n*

expedite *v* hasten the progress of. **expedition** *n* 1 organized journey, esp. for exploration. 2 people and equipment comprising an expedition. 3 pleasure trip or excursion. **expeditionary** *adj* relating to an expedition, esp. a military one. **expeditious** *adj* done quickly and efficiently.

expel ⓿ *v* –pelling, –pelled 1 drive out with force. 2 dismiss from a school etc. permanently. **expulsion** *n*

expend ⓿ *v* spend, use up. **expendable** *adj* able to be sacrificed to achieve an objective. **expenditure** *n* 1 something expended, esp. money. 2 amount expended. **expense** *n* 1 cost. 2 (cause of) spending. ◆ *pl* 3 charges, outlay incurred. **expensive** *adj* high-priced.

experience ⓿ *n* 1 direct personal participation. 2 particular incident, feeling, etc. that a person has undergone. 3 accumulated knowledge. ◆ *v* 4 participate in. 5 be affected by (an emotion). **experienced** *adj* skilful from extensive participation.

experiment ⓿ *n* 1 test to provide evidence to prove or disprove a theory. 2 attempt at something new. ◆ *v* 3 carry out an experiment. **experimental** *adj* **experimentation** *n*

expert ⓿ *n* 1 person with extensive skill or knowledge in a particular field. ◆ *adj* 2 skilful or knowledgeable. **expertise** [eks-per-**teez**] *n* special skill or knowledge.

expiate *v* make amends for.

expire ⓿ *v* 1 finish or run out. 2 breathe out. 3 *Lit* die. **expiration** *n* **expiry** *n* end,

——————————— THESAURUS ———————————

expound on, flesh out

expatriate *adj* 1 = **exiled**, banished, emigrant, émigré ◆ *n* 2 = **exile**, emigrant, émigré, refugee

expect *v* 1 = **think**, assume, believe, imagine, presume, reckon, suppose, surmise, trust 2 = **look forward to**, anticipate, await, contemplate, envisage, hope for, predict, watch for 3 = **require**, call for, demand, insist on, want

expedient *n* 1 = **means**, contrivance, device, makeshift, measure, method, resort, scheme, stopgap ◆ *adj* 2 = **advantageous**, appropriate, beneficial, convenient, effective, helpful, opportune, practical, suitable, useful ≠ **ineffective**

expel *v* 1 = **drive out**, belch, cast out, discharge, eject, remove, spew 2 = **dismiss**, ban, banish, drum out, evict, exclude, exile, throw out, turf out (*inf*) ≠ **admit**

expend *v* = **spend**, consume, dissipate, exhaust, go through, pay out, use (up)

experience *n* 1 = **participation**, contact, exposure, familiarity, involvement 2 = **event**, adventure, affair, encounter, episode, happening, incident, occurrence 3 = **knowledge**, practice, training ◆ *v* 4 = **undergo**, encounter, endure, face, feel, go through, live through, sample, taste

experiment *n* 1 = **test**, examination, experimentation, investigation, procedure, proof, research 2 = **trial**, trial run ◆ *v* 3 = **test**, examine, investigate, put to the test, research, sample, try, verify

expert *n* 1 = **master**, authority, connoisseur, dab hand (*Brit inf*), fundi (*S Afr*), guru, mana (*NZ*), past master, professional, specialist, virtuoso ≠ **amateur** ◆ *adj* 2 = **skilful**, adept, adroit, experienced, masterly, practised, professional, proficient, qualified, virtuoso ≠ **inexperienced**

esp. of a contract period.

explain ⊕ v 1 make clear and intelligible. 2 account for. **explanation** n **explanatory** adj

expletive n swearword.

explicable adj able to be explained. **explication** n

explicit ⊕ adj 1 precisely and clearly expressed. 2 shown in realistic detail. **explicitly** adv

explode ⊕ v 1 burst with great violence, blow up. 2 react suddenly with emotion. 3 increase rapidly. 4 show (a theory etc.) to be baseless. **explosion** n **explosive** adj 1 tending to explode. ◆ n 2 substance that causes explosions.

exploit ⊕ v 1 take advantage of for one's own purposes. 2 make the best use of. ◆ n 3 notable feat or deed. **exploitation** n **exploiter** n

explore ⊕ v 1 investigate. 2 travel into (unfamiliar regions), esp. for scientific purposes. **exploration** n **exploratory** adj **explorer** n

exponent ⊕ n 1 person who advocates an idea, cause, etc. 2 skilful performer, esp. a musician.

export n 1 selling or shipping of goods to a

foreign country. 2 product shipped or sold to a foreign country. ◆ v 3 sell or ship (goods) to a foreign country.

expose ⊕ v 1 uncover or reveal. 2 make vulnerable, leave unprotected. 3 subject (a photographic film) to light. **expose oneself** display one's sexual organs in public. **exposure** n 1 exposing. 2 lack of shelter from the weather, esp. the cold. 3 appearance before the public, as on television.

exposé [iks-**pose**–ay] n bringing of a crime, scandal, etc. to public notice.

expound ⊕ v explain in detail. **exposition** n 1 explanation. 2 large public exhibition.

express ⊕ v 1 put into words. 2 show (an emotion). 3 indicate by a symbol or formula. 4 squeeze out (juice etc.). ◆ adj 5 explicitly stated. 6 (of a purpose) particular. 7 of or for rapid transportation of people, mail, etc. ◆ n 8 fast train or bus stopping at only a few stations. ◆ adv 9 by express delivery. **expression** n 1 expressing. 2 word or phrase. 3 showing or communication of emotion. 4 look on the face that indicates mood. 5 Maths variable, function, or some combination of these. **expressionless** adj **expressive** adj

———— THESAURUS ————

expire v 1 = **finish**, cease, close, come to an end, conclude, end, lapse, run out, stop, terminate 2 = **breathe out**, emit, exhale, expel 3 Lit = **die**, cark (Aust & NZ sl) depart, kick the bucket (inf), pass away or on, perish

explain v 1 = **make clear** or **plain**, clarify, clear up, define, describe, elucidate, expound, resolve, teach 2 = **account for**, excuse, give a reason for, justify

explicit adj 1 = **clear**, categorical, definite, frank, precise, specific, straightforward, unambiguous ≠ **uncertain**

explode v 1 = **blow up**, burst, detonate, discharge, erupt, go off, set off, shatter 4 = **disprove**, debunk, discredit, give the lie to, invalidate, refute, repudiate

exploit v 1 = **take advantage of**, abuse, manipulate, milk, misuse, play on or upon

2 = **make the best use of**, capitalize on, cash in on (inf), profit by or from, use, utilize ◆ n 3 = **feat**, accomplishment, achievement, adventure, attainment, deed, escapade, stunt

explore v 1 = **investigate**, examine, fossick (Aust & NZ), inquire into, inspect, look into, probe, research, search 3 = **travel**, reconnoitre, scout, survey, tour

exponent n 1 = **advocate**, backer, champion, defender, promoter, proponent, supporter, upholder 2 = **performer**, player

expose v 1 = **uncover**, display, exhibit, present, reveal, show, unveil ≠ **cover** 2 = **make vulnerable**, endanger, imperil, jeopardize, lay open, leave open, subject

expound v = **explain**, describe, elucidate, interpret, set forth, spell out, unfold

expropriate v deprive an owner of (property). **expropriation** n

expunge v delete, erase, blot out.

expurgate v remove objectionable parts from (a book etc.).

exquisite 🛈 adj 1 of extreme beauty or delicacy. 2 intense in feeling. **exquisitely** adv

extend 🛈 v 1 draw out or be drawn out, stretch. 2 last for a certain time. 3 (foll. by to) include. 4 increase in size or scope. 5 offer, e.g. *extend one's sympathy*. **extendable** adj **extension** n 1 room or rooms added to an existing building. 2 additional telephone connected to the same line as another. 3 extending. **extensive** adj having a large extent, widespread. **extensor** n muscle that extends a part of the body. **extent** n range over which something extends, area.

extenuate v make (an offence or fault) less blameworthy.

exterior 🛈 n 1 part or surface on the outside. 2 outward appearance. ◆ adj 3 of, on, or coming from the outside.

exterminate 🛈 v destroy (animals or people) completely. **extermination** n

external 🛈 adj of, situated on, or coming from the outside. **externally** adv

extinct 🛈 adj 1 having died out. 2 (of a volcano) no longer liable to erupt. **extinction** n

extinguish 🛈 v 1 put out (a fire or light). 2 remove or destroy entirely. **extinguisher** n

extol 🛈 v –tolling, –tolled praise highly.

extort 🛈 v get (something) by force or threats. **extortion** n **extortionate** adj (of prices) excessive.

extra 🛈 adj 1 more than is usual, expected or needed. ◆ n 2 additional person or thing. 3 something for which an additional charge is made. 4 *Films* actor hired for crowd scenes. ◆ adv 5 unusually or exceptionally.

extra– prefix outside or beyond an area or scope, e.g. *extrasensory; extraterritorial*.

extract 🛈 v 1 pull out by force. 2 remove.

express v 1 = **state**, articulate, communicate, declare, phrase, put into words, say, utter, voice, word 2 = **show**, convey, exhibit, intimate, make known, reveal 3 = **represent**, indicate, signify, stand for, symbolize ◆ adj 5 = **explicit**, categorical, clear, definite, distinct, plain, unambiguous 6 = **specific**, clear-cut, especial, particular, singular, special 7 = **fast**, direct, high-speed, nonstop, rapid, speedy, swift

exquisite adj 1 = **beautiful**, attractive, comely, dainty, delicate, elegant, fine, lovely, pleasing ≠ **ugly** 2 = **intense**, acute, keen, sharp

extend v 1 = **make longer**, drag out, draw out, lengthen, prolong, spin out, spread out, stretch ≠ **cut** 2 = **last**, carry on, continue, go on 4 = **widen**, add to, augment, broaden, enhance, enlarge, expand, increase, supplement ≠ **cut** 5 = **offer**, confer, impart, present, proffer ≠ **withdraw**

exterior n 1 = **outside**, coating, covering, facade, face, shell, skin, surface ≠ **inside** ◆ adj 3 = **outside**, external, outer, outermost, outward, surface ≠ **inside**

exterminate v = **destroy**, abolish, annihilate, eliminate, eradicate

external adj = **outer**, exterior, outermost, outside, outward, surface ≠ **inside**

extinct adj 1 = **dead**, defunct, gone, lost, vanished ≠ **living**

extinguish v 1 = **put out**, blow out, douse, quench, smother, snuff out, stifle 2 = **destroy**, annihilate, eliminate, end, eradicate, exterminate, remove, wipe out

extol v = **praise**, acclaim, commend, eulogize, exalt, glorify, sing the praises of

extort v = **force**, blackmail, bully, coerce, extract, squeeze

extra adj 1 a = **additional**, added, ancillary, auxiliary, further, more, supplementary ≠ **needed** b = **surplus**, excess, leftover, redundant, spare, superfluous, unused ◆ n 2 = **addition**, accessory, attachment,

3 derive. 4 copy out (an article, passage, etc.) from a publication. ◆ *n* 5 something extracted, such as a passage from a book etc. 6 preparation containing the concentrated essence of a substance, e.g. *beef extract.* **extraction** *n* **extractor** *n*

extramural *adj* connected with but outside the normal courses of a university or college.

extraneous ❶ [iks–train–ee–uss] *adj* irrelevant.

extraordinary ❶ *adj* 1 very unusual. 2 (of a meeting) specially arranged to deal with a particular subject. **extraordinarily** *adv*

extrapolate *v* 1 infer (something not known) from the known facts. 2 *Maths* estimate (a value of a function or measurement) beyond the known values by the extension of a curve. **extrapolation** *n*

extrasensory *adj* **extrasensory perception** supposed ability to obtain information other than through the normal senses.

extravagant ❶ *adj* 1 spending money excessively. 2 going beyond reasonable limits. **extravagance** *n* **extravaganza** *n* elaborate and lavish entertainment, display, etc.

extreme ❶ *adj* 1 of a high or the highest degree or intensity. 2 severe. 3 immoderate. 4 farthest or outermost. ◆ *n* 5 either of the two limits of a scale or range. **extremely** *adv* **extremist** *n* 1 person who favours immoderate methods. ◆ *adj* 2 holding extreme opinions. **extremity** *n, pl* **–ties** 1 farthest point. 2 extreme condition, as of misfortune. ◆ *pl* 3 hands and feet.

extricate ❶ *v* free from complication or difficulty.

extrovert ❶ *adj* 1 lively and outgoing. 2 concerned more with external reality than inner feelings. ◆ *n* 3 extrovert person.

extrude *v* squeeze or force out. **extrusion** *n*

exuberant ❶ *adj* 1 high–spirited. 2 growing luxuriantly. **exuberance** *n*

exude *v* 1 (of a liquid or smell) seep or flow out slowly and steadily. 2 make apparent by mood or behaviour, e.g. *exude confidence.*

THESAURUS

bonus, extension, supplement ≠ **essential** ◆ *adv* 5 = **exceptionally**, especially, extraordinarily, extremely, particularly, remarkably, uncommonly, unusually

extract *v* 1 = **pull out**, draw, pluck out, pull, remove, take out, uproot, withdraw 3 = **derive**, draw, elicit, glean, obtain ◆ *n* 5 = **passage**, citation, clipping, cutting, excerpt, quotation, selection 6 = **essence**, concentrate, distillation, juice

extraneous *adj* = **irrelevant**, beside the point, immaterial, inappropriate, off the subject, unconnected, unrelated

extraordinary *adj* 1 = **unusual**, amazing, exceptional, fantastic, outstanding, phenomenal, remarkable, strange, uncommon ≠ **ordinary**

extravagant *adj* 1 = **wasteful**, lavish, prodigal, profligate, spendthrift ≠ **sparing** 2 = **excessive**, outrageous, over the top (*sl*), preposterous, reckless, unreasonable

≠ **conservative**

extreme *adj* 1 = **maximum**, acute, great, highest, intense, severe, supreme, ultimate, utmost ≠ **common** 2 = **severe**, drastic, harsh, radical, rigid, strict, uncompromising 3 = **excessive**, fanatical, immoderate, radical ≠ **moderate** 4 = **farthest**, far–off, most distant, outermost, remotest ≠ **nearest** ◆ *n* 5 = **limit**, boundary, edge, end, extremity, pole

extricate *v* = **free**, disengage, disentangle, get out, release, remove, rescue, wriggle out of

extrovert *adj* 1 = **outgoing**, exuberant, gregarious, sociable

exuberant *adj* 1 = **high–spirited**, animated, cheerful, ebullient, energetic, enthusiastic, lively, spirited, vivacious ≠ **dull** 2 = **luxuriant**, abundant, copious, lavish, plentiful, profuse

exult ❶ *v* be joyful or jubilant. **exultation** *n* **exultant** *adj*

eye ❶ *n* **1** organ of sight. **2** external part of an eye. **3** (*often pl*) ability to see. **4** attention, e.g. *his new shirt caught my eye.* **5** ability to judge or appreciate, e.g. *a good eye for detail.* **6** one end of a sewing needle. **7** small area of calm at the centre of a hurricane. **8** dark spot on a potato from which a stem grows. ◆ *v* **eyeing** *or* **eying, eyed 9** look at carefully or warily. **eyelet** *n* **1** small hole for a lace or cord to be passed through. **2** ring that strengthens this. **eyeball** *n* ball–shaped part of the eye. **eyebrow** *n* line of hair on the bony ridge above the eye. **1 eyelash** *n* short hair that grows out from the eyelid. **eyelid** *n* fold of skin that covers the eye when it is closed. **eyeliner** *n* cosmetic used to outline the eyes. **eye–opener** *n Informal* something startling or revealing. **eye shadow** coloured cosmetic worn on the upper eyelids. **eyesight** *n* ability to see. **eyesore** *n* ugly object. **eyetooth** *n* canine tooth. **eyewitness** *n* person who was present at an event and can describe what happened.

eyrie *n* **1** nest of an eagle. **2** high isolated place.

———————————— THESAURUS ————————————

exult *v* = **be joyful**, be overjoyed, celebrate, jump for joy, rejoice

eye *n* **1** = **eyeball**, optic (*inf*) **5** = **appreciation**, discernment, discrimination, judgment, perception, recognition, taste ◆ *v* **9** = **look at**, check out (*inf*), contemplate, inspect, study, survey, view, watch

F f

F Fahrenheit.

fable ❶ *n* **1** story with a moral. **2** false or fictitious account. **3** legend. **fabled** *adj* made famous in legend. **fabulous** *adj* amazing.

fabric ❶ *n* **1** knitted or woven cloth. **2** framework or structure.

face ❶ *n* **1** front of the head. **2** facial expression. **3** distorted expression. **4** outward appearance. **5** front or main side. **6** dial of a clock. **7** exposed area of coal or ore in a mine. **8** dignity, self-respect. ♦ *v* **9** look or turn towards. **10** be opposite. **11** be confronted by. **12** provide with a surface. **faceless** *adj* impersonal, anonymous. **face–lift** *n* operation to tighten facial skin, to remove wrinkles. **face–saving** *adj* maintaining dignity or self-respect. **face up to** *v* accept (an unpleasant fact or reality). **face value**

apparent worth or meaning.

facetious ❶ [fas–**see**–shuss] *adj* funny or trying to be funny, esp. at inappropriate times.

facia *n*, *pl* **–ciae** same as FASCIA.

facile ❶ [fas–sile] *adj* (of a remark, argument, etc.) superficial and showing lack of real thought.

facsimile ❶ [fak–**sim**–ill–ee] *n* exact copy.

fact ❶ *n* **1** event or thing known to have happened or existed. **2** provable truth. **facts of life** details of sex and reproduction. **factual** *adj*

faction ❶ *n* **1** (dissenting) minority group within a larger body. **2** dissension. **factious** *adj* of or producing factions.

factor ❶ *n* **1** element contributing to a result. **2** *Maths* one of the integers multiplied together to give a given number. **3** *Scot* property manager.

THESAURUS

fable *n* **1** = **story**, allegory, legend, myth, parable, tale **2, 3** = **fiction**, fabrication, fantasy, invention, tall story (*inf*), urban legend, urban myth, yarn (*inf*) ≠ **fact**

fabric *n* **1** = **cloth**, material, stuff, textile, web **2** = **framework**, constitution, construction, foundations, make–up, organization, structure

face *n* **1** = **countenance**, features, mug (*sl*), visage **2** = **expression**, appearance, aspect, look **3** = **scowl**, frown, grimace, pout, smirk **4** = **side**, exterior, front, outside, surface **8** *As in* **save** *or* **lose face** = **self–respect**, authority, dignity, honour, image, prestige, reputation, standing, status ♦ *v* **10** = **look onto**, be opposite, front onto, overlook **11** = **confront**, brave, come up against, deal with, encounter,

experience, meet, oppose, tackle **12** = **coat**, clad, cover, dress, finish

facetious *adj* = **funny**, amusing, comical, droll, flippant, frivolous, humorous, jocular, playful, tongue in cheek

facile *adj* = **superficial**, cursory, glib, hasty, shallow, slick

facsimile *n* = **copy**, carbon copy, duplicate, fax, photocopy, print, replica, reproduction, transcript

fact *n* **1** = **event**, act, deed, *fait accompli*, happening, incident, occurrence, performance **2** = **truth**, certainty, reality ≠ **lie**

faction *n* **1** = **group**, bloc, cabal, clique, contingent, coterie, gang, party, set, splinter group **2** = **dissension**, conflict, disagreement, discord, disunity, division,

factorial *n* product of all the integers from one to a given number.

factory 🛈 *n, pl* **–ries** building where goods are manufactured.

faculty 🛈 *n, pl* **–ties 1** physical or mental ability. **2** department in a university or college.

fad 🛈 *n* **1** short–lived fashion. **2** whim.

fade 🛈 *v* **1** (cause to) lose brightness, colour, or strength. **2** vanish slowly.

faeces [**fee**–seez] *pl n* waste matter discharged from the anus. **faecal** [**fee**–kl] *adj*

fag[1] *n* **1** *Informal* boring task. **2** young public schoolboy who does menial chores for a senior boy. ◆ *v* **3** do menial chores in a public school.

fag[2] *n Slang* cigarette. **fag end 1** last and worst part. **2** *Slang* cigarette stub.

faggot *n* **1** ball of chopped liver, herbs, and bread. **2** bundle of sticks for fuel.

Fahrenheit [**far**–ren–hite] *adj* of a temperature scale with the freezing point of water at 32° and the boiling point at 212°.

fail 🛈 *v* **1** be unsuccessful. **2** stop operating. **3** be or judge to be below the required standard in a test. **4** disappoint or be useless to (someone). **5** neglect or be unable to do (something). ◆ *n* **6** instance of not passing an exam or test. **without fail** regularly. **failing** *n* **1** weak point. ◆ *prep* **2** in the absence of. **failure** *n* **1** act or instance of failing. **2** unsuccessful person or thing.

faint 🛈 *adj* **1** lacking clarity, brightness, or volume. **2** feeling dizzy or weak. **3** lacking conviction or force. ◆ *v* **4** lose consciousness temporarily. ◆ *n* **5** temporary loss of consciousness.

fair[1] 🛈 *adj* **1** unbiased and reasonable. **2** light in colour. **3** beautiful. **4** quite good, e.g. *a fair attempt.* **5** quite large, e.g. *a fair amount of money.* **6** (of weather) fine. ◆ *adv* **7** fairly. **fairly** *adv* **1** moderately. **2** to a great degree or extent. **3** as deserved, reasonably. **fairness** *n* **fairway** *n Golf* smooth area between the tee and the green.

fair[2] 🛈 *n* **1** travelling entertainment with sideshows, rides, and amusements. **2** exhibition of commercial or industrial products. **tairground** *n* open space used for a fair.

THESAURUS

infighting, rebellion ≠ **accord**

factor *n* **1** = **element**, aspect, cause, component, consideration, influence, item, part

factory *n* = **works**, mill, plant

faculty *n* **1** = **ability**, aptitude, capacity, facility, power, propensity, skill **2** = **department**, school ≠ **failing**

fad *n* **1** = **craze**, fashion, mania, rage, trend, vogue **2** = **whim**

fade *v* **1** = **pale**, bleach, discolour, lose colour, wash out **2** = **dwindle**, decline, die away, disappear, dissolve, melt away, vanish, wane

fail *v* **1** = **be unsuccessful**, bite the dust, break down, come to grief, come unstuck, fall, fizzle out (*inf*), flop (*inf*), founder, miscarry, misfire ≠ **succeed 2** = **give out**, cark (*Aust & NZ sl*), conk out (*inf*), cut out, die, peter out, stop working **4, 5**

= **disappoint**, abandon, desert, forget, forsake, let down, neglect, omit **without fail 1** = **regularly**, like clockwork, religiously **2** = **dependably**, conscientiously, constantly, without exception

faint *adj* **1** = **dim**, distant, faded, indistinct, low, muted, soft, subdued, vague ≠ **clear 2** = **dizzy**, exhausted, giddy, light–headed, muzzy, weak, woozy (*inf*) ≠ **fresh 3** = **slight**, feeble, remote, unenthusiastic, weak ◆ *v* **4** = **pass out**, black out, collapse, flake out (*inf*), keel over (*inf*), lose consciousness, swoon (*lit*) ◆ *n* **5** = **blackout**, collapse, swoon (*lit*), unconsciousness

fair[1] *adj* **1** = **unbiased**, above board, equitable, even–handed, honest, impartial, just, lawful, legitimate, proper, unprejudiced ≠ **unfair 2** = **light**, blond,

fairy ⊕ *n, pl* **fairies** 1 imaginary small
creature with magic powers. 2 *Offens* male
homosexual. **fairy godmother** person who
helps in time of trouble. **fairyland** *n* fairy
lights small coloured electric bulbs used as
decoration. **fairy tale, story** 1 story about
fairies or magic. 2 unbelievable story or
explanation.

faith ⊕ *n* 1 strong belief, esp. without
proof. 2 religion. 3 complete confidence
or trust. 4 allegiance to a person or cause.
faithful *adj* 1 loyal. 2 consistently reliable.
4 accurate in detail. **faithfully** *adv* **faithless**
adj disloyal or dishonest.

fake ⊕ *v* 1 cause something not genuine to
appear real or more valuable by fraud. 2
pretend to have (an illness, emotion, etc.).
♦ *n* 3 person, thing, or act that is not
genuine. ♦ *adj* 4 not genuine.

falcon *n* small bird of prey. **falconry** *n* 1 art
of training falcons. 2 sport of hunting with
falcons.

fall ⊕ *v* **falling, fell, fallen** 1 drop from a
higher to a lower place through the force
of gravity. 2 collapse to the ground. 3
decrease in number or quality. 4 slope
downwards. 5 die in battle. 6 be captured.
7 pass into a specified condition. 8 (of the
face) take on a sad expression. 9 occur. 10
yield to temptation. ♦ *n* 11 falling. 12
thing or amount that falls. 13 decrease in
value or number. 14 decline in power or
influence. 15 capture or overthrow. 16 *US*
autumn. ♦ *pl* 17 waterfall. 18 **fall for** *v* 1
Informal fall in love with. 2 be deceived by
(a lie or trick). **fall guy** 1 *Informal* victim of
a confidence trick. 2 scapegoat. **fallout** *n*
radioactive particles spread as a result of a
nuclear explosion.

fallacy ⊕ *n, pl* –**cies** 1 false belief. 2
unsound reasoning. **fallacious** *adj*

fallow ⊕ *adj* (of land) ploughed but left
unseeded to regain fertility.

false ⊕ *adj* 1 not true or correct. 2 artificial,

blonde, fair–haired, flaxen–haired,
towheaded 3 = **beautiful**, bonny, comely,
handsome, lovely, pretty ≠ **homely**
4 = **respectable**, adequate, average,
decent, moderate, O.K. *or* okay (*inf*),
passable, reasonable, satisfactory, tolerable
6 = **fine**, bright, clear, cloudless, dry,
sunny, unclouded

fair² *n* 1 = **carnival**, bazaar, festival, fete,
gala, show

fairy *n* 1 = **sprite**, brownie, elf, leprechaun,
peri, pixie

faith *n* 1, 3 = **confidence**, assurance,
conviction, credence, credit, dependence,
reliance, trust ≠ **doubt** 2 = **religion**, belief,
church, communion, creed,
denomination, dogma, persuasion
≠ **agnosticism** 4 = **allegiance**, constancy,
faithfulness, fidelity, loyalty

fake *v* 1 = **counterfeit**, copy, fabricate,
forge 2 = **sham**, feign, pretend, put on,
simulate ♦ *n* 3 = **impostor**, charlatan,
copy, forgery, fraud, hoax, imitation,
reproduction, sham ♦ *adj* 4 = **artificial**,
counterfeit, false, forged, imitation, mock,

phoney *or* phony (*inf*), sham ≠ **real**

fall *v* 1, 2 = **descend**, cascade, collapse,
dive, drop, plummet, plunge, sink,
subside, tumble ≠ **rise** 3 = **decrease**,
decline, diminish, drop, dwindle, go
down, lessen, slump, subside ≠ **increase**
4 = **slope**, fall away, incline 5 = **die**, be
killed, cark (*Aust & NZ sl*), meet one's end,
perish ≠ **survive** 6 = **be overthrown**,
capitulate, pass into enemy hands,
succumb, surrender ≠ **triumph** 9 = **occur**,
befall, chance, come about, come to pass,
happen, take place 10 = **lapse**, err, go
astray, offend, sin, transgress, trespass ♦ *n*
11 = **descent**, dive, drop, nose dive,
plummet, plunge, slip, tumble
13 = **decrease**, cut, decline, dip, drop,
lessening, lowering, reduction, slump 14,
15 = **collapse**, capitulation, defeat,
destruction, downfall, overthrow, ruin

fallacy *n* 1 = **error**, delusion, falsehood,
flaw, misapprehension, misconception,
mistake, untruth

fallow *adj* = **uncultivated**, dormant, idle,
inactive, resting, unplanted, unused

fake. 3 deceptive, e.g. *false promises.*
falsely *adv* **falseness** *n* **falsity** *n* **falsehood**
n 1 quality of being untrue. 2 lie.

falsetto *n, pl* –tos voice pitched higher
than one's natural range.

falter ⊕ *v* 1 be hesitant, weak, or unsure. 2
lose power momentarily. 3 utter
hesitantly. 4 move unsteadily.

fame ⊕ *n* state of being widely known or
recognized. **famed** *adj* famous.

familiar ⊕ *adj* 1 well-known. 2 intimate,
friendly. 4 too friendly. ♦ *n* 5 demon
supposed to attend a witch. 6 friend.
familiarly *adv* **familiarity** *n* **familiarize** *v*
acquaint fully with a particular subject.

family ⊕ *n, pl* –lies 1 group of parents and
their children. 2 one's spouse and
children. 3 group descended from a
common ancestor. 5 group of related
objects or beings. ♦ *adj* 6 suitable for
parents and children together. **familial** *adj*
family planning control of the number of
children in a family by the use of
contraception.

famine ⊕ *n* severe shortage of food.

fan¹ ⊕ *n* 1 hand-held or mechanical object
used to create a current of air for
ventilation or cooling. ♦ *v* fanning, fanned
2 blow or cool with a fan. 3 spread out
like a fan.

fan² ⊕ *n Informal* devotee of a pop star,
sport, or hobby.

fanatic ⊕ *n* person who is excessively
enthusiastic about something. **fanatical**
adj **fanatically** *adv* **fanaticism** *n*

fancy ⊕ *adj* –cier, –ciest 1 elaborate, not
plain. 2 (of prices) higher than usual. ♦ *n,
pl* –cies 3 sudden irrational liking or desire.
4 uncontrolled imagination. ♦ *v* –cying,
–cied 5 *Informal* be sexually attracted to. 6
Informal have a wish for. 7 picture in the
imagination. 8 suppose. **fancy oneself**
Informal have a high opinion of oneself.
fanciful *adj* 1 not based on fact. 2
excessively elaborate. **fancy dress** party
costume representing a historical figure,
animal, etc. **fancy-free** *adj* not in love.

fanfare *n* short loud tune played on brass

————— THESAURUS —————

false *adj* 1 = **incorrect**, erroneous, faulty,
inaccurate, inexact, invalid, mistaken,
wrong ≠ **right** 2 = **artificial**, bogus,
counterfeit, fake, forged, imitation, sham,
simulated ≠ **real** 3 = **untrue**, deceitful,
deceptive, fallacious, fraudulent,
hypocritical, lying, misleading, trumped
up, unreliable, unsound, untruthful ≠ **true**

falter *v* 1 = **hesitate**, vacillate, waver ≠ **last**
3 = **stutter**, stammer 4 = **stumble**, totter

fame *n* = **prominence**, celebrity, glory,
honour, renown, reputation, repute,
stardom

familiar *adj* 1 = **well-known**, recognizable
≠ **unusual** 2 = **common**, accustomed,
customary, frequent, ordinary, routine
3 = **friendly**, amicable, close, easy,
intimate, relaxed ≠ **cold** 4 = **disrespectful**,
bold, forward, impudent, intrusive,
presumptuous

family *n* 1, 2 = **relations**, folk (*inf*),
household, kin, kith and kin, one's nearest
and dearest, one's own flesh and blood,

relatives 4 = **clan**, dynasty, house, race,
tribe 5 = **group**, class, genre, network,
subdivision, system

famine *n* = **hunger**, dearth, scarcity,
starvation

fan¹ *n* 1 = **blower**, air conditioner,
ventilator ♦ *v* 2 = **blow**, air-condition,
cool, refresh, ventilate

fan² *n Inf* = **supporter**, admirer, aficionado,
buff (*inf*), devotee, enthusiast, follower,
lover

fanatic *n* = **extremist**, activist, bigot,
militant, zealot

fancy *adj* 1 = **elaborate**, baroque,
decorative, embellished, extravagant,
intricate, ornamental, ornate ≠ **common** ♦
n 3 = **whim**, caprice, desire, humour, idea,
impulse, inclination, notion, thought, urge
4 = **delusion**, chimera, daydream, dream,
fantasy, vision ♦ *v* 5 *Inf* = **be attracted to**,
be captivated by, like, lust after, take a
liking to, take to 6 *Inf* = **wish for**, crave,
desire, hanker after, hope for, long for,

instruments.

fang n 1 snake's tooth which injects poison.
2 long pointed tooth.

fantasy ❶ n, pl **–sies** 1 far–fetched notion.
2 imagination unrestricted by reality. 3
daydream. 4 fiction with a large fantasy
content. **fantasize** v indulge in daydreams.

far ❶ adv farther or further, farthest or
furthest 1 at, to, or from a great distance.
2 at or to a remote time. 3 very much. ◆
adj 4 remote in space or time. 5 Far East
East Asia. **far–fetched** adj hard to believe.

✔ WORD TIP

Farther is often used, rather than
further, when distance, not time or
effort, is involved.

---

farce ❶ n 1 boisterous comedy. 2 ludicrous
situation. **farcical** adj ludicrous.

fare ❶ n 1 charge for a passenger's
journey. 2 passenger. 3 food provided. ◆ v
4 get on (as specified), e.g. *we fared badly*.

farm ❶ n 1 area of land for growing crops
or rearing livestock. 2 area of land or
water for growing or rearing a specified
animal or plant, e.g. *fish farm*. ◆ v 3
cultivate (land). 4 rear (stock). **farmer** n
farmhouse n **farm out** v send (work) to be
done by others. **farmstead** n farm and its
buildings. **farmyard** n

fart *Taboo* ◆ n 1 emission of gas from the
anus. ◆ v 2 emit gas from the anus.

farther, farthest adv, adj see FAR.

farthing n former British coin equivalent to
a quarter of a penny.

fascia [**fay**–shya] n, pl **–ciae**, **–cias** 1 outer
surface of a dashboard. 2 flat surface
above a shop window.

fascinate ❶ v 1 attract and interest
strongly. 2 make motionless from fear or
awe. **fascinating** adj **fascination** n

fascism [**fash**–iz–zum] n right–wing
totalitarian political system characterized
by state control and extreme nationalism.
fascist adj, n

fashion ❶ n 1 style in clothes, hairstyle,
etc., popular at a particular time. 2 way
something happens or is done. ◆ v 3 form
or make into a particular shape.
fashionable adj currently popular.
fashionably adv

fast¹ ❶ adj 1 (capable of) acting or moving
quickly. 2 done in or lasting a short time.
3 adapted to or allowing rapid movement.
4 (of a clock or watch) showing a time
later than the correct time. 5 dissipated. 6
firmly fixed, fastened, or shut. ◆ adv 7
quickly. 8 soundly, deeply, e.g. *fast asleep*.
9 tightly and firmly. **fast food** food, such
as hamburgers, prepared and served very
quickly.

THESAURUS

thirst for, yearn for 7, 8 = **suppose**,
believe, conjecture, imagine, reckon,
think, think likely

fantasy n 1, 3 = **daydream**, dream, flight
of fancy, illusion, mirage, pipe dream,
reverie, vision 2 = **imagination**, creativity,
fancy, invention, originality

far adv 1 = **a long way**, afar, a good way, a
great distance, deep, miles 3 = **much**,
considerably, decidedly, extremely,
greatly, incomparably, very much ◆ adj
4 = **remote**, distant, faraway, far-flung,
far-off, outlying, out–of–the–way ≠ **close**

farce n 1 = **comedy**, buffoonery, burlesque,
satire, slapstick 2 = **mockery**, joke,
nonsense, parody, sham, travesty

fare n 1 = **charge**, price, ticket money
3 = **food**, provisions, rations, sustenance,
victuals ◆ v 4 = **get on**, do, get along,
make out, manage, prosper

farm n 1 = **smallholding**, croft (*Scot*),
farmstead, grange, homestead, plantation,
ranch (*chiefly N Amer*) ◆ v 3 = **cultivate**,
plant, work

fascinate v 1 = **entrance**, absorb, beguile,
captivate, engross, enthral, hold
spellbound, intrigue 2 = **transfix**, rivet

fashion n 1 = **style**, craze, custom, fad,
look, mode, rage, trend, vogue
2 = **method**, manner, mode, style, way ◆
v 3 = **make**, construct, create, forge, form,
manufacture, mould, shape

fast² ❶ *v* **1** go without food, esp. for religious reasons. ◆ *n* **2** period of fasting.

fasten ❶ *v* **1** make or become firmly fixed or joined. **2** close by fixing in place or locking. **3** (foll. by *on*) direct (one's attention) towards. **fastener, fastening** *n* device that fastens.

fastidious *adj* **1** very fussy about details. **2** excessively concerned with cleanliness.

fat ❶ *adj* **fatter, fattest 1** having excess flesh on the body. **2** (of meat) containing a lot of fat. **3** thick. **4** profitable. ◆ *n* **5** extra flesh on the body. **6** oily substance obtained from animals or plants. **fatten** *v* (cause to) become fat. **fatty** *adj* containing fat. **fathead** *n Informal* stupid person.

fate ❶ *n* **1** power supposed to predetermine events. **2** inevitable fortune that befalls a person or thing. **fated** *adj* **1** destined. **2** doomed to death or destruction. **fateful** *adj* having important, usu. disastrous, consequences.

father ❶ *n* **1** male parent. **2** person who founds a line or family. **3** man who starts,

creates, or invents something. **4** (F–) God. **5** (F–) title of some priests. ◆ *v* **6** be the father of (offspring). **fatherhood** *n* **fatherless** *adj* **fatherly** *adj* **father-in-law** *n, pl* **fathers-in-law** father of one's husband or wife. **fatherland** *n* one's native country.

fathom ❶ *n* **1** unit of measurement of the depth of water, equal to six feet. ◆ *v* **2** understand. **fathomless** *adj* too deep or difficult to fathom.

fatigue ❶ [fat-**eeg**] *n* **1** extreme physical or mental tiredness. **2** weakening of a material due to stress. **3** soldier's nonmilitary duty. ◆ *v* **4** tire out.

fatuous ❶ *adj* foolish.

fault ❶ *n* **1** responsibility for something wrong. **2** defect or flaw. **3** mistake or error. **4** *Geology* break in layers of rock. **5** *Tennis, squash, etc.* invalid serve. ◆ *v* **6** criticize or blame. **at fault** guilty of error. **find fault with** seek out minor imperfections in. **to a fault** excessively. **faulty** *adj* **faultless** *adj*

———————— THESAURUS ————————

fast¹ *adj* **1–3 = quick,** brisk, fleet, flying, hasty, nippy (*Brit inf*), rapid, speedy, swift **5 = dissipated,** dissolute, extravagant, loose, profligate, reckless, self-indulgent, wanton, wild **6 = fixed,** close, fastened, firm, immovable, secure, sound, steadfast, tight ◆ *adv* **8 = quickly,** hastily, hurriedly, in haste, like lightning, rapidly, speedily, swiftly ≠ **slowly 9 = soundly,** deeply, firmly, fixedly, securely, tightly

fast² *v* **1 = go hungry,** abstain, deny oneself, go without food ◆ *n* **2 = fasting,** abstinence

fasten *v* **1, 2 = fix,** affix, attach, bind, connect, join, link, secure, tie

fat *adj* **1 = overweight,** corpulent, heavy, obese, plump, podgy, portly, rotund, stout, tubby ≠ **thin 2 = fatty,** adipose, greasy, oily, oleaginous ◆ *n* **5 = fatness,** blubber, bulk, corpulence, flab, flesh, obesity, paunch

fate *n* **1 = destiny,** chance, divine will, fortune, kismet, nemesis, predestination,

providence **2 = fortune,** cup, horoscope, lot, portion, stars

father *n* **1 = daddy** (*inf*), dad (*inf*), old man (*inf*), pa (*inf*), papa (*old-fashioned inf*), pater, pop (*inf*) **2 = forefather,** ancestor, forebear, predecessor, progenitor **3 = founder,** architect, author, creator, inventor, maker, originator, prime mover **5** (with cap.) **= priest,** padre (*inf*), pastor ◆ *v* **6 = sire,** beget, get, procreate

fathom *v* **2 = understand,** comprehend, get to the bottom of, grasp, interpret

fatigue *n* **1 = tiredness,** heaviness, languor, lethargy, listlessness ◆ *v* **4 = tire,** drain, exhaust, knacker (*sl*), take it out of (*inf*), weaken, wear out, weary ≠ **rest**

fatuous *adj* **= foolish,** brainless, idiotic, inane, ludicrous, mindless, moronic, silly, stupid, witless

fault *n* **1 = responsibility,** accountability, culpability, liability **2 = flaw,** blemish, defect, deficiency, failing, imperfection, shortcoming, weakness, weak point

faun *n* (in Roman legend) creature with a human face and torso and a goat's horns and legs.

fauna *n, pl* **–nas, –nae** animals of a given place or time.

faux pas [**foe pah**] *n, pl* **faux pas** social blunder.

favour ❶ *n* 1 approving attitude. 2 act of goodwill or generosity. 3 partiality. ◆ *v* 4 prefer. 5 regard or treat with especial kindness. 6 support or advocate. **favourable** *adj* **favourite** *n* favoured person or thing.

fawn¹ ❶ *n* 1 young deer. ◆ *adj* 2 light yellowish–brown.

fawn² ❶ *v* 1 (foll. by *on*) seek attention from (someone) by insincere flattery. 2 (of a dog) try to please by a show of extreme affection.

fax *n* 1 electronic system for sending facsimiles of documents by telephone. 2 document sent by this system. ◆ *v* 3 send (a document) by this system.

FBI *US* Federal Bureau of Investigation.

fear ❶ *n* 1 distress or alarm caused by impending danger or pain. 2 something that causes distress. ◆ *v* 3 be afraid of (something or someone). **fear for** feel anxiety about something. **fearful** *adj* 1 feeling fear. 2 causing fear. 3 *Informal* very unpleasant. **fearfully** *adv* **fearless** *adj* **fearsome** *adj* terrifying.

feasible ❶ *adj* able to be done, possible. **feasibly** *adv* **feasibility** *n*

feast ❶ *n* 1 lavish meal. 2 something extremely pleasing. 3 annual religious celebration. ◆ *v* 4 eat a feast. 5 (foll. by *on*) eat a large amount of.

feat ❶ *n* remarkable, skilful, or daring action.

feather *n* 1 one of the barbed shafts forming the plumage of birds. ◆ *v* 2 fit or cover with feathers. 3 turn (an oar) edgeways. **feather in one's cap** achievement one can be pleased with. **feather one's nest** make one's life comfortable. **feathered** *adj* **feathery** *adj* **featherweight** *n* 1 boxer weighing up to

———————— THESAURUS ————————

≠ credit 3 = **mistake**, blunder, error, indiscretion, lapse, oversight, slip ◆ *v* 6 = **criticize**, blame, censure, find fault with, hold (someone) responsible, impugn **at fault** = **guilty**, answerable, blamable, culpable, in the wrong, responsible, to blame **find fault with** = **criticize**, carp at, complain, pick holes in, pull to pieces, quibble, take to task **to a fault** = **excessively**, immoderately, in the extreme, overmuch, unduly

favour *n* 1 = **approval**, approbation, backing, good opinion, goodwill, patronage, support ≠ **disapproval** 2 = **good turn**, benefit, boon, courtesy, indulgence, kindness, service ≠ **wrong** ◆ *v* 4, 5 = **prefer**, incline towards, indulge, reward, side with, smile upon 6 = **support**, advocate, approve, champion, commend, encourage ≠ **oppose**

fawn¹ *adj* 2 = **beige**, buff, greyish–brown, neutral

fawn² *v* 1 (foll. by *on*) = **ingratiate oneself**, crawl, creep, curry favour, dance attendance, flatter, grovel, kowtow, pander to

fear *n* 1 = **dread**, alarm, apprehensiveness, fright, horror, panic, terror, trepidation 2 = **bugbear**, bête noire, bogey, horror, nightmare, spectre ◆ *v* 3 = **be afraid**, dread, shake in one's shoes, shudder at, take fright, tremble at **fear for** = **worry about**, be anxious about, feel concern for

feasible *adj* = **possible**, achievable, attainable, likely, practicable, reasonable, viable, workable

feast *n* 1 = **banquet**, dinner, repast, spread (*inf*), treat 2 = **treat**, delight, enjoyment, gratification, pleasure 3 = **festival**, celebration, fete, holiday, holy day, red–letter day, saint's day ◆ *v* 4 = **eat one's fill**, gorge, gormandize, indulge, overindulge, pig out (*sl*)

feat *n* = **accomplishment**, achievement, act, attainment, deed, exploit, performance

126lb (professional) or 57kg (amateur). **2** insignificant person or thing.

feature ❶ *n* **1** part of the face, such as the eyes. **2** prominent or distinctive part. **3** special article in a newspaper or magazine. **4** main film in a cinema programme. ◆ *v* **5** have as a feature or be a feature in. **6** give prominence to. **featureless** *adj*

Feb. February.

February *n* second month of the year.

feckless ❶ *adj* ineffectual or irresponsible.

federal *adj* **1** of a system in which power is divided between one central government and several regional governments. **2** of the central government of a federation. **federalism** *n* **federalist** *n* **federate** *v* unite in a federation. **federation** *n* **1** union of several states, provinces, etc. **2** association.

fee ❶ *n* **1** charge paid to be allowed to do something. **2** payment for professional services.

feeble ❶ *adj* **1** lacking physical or mental power. **2** unconvincing. **feebleness** *n* **feebly** *adv* **feeble–minded** *adj* unable to think or understand effectively.

feed ❶ *v* **feeding, fed** **1** give food to. **2** give (something) as food. **3** eat. **4** supply or prepare food for. **5** supply (what is needed). ◆ *n* **6** act of feeding. **7** food, esp. for babies or animals. **8** *Informal* meal. **feedback** *n* **1** information received in

response to something done. **2** return of part of the output of an electrical circuit or loudspeaker to its source.

feel ❶ *v* **feeling, felt** **1** have a physical or emotional sensation of. **2** become aware of or examine by touch. **3** believe. ◆ *n* **4** act of feeling. **5** impression. **6** way something feels. **7** sense of touch. **8** instinctive aptitude. **feeler** *n* **1** organ of touch in some animals. **2** remark made to test others' opinion. **feeling** *n* **1** emotional reaction. **2** intuitive understanding. **3** opinion. **4** sympathy, understanding. **5** ability to experience physical sensations. **6** sensation experienced. ◆ *pl* **7** emotional sensitivities. **feel like** wish for, want.

✓ **WORD TIP**

Feel is followed by an adjective when it refers back to the subject: *I feel sick*. Otherwise it is followed by an adverb: *She feels strongly about it*.

feet *n* plural of FOOT.

feign [**fane**] *v* pretend.

feint [**faint**] *n* **1** sham attack or blow meant to distract an opponent. ◆ *v* **2** make a feint.

felicity *n* **1** happiness. **2** (*pl* **–ties**) appropriate expression or style. **felicitations** *pl n* congratulations.

═══════ THESAURUS ═══════

feature *n* **2** = **aspect**, characteristic, facet, factor, hallmark, peculiarity, property, quality, trait **3** = **article**, column, item, piece, report, story **4** = **highlight**, attraction, main item, speciality ◆ *v* **6** = **spotlight**, emphasize, foreground, give prominence to, play up, present, star

feckless *adj* = **irresponsible**, good–for–nothing, hopeless, incompetent, ineffectual, shiftless, worthless

fee *n* = **charge**, bill, payment, remuneration, toll

feeble *adj* **1** = **weak**, debilitated, doddering, effete, frail, infirm, puny, sickly, weedy (*inf*) ≠ **strong** **2** = **flimsy**, inadequate, insufficient, lame, paltry,

pathetic, poor, tame, thin, unconvincing ≠ **successful**

feed *v* **1, 2, 4** = **cater for**, nourish, provide for, provision, supply, sustain, victual, wine and dine **3** = **eat**, devour, exist on, live on, partake of ◆ *n* **7** = **food**, fodder, pasturage, provender **8** *Inf* = **meal**, feast, nosh (*sl*), repast, spread (*inf*)

feel *v* **1** = **experience**, be aware of, notice, observe, perceive **2** = **touch**, caress, finger, fondle, handle, manipulate, paw, stroke **3** = **sense**, be convinced, intuit **4** = **believe**, consider, deem, hold, judge, think ◆ *n* **5** = **impression**, air, ambience, atmosphere, feeling, quality, sense **6** = **texture**, finish, surface, touch

felicitous adj

feline adj 1 of cats. 2 catlike. ♦ n 3 member of the cat family.

fell¹ ❶ v 1 cut down (a tree). 2 knock down.

fell² n Scot & N English a mountain, hill, or moor.

fellow ❶ n 1 Old-fashioned man or boy. 2 comrade or associate. 3 person in the same group or condition. 4 member of a learned society or the governing body of a college. ♦ adj 5 in the same group or condition. **fellowship** n 1 sharing of aims or interests. 2 group with shared aims or interests. 3 feeling of friendliness. 4 paid research post in a college or university.

felon n Criminal law (formerly) person guilty of a felony. **felony** n, pl **–nies** serious crime. **felonious** adj

felt n matted fabric made by bonding fibres by pressure. **felt-tip pen** pen with a writing point made from pressed fibres.

female adj 1 of the sex which bears offspring. 2 (of plants) producing fruits. ♦ n 3 female person or animal.

feminine ❶ adj 1 having qualities traditionally regarded as suitable for, or typical of, women. 2 of women. 3 belonging to a particular class of grammatical inflection in some languages. **femininity** n **feminism** n advocacy of equal rights for women. **feminist** n, adj

fen ❶ n low-lying flat marshy land.

fence ❶ n 1 barrier of posts linked by wire or wood, enclosing an area. 2 Slang dealer in stolen property. ♦ v 3 enclose with or as if with a fence. 4 fight with swords as a sport. 5 avoid a question. **fencing** n 1 sport of fighting with swords. 2 material for making fences.

fend v fend for oneself provide for oneself. **fend off** v defend oneself against (verbal or physical attack).

fennel n fragrant plant whose seeds, leaves, and root are used in cookery.

feral adj wild.

ferment ❶ n 1 commotion, unrest. ♦ v 2 undergo or cause to undergo fermentation. **fermentation** n reaction in which an organic molecule splits into simpler substances, esp. the conversion of sugar to alcohol.

fern n flowerless plant with fine fronds.

ferocious ❶ adj savagely fierce or cruel. **ferocity** n

ferret n 1 tamed polecat used to catch rabbits or rats. ♦ v **ferreting, ferreted** 2 hunt with ferrets. 3 search around. **ferret out** v find by searching.

ferric, ferrous adj of or containing iron.

ferry ❶ n, pl **–ries** 1 boat for transporting people and vehicles. ♦ v **–rying, –ried** 2 carry by ferry. 3 convey (goods or people).

fertile ❶ adj 1 capable of producing young, crops, or vegetation. 2 highly productive, e.g. a fertile mind. **fertility** n **fertilize** v 1 provide (an animal or plant) with sperm or pollen to bring about

fell¹ v 1 = **cut down**, cut, hew 2 = **knock down**, demolish, level

fellow n 1 Old-fashioned = **man**, bloke (Brit inf), chap (inf), character, guy (inf), individual, person 2, 3 = **associate**, colleague, companion, comrade, partner, peer

feminine adj 1, 2 = **womanly**, delicate, gentle, ladylike, soft, tender ≠ **rough**

fen n = **marsh**, bog, morass, quagmire, slough, swamp

fence n 1 = **barrier**, barricade, defence, hedge, palisade, railings, rampart, wall ♦ v 3 = **enclose**, bound, confine, encircle, pen, protect, surround 5 = **evade**, dodge, equivocate, flannel (Brit inf), parry

ferment n 1 = **commotion**, disruption, excitement, frenzy, furore, stir, tumult, turmoil, unrest, uproar ≠ **quiet**

ferocious adj = **fierce**, bloodthirsty, brutal, cruel, predatory, rapacious, ravening, ruthless, savage, vicious, violent, wild ≠ **calm**

ferry n 1 = **ferry boat**, packet, packet boat ♦ v 2, 3 = **carry**, chauffeur, convey, run, ship, shuttle, transport fertilization. 2 supply (soil) with nutrients. **fertilization** n **fertilizer** n substance added to the soil to increase its productivity.

fervent ⊕ fervid adj intensely passionate and sincere. **fervour** n intensity of feeling.

fester ⊕ v 1 grow worse and increasingly hostile. 2 (of a wound) form pus. 3 rot and decay.

festival ⊕ n 1 organized series of special events or performances. 2 day or period of celebration. **festive** adj of or like a celebration. **festivity** n, pl –ties 1 happy celebration. ◆ pl 2 celebrations.

festoon ⊕ v hang decorations in loops.

fete [fate] n 1 gala, bazaar, etc., usu. held outdoors. ◆ v 2 honour or entertain regally.

fetid adj stinking.

fetish ⊕ n 1 form of behaviour in which sexual pleasure is derived from looking at or handling an inanimate object. 2 thing with which one is excessively concerned. 3 object believed to have magical powers. **fetishism** n **fetishist** n

fetter n 1 chain or shackle for the foot. ◆ pl 2 restrictions. ◆ v 3 restrict. 4 bind in fetters.

fettle n state of health or spirits.

fetus [fee-tuss] n, pl –tuses embryo of a mammal in the later stages of development. **fetal** adj

feud ⊕ n 1 long bitter hostility between two people or groups. ◆ v 2 carry on a feud.

fever ⊕ n 1 (illness causing) high body temperature. 2 nervous excitement. **fevered** adj **feverish** adj 1 suffering from fever. 2 in a state of nervous excitement.

few ⊕ adj not many. **a few** a small number. **quite a few, a good few** several.

✓ **WORD TIP**

Few(er) is used of things that can be counted: *Fewer than five visits.* Compare *less,* which is used for quantity: *It uses less sugar.*

---

fez n, pl **fezzes** brimless tasselled cap, orig. from Turkey.

fiancé [fee-on-say] n man engaged to be married. **fiancée** n fem

fiasco ⊕ n, pl –cos, –coes ridiculous or humiliating failure.

fib ⊕ n 1 trivial lie. ◆ v **fibbing, fibbed** 2 tell a lie. **fibber** n

fibre ⊕ n 1 thread that can be spun into yarn. 2 threadlike animal or plant tissue. 3 fibrous material in food. 4 strength of character. 5 essential substance or nature. **fibrous** adj **fibreglass** n material made of fine glass fibres, used as insulation. **fibre optics** transmission of information by light

---

THESAURUS

fertile adj = **productive**, abundant, fecund, fruitful, luxuriant, plentiful, prolific, rich, teeming ≠ **poor**

fervent, fervid adj = **intense**, ardent, devout, earnest, enthusiastic, heartfelt, impassioned, passionate, vehement

fester v 1 = **intensify**, aggravate, smoulder 2 = **suppurate**, ulcerate 3 = **putrefy**, decay

festival n 1 = **celebration**, carnival, entertainment, fête, gala, jubilee 2 = **holy day**, anniversary, commemoration, feast, fete, fiesta, holiday, red-letter day, saint's day

festoon v = **decorate**, array, deck, drape, garland, hang, swathe, wreathe

fetish n 1, 2 = **fixation**, mania, obsession,

thing (inf) 3 = **talisman**, amulet

feud n 1 = **hostility**, argument, conflict, disagreement, enmity, quarrel, rivalry, row, vendetta ◆ v 2 = **quarrel**, bicker, clash, contend, dispute, fall out, row, squabble, war

fever n 1 = **delirium** 2 = **excitement**, agitation, ferment, fervour, frenzy, restlessness

few adj = **not many**, meagre, negligible, rare, scanty, scarcely any, sparse, sporadic ≠ **many**

fiasco n = **flop** (inf), catastrophe, cock-up (Brit sl), debacle, disaster, failure, mess, washout (inf)

fib n 1 = **lie**, fiction, story, untruth, white lie

along very thin flexible fibres of glass.

fickle ⊕ *adj* changeable, inconstant. **fickleness** *n*

fiction ⊕ *n* **1** literary works of the imagination, such as novels. **2** invented story. **fictional** *adj* **fictionalize** *v* turn into fiction. **fictitious** *adj* **1** not genuine. **2** of or in fiction.

fiddle ⊕ *n* **1** violin. **2** *Informal* dishonest action or scheme. ♦ *v* **3** play the violin. **4** falsify (accounts). **5** move or touch something restlessly. **fiddling** *adj* trivial. **fiddly** *adj* awkward to do or use. **fiddlesticks** *interj* expression of annoyance or disagreement.

fidelity ⊕ *n* **1** faithfulness. **2** accuracy in detail. **3** quality of sound reproduction.

fidget ⊕ *v* **1** move about restlessly. ♦ *n* **2** person who fidgets. ♦ *pl* **3** restlessness. **fidgety** *adj*

field ⊕ *n* **1** enclosed piece of agricultural land. **2** marked off area for sports. **3** area rich in a specified natural resource. **4** all the competitors in a competition. **5** all the

competitors except the favourite. **6** battlefield. **7** sphere of knowledge or activity. **8** place away from the laboratory or classroom where practical work is done. **9** background, as of a flag. **10** area over which electric, gravitational, or magnetic force is exerted. ♦ *v* **11** *Sport* catch and return (a ball). **12** send (a player or team) on to the field. **13** play as a fielder. **14** deal with (a question) successfully. **fielder** *n Sport* player whose task is to field the ball. **field day** day or time of exciting activity. **field glasses** binoculars. **field marshal** army officer of the highest rank. **field sports** hunting, shooting, and fishing. **fieldwork** *n* investigation made in the field as opposed to the classroom or the laboratory.

fiend ⊕ [feend] *n* **1** evil spirit. **2** cruel or wicked person. **3** *Informal* person devoted to something, e.g. *fitness fiend*. **fiendish** *adj*

fierce ⊕ *adj* **1** wild or aggressive. **2** intense or strong. **fiercely** *adv* **fierceness** *n*

fibre *n* = **thread**, filament, pile, strand, texture, wisp **4** *As in moral fibre* = **strength of character**, resolution, stamina, strength, toughness **5** = **essence**, nature, quality, spirit, substance

fickle *adj* = **changeable**, capricious, faithless, inconstant, irresolute, temperamental, unfaithful, variable, volatile

fiction *n* **1** = **tale**, fantasy, legend, myth, novel, romance, story, yarn (*inf*) **2** = **lie**, cock and bull story (*inf*), fabrication, falsehood, invention, tall story, untruth, urban legend, urban myth

fiddle *n* **1** = **violin 2** *Inf* = **fraud**, fix, racket, scam (*sl*), swindle ♦ *v* **4** = **cheat**, cook the books (*inf*), diddle (*inf*), fix, swindle, wangle (*inf*) **5** = **fidget**, finger, interfere with, mess about *or* around, play, tamper with, tinker

fidelity *n* **1** = **loyalty**, allegiance, constancy, dependability, devotion, faithfulness, staunchness, trustworthiness

≠ **infidelity 2** = **accuracy**, closeness, correspondence, exactness, faithfulness, precision, scrupulousness ≠ **inaccuracy**

fidget *v* **1** = **move restlessly**, fiddle (*inf*), fret, squirm, twitch ♦ *pl n* **3** = **restlessness**, fidgetiness, jitters (*inf*), nervousness, unease, uneasiness

field *n* **1** = **meadow**, grassland, green, lea (*poet*), pasture **4** = **competitors**, applicants, candidates, competition, contestants, entrants, possibilities, runners **7** = **speciality**, area, department, discipline, domain, line, province, territory ♦ *v* **11** *Sport* = **retrieve**, catch, pick up, return, stop **14** = **deal with**, deflect, handle, turn aside

fiend *n* **1** = **demon**, devil, evil spirit **2** = **brute**, barbarian, beast, ghoul, monster, ogre, savage **3** *Inf* = **enthusiast**, addict, fanatic, freak (*inf*), maniac

fierce *adj* **1** = **wild**, brutal, cruel, dangerous, ferocious, fiery, furious, menacing, powerful, raging, savage,

fiery ⊕ *adj* **fierier, fieriest 1** consisting of or like fire. **2** easily angered. **3** (of food) very spicy.

fiesta *n* religious festival, carnival.

fifteen *adj, n* five and ten. **fifteenth** *adj, n*

fig *n* **1** soft pear–shaped fruit. **2** tree bearing it.

fight ⊕ *v* **fighting, fought 1** struggle (against) in battle or physical combat. **2** struggle to overcome someone or obtain something. **3** carry on (a battle or contest). **4** make (one's way) somewhere with difficulty. ♦ *n* **5** aggressive conflict between two (groups of) people. **6** quarrel or contest. **7** resistance. **8** boxing match. **fighter** *n* **1** boxer. **2** determined person. **3** aircraft designed to destroy other aircraft. **fight off** *v* **1** drive away (an attacker). **2** struggle to avoid.

figment *n* **figment of one's imagination** imaginary thing.

figure ⊕ *n* **1** numerical symbol. **2** amount expressed in numbers. **3** bodily shape. **4** well–known person. **5** representation in painting or sculpture of a human form. **6** diagram or illustration. **7** set of movements in dancing or skating. **8** *Maths* any combination of lines, planes, points, or curves. ♦ *v* **9** calculate (sums or amounts). **10** *US & Aust* consider, conclude. **11** (usu. foll. by *in*) be included (in). **figure of speech** expression in which words do not have their literal meaning. **figurative** *adj* (of language) abstract, imaginative, or symbolic. **figuratively** *adv* **figurine** *n* statuette. **figurehead** *n* **1** nominal leader. **2** carved bust at the bow of a ship. **figure out** *v* solve or understand.

filament *n* **1** fine wire in a light bulb that gives out light. **2** fine thread.

filch ⊕ *v* steal (small amounts).

file¹ ⊕ *n* **1** box or folder used to keep documents in order. **2** documents in a file. **3** information about a person or subject. **4** line of people one behind the other. **5** *Computers* organized collection of related material. ♦ *v* **6** place (a document) in a file. **7** place (a legal document) on official record. **8** bring a lawsuit, esp. for divorce. **9** walk or march in a line.

file² ⊕ *n* **1** tool with a roughened blade for smoothing or shaping. ♦ *v* **2** shape or smooth with a file. **filings** *pl n* shavings removed by a file.

filial *adj* of or befitting a son or daughter.

filibuster *n* **1** obstruction of legislation by

stormy, strong, tempestuous, vicious, violent ≠ **tranquil 2** = **intense**, cut–throat, keen, relentless, strong

fiery *adj* **1** = **burning**, ablaze, afire, aflame, blazing, flaming, on fire **2** = **excitable**, fierce, hot–headed, impetuous, irascible, irritable, passionate

fight *v* **1** = **battle**, box, clash, combat, do battle, grapple, spar, struggle, tussle, wrestle **2** = **oppose**, contest, defy, dispute, make a stand against, resist, stand up to, withstand **3** = **engage in**, carry on, conduct, prosecute, wage ♦ *n* **5**, **6** = **battle**, clash, conflict, contest, dispute, duel, encounter, struggle, tussle **7** = **resistance**, belligerence, militancy, pluck, spirit

figure *n* **1** = **number**, character, digit, numeral, symbol **2** = **amount**, cost, price, sum, total, value **3** = **shape**, body, build, frame, physique, proportions **4** = **character**, big name, celebrity, dignitary, personality **5**, **6** = **diagram**, design, drawing, illustration, representation, sketch ♦ *v* **9** = **calculate**, compute, count, reckon, tally, tot up, work out **11** (usu. foll. by *in*) = **feature**, act, appear, be featured, contribute to, play a part

filch *v* = **steal**, embezzle, misappropriate, pilfer, pinch (*inf*), take, thieve, walk off with

file¹ *n* **1** = **folder**, case, data, documents, dossier, information, portfolio **4** = **line**, column, queue, row ♦ *v* **6** = **put in place**, document, enter, pigeonhole **7** = **register**, record **9** = **march**, parade, troop

file² *v* **2** = **smooth**, abrade, polish, rasp,

making long speeches. **2** person who filibusters. ◆ v **3** obstruct (legislation) with such delaying tactics.

filigree n **1** delicate ornamental work of gold or silver wire. ◆ adj **2** made of filigree.

fill ❶ v **1** make or become full. **2** occupy completely. **3** plug (a gap). **4** satisfy (a need). **5** hold and perform the duties of (a position). **6** appoint to (a job or position). **one's fill** sufficient for one's needs or wants. **1 filling** n **1** substance that fills a gap or cavity, esp. in a tooth. ◆ adj **2** (of food) substantial and satisfying. **filling station** garage selling petrol, oil, etc.

fillet n **1** boneless piece of meat or fish. ◆ v **filleting, filleted 2** remove the bones from.

fillip n something that adds stimulation or enjoyment.

filly n, pl **–lies** young female horse.

film ❶ n **1** sequence of images projected on a screen, creating the illusion of movement. **2** story told in such a sequence of images. **3** thin strip of light–sensitive cellulose used to make photographic negatives and transparencies. **4** thin sheet or layer. ◆ v **5** photograph with a movie or video camera. **6** make a film of (a scene, story, etc.). **7** cover or become covered with a thin layer. ◆ adj **8** connected with films or the cinema. **filmy** adj very thin, delicate.

filth ❶ n **1** disgusting dirt. **2** offensive material or language. **filthy** adj **filthily** adv **filthiness** n

fin n **1** projection from a fish's body enabling it to balance and swim. **2** vertical tailplane of an aircraft.

final ❶ adj **1** at the end. **2** having no possibility of further change, action, or discussion. ◆ n **3** deciding contest between winners of previous rounds in a competition. ◆ pl **4** last examinations in an educational course. **finally** adv **finality** n **finalist** n competitor in a final. **finalize** v put into final form. **finale** [fin–**nah**–lee] n concluding part of a dramatic performance or musical work.

finance ❶ v **1** provide or obtain funds for. ◆ n **2** management of money, loans, or credits. **3** (provision of) funds. ◆ pl **4** money resources. **financial** adj **financially** adv **financier** n person involved in large–scale financial business. **financial year** twelve–month period used for financial calculations.

finch n, pl **finches** small songbird with a short strong beak.

find ❶ v **finding, found 1** discover by chance. **2** discover by search or effort. **3** become aware of. **4** consider to have a particular quality. **5** experience (a particular feeling). **6** Law pronounce (the defendant) guilty or not guilty. **7** provide, esp. with difficulty. ◆ n **8** person or thing

──────┤ T H E S A U R U S ├──────

rub, scrape, shape

fill v **1** = **stuff**, cram, crowd, glut, pack, stock, supply, swell **2** = **saturate**, charge, imbue, impregnate, pervade, suffuse **3** = **plug**, block, bung, close, cork, seal, stop **5** = **perform**, carry out, discharge, execute, fulfil, hold, occupy **one's fill** = **sufficient**, all one wants, ample, enough, plenty

film n **1, 2** = **movie**, flick (sl), motion picture **4** = **layer**, coating, covering, dusting, membrane, skin, tissue ◆ v **5, 6** = **photograph**, shoot, take, video, videotape

filth n **1** = **dirt**, excrement, grime, muck, refuse, sewage, slime, sludge, squalor **2** = **obscenity**, impurity, indecency, pornography, smut, vulgarity

final adj **1** = **last**, closing, concluding, latest, terminal, ultimate ≠ **first 2** = **conclusive**, absolute, decided, definite, definitive, incontrovertible, irrevocable, settled

finance v **1** = **fund**, back, bankroll (US), guarantee, pay for, subsidize, support, underwrite ◆ n **2** = **economics**, accounts, banking, business, commerce, investment, money

found, esp. when valuable. **finder** n
finding n conclusion from an
investigation. **find out** v 1 gain knowledge
of. 2 detect (a crime, deception, etc.).
fine¹ ❶ adj 1 very good. 2 (of weather)
clear and dry. 3 in good health. 4
satisfactory. 5 of delicate workmanship. 6
thin or slender. 7 subtle or abstruse, e.g. *a
fine distinction*. **finely** adv **fineness** n **finery**
n showy clothing. **fine art** art produced to
appeal to the sense of beauty. **fine–tune** v
make small adjustments to (something) so
that it works really well.
fine² ❶ n 1 payment imposed as a penalty.
♦ v 2 impose a fine on.
finger ❶ n 1 one of the four long jointed
parts of the hand. 2 part of a glove that
covers a finger. 3 quantity of liquid in a
glass as deep as a finger is wide. ♦ v 4
touch or handle with the fingers.
fingering n technique of using the fingers
in playing a musical instrument.
fingerboard n part of a stringed
instrument against which the strings are
pressed. **fingerprint** n 1 impression of the

ridges on the tip of the finger. ♦ v 2 take
the fingerprints of (someone).
finicky adj 1 excessively particular, fussy. 2
overelaborate.
finish ❶ v 1 bring to an end, stop. 2 use
up. 3 bring to a desired or completed
condition. 4 put a surface texture on
(wood, cloth, or metal). 5 defeat or
destroy. ♦ n 6 end, last part. 7 death or
defeat. 8 surface texture.
finite ❶ adj having limits in space, time, or
size.
fiord n same as FJORD.
fir n pyramid–shaped tree with needle–like
leaves and erect cones.
fire ❶ n 1 state of combustion producing
heat, flames, and smoke. 2 burning coal or
wood, or a gas or electric device, used to
heat a room. 3 uncontrolled destructive
burning. 4 shooting of guns. 5 intense
passion, ardour. ♦ v 6 operate (a weapon)
so that a bullet or missile is released. 7
Informal dismiss from employment. 8 bake
(ceramics etc.) in a kiln. 9 excite. **firearm** n
rifle, pistol, or shotgun. 1 **firebrand** n

find v 1 = **discover**, come across,
encounter, hit upon, locate, meet,
recognize, spot, uncover ≠ **lose** 2,
3 = **realise**, detect, discover, learn, note,
notice, observe, perceive ♦ n
8 = **discovery**, acquisition, asset, bargain,
catch, good buy
fine¹ adj 1 = **excellent**, accomplished,
exceptional, exquisite, first–rate,
magnificent, masterly, outstanding,
splendid, superior ≠ **poor** 2 = **sunny**,
balmy, bright, clear, clement, cloudless,
dry, fair, pleasant ≠ **dull** 4 = **satisfactory**,
acceptable, all right, convenient, good,
O.K. or okay (*inf*), suitable 5 = **delicate**,
dainty, elegant, expensive, exquisite,
fragile, quality ≠ **heavy** 6 = **slender**,
diaphanous, flimsy, gauzy, gossamer,
light, sheer, thin 7 = **subtle**, abstruse,
acute, hairsplitting, minute, nice, precise,
sharp
fine² n 1 = **penalty**, damages, forfeit,

punishment ♦ v 2 = **penalize**, mulct,
punish
finger v 4 = **touch**, feel, fiddle with (*inf*),
handle, manipulate, maul, paw (*inf*), toy
with
finish v 1 = **stop**, cease, close, complete,
conclude, end, round off, terminate, wind
up, wrap up (*inf*) ≠ **start** 2 = **consume**,
devour, dispose of, eat, empty, exhaust,
use up 3 = **perfect**, polish, refine 4 = **coat**,
gild, lacquer, polish, stain, texture, veneer,
wax 5 = **destroy**, bring down, defeat,
dispose of, exterminate, overcome, put an
end to, put paid to, rout, ruin ♦ n 6 = **end**,
cessation, close, completion, conclusion,
culmination, denouement, finale, run–in
≠ **beginning** 7 = **defeat**, annihilation,
curtains (*inf*), death, end, end of the road,
ruin 8 = **surface**, lustre, patina, polish,
shine, smoothness, texture
finite adj = **limited**, bounded,
circumscribed, delimited, demarcated,

person who causes unrest. **fire brigade** organized body of people whose job is to put out fires. **fire drill** rehearsal of procedures for escape from a fire. **fire engine** vehicle with apparatus for extinguishing fires. **fire escape** metal staircase or ladder down the outside of a building for escape in the event of fire. **firefighter** *n* member of a fire brigade. **firefly** *n, pl* **-flies** beetle that glows in the dark. **fireguard** *n* protective grating in front of a fire. **fireplace** *n* recess in a room for a fire. **fire power** *Mil* amount a weapon or unit can fire. **fire station** building where firefighters are stationed. **firework** *n* **1** device containing chemicals that is ignited to produce spectacular explosions and coloured sparks. ◆ *pl* **2** show of fireworks. **3** *Informal* outburst of temper. **firing squad** group of soldiers ordered to execute an offender by shooting.

firm ⊕ *adj* **1** not soft or yielding. **2** securely in position. **3** definite. **4** having determination or strength. ◆ *adv* **5** in an unyielding manner, e.g. *hold firm*. ◆ *v* **6** make or become firm. **firmly** *adv* **firmness** *n*

fiscal *adj* of government finances, esp. taxes.

fish *n, pl* **fish, fishes 1** cold-blooded vertebrate with gills, that lives in water. **2** its flesh as food. ◆ *v* **3** try to catch fish. **4** fish in (a particular area of water). **5** (foll. by *for*) grope for and find with difficulty. **6**

(foll. by *for*) seek indirectly. **fisherman** *n* person who catches fish for a living or for pleasure. **fishery** *n, pl* **-eries** area of the sea used for fishing. **fishy** *adj* **1** of or like fish. **2** *Informal* suspicious or questionable. **fishmeal** dried ground fish used as animal feed or fertilizer. **fishmonger** *n* seller of fish. **fishnet** *n* open mesh fabric resembling netting. **fishwife** *n, pl* coarse scolding woman.

fissure ⊕ [**fish**-er] *n* long narrow cleft or crack.

fist *n* clenched hand. **fisticuffs** *pl n* fighting with the fists.

fit¹ ⊕ *v* **fitting, fitted 1** be appropriate or suitable for. **2** be of the correct size or shape (for). **3** adjust so as to make appropriate. **4** try (clothes) on and note any adjustments needed. **5** make competent or ready. **6** correspond with the facts or circumstances. ◆ *adj* **7** appropriate. **8** in good health. **9** worthy or deserving. ◆ *n* **10** way in which something fits. **fitness** *n* **fitter** *n* **1** person skilled in the installation and adjustment of machinery. **2** person who fits garments. **fitting** *adj* **1** appropriate, suitable. ◆ *n* **2** accessory or part. **3** trying on of clothes for size. ◆ *pl* **4** furnishings and accessories in a building. **fitment** *n* detachable part of the furnishings of a room. **fit in** *v* **1** give a place or time to. **2** belong or conform. **fit out** *v* provide with the necessary equipment.

fit² ⊕ *n* **1** sudden attack or convulsion, such

restricted

fire *n* **1, 3** = **flames**, blaze, combustion, conflagration, inferno **4** = **bombardment**, barrage, cannonade, flak, fusillade, hail, salvo, shelling, sniping, volley **5** = **passion**, ardour, eagerness, enthusiasm, excitement, fervour, intensity, sparkle, spirit, verve, vigour ◆ *v* **6** = **shoot**, detonate, discharge, explode, let off, pull the trigger, set off, shell **7** *Inf* = **dismiss**, cashier, discharge, make redundant, sack (*inf*), show the door **9** = **inspire**, animate,

enliven, excite, galvanize, impassion, inflame, rouse, stir

firm *adj* **1** = **hard**, dense, inflexible, rigid, set, solid, solidified, stiff, unyielding ≠ **soft** **2** = **secure**, embedded, fast, fixed, immovable, rooted, stable, tight, unshakable ≠ **loose 3** = **definite 4** = **determined**, adamant, inflexible, resolute, resolved, set on, unbending, unshakable, unyielding ≠ **wavering**

fissure *n* = **crack**, breach, cleft, crevice, fault, fracture, opening, rift, rupture, split

as an epileptic seizure. 2 sudden short
burst or spell.

five *adj, n* one more than four. **fiver** *n*
Informal five–pound note.

fix ❶ *v* 1 make or become firm, stable, or
secure. 2 repair. 3 place permanently. 4
settle definitely. 5 direct (the eyes etc.)
steadily. 6 *Informal* unfairly influence the
outcome of. ◆ *n* 7 *Informal* difficult
situation. 8 ascertaining of the position of
a ship by radar etc. 9 *Slang* injection of a
narcotic drug. **fixed** *adj* **fixedly** *adv*
steadily. **fix up** *v* 1 arrange. 2 provide
(with).

fizz ❶ *v* 1 make a hissing or bubbling noise.
2 give off small bubbles. ◆ *n* 3 hissing or
bubbling noise. 4 releasing of small
bubbles of gas by a liquid. 5 effervescent
drink. **fizzy** *adj* **fizziness** *n*

fizzle *v* make a weak hissing or bubbling
sound. **fizzle out** *v Informal* come to
nothing, fail.

fjord [fee–**ord**] *n* long narrow inlet of the
sea between cliffs, esp. in Norway.

FL Florida.

flabby ❶ *adj* **–bier, –biest** 1 having flabby
flesh. 2 loose or limp.

flag[1] ❶ *n* 1 piece of cloth attached to a
pole as an emblem or signal. ◆ *v* **flagging,
flagged** 2 mark with a flag or sticker. 3
(often foll. by *down*) signal (a vehicle) to
stop by waving the arm. **flag day** day on
which small stickers are sold in the streets
for charity. **flagpole, flagstaff** *n* pole for a
flag. **flagship** *n* 1 admiral's ship. 2 most
important product of an organization.

flag[2] ❶ *v* **flagging, flagged** lose enthusiasm
or vigour.

flag[3], **flagstone** *n* flat paving–stone.

flagon *n* 1 wide bottle for wine or cider. 2
narrow–necked jug for liquid.

flagrant ❶ [**flayg**–rant] *adj* openly
outrageous. **flagrancy** *n*

flail ❶ *v* 1 wave about wildly. 2 beat or
thrash. ◆ *n* 3 tool formerly used for
threshing grain by hand.

flair ❶ *n* 1 natural ability. 2 stylishness.

flak *n* 1 anti–aircraft fire. 2 *Informal* severe
criticism.

flake ❶ *n* 1 small thin piece, esp. chipped
off something. 2 *Aust, NZ & US informal*
unreliable person. ◆ *v* 3 peel off in flakes.

fit[1] *v* 1, 2 = **suit**, accord, belong, conform,
correspond, match, meet, tally 3 = **adapt**,
adjust, alter, arrange, customize, modify,
shape, tweak (*inf*) 5 = **equip**, arm, fit out,
kit out, prepare, provide ◆ *adj*
7 = **appropriate**, apt, becoming, correct,
fitting, proper, right, seemly, suitable
≠ **inadequate** 8 = **healthy**, able–bodied,
hale, in good shape, robust, strapping,
trim, well ≠ **unfit**

fit[2] *n* 1 = **seizure**, attack, bout, convulsion,
paroxysm, spasm 2 = **outbreak**, bout,
burst, outburst, spell

fix *v* 1 = **fasten**, attach, bind, connect, link,
secure, stick, tie 2 = **repair**, correct, mend,
patch up, put to rights, see to 3 = **place**,
embed, establish, implant, install, locate,
plant, position, set 4 = **decide**, agree on,
arrange, arrive at, determine, establish,
set, settle, specify 5 = **focus**, direct 6 *Inf*
= **rig**, fiddle (*inf*), influence, manipulate ◆

n 7 *Inf* = **predicament**, difficulty, dilemma,
embarrassment, mess, pickle (*inf*), plight,
quandary

fizz *v* 1, 2 = **bubble**, effervesce, fizzle, froth,
hiss, sparkle, sputter

flabby *adj* 1 = **baggy** 2 = **limp**, drooping,
flaccid, floppy, loose, pendulous, sagging
≠ **hard**

flag[1] *n* 1 = **banner**, colours, ensign,
pennant, pennon, standard, streamer ◆ *v*
2 = **mark**, indicate, label, note 3 (often
foll. by *down*) = **hail**, signal, warn, wave

flag[2] *v* = **weaken**, abate, droop, fade,
languish, peter out, sag, wane, weary, wilt

flagrant *adj* = **outrageous**, barefaced,
blatant, brazen, glaring, heinous,
scandalous, shameless

flail *v* 1 = **windmill** 2 = **thrash**, beat, thresh

flair *n* 1 = **ability**, aptitude, faculty, feel,
genius, gift, knack, mastery, talent
2 = **style**, chic, dash, discernment,

flaky adj **flake out** v Informal collapse or fall asleep from exhaustion.

flambé [flahm–bay] v **flambéing, flambéed** cook or serve (food) in flaming brandy.

flamboyant ⊕ adj **1** behaving in a very noticeable, extravagant way. **2** very bright and showy. **flamboyance** n

flame ⊕ n **1** luminous burning gas coming from burning material. ♦ v **2** burn brightly. **3** become bright red. **old flame** Informal former sweetheart.

flamenco n, pl **–cos 1** rhythmical Spanish dance accompanied by a guitar and vocalist. **2** music for this dance.

flamingo n, pl **–gos, –goes** large pink wading bird with a long neck and legs.

flammable adj easily set on fire.

✓ **WORD TIP**

This now replaces inflammable in labelling and packaging because inflammable was often mistaken to mean 'not flammable'.

---

flan n open sweet or savoury tart.

flange n projecting rim or collar.

flank ⊕ n **1** part of the side between the hips and ribs. **2** side of a body of troops. ♦ v **3** be at or move along the side of.

flannel n **1** small piece of cloth for washing the face. **2** soft woollen fabric for clothing. **3** Informal evasive talk. ♦ pl **4** trousers made of flannel. ♦ v **–nelling, –nelled 5** Informal talk evasively. **flannelette** n cotton

imitation of flannel.

flap ⊕ v **flapping, flapped 1** move back and forwards or up and down. ♦ n **2** action or sound of flapping. **3** piece of something attached by one edge only. **4** Informal state of excitement or panic.

flapjack n chewy biscuit made with oats.

flare ⊕ v **1** blaze with a sudden unsteady flame. **2** Informal (of temper, violence, or trouble) break out suddenly. **3** (of a skirt or trousers) become wider towards the hem. ♦ n **4** sudden unsteady flame. **5** signal light. ♦ pl **6** flared trousers. **flared** adj (of a skirt or trousers) becoming wider towards the hem.

flash ⊕ n **1** sudden burst of light or flame. **2** sudden occurrence (of intuition or emotion). **3** very short time. **4** brief unscheduled news announcement. **5** Photog small bulb that produces an intense flash of light. ♦ adj **6** (also **flashy**) vulgarly showy. ♦ v **7** (cause to) burst into flame. **8** (cause to) emit light suddenly or intermittently. **9** move very fast. **10** come rapidly (to mind or view). **11** Informal display ostentatiously. **12** Slang expose oneself indecently. **flasher** n Slang man who exposes himself indecently. **flashback** n scene in a book, play, or film, that shows earlier events. **flash flood** sudden short–lived flood. **flashlight** n US torch. **flash point 1** critical point beyond which a situation will inevitably erupt into violence. **2** lowest temperature at which vapour given off by a liquid can ignite.

─── THESAURUS ───

elegance, panache, stylishness, taste

flake n **1** = **chip**, layer, peeling, scale, shaving, sliver, wafer ♦ v **3** = **chip**, blister, peel off

flamboyant adj **1** = **theatrical**, dashing, extravagant, ostentatious, swashbuckling **2** = **showy**, brilliant, colourful, dazzling, elaborate, florid, glamorous, glitzy (sl), ornate

flame n **1** = **fire**, blaze ♦ v **2** = **burn**, blaze, flare, flash, glare, glow, shine

flank n **1** = **side**, hip, loin, thigh

flap v **1** = **flutter**, beat, flail, shake, thrash, vibrate, wag, wave ♦ n **2** = **flutter**, beating, shaking, swinging, swish, waving **4** Inf = **panic**, agitation, commotion, fluster, state (inf), sweat (inf), tizzy (inf)

flare v **1** = **blaze**, burn up, flicker, glare ♦ n **4** = **flame**, blaze, burst, flash, flicker, glare

flash n **1** = **gleam**, blaze, burst, dazzle, flare, flicker, shimmer, spark, streak **3** = **moment**, instant, jiffy (inf), second, split second, trice, twinkling of an eye ♦ adj **6** (also **flashy**) = **showy**, flamboyant,

flask *n* **1** same as VACUUM FLASK. **2** flat bottle for carrying alcoholic drink in the pocket. **3** narrow-necked bottle.

flat¹ ⊕ *adj* **flatter, flattest 1** level and horizontal. **2** even and smooth. **3** (of a tyre) deflated. **4** outright. **5** fixed. **6** without variation or emotion. **7** (of a drink) no longer fizzy. **8** (of a battery) with no electrical charge. **9** *Music* below the true pitch. ◆ *adv* **10** in or into a flat position. **11** completely or absolutely. **12** exactly. **13** *Music* too low in pitch. ◆ *n* **14** flat surface. **15** *Music* symbol lowering the pitch of a note by a semitone. **16** punctured car tyre. **17** level ground. **18** mudbank exposed at low tide. **flat out** with maximum speed or effort. **flatly** *adv* **flatness** *n* **flatten** *v* **flatfish** *n* sea fish, such as the sole, which has a flat body. **1 flat racing** horse racing over level ground with no jumps.

flat² ⊕ *n* set of rooms for living in which are part of a larger building. **flatmate** *n* person with whom one shares a flat.

flatter ⊕ *v* **1** praise insincerely. **2** show to advantage. **3** make (a person) appear more attractive in a picture than in reality. **flatterer** *n* **flattery** *n*

flattie *n* NZ & S Afr informal flat tyre.

flatulent *adj* suffering from or caused by too much gas in the intestines. **flatulence** *n*

flaunt ⊕ *v* display (oneself or one's possessions) arrogantly.

> ✔ **WORD TIP**
> Be careful not to confuse this with *flout* meaning 'disobey'.

flavour ⊕ *n* **1** distinctive taste. **2** distinctive characteristic or quality. ◆ *v* **3** give flavour to. **flavouring** *n* substance used to flavour food.

flaw ⊕ *n* **1** imperfection or blemish. **2** mistake that makes a plan or argument invalid. **flawed** *adj* **flawless** *adj*

flax *n* **1** plant grown for its stem fibres and seeds. **2** its fibres, spun into linen thread. **flaxen** *adj* (of hair) pale yellow.

flay *v* **1** strip the skin off. **2** criticize severely.

flea *n* small wingless jumping bloodsucking insect. **flea market** market for cheap goods. **fleapit** *n* Informal shabby cinema or theatre.

fleck *n* **1** small mark, streak, or speck. ◆ *v* **2** speckle.

THESAURUS

garish, gaudy, glitzy (*sl*), jazzy (*inf*), ostentatious, snazzy (*inf*), tacky (*inf*), tasteless, vulgar ◆ *v* **7** = **blaze**, flare **8** = **gleam**, flicker, glare, shimmer, sparkle, twinkle **9** = **speed**, dart, dash, fly, race, shoot, streak, whistle, zoom **11** *Inf* = **show**, display, exhibit, expose, flaunt, flourish

flat¹ *adj* **1, 2** = **even**, horizontal, level, levelled, low, smooth ≠ **broken**
3 = **punctured**, blown out, burst, collapsed, deflated, empty **4** = **absolute**, categorical, downright, explicit, out-and-out, positive, unequivocal, unqualified **6** = **dull**, boring, dead, lacklustre, lifeless, monotonous, tedious, tiresome, uninteresting ≠ **exciting** ◆ *adv*
11 = **completely**, absolutely, categorically, exactly, point blank, precisely, utterly **flat**

out = **at full speed**, all out, at full tilt, for all one is worth, hell for leather (*inf*)

flat² *n* = **apartment**, rooms

flatter *v* **1** = **praise**, butter up, compliment, pander to, soft-soap (*inf*), sweet-talk (*inf*), wheedle **2** = **suit**, become, do something for, enhance, set off, show to advantage

flaunt *v* = **show off**, brandish, display, exhibit, flash about, flourish, parade, sport (*inf*)

flavour *n* **1** = **taste**, aroma, flavouring, piquancy, relish, savour, seasoning, smack, tang, zest ≠ **blandness 2** = **quality**, character, essence, feel, feeling, style, tinge, tone ◆ *v* **3** = **season**, ginger up, imbue, infuse, leaven, spice

flaw *n* **1** = **weakness**, blemish, chink in one's armour, defect, failing, fault, imperfection, weak spot

flee v fleeing, fled run away (from).

fleece n 1 sheep's coat of wool. 2 sheepskin used as a lining for coats etc. 3 warm polyester fabric. 4 jacket or top made of this fabric. ◆ v 5 defraud or overcharge. **fleecy** adj made of or like fleece.

fleet[1] n 1 number of warships organized as a unit. 2 number of vehicles under the same ownership.

fleet[2] adj swift in movement. **fleeting** adj rapid and soon passing.

flesh n 1 soft part of a human or animal body. 2 Informal excess fat. 3 meat of animals as opposed to fish or fowl. 4 thick soft part of a fruit or vegetable. 5 human body as opposed to the soul. **in the flesh** in person, actually present. **one's own flesh and blood** one's family. **flesh-coloured** adj yellowish–pink. **fleshy** adj 1 plump. 2 like flesh. **flesh wound** wound affecting only superficial tissue.

flex n 1 flexible insulated electric cable. ◆ v 2 bend. **flexible** adj 1 easily bent. 2 adaptable. **flexibly** adv **flexibility** n **flexitime** n system permitting variation in starting and finishing times of work.

flick v 1 touch or move with the finger or hand in a quick movement. 2 move with a short sudden movement, often repeatedly. ◆ n 3 tap or quick stroke. ◆ pl 4 Slang the cinema. **flick through** v look at (a book or magazine) quickly or idly.

flicker v 1 shine unsteadily or intermittently. 2 move quickly to and fro. ◆ n 3 unsteady brief light. 4 brief faint indication.

flight[1] n 1 journey by air. 2 act or manner of flying through the air. 3 group of birds or aircraft flying together. 4 aircraft flying on a scheduled journey. 5 set of stairs between two landings. 6 stabilizing feathers or plastic fins on an arrow or dart. **flight deck 1** crew compartment in an airliner. **2** runway deck on an aircraft carrier. **flight recorder** electronic device in an aircraft storing information about its flight.

flight[2] n act of running away.

flimsy adj –sier, –siest 1 not strong or substantial. 2 thin. 3 not very convincing. **flimsily** adv **flimsiness** n

flinch v draw back or wince, as from pain. **flinch from** v shrink from or avoid.

fling v flinging, flung 1 throw, send, or move forcefully or hurriedly. ◆ n 2 spell of self–indulgent enjoyment. 3 brief romantic or sexual relationship.

flee v = **run away**, bolt, depart, escape, fly, make one's getaway, scarper (Brit sl), take flight, take off (inf), take to one's heels, turn tail

fleet[1] n 1 = **navy**, armada, flotilla, task force

fleet[2] adj = **swift**, fast, flying, mercurial, meteoric, nimble, nimble–footed, quick, rapid, speedy, winged

flesh n 1 = **meat**, tissue 2 = **fat**, brawn, weight 5 = **physical nature**, carnality, flesh and blood, human nature **one's own flesh and blood = family**, blood, kin, kinsfolk, kith and kin, relations, relatives

flick v 1 = **strike**, dab, flip, hit, tap, touch **flick through = browse**, flip through, glance at, skim, skip, thumb

flicker v 1 = **twinkle**, flare, flash, glimmer, gutter, shimmer, sparkle 2 = **flutter**, quiver, vibrate, waver ◆ n 3 = **glimmer**, flare, flash, gleam, spark 4 = **trace**, breath, glimmer, iota, spark

flight[1] n 1 = **journey**, trip, voyage 2 = **aviation**, aeronautics, flying 3 = **flock**, cloud, formation, squadron, swarm, unit

flight[2] n = **escape**, departure, exit, exodus, fleeing, getaway, retreat, running away

flimsy adj 1 = **fragile**, delicate, frail, insubstantial, makeshift, rickety, shaky ≠ **strong** 2 = **thin**, gauzy, gossamer, light, sheer, transparent 3 = **unconvincing**, feeble, implausible, inadequate, pathetic, poor, unsatisfactory, weak

flinch v = **recoil**, cower, cringe, draw back, quail, shirk, shrink, shy away, wince

fling v 1 = **throw**, cast, catapult, heave, hurl, propel, sling, toss ◆ n 2 = **binge** (inf),

flint n 1 hard grey stone. 2 piece of this. 3 small piece of an iron alloy, used in cigarette lighters. **flinty** adj 1 cruel. 2 of or like flint.

flip ⊕ v **flipping, flipped** 1 throw (something small or light) carelessly. 2 turn (something) over. 3 (also **flip one's lid**) Slang fly into an emotional state. ◆ n 4 snap or tap. ◆ adj 5 Informal flippant. **flipper** n 1 limb of a sea animal adapted for swimming. 2 one of a pair of paddle–like rubber devices worn on the feet to help in swimming. **flip–flop** n rubber–soled sandal held on by a thong between the big toe and the next toe.

flirt ⊕ v 1 behave as if sexually attracted to someone. 2 consider lightly, toy (with). ◆ n 3 person who flirts. **flirtation** n **flirtatious** adj

flit v **flitting, flitted** 1 move lightly and rapidly. 2 Scot move house. 3 Informal depart hurriedly and secretly. ◆ n 4 act of flitting.

float ⊕ v 1 rest on the surface of a liquid. 2 move lightly and freely. 3 move about aimlessly. 4 launch (a company). 5 offer for sale on the stock market. 6 allow (a currency) to fluctuate against other currencies. ◆ n 7 light object used to help someone or something float. 8 indicator on a fishing line that moves when a fish

bites. 9 decorated lorry in a procession. 10 small delivery vehicle. 11 sum of money used for minor expenses or to provide change. **floating** adj 1 moving about, changing, e.g. floating population. 2 (of a voter) not committed to one party.

flock ⊕ n 1 number of animals of one kind together. 2 large group of people. 3 Christianity congregation. ◆ v 4 gather in a crowd.

floe n sheet of floating ice.

flog ⊕ v **flogging, flogged** 1 beat with a whip or stick. 2 Slang sell. **flogging** n

flood ⊕ n 1 overflow of water onto a normally dry area. 2 large amount of water. 3 rising of the tide. ◆ v 4 cover or become covered with water. 5 fill to overflowing. 6 come in large numbers or quantities. **floodgate** n gate used to control the flow of water. **floodlight** n 1 lamp that casts a broad intense beam of light. ◆ v **–lighting, –lit** 2 illuminate by floodlight.

floor ⊕ n 1 lower surface of a room. 2 level of a building. 3 flat bottom surface. 4 (right to speak in) a legislative hall. ◆ v 5 knock down. 6 Informal disconcert or defeat. **floored** adj covered with a floor. **flooring** n material for floors. **floor show** entertainment in a nightclub.

flop ⊕ v **flopping, flopped** 1 bend, fall, or

bash, good time, party, rave–up (Brit sl), spree

flip v 1, 2 = **toss**, flick, spin, throw ◆ n 4 = **snap**

flirt v 1 = **chat up** (inf), lead on, make advances, make eyes at, make sheep's eyes at, philander 2 = **toy with**, consider, dabble in, entertain, expose oneself to, give a thought to, play with, trifle with ◆ n 3 = **tease**, coquette, heart–breaker, philanderer

float v 1 = **be buoyant**, bob, sail ≠ **settle** 2 = **glide**, hang, hover, move gently, slide, slip along 3 = **drift** 4 = **launch**, get going, promote, set up ≠ **cancel**

flock n 1 = **herd**, colony, drove, flight,

gaggle, skein 2 = **crowd**, collection, company, gathering, group, herd, host, mass 3 Christianity = **congregation** ◆ v 4 = **gather**, collect, congregate, converge, crowd, herd, huddle, mass, throng

flog v 1 = **beat**, flagellate, flay, lash, scourge, thrash, trounce, whack, whip

flood n 1 = **overflow**, deluge, downpour, inundation 2 = **torrent**, flow, rush, stream 3 = **tide**, spate ◆ v 4 = **immerse**, drown, engulf, inundate, overwhelm, pour over, submerge, surge, swamp 5 = **overflow**, fill, saturate

floor n 2 = **tier**, level, stage, storey ◆ v 5 = **knock down**, deck (sl), prostrate 6 Inf = **disconcert**, baffle, bewilder, confound, collapse loosely or carelessly. **2** *Informal* fail. ◆ *n* **3** *Informal* failure. **4** flopping movement. **floppy** *adj* hanging downwards, loose. **floppy disk** *Computers* flexible magnetic disk that stores information.

flora *n* plants of a given place or time.

floret *n* small flower forming part of a composite flower head.

florid ❶ *adj* **1** with a red or flushed complexion. **2** ornate.

floss *n* fine silky fibres.

flotilla *n* small fleet or fleet of small ships.

flotsam ❶ *n* floating wreckage. **flotsam and jetsam 1** odds and ends. **2** homeless or vagrant people.

flounce¹ *v* **1** go with emphatic movements. ◆ *n* **2** flouncing movement.

flounce² *n* ornamental frill on a garment.

flounder¹ ❶ *v* **1** move with difficulty, as in mud. **2** behave or speak in a bungling or hesitating manner.

flounder² *n* edible flatfish.

flour *n* **1** powder made by grinding grain, esp. wheat. ◆ *v* **2** sprinkle with flour. **floury** *adj*

flourish ❶ *v* **1** be active, successful, or widespread. **2** be at the peak of development. **3** wave (something)

dramatically. ◆ *n* **4** dramatic waving motion. **5** ornamental curly line in writing. **flourishing** *adj*

flow ❶ *v* **1** (of liquid) move in a stream. **2** (of blood or electricity) circulate. **3** proceed smoothly. **4** hang loosely. **5** be abundant. ◆ *n* **6** act, rate, or manner of flowing. **7** continuous stream or discharge. **flow chart** diagram showing a sequence of operations in a process.

flower ❶ *n* **1** part of a plant that produces seeds. **2** plant grown for its colourful flowers. **3** best or finest part. ◆ *v* **4** produce flowers, bloom. **5** reach full growth or maturity. **in flower** with flowers open. **flowered** *adj* decorated with a floral design. **flowery** *adj* **1** decorated with a floral design. **2** (of language or style) elaborate. **flowerbed** *n* piece of ground for growing flowers.

fl. oz. fluid ounce(s).

flu *n* short for INFLUENZA.

fluctuate ❶ *v* change frequently and erratically. **fluctuation** *n*

flue *n* passage or pipe for smoke or hot air.

fluent ❶ *adj* **1** able to speak or write with ease. **2** spoken or written with ease. **fluency** *n*

fluff ❶ *n* **1** soft fibres. **2** *Informal* mistake. ◆

─────┤ THESAURUS ├─────

defeat, dumbfound, perplex, puzzle, stump, throw (*inf*)

flop *v* **1** = **fall**, collapse, dangle, droop, drop, sag, slump **2** *Inf* = **fail**, come unstuck, fall flat, fold (*inf*), founder, go belly–up (*sl*), misfire ≠ **work** ◆ *n* **3** *Inf* = **failure**, debacle, disaster, fiasco, nonstarter, washout (*inf*) ≠ **hit**

florid *adj* **1** = **flushed**, blowsy, rubicund, ruddy ≠ **pale 2** = **ornate**, baroque, flamboyant, flowery, high–flown, overelaborate ≠ **plain**

flotsam *n* = **debris**, detritus, jetsam, junk, odds and ends, wreckage

flounder¹ *v* **1** = **struggle**, fumble, grope, stumble, thrash, toss

flourish *v* **1, 2** = **thrive**, bloom, blossom, boom, flower, grow, increase, prosper,

succeed ≠ **fail 3** = **wave**, brandish, display, flaunt, shake, wield ◆ *n* **4** = **wave 5** = **ornamentation**, curlicue, decoration, embellishment, plume, sweep

flow *v* **1** = **pour**, cascade, flood, gush, rush, stream, surge, sweep **2** = **run**, circulate, course, move, roll **3** = **issue**, arise, emanate, emerge, proceed, result, spring ◆ *n* **6** = **course**, current, drift, flood, flux, outpouring, spate, tide **7** = **stream**

flower *n* **1, 2** = **bloom**, blossom, efflorescence **3** = **elite**, best, cream, pick ◆ *v* **4** = **bloom**, blossom, flourish, open, unfold **5** = **mature**

fluctuate *v* = **change**, alternate, oscillate, seesaw, shift, swing, vary, veer, waver

fluent *adj* **1** = **flowing**, articulate, natural, smooth, voluble, well–versed ≠ **halting**

v **3** make or become soft and puffy. **4** *Informal* make a mistake. **fluffy** *adj*

fluid ❶ *n* **1** substance able to flow and change its shape; a liquid or a gas. ♦ *adj* **2** able to flow or change shape easily. **fluidity** *n* **fluid ounce** one twentieth of a pint.

fluke ❶ *n* accidental stroke of luck. **fluky** *adj*

flummox *v* puzzle or confuse.

flunky, flunkey *n, pl* **flunkies, flunkeys 1** servile person. **2** manservant who wears a livery.

fluoride *n* compound containing fluorine. **fluoridate** *v* add fluoride to (water) as protection against tooth decay. **fluoridation** *n*

flurry ❶ *n, pl* **-ries 1** sudden commotion. **2** gust of rain or wind or fall of snow. ♦ *v* **-rying, -ried 3** confuse.

flush¹ ❶ *v* **1** blush or cause to blush. **2** send water through (a toilet or pipe) so as to clean it. **3** elate. ♦ *n* **4** blush. **5** rush of water. **6** excitement or elation. **flushed** *adj*

flush² ❶ *adj* **1** level with the surrounding surface. **2** *Informal* having plenty of money.

fluster ❶ *v* **1** make nervous or upset. ♦ *n* **2** nervous or upset state.

flute *n* **1** wind instrument consisting of a tube with sound holes and a mouth hole in the side. **2** tall narrow wineglass. **fluted**

adj having decorative grooves.

flutter ❶ *v* **1** wave rapidly. **2** flap the wings. **3** move quickly and irregularly. **4** (of the heart) beat abnormally quickly. ♦ *n* **5** flapping movement. **6** nervous agitation. **7** *Informal* small bet. **8** abnormally fast heartbeat.

flux *n* **1** constant change or instability. **2** flow or discharge. **3** substance mixed with metal to assist in fusion.

fly¹ ❶ *v* **flying, flew, flown 1** move through the air on wings or in an aircraft. **2** control the flight of. **3** float, flutter, display, or be displayed in the air. **4** transport or be transported by air. **5** move quickly or suddenly. **6** (of time) pass rapidly. **7** flee. ♦ *n, pl* **flies 8** (often pl) fastening at the front of trousers. **9** flap forming the entrance to a tent. ♦ *pl* **10** space above a stage, used for storage. **flyer, flier** *n* **1** small advertising leaflet. **2** aviator. **fly-by-night** *adj Informal* unreliable or untrustworthy. **flyleaf** *n* blank leaf at the beginning or end of a book. **flyover** *n* road passing over another by a bridge. **fly-past** *n* ceremonial flight of aircraft. **flywheel** *n* heavy wheel regulating the speed of a machine.

fly² *n, pl* **flies** two-winged insect. **flycatcher** *n* small insect-eating songbird. **fly-fishing** *n* fishing with an artificial fly as a lure. **flypaper** *n* paper with a sticky poisonous coating, used to kill flies. **flyweight** *n*

2 = **effortless**, easy

fluff *n* **1** = **fuzz**, down, nap, pile ♦ *v* **4** *Inf* = **mess up** (*inf*), bungle, make a mess off, muddle, spoil

fluid *n* **1** = **liquid**, liquor, solution ≠ **set** ♦ *adj* **2** = **liquid**, flowing, liquefied, melted, molten, runny, watery

fluke *n* = **stroke of luck**, accident, chance, coincidence, lucky break, quirk of fate, serendipity

flurry *n* **1** = **commotion**, ado, bustle, disturbance, excitement, flutter, fuss, stir **2** = **gust**, squall

flush¹ *v* **1** = **blush**, colour, glow, go red, redden **2** = **rinse out**, cleanse, flood, hose

down, wash out ♦ *n* **4** = **blush**, colour, glow, redness, rosiness

flush² *adj* **1** = **level**, even, flat, square, true **2** *Inf* = **wealthy**, in the money (*inf*), moneyed, rich, well-heeled (*inf*), well-off

fluster *v* **1** = **upset**, agitate, bother, confuse, disturb, perturb, rattle (*inf*), ruffle, unnerve ♦ *n* **2** = **turmoil**, disturbance, dither, flap (*inf*), flurry, flutter, furore, state (*inf*)

flutter *v* **2** = **beat**, flap **3** = **tremble**, quiver, ripple, waver **4** = **palpitate** ♦ *n* **5** = **vibration**, quiver, shiver, shudder, tremble, tremor, twitching **6** = **agitation**, commotion, confusion, dither, excitement, boxer weighing up to 112lb (professional) or 51kg (amateur).

foal n 1 young of a horse or related animal. ◆ v 2 give birth to a foal.

foam ❶ n 1 mass of small bubbles on a liquid. 2 frothy saliva. 3 light spongelike solid used for insulation, packing, etc. ◆ v 4 produce foam. **foamy** adj

fob n 1 short watch chain. 2 small pocket in a waistcoat.

focus ❶ n, pl **–cuses, –ci** [–sye] 1 point at which light or sound waves converge. 2 state of an optical image when it is clearly defined. 3 state of an instrument producing such an image. 4 centre of interest or activity. ◆ v **–cusing, –cused** or **–cussing, –cussed** 5 bring or come into focus. 6 concentrate (on). **focal** adj of or at a focus.

fodder n feed for livestock.

foe ❶ n enemy, opponent.

fog ❶ n 1 mass of condensed water vapour in the lower air, often greatly reducing visibility. ◆ v **fogging, fogged** 2 cover with steam. **foggy** adj **foghorn** n large horn sounded to warn ships in fog.

fogey, fogy n, pl **–geys, –gies** old-fashioned person.

foible n minor weakness or slight peculiarity.

foil¹ ❶ v ruin (someone's plan).

foil² ❶ n 1 metal in a thin sheet. 2 anything which sets off another thing to advantage.

foil³ n light slender flexible sword tipped with a button.

foist ❶ v (foll. by on or upon) force or impose on.

fold¹ ❶ v 1 bend so that one part covers another. 2 interlace (the arms). 3 clasp (in the arms). 4 Cooking mix gently. 5 Informal fail or go bankrupt. ◆ n 6 folded piece or part. 7 mark, crease, or hollow made by folding. **folder** n piece of folded cardboard for holding loose papers.

fold² n 1 enclosure for sheep. 2 church or its members.

foliage n leaves.

folio n, pl **–lios** 1 sheet of paper folded in half to make two leaves of a book. 2 book made up of such sheets. 3 page number.

folk ❶ n 1 people in general. 2 race of people. 3 pl 4 relatives. **folksy** adj simple and unpretentious. **folk dance** traditional country dance. **folklore** n traditional beliefs and stories of a people. 1 **folk song** 1 song handed down among the common people. 2 modern song like this. **folk singer**

follicle n small cavity in the body, esp. one from which a hair grows.

follow ❶ v 1 go or come after. 2 be a logical or natural consequence of. 3 keep

───────┤ THESAURUS ├───────

fluster, state (inf) 8 = **palpitation**

fly¹ v 1 = **take wing**, flit, flutter, hover, sail, soar, wing 2 = **pilot**, control, manoeuvre, operate 3 = **display**, flap, float, flutter, show, wave 5 = **rush**, career, dart, dash, hurry, race, shoot, speed, sprint, tear 6 = **pass**, elapse, flit, glide, pass swiftly, roll on, run its course, slip away 7 = **flee**, escape, get away, run for it, skedaddle (inf), take to one's heels

foam n 1 = **froth**, bubbles, head, lather, spray, spume, suds ◆ v 4 = **bubble**, boil, effervesce, fizz, froth, lather

focus n 4 = **centre**, focal point, heart, hub, target ◆ v 6 = **concentrate**, aim, centre, direct, fix, pinpoint, spotlight, zoom in

foe n = **enemy**, adversary, antagonist, opponent, rival

fog n 1 = **mist**, gloom, miasma, murk, peasouper (inf), smog

foil¹ v = **thwart**, balk, counter, defeat, disappoint, frustrate, nullify, stop

foil² n 2 = **contrast**, antithesis, complement

foist v (foll. by on or upon) = **impose**, fob off, palm off, pass off, sneak in, unload

fold¹ v 1 = **bend**, crease, double over 5 Inf = **go bankrupt**, collapse, crash, fail, go bust (inf), go to the wall, go under, shut down ◆ n 7 = **crease**, bend, furrow, overlap, pleat, wrinkle

folk n 1 = **people** 2 = **race**, clan, tribe ◆ pl 4 = **family**, kin, kindred to the course or track of. **4** act in accordance with. **5** accept the ideas or beliefs of. **6** understand. **7** have a keen interest in. **follower** n disciple or supporter. **following** adj **1** about to be mentioned. **2** next in time. ♦ n **3** group of supporters. ♦ prep **4** as a result of. **5** follow up v **1** investigate. **2** do a second, often similar, thing after (a first). **follow–up** n something done to reinforce an initial action.

folly ❶ n, pl **–lies 1** foolishness. **2** foolish action or idea. **3** useless extravagant building.

foment [foam–**ent**] v encourage or stir up (trouble).

fond ❶ adj **1** tender, loving. **2** unlikely to be realized, e.g. *a fond hope*. **fond of** having a liking for. **fondness** n

fondant n (sweet made from) flavoured paste of sugar and water.

fondle ❶ v caress.

font n bowl in a church for baptismal water.

fontanelle n soft membranous gap between the bones of a baby's skull.

food ❶ n what one eats, solid nourishment. **foodie** n Informal gourmet. **foodstuff** n substance used as food.

fool¹ ❶ n **1** person lacking sense or judgment. **2** person made to appear ridiculous. **3** Hist jester, clown. ♦ v **4** deceive (someone). **foolish** adj unwise, silly, or absurd. **foolishness** n **fool around** v act or play irresponsibly or aimlessly. **foolproof** adj unable to fail.

fool² n dessert of puréed fruit mixed with cream.

foot n, pl **feet 1** part of the leg below the ankle. **2** unit of length of twelve inches (0.3048 metre). **3** lowest part of anything. **4** unit of poetic rhythm. **foot the bill** pay the entire cost. **footage** n amount of film used. **foot–and–mouth disease** infectious viral disease of sheep, cattle, etc. **football** n game played by two teams kicking a ball in an attempt to score goals. **footbridge** n bridge for pedestrians. **footfall** n sound of a footstep. **foothills** pl n hills at the foot of a mountain. **foothold** n **1** secure position from which progress may be made. **2** small place giving a secure grip for the foot. **footlights** pl n lights across the front of a stage. **footloose** adj free from ties. **footman** n male servant in uniform. **footnote** n note printed at the foot of a page. **footpath** n **1** narrow path for walkers only. **2** Aust raised space alongside

follow v **1** = **come after**, come next, succeed, supersede, supplant, take the place of ≠ **lead 2** = **accompany**, attend, escort, tag along **3** = **result**, arise, develop, ensue, flow, issue, proceed, spring **4** = **pursue**, chase, dog, hound, hunt, shadow, stalk, track, trail ≠ **avoid 5** = **obey**, be guided by, conform, heed, observe ≠ **reject 7** = **understand**, appreciate, catch on (inf), comprehend, fathom, grasp, realize, take in **8** = **be interested in**, cultivate, keep abreast of, support

folly n **1** = **foolishness**, imprudence, indiscretion, lunacy, madness, nonsense, rashness, stupidity

fond adj **1** = **loving**, adoring, affectionate, amorous, caring, devoted, doting,

indulgent, tender, warm ≠ **indifferent 2** = **foolish**, deluded, delusive, empty, naive, overoptimistic, vain ≠ **sensible fond of** = **keen on**, addicted to, attached to, enamoured of, having a soft spot for, hooked on, into (inf), partial to

fondle v = **caress**, cuddle, dandle, pat, pet, stroke

food n = **nourishment**, cuisine, diet, fare, grub (sl), nutrition, rations, refreshment

fool¹ n **1** = **simpleton**, blockhead, dunce, halfwit, idiot, ignoramus, imbecile (inf), numbskull or numbskull, twit (inf, chiefly Brit) ≠ **expert 2** = **dupe**, fall guy (inf), laughing stock, mug (Brit sl), stooge (sl), sucker (sl) **3** Hist = **clown**, buffoon, harlequin, jester ♦ v **4** = **deceive**, beguile, con (inf), delude, dupe, hoodwink, a road, for pedestrians. **footplate** n platform in the cab of a locomotive for the driver. **footprint** n mark left by a foot. **footstep** n **1** step in walking. **2** sound made by walking. **footstool** n low stool used to rest the feet on while sitting. **footwear** n anything worn to cover the feet. **footwork** n skilful use of the feet, as in sport or dancing.

footle v Informal loiter aimlessly. **footling** adj trivial.

for prep **1** indicating a person intended to benefit from or receive something, span of time or distance, person or thing represented by someone, etc., e.g. a gift for you; for five miles; playing for his country. ◆ conj **2** because. **for it** Informal liable to punishment or blame.

forage ❶ v **1** search about (for). ◆ n **2** food for cattle or horses.

foray ❶ n **1** brief raid or attack. **2** first attempt or new undertaking.

forbear ❶ v cease or refrain (from doing something). **forbearance** n tolerance, patience.

forbid ❶ v prohibit, refuse to allow. **forbidden** adj **forbidding** adj severe, threatening.

force ❶ n **1** strength or power. **2** compulsion. **3** Physics influence tending to produce a change in a physical system. **4** mental or moral strength. **5** person or thing with strength or influence. **6** vehemence or intensity. **7** group of people organized for a particular task or duty. ◆ v **8** compel, make (someone) do something. **9** acquire or produce through effort, strength, etc. **10** propel or drive. **11** break open. **12** impose or inflict. **13** cause to grow at an increased rate. **in force 1** having legal validity. **2** in great numbers. **forced** adj **1** compulsory. **2** false or unnatural. **3** due to an emergency. **forceful** adj **1** emphatic and confident. **2** effective. **forcefully** adv **forcible** adj **1** involving physical force or violence. **2** strong and emphatic. **forcibly** adv

forceps pl n surgical pincers.

ford n **1** shallow place where a river may be crossed. ◆ v **2** cross (a river) at a ford.

fore adj **1** in, at, or towards the front. ◆ n **2** front part. **to the fore** in a conspicuous position.

forearm[1] n arm from the wrist to the elbow.

forearm[2] v prepare beforehand.

forebear ❶ n ancestor.

forecast ❶ v **-casting, -cast** or **-casted 1** predict (weather, events, etc.). ◆ n **2** prediction.

forecastle [**foke**–sl] n raised front part of a ship.

mislead, take in, trick

forage v **1** = **search**, cast about, explore, hunt, rummage, scour, seek ◆ n **2** = **fodder**, feed, food, provender

foray n **1** = **raid**, incursion, inroad, invasion, sally, sortie, swoop

forbear v = **refrain**, abstain, cease, desist, hold back, keep from, restrain oneself, stop

forbid v = **prohibit**, ban, disallow, exclude, outlaw, preclude, rule out, veto

force n **1** = **power**, energy, impulse, might, momentum, pressure, strength, vigour ≠ **weakness 2** = **compulsion**, arm–twisting (inf), coercion, constraint, duress, pressure, violence **6** = **intensity**, emphasis, fierceness, vehemence, vigour **7** = **army**, host, legion, patrol, regiment, squad, troop, unit ◆ v **8** = **compel**, coerce, constrain, dragoon, drive, impel, make, oblige, press, pressurize **10** = **push**, propel, thrust **11** = **break open**, blast, prise, wrench, wrest **in force 1** = **valid**, binding, current, effective, in operation, operative, working **2** = **in great numbers**, all together, in full strength

forebear n = **ancestor**, father, forefather, forerunner, predecessor

forecast v **1** = **predict**, anticipate, augur, divine, foresee, foretell, prophesy ◆ n **2** = **prediction**, conjecture, guess, prognosis, prophecy

foreclose v take possession of (property bought with borrowed money which has not been repaid). **foreclosure** n

forecourt n courtyard or open space In front of a building.

forefather ⊕ n ancestor.

forefinger n finger next to the thumb.

forefront ⊕ n 1 most active or prominent position. 2 very front.

foregoing ⊕ adj going before, preceding. **foregone conclusion** inevitable result.

foreground n part of a view, esp. in a picture, nearest the observer.

forehand n Tennis etc. stroke played with the palm of the hand facing forward.

forehead n part of the face above the eyebrows.

foreign ⊕ adj 1 not of, or in, one's own country. 2 relating to or connected with other countries. 3 unfamiliar, strange. 4 in an abnormal place or position, e.g. foreign matter. **foreigner** n

foreman n 1 person in charge of a group of workers. 2 leader of a jury.

foremost ⊕ adj, adv first in time, place, or importance.

forensic adj used in or connected with courts of law. **forensic medicine** use of medical knowledge for the purposes of the law.

forerunner ⊕ n person or thing that goes before, precursor.

foresee ⊕ v see or know beforehand. **foreseeable** adj

foreshadow ⊕ v show or indicate beforehand.

foresight ⊕ n ability to anticipate and provide for future needs.

foreskin n fold of skin covering the tip of the penis.

forest n large area with a thick growth of trees. **forestry** n 1 science of planting and caring for trees. 2 management of forests. **forester** n person skilled in forestry.

forestall v prevent or guard against in advance.

foretaste n early limited experience of something to come.

foretell ⊕ v tell or indicate beforehand.

forethought ⊕ n thoughtful planning for future events.

forever, **for ever** adv 1 without end. 2 at all times. 3 Informal for a long time.

forewarn ⊕ v warn beforehand.

foreword n introduction to a book.

forfeit ⊕ n [for fit] n 1 thing lost or given up

THESAURUS

forefather n = **ancestor**, father, forebear, forerunner, predecessor

forefront n 1 = **foreground**, centre, fore, prominence 2 = **lead**, front, spearhead, vanguard

foregoing adj = **preceding**, above, antecedent, anterior, former, previous, prior

foreign adj 1, 2 = **external**, exotic, imported, remote 3 = **alien**, strange, unfamiliar, unknown ≠ **domestic**

foremost adj = **leading**, chief, highest, paramount, pre–eminent, primary, prime, principal, supreme

forerunner n = **precursor**, harbinger, herald, prototype

foresee v = **predict**, anticipate, envisage, forecast, foretell, prophesy

foreshadow v = **indicate**, augur,

forebode, portend, prefigure, presage, promise, signal

foresight n = **forethought**, anticipation, far–sightedness, precaution, preparedness, prescience, prudence

foretell v = **predict**, forecast, forewarn, presage, prognosticate, prophesy

forethought n = **anticipation**, far–sightedness, foresight, precaution, providence, provision, prudence

forever, **for ever** adv 1 = **evermore**, always, endlessly, eternally, for all time, for keeps, in perpetuity 2 = **constantly**, all the time, continually, incessantly, interminably, perpetually, twenty–four–seven (inf), unremittingly 3 Inf = **till the cows come home** (inf), till Doomsday

forewarn v = **caution**, advise, alert, apprise, give fair warning, put on guard,

as a penalty for a fault or mistake. ◆ *v* 2
lose as a forfeit. ◆ *adj* 3 lost as a forfeit.
forfeiture *n*

forge¹ ❶ *n* 1 place where metal is worked,
smithy. 2 furnace for melting metal. ◆ *v* 3
make a fraudulent imitation of
(something). 4 shape (metal) by heating
and hammering it. 5 create (an alliance
etc.).

forge² *v* advance steadily. **forge ahead**
increase speed or take the lead.

forget ❶ *v* –getting, –got, –gotten 1 fail to
remember. 2 neglect. 3 leave behind by
mistake. **forgetful** *adj* tending to forget.
forget-me-not *n* plant with clusters of
small blue flowers.

forgive ❶ *v* –giving, –gave, –given cease
to blame or hold resentment against,
pardon. **forgiveness** *n*

forgo ❶ *v* do without or give up.

fork ❶ *n* 1 tool for eating food, with
prongs and a handle. 2 large similarly–
shaped tool for digging or lifting. 3 point
where a road, river, etc. divides into
branches. 4 one of the branches. ◆ *v* 5
pick up, dig, etc. with a fork. 6 branch. 7
take one or other branch at a fork in the
road. **forked** *adj* **fork–lift truck** vehicle
with a forklike device at the front which
can be raised or lowered to move loads.
fork out *v Informal* pay.

forlorn ❶ *adj* lonely and unhappy. **forlorn
hope** hopeless enterprise.

form ❶ *n* 1 shape or appearance. 2 mode
in which something appears. 3 type or
kind. 4 printed document with spaces for
details. 5 physical or mental condition. 6
previous record of an athlete, racehorse,
etc. 7 class in school. 8 procedure or
etiquette. 9 bench. 10 hare's nest. ◆ *v* 11
give a (particular) shape to or take a
(particular) shape. 12 come or bring into
existence. 13 make or be made. 14 train.
15 acquire or develop. 16 be an element
of. **formation** *n* structure or shape.
formless *adj*

formal ❶ *adj* 1 of or characterized by
established conventions of ceremony and
behaviour. 2 of or for formal occasions. 3
stiff in manner. 4 organized. 5
symmetrical. **formally** *adv* **formality** *n, pl*
–ties 1 requirement of custom or
etiquette. 2 necessary procedure without
real importance. **formalize** *v* make official

tip off

forfeit *n* 1 = **penalty**, damages, fine,
forfeiture, loss, mulct ◆ *v* 2 = **lose**, be
deprived of, be stripped of, give up,
relinquish, renounce, say goodbye to,
surrender

forge¹ *v* 3 = **fake**, copy, counterfeit, falsify,
feign, imitate 4 = **shape**, fashion, mould,
work 5 = **create**, construct, devise, form,
frame, make

forget *v* 1 = **omit**, overlook 2 = **neglect**,
lose sight of 3 = **leave behind**

forgive *v* = **excuse**, absolve, acquit,
condone, exonerate, let bygones be
bygones, let off (*inf*), pardon

forgo *v* = **give up**, abandon, do without,
relinquish, renounce, resign, surrender,
waive, yield

fork *v* 6 = **branch**, bifurcate, diverge,
divide, part, split

forlorn *adj* = **miserable**, disconsolate,
down in the dumps (*inf*), helpless,
hopeless, pathetic, pitiful, unhappy,
woebegone, wretched ≠ **happy**

form *n* 1 = **shape**, appearance, structure
2 = **formation**, configuration, pattern
3 = **type**, kind, sort, style, variety
4 = **document**, application, paper, sheet
5 = **condition**, fettle, fitness, health, shape,
trim 7 = **class**, grade, rank 8 = **procedure**,
convention, custom, etiquette, protocol ◆
v 11 = **arrange**, combine, draw up,
organize 12 = **take shape**, appear,
become visible, come into being,
crystallize, grow, materialize, rise
13 = **make**, build, construct, create,
fashion, forge, mould, produce, shape
15 = **develop**, acquire, contract, cultivate,
pick up 16 = **constitute**, compose,
comprise, make up

or formal.

format ❶ *n* 1 size and shape of a publication. 2 style in which something is arranged.

former ❶ *adj* of an earlier time, previous. **the former** first mentioned of two. **formerly** *adv*

Formica *n* ® kind of laminated sheet used to make heat-resistant surfaces.

formidable ❶ *adj* 1 frightening because difficult to overcome or manage. 2 extremely impressive.

formula ❶ *n, pl* **-las, -lae** 1 group of numbers, letters, or symbols expressing a scientific or mathematical rule. 2 method or rule for doing or producing something. 3 set form of words used in religion, law, etc. 4 specific category of car in motor racing. **formulaic** *adj* **formulate** *v* plan or describe precisely and clearly. **formulation** *n*

forsake ❶ *v* **-saking, -sook, -saken** 1 withdraw support or friendship from. 2 give up, renounce.

forswear *v* **-swearing, -swore, -sworn**

renounce or reject.

fort ❶ *n* fortified building or place. **hold the fort** *Informal* keep things going during someone's absence.

forte¹ ❶ [**for**-tay] *n* thing at which a person excels.

forte² [**for**-tay] *adv Music* loudly.

forth ❶ *adv* forwards, out, or away.

forthright ❶ *adj* direct and outspoken.

fortify ❶ *v* **-fying, -fied** 1 make (a place) defensible, as by building walls. 2 strengthen. 3 add vitamins etc. to (food). 4 add alcohol to (wine) to make sherry or port. **fortification** *n*

fortitude ❶ *n* courage in adversity or pain.

fortnight *n* two weeks. **fortnightly** *adv, adj*

fortress ❶ *n* large fort or fortified town.

fortuitous [for-**tyew**-it-uss] *adj* happening by (lucky) chance.

fortune ❶ *n* 1 luck, esp. when favourable. 2 power regarded as influencing human destiny. 3 wealth, large sum of money. ♦ *pl* 4 person's destiny. **fortunate** *adj* having good luck. **fortune-teller** *n* person who claims to predict the future of others.

THESAURUS

formal *adj* 1 = **conventional**, correct, solemn 2 = **official**, ceremonial, ritualistic 3 = **stiff**, affected, precise, unbending ≠ **relaxed**

format *n* 1 = **layout**, construction, form, make-up, plan 2 = **arrangement**, appearance, look, style, type

former *adj* = **previous**, earlier, erstwhile, one-time, prior ≠ **coming**

formidable *adj* 1 = **intimidating**, daunting, dismaying, fearful, frightful, terrifying ≠ **encouraging** 2 = **impressive**, awesome, great, mighty, powerful, redoubtable, terrific, tremendous

formula *n* 2 = **method**, blueprint, precept, principle, procedure, recipe, rule

forsake *v* 1 = **desert**, abandon, disown, leave in the lurch, strand 2 = **give up**, forgo, relinquish, renounce, set aside, surrender, yield

fort *n* = **fortress**, blockhouse, camp, castle, citadel, fortification, garrison, stronghold

hold the fort *Inf* = **carry on**, keep things on an even keel, stand in, take over the reins

forte¹ *n* = **speciality**, gift, long suit (*inf*), métier, strength, strong point, talent

forth *adv* = **forward**, ahead, away, onward, out, outward

forthright *adj* = **outspoken**, blunt, candid, direct, frank, open, plain-spoken, straightforward, upfront (*inf*)

fortify *v* 1 = **protect**, buttress, reinforce, shore up 2 = **strengthen**, augment, support

fortitude *n* = **courage**, backbone, bravery, fearlessness, grit, perseverance, resolution, strength, valour

fortress *n* = **castle**, citadel, fastness, fort, redoubt, stronghold

fortune *n* 1 = **luck**, chance 2 = **fate**, destiny, kismet, providence 3 = **wealth**, affluence, opulence, possessions, property, prosperity, riches, treasure ≠ **poverty** ♦ *pl*

forty *adj, n, pl* **–ties** four times ten. **fortieth** *adj, n*

forum *n* meeting or medium for open discussion or debate.

forward ❶ *adj* 1 directed or moving ahead. 2 in, at, or near the front. 3 presumptuous. 4 well developed or advanced. 5 relating to the future. ◆ *n* 6 attacking player in various team games, such as football or hockey. ◆ *adv* 7 forwards. ◆ *v* 8 send (a letter etc.) on to an ultimate destination. 9 advance or promote. **forwards** *adv* 1 towards or at a place further ahead in space or time. 2 towards the front.

fossick *v Aust & NZ* search, esp. for gold or precious stones.

fossil *n* hardened remains of a prehistoric animal or plant preserved in rock. **fossilize** *v* 1 turn into a fossil. 2 become out–of–date or inflexible.

foster ❶ *v* 1 promote the growth or development of. 2 bring up (a child not one's own). ◆ *adj* 3 of or involved in fostering a child, e.g. *foster parents.*

foul ❶ *adj* 1 loathsome or offensive. 2 stinking or dirty. 3 (of language) obscene or vulgar. 4 unfair. ◆ *n* 5 *Sport* violation of the rules. ◆ *v* 6 make dirty or polluted. 7 make or become entangled or clogged. 8 *Sport* commit a foul against (an opponent). **fall foul of** come into conflict with. **foul–mouthed** *adj* habitually using foul language. **foul play** unfair conduct, esp. involving violence.

found¹ ❶ *v* 1 establish or bring into being. 2 lay the foundation of. 3 (foll. by *on* or *upon*) have a basis (in). **founder** *n* **founder member** one of the original members of a club or organization, often someone involved in setting it up.

found² *v* 1 cast (metal or glass) by melting and setting in a mould. 2 make (articles) by this method.

founder ❶ *v* 1 break down or fail. 2 (of a ship) sink. 3 stumble or fall.

foundling ❶ *n* abandoned baby.

fount *n* 1 *Lit* fountain. 2 source.

fountain ❶ *n* 1 jet of water. 2 structure from which such a jet spurts. 3 source. **fountainhead** *n* original source. **fountain pen** pen supplied with ink from a container inside it.

four *adj, n* 1 one more than three. ◆ *n* 2

——————— THESAURUS ———————

4 = **destiny**, lot

forward *adj* 1 = **leading**, advance, head 2 = **front**, first, foremost 3 = **presumptuous**, bold, brash, brazen, cheeky, familiar, impertinent, impudent, pushy (*inf*) ≠ **retiring** 4 = **well–developed**, advanced, precocious, premature ◆ *adv* 7 = **forth**, ahead, on, onward ≠ **backward(s)** ◆ *v* 8 = **send**, dispatch, post, send on 9 = **promote**, advance, assist, expedite, further, hasten, hurry ≠ **bar**

foster *v* 1 = **promote**, cultivate, encourage, feed, nurture, stimulate, support, uphold ≠ **oppose** 2 = **bring up**, mother, nurse, raise, rear, take care of

foul *adj* 1 = **offensive**, abhorrent, despicable, detestable, disgraceful, scandalous, shameful, wicked ≠ **attractive** 2 = **dirty**, fetid, filthy, malodorous,

nauseating, putrid, repulsive, squalid, stinking, unclean ≠ **clean** 3 = **obscene**, abusive, blue, coarse, indecent, lewd, profane, scurrilous, vulgar 4 = **unfair**, crooked, dishonest, fraudulent, shady (*inf*), underhand, unscrupulous ◆ *v* 7 = **dirty**, besmirch, contaminate, defile, pollute, stain, sully, taint ≠ **clear**

found¹ *v* 1 = **establish**, constitute, create, inaugurate, institute, organize, originate, set up, start

① **founder** *n* = **initiator**, architect, author, beginner, father, inventor, originator

② **founder** *v* 1 = **fail**, break down, collapse, come to grief, come unstuck, fall through, miscarry, misfire 2 = **sink**, be lost, go down, go to the bottom, submerge 3 = **stumble**, lurch, sprawl, stagger, trip

fountain *n* 1 = **jet**, spout, spray, spring

(crew of) four–oared rowing boat. **on all
fours** on hands and knees. **four–letter
word** short obscene word referring to sex
or excrement. **four–poster** *n* bed with four
posts supporting a canopy. **foursome** *n*
group of four people.

fowl *n* 1 domestic cock or hen. 2 any bird
used for food or hunted as game.

fox *n* 1 reddish–brown bushy–tailed animal
of the dog family. 2 its fur. 3 cunning
person. ◆ *v* 4 *Informal* perplex or deceive.
foxy *adj* of or like a fox, esp. in craftiness.

foxglove *n* tall plant with purple or white
flowers. **foxtrot** *n* 1 ballroom dance with
slow and quick steps. 2 music for this.

foyer ❶ [**foy**–ay] *n* entrance hall in a
theatre, cinema, or hotel.

fracas ❶ [**frak**–ah] *n, pl* –**cas** noisy quarrel.

fraction ❶ *n* 1 numerical quantity that is
not a whole number. 2 fragment, piece. 3
Chem substance separated by distillation.
fractional *adj*

fracture ❶ *n* 1 breaking, esp. of a bone. ◆
v 2 break.

fragile ❶ *adj* 1 easily broken or damaged.
2 in a weakened physical state. **fragility** *n*

fragrant ❶ *adj* sweet–smelling. **fragrance**
n 1 pleasant smell. 2 perfume, scent.

frail ❶ *adj* 1 physically weak. 2 easily

damaged. **frailty** *n, pl* –**ties** physical or
moral weakness.

frame ❶ *n* 1 structure giving shape or
support. 2 enclosing case or border, as
round a picture. 3 person's build. 4
individual exposure on a strip of film. 5
individual game of snooker in a match. ◆ *v*
6 put together, construct. 7 put into
words. 8 put into a frame. 9 *Slang*
incriminate (a person) on a false charge. **5
frame of mind** mood or attitude. **frame–
up** *n Slang* false incrimination. **framework**
n supporting structure.

franc *n* monetary unit of France,
Switzerland, Belgium, and various African
countries.

franchise *n* 1 right to vote. 2 authorization
to sell a company's goods.

frank ❶ *adj* 1 honest and straightforward
in speech or attitude. ◆ *n* 2 official mark
on a letter permitting delivery. ◆ *v* 3 put
such a mark on (a letter). **frankly** *adv*

frankfurter *n* smoked sausage.

frankincense *n* aromatic gum resin
burned as incense.

frantic ❶ *adj* 1 distracted with rage, grief,
joy, etc. 2 hurried and disorganized.
frantically *adv*

fraternal *adj* of a brother, brotherly.

———————— THESAURUS ————————

2 = **fount**, font, well 3 = **source**, cause,
derivation, fount, fountainhead, origin,
wellspring

foyer *n* = **entrance hall**, antechamber,
anteroom, lobby, reception area, vestibule

fracas *n* = **brawl**, affray (*Law*), disturbance,
mêlée, riot, rumpus, scuffle, skirmish

fraction *n* 1 = **percentage** 2 = **piece**, part,
portion, section, segment, share, slice

fracture *n* 1 = **break**, crack ◆ *v* 2 = **break**,
crack, rupture, split

fragile *adj* 1 = **delicate**, breakable, brittle,
dainty, fine, flimsy, frangible ≠ **lasting**
2 = **weak**, frail

fragrant *adj* = **aromatic**, balmy, odorous,
perfumed, redolent, sweet–scented,
sweet–smelling

frail *adj* 1 = **weak**, feeble, fragile, infirm,

puny ≠ **strong** 2 = **delicate**, flimsy,
insubstantial, vulnerable

frame *n* 1 = **casing**, construction,
framework, shell, structure 3 = **physique**,
anatomy, body, build, carcass ◆ *v*
6 = **construct**, assemble, build, make,
manufacture, put together 7 = **devise**,
compose, draft, draw up, formulate, map
out, sketch 8 = **mount**, case, enclose,
surround **frame of mind** = **mood**, attitude,
disposition, humour, outlook, state,
temper

frank *adj* 1 = **honest**, blunt, candid, direct,
forthright, open, outspoken, plain–spoken,
sincere, straightforward, truthful

frantic *adj* 1 = **distraught**, at the end of
one's tether, berserk, beside oneself,
desperate, distracted, fraught (*inf*), furious,

fraternity n 1 group of people with shared interests, aims, etc. 2 brotherhood. 3 US male social club at college. **fraternize** v associate on friendly terms. **fraternization** n **fratricide** n 1 crime of killing one's brother. 2 person who does this.

fraud ❶ n 1 (criminal) deception, swindle. 2 person who acts in a deceitful way. **fraudulent** adj **fraudulence** n

fraught [frawt] adj tense or anxious. **fraught with** involving, filled with.

fray¹ n noisy quarrel or conflict.

fray² ❶ v 1 make or become ragged at the edge. 2 become strained.

frazzle n Informal exhausted state.

freak ❶ n 1 abnormal person or thing. 2 person who is excessively enthusiastic about something. ◆ adj 3 abnormal. **freakish** adj **freak out** v Informal (cause to) be in a heightened emotional state.

freckle n small brown spot on the skin. **freckled** adj marked with freckles.

free ❶ adj **freer, freest** 1 able to act at will, not compelled or restrained. 2 not subject (to). 3 independent. 4 provided without charge. 5 generous, lavish. 6 not in use. 7 (of a person) not busy. 8 not fixed or joined. ◆ v **freeing, freed** 9 release, liberate. 10 remove (obstacles, pain, etc.) from. 11 make available or usable. **a free hand** unrestricted freedom to act. **freely** adv **free fall** part of a parachute descent before the parachute opens. **free-for-all** n

Informal brawl. **freehand** adj drawn without guiding instruments. **freehold** n tenure of land for life without restrictions. **freeholder** n **freelance** adj, n (of) a self-employed person doing specific pieces of work for various employers. **freeloader** n *Slang* habitual scrounger. **free-range** adj kept or produced in natural conditions. **freeway** n *Chiefly US* motorway. **freewheel** v travel downhill on a bicycle without pedalling.

✓ **WORD TIP**

Free of means 'not subject to': *free of charge. Free from* suggests a change of circumstances: *They were free from danger.*

---

freeze ❶ v **freezing, froze, frozen** 1 change from a liquid to a solid by the reduction of temperature, as water to ice. 2 preserve (food etc.) by extreme cold. 3 (cause to) be very cold. 4 become motionless with fear, shock, etc. 5 fix (prices or wages) at a particular level. 6 ban the exchange or collection of (loans, assets, etc.) ◆ n 7 period of very cold weather. 8 freezing of prices or wages. **freezer** n insulated cabinet for cold-storage of perishable foods. **freeze-dry** v preserve (food) by rapid freezing and drying in a vacuum. **freezing** adj *Informal* very cold.

wild 2 = **hectic**, frenetic, frenzied ≠ **together** (sl)

fraud n 1 = **deception**, chicanery, deceit, double-dealing, duplicity, sharp practice, swindling, treachery, trickery ≠ **virtue** 2 = **impostor**, charlatan, fake, hoaxer, phoney or phony (inf), pretender, swindler

fray² v 1 = **wear thin**, wear

freak n 1 = **oddity**, aberration, anomaly, malformation, monstrosity, weirdo or weirdie (inf) 2 = **enthusiast**, addict, aficionado, buff (inf), devotee, fan, fanatic, fiend (inf), nut (sl) ◆ adj 3 = **abnormal**, exceptional, unparalleled, unusual

free adj 1 = **allowed**, able, clear, permitted, unimpeded, unrestricted 2, 3 = **at liberty**, at large, footloose, independent, liberated, loose, on the loose, unfettered ≠ **secured** 4 = **complimentary**, for free (inf), for nothing, free of charge, gratis, gratuitous, on the house, unpaid, without charge 5 = **generous**, lavish, liberal, unsparing, unstinting ≠ **mean** 6 = **available**, empty, spare, unoccupied, unused, vacant 7 = **idle**, unemployed ◆ v 9 = **release**, deliver, let out, liberate, loose, set free, turn loose, unchain, untie ≠ **limit** 10 = **clear**, cut loose, disengage,

freight ❶ [frate] n 1 commercial transport of goods. 2 cargo transported. 3 cost of this. ♦ v 4 send by freight. **freighter** n ship or aircraft for transporting goods.

frenetic [frin–net–ik] adj uncontrolled, excited.

frenzy ❶ n, pl –zies 1 violent mental derangement. 2 wild excitement. **frenzied** adj

frequent ❶ adj 1 happening often. 2 habitual. ♦ v 3 visit habitually. **frequently** adv **frequency** n, pl –cies 1 rate of occurrence. 2 Physics number of times a wave repeats itself in a given time.

fresco n, pl –coes, –cos watercolour painting done on wet plaster on a wall.

fresh ❶ adj 1 newly made, acquired, etc. 2 novel, original. 3 most recent. 4 further, additional. 5 (of food) not preserved. 6 (of water) not salty. 7 (of weather) brisk or invigorating. 8 not tired. 9 Informal impudent. **freshly** adv **freshness** n **freshen** v make or become fresh or fresher. **fresher, freshman** n first–year student.

fret¹ ❶ v **fretting, fretted** be worried. **fretful** adj irritable.

fret² n small bar on the fingerboard of a guitar etc.

Fri. Friday.

friable adj easily crumbled.

friar n member of a male Roman Catholic religious order. **friary** n, pl –ries house of friars.

fricassee n stewed meat served in a thick white sauce.

friction ❶ n 1 resistance met with by a body moving over another. 2 rubbing. 3 clash of wills or personalities. **frictional** adj

Friday n sixth day of the week.

fridge n apparatus in which food and drinks are kept cool.

friend ❶ n 1 person whom one knows well and likes. 2 supporter or ally. **friendly** adj 1 showing or expressing liking. 2 not hostile, on the same side. ♦ n, pl –lies 3 Sport match played for its own sake and not as part of a competition. **–friendly** combining form good or easy for the person or thing specified, e.g. user–friendly. **friendliness** n **friendless** adj **friendship** n

frieze [freeze] n ornamental band on a wall.

frigate [frig–it] n medium–sized fast warship.

fright ❶ n 1 sudden fear or alarm. 2

═══ THESAURUS ═══

disentangle, extricate, rescue

freeze v 1 = **ice over** or **up**, harden, stiffen 3 = **chill** 5, 6 = **suspend**, fix, hold up, inhibit, stop

freight n 1 = **transportation**, carriage, conveyance, shipment 2 = **cargo**, burden, consignment, goods, load, merchandise, payload

frenzy n 1 = **fury**, derangement, hysteria, paroxysm, passion, rage, seizure ≠ **calm**

frequent adj 1 = **persistent**, recurrent, repeated 2 = **habitual**, common, customary, everyday, familiar, usual ≠ **few** ♦ v 3 = **visit**, attend, hang out at (inf), haunt, patronize ≠ **avoid**

fresh adj 1 = **new**, different ≠ **old** 2 = **novel**, original 3 = **recent**, modern, up–to–date 4 = **additional**, added, auxiliary, extra, further, more, other,

supplementary 5 = **natural**, unprocessed ≠ **frozen** 7 = **invigorating**, bracing, brisk, clean, cool, crisp, pure, refreshing, unpolluted ≠ **warm** 8 = **lively**, alert, energetic, keen, refreshed, sprightly, spry, vigorous ≠ **exhausted** 9 Inf = **cheeky**, disrespectful, familiar, forward, impudent, insolent, presumptuous ≠ **well–mannered**

fret¹ v = **worry**, agonize, brood, lose sleep over, obsess about, upset or distress oneself

friction n 2 = **rubbing**, abrasion, chafing, grating, rasping, resistance, scraping 3 = **hostility**, animosity, bad blood, conflict, disagreement, discord, dissension, resentment

friend n 1 = **companion**, buddy (inf), chum (inf), comrade, mate (inf), pal, playmate ≠ **rival** 2 = **supporter**, ally, associate, sudden alarming shock. **3 frighten** v **1** scare or terrify. **2** force (someone) to do something from fear. **frightening** adj **frightful** adj **1** horrifying. **2** Informal very great. **frightfully** adv

frigid ✪ [frij–id] adj **1** (of a woman) sexually unresponsive. **2** very cold. **3** excessively formal. **frigidity** n

frill n **1** gathered strip of fabric attached at one edge. ◆ pl **2** superfluous decorations or details. **frilly** adj

fringe ✪ n **1** hair cut short and hanging over the forehead. **2** ornamental edge of hanging threads, tassels, etc. **3** outer edge. **4** less important parts of an activity or group. ◆ v **5** decorate with a fringe. ◆ adj **6** (of theatre) unofficial or unconventional. **fringed** adj **fringe benefit** benefit given in addition to a regular salary.

frisk ✪ v **1** move or leap playfully. **2** Informal search (a person) for concealed weapons etc. **frisky** adj lively or high–spirited. **friskily** adv

frisson [frees–sonn] n shiver of fear or excitement.

fritter ✪ n piece of food fried in batter.

frivolous ✪ adj **1** not serious or sensible. **2** enjoyable but trivial. **frivolity** n

frizz v form (hair) into stiff wiry curls. **frizzy** adj

frock n dress. **frock coat** man's skirted coat as worn in the 19th century.

frog n smooth–skinned tailless amphibian with long back legs used for jumping. **frog**

in one's throat phlegm on the vocal cords, hindering speech. **frogman** n swimmer with a rubber suit and breathing equipment for working underwater. **frogmarch** v force (a resisting person) to move by holding his arms. **frogspawn** n jelly–like substance containing frog's eggs.

frolic ✪ v **–icking, –icked 1** run and play in a lively way. ◆ n **2** lively and merry behaviour. **frolicsome** adj playful.

from prep indicating the point of departure, source, distance, cause, change of state, etc.

✓ **WORD TIP**

The use of off to mean from is very informal: They bought milk from (rather than off) a farmer.

---

frond n long leaf or leaflike part of a fern, palm, or seaweed.

front ✪ n **1** fore part. **2** position directly before or ahead. **3** seaside promenade. **4** battle line or area. **5** Meteorol dividing line between two different air masses. **6** outward appearance. **7** Informal cover for another, usu. criminal, activity. **8** group with a common goal. ◆ adj **9** of or at the front. ◆ v **10** face (onto). **11** be the presenter of (a television show). **frontal** adj **frontage** n facade of a building. **front bench** parliamentary leaders of the government or opposition. **front–bencher** n **frontrunner** n Informal person regarded as most likely to win a race, election, etc.

patron, well–wisher

fright n **1, 2 = fear**, alarm, consternation, dread, horror, panic, scare, shock, trepidation ≠ **courage**

frigid adj **1 = unresponsive 2 = cold**, arctic, frosty, frozen, glacial, icy, wintry ≠ **hot 3 = formal**, aloof, austere, forbidding, unapproachable, unfeeling

fringe n **2 = border**, edging, hem, trimming **3 = edge**, borderline, limits, margin, outskirts, perimeter, periphery ◆ adj **6 = unofficial**, unconventional,

unorthodox

frisk v **1 = frolic**, caper, cavort, gambol, jump, play, prance, skip, trip **2** Inf **= search**, check, inspect, run over, shake down (US sl)

frivolous adj **1 = flippant**, childish, foolish, idle, juvenile, puerile, silly, superficial ≠ **serious 2 = trivial**, footling (inf), minor, petty, shallow, trifling, unimportant ≠ **important**

frolic v **1 = play**, caper, cavort, frisk, gambol, lark, make merry, romp, sport ◆ n

frost ⊕ n 1 white frozen dew or mist. 2 atmospheric temperature below freezing point. ◆ v 3 become covered with frost. **frosted** adj (of glass) having a rough surface to make it opaque. **frosting** n Chiefly US sugar icing. **frosty** adj 1 characterized by or covered by frost. 2 unfriendly. **frostily** adv **frostiness** n **frostbite** n destruction of tissue, esp. of the fingers or ears, by cold.

froth ⊕ n 1 mass of small bubbles. ◆ v 2 foam. **frothy** adj

frown ⊕ v 1 wrinkle one's brows in worry, anger, or thought. 2 look disapprovingly (on). ◆ n 3 frowning expression.

frugal ⊕ adj 1 thrifty, sparing. 2 meagre and inexpensive. **frugality** n

fruit ⊕ n 1 part of a plant containing seeds, esp. if edible. 2 any plant product useful to man. 3 (often pl) result of an action or effort. ◆ v 4 bear fruit. **fruiterer** n person who sells fruit. **fruitful** adj useful or productive. **fruitless** adj useless or unproductive. **fruity** adj 1 of or like fruit. 2 (of a voice) mellow. 3 Informal mildly bawdy. **fruit machine** coin-operated gambling machine.

frump n dowdy woman. **frumpy** adj

frustrate ⊕ v 1 upset or anger. 2 hinder or prevent. **frustrated** adj **frustrating** adj **frustration** n

fry[1] v **frying, fried** 1 cook or be cooked in fat or oil. ◆ n, pl **fries** 2 (also **fry-up**) dish of fried food. ◆ pl 3 potato chips.

fry[2] pl n young fishes. **small fry** young or insignificant people.

ft. 1 foot. 2 feet.

fuchsia [fyew-sha] n ornamental shrub with hanging flowers.

fuddle v cause to be intoxicated or confused.

fuddy-duddy ⊕ adj, n, pl **-dies** Informal old-fashioned (person).

fudge[1] n soft caramel-like sweet.

fudge[2] ⊕ v avoid making a firm statement or decision.

fuel ⊕ n 1 substance burned or treated to produce heat or power. 2 something that intensifies (a feeling etc.). ◆ v **fuelling, fuelled** 3 provide with fuel.

fugitive ⊕ [fyew-jit-iv] n 1 person who flees, esp. from arrest or pursuit. ◆ adj 2 fleeing. 3 transient.

fugue [fyewg] n musical composition in which a theme is repeated in different parts.

THESAURUS

2 = **revel**, antic, game, lark, romp, spree
front n 1 = **foreground**, frontage
2 = **forefront**, head, lead, vanguard
4 = **front line** 6 = **exterior**, facade, face
7 Inf = **cover**, blind, cover-up, disguise, mask, pretext ◆ adj 9 = **foremost**, first, head, lead, leading, topmost ≠ **back** ◆ v
10 = **face onto**, look over or onto, overlook
frost n 1 = **hoarfrost**, rime 2 = **freeze**
froth n 1 = **foam**, bubbles, effervescence, head, lather, scum, spume, suds ◆ v
2 = **fizz**, bubble over, come to a head, effervesce, foam, lather
frown v 1 = **scowl**, glare, glower, knit one's brows, look daggers, lour or lower
2 = **disapprove of**, discourage, dislike, look askance at, take a dim view of
frugal adj 1 = **thrifty**, abstemious, careful,

economical, niggardly, parsimonious, prudent, sparing ≠ **excessive**
fruit n 2 = **produce**, crop, harvest, product, yield 3 (often pl) = **result**, advantage, benefit, consequence, effect, end result, outcome, profit, return, reward
frustrate v 2 = **thwart**, balk, block, check, counter, defeat, disappoint, foil, forestall, nullify, stymie ≠ **further**
fuddy-duddy n Inf = **conservative**, (old) fogey, square (inf), stick-in-the-mud (inf), stuffed shirt (inf)
fudge[2] v = **misrepresent**, equivocate, flannel (Brit inf)
fuel n = **incitement**, provocation
fugitive n 1 = **runaway**, deserter, escapee, refugee ◆ adj 3 = **momentary**, brief, ephemeral, fleeting, passing, short-lived, temporary, transient, transitory

fulcrum *n, pl* **–crums, –cra** pivot about which a lever turns.

fulfil ⦸ *v* **–filling, –filled 1** bring about the achievement of (a desire or promise). **2** carry out (a request or order). **3** do what is required. **fulfilment** *n* **fulfil oneself** *v* achieve one's potential.

full ⦸ *adj* **1** containing as much or as many as possible. **2** abundant in supply. **3** having had enough to eat. **4** plump. **5** complete, whole. **6** (of a garment) of ample cut. **7** (of a sound or flavour) rich and strong. ◆ *adv* **8** completely. **9** directly. **10** very. **fully** *adv* **fullness** *n* **in full** without shortening. **full–blooded** *adj* vigorous or enthusiastic. **full–blown** *adj* fully developed. **1 full moon** phase of the moon when it is visible as a fully illuminated disc. **full–scale** *adj* **1** (of a plan) of actual size. **2** using all resources. **full stop** punctuation mark (.) at the end of a sentence and after abbreviations.

fulminate *v* (foll. by *against*) criticize or denounce angrily.

fulsome ⦸ *adj* distastefully excessive or insincere.

fumble ⦸ *v* **1** handle awkwardly. **2** say awkwardly. ◆ *n* **3** act of fumbling.

fume ⦸ *v* **1** be very angry. **2** give out smoke or vapour. **3** *pl n* **4** pungent smoke or vapour.

fun ⦸ *n* enjoyment or amusement. **make fun of** mock or tease. **funny** *adj* **1** comical, humorous. **2** odd. **funny bone** part of the elbow where the nerve is near the surface. **funnily** *adv*

function ⦸ *n* **1** purpose something exists for. **2** way something works. **3** large or formal social event. **4** *Maths* quantity whose value depends on the varying value of another. **5** sequence of operations performed by a computer at a key stroke. ◆ *v* **6** operate or work. **7** (foll. by *as*) fill the role of. **functional** *adj* **1** of or as a function. **2** practical rather than decorative. **3** in working order. **functionary** *n, pl* **–aries** official.

fund ⦸ *n* **1** stock of money for a special purpose. **2** supply or store. ◆ *pl* **3** money resources. ◆ *v* **4** provide money to. **funding** *n*

fundamental ⦸ *adj* **1** essential or primary. **2** basic. ◆ *n* **3** basic rule or fact. **fundamentally** *adv* **fundamentalism** *n* literal or strict interpretation of a religion. **fundamentalist** *n, adj*

fulfil *v* **1** = **achieve**, accomplish, realise **2** = **carry out**, complete, perform, satisfy ≠ **neglect 3** = **comply with**, answer, conform to, fill, meet, obey, observe

full *adj* **1** = **filled**, brimming, complete, loaded, saturated, stocked ≠ **empty 2** = **extensive**, abundant, adequate, ample, generous, plentiful ≠ **limited 3** = **satiated**, replete **4** = **plump**, buxom, curvaceous, rounded, voluptuous **5** = **comprehensive**, exhaustive **6** = **voluminous**, baggy, capacious, large, loose, puffy ≠ **tight 7** = **rich**, clear, deep, distinct, loud, resonant, rounded ≠ **thin in full** = **completely**, in its entirety, in total, without exception

fulsome *adj* = **extravagant**, excessive, immoderate, inordinate, insincere, sycophantic, unctuous

fumble *v* **1** = **grope**, feel around, flounder, scrabble

fume *v* **1** (*inf*) = **rage**, rant, see red (*inf*), seethe, smoulder, storm ◆ *pl n* **4** = **smoke**, exhaust, gas, pollution, smog, vapour

fun *n* = **enjoyment**, amusement, entertainment, jollity, merriment, mirth, pleasure, recreation, sport ≠ **depression make fun of** = **mock**, lampoon, laugh at, parody, poke fun at, ridicule, satirize, send up (*Brit inf*)

function *n* **1** = **purpose**, business, duty, job, mission, *raison d'être*, responsibility, role, task **3** = **reception**, affair, do (*inf*), gathering, social occasion ◆ *v* **6** = **work**, go, operate, perform, run **7** (foll. by *as*) = **act as**, behave as, do duty as

fund *n* **1** = **kitty**, pool **2** = **reserve**, stock, store, supply ◆ *v* **4** = **finance**, pay for,

fundi n S Afr expert or boffin.

funeral ❶ n ceremony of burying or cremating a dead person.

fungus n, pl **-gi, -guses** plant without leaves, flowers, or roots, such as a mushroom or mould. **fungal, fungous** adj **fungicide** n substance that destroys fungi.

funk n style of dance music with a strong beat. **funky** adj **funkier, funkiest** (of music) having a strong beat.

funnel ❶ n 1 cone-shaped tube for pouring liquids into a narrow opening. 2 chimney of a ship or locomotive. ◆ v **-nelling, -nelled** 3 (cause to) move through or as if through a funnel.

fur n 1 soft hair of a mammal. 2 animal skin with the fur left on. 3 garment made of this. 4 whitish coating on the tongue or inside a kettle. ◆ v 5 cover or become covered with fur. **furry** adj **furrier** n dealer in furs.

furious ❶ adj 1 very angry. 2 violent or unrestrained.

furl v roll up and fasten (a sail, umbrella, or flag).

furlong n eighth of a mile.

furnace n enclosed chamber containing a very hot fire.

furnish ❶ v 1 provide (a house or room) with furniture. 2 supply, provide. **furnishings** pl n furniture, carpets, and fittings. **furniture** n large movable articles such as chairs and wardrobes.

furore ❶ [fyew–**ror**–ee] n very excited or angry reaction.

furrow ❶ n 1 trench made by a plough. 2 groove, esp. a wrinkle on the forehead. ◆ v 3 make or become wrinkled. 4 make furrows in.

further ❶ adv 1 in addition. 2 to a greater distance or extent. ◆ adj 3 additional. 4 more distant. ◆ v 5 assist the progress of. **further education** education beyond school other than at a university. **furthest** adv 1 to the greatest distance or extent. ◆ adj 2 most distant. **furtherance** n **furthermore** adv besides. **furthermost** adj most distant.

furtive ❶ adj sly and secretive. **furtively** adv

fury ❶ n, pl **-ries** 1 wild anger. 2 uncontrolled violence.

fuse[1] n cord containing an explosive for detonating a bomb.

fuse[2] n 1 safety device for electric circuits, containing a wire that melts and breaks

──── | THESAURUS | ────

subsidize, support

fundamental adj 1 = **essential**, cardinal, central, key, primary, principal ≠ **extra** 2 = **basic**, elementary, rudimentary, underlying ◆ n 3 = **principle**, axiom, cornerstone, law, rudiment, rule

funeral n = **burial**, cremation, interment, obsequies

funnel v 3 = **channel**, conduct, convey, direct, filter, move, pass, pour

furious adj 1 = **angry**, beside oneself, enraged, fuming, incensed, infuriated, livid (inf), raging, up in arms ≠ **pleased** 2 = **violent**, fierce, intense, savage, turbulent, unrestrained, vehement

furnish v 1 = **decorate**, equip, fit out, stock 2 = **supply**, give, grant, hand out, offer, present, provide

furore n = **commotion**, disturbance, hullaballoo, outcry, stir, to-do, uproar

furrow n 1 = **groove**, channel, hollow, line, rut, seam, trench 2 = **wrinkle**, crease ◆ v 3 = **wrinkle**, corrugate, crease, draw together, knit

further adv 1 = **in addition**, additionally, also, besides, furthermore, into the bargain, moreover, to boot ◆ adj 3 = **additional**, extra, fresh, more, new, other, supplementary ◆ v 5 = **promote**, advance, assist, encourage, forward, help, lend support to, work for ≠ **stop**

furtive adj = **sly**, clandestine, conspiratorial, secretive, sneaky, stealthy, surreptitious, underhand, under-the-table

fury n 1 = **anger**, frenzy, impetuosity, madness, passion, rage, wrath ≠ **calm** 2 = **violence**, ferocity, fierceness, force, intensity, savagery, severity, vehemence the connection when the circuit is overloaded. ◆ *v* 2 (cause to) fail as a result of a blown fuse. 3 equip (a plug) with a fuse. 4 join or combine. 5 unite by melting. 6 melt with heat.

fuselage [**fyew**–zill–lahzh] *n* body of an aircraft.

fuss ❶ *n* 1 needless activity or worry. 2 complaint or objection. 3 great display of attention. ◆ *v* 4 make a fuss. **fussy** *adj* 1 inclined to fuss. 2 overparticular. 3 overelaborate. **fussily** *adv* **fussiness** *n*

fusty ❶ *adj* –**tier**, –**tiest** 1 stale–smelling. 2 behind the times.

futile ❶ *adj* unsuccessful or useless. **futility** *n*

futon [**foo**–tonn] *n* Japanese padded quilt, laid on the floor as a bed.

future ❶ *n* 1 time to come. 2 what will happen. 3 prospects. ◆ *adj* 4 yet to come or be. 5 of or relating to time to come. 6 (of a verb tense) indicating that the action specified has not yet taken place. **futuristic** *adj* of a design appearing to belong to some future time.

fuzz¹ *n* mass of fine or curly hairs or fibres. **fuzzy** *adj* **fuzzier, fuzziest** 1 of, like, or covered with fuzz. 2 blurred or indistinct. 3 (of hair) tightly curled. **fuzzily** *adv* **fuzziness** *n*

fuzz² *n Slang* police.

———— THESAURUS ————

≠ **peace**

fuss *n* 1 = **bother**, ado, commotion, excitement, hue and cry, palaver, stir, to–do 2 = **argument**, complaint, furore, objection, row, squabble, trouble ◆ *v* 4 = **worry**, fidget, flap (*inf*), fret, get worked up, take pains

fusty *adj* 1 = **stale**, airless, damp, mildewed, mouldering, mouldy, musty,

stuffy

futile *adj* = **useless**, fruitless, ineffectual, unavailing, unprofitable, unsuccessful, vain, worthless ≠ **successful**

future *n* 1 = **time to come**, hereafter 3 = **prospect**, expectation, outlook ◆ *adj* 4, 5 = **forthcoming**, approaching, coming, fated, impending, later, subsequent, to come ≠ **late**

G g

g 1 gram(s). **2** (acceleration due to) gravity.
GA Georgia.
gabardine, gaberdine *n* strong twill cloth used esp. for raincoats.
gabble ⊕ *v* **1** speak rapidly and indistinctly. ♦ *n* **2** rapid indistinct speech.
gable *n* triangular upper part of a wall between sloping roofs. **gabled** *adj*
gad *v* **gadding, gadded. gad about, around** go around in search of pleasure.
gadget ⊕ *n* small mechanical device or appliance. **gadgetry** *n* gadgets.
gaffe ⊕ *n* social blunder.
gaffer ⊕ *n* **1** *Informal* foreman or boss. **2** old man.
gag¹ ⊕ *v* **gagging, gagged 1** choke or retch. **2** stop up the mouth of (a person) with cloth etc. **3** deprive of free speech. ♦ *n* **4** cloth etc. put into or tied across the mouth.

gag² ⊕ *n* *Informal* joke.
gaggle *n* **1** *Informal* disorderly crowd. **2** flock of geese.
gain ⊕ *v* **1** acquire or obtain. **2** increase or improve. **3** reach. **4** (of a watch or clock) be or become too fast. ♦ *n* **5** profit or advantage. **6** increase or improvement. **gainful** *adj* useful or profitable. **gainfully** *adv* **gain on, upon** *v* get nearer to or catch up with.
gainsay ⊕ *v* **–saying, –said** deny or contradict.
gait ⊕ *n* manner of walking.
gala ⊕ *n* [**gah**–la] **1** festival. **2** competitive sporting event.
galaxy *n*, *pl* **–axies 1** system of stars. **2** gathering of famous people. **galactic** *adj*
gale ⊕ *n* **1** strong wind. **2** *Informal* loud outburst.
gall¹ ⊕ *n* [**gawl**] **1** *Informal* impudence.

THESAURUS

gabble *v* **1** = **prattle**, babble, blabber, gibber, gush, jabber, spout ♦ *n* **2** = **gibberish**, babble, blabber, chatter, drivel, prattle, twaddle
gadget *n* = **device**, appliance, contraption (*inf*), contrivance, gizmo (*sl, chiefly US*), instrument, invention, thing, tool
gaffe *n* = **blunder**, bloomer (*inf*), clanger (*inf*), faux pas, howler, indiscretion, lapse, mistake, slip, solecism
gaffer *n* **1** *Inf* = **manager**, boss (*inf*), foreman, overseer, superintendent, supervisor **2** = **old man**, granddad, greybeard, old boy (*inf*), old fellow, old–timer (*US*)
gag¹ *v* **1** = **retch**, heave, puke (*sl*), spew, throw up (*inf*), vomit **2** = **suppress**, curb, muffle, muzzle, quiet, silence, stifle, stop

up
gag² *n* *Inf* = **joke**, crack (*sl*), funny (*inf*), hoax, jest, wisecrack (*inf*), witticism
gain *v* **1** = **acquire**, attain, capture, collect, gather, get, land, secure ≠ **lose**
2 = **improve**, advance, increase, pick up, profit ≠ **lose 3** = **reach**, arrive at, attain, come to, get to ♦ *n* **5** = **profit**, advantage, benefit, dividend, return, yield ≠ **loss**
6 = **increase**, advance, growth, improvement, progress, rise
gainsay *v* = **contradict**, contravene, controvert, deny, disagree with, dispute, rebut, retract
gait *n* = **walk**, bearing, carriage, pace, step, stride, tread
gala *n* **1** = **festival**, carnival, celebration, festivity, fete, jamboree, pageant

2 bitter feeling. 3 bile. **gall bladder** sac attached to the liver, storing bile. **gallstone** *n* hard mass formed in the gall bladder or its ducts.

gall² ❶ [gawl] *v* 1 annoy. 2 make sore by rubbing. ◆ *n* 3 sore caused by rubbing. **galling** *adj* annoying or bitterly humiliating.

gallant ❶ *adj* 1 brave and noble. 2 (of a man) attentive to women. **gallantry** *n* 1 showy, attentive treatment of women. 2 bravery.

galleon *n* large three–masted sailing ship of the 15th-17th centuries.

gallery *n, pl* **–ries** 1 room or building for displaying works of art. 2 balcony in a church, theatre, etc. 3 passage in a mine. 4 long narrow room for a specific purpose, e.g. *shooting gallery.*

galley *n* 1 kitchen of a ship or aircraft. 2 *Hist* ship propelled by oars, usu. rowed by slaves. **galley slave** 1 slave forced to row in a galley. 2 *Informal* drudge.

gallivant ❶ *v* go about in search of pleasure.

gallon *n* liquid measure of eight pints, equal to 4.55 litres.

gallop ❶ *n* 1 horse's fastest pace. 2 galloping. ◆ *v* **galloping, galloped** 3 go or ride at a gallop. 4 move or progress rapidly.

gallows *n* wooden structure used for hanging criminals.

galore ❶ *adv* in abundance.

galoshes *pl n* waterproof overshoes.

gambit *n* 1 opening line or move intended to secure an advantage. 2 *Chess* opening move involving the sacrifice of a pawn.

gamble ❶ *v* 1 play games of chance to win money. 2 act on the expectation of something. ◆ *n* 3 risky undertaking. 4 bet or wager. **gambler** *n* **gambling** *n*

gambol ❶ *v* **–bolling, –bolled** 1 jump about playfully, frolic. ◆ *n* 2 frolic.

game¹ ❶ *n* 1 amusement or pastime. 2 contest for amusement. 3 single period of play in a contest. 4 animals or birds hunted for sport or food. 5 their flesh. 6 scheme or trick. ◆ *v* 7 gamble. ◆ *adj* 8 brave. 9 willing. **gamely** *adv* **gaming** *n* gambling. **gamekeeper** *n* person employed to breed game and prevent poaching. **gamesmanship** *n* art of winning by cunning practices without actually cheating.

game² ❶ *adj Brit, Aust & NZ* lame, crippled.

———————————— THESAURUS ————————————

gale *n* 1 = **storm**, blast, cyclone, hurricane, squall, tempest, tornado, typhoon 2 *Inf* = **outburst**, burst, eruption, explosion, fit, howl, outbreak, paroxysm, peal, shout, shriek, storm

gall¹ *n* 1 *Inf* = **impudence**, brazenness, cheek (*inf*), chutzpah (*US & Canad inf*), effrontery, impertinence, insolence, nerve (*inf*) 2 = **bitterness**, acrimony, animosity, bile, hostility, rancour

gall² *v* 1 = **annoy**, exasperate, irk, irritate, provoke, rankle, vex 2 = **scrape**, abrade, chafe, irritate

gallant *adj* 1 = **brave**, bold, courageous, heroic, honourable, intrepid, manly, noble, valiant ≠ **cowardly** 2 = **courteous**, attentive, chivalrous, gentlemanly, gracious, noble, polite ≠ **discourteous**

gallivant *v* = **wander**, gad about, ramble, roam, rove

gallop *v* 3, 4 = **run**, bolt, career, dash, hurry, race, rush, speed, sprint

galore *adv* = **in abundance**, all over the place, aplenty, everywhere, in great quantity, in numbers, in profusion, to spare

gamble *v* 1 = **bet**, game, have a flutter (*inf*), play, punt, wager 2 = **risk**, chance, hazard, speculate, stick one's neck out (*inf*), take a chance ◆ *n* 3 = **risk**, chance, leap in the dark, lottery, speculation, uncertainty, venture ≠ **certainty** 4 = **bet**, flutter (*inf*), punt, wager

gambol *v* = **frolic**, caper, cavort, frisk, hop, jump, prance, skip ◆ *n* 2 = **frolic**, caper, hop, jump, prance, skip

game¹ *n* 1 = **pastime**, amusement, distraction, diversion, entertainment, lark,

gammon n cured or smoked ham.

gamut 1 n whole range or scale (of music, emotions, etc.).

gander n 1 male goose. 2 *Informal* quick look.

gang 1 n 1 (criminal) group. 2 organized group of workmen. **gangland** n criminal underworld. **gang up** v form an alliance (against).

gangling 1 adj lanky and awkward.

gangplank n portable bridge for boarding or leaving a ship.

gangrene n decay of body tissue as a result of disease or injury. **gangrenous** adj

gangster 1 n member of a criminal gang.

gangway n 1 passage between rows of seats. 2 gangplank.

gannet n 1 large sea bird. 2 *Slang* greedy person.

gantry n, pl –**tries** structure supporting something such as a crane or rocket.

gaol [jayl] n same as JAIL.

gap 1 n 1 break or opening. 2 interruption or interval. 3 divergence or difference. **gappy** adj

gape 1 v 1 stare in wonder. 2 open the mouth wide. 3 be or become wide open.

gaping adj

garage n 1 building used to house cars. 2 place for the refuelling, sale, and repair of cars. ♦ v 3 put or keep a car in a garage.

garb n 1 clothes. ♦ v 2 clothe.

garbage 1 n rubbish.

garden n 1 piece of land for growing flowers, fruit, or vegetables. ♦ pl 2 ornamental park. ♦ v 3 cultivate a garden. **gardener** n **gardening** n **garden centre** place selling plants and gardening equipment.

gargantuan adj huge.

gargle v 1 wash the throat with (a liquid) by breathing out slowly through the liquid. ♦ n 2 liquid used for gargling.

gargoyle n waterspout carved in the form of a grotesque face, esp. on a church.

garish 1 adj crudely bright or colourful.

garland 1 n 1 wreath of flowers worn or hung as a decoration. ♦ v 2 decorate with garlands.

garlic n pungent bulb of a plant of the onion family, used in cooking.

garment n 1 article of clothing. ♦ pl 2 clothes.

garner 1 v collect or store.

---

recreation, sport ≠ **work** 2 = **match**, competition, contest, event, head-to-head, meeting, tournament 4 = **wild animals**, prey, quarry 6 = **scheme**, design, plan, plot, ploy, stratagem, tactic, trick ♦ adj 8 = **brave**, courageous, gallant, gritty, intrepid, persistent, plucky, spirited ≠ **fearful** 9 = **willing**, desirous, eager, interested, keen, prepared, ready

game² adj = **disabled**, bad, crippled, deformed, gammy (*Brit sl*), incapacitated, injured, lame, maimed

gamut n = **range**, area, catalogue, compass, field, scale, scope, series, sweep

gang n = **group**, band, clique, club, company, coterie, crowd, mob, pack, squad, team

gangling adj = **tall**, angular, awkward, lanky, rangy, rawboned, spindly

gangster n = **racketeer**, crook (*inf*), hood

(*US sl*), hoodlum (*chiefly US*), mobster (*US sl*)

gap n 1 = **opening**, break, chink, cleft, crack, hole, space 2 = **interval**, breathing space, hiatus, interlude, intermission, interruption, lacuna, lull, pause, respite 3 = **difference**, disagreement, disparity, divergence, inconsistency

gape v 1 = **stare**, gawk, gawp (*Brit sl*), goggle, wonder 3 = **open**, crack, split, yawn

garbage n = **waste**, refuse, rubbish, trash (*chiefly US*)

garish adj = **gaudy**, brash, brassy, flashy, loud, showy, tacky (*inf*), tasteless, vulgar

garland n 1 = **wreath**, bays, chaplet, crown, festoon, honours, laurels ♦ v 2 = **adorn**, crown, deck, festoon, wreathe

garner v = **collect**, accumulate, amass, gather, hoard, save, stockpile, store, stow

garnet n red semiprecious stone.

garnish ❶ v 1 decorate (food). ◆ n 2 decoration for food.

garret n attic in a house.

garrison ❶ n 1 troops stationed in a town or fort. 2 fortified place. ◆ v 3 station troops in.

garrotte, garotte n 1 Spanish method of execution by strangling. 2 cord or wire used for this. ◆ v 3 kill by this method.

garrulous ❶ adj talkative.

garter n band worn round the leg to hold up a sock or stocking.

gas n, pl **gases**, **gasses** 1 airlike substance that is not liquid or solid. 2 fossil fuel in the form of a gas, used for heating. 3 gaseous anaesthetic. 4 Chiefly US petrol. ◆ v **gassing**, **gassed** 5 poison or render unconscious with gas. 6 Informal talk idly or boastfully. **gassy** adj filled with gas. **gaseous** adj of or like gas. **gasbag** n Informal person who talks too much. **gas chamber** airtight room which is filled with poison gas to kill people or animals. **gas mask** mask with a chemical filter to protect the wearer against poison gas.

gash ❶ v 1 make a long deep cut in. ◆ n 2 long deep cut.

gasket n piece of rubber etc. placed between the faces of a metal joint to act as a seal.

gasp ❶ v 1 draw in breath sharply or with difficulty. 2 utter breathlessly. ◆ n 3 convulsive intake of breath.

gastric adj of the stomach. **gastritis** n inflammation of the stomach lining.

gastroenteritis n inflammation of the stomach and intestines.

gastronomy n art of good eating. **gastronomic** adj

gate ❶ n 1 movable barrier, usu. hinged, in a wall or fence. 2 opening with a gate. 3 any entrance or way in. 4 (entrance money paid by) those attending a sporting event. **gate-crash** v enter (a party) uninvited. **gatehouse** n building at or above a gateway. **gateway** n 1 entrance with a gate. 2 means of access, e.g. Bombay, gateway to India.

gâteau [**gat**-toe] n, pl **-teaux** [-toes] rich elaborate cake.

gather ❶ v 1 assemble. 2 collect gradually. 3 increase gradually. 4 learn from information given. 5 pick or harvest. 6 draw (material) into small tucks or folds. **gathering** n assembly.

gaudy ❶ adj **gaudier**, **gaudiest** vulgarly bright or colourful.

───────────── THESAURUS ─────────────

away

garnish v 1 = **decorate**, adorn, embellish, enhance, ornament, set off, trim ≠ **strip** ◆ n 2 = **decoration**, adornment, embellishment, enhancement, ornamentation, trimming

garrison n 1 = **troops**, armed force, command, detachment, unit 2 = **fort**, base, camp, encampment, fortification, fortress, post, station, stronghold ◆ v 3 = **station**, assign, position, post, put on duty

garrulous adj = **talkative**, chatty, gossiping, loquacious, prattling, verbose, voluble ≠ **reserved**

gash v 1 = **cut**, gouge, lacerate, slash, slit, split, tear, wound ◆ n 2 = **cut**, gouge, incision, laceration, slash, slit, split, tear,

wound

gasp v 1 = **gulp**, blow, catch one's breath, choke, pant, puff ◆ n 3 = **gulp**, exclamation, pant, puff, sharp intake of breath

gate n 1–3 = **barrier**, door, entrance, exit, gateway, opening, passage, portal

gather v 1, 2 = **assemble**, accumulate, amass, collect, garner, mass, muster, stockpile ≠ **separate** 3 = **intensify**, deepen, expand, grow, heighten, increase, rise, swell, thicken 4 = **learn**, assume, conclude, deduce, hear, infer, surmise, understand 5 = **pick**, cull, garner, glean, harvest, pluck, reap, select 6 = **fold**, pleat, tuck

gaudy adj = **garish**, bright, flashy, loud, showy, tacky (inf), tasteless, vulgar

gauge ❶ [**gayj**] v 1 estimate or judge. 2 measure the amount or condition of. ♦ n 3 measuring instrument. 4 scale or standard of measurement. 5 distance between the rails of a railway track.

gaunt ❶ adj 1 lean and haggard.

gauntlet n 1 heavy glove with a long cuff. 2 medieval armoured glove. **throw down the gauntlet** offer a challenge.

gauze n transparent loosely-woven fabric, often used for surgical dressings. **gauzy** adj

gavel [**gav-**el] n small hammer banged on a table by a judge, auctioneer, or chairman to call for attention.

gay ❶ adj 1 homosexual. 2 carefree and merry. 3 colourful. ♦ n 4 homosexual.

> ✔ **WORD TIP**
> The meaning 'homosexual' is now the most frequent use of gay, which retains the meaning 'happy' only in older books.

gaze ❶ v 1 look fixedly. ♦ n 2 fixed look.

gazebo [gaz-**zee**-boh] n, pl -**bos**, -**boes** summerhouse with a good view.

gazelle n small graceful antelope.

gazette ❶ n official publication containing announcements. **gazetteer** n (part of) a book that lists and describes places.

GB Great Britain.

GBH grievous bodily harm.

GCE General Certificate of Education.

GCSE General Certificate of Secondary Education.

gear ❶ n 1 set of toothed wheels connecting with another or with a rack to change the direction or speed of transmitted motion. 2 mechanism for transmitting motion by gears. 3 setting of a gear to suit engine speed, e.g. first gear. 4 clothing or belongings. 5 equipment. ♦ v 6 prepare or organize for something. **in, out of gear** with the gear mechanism engaged or disengaged. **gearbox** n case enclosing a set of gears in a motor vehicle. **gear up** v prepare for an activity.

geese n plural of GOOSE.

geezer n Informal man.

geisha [**gay**-sha] n, pl -**sha**, -**shas** (in Japan) professional female companion for men.

gel [**jell**] n 1 jelly-like substance, esp. one used to secure a hairstyle. ♦ v **gelling, gelled** 2 form a gel. 3 Informal take on a definite form.

gelatine [**jel**-at-teen], **gelatin** n 1 substance made by boiling animal bones. 2 edible jelly made of this. **gelatinous** [jel-**at**-in-uss] adj of or like jelly.

geld v castrate. **gelding** n castrated horse.

gelignite n type of dynamite used for blasting.

THESAURUS

gauge v 1 = **judge**, adjudge, appraise, assess, estimate, evaluate, guess, rate, reckon, value 2 = **measure**, ascertain, calculate, check, compute, count, determine, weigh ♦ n 3, 4 = **indicator**, criterion, guide, guideline, measure, meter, standard, test, touchstone, yardstick

gaunt adj = **thin**, angular, bony, haggard, lean, pinched, scrawny, skinny, spare

gay adj 1 = **homosexual**, lesbian, queer (inf, derog) 2 = **cheerful**, blithe, carefree, jovial, light-hearted, lively, merry, sparkling ≠ **serious** 3 = **colourful**, bright, brilliant,

flamboyant, flashy, rich, showy, vivid ≠ **conservative** ♦ n 4 = **homosexual**, lesbian

gaze v 1 = **stare**, gape, look, regard, view, watch, wonder ♦ n 2 = **stare**, fixed look, look

gazette n = **newspaper**, journal, news-sheet, paper, periodical

gear n 1 = **cog**, cogwheel, gearwheel 2 = **mechanism**, cogs, machinery, works 4 = **clothing**, clothes, costume, dress, garments, outfit, togs, wear 5 = **equipment**, accoutrements, apparatus, instruments, paraphernalia, supplies, tackle, tools ♦ v 6 = **equip**, adapt, adjust,

gem ❶ *n* 1 precious stone or jewel. 2 highly valued person or thing.

gen *n Informal* information. **gen up on** *v* **genning, genned** *Informal* make or become fully informed about.

gender *n* 1 state of being male or female. 2 *Grammar* classification of nouns in certain languages as masculine, feminine, or neuter.

gene [jean] *n* part of a cell which determines inherited characteristics.

genealogy [jean–ee–**al**–a–gee] *n, pl* **–gies** (study of) the history and descent of a family or families.

general ❶ *adj* 1 common or widespread. 2 of or affecting all or most. 3 not specific. 4 including or dealing with various or miscellaneous items. 5 highest in authority or rank, e.g. *general manager.* ◆ *n* 6 very senior army officer. **in general** mostly or usually. **generally** *adv* **generality** *n, pl* **–ties** 1 general principle. 2 state of being general. **generalize** *v* 1 draw general conclusions. 2 speak in generalities. 3 make widely known or used. **generalization** *n* **general election** election in which representatives are chosen for every constituency. **general practitioner** nonspecialist doctor serving a local area.

generate ❶ *v* produce or bring into being. **generation** *n* all the people born about the same time. **generative** *adj* capable of producing. **generator** *n* machine for converting mechanical energy into electrical energy.

generous ❶ *adj* 1 free in giving. 2 free from pettiness. 3 plentiful. **generosity** *n*

genesis ❶ [**jen**–iss–iss] *n, pl* **–eses** [–iss–eez] beginning or origin.

genial ❶ [**jean**–ee–al] *adj* cheerful and friendly. **genially** *adv* **geniality** *n*

genie [**jean**–ee] *n* (in fairy tales) servant who appears by magic and grants wishes.

genital *adj* of the sexual organs or reproduction. **genitals, genitalia** [jen–it–**ail**–ya] *pl n* external sexual organs.

genius ❶ [**jean**–yuss] *n* (person with) exceptional ability in a particular field.

genocide [**jen**–no–side] *n* murder of a race of people.

genre ❶ [**zhohn**–ra] *n* style of literary, musical, or artistic work.

gent *n Informal* gentleman. **gents** *n* men's public toilet.

genteel ❶ *adj* affectedly proper and polite. **genteelly** *adv*

gentile *adj, n* non–Jewish (person).

gentle ❶ *adj* 1 mild or kindly. 2 not rough

——————{ THESAURUS }——————

fit

gem *n* 1 = **precious stone**, jewel, stone 2 = **prize**, jewel, masterpiece, pearl, treasure

general *adj* 1 = **common**, accepted, broad, extensive, popular, prevalent, public, universal, widespread ≠ **private** 2, 4 = **universal**, across–the–board, blanket, collective, comprehensive, indiscriminate, miscellaneous, overall, overarching, sweeping, total ≠ **special** 3 = **imprecise**, approximate, ill–defined, indefinite, inexact, loose, unspecific, vague ≠ **specific**

generate *v* = **produce**, breed, cause, create, engender, give rise to, make, propagate ≠ **end**

generous *adj* 1 = **liberal**, beneficent, bountiful, charitable, hospitable, kind,

lavish, open–handed, unstinting ≠ **mean** 2 = **unselfish**, big–hearted, good, high–minded, lofty, magnanimous, noble 3 = **plentiful**, abundant, ample, copious, full, lavish, liberal, rich, unstinting ≠ **meagre**

genesis *n* = **beginning**, birth, creation, formation, inception, origin, start

genial *adj* = **cheerful**, affable, agreeable, amiable, congenial, friendly, good–natured, jovial, pleasant, warm

genius *n* = **master**, brainbox, expert, fundi (*S Afr*), hotshot (*inf*), maestro, mastermind, virtuoso, whiz (*inf*) ≠ **idiot**

genre *n* = **type**, category, class, group, kind, sort, species, style

genteel *adj* = **refined**, courteous, cultured, elegant, gentlemanly, ladylike, polite, or severe. 3 gradual. 4 easily controlled, tame. **gentleness** n **gently** adv **gentleman** n 1 polite well–bred man. 2 man of high social position. 3 polite name for a man. **gentlemanly** adj **gentlewoman** n fem

gentry ❶ n people just below the nobility in social rank. **gentrification** n taking–over of a traditionally working–class area by middle–class incomers. **gentrify** v

genuine ❶ adj 1 not fake, authentic. 2 sincere. **genuinely** adv **genuineness** n

genus [**jean**–uss] n, pl **genera** 1 group into which a family of animals or plants is divided. 2 kind, type.

geography n study of the earth's physical features, climate, population, etc. **geographer** n **geographical, geographic** adj

geology n study of the earth's origin, structure, and composition. **geological** adj **geologist** n

geometry n branch of mathematics dealing with points, lines, curves, and surfaces. **geometric, geometrical** adj

geranium n cultivated plant with red, pink, or white flowers.

gerbil [**jer**–bill] n burrowing desert rodent of Asia and Africa.

geriatrics n branch of medicine dealing with old age and its diseases. **geriatric** adj, n old (person).

germ ❶ n 1 microbe, esp. one causing

disease. 2 beginning from which something may develop. 3 simple structure that can develop into a complete organism. **germicide** n substance that kills germs.

germinate ❶ v (cause to) sprout or begin to grow. **germination** n **germinal** adj of or in the earliest stage of development.

gestation n 1 (period of) carrying of young in the womb between conception and birth. 2 developing of a plan or idea in the mind.

gesticulate ❶ v make expressive movements with the hands and arms. **gesticulation** n

gesture ❶ n 1 movement to convey meaning. 2 thing said or done to show one's feelings. ♦ v 3 gesticulate.

get ❶ v **getting, got** 1 obtain or receive. 2 bring or fetch. 3 contract (an illness). 4 capture or seize. 5 (cause to) become as specified, e.g. *get wet*. 6 understand. 7 (often foll. by *to*) come (to) or arrive (at). 8 go on board (a plane, bus, etc.). 9 persuade. 10 receive a broadcast signal. 11 *Informal* annoy. 12 *Informal* have the better of. 13 be revenged on. **get across** v (cause to) be understood. **get at** v 1 gain access to. 2 imply or mean. 3 criticize. **getaway** adj, n (used in) escape. **get by** v manage in spite of difficulties. **get off** v (cause to) avoid the consequences of, or punishment

————————| THESAURUS |————————

respectable, urbane, well–mannered

gentle adj 1 = **mild**, compassionate, humane, kindly, meek, placid, sweet–tempered, tender ≠ **hard** 2 = **moderate**, light, mild, muted, slight, soft, soothing ≠ **powerful** 3 = **gradual**, easy, imperceptible, light, mild, moderate, slight, slow ≠ **sudden** 4 = **tame**, biddable, broken, docile, manageable, placid, tractable

gentry n = **upper class**, aristocracy, elitey, upper crust (inf)

genuine adj 1 = **authentic**, actual, bona fide, legitimate, real, the real McCoy, true, veritable ≠ **false** 2 = **sincere**, candid,

earnest, frank, heartfelt, honest, unaffected, unfeigned ≠ **insincere**

germ n 1 = **microbe**, bacterium, bug (inf), microorganism, virus 2 = **beginning**, embryo, origin, root, rudiment, seed, source, spark 3 = **embryo**, seed

germinate v = **sprout**, bud, develop, generate, grow, originate, shoot, swell, vegetate

gesticulate v = **signal**, gesture, indicate, make a sign, motion, sign, wave

gesture n 1 = **signal**, action, gesticulation, indication, motion, sign 2 = **signal**, indication, sign ♦ v 3 = **signal**, gesticulate, indicate, motion, sign, wave

for, an action. **get off with** v Informal start
a romantic or sexual relationship with. 1
get over v recover from. **get through** v 1
(cause to) succeed. 2 use up (money or
supplies). **get through to** v 1 make (a
person) understand. 2 contact by
telephone. **get–up** n Informal costume. **get
up to** v be involved in.

geyser [geez–er] n 1 spring that discharges
steam and hot water. 2 domestic gas
water heater.

ghastly ❶ adj –lier, –liest 1 Informal
unpleasant. 2 deathly pale. 3 Informal
unwell. 4 Informal horrible. **ghastliness** n

gherkin n small pickled cucumber.

ghetto n, pl –tos, –toes slum area
inhabited by a deprived minority. **ghetto–
blaster** n Informal large portable cassette
recorder or CD player.

ghost ❶ n 1 disembodied spirit of a dead
person. 2 faint trace. ◆ v 3 ghostwrite.
ghostly adj **ghost town** deserted town.
ghostwrite v write (a book or article) on
behalf of another person who is credited
as the author. **ghostwriter** n

ghoul [gool] n 1 person with morbid
interests. 2 demon that eats corpses.
ghoulish adj

giant ❶ n 1 mythical being of superhuman
size. 2 very large person or thing. ◆ adj 3
huge.

gibber [jib–ber] v speak or utter rapidly
and unintelligibly. **gibberish** n rapid
unintelligible talk.

gibbon [gib–bon] n agile tree–dwelling ape
of S Asia.

gibe ❶ [jibe] v, n same as JIBE¹.

giblets [jib–lets] pl n gizzard, liver, heart,
and neck of a fowl.

gidday, g'day interj Aust & NZ expression
of greeting.

giddy ❶ adj –dier, –diest having or causing
a feeling of dizziness. **giddily** adv
giddiness n

gift ❶ n 1 present. 2 natural talent. ◆ v 3
make a present of. **gifted** adj talented.

gig n 1 single performance by pop or jazz
musicians. ◆ v **gigging, gigged** 2 play a
gig or gigs.

gigantic ❶ adj enormous.

giggle ❶ v 1 laugh nervously or foolishly. ◆
n 2 such a laugh. **giggly** adj

gild ❶ v **gilding, gilded** or **gilt** 1 put a thin
layer of gold on. 2 make falsely attractive.

gill [jill] n liquid measure of quarter of a
pint, equal to 0.142 litres.

get v 1 = **obtain**, acquire, attain, gain, land,
net, pick up, procure, receive, secure, win
2 = **bring**, fetch 3 = **contract**, catch, come
down with, fall victim to, take 4 = **capture**,
grab, lay hold of, nab (inf), seize, take
5 = **become**, come to be, grow, turn
6 = **understand**, catch, comprehend,
fathom, follow, perceive, see, take in, work
out 9 = **persuade**, convince, induce,
influence, prevail upon 11 Inf = **annoy**,
bug (inf), gall, irritate, upset, vex

ghastly Inf adj 1 = **horrible**, dreadful,
frightful, gruesome, hideous, horrendous,
loathsome, shocking, terrible, terrifying
≠ **lovely**

ghost n 1 = **spirit**, apparition, phantom,
soul, spectre, spook (inf), wraith 2 = **trace**,
glimmer, hint, possibility, semblance,
shadow, suggestion

giant n 1, 2 = **ogre**, colossus, monster, titan
◆ adj 3 = **huge**, colossal, enormous,
gargantuan, gigantic, immense,
mammoth, titanic, vast ≠ **tiny**

gibe v, n see JIBE¹

giddy adj = **dizzy**, dizzying, faint, light–
headed, reeling, unsteady, vertiginous

gift n 1 = **donation**, bequest, bonus,
contribution, grant, hand–out, legacy,
offering, present 2 = **talent**, ability,
capability, capacity, flair, genius, knack,
power

gigantic adj = **enormous**, colossal, giant,
huge, immense, mammoth, stupendous,
titanic, tremendous

giggle v 1, n 2 = **laugh**, cackle, chortle,
chuckle, snigger, titter, twitter

gild v 2 = **embellish**, adorn, beautify,
brighten, coat, dress up, embroider,

gimmick ● *n* something designed to attract attention or publicity. **gimmickry** *n* **gimmicky** *adj*

gin *n* alcoholic drink flavoured with juniper berries.

ginger *n* 1 root of a tropical plant, used as a spice. 2 light orange–brown colour. **gingery** *adj* **ginger ale, beer** fizzy ginger–flavoured soft drink. **gingerbread** *n* moist cake flavoured with ginger. **ginger group** group within a larger group that agitates for a more active policy.

gingerly ● *adv* cautiously.

gingham *n* cotton cloth, usu. checked or striped.

gingivitis [jin–jiv–**vite**–iss] *n* inflammation of the gums.

ginseng [**jin**–seng] *n* (root of) a plant believed to have tonic and energy–giving properties.

Gipsy *n, pl* –**sies** same as GYPSY.

giraffe *n* African ruminant mammal with a spotted yellow skin and long neck and legs.

gird ● *v* **girding, girded** *or* **girt** 1 put a belt round. 2 secure with or as if with a belt. 3 surround. **gird (up) one's loins** prepare for action.

girdle ● *n* 1 woman's elastic corset. 2 belt. 3 *Anat* encircling structure or part. ◆ *v* 4 surround or encircle.

girl ● *n* 1 female child. 2 young woman. 3 girlfriend. 4 *Informal* any woman. **girlhood** *n* **girlish** *adj* **girlie** *adj Informal* featuring

photographs of naked or scantily clad women. **girlfriend** *n* 1 girl or woman with whom a person is romantically or sexually involved. 2 female friend.

giro [**jire**–oh] *n, pl* –**ros** 1 system of transferring money within a post office or bank directly from one account to another. 2 *Informal* social security payment by giro cheque.

girth ● *n* 1 measurement round something. 2 band round a horse to hold the saddle in position.

gist ● [**jist**] *n* substance or main point of a matter.

give ● *v* **giving, gave, given** 1 present (something) to another person. 2 transfer in exchange or payment. 3 impart. 4 attribute. 5 administer. 6 be a source of. 7 utter or emit. 8 sacrifice or devote. 9 organize or host. 10 concede. 11 yield or break under pressure. ◆ *n* 12 resilience or elasticity. **give away** *v* 1 donate as a gift. 2 reveal. 3 **giveaway** *n* 1 something that reveals hidden feelings or intentions. ◆ *adj* 2 very cheap or free. **give in** *v* admit defeat. **give off** *v* emit. **give out** *v* 1 distribute. 2 emit. 3 come to an end or fail. **give over** *v* 1 set aside for a specific purpose. 2 *Informal* cease. **give up** *v* 1 abandon. 2 acknowledge defeat.

glacé [**glass**–say] *adj* preserved in a thick sugary syrup.

glacier *n* slow–moving mass of ice formed by accumulated snow. **glacial** *adj* 1 of ice

enhance, ornament

gimmick *n* = **stunt**, contrivance, device, dodge, ploy, scheme

gingerly *adv* = **cautiously**, carefully, charily, circumspectly, hesitantly, reluctantly, suspiciously, timidly, warily ≠ **boldly**

gird *v* 3 = **surround**, encircle, enclose, encompass, enfold, hem in, ring

girdle *n* 2 = **belt**, band, cummerbund, sash, waistband ◆ *v* 4 = **surround**, bound, encircle, enclose, encompass, gird, ring

girl *n* 1, 2 = **female child**, damsel (*arch*),

daughter, lass, lassie (*inf*), maid (*arch*), maiden (*arch*), miss

girth *n* 1 = **circumference**, bulk, measure, size

gist *n* = **point**, core, essence, force, idea, meaning, sense, significance, substance

give *v* 1 = **present**, award, contribute, deliver, donate, grant, hand over *or* out, provide, supply ≠ **take** 3, 7 = **announce**, communicate, issue, notify, pronounce, transmit, utter 6 = **produce**, cause, engender, make, occasion 8 = **devote**, hand over, relinquish 10 = **concede**, allow, or glaciers. **2** very cold. **3** unfriendly. **glaciation** n

glad ⊕ adj **gladder, gladdest 1** pleased and happy. **2** causing happiness. **glad to** very willing to (do something). **the glad eye gladly** adv **gladden** v make glad. **glad rags** Informal best clothes.

glade n open space in a forest.

gladiator n (in ancient Rome) man trained to fight in arenas to provide entertainment.

gladiolus n, pl **-lus, -li, -luses** garden plant with sword–shaped leaves.

glamour ⊕ n alluring charm or fascination. **glamorous** adj alluring. **glamorize** v

glance ⊕ v **1** look rapidly or briefly. **2** glint or gleam. ◆ n **3** brief look. **glancing** adj hitting at an oblique angle. **glance off** v strike and be deflected off (an object) at an oblique angle.

gland n organ that produces and secretes substances in the body. **glandular** adj

glare ⊕ v **1** stare angrily. **2** be unpleasantly bright. ◆ n **3** angry stare. **4** unpleasant brightness. **glaring** adj **1** conspicuous. **2** unpleasantly bright. **glaringly** adv

glass n **1** hard brittle, usu. transparent substance consisting of metal silicates or similar compounds. **2** tumbler. **3** its

contents. **4** objects made of glass. **5** mirror. **6** barometer. ◆ pl **7** spectacles. **glassy** adj **1** like glass. **2** expressionless. **glassiness** n **glasshouse** n **1** greenhouse. **2** Informal army prison.

glaucoma n eye disease.

glaze ⊕ v **1** fit or cover with glass. **2** cover with a protective shiny coating. ◆ n **3** transparent coating. **4** substance used for this. **glazier** n person who fits windows with glass.

gleam ⊕ n **1** small beam or glow of light. **2** brief or faint indication. ◆ v **3** emit a gleam. **gleaming** adj

glean v **1** gather (facts etc.) bit by bit. **2** gather (the useful remnants of a crop) after harvesting.

glee ⊕ n triumph and delight. **gleeful** adj

glen n deep narrow valley.

glib ⊕ adj **glibber, glibbest** fluent but insincere or superficial.

glide ⊕ v **1** move easily and smoothly. **2** pass gradually and imperceptibly. ◆ n **3** smooth easy movement. **glider** n aircraft without an engine which floats on air currents. **gliding** n sport of flying gliders.

glimmer ⊕ v **1** shine faintly, flicker. ◆ n **2** faint gleam. **3** faint indication.

━━━━━━━━ THESAURUS ━━━━━━━━

grant **11** = **surrender**, yield
glad adj **1** = **happy**, contented, delighted, gratified, joyful, overjoyed, pleased ≠ **sad** **2** = **pleasing**, cheerful, cheering, gratifying, pleasant
glamour n = **charm**, allure, appeal, attraction, beauty, enchantment, fascination, prestige
glance v **1** = **peek**, glimpse, look, peep, scan, view ≠ **study 2** = **gleam**, flash, glimmer, glint, glisten, glitter, reflect, shimmer, shine, twinkle ◆ n **3** = **peek**, dekko (sl), glimpse, look, peep, view ≠ **examination**
glare v **1** = **scowl**, frown, glower, look daggers, lour or lower **2** = **dazzle**, blaze, flame, flare ◆ n **3** = **scowl**, black look, dirty look, frown, glower, lour or lower

4 = **dazzle**, blaze, brilliance, flame, glow
glaze v **2** = **coat**, enamel, gloss, lacquer, polish, varnish ◆ n **3, 4** = **coat**, enamel, finish, gloss, lacquer, lustre, patina, polish, shine, varnish
gleam n **1** = **glow**, beam, flash, glimmer, ray, sparkle **2** = **trace**, flicker, glimmer, hint, inkling, suggestion ◆ v **3** = **shine**, flash, glimmer, glint, glisten, glitter, glow, shimmer, sparkle
glee n = **delight**, elation, exhilaration, exuberance, exultation, joy, merriment, triumph
glib adj = **smooth**, easy, fluent, insincere, plausible, quick, ready, slick, suave, voluble
glide v **1** = **slide**, coast, drift, float, flow, roll, run, sail, skate, slip **2** = **slip**, drift, slide

glimpse ❶ *n* 1 brief or incomplete view. ◆ *v* 2 catch a glimpse of.

glint ❶ *v* 1 gleam brightly. ◆ *n* 2 bright gleam.

glisten ❶ *v* gleam by reflecting light.

glitter ❶ *v* 1 shine with bright flashes. 2 be showy. ◆ *n* 3 sparkle or brilliance. 4 tiny pieces of shiny decorative material.

gloat ❶ *v* (often foll. by *over*) regard one's own good fortune or the misfortune of others with smug or malicious pleasure.

globe ❶ *n* 1 sphere with a map of the earth on it. 2 spherical object. 3 *S Afr* light bulb. **the globe** the earth. **global** *adj* 1 worldwide. 2 total or comprehensive. **globally** *adv* **globetrotter** *n* habitual worldwide traveller. **globetrotting** *n, adj*

globule ❶ *n* small round drop. **globular** *adj*

glockenspiel *n* percussion instrument consisting of small metal bars played with hammers.

gloom ❶ *n* 1 melancholy or depression. 2 darkness. **gloomy** *adj* **gloomier, gloomiest. gloomily** *adv*

glory ❶ *n, pl* **–ries** 1 praise or honour. 2 splendour. 3 praiseworthy thing. ◆ *v* – **rying, –ried** 4 (foll. by *in*) triumph or exalt. **glorify** *v* 1 make (something) seem more worthy than it is. 2 praise. 3 **glorification** *n* **glorious** *adj* 1 brilliantly beautiful. 2 delightful. 3 full of or conferring glory. **gloriously** *adv* **glory hole** *Informal* untidy cupboard or storeroom.

gloss[1] ❶ *n* 1 surface shine or lustre. 2 paint or cosmetic giving a shiny finish. **glossy** *adj* **–sier, –siest** 1 smooth and shiny. 2 (of a magazine) printed on shiny paper. **glossily** *adv* **glossiness** *n* **gloss over** *v* (try to) cover up or pass over (a fault or error).

gloss[2] ❶ *n* 1 explanatory comment added to the text of a book. ◆ *v* 2 add glosses to.

glove *n* covering for the hand with individual sheaths for each finger and the thumb. **gloved** *adj* covered by a glove or gloves. **glove compartment** small storage

━━━━ THESAURUS ━━━━

glimmer *v* 1 = **flicker**, blink, gleam, glisten, glitter, glow, shimmer, shine, sparkle, twinkle ◆ *n* 2 = **gleam**, blink, flicker, glow, ray, shimmer, sparkle, twinkle 3 = **trace**, flicker, gleam, hint, inkling, suggestion

glimpse *n* 1 = **look**, glance, peek, peep, sight, sighting ◆ *v* 2 = **catch sight of**, espy, sight, spot, spy, view

glint *v* 1 = **gleam**, flash, glimmer, glitter, shine, sparkle, twinkle ◆ *n* 2 = **gleam**, flash, glimmer, glitter, shine, sparkle, twinkle, twinkling

glisten *v* = **gleam**, flash, glance, glare, glimmer, glint, glitter, shimmer, shine, sparkle, twinkle

glitter *v* 1 = **shine**, flash, glare, gleam, glimmer, glint, glisten, shimmer, sparkle, twinkle ◆ *n* 3 = **shine**, brightness, flash, glare, gleam, radiance, sheen, shimmer, sparkle 4 = **glamour**, display, gaudiness, pageantry, show, showiness, splendour, tinsel

gloat *v* (often foll. by *over*) = **relish**, crow, drool, exult, glory, revel in, rub it in (*inf*),

triumph

globe *n* 2 = **sphere**, ball, orb **the globe** = **earth**, planet, world

globule *n* = **droplet**, bead, bubble, drop, particle, pearl, pellet

gloom *n* 1 = **depression**, dejection, despondency, low spirits, melancholy, sorrow, unhappiness, woe ≠ **delight** 2 = **darkness**, blackness, dark, dusk, murk, obscurity, shade, shadow, twilight ≠ **light**

glory *n* 1 = **honour**, dignity, distinction, eminence, fame, praise, prestige, renown ≠ **shame** 2 = **splendour**, grandeur, greatness, magnificence, majesty, nobility, pageantry, pomp ◆ *v* 4 (foll. by *in*) = **triumph**, exalt, pride oneself, relish, revel, take delight

gloss[1] *n* 1, 2 = **shine**, brightness, gleam, lustre, patina, polish, sheen, veneer

gloss[2] *n* 1 = **comment**, annotation, commentary, elucidation, explanation, footnote, interpretation, note, translation ◆ *v* 2 = **interpret**, annotate, comment, elucidate, explain, translate area in the dashboard of a car.

glow ● v 1 emit light and heat without flames. 2 shine. 3 have a feeling of wellbeing or satisfaction. 4 (of a colour) look warm. 5 be hot. ◆ n 6 glowing light. 7 warmth of colour. 8 feeling of wellbeing. **glow–worm** n insect giving out a green light.

glower ● [rhymes with **power**] v, n scowl.

glucose n kind of sugar found in fruit.

glue ● n 1 natural or synthetic sticky substance used as an adhesive. ◆ v **gluing** or **glueing, glued** 2 fasten with glue. 3 (foll. by to) pay full attention to, e.g. her eyes were glued to the TV. **gluey** adj **glue–sniffing** n inhaling of glue fumes for intoxicating or hallucinatory effects.

glum ● adj **glummer, glummest** sullen or gloomy.

glut ● n 1 excessive supply. ◆ v **glutting, glutted** 2 oversupply.

glutton ● n 1 greedy person. 2 person with a great capacity for something. **gluttonous** adj **gluttony** n

glycerine, glycerin n colourless sweet liquid used widely in chemistry and industry.

GMT Greenwich Mean Time.

gnarled ● adj rough, twisted, and knobbly.

gnash v grind (the teeth) together in anger or pain.

gnat n small biting two–winged fly.

gnaw ● v gnawing, gnawed, gnawed or gnawn 1 bite or chew steadily. 2 (foll. by at) cause constant distress (to).

gnome n imaginary creature like a little old man.

gnu [noo] n oxlike S African antelope.

go ● v going, went, gone 1 move to or from a place. 2 be in regular attendance at. 3 depart. 4 function. 5 be, do, or become as specified. 6 contribute to a result, e.g. it just goes to show. 7 be allotted to a specific purpose or recipient. 8 be sold. 9 blend or harmonize. 10 fail or break down. 11 elapse. 12 be got rid of. 13 attend. 14 reach or exceed certain limits, e.g. she's gone too far this time. 15 be acceptable. 16 n 17 attempt. 18 verbal attack. 19 turn. 20 Informal energy or vigour. **make a go of** be successful at. **go back on** v break (a promise etc.). **go–between** n intermediary. **go for** v 1 Informal choose. 2 attack. 3 apply to equally. **go–getter** n energetically ambitious person. **go off** v 1 explode. 2 ring or sound. 3 Informal become stale or rotten. 4 Informal stop liking. **go out** v 1 go to entertainments or social functions. 2 be romantically involved (with). 3 be extinguished. **go over** v examine or check. **go–slow** n deliberate slowing of work–rate as an industrial protest. **go through** v 1 suffer or undergo. 2 examine or search.

goad ● v 1 provoke (someone) to take

——————| T H E S A U R U S |——————

glow v 1 = **smoulder**, burn 2 = **shine**, brighten, burn, gleam, glimmer, redden ◆ n 6 = **light**, burning, gleam, glimmer, luminosity, phosphorescence ≠ **dullness** 7 = **radiance**, brightness, brilliance, effulgence, splendour, vividness ≠ **dullness**

① **glower** v = **scowl**, frown, give a dirty look, glare, look daggers, lour or lower

② **glower** n = **scowl**, black look, dirty look, frown, glare, lour or lower

glue n 1 = **adhesive**, cement, gum, paste

glum adj = **gloomy**, crestfallen, dejected, doleful, low, morose, pessimistic, sullen

glut n 1 = **surfeit**, excess, oversupply, plethora, saturation, superfluity, surplus ≠ **lack** ◆ v 2 = **saturate**, choke, clog, deluge, flood, inundate, overload, oversupply

glutton n 1 = **gourmand**, gannet (sl), pig (inf)

gnarled adj = **twisted**, contorted, knotted, knotty, rough, rugged, weather–beaten, wrinkled

gnaw v 1 = **bite**, chew, munch, nibble

go v 1 = **move**, advance, journey, make for, pass, proceed, set off, travel ≠ **remain** 3 = **leave**, depart, make tracks, move out, some kind of action, usu. in anger. ◆ n 2 spur or provocation. 3 spiked stick for driving cattle.

goal ❶ n 1 Sport posts through which the ball or puck has to be propelled to score. 2 score made in this way. 3 aim or purpose. **goalie** n Informal goalkeeper. **goalkeeper** n player whose task is to stop shots entering the goal. **goalpost** n one of the two posts supporting the crossbar of a goal. **move the goalposts** change the aims of an activity to ensure the desired result.

goat n sure–footed ruminant animal with horns. **get someone's goat** Slang annoy someone. **goatee** n pointed tuftlike beard.

gobble¹ ❶ v eat hastily and greedily.

gobble² n 1 rapid gurgling cry of the male turkey. ◆ v 2 make this noise.

gobbledegook ❶ **gobbledygook** n unintelligible (official) language or jargon.

goblet n drinking cup without handles.

goblin n (in folklore) small malevolent creature.

god n 1 spirit or being worshipped as having supernatural power. 2 object of worship, idol. 3 (G–) (in monotheistic religions) the Supreme Being, creator and ruler of the universe. **the gods** top balcony in a theatre. **goddess** n fem **godlike** adj **godly** adj devout or pious. **godliness** n **god–fearing** adj pious and devout. **godforsaken** adj desolate or dismal. **godsend** n something unexpected but welcome.

gogga n S Afr informal any small insect.

goggle v 1 (of the eyes) bulge. 2 stare. **goggles** pl n protective spectacles.

go–kart n small low–powered racing car.

gold n 1 yellow precious metal. 2 coins or articles made of this. 3 colour of gold. ◆ adj 4 made of gold. 5 gold–coloured. **gold–digger** n 1 Informal woman who uses her sexual attractions to get money from a man. **goldfinch** n kind of finch, the male of which has yellow–and–black wings. **goldfish** n orange fish kept in ponds or aquariums. **gold leaf** thin gold sheet used for gilding. **gold medal** medal given to the winner of a competition or race.

golf n 1 outdoor game in which a ball is struck with clubs into a series of holes. ◆ v 2 play golf. **golfer** n

gondola n 1 long narrow boat used in Venice. 2 suspended cabin of a cable car, airship, etc. **gondolier** n person who propels a gondola.

gong n 1 rimmed metal disc that produces a note when struck. 2 Slang medal.

good ❶ adj better, best 1 giving pleasure. 2 morally excellent. 3 beneficial. 4 kindly. 5 talented. 6 well behaved. 7 valid. 8 reliable. 9 financially sound. 10 complete or full. ◆ n 11 benefit. 12 positive moral qualities. ◆ pl 13 merchandise. 14 property. **as good as** virtually. **for good** permanently. **goodness** n **goodly** adj considerable. **goody** n 1 Informal hero in a book or film. 2 enjoyable thing. **goody–goody** adj, n smugly virtuous (person). **good–for–nothing** adj, n irresponsible or worthless (person). **Good Samaritan**

slope off, withdraw 4 = **function**, move, operate, perform, run, work ≠ **break (down)** 6 = **contribute**, lead to, serve, tend, work towards 9 = **harmonize**, agree, blend, chime, complement, correspond, fit, match, suit 11 = **elapse**, expire, flow, lapse, pass, slip away ◆ n 17, 19 = **attempt**, bid, crack (inf), effort, shot (inf), try, turn 20 Inf = **energy**, drive, force, life, spirit, verve, vigour, vitality, vivacity

goad v 1 = **provoke**, drive, egg on, exhort,

incite, prod, prompt, spur ◆ n 2 = **provocation**, impetus, incentive, incitement, irritation, spur, stimulus, urge

goal n 3 = **aim**, ambition, end, intention, object, objective, purpose, target

gobble¹ v = **devour**, bolt, cram, gorge, gulp, guzzle, stuff, swallow, wolf

gobbledegook, gobbledygook n = **nonsense**, babble, cant, gabble, gibberish, hocus–pocus, jargon, mumbo jumbo, twaddle

person who helps another in distress.
goodwill n 1 kindly feeling. 2 value of a
business in reputation etc. over and above
its tangible assets.

> ✓ **WORD TIP**
> Note that *good* is an adjective. To
> modify a verb, use *well: She did well.*

goodbye ❶ *interj, n* expression used on
parting.
gooey *adj* **gooier, gooiest** *Informal* sticky
and soft.
goose *n, pl* **geese** 1 web–footed bird like a
large duck. 2 female of this bird. **goose
flesh, pimples** bumpy condition of the
skin and bristling of the hair due to cold or
fright. **goose step** march step in which
the leg is raised rigidly.
gooseberry n 1 edible yellowy–green
berry. 2 *Informal* unwanted third person

accompanying a couple.
gore¹ ❶ *n* blood from a wound.
gore² ❶ *v* pierce with horns.
gorge ❶ *n* 1 deep narrow valley. ◆ *v* 2 eat
greedily. **make one's gorge rise** cause
feelings of disgust or nausea.
gorgeous ❶ *adj* 1 strikingly beautiful or
attractive. 2 *Informal* very pleasant.
gorilla *n* largest of the apes, found in
Africa.
gormless *adj Informal* stupid.
gorse *n* prickly yellow–flowered shrub.
gosling *n* young goose.
gospel ❶ *n* 1 (G–) any of the first four
books of the New Testament. 2
unquestionable truth. 3 Black religious
music originating in the churches of the
Southern US.
gossamer *n* 1 very fine fabric. 2 filmy
cobweb.
gossip ❶ *n* 1 idle talk, esp. about other

——————| T H E S A U R U S |——————

good *adj* 1 = **excellent**, acceptable,
admirable, fine, first–class, first–rate, great,
pleasing, satisfactory, splendid, superior
≠ **bad** 2 = **honourable**, admirable, ethical,
honest, moral, praiseworthy, righteous,
trustworthy, upright, virtuous, worthy
≠ **bad** 3 = **favourable**, advantageous,
beneficial, convenient, fitting, helpful,
profitable, suitable, useful, wholesome
≠ **disadvantageous** 4 = **kind**, altruistic,
benevolent, charitable, friendly, humane,
kind–hearted, kindly, merciful, obliging
≠ **bad** 5 = **expert**, able, accomplished,
adept, adroit, clever, competent,
proficient, skilled, talented ≠ **useless**
6 = **well–behaved**, dutiful, obedient,
orderly, polite, well–mannered ≠ **rude**
7 = **valid**, authentic, bona fide, genuine,
legitimate, proper, real, true ≠ **false**
10 = **full**, adequate, ample, complete,
considerable, extensive, large, substantial,
sufficient ◆ *n* 11 = **benefit**, advantage,
gain, interest, profit, use, usefulness,
welfare, wellbeing ≠ **harm** 12 = **virtue**,
excellence, goodness, merit, morality,
rectitude, right, righteousness, worth

≠ **evil** ◆ *pl* 13 = **merchandise**,
commodities, stock, stuff, wares
14 = **property**, belongings, chattels,
effects, gear, paraphernalia, possessions,
things, trappings **for good**
= **permanently**, finally, for ever,
irrevocably, once and for all
① **goodbye** *interj* = **farewell**, adieu
② **goodbye** *n* = **parting**, adieu, farewell,
leave–taking
gore¹ *n* = **blood**, bloodshed, butchery,
carnage, slaughter
gore² *v* = **pierce**, impale, transfix, wound
gorge *n* 1 = **ravine**, canyon, chasm, cleft,
defile, fissure, pass ◆ *v* 2 = **overeat**, cram,
devour, feed, glut, gobble, gulp, guzzle,
stuff, wolf
gorgeous *adj* 1 = **beautiful**, dazzling,
elegant, magnificent, ravishing, splendid,
stunning (*inf*), sumptuous, superb ≠ **cheap**
2 *Inf* = **pleasing**, delightful, enjoyable,
exquisite, fine, glorious, good, lovely
≠ **awful**
gospel *n* 1 = **doctrine**, credo, creed,
message, news, revelation, tidings
2 = **truth**, certainty, fact, the last word

people. 2 person who engages in gossip.
♦ v gossiping, gossiped 3 engage in
gossip. gossipy adj

gouge ❶ [gowj] v 1 scoop or force out. 2
cut (a hole or groove) in (something). ♦ n
3 hole or groove. 4 chisel with a curved
cutting edge.

goulash [goo–lash] n rich stew seasoned
with paprika.

gourd [goord] n 1 fleshy fruit of a climbing
plant. 2 its dried shell, used as a container.

gourmand [goor–mand] n person who is
very keen on food and drink.

gourmet ❶ [goor–may] n connoisseur of
food and drink.

gout [gowt] n disease causing
inflammation of the joints.

govern ❶ v 1 rule, direct, or control. 2
exercise restraint over (temper etc.).
governance n governing. governess n
woman teacher in a private household.
government n 1 executive policy–making
body of a state. 2 exercise of political
authority over a country or state. 3 system
by which a country or state is ruled.
governmental adj governor n 1 official
governing a province or state. 2 senior

administrator of a society, institution, or
prison.

gown ❶ n 1 woman's long formal dress. 2
surgeon's overall. 3 official robe worn by
judges, clergymen, etc.

GP general practitioner.

grab ❶ v grabbing, grabbed 1 grasp
suddenly, snatch. ♦ n 2 sudden snatch. 3
mechanical device for gripping.

grace ❶ n 1 beauty and elegance. 2 polite,
kind behaviour. 3 goodwill or favour. 4
courtesy or decency. 5 delay granted. 6
short prayer of thanks for a meal. 7 (G–)
title of a duke, duchess, or archbishop (in
Greek mythology) three sister goddesses,
givers of charm and beauty. ♦ v 8 honour.
9 add grace to. graceful adj gracefully adv
graceless adj gracious adj 1 kind and
courteous. 2 condescendingly polite. 3
elegant. graciously

grade ❶ n 1 place on a scale of quality,
rank, or size. 2 mark or rating. 3 US & Aust
class in school. ♦ v 4 arrange in grades. 5
assign a grade to. make the grade
succeed. gradation n 1 (stage in) a series
of degrees or steps. 2 arrangement in
stages.

————— THESAURUS —————

gossip n 1 = idle talk, blether, chinwag
(Brit inf), chitchat, hearsay, scandal, small
talk, tittle–tattle 2 = busybody, chatterbox
(inf), chatterer, gossipmonger,
scandalmonger, tattler, telltale ♦ v
3 = chat, blether, gabble, jaw (sl), prate,
prattle, tattle

gouge v 1, 2 = scoop, chisel, claw, cut, dig
(out), hollow (out) ♦ n 3 = gash, cut,
furrow, groove, hollow, scoop, scratch,
trench

gourmet n = connoisseur, bon vivant,
epicure, foodie (inf), gastronome

govern v 1 = rule, administer, command,
control, direct, guide, handle, lead,
manage, order 2 = restrain, check,
control, curb, discipline, hold in check,
master, regulate, subdue, tame

gown n 1 = dress, frock 3 = robe, costume,
garb, garment, habit

grab v 1 = snatch, capture, catch, catch or
take hold of, clutch, grasp, grip, pluck,
seize, snap up

grace n 1 = elegance, attractiveness,
beauty, charm, comeliness, ease,
gracefulness, poise, polish, refinement,
tastefulness ≠ awkwardness 2,
4 = manners, consideration, decency,
decorum, etiquette, propriety, tact ≠ bad
manners 3 = goodwill, benefaction,
benevolence, favour, generosity,
goodness, kindliness, kindness ≠ ill will
5 = indulgence, mercy, pardon, reprieve
6 = prayer, benediction, blessing, thanks,
thanksgiving ♦ v 8 = honour, dignify,
favour ≠ ruin 9 = enhance, adorn,
decorate, embellish, enrich, ornament, set
off

grade n 1–3 = level, category (US & Aust),
class, degree, echelon, group, rank, stage

gradient ⊙ *n* (degree of) slope.
gradual ⊙ *adj* occurring, developing, or moving in small stages. **gradually** *adv*
graduate ⊙ *v* 1 receive a degree or diploma. 2 group by type or quality. 3 mark (a container etc.) with units of measurement. ◆ *n* 4 holder of a degree. **graduation** *n*
graffiti [graf–**fee**–tee] *pl n* words or drawings scribbled or sprayed on walls etc.

✓ WORD TIP

English does not have a singular form for this word and tends to use *graffiti* for both singular and multiple examples.

---

graft¹ ⊙ *n* 1 surgical transplant of skin or tissue. 2 shoot of a plant set in the stalk of another. ◆ *v* 3 transplant (living tissue) surgically. 4 insert (a plant shoot) in another stalk.
graft² *Informal* ◆ *n* 1 hard work. 2 obtaining of money by misusing one's position. ◆ *v* 3 work hard.
grain ⊙ *n* 1 seedlike fruit of a cereal plant. 2 cereal plants in general. 3 small hard particle. 4 very small amount. 5 arrangement of fibres, as in wood. 6 texture or pattern resulting from this. **go against the grain** be contrary to one's natural inclination. **grainy** *adj*
gram, gramme *n* metric unit of mass equal to one thousandth of a kilogram.

grammar *n* 1 branch of linguistics dealing with the form, function, and order of words. 2 use of words. 3 book on the rules of grammar. **grammatical** *adj* according to the rules of grammar. **grammar school** esp. formerly, a secondary school providing an education with a strong academic bias.
gramophone *n* old–fashioned type of record player.
gran *n Informal* grandmother.
granary *n, pl* –**ries** storehouse for grain.
grand ⊙ *adj* 1 large or impressive, imposing. 2 dignified or haughty. 3 *Informal* excellent. 4 (of a total) final. ◆ *n* 5 *Slang* thousand pounds or dollars. 6 grand piano. **grandchild** *n* child of one's child. **granddaughter** *n* female grandchild. **grandfather** *n* male grandparent. **grandfather clock** tall standing clock with a pendulum and wooden case. **grandmother** *n* female grandparent. **grandparent** *n* parent of one's parent. **grand piano** large harp–shaped piano with the strings set horizontally. **grand slam** winning of all the games or major tournaments in a sport in one season. **grandson** *n* male grandchild. **grandstand** *n* terraced block of seats giving the best view at a sports ground.
granite [**gran**–nit] *n* very hard igneous rock often used in building.
grant ⊙ *v* 1 consent to fulfil (a request). 2 give formally. 3 admit. ◆ *n* 4 sum of money provided by a government for a

---

THESAURUS

◆ *v* 4, 5 = **classify**, arrange, class, group, order, range, rank, rate, sort
gradient *n* = **slope**, bank, declivity, grade, hill, incline, rise
gradual *adj* = **steady**, gentle, graduated, piecemeal, progressive, regular, slow, unhurried
graduate *v* 2 = **classify**, arrange, grade, group, order, rank, sort 3 = **mark off**, calibrate, grade, measure out, proportion, regulate
graft¹ *n* 2 = **shoot**, bud, implant, scion,

splice, sprout ◆ *v* 3, 4 = **transplant**, affix, implant, ingraft, insert, join, splice
grain *n* 1 = **seed**, grist, kernel 2 = **cereals**, corn 4 = **bit**, fragment, granule, modicum, morsel, particle, piece, scrap, speck, trace 5, 6 = **texture**, fibre, nap, pattern, surface, weave
grand *adj* 1 = **impressive**, grandiose, great, imposing, large, magnificent, regal, splendid, stately, sublime ≠ **unimposing** 3 *Inf* = **excellent**, fine, first–class, great (*inf*), outstanding, smashing (*inf*), splendid,

specific purpose, such as education. **take for granted 1** accept as true without proof. **2** take advantage of without due appreciation.

granule ⊕ *n* small grain. **granular** *adj* of or like grains. **granulated** *adj* (of sugar) in the form of coarse grains.

grape *n* small juicy green or purple berry, eaten raw or used to produce wine, raisins, currants, or sultanas. **grapevine** *n* **1** grape–bearing vine. **2** *Informal* unofficial way of spreading news.

grapefruit *n* large round yellow citrus fruit.

graph *n* drawing showing the relation of different numbers or quantities plotted against a set of axes.

graphic ⊕ *adj* **1** vividly descriptive. **2** of or using drawing, painting, etc. **graphics** *pl n* diagrams, graphs, etc., esp. as used on a television programme or computer screen. **graphically** *adv*

graphite *n* soft black form of carbon, used in pencil leads.

grapple ⊕ *v* **1** try to cope with (something difficult). **2** come to grips with (a person). **grappling iron** grapnel.

grasp ⊕ *v* **1** grip something firmly. **2** understand. **3** try to seize. ◆ *n* **4** grip or clasp. **5** understanding. **6** total rule or possession. **grasping** *adj* greedy or avaricious.

grass *n* **1** common type of plant with jointed stems and long narrow leaves, including cereals and bamboo. **2** lawn. **3** pasture land. **4** *Slang* marijuana. **5** *Slang* person who informs, esp. on criminals. ◆ *v* **6** cover with grass. **7** (often foll. by *on*) *Slang* inform on. **grassy** *adj* **–sier, –siest**. **grasshopper** *n* jumping insect with long hind legs. **grass roots 1** ordinary members of a group, as distinct from its leaders. **2** essentials. **grassroots** *adj* **grass widow** wife whose husband is absent for a time.

grate[1] ⊕ *v* **1** rub into small bits on a rough surface. **2** scrape with a harsh rasping noise. **3** annoy. **grater** *n* **grating** *adj* **1** harsh or rasping. **2** annoying.

grate[2] *n* framework of metal bars for holding fuel in a fireplace. **grating** *n* framework of metal bars covering an opening.

grateful ⊕ *adj* feeling or showing gratitude. **gratefully** *adv*

gratify ⊕ *v* **–fying, –fied 1** satisfy or please. **2** indulge (a desire or whim). **gratification** *n*

gratis *adv, adj* free, for nothing.

THESAURUS

wonderful ≠ **terrible**

grant *v* **1 = consent to**, accede to, agree to, allow, permit **2 = give**, allocate, allot, assign, award, donate, hand out, present **3 = admit**, acknowledge, concede ◆ *n* **4 = award**, allowance, donation, endowment, gift, hand–out, present, subsidy

granule *n* **= grain**, atom, crumb, fragment, molecule, particle, scrap, speck

graphic *adj* **1 = vivid**, clear, detailed, explicit, expressive, lively, lucid, striking ≠ **vaguely 2 = pictorial**, diagrammatic, visual ≠ **impressionistic**

grapple *v* **1 = deal with**, address oneself to, confront, get to grips with, tackle, take on, wrestle **2 = grip**, clutch, grab, grasp, seize, struggle, wrestle

grasp *v* **1, 3 = grip**, catch, clasp, clinch, clutch, grab, grapple, hold, lay or take hold of, seize, snatch **2 = understand**, catch on, catch or get the drift of, comprehend, get, realize, see, take in ◆ *n* **4 = grip**, clasp, clutches, embrace, hold, possession, tenure **5 = understanding**, awareness, comprehension, grip, knowledge, mastery **6 = control**, power, reach, scope

grate[1] *v* **1 = scrape**, creak, grind, rasp, rub, scratch **3 = annoy**, exasperate, get on one's nerves (*inf*), irritate, jar, rankle, set one's teeth on edge

grateful *adj* **= thankful**, appreciative, beholden, indebted, obliged

gratify *v* **= please**, delight, give pleasure, gladden, humour, requite, satisfy

gratitude *n* feeling of being thankful for a favour or gift.

gratuitous ⊕ *adj* 1 unjustified, e.g. *gratuitous violence*. 2 given free.

grave¹ ⊕ *n* hole for burying a corpse. **gravestone** *n* stone marking a grave. **graveyard** *n* cemetery.

grave² ⊕ *adj* 1 causing concern. 2 serious and solemn. 3 important.

grave³ [rhymes with **halve**] *n* accent (`) over a vowel to indicate a special pronunciation.

gravel *n* mixture of small stones and coarse sand. **gravelly** *adj* 1 covered with gravel. 2 rough-sounding.

graven *adj* carved or engraved.

gravitate *v* 1 be influenced or drawn towards. 2 *Physics* move by gravity. **gravitation** *n* **gravitational** *adj*

gravity ⊕ *n, pl* **-ties** 1 force of attraction of one object for another, esp. of objects to the earth. 2 seriousness or importance. 3 solemnity.

gravy *n, pl* **-vies** 1 juices from meat in cooking. 2 sauce made from these.

graze¹ ⊕ *v* feed on grass.

graze² ⊕ *v* 1 scratch or scrape the skin. 2 touch lightly in passing. ◆ *n* 3 slight scratch or scrape.

grease *n* 1 soft melted animal fat. 2 any thick oily substance. ◆ *v* 3 apply grease to. **greasy** *adj* **greasier**, **greasiest** covered with or containing grease. **greasiness** *n* **greasepaint** *n* theatrical make-up.

great ⊕ *adj* 1 large in size or number. 2 important. 3 pre-eminent. 4 *Informal* excellent. **great-** *prefix* one generation older or younger than, e.g. *great-grandfather*. **greatly** *adv* **greatness** *n* **greatcoat** *n* heavy overcoat.

greed ⊕ *n* excessive desire for food, wealth, etc. **greedy** *adj* **greedily** *adv* **greediness** *n*

green ⊕ *adj* 1 of a colour between blue and yellow. 2 characterized by green plants or foliage. 3 (G-) of or concerned with environmental issues. 4 unripe. 5 envious or jealous. 6 immature or gullible. ◆ *n* 7 colour between blue and yellow. 8 area of grass kept for a special purpose. ◆ *pl* 9 green vegetables. ◆ *v* 10 make or become green. **greenness** *n* **greenery** *n*

THESAURUS

gratitude *n* = **thankfulness**, appreciation, gratefulness, indebtedness, obligation, recognition, thanks

gratuitous *adj* 1 = **unjustified**, baseless, causeless, groundless, needless, superfluous, uncalled-for, unmerited, unnecessary, unwarranted, wanton 2 = **voluntary**, complimentary, free, gratis, spontaneous, unasked-for, unpaid, unrewarded

grave¹ *n* = **tomb**, burying place, crypt, mausoleum, pit, sepulchre, vault

grave² 1 *adj* = **critical**, acute, dangerous, pressing, serious, severe, threatening ≠ **mild** 2 = **serious**, dignified, dour, earnest, sober, solemn, sombre, unsmiling ≠ **happy** 3 = **important**, serious, urgent

gravity *n* 2 = **importance**, acuteness, momentousness, perilousness, seriousness, severity, significance, urgency, weightiness ≠ **insignificance** 3 = **solemnity**, dignity,

earnestness, seriousness, sobriety ≠ **happines**

graze¹ *v* = **feed**, browse, crop, pasture

graze² *v* 1 = **scratch**, abrade, chafe, scrape, skin 2 = **touch**, brush, glance off, rub, scrape, shave, skim ◆ *n* 3 = **scratch**, abrasion, scrape

great *adj* 1 = **large**, big, enormous, gigantic, huge, immense, prodigious, vast, voluminous ≠ **little** 2 = **important**, critical, crucial, momentous, serious, significant ≠ **trivial** 3 = **famous**, eminent, illustrious, noteworthy, outstanding, prominent, remarkable, renowned 4 *Inf* = **excellent**, fantastic (*inf*), fine, marvellous (*inf*), superb, terrific (*inf*), tremendous (*inf*), wonderful ≠ **poor**

greed *n* = **gluttony**, acquisitiveness, avarice, avidity, covetousness, craving, desire, edacity, esurience, gormandizing, hunger, longing, selfishness, voracity vegetation. **green belt** protected area of open country around a town. **green fingers** skill in gardening. **greenfly** n green aphid, a common garden pest. **greengage** n sweet green plum. **greengrocer** n shopkeeper selling vegetables and fruit. **greenhorn** n novice. **greenhouse** n glass building for rearing plants. **greenhouse effect** rise in the temperature of the earth caused by heat absorbed from the sun being unable to leave the atmosphere. **green light 1** signal to go. **2** permission to proceed with something. **greenroom** n room for actors when offstage.

greet 🟢 v **1** meet with expressions of welcome. **2** receive in a specified manner. **3** be immediately noticeable to. **greeting** n

gregarious 🟢 adj **1** fond of company. **2** (of animals) living in flocks or herds.

gremlin n imaginary being blamed for mechanical malfunctions.

grenade n small bomb thrown by hand or fired from a rifle. **grenadier** n soldier of a regiment formerly trained to throw grenades.

grenadine [gren–a–**deen**] n syrup made from pomegranates.

grey 🟢 adj **1** of a colour between black and white. **2** (of hair) partly turned white. **3** dismal or dark. **4** dull or boring. ◆ n **5** grey colour. **6** grey or white horse. **greying** adj (of hair) turning grey. **greyish** adj

greyness n **grey matter** Informal brains.

greyhound n swift slender dog used in racing.

grid n **1** network of horizontal and vertical lines, bars, etc. **2** national network of electricity supply cables.

griddle n flat iron plate for cooking.

gridiron n **1** frame of metal bars for grilling food. **2** American football pitch.

grief 🟢 n deep sadness. **grieve** v (cause to) feel grief. **grievance** n real or imaginary cause for complaint. **grievous** adj **1** very severe or painful. **2** very serious.

grill n **1** device on a cooker that radiates heat downwards. **2** grilled food. **3** gridiron. ◆ v **4** cook under a grill. **5** question relentlessly. **grilling** n relentless questioning

grille, grill n grating over an opening.

grim 🟢 adj grimmer, grimmest **1** stern. **2** harsh or forbidding. **3** very unpleasant. **grimly** adv **grimness** n

grimace 🟢 n **1** ugly or distorted facial expression of pain, disgust, etc. ◆ v **2** make a grimace.

grime 🟢 n **1** ingrained dirt. ◆ v **2** make very dirty. **grimy** adj **griminess** n

grin v grinning, grinned **1** smile broadly, showing the teeth. ◆ n **2** broad smile.

grind 🟢 v grinding, ground **1** crush or rub to a powder. **2** smooth or sharpen by friction. **3** scrape together with a harsh noise. **4** oppress. **5** n **6** Informal hard work.

———————————————— THESAURUS ————————————————

≠ **generosity**

green adj **2** = **leafy**, grassy, verdant **3** (with cap.) = **ecological**, conservationist, environment–friendly, non–polluting, ozone–friendly **5** = **jealous**, covetous, envious, grudging, resentful **6** = **inexperienced**, gullible, immature, naive, new, raw, untrained, wet behind the ears (inf) ◆ n **8** = **lawn**, common, sward, turf

greet v **1, 2** = **welcome**, accost, address, compliment, hail, meet, receive, salute

gregarious adj **1** = **outgoing**, affable, companionable, convivial, cordial, friendly,

sociable, social

grey adj **3** = **dismal**, dark, depressing, dim, drab, dreary, dull, gloomy **4** = **characterless**, anonymous, colourless, dull

grief n = **sadness**, anguish, distress, heartache, misery, regret, remorse, sorrow, suffering, woe ≠ **delight**

grim adj **1, 2** = **forbidding**, formidable, harsh, merciless, ruthless, severe, sinister, stern, terrible ≠ **easy**

grimace n **1** = **scowl**, face, frown, sneer ◆ v **2** = **scowl**, frown, lour or lower, make a face or faces, sneer

7 act or sound of grinding. **grind out** v produce in a routine or uninspired manner. **grindstone** n stone used for grinding.

grip ❶ n 1 firm hold or grasp. 2 way in which something is grasped. 3 mastery or understanding. 4 US travelling bag. 5 handle. ◆ v **gripping, gripped** 6 grasp or hold tightly. 7 hold the interest or attention of. **gripping** adj

gripe v 1 Informal complain persistently. ◆ n 2 Informal complaint. 3 sudden intense bowel pain.

grisly ❶ adj –lier, –liest horrifying or ghastly.

grist n grain for grinding. **grist to one's mill** something which can be turned to advantage.

gristle n tough stringy animal tissue found in meat. **gristly** adj

grit ❶ n 1 rough particles of sand. 2 courage. ◆ pl 3 coarsely ground grain. ◆ v **gritting, gritted** 4 spread grit on (an icy road etc.). 5 clench or grind (the teeth). **gritty** adj –tier, –tiest

grizzle v Informal whine or complain.

grizzled adj grey–haired.

grizzly n, pl –zlies large American bear (also **grizzly bear**).

groan ❶ n 1 deep sound of grief or pain. 2 Informal complaint. ◆ v 3 utter a groan. 4 Informal complain.

grocer n shopkeeper selling foodstuffs. **grocery** n, pl –ceries 1 business or premises of a grocer. ◆ pl 2 goods sold by a grocer.

grog n spirit, usu. rum, and water.

groin n 1 place where the legs join the abdomen.

groom ❶ n 1 person who looks after horses. 2 bridegroom. 3 officer in a royal household. ◆ v 4 make or keep one's clothes and appearance neat and tidy. 5 brush or clean a horse. 6 train (someone) for a future role.

groove ❶ n long narrow channel in a surface.

grope ❶ v feel about or search uncertainly.

gross ❶ adj 1 flagrant. 2 vulgar. 3 Slang disgusting or repulsive. 4 repulsively fat. 5 total, without deductions. ◆ n 6 twelve dozen. ◆ v 7 make as total revenue before deductions. **grossly** adv

grotesque ❶ [grow–**tesk**] adj 1 strangely

──────THESAURUS──────

grime n 1 = **dirt**, filth, grot (sl), smut, soot

grind v 1 = **crush**, abrade, granulate, grate, mill, pound, powder, pulverize, triturate 2 = **smooth**, polish, sand, sharpen, whet 3 = **scrape**, gnash, grate ◆ n 6 Inf = **hard work**, chore, drudgery, labour, sweat (inf), toil

grip n 1 = **control**, clasp, clutches, domination, hold, influence, mana (NZ), possession, power 3 = **understanding**, command, comprehension, grasp, mastery ◆ v 6 = **grasp**, clasp, clutch, hold, seize, take hold of 7 = **engross**, absorb, enthral, entrance, fascinate, hold, mesmerize, rivet

grisly adj = **gruesome**, appalling, awful, dreadful, ghastly, horrible, macabre, shocking, terrifying

grit n 1 = **gravel**, dust, pebbles, sand 2 = **courage**, backbone, determination, fortitude, guts (inf), perseverance, resolution, spirit, tenacity ◆ v 5 = **grind**, clench, gnash, grate

groan n 1 = **moan**, cry, sigh, whine 2 Inf = **complaint**, gripe (inf), grouse, grumble, objection, protest ◆ v 3 = **moan**, cry, sigh, whine 4 Inf = **complain**, bemoan, gripe (inf), grouse, grumble, lament, object

groom n 1 = **stableman**, hostler or ostler (arch), stableboy ◆ v 4 = **smarten up**, clean, preen, primp, spruce up, tidy 5 = **rub down**, brush, clean, curry, tend 6 = **train**, coach, drill, educate, make ready, nurture, prepare, prime, ready

groove n = **indentation**, channel, cut, flute, furrow, hollow, rut, trench, trough

grope v = **feel**, cast about, fish, flounder, forage, fumble, scrabble, search

gross adj 1 = **blatant**, flagrant, grievous, heinous, rank, sheer, unmitigated, utter distorted. 2 absurd. ◆ n 3 grotesque person or thing. 4 artistic style mixing distorted human, animal, and plant forms. **grotesquely** adv

grotto n, pl **-toes, -tos** small picturesque cave.

grotty adj **-tier, -tiest** Informal nasty or in bad condition.

grouch Informal ◆ v 1 grumble or complain. ◆ n 2 person who is always complaining. 3 persistent complaint. **grouchy** adj

ground ① n 1 surface of the earth. 2 soil. 3 area used for a specific purpose, e.g. rugby ground. 4 position in an argument or controversy. 5 background colour of a painting. ◆ pl 6 enclosed land round a house. 7 reason or motive. 8 coffee dregs. ◆ adj 9 on or of the ground. ◆ v 10 base or establish. 11 instruct in the basics. 12 ban an aircraft or pilot from flying. 13 run (a ship) aground. 14 place on the ground. **groundless** adj without reason. **grounding** n basic knowledge of a subject. **ground-breaking** adj innovative. **ground floor** floor of a building level with the ground. **groundnut** n peanut. **groundsheet** n

waterproof sheet put on the ground under a tent. **groundsman** n person employed to maintain a sports ground or park. **groundswell** n rapidly developing general feeling or opinion. **groundwork** n preliminary work.

group ① n 1 number of people or things regarded as a unit. 2 small band of musicians or singers. ◆ v 3 place or form into a group.

grouse¹ n 1 stocky game bird. 2 its flesh.

grouse² ① v 1 grumble or complain. ◆ n 2 complaint.

grout n 1 thin mortar. ◆ v 2 fill up with grout.

grove ① n small group of trees.

grovel ① [grov-el] v **-elling, -elled** 1 behave humbly in order to win a superior's favour. 2 crawl on the floor.

grow ① v **growing, grew, grown** 1 develop physically. 2 (of a plant) exist. 3 cultivate (plants). 4 increase in size or degree. 5 originate. 6 become gradually, e.g. it was growing dark. **growth** n 1 growing. 2 increase. 3 something grown or growing. 4 tumour. **grown-up** adj, n adult. **grow up** v mature.

THESAURUS

≠ **qualified** 2 = **vulgar**, coarse, crude, indelicate, obscene, offensive ≠ **pure** 4 = **fat**, corpulent, hulking, obese, overweight 5 = **total**, aggregate, before deductions, before tax, entire, whole ≠ **net** ◆ v 7 = **earn**, bring in, make, rake in (inf), take

grotesque adj 1 = **deformed**, distorted 2 = **unnatural**, bizarre, fantastic, freakish, outlandish, preposterous, strange

ground n 1, 2 = **earth**, dry land, land, soil, terra firma, terrain, turf 3 = **stadium**, arena, field, park (inf), pitch ◆ pl 6 = **land**, estate, fields, gardens, terrain, territory 7 = **reason**, basis, cause, excuse, foundation, justification, motive, occasion, pretext, rationale 8 = **dregs**, deposit, lees, sediment ◆ v 10 = **base**, establish, fix, found, set, settle 11 = **instruct**, acquaint with, familiarize with, initiate, teach, train,

tutor

group n 1 = **set**, band, bunch, cluster, collection, crowd, gang, pack, party ◆ v 3 = **arrange**, bracket, class, classify, marshal, order, sort

grouse² v 1 = **complain**, bellyache (sl), carp, gripe (inf), grumble, moan, whine, whinge (inf) ◆ n 2 = **complaint**, grievance, gripe (inf), grouch (inf), grumble, moan, objection, protest

grove n = **wood**, coppice, copse, covert, plantation, spinney, thicket

grovel v 1 = **humble oneself**, abase oneself, bow and scrape, crawl, creep, cringe, demean oneself, fawn, kowtow, toady ≠ **be proud** 2 = **crawl**, creep ≠ **be proud**

grow v 1 = **increase**, develop, enlarge, expand, get bigger, multiply, spread, stretch, swell ≠ **decrease** 3 = **cultivate**,

growl v 1 make a low rumbling sound. 2 utter with a growl. ◆ n 3 growling sound.

grub ❶ n 1 legless insect larva. 2 *Slang* food. ◆ v **grubbing, grubbed** 3 search carefully for something by digging or by moving things about. 4 dig up the surface of (soil).

grubby ❶ adj **–bier, –biest** dirty. **grubbiness** n

grudge ❶ v 1 be unwilling to give or allow. ◆ n 2 resentment.

gruel n thin porridge.

gruelling ❶ adj exhausting or severe.

gruesome ❶ adj causing horror and disgust.

gruff ❶ adj rough or surly in manner or voice. **gruffly** adv **gruffness** n

grumble ❶ v 1 complain. 2 rumble. ◆ n 3 complaint. 4 rumble. **grumbling** adj, n

grumpy ❶ adj **grumpier, grumpiest** bad–tempered. **grumpily** adv **grumpiness** n

grunt v 1 make a low short gruff sound,

like a pig. ◆ n 2 pig's sound. 3 gruff noise.

G–string n small strip of cloth covering the genitals and attached to a waistband.

guarantee ❶ n 1 formal assurance, esp. in writing, that a product will meet certain standards. 2 something that makes a specified condition or outcome certain. 3 v **–teeing, –teed** 5 give a guarantee. 6 secure against risk etc. 7 ensure. **guarantor** n person who gives or is bound by a guarantee.

guard ❶ v 1 watch over to protect or to prevent escape. ◆ n 2 person or group that guards. 3 official in charge of a train. 4 protection. 5 screen for enclosing anything dangerous. 6 posture of defence in sports such as boxing or fencing. ◆ pl 7 (G–) regiment with ceremonial duties. **guarded** adj cautious or noncommittal. **guard against** v take precautions against. **guardian** n keeper or protector. **guardsman** n member of the Guards.

──────── THESAURUS ────────

breed, farm, nurture, produce, propagate, raise 4 = **improve**, advance, flourish, progress, prosper, succeed, thrive 5 = **originate**, arise, issue, spring, stem 6 = **become**, come to be, get, turn

grub n 1 = **larva**, caterpillar, maggot 2 *Sl* = **food**, nosh (*sl*), rations, sustenance, tucker (*Aust & NZ inf*), victuals ◆ v 3 = **search**, ferret, forage, fossick (*Aust & NZ*), hunt, rummage, scour, uncover, unearth 4 = **dig up**, burrow, pull up, root (*inf*)

grubby adj = **dirty**, filthy, grimy, messy, mucky, scruffy, scungy (*Aust & NZ inf*), seedy, shabby, sordid, squalid, unwashed

grudge v 1 = **resent**, begrudge, complain, covet, envy, mind ≠ **welcome** ◆ n 2 = **resentment**, animosity, antipathy, bitterness, dislike, enmity, grievance, rancour ≠ **goodwill**

gruelling adj = **exhausting**, arduous, backbreaking, demanding, laborious, punishing, severe, strenuous, taxing, tiring

gruesome adj = **horrific**, ghastly, grim, grisly, horrible, macabre, shocking, terrible

gruff adj a = **surly**, bad–tempered, brusque, churlish, grumpy, rough, rude, sullen, ungracious ≠ **pleasant** b = **hoarse**, croaking, guttural, harsh, husky, low, rasping, rough, throaty ≠ **smooth**

grumble v 1 = **complain**, bleat, carp, gripe (*inf*), grouch (*inf*), grouse, moan, whine, whinge (*inf*) 2 = **rumble**, growl, gurgle, murmur, mutter, roar ◆ n 3 = **complaint**, grievance, gripe (*inf*), grouch (*inf*), grouse, moan, objection, protest 4 = **rumble**, growl, gurgle, murmur, muttering, roar

grumpy adj = **irritable**, bad–tempered, cantankerous, crotchety (*inf*), peevish, sulky, sullen, surly, testy

guarantee n 1 = **assurance**, bond, certainty, pledge, promise, security, surety, warranty, word of honour ◆ v 5– 7 = **ensure**, assure, certify, make certain, pledge, promise, secure, vouch for, warrant

guard v 1 = **watch over**, defend, mind, preserve, protect, safeguard, secure, shield ◆ n 2 = **protector**, custodian, defender, lookout, picket, sentinel, sentry, warder,

guava [gwah–va] n yellow–skinned tropical American fruit.

guerrilla ❶ guerilla n member of an unofficial armed force fighting regular forces.

guess ❶ v 1 estimate or draw a conclusion without proper knowledge. 2 estimate correctly by guessing. 3 *Chiefly US* suppose. ◆ n 4 estimate or conclusion reached by guessing. **guesswork** n process or results of guessing.

guest ❶ n 1 person entertained at another's house or at another's expense. 2 invited performer or speaker. 3 customer at a hotel or restaurant. ◆ v 4 appear as a visiting player or performer. **guesthouse** n boarding house.

guffaw n 1 crude noisy laugh. ◆ v 2 laugh in this way.

guide ❶ n 1 person who conducts tour expeditions. 2 person who shows the way. 3 book of instruction or information. 4 model for behaviour. 5 something used to gauge something or to help in planning one's actions. 6 (G–) member of an organization for girls equivalent to the Scouts. ◆ v 7 act as a guide for. 8 control,

supervise, or influence. **guidance** n leadership, instruction, or advice. **guided missile** missile whose flight is controlled electronically. **guide dog** dog trained to lead a blind person. **guideline** n set principle for doing something.

guild ❶ n 1 organization or club. 2 *Hist* society of men in the same trade or craft.

guile ❶ [gile] n cunning or deceit. ◆ *adj*, *adj*

guillotine n 1 machine for beheading people. 2 device for cutting paper or sheet metal. 3 method of preventing lengthy debate in parliament by fixing a time for taking the vote. ◆ v 4 behead by guillotine. 5 limit debate by the guillotine.

guilt ❶ n 1 fact or state of having done wrong. 2 remorse for wrongdoing. **guiltless** adj innocent. **guilty** adj 1 responsible for an offence or misdeed. 2 feeling or showing guilt. **guiltily** adv

guinea n 1 former British monetary unit worth 21 shillings (1.05 pounds). 2 former gold coin of this value. **guinea fowl** bird related to the pheasant. **guinea pig** 1 tailless S American rodent, commonly kept as a pet. 2 *Informal* person used for

──┤ THESAURUS ├──

watch, watchman 4, 5 = **protection**, buffer, defence, safeguard, screen, security, shield

guerrilla, guerilla n = **freedom fighter**, partisan, underground fighter

guess v 1 = **estimate**, conjecture, hypothesize, predict, speculate, work out ≠ **know** 3 *Chiefly US* = **suppose**, believe, conjecture, fancy, imagine, judge, reckon, suspect, think ≠ **know** ◆ n
4 = **supposition**, conjecture, hypothesis, prediction, shot in the dark, speculation, theory ≠ **fact**

guest n 1, 3 = **visitor**, boarder, caller, company, lodger, visitant

guide n 1, 2 = **escort**, adviser, conductor, counsellor, guru, leader, mentor, teacher, usher 3 = **guidebook**, catalogue, directory, handbook, instructions, key, manual
4 = **model**, example, ideal, inspiration,

paradigm, standard 5 = **pointer**, beacon, guiding light, landmark, lodestar, marker, sign, signpost ◆ v 7 = **lead**, accompany, conduct, direct, escort, shepherd, show the way, usher 8 = **supervise**, advise, command, control, counsel, direct, handle, influence, instruct, manage, manoeuvre, oversee, steer, superintend, teach, train

guild n 1 = **society**, association, brotherhood, club, company, corporation, fellowship, fraternity, league, lodge, order, organization, union

guile n = **cunning**, artifice, cleverness, craft, deceit, slyness, trickery, wiliness

guilt n 1 = **culpability**, blame, guiltiness, misconduct, responsibility, sinfulness, wickedness, wrongdoing ≠ **virtue**
2 = **remorse**, contrition, guilty conscience, regret, self–reproach, shame, stigma

experimentation.

guise ❶ [rhymes with **size**] *n* 1 false appearance. 2 external appearance.

guitar *n* stringed instrument with a flat back and a long neck, played by plucking or strumming. **guitarist** *n*

gulf ❶ *n* 1 large deep bay. 2 chasm. 3 large difference in opinion or understanding.

gull *n* long-winged sea bird.

gullet *n* muscular tube through which food passes from the mouth to the stomach.

gullible ❶ *adj* easily tricked. **gullibility** *n*

gully ❶ *n, pl* –**lies** channel cut by running water.

gulp ❶ *v* 1 swallow hastily. 2 gasp. ◆ *n* 3 gulping. 4 thing gulped.

gum¹ *n* firm flesh in which the teeth are set.

gum² ❶ *n* 1 sticky substance obtained from certain plants. 2 adhesive. 3 chewing gum. 4 gumdrop. 5 gumtree. ◆ *v* gumming, gummed 6 stick with gum. **gummy** *adj* –**mier**, –**miest**. **gumboots** *pl n* Wellington boots. **gumdrop** *n* hard jelly-like sweet. **gumtree** *n* eucalyptus tree.

gumption ❶ *n Informal* 1 resourcefulness. 2 courage.

gun ❶ *n* 1 weapon with a metal tube from which missiles are fired by explosion. 2

device from which a substance is ejected under pressure. ◆ *v* gunning, gunned 3 cause (an engine) to run at high speed. **jump the gun** act prematurely. **gunner** *n* artillery soldier. **gunnery** *n* use or science of large guns. **gunboat** *n* small warship. **gun down** *v* shoot (a person). **gun for** *v* seek or pursue vigorously. **gunman** *n* armed criminal. **gunmetal** *n* 1 alloy of copper, tin, and zinc. ◆ *adj* 2 dark grey. **gunpowder** *n* explosive mixture of potassium nitrate, sulphur, and charcoal. **gunshot** *n* shot or range of a gun.

gunge *n Informal* sticky unpleasant substance. **gungy** *adj* –**gier**, –**giest**

gunwale, gunnel [**gun**–nel] *n* top of a ship's side.

guppy *n, pl* –**pies** small colourful aquarium fish.

gurgle ❶ *v, n* (make) a bubbling noise.

guru ❶ *n* 1 Hindu or Sikh religious teacher or leader. 2 leader or adviser.

gush ❶ *v* 1 flow out suddenly and profusely. 2 express admiration effusively. ◆ *n* 3 sudden copious flow. 4 sudden surge of strong feeling.

gusset *n* piece of material sewn into a garment to strengthen it.

gust ❶ *n* 1 sudden blast of wind.

─────── THESAURUS ───────

≠ **pride**

guise *n* 1 = **disguise**, pretence, semblance 2 = **form**, appearance, aspect, demeanour, mode, shape

gulf *n* 1 = **bay**, bight, sea inlet 2 = **chasm**, abyss, gap, opening, rift, separation, split, void

gullible *adj* = **naive**, born yesterday, credulous, innocent, simple, trusting, unsuspecting, wet behind the ears (*inf*)

gully *n* = **channel**, ditch, gutter, watercourse

gulp *v* 1 = **swallow**, devour, gobble, guzzle, quaff, swig (*inf*), swill, wolf 2 = **gasp**, choke, swallow ◆ *n* 4 = **swallow**, draught, mouthful, swig (*inf*)

gum² *n* 1 = **resin** 2 = **glue**, adhesive, cement, paste ◆ *v* 6 = **stick**, affix, cement,

glue, paste

gumption *n Inf* 1 = **resourcefulness**, acumen, astuteness, common sense, enterprise, initiative, mother wit, savvy (*sl*), wit(s)

gun *n* 1 = **firearm**, handgun, piece (*sl*), shooter (*sl*)

① **gurgle** *v* = **murmur**, babble, bubble, lap, plash, purl, ripple, splash

② **gurgle** *n* = **murmur**, babble, purl, ripple

guru *n* 2 = **teacher**, authority, leader, mana (*NZ*), master, mentor, sage, Svengali, tutor

gush *v* 1 = **flow**, cascade, flood, pour, run, rush, spout, spurt, stream 2 = **enthuse**, babble, chatter, effervesce, effuse, overstate, spout ◆ *n* 3, 4 = **stream**, cascade, flood, flow, jet, rush, spout,

◆ *v* 2 blow in gusts. **gusty** *adj*

gusto ❶ *n* enjoyment or zest.

gut ❶ *n* 1 intestine. 2 *Informal* fat stomach. 3 short for CATGUT. ◆ *pl* 4 internal organs. 5 *Informal* courage. 6 *v* **gutting, gutted** 7 remove the guts from. 8 (of a fire) destroy the inside of (a building). ◆ *adj* 9 basic or instinctive, e.g. *a gut reaction.* **gutsy** *adj* – **sier, –siest** *Informal* 1 courageous. 2 vigorous or robust, e.g. *a gutsy performance.* **gutted** *adj Informal* disappointed and upset.

gutter ❶ *n* 1 shallow channel for carrying away water from a roof or roadside. ◆ *v* 2 (of a candle) burn unsteadily, with wax running down the sides. **the gutter** degraded or criminal environment. **guttering** *n* material for gutters. **gutter press** newspapers that rely on sensationalism. **guttersnipe** *n* neglected slum child.

guttural ❶ *adj* 1 (of a sound) produced at the back of the throat. 2 (of a voice) harsh–sounding.

guy¹ ❶ *n* 1 *Informal* man or boy. 2 effigy of Guy Fawkes burnt on Nov. 5th (**Guy Fawkes Day**).

guy² *n* rope or chain to steady or secure something. **guyrope** *n*

guzzle ❶ *v* eat or drink greedily.

gym *n* 1 gymnasium. 2 gymnastics.

gymkhana [jim–**kah**–na] *n* horse–riding competition.

gymnasium *n* large room with equipment for physical training. **gymnast** *n* expert in gymnastics. **gymnastic** *adj* **gymnastics** *pl n* exercises to develop strength and agility.

gynaecology [guy–nee–**kol**–la–jee] *n* branch of medicine dealing with diseases and conditions specific to women. **gynaecologist** *n*

gypsum *n* chalklike mineral used to make plaster of Paris.

Gypsy ❶ *n, pl* **–sies** member of a travelling people found throughout Europe.

gyrate [jire–**rate**] *v* rotate or spiral about a point or axis. **gyration** *n*

gyroscope [**jire**–oh–skohp] *n* disc rotating on an axis that can turn in any direction, so the disc maintains the same position regardless of the movement of the surrounding structure.

THESAURUS

spurt, torrent

gust *n* 1 = **blast**, blow, breeze, puff, rush, squall ◆ *v* 2 = **blow**, blast, squall

gusto *n* = **relish**, delight, enjoyment, enthusiasm, fervour, pleasure, verve, zeal

gut *n* 2 *Inf* = **paunch**, belly, potbelly, spare tyre (*Brit sl*) ◆ *pl* 4 = **intestines**, belly, bowels, entrails, innards (*inf*), insides (*inf*), stomach, viscera 5 *Inf* = **courage**, audacity, backbone, bottle (*sl*), daring, mettle, nerve, pluck, spirit ◆ *v* 7 = **disembowel**, clean 8 = **ravage**, clean out, despoil, empty ◆ *adj* 9 As in **gut reaction**

= **instinctive**, basic, heartfelt, intuitive, involuntary, natural, spontaneous, unthinking, visceral

gutter *n* 1 = **drain**, channel, conduit, ditch, sluice, trench, trough

guttural *adj* = **throaty**, deep, gravelly, gruff, hoarse, husky, rasping, rough, thick

guy¹ *n* 1 *Inf* = **man**, bloke (*Brit inf*), chap, fellow, lad, person

guzzle *v* = **devour**, bolt, cram, drink, gobble, stuff (oneself), swill, wolf

Gypsy *n* = **traveller**, Bohemian, nomad, rambler, roamer, Romany, rover, wanderer

H h

haberdasher *n Brit, Aust & NZ* dealer in small articles used for sewing. **haberdashery** *n*

habit 𝕋 *n* 1 established way of behaving. 2 addiction to a drug. 3 costume of a monk or nun. **habitual** *adj* done regularly and repeatedly.

habitable *adj* fit to be lived in. **habitat** *n* natural home of an animal or plant. **habitation** *n* (occupation of) a dwelling place.

hack¹ 𝕋 *v* cut or chop violently *Brit and NZ informal* tolerate.

hack² 𝕋 *n* 1 (inferior) writer or journalist. 2 horse kept for riding.

hackles *pl n* **make one's hackles rise** make one feel angry or hostile.

hackneyed 𝕋 *adj* (of a word or phrase) unoriginal and overused.

hacksaw *n* small saw for cutting metal.

haddock *n* edible sea fish.

haemoglobin [hee–moh–**globe**–in] *n* protein found in red blood cells which carries oxygen.

haemophilia [hee–moh–**fill**–lee–a] *n* hereditary illness in which the blood does not clot. **haemophiliac** *n*

haemorrhage [**hem**–or–ij] *n* 1 heavy bleeding. ◆ *v* 2 bleed heavily.

haemorrhoids [**hem**–or–oydz] *pl n* swollen veins in the anus (also **piles**).

hag 𝕋 *n* ugly old woman. **hag–ridden** *adj* distressed or worried.

haggard 𝕋 *adj* looking tired and ill.

haggis *n* Scottish dish made from sheep's offal, oatmeal, suet, and seasonings, boiled in a bag made from the sheep's stomach.

haggle 𝕋 *v* bargain or wrangle over a price.

hail¹ 𝕋 *n* 1 (shower of) small pellets of ice. 2 large number of insults, missiles, blows, etc. ◆ *v* 3 fall as or like hail. **hailstone** *n*

hail² 𝕋 *v* 1 call out to, greet. 2 stop (a taxi) by waving. 3 acknowledge publicly. **hail from** *v* come originally from.

hair 𝕋 *n* 1 threadlike growth on the skin. 2 such growths collectively, esp. on the head. **hairy** *adj* 1 covered with hair. 2 *Slang* dangerous or exciting. **hairiness** *n* **hairdo** *n Informal* hairstyle. **hairdresser** *n* person who cuts and styles hair. **hairgrip** *n*

THESAURUS

habit *n* 1 = **mannerism**, custom, practice, proclivity, propensity, quirk, tendency, way 2 = **addiction**, dependence

hack¹ *v* = **cut**, chop, hew, lacerate, mangle, mutilate, slash

hack² *n* 1 = **scribbler**, literary hack 2 = **horse**, crock, nag

hackneyed *adj* = **unoriginal**, clichéd, commonplace, overworked, stale, stereotyped, stock, threadbare, tired, trite

hag *n* = **witch**, crone, harridan

haggard *adj* = **gaunt**, careworn, drawn, emaciated, pinched, thin, wan

haggle *v* = **bargain**, barter, beat down

hail¹ *n* 1 = **shower**, rain, storm 2 = **barrage**, bombardment, downpour, volley ◆ *v* 3 = **shower**, batter, beat down upon, bombard, pelt, rain, rain down on

hail² *v* 1 = **salute**, greet, welcome ≠ **cut** (*inf*) 2 = **flag down**, signal to, wave down 3 = **acclaim**, acknowledge, applaud, cheer, honour ≠ **condemn hail from** = **come from**, be a native of, be born in, originate in small, tightly bent metal hairpin. **hairline** n 1 edge of hair at the top of the forehead. ◆ adj 2 very fine or narrow. **hairpin** n U–shaped wire used to hold the hair in place. **hairpin bend** very sharp bend in a road. **hair–raising** adj frightening or exciting. **hairsplitting** n, adj making petty distinctions. **hairstyle** n cut and arrangement of a person's hair.

hale ⊕ adj healthy, robust.

half ⊕ n, pl **halves** 1 either of two equal parts. 2 Informal half–pint of beer etc. 3 half–price ticket. ◆ adj 4 denoting one of two equal parts. ◆ adv 5 to the extent of half. 6 partially. **half–baked** adj Informal not properly thought out. **half–brother**, **half–sister** n brother or sister related through one parent only. **half–caste** n Offens person with parents of different races. **half–cocked** adj go off **half–cocked**, (at) **half–cock** fail because of inadequate preparation. **half–hearted** adj unenthusiastic. **half–life** n time taken for half the atoms in radioactive material to decay. **half–time** n Sport short rest period between two halves of a game. **halfway** adv, adj at or to half the distance. **halfwit** n foolish or stupid person.

halibut n large edible flatfish.

halitosis n unpleasant–smelling breath.

hall ⊕ n 1 (also **hallway**) entrance passage. 2 large room or building for public meetings, dances, etc. 3 large country house.

hallelujah [hal–ee–**loo**–ya] interj exclamation of praise to God.

hallmark ⊕ n 1 typical feature. 2 mark indicating the standard of tested gold and silver.

hallo interj same as HELLO.

hallowed adj regarded as holy.

hallucinate v seem to see something that is not really there. **hallucination** n **hallucinatory** adj **hallucinogenic** adj

halo ⊕ [**hay**–loh] n, pl –**loes**, –**los** 1 ring of light round the head of a sacred figure. 2 circle of refracted light round the sun or moon.

halt ⊕ v 1 come or bring to a stop. ◆ n 2 temporary stop. 3 minor railway station without a building. **halting** adj hesitant, uncertain.

halter n strap round a horse's head with a rope to lead it with. **halterneck** n woman's top or dress with a strap fastened at the back of the neck.

halve ⊕ v 1 divide in half. 2 reduce by half.

ham[1] n smoked or salted meat from a pig's thigh. **ham–fisted** adj clumsy.

ham[2] Informal ◆ n 1 amateur radio operator. 2 actor who overacts. ◆ v hamming, hammed 3 ham it up overact.

hamburger n minced beef shaped into a flat disc, cooked and usu. served in a bread roll.

hamlet n small village.

hammer ⊕ n 1 tool with a heavy metal head and a wooden handle, used to drive

———— THESAURUS ————

hair n 2 = **locks**, head of hair, mane, mop, shock, tresses

hale adj = **healthy**, able–bodied, fit, flourishing, in the pink, robust, sound, strong, vigorous, well

half n 1 = **equal part**, fifty per cent, hemisphere, portion, section ◆ adj 4 = **partial**, halved, limited, moderate ◆ adv 6 = **partially**, in part, partly

hall n 1 = **entrance hall**, corridor, entry, foyer, lobby, passage, passageway, vestibule 2 = **meeting place**, assembly room, auditorium, chamber, concert hall

hallmark n 1 = **indication**, sure sign, telltale sign 2 = **seal**, device, endorsement, mark, sign, stamp, symbol

halo n = **ring of light**, aura, corona, nimbus, radiance

halt v 1 a = **stop**, break off, cease, come to an end, desist, rest, stand still, wait ≠ start b = **hold back**, block, bring to an end, check, curb, cut short, end, nip in the bud, terminate ≠ encourage ◆ n 2 = **stop**, close, end, pause, standstill, stoppage

halve v 1 = **bisect**, cut in half, divide equally, share equally, split in two in nails etc. **2** part of a gun which causes the bullet to be fired. **3** heavy metal ball on a wire, thrown as a sport. **4** auctioneer's mallet. **5** striking mechanism in a piano. ◆ v **6** hit (as if) with a hammer. **7** *Informal* punish or defeat utterly. **go at it hammer and tongs** do something, esp. argue, very vigorously. **hammerhead** n shark with a wide flattened head. **hammertoe** n condition in which a toe is permanently bent at the joint.

hammock n hanging bed made of canvas or net.

hamper¹ ❶ v make it difficult for (someone or something) to move or progress.

hamper² n **1** large basket with a lid. **2** selection of food and drink packed as a gift.

hamster n small rodent with a short tail and cheek pouches.

> ✓ **WORD TIP**
> Note the spelling. There is no 'p'.

hamstring n **1** tendon at the back of the knee. ◆ v **2** make it difficult for (someone) to take any action.

hand ❶ n **1** part of the body at the end of the arm, consisting of a palm, four fingers, and a thumb. **2** style of handwriting. **3** round of applause. **4** manual worker. **5** pointer on a dial, esp. on a clock. **6** cards dealt to a player in a card game. **7** unit of length of four inches used to measure horses. ◆ v **8** pass, give. **have a hand in** be involved in. **lend a hand** help. **out of hand 1** beyond control. **2** definitely and finally. **to hand, at hand, on hand** nearby. **win hands down** win easily. **handbag** n woman's small bag for carrying personal articles in. **handbook** n small reference or instruction book. **handcuff** n **1** one of a linked pair of metal rings designed to be locked round a prisoner's wrists by the police. ◆ v **2** put handcuffs on. **hand–out** n **1** clothing, food, or money given to a needy person. **2** written information given out at a talk etc. **hands–on** adj involving practical experience of equipment. **handstand** n act of supporting the body on the hands in an upside–down position. **handwriting** n (style of) writing by hand.

handicap ❶ n **1** physical or mental disability. **2** something that makes progress difficult. **3** contest in which the competitors are given advantages or disadvantages in an attempt to equalize their chances. **4** advantage or disadvantage given. ◆ v **5** make it difficult for (someone) to do something.

handle ❶ n **1** part of an object that is held so that it can be used. ◆ v **2** hold, feel, or move with the hands. **3** control or deal with. **handler** n person who controls an animal. **handlebars** pl n curved metal bar used to steer a cycle.

handsome ❶ adj **1** (esp. of a man) good–

—————————————— THESAURUS ——————————————

hammer v **6** = **hit**, bang, beat, drive, knock, strike, tap **7** *Inf* = **defeat**, beat, drub, run rings around (*inf*), thrash, trounce, wipe the floor with (*inf*)

hamper¹ v = **hinder**, frustrate, hamstring, handicap, impede, interfere with, obstruct, prevent, restrict ≠ **help**

hand n **1** = **palm**, fist, mitt (*sl*), paw (*inf*) **2** = **penmanship**, calligraphy, handwriting, script **3** = **round of applause**, clap, ovation **4** = **worker**, artisan, craftsman, employee, hired man, labourer, operative, workman ◆ v **8** = **give**, deliver,

hand over, pass **to**, **at** *or* **on hand** = **nearby**, at one's fingertips, available, close, handy, near, ready, within reach

handicap n **1** = **disability**, defect, impairment **2** = **disadvantage**, barrier, drawback, hindrance, impediment, limitation, obstacle, restriction, stumbling block ≠ **benefit 3** = **advantage**, head start ◆ v **5** = **hinder**, burden, encumber, hamper, hamstring, hold back, impede, limit, restrict ≠ **help**

handle n **1** = **grip**, haft, hilt, stock ◆ v **2** = **hold**, feel, finger, grasp, pick up, looking. 2 large or generous, e.g. *a handsome profit.*

hang ❶ *v* hanging, hung 1 attach or be attached at the top with the lower part free. 2 (*past* hanged) suspend or be suspended by the neck until dead. 3 fasten to a wall. **get the hang of** *Informal* begin to understand. **hanger** *n* curved piece of wood, wire, or plastic, with a hook, for hanging up clothes (also **coat hanger**) 1 **hang back** *v* hesitate, be reluctant. **hangman** *n* man who executes people by hanging. **hangover** *n* headache and nausea as a result of drinking too much alcohol. **hang-up** *n Informal* emotional or psychological problem.

hangar *n* large shed for storing aircraft.

hanker ❶ *v* (foll. by *after*) desire intensely.

hanky, hankie *n*, *pl* **hankies** *Informal* handkerchief.

haphazard ❶ *adj* not organized or planned.

hapless *adj* unlucky.

happen ❶ *v* 1 take place, occur. 2 chance (to be or do something). **happening** *n* event, occurrence.

happy ❶ *adj* –pier, –piest 1 feeling or causing joy. 2 lucky, fortunate. **happily** *adv* **happiness** *n* **happy-go-lucky** *adj*

carefree and cheerful.

harangue ❶ *v* 1 address angrily or forcefully. ◆ *n* 2 angry or forceful speech.

harass ❶ *v* annoy or trouble constantly. **harassed** *adj* **harassment** *n*

harbour ❶ *n* 1 sheltered port. ◆ *v* 2 maintain secretly in the mind. 3 give shelter or protection to.

hard ❶ *adj* 1 firm, solid, or rigid. 2 difficult. 3 requiring a lot of effort. 4 unkind, unfeeling. 5 causing pain, sorrow, or hardship. 6 (of water) containing calcium salts which stop soap lathering freely. 7 (of a drug) strong and addictive. ◆ *adv* 8 with great energy or effort. 9 with great intensity. **hard of hearing** unable to hear properly. **hard up** *Informal* short of money. **harden** *v* **hardness** *n* **hardship** *n* 1 suffering. 2 difficult circumstances. **hard-bitten** *adj* tough and determined. **hard-boiled** *adj* 1 (of an egg) boiled until solid. 2 *Informal* tough, unemotional. **hard copy** computer output printed on paper. 1 **hard-headed** *adj* shrewd, practical. **hardhearted** *adj* unsympathetic, uncaring. **hard sell** aggressive sales technique. **hard shoulder** surfaced verge at the edge of a motorway for emergency stops.

hardy ❶ *adj* **hardier, hardiest** able to

touch 3 = **control**, cope with, deal with, direct, guide, manage, manipulate, manoeuvre

handsome *adj* 1 = **good-looking**, attractive, comely, dishy (*inf, chiefly Brit*), elegant, gorgeous, personable ≠ **ugly** 2 = **generous**, abundant, ample, considerable, large, liberal, plentiful, sizable *or* sizeable ≠ **mean**

hang *v* 1 = **suspend**, dangle, droop 2 = **execute**, lynch, string up (*inf*) **get the hang of** *Inf* = **grasp**, comprehend, understand

hanker *v* (foll. by *after*) = **desire**, crave, hunger, itch, long, lust, pine, thirst, yearn

haphazard *adj* = **unsystematic**, aimless, casual, disorganized, hit or miss (*inf*), indiscriminate, slapdash

happen *v* 1 = **occur**, come about, come to pass, develop, result, take place, transpire (*inf*) 2 = **chance**, turn out

happy *adj* 1 = **joyful**, blissful, cheerful, content, delighted, ecstatic, elated, glad, jubilant, merry, overjoyed, pleased, thrilled 2 = **fortunate**, advantageous, auspicious, favourable, lucky, timely ≠ **unhappy**

harangue *v* 1 = **rant**, address, declaim, exhort, hold forth, lecture, spout (*inf*) ◆ *n* 2 = **speech**, address, declamation, diatribe, exhortation, tirade

harass *v* = **annoy**, bother, harry, hassle (*inf*), hound, persecute, pester, plague, trouble, vex

harbour *n* 1 = **port**, anchorage, haven ◆ *v* 2 = **maintain**, cling to, entertain, foster, hold, nurse, nurture, retain 3 = **shelter**, stand difficult conditions. **hardiness** n

hare n 1 animal like a large rabbit, with longer ears and legs. ◆ v 2 (usu. foll. by *off*) run (away) quickly. **harebell** n blue bell-shaped flower. **harebrained** adj foolish or impractical. **harelip** n slight split in the upper lip.

harem n (apartments of) a Muslim man's wives and concubines.

hark v Old-fashioned listen. **hark back** v return (to an earlier subject).

harlequin n 1 stock comic character with a diamond-patterned costume and mask. ◆ adj 2 in many colours.

harlot n Lit prostitute.

harm ⊙ v 1 injure physically, mentally, or morally. ◆ n 2 physical, mental, or moral injury. **harmful** adj **harmless** adj

harmony ⊙ n, pl **-nies** 1 peaceful agreement and cooperation. 2 pleasant combination of notes sounded at the same time. **harmonious** adj **harmonic** adj of harmony. **harmonics** n science of musical sounds. **harmonize** v blend well together.

harness ⊙ n 1 arrangement of straps for attaching a horse to a cart or plough. 2 set of straps fastened round someone's body to attach something, e.g. *a safety harness*. ◆ v 3 put a harness on. 4 control (something) in order to make use of it.

harp n large triangular stringed instrument played with the fingers. **harpist** n **harp on about** v talk continuously.

harpoon n 1 barbed spear attached to a rope used for hunting whales. ◆ v 2 spear with a harpoon.

harrier n cross-country runner.

harrow n 1 implement used to break up lumps of soil. ◆ v 2 draw a harrow over.

harry ⊙ v **-rying, -ried** keep asking (someone) to do something, pester.

harsh ⊙ adj 1 severe and difficult to cope with. 2 unkind, unsympathetic. 3 extremely hard, bright, or rough. **harshly** adv **harshness** n

harvest ⊙ n 1 (season for) the gathering of crops. 2 crops gathered. ◆ v 3 gather (a ripened crop). **harvester** n

has v third person singular of the present

hide, protect, provide refuge, shield

hard adj 1 = **tough**, firm, inflexible, rigid, rocklike, solid, stiff, strong, unyielding ≠ **soft** 2 = **difficult**, complicated, intricate, involved, knotty, perplexing, puzzling, thorny ≠ **easy** 3 = **strenuous**, arduous, backbreaking, exacting, exhausting, laborious, rigorous, tough 4 = **harsh**, callous, cold, cruel, hardhearted, pitiless, stern, unfeeling, unkind, unsympathetic ≠ **kind** 5 = **grim**, disagreeable, distressing, grievous, intolerable, painful, unpleasant ◆ adv 8, 9 = **energetically**, fiercely, forcefully, forcibly, heavily, intensely, powerfully, severely, sharply, strongly, vigorously, violently, with all one's might, with might and main

hardy adj = **strong**, robust, rugged, sound, stout, sturdy, tough ≠ **soft**

harm v 1 = **injure**, abuse, damage, hurt, ill-treat, maltreat, ruin, spoil, wound ≠ **heal** ◆ n 2 = **injury**, abuse, damage,

hurt, ill, loss, mischief, misfortune ≠ **good**

harmony n 1 = **agreement**, accord, amicability, compatibility, concord, cooperation, friendship, peace, rapport, sympathy ≠ **opposition** 2 = **tunefulness**, euphony, melody, tune, unison ≠ **cacophony**

harness n 1 = **tack** 2 = **equipment**, gear, tackle ◆ v 4 = **exploit**, channel, control, employ, mobilize, utilize

harry v = **pester**, badger, bother, chivvy, harass, hassle (*inf*), plague

harsh adj 1, 2 = **severe**, austere, cruel, Draconian, drastic, hard, pitiless, punitive, ruthless, stern, tough ≠ **loving** 3 = **raucous**, discordant, dissonant, grating, guttural, rasping, rough, strident ≠ **soft**

harvest n 1 = **gathering**, harvesting, harvest-time, reaping 2 = **crop**, produce, yield ◆ v 3 = **gather**, mow, pick, pluck, reap tense of HAVE. **has–been** n Informal person who is no longer popular or successful.

hash ⊕ n dish of diced cooked meat and vegetables reheated. **make a hash of** Informal spoil, do badly.

hashish [hash–eesh] n drug made from the cannabis plant, smoked for its intoxicating effects.

hassle ⊕ Informal ♦ n 1 trouble, bother. 2 long argument. ♦ v 3 bother or annoy.

hassock n cushion for kneeling on in church.

haste ⊕ n (excessive) quickness. **hasten** v (cause to) hurry. **hasty** adj (too) quick. **hastily** adv

hat n covering for the head, often with a brim, usu. worn to give protection from the weather. **keep something under one's hat** keep something secret. **hat trick** any three successive achievements, esp. in sport.

hatch[1] ⊕ v 1 (cause to) emerge from an egg. 2 devise (a plot).

hatch[2] n 1 hinged door covering an opening in a floor or wall. 2 opening in the wall between a kitchen and a dining area. 3 door in an aircraft or spacecraft. **hatchback** n car with a lifting door at the back. **hatchway** n opening in the deck of a ship.

hatchet n small axe. **bury the hatchet** become reconciled. **hatchet job** malicious verbal or written attack. **hatchet man** Informal person carrying out unpleasant tasks for an employer.

hate ⊕ v 1 dislike intensely. 2 be unwilling (to do something). ♦ n 3 Intense dislike. 4 person or thing hated. **hateful** adj causing or deserving hate. **hater** n **hatred** n intense dislike.

haughty ⊕ adj –tier, –tiest proud, arrogant. **haughtily** adv **haughtiness** n

haul ⊕ v 1 pull or drag with effort. ♦ n 2 amount gained by effort or theft. **long haul** something that takes a lot of time and effort. **haulage** n (charge for) transporting goods. **haulier** n firm or person that transports goods by road.

haunch n human hip or fleshy hindquarter of an animal.

haunt ⊕ v 1 visit in the form of a ghost. 2 remain in the memory or thoughts of. ♦ n 3 place visited frequently. **haunted** adj 1 frequented by ghosts. 2 worried. **haunting** adj memorably beautiful or sad.

have ⊕ v **has, having, had** 1 possess, hold. 2 receive, take, or obtain. 3 experience or be affected by. 4 (foll. by to) be obliged, must, e.g. I had to go. 5 cause to be done. 6 give birth to. 7 Slang cheat or outwit.

hash n make a hash of Inf = **mess up**, botch, bungle, make a pig's ear of (inf), mishandle, mismanage, muddle

hassle Inf n 1 = **trouble**, bother, difficulty, grief (inf), inconvenience, problem 2 = **argument**, bickering, disagreement, dispute, fight, quarrel, row, squabble ♦ v 3 = **bother**, annoy, badger, bug (inf), harass, hound, pester

haste n = **speed**, alacrity, hurry, impetuosity, quickness, rapidity, rush, swiftness, urgency, velocity ≠ **slowness**

hatch[1] v 1 = **incubate**, breed, bring forth, brood 2 = **devise**, conceive, concoct, contrive, cook up (inf), design, dream up (inf), think up

hate v 1 = **detest**, abhor, despise, dislike, loathe, recoil from ≠ **like** 2 = **be unwilling**, be loath, be reluctant, be sorry, dislike, feel disinclined, shrink from ≠ **like** 3 = **dislike**, animosity, antipathy, aversion, detestation, enmity, hatred, hostility, loathing ≠ **liking**

haughty adj = **proud**, arrogant, conceited, contemptuous, disdainful, imperious, scornful, snooty (inf), stuck–up (inf), supercilious

haul v 1 = **drag**, draw, heave, lug, pull, tug ♦ n 2 = **yield**, booty, catch, gain, harvest, loot, spoils, takings

haunt v 2 = **plague**, obsess, possess, prey on, recur, stay with, torment, trouble, weigh on ♦ n 3 = **meeting place**, rendezvous, stamping ground

8 used to form past tenses (with a past participle), e.g. *we have looked; she had done enough*. **have it out** *Informal* settle a matter by argument. **have on** *v* 1 wear. 2 *Informal* tease or trick. **have up** *v* bring to trial.

haven ❶ *n* place of safety.

haversack *n* canvas bag carried on the back or shoulder.

havoc ❶ *n* disorder and confusion.

hawk¹ *n* 1 bird of prey with a short hooked bill and very good eyesight. 2 *Politics* supporter or advocate of warlike policies. **hawkish, hawklike** *adj* **hawk–eyed** *adj* having very good eyesight.

hawk² *v* offer (goods) for sale in the street or door–to–door.

hawker *n* a person who travels from place to place selling goods.

hawthorn *n* thorny shrub or tree.

hay *n* grass cut and dried as fodder. **hay fever** allergy to pollen, causing sneezing and watery eyes. **haystack** *n* large pile of stored hay. **haywire** *adj* **go haywire** *Informal* not function properly.

hazard ❶ *n* 1 something that could be dangerous. ◆ *v* 2 put in danger. 3 make (a guess).

hazardous *adj* involving great risk.

haze ❶ *n* mist, often caused by heat. **hazy** *adj* 1 not clear, misty. 2 confused or vague.

hazel *n* 1 small tree producing edible nuts. ◆ *adj* 2 (of eyes) greenish–brown. **hazelnut** *n*

he *pron* refers to: 1 male person or animal. 2 person or animal of unspecified sex.

✓ **WORD TIP**

Try to avoid the use of *he* as a pronoun of general reference. It can appear sexist if the reference is to both men and women.

---

head ❶ *n* 1 upper or front part of the body, containing the sense organs and the brain. 2 mind and mental abilities. 3 upper or most forward part of anything. 4 person in charge of a group, organization, or school. 5 pus–filled tip of a spot or boil. 6 white froth on beer. 7 (*pl* **head**) person or animal considered as a unit. 8 headline or heading. 9 *Informal* headache. ◆ *adj* 10 chief, principal. ◆ *v* 11 be at the top or front of. 12 be in charge of. 13 move (in a particular direction). 14 hit (a ball) with the head. 15 provide with a heading. **go to one's head** make one drunk or conceited. **head over heels (in love)** very much in love. **not make head nor tail of** not understand. **heads** *adv Informal* with the side of a coin which has a portrait of a head on it uppermost. **heading** *n* title printed at the top of a page. **heady** *adj* intoxicating or exciting. **headache** *n* 1 continuous pain in the head. 2 cause of worry or annoyance. **headdress** *n* decorative head covering. **head–hunt** *v* (of a company) approach and offer a job to (a person working for a rival company). **head–hunter** *n* **headland** *n* area of land jutting out into the sea. **headlight** *n* powerful light on the front of a vehicle. **headline** *n* 1 title at the top of a

---

——————— THESAURUS ———————

have *v* 1 = **possess**, hold, keep, obtain, own, retain 2 = **receive**, accept, acquire, gain, get, obtain, procure, secure, take 3 = **experience**, endure, enjoy, feel, meet with, suffer, sustain, undergo 4 (foll. by *to*) = **be obliged**, be bound, be compelled, be forced, have got to, must, ought, should 6 = **give birth to**, bear, beget, bring forth, deliver 7 *Sl* = **cheat**, deceive, dupe, fool, outwit, swindle, take in (*inf*), trick

haven *n* = **sanctuary**, asylum, refuge, retreat, sanctum, shelter

havoc *n* = **disorder**, chaos, confusion, disruption, mayhem, shambles

hazard *n* 1 = **danger**, jeopardy, peril, pitfall, risk, threat ◆ *v* 2 = **jeopardize**, endanger, expose, imperil, risk, threaten 3 = **conjecture**, advance, offer, presume, throw out, venture, volunteer

haze *n* = **mist**, cloud, fog, obscurity,

newspaper article, esp. on the front page. ◆ *pl* **2** main points of a news broadcast. **headlong** *adv, adj* **1** with the head first. **2** hastily. **3** **headphones** *pl n* two small loudspeakers held against the ears by a strap. **headquarters** *pl n* centre from which operations are directed. **head start** advantage in a competition. **headstone** *n* memorial stone on a grave. **headstrong** *adj* self–willed, obstinate. **headway** *n* progress. **headwind** *n* wind blowing against the course of an aircraft or ship.

heal ● *v* make or become well.

health ● *n* normal (good) condition of someone's body. **healthy** *adj* **healthier, healthiest** **1** having good health. **2** of or producing good health. **3** functioning well, sound.

heap ● *n* **1** pile of things one on top of another. **2** (also **heaps**) large number or quantity. ◆ *v* **3** gather into a pile. **4** (foll. by *on*) give liberally (to).

hear ● *v* **hearing, heard** **1** perceive (a sound) by ear. **2** listen to. **3** learn or be informed. **4** *Law* try (a case). **hear! hear!** **4** *Law* try (a case). **hear! hear!**

exclamation of approval or agreement. **hearing** *n* **1** ability to hear. **2** trial of a case. **within hearing** close enough to be heard.

hearken *v Obs* listen.

hearse *n* funeral car used to carry a coffin.

heart ● *n* **1** organ that pumps blood round the body. **2** centre of emotions, esp. love. **3** courage, spirit. **4** central or most important part. **5** figure representing a heart. **6** playing card with red heart heart–shaped symbols. **break someone's heart** cause someone great grief. **by heart** from memory. **set one's heart on something** greatly desire something. **take something to heart** be upset about something. **hearten** *v* encourage, make cheerful. **heartless** *adj* cruel, unkind. **hearty** *adj* **1** substantial, nourishing. **2** friendly, enthusiastic. **heartily** *adv* **heart attack** sudden severe malfunction of the heart. **heart failure** sudden stopping of the heartbeat. **heart–rending** *adj* causing great sorrow. **heart–throb** *n Slang* very attractive man, esp. a film or pop star.

vapour

head *n* **1** = **skull**, crown, loaf (*sl*), nut (*sl*), pate **2** = **mind**, brain, brains (*inf*), intellect, intelligence, thought, understanding **3** = **top**, crest, crown, peak, pinnacle, summit, tip **4** = **leader**, boss (*inf*), captain, chief, commander, director, manager, master, principal, supervisor ◆ *adj* **10** = **chief**, arch, first, leading, main, pre–eminent, premier, prime, principal, supreme ◆ *v* **11** = **lead**, be *or* go first, cap, crown, lead the way, precede, top **12** = **be in charge of**, command, control, direct, govern, guide, lead, manage, run **13** = **make for**, aim, go to, make a beeline for, point, set off for, set out, start towards, steer, turn **go to one's head** = **excite**, intoxicate, make conceited, puff up **head over heels** = **completely**, intensely, thoroughly, uncontrollably, utterly, wholeheartedly

heal *v* = **cure**, make well, mend,

regenerate, remedy, restore, treat ≠ **hurt**

health *n* **a** = **condition**, constitution, fettle, shape, state **b** = **wellbeing**, fitness, good condition, healthiness, robustness, soundness, strength, vigour ≠ **disease**

heap *n* **1** = **pile**, accumulation, collection, hoard, lot, mass, mound, stack **2** (also **heaps**) = **a lot**, great deal, load(s) (*inf*), lots (*inf*), mass, plenty, pot(s) (*inf*), stack(s), tons ◆ *v* **3** = **pile**, accumulate, amass, collect, gather, hoard, stack **4** (foll. by *on*) = **confer**, assign, bestow, load, shower upon

hear *v* **1** = **perceive**, catch, overhear **2** = **listen to 3** = **learn**, ascertain, discover, find out, gather, get wind of (*inf*), pick up **4** *Law* = **try**, examine, investigate, judge

heart *n* **2** = **nature**, character, disposition, soul, temperament **3** = **courage**, bravery, fortitude, pluck, purpose, resolution, spirit, will **4** = **centre**, core, hub, middle, nucleus, quintessence **by heart** = **by**

hearth *n* floor of a fireplace.

heat ❶ *v* 1 make or become hot. ◆ *n* 2 state of being hot. 3 energy transferred as a result of a difference in temperature. 4 hot weather. 5 intensity of feeling. 6 preliminary eliminating contest in a competition. **on, in heat** (of some female animals) ready for mating. **heated** *adj* angry and excited. **heater** *n*

heath *n* area of open uncultivated land.

heathen ❶ *adj*, *n* (of) a person who does not believe in an established religion.

heather *n* low-growing plant with small purple, pinkish, or white flowers, growing on heaths and mountains.

heave ❶ *v* 1 lift with effort. 2 throw (something heavy). 3 utter (a sigh). 4 rise and fall. 5 vomit. ◆ *n* 6 heaving.

heaven ❶ *n* 1 place believed to be the home of God, where good people go when they die. 2 place or state of bliss. **the heavens** sky. **heavenly** *adj* 1 of or like heaven. 2 of or occurring in space. 3 wonderful or beautiful.

heavy ❶ *adj* **heavier, heaviest** 1 of great weight. 2 having a high density. 3 great in degree or amount. 4 *Informal* (of a

situation) serious. **heavily** *adv* **heaviness** *n* **heavy industry** large-scale production of raw material or machinery. **heavy metal** very loud rock music featuring guitar riffs. **heavyweight** *n* boxer weighing over 175lb (professional) or 81kg (amateur).

heckle ❶ *v* interrupt (a public speaker) with comments, questions, or taunts. **heckler** *n*

hectare *n* one hundred ares or 10 000 square metres (2.471 acres).

hectic ❶ *adj* rushed or busy.

hedge ❶ *n* 1 row of bushes forming a barrier or boundary. ◆ *v* 2 be evasive or noncommittal. 3 (foll. by *against*) protect oneself (from). **hedgerow** *n* bushes forming a hedge.

hedonism *n* doctrine that pleasure is the most important thing in life. **hedonist** *n* **hedonistic** *adj*

heed ❶ *n* 1 careful attention. ◆ *v* 2 pay careful attention to. **heedless** *adj* **heedless of** taking no notice of.

heel¹ ❶ *n* 1 back part of the foot. 2 part of a shoe supporting the heel. 3 *Slang* contemptible person. ◆ *v* 4 repair the heel of (a shoe).

———————— THESAURUS ————————

memory, by rote, off pat, parrot–fashion (*inf*), pat, word for word

heat *v* 1 = **warm up**, make hot, reheat ≠ **cool** ◆ *n* 2 = **hotness**, high temperature, warmth ≠ **cold** 5 = **passion**, excitement, fervour, fury, intensity, vehemence ≠ **composure**

① **heathen** *adj* = **pagan**, godless, idolatrous, irreligious

② **heathen** *n* = **pagan**, infidel, unbeliever

heave *v* 1 = **lift**, drag (up), haul (up), hoist, pull (up), raise, tug 2 = **throw**, cast, fling, hurl, pitch, send, sling, toss 3 = **sigh**, groan, puff 5 = **vomit**, be sick, gag, retch, spew, throw up (*inf*)

heaven *n* 1 = **paradise**, bliss, Elysium *or* Elysian fields (*Greek myth*), hereafter, life everlasting, next world, nirvana (*Buddhism, Hinduism*), Zion (*Christianity*)
2 = **happiness**, bliss, ecstasy, paradise,

rapture, seventh heaven, utopia **the heavens** = **sky**, ether, firmament

heavy *adj* 1 = **weighty**, bulky, hefty, massive, ponderous ≠ **light**
3 = **considerable**, abundant, copious, excessive, large, profuse ≠ **light**

heckle *v* = **jeer**, barrack (*inf*), boo, disrupt, interrupt, shout down, taunt

hectic *adj* = **frantic**, animated, chaotic, feverish, frenetic, heated, turbulent

hedge *n* 1 = **hedgerow** ◆ *v* 2 = **dodge**, duck, equivocate, evade, flannel (*Brit inf*), prevaricate, sidestep, temporize 3 (foll. by *against*) = **insure**, cover, guard, protect, safeguard, shield

heed *n* 1 = **care**, attention, caution, mind, notice, regard, respect, thought ≠ **neglect**
◆ *v* 2 = **pay attention to**, bear in mind, consider, follow, listen to, note, obey, observe, take notice of ≠ **ignore**

heel² ❶ v (foll. by *over*) lean to one side.

hefty ❶ adj **heftier**, **heftiest** large, heavy, or strong.

heifer [hef–fer] n young cow.

height ❶ n 1 distance from base to top. 2 distance above sea level. 3 highest degree or topmost point. **heighten** v make or become higher or more intense.

heinous adj evil and shocking.

heir ❶ n person entitled to inherit property or rank. **heiress** n fem **heirloom** n object that has belonged to a family for generations.

helicopter n aircraft lifted and propelled by rotating overhead blades. **heliport** n airport for helicopters.

helium [heel–ee–um] n Chem very light colourless odourless gas.

helix [heel–iks] n, pl **helices**, **helixes** spiral.

hell ❶ n 1 place believed to be where wicked people go when they die. 2 place or state of suffering or punishment. **hell for leather** at great speed. **hellish** adj **hellbent** adj (foll. by *on*) intent.

hello ❶ interj expression of greeting or surprise.

helm ❶ n tiller or wheel for steering a ship. **at the helm** in charge or in control.

helmet n hard hat worn for protection.

help ❶ v 1 make something easier, better, or quicker for (someone). 2 improve (a situation). 3 refrain from, e.g. *I can't help smiling.* ◆ n 4 assistance or support. **help oneself** 1 take something, esp. food or drink, without being served. 2 Informal steal something. **helper** n **helpful** adj **helping** n single portion of food. **helpless** adj weak or incapable. **helpline** n telephone line set aside for callers to contact an organization for help with a problem. **helpmate** n companion and helper, esp. a husband or wife.

helter-skelter ❶ adj 1 haphazard and careless. ◆ adv 2 in a haphazard and careless manner. ◆ n 3 high spiral slide at a fairground.

hem ❶ n 1 bottom edge of a garment, folded under and stitched down. ◆ v **hemming**, **hemmed** 2 provide with a hem. **hem in** v surround and prevent from moving.

hemisphere n half of a sphere, esp. the

THESAURUS

heel¹ n 3 SI = **swine**, bounder (*old–fashioned Brit sl*), cad (*Brit inf*), rotter (*sl, chiefly Brit*)

heel² (foll. by *over*) v = **lean over**, keel over, list, tilt

hefty adj = **big**, burly, hulking, massive, muscular, robust, strapping, strong ≠ **little**

height n 1, 2 = **altitude**, elevation, highness, loftiness, stature, tallness ≠ **shortness** 3 a = **culmination**, climax, limit, maximum, ultimate ≠ **nadir** b = **peak**, apex, crest, crown, pinnacle, summit, top, zenith ≠ **base**

heir n = **successor**, beneficiary, heiress (*fem*), inheritor, next in line

hell n 1 = **underworld**, abyss, fire and brimstone, Hades (*Greek myth*), hellfire, inferno, nether world 2 = **torment**, agony, anguish, misery, nightmare, ordeal, suffering, wretchedness

hello interj = **hi** (*inf*), gidday (*Aust & NZ*), good afternoon, good evening, good morning, greetings, how do you do?, welcome

helm n = **tiller**, rudder, wheel **at the helm** = **in charge**, at the wheel, in command, in control, in the driving seat, in the saddle

help v 1 = **aid**, abet, assist, cooperate, lend a hand, succour, support ≠ **fight** 2 = **improve**, alleviate, ameliorate, ease, facilitate, mitigate, relieve ≠ **aggravate** 3 = **refrain from**, avoid, keep from, prevent, resist ◆ n 4 = **assistance**, advice, aid, cooperation, guidance, helping hand, support

helter–skelter adj 1 = **haphazard**, confused, disordered, higgledy–piggledy (*inf*), hit–or–miss, jumbled, muddled, random, topsy–turvy ◆ adv 2 = **carelessly**, anyhow, hastily, headlong, hurriedly, pell–mell, rashly, recklessly, wildly

hem n 1 = **edge**, border, fringe, margin,

earth. **hemispherical** *adj*
hemlock *n* poison made from a plant with spotted stems and small white flowers.
hemp *n* **1** (also **cannabis**) Asian plant with tough fibres. **2** its fibre, used to make canvas and rope. **3** narcotic drug obtained from hemp.
hen *n* **1** female domestic fowl. **2** female of any bird. **hen night**, **party** party for women only. **henpecked** *adj* (of a man) dominated by his wife.
hence ✪ *conj* **1** for this reason. ◆ *adv* **2** from this time. **henceforth** *adv* from now on.
henchman ✪ *n* attendant or follower.
henna *n* reddish dye made from a shrub or tree.
hepatitis *n* inflammation of the liver.
heptagon *n* geometric figure with seven sides.
her *pron* **1** refers to a female person or animal or anything personified as feminine when the object of a sentence or clause. ◆ *adj* **2** belonging to her.
herald ✪ *n* **1** person who announces important news. **2** forerunner. ◆ *v* **3** signal the approach of. **heraldry** *n* study of coats of arms and family trees. **heraldic** *adj*
herb *n* plant used for flavouring in cookery, and in medicine. **herbal** *adj* **herbalist** *n* person who grows or specializes in the use of medicinal herbs. **herbaceous** *adj* (of a plant) soft-stemmed. **herbicide** *n* chemical used to destroy plants, esp. weeds.
herbivore *n* animal that eats only plants.

herbivorous [her-**biv**-or-uss] *adj*
herd ✪ *n* **1** group of animals feeding and living together. **2** large crowd of people. ◆ *v* **3** collect into a herd. **herdsman** *n* man who looks after a herd of animals.
here *adv* in, at, or to this place or point. **hereabouts** *adv* near here. **hereafter** *adv* after this point or time. **the hereafter** life after death. **hereby** *adv* by means of or as a result of this. **herein** *adv* in this place, matter, or document. **herewith** *adv* with this.
heredity ✪ [hir-**red**-it-ee] *n* passing on of characteristics from one generation to another. **hereditary** *adj* **1** passed on genetically from one generation to another. **2** passed on by inheritance.
heresy ✪ [**herr**-iss-ee] *n, pl* -**sies** opinion contrary to accepted opinion or belief. **heretic** [**herr**-it-ik] *n* person who holds unorthodox opinions. **heretical** [hir-**ret**-ik-al] *adj*
heritage ✪ *n* **1** something inherited. **2** anything from the past, considered as the inheritance of present-day society.
hermaphrodite [her-**maf**-roe-dite] *n* animal, plant, or person with both male and female reproductive organs.
hermetic *adj* sealed so as to be airtight. **hermetically** *adv*
hermit ✪ *n* person living in solitude, esp. for religious reasons. **hermitage** *n* home of a hermit.
hernia *n* protrusion of an organ or part through the lining of the surrounding

──── THESAURUS ────

trimming
hence *conj* **1** = **therefore**, ergo, for this reason, on that account, thus
henchman *n* = **attendant**, associate, bodyguard, follower, minder (*sl*), right-hand man, sidekick (*sl*), subordinate, supporter
herald *n* **1** = **messenger**, crier **2** = **forerunner**, harbinger, indication, omen, precursor, sign, signal, token ◆ *v* **3** = **indicate**, foretoken, portend, presage, promise, show, usher in

herd *n* **1** = **flock**, drove **2** = **crowd**, collection, horde, mass, mob, multitude, swarm, throng ◆ *v* **3** = **congregate**, assemble, collect, flock, gather, huddle, muster, rally
heredity *n* = **genetics**, constitution, genetic make-up, inheritance
heresy *n* = **unorthodoxy**, apostasy, dissidence, heterodoxy, iconoclasm
heritage *n* **1** = **inheritance**, bequest, birthright, endowment, legacy
hermit *n* = **recluse**, anchorite, loner (*inf*),

body cavity.

hero ● *n, pl* **heroes 1** principal character in a film, book, etc. **2** man greatly admired for his exceptional qualities or achievements. **heroine** *n fem* **heroic** *adj* **1** courageous. **2** of or like a hero. **heroics** *pl n* extravagant behaviour. **heroically** *adv* **heroism** [**herr**–oh–izz–um] *n*

heroin *n* highly addictive drug derived from morphine.

heron *n* long–legged wading bird.

herring *n* important food fish of northern seas. **herringbone** *n* pattern of zigzag lines.

hertz *n, pl* **hertz** *Physics* unit of frequency.

hesitate ● *v* **1** be slow or uncertain in doing something. **2** be reluctant (to do something). **hesitation** *n* **hesitant** *adj* undecided or wavering. **hesitancy** *n*

hessian *n* coarse jute fabric.

heterogeneous [het–er–oh–**jean**–ee–uss] *adj* composed of diverse elements. **heterogeneity** *n*

heterosexual *n, adj* (person) sexually attracted to members of the opposite sex.

hew ● *v* **hewing, hewed, hewed** *or* **hewn 1** cut with an axe. **2** carve from a substance.

hexagon *n* geometrical figure with six sides. **hexagonal** *adj*

hey *interj* expression of surprise or for catching attention.

heyday ● *n* time of greatest success, prime.

HI Hawaii.

hiatus ● [hie–**ay**–tuss] *n, pl* **-tuses, -tus** pause or interruption in continuity.

hibernate *v* (of an animal) pass the winter as if in a deep sleep. **hibernation** *n*

hiccup, hiccough *n* **1** spasm of the breathing organs with a sharp coughlike sound. **2** *Informal* small problem, hitch. ◆ *v* **3** make a hiccup.

hickory *n, pl* **-ries 1** N American nut–bearing tree. **2** its wood.

hide[1] ● *v* **hiding, hid, hidden 1** put (oneself or an object) somewhere difficult to see or find. **2** keep secret. ◆ *n* **3** place of concealment, esp. for a bird–watcher. **hiding** *n* state of concealment, e.g. *in hiding.* **hide–out** *n* place to hide in.

hide[2] ● *n* skin of an animal. **hiding** *n Slang* severe beating. **hidebound** *adj* unwilling to accept new ideas.

hideous ● [**hid**–ee–uss] *adj* ugly, revolting.

hierarchy ● [**hire**–ark–ee] *n, pl* **-chies** system of people or things arranged in a graded order. **hierarchical** *adj*

hieroglyphic [hire–oh–**gliff**–ik] *adj* **1** of a form of writing using picture symbols, as used in ancient Egypt. ◆ *n* **2** symbol that is difficult to decipher. **3** (also **hieroglyph**) symbol representing an object, idea, or sound.

———— THESAURUS ————

monk

hero *n* **1** = **leading man**, protagonist **2** = **idol**, champion, conqueror, star, superstar, victor

hesitate *v* **1** = **waver**, delay, dither, doubt, hum and haw, pause, vacillate, wait ≠ **decide 2** = **be reluctant**, balk, be unwilling, demur, hang back, scruple, shrink from, think twice ≠ **resolve**

hew *v* **1** = **cut**, axe, chop, hack, lop, split **2** = **carve**, fashion, form, make, model, sculpt, sculpture, shape, smooth

heyday *n* = **prime**, bloom, pink, prime of life, salad days

hiatus *n* = **pause**, break, discontinuity,

gap, interruption, interval, respite, space

hide[1] *v* **1 a** = **go into hiding**, go to ground, go underground, hole up, lie low, take cover **b** = **conceal**, camouflage, cloak, cover, disguise, mask, obscure, secrete, shroud, stash (*inf*), veil ≠ **display 2** = **suppress**, draw a veil over, hush up, keep dark, keep secret, keep under one's hat, withhold ≠ **admit**

hide[2] *n* = **skin**, pelt

hideous *adj* = **ugly**, ghastly, grim, grisly, grotesque, gruesome, monstrous, repulsive, revolting, unsightly ≠ **beautiful**

hierarchy *n* = **grading**, pecking order, ranking

hi–fi n 1 set of high–quality sound–reproducing equipment. ♦ adj 2 high–fidelity.

high ⊕ adj 1 of a great height. 2 far above ground or sea level. 3 being at its peak. 4 greater than usual in intensity or amount. 5 (of a sound) acute in pitch. 6 (of food) slightly decomposed. 7 of great importance, quality, or rank. 8 Informal under the influence of alcohol or drugs. ♦ adv 9 at or to a high level. 10 **highly** adv **highly strung** nervous and easily upset. **Highness** n title used to address or refer to a royal person. **higher education** education at colleges and universities. **high–fidelity** adj able to reproduce sound with little or no distortion. **high–flown** adj (of language) extravagant or pretentious. **high–handed** adj excessively forceful. **high–rise** adj (of a building) having many storeys. **high tea** early evening meal consisting of a cooked dish, bread, cakes, and tea. **high time** latest possible time.

hijack ⊕ v seize control of (an aircraft or other vehicle) while travelling. **hijacker** n

hike ⊕ n 1 long walk in the country, esp. for pleasure. ♦ v 2 go for a long walk. 3 (foll. by up) pull (up) or raise. **hiker** n

hill ⊕ n raised part of the earth's surface, less high than a mountain. **hilly** adj **hillock** n small hill. **hillbilly** n US unsophisticated country person.

hilt ⊕ n handle of a sword or knife.

him pron refers to a male person or animal when the object of a sentence or clause.

hind¹ adj **hinder**, **hindmost** situated at the back.

hind² n female deer.

hinder ⊕ v get in the way of. **hindrance** n

hinge ⊕ n 1 device for holding together two parts so that one can swing freely. ♦ v 2 (foll. by on) depend (on). 3 fit a hinge to.

hint ⊕ n 1 indirect suggestion. 2 piece of advice. 3 small amount. ♦ v 4 suggest indirectly.

hinterland n land lying behind a coast or near a city, esp. a port.

hip¹ n either side of the body between the waist and the thigh.

hip² n rosehip.

hip³ adj **hipper**, **hippest** Slang aware of or following the latest trends.

hippie adj, n same as HIPPY.

hippopotamus n, pl **-muses**, **-mi** large African mammal with thick wrinkled skin, living near rivers.

hire ⊕ v 1 pay to have temporary use of. 2 employ for wages. ♦ n 3 hiring. **for hire** available to be hired. **hireling** n person

---

THESAURUS

high adj 1, 2 = **tall**, elevated, lofty, soaring, steep, towering ≠ **low** 4 = **extreme**, excessive, extraordinary, great, intensified, sharp, strong ≠ **low** 5 = **high–pitched**, acute, penetrating, piercing, piping, sharp, shrill, strident ≠ **low** 7 = **important**, arch, chief, eminent, exalted, powerful, superior ≠ **insignificant** 8 Inf = **intoxicated**, stoned (sl), tripping (inf) ♦ adv 9 = **aloft**, at great height, far up, way up

hijack v = **seize**, commandeer, expropriate, take over

hike n 1 = **walk**, march, ramble, tramp, trek ♦ v 2 = **walk**, back–pack, ramble, tramp 3 (foll. by up) = **raise**, hitch up, jack up, lift, pull up

hill n = **mount**, fell, height, hillock, hilltop, knoll, mound, tor

hilt n = **handle**, grip, haft, handgrip

hinder v = **obstruct**, block, check, delay, encumber, frustrate, hamper, handicap, hold up or back, impede, interrupt, stop

hinder, hindmost adj = **last**, final, furthest, furthest behind, rearmost, trailing

hinge v 2 (foll. by on) = **depend on**, be contingent on, hang on, pivot on, rest on, revolve around, turn on

hint n 1 = **indication**, allusion, clue, implication, innuendo, insinuation, intimation, suggestion 2 = **advice**, help, pointer, suggestion, tip 3 = **trace**, dash, suggestion, suspicion, tinge, touch, undertone ♦ v 4 = **suggest**, imply, who works only for wages. **hire–purchase** n system of purchase by which the buyer pays for goods by instalments.

hirsute [**her**–suit] adj hairy.

his pron, adj (something) belonging to him.

hiss ❶ n 1 sound like that of a long s (as an expression of contempt). ◆ v 2 utter a hiss. 3 show derision or anger towards.

history ❶ n, pl –ries 1 (record or account of) past events and developments. 2 study of these. 3 record of someone's past. **historian** n writer of history. **historic** adj famous or significant in history. **historical** adj 1 occurring in the past. 2 based on history. **historically** adv

histrionic adj excessively dramatic. **histrionics** pl n excessively dramatic behaviour.

hit ❶ v hitting, hit 1 strike, touch forcefully. 2 come into violent contact with. 3 affect badly. 4 reach (a point or place). ◆ n 5 hitting. 6 successful record, film, etc. **hit it off** Informal get on well together. **hit the road** Informal start a journey. **hit-and-miss** adj sometimes successful and sometimes not. **hit man** hired assassin. **hit on** v think of (an idea).

hitch ❶ n 1 minor problem. ◆ v 2 Informal obtain (a lift) by hitchhiking. 3 fasten with a knot or tie. 4 (foll. by up) pull up with a jerk. **hitchhike** v travel by obtaining free lifts. **hitchhiker** n

hither adv Old-fashioned to or towards this place. **hitherto** adv until this time.

HIV human immunodeficiency virus, the cause of AIDS.

hive n same as BEEHIVE. **hive off** v separate from a larger group.

hives n allergic reaction in which itchy red or whitish patches appear on the skin.

HM Her (or His) Majesty.

HMS Her (or His) Majesty's Ship.

hoard ❶ n 1 store hidden away for future use. ◆ v 2 save or store. **hoarder** n

---

✓ **WORD TIP**

Do not confuse hoard with horde, which means 'a large group'.

---

hoarding n large board for displaying advertisements.

hoarse ❶ adj 1 (of a voice) rough and unclear. 2 having a rough and unclear voice. **hoarsely** adv **hoarseness** n

THESAURUS

indicate, insinuate, intimate

hire v 1 = **rent**, charter, engage, lease, let 2 = **employ**, appoint, commission, engage, sign up, take on ◆ n 3 = **rental**

hiss n 1 a = **sibilation**, buzz, hissing b = **catcall**, boo, jeer ◆ v 2 = **whistle**, sibilate, wheeze, whirr, whiz 3 = **jeer**, boo, deride, hoot, mock

history n 1 a = **chronicle**, account, annals, narrative, recital, record, story b = **the past**, antiquity, olden days, yesterday, yesteryear

hit v 1 = **strike**, bang, beat, clout (inf), knock, slap, smack, thump, wallop (inf), whack 2 = **collide with**, bang into, bump, clash with, crash against, run into, smash into 3 = **affect**, damage, devastate, impact on, influence, leave a mark on, overwhelm, touch 4 = **reach**, accomplish, achieve, arrive at, attain, gain ◆ n

5 = **stroke**, belt (inf), blow, clout (inf), knock, rap, slap, smack, wallop (inf) 6 = **success**, sensation, smash (inf), triumph, winner **hit it off** Inf = **get on (well) with**, be on good terms, click (sl), get on like a house on fire (inf)

hitch n 1 = **problem**, catch, difficulty, drawback, hindrance, hold–up, impediment, obstacle, snag ◆ v 2 Inf = **hitchhike**, thumb a lift 3 = **fasten**, attach, connect, couple, harness, join, tether, tie 4 (foll. by up) = **pull up**, jerk, tug, yank

hoard n 1 = **store**, accumulation, cache, fund, pile, reserve, stash, stockpile, supply, treasure–trove ◆ v 2 = **save**, accumulate, amass, collect, gather, lay up, put by, stash away (inf), stockpile, store

hoarse adj 1 = **rough**, croaky, grating, gravelly, gruff, guttural, husky, rasping,

hoary *adj* **hoarier, hoariest 1** grey or white(–haired). **2** very old.

hoax ❶ *n* **1** deception or trick. ◆ *v* **2** deceive or play a trick upon.

hob *n* flat top part of a cooker, or a separate flat surface, containing gas or electric rings for cooking on.

hobble *v* **1** walk lamely. **2** tie the legs of (a horse) together.

hobby ❶ *n, pl* **–bies** activity pursued in one's spare time. **hobbyhorse** *n* **1** favourite topic. **2** toy horse.

hobgoblin *n* mischievous goblin.

hobnob ❶ *v* **–nobbing, –nobbed** (foll. by *with*) be on friendly terms (with).

hobo *n, pl* **–bos** *US & Aust* tramp or vagrant.

hock[1] *n* joint in the back leg of an animal such as a horse that corresponds to the human ankle.

hock[2] *n* white German wine.

hockey *n* **1** team game played on a field with a ball and curved sticks. **2** *US* ice hockey.

hod *n* open wooden box attached to a pole, for carrying bricks or mortar.

hoe *n* **1** long–handled tool used for loosening soil or weeding. ◆ *v* **2** scrape or weed with a hoe.

hog *n* **1** castrated male pig. **2** *Informal*

greedy person. ◆ *v* **hogging, hogged 3** *Informal* take more than one's share of.

hogshead *n* large cask. **hogwash** *n* *Informal* nonsense.

hoist ❶ *v* **1** raise or lift up. ◆ *n* **2** device for lifting things.

hold[1] ❶ *v* **holding, held 1** keep or support in or with the hands or arms. **2** arrange for (a meeting, party, etc.) to take place. **3** consider to be as specified, e.g. *who are you holding responsible?* **4** maintain in a specified position or state. **5** have the capacity for. **6** *Informal* wait, esp. on the telephone. **7** reserve (a room etc.). **8** restrain or keep back. **9** own, possess. **10** (cause to) remain committed to (a promise etc.). **11** believe. ◆ *n* **12** act or way of holding. **13** controlling influence. **14** something to hold onto for support. **holder** *n* **holding** *n* property, such as land or stocks and shares. **holdall** *n* large strong travelling bag. **hold–up** *n* **1** armed robbery. **2** delay.

hold[2] *n* cargo compartment in a ship or aircraft.

hole ❶ *n* **1** area hollowed out in a solid. **2** opening or hollow. **3** animal's burrow. **4** *Informal* unattractive place. **5** *Informal* difficult situation. ◆ *v* **6** make holes in. **7** hit (a golf ball) into the target hole.

══════╡ THESAURUS ╞══════

raucous, throaty

hoax *n* **1** = **trick**, con (*inf*), deception, fraud, practical joke, prank, spoof (*inf*), swindle ◆ *v* **2** = **deceive**, con (*sl*), dupe, fool, hoodwink, swindle, take in (*inf*), trick

hobby *n* = **pastime**, diversion, (leisure) activity, leisure pursuit, relaxation

hobnob *v* (foll. by *with*) = **socialize**, associate, consort, fraternize, hang about, hang out (*inf*), keep company, mingle, mix

hoist *v* **1** = **raise**, elevate, erect, heave, lift ◆ *n* **2** = **lift**, crane, elevator, winch

hold[1] *v* **1** = **grasp**, clasp, cling, clutch, cradle, embrace, enfold, grip **2** = **convene**, call, conduct, preside over, run ≠ **cancel 5** = **accommodate**, contain, have a

capacity for, seat, take **8** = **restrain**, confine, detain, impound, imprison ≠ **release 9** = **own**, have, keep, maintain, occupy, possess, retain ≠ **give 11** = **consider**, assume, believe, deem, judge, presume, reckon, regard, think ≠ **deny** ◆ *v* **12** = **grip**, clasp, grasp **13** = **control**, influence, mana (*NZ*), mastery **14** = **foothold**, footing, support

hole *n* **1** = **cavity**, cave, cavern, chamber, hollow, pit **2** = **opening**, aperture, breach, crack, fissure, gap, orifice, perforation, puncture, tear, vent **3** = **burrow**, den, earth, lair, shelter **4** *Inf* = **hovel**, dive (*sl*), dump (*inf*), slum **5** *Inf* = **predicament**, dilemma, fix (*inf*), hot water (*inf*), jam (*inf*), mess, scrape (*inf*), spot (*inf*), tight spot

holiday ❶ n 1 time spent away from home for rest or recreation. 2 day or other period of rest from work or studies

holistic adj considering the complete person, physically and mentally, in the treatment of an illness. **holism** n

hollow ❶ adj 1 having a hole or space inside. 2 (of a sound) as if echoing in a hollow place. 3 without any real value or worth. ◆ n 4 cavity or space. 5 dip in the land. ◆ v 6 form a hollow in.

holly n evergreen tree with prickly leaves and red berries.

hollyhock n tall garden plant with spikes of colourful flowers.

holocaust ❶ n destruction or loss of life on a massive scale.

hologram n three–dimensional photographic image.

holster n leather case for a pistol, hung from a belt.

holy ❶ adj –lier, –liest 1 of God or a god. 2 devout or virtuous. **holier–than–thou** adj self–righteous. **Holy Grail** (in medieval legend) the bowl used by Jesus Christ at the Last Supper.

homage ❶ n show of respect or honour towards someone or something.

home ❶ n 1 place where one lives. 2 institution for the care of the elderly, orphans, etc. ◆ adj 3 of one's home, birthplace, or native country. 4 Sport played on one's own ground. ◆ adv 5 to or at home. ◆ v 6 (foll. by in or in on) direct towards (a point or target). **at home** at ease. **bring home to** make clear to. **home and dry** Informal safe or successful. **homeless** adj 1 having nowhere to live. ◆ pl n 2 people who have nowhere to live. **homelessness** n **homely** adj 1 simple, ordinary, and comfortable. 2 US unattractive. **homeward** adj, adv **homewards** adv **home–brew** n beer made at home. **home–made** adj made at home or on the premises. **home truths** unpleasant facts told to a person about himself or herself.

homeopathy [home–ee–**op**–ath–ee] n treatment of disease by small doses of a drug that produces symptoms of the disease in healthy people. **homeopath** n person who practises homeopathy. **homeopathic** adj

homework n school work done at home.

homicide ❶ n 1 killing of a human being. 2 person who kills someone. **homicidal** adj

homily ❶ n, pl –lies speech telling people how they should behave.

holiday n 1 = **vacation**, break, leave, recess, time off 2 = **festival**, celebration, feast, fete, gala

hollow adj 1 = **empty**, unfilled, vacant, void ≠ **full** 2 = **toneless**, deep, dull, low, muted, reverberant ≠ **vibrant** 3 = **worthless**, fruitless, futile, meaningless, pointless, useless, vain ≠ **valuable** ◆ n 4 = **cavity**, basin, bowl, crater, depression, hole, pit, trough ≠ **bump** 5 = **valley**, dale, dell, dingle, glen ≠ **hill** ◆ v 6 = **scoop**, dig, channel, excavate, gouge

holocaust n = **genocide**, annihilation, conflagration, destruction, devastation, massacre

holy adj 1 = **sacred**, blessed, consecrated, hallowed, sacrosanct, sanctified, venerable ≠ **unholy** 2 = **devout**, god–fearing, godly, pious, pure, religious, righteous, saintly, virtuous ≠ **worldly**

homage n = **respect**, adoration, adulation, deference, devotion, honour, reverence, worship ≠ **contempt**

home n 1 = **dwelling**, abode, domicile, habitation, house, pad (sl), residence ◆ adj 3 = **domestic**, familiar, internal, local, native **at home** = **at ease**, comfortable, familiar, relaxed **bring home to** = **make clear**, drive home, emphasize, impress upon, press home

homicide n 1 = **murder**, bloodshed, killing, manslaughter, slaying 2 = **murderer**, killer, slayer

homily n = **sermon**, address, discourse, lecture, preaching

homogeneous ⊕ [home–oh–**jean**–ee–uss] *adj* formed of similar parts. **homogeneity** *n* **homogenize** *v* 1 break up fat globules in (milk or cream) to distribute them evenly. 2 make homogeneous.

homonym *n* word spelt or pronounced the same as another, but with a different meaning.

homosexual ⊕ *n, adj* (person) sexually attracted to members of the same sex. **homosexuality** *n*

hone ⊕ *v* sharpen.

honest ⊕ *adj* 1 truthful and moral. 2 open and sincere. **honestly** *adv* **honesty** *n*

honey *n* 1 sweet edible sticky substance made by bees from nectar. 2 term of endearment. **honeycomb** *n* waxy structure of six–sided cells in which honey is stored by bees in a beehive. **honeymoon** *n* holiday taken by a newly married couple. **honeysuckle** *n* climbing shrub with sweet–smelling flowers.

honk *n* 1 sound made by a car horn. 2 sound made by a goose. ◆ *v* 3 (cause to) make this sound.

honour ⊕ *n* 1 sense of honesty and fairness. 2 (award given out of) respect. 3 pleasure or privilege. ◆ *pl* 4 university degree of a higher standard than an ordinary degree. ◆ *v* 5 give praise and attention to. 6 give an award to

(someone) out of respect. 7 accept or pay (a cheque or bill). 8 keep (a promise). **do the honours** act as host or hostess by pouring drinks or giving out food. **honourable** *adj* worthy of respect or esteem. **honourably** *adv* **honorary** *adj* 1 held or given only as an honour. 2 unpaid. **honorific** *adj* showing respect.

hood *n* 1 head covering, often attached to a coat or jacket. 2 folding roof of a convertible car or a pram. 3 *US & Aust* car bonnet. **hooded** *adj* 1 (of a garment) having a hood. 2 (of eyes) having heavy eyelids that appear to be half–closed.

hoodlum *n Slang* violent criminal, gangster.

hoof *n, pl* **hooves, hoofs** horny covering of the foot of a horse, deer, etc. **hoof it** *Slang* walk.

hook ⊕ *n* 1 curved piece of metal, plastic, etc., used to hang, hold, or pull something. 2 short swinging punch. ◆ *v* 3 fasten or catch (as if) with a hook. **hooked** *adj* 1 bent like a hook. 2 (foll. by *on*) *Slang* addicted (to) or obsessed (with). **hooker** *n* 1 *Slang* prostitute. 2 *Rugby* player who uses his feet to get the ball in a scrum. **hook–up** *n* linking of radio or television stations. **hookworm** *n* blood–sucking worm with hooked mouthparts.

hooligan ⊕ *n* rowdy young person. **hooliganism** *n*

——— THESAURUS ———

homogeneous *adj* = **uniform**, akin, alike, analogous, comparable, consistent, identical, similar, unvarying

① **homosexual** *n* = **gay**, lesbian
② **homosexual** *adj* = **gay**, lesbian

hone *v* = **sharpen**, edge, file, grind, point, polish, whet

honest *adj* 1 = **trustworthy**, ethical, honourable, law–abiding, reputable, scrupulous, truthful, upright, virtuous ≠ **bad** 2 = **open**, candid, direct, forthright, frank, plain, sincere, upfront (*inf*) ≠ **false**

honour *n* 1 = **integrity**, decency, fairness, goodness, honesty, morality, probity, rectitude ≠ **degradation** 2 a = **tribute**,

accolade, commendation, homage, praise, recognition b = **prestige**, credit, dignity, distinction, fame, glory, renown, reputation, respect ≠ **shame** 3 = **privilege**, compliment, credit, pleasure ◆ *v* 5 = **respect**, adore, appreciate, esteem, prize, value 6 = **acclaim**, commemorate, commend, decorate, praise 7 = **pay**, accept, acknowledge, pass, take ≠ **refuse** 8 = **fulfil**, be true to, carry out, discharge, keep, live up to, observe

hook *n* 1 = **fastener**, catch, clasp, link, peg ◆ *v* 3 a = **fasten**, clasp, fix, secure b = **catch**, ensnare, entrap, snare, trap

hooligan *n* = **delinquent**, lager lout,

hoon n Aust & NZ slang loutish youth who drives irresponsibly.

hoop ❶ n rigid circular band, used esp. as a child's toy or for animals to jump through in the circus. **jump, be put through the hoops** go through an ordeal or test.

hooray interj same as HURRAH.

hoot ❶ n 1 sound of a car horn. 2 cry of an owl. 3 cry of derision. 4 Informal amusing person or thing. ◆ v 5 sound (a car horn). 6 jeer or yell contemptuously (at someone). **hooter** n 1 device that hoots. 2 Slang nose.

Hoover n 1 ® vacuum cleaner. ◆ v 2 (h–) clean with a vacuum cleaner.

hop¹ ❶ v hopping, hopped 1 jump on one foot. 2 move in short jumps. 3 Informal move quickly. ◆ n 4 instance of hopping. 5 Informal dance. 6 short journey, esp. by air. **catch someone on the hop** Informal catch someone unprepared.

hop² n (often pl) climbing plant, the dried flowers of which are used to make beer.

hope ❶ v 1 want (something) to happen or be true. ◆ n 2 expectation of something desired. 3 thing that gives cause for hope or is desired. **hopeful** adj 1 having, expressing, or inspiring hope. ◆ n 2 person considered to be on the brink of success. **hopefully** adv 1 in a hopeful manner. 2 it is hoped. **hopeless** adj

> ✓ **WORD TIP**
>
> Although many people dislike the use of *hopefully* as in *I'll see you in June, hopefully*, it is now well established.

hopper n container for storing substances such as grain or sand.

hopscotch n children's game of hopping in a pattern drawn on the ground.

horde ❶ n large crowd.

> ✓ **WORD TIP**
>
> Do not confuse *horde* with *hoard*, which means 'to store hidden away for future use'.

horizon ❶ n 1 apparent line that divides the earth and the sky. ◆ pl 2 limits of scope, interest, or knowledge. **horizontal** adj parallel to the horizon, level, flat.

hormone n 1 substance secreted by certain glands which stimulates certain organs of the body. 2 synthetic substance with the same effect. **hormonal** adj

horn n 1 one of a pair of bony growths sticking out of the heads of cattle, sheep, etc. 2 substance of which horns are made. 3 musical instrument with a tube or pipe of brass fitted with a mouthpiece. 4 device on a vehicle sounded as a warning. **horned** adj **horny** adj 1 of or like horn. 2 Slang (easily) sexually aroused. **hornpipe** n (music for) a solo dance, traditionally performed by sailors.

hornet n large wasp with a severe sting.

horoscope n 1 prediction of a person's future based on the positions of the planets, sun, and moon at his or her birth.

horrendous adj very unpleasant and shocking.

horror ❶ n (thing or person causing) terror or hatred. **horrible** adj disagreeable, unpleasant.

———— THESAURUS ————

ruffian, vandal, yob or yobbo (Brit sl)

hoop n = **ring**, band, circlet, girdle, loop, round, wheel

hoot n 1 = **toot** 2 = **cry**, call 3 = **catcall**, boo, hiss, jeer ◆ v 6 = **jeer**, boo, hiss, howl down

hop¹ v 2 = **jump**, bound, caper, leap, skip, spring, trip, vault ◆ v 4 = **jump**, bounce, bound, leap, skip, spring, step, vault

hope v 1 = **desire**, aspire, cross one's fingers, long, look forward to, set one's heart on ◆ n 2 = **belief**, ambition, assumption, confidence, desire, dream, expectation, longing

horde n = **crowd**, band, drove, gang, host, mob, multitude, pack, swarm, throng

horizon n 1 = **skyline**, vista

horror n = **terror**, alarm, aversion,

hors d'oeuvre [or durv] n appetizer
served before a main meal.

horse ❶ n 1 large animal with hooves, a
mane, and a tail, used for riding and
pulling carts etc. 2 piece of gymnastic
equipment used for vaulting over.
(straight) from the horse's mouth from
the original source. **horsey, horsy** adj 1
very keen on horses. 2 of or like a horse.
horse around v Informal play roughly or
boisterously. **horse chestnut** tree with
broad leaves and inedible large brown
shiny nuts in spiky cases. **horsefly** n large
bloodsucking fly. **horsehair** n hair from
the tail or mane of a horse. **horse laugh**
loud coarse laugh. **horseman**,
horsewoman n person riding a horse.
horseplay n rough or rowdy play.
horsepower n unit of power (equivalent
to 745.7 watts), used to measure the
power of an engine. **horseradish** n
strong–tasting root of a plant, usu. made
into a sauce. **horseshoe** n protective U–
shaped piece of iron nailed to a horse's
hoof, regarded as a symbol of good luck.

horticulture n art or science of cultivating
gardens. **horticultural** adj

hose¹ n 1 flexible pipe for conveying liquid.
♦ v 2 water with a hose.

hose² n stockings, socks, and tights.
hosiery n stockings, socks, and tights
collectively.

hospice [hoss–piss] n nursing home for
the terminally ill.

hospital n place where people who are ill
are looked after and treated. **hospitalize** v
send or admit to hospital for treatment.
hospitalization n

hospitality ❶ n kindness in welcoming
strangers or guests. **hospitable** adj
welcoming to strangers or guests.

host¹ ❶ n 1 (fem **hostess**) person who
entertains guests, esp. in his own home. 2
place or country providing the facilities for
an event. 3 compere of a show. 4 animal
or plant on which a parasite lives. ♦ v 5 be
the host of.

host²❶ n large number.

hostage ❶ n person who is illegally held
prisoner until certain demands are met by
other people.

hostel n building providing
accommodation at a low cost for
travellers, homeless people, etc.

hostile ❶ adj 1 unfriendly. 2 (foll. by to)
opposed (to). 3 of an enemy. **hostility** n,
pl **–ties** 1 unfriendly and aggressive
feelings or behaviour. ♦ pl 2 acts of
warfare.

hot ❶ adj **hotter, hottest** 1 having a high
temperature. 2 strong, spicy. 3 (of news)
very recent. 4 (of a contest) fiercely
fought. 5 (of a temper) quick to rouse. 6
liked very much, e.g. a hot favourite. 7
Slang stolen. **in hot water** Informal in
trouble. **hotly** adv **hot air** Informal empty
talk. **hot–blooded** adj passionate or
excitable. **hot dog** long roll split
lengthways with a hot frankfurter inside.
hot–headed adj rash, having a hot
temper. **hotline** n direct telephone link for
emergency use.

──┤ T H E S A U R U S ├──

consternation, detestation, disgust, dread,
fear, fright, hatred, loathing, odium,
panic, repugnance, revulsion ≠ **liking**

horse n 1 = **nag**, colt, filly, gee–gee (sl),
mare, mount, stallion, steed (arch or lit)

hospitality n = **welcome**, conviviality,
cordiality, friendliness, neighbourliness,
sociability, warmth

host¹ n 1 = **master of ceremonies**,
entertainer, innkeeper, landlord or
landlady, proprietor 3 = **presenter**,

anchorman or anchorwoman, compere
(Brit) ♦ v 5 = **present**, compere (Brit), front
(inf), introduce

host² n = **multitude**, army, array, drove,
horde, legion, myriad, swarm, throng

hostage n = **prisoner**, captive, pawn

hostile adj 1 = **unfriendly**, antagonistic,
belligerent, contrary, ill–disposed,
opposed, rancorous ≠ **warm** 2 (foll. by to)
= **inhospitable**, adverse, unsympathetic,
unwelcoming ≠ **congenial**

hotchpotch ❶ n jumbled mixture.
hotel n commercial establishment providing lodging and meals. **hotelier** n owner or manager of a hotel.
hound ❶ n 1 hunting dog. ♦ v 2 pursue relentlessly.
hour n 1 twenty–fourth part of a day, sixty minutes. 2 time of day. ♦ pl 3 period regularly appointed for work or business. **hourly** adj, adv 1 (happening) every hour. 2 frequent(ly). **hourglass** n device with two glass compartments, containing a quantity of sand that takes an hour to trickle from the top section to the bottom one.
house ❶ n 1 building used as a home. 2 building used for some specific purpose, e.g. the opera house. 3 business firm. 4 law–making body or the hall where it meets. 5 family or dynasty. 6 theatre or cinema audience. ♦ v 7 give accommodation to. 8 contain or cover. **get on like a house on fire** Informal get on very well together. **on the house** Informal provided free by the management. **housing** n 1 (providing of) houses. 2 protective case or covering of a machine. **house arrest** confinement to one's home rather than in prison. **houseboat** n stationary boat used as a home.

housecoat n woman's long loose coat–shaped garment for wearing at home.
household n all the people living in a house. **householder** n person who owns or rents a house. **housekeeper** n person employed to run someone else's household. **housekeeping** n (money for) running a household. **housemaid** n female servant employed to do housework. **house–train** v train (a pet) to urinate and defecate outside. **house–warming** n party to celebrate moving into a new home. **housewife** n woman who runs her own household and does not have a job. **housework** n work of running a home, such as cleaning, cooking, and shopping.
hovel ❶ n small dirty house or hut.
hover ❶ v 1 (of a bird etc.) remain suspended in one place in the air. 2 loiter. 3 be in a state of indecision. **hovercraft** n vehicle which can travel over both land and sea on a cushion of air.
how adv 1 in what way, by what means. 2 to what degree, e.g. I know how hard it is. **however** adv 1 nevertheless. 2 by whatever means. 3 no matter how, e.g. however much it hurt, he could do it.
howl ❶ n 1 loud wailing cry. 2 loud burst of laughter. ♦ v 3 utter a howl. **howler** n Informal stupid mistake.

———— THESAURUS ————

hot adj 1 = **heated**, boiling, roasting, scalding, scorching, searing, steaming, sultry, sweltering, torrid, warm ≠ **cold** 2 = **spicy**, biting, peppery, piquant, pungent, sharp ≠ **mild** 3 = **new**, fresh, just out, latest, recent, up to the minute ≠ **old** 4 = **passionate**, fierce, fiery, intense, raging, stormy, violent 6 = **popular**, approved, favoured, in demand, in vogue, sought–after ≠ **unpopular**
hotchpotch n = **mixture**, farrago, jumble, medley, melange, mess, mishmash, potpourri
hound v 2 = **harass**, badger, goad, harry, impel, persecute, pester, provoke
house n 1 = **home**, abode, domicile, dwelling, habitation, homestead, pad (sl),

residence 3 = **firm**, business, company, organization, outfit (inf) 4 = **assembly**, Commons, legislative body, parliament 5 = **dynasty**, clan, family, tribe ♦ v 7 = **accommodate**, billet, harbour, lodge, put up, quarter, take in 8 = **contain**, cover, keep, protect, sheathe, shelter, store **on the house** Inf = **free**, for nothing, gratis
hovel n = **hut**, cabin, den, hole, shack, shanty, shed
hover v 1 = **float**, drift, flutter, fly, hang 2 = **linger**, hang about 3 = **waver**, dither, fluctuate, oscillate, vacillate
howl n 1 = **cry**, bawl, bay, clamour, groan, roar, scream, shriek, wail ♦ v 3 = **cry**, bawl, bellow, roar, scream, shriek, wail, weep, yell

HP, h.p. 1 hire–purchase. **2** horsepower.
HQ headquarters.
HRH Her (or His) Royal Highness.
hub ❶ *n* **1** centre of a wheel, through which the axle passes. **2** central point of activity.
hubbub *n* confused noise of many voices.
huddle ❶ *v* **1** hunch (oneself) through cold or fear. **2** crowd closely together. ◆ *n* **3** small group. **4** *Informal* impromptu conference.
hue ❶ *n* colour, shade.
huff *n* **1** passing mood of anger or resentment. ◆ *v* **2** blow or puff heavily. **huffy** *adj* **huffily** *adv*
hug ❶ *v* **hugging, hugged 1** clasp tightly in the arms, usu. with affection. **2** keep close to (the ground, kerb, etc.). ◆ *n* **3** tight or fond embrace.
huge ❶ *adj* very big. **hugely** *adv*
hulk ❶ *n* **1** body of an abandoned ship. **2** *Offens* large heavy person or thing. **hulking** *adj* bulky, unwieldy.
hull ❶ *n* **1** main body of a boat. **2** leaves round the stem of a strawberry, raspberry, etc. ◆ *v* **3** remove the hulls from.

hullabaloo *n, pl* **–loos** loud confused noise or clamour.
hum ❶ *v* **humming, hummed 1** make a low continuous vibrating sound. **2** sing with the lips closed. **3** *Slang* (of a place) be very busy. ◆ *n* **4** humming sound.
hummingbird *n* very small American bird whose powerful wings make a humming noise as they vibrate.
human ❶ *adj* **1** of or typical of people. ◆ *n* **2** human being. **humanly** *adv* by human powers or means. **human being** man, woman, or child. **humane** *adj* kind or merciful. **humanity** *n* human race.
humble ❶ *adj* **1** conscious of one's failings. **2** modest, unpretentious. **3** unimportant. ◆ *v* **4** cause to feel humble, humiliate. **humbly** *adv*
humbug ❶ *n* **1** hard striped peppermint sweet. **2** nonsense. **3** dishonest person.
humdrum ❶ *adj* ordinary, dull.
humid ❶ *adj* damp and hot. **humidity** *n* **humidify** *v* **–fying, –fied. humidifier** *n* device for increasing the amount of water vapour in the air in a room.
humiliate ❶ *v* lower the dignity or hurt

———————— THESAURUS ————————

hub *n* **2 = centre**, core, focal point, focus, heart, middle, nerve centre
huddle *v* **1 = curl up**, crouch, hunch up **2 = crowd**, cluster, converge, flock, gather, press, throng ◆ *n* **4** *Inf* **= conference**, confab (*inf*), discussion, meeting, powwow
hue *n* **= colour**, dye, shade, tinge, tint, tone
hug *v* **1 = clasp**, cuddle, embrace, enfold, hold close, squeeze, take in one's arms ◆ *n* **3 = embrace**, bear hug, clasp, clinch (*sl*), squeeze
huge *adj* **= enormous**, colossal, gigantic, immense, large, mammoth, massive, monumental, tremendous, vast
hulk *n* **1 = wreck**, frame, hull, shell, shipwreck **2** *Offens* **= oaf**, lout, lubber, lump (*inf*)
hull *n* **1 = frame**, body, casing, covering, framework
hum *v* **1 = drone**, buzz, murmur, purr,

throb, thrum, vibrate, whir **3** *Sl* **= be busy**, bustle, buzz, pulsate, pulse, stir
human *adj* **= mortal**, manlike ◆ *n* **2 = human being**, creature, individual, man *or* woman, mortal, person, soul
humble *adj* **1 = modest**, meek, self–effacing, unassuming, unostentatious, unpretentious ≠ **lordly 2 = modest**, lowly, mean, obscure, ordinary, plebeian, poor, simple, undistinguished ≠ **important** ◆ *v* **4 = humiliate**, chasten, crush, disgrace, put (someone) in their place, subdue, take down a peg (*inf*) ≠ **raise**
humbug *n* **2 = nonsense**, baloney (*inf*), cant, claptrap (*inf*), hypocrisy, kak (*S Afr sl*), quackery, rubbish **3 = fraud**, charlatan, con man (*inf*), faker, impostor, phoney *or* phony (*inf*), swindler, trickster
humdrum *adj* **= dull**, banal, boring, dreary, monotonous, mundane, ordinary, tedious, tiresome, uneventful

the pride of. **humiliating** adj **humiliation** n
humility ❶ n quality of being humble.
hummock n very small hill.
humour ❶ n 1 ability to say or perceive things that are amusing. 2 amusing quality in a situation, film, etc. 3 state of mind, mood. 4 Old–fashioned fluid in the body. ◆ v 5 be kind and indulgent to. **humorous** adj **humorist** n writer or entertainer who uses humour in his or her work.
hump ❶ n 1 raised piece of ground. 2 large lump on the back of an animal or person. ◆ v 3 Slang carry or heave. **hump–back, humpbacked bridge** road bridge with a sharp slope on each side.
humus [**hew**–muss] n decomposing vegetable and animal mould in the soil.
hunch ❶ n 1 feeling or suspicion not based on facts. ◆ v 2 draw (one's shoulders) up or together. **hunchback** n Offens person with an abnormal curvature of the spine.
hundred adj, n 1 ten times ten. ◆ n 2 (often pl) large but unspecified number. **hundredth** adj, n **hundredweight** n Brit unit of weight of 112 pounds (50.8 kilograms).

hunger ❶ n 1 discomfort or weakness from lack of food. 2 desire or craving. ◆ v 3 (foll. by for) want very much. **hunger strike** refusal of all food, as a means of protest. **hungry** adj having a desire or craving (for).
hunk ❶ n 1 large piece. 2 Slang sexually attractive man.
hunt ❶ v 1 seek out and kill (wild animals) for food or sport. 2 (foll. by for) search (for). ◆ n 3 hunting. 4 (party organized for) hunting wild animals for sport. **hunter** n person or animal that hunts wild animals for food or sport. **huntsman** n man who hunts wild animals, esp. foxes.
hurdle ❶ n 1 Sport light barrier for jumping over in some races. 2 problem or difficulty. ◆ pl 3 race involving hurdles. ◆ v 4 jump over (something). **hurdler** n
hurdy–gurdy n, pl –dies mechanical musical instrument, such as a barrel organ.
hurl ❶ v throw or utter forcefully.
hurly–burly n loud confusion.
hurrah, hurray interj exclamation of joy or applause.

— THESAURUS —

humid adj = **damp**, clammy, dank, moist, muggy, steamy, sticky, sultry, wet
humiliate v = **embarrass**, bring low, chasten, crush, degrade, humble, mortify, put down, put (someone) in their place, shame
humility n = **modesty**, humbleness, lowliness, meekness, submissiveness, unpretentiousness
humour n 1, 2 = **funniness**, amusement, comedy, drollery, facetiousness, fun, jocularity, ludicrousness ≠ **grief** 3 = **mood**, disposition, frame of mind, spirits, temper ◆ v 5 = **indulge**, accommodate, flatter, go along with, gratify, mollify, pander to ≠ **oppose**
hump n 1 = **lump**, bulge, bump, mound, projection, protrusion, protuberance, swelling ◆ v 3 Sl = **carry**, heave, hoist, lug, shoulder
hunch n 1 = **feeling**, idea, impression,

inkling, intuition, premonition, presentiment, suspicion ◆ v 2 = **draw in**, arch, bend, curve
hunger n 1 = **appetite**, emptiness, hungriness, ravenousness 2 = **desire**, ache, appetite, craving, itch, lust, thirst, yearning ◆ v 3 = **want**, ache, crave, desire, hanker, itch, long, thirst, wish, yearn
hunk n 1 = **lump**, block, chunk, mass, nugget, piece, slab, wedge
hunt v 1 = **stalk**, chase, hound, pursue, track, trail 2 (foll. by for) = **search**, ferret about, forage, fossick (Aust & NZ), look, scour, seek ◆ n 3 = **search**, chase, hunting, investigation, pursuit, quest
hurdle n 1 = **fence**, barricade, barrier 2 = **obstacle**, barrier, difficulty, handicap, hazard, hindrance, impediment, obstruction, stumbling block
hurl v = **throw**, cast, fling, heave, launch,

hurricane ⊕ *n* very strong, often destructive, wind or storm. **hurricane lamp** paraffin lamp with a glass covering.

hurry ⊕ *v* **–rying, –ried 1** (cause to) move or act very quickly. ◆ *n* **2** doing something quickly or the need to do something quickly. **hurriedly** *adv*

hurt ⊕ *v* **hurting, hurt 1** cause physical or mental pain to. **2** be painful. **3** *Informal* feel pain. ◆ *n* **4** physical or mental pain. **hurtful** *adj* unkind.

hurtle ⊕ *v* move quickly or violently.

husband ⊕ *n* **1** woman's partner in marriage. ◆ *v* **2** use economically. **husbandry** *n* **1** farming. **2** management of resources.

hush ⊕ *v* **1** make or be silent. ◆ *n* **2** stillness or silence. **hush–hush** *adj Informal* secret. **hush up** *v* suppress information about.

husk *n* **1** outer covering of certain seeds and fruits. ◆ *v* **2** remove the husk from.

husky[1] *adj* **huskier, huskiest 1** slightly hoarse. **2** *Informal* big and strong. **huskily** *adv*

husky[2] *n, pl* **huskies** Arctic sledge dog with thick hair and a curled tail.

hussy *n, pl* **–sies** immodest or promiscuous woman.

hustings *pl n* political campaigns and speeches before an election.

hustle ⊕ *v* **1** push about, jostle. ◆ *n* **2** lively activity or bustle.

hut ⊕ *n* small house, shelter, or shed.

hutch *n* cage for pet rabbits etc.

hyacinth *n* sweet–smelling spring flower that grows from a bulb.

hybrid ⊕ *n* **1** offspring of two plants or animals of different species. **2** anything of mixed origin. ◆ *adj* **3** of mixed origin.

hydrangea *n* ornamental shrub with clusters of pink, blue, or white flowers.

hydrant *n* outlet from a water main with a nozzle for a hose.

hydraulic *adj* operated by force forced through a pipe by a liquid such as water or oil. **hydraulics** *n* study of the mechanical properties of fluids as they apply to practical engineering.

hydrochloric acid *n* strong colourless acid used in many industrial and laboratory processes.

hydroelectric *adj* of the generation of electricity by water pressure.

hydrofoil *n* fast light boat with its hull raised out of the water on one or more pairs of fins.

hydrogen *n Chem* light flammable colourless gas that combines with oxygen to form water. **hydrogen bomb** extremely powerful bomb in which energy is released by fusion of hydrogen nuclei to

————————— THESAURUS —————————

let fly, pitch, propel, sling, toss

hurricane *n* = **storm**, cyclone, gale, tempest, tornado, twister (*US inf*), typhoon

hurry *v* **1** = **rush**, dash, fly, get a move on (*inf*), make haste, scoot, scurry, step on it (*inf*) ≠ **slowness** ◆ *n* **2** = **haste**, flurry, quickness, rush, speed, urgency

hurt *v* **1 a** = **harm**, bruise, damage, disable, impair, injure, mar, spoil, wound ≠ **restored b** = **upset**, annoy, distress, grieve, pain, sadden, wound ≠ **calmed 2** = **ache**, be sore, be tender, burn, smart, sting, throb ◆ *n* **4** = **distress**, discomfort, pain, pang, soreness, suffering ≠ **delight** ◆ *adj* **a** = **injured**, bruised, crook (*Aust & NZ sl*), cut, damaged, harmed, scarred,

wounded **b** = **upset**, aggrieved, crushed, offended, wounded

hurtle *v* = **rush**, charge, crash, fly, plunge, race, shoot, speed, stampede, tear

husband *n* **1** = **partner**, better half (*hum*), mate, spouse ◆ *v* **2** = **economize**, budget, conserve, hoard, save, store ≠ **spend**

hush *v* **1** = **quieten**, mute, muzzle, shush, silence ◆ *n* **2** = **quiet**, calm, peace, silence, stillness, tranquillity

hustle *v* **1** = **jostle**, elbow, force, jog, push, shove

hut *n* = **shed**, cabin, den, hovel, lean–to, shanty, shelter

hybrid *n* **1** = **crossbreed**, cross, half–breed, mongrel **2** = **mixture**, amalgam, give helium nuclei. **hydrogen peroxide** colourless liquid used as a hair bleach and as an antiseptic.

hydrophobia *n* 1 rabies. 2 fear of water.

hyena *n* scavenging doglike mammal of Africa and S Asia.

hygiene ❶ *n* 1 principles and practice of health and cleanliness. 2 **hygienic** *adj*

hymen *n* membrane partly covering the opening of a girl's vagina, which breaks before puberty or at the first occurrence of sexual intercourse.

hymn ❶ *n* Christian song of praise sung to God or a saint. **hymnal** *n* book of hymns (also **hymn book**).

hype ❶ *n* 1 intensive or exaggerated publicity or sales promotion. ◆ *v* 2 promote (a product) using intensive or exaggerated publicity.

hyperbole [hie–**per**–bol–ee] *n* deliberate exaggeration for effect. **hyperbolic** *adj*

hypermarket *n* huge self–service store.

hypertension *n* very high blood pressure.

hyphen *n* punctuation mark (–) indicating that two words or syllables are connected. **hyphenated** *adj* (of two words or syllables) having a hyphen between them. **hyphenation** *n*

hypnosis *n* artificially induced state of relaxation in which the mind is more than usually receptive to suggestion. **hypnotic** *adj* of or (as if) producing hypnosis.

hypnotism *n* inducing hypnosis in someone. **hypnotist** *n* **hypnotize** *v*

hypochondria *n* undue preoccupation with one's health. **hypochondriac** *n*

hypocrisy ❶ [hip–**ok**–rass–ee] *n, pl* **–sies** (instance of) pretence of having standards or beliefs that are contrary to one's real character or actual behaviour. **hypocrite** [**hip**–oh–krit] *n* person who pretends to be what he or she is not. **hypocritical** *adj*

hypodermic *adj, n* (denoting) a syringe or needle used to inject a drug beneath the skin.

hypotenuse [hie–**pot**–a–news] *n* side of a right–angled triangle opposite the right angle.

hypothermia *n* condition in which a person's body temperature is dangerously low as a result of prolonged exposure to severe cold.

hypothesis ❶ [hie–**poth**–iss–iss] *n, pl* **–ses** [–seez] suggested but unproved explanation of something. **hypothetical** *adj* based on assumption rather than fact or reality.

hysterectomy *n, pl* **–mies** surgical removal of the womb.

hysteria ❶ *n* state of uncontrolled excitement, anger, or panic. **hysterical** *adj* 1 **hysterics** *pl n* 1 attack of hysteria. 2 *Informal* uncontrollable laughter.

——— THESAURUS ———

composite, compound, cross

hygiene *n* 1 = **cleanliness**, sanitation

hymn *n* = **song of praise**, anthem, carol, chant, paean, psalm

hype *n* 1 = **publicity**, ballyhoo (*inf*), brouhaha, plugging (*inf*), promotion, razzmatazz (*sl*)

hypocrisy *n* = **insincerity**, cant,

deceitfulness, deception, duplicity, pretence

hypothesis *n* = **assumption**, postulate, premise, proposition, supposition, theory, thesis

hysteria *n* = **frenzy**, agitation, delirium, hysterics, madness, panic

I i

I[1] *pron* used by a speaker or writer to refer to himself or herself as the subject of a verb.
I[2] **the Roman numeral for one.**
IA Iowa.
ibis [**ibe**–iss] *n* large wading bird with long legs.
ice *n* 1 frozen water. 2 portion of ice cream. ◆ *v* 3 (foll. by *up* or *over*) become covered with ice. 4 cover with icing. **break the ice** create a relaxed atmosphere, esp. between people meeting for the first time. **iced** *adj* 1 covered with icing. 2 (of a drink) containing ice. **icy** *adj* **icier, iciest** 1 very cold. 2 covered with ice. 3 aloof and unfriendly. **icily** *adv* **iciness** *n* **iceberg** *n* large floating mass of ice. **icebox** *n US* refrigerator. **ice cream** sweet creamy frozen food. **ice floe** sheet of ice floating in the sea. **ice hockey** team game like hockey played on ice with a puck. **ice pick** pointed tool for breaking ice. **ice skate** boot with a steel blade fixed to the sole, to enable the wearer to glide over ice. **ice–skate** *v* **ice–skater** *n*
icon *n* 1 picture of Christ or another religious figure, regarded as holy in the Orthodox Church. 2 picture on a computer screen representing a function that can be activated by moving the cursor over it.
ID 1 Idaho. 2 identification.
idea ⊕ *n* 1 plan or thought formed in the mind. 2 thought of something. 3 belief or opinion. **ideal** *n* 1 idea of perfection. 2 perfect person or thing.
identity ⊕ *n, pl* –ties 1 state of being a specified person or thing. 2 individuality or personality. 3 state of being the same. **identical** *adj* very same. **identify** *v* establish identity of.
ideology *n, pl* –gies body of ideas and beliefs of a group, nation, etc. **ideological** *adj* **ideologist** *n*
idiom ⊕ *n* 1 group of words which when used together have a different meaning from the words individually, e.g. *raining cats and dogs*. 2 way of expression natural or peculiar to a language or group. **idiomatic** *adj* **idiomatically** *adv*
idiosyncrasy ⊕ *n, pl* –sies personal peculiarity of mind, habit, or behaviour.
idiot ⊕ *n* 1 foolish or stupid person. 2 *Offens* mentally retarded person. **idiotic** *adj* **idiotically** *adv*
idle ⊕ *adj* 1 not doing anything. 2 not willing to work, lazy. 3 not being used. 4 useless or meaningless, e.g. *an idle threat.*

THESAURUS

idea *n* 1 = **intention**, aim, object, objective, plan, purpose 2 = **thought**, concept, impression, perception 3 = **belief**, conviction, notion, opinion, teaching, view
identity *n* 1, 2 = **existence**, individuality, personality, self 3 = **sameness**, correspondence, unity
idiom *n* 1 = **phrase**, expression, turn of phrase 2 = **language**, jargon, parlance, style, vernacular
idiosyncrasy *n* = **peculiarity**, characteristic, eccentricity, mannerism, oddity, quirk, trick
idiot *n* 1 = **fool**, chump, cretin, dunderhead, halfwit, imbecile, moron, nincompoop, numbskull *or* numskull, simpleton, twit (*inf, chiefly Brit*)

◆ *v* **5** (usu. foll. by *away*) spend (time) doing very little. **6** (of an engine) run slowly with the gears disengaged. **idleness** *n* **idler** *n* **idly** *adv*

idol ❶ *n* **1** object of excessive devotion. **2** image of a god as an object of worship. **idolatry** *n* worship of idols. **idolatrous** *adj* **idolize** *v* love or admire excessively.

idyll [id–ill] *n* scene or time of great peace and happiness. **idyllic** *adj*

i.e. that is to say.

if ❶ *conj* **1** on the condition or supposition that. **2** whether. **3** even though. ◆ *n* **4** uncertainty or doubt, e.g. *no ifs, ands, or buts*. **iffy** *adj Informal* doubtful, uncertain.

igloo *n, pl* **–loos** dome–shaped Inuit house made of snow and ice.

ignite ❶ *v* catch fire or set fire to.

ignoble *adj* dishonourable. **ignobly** *adv*

ignominy ❶ [ig–nom–in–ee] *n* humiliating disgrace. **ignominious** *adj*

ignore ❶ *v* refuse to notice, disregard deliberately. **ignorant** *adj* lacking knowledge.

iguana *n* large tropical American lizard.

IL Illinois.

ill ❶ *adj* **1** not in good health. **2** harmful or unpleasant, e.g. *ill effects.* ◆ *n* **3** evil, harm ◆ *adv* **4** badly. **5** hardly, with difficulty, e.g. *I can ill afford to lose him.* **ill at ease** uncomfortable, unable to relax. **Illness** *n* **ill–advised** *adj* **1** badly thought out. **2** unwise. **ill–disposed** *adj* (often foll. by *towards*) unfriendly, unsympathetic. **ill–fated** *adj* doomed to end unhappily. **ill–gotten** *adj* obtained dishonestly. **ill health** *n* condition of being unwell. **ill–mannered** *adj* having bad manners. **ill–treat** *v* treat cruelly. **ill will** unkind feeling, hostility.

illegal ❶ *adj* against the law. **illegally** *adv* **illegality** *n, pl* **–ties**

illegible ❶ *adj* unable to be read or deciphered.

illegitimate ❶ *adj* **1** born of parents not married to each other. **2** not lawful. **illegitimacy** *n*

illicit ❶ *adj* **1** illegal. **2** forbidden or disapproved of by society.

Idle *adj* **1** = **inactive**, redundant, unemployed, unoccupied ≠ **working 2** = **lazy**, good–for–nothing, indolent, lackadaisical, shiftless, slothful, sluggish ≠ **working 3** = **unused**, vacant **4** = **useless**, fruitless, futile, groundless, ineffective, pointless, unavailing, unsuccessful, vain, worthless ≠ **effective** ◆ *v* **5** (usu. foll. by *away*) = **laze**, dally, dawdle, kill time, loaf, loiter, lounge, potter

idol *n* **1** = **hero**, beloved, darling, favourite, pet, pin–up (*sl*) **2** = **graven image**, deity, god

if *conj* **1** = **provided**, assuming, on condition that, providing, supposing

ignite *v* **a** = **catch fire**, burn, burst into flames, flare up, inflame, take fire **b** = **set fire to**, kindle, light, set ablaze, set alight, torch

ignominy *n* = **disgrace**, discredit, dishonour, disrepute, humiliation, infamy, obloquy, shame, stigma

ignore *v* = **overlook**, discount, disregard,

neglect, pass over, reject, take no notice of, turn a blind eye to ≠ **note**

ill *adj* **1** = **unwell**, ailing, crook (*Aust & NZ sl*), diseased, indisposed, infirm, off colour, poorly (*inf*), sick, under the weather (*inf*), unhealthy ≠ **well 2** = **harmful**, bad, damaging, deleterious, detrimental, evil, foul, injurious, unfortunate ≠ **good** ◆ *n* **3** = **harm**, affliction, hardship, hurt, injury, misery, misfortune, trouble, unpleasantness, woe ≠ **good** ◆ *adv* **4** = **badly**, inauspiciously, poorly, unfavourably, unfortunately, unluckily **5** = **hardly**, barely, by no means, scantily ≠ **well**

illegal *adj* = **unlawful**, banned, criminal, felonious, forbidden, illicit, outlawed, prohibited, unauthorized, unlicensed ≠ **legal**

illegible *adj* = **indecipherable**, obscure, scrawled, unreadable

illegitimate *adj* **1** = **born out of wedlock**, bastard **2** = **unlawful**, illegal, illicit,

illiterate ❶ *n, adj* (person) unable to read or write. **illiteracy** *n*

illogical ❶ *adj* **1** unreasonable. **2** not logical.

illuminate ❶ *v* **1** light up. **2** make clear, explain. **3** decorate with lights. **4** *Hist* decorate (a manuscript) with designs of gold and bright colours. **illumination** *n* **illuminating** *adj*

illusion ❶ *n* deceptive appearance or belief. **illusionist** *n* conjuror. **illusory** *adj* seeming to be true, but actually false.

illustrate ❶ *v* **1** explain by use of examples. **2** provide (a book or text) with pictures. **3** be an example of. **illustration** *n* **1** picture or diagram. **2** example. **illustrative** *adj* **illustrator** *n*

illustrious ❶ *adj* famous and distinguished.

image ❶ *n* **1** mental picture of someone or something. **2** impression people have of a person, organization, etc. **3** representation

of a person or thing in a work of art. **4** optical reproduction of someone or something, for example in a mirror. **5** person or thing that looks almost exactly like another. **6** figure of speech, esp. a metaphor or simile. **imagery** *n* images collectively, esp. in the arts.

imagine ❶ *v* **1** form a mental image of. **2** think, believe, or guess. **imaginable** *adj* **imaginary** *adj* existing only in the imagination. **imagination** *n* **1** ability to make mental images of things that may not exist in real life. **2** creative mental ability. **imaginative** *adj* having or showing a lot of creative mental ability. **imaginatively** *adv*

imbalance *n* lack of balance or proportion.

imbecile ❶ [**imb**–ess–eel] *n* **1** stupid person. ◆ *adj* **2** (also **imbecilic**) stupid or senseless. **imbecility** *n*

imbibe ❶ *v* **1** drink (alcoholic drinks). **2** *Lit* absorb (ideas etc.).

————— THESAURUS —————

improper, unauthorized ≠ **legal**

illicit *adj* **1** = **illegal**, criminal, felonious, illegitimate, prohibited, unauthorized, unlawful, unlicensed ≠ **legal**
2 = **forbidden**, clandestine, furtive, guilty, immoral, improper

illiterate *adj* = **uneducated**, ignorant, uncultured, untaught, untutored ≠ **aware**

illogical *adj* = **irrational**, absurd, inconsistent, invalid, meaningless, senseless, shonky (*Aust & NZ inf*), unreasonable, unscientific, unsound

illuminate *v* **1** = **light up**, brighten ≠ **obscure** **2** = **clarify**, clear up, elucidate, enlighten, explain, interpret, make clear, shed light on ≠ **obscure**

illusion *n* **a** = **fantasy**, chimera, daydream, figment of the imagination, hallucination, mirage, will-o'-the-wisp **b** = **misconception**, deception, delusion, error, fallacy, misapprehension ≠ **fact**

illustrate *v* **1** = **demonstrate**, bring home, elucidate, emphasize, explain, point up, show

illustrious *adj* = **famous**, celebrated,

distinguished, eminent, glorious, great, notable, prominent, renowned

image *n* **1, 2** = **concept**, idea, impression, mental picture, perception
3 = **representation**, effigy, figure, icon, idol, likeness, picture, portrait, statue
5 = **replica**, counterpart, (dead) ringer (*sl*), doppelgänger, double, facsimile, spitting image (*inf*)

imagine *v* **1** = **envisage**, conceive, conceptualize, conjure up, picture, plan, think of, think up, visualize **2** = **believe**, assume, conjecture, fancy, guess (*inf*, *chiefly US & Canad*), infer, suppose, surmise, suspect, take it, think

imbecile *n* **1** = **idiot**, chump, cretin, fool, halfwit, moron, numbskull *or* numskull, thickhead, twit (*inf, chiefly Brit*) ◆ *adj* **2** (also **imbecilic**) = **stupid**, asinine, fatuous, feeble–minded, foolish, idiotic, moronic, thick, witless

imbibe *v* **1** = **drink**, consume, knock back (*inf*), quaff, sink (*inf*), swallow, swig (*inf*)
2 *Lit* = **absorb**, acquire, assimilate, gain, gather, ingest, receive, take in

imbue v **–buing, –bued** (usu. foll. by *with*) fill or inspire with (ideals or principles).

imitate ● v **1** take as a model. **2** copy the voice and mannerisms of, esp. for entertainment. **imitation** n **1** copy of an original. **2** imitating. **imitative** adj **imitator** n

immaculate ● adj **1** completely clean or tidy. **2** completely flawless. **immaculately** adv

immaterial ● adj not important, not relevant.

immature ● adj **1** not fully developed. **2** lacking wisdom or stability because of youth.

immediate ● adj **1** occurring at once. **2** next or nearest in time, space, or relationship. **immediately** adv **immediacy** n

immense ● adj extremely large. **immensely** adv to a very great degree. **immensity** n

immerse ● v **1** involve deeply, engross. **2** plunge (something or someone) into liquid. **immersion** n

imminent ● adj about to happen.

imminence n

immobile ● adj **1** not moving. **2** unable to move. **immobility** n **immobilize** v make unable to move or work

immolate v kill as a sacrifice.

immoral ● adj **1** morally wrong, corrupt. **2** sexually depraved or promiscuous. **immorality** n

> ✓ **WORD TIP**
> Do not confuse *immoral* with *amoral*, which means 'having no moral standards'.

immortal ● adj **1** living forever. **2** famous for all time. ◆ n **3** person whose fame will last for all time. **4** immortal being. **immortality** n **immortalize** v

immune ● adj **1** protected against a specific disease. **2** (foll. by *to*) secure (against). **3** (foll. by *from*) exempt (from). **immunity** n, pl **–ties 1** ability to resist disease. **2** freedom from prosecution, tax, etc. **immunize** v make immune to a disease. **immunization** n

imp ● n **1** (in folklore) mischievous small

———— THESAURUS ————

imitate v **1 = follow**, emulate, mirror, simulate **2 = copy**, ape, echo, mimic, repeat

immaculate adj **1 = clean**, neat, spick-and-span, spotless, spruce, squeaky-clean ≠ **dirty 2 = pure**, above reproach, faultless, flawless, impeccable, perfect, unblemished, unexceptionable, untarnished ≠ **corrupt**

immaterial adj = **irrelevant**, extraneous, inconsequential, inessential, insignificant, of no importance, trivial, unimportant ≠ **important**

immature adj **1 = young**, adolescent, undeveloped, unformed, unripe **2 = childish**, callow, inexperienced, infantile, juvenile, puerile

immediate adj **1 = instant**, instantaneous ≠ **late 2 = nearest**, close, direct, near, next ≠ **far**

immense adj = **huge**, colossal, enormous, extensive, gigantic, great, massive, monumental, stupendous, tremendous, vast

immerse v **1 = engross**, absorb, busy, engage, involve, occupy, take up **2 = plunge**, bathe, dip, douse, duck, dunk, sink, submerge

imminent adj = **near**, at hand, close, coming, forthcoming, gathering, impending, in the pipeline, looming

immobile adj = **stationary**, at a standstill, at rest, fixed, immovable, motionless, rigid, rooted, static, still, stock-still, unmoving ≠ **mobile**

immoral adj **1 = wicked**, bad, corrupt, sinful, unethical, unprincipled, wrong **2 = depraved**, debauched, dissolute, indecent

immortal adj **1 = eternal**, deathless, enduring, everlasting, imperishable, lasting, perennial, undying ≠ **passing** ◆ n creature with magical powers. **2** mischievous child.

impact ❶ *n* **1** strong effect. **2** (force of) a collision. ◆ *v* **3** press firmly into something.

impair ❶ *v* weaken or damage. **impairment** *n*

impala [imp–**ah**–la] *n* southern African antelope.

impale *v* pierce with a sharp object.

impart ❶ *v* **1** communicate (information). **2** give.

impartial ❶ *adj* not favouring one side or the other. **impartially** *adv* **impartiality** *n*

impassable ❶ *adj* (of a road etc.) impossible to travel through or over.

impasse ❶ [**am**–pass] *n* situation in which progress is impossible.

impassioned ❶ *adj* full of emotion.

impassive *adj* showing no emotion, calm.

impatient ❶ *adj* **1** irritable at any delay or difficulty. **2** restless (to have or do something). **impatience** *n*

impeach ❶ *v* charge with a serious crime against the state. **impeachment** *n*

impeccable ❶ *adj* without fault, excellent. **impeccably** *adv*

impede ❶ *v* hinder in action or progress. **impediment** *n* something that makes action, speech, or progress difficult. **impedimenta** *pl n* objects impeding progress, esp. baggage or equipment.

impel ❶ *v* **–pelling, –pelled** push or force (someone) to do something.

impending ❶ *adj* (esp. of something bad) about to happen.

imperative ❶ *adj* **1** extremely urgent, vital. **2** *Grammar* denoting a mood of verbs used in commands. ◆ *n* **3** *Grammar* imperative mood.

imperfect ❶ *adj* **1** having faults or mistakes. **2** not complete. **3** *Grammar* denoting a tense of verbs describing continuous, incomplete, or repeated past

3 = **great**, genius, hero **4** = **god**, goddess

immune *adj* **1** = **protected**, clear, free, resistant **2** = **invulnerable**, proof (against), safe, unaffected **3** = **exempt**

imp *n* **1** = **demon**, devil, sprite **2** = **rascal**, brat, minx, rogue, scamp

impact *n* **1** = **effect**, consequences, impression, influence, repercussions, significance **2** = **collision**, blow, bump, contact, crash, jolt, knock, smash, stroke, thump

impair *v* = **worsen**, blunt, damage, decrease, diminish, harm, hinder, injure, lessen, reduce, undermine, weaken

impart *v* **1** = **communicate**, convey, disclose, divulge, make known, pass on, relate, reveal, tell **2** = **give**, accord, afford, bestow, confer, grant, lend, yield

impartial *adj* = **neutral**, detached, disinterested, equitable, even–handed, fair, just, objective, open–minded, unbiased, unprejudiced

impassable *adj* = **blocked**, closed, impenetrable, obstructed

impasse *n* = **deadlock**, dead end,

stalemate, standoff, standstill

impassioned *adj* = **intense**, animated, fervent, fiery, heated, inspired, passionate, rousing, stirring

impatient *adj* **1** = **irritable**, demanding, hot–tempered, intolerant, quick–tempered, snappy, testy ≠ **tolerant** **2** = **restless**, eager, edgy, fretful, straining at the leash

impeach *v* = **charge**, accuse, arraign, indict

impeccable *adj* = **faultless**, blameless, flawless, immaculate, irreproachable, perfect, squeaky–clean, unblemished, unimpeachable

impede *v* = **hinder**, block, check, disrupt, hamper, hold up, obstruct, slow (down), thwart

impel *v* = **force**, compel, constrain, drive, induce, oblige, push, require

impending *adj* = **looming**, approaching, coming, forthcoming, gathering, imminent, in the pipeline, near, upcoming

imperative *adj* **1** = **urgent**, crucial, essential, pressing, vital ≠ **unnecessary**

actions. ◆ n 4 *Grammar* imperfect tense.
imperfection n
imperial ❶ *adj* 1 of or like an empire or
emperor. 2 denoting a system of weights
and measures formerly used in Britain.
imperialism n rule by one country over
many others. **imperialist** *adj, n*
imperil ❶ *v* **-illing, -illed** put in danger.
imperious *adj* proud and domineering.
impersonal ❶ *adj* 1 not relating to any
particular person, objective. 2 lacking
human warmth or sympathy. 3 *Grammar*
(of a verb) without a personal subject, e.g.
it is snowing.
impersonate ❶ *v* 1 pretend to be
(another person). 2 copy the voice and
mannerisms of, esp. for entertainment.
impersonation n **impersonator** n
impertinent ❶ *adj* disrespectful or rude.
impertinence n
imperturbable ❶ *adj* calm, not excitable.
impervious ❶ *adj* (foll. by *to*) 1 not letting
(water etc.) through. 2 not influenced by

(a feeling, argument, etc.).
impetigo [imp–it–**tie**–go] n contagious
skin disease.
impetuous ❶ *adj* done or acting without
thought, rash. **impetuosity** n
impetus ❶ [imp–ee–uss] n, *pl* **–tuses** 1
incentive, impulse. 2 force that starts a
body moving.
impinge ❶ *v* (foll. by *on*) affect or restrict.
impious ❶ [imp–ee–uss] *adj* showing a
lack of respect or reverence.
implacable ❶ *adj* not prepared to be
appeased, unyielding. **implacably** *adv*
implant ❶ n 1 *Med* something put into
someone's body, usu. by surgical
operation. ◆ *v* 2 put (something) into
someone's body, usu. by surgical
operation. 3 fix firmly in someone's mind.
implantation n
implement ❶ *v* 1 carry out (instructions
etc.). ◆ n 2 tool, instrument.
implementation n
implore ❶ *v* beg earnestly.

imperfect *adj* 1 = **flawed**, damaged,
defective, faulty, impaired, limited,
2 = **incomplete**, unfinished
imperial *adj* 1 = **royal**, kingly, majestic,
princely, queenly, regal, sovereign
imperil *v* = **endanger**, expose, jeopardize,
risk
impersonal *adj* 2 = **detached**, aloof, cold,
dispassionate, formal, inhuman, neutral,
remote ≠ **personal**
impersonate *v* 1 = **pretend to be**,
masquerade as, pass oneself off as, pose as
(*inf*) 2 = **imitate**, ape, do (*inf*), mimic, take
off (*inf*)
impertinent *adj* = **rude**, brazen, cheeky
(*inf*), disrespectful, impolite, impudent,
insolent, presumptuous ≠ **mannerly**
imperturbable *adj* = **calm**, collected,
composed, cool, nerveless, self–possessed,
serene, unexcitable, unflappable (*inf*),
unruffled
impervious *adj* 1 (foll. by *to*) = **sealed**,
impassable, impenetrable, impermeable,
resistant 2 = **unaffected**, immune,

invulnerable, proof against, unmoved,
untouched
impetuous *adj* = **rash**, hasty, impulsive,
precipitate, unthinking
impetus n 1 = **incentive**, catalyst, goad,
impulse, motivation, push, spur, stimulus
2 = **force**, energy, momentum, power
impinge *v* (foll. by *on*) = **affect**, bear upon,
have a bearing on, impact, influence,
relate to, touch
impious *adj* = **sacrilegious**, blasphemous,
godless, irreligious, irreverent, profane,
sinful, ungodly, unholy, wicked
implacable *adj* = **unyielding**, inflexible,
intractable, merciless, pitiless, unbending,
uncompromising, unforgiving
implant *v* 2 = **insert**, fix, graft 3 = **instil**,
inculcate, infuse
implement *v* 1 = **carry out**, bring about,
complete, effect, enforce, execute, fulfil,
perform, realize ≠ **delay** ◆ n 2 = **tool**,
apparatus, appliance, device, gadget,
instrument, utensil
implore *v* = **beg**, beseech, entreat,

imply ⊕ v –plying, –plied 1 indicate by
hinting, suggest. 2 involve as a necessary
consequence.
import ⊕ v 1 bring in (goods) from
another country. ♦ n 2 something
imported. 3 importance. 4 meaning.
importation n **importer** n
important ⊕ adj 1 of great significance or
value. 2 having influence or power.
importance n
impose ⊕ v 1 force the acceptance of. 2
(foll. by on) take unfair advantage (of).
imposing adj grand, impressive.
imposition n unreasonable demand.
impossible ⊕ adj 1 not able to be done or
to happen. 2 absurd or unreasonable.
impossibly adv **impossibility** n, pl –ties
impotent ⊕ [imp–a–tent] adj 1 powerless.
2 (of a man) incapable of sexual
intercourse. **impotence** n
impound v take legal possession of,
confiscate.
impoverish ⊕ v make poor or weak.

impoverishment n
impractical ⊕ adj not sensible.
impregnable ⊕ adj impossible to break
into.
impregnate ⊕ v 1 saturate, spread all
through. 2 make pregnant. **impregnation**
n
impresario n, pl –ios person who runs
theatre performances, concerts, etc.
impress ⊕ v 1 affect strongly, usu.
favourably. 2 stress, emphasize. 3 imprint,
stamp. **impression** n 1 effect, esp. a
strong or favourable one. 2 vague idea. 3
impersonation for entertainment. 4 mark
made by pressing. **impressionable** adj
easily impressed or influenced. **impressive**
adj making a strong impression, esp.
through size, importance, or quality.
imprint ⊕ n 1 mark made by printing or
stamping. 2 publisher's name and address
on a book. ♦ v 3 produce (a mark) by
printing or stamping.
imprison ⊕ v put or confine in prison.

————— THESAURUS —————

importune, plead with, pray
imply v 1 = **hint**, insinuate, intimate,
signify, suggest 2 = **entail**, indicate,
involve, mean, point to, presuppose
import v 1 = **bring in**, introduce ♦ n
3 = **importance**, consequence, magnitude,
moment, significance, substance, weight
4 = **meaning**, drift, gist, implication,
intention, sense, significance, thrust
important adj 1 = **significant**, far–
reaching, momentous, seminal, serious,
substantial, urgent, weighty ≠ **minor**
2 = **powerful**, eminent, high–ranking,
influential, noteworthy, pre–eminent,
prominent
impose v 1 = **establish**, decree, fix,
institute, introduce, levy, ordain 2 (foll. by
on) = **inflict**, saddle (someone) with, take
advantage of
impossible adj 1 = **inconceivable**,
impracticable, out of the question,
unachievable, unattainable, unobtainable,
unthinkable ≠ **possible** 2 = **absurd**,
ludicrous, outrageous, preposterous,

unreasonable
impotent adj 1 = **powerless**, feeble, frail,
helpless, incapable, incapacitated,
incompetent, ineffective, paralysed, weak
impoverish v = **bankrupt**, beggar, break,
ruin
impractical adj = **unworkable**, impossible,
impracticable, inoperable, nonviable,
unrealistic, wild ≠ **possible**
impregnable adj = **invulnerable**,
impenetrable, indestructible, invincible,
secure, unassailable, unbeatable,
unconquerable
impregnate v 1 = **saturate**, infuse,
permeate, soak, steep, suffuse 2 = **fertilize**,
inseminate, make pregnant
impress v 1 = **excite**, affect, inspire, make
an impression, move, stir, strike, touch
2 = **stress**, bring home to, emphasize, fix,
inculcate, instil into 3 = **imprint**, emboss,
engrave, indent, mark, print, stamp
imprint n 1 = **mark**, impression,
indentation, sign, stamp ♦ v 3 = **fix**,
engrave, etch, impress, print, stamp

imprisonment n

improbable ⊕ adj not likely to be true or to happen. **improbability** n, pl **-ties**

impromptu ⊕ adj without planning or preparation.

improper ⊕ adj 1 indecent. 2 incorrect or irregular. **improper fraction** fraction in which the numerator is larger than the denominator, as in ⅚.

improve ⊕ v make or become better. **improvement** n

improvident ⊕ adj not planning for future needs. **improvidence** n

improvise ⊕ v 1 make use of whatever materials are available. 2 make up (a piece of music, speech, etc.) as one goes along. **improvisation** n

impudent ⊕ adj cheeky, disrespectful. **impudence** n

impugn [imp–**yoon**] v challenge the truth or validity of.

impulse ⊕ n 1 sudden urge to do something. 2 short electrical signal passing along a wire or nerve or through the air.

on impulse suddenly and without planning. **impulsive** adj acting or done without careful consideration. **impulsively** adv

impunity ⊕ [imp–**yoon**–it–ee] n with impunity without punishment.

impure ⊕ adj 1 having dirty or unwanted substances mixed in. 2 immoral, obscene. **impurity** n

impute v attribute responsibility to. **imputation** n

in prep 1 indicating position inside, state or situation, etc., e.g. in the net; in tears. ◆ adv 2 indicating position inside, entry into, etc., e.g. she stayed in; come in. ◆ adj 3 fashionable. **inward** adj 1 directed towards the middle. 2 situated within. 3 spiritual or mental. ◆ adv 4 (also **inwards**) towards the inside or middle. **inwardly** adv

IN Indiana.

inability n lack of means or skill to do something.

inaccurate ⊕ adj not correct. **inaccuracy** n, pl **-cies**

─── THESAURUS ───

imprison v = **jail**, confine, detain, incarcerate, intern, lock up, put away, send down (inf)

improbable adj = **doubtful**, dubious, fanciful, far–fetched, implausible, questionable, unconvincing, unlikely, weak ≠ **likely**

impromptu adj = **unprepared**, ad–lib, extemporaneous, improvised, offhand, off the cuff (inf), spontaneous, unrehearsed, unscripted ≠ **planned**

improper adj 1 = **indecent**, risqué, smutty, suggestive, unbecoming, unseemly, untoward, vulgar ≠ **decent**
2 = **inappropriate**, out of place, uncalled–for, unfit, unsuitable, unwarranted ≠ **appropriate**

improve v a = **enhance**, ameliorate, better, correct, help, rectify, touch up, upgrade ≠ **damage** b = **progress**, advance, develop, make strides, pick up, rally, rise

improvident adj = **imprudent**, careless, negligent, prodigal, profligate, reckless,

short–sighted, spendthrift, thoughtless, wasteful

improvise v 1 = **concoct**, contrive, devise, throw together 2 = **extemporize**, ad–lib, busk, invent, play it by ear (inf), speak off the cuff (inf), wing it (inf)

impudent adj = **bold**, audacious, brazen, cheeky (inf), impertinent, insolent, presumptuous, rude, shameless

impulse n 1 = **urge**, caprice, feeling, inclination, notion, whim, wish

impunity n with impunity = **without punishment**, at liberty, with freedom, with immunity, with licence, with permission

impure adj 1 a = **unclean**, contaminated, defiled, dirty, infected, polluted, tainted ≠ **clean** b = **unrefined**, adulterated, debased, mixed 2 = **immoral**, corrupt, indecent, lascivious, lewd, licentious, obscene, unchaste ≠ **moral**

inaccurate adj = **incorrect**, defective, erroneous, faulty, imprecise, mistaken,

inadequate ⊕ *adj* **1** not enough. **2** not good enough. **inadequacy** *n*

inane ⊕ *adj* senseless, silly. **inanity** *n*

inanimate ⊕ *adj* not living.

inappropriate *adj* not suitable.

inarticulate *adj* unable to express oneself clearly or well.

inaugurate ⊕ *v* **1** open or begin the use of, esp. with ceremony. **2** formally establish (a new leader) in office. **inaugural** *adj* **inauguration** *n*

inauspicious *adj* unlucky, likely to have an unfavourable outcome.

inborn ⊕ *adj* existing from birth, natural.

incalculable ⊕ *adj* too great to be estimated.

incandescent *adj* glowing with heat. **incandescence** *n*

incantation ⊕ *n* ritual chanting of magic words or sounds.

incapable *adj* **1** (foll. by *of*) unable (to do something). **2** incompetent.

incapacitate ⊕ *v* deprive of strength or ability. **incapacity** *n*

incarcerate ⊕ *v* imprison. **incarceration** *n*

incarnate ⊕ *adj* in human form. **incarnation** *n*

incendiary [in–**send**–ya–ree] *adj* **1** (of a bomb, attack, etc.) designed to cause fires. ◆ *n, pl* **–aries 2** bomb designed to cause fires.

incense[1] ⊕ *v* make very angry.

incense[2] *n* substance that gives off a sweet perfume when burned.

incentive ⊕ *n* something that encourages effort or action.

inception ⊕ *n* beginning.

incessant ⊕ *adj* never stopping.

incest *n* sexual intercourse between two people too closely related to marry. **incestuous** *adj*

inch *n* **1** unit of length equal to one twelfth of a foot or 2.54 centimetres. ◆ *v* **2** move slowly and gradually.

incident ⊕ *n* **1** something that happens. **2** event involving violence. **incidental** *adj* occurring in connection with or resulting from something more important.

——————— THESAURUS ———————

out, shonky (*Aust & NZ inf*), unreliable, unsound, wrong

inadequate *adj* **1** = **insufficient**, meagre, scant, sketchy, sparse ≠ **sufficient 2** = **deficient**, faulty, found wanting, incapable, incompetent, not up to scratch (*inf*), unqualified ≠ **fit**

inane *adj* = **senseless**, empty, fatuous, frivolous, futile, idiotic, mindless, silly, stupid, vacuous

inanimate *adj* = **lifeless**, cold, dead, defunct, extinct, inert

inaugurate *v* **1** = **launch**, begin, commence, get under way, initiate, institute, introduce, set in motion **2** = **invest**, induct, install

inborn *adj* = **natural**, congenital, hereditary, inbred, ingrained, inherent, innate, instinctive, intuitive, native

incalculable *adj* = **countless**, boundless, infinite, innumerable, limitless, numberless, untold, vast

incantation *n* = **chant**, charm, formula,

invocation, spell

incapacitate *v* = **disable**, cripple, immobilize, lay up (*inf*), paralyse, put out of action (*inf*)

incarcerate *v* = **imprison**, confine, detain, impound, intern, jail *or* gaol, lock up, throw in jail

incarnate *adj* = **personified**, embodied, typified

incense[1] *v* = **anger**, enrage, inflame, infuriate, irritate, madden, make one's hackles rise, rile (*inf*)

incentive *n* = **encouragement**, bait, carrot (*inf*), enticement, inducement, lure, motivation, spur, stimulus

inception *n* = **beginning**, birth, commencement, dawn, initiation, origin, outset, start

incessant *adj* = **endless**, ceaseless, constant, continual, eternal, interminable, never–ending, nonstop, perpetual, unceasing, unending

incident *n* **1** = **happening**, adventure,

incinerate ❶ v burn to ashes. **incineration** n **incinerator** n furnace for burning rubbish.

incipient ❶ adj just starting to appear or happen.

incise v cut into with a sharp tool. **incision** n **incisive** adj direct and forceful. **incisor** n front tooth, used for biting into food.

incite ❶ v stir up, provoke. **incitement** n

inclement ❶ adj (of weather) stormy or severe. **inclemency** n

incline ❶ v 1 lean, slope. 2 (cause to) have a certain disposition or tendency. ♦ n 3 slope. **inclination** n 1 liking, tendency, or preference. 2 slope.

include ❶ v 1 have as part of the whole. 2 put in as part of a set or group. **inclusion** n **inclusive** adj including everything (specified). **inclusively** adv

incognito ❶ [in–kog–**nee**–toe] adj, adv 1 having adopted a false identity. ♦ n, pl –tos 2 false identity.

incoherent ❶ adj unclear and impossible to understand. **incoherence** n

income ❶ n amount of money earned from work, investments, etc. **income tax** personal tax levied on annual income.

incoming ❶ adj 1 coming in. 2 about to come into office.

incomparable ❶ adj beyond comparison, unequalled. **incomparably** adv

incompatible ❶ adj inconsistent or conflicting. **incompatibility** n

incompetent ❶ adj not having the necessary ability or skill to do something. **incompetence** n

inconceivable ❶ adj extremely unlikely, unimaginable.

inconclusive ❶ adj not giving a final decision or result.

——————| THESAURUS |——————

episode, event, fact, matter, occasion, occurrence 2 = **disturbance**, clash, commotion, confrontation, contretemps, scene

incinerate v = **burn up**, carbonize, char, cremate, reduce to ashes

incipient adj = **beginning**, commencing, developing, embryonic, inchoate, nascent, starting

incite v = **provoke**, encourage, foment, inflame, instigate, spur, stimulate, stir up, urge, whip up

inclement adj = **stormy**, foul, harsh, intemperate, rough, severe, tempestuous ≠ **fine**

incline v 1 = **slope**, lean, slant, tilt, tip, veer 2 = **predispose**, influence, persuade, prejudice, sway ♦ n 3 = **slope**, ascent, descent, dip, grade, gradient, rise

include v 1 = **contain**, comprise, cover, embrace, encompass, incorporate, involve, subsume, take in ≠ **exclude** 2 = **introduce**, add, enter, insert

incognito adj 1 = **in disguise**, disguised, under an assumed name, unknown, unrecognized

incoherent adj = **unintelligible**, confused, disjointed, disordered, inarticulate, inconsistent, jumbled, muddled, rambling, stammering, stuttering

income n = **revenue**, earnings, pay, proceeds, profits, receipts, salary, takings, wages

incoming adj 1 = **arriving**, approaching, entering, homeward, landing, returning ≠ **leaving** 2 = **new**

incomparable adj = **unequalled**, beyond compare, inimitable, matchless, peerless, superlative, supreme, transcendent, unmatched, unparalleled, unrivalled

incompatible adj = **inconsistent**, conflicting, contradictory, incongruous, mismatched, unsuited

incompetent adj = **inept**, bungling, floundering, incapable, ineffectual, inexpert, unfit, useless

inconceivable adj = **unimaginable**, beyond belief, incomprehensible, incredible, mind–boggling (inf), out of the question, unbelievable, unheard–of, unthinkable

inconclusive adj = **indecisive**, ambiguous, indeterminate, open, unconvincing, undecided, up in the air (inf), vague

incongruous ❶ *adj* inappropriate or out of place. **incongruity** *n*, *pl* **–ties**

inconsequential *adj* unimportant, insignificant.

incontinent *adj* unable to control one's bladder or bowels. **incontinence** *n*

incontrovertible ❶ *adj* impossible to deny or disprove.

inconvenience ❶ *n* 1 trouble or difficulty. ♦ *v* 2 cause trouble or difficulty to. **inconvenient** *adj*

incorporate ❶ *v* include or be included as part of a larger unit. **incorporation** *n*

incorrigible ❶ *adj* beyond correction or reform.

increase ❶ *v* 1 make or become greater in size, number, etc. ♦ *n* 2 rise in number, size, etc. 3 amount by which something increases. **increasingly** *adv*

incredible ❶ *adj* 1 hard to believe or imagine. 2 *Informal* marvellous, amazing. **incredibly** *adv*

incredulous ❶ *adj* not willing to believe something. **incredulity** *n*

increment ❶ *n* increase in money or value, esp. a regular salary increase. **incremental** *adj*

incriminate ❶ *v* make (someone) seem guilty of a crime. **incriminating** *adj*

incubate [in–cube–ate] *v* 1 (of a bird) hatch (eggs) by sitting on them. 2 grow (bacteria). 3 (of bacteria) remain inactive in an animal or person before causing disease. **incubation** *n* **incubator** *n* 1 heated enclosed apparatus for rearing premature babies. 2 apparatus for artificially hatching birds' eggs.

inculcate *v* fix in someone's mind by constant repetition.

incumbent *n* 1 person holding a particular office or position. ♦ *adj* 2 **it is incumbent on** it is the duty of. **incumbency** *n*, *pl* **–cies**

incur ❶ *v* **–curring**, **–curred** cause (something unpleasant) to happen.

indebted ❶ *adj* 1 owing gratitude for help or favours. 2 owing money. **indebtedness** *n* the state of owing money.

——— THESAURUS ———

incongruous *adj* = **inappropriate**, discordant, improper, incompatible, out of keeping, out of place, unbecoming, unsuitable

incontrovertible *adj* = **indisputable**, certain, established, incontestable, indubitable, irrefutable, positive, sure, undeniable, unquestionable

inconvenience *n* 1 = **trouble**, awkwardness, bother, difficulty, disadvantage, disruption, disturbance, fuss, hindrance, nuisance ♦ *v* 2 = **trouble**, bother, discommode, disrupt, disturb, put out, upset

incorporate *v* = **include**, absorb, assimilate, blend, combine, integrate, merge, subsume

incorrigible *adj* = **incurable**, hardened, hopeless, intractable, inveterate, irredeemable, unreformed

increase *v* 1 = **grow**, advance, boost, develop, enlarge, escalate, expand, extend, multiply, raise, spread, swell

≠ **decline** ♦ *n* 2 = **growth**, development, enlargement, escalation, expansion, extension, gain, increment, rise, upturn ≠ **reduce**

incredible *adj* 1 = **implausible**, beyond belief, far–fetched, improbable, inconceivable, preposterous, unbelievable, unimaginable, unthinkable 2 *Inf* = **amazing**, astonishing, astounding, extraordinary, prodigious, sensational (*inf*), wonderful

incredulous *adj* = **disbelieving**, distrustful, doubtful, dubious, sceptical, suspicious, unbelieving, unconvinced

increment *n* = **increase**, accrual, addition, advancement, augmentation, enlargement, gain, step up, supplement

incriminate *v* = **implicate**, accuse, blame, charge, impeach, inculpate, involve

incur *v* = **earn**, arouse, bring (upon oneself), draw, expose oneself to, gain, meet with, provoke

indebted *adj* 1 = **grateful**, beholden,

indecent ❶ *adj* 1 morally or sexually offensive. 2 unsuitable or unseemly, e.g. *indecent haste.* **indecency** *n*

indeed ❶ *adv* 1 really, certainly. ◆ *interj* 2 expression of indignation or surprise.

indefatigable *adj* never getting tired.

indefensible ❶ *adj* 1 unable to be justified. 2 impossible to defend.

indefinite ❶ *adj* 1 without exact limits, e.g. *for an indefinite period.* 2 vague, unclear. **indefinite article** *Grammar* the word *a* or *an.* **indefinitely** *adv*

indelible ❶ *adj* 1 impossible to erase or remove. 2 making indelible marks. **indelibly** *adv*

indelicate ❶ *adj* offensive or embarrassing.

indemnity ❶ *n, pl* **-ties** 1 insurance against loss or damage. 2 compensation for loss or damage.

indent *v* 1 start (a line of writing) further from the margin than the other lines. 2 order (goods) using a special order form. **indentation** *n* dent in a surface or edge.

independent ❶ *adj* 1 free from the control or influence of others. 2 separate. 3 financially self-reliant. 4 capable of acting for oneself or on one's own. ◆ *n* 5 politician who does represent any political party. **independence** *n*

indescribable ❶ *adj* too intense or extreme for words. **indescribably** *adv*

indeterminate ❶ *adj* uncertain in extent, amount, or nature. **indeterminacy** *n*

index *n, pl* **indices** [in-diss-eez] 1 alphabetical list of names or subjects dealt with in a book. 2 file or catalogue used to find things. ◆ *v* 3 provide (a book) with an index. 4 enter in an index. 5 make index-linked. **index finger** finger next to the thumb. **index-linked** *adj* (of pensions, wages, etc.) rising or falling in line with the cost of living.

indicate ❶ *v* 1 be a sign or symptom of. 2 point out. 3 state briefly. 4 (of a measuring instrument) show a reading of. **indication** *n* **indicative** *adj* (foll. by *of*) suggesting. 2 *Grammar* denoting a mood of verbs used to make a statement. ◆ *n* 3 *Grammar* indicative mood. **indicator** *n* 1 something acting as a sign or indication. 2 flashing light on a vehicle showing the driver's intention to turn. 3 dial or gauge.

indict ❶ [in-dite] *v* formally charge with a

THESAURUS

obligated, obliged, under an obligation 2 = **in debt**, owing money

indecent *adj* 1 = **lewd**, crude, dirty, filthy, immodest, improper, impure, licentious, pornographic, salacious, scungy (*Aust & NZ inf*) ≠ **pure** 2 = **unbecoming**, in bad taste, indecorous, unseemly, vulgar ≠ **seemly**

indeed *adv* = **really**, actually, certainly, in truth, truly, undoubtedly

indefensible *adj* 1 = **unforgivable**, inexcusable, unjustifiable, unpardonable, untenable, unwarrantable, wrong

indefinite *adj* = **unclear**, doubtful, equivocal, ill-defined, imprecise, indeterminate, inexact, uncertain, unfixed, vague ≠ **clear**

indelible *adj* 1 = **permanent**, enduring, indestructible, ineradicable, ingrained, lasting

indelicate *adj* = **offensive**, coarse, crude, embarrassing, immodest, risqué, rude, suggestive, tasteless, vulgar

indemnity *n* 1 = **insurance**, guarantee, protection, security 2 = **compensation**, redress, reimbursement, remuneration, reparation, restitution

independent *adj* 1 = **free**, autonomous, liberated, self-determining, self-governing, separate, sovereign, unconstrained, uncontrolled ≠ **controlled** 3 = **self-sufficient**, liberated, self-contained, self-reliant, self-supporting

indescribable *adj* = **unutterable**, beyond description, beyond words, indefinable, inexpressible

indeterminate *adj* = **uncertain**, imprecise, indefinite, inexact, undefined, unfixed, unspecified, unstipulated, vague

indicate *v* 1 = **signify**, betoken, denote,

crime. **indictable** adj **indictment** n

indifferent ⊙ adj **1** showing no interest or concern. **2** of poor quality. **indifference** n

indigenous [in–**dij**–in–uss] adj born in or natural to a country.

indigent adj extremely poor. **indigence** n

indigestion ⊙ n (discomfort or pain caused by) difficulty in digesting food. **indigestible** adj

indigo adj **1** deep violet–blue. ♦ n **2** dye of this colour.

indirect ⊙ adj **1** done or caused by someone or something else. **2** not by a straight route. **indirect object** Grammar person or thing indirectly affected by the action of a verb, e.g. Amy in I bought Amy a bag. **indirect tax** tax, such as VAT, added to the price of something.

indiscreet ⊙ adj incautious or tactless in revealing secrets. **indiscretion** n

indiscriminate ⊙ adj showing lack of careful thought.

indispensable ⊙ adj absolutely essential.

indisposed ⊙ adj **1** unwell, ill. **2** unwilling. **indisposition** n

indisputable ⊙ adj beyond doubt. **indisputably** adv

indissoluble adj permanent.

individual ⊙ adj **1** characteristic of or meant for a single person or thing. **2** separate, distinct. **3** distinctive, unusual. ♦ n **4** single person or thing. **individually** adv **individuality** n **individualism** n principle of living one's life in one's own way. **individualist** n **individualistic** adj

indoctrinate ⊙ v teach (someone) to accept a doctrine or belief uncritically. **indoctrination** n

indolent ⊙ adj lazy. **indolence** n

indoor adj inside a building. **indoors** adv

indubitable ⊙ adj beyond doubt, certain. **indubitably** adv

induce ⊙ v **1** persuade or influence. **2** cause. **3** Med cause (a woman) to go into

---

THESAURUS

imply, manifest, point to, reveal, suggest **2 = point out**, designate, specify **4 = show**, display, express, read, record, register

indict v **= charge**, accuse, arraign, impeach, prosecute, summon

indifferent adj **1 = unconcerned**, aloof, callous, cold, cool, detached, impervious, inattentive, uninterested, unmoved, unsympathetic ≠ **interested 2 = mediocre**, moderate, no great shakes (inf), ordinary, passable, so–so (inf), undistinguished ≠ **fine**

indigestion n **= heartburn**, dyspepsia, upset stomach

indirect adj **1 = incidental**, secondary, subsidiary, unintended **2 = circuitous**, long–drawn–out, meandering, oblique, rambling, roundabout, tortuous, wandering ≠ **direct**

indiscreet adj **= tactless**, impolitic, imprudent, incautious, injudicious, naive, rash, reckless, unwise

indiscriminate adj **= random**, careless, desultory, general, uncritical,

undiscriminating, unsystematic, wholesale

indispensable adj **= essential**, crucial, imperative, key, necessary, needed, requisite, vital

indisposed adj **1 = ill**, ailing, crook (Aust & NZ sl), poorly (inf), sick, under the weather, unwell ≠ **well**

indisputable adj **= undeniable**, beyond doubt, certain, incontestable, incontrovertible, indubitable, irrefutable, unquestionable

individual adj **1 = personal**, characteristic, exclusive, own, special, specific ≠ **general 3 = distinctive**, idiosyncratic, munted (NZ sl), particular, peculiar, singular, unique ≠ **ordinary** ♦ n **4 = person**, being, character, creature, soul, unit

indoctrinate v **= train**, brainwash, drill, ground, imbue, initiate, instruct, school, teach

indolent adj **= lazy**, idle, inactive, inert, languid, lethargic, listless, slothful, sluggish, workshy

indubitable adj **= certain**, incontestable, incontrovertible, indisputable, irrefutable, labour or bring on (labour) by the use of drugs etc. **inducement** n something used to persuade someone to do something.

induct v formally install (someone, esp. a clergyman) in office.

indulge ⊕ v **1** allow oneself pleasure. **2** allow (someone) to have or do everything he or she wants. **indulgence** n **1** something allowed because it gives pleasure. **2** act of indulging oneself or someone else. **3** liberal or tolerant treatment. **indulgent** adj **indulgently** adv

industry ⊕ n, pl **-tries 1** manufacture of goods. **2** branch of this, e.g. the music industry. **3** quality of working hard. **industrial** adj of, used in, or employed in industry. **industrious** adj hard-working.

inedible adj not fit to be eaten.

ineffable adj too great for words.

ineligible ⊕ adj not qualified for or entitled to something.

inept ⊕ adj awkward, clumsy, lacking skill. **ineptitude** n

inert ⊕ adj **1** without the power of motion

or resistance. **2** chemically unreactive.

inescapable ⊕ adj unavoidable.

inestimable ⊕ adj too great to be estimated.

inevitable ⊕ adj unavoidable, sure to happen. **the inevitable** something that cannot be prevented. **inevitably** adv **inevitability** n

inexorable ⊕ adj unable to be prevented from continuing or progressing. **inexorably** adv

inexplicable ⊕ adj impossible to explain. **inexplicably** adv

infallible ⊕ adj never wrong. **infallibly** adv **infallibility** n

infamous ⊕ [in-fam-uss] adj well-known for something bad. **infamy** n

infant ⊕ n very young child. **Infancy** n **1** early childhood. **2** early stage of development. **infantile** adj childish.

infantry n soldiers who fight on foot.

infect ⊕ v **1** affect with a disease. **2** affect with a feeling. **infection** n **infectious** adj **1** (of a disease) spreading without actual

obvious, sure, undeniable, unquestionable

induce v **1** = **persuade**, convince, encourage, incite, influence, instigate, prevail upon, prompt, talk into ≠ **stop 2** = **cause**, bring about, effect, engender, generate, give rise to, lead to, occasion, produce ≠ **stop**

indulge v **1** = **gratify**, feed, give way to, pander to, satisfy, yield to **2** = **spoil**, cosset, give in to, go along with, humour, mollycoddle, pamper

industry n **1, 2** = **business**, commerce, manufacturing, production, trade **3** = **effort**, activity, application, diligence, labour, tirelessness, toil, zeal

ineligible adj = **unqualified**, disqualified, ruled out, unacceptable, unfit, unsuitable

inept adj = **incompetent**, bumbling, bungling, clumsy, inexpert, maladroit ≠ **able**

inert adj **1** = **inactive**, dead, dormant, immobile, lifeless, motionless, static, still, unresponsive ≠ **moving 2** = **unreactive**

inescapable adj = **unavoidable**, certain, destined, fated, ineluctable, inevitable, inexorable, sure

inestimable adj = **incalculable**, immeasurable, invaluable, precious, priceless, prodigious

inevitable adj = **unavoidable**, assured, certain, destined, fixed, ineluctable, inescapable, inexorable, sure

inexorable adj = **unrelenting**, inescapable, relentless, remorseless, unbending, unyielding

inexplicable adj = **unaccountable**, baffling, enigmatic, incomprehensible, insoluble, mysterious, mystifying, strange, unfathomable, unintelligible

infallible adj = **sure**, certain, dependable, foolproof, reliable, sure-fire (inf), trustworthy, unbeatable, unfailing ≠ **unreliable**

infamous adj = **notorious**, disreputable, ignominious, ill-famed

infant n = **baby**, babe, bairn (Scot), child,

contact. **2** spreading from person to person, e.g. *infectious enthusiasm.*

infer ❶ *v* **–ferring, –ferred** work out from evidence. **inference** *n*

> ✓ **WORD TIP**
> Someone *infers* something by 'reading between the lines' of a remark. Do not confuse with *imply,* which means 'to hint'.

inferior ❶ *adj* **1** lower in quality, position, or status. ♦ *n* **2** person of lower position or status. **inferiority** *n*

infernal ❶ *adj* **1** of hell. **2** *Informal* irritating.

inferno *n, pl* **–nos** intense raging fire.

infertile ❶ *adj* **1** unable to produce offspring. **2** (of soil) barren, not productive. **infertility** *n*

infest ❶ *v* inhabit or overrun in unpleasantly large numbers. **infestation** *n*

infidelity *n, pl* **–ties** (act of) sexual unfaithfulness to one's husband, wife, or lover.

infiltrate ❶ *v* enter gradually and secretly. **infiltration** *n* **infiltrator** *n*

infinite ❶ [in–fin–it] *adj* without any limit or end. **infinitely** *adv* **infinity** *n* endless space, time, or number.

infinitive *n Grammar* form of a verb not showing tense, person, or number, e.g. *to sleep.*

infirm ❶ *adj* physically or mentally weak. **infirmity** *n, pl* **–ties**

inflame ❶ *v* make angry or excited. **inflamed** *adj* (of part of the body) red, swollen, and painful because of infection. **inflammation** *n*

inflate ❶ *v* **1** expand by filling with air or gas. **2** cause economic inflation in. **inflatable** *adj* **1** able to be inflated. ♦ *n* **2** plastic or rubber object which can be inflated.

inflection, inflexion *n* **1** change in the pitch of the voice. **2** *Grammar* change in the form of a word to show grammatical use.

inflexible ❶ *adj* **1** unwilling to be persuaded, obstinate. **2** incapable of being bent. **inflexibly** *adv* **inflexibility** *n*

inflict ❶ *v* impose (something unpleasant) on. **infliction** *n*

————— THESAURUS —————

toddler, tot

infect *v* **1** = **contaminate**, affect, blight, corrupt, defile, poison, pollute, taint

infer *v* = **deduce**, conclude, derive, gather, presume, surmise, understand

inferior *adj* **1** = **lower**, lesser, menial, minor, secondary, subordinate, subsidiary ≠ **higher** ♦ *n* **2** = **underling**, junior, menial, subordinate

infernal *adj* **1** = **devilish**, accursed, damnable, damned, diabolical, fiendish, hellish, satanic

infertile *adj* = **barren**, sterile, unfruitful, unproductive ≠ **productive**

infest *v* = **overrun**, beset, invade, penetrate, permeate, ravage, swarm, throng

infiltrate *v* = **penetrate**, filter through, insinuate oneself, make inroads (into), percolate, permeate, pervade, sneak in

(*inf*)

infinite *adj* = **never–ending**, boundless, eternal, everlasting, illimitable, immeasurable, inexhaustible, limitless, measureless, unbounded ≠ **limited**

infirm *adj* = **frail**, ailing, debilitated, decrepit, doddering, enfeebled, failing, feeble, weak ≠ **strong**

inflame *v* = **enrage**, anger, arouse, excite, incense, infuriate, madden, provoke, rouse, stimulate ≠ **cool**

inflate *v* **1** = **expand**, bloat, blow up, dilate, distend, enlarge, increase, puff up *or* out, pump up, swell ≠ **deflate**

inflexible *adj* **1** = **obstinate**, implacable, intractable, obdurate, resolute, set in one's ways, steadfast, stubborn, unbending, uncompromising ≠ **yielding** **2** = **inelastic**, hard, rigid, stiff, taut ≠ **yielding**

inflict *v* = **impose**, administer, apply,

influence ⊕ n 1 effect of one person or thing on another. 2 (person with) the power to have such an effect. ◆ v 3 have an effect on. **influential** adj

influenza n contagious viral disease causing headaches, muscle pains, and fever.

influx ⊕ n arrival or entry of many people or things.

inform ⊕ v 1 tell. 2 give incriminating information to the police. **informant** n person who gives information. **information** n knowledge or facts. **informative** adj giving useful information. **information superhighway** worldwide network of computers transferring information at high speed. **information technology** use of computers and electronic technology to store and communicate information. **informer** n person who informs to the police.

informal ⊕ adj 1 relaxed and friendly. 2 appropriate for everyday life or use. **informally** adv **informality** n

infrared adj of or using rays below the red end of the visible spectrum.

infrastructure n basic facilities, services, and equipment needed for a country or

organization to function properly.

infringe ⊕ v break (a law or agreement). **infringement** n

infuriate ⊕ v make very angry.

infuse v 1 fill (with an emotion or quality). 2 soak to extract flavour. **infusion** n 1 infusing. 2 liquid obtained by infusing.

ingenious ⊕ [in–**jean**–ee–uss] adj showing cleverness and originality. **ingenuity** [in–jen–**new**–it–ee] n

ingenuous ⊕ [in–**jen**–new–uss] adj unsophisticated and trusting.

ingot n oblong block of cast metal.

ingrained adj firmly fixed.

ingratiate ⊕ v try to make (oneself) popular with someone. **ingratiating** adj

ingredient ⊕ n component of a mixture or compound.

inhabit ⊕ v –habiting, –habited live in. **inhabitant** n

inhale ⊕ v breathe in (air, smoke, etc.). **inhalation** n **inhalant** n medical preparation inhaled to help breathing problems. **inhaler** n container for an inhalant.

inherent ⊕ adj existing as an inseparable part.

inherit ⊕ v –heriting, –herited 1 receive

deliver, levy, mete or deal out, visit, wreak

influence n 1 = **effect**, hold, magnetism, power, spell, sway, weight 2 = **power**, ascendancy, authority, clout (inf), control, domination, importance, leverage, mana (NZ), mastery, prestige, pull (inf) ◆ v 3 = **affect**, control, direct, guide, manipulate, sway

influx n = **arrival**, incursion, inrush, inundation, invasion, rush

inform v 1 = **tell**, advise, communicate, enlighten, instruct, notify, teach, tip off 2 = **betray**, blow the whistle on (inf), denounce, grass (Brit sl), incriminate, inculpate, shop (sl, chiefly Brit), squeal (sl)

informal adj 1 = **relaxed**, casual, colloquial, cosy, easy, familiar, natural, simple, unofficial ≠ **formal**

infringe v = **break**, contravene, disobey,

transgress, violate

infuriate v = **enrage**, anger, exasperate, incense, irritate, madden, provoke, rile

ingenious adj = **creative**, bright, brilliant, clever, crafty, inventive, original, resourceful, shrewd

ingenuous adj = **naive**, artless, guileless, honest, innocent, open, plain, simple, sincere, trusting, unsophisticated

ingratiate v = **pander to**, crawl, curry favour, fawn, flatter, grovel, insinuate oneself, toady

ingredient n = **component**, constituent, element, part

inhabit v = **live**, abide, dwell, occupy, populate, reside

inhale v = **breathe in**, draw in, gasp, respire, suck in

inherent adj = **innate**, essential, hereditary,

(money etc.) from someone who has died.
2 receive (a characteristic) from an earlier
generation. 3 receive from a predecessor.
inheritance *n* **inheritor** *n*

inhibit ❶ *v* –**hibiting**, –**hibited 1** restrain
(an impulse or desire). 2 hinder or prevent
(action). **inhibited** *adj* **inhibition** *n* feeling
of fear or embarrassment that stops one
from behaving naturally.

inhospitable ❶ *adj* 1 not welcoming,
unfriendly. 2 difficult to live in, harsh.

inhuman ❶ *adj* 1 cruel or brutal. 2 not
human.

inhumane ❶ *adj* cruel or brutal.
inhumanity *n*

inimical ❶ *adj* unfavourable or hostile.

inimitable ❶ *adj* impossible to imitate,
unique.

iniquity ❶ *n, pl* –**ties 1** injustice or
wickedness. 2 wicked act. **iniquitous** *adj*

initial ❶ *adj* 1 first, at the beginning. ♦ *n* 2
first letter, esp. of a person's name. ♦ *v*

–**tialling**, –**tialled 3** sign with one's initials.
initially *adv*

initiate ❶ *v* 1 begin or set going. 2 admit
(someone) into a closed group. 3 instruct
in the basics of something. ♦ *n* 4 recently
initiated person. **initiation** *n* **initiator** *n*

inject ❶ *v* 1 put (a fluid) into the body
with a syringe. 2 introduce (a new
element), e.g. *try to inject a bit of humour.*
injection *n*

injunction ❶ *n* court order not to do
something.

injustice ❶ *n* 1 unfairness. 2 unfair action.

ink *n* 1 coloured liquid used for writing or
printing. ♦ *v* 2 (foll. by *in*) mark in ink
(something already marked in pencil).
inky *adj* 1 dark or black. 2 covered in ink.

inkling ❶ *n* slight idea or suspicion.

inland ❶ *adj, adv* in or towards the interior
of a country, away from the sea. **Inland
Revenue** government department that
collects taxes.

inborn, inbred, ingrained, inherited,
intrinsic, native, natural

inherit *v* 1 = **be left**, come into, fall heir to,
succeed to

inhibit *v* 1 = **restrain**, check, constrain,
curb, discourage, hold back *or* in
2 = **hinder**, check, frustrate, hold back,
impede, obstruct, prevent ≠ **allow**

inhospitable *adj* 1 = **unfriendly**, cool,
uncongenial, unreceptive, unsociable,
unwelcoming, xenophobic ≠ **welcoming**
2 = **bleak**, barren, desolate, forbidding,
godforsaken, hostile

inhuman *adj* 1 = **cruel**, barbaric, brutal,
cold–blooded, heartless, merciless, pitiless,
ruthless, savage, unfeeling

inhumane *adj* = **cruel**, brutal, heartless,
pitiless, unfeeling, unkind, unsympathetic

inimical *adj* = **hostile**, adverse,
antagonistic, ill–disposed, opposed,
unfavourable, unfriendly, unwelcoming

inimitable *adj* = **unique**, consummate,
incomparable, matchless, peerless,
unparalleled, unrivalled

iniquity *n* = **wickedness**, abomination,

evil, injustice, sin, wrong

initial *adj* 1 = **first**, beginning, incipient,
introductory, opening, primary ≠ **last**

initiate *v* 1 = **begin**, commence, get under
way, kick off (*inf*), launch, open, originate,
set in motion, start 2 = **induct**,
indoctrinate, introduce, invest
3 = **instruct**, acquaint with, coach,
familiarize with, teach, train ♦ *n*
4 = **novice**, beginner, convert, entrant,
learner, member, probationer

inject *v* 1 = **vaccinate**, inoculate
2 = **introduce**, bring in, infuse, insert, instil

injunction *n* = **order**, command,
exhortation, instruction, mandate,
precept, ruling

injustice *n* 1 = **unfairness**, bias,
discrimination, inequality, inequity,
iniquity, oppression, partisanship,
prejudice, wrong ≠ **right**

inkling *n* = **suspicion**, clue, conception,
hint, idea, indication, intimation, notion,
suggestion, whisper

inland *adj* = **interior**, domestic, internal,
upcountry

inlay n inlaid substance or pattern.
inlet ⊕ n 1 narrow strip of water extending from the sea into the land. 2 valve etc. through which liquid or gas enters.
inmate n person living in an institution such as a prison.
inmost ⊕ adj innermost.
inn n pub or small hotel, esp. in the country. **innkeeper** n
innards pl n Informal 1 internal organs. 2 working parts of a machine.
innate ⊕ adj being part of someone's nature, inborn.
inner ⊕ adj 1 happening or located inside. 2 relating to private feelings, e.g. the inner self. **innermost** adj furthest inside. **inner city** parts of a city near the centre, esp. having social and economic problems.
innings n 1 Sport player's or side's turn of batting. 2 period of opportunity.
innocent ⊕ adj 1 not guilty of a crime. 2 without experience of evil. 3 without malicious intent. ◆ n 4 innocent person, esp. a child. **innocence** n
innocuous adj not harmful. **innocuously** adv

innuendo ⊕ n, pl **-does** (remark making) an indirect reference to something rude or unpleasant.
innumerable ⊕ adj too many to be counted.
inoculate v protect against disease by injecting with a vaccine. **inoculation** n
inoperable adj (of a tumour or cancer) unable to be surgically removed.
inordinate ⊕ adj excessive.
inorganic ⊕ adj 1 not having the characteristics of living organisms. 2 of chemical substances that do not contain carbon.
input n 1 resources put into a project etc. 2 data fed into a computer. ◆ v **-putting**, **-put** 3 enter (data) in a computer.
inquest ⊕ n official inquiry into a sudden death.
inquire ⊕ v seek information or ask (about). **inquirer** n **inquiry** n, pl **-ries** 1 question. 2 investigation.
inquisition ⊕ n thorough investigation. **inquisitor** n **inquisitorial** adj
inquisitive ⊕ adj excessively curious about other people's affairs. **inquisitively** adv

——— THESAURUS ———

inlet n 1 = **bay**, bight, creek, firth or frith (Scot), fjord, passage
inmost adj = **deepest**, basic, central, essential, innermost, intimate, personal, private, secret
innate adj = **inborn**, congenital, constitutional, essential, inbred, ingrained, inherent, instinctive, intuitive, native, natural
inner adj 1 = **inside**, central, interior, internal, inward, middle ≠ **outside** 2 = **hidden**, intimate, personal, private, repressed, secret, unrevealed ≠ **revealed**
innocent adj 1 = **not guilty**, blameless, guiltless, honest, in the clear, uninvolved ≠ **guilty** 2 = **naive**, artless, childlike, credulous, gullible, ingenuous, open, simple, unworldly ≠ **worldly** 3 = **harmless**, innocuous, inoffensive, unobjectionable, well-intentioned, well-meant ≠ **offensive**
innuendo n = **insinuation**, aspersion, hint,

implication, imputation, intimation, overtone, suggestion, whisper
innumerable adj = **countless**, beyond number, incalculable, infinite, multitudinous, myriad, numberless, numerous, unnumbered, untold
inordinate adj = **excessive**, disproportionate, extravagant, immoderate, intemperate, preposterous, unconscionable, undue, unreasonable, unwarranted
inorganic adj 1 = **artificial**, chemical, man-made
inquest n = **inquiry**, inquisition, investigation, probe
inquire v = **investigate**, ask, examine, explore, look into, make inquiries, probe, query, question, research
inquisition n = **investigation**, cross-examination, examination, grilling (inf), inquest, inquiry, questioning,

insane ⊕ *adj* 1 mentally ill. 2 stupidly irresponsible. **insanely** *adv* **insanity** *n*

insatiable ⊕ [in-**saysh**-a-bl] *adj* unable to be satisfied.

inscribe ⊕ *v* write or carve words on. **inscription** *n* words inscribed.

inscrutable ⊕ *adj* mysterious, enigmatic.

insect *n* small animal with six legs and usu. wings, such as an ant or fly. **insecticide** *n* substance for killing insects. **insectivorous** *adj* insect-eating.

insecure ⊕ *adj* 1 anxious, not confident. 2 not safe or well-protected.

insensible ⊕ *adj* 1 unconscious, without feeling. 2 (foll. by *to* or *of*) not aware (of) or affected (by). **insensibility** *n*

insensitive ⊕ *adj* unaware of or ignoring other people's feelings. **insensitivity** *n*

insert ⊕ *v* 1 put inside or include. ◆ *n* 2 something inserted. **insertion** *n*

inset *n* small picture inserted within a larger one.

inshore *adj* 1 close to the shore. ◆ *adj, adv* 2 towards the shore.

inside ⊕ *prep* 1 in or to the interior of. ◆ *adj* 2 on or of the inside. 3 by or from someone within an organization, e.g. *inside information.* ◆ *adv* 4 on, in, or to the inside, indoors. 5 *Slang* in(to) prison. ◆ *n* 6 inner side, surface, or part. ◆ *pl* 7 *Informal* stomach and bowels. **inside out** with the inside facing outwards. **know inside out** know thoroughly. **insider** *n* member of a group who has privileged knowledge about it.

> ✓ **WORD TIP**
> Avoid using the expression *inside of,* as the second preposition *of* is superfluous.

insidious ⊕ *adj* subtle or unseen but dangerous.

insight ⊕ *n* deep understanding.

insignia ⊕ *n, pl* –**nias**, –**nia** badge or emblem of honour or office.

insignificant ⊕ *adj* not important. **insignificance** *n*

━━━━━━━━ THESAURUS ━━━━━━━━

third degree (*inf*)

inquisitive *adj* 1 = **prying**, curious, nosy (*inf*), probing 2 = **inquiring**, curious, questioning

insane *adj* 1 = **mad**, crazed, crazy, demented, deranged, mentally ill, out of one's mind ≠ **sound** 2 = **stupid**, daft (*inf*), foolish, idiotic, impractical, irrational, irresponsible, preposterous, senseless ≠ **sensible**

insatiable *adj* = **unquenchable**, greedy, intemperate, rapacious, ravenous, voracious

inscribe *v* = **carve**, cut, engrave, etch, impress, imprint

inscrutable *adj* a = **mysterious**, hidden, incomprehensible, inexplicable, unexplainable, unfathomable, unintelligible ≠ **clear** b = **enigmatic**, blank, deadpan, impenetrable, poker-faced (*inf*), unreadable ≠ **open**

insecure *adj* 1 = **anxious**, afraid, uncertain, unsure ≠ **secure** 2 = **unsafe**, defenceless,

exposed, unguarded, unprotected, vulnerable, wide-open ≠ **protected**

insensible *adj* 2 (foll. by *to* or *of*) = **unaware**, impervious, oblivious, unaffected, unconscious, unmindful

insensitive *adj* = **unfeeling**, callous, hardened, indifferent, thick-skinned, tough, uncaring, unconcerned

insert *v* 1 = **enter**, embed, implant, introduce, place, put, stick in ≠ **remove**

inside *adj* 2 = **inner**, interior, internal, inward ≠ **outside** 3 = **confidential**, classified, exclusive, internal, private, restricted, secret ◆ *adv* 4 = **indoors**, under cover, within ◆ *n* 6 = **interior**, contents ◆ *pl* 7 *Inf* = **stomach**, belly, bowels, entrails, guts, innards (*inf*), viscera, vitals

insidious *adj* = **stealthy**, deceptive, sly, smooth, sneaking, subtle, surreptitious

insight *n* = **understanding**, awareness, comprehension, discernment, judgment, observation, penetration, perception, perspicacity, vision

insincere ❶ *adj* showing false feelings, not genuine. **insincerely** *adv* **insincerity** *n, pl* **-ties**

insinuate ❶ *v* 1 suggest indirectly. 2 work (oneself) into a position by gradual manoeuvres. **insinuation** *n*

insipid ❶ *adj* lacking interest, spirit, or flavour.

insist ❶ *v* demand or state firmly. **insistent** *adj* 1 making persistent demands. 2 demanding attention. **insistence** *n*

insole *n* inner sole of a shoe or boot.

insolent ❶ *adj* rude and disrespectful. **insolence** *n*

insoluble ❶ *adj* 1 incapable of being solved. 2 incapable of being dissolved.

insolvent ❶ *adj* unable to pay one's debts **insolvency** *n*

insomnia ❶ *n* inability to sleep. **insomniac** *n*

inspect *v* check closely or officially. **inspection** *n* **inspector** *n* 1 person who inspects. 2 high-ranking police officer.

inspire ❶ *v* 1 fill with enthusiasm, stimulate. 2 arouse (an emotion). **inspiration** *n* 1 creative influence or stimulus. 2 brilliant idea. **inspirational** *adj*

install ❶ *v* 1 put in and prepare (equipment) for use. 2 place (a person) formally in a position or rank. **installation** *n* 1 installing. 2 equipment installed. 3 place containing equipment for a particular purpose, e.g. *oil installations*.

instalment ❶ *n* any of the portions of a thing presented or a debt paid in successive parts.

instance ❶ *n* 1 particular example. ♦ *v* 2 mention as an example. **for instance** as an example.

instant ❶ *n* 1 very brief time. 2 particular moment. ♦ *adj* 3 happening at once. 4 (of foods) requiring little preparation. **instantly** *adv*

instead ❶ *adv* as a replacement or

THESAURUS

insignia *n* = **badge**, crest, emblem, symbol

insignificant *adj* = **unimportant**, inconsequential, irrelevant, meaningless, minor, nondescript, paltry, petty, trifling, trivial

insincere *adj* = **deceitful**, dishonest, disingenuous, duplicitous, false, hollow, hypocritical, lying, two-faced, untruthful

insinuate *v* 1 = **imply**, allude, hint, indicate, intimate, suggest 2 = **ingratiate**, curry favour, get in with, worm *or* work one's way in

insipid *adj* a = **bland**, anaemic, characterless, colourless, prosaic, uninteresting, vapid, wishy-washy (*inf*) ≠ **interesting** b = **tasteless**, bland, flavourless, unappetizing, watery ≠ **tasty**

insist *v* a = **demand**, lay down the law, put one's foot down (*inf*), require b = **state**, assert, aver, claim, maintain, reiterate, repeat, swear, vow

insolent *adj* = **rude**, bold, contemptuous, impertinent, impudent, insubordinate, insulting

insoluble *adj* 1 = **inexplicable**, baffling,

impenetrable, indecipherable, mysterious, unaccountable, unfathomable, unsolvable ≠ **comprehensible**

insolvent *adj* = **bankrupt**, broke (*inf*), failed, gone bust (*inf*), gone to the wall, in receivership, munted (*NZ sl*), ruined

insomnia *n* = **sleeplessness**, wakefulness

inspect *v* = **examine**, check, go over *or* through, investigate, look over, scrutinize, survey, vet

inspire *v* 1 = **stimulate**, animate, encourage, enliven, galvanize, gee up, influence, spur ≠ **depress** 2 = **arouse**, enkindle, excite, give rise to, produce

install *v* 1 = **set up**, fix, lay, lodge, place, position, put in, station 2 = **induct**, establish, inaugurate, institute, introduce, invest

instalment *n* = **portion**, chapter, division, episode, part, repayment, section

instance *n* 1 = **example**, case, illustration, occasion, occurrence, situation ♦ *v* 2 = **quote**, adduce, cite, mention, name, specify

instant *n* 1 = **second**, flash, jiffy (*inf*),

substitute.

instep n 1 part of the foot forming the arch between the ankle and toes. 2 part of a shoe etc. covering this.

instigate ⊕ v cause to happen. **instigation** n **instigator** n

instil ⊕ v –stilling, –stilled introduce (an idea etc.) gradually into someone's mind.

instinct ⊕ n inborn tendency to behave in a certain way. **instinctive** adj **instinctively** adv

institute ⊕ n 1 organization set up for a specific purpose, esp. research or teaching. ◆ v 2 start or establish. **institution** n large important organization such as a university or bank.

instruct ⊕ v 1 order to do something. 2 teach (someone) how to do something. **instruction** n 1 order to do something. 2 teaching. ◆ pl 3 information on how to do or use something. **instructive** adj informative or helpful. **instructor** n

instrument ⊕ n 1 tool used for particular work. 2 object played to produce a musical sound. 3 measuring device to show height, speed, etc. 4 Informal someone or something used to achieve an aim. **instrumental** adj 1 (foll. by in) having an important function (in). 2 played by or composed for musical instruments. **instrumentalist** n player of a musical instrument. **instrumentation** n 1 set of instruments in a car etc. 2 arrangement of music for instruments.

insubordinate ⊕ adj not submissive to authority. **insubordination** n

insufferable ⊕ adj unbearable.

insular ⊕ adj not open to new ideas, narrow–minded. **insularity** n

insulate ⊕ v 1 prevent or reduce the transfer of electricity, heat, or sound by surrounding or lining with a nonconducting material. 2 isolate or set apart. **insulation** n **insulator** n

insulin n hormone produced in the pancreas that controls the amount of sugar in the blood.

insult ⊕ v 1 behave rudely to, offend. ◆ n

moment, split second, trice, twinkling of an eye (inf) 2 = **juncture**, moment, occasion, point, time ◆ adj 3 = **immediate**, direct, instantaneous, on–the–spot, prompt, quick, split–second 4 = **precooked**, convenience, fast, ready–mixed

instead adv = **rather**, alternatively, in lieu, in preference, on second thoughts, preferably **instead of** = **in place of**, in lieu of, rather than

instigate v = **provoke**, bring about, incite, influence, initiate, prompt, set off, start, stimulate, trigger

instil v = **introduce**, engender, imbue, implant, inculcate, infuse, insinuate

instinct n = **intuition**, faculty, gift, impulse, knack, predisposition, proclivity, talent, tendency

institute n 1 = **society**, academy, association, college, foundation, guild, institution, school ◆ v 2 = **establish**, fix, found, initiate, introduce, launch,

organize, originate, pioneer, set up, start ≠ **end**

instruct v 1 = **order**, bid, charge, command, direct, enjoin, tell 2 = **teach**, coach, drill, educate, ground, school, train, tutor

instrument n 1 = **tool**, apparatus, appliance, contraption (inf), device, gadget, implement, mechanism 4 Inf = **means**, agency, agent, mechanism, medium, organ, vehicle

insubordinate adj = **disobedient**, defiant, disorderly, mutinous, rebellious, recalcitrant, refractory, undisciplined, ungovernable, unruly

insufferable adj = **unbearable**, detestable, dreadful, impossible, insupportable, intolerable, unendurable

insular adj = **narrow–minded**, blinkered, circumscribed, inward–looking, limited, narrow, parochial, petty, provincial

insulate v 2 = **isolate**, close off, cocoon, cushion, cut off, protect, sequester, shield

2 insulting remark or action. **insulting** *adj*

insuperable ⊕ *adj* impossible to overcome.

insurrection ⊕ *n* rebellion.

intact ⊕ *adj* not changed or damaged in any way.

intake *n* amount or number taken in.

integer *n* positive or negative whole number or zero.

integral ⊕ *adj* 1 being an essential part of a whole. ◆ *n* 2 *Maths* sum of a large number of very small quantities.

integrity ⊕ *n* 1 quality of having high moral principles. 2 quality of being united.

intellect ⊕ *n* power of thinking and reasoning. **intellectual** *adj* 1 of or appealing to the intellect. 2 clever, intelligent. ◆ *n* 3 intellectual person.

intelligent ⊕ *adj* 1 able to understand, learn, and think things out quickly. 2 (of a computerized device) able to initiate or modify action in the light of ongoing events. **intelligence** *n* 1 quality of being

intelligent. 2 secret government or military information. 3 people or department collecting such information.

intemperate ⊕ *adj* 1 unrestrained, uncontrolled. 2 drinking alcohol to excess. **intemperance** *n*

intend ⊕ *v* 1 propose or plan (to do something). 2 have as one's purpose.

intense ⊕ *adj* 1 of great strength or degree. 2 deeply emotional. **intensity** *n* **intensify** *v* **-fying, -fied** make or become more intense. **intensification** *n*

intent ⊕ *n* 1 intention. ◆ *adj* 2 paying close attention. **intent on doing something** determined to do something.

inter ⊕ [in-**ter**] *v* **-terring, -terred** bury (a corpse). **interment** *n*

Inter- *prefix* between or among, e.g. *international*.

interact *v* act on or in close relation with each other. **interaction** *n* **interactive** *adj*

intercede ⊕ *v* try to end a dispute between two people or groups.

— THESAURUS —

insult *v* 1 = **offend**, abuse, affront, call names, put down, slander, slight, snub ≠ **praise** ◆ *n* 2 = **abuse**, affront, aspersion, insolence, offence, put-down, slap in the face (*inf*), slight, snub

insuperable *adj* = **insurmountable**, impassable, invincible, unconquerable

insurrection *n* = **rebellion**, coup, insurgency, mutiny, revolt, revolution, riot, uprising

intact *adj* = **undamaged**, complete, entire, perfect, sound, unbroken, unharmed, unimpaired, unscathed, whole

integral *adj* 1 = **essential**, basic, component, constituent, fundamental, indispensable, intrinsic, necessary ≠ **unnecessary**

integrity *n* 1 = **honesty**, goodness, honour, incorruptibility, principle, probity, purity, rectitude, uprightness, virtue ≠ **corruption** 2 = **soundness**, coherence, cohesion, completeness, unity, wholeness ≠ **fragility**

intellect *n* = **intelligence**, brains (*inf*),

judgment, mind, reason, sense, understanding

intelligent *adj* 1 = **clever**, brainy (*inf*), bright, enlightened, perspicacious, quick-witted, sharp, smart, well-informed ≠ **stupid**

intemperate *adj* 1 = **excessive**, extreme, immoderate, profligate, self-indulgent, unbridled, unrestrained, wild

intend *v* = **plan**, aim, have in mind or view, mean, propose, purpose

intense *adj* 1 = **extreme**, acute, deep, excessive, fierce, great, powerful, profound, severe ≠ **moderate** 2 = **passionate**, ardent, fanatical, fervent, fierce, heightened, impassioned, vehement ≠ **cool**

intent *n* 1 = **intention**, aim, design, end, goal, meaning, object, objective, plan, purpose ≠ **chance** ◆ *adj* 2 = **intense**, absorbed, attentive, engrossed, preoccupied, rapt, steadfast, watchful ≠ **casual**

inter *v* = **bury**, entomb, lay to rest

intercession n

intercept ⊙ v seize or stop in transit. **interception** n

interchange ⊙ v 1 (cause to) exchange places. ◆ n 2 motorway junction. **interchangeable** adj

intercom n internal communication system with loudspeakers.

intercontinental adj travelling between or linking continents.

intercourse ⊙ n 1 sexual intercourse. 2 communication or dealings between people or groups.

interest ⊙ n 1 desire to know or hear more about something. 2 something in which one is interested. 3 (often pl) advantage, benefit. 4 sum paid for the use of borrowed money. 5 (often pl) right or share. ◆ v 6 arouse the interest of. **interested** adj 1 feeling or showing interest. 2 involved in or affected by something. **interesting** adj

interface ⊙ n 1 area where two things interact or link. 2 circuit linking a computer and another device.

interfere ⊙ v 1 try to influence other people's affairs where one is not involved or wanted. 2 (foll. by with) clash (with). 3 (foll. by with) Euphemistic abuse (a child) sexually. **interfering** adj **interference** n 1 interfering. 2 Radio interruption of reception by atmospherics or unwanted signals.

interim ⊙ adj temporary or provisional.

interior ⊙ n 1 inside. 2 inland region. ◆ adj 3 inside, inner. 4 mental or spiritual.

interject v make (a remark) suddenly or as an interruption. **interjection** n

interlock v join firmly together.

interloper ⊙ [in–ter–lope–er] n person in a place or situation where he or she has no right to be.

interlude ⊙ n short rest or break in an activity or event.

intermarry v (of families, races, or religions) become linked by marriage. **intermarriage** n

intermediate ⊙ adj coming between two points or extremes.

interminable ⊙ adj seemingly endless because boring.

intermission ⊙ n interval between parts

intercede v = **mediate**, arbitrate, intervene, plead

intercept v = **seize**, block, catch, cut off, head off, interrupt, obstruct, stop

interchange v 1 = **switch**, alternate, exchange, reciprocate, swap ◆ n 2 = **junction**, intersection

intercourse n 1 = **sexual intercourse**, carnal knowledge, coitus, copulation, sex (inf) 2 = **communication**, commerce, contact, dealings

interest n 1 = **curiosity**, attention, concern, notice, regard 2 = **hobby**, activity, diversion, pastime, preoccupation, pursuit 3 (often pl) = **advantage**, benefit, good, profit 5 (often pl) = **stake**, claim, investment, right, share ◆ v 6 = **arouse one's curiosity**, attract, catch one's eye, divert, engross, fascinate, intrigue ≠ **bore**

interface n 1 = **connection**, border, boundary, frontier, link

interfere v 1 = **intrude**, butt in, intervene, meddle, stick one's oar in (inf), tamper 2 (foll. by with) = **conflict**, clash, hamper, handicap, hinder, impede, inhibit, obstruct

interim adj 1 = **temporary**, acting, caretaker, improvised, makeshift, provisional, stopgap

interior n 1 = **inside**, centre, core, heart ≠ **outside** ◆ adj 3 = **inside**, inner, internal, inward 4 = **mental**, hidden, inner, intimate, personal, private, secret, spiritual

interloper n = **trespasser**, gate–crasher (inf), intruder, meddler

interlude n = **interval**, break, breathing space, delay, hiatus, intermission, pause, respite, rest, spell, stoppage

intermediate adj = **middle**, halfway, in–between (inf), intervening, mid, midway, transitional

interminable adj = **endless**, ceaseless,

of a play, film, etc.

intern ❶ v 1 imprison, esp. during a war. ◆ n 2 Chiefly US trainee doctor in a hospital. **internment** n **internee** n person who is interned.

internal ❶ adj 1 of or on the inside. 2 within a country or organization. 3 spiritual or mental. **internal–combustion engine** engine powered by the explosion of a fuel–and–air mixture within the cylinders.

international ❶ adj 1 of or involving two or more countries. ◆ n 2 game or match between teams of different countries. 3 player in such a match.

internecine adj mutually destructive.

interplanetary adj of or linking planets.

interplay n action and reaction of two things upon each other.

interpolate [in–**ter**–pole–ate] v insert (a comment or passage) into (a conversation or text). **interpolation** n

interpose ❶ v 1 insert between or among things. 2 say as an interruption.

interpret ❶ v 1 explain the meaning of. 2 translate orally from one language into another. 3 convey the meaning of (a poem, song, etc.) in performance. **interpretation** n **interpreter** n

interrogate ❶ v question closely.

interrogation n **interrogative** adj 1 questioning. ◆ n 2 word used in asking a question, such as how or why. **interrogator** n

interrupt ❶ v 1 break into (a conversation etc.). 2 stop (a process or activity) temporarily. **interruption** n

intersect v 1 (of roads) meet and cross. 2 divide by passing across or through. **intersection** n

interstellar adj between or among stars.

interstice [in–**ter**–stiss] n small crack or gap between things.

intertwine v twist together.

interval ❶ n 1 time between two particular moments or events. 2 break between parts of a play, concert, etc. 3 difference in pitch between musical notes. **at intervals** 1 repeatedly. 2 with spaces left between.

intervene ❶ v 1 involve oneself in a situation, esp. to prevent conflict. 2 happen so as to stop something. **intervention** n

interview ❶ n 1 formal discussion, esp. between a job–seeker and an employer. 2 questioning of a well–known person about his or her career, views, etc., by a reporter. ◆ v 3 conduct an interview with. **interviewee** n **interviewer** n

——— THESAURUS ———

everlasting, infinite, long–drawn–out, long–winded, never–ending, perpetual, protracted

intermission n = **interval**, break, interlude, pause, recess, respite, rest, stoppage

intern v 1 = **imprison**, confine, detain, hold, hold in custody

internal adj 1 = **inner**, inside, interior ≠ **outside** 2 = **domestic**, civic, home, in–house, intramural

international adj 1 = **universal**, cosmopolitan, global, intercontinental, worldwide

interpose v 1 = **insert** 2 = **interrupt**, interject, put one's oar in

interpret v 1 = **explain**, decipher, decode,

elucidate, make sense of 2 = **translate**, construe 3 = **render**

interrogate v = **question**, cross–examine, examine, grill (inf), investigate, pump, quiz

interrupt v 1 = **intrude**, barge in (inf), break in, butt in, disturb, heckle, interfere (with) 2 = **suspend**, break off, cut short, delay, discontinue, hold up, lay aside, stop

interval n 1 = **break**, delay, gap, pause, respite, rest, space, spell 2 = **interlude**, intermission

intervene v 1 = **step in** (inf), arbitrate, intercede, interfere, intrude, involve oneself, mediate, take a hand (inf) 2 = **happen**, befall, come to pass, ensue, occur, take place

interview n 2 = **meeting**, audience,

intestate *adj* not having made a will.
intestacy *n*

intestine ❶ *n* (often pl) lower part of the alimentary canal between the stomach and the anus. **intestinal** *adj*

intimate¹ ❶ *adj* 1 having a close personal relationship. 2 personal or private. 3 (of knowledge) extensive and detailed. 4 (foll. by *with*) *Euphemistic* having a sexual relationship (with). 5 having a friendly quiet atmosphere. ◆ *n* 6 close friend. **intimately** *adv* **intimacy** *n*

intimate² ❶ *v* 1 hint at or suggest. 2 announce. **intimation** *n*

intimidate ❶ *v* subdue or influence by fear. **intimidating** *adj* **intimidation** *n*

into *prep* 1 indicating motion towards the centre, result of a change, division, etc., e.g. *into the valley; turned into a madman; cut into pieces.* 2 *Informal* interested in.

intolerable *adj* more than can be endured.

intolerant *adj* refusing to accept practices and beliefs different from one's own. **intolerance** *n*

intone ❶ *v* speak or recite in an unvarying tone of voice.

intoxicate *v* 1 make drunk. 2 excite to excess. **intoxicant** *n* intoxicating drink. **intoxication** *n*

intractable *adj* 1 (of a person) difficult to control. 2 (of a problem or issue) difficult to deal with.

intransigent ❶ *adj* refusing to change one's attitude. **intransigence** *n*

intravenous [in–tra–**vee**–nuss] *adj* into a vein.

intrepid ❶ *adj* fearless, bold. **intrepidity** *n*

intricate ❶ *adj* 1 involved or complicated. 2 full of fine detail. **intricately** *adv* **intricacy** *n*, *pl* –**cies**

intrigue ❶ *v* 1 make interested or curious. 2 plot secretly. ◆ *n* 3 secret plotting. 4 secret love affair. **intriguing** *adj*

intrinsic ❶ *adj* essential to the basic nature of something. **intrinsically** *adv*

introduce ❶ *v* 1 present (someone) by name (to another person). 2 present (a radio or television programme). 3 bring forward for discussion. 4 bring into use. 5 insert. **introduction** *n* 1 presentation of

conference, consultation, dialogue, press conference, talk ◆ *v* 3 = **question**, examine, interrogate, talk to

intestine *n* (often pl) = **guts**, bowels, entrails, innards (*inf*), insides (*inf*), viscera

intimate¹ *adj* 1 = **close**, bosom, confidential, dear, near, thick (*inf*) ≠ **remote** 2 = **private**, confidential, personal, secret ≠ **known** 3 = **detailed**, deep, exhaustive, first–hand, immediate, in–depth, profound, thorough 5 = **snug**, comfy (*inf*), cosy, friendly, warm ◆ *n* 6 = **friend**, close friend, cobber (*Aust or old–fashioned NZ inf*), confidant *or* confidante, (constant) companion, crony

intimate² *v* 1 = **suggest**, hint, imply, indicate, insinuate 2 = **announce**, communicate, declare, make known, state

intimidate *v* = **frighten**, browbeat, bully, coerce, daunt, overawe, scare, subdue, terrorize, threaten

intone *v* = **recite**, chant

intransigent *adj* = **uncompromising**, hard–line, intractable, obdurate, obstinate, stiff–necked, stubborn, unbending, unyielding

intrepid *adj* = **fearless**, audacious, bold, brave, courageous, daring, gallant, plucky, stouthearted, valiant

intricate *adj* 1 = **complicated**, complex, convoluted, involved, labyrinthine, tangled, tortuous 2 = **elaborate**, fancy

intrigue *v* 1 = **interest**, attract, fascinate, rivet, titillate 2 = **plot**, connive, conspire, machinate, manoeuvre, scheme ◆ *n* 3 = **plot**, chicanery, collusion, conspiracy, machination, manoeuvre, scheme, stratagem, wile 4 = **affair**, amour, intimacy, liaison, romance

intrinsic *adj* = **inborn**, basic, built–in, congenital, constitutional, essential, fundamental, inbred, inherent, native, one person to another. **2** preliminary part or treatment. **introductory** *adj*

introvert *n* person concerned more with his or her thoughts and feelings than with the outside world. **introverted** *adj* **introversion** *n*

intrude ⊕ *v* come in or join in without being invited. **intruder** *n* **intrusion** *n* **intrusive** *adj*

intuition ⊕ *n* instinctive knowledge or insight without conscious reasoning. **intuitive** *adj* **intuitively** *adv*

inundate ⊕ *v* **1** flood. **2** overwhelm. **inundation** *n*

inured *adj* accustomed, esp. to hardship or danger.

invade ⊕ *v* **1** enter (a country) by military force. **2** enter in large numbers. **3** disturb (someone's privacy). **invader** *n*

invalid¹ ⊕ *adj, n* **1** disabled or chronically ill (person). ◆ *v* **2** (often foll. by *out*) dismiss from active service because of illness or injury. **invalidity** *n*

invalid² ⊕ *adj* **1** having no legal force. **2** (of an argument etc.) not valid because based on a mistake. **invalidate** *v* make or show to be invalid.

invaluable ⊕ *adj* of very great value or worth

invasion ⊕ *n* **1** invading. **2** intrusion, e.g. *an invasion of privacy*.

invective ⊕ *n* abusive speech or writing.

inveigle *v* coax by cunning or trickery.

invent ⊕ *v* **1** think up or create (something new). **2** make up (a story, excuse, etc.). **invention** *n* **1** something invented. **2** ability to invent. **inventive** *adj* creative and resourceful. **inventiveness** *n* **inventor** *n*

inventory ⊕ *n, pl* **-tories** detailed list of goods or furnishings.

invert ⊕ *v* turn upside down or inside out. **inversion** *n* **inverted commas** quotation marks.

invertebrate *n* animal with no backbone.

invest ⊕ *v* **1** spend (money, time, etc.) on something with the expectation of profit.

── THESAURUS ──

natural

introduce *v* **1** = **present**, acquaint, familiarize, make known **3** = **bring up**, advance, air, broach, moot, put forward, submit **4** = **bring in**, establish, found, initiate, institute, launch, pioneer, set up, start **5** = **insert**, add, inject, put in, throw in (*Inf*)

intrude *v* = **interfere**, butt in, encroach, infringe, interrupt, meddle, push in, trespass

intuition *n* = **instinct**, hunch, insight, perception, presentiment, sixth sense

inundate *v* **1** = **flood**, drown, engulf, immerse, overflow, submerge, swamp **2** = **overwhelm**, overrun

invade *v* **1** = **attack**, assault, burst in, descend upon, encroach, infringe, make inroads, occupy, raid, violate **2** = **infest**, overrun, permeate, pervade, swarm over

① **invalid¹** *adj* = **disabled**, ailing, bedridden, frail, ill, infirm, sick

② **invalid¹** *n* = **patient**, convalescent, valetudinarian

invalid² *adj* **1** = **null and void**, inoperative, void ≠ **valid 2** = **unsound**, fallacious, false, illogical, irrational, shonky (*Aust & NZ inf*), unfounded, worthless ≠ **valid**

invaluable *adj* = **precious**, inestimable, priceless, valuable, worth one's *or* its weight in gold

invasion *n* **1** = **attack**, assault, campaign, foray, incursion, inroad, offensive, onslaught, raid **2** = **intrusion**, breach, encroachment, infraction, infringement, usurpation, violation

invective *n* = **abuse**, censure, denunciation, diatribe, tirade, tongue–lashing, vilification, vituperation

invent *v* **1** = **create**, coin, conceive, design, devise, discover, formulate, improvise, originate, think up **2** = **make up**, concoct, cook up (*inf*), fabricate, feign, forge, manufacture, trump up

inventory *n* = **list**, account, catalogue, file, record, register, roll, roster

invert *v* = **overturn**, reverse, transpose, upset, upturn

2 (foll. by *with*) give (power or rights) to. **investment** *n* 1 money invested. 2 something invested in. **investor** *n* **invest in** *v* buy.

investigate ❶ *v* inquire into, examine. **investigation** *n* **investigative** *adj* **investigator** *n*

inveterate ❶ *adj* firmly established in a habit or condition.

invidious *adj* likely to cause resentment.

invigilate ❶ *v* supervise people sitting an examination. **invigilator** *n*

invigorate ❶ *v* give energy to, refresh.

invincible ❶ *adj* impossible to defeat. **invincibility** *n*

inviolable ❶ *adj* unable to be broken or violated.

invisible ❶ *adj* not able to be seen. **invisibility** *n*

invite ❶ *v* 1 request the company of. 2 ask politely to. 3 encourage or provoke, e.g. *the two works inevitably invite comparison.* ◆ *n* 4 *Informal* invitation. **inviting** *adj* tempting, attractive. **invitation** *n*

invoice *v, n* (present with) a bill for goods or services supplied.

invoke ❶ *v* 1 put (a law or penalty) into operation. 2 prompt or cause (a certain

feeling). 3 call on (a god or spirit) for help, inspiration, etc. **invocation** *n*

involuntary ❶ *adj* not done consciously, unintentional. **involuntarily** *adv*

involve ❶ *v* 1 include as a necessary part. 2 affect, concern. 3 implicate (a person). **involved** *adj* 1 complicated. 2 concerned, taking part. **involvement** *n*

inward *adj, adv* see IN.

iodine *n Chem* bluish–black element used in medicine and photography. **iodize** *v* treat with iodine.

ion *n* electrically charged atom. **ionize** *v* change into ions. **ionosphere** *n* region of ionized air in the upper atmosphere that reflects radio waves.

IOU *n* signed paper acknowledging debt.

IQ intelligence quotient.

ire *n Lit* anger.

iridescent *adj* having shimmering changing colours like a rainbow. **iridescence** *n*

iris *n* 1 coloured circular membrane of the eye containing the pupil. 2 tall plant with purple, yellow, or white flowers.

irk *v* irritate, annoy. **irksome** *adj* irritating, annoying.

iron ❶ *n* 1 strong silvery–white metallic

——————[THESAURUS]——————

invest *v* **1** = **spend**, advance, devote, lay out, put in, sink **2** (foll. by *with*) = **empower**, authorize, charge, license, sanction, vest

investigate *v* = **examine**, explore, go into, inquire into, inspect, look into, probe, research, study

inveterate *adj* = **long–standing**, chronic, confirmed, deep–seated, dyed–in–the–wool, entrenched, habitual, hardened, incorrigible, incurable

invigilate *v* = **watch over**, conduct, keep an eye on, oversee, preside over, run, superintend, supervise

invigorate *v* = **refresh**, energize, enliven, exhilarate, fortify, galvanize, liven up, revitalize, stimulate

invincible *adj* = **unbeatable**, impregnable, indestructible, indomitable, insuperable,

invulnerable, unassailable, unconquerable

inviolable *adj* = **sacrosanct**, hallowed, holy, inalienable, sacred, unalterable

invisible *adj* = **unseen**, imperceptible, indiscernible ≠ **seen**

invite *v* **1** = **request**, ask, beg, bid, summon **2** = **ask for** (*inf*) **3** = **encourage**, attract, court, entice, provoke, tempt

invoke *v* **1** = **apply**, implement, initiate, put into effect, resort to, use **3** = **call upon**, appeal to, beg, beseech, entreat, implore, petition, pray, supplicate

involuntary *adj* = **unintentional**, automatic, instinctive, reflex, spontaneous, unconscious, uncontrolled, unthinking ≠ **voluntary**

involve *v* **1** = **entail**, imply, mean, necessitate, presuppose, require **2** = **concern**, affect, draw in, implicate, element, widely used for structural and engineering purposes. **2** appliance used, when heated, to press clothes. **3** metal–headed golf club. ♦ *pl* **4** chains, restraints. ♦ *adj* **5** made of iron. **6** strong, inflexible, e.g. *iron will*. ♦ *v* **7** smooth (clothes or fabric) with an iron. **ironing** *n* clothes to be ironed. **ironing board** long cloth–covered board with folding legs, for ironing clothes on. **iron out** *v* settle (a problem) through discussion.

irony ❶ *n, pl* –**nies 1** mildly sarcastic use of words to imply the opposite of what is said. **2** aspect of a situation that is odd or amusing because the opposite of what one would expect.

irradiate *v* subject to or treat with radiation. **irradiation** *n*

irrational ❶ *adj* not based on or not using logical reasoning.

irregular ❶ *adj* **1** not regular or even. **2** not conforming to accepted practice. **3** (of a word) not following the typical pattern of formation in a language. **irregularly** *adv* **irregularity** *n, pl* –**ties**

irrelevant ❶ *adj* not connected with the matter in hand. **irrelevance** *n*

irreparable ❶ *adj* not able to be repaired or put right.

irresistible ❶ *adj* too attractive or strong to resist. **irresistibly** *adv*

irrevocable ❶ *adj* not possible to change or undo. **irrevocably** *adv*

irrigate ❶ *v* supply (land) with water by artificial channels or pipes. **irrigation** *n*

irritate ❶ *v* **1** annoy, anger. **2** cause (a body part) to itch or become inflamed. **irritable** *adj* easily annoyed. **irritably** *adv* **irritant** *n, adj* (person or thing) causing irritation. **irritation** *n*

is *v* third person singular present tense of BE.

Islam *n* **1** Muslim religion teaching that there is one God and that Mohammed is his prophet. **2** Muslim countries and civilization. **Islamic** *adj*

island ❶ *n* piece of land surrounded by water. **islander** *n* person who lives on an island.

isle *n Poetic* island. **islet** *n* small island.

isobar [**ice**–oh–bar] *n* line on a map connecting places of equal atmospheric pressure.

——————— THESAURUS ———————

touch

iron *adj* **5** = **ferrous**, ferric **6** = **Inflexible**, adamant, hard, implacable, indomitable, steely, strong, tough, unbending ≠ **flexible**

irony *n* **1** = **sarcasm**, mockery, satire **2** = **paradox**, incongruity

irrational *adj* = **illogical**, absurd, crazy, nonsensical, preposterous, unreasonable ≠ **sound**

irregular *adj* **1 a** = **variable**, erratic, fitful, haphazard, occasional, random, spasmodic, sporadic, unsystematic ≠ **steady b** = **uneven**, asymmetrical, bumpy, crooked, jagged, lopsided, ragged, rough ≠ **even** **2** = **unconventional**, abnormal, exceptional, extraordinary, munted (*NZ sl*), peculiar, unofficial, unorthodox, unusual ≠ **standard**

irrelevant *adj* = **unconnected**, beside the point, extraneous, immaterial, impertinent, inapplicable, inappropriate, neither here nor there, unrelated

irreparable *adj* = **beyond repair**, incurable, irremediable, irretrievable, irreversible

irresistible *adj* = **overwhelming**, compelling, compulsive, overpowering, urgent

irrevocable *adj* = **fixed**, fated, immutable, irreversible, predestined, predetermined, settled, unalterable

irrigate *v* = **water**, flood, inundate, moisten, wet

irritate *v* **1** = **annoy**, anger, bother, exasperate, get on one's nerves (*inf*), infuriate, needle (*inf*), nettle, rankle with, try one's patience ≠ **calm 2** = **rub**, chafe, inflame, pain

island *n* = **isle**, ait or eyot (*dial*), atoll, cay or key, islet

isolate ❶ v 1 place apart or alone. 2 *Chem* obtain (a substance) in uncombined form. **isolation** n **isolationism** n policy of not participating in international affairs. **isolationist** n, adj

isomer [ice–oh–mer] n substance whose molecules contain the same atoms as another but in a different arrangement.

isometric adj relating to muscular contraction without shortening of the muscle. **isometrics** pl n isometric exercises.

isotope n one of two or more atoms with the same number of protons in the nucleus but a different number of neutrons.

issue ❶ n 1 topic of interest or discussion. 2 reason for quarrelling. 3 particular edition of a magazine or newspaper. 4 outcome or result. 5 *Law* child or children. ♦ v 6 make (a statement etc.) publicly. 7 supply officially (with). 8 produce and make available. **take issue with** disagree with.

isthmus [iss–muss] n, pl –muses narrow strip of land connecting two areas of land.

it pron 1 refers to a nonhuman, animal, plant, or inanimate object. 2 refers to a thing mentioned or being discussed. 3 used as the subject of impersonal verbs, e.g. *it's windy.* 4 *Informal* crucial or ultimate point. **its** adj, pron belonging to it. **it's 1** it is. **2** it has. **itself** pron emphatic form of IT.

✓ **WORD TIP**
Beware of mistaking the possessive *its* (no apostrophe) as in *The cat has hurt its paw,* for the abbreviation *it's* meaning *it is* or *it has: It's been a long time.*

---

italic adj (of printing type) sloping to the right. **italics** pl n this type, used for emphasis. **italicize** v put in italics.

itch ❶ n 1 skin irritation causing a desire to scratch. 2 restless desire. ♦ v 3 have an itch. **itchy** adj

item ❶ n 1 single thing in a list or collection. 2 piece of information. **itemize** v make a list of.

itinerant ❶ adj travelling from place to place. **itinerary** n detailed plan of a journey.

ivory n 1 hard white bony substance forming the tusks of elephants. ♦ adj 2 yellowish–white. **ivory tower** remoteness from the realities of everyday life.

ivy n, pl **ivies** evergreen climbing plant.

THESAURUS

isolate v 1 = **separate**, cut off, detach, disconnect, insulate, segregate, set apart

issue n 1 = **topic**, matter, point, question, subject 2 = **problem**, bone of contention 3 = **edition**, copy, number, printing 4 = **outcome**, consequence, effect, end result, result, upshot 5 *Law* = **children**, descendants, heirs, offspring, progeny ≠ **parent** ♦ v 6 = **announce**, broadcast 8 = **give out**, circulate, deliver, distribute, publish, put out, release ≠ **withdraw** **take issue with** = **disagree with**, challenge, dispute, object to, oppose, raise an objection to, take exception to

itch n 1 = **irritation**, itchiness, prickling, tingling 2 = **desire**, craving, hankering, hunger, longing, lust, passion, yearning, yen (*inf*) ♦ v 3 a = **prickle**, irritate, tickle, tingle b = **long**, ache, crave, hanker, hunger, lust, pine, yearn

item n 1 = **detail**, article, component, entry, matter, particular, point, thing 2 = **report**, account, article, bulletin, dispatch, feature, note, notice, paragraph, piece

itinerant adj = **wandering**, migratory, nomadic, peripatetic, roaming, roving, travelling, vagrant

J j

jab ⊕ *v* **jabbing, jabbed 1** poke sharply. ♦ *n*
2 quick punch or poke. **3** *Informal*
injection.

jabber ⊕ *v* talk rapidly or incoherently.

jack *n* **1** device for raising a motor vehicle
or other heavy object. **2** playing card with
a picture of a pageboy. **3** *Bowls* small
white bowl aimed at by the players. **4**
socket in electrical equipment into which a
plug fits. **5** flag flown at the bow of a ship,
showing nationality.

jackal *n* doglike wild animal of Africa and
Asia.

jackass *n* **1** fool. **2** male of the ass.
laughing jackass same as KOOKABURRA.

jackboot *n* high military boot.

jackdaw *n* black- and grey bird of the
crow family.

jacket ⊕ *n* **1** short coat. **2** skin of a baked
potato. **3** outer paper cover on a hardback
book.

jackknife *v* **1** (of an articulated lorry) go
out of control so that the trailer swings
round at a sharp angle to the cab. ♦ *n* **2**
large clasp knife.

jackpot ⊕ *n* largest prize that may be won
in a game. **hit the jackpot** be very

successful through luck.

Jacuzzi [jak–**oo**–zee] *n* ® circular bath
with a device that swirls the water.

jade *n* **1** ornamental semiprecious stone,
usu. dark green. ♦ *adj* **2** bluish–green.

jaded ⊕ *adj* tired and unenthusiastic.

jaguar *n* large S American spotted cat.

jail ⊕ *n* **1** prison. ♦ *v* **2** send to prison. **jailer**
n **jailbird** *n* *Informal* person who has often
been in prison.

jam¹ ⊕ *v* **jamming, jammed 1** pack tightly
into a place. **2** crowd or congest. **3** make
or become stuck. **4** *Radio* block (another
station) with impulses of equal
wavelength. **5** play a jam session. ♦ *n* **6**
hold–up of traffic. **7** *Informal* awkward
situation. **jam on the brakes** apply brakes
fiercely. **jam–packed** *adj* filled to capacity.
jam session informal rock or jazz
performance.

jam² *n* food made from fruit boiled with
sugar.

jamb *n* side post of a door or window
frame.

jamboree ⊕ *n* large gathering or
celebration.

Jan. January.

THESAURUS

jab *v* **1** = **poke**, dig, lunge, nudge, prod,
punch, stab, thrust ♦ *n* **2** = **poke**, dig,
lunge, nudge, prod, punch, stab, thrust

jabber *v* **1** = **chatter**, babble, blether,
gabble, mumble, prate, rabbit (on) (*Brit
inf*), ramble, yap (*inf*)

jacket *n* **3** = **cover**, wrapper

jackpot *n* = **prize**, award, bonanza, reward,
winnings

jaded *adj* = **tired**, exhausted, fatigued,
spent, weary ≠ **fresh**

jail *n* **1** = **prison**, nick (*Brit sl*), penitentiary
(*US*), reformatory, slammer (*sl*) ♦ *v*
2 = **imprison**, confine, detain, incarcerate,
lock up, send down

jam¹ *v* **1** = **pack**, cram, force, press, ram,
squeeze, stuff, wedge **2** = **crowd**, congest,
crush, throng **3** = **stick**, block, clog,
obstruct, stall ♦ *n* **7** *Inf* = **predicament**,
deep water, fix (*inf*), hole (*sl*), hot water,
pickle (*inf*), tight spot, trouble

jamboree *n* = **festival**, carnival,

jangle ⊙ v 1 (cause to) make a harsh ringing noise. 2 (of nerves) be upset or irritated.

janitor ⊙ n caretaker of a school or other building.

January n first month of the year.

jar¹ ⊙ n wide-mouthed container, usu. round and made of glass.

jar² ⊙ v jarring, jarred 1 have a disturbing or unpleasant effect. 2 jolt or bump. ♦ n 3 jolt or shock.

jargon ⊙ n specialized technical language of a particular subject.

jasmine n shrub with sweet-smelling yellow or white flowers.

jaundice n disease marked by yellowness of the skin. **jaundiced** adj 1 (of an attitude or opinion) bitter or cynical. 2 having jaundice.

jaunt ⊙ n short journey for pleasure.

jaunty ⊙ adj -tier, -tiest 1 sprightly and cheerful. 2 smart. **jauntily** adv

javelin n light spear thrown in sports competitions.

jaw ⊙ n 1 one of the bones in which the teeth are set. ♦ pl 2 mouth. 3 gripping part of a tool. 4 narrow opening of a gorge or valley. ♦ v 5 Slang talk lengthily.

jay n bird with a pinkish body and blue-and-black wings.

jazz n kind of music with an exciting rhythm, usu. involving improvisation. **jazzy** adj flashy or showy. **jazz up** v make more lively.

jealous ⊙ adj 1 fearful of losing a partner or possession to a rival. 2 envious. 3 suspiciously watchful. **jealousy** n, pl -sies

jeans ⊙ pl n casual denim trousers.

Jeep n ® four-wheel-drive motor vehicle.

jeer ⊙ v 1 scoff or deride. ♦ n 2 cry of derision.

jell ⊙ v 1 form into a jelly-like substance. 2 take on a definite form.

jelly n, pl -lies 1 soft food made of liquid set with gelatine. 2 jam made from fruit juice and sugar. **jellied** adj prepared in a jelly.

jemmy n, pl -mies short steel crowbar used by burglars.

jeopardy ⊙ n danger. **jeopardize** v place in danger.

jerk ⊙ v 1 move or throw abruptly. ♦ n 2 sharp or abruptly stopped movement. 3 Slang contemptible person. **jerky** adj sudden or abrupt. **jerkily** adv **jerkiness** n

jerkin n sleeveless jacket.

——————— THESAURUS ———————

celebration, festivity, fete, revelry

jangle v 1 = **rattle**, chime, clank, clash, clatter, jingle, vibrate

janitor n = **caretaker**, concierge, custodian, doorkeeper, porter

jar¹ n 1 = **pot**, container, crock, jug, pitcher, urn, vase

jar² v 1 = **irritate**, annoy, get on one's nerves (inf), grate, irk, nettle, offend 2 = **jolt**, bump, convulse, rattle, rock, shake, vibrate ♦ n 3 = **jolt**, bump, convulsion, shock, vibration

jargon n = **parlance**, argot, idiom, usage

jaunt n = **outing**, airing, excursion, expedition, ramble, stroll, tour, trip

jaunty adj 1 = **sprightly**, buoyant, carefree, high-spirited, lively, perky, self-confident, sparky

jaw v 5 Sl = **talk**, chat, chatter, gossip, spout

jealous adj 1 = **possessive**, mistrustful, protective 2 = **envious**, covetous, desirous, green, grudging, resentful ≠ **satisfied** 3 = **suspicious**, vigilant, wary, watchful ≠ **trusting**

jeans pl n = **denims**

jeer v 1 = **mock**, barrack, deride, gibe, heckle, ridicule, scoff, taunt ≠ **praise** ♦ n 2 = **mockery**, abuse, boo, catcall, derision, gibe, ridicule, taunt

jell v 1 = **solidify**, congeal, harden, set, thicken 2 = **take shape**, come together, crystallize, materialize

jeopardy n = **danger**, insecurity, peril, risk, vulnerability

jerk v 1 = **tug**, jolt, lurch, pull, thrust, twitch, wrench, yank ♦ n 2 = **tug**, jolt, lurch, pull, thrust, twitch, wrench, yank

jersey *n* 1 knitted jumper. 2 machine–knitted fabric. 3 (J–) breed of cow.

jest ❶ *n, v* joke. **jester** *n Hist* professional clown at court.

jet¹ ❶ *n* 1 aircraft driven by jet propulsion. 2 stream of liquid or gas, esp. one forced from a small hole. 3 nozzle from which gas or liquid is forced. ◆ *v* **jetting, jetted** 4 fly by jet aircraft. **jet lag** fatigue caused by crossing time zones in an aircraft. **jet propulsion** propulsion by thrust provided by a jet of gas or liquid. **jet–propelled** *adj* **jet set** rich and fashionable people who travel the world for pleasure.

jet² *n* hard black mineral. **jet–black** *adj* glossy black.

jetsam *n* goods thrown overboard to lighten a ship.

jetty ❶ *n, pl* **–ties** small pier.

Jew *n* 1 person whose religion is Judaism. 2 descendant of the ancient Hebrews. **Jewish** *adj* **jew's–harp** *n* musical instrument held between the teeth and played by plucking a metal strip with one's finger.

jewel ❶ *n* 1 precious stone. 2 special person or thing. **jeweller** *n* dealer in jewels. **jewellery** *n* objects decorated with precious stones.

jib¹ *n* triangular sail set in front of a mast.

jib² ❶ *v* **jibbing, jibbed** (of a horse, person, etc.) stop and refuse to go on. **jib at** *v* object to (a proposal etc.).

jib³ *n* projecting arm of a crane or derrick.

jibe¹ ❶ *n, v* taunt or jeer.

jibe² *v* same as GYBE.

jig ❶ *n* 1 type of lively dance. 2 music for it. 3 device that holds a component in place for cutting etc. ◆ *v* **jigging, jigged** 4 make jerky up–and–down movements.

jilt *v* leave or reject (one's lover).

jingle ❶ *n* 1 catchy verse or song used in a radio or television advert. 2 gentle ringing noise. ◆ *v* 3 (cause to) make a gentle ringing sound.

jingoism *n* aggressive nationalism. **jingoistic** *adj*

jinks *pl n* **high jinks** boisterous merrymaking.

jinx ❶ *n* 1 person or thing bringing bad luck. ◆ *v* 2 be or put a jinx on.

jitters ❶ *pl n* worried nervousness. **jittery** *adj* nervous.

jive *n* 1 lively dance of the 1940s and '50s. ◆ *v* 2 dance the jive.

job ❶ *n* 1 occupation or paid employment. 2 task to be done. 3 *Informal* difficult task. 4 *Informal* crime, esp. robbery. **jobbing** *adj* doing individual jobs for payment. **jobless** *adj, pl n* unemployed (people). **job lot** assortment sold together. **job sharing** splitting one post between two people working part–time.

jockey *n* 1 (professional) rider of

━━━━━━━ THESAURUS ━━━━━━━

① **jest** *n* = **joke**, bon mot, crack (*sl*), jape, pleasantry, prank, quip, wisecrack (*inf*), witticism
② **jest** *v* = **joke**, kid (*inf*), mock, quip, tease
jet¹ *n* 2 = **stream**, flow, fountain, gush, spout, spray, spring 3 = **nozzle**, atomizer, sprayer, sprinkler ◆ *v* 4 = **fly**, soar, zoom
jetty *n* = **pier**, dock, quay, wharf
jewel *n* 1 = **gemstone**, ornament, rock (*sl*), sparkler (*inf*) 2 = **rarity**, collector's item, find, gem, humdinger (*sl*), pearl, treasure, wonder
jib² *v* = **refuse**, balk, recoil, retreat, shrink, stop short

① **jibe¹** *n* = **taunt**, jeering, mockery, ridicule, scoffing, scorn, sneering
② **jibe¹** *v* = **taunt**, jeer, make fun of, mock, poke fun at, ridicule, scoff, scorn, sneer
jig *v* 4 = **skip**, bob, bounce, caper, prance, wiggle
jingle *n* 1 = **song**, chorus, ditty, melody, tune 2 = **rattle**, clink, reverberation, ringing, tinkle ◆ *v* 3 = **ring**, chime, clink, jangle, rattle, tinkle
jinx *n* 1 = **curse**, hex (*US & Canad inf*), hoodoo (*inf*), nemesis ◆ *v* 2 = **curse**, bewitch, hex (*US & Canad inf*)
jitters *pl n* = **nerves**, anxiety, butterflies (in one's stomach) (*inf*), cold feet (*inf*),

racehorses. ♦ v 2 **jockey for position** manoeuvre to obtain an advantage.

jockstrap n belt with a pouch to support the genitals, worn by male athletes.

jocular ❶ adj 1 fond of joking. 2 meant as a joke. **jocularity** n

jodhpurs pl n riding trousers, loose–fitting above the knee but tight below.

jog ❶ v **jogging, jogged** 1 run at a gentle pace, esp. for exercise. 2 nudge slightly. ♦ n 3 slow run. **jogger** n **jogging** n

join ❶ v 1 become a member (of). 2 come into someone's company. 3 take part (in). 4 come or bring together. ♦ n 5 place where two things are joined. **join up** v enlist in the armed services.

joint ❶ adj 1 shared by two or more. ♦ n 2 place where bones meet but can move. 3 junction of two or more parts or objects. 4 piece of meat for roasting. 5 *Slang* house or place, esp. a disreputable bar or nightclub. 6 *Slang* marijuana cigarette. ♦ v 7 divide meat into joints. **out of joint** 1 disorganized. 2 dislocated. **jointly** adv

joist n horizontal beam that helps support a floor or ceiling.

joke ❶ n 1 thing said or done to cause laughter. 2 amusing or ridiculous person or thing. ♦ v 3 make jokes. **jokey** adj **joker** n 1 person who jokes. 2 *Slang* fellow. 3 extra card in a pack, counted as any other in some games.

jolly ❶ adj **–lier, –liest** 1 (of a person) happy and cheerful. 2 (of an occasion) merry and festive. ♦ v **–lying, –lied** 3 **jolly along** try to keep (someone) cheerful by flattery or coaxing. **jollity** n **jollification** n merrymaking.

jolt ❶ n 1 unpleasant surprise or shock. 2 sudden jerk or bump. ♦ v 3 surprise or shock. 4 move or shake with a jerk.

joss stick n stick of incense giving off a sweet smell when burnt.

jostle ❶ v knock or push against.

jot ❶ v **jotting, jotted** 1 write briefly. ♦ n 2 very small amount. **jotter** n notebook. **jottings** pl n notes jotted down.

joule [jool] n *Physics* unit of work or energy.

journal ❶ n 1 daily newspaper or magazine. 2 daily record of events. **journalese** n superficial style of writing, found in some newspapers. **journalism** n writing in or editing of newspapers and

——————— THESAURUS ———————

fidgets, nervousness, the shakes (*inf*)

job n 1 = **occupation**, business, calling, career, employment, livelihood, profession, vocation 2 = **task**, assignment, chore, duty, enterprise, errand, undertaking, venture, work

jocular adj = **humorous**, amusing, droll, facetious, funny, joking, jovial, playful, sportive, teasing, waggish

jog v 1 = **run**, canter, lope, trot 2 = **nudge**, prod, push, shake, stir

join v 1 = **enrol**, enlist, enter, sign up 4 = **connect**, add, append, attach, combine, couple, fasten, link, unite ≠ **separate**

joint adj 1 = **shared**, collective, combined, communal, cooperative, joined, mutual, united ♦ n 3 = **junction**, connection, hinge, intersection, nexus, node ♦ v 7 = **divide**, carve, cut up, dissect, segment, sever

joke n 1 = **jest**, gag (*inf*), jape, prank, pun, quip, wisecrack (*inf*), witticism 2 = **laughing stock**, buffoon, clown ♦ v 3 = **jest**, banter, kid (*inf*), mock, play the fool, quip, taunt, tease

jolly adj 1 = **happy**, cheerful, chirpy (*inf*), genial, jovial, merry, playful, sprightly, upbeat (*inf*)

jolt n 1 = **surprise**, blow, bolt from the blue, bombshell, setback, shock 2 = **jerk**, bump, jar, jog, jump, lurch, shake, start ♦ v 3 = **surprise**, discompose, disturb, perturb, stagger, startle, stun 4 = **jerk**, jar, jog, jostle, knock, push, shake, shove

jostle v = **push**, bump, elbow, hustle, jog, jolt, shake, shove

jot v 1 = **note down**, list, record, scribble ♦ n 2 = **bit**, fraction, grain, morsel, scrap, speck magazines. **journalist** n **journalistic** adj

journey ❶ n 1 act or process of travelling from one place to another. ◆ v 2 travel.

journeyman n qualified craftsman employed by another.

jovial ❶ adj happy and cheerful. **jovially** adv **joviality** n

jowl n 1 lower jaw. pl 2 cheeks.

joy ❶ n 1 feeling of great delight or pleasure. 2 cause of this feeling. **joyful** adj **joyless** adj **joyous** adj extremely happy and enthusiastic. **joyriding** n driving for pleasure, esp. in a stolen car. **joyride** n **joyrider** n **joystick** n control device for an aircraft or computer.

JP Justice of the Peace.

jubilant ❶ adj feeling or expressing great joy. **jubilation** n

jubilee ❶ n special anniversary, esp. 25th (**silver jubilee**) or 50th (**golden jubilee**).

judder v 1 vibrate violently. ◆ n 2 violent vibration.

judge ❶ n 1 public official who tries cases and passes sentence in a court of law. 2 person who decides the outcome of a contest. ◆ v 3 act as a judge. 4 appraise critically. 5 consider something to be the case. **judgment, judgement** n 1 opinion reached after careful thought. 2 verdict of a judge. 3 ability to appraise critically. **Judgmental, judgemental** adj

✓ WORD TIP
The alternative spellings with or without an 'e' between 'g' and 'm' are equally acceptable.

judicial ❶ adj 1 of or by a court or judge. 2 showing or using judgment. **judicially** adv

judo n sport in which two opponents try to throw each other to the ground.

jug ❶ n container for liquids, with a handle and small spout.

juggernaut n 1 large heavy lorry. 2 any irresistible destructive force.

juggle ❶ v 1 throw and catch (several objects) so that most are in the air at the same time. 2 manipulate (figures, situations, etc.) to suit one's purposes. **juggler** n

juice ❶ n 1 liquid part of vegetables, fruit, or meat. 2 Informal petrol. ◆ pl 3 fluids secreted by an organ of the body. **juicy** adj 1 full of juice. 2 interesting.

jujitsu n Japanese art of wrestling and self-defence.

jukebox n coin-operated machine for playing records, CDs, or videos.

July n seventh month of the year.

jumble ❶ n 1 confused heap or state. 2 articles for a jumble sale. ◆ v 3 mix in a disordered way. **jumble sale** sale of

———————— THESAURUS ————————

journal n 1 = **newspaper**, daily, gazette, magazine, monthly, periodical, weekly 2 = **diary**, chronicle, day-to-day account, log, record

journey n 1 = **trip**, excursion, expedition, odyssey, pilgrimage, tour, trek, voyage ◆ v 2 = **travel**, go, proceed, roam, rove, tour, traverse, trek, voyage, wander

jovial adj = **cheerful**, animated, cheery, convivial, happy, jolly, merry, mirthful

joy n 1 = **delight**, bliss, ecstasy, elation, gaiety, glee, pleasure, rapture, satisfaction ≠ **despair**

jubilant adj = **overjoyed**, elated, enraptured, euphoric, exuberant, exultant, thrilled, triumphant

jubilee n = **celebration**, festival, festivity, holiday

judge n 1 = **magistrate**, beak (Brit sl), justice 2 = **referee**, adjudicator, arbiter, arbitrator, moderator, umpire connoisseur, expert ◆ v 3 = **adjudicate**, arbitrate, decide, mediate, referee, umpire 5 = **consider**, appraise, assess, esteem, estimate, evaluate, rate, value

judicial adj 1 = **legal**, official

jug n = **container**, carafe, crock, ewer, jar, pitcher, urn, vessel

juggle v 2 = **manipulate**, alter, change, manoeuvre, modify

juice n 1 = **liquid**, extract, fluid, liquor, nectar, sap miscellaneous second–hand items.

jumbo ① *adj* **1** *Informal* very large. ◆ *n* **2** (also **jumbo jet**) large jet airliner.

jump ① *v* **1** leap or spring into the air using the leg muscles. **2** move quickly and suddenly. **3** jerk with surprise. **4** increase suddenly. **5** change the subject abruptly. **6** *Informal* attack without warning. **7** pass over or miss out (intervening material). ◆ *n* **8** act of jumping. **9** sudden rise. **10** break in continuity. **jump the gun** act prematurely. **jump the queue** not wait one's turn. **jumpy** *adj* nervous. **jump at** *v* accept (a chance etc.) gladly. **jumped–up** *adj* arrogant because of recent promotion. **jump on** *v* attack suddenly and forcefully.

junction ① *n* place where routes, railway lines, or roads meet.

juncture ① *n* point in time, esp. a critical one.

June *n* sixth month of the year.

jungle *n* **1** tropical forest of dense tangled vegetation. **2** confusion or mess. **3** place of intense struggle for survival.

junior ① *adj* **1** of lower standing. **2** younger. ◆ *n* **3** junior person.

juniper *n* evergreen shrub with purple berries.

junk[1] ① *n* **1** discarded or useless objects. **2** *Informal* rubbish. **3** *Slang* narcotic drug, esp. heroin. **junkie, junky** *n, pl* **junkies** *Slang* drug addict. **junk food** snack food of low nutritional value. **junk mail** unwanted mail advertising goods or services.

junk[2] *n* flat–bottomed Chinese sailing boat.

junket *n* **1** excursion by public officials paid for from public funds. **2** sweetened milk set with rennet.

junta *n* group of military officers holding power in a country, esp. after a coup.

jurisdiction ① *n* **1** right or power to administer justice and apply laws. **2** extent of this right or power.

jury *n, pl* **–ries** group of people sworn to deliver a verdict in a court of law. **juror** *n* member of a jury.

just ① *adv* **1** very recently. **2** at this instant. **3** merely, only. **4** exactly. **5** barely. **6** really. ◆ *adj* **7** fair or impartial in action or judgment. **8** proper or right. **justice** *n* **1** quality of being just. **2** judicial proceedings. **3** magistrate. **justify** *v* prove right or reasonable.

jut ① *v* **jutting, jutted** project or stick out.

jute *n* plant fibre, used for rope, canvas, etc.

————— THESAURUS —————

jumble *n* **1** = **muddle**, clutter, confusion, disarray, disorder, mess, mishmash, mixture ◆ *v* **3** = **mix**, confuse, disorder, disorganize, mistake, muddle, shuffle

jumbo *adj* **1** *Inf* = **giant**, gigantic, huge, immense, large, oversized

jump *v* **1** = **leap**, bounce, bound, hop, hurdle, skip, spring, vault **3** = **recoil**, flinch, jerk, start, wince **4** = **increase**, advance, ascend, escalate, rise, surge **7** = **miss**, avoid, evade, omit, skip ◆ *n* **8** = **leap**, bound, hop, skip, spring, vault **9** = **rise**, advance, increase, increment, upsurge, upturn **10** = **interruption**, break, gap, hiatus, lacuna, space

junction *n* = **connection**, coupling, linking, union

juncture *n* = **moment**, occasion, point, time

junior *adj* **1** = **lower**, inferior, lesser, minor, secondary, subordinate **2** = **younger**

junk[1] *n* **1, 2** = **rubbish**, clutter, debris, litter, odds and ends, refuse, scrap, trash, waste

jurisdiction *n* **1, 3** = **authority**, command, control, influence, power, rule **2** = **range**, area, bounds, compass, field, province, scope, sphere

just *adv* **1** = **recently**, hardly, lately, only now, scarcely **3** = **merely**, by the skin of one's teeth, only, simply, solely **4** = **exactly**, absolutely, completely, entirely, perfectly, precisely ◆ *adj* **7** = **fair**, conscientious, equitable, fair–minded, good, honest, upright, virtuous ≠ **unfair** **8** = **fitting**, appropriate, apt, deserved, due, justified, merited, proper, rightful ≠ **inappropriate**

jut *v* = **stick out**, bulge, extend, overhang,

juvenile ❶ *adj* **1** young. **2** of or suitable for young people. **3** immature and rather silly. ◆ *n* **4** young person or child. **juvenile delinquent** young person guilty of a crime.

juxtapose *v* put side by side. **juxtaposition** *n*

poke, project, protrude
juvenile *adj* **1** = **young**, youthful ≠ **adult**
3 = **immature**, babyish, callow, childish,
inexperienced, infantile, puerile ◆ *n*
4 = **child**, adolescent, boy, girl, infant,
minor, youth ≠ **adult**

K k

kaftan *n* **1** long loose Eastern garment. **2** woman's dress resembling this.

kak *n* S Afr slang **1** faeces. **2** rubbish.

kaleidoscope *n* tube–shaped toy containing loose coloured pieces reflected by mirrors so that intricate patterns form when the tube is twisted. **kaleidoscopic** *adj*

kamikaze ⊕ [kam–mee–**kah**–zee] *n* **1** (in World War II) Japanese pilot who performed a suicide mission. ◆ *adj* **2** (of an action) undertaken in the knowledge that it will kill or injure the person performing it.

kangaroo *n, pl* **–roos** Australian marsupial which moves by jumping with its powerful hind legs. **kangaroo court** unofficial court set up by a group to discipline its members.

karate *n* Japanese system of unarmed combat using blows with the feet, hands, elbows, and legs.

karma *n* Buddhism, Hinduism person's actions affecting his or her fate in the next reincarnation.

kayak *n* **1** Inuit canoe made of sealskins stretched over a frame. **2** fibreglass or canvas–covered canoe of this design.

kebab *n* **1** dish of small pieces of meat grilled on skewers. **2** (also **doner kebab**) grilled minced lamb served in a split slice of unleavened bread.

kedgeree *n* dish of fish with rice and eggs.

keel *n* main lengthways timber or steel support along the base of a ship. **keel over** *v* **1** turn upside down. **2** Informal collapse suddenly.

keen¹ ⊕ *adj* **1** eager or enthusiastic. **2** intense or strong. **3** intellectually acute. **4** (of the senses) capable of recognizing small distinctions. **5** sharp. **6** cold and penetrating. **7** competitive. **keenly** *adv* **keenness** *n*

keep ⊕ *v* **keeping, kept 1** have or retain possession of. **2** take temporary charge of. **3** store. **4** stay or cause to stay (in, on, or at a place or position). **5** continue or persist. **6** support financially. **7** detain (someone). **8** look after or maintain. **9** (of food) remain good. ◆ *n* **10** cost of food and everyday expenses. **11** central tower of a castle. **keeper** *n* **1** person who looks after animals in a zoo. **2** person in charge of a museum or collection. **3** short for GOALKEEPER. **keeping** *n* care or charge. **in, out of keeping with** appropriate *or* inappropriate for. **keep fit** exercises designed to promote physical fitness. **keepsake** *n* gift treasured for the sake of the giver. **keep up** *v* maintain at the current level. **keep up with** *v* maintain a pace set by (someone).

THESAURUS

kamikaze *adj* **2** = **self–destructive**, foolhardy, suicidal

keen *adj* **1** = **eager**, ardent, avid, enthusiastic, impassioned, zealous **2** = **intense 3** = **astute**, canny, clever, perceptive, quick, shrewd, wise ≠ **indifferent 5** = **sharp**, cutting, incisive, razor–like ≠ **dull**

keep *v* **1** = **retain**, conserve, control, hold, maintain, possess, preserve **2** = **look after**, care for, guard, maintain, manage, mind, protect, tend, watch over **3** = **store**, carry, deposit, hold, place, stack, stock **6** = **support**, maintain, provide for,

keg ⊕ *n* small metal beer barrel.

kelp *n* large brown seaweed.

ken *v* **kenning, kenned** or **kent** *Scot* know. **beyond one's ken** beyond one's range of knowledge.

kennel *n* **1** hutlike shelter for a dog. ♦ *pl* **2** place for breeding, boarding, or training dogs.

kerb *n* stone edging to a footpath.

kernel ⊕ *n* **1** seed of a nut, cereal, or fruit stone. **2** central and essential part of something.

kerosene *n Chiefly US* paraffin.

kestrel *n* type of small falcon.

ketchup *n* thick cold sauce, usu. made of tomatoes.

kettle *n* container with a spout and handle used for boiling water. **kettledrum** *n* large bowl-shaped metal drum.

key ⊕ *n* **1** device for operating a lock by moving a bolt. **2** device turned to wind a clock, operate a machine, etc. **3** any of a set of levers or buttons pressed to operate a typewriter, computer, or musical keyboard instrument. **4** *Music* set of related notes. **5** something crucial in providing an explanation or interpretation. **6** means of achieving a desired end. **7** list of explanations of codes, symbols, etc. ♦ *adj* **8** of great importance. ♦ *v* **9** (also **key in**) enter (text) using a keyboard. **keyed up** very excited or nervous.

kg kilogram(s).

khaki *adj* **1** dull yellowish-brown. ♦ *n* **2** hard-wearing fabric of this colour used for military uniforms.

kibbutz *n*, *pl* **kibbutzim** communal farm or factory in Israel.

kick ⊕ *v* **1** drive, push, or strike with the foot. **2** (of a gun) recoil when fired. **3** *Informal* object or resist. **4** *Informal* free oneself of (an addiction). **5** *Rugby* score with a kick. ♦ *n* **6** thrust or blow with the foot. **7** recoil of a gun. **8** *Informal* excitement or thrill. **kickback** *n* money paid illegally for favours done. **kick off** *v* **1** start a game of football. **2** *Informal* begin. **kick out** *v* dismiss or expel forcibly. **kick-start** *v* **1** start (a motorcycle) by kicking a pedal. **2 kick up** *v Informal* create (a fuss).

kid¹ ⊕ *n* **1** (also **kiddie**) *Informal* child. **2** young goat. **3** leather made from the skin of a young goat. **treat, handle someone with kid gloves** treat someone with great tact in order not to upset them.

kid² ⊕ *v* **kidding, kidded** *Informal* tease or deceive (someone).

kidnap ⊕ *v* **-napping, -napped** seize and hold (a person) to ransom. **kidnapper** *n*

kidney *n* **1** either of the pair of organs that filter waste products from the blood to produce urine. **2** animal kidney used as food. **kidney bean** reddish-brown kidney-shaped bean, edible when cooked.

kill ⊕ *v* **1** cause the death of. **2** *Informal* cause (someone) pain or discomfort. **3** put an end to. **4** pass (time). ♦ *n* **5** act of killing. **6** animals or birds killed in a hunt. **killer** *n* killing *Informal* ♦ *adj* **1** very tiring. **2** very funny. ♦ *n* **3** sudden financial

————— THESAURUS —————

subsidize, sustain **7 = detain**, delay, hinder, hold back, keep back, obstruct, prevent, restrain ♦ *n* **10 = board**, food, living, maintenance **11 = tower**, castle

keg *n* = **barrel**, cask, drum, vat

kernel *n* **2 = essence**, core, germ, gist, nub, pith, substance

key¹ *n* **1 = opener**, latchkey **5 = answer**, explanation, solution ♦ *adj* **8 = essential**, crucial, decisive, fundamental, important, leading, main, major, pivotal, principal ≠ **minor** ♦ *v* **9** (also **key in**) = **type**, enter,

input, keyboard

kick *v* **1 = boot**, punt **4** *Inf* = **give up**, abandon, desist from, leave off, quit, stop ♦ *n* **8** *Inf* = **thrill**, buzz (*sl*), pleasure, stimulation

kid¹ *n* **1** (also **kiddie**) *Inf* = **child**, baby, bairn, infant, teenager, tot, youngster, youth

kid² *v Inf* = **tease**, delude, fool, hoax, jest, joke, pretend, trick, wind up (*Brit sl*)

kidnap *v* = **abduct**, capture, hijack, hold to ransom, seize success. **killjoy** *n* person who spoils others' pleasure.

kiln *n* oven for baking, drying, or processing pottery, bricks, etc.

kilo *n* short for KILOGRAM.

kilo– *combining form* one thousand, e.g. *kilometre*.

kilogram, kilogramme *n* one thousand grams.

kilohertz *n* one thousand hertz.

kilt *n* knee–length pleated tartan skirt worn orig. by Scottish Highlanders.

kimono *n, pl* **–nos 1** loose wide–sleeved Japanese robe, fastened with a sash. **2** European dressing gown resembling this.

kin ❶ **kinsfolk** *n* person's relatives collectively. **kinship** *n*

kind¹ ❶ *adj* considerate, friendly, and helpful. **kindness** *n* **kindly** *adj* **–lier, –liest 1** having a warm–hearted nature. **2** pleasant or agreeable. ◆ *adv* **3** in a considerate way. **4** please, e.g. *will you kindly be quiet!* **kindliness** *n* **kind–hearted** *adj*

kind² ❶ *n* **1** class or group with common characteristics. **2** essential nature or character. **in kind 1** (of payment) in goods rather than money. **2** with something similar. **kind of** to a certain extent.

kindergarten *n* class or school for children of about four to six years old.

kindle ❶ *v* **1** set (a fire) alight. **2** (of a fire) start to burn. **3** arouse or be aroused. **kindling** *n* dry wood or straw for starting fires.

kindy, kindie *n, pl* **–dies** *Aust & NZ informal* kindergarten.

kinetic [kin–**net**–ik] *adj* relating to or caused by motion.

king ❶ *n* **1** male ruler of a monarchy. **2** ruler or chief. **3** best or most important of its kind. **4** piece in chess that must be defended. **5** playing card with a picture of a king on it. **kingship** *n* **kingdom** *n* **1** state ruled by a king or queen. **2** division of the natural world. **king–size, king–sized** *adj* larger than standard size.

kingfisher *n* small bird with a bright greenish–blue and orange plumage, that dives for fish.

kink ❶ *n* **1** twist or bend in rope, wire, hair, etc. **2** *Informal* quirk in someone's personality. **kinky** *adj* **1** *Slang* given to unusual sexual practices. **2** full of kinks.

kiosk ❶ *n* **1** small booth selling drinks, cigarettes, newspapers, etc. **2** public telephone box.

kip *n, v* **kipping, kipped** *Informal* sleep.

kipper *n* cleaned, salted, and smoked herring.

kirk *n Scot* church.

kismet *n* fate or destiny.

kiss ❶ *v* **1** touch with the lips in affection or greeting. **2** join lips with a person in love or desire. ◆ *n* **3** touch with the lips. **kiss of life** mouth–to–mouth resuscitation.

klst *n S Afr* large wooden chest.

kit ❶ *n* **1** outfit or equipment for a specific purpose. **2** set of pieces of equipment sold ready to be assembled. **kit out** *v* **kitting,**

———————— THESAURUS ————————

kill *v* **1** = **slay**, assassinate, butcher, destroy, execute, exterminate, liquidate, massacre, murder, slaughter **3** = **suppress**, extinguish, halt, quash, quell, scotch, smother, stifle, stop

kin, kinsfolk *n* = **family**, kindred, relations, relatives

kind¹ *adj* = **considerate**, benign, charitable, compassionate, courteous, friendly, generous, humane, kindly, obliging, philanthropic, tender–hearted ≠ **severe**

kind² *n* **1** = **class**, brand, breed, family, set,

sort, species, variety

kindle *v* **1** = **set fire to**, ignite, inflame, light ≠ **quell 3** = **arouse**, awaken, induce, inspire, provoke, rouse, stimulate, stir

king *n* **1** = **ruler**, emperor, monarch, sovereign

kink *n* **1** = **twist**, bend, coil, wrinkle **2** *Inf* = **quirk**, eccentricity, fetish, foible, idiosyncrasy, vagary, whim

kiosk **1** = **booth**, bookstall, counter, newsstand, stall, stand

kiss *v* **1, 2** = **osculate**, neck (*inf*), peck (*inf*)

kitted provide with clothes or equipment needed for a particular activity.

kitchen n room used for cooking. **kitchenette** n small kitchen. **kitchen garden** garden for growing vegetables, herbs, etc.

kite n 1 light frame covered with a thin material flown on a string in the wind. 2 large hawk with a forked tail.

kitsch n art or literature with popular sentimental appeal.

kitten n young cat. **kittenish** adj lively and flirtatious.

kitty n, pl **-ties** 1 communal fund. 2 total amount wagered in certain gambling games.

kiwi n 1 NZ flightless bird with a long beak and no tail. 2 Informal New Zealander. **kiwi fruit** edible fruit with a fuzzy brownish skin and green flesh.

klaxon n loud horn used on emergency vehicles as a warning signal.

kleptomania n compulsive tendency to steal. **kleptomaniac** n

kloof n S Afr mountain pass or gorge.

km kilometre(s).

knack ⊕ n 1 skilful way of doing something. 2 innate ability.

knacker n buyer of old horses for killing

knapsack n soldier's or traveller's bag worn strapped on the back.

knave ⊕ n 1 jack at cards. 2 Obs dishonest man.

knead ⊕ v 1 work (dough) into a smooth mixture with the hands. 2 squeeze or press with the hands.

knee n 1 joint between thigh and lower leg. 2 lap. 3 part of a garment covering the knee. ◆ v kneeing, kneed 4 strike or push with the knee. **kneecap** n 1 bone in front of the knee. ◆ v 2 shoot in the kneecap. **kneejerk** adj (of a reply or reaction) automatic and predictable. **knees-up** n Informal party.

kneel ⊕ v kneeling, kneeled or knelt fall or rest on one's knees.

knell ⊕ n 1 sound of a bell, esp. at a funeral or death. 2 portent of doom.

knickers ⊕ pl n woman's or girl's undergarment covering the lower trunk and having legs or legholes.

knick-knack ⊕ n trifle or trinket.

knife n, pl **knives** 1 cutting tool or weapon consisting of a sharp-edged blade with a handle. ◆ v 2 cut or stab with a knife.

knight n 1 man who has been given a knighthood. 2 Hist man who served his lord as a mounted armoured soldier. 3 chess piece shaped like a horse's head. ◆ v 4 award a knighthood to. **knighthood** n honorary title given to a man by the British sovereign.

knit ⊕ v knitting, knitted or knit 1 make (a garment) by interlocking a series of loops in wool or other yarn. 2 join closely together. 3 draw (one's eyebrows) together. **knitting** n **knitwear** n knitted clothes, such as sweaters.

knob ⊕ n 1 rounded projection, such as a switch on a radio. 2 rounded handle on a door or drawer. 3 small amount of butter.

——————————— THESAURUS ———————————

◆ n 3 = **osculation**, peck (inf), smacker (sl)

kit n 1 = **equipment**, apparatus, gear, paraphernalia, tackle, tools

knack n 1 = **skill**, trick 2 = **gift**, ability, aptitude, capacity, expertise, facility, propensity, skill, talent

knave n 2 Obs = **rogue**, blackguard, bounder (old-fashioned Brit sl), rascal, rotter (sl, chiefly Brit), scoundrel, villain

knead v 2 = **squeeze**, form, manipulate, massage, mould, press, rub, shape, work

kneel v = **genuflect**, stoop

knell n 1 = **ringing**, chime, peal, sound, toll

knickers pl n = **underwear**, bloomers, briefs, broekies (S Afr inf), drawers, panties, smalls

knick-knack n = **trinket**, bagatelle, bauble, bric-a-brac, plaything, trifle

knife n 1 = **blade**, cutter ◆ v 2 = **cut**, lacerate, pierce, slash, stab, wound

knit v 2 = **join**, bind, fasten, intertwine, link, tie, unite, weave 3 = **wrinkle**, crease,

knobbly *adj* covered with small bumps.

knock ⊕ *v* 1 give a blow or push to. 2 rap audibly with the knuckles. 3 make or drive by striking. 4 *Informal* criticize adversely. 5 (of an engine) make a regular banging noise as a result of a fault. ◆ *n* 6 blow or rap. 7 knocking sound. **knocker** *n* metal fitting for knocking on a door. **knock about, around** *v* 1 wander or spend time aimlessly. 2 hit or kick brutally. **knockabout** *adj* (of comedy) boisterous. **knock back** *v Informal* 1 drink quickly. 2 cost. 3 reject or refuse. **knock down** *v* 1 demolish. 2 reduce the price of. **knockdown** *adj* (of a price) very low. **knock-knees** *pl n* legs that curve in at the knees. **knock off** *v* 1 *Informal* cease work. 2 *Informal* make or do (something) hurriedly or easily. 3 take (a specified amount) off a price. 4 *Informal* steal. **knock out** *v* 1 render (someone) unconscious. 2 *Informal* overwhelm or amaze. 3 defeat in a knockout competition. **knockout** *n* 1 blow that renders an opponent unconscious. 2 competition from which competitors are progressively eliminated. 3 *Informal* overwhelmingly attractive person or thing. **knock up** *v* 1 *Informal* assemble (something) quickly. 2 *Informal* waken.

knoll *n* small rounded hill.

knot ⊕ *n* 1 fastening made by looping and pulling tight strands of string, cord, or rope. 2 tangle (of hair). 3 small cluster or huddled group. 4 round lump or spot in timber. 5 feeling of tightness, caused by tension or nervousness. 6 unit of speed used by ships, equal to one nautical mile

per hour. ◆ *v* **knotting, knotted** 7 tie with or into a knot. **knotty** *adj* 1 full of knots. 2 puzzling or difficult.

know ⊕ *v* **knowing, knew, known** 1 be or feel certain of the truth of (information etc.). 2 be acquainted with. 3 have a grasp of or understand (a skill or language). 4 be aware of. **in the know** *Informal* informed or aware. **knowing** *adj* suggesting secret knowledge. **knowingly** *adv* 1 deliberately. 2 in a way that suggests secret knowledge. **knowledge** *n* facts or experiences known by a person. **know-all** *n Offens* person who acts as if knowing more than other people. **know-how** *n Informal* ingenuity, aptitude, or skill.

knuckle *n* 1 bone at the finger joint. 2 knee joint of a calf or pig. **near the knuckle** *Informal* rather rude or offensive. **knuckle-duster** *n* metal appliance worn on the knuckles to add force to a blow. **knuckle under** *v* yield or submit.

KO knockout.

koala *n* tree-dwelling Australian marsupial with dense grey fur.

kohl *n* cosmetic powder used to darken the edges of the eyelids.

Koran *n* sacred book of Islam.

kosher [koh-sher] *adj* 1 conforming to Jewish religious law, esp. (of food) to Jewish dietary law. 2 *Informal* legitimate or authentic. ◆ *n* 3 kosher food.

kowtow *v* be servile (towards).

krypton *n Chem* colourless gas present in the atmosphere and used in fluorescent lights.

KS Kansas.

——————— THESAURUS ———————

furrow, knot, pucker

knob *n* 1 = **lump**, bump, hump, knot, projection, protrusion, protuberance, snag, stud, swell

knock *v* 1 = **hit**, belt (*inf*), cuff, punch, smack, strike, thump 2 = **rap** 4 *Inf* = **criticize**, abuse, belittle, censure, condemn, denigrate, deprecate, disparage, find fault, run down ◆ *n* 6 = **blow**, clip, clout (*inf*), cuff, rap, slap,

smack, thump

knot *n* 1 = **connection**, bond, joint, ligature, loop, tie 3 = **cluster**, bunch, clump, collection ◆ *v* 7 = **tie**, bind, loop, secure, tether

know *v* 1 = **understand**, comprehend, feel certain, notice, perceive, realize, recognize, see 2 = **be acquainted with**, be familiar with, have dealings with, have knowledge of, recognize ≠ **be ignorant of**

kudos *n* fame or credit.
kugel [**koog**–el] *n S Afr* rich, fashion–conscious, materialistic young woman.
kumara *n NZ* tropical root vegetable with yellow flesh.
kung fu *n* Chinese martial art combining hand, foot, and weapon techniques.
KY Kentucky.

——————{ THESAURUS }——————

knowledge *n* = **learning**, education, enlightenment, erudition, instruction, intelligence, scholarship, schooling, science, tuition, wisdom
known *adj* = **famous**, acknowledged, admitted, avowed, celebrated, common, confessed, familiar, manifest, noted, obvious, patent, plain, popular, published, recognized, well-known

L l

l litre.

LA Louisiana.

lab *n Informal* short for LABORATORY.

label ⊕ *n* **1** piece of card or other material fixed to an object to show its ownership, destination, etc. ◆ *v* **-elling, -elled** **2** give a label to.

laboratory *n, pl* **-ries** building or room designed for scientific research or for the teaching of practical science.

labrador *n* large retriever dog with a usu. gold or black coat.

laburnum *n* ornamental tree with yellow hanging flowers.

labyrinth ⊕ [**lab**–er–inth] *n* **1** complicated network of passages. **2** interconnecting cavities in the internal ear. **labyrinthine** *adj*

lace ⊕ *n* **1** delicate decorative fabric made from threads woven into an open weblike pattern. **2** cord drawn through eyelets and tied. ◆ *v* **3** fasten with laces. **4** thread a cord or string through holes in something. **5** add a small amount of alcohol, a drug, etc. to (food or drink). **lacy** *adj* fine, like lace.

lacerate ⊕ [**lass**–er–rate] *v* tear (flesh). **laceration** *n*

lachrymose *adj* **1** tearful. **2** sad.

lack ⊕ *n* **1** shortage or absence of something needed or wanted. ◆ *v* **2** need or be short of (something).

lackadaisical ⊕ *adj* **1** lazy and careless in a dreamy way.

lackey ⊕ *n* **1** servile follower. **2** uniformed male servant.

lacklustre ⊕ *adj* lacking brilliance or vitality.

laconic ⊕ *adj* using only a few words, terse. **laconically** *adv*

lacquer *n* **1** hard varnish for wood or metal. **2** clear sticky substance sprayed onto the hair to hold it in place.

lacrosse *n* sport in which teams catch and throw a ball using long sticks with a pouched net at the end, in an attempt to score goals.

lad ⊕ *n* boy or young man.

ladder *n* **1** frame of two poles connected

THESAURUS

label *n* **1** = **tag**, marker, sticker, ticket ◆ *v* **3** = **tag**, mark, stamp

labyrinth *n* **1, 2** = **maze**, intricacy, jungle, tangle

lace *n* **1** = **netting**, filigree, openwork **2** = **cord**, bootlace, shoelace, string, tie ◆ *v* **3** = **fasten**, bind, do up, thread, tie **4** = **intertwine**, interweave, twine **5** = **mix in**, add to, fortify, spike

lacerate *v* = **tear**, claw, cut, gash, mangle, rip, slash, wound

lack *n* **1** = **shortage**, absence, dearth, deficiency, need, scarcity, want ≠ **excess** ◆ *v* **2** = **need**, be deficient in, be short of,

be without, miss, require, want ≠ **have**

lackadaisical *adj* **1** = **lethargic**, apathetic, dull, half–hearted, indifferent, languid, listless **2** = **lazy**, abstracted, dreamy, idle, indolent, inert

lackey *n* **1** = **hanger–on**, flatterer, minion, sycophant, toady, yes man **2** = **manservant**, attendant, flunky, footman, valet

lacklustre *adj* = **flat**, drab, dull, leaden, lifeless, muted, prosaic, uninspired, vapid

laconic *adj* = **terse**, brief, concise, curt, monosyllabic, pithy, short, succinct

lad *n* = **boy**, fellow, guy (*inf*), juvenile, kid

by horizontal steps used for climbing. **2**
line of stitches that have come undone in
tights or stockings. ♦ *v* **3** have or cause to
have such a line of undone stitches.

laden ❶ *adj* **1** loaded. **2** burdened.

ladle *n* **1** spoon with a long handle and a
large bowl, used for serving soup etc. ♦ *v*
2 serve out.

lady ❶ *n*, *pl* **–dies 1** woman regarded as
having characteristics of good breeding or
high rank. **2** polite term of address for a
woman. **3** (**L–**) title of some female
members of the nobility. **lady–in–waiting**
n, *pl* **ladies–in–waiting** female servant of a
queen or princess. **ladykiller** *n Informal*
man who is or thinks he is irresistible to
women. **ladylike** *adj* polite and dignified.

lag¹ ❶ *v* **lagging, lagged 1** go too slowly,
fall behind. ♦ *n* **2** delay between events.
laggard *n* person who lags behind.

lag² *v* **lagging, lagged** wrap (a boiler, pipes,
etc.) with insulating material. **lagging** *n*
insulating material.

lag³ *n* **old lag** *Slang* convict.

lager *n* light–bodied beer.

lagoon *n* body of water cut off from the
open sea by coral reefs or sand bars.

laid *v* past of LAY¹. **laid–back** *adj Informal*
relaxed.

lair ❶ *n* resting place of an animal.

laird *n* Scottish landowner.

laissez–faire ❶ [less–ay–**fair**] *n* principle
of nonintervention, esp. by a government
in commercial affairs.

laity [**lay**–it–ee] *n* people who are not
members of the clergy.

lake ❶ *n* expanse of water entirely
surrounded by land. **lakeside** *n*

lama *n* Buddhist priest in Tibet or
Mongolia.

lamb *n* **1** young sheep. **2** its meat. ♦ *v* **3** (of
sheep) give birth to a lamb or lambs.

lambast, lambaste *v* **1** beat or thrash. **2**
reprimand severely.

lame ❶ *adj* **1** having an injured or disabled
leg or foot. **2** (of an excuse) unconvincing.
♦ *v* **3** make lame. **lamely** *adv* **lameness** *n*
lame duck person or thing unable to cope
without help.

lamé [lah–**may**] *n*, *adj* (fabric) interwoven
with gold or silver thread.

lament ❶ *v* **1** feel or express sorrow (for).
♦ *n* **2** passionate expression of grief. **3**
lamentable *adj* very disappointing.
lamentation *n*

laminate *v* **1** make (a sheet of material) by
sticking together thin sheets. **2** cover with
a thin sheet of material. ♦ *n* **3** laminated
sheet.

lamington *n Aust & NZ* sponge cake
coated with a sweet frosting.

lamp *n* device which produces light from
electricity, oil, or gas. **lamppost** *n* post
supporting a lamp in the street.
lampshade *n*

lampoon ❶ *n* **1** humorous satire ridiculing
someone. ♦ *v* **2** satirize or ridicule.

lamprey *n* eel–like fish with a round

——— THESAURUS ———

(*inf*), youngster, youth

laden *adj* = **loaded**, burdened, charged,
encumbered, full, weighed down

lady *n* **1** = **gentlewoman**, dame
2 = **woman**, female

lag¹ *v* **1** = **hang back**, dawdle, delay, linger,
loiter, straggle, tarry, trail

lair *n* **1** = **nest**, burrow, den, earth, hole

laissez–faire *n* = **nonintervention**, free
enterprise, free trade

lake *n* = **pond**, lagoon, loch (*Scot*), lough
(*Irish*), mere, reservoir, tarn

lame *adj* **1** = **disabled**, crippled, game,

handicapped, hobbling, limping
2 = **unconvincing**, feeble, flimsy,
inadequate, pathetic, poor, thin,
unsatisfactory, weak

lament *v* **1** = **bemoan**, bewail, complain,
deplore, grieve, mourn, regret, sorrow,
wail, weep ♦ *n* **2** = **complaint**,
lamentation, moan, wailing **3** = **dirge**,
elegy, requiem, threnody

lampoon *n* **1** = **satire**, burlesque,
caricature, parody, send–up (*Brit inf*), skit,
takeoff (*inf*) ♦ *v* **2** = **ridicule**, caricature,
make fun of, mock, parody, satirize, send

sucking mouth.

lance *n* **1** long spear used by a mounted soldier. ◆ *v* **2** pierce (a boil or abscess) with a lancet. **lancer** *n* formerly, cavalry soldier armed with a lance. **lance corporal** noncommissioned army officer of the lowest rank.

land ⊕ *n* **1** solid part of the earth's surface. **2** ground, esp. with reference to its type or use. **3** rural or agricultural area. **4** property consisting of land. **5** country or region. ◆ *v* **6** come or bring to earth after a flight, jump, or fall. **7** go or take from a ship at the end of a voyage. **8** come to or touch shore. **9** come or bring to some point or condition. **10** *Informal* obtain. **11** take (a hooked fish) from the water. **12** *Informal* deliver (a punch). **landed** *adj* possessing or consisting of lands. **landward** *adj* **1** nearest to or facing the land. ◆ *adv* **2** (also **landwards**) towards land. **landfall** *n* ship's first landing after a voyage. **landlocked** *adj* entirely surrounded by land. **landlord** *n* person who rents out land, houses, etc. **landmark** *n* prominent object in or feature of a landscape. **landscape** *n* extensive piece of inland scenery seen from one place. **land up** *v* arrive at a final point or condition.

lane ⊕ *n* **1** narrow road. **2** area of road for one stream of traffic. **3** specified route followed by ships or aircraft. **4** strip of a running track or swimming pool for use by one competitor.

language ⊕ *n* **1** system of sounds, symbols, etc. for communicating thought. **2** particular system used by a nation or people. **3** system of words and symbols for computer programming.

languish ⊕ *v* **1** suffer neglect or hardship. **2** lose or diminish in strength or vigour. **3** pine (for).

lank ⊕ *adj* **1** (of hair) straight and limp. **2** thin or gaunt. **lanky** *adj* ungracefully tall and thin.

lantern *n* light in a transparent protective case.

lap¹ *n* part between the waist and knees of a person when sitting. **in the lap of luxury** in conditions of great comfort and wealth. **laptop** *adj* (of a computer) small enough to fit on a user's lap.

lap² ⊕ *n* **1** single circuit of a racecourse or track. **2** stage of a journey. ◆ *v* **lapping, lapped 3** overtake an opponent so as to be one or more circuits ahead.

lap³ ⊕ *v* **lapping, lapped** (of waves) beat softly against (a shore etc.). **lap up** *v* **1** drink by scooping up with the tongue. **2** accept (information or attention) eagerly.

lapel [lap–**pel**] *n* part of the front of a coat or jacket folded back towards the shoulders.

lapwing *n* plover with a tuft of feathers on the head.

larceny *n, pl* **–nies** *Law* theft.

larch *n* deciduous coniferous tree.

lard *n* **1** soft white fat obtained from a pig.

——————— THESAURUS ———————

up (*Brit inf*), take off (*inf*)

land *n* **1** = **ground**, dry land, earth, terra firma **2** = **soil**, dirt, ground, loam **3** = **countryside**, farmland **4** = **property**, estate, grounds, realty **5** = **country**, district, nation, province, region, territory, tract ◆ *v* **6** = **alight**, arrive, come to rest, touch down **7** = **disembark 8** = **dock 10** *Inf* = **obtain**, acquire, gain, get, secure, win

lane *n* **1** = **road**, alley, footpath, passageway, path, pathway, street, way

language *n* **1** = **speech**, communication,

discourse, expression, parlance, talk **2** = **tongue**, dialect, patois, vernacular

languish *v* **1** = **waste away**, be abandoned, be neglected, rot, suffer ≠ **thrive 2** = **decline**, droop, fade, fail, faint, flag, weaken, wilt, wither ≠ **thrive 3** = **pine**, desire, hanker, hunger, long, yearn

lank *adj* **1** = **limp**, lifeless, straggling **2** = **thin**, emaciated, gaunt, lean, scrawny, skinny, slender, slim, spare

lap² *n* **1** = **circuit**, circle, loop, orbit, tour

lap³ *v* = **ripple**, gurgle, plash, purl, splash,

◆ v 2 insert strips of bacon in (meat) before cooking. 3 decorate (speech or writing) with strange words unnecessarily.
larder n storeroom for food.
large ❶ adj great in size, number, or extent. **at large 1** in general. **2** free, not confined. **3** fully. **largely** adv **largish** adj **large–scale** adj wide–ranging or extensive.
largo n, pl **–gos**, adv Music (piece to be played) in a slow and dignified manner.
lark¹ n small brown songbird, skylark.
lark² ❶ n Informal **1** harmless piece of mischief or fun. **2** unnecessary activity or job. **lark about** v play pranks.
larrikin n Aust or NZ old–fashioned slang mischievous or unruly person.
larva n, pl **–vae** insect in an immature stage, often resembling a worm. **larval** adj
larynx n, pl **larynges** part of the throat containing the vocal cords. **laryngeal** adj **laryngitis** n inflammation of the larynx.
lasagne, lasagna [laz–**zan**–ya] n **1** pasta in wide flat sheets. **2** dish made from layers of lasagne, meat, and cheese.
lascivious [lass–**iv**–ee–uss] adj showing or producing sexual desire.
laser [**lay**–zer] n device that produces a very narrow intense beam of light, used for cutting very hard materials and in surgery etc.
lash¹ ❶ n **1** eyelash. **2** sharp blow with a whip. ◆ v **3** hit with a whip. **4** (of rain or

waves) beat forcefully against. **5** attack verbally, scold. **6** flick or wave sharply to and fro. **lash out** v **1** make a sudden physical or verbal attack. **2** Informal spend (money) extravagantly.
lash² ❶ v fasten or bind tightly with cord etc.
lashings pl n Old–fashioned large amounts.
lass ❶ lassie n girl.
lassitude n physical or mental weariness.
lasso [lass–**oo**] n, pl **–sos**, **–soes 1** rope with a noose for catching cattle and horses. ◆ v **–soing**, **–soed 2** catch with a lasso.
last¹ ❶ adj, adv **1** coming at the end or after all others. **2** most recent(ly). ◆ adj **3** only remaining. ◆ n **4** last person or thing. **lastly** adv **last–ditch** adj done as a final resort. **last post** army bugle–call played at sunset or funerals. **last straw** small irritation or setback that, coming after others, is too much to bear. **last word 1** final comment in an argument. **2** most recent or best example of something.
last² ❶ v **1** continue. **2** be sufficient for (a specified amount of time). **3** remain fresh, uninjured, or unaltered. **lasting** adj
last³ n model of a foot on which shoes and boots are made or repaired.
latch ❶ n **1** fastening for a door with a bar and lever. **2** lock which can only be opened from the outside with a key. ◆ v **3**

———— THESAURUS ————

swish, wash **lap up 1 = drink**, lick, sip, sup
large adj **1 = big**, considerable, enormous, gigantic, great, huge, immense, massive, monumental, sizable or sizeable, substantial, vast ≠ **little at large 1 = in general**, as a whole, chiefly, generally, in the main, mainly **2 = free**, at liberty, on the loose, on the run, unconfined **3 = fully**, at length, exhaustively, greatly, in full detail
lark² Inf n **1 = prank**, caper, escapade, fun, game, jape, mischief **lark about** ◆ v **= play**, caper, cavort, have fun, make mischief
lash¹ n **2 = blow**, hit, stripe, stroke, swipe

(inf) ◆ v **3 = whip**, beat, birch, flog, scourge, thrash **4 = pound**, beat, buffet, dash, drum, hammer, smack, strike **5 = censure**, attack, blast, criticize, put down, rouse on (Aust), scold, slate (inf, chiefly Brit), tear into (inf), upbraid
lash² v **= fasten**, bind, make fast, secure, strap, tie
lass, lassie n **= girl**, damsel, maid, maiden, young woman
last¹ adj **1 = final**, at the end, closing, concluding, hindmost, rearmost, terminal, ultimate ≠ **first 2 = most recent**, latest
last² v **1 = continue**, abide, carry on, endure, keep on, persist, remain

fasten with a latch. **latch onto** v become
attached to (a person or idea).

late ⊕ adj **1** after the normal or expected
time. **2** towards the end of a period. **3**
being at an advanced time. **4** recently
dead. **5** recent. **6** former. ◆ adv **7** after the
normal or expected time. **8** at a relatively
advanced age. **9** recently. **lately** adv in
recent times. **lateness** n **latish** adj, adv

latent ⊕ adj hidden and not yet
developed. **latency** n

lateral ⊕ [lat–ter–al] adj of or relating to
the side or sides.

latex n milky fluid found in some plants,
esp. the rubber tree, used in making
rubber.

lath n thin strip of wood used to support
plaster, tiles, etc.

lathe n machine for turning wood or metal
while it is being shaped.

lather ⊕ n **1** froth of soap and water. **2**
frothy sweat. **3** Informal state of agitation.
◆ v **4** make frothy. **5** rub with soap until
lather appears.

Latin n **1** language of the ancient Romans.
◆ adj **2** of or in Latin. **3** of a people whose
language derives from Latin. **Latin
America** parts of South and Central
America whose official language is Spanish
or Portuguese.

latitude ⊕ n **1** angular distance measured
in degrees N or S of the equator. **2** scope

for freedom of action or thought. ◆ pl **3**
regions considered in relation to their
distance from the equator.

latrine n toilet in a barracks or camp.

latter ⊕ adj **1** second of two. **2** later. **3**
recent. **latterly** adv **latter–day** adj modern.

✓ **WORD TIP**
Latter is used for the last mentioned of
two items. When there are more, use
last–named.

lattice ⊕ [lat–iss] n **1** framework of
intersecting strips of wood, metal, etc. **2**
gate, screen, etc. formed of such a
framework.

laud v praise or glorify. **laudable** adj
praiseworthy. **laudatory** adj praising or
glorifying.

laudanum [lawd–a–num] n opium–based
sedative.

laugh ⊕ v **1** make inarticulate sounds with
the voice expressing amusement,
merriment, or scorn. **2** utter or express
with laughter. ◆ n **3** act or instance of
laughing. **4** Informal person or thing
causing amusement. **laughable** adj
ridiculously inadequate. **laughter** n sound
or action of laughing. **laughing stock**
object of general derision. **laugh off** v treat
(something serious or difficult) lightly.

launch¹ ⊕ v **1** put (a ship or boat) into the

———— THESAURUS ————

3 = **survive**, stand up
latch n **1** = **fastening**, bar, bolt, catch,
hasp, hook, lock ◆ v **3** = **fasten**, bar, bolt,
make fast, secure
late adj **1** = **overdue**, behind, behindhand,
belated, delayed, last–minute, tardy
≠ **timely 4** = **dead**, deceased, defunct,
departed, former, past ≠ **existing**
5 = **recent**, advanced, fresh, modern, new
≠ **old** ◆ adv **7** = **belatedly**, at the last
minute, behindhand, behind time,
dilatorily, tardily ≠ **early**
latent adj = **hidden**, concealed, dormant,
invisible, potential, undeveloped,
unrealized

lateral adj = **sideways**, edgeways, flanking
lather n **1** = **froth**, bubbles, foam,
soapsuds, suds **3** Inf = **fluster**, dither, flap
(inf), fuss, state (inf), sweat, tizzy (inf) ◆ v
4 = **froth**, foam **5** = **soap**
latitude n **2** = **scope**, elbowroom,
freedom, laxity, leeway, liberty, licence,
play, space
latter adj **1** = **second 2** = **later**, closing,
concluding, last, last–mentioned ≠ **earlier**
lattice n = **grid**, grating, grille, trellis
laugh v **1** = **chuckle**, be in stitches, chortle,
giggle, guffaw, snigger, split one's sides,
titter ◆ n **3** = **chuckle**, chortle, giggle,
guffaw, snigger, titter **4** Inf a = **clown**,

water, esp. for the first time. **2** begin (a campaign, project, etc.). **3** put a new product on the market. **4** send (a missile or spacecraft) into space or the air. ♦ *n* **5** launching. **launch into** *v* start doing something enthusiastically.

launch² *n* open motorboat.

laureate [lor–ee–at] *adj* see POET LAUREATE.

laurel *n* **1** glossy–leaved shrub, bay tree. ♦ *pl* **2** wreath of laurel, an emblem of victory or merit.

lava *n* molten rock thrown out by volcanoes, which hardens as it cools.

lavatory ⊕ *n, pl* **–ries** toilet.

lavender *n* **1** shrub with fragrant flowers. ♦ *adj* **2** bluish–purple.

lavish ⊕ *adj* **1** great in quantity or richness. **2** giving or spending generously. **3** extravagant. ♦ *v* **4** give or spend generously.

law ⊕ *n* **1** rule binding on a community. **2** system of such rules. **3** *Informal* police. **4** invariable sequence of events in nature. **5** general principle deduced from facts. **lawful** *adj* allowed by law. **lawfully** *adv* **lawless** *adj* breaking the law, esp. in a violent way. **lawlessness** *n* **law–abiding** *adj* obeying the laws. **lawsuit** *n* court case brought by one person or group against another.

lawn *n* area of tended and mown grass. **lawn mower** machine for cutting grass.

lawn tennis tennis, esp. when played on a grass court.

lawyer ⊕ *n* professionally qualified legal expert.

lax ⊕ *adj* not strict. **laxity** *n*

lay¹ ⊕ *v* **laying, laid 1** cause to lie. **2** devise or prepare. **3** set in a particular place or position. **4** attribute (blame). **5** put forward (a plan, argument, etc.). **6** (of a bird or reptile) produce eggs. **7** place (a bet). **8** arrange (a table) for a meal. **lay waste** devastate. **lay–by** *n* stopping place for traffic beside a road. **1 lay off** *v* dismiss staff during a slack period. **lay–off** *n* **lay on** *v* provide or supply. **lay out** *v* **1** arrange or spread out. **2** prepare (a corpse) for burial. **3** *Informal* spend money, esp. lavishly. **4** *Informal* knock unconscious. **layout** *n* arrangement, esp. of matter for printing or of a building.

✓ **WORD TIP**

Lay and *lie* are often confused. *Lay* takes an object: *He laid down his weapon; lie* does not take an object: *I'm going to lie down.*

---

lay² ⊕ *v* past tense of LIE². **layabout** *n* lazy person.

lay³ ⊕ *adj* **1** of or involving people who are not clergymen. **2** nonspecialist. **layman** *n* **1** person who is not a member of the

---

card (*inf*), entertainer, hoot (*inf*), scream (*inf*) **b** = **joke**, hoot (*inf*), lark

launch¹ *v* **2** = **begin**, commence, embark upon, inaugurate, initiate, instigate, introduce, open, start **4** = **propel**, discharge, dispatch, fire, project, send off, set in motion

lavatory *n* = **toilet**, bathroom, cloakroom (*Brit*), latrine, loo (*Brit inf*), powder room, privy, (public) convenience, washroom, water closet, W.C.

lavish *adj* **1** = **plentiful**, abundant, copious, profuse, prolific ≠ **meagre 2** = **generous**, bountiful, free, liberal, munificent, open–handed, unstinting ≠ **stingy**

3 = **extravagant**, exaggerated, excessive, immoderate, prodigal, unrestrained, wasteful, wild ≠ **sparing** ♦ *v* **4** = **spend**, deluge, dissipate, expend, heap, pour, shower, squander, waste ≠ **withhold**

law *n* **1** = **rule**, act, command, commandment, decree, edict, order, ordinance, regulation, statute
2 = **constitution**, charter, code
5 = **principle**, axiom, canon, precept

lawyer *n* = **legal adviser**, advocate, attorney, barrister, counsel, counsellor, solicitor

lax *adj* = **slack**, careless, casual, lenient, negligent, overindulgent, remiss, slapdash, clergy. 2 person without specialist knowledge.

lay⁴ **⊕** n short narrative poem designed to be sung.

layette n clothes for a newborn baby.

lazy **⊕** adj **lazier, laziest 1** not inclined to work or exert oneself. **2** done in a relaxed manner without much effort. **3** (of movement) slow and gentle. **lazily** adv **laziness** n **lazybones** n Informal lazy person.

lbw Cricket leg before wicket.

lead¹ **⊕** v **leading, led 1** guide or conduct. **2** cause to feel, think, or behave in a certain way. **3** be the most important person or thing in. **4** be, go, or play first. **5** (of a road, path, etc.) go towards. **6** control or direct. **7** (foll. by to) result in. **8** pass or spend (one's life). ◆ n **9** first or most prominent place. **10** example or leadership. **11** amount by which a person or group is ahead of another. **12** clue. **13** length of leather or chain attached to a dog's collar to control it. **14** principal role or actor in a film, play, etc. **15** cable bringing current to an electrical device. ◆ adj **16** acting as a leader or lead. **leader** n person who leads. **leading** adj **1** principal. **2** in the first position. **leading question** question worded to prompt the answer desired. **lead–in** n introduction to a subject.

lead² n **1** soft heavy grey metal. **2** (in a pencil) graphite. **leaded** adj (of windows) made from many small panes of glass held together by lead strips. **leaden** adj **1** heavy or sluggish. **2** dull grey. **3** made from lead.

leaf **⊕** n, pl **leaves 1** flat usu. green blade attached to the stem of a plant. **2** single sheet of paper in a book. **3** very thin sheet of metal. **4** extending flap on a table. **leafy** adj **leafless** adj **leaf through** v turn pages without reading them.

league¹ **⊕** n **1** association promoting the interests of its members. **2** association of sports clubs organizing competitions between its members. **3** Informal class or level.

league² n Obs measure of distance, about three miles.

slipshod ≠ severe

lay¹ v **1, 3 = place**, deposit, leave, plant, position, put, set, set down, spread **2 = devise**, concoct, contrive, design, hatch, plan, plot, prepare, work out **4 = attribute**, allocate, allot, ascribe, assign, impute **5 = put forward**, advance, bring forward, lodge, offer, present, submit **6 = produce**, bear, deposit **7 = bet**, gamble, give odds, hazard, risk, stake, wager **8 = arrange**, organize, set out

lay³ adj **1 = nonclerical**, secular **2 = nonspecialist**, amateur, inexpert, nonprofessional

lay⁴ n = **poem**, ballad, lyric, ode, song

lazy adj **1 = idle**, inactive, indolent, inert, slack, slothful, slow, workshy ≠ active **3 = lethargic**, drowsy, languid, languorous, sleepy, slow–moving, sluggish, somnolent, torpid ≠ quick

lead¹ v **1 = guide**, conduct, escort, pilot, precede, show the way, steer, usher

2 = cause, dispose, draw, incline, induce, influence, persuade, prevail, prompt **3 = command**, direct, govern, head, manage, preside over, supervise **4 = be ahead (of)**, blaze a trail, come first, exceed, excel, outdo, outstrip, surpass, transcend **7** (foll. by to) **= result in**, bring on, cause, contribute to, produce **8 = live**, experience, have, pass, spend, undergo ◆ n **9 = first place**, precedence, primacy, priority, supremacy, vanguard **10 = example**, direction, guidance, leadership, model **11 = advantage**, edge, margin, start **12 = clue**, hint, indication, suggestion **14 = leading role**, principal, protagonist, title role ◆ adj **16 = main**, chief, first, foremost, head, leading, premier, primary, prime, principal

leaf n **1 = frond**, blade **2 = page**, folio, sheet **leaf through** ◆ v = **skim**, browse, flip, glance, riffle, thumb (through)

league¹ n **1 = association**, alliance,

leak ❶ *n* **1** hole or defect that allows the escape or entrance of liquid, gas, radiation, etc. **2** liquid etc. that escapes or enters. **3** disclosure of secrets. ♦ *v* **4** let liquid etc. in or out. **5** (of liquid etc.) find its way through a leak. **6** disclose secret information. **leakage** *n* act or instance of leaking. **leaky** *adj*

lean¹ ❶ *v* **leaning, leaned** *or* **leant 1** rest against. **2** bend or slope from an upright position. **3** tend (towards). **leaning** *n* tendency. **lean on** *v* **1** *Informal* threaten or intimidate. **2** depend on for help or advice. **lean–to** *n* shed built against an existing wall.

lean² ❶ *adj* **1** thin but healthy–looking. **2** (of meat) lacking fat. **3** unproductive. ♦ *n* **4** lean part of meat. **leanness** *n*

leap ❶ *v* **leaping, leapt** *or* **leaped 1** make a sudden powerful jump. ♦ *n* **2** sudden powerful jump. **3** abrupt increase, as in costs or prices. **leapfrog** *n* game in which a player vaults over another bending down. **leap year** year with February 29th as an extra day.

learn ❶ *v* **learning, learned** *or* **learnt 1** gain skill or knowledge by study, practice, or teaching. **2** memorize (something). **3** find out or discover. **learned** *adj* **1** erudite, deeply read. **2** showing much learning. **learner** *n* **learning** *n* knowledge got by study.

lease ❶ *n* **1** contract by which land or property is rented for a stated time by the owner to a tenant. ♦ *v* **2** let or rent by lease. **leasehold** *n, adj* (land or property) held on lease. **leaseholder** *n*

leash ❶ *n* lead for a dog.

least ❶ *adj* **1** superlative of LITTLE. **2** smallest. ♦ *n* **3** smallest one. ♦ *adv* **4** in the smallest degree.

leather *n* **1** material made from specially treated animal skins. ♦ *adj* **2** made of leather. ♦ *v* **3** beat or thrash. **leathery** *adj* like leather, tough.

leave¹ ❶ *v* **leaving, left 1** go away from. **2** allow to remain, accidentally or deliberately. **3** cause to be or remain in a specified state. **4** discontinue membership of. **5** permit. **6** entrust. **7** bequeath. **leave out** *v* exclude or omit.

leave² ❶ *n* **1** permission to be absent from work or duty. **2** period of such absence. **3** permission to do something. **4** formal parting.

leaven [lev–ven] *n* **1** substance that causes

═════════ THESAURUS ═════════

coalition, confederation, consortium, federation, fraternity, group, guild, partnership, union **3** *Inf* = **class**, category, level

leak *n* **1** = **hole**, aperture, chink, crack, crevice, fissure, opening, puncture **2** = **leakage**, drip, percolation, seepage **3** = **disclosure**, divulgence ♦ *v* **5** = **escape**, drip, exude, ooze, pass, percolate, seep, spill, trickle **6** = **disclose**, divulge, give away, let slip, make known, make public, pass on, reveal, tell

lean¹ *v* **1** = **rest**, be supported, prop, recline, repose **2** = **bend**, heel, incline, slant, slope, tilt, tip **3** = **tend**, be disposed to, be prone to, favour, prefer **lean on 2** = **depend on**, count on, have faith in, rely on, trust

lean² *adj* **1** = **trim**, angular, bony, rangy,

skinny, slender, slim, spare, thin, wiry ≠ **fat 3** = **poor**, barren, meagre, scanty, unfruitful, unproductive ≠ **rich**

leap *v* **1** = **jump**, bounce, bound, hop, skip, spring ♦ *n* **2** = **jump**, bound, spring, vault **3** = **rise**, change, escalation, increase, surge, upsurge, upswing

learn *v* **1** = **master**, grasp, pick up **2** = **memorize**, commit to memory, get off pat, learn by heart **3** = **discover**, ascertain, detect, discern, find out, gather, hear, understand

lease *v* **2** = **hire**, charter, let, loan, rent

leash *n* = **lead**, rein, tether

least *adj* **1, 2** = **smallest**, fewest, lowest, meanest, minimum, poorest, slightest, tiniest

leave¹ *v* **1** = **depart**, decamp, disappear, exit, go, go away, make tracks, move, pull dough to rise. 2 influence that produces a gradual change. ◆ v 3 raise with leaven. 4 spread through and influence (something).

lecherous ⊕ [letch–er–uss] adj (of a man) having or showing excessive sexual desire. **lecher** n **lechery** n

lectern n sloping reading desk, esp. in a church.

lecture ⊕ n 1 informative talk to an audience on a subject. 2 lengthy rebuke or scolding. ◆ v 3 give a talk. 4 scold. **lecturer** n **lectureship** n appointment as a lecturer.

ledge ⊕ n 1 narrow shelf sticking out from a wall. 2 shelflike projection from a cliff etc.

ledger n book of debit and credit accounts of a firm.

lee n sheltered part or side. **leeward** adj, n 1 (on) the lee side. ◆ adv 2 towards this side. **leeway** n room for free movement within limits.

leech n 1 species of bloodsucking worm. 2 person who lives off others.

leek n vegetable of the onion family with a long bulb and thick stem.

leer ⊕ v 1 look or grin at in a sneering or suggestive manner. ◆ n 2 sneering or suggestive look or grin.

lees ⊕ pl n sediment of wine.

left¹ ⊕ adj 1 of the side that faces west when the front faces north. ◆ adv 2 on or towards the left. ◆ n 3 left hand or part. 4 *Politics* people supporting socialism rather than capitalism. **leftist** n, adj (person) of the political left. **left–handed** adj more adept with the left hand than with the right. **left–wing** adj 1 socialist. 2 belonging to the more radical part of a political party.

left² v past of LEAVE¹.

leg ⊕ n 1 one of the limbs on which a person or animal walks, runs, or stands. 2 part of a garment covering the leg. 3 structure that supports, such as one of the legs of a table. 4 stage of a journey. 5 *Sport* (part of) one game or race in a series. **pull someone's leg** tease someone. **leggy** adj having long legs. **legless** adj 1 without legs. 2 *Slang* very drunk. **leggings** pl n 1 covering of leather or other material for the legs. 2 close–fitting trousers for women or children.

——————— THESAURUS ———————

out, quit, retire, slope off, withdraw ≠ **come** 2 = **forget**, leave behind, mislay 3 = **cause**, deposit, generate, produce, result in 4 = **give up**, abandon, drop, relinquish, renounce, surrender ≠ **continue with** 6 = **entrust**, allot, assign, cede, commit, consign, give over, refer 7 = **bequeath**, hand down, will

leave² n 1, 2 = **holiday**, furlough, leave of absence, sabbatical, time off, vacation 3 = **permission**, allowance, authorization, concession, consent, dispensation, freedom, liberty, sanction ≠ **refusal** 4 = **departure**, adieu, farewell, goodbye, leave–taking, parting, retirement, withdrawal ≠ **arrival**

lecherous adj = **lustful**, lascivious, lewd, libidinous, licentious, prurient, randy (inf, chiefly Brit), salacious

lecture n 1 = **talk**, address, discourse,

instruction, lesson, speech 2 = **telling off** (inf), dressing–down (inf), rebuke, reprimand, reproof, scolding, talking–to (inf) ◆ v 3 = **talk**, address, discourse, expound, hold forth, speak, spout, teach 4 = **tell off** (inf), admonish, berate, castigate, censure, reprimand, reprove, rouse on (Aust), scold

ledge n 1 = **shelf**, mantle, projection, sill 2 = **ridge**, step

leer n, v = **grin**, gloat, goggle, ogle, smirk, squint, stare

lees pl n = **sediment**, deposit, dregs, grounds

left¹ adj 1 = **left–hand**, larboard (Naut), port

leg n 1 = **limb**, lower limb, member, pin (inf), stump (inf) 3 = **support**, brace, prop, upright 4 = **stage**, lap, part, portion, section, segment, stretch **pull someone's leg** = **tease**, fool, kid (inf), make fun of,

legacy ❶ n, pl –cies 1 thing left in a will. 2 thing handed down to a successor.

legal ❶ adj 1 established or permitted by law. 2 relating to law or lawyers. **legally** adv **legality** n **legalize** v make legal. **legalization** n

legate n messenger or representative, esp. from the Pope. **legation** n 1 diplomatic minister and his staff. 2 official residence of a diplomatic minister.

legatee n recipient of a legacy.

legato [leg–ah–toe] n, pl –tos, adv Music (piece to be played) smoothly.

legend ❶ n 1 traditional story or myth. 2 traditional literature. 3 famous person or event. 4 stories about such a person or event. 5 inscription. **legendary** adj 1 famous. 2 of or in legend.

legible ❶ adj easily read. **legibility** n **legibly** adv

legion ❶ n 1 large military force. 2 large number. 3 association of veterans. 4 infantry unit in the Roman army. **legionary** adj, n **legionnaire** n member of a legion. **legionnaire's disease** serious bacterial disease similar to pneumonia.

legislate v make laws. **legislation** n 1 legislating. 2 laws made. **legislative** adj **legislator** n maker of laws. **legislature** n body of people that makes, amends, or repeals laws.

legitimate ❶ adj 1 authorized by or in accordance with law. 2 fairly deduced. 3 born to parents married to each other. ♦ v 4 make legitimate. **legitimacy** n **legitimately** adv **legitimize** v make legitimate, legalize. **legitimization** n

legume n 1 pod of a plant of the pea or bean family. ♦ pl 2 peas or beans. **leguminous** adj (of plants) pod–bearing.

leisure ❶ n time for relaxation or hobbies. **at one's leisure** when one has time. **leisurely** adj 1 deliberate, unhurried. ♦ adv 2 slowly.

lekker adj S Afr slang 1 attractive or nice. 2 tasty.

lemming n rodent of arctic regions, reputed to run into the sea and drown during mass migrations.

lemon n 1 yellow oval fruit that grows on trees. 2 Slang useless or defective person or thing. ♦ adj 3 pale–yellow. **lemonade** n lemon–flavoured soft drink, often fizzy. **lemon curd** creamy spread made of lemons, butter, etc.

lemur n nocturnal animal like a small monkey, found in Madagascar.

length ❶ n 1 extent or measurement from end to end. 2 period of time for which something happens. 3 quality of being long. 4 piece of something narrow and long. **at length** 1 at last. 2 in full detail. **lengthy** adj very long or tiresome. **lengthily** adv **lengthen** v make or become longer. **lengthways, lengthwise** adj, adv

lenient ❶ [lee–nee–ent] adj tolerant, not

THESAURUS

---

trick, wind up (Brit sl)

legacy n = **bequest**, estate, gift, heirloom, inheritance

legal adj 1 = **lawful**, allowed, authorized, constitutional, legitimate, licit, permissible, sanctioned, valid 2 = **judicial**, forensic, judiciary, juridical

legend n 1 = **myth**, fable, fiction, folk tale, saga, story, tale 3 = **celebrity**, luminary, megastar (inf), phenomenon, prodigy 5 = **inscription**, caption, motto

legible adj = **readable**, clear, decipherable, distinct, easy to read, neat

legion n 1 = **army**, brigade, company, division, force, troop 2 = **multitude**, drove, horde, host, mass, myriad, number, throng

legitimate adj 1 = **lawful**, authentic, authorized, genuine, kosher (inf), legal, licit, rightful ≠ **illegal** 2 = **reasonable**, admissible, correct, justifiable, logical, sensible, valid, warranted, well–founded ≠ **unfair** ♦ v 4 = **legitimize**, authorize, legalize, permit, pronounce lawful, sanction

leisure n = **spare time**, ease, freedom, free time, liberty, recreation, relaxation, rest

length n 1 = **distance**, extent, longitude,

strict or severe. **leniency** n

lens n, pl **lenses 1** piece of glass or similar material with one or both sides curved, used to bring together or spread light rays in cameras, spectacles, telescopes, etc. **2** transparent structure in the eye that focuses light.

lent v past of LEND.

Lent n period from Ash Wednesday to Easter Saturday.

lentil n edible seed of a leguminous Asian plant.

leopard n large spotted carnivorous animal of the cat family.

leotard n tight–fitting garment covering most of the body, worn for dancing or exercise.

leper n **1** person suffering from leprosy. **2** ignored or despised person.

leprechaun n mischievous elf of Irish folklore.

lesbian ⊕ n **1** homosexual woman. ♦ adj **2** of homosexual women. **lesbianism** n

lesion n **1** structural change in an organ of the body caused by illness or injury. **2** injury or wound.

less ⊕ adj **1** smaller in extent, degree, or duration. **2** not so much. **3** comparative of LITTLE. ♦ pron **4** smaller part or quantity. ♦ adv **5** to a smaller extent or degree. ♦ prep **6** after deducting, minus. **lessen** v make or become smaller or not as much. **lesser** adj not as great in quantity, size, or worth.

✓ **WORD TIP**

Avoid confusion with *few(er)*. *Less* is used with amounts that cannot be counted: *less time; less fuss*. *Few(er)* is used of things that can be counted.

---

lesson ⊕ n **1** single period of instruction in a subject. **2** content of this. **3** experience that teaches. **4** portion of Scripture read in church.

lest conj **1** so as to prevent any possibility that. **2** for fear that.

let¹ ⊕ v **letting, let 1** allow, enable, or cause. **2** used as an auxiliary to express a proposal, command, threat, or assumption. **3** grant use of for rent, lease. **4** allow to escape. **let alone** not to mention. **let down** v **1** disappoint. **2** lower. **3** deflate. **letdown** n disappointment. **let off** v **1** excuse from (a duty or punishment). **2** fire or explode (a weapon). **3** emit (gas, steam, etc.). **let on** v Informal reveal (a secret). **let out** v **1** emit. **2** release. **let up** v diminish or stop. **let–up** n lessening.

let² n **1** Tennis minor infringement or obstruction of the ball requiring a replay of the point. **2** hindrance.

lethal ⊕ adj deadly.

lethargy ⊕ n **1** sluggishness or dullness. **2** abnormal lack of energy. **lethargic** adj **lethargically** adv

---

─────────── THESAURUS ───────────

measure, reach, span **2 = duration**, period, space, span, stretch, term **4 = piece**, measure, portion, section, segment **at length 1 = at last**, at long last, eventually, finally, in the end **2 = in detail**, completely, fully, in depth, thoroughly, to the full

lenient adj **= merciful**, compassionate, forbearing, forgiving, indulgent, kind, sparing, tolerant

lesbian adj **2 = homosexual**, gay

less adj **1 = smaller**, shorter ♦ prep **6 = minus**, excepting, lacking, subtracting, without

lesson n **1 = class**, coaching, instruction, period, schooling, teaching, tutoring **3 = example**, deterrent, message, moral

let¹ v **1 = allow**, authorize, entitle, give permission, give the go–ahead, permit, sanction, tolerate **3 = lease**, hire, rent

let² n **2 = hindrance**, constraint, impediment, interference, obstacle, obstruction, prohibition, restriction

lethal adj **= deadly**, dangerous, destructive, devastating, fatal, mortal, murderous, virulent

lethargy n **= sluggishness**, apathy, drowsiness, inertia, languor, lassitude,

letter ❶ n 1 written message, usu. sent by post. 2 alphabetical symbol. 3 strict meaning (of a law etc.). ◆ pl 4 literary knowledge or ability. **lettered** adj learned. **lettering** n **letter box** 1 slot in a door through which letters are delivered. 2 box in a street or post office where letters are posted. **letterhead** n printed heading on stationery giving the sender's name and address.

lettuce n plant with large green leaves used in salads.

leukaemia [loo-**kee**-mee-a] n disease caused by uncontrolled overproduction of white blood cells.

level ❶ adj 1 horizontal. 2 having an even surface. 3 of the same height as something else. 4 equal to or even with (someone or something else). 5 not going above the top edge of (a spoon etc.). ◆ v -elling, -elled 6 make even or horizontal. 7 make equal in position or status. 8 direct (a gun, accusation, etc.) at. 9 raze to the ground. ◆ n 10 horizontal line or surface. 11 device for showing or testing if something is horizontal. 12 position on a scale. 13 standard or grade. 14 flat area of land. **on the level** Informal honest or trustworthy. **level crossing** point where a railway line and road cross. **level-headed** adj not apt to be carried away by emotion.

lever ❶ n 1 handle used to operate machinery. 2 bar used to move a heavy object or to open something. 3 rigid bar pivoted about a fulcrum to transfer a force to a load. 4 means of exerting pressure to achieve an aim. ◆ v 5 prise or move with a lever. **leverage** n 1 action or power of a lever. 2 influence or strategic advantage.

leveret [**lev**-ver-it] n young hare.

leviathan [lev-**vie**-ath-an] n 1 sea monster. 2 anything huge or formidable.

levitation n raising of a solid body into the air supernaturally. **levitate** v rise or cause to rise into the air.

levity ❶ n, pl -ties inclination to make a joke of serious matters.

levy ❶ [**lev**-vee] v **levying, levied** 1 impose and collect (a tax). 2 raise (troops). ◆ n, pl **levies** 3 imposition or collection of taxes. 4 money levied.

lewd ❶ adj lustful or indecent.

lexicon n 1 dictionary. 2 vocabulary of a language. **lexical** adj relating to the vocabulary of a language. **lexicographer** n writer of dictionaries. **lexicography** n

liable ❶ adj 1 legally obliged or responsible. 2 given to or at risk from a condition. **liability** n 1 hindrance or disadvantage. 2 state of being liable. 3 financial obligation.

——————| THESAURUS |——————

listlessness, sleepiness, sloth

letter n 1 = **message**, communication, dispatch, epistle, line, missive, note 2 = **character**, sign, symbol

level adj 1 = **horizontal**, flat ≠ uneven 2 = **even**, consistent, plain, smooth, uniform 4 = **equal**, balanced, commensurate, comparable, equivalent, even, neck and neck, on a par, proportionate ◆ v 6 = **flatten**, even off or out, plane, smooth 7 = **equalize**, balance, even up 8 = **direct**, aim, focus, point, train 9 = **destroy**, bulldoze, demolish, devastate, flatten, knock down, pull down, raze, tear down ≠ build ◆ n 13 = **position**, achievement, degree, grade, rank, stage, standard, standing, status **on the level** Inf = **honest**, above board, fair, genuine, square, straight

lever n 1, 2 = **handle**, bar ◆ v 5 = **prise**, force

levity n = **light-heartedness**, facetiousness, flippancy, frivolity, silliness, skittishness, triviality

levy v 1 = **impose**, charge, collect, demand, exact 2 = **conscript**, call up, mobilize, muster, raise ◆ n 3 = **imposition**, assessment, collection, exaction, gathering 4 = **tax**, duty, excise, fee, tariff, toll

lewd adj = **indecent**, bawdy, lascivious, libidinous, licentious, lustful, obscene, pornographic, smutty, wanton

✓ **WORD TIP**

The use of *liable* to mean 'likely' is informal. It generally means 'responsible for': *He was liable for any damage.*

liar ❶ *n* person who tells lies.

lib *n Informal* short for LIBERATION.

libel ❶ *n* 1 published statement falsely damaging a person's reputation. ♦ *v* **–belling, –belled** 2 falsely damage the reputation of (someone). **libellous** *adj*

liberal ❶ *adj* 1 having social and political views that favour progress and reform. 2 generous in behaviour or temperament. 3 tolerant. 4 abundant. 5 (of education) designed to develop general cultural interests. ♦ *n* 6 person who has liberal ideas or opinions. **liberally** *adv* **liberalism** *n* belief in democratic reforms and individual freedom. **liberality** *n* generosity. **liberalize** *v* make (laws, a country, etc.) less restrictive. **liberalization** *n*

liberate ❶ *v* set free. **liberation** *n* **liberator** *n*

libertine ❶ [lib–er–teen] *n* morally dissolute person.

liberty ❶ *n, pl* **–ties** 1 freedom. 2 act or comment regarded as forward or socially unacceptable. **at liberty** 1 free. 2 having the right. **take liberties** be presumptuous.

libido [lib–**ee**–doe] *n, pl* **–dos** 1 psychic energy. 2 emotional drive, esp. of sexual origin. **libidinous** *adj* lustful.

library *n, pl* **–braries** 1 room or building where books are kept. 2 collection of books, records, etc. for consultation or borrowing. **librarian** *n* keeper of or worker in a library. **librarianship** *n*

libretto *n, pl* **–tos, –ti** words of an opera. **librettist** *n*

lice *n* a plural of LOUSE.

licence ❶ *n* 1 document giving official permission to do something. 2 formal permission. 3 disregard of conventions for effect, e.g. *poetic licence.* 4 excessive liberty. **license** *v* grant a licence to. **licensed** *adj* **licensee** *n* holder of a licence, esp. to sell alcohol.

✓ **WORD TIP**

Note the *–ce* ending for the noun *licence*, with *–se* for the verb *license*.

licentious ❶ *adj* sexually unrestrained or promiscuous.

lichen *n* small flowerless plant forming a

──── THESAURUS ────

liable *adj* 1 = **responsible**, accountable, answerable, obligated 2 = **vulnerable**, exposed, open, subject, susceptible

liar *n* = **falsifier**, fabricator, fibber, perjurer

libel *n* 1 = **defamation**, aspersion, calumny, denigration, smear ♦ *v* 2 = **defame**, blacken, malign, revile, slur, smear, vilify

liberal *adj* 1 = **progressive**, libertarian, radical, reformist ≠ **conservative** 2 = **generous**, beneficent, bountiful, charitable, kind, open–handed, open–hearted, unstinting ≠ **stingy** 3 = **tolerant**, broad–minded, indulgent, permissive ≠ **intolerant** 4 = **abundant**, ample, bountiful, copious, handsome, lavish, munificent, plentiful, profuse, rich ≠ **small**

liberate *v* = **free**, deliver, emancipate, let loose, let out, release, rescue, set free

libertine *n* = **reprobate**, debauchee, lecher, profligate, rake, roué, sensualist, voluptuary, womanizer

liberty *n* 1 = **freedom**, autonomy, emancipation, immunity, independence, liberation, release, self–determination, sovereignty ≠ **restraint** 2 = **impertinence**, impropriety, impudence, insolence, presumption **at liberty** 1 = **free**, on the loose 2 = **unrestricted**

licence *n* 1 = **certificate**, charter, permit, warrant 2 = **permission**, authority, authorization, blank cheque, carte blanche, dispensation, entitlement, exemption, immunity, leave, liberty, right ≠ **restriction** 3 = **freedom**, independence, latitude, leeway, liberty ≠ **restraint** 4 = **laxity**, excess, immoderation, crust on rocks, trees, etc.

licit *adj* lawful, permitted.

lick ❶ *v* 1 pass the tongue over. 2 touch lightly or flicker round. 3 *Slang* defeat. ◆ *n* 4 licking. 5 small amount (of paint etc.). 6 *Informal* fast pace.

licorice *n* same as LIQUORICE.

lid *n* 1 movable cover. 2 short for EYELID.

lido [**lee**–doe] *n, pl* –dos open-air centre for swimming and water sports.

lie¹ ❶ *v* lying, lied 1 make a deliberately false statement. ◆ *n* 2 deliberate falsehood. white lie see WHITE.

lie² ❶ *v* lying, lay, lain 1 place oneself or be in a horizontal position. 2 be situated. 3 be or remain in a certain state or position. 4 exist or be found. ◆ *n* 5 way something lies. lie-down *n* rest. lie in *v* remain in bed late into the morning. lie-in *n* long stay in bed in the morning.

> ### ✓ WORD TIP
> Note that the past of *lie* is *lay*: *She lay on the beach all day.* Do not confuse with the main verb *lay* meaning 'put'.

lieu [**lyew**] *n* in lieu of instead of.

lieutenant [lef–**ten**–ant] *n* 1 junior officer in the army or navy. 2 main assistant.

life ❶ *n, pl* lives 1 state of living beings, characterized by growth, reproduction, and response to stimuli. 2 period between birth and death or between birth and the present time. 3 way of living. 4 amount of time something is active or functions. 5 biography. 6 liveliness or high spirits. 7 living beings collectively. **lifeless** *adj* 1 dead. 2 not lively or exciting. 3 unconscious. **lifelike** *adj* **lifelong** *adj* lasting all of a person's life. **life belt, jacket** buoyant device to keep afloat a person in danger of drowning. 1 **lifeboat** *n* boat used for rescuing people at sea. **life cycle** series of changes undergone by each generation of an animal or plant. **lifeline** *n* 1 means of contact or support. 2 rope used in rescuing a person in danger. **life science** any science concerned with living organisms, such as biology, botany, or zoology. **lifestyle** *n* particular attitudes, habits, etc. **life-support** *adj* (of equipment or treatment) necessary to keep a person alive. **lifetime** *n* length of time a person is alive.

lift ❶ *v* 1 move upwards in position, status, volume, etc. 2 revoke or cancel. 3 take (plants) out of the ground for harvesting. 4 disappear. 5 make or become more cheerful. ◆ *n* 6 cage raised and lowered in a vertical shaft to transport people or goods. 7 ride in a car etc. as a passenger. 8 *Informal* feeling of cheerfulness. 9 lifting. **liftoff** *n* moment a rocket leaves the ground.

———————— THESAURUS ————————

indulgence, irresponsibility ≠ **moderation**

licentious *adj* = **promiscuous**, abandoned, debauched, dissolute, immoral, lascivious, lustful, sensual, wanton

lick *v* 1 = **taste**, lap, tongue 2 = **flicker**, dart, flick, play over, ripple, touch 3 *Sl* = **beat**, defeat, master, outdo, outstrip, overcome, rout, trounce, vanquish ◆ *n* 5 = **dab**, bit, stroke, touch 6 *Inf* = **pace**, clip (inf), rate, speed

lie¹ *v* 1 = **fib**, dissimulate, equivocate, fabricate, falsify, prevaricate, tell untruths ◆ *n* 3 = **falsehood**, deceit, fabrication, fib, fiction, invention, prevarication, untruth

lie² *v* 1 = **recline**, loll, lounge, repose, rest, sprawl, stretch out 2 = **be situated**, be, be placed, exist 3 = **be**, remain 4 = **exist**

life *n* 1 = **being**, sentience, vitality 2 = **existence**, being, lifetime, span, time 3 = **behaviour**, conduct, life style, way of life 5 = **biography**, autobiography, confessions, history, life story, memoirs, story 6 = **liveliness**, animation, energy, high spirits, spirit, verve, vigour, vitality, vivacity, zest

lift *v* 1 = **raise**, draw up, elevate, hoist, pick up, uplift, upraise ≠ **drop** 2 = **revoke**, annul, cancel, countermand, end, remove, rescind, stop, terminate ≠ **establish** 4 = **disappear**, be dispelled, disperse,

ligament n band of tissue joining bones.

light¹ ❶ n 1 electromagnetic radiation by which things are visible. 2 source of this, lamp. 3 anything that lets in light, such as a window. 4 aspect or view. 5 mental vision. 6 means of setting fire to. ◆ pl 7 traffic lights. ◆ adj 8 bright. 9 (of a colour) pale. ◆ v **lighting, lighted** or **lit** 10 ignite. 11 illuminate or cause to illuminate. **lighten** v make less dark. **lighting** n apparatus for and use of artificial light in theatres, films, etc. **light bulb** glass part of an electric lamp. **lighthouse** n tower with a light to guide ships. **1 light year** Astronomy distance light travels in one year, about six million million miles.

light² ❶ adj 1 not heavy, weighing relatively little. 2 relatively low in strength, amount, density, etc. 3 not clumsy. 4 not serious or profound. 5 easily digested. ◆ adv 6 with little equipment or luggage. ◆ v **lighting, lighted, lit** 7 (esp. of birds) settle after flight. 8 come (upon) by chance. **lightly** adv **lightness** n **lighten** v 1 make less heavy or burdensome. 2 make more cheerful or lively. **light-fingered** adj skilful

at stealing. **light-headed** adj feeling faint, dizzy. **light-hearted** adj carefree.

lightweight n, adj 1 (person) of little importance. ◆ n 2 boxer weighing not more than 135lb (professional) or 60kg (amateur).

lighter n device for lighting cigarettes etc.

like¹ ❶ prep, conj, adj, pron indicating similarity, comparison, etc. **liken** v compare. **likeness** n 1 resemblance. 2 portrait. **likewise** adv similarly.

like² ❶ v 1 find enjoyable. 2 be fond of. 3 prefer, choose, or wish. **likeable, likable** adj **likely** adj probable. **liking** n 1 fondness. 2 preference.

lilac n 1 shrub with pale mauve or white flowers. ◆ adj 2 light-purple.

lilt n 1 pleasing musical quality in speaking. 2 jaunty rhythm. 3 graceful rhythmic motion. **lilting** adj

lily n, pl **lilies** plant which grows from a bulb and has large, often white, flowers.

limb ❶ n 1 arm, leg, or wing. 2 main branch of a tree.

limber adj pliant or supple. **limber up** v loosen stiff muscles by exercising.

limbo¹ n **in limbo** not knowing the result

—————| THESAURUS |—————

dissipate, vanish ◆ n 6 = **elevator** (chiefly US) 7 = **ride**, drive, run 8 Inf = **boost**, encouragement, fillip, gee–up, pick–me–up, shot in the arm (inf) ≠ **blow**

light¹ n 1 = **brightness**, brilliance, glare, gleam, glint, glow, illumination, luminosity, radiance, shine ≠ **dark** 2 = **lamp**, beacon, candle, flare, lantern, taper, torch 4 = **aspect**, angle, context, interpretation, point of view, slant, vantage point, viewpoint 6 = **match**, flame, lighter ◆ adj 8 = **bright**, brilliant, illuminated, luminous, lustrous, shining, well–lit ≠ **dark** 9 = **pale**, bleached, blond, blonde, faded, fair, pastel ≠ **deep** ◆ v 10 = **ignite**, inflame, kindle ≠ **put out** 11 = **illuminate**, brighten, illuminate, irradiate, light up ≠ **cloud**

light² adj 1 = **insubstantial**, airy, buoyant, flimsy, portable, slight ≠ **heavy** 2 = **weak**, faint, gentle, indistinct, mild, moderate,

slight, soft ≠ **strong** 3 = **nimble**, agile, graceful, lithe, sprightly, sylphlike ≠ **clumsy** 4 = **insignificant**, inconsequential, inconsiderable, scanty, slight, small, trifling, trivial ≠ **serious** 5 = **digestible**, frugal, modest ≠ **rich** ◆ v 7 = **settle**, alight, land, perch 8 = **come across**, chance upon, discover, encounter, find, happen upon, hit upon, stumble on

like¹ adj = **similar**, akin, alike, analogous, corresponding, equivalent, identical, parallel, same ≠ **different**

like² v 1 = **enjoy**, be fond of, be keen on, be partial to, delight in, go for, love, relish, revel in ≠ **hate** 2 = **admire**, appreciate, approve, cherish, esteem, hold dear, prize, take to ≠ **hate** 3 = **wish**, care to, choose, desire, fancy, feel inclined, prefer, want

limb n 1 = **part**, appendage, arm, extremity, leg, member, wing 2 = **branch**, or next stage of something and powerless to influence it.

limbo² *n, pl* **–bos** West Indian dance in which dancers lean backwards to pass under a bar.

lime¹ *n* calcium compound used as a fertilizer or in making cement. **limelight** *n* glare of publicity. **limestone** *n* sedimentary rock used in building.

lime² *n* small green citrus fruit. **lime–green** *adj* greenish–yellow.

lime³ *n* deciduous tree with heart–shaped leaves and fragrant flowers.

limerick [**lim**–mer–ik] *n* humorous verse of five lines.

limit ❶ *n* **1** ultimate extent, degree, or amount of something. **2** boundary or edge. ♦ *v* **–iting, –ited 3** restrict or confine. **limitation** *n* **limitless** *adj* **limited company** company whose shareholders' liability for debts is restricted.

limousine *n* large luxurious car.

limp¹ ❶ *v* **1** walk with an uneven step. ♦ *n* **2** limping walk.

limp² ❶ *adj* without firmness or stiffness.

limpet *n* shellfish which sticks tightly to rocks.

limpid *adj* **1** clear or transparent. **2** easy to understand. **limpidity** *n*

linchpin, lynchpin *n* **1** pin to hold a wheel on its axle. **2** essential person or thing.

linctus *n, pl* **–tuses** syrupy cough medicine.

line¹ ❶ *n* **1** long narrow mark. **2** indented mark or wrinkle. **3** continuous length without breadth. **4** boundary or limit. **5** mark on a sports ground showing divisions of a pitch or track. **6** edge or contour of a shape. **7** string or wire for a particular use. **8** telephone connection. **9** wire or cable for transmitting electricity. **10** shipping company. **11** railway track. **12** course or direction of movement. **13** course or method of action. **14** prescribed way of thinking. **15** field of interest or activity. **16** row or queue of people. **17** class of goods. **18** row of words. **19** unit of verse. **20** military formation. ♦ *pl* **21** words of a theatrical part. **22** school punishment of writing out a sentence a specified number of times. ♦ *v* **23** mark with lines. **24** be or form a border or edge. **in line for** likely to receive. **in line with** in accordance with. **line–up** *n* people or things assembled for a particular purpose. **line up** *v* form or organize a line–up.

line² ❶ *v* **1** give a lining to. **2** cover the inside of.

linen *n* **1** cloth or thread made from flax. **2** sheets, tablecloths, etc.

liner¹ *n* large passenger ship or aircraft.

liner² *n* something used as a lining.

linger ❶ *v* **1** delay or prolong departure. **2** continue in a weakened state for a long time before dying or disappearing. **3** spend a long time doing something.

lingerie [**lan**–zher–ee] *n* women's

---

bough, offshoot, projection, spur

limit *n* **1** = **end**, breaking point, deadline, ultimate **2** = **boundary**, border, edge, frontier, perimeter ♦ *v* **3** = **restrict**, bound, check, circumscribe, confine, curb, ration, restrain

limp¹ *v* **1, 2** = **hobble**, falter, hop, shamble, shuffle ♦ *n* **3** = **lameness**, hobble

limp² *adj* **1** = **floppy**, drooping, flabby, flaccid, pliable, slack, soft ≠ **hard**

line¹ *n* **1** = **stroke**, band, groove, mark, score, scratch, streak, stripe **2** = **wrinkle**, crease, crow's foot, furrow, mark

4 = **boundary**, border, borderline, edge, frontier, limit **7** = **string**, cable, cord, rope, thread, wire **12** = **trajectory**, course, direction, path, route, track

15 = **occupation**, area, business, calling, employment, field, job, profession, specialization, trade **16** = **row**, column, file, procession, queue, rank ♦ *pl n*

21 = **words**, part, script ♦ *v* **23** = **mark**, crease, furrow, rule, score **24** = **border**, bound, edge, fringe **in line for** = **due for**, in the running for

line² *v* = **fill**, ceil, cover, face, interline

underwear or nightwear.

linguist *n* 1 person skilled in foreign languages. 2 person who studies linguistics. **linguistic** *adj* of languages. **linguistics** *n* scientific study of language.

liniment *n* medicated liquid rubbed on the skin to relieve pain or stiffness.

lining *n* 1 layer of cloth attached to the inside of a garment etc. 2 inner covering of anything.

link ❶ *n* 1 any of the rings forming a chain. 2 person or thing forming a connection. ◆ *v* 3 connect with or as if with links. 4 connect by association. **linkage** *n* **link–up** *n* joining together of two systems or groups.

links *pl n* golf course, esp. one by the sea.

linnet *n* songbird of the finch family.

lino *n* short for LINOLEUM.

linoleum *n* floor covering of hessian or jute with a smooth decorative coating of powdered cork.

linseed *n* seed of the flax plant.

lint *n* soft material for dressing a wound.

lintel *n* horizontal beam at the top of a door or window.

lion *n* large animal of the cat family, the male of which has a shaggy mane. **lioness** *n fem* **the lion's share** the biggest part. **lionize** *v* treat as a celebrity.

lip ❶ *n* 1 either of the fleshy edges of the mouth. 2 rim of a jug etc. 3 *Slang* impudence. **lip–reading** *n* method of understanding speech by interpreting lip

movements. **lip service** insincere tribute or respect. **lipstick** *n* cosmetic in stick form, for colouring the lips.

liqueur [lik–**cure**] *n* flavoured and sweetened alcoholic spirit.

liquid ❶ *n* 1 substance in a physical state which can change shape but not size. ◆ *adj* 2 of or being a liquid. 3 flowing smoothly. 4 (of assets) in the form of money or easily converted into money. **liquidize** *v* make or become liquid. **liquidizer** *n* kitchen appliance that liquidizes food. **liquidity** *n* state of being able to meet financial obligations.

liquidate ❶ *v* 1 pay (a debt). 2 dissolve a company and share its assets among creditors. 3 wipe out or kill. **liquidation** *n* **liquidator** *n* official appointed to liquidate a business.

liquor ❶ *n* 1 alcoholic drink, esp. spirits. 2 liquid in which food has been cooked.

liquorice [**lik**–ker–iss] *n* black substance used in medicine and as a sweet.

lira *n, pl* –re, –ras monetary unit of Italy and Turkey.

lisp *n* 1 speech defect in which *s* and *z* are pronounced *th*. ◆ *v* 2 speak or utter with a lisp.

lissom, lissome *adj* supple, agile.

list¹ ❶ *n* 1 item–by–item record of names or things, usu. written one below another. ◆ *v* 2 make a list of. 3 include in a list.

list² ❶ *v* 1 (of a ship) lean to one side. ◆ *n* 2 leaning to one side.

———————| THESAURUS |———————

linger *v* 1 = **stay**, hang around, loiter, remain, stop, tarry, wait 3 = **delay**, dally, dawdle, drag one's feet *or* heels, idle, take one's time

link *n* 2 = **connection**, affinity, association, attachment, bond, relationship, tie–up ◆ *v* 3 = **connect**, attach, bind, couple, fasten, join, tie, unite ≠ **separate** 4 = **associate**, bracket, connect, identify, relate

lip *n* 2 = **edge**, brim, brink, margin, rim 3 *Sl* = **impudence**, backchat (*inf*), cheek (*inf*), effrontery, impertinence, insolence

liquid *n* 1 = **fluid**, juice, solution ◆ *adj*

2 = **fluid**, aqueous, flowing, melted, molten, runny 4 *Of assets* = **convertible**, negotiable

liquidate *v* 1 = **pay**, clear, discharge, honour, pay off, settle, square
2 = **dissolve**, abolish, annul, cancel, terminate 3 = **kill**, destroy, dispatch, eliminate, exterminate, get rid of, murder, wipe out (*inf*)

liquor *n* 1 = **alcohol**, booze (*inf*), drink, hard stuff (*inf*), spirits, strong drink
2 = **juice**, broth, extract, liquid, stock

list¹ *n* 1 = **inventory**, catalogue, directory,

listen ❶ v 1 concentrate on hearing something. 2 heed or pay attention to. **listener** n **listen in** v listen secretly, eavesdrop.

listless ❶ adj lacking interest or energy.

litany n, pl **-nies** 1 prayer with responses from the congregation. 2 any tedious recital.

literal ❶ adj 1 according to the explicit meaning of a word or text, not figurative. 2 (of a translation) word for word. 3 actual, true. **literally** adv

> ✓ **WORD TIP**
> Note that *literally* means much the same as 'actually'. It is very loosely used to mean 'just about' but this can be ambiguous.

literate ❶ adj 1 able to read and write. 2 educated. **literati** pl n literary people.

literature ❶ n 1 written works such as novels, plays, and poetry. 2 books and writings of a country, period, or subject.

lithe ❶ adj flexible or supple, pliant.

lithium n Chem chemical element, the lightest known metal.

lithography [lith–**og**–ra–fee] n method of printing from a metal or stone surface in which the printing areas are made receptive to ink. **lithograph** n 1 print

made by lithography. ◆ v 2 reproduce by lithography.

litmus n blue dye turned red by acids and restored to blue by alkalis. **litmus test** something which is regarded as a simple and accurate test of a particular thing.

litre n unit of liquid measure equal to 1.76 pints.

litter ❶ n 1 untidy rubbish dropped in public places. 2 group of young animals produced at one birth. 3 straw etc. as bedding for an animal. 4 dry material to absorb a cat's excrement. 5 bed or seat on parallel sticks for carrying people. ◆ v 6 strew with litter. 7 scatter or be scattered about untidily. 8 give birth to young.

little ❶ adj 1 small or smaller than average. 2 young. ◆ adv 3 not a lot. 4 hardly. 5 not much or often. ◆ n 6 small amount, extent, or duration.

liturgy n, pl **-gies** prescribed form of public worship. **liturgical** adj

live[1] ❶ v 1 be alive. 2 remain in life or existence. 3 exist in a specified way, e.g. *we live well*. 4 reside. 5 continue or last. 6 subsist. 7 enjoy life to the full. **liver** n person who lives in a specified way. **live down** v wait till people forget a past mistake or misdeed. **live–in** adj resident. **live up to** v meet (expectations). **live with** v tolerate.

THESAURUS

index, record, register, roll, series, tally ◆ v 2, 3 = **itemize**, catalogue, enter, enumerate, record, register, tabulate

list[2] v 1 = **lean**, careen, heel over, incline, tilt, tip ◆ n 2 = **tilt**, cant, leaning, slant

listen v 1 = **hear**, attend, lend an ear, prick up one's ears 2 = **pay attention**, heed, mind, obey, observe, take notice

listless adj = **languid**, apathetic, indifferent, indolent, lethargic, sluggish

literal adj 1 = **explicit**, precise, strict 2 = **exact**, accurate, close, faithful, verbatim, word for word 3 = **actual**, bona fide, genuine, plain, real, simple, true, unvarnished

literate adj 2 = **educated**, informed,

knowledgeable

literature n = **writings**, lore

lithe adj = **supple**, flexible, limber, lissom(e), loose–limbed, pliable

litter n 1 = **rubbish**, debris, detritus, garbage (chiefly US), muck, refuse, trash 2 = **brood**, offspring, progeny, young ◆ v 6 = **clutter**, derange, disarrange, disorder, mess up 7 = **scatter**, strew

little adj 1 = **small**, diminutive, miniature, minute, petite, short, tiny, wee ≠ **great** 2 = **young**, babyish, immature, infant, undeveloped ◆ adv 4 = **hardly**, barely ≠ **much** 5 = **rarely**, hardly ever, not often, scarcely, seldom ≠ **much** ◆ n 6 = **bit**, fragment, hint, particle, speck, spot,

live² ❼ *adj* 1 living, alive. 2 (of a broadcast) transmitted during the actual performance. 3 (of a performance) done in front of an audience. 4 (of a wire, circuit, etc.) carrying an electric current. 5 causing interest or controversy. 6 capable of exploding. 7 glowing or burning. ◆ *adv* 8 in the form of a live performance. **lively** *adj* 1 full of life or vigour. 2 animated. 3 vivid. **liveliness** *n* **liven up** *v* make (more) lively.

livelihood ❼ *n* occupation or employment.

liver *n* 1 organ secreting bile. 2 animal liver as food. **liverish** *adj* 1 having a disorder of the liver. 2 touchy or irritable.

livery ❼ *n, pl* **–eries** 1 distinctive dress, esp. of a servant or servants. 2 distinctive design or colours of a company. **liveried** *adj* **livery stable** stable where horses are kept at a charge or hired out.

livestock *n* farm animals.

livid ❼ *adj* 1 *Informal* angry or furious. 2 bluish–grey.

lizard *n* four–footed reptile with a long body and tail.

llama *n* woolly animal of the camel family used as a beast of burden in S America.

load ❼ *n* 1 burden or weight. 2 amount carried. 3 source of worry. 4 amount of electrical energy drawn from a source. ◆ *pl* 5 *Informal* lots. ◆ *v* 6 put a load on or into. 7 burden or oppress. 8 cause to be biased. 9 put ammunition into (a weapon). 10 put film into (a camera). 11 transfer (a program) into computer memory. **loaded** *adj* 1 (of a question) containing a hidden trap or implication. 2 (of dice) dishonestly weighted. 3 *Slang* wealthy.

loaf¹ ❼ *n, pl* **loaves** 1 shaped mass of baked bread. 2 shaped mass of food. 3 *Slang* head, esp. as the source of common sense, e.g. *use your loaf.*

loaf² ❼ *v* idle, loiter. **loafer** *n*

loam *n* fertile soil.

loan ❼ *n* 1 money lent at interest. 2 lending. 3 thing lent. ◆ *v* 4 lend. **loan shark** person who lends money at an extremely high interest rate.

loath ❼ **loth** [rhymes with **both**] *adj* unwilling or reluctant (to).

✓ **WORD TIP**
Distinguish between *loath* 'reluctant' and *loathe* 'be disgusted by'.

---

touch, trace ≠ **much**

live¹ *v* 1 = **exist**, be, be alive, breathe 4 = **dwell**, abide, inhabit, lodge, occupy, reside, settle 5 = **persist**, last, prevail 6 = **survive**, endure, get along, make ends meet, subsist, support oneself 7 = **thrive**, flourish, prosper

live² *adj* 1 = **living**, alive, animate, breathing 5 = **topical**, burning, controversial, current, hot, pertinent, pressing, prevalent 7 = **burning**, active, alight, blazing, glowing, hot, ignited, smouldering

livelihood *n* = **occupation**, bread and butter (*inf*), employment, job, living, work, yakka (*Aust & NZ inf*)

livery *n* 1 = **costume**, attire, clothing, dress, garb, regalia, suit, uniform

livid *adj* 1 *Inf* = **angry**, beside oneself,

enraged, fuming, furious, incensed, indignant, infuriated, outraged ≠ **happy** 2 = **discoloured**, black–and–blue, bruised, contused, purple

load *n* 1 = **cargo**, consignment, freight, shipment 3 = **burden**, albatross, encumbrance, millstone, onus, trouble, weight, worry ◆ *v* 6 = **fill**, cram, freight, heap, pack, pile, stack, stuff 7 = **burden**, encumber, oppress, saddle with, weigh down, worry 9 *Firearms* = **make ready**, charge, prime

loaf¹ *n* 2 = **lump**, block, cake, cube, slab 3 *Sl* = **head**, gumption (*Brit inf*), nous (*Brit sl*), sense

loaf² *v* = **idle**, laze, lie around, loiter, lounge around, take it easy

loan *n* 1–3 = **advance**, credit ◆ *v* 4 = **lend**, advance, let out

lob *Sport* ◆ *n* **1** ball struck or thrown in a high arc. ◆ *v* **lobbing, lobbed 2** strike or throw (a ball) in a high arc.

lobby ❶ *n, pl* **-bies 1** corridor into which rooms open. **2** group which tries to influence legislators. **3** hall in a legislative building to which the public has access. ◆ *v* **4** try to influence (legislators) in the formulation of policy. **lobbyist** *n*

lobe *n* **1** rounded projection. **2** soft hanging part of the ear. **3** subdivision of *a* body organ.

lobelia *n* garden plant with blue, red, or white flowers.

lobster *n* shellfish with a long tail and claws, which turns red when boiled.

local ❶ *adj* **1** of or existing in a particular place. **2** confined to a particular place. ◆ *n* **3** person belonging to a particular district. **4** *Informal* pub close to one's home. **locally** *adv* **locality** *n* neighbourhood or area. **localize** *v* restrict to a particular place. **locale** [loh-**kahl**] *n* scene of an event. **local anaesthetic** anaesthetic which produces loss of feeling in one part of the body. **local authority** governing body of a county or district. **local government** government of towns, counties, and districts by locally elected political bodies.

locate ❶ *v* **1** discover the whereabouts of. **2** situate or place. **location** *n* **1** site or position. **2** act of discovering where something is. **3** site of a film production away from the studio. **4** *S Afr* Black African or coloured township.

loch *n Scot* **1** lake. **2** long narrow bay.

lock¹ ❶ *n* **1** appliance for fastening a door, case, etc. **2** section of a canal shut off by gates between which the water level can be altered to aid boats moving from one level to another. **3** extent to which a vehicle's front wheels will turn. **4** interlocking of parts. **5** mechanism for firing a gun. **6** wrestling hold. ◆ *v* **7** fasten or become fastened securely. **8** become or cause to become fixed or united. **9** become or cause to become immovable. **10** embrace closely. **lockout** *n* closing of a workplace by an employer to force workers to accept terms. **locksmith** *n* person who makes and mends locks. **lockup** *n* **1** prison. **2** garage or storage place away from the main premises.

lock² ❶ *n* strand of hair.

locket *n* small hinged pendant for a portrait etc.

locomotive *n* **1** self-propelled engine for pulling trains. ◆ *adj* **2** of locomotion. **locomotion** *n* action or power of moving.

locum *n* temporary stand-in for a doctor or clergyman.

locus [**loh**-kuss] *n, pl* **loci** [**loh**-sigh] **1** area or place where something happens. **2** *Maths* set of points or lines satisfying one or more specified conditions.

locust *n* destructive African insect that flies in swarms and eats crops.

lodge ❶ *n* **1** gatekeeper's house. **2** house or cabin used occasionally by hunters, skiers, etc. **3** porters' room in a university or college. **4** local branch of some societies. ◆ *v* **5** live in another's house at a fixed charge. **6** stick or become stuck (in a place). **7** make (a complaint etc.) formally.

——— THESAURUS ———

loath, loth *adj* = **unwilling**, averse, disinclined, opposed, reluctant

lobby *n* **1** = **corridor**, entrance hall, foyer, hallway, passage, porch, vestibule **2** = **pressure group** ◆ *v* **4** = **campaign**, influence, persuade, press, pressure, promote, push, urge

local *adj* **1** = **regional**, provincial **2** = **restricted**, confined, limited ◆ *n* **3** = **resident**, inhabitant, native

locate *v* **1** = **find**, come across, detect, discover, pin down, pinpoint, track down, unearth **2** = **place**, establish, fix, put, seat, set, settle, situate

lock¹ *n* **1** = **fastening**, bolt, clasp, padlock ◆ *v* **7** = **fasten**, bolt, close, seal, secure, shut **8** = **unite**, engage, entangle, entwine, join, link **9** = **clench**, freeze **10** = **embrace**, clasp, clutch, encircle, enclose, grasp, hug, press

lodger *n* **lodging** *n* 1 temporary residence. ◆ *pl* 2 rented room or rooms in another person's house.

loft *n* 1 space between the top storey and roof of a building. 2 gallery in a church etc. ◆ *v* 3 *Sport* strike, throw, or kick (a ball) high into the air.

log[1] **◐** *n* 1 portion of a felled tree stripped of branches. 2 detailed record of a journey of a ship, aircraft, etc. ◆ *v* **logging, logged** 3 saw logs from a tree. 4 record in a log. **logging** *n* work of cutting and transporting logs. **logbook** *n* book recording the details about a car or a ship's journeys. **log in, out** *v* gain entrance to or leave a computer system by keying in a special command.

log[2] *n* short for LOGARITHM.

loganberry *n* purplish–red fruit, similar to a raspberry.

logarithm *n* one of a series of arithmetical functions used to make certain calculations easier.

loggerheads ◐ *pl n* **at loggerheads** quarrelling, disputing.

logic ◐ *n* 1 philosophy of reasoning. 2 reasoned thought or argument. **logical** *adj* 1 of logic. 2 capable of or using clear valid reasoning. 3 reasonable. **logically** *adv*

logistics *n* detailed planning and organization of a large, esp. military, operation. **logistical, logistic** *adj*

logo [**loh**–go] *n, pl* **–os** company emblem or similar device.

loin *n* 1 part of the body between the ribs and the hips. 2 cut of meat from this part of an animal. ◆ *pl* 3 hips and inner thighs. **loincloth** *n* piece of cloth covering the loins only.

loiter ◐ *v* stand or wait aimlessly or idly.

loll ◐ *v* 1 lounge lazily. 2 hang loosely.

lollipop *n* boiled sweet on a small wooden stick. **lollipop man, lady** *Informal* person holding a circular sign on a pole, who controls traffic so that children may cross the road safely.

lolly *n, pl* **–ies** 1 *Informal* lollipop or ice lolly. 2 *Aust & NZ informal* sweet. 3 *Slang* money.

lone ◐ *adj* solitary. **lonely** *adj* 1 sad because alone. 2 resulting from being alone. 3 unfrequented. **loneliness** *n* **loner** *n Informal* person who prefers to be alone. **lonesome** *adj* lonely.

long[1] **◐** *adj* 1 having length, esp. great length, in space or time. ◆ *adv* 2 for an extensive period. **long–distance** *adj* going between places far apart. **long face** glum expression. **longhand** *n* ordinary writing, not shorthand or typing. **long johns** *Informal* long underpants. **long–life** *adj* (of milk, batteries, etc.) lasting longer than the regular kind. **long–lived** *adj* living or lasting for a long time. **long–range** *adj* 1 extending into the future. 2 (of vehicles, weapons, etc.) designed to cover great distances. **long shot** competitor, undertaking, or bet with little chance of success. **long–sighted** *adj* able to see distant objects in focus but not nearby

THESAURUS

lock[2] *n* = **strand**, curl, ringlet, tress, tuft

lodge *n* 1 = **gatehouse** 2 = **cabin**, chalet, cottage, hut, shelter 4 = **society**, branch, chapter, club, group ◆ *v* 5 = **stay**, board, room 6 = **stick**, come to rest, imbed, implant 7 = **register**, file, put on record, submit

log[1] *n* 1 = **stump**, block, chunk, trunk 2 = **record**, account, journal, logbook ◆ *v* 3 = **chop**, cut, fell, hew 4 = **record**, chart, note, register, set down

loggerheads *pl n* **at loggerheads** = **quarrelling**, at daggers drawn, at each other's throats, at odds, feuding, in dispute, opposed

logic *n* 3 = **reason**, good sense, sense

loiter *v* = **linger**, dally, dawdle, dilly–dally (*inf*), hang about *or* around, idle, loaf, skulk

loll *v* 1 = **lounge**, loaf, outspan (*S Afr*), recline, relax, slouch, slump, sprawl 2 = **droop**, dangle, drop, flap, flop, hang, sag

lone *adj* 1 = **solitary**, one, only, single, sole,

ones. **long–standing** *adj* existing for a long time. **long–suffering** *adj* enduring trouble or unhappiness without complaint. **long–term** *adj* lasting or effective for a long time. **long wave** radio wave with a wavelength of over 1000 metres. **long–winded** *adj* speaking or writing at tedious length.

long² **⊕** *v* have a strong desire (for). **longing** *n* yearning.

longevity [lon–**jev**–it–ee] *n* long life.

longitude *n* distance east or west from a standard meridian. **longitudinal** *adj* 1 of length or longitude. 2 lengthways.

loo *n Informal* toilet.

look **⊕** *v* 1 direct the eyes or attention (towards). 2 have the appearance of being. 3 face in a particular direction. 4 search (for). 5 hope (for). **♦** *n* 6 instance of looking. 7 (often pl) appearance. **look after** *v* take care of. **lookalike** *n* person who is the double of another. **look down on** *v* treat as inferior or unimportant. **look forward to** *v* anticipate with pleasure. **look on** *v* 1 be a spectator. 2 consider or regard. **lookout** *n* 1 guard. 2 place for watching. 3 *Informal* worry or concern. 4 chances or prospect. **look out** *v* be careful. **look up** *v* 1 discover or confirm by

checking in a book. 2 improve. 3 visit. **look up to** *v* respect.

loom¹ *n* machine for weaving cloth.

loom² **⊕** *v* 1 appear dimly. 2 seem ominously close.

loony *Slang* **♦** *adj* **loonier, looniest** 1 foolish or insane. **♦** *n, pl* **loonies** 2 foolish or insane person.

loop **⊕** *n* 1 rounded shape made by a curved line or rope crossing itself. **♦** *v* 2 form or fasten with a loop. **loophole** *n* means of evading a rule without breaking it.

loose **⊕** *adj* 1 not tight, fastened, fixed, or tense. 2 vague. 3 dissolute or promiscuous. **♦** *adv* 4 in a loose manner. **♦** *v* 5 free. 6 unfasten. 7 slacken. 8 let fly (an arrow, bullet, etc.). **at a loose end** bored, with nothing to do. **loosely** *adv* **looseness** *n* **loosen** *v* make loose. **loosen up** *v* relax, stop worrying. **loose–leaf** *adj* allowing the addition or removal of pages.

> ✓ **WORD TIP**
> Note the difference in spelling between the adjective *loose* and the verb *lose*.

loot **⊕** *n, v* 1 plunder. **♦** *n* 2 *Informal*

——————— THESAURUS ———————

unaccompanied

long¹ *adj* 1 a = **elongated**, expanded, extensive, far–reaching, lengthy, spread out, stretched ≠ **little** b = **prolonged**, interminable, lengthy, lingering, long–drawn–out, protracted, sustained ≠ **short**

long² *v* = **desire**, crave, hanker, itch, lust, pine, want, wish, yearn

look *v* 1 = **see**, behold, contemplate, examine, eye, gaze, glance, observe, scan, study, survey, view, watch 2 = **seem**, appear, look like, strike one as 3 = **face**, front, overlook 4 = **search**, forage, fossick (*Aust & NZ*), hunt, seek 5 = **hope**, anticipate, await, expect, reckon on **♦** *n* 6 = **glimpse**, examination, gaze, glance, inspection, observation, peek,

sight, view 7 (often pl) = **appearance**, air, aspect, bearing, countenance, demeanour, expression, manner, semblance

loom² *v* 1 = **appear**, bulk, emerge, hover, take shape 2 = **threaten**, impend, menace

loop *n* 1 = **curve**, circle, coil, curl, ring, spiral, twirl, twist, whorl **♦** *v* 5 = **twist**, coil, curl, knot, roll, spiral, turn, wind round

loose *adj* 1 a = **slack**, easy, relaxed, sloppy ≠ **tight** b = **free**, insecure, unattached, unbound, unfastened, unfettered, unrestricted, untied ≠ **bind** 2 = **vague**, ill–defined, imprecise, inaccurate, indistinct, inexact, rambling, random ≠ **clear** 3 = **promiscuous**, abandoned, debauched, dissipated, dissolute, fast, immoral, profligate ≠ **moral** **♦** *v* 5, money. **looting** n

lop v **lopping, lopped 1** cut away twigs and branches. **2** chop off.

lope v run with long easy strides.

lopsided ⊕ adj greater in height, weight, or size on one side.

loquacious adj talkative. **loquacity** n

lord ⊕ n **1** person with power over others, such as a monarch or master. **2** male member of the nobility. **3** Hist feudal superior. **4** (L–) God or Jesus. **5** (L–) title given to certain male officials and peers. **lord it over** act in a superior manner towards. **lordly** adj imperious, proud. **Lordship** n title of some male officials and peers.

lore ⊕ n body of traditions on a subject.

lorry n, pl –**ries** large vehicle for transporting loads by road.

lose ⊕ v **losing, lost 1** come to be without, esp. by accident or carelessness. **2** fail to keep or maintain. **3** be deprived of. **4** fail to get or make use of. **5** be defeated in a competition etc. **6** fail to perceive or understand. **7** go astray or allow to go astray. **8** be or become engrossed, e.g. *lost in thought.* **9** die or be destroyed. **10** (of a clock etc.) run slow (by a specified amount). **loser** n **1** person or thing that loses. **2** Informal person who seems

destined to fail.

✔ **WORD TIP**

Note the difference in spelling between the verb *lose* and the adjective *loose.*

---

loss n **1** losing. **2** that which is lost. **lost** adj unable to find one's way.

lot ⊕ pron **1** great number. ◆ n **2** collection of people or things. **3** fate or destiny. **4** one of a set of objects drawn at random to make a selection or choice. **5** item at auction. ◆ pl **6** Informal great numbers or quantities. **a lot** Informal a great deal.

lotion ⊕ n medical or cosmetic liquid for use on the skin.

lottery ⊕ n, pl –**teries 1** method of raising money by selling tickets that win prizes by chance. **2** gamble.

lotus n **1** legendary plant whose fruit induces forgetfulness. **2** Egyptian water lily.

loud ⊕ adj **1** relatively great in volume. **2** capable of making much noise. **3** insistent and emphatic. **4** unpleasantly patterned or colourful. **loudly** adv **loudness** n **loudspeaker** n instrument for converting electrical signals into sound.

lounge ⊕ n **1** living room in a private

| T H E S A U R U S |

6 = free, detach, disconnect, liberate, release, set free, unfasten, unleash, untie

① **loot** n **1 = plunder**, booty, goods, haul, prize, spoils, swag (sl)

② **loot** v **1 = plunder**, despoil, pillage, raid, ransack, ravage, rifle, rob, sack

lopsided adj **= crooked**, askew, asymmetrical, awry, cockeyed, disproportionate, skewwhiff (Brit inf), squint, unbalanced, uneven, warped

lord n **1 = master**, commander, governor, leader, liege, overlord, ruler, superior **2 = nobleman**, earl, noble, peer, viscount **4** (with cap.) **= Jesus Christ**, Christ, God, Jehovah, the Almighty **lord it over = order around**, boss around (inf), domineer, pull rank, put on airs, swagger

lore n **= traditions**, beliefs, doctrine, sayings, teaching, wisdom

lose v **1 = mislay**, drop, forget, misplace **2, 5 = forfeit**, miss, pass up (inf), yield **3 = be deprived of 6 = be defeated**, come to grief, lose out

lot n **2 = collection**, assortment, batch, bunch (inf), consignment, crowd, group, quantity, set **3 = destiny**, accident, chance, doom, fate, fortune **a lot** Inf **= plenty**, abundance, a great deal, heap(s), load(s) (inf), masses (inf), piles (inf), scores, stack(s)

lotion n **= cream**, balm, embrocation, liniment, salve, solution

lottery n **1 = raffle**, draw, sweepstake **2 = gamble**, chance, hazard, risk, house. **2** more expensive bar in a pub. **3** area for waiting in an airport. ◆ *v* **4** sit, lie, or stand in a relaxed manner. **lounge suit** man's suit for daytime wear.

lour *v* same as LOWER².

louse *n* **1** (*pl* **lice**) wingless parasitic insect. **2** (*pl* **louses**) unpleasant person. **lousy** *adj* **1** *Slang* mean or unpleasant. **2** bad, inferior. **3** unwell.

lout ❶ *n* crude, oafish, or aggressive person. **loutish** *adj*

louvre [loo–ver] *n* one of a set of parallel slats slanted to admit air but not rain. **louvred** *adj*

love ❶ *v* **1** have a great affection for. **2** feel sexual passion for. **3** enjoy (something) very much. ◆ *n* **4** great affection. **5** sexual passion. **6** wholehearted liking for something. **7** beloved person. **8** *Tennis, squash, etc.* score of nothing. **fall in love** become in love. **in love (with)** feeling a strong emotional (and sexual) attraction (for). **make love (to)** have sexual intercourse (with). **lovable, loveable** *adj* **loveless** *adj* **lovely** *adj* **–lier, –liest 1** very attractive. **2** highly enjoyable. **lover** *n* **1** person having a sexual relationship outside marriage. **2** person in love. **3** someone who loves a specified person or

thing. **loving** *adj* affectionate, tender. **love affair** romantic or sexual relationship between two people who are not married to each other. **lovebird** *n* small parrot. **love child** *Euphemistic* child of an unmarried couple. **love life** person's romantic or sexual relationships. **lovelorn** *adj* miserable because of unhappiness in love. **lovemaking** *n*

low¹ ❶ *adj* **1** not tall, high, or elevated. **2** of little or less than the usual amount, degree, quality, or cost. **3** coarse or vulgar. **4** dejected. **5** ill. **6** not loud. **7** deep in pitch. **8** (of a gear) providing a relatively low speed. ◆ *adv* **9** in or to a low position, level, or degree. ◆ *n* **10** low position, level, or degree. **11** area of low atmospheric pressure, depression. **lowly** *adj* modest, humble. **lowliness** *n* **lowbrow** *n, adj* (person) with nonintellectual tastes and interests. **lowdown** *n Informal* inside information. **low–down** *adj Informal* mean, underhand, or dishonest. **low–key** *adj* subdued, restrained, not intense. **lowland** *n* **1** low–lying country. ◆ *pl* **2** (L–) less mountainous parts of Scotland. **low profile** position or attitude avoiding prominence or publicity.

low² *n* **1** cry of cattle, moo. ◆ *v* **2** moo.

——————— THESAURUS ———————

toss–up (*inf*)

loud *adj* **1** = **noisy**, blaring, booming, clamorous, deafening, ear–splitting, forte (*Music*), resounding, thundering, tumultuous, vociferous ≠ **low 4** = **garish**, brash, flamboyant, flashy, gaudy, glaring, lurid, showy ≠ **conservative**

lounge *v* **4** = **relax**, laze, lie about, loaf, loiter, loll, outspan (*S Afr*), sprawl, take it easy

lout *n* = **oaf**, boor, dolt, yob *or* yobbo (*Brit sl*)

love *v* **1** = **adore**, cherish, dote on, hold dear, idolize, prize, treasure, worship ≠ **hate 3** = **enjoy**, appreciate, delight in, like, relish, savour, take pleasure in ≠ **hate** ◆ *n* **4** = **affection**, adoration, attachment, devotion, infatuation, tenderness, warmth

5 = **passion**, ardour ≠ **hate 6** = **liking**, devotion, enjoyment, fondness, inclination, partiality, relish, soft spot, taste, weakness **7** = **beloved**, darling, dear, dearest, lover, sweetheart, truelove ≠ **enemy in love (with)** = **enamoured**, besotted, charmed, enraptured, infatuated, smitten

low¹ *adj* **1** = **small**, little, short, squat, stunted ≠ **towering 2** = **inferior**, deficient, inadequate, poor, second–rate, shoddy **3** = **coarse**, common, crude, disreputable, rough, rude, undignified, vulgar **4** = **dejected**, depressed, despondent, disheartened, downcast, down in the dumps (*inf*), fed up, gloomy, glum, miserable ≠ **high 5** = **ill**, debilitated, frail, stricken, weak ≠ **strong 6** = **quiet**, gentle,

lower¹ ❶ *adj* 1 below one or more other things. 2 smaller or reduced in amount or value. ◆ *v* 3 cause or allow to move down. 4 behave in a way that damages one's respect. 5 lessen. **lower case** small, as distinct from capital, letters.

lower² ❶ , **lour** *v* (of the sky or weather) look gloomy or threatening. **lowering** *adj*

loyal ❶ *adj* faithful to one's friends, country, or government. **loyally** *adv* **loyalty** *n* **loyalist** *n*

lozenge *n* 1 medicated tablet held in the mouth until it dissolves. 2 four–sided diamond–shaped figure.

LP *n* record playing approximately 20-25 minutes each side.

L–plate *n* sign on a car being driven by a learner driver.

LSD lysergic acid diethylamide, a hallucinogenic drug.

lubricate ❶ [loo–brik–ate] *v* oil or grease to lessen friction. **lubricant** *n* lubricating substance, such as oil. **lubrication** *n*

lucerne *n* fodder plant like clover, alfalfa.

lucid ❶ *adj* 1 clear and easily understood. 2 able to think clearly. 3 bright and clear. **lucidity** *n*

luck ❶ *n* 1 fortune, good or bad. 2 good fortune. **lucky** *adj* having or bringing good luck. **lucky dip** game in which prizes are picked from a tub at random. **luckily** *adv* fortunately. **luckless** *adj* having bad luck.

lucrative ❶ *adj* very profitable.

ludicrous ❶ *adj* absurd or ridiculous.

lug¹ *v* lugging, lugged carry or drag with great effort.

lug² *n* 1 projection serving as a handle. 2 *Informal* ear.

luggage ❶ *n* traveller's cases, bags, etc.

lugubrious ❶ *adj* mournful, gloomy.

lukewarm ❶ *adj* 1 moderately warm, tepid. 2 indifferent or half–hearted.

lull ❶ *v* 1 soothe (someone) by soft sounds or motions. 2 calm (fears or suspicions) by deception. ◆ *n* 3 brief time of quiet in a storm etc.

lumbago [lum–**bay**–go] *n* pain in the lower back. **lumbar** *adj* relating to the

————— THESAURUS —————

hushed, muffled, muted, soft, subdued, whispered ≠ **loud**

lower¹ *adj* 1 = **under**, inferior, junior, lesser, minor, secondary, second–class, smaller, subordinate 2 = **reduced**, curtailed, decreased, diminished, lessened ≠ **higher** ◆ *v* 3 = **drop**, depress, fall, let down, sink, submerge, take down ≠ **raise** 5 = **lessen**, cut, decrease, diminish, minimize, prune, reduce, slash ≠ **increase**

lower², **lour** *v* = **darken**, be brewing, blacken, cloud up *or* over, loom, menace, threaten

loyal *adj* = **faithful**, constant, dependable, devoted, dutiful, staunch, steadfast, true, trustworthy, truthful, unwavering

lubricate *v* = **oil**, grease, smear

lucid *adj* 1 = **clear**, comprehensible, explicit, intelligible, transparent ≠ **confused** 2 = **clear–headed**, all there, *compos mentis*, in one's right mind, rational, sane ≠ **confused** 3 = **translucent**, clear, crystalline, diaphanous, glassy,

limpid, pellucid, transparent

luck *n* 1 = **fortune**, accident, chance, destiny, fate 2 = **good fortune**, advantage, blessing, godsend, prosperity, serendipity, success, windfall

lucrative *adj* = **profitable**, advantageous, fruitful, productive, remunerative, well–paid

ludicrous *adj* = **ridiculous**, absurd, crazy, farcical, laughable, nonsensical, outlandish, preposterous, silly

luggage *n* = **baggage**, bags, cases, gear, impedimenta, paraphernalia, suitcases, things

lugubrious *adj* = **gloomy**, doleful, melancholy, mournful, sad, serious, sombre, sorrowful, woebegone

lukewarm *adj* 1 = **tepid**, warm 2 = **half–hearted**, apathetic, cool, indifferent, unenthusiastic, unresponsive

lull *v* 1 = **calm**, allay, pacify, quell, soothe, subdue, tranquillize ◆ *n* 3 = **respite**, calm, hush, let–up (*inf*), pause, quiet, silence lower back.

lumber¹ ❶ n 1 unwanted disused household articles. 2 *Chiefly US* sawn timber. ♦ v 3 *Informal* burden with something unpleasant. **lumberjack** n *US* man who fells trees and prepares logs for transport.

lumber² ❶ v move heavily and awkwardly. **lumbering** adj

luminous ❶ adj reflecting or giving off light. **luminosity** n **luminary** n 1 famous person. 2 *Lit* heavenly body giving off light. **luminescence** n emission of light at low temperatures by any process other than burning. **luminescent** adj

lump¹ ❶ n 1 shapeless piece or mass. 2 swelling. 3 *Informal* awkward or stupid person. ♦ v 4 consider as a single group. **lump in one's throat** tight dry feeling in one's throat, usu. caused by great emotion. **lumpy** adj **lump sum** relatively large sum of money paid at one time.

lump² v **lump it** *Informal* tolerate or put up with it.

lunar adj relating to the moon.

lunatic ❶ adj 1 foolish and irresponsible. ♦ n 2 foolish or annoying person. 3 *Old–fashioned* insane person. **lunacy** n

lunch n 1 meal taken in the middle of the day. ♦ v 2 eat lunch. **luncheon** n formal lunch. **luncheon meat** tinned ground mixture of meat and cereal.

lung n organ that allows an animal or bird to breathe air: humans have two lungs in the chest.

lunge ❶ n 1 sudden forward motion. 2 thrust with a sword. ♦ v 3 move with or make a lunge.

lupin n garden plant with tall spikes of flowers.

lurch¹ ❶ v 1 tilt or lean suddenly to one side. 2 stagger. ♦ n 3 lurching movement.

lurch² n **leave someone in the lurch** abandon someone in difficulties.

lure ❶ v 1 tempt or attract by the promise of reward. ♦ n 2 person or thing that lures. 3 brightly–coloured artificial angling bait.

lurid ❶ adj 1 vivid in shocking detail, sensational. 2 glaring in colour.

lurk ❶ v 1 lie hidden or move stealthily, esp. for sinister purposes. 2 be latent.

luscious ❶ [lush–uss] adj 1 extremely pleasurable to taste or smell. 2 very attractive.

lush ❶ adj 1 (of grass etc.) growing thickly and healthily. 2 opulent.

lust ❶ n 1 strong sexual desire. 2 any

lumber¹ n 1 = **junk**, clutter, jumble, refuse, rubbish, trash ♦ v 3 *Inf* = **burden**, encumber, land, load, saddle

lumber² v = **plod**, shamble, shuffle, stump, trudge, trundle, waddle

luminous adj = **bright**, glowing, illuminated, luminescent, lustrous, radiant, shining

lump¹ n 1 = **piece**, ball, chunk, hunk, mass, nugget 2 = **swelling**, bulge, bump, growth, hump, protrusion, tumour ♦ v 4 = **group**, collect, combine, conglomerate, consolidate, mass, pool

lunatic adj 1 = **irrational**, crackbrained, crackpot (*inf*), crazy, daft, deranged, insane, mad ♦ n 3 *Old–fashioned* = **madman**, maniac, nutcase (*sl*), psychopath

lunge n 1 = **pounce**, charge, spring, swing 2 = **thrust**, jab ♦ v 3 a = **pounce**, charge, dive, leap b = **thrust**, jab

lurch¹ v 1 = **tilt**, heave, heel, lean, list, pitch, rock, roll 2 = **stagger**, reel, stumble, sway, totter, weave

lure v 1 = **tempt**, allure, attract, draw, ensnare, entice, invite, seduce ♦ n 2 = **temptation**, allurement, attraction, bait, carrot (*inf*), enticement, incentive, inducement

lurid adj 1 = **sensational**, graphic, melodramatic, shocking, vivid ≠ **controlled** 2 = **glaring**, intense ≠ **pale**

lurk v 1 = **hide**, conceal oneself, lie in wait, prowl, skulk, slink, sneak

luscious adj 1 = **delicious**, appetizing, juicy, mouth–watering, palatable, strong desire. ◆ v **3** have passionate desire (for). **lustful** adj **lusty** adj vigorous, healthy. **lustily** adv

lustre ❶ n **1** gloss, sheen. **2** splendour or glory. **3** metallic pottery glaze. **lustrous** adj shining, luminous.

lute n ancient guitar–like musical instrument with a body shaped like a half pear.

luxury ❶ n, pl **–ries 1** enjoyment of rich, very comfortable living. **2** enjoyable but not essential thing. ◆ adj **3** of or providing luxury. **luxurious** adj full of luxury, sumptuous.

lychee [lie–**chee**] n Chinese fruit with a whitish juicy pulp.

Lycra n ® elastic fabric used for tight–fitting garments, such as swimsuits.

lymph n colourless bodily fluid consisting mainly of white blood cells. **lymphatic** adj

lynch v put to death without a trial.

lynx n animal of the cat family with tufted ears and a short tail.

lyre n ancient musical instrument like a U–shaped harp.

lyric adj **1** (of poetry) expressing personal emotion in songlike style. **2** like a song. ◆ n **3** short poem in a songlike style. ◆ pl **4** words of a popular song. **lyrical** adj **1** lyric. **2** enthusiastic. **lyricist** n person who writes the words of songs or musicals.

succulent, sweet, toothsome

lush adj **1** = **abundant**, dense, flourishing, green, rank, verdant **2** = **luxurious**, elaborate, extravagant, grand, lavish, opulent, ornate, palatial, plush (inf), sumptuous

lust n **1** = **lechery**, lasciviousness, lewdness, sensuality **2** = **desire**, appetite, craving, greed, longing, passion, thirst ◆ v **3** = **desire**, covet, crave, hunger for or

after, want, yearn

lustre n **1** = **sparkle**, gleam, glint, glitter, gloss, glow, sheen, shimmer, shine **2** = **glory**, distinction, fame, honour, prestige, renown

luxury n **1** = **opulence**, affluence, hedonism, richness, splendour, sumptuousness ≠ want **2** = **extravagance**, extra, frill, indulgence, treat ≠ **necessity**

M m

m 1 metre(s). **2** mile(s). **3** minute(s).
m 1 male. **2** married. **3** month.
MA 1 Master of Arts. **2** Massachusetts.
mac *n Informal* mackintosh.
macabre ❶ [mak–**kahb**–ra] *adj* strange and horrible, gruesome.
macaroni *n* pasta in short tube shapes.
macaroon *n* small biscuit or cake made with ground almonds.
macaw *n* large tropical American parrot.
mace¹ *n* **1** ceremonial staff of office. **2** medieval weapon with a spiked metal head.
mace² *n* spice made from the dried husk of the nutmeg.
machete [mash–**ett**–ee] *n* broad heavy knife used for cutting or as a weapon.
Machiavellian ❶ [mak–ee–a–**vel**–yan] *adj* unprincipled, crafty, and opportunist.
machine ❶ *n* **1** apparatus, usu. powered by electricity, designed to perform a particular task. **2** vehicle, such as a car or aircraft. **3** controlling system of an organization. ◆ *v* **4** make or produce by machine. **machinery** *n* machines or

machine parts collectively. **machinist** *n* person who operates a machine. **machine gun** automatic gun that fires rapidly and continuously. **machine–readable** *adj* (of data) in a form suitable for processing by a computer.
macho ❶ [**match**–oh] *adj* strongly or exaggeratedly masculine.
mackerel *n* edible sea fish with blue and silver stripes.
mackintosh *n* **1** waterproof raincoat of rubberized cloth. **2** any raincoat.
macramé [mak–**rah**–mee] *n* ornamental work of knotted cord.
macrocosm *n* **1** the universe. **2** any large complete system.
mad ❶ *adj* **madder, maddest 1** mentally deranged, insane. **2** very foolish. **3** *Informal* angry. **4** frantic. **5** (foll. by *about* or *on*) very enthusiastic (about). **like mad** *Informal* with great energy, enthusiasm, or haste. **madly** *adv* **1** madness *n* **madden** *v* infuriate or irritate. **maddening** *adj* **madman, madwoman** *n*
madam *n* **1** polite form of address to a

THESAURUS

macabre *adj* = **gruesome**, dreadful, eerie, frightening, ghastly, ghostly, ghoulish, grim, grisly, morbid
Machiavellian *adj* = **scheming**, astute, crafty, cunning, cynical, double–dealing, opportunist, sly, underhand, unscrupulous
machine *n* **1** = **appliance**, apparatus, contraption, contrivance, device, engine, instrument, mechanism, tool **3** = **system**, machinery, organization, setup (*inf*), structure
macho *adj* = **manly**, chauvinist, masculine, virile

mad *adj* **1** = **insane**, crazy (*inf*), demented, deranged, *non compos mentis*, nuts (*sl*), of unsound mind, out of one's mind, psychotic, raving, unhinged, unstable ≠ **rational 2** = **foolish**, absurd, asinine, daft (*inf*), foolhardy, irrational, nonsensical, preposterous, senseless, wild ≠ **sound 3** *Inf* = **angry**, berserk, enraged, furious, incensed, livid (*inf*), pissed (*taboo sl*), pissed off (*taboo sl*), wild ≠ **calm**
4 = **frenzied**, excited, frenetic, uncontrolled, unrestrained, wild
5 = **enthusiastic**, ardent, avid, crazy (*inf*),

woman. 2 *Informal* precocious or
conceited girl.
madcap ❶ *adj* foolish or reckless.
made *v* past of MAKE.
Madonna *n* 1 the Virgin Mary. 2 picture or
statue of her.
madrigal *n* 16th-17th-century part song
for unaccompanied voices.
maelstrom ❶ [**male**–strom] *n* 1 great
whirlpool. 2 turmoil.
maestro ❶ [**my**–stroh] *n, pl* –**tri, –tros** 1
outstanding musician or conductor. 2 any
master of an art.
magazine ❶ *n* 1 periodical publication
with articles by different writers. 2
television or radio programme made up of
short nonfictional items. 3 appliance for
automatically supplying cartridges to a
gun or slides to a projector. 4 storehouse
for explosives or arms.
magenta [maj–**jen**–ta] *adj* deep purplish–
red.
maggot *n* larva of an insect. **maggoty** *adj*
magic ❶ *n* 1 supposed art of invoking
supernatural powers to influence events. 2
mysterious quality or power. ◆ *adj* 3 (also
magical) of, using, or like magic. 4
Informal wonderful, marvellous. **magically**

adv **magician** *n* 1 conjuror. 2 person with
magic powers.
magistrate ❶ *n* 1 public officer
administering the law. 2 justice of the
peace. **magisterial** *adj* 1 commanding or
authoritative. 2 of a magistrate.
magnanimous ❶ *adj* noble and
generous. **magnanimity** *n*
magnate ❶ *n* influential or wealthy
person, esp. in industry.
magnesium *n Chem* silvery–white metallic
element.
magnet *n* piece of iron or steel capable of
attracting iron and pointing north when
suspended. **magnetic** *adj* 1 having the
properties of a magnet. 2 powerfully
attractive. **magnetically** *adv* **magnetism** *n*
1 magnetic property. 2 powerful personal
charm. 3 science of magnetic properties.
magnetize *v* 1 make into a magnet. 2
attract strongly. **magnetic tape** plastic
strip coated with a magnetic substance for
recording sound or video signals.
magnificent ❶ *adj* 1 splendid or
impressive. 2 excellent. **magnificently** *adv*
magnificence *n*
magnify ❶ *v* –**fying, –fied** 1 increase in
apparent size, as with a lens.

fanatical, impassioned, infatuated, wild
≠ **uncaring** like mad *Inf* = **energetically**,
enthusiastically, excitedly, furiously,
rapidly, speedily, violently, wildly
madcap *adj* = **reckless**, crazy, foolhardy,
hare–brained, imprudent, impulsive, rash,
thoughtless
maelstrom *n* 1 = **whirlpool**, vortex
2 = **turmoil**, chaos, confusion, disorder,
tumult, upheaval
maestro *n* 1 = **virtuoso** 2 = **master**,
expert, fundi (*S Afr*), genius
magazine *n* 1 = **journal**, pamphlet,
periodical 2 = **storehouse**, arsenal, depot,
store, warehouse
magic *n* 1 = **sorcery**, black art,
enchantment, necromancy, witchcraft,
wizardry 2 = **conjuring**, illusion,
legerdemain, prestidigitation, sleight of

hand, trickery 3 = **charm**, allurement,
enchantment, fascination, glamour,
magnetism, power ◆ *adj* 4 (also **magical**)
= **miraculous**, bewitching, charming,
enchanting, entrancing, fascinating,
spellbinding 5 *Inf* = **marvellous**
magistrate *n* 1 = **judge** 2 = **justice of the
peace**, J.P., justice
magnanimous *adj* = **generous**, big–
hearted, bountiful, charitable, kind, noble,
selfless, unselfish
magnate *n* = **tycoon**, baron, big hitter
(*inf*), captain of industry, heavy hitter (*inf*),
mogul, plutocrat
magnificent *adj* 1 = **splendid**, glorious,
gorgeous, imposing, impressive, majestic,
regal, sublime, sumptuous ≠ **ordinary**
2 = **excellent**, brilliant, fine, outstanding,
splendid, superb

2 exaggerate. **magnification** n

magnitude ❶ n relative importance or size.

magnolia n shrub or tree with showy white or pink flowers.

magnum n large wine bottle holding about 1.5 litres.

magpie n black-and-white bird.

maharajah n former title of some Indian princes. **maharani** n fem

mahogany n hard reddish-brown wood of several tropical trees.

maiden ❶ n 1 Lit young unmarried woman. ◆ adj 2 unmarried. 3 first, e.g. maiden voyage. **maid** n female servant. **maidenly** adj **maidenhair** n fern with delicate fronds. **maiden name** woman's surname before marriage. **maiden over** Cricket over in which no runs are scored.

mail¹ ❶ n 1 letters and packages transported and delivered by the post office. 2 postal system. 3 single collection or delivery of mail. 4 train, ship, or aircraft carrying mail. 5 same as E-MAIL. ◆ v 6 send by mail. **mailbox** n Aust, Canad & US box into which letters and parcels are delivered. ◆ n **mail order** system of buying goods by post. **mailshot** n posting of advertising material to many selected people at once.

mail² n flexible armour of interlaced rings or links.

maim ❶ v cripple or mutilate.

main ❶ adj 1 chief or principal. ◆ n 2 principal pipe or line carrying water, gas, or electricity. ◆ pl 3 main distribution network for water, gas, or electricity. **in the main** on the whole. **mainly** adv for the most part, chiefly. **mainframe** n, adj Computers (denoting) a high-speed general-purpose computer. **mainland** n stretch of land which forms the main part of a country. **mainmast** n chief mast of a ship. **mainsail** n largest sail on a mainmast. **mainspring** n 1 chief cause or motive. 2 chief spring of a watch or clock. **mainstay** n 1 chief support. 2 rope securing a mainmast. **mainstream** adj (of) a prevailing cultural trend.

maintain ❶ v 1 continue or keep in existence. 2 keep up or preserve. 3 support financially. 4 assert. **maintenance** n 1 maintaining. 2 upkeep of a building, car, etc. 3 provision of money for a separated or divorced spouse.

maisonette n flat with more than one floor.

maize n type of corn with spikes of yellow grains.

majesty ❶ n, pl -ties 1 stateliness or grandeur. 2 supreme power. **majestic** adj **majestically** adv

major ❶ adj 1 greater in number, quality,

magnify v 1 = **enlarge**, amplify, blow up (inf), boost, dilate, expand, heighten, increase ≠ **reduce** 2 = **exaggerate**, inflate, intensify, overemphasize, overplay, overstate ≠ **understate**

magnitude n a = **importance**, consequence, greatness, moment, note, significance, weight ≠ **insignificance** b = **size**, amount, amplitude, extent, mass, quantity, volume

maiden n 1 Lit = **girl**, damsel, lass, lassie (inf), maid, virgin, wench ◆ adj 2 = **unmarried**, unwed 3 = **first**, inaugural, initial, introductory

mail¹ n 1 = **letters**, correspondence 1–3 = **post** ◆ v 6 = **post**, dispatch, forward, send

maim v = **cripple**, disable, hurt, injure, mutilate, wound

main adj 1 = **chief**, central, essential, foremost, head, leading, pre-eminent, primary, principal ≠ **least** ◆ n 2 = **conduit**, cable, channel, duct, line, pipe **in the main** = **on the whole**, for the most part, generally, in general, mainly

maintain v 1 = **continue**, carry on, perpetuate, prolong, retain, sustain ≠ **end** 2 = **keep up**, care for, preserve 3 = **look after**, provide for, support, take care of 4 = **assert**, avow, claim, contend, declare, insist, profess, state ≠ **disavow**

majesty n 1 = **grandeur**, glory,

or extent. **2** significant or serious. ◆ *n* **3** middle–ranking army officer. **4** scale in music. **5** *US & Aust* principal field of study at a university etc. ◆ *v* **6** (foll. by *in*) *US, Canadian, Aust & NZ* do one's principal study in (a particular subject). **majority** *n* greater number.

make ❶ *v* **making, made 1** create, construct, or establish. **2** cause to do or be. **3** bring about or produce. **4** perform (an action). **5** serve as or become. **6** amount to. **7** earn. ◆ *n* **8** brand, type, or style. **make do** manage with an inferior alternative. **make it** *Informal* be successful. **on the make** *Informal* out for profit or conquest. **maker** *n* **making** *n* **1** creation or production. ◆ *pl* **2** necessary requirements or qualities. **make–believe** *n* fantasy or pretence. **make for** *v* head towards. **make off with** *v* steal or abduct. **1 makeshift** *adj* serving as a temporary substitute. **make up** *v* **1** form or constitute. **2** prepare. **3** invent. **4** supply what is lacking, complete. **5** (foll. by *for*) compensate (for). **6** settle a quarrel. **7** apply cosmetics. **make–up** *n* **1** cosmetics. **2** way something is made. **3** mental or physical constitution.

makeweight *n* something unimportant added to make up a lack.

mal– *combining form* bad or badly, e.g. *malformation.*

maladjusted ❶ *adj Psychol* unable to meet the demands of society. **maladjustment** *n*

malady ❶ *n, pl* **–dies** disease or illness.

malaise ❶ [mal–**laze**] *n* vague feeling of unease, illness, or depression.

malapropism *n* comical misuse of a word by confusion with one which sounds similar.

malaria *n* infectious disease caused by the bite of some mosquitoes. **malarial** *adj*

malcontent ❶ *n* discontented person.

male ❶ *adj* **1** of the sex which can fertilize female reproductive cells. ◆ *n* **2** male person or animal.

malevolent ❶ [mal–**lev**–a–lent] *adj* wishing evil to others. **malevolence** *n*

malice ❶ [**mal**–iss] *n* desire to cause harm to others. **malicious** *adj* **maliciously** *adv*

malign ❶ [mal–**line**] *v* **1** slander or defame. ◆ *adj* **2** evil in influence or effect.

malinger *v* feign illness to avoid work. **malingerer** *n*

mall [**mawl**] *n* street or shopping area

——————— THESAURUS ———————

magnificence, nobility, pomp, splendour, stateliness

major *adj* **1** = **main**, bigger, chief, greater, higher, leading, senior, supreme ≠ **smaller 2** = **important**, critical, crucial, great, notable, outstanding, serious, significant ≠ **trivial**

make *v* **1** = **create**, assemble, build, construct, fashion, form, manufacture, produce, put together, synthesize **2** = **force**, cause, compel, constrain, drive, impel, induce, oblige, prevail upon, require **3** = **produce**, accomplish, bring about, cause, create, effect, generate, give rise to, lead to **4** = **perform**, carry out, do, effect, execute **6** = **amount to**, add up to, compose, constitute, form **7** = **earn**, clear, gain, get, net, obtain, win ◆ *n* **8** = **brand**, kind, model, sort, style, type, variety

maladjusted *adj Psychol* = **disturbed**,

alienated, neurotic, unstable

malady *n* = **disease**, affliction, ailment, complaint, disorder, illness, infirmity, sickness

malaise *n* **2** = **unease**, anxiety, depression, disquiet, melancholy

malcontent *n* = **troublemaker**, agitator, mischief–maker, rebel, stirrer (*inf*)

male *adj* **1** = **masculine**, manly, virile

malevolent *adj* = **spiteful**, hostile, ill– natured, malicious, malign, vengeful, vindictive

malice *n* = **spite**, animosity, enmity, evil intent, hate, hatred, ill will, malevolence, vindictiveness

malign *v* **1** = **disparage**, abuse, defame, denigrate, libel, run down, slander, smear, vilify ≠ **praise** ◆ *adj* **2** = **evil**, bad, destructive, harmful, hostile, injurious, malevolent, malignant, pernicious, wicked closed to vehicles.

mallard n wild duck.

malleable ⊕ [mal-lee–a–bl] adj 1 capable of being hammered or pressed into shape. 2 easily influenced. **malleability** n

mallet n 1 (wooden) hammer. 2 stick with a head like a hammer, used in croquet or polo.

malnutrition n inadequate nutrition.

malodorous ⊕ [mal–**lode**–or–uss] adj bad-smelling.

malpractice ⊕ n immoral, illegal, or unethical professional conduct.

malt n 1 grain, such as barley, prepared for use in making beer or whisky.

maltreat ⊕ v treat badly. **maltreatment** n

mammal n animal of the type that suckles its young. **mammalian** adj

mammary adj of the breasts or milk-producing glands.

mammon n wealth regarded as a source of evil.

mammoth ⊕ n 1 extinct elephant-like mammal. ♦ adj 2 colossal.

man ⊕ n, pl **men** 1 adult male. 2 human being or person. 3 mankind. 4 manservant. 5 piece used in chess etc. ♦ v **manning, manned** 6 supply with sufficient people for operation or defence. **manhood** n **mankind** n human beings collectively. **manly** adj (possessing qualities) appropriate to a man. **manliness** n **mannish** adj like a man. **man–hour** n work done by one person in one hour. **man–made** adj made artificially.

mana n NZ authority, influence.

manacle ⊕ [man–a–kl] n, v handcuff or fetter.

manage ⊕ v 1 succeed in doing. 2 be in charge of, administer. 3 handle or control. 4 cope with (financial) difficulties. **manageable** adj **management** n 1 managers collectively. 2 administration or organization. **manager, manageress** n person in charge of a business, institution, actor, sports team, etc. **managerial** adj

—————— THESAURUS ——————

≠ good

malleable adj 1 = **workable**, ductile, plastic, soft, tensile 2 = **manageable**, adaptable, biddable, compliant, impressionable, pliable, tractable

malodorous adj = **smelly**, fetid, mephitic, nauseating, noisome, offensive, putrid, reeking, stinking

malpractice n = **misconduct**, abuse, dereliction, mismanagement, negligence

maltreat v = **abuse**, bully, harm, hurt, ill-treat, injure, mistreat

mammoth adj 2 = **colossal**, enormous, giant, gigantic, huge, immense, massive, monumental, mountainous, prodigious

man n 1 = **male**, bloke (Brit inf), chap (inf), gentleman, guy (inf) 2 = **human**, human being, individual, person, soul 3 = **mankind**, Homo sapiens, humanity, humankind, human race, people 4 = **manservant**, attendant, retainer, servant, valet ♦ v 6 = **staff**, crew, garrison, occupy, people

① **manacle** n = **handcuff**, bond, chain,

mandarin n 1 high–ranking government official. 2 kind of small orange.

mandate ⊕ n 1 official or authoritative command. 2 authorization or instruction from an electorate to its representative or government. ◆ v 3 give authority to. **mandatory** adj compulsory.

mandible n lower jawbone or jawlike part.

mandolin n musical instrument with four pairs of strings.

mane n long hair on the neck of a horse, lion, etc.

manfully ⊕ adv bravely and determinedly.

manganese n Chem brittle greyish–white metallic element.

mange n skin disease of domestic animals.

manger n eating trough in a stable or barn.

mangle¹ ⊕ v 1 destroy by crushing and twisting. 2 spoil.

mangle² n 1 machine with rollers for squeezing water from washed clothes. ◆ v 2 put through a mangle.

mango n, pl **–goes, –gos** tropical fruit with sweet juicy yellow flesh.

mangrove n tropical tree with exposed roots, which grows beside water.

mania ⊕ n 1 extreme enthusiasm. 2 madness. **maniac** n 1 mad person. 2 Informal person who has an extreme enthusiasm for something. **maniacal** [man–**eye**–a–kl] adj

manicure n 1 cosmetic care of the fingernails and hands. ◆ v 2 care for (the fingernails and hands) in this way. **manicurist** n

manifest ⊕ adj 1 easily noticed, obvious. ◆ v 2 show plainly. 3 be evidence of. ◆ n 4 list of cargo or passengers for customs. **manifestation** n

manifold ⊕ adj 1 numerous and varied. ◆ n 2 pipe with several outlets, esp. in an internal–combustion engine.

manila, manilla n strong brown paper used for envelopes.

manipulate ⊕ v 1 handle skilfully. 2 control cleverly or deviously. **manipulation** n **manipulative** adj **manipulator** n

manna n Bible miraculous food which sustained the Israelites in the wilderness. 2 windfall.

mannequin n 1 woman who models clothes at a fashion show. 2 life–size dummy of the human body used to fit or display clothes.

manner ⊕ n 1 way a thing happens or is done. 2 person's bearing or behaviour. 3 type or kind. ◆ pl 4 (polite) social behaviour. **mannered** adj affected.

——— THESAURUS ———

fetter, iron, shackle

② **manacle** v = **handcuff**, bind, chain, fetter, put in chains, shackle

manage v 1 = **succeed**, accomplish, arrange, contrive, effect, engineer 2 = **administer**, be in charge (of), command, conduct, direct, handle, run, supervise 3 = **handle**, control, manipulate, operate, use 4 = **cope**, carry on, get by (inf), make do, muddle through, survive

mandate n 1 = **command**, commission, decree, directive, edict, instruction, order

manfully adv = **bravely**, boldly, courageously, determinedly, gallantly, hard, resolutely, stoutly, valiantly

mangle v 1 = **crush**, deform, destroy, disfigure, distort, mutilate, tear 2 = **spoil**,

ruin, wreck

mania n 1 = **obsession**, craze, fad (inf), fetish, fixation, passion, preoccupation, thing (inf) 2 = **madness**, delirium, dementia, derangement, insanity, lunacy

manifest adj 1 = **obvious**, apparent, blatant, clear, conspicuous, evident, glaring, noticeable, palpable, patent ≠ **masked** ◆ v 2 = **display**, demonstrate, exhibit, expose, express, reveal, show ≠ **hide**

manifold adj 1 = **numerous**, assorted, copious, diverse, many, multifarious, multiple, varied, various

manipulate v 1 = **work**, handle, operate, use 2 = **influence**, control, direct, engineer, manoeuvre

mannerism n person's distinctive habit or trait.

manoeuvre ❶ [man–**noo**–ver] n 1 skilful movement. 2 contrived, complicated, and possibly deceptive plan or action. ◆ pl 3 military or naval exercises. ◆ v 4 manipulate or contrive skilfully or cunningly. **manoeuvrable** adj

manor n large country house and its lands. **manorial** adj

manse n house provided for a minister in some religious denominations.

mansion ❶ n large house.

mantle ❶ n 1 loose cloak. 2 covering. 3 responsibilities and duties which go with a particular job or position.

mantra n Hinduism, Buddhism any sacred word or syllable used as an object of concentration.

manual ❶ adj 1 of or done with the hands. 2 by human labour rather than automatic means. ◆ n 3 handbook. 4 organ keyboard. **manually** adv

manufacture ❶ v 1 process or make (goods) on a large scale using machinery. 2 invent or concoct (an excuse etc.). ◆ n 3 process of manufacturing goods. **manufacturer** n

manure ❶ n 1 animal excrement used as a fertilizer.

manuscript n 1 book or document, orig. one written by hand. 2 copy for printing.

many ❶ adj more, most 1 numerous. ◆ n 2 large number.

map n 1 representation of the earth's surface or some part of it, showing geographical features. ◆ v mapping, mapped 2 make a map of. **map out** v plan.

maple n tree with broad leaves, a variety of which (**sugar maple**) yields sugar.

mar ❶ v marring, marred spoil or impair.

Mar. March.

maraca [mar–**rak**–a] n shaken percussion instrument made from a gourd containing dried seeds etc.

marathon n 1 long–distance race of 26 miles 385 yards (42.195 kilometres). 2 long or arduous task.

marble n 1 kind of limestone with a mottled appearance, which can be highly polished. 2 small glass ball used in playing marbles. ◆ pl 3 game of rolling these at one another. **marbled** adj having a mottled appearance like marble.

march ❶ v 1 walk with a military step. 2 make (a person or group) proceed. 3 progress steadily. ◆ n 4 action of

manner n 1 = **way**, method, mode 2 = **behaviour**, air, aspect, bearing, conduct, demeanour 3 = **type**, brand, category, form, kind, sort, variety

manoeuvre n 1 = **movement**, exercise, operation 2 = **stratagem**, dodge, intrigue, machination, ploy, ruse, scheme, subterfuge, tactic, trick ◆ v 4 = **manipulate**, contrive, engineer, machinate, pull strings, scheme, wangle (inf)

mansion n = **residence**, hall, manor, seat, villa

mantle n 1 = **cloak**, cape, hood, shawl, wrap 2 = **covering**, blanket, canopy, curtain, pall, screen, shroud, veil

manual adj 1 = **hand–operated** 2 = **human**, physical ◆ n 3 = **handbook**, bible, guide, instructions

manufacture v 1 = **make**, assemble, build, construct, create, mass–produce, produce, put together, turn out 2 = **concoct**, cook up (inf), devise, fabricate, invent, make up, think up, trump up ◆ n 3 = **making**, assembly, construction, creation, production

manure n 1 = **compost**, droppings, dung, excrement, fertilizer, kak (S Afr sl), muck, ordure

many adj 1 = **numerous**, abundant, countless, innumerable, manifold, myriad, umpteen (inf), various ◆ n 2 = **a lot**, heaps (inf), lots (inf), plenty, scores

mar v = **spoil**, blemish, damage, detract from, disfigure, hurt, impair, ruin, scar, stain, taint, tarnish marching. **5** steady progress. **6** distance covered by marching. **7** piece of music, as for a march. **marcher** *n*

March *n* third month of the year.

marchioness [marsh–on–**ness**] *n* **1** woman holding the rank of marquis. **2** wife or widow of a marquis.

mare *n* female horse or zebra. **mare's nest** discovery which proves worthless.

margarine *n* butter substitute made from animal or vegetable fats.

margin ❶ *n* **1** edge or border. **2** blank space round a printed page. **3** additional amount or one greater than necessary. **marginal** *adj* **1** insignificant, unimportant. **2** near a limit. **3** *Politics* (of a constituency) won by only a small margin. ♦ *n* **4** *Politics* marginal constituency. **marginally** *adv*

marigold *n* plant with yellow or orange flowers.

marijuana ❶ [mar–ree–**wah**–na] *n* dried flowers and leaves of the cannabis plant, used as a drug, esp. in cigarettes.

marina *n* harbour for yachts and other pleasure boats.

marinade *n* **1** seasoned liquid in which fish or meat is soaked before cooking. ♦ *v* **2** same as MARINATE. **marinate** *v* soak in marinade.

marine ❶ *adj* **1** of the sea or shipping. **2** *n* **3** soldier trained for land and sea combat.

4 country's shipping or fleet. **mariner** *n* sailor.

marionette *n* puppet worked with strings.

marital ❶ *adj* relating to marriage.

maritime ❶ *adj* **1** relating to shipping. **2** of, near, or living in the sea.

mark ❶ *n* **1** line, dot, scar, etc. visible on a surface. **2** distinguishing sign or symbol. **3** written or printed symbol. **4** letter or number used to grade academic work. **5** indication of position. **6** indication of some quality. **7** target or goal. ♦ *v* **8** make a mark on. **9** characterize or distinguish. **10** indicate. **11** pay attention to. **12** notice or watch. **13** grade (academic work). **14** stay close to (a sporting opponent) to hamper his or her play. **15 marked** *adj* noticeable. **markedly** *adv* **marker** *n*

market ❶ *n* **1** assembly or place for buying and selling. **2** demand for goods. ♦ *v* –**keting**, –**keted 3** offer or produce for sale. **on the market** for sale. **marketable** *adj* **marketing** *n* part of a business that controls the way that goods or services are sold. **market garden** place where fruit and vegetables are grown for sale. **marketplace** *n* **1** market. **2** commercial world. **market research** research into consumers' needs and purchases.

marmalade *n* jam made from citrus fruits.

marmoset *n* small bushy–tailed monkey.

——————— THESAURUS ———————

march *v* **1 = walk**, pace, parade, stride, strut **3 = file** ♦ *n* **4 = walk**, routemarch, trek **5 = progress**, advance, development, evolution, progression

margin *n* **1 = edge**, border, boundary, brink, perimeter, periphery, rim, side, verge

marijuana *n* **= cannabis**, dope (*sl*), grass (*sl*), hemp, pot (*sl*)

marine *adj* **1 = nautical**, maritime, naval, seafaring, seagoing

marital *adj* **= matrimonial**, conjugal, connubial, nuptial

maritime *adj* **1 = nautical**, marine, naval, oceanic, seafaring **2 = coastal**, littoral, seaside

mark *n* **1 = spot**, blemish, blot, line, scar, scratch, smudge, stain, streak **2 = sign**, badge, device, emblem, flag, hallmark, label, token **3 = symbol 6 = criterion**, measure, norm, standard, yardstick **7 = target**, aim, goal, object, objective, purpose ♦ *v* **8 = scar**, blemish, blot, scratch, smudge, stain, streak **9 = distinguish**, brand, characterize, denote, exemplify, flag, identify, illustrate, label, show, stamp **11 = pay attention**, attend, mind, pay heed **12 = observe**, note, notice, watch **13 = grade**, appraise, assess, correct, evaluate

market *n* **1 = fair**, bazaar, mart ♦ *v* **3 = sell**, retail, vend

maroon¹ *adj* reddish–purple.

maroon² ❶ *v* 1 abandon ashore, esp. on an island. 2 isolate without resources.

marquee *n* large tent used for a party or exhibition.

marquetry *n* ornamental inlaid work of wood.

marquis *n* (in various countries) nobleman of the rank above a count.

marrow *n* 1 fatty substance inside bones. 2 long thick striped green vegetable with whitish flesh.

marry ❶ *v* **–rying, –ried** 1 take as a husband or wife. 2 join or give in marriage. 3 unite closely. **marriage** *n* 1 state of being married. 2 wedding. **marriageable** *adj*

marsh ❶ *n* low–lying wet land. **marshy** *adj*

marshal ❶ *n* 1 officer of the highest rank. 2 official who organizes ceremonies or events. 3 *US* law officer. ♦ *v* **–shalling, –shalled** 4 arrange in order. 5 assemble. 6 conduct with ceremony.

marshmallow *n* spongy pink or white sweet.

marsupial [mar–**soop**–ee–al] *n* animal that carries its young in a pouch, such as a kangaroo.

marten *n* 1 weasel–like animal.

martial ❶ *adj* of war, warlike. **martial art** any of various philosophies and techniques of self–defence, orig. Eastern, such as karate. **martial law** law enforced by military authorities in times of danger or emergency.

martin *n* bird with a slightly forked tail.

martinet ❶ *n* person who maintains strict discipline.

martyr *n* 1 person who dies or suffers for his or her beliefs. ♦ *v* 2 make a martyr of. **be a martyr to** be constantly suffering from. **martyrdom** *n*

marvel ❶ *v* **–velling, –velled** 1 be filled with wonder. ♦ *n* 2 wonderful thing. **marvellous** *adj* 1 amazing. 2 wonderful.

marzipan *n* paste of ground almonds, sugar, and egg whites.

mascara *n* cosmetic for darkening the eyelashes.

mascot *n* person, animal, or thing supposed to bring good luck.

masculine ❶ *adj* 1 relating to males. 2 manly. 3 *Grammar* of the gender of nouns that includes some male animate things. **masculinity** *n*

mash *n* 1 *Informal* mashed potatoes. 2 bran or meal mixed with warm water as food for horses etc. ♦ *v* 3 crush into a soft mass.

mask ❶ *n* 1 covering for the face, as a disguise or protection. 2 behaviour that hides one's true feelings. ♦ *v* 3 cover with a mask. 4 hide or disguise.

masochism [**mass**–oh–kiz–zum] *n* condition in which (sexual) pleasure is obtained from feeling pain or from being humiliated. **masochist** *n* **masochistic** *adj*

mason *n* person who works with stone. **masonry** *n* stonework.

masquerade ❶ [mask–er–**aid**] *n* 1 deceptive show or pretence. 2 party at which masks and costumes are worn. ♦ *v* 3 pretend to be someone or something

maroon² *v* 1 = **abandon**, desert, leave 2 = **strand**, leave high and dry (*inf*)

marry *v* 1 = **wed**, get hitched (*sl*), tie the knot (*inf*) 3 = **unite**, ally, bond, join, knit, link, merge, unify, yoke

marsh *n* = **swamp**, bog, fen, morass, quagmire, slough

marshal *v* 4 = **arrange**, align, array, draw up, line up, order, organize 5 = **group**, deploy 6 = **conduct**, escort, guide, lead, shepherd, usher

martial *adj* = **military**, bellicose, belligerent, warlike

martinet *n* = **disciplinarian**, stickler

marvel *v* 1 = **wonder**, be amazed, be awed, gape ♦ *n* 2 = **wonder**, miracle, phenomenon, portent, prodigy

masculine *adj* 1 = **male**, manlike, mannish 2 = **manly**, virile

mask *n* 1 = **disguise**, camouflage, cover, veil 2 = **front**, facade, guise, screen ♦ *v* 4 = **disguise**, camouflage, cloak, conceal, else.

mass ❶ n 1 coherent body of matter. 2 large quantity or number. 3 *Physics* amount of matter in a body. ◆ adj 4 large–scale. 5 involving many people. ◆ v 6 form into a mass. **the masses** ordinary people. **massive** adj large and heavy. **mass–market** adj for or appealing to a large number of people. **mass media** means of communication to many people, such as television and newspapers. **mass–produce** v manufacture (standardized goods) in large quantities.

Mass n service of the Eucharist, esp. in the RC Church.

massacre ❶ [mass–a–ker] n 1 indiscriminate killing of large numbers of people. ◆ v 2 kill in large numbers.

massage ❶ [mass–ahzh] n 1 rubbing and kneading of parts of the body to reduce pain or stiffness. ◆ v 2 give a massage to. **masseur**, (*fem*) **masseuse** n person who gives massages.

mast n tall pole for supporting something, esp. a ship's sails. **masthead** n 1 *Naut* head of a mast. 2 name of a newspaper printed at the top of the front page.

mastectomy [mass–tek–tom–ee] n, pl –mies surgical removal of a breast.

master ❶ n 1 person in control, such as an employer or an owner of slaves or animals. 2 expert. 3 great artist. 4 original thing from which copies are made. 5 male teacher. ◆ adj 6 overall or controlling. 7 main or principal. ◆ v 8 acquire knowledge of or skill in. 9 overcome. **masterful** adj 1 domineering. 2 showing great skill. **masterly** adj showing great skill. **mastery** n 1 expertise. 2 control or command. **master key** key that opens all the locks of a set. **mastermind** v 1 plan and direct (a complex task). ◆ n 2 person who plans and directs a complex task. **masterpiece** n outstanding work of art.

masticate v chew. **mastication** n

mastiff n large dog.

masturbate v fondle the genitals (of). **masturbation** n

mat ❶ n 1 piece of fabric used as a floor covering or to protect a surface. 2 thick tangled mass. ◆ v **matting, matted** 3 tangle or become tangled into a dense mass.

matador n man who kills the bull in bullfights.

match[1] ❶ n 1 contest in a game or sport. 2 person or thing exactly like, equal to, or in harmony with another. 3 marriage. ◆ v 4 be exactly like, equal to, or in harmony with. 5 put in competition (with). 6 find a

cover, hide, obscure, screen, veil

masquerade n 1 = **pretence**, cloak, cover–up, deception, disguise, mask, pose, screen, subterfuge 2 = **masked ball**, fancy dress party, revel ◆ v 3 = **pose**, disguise, dissemble, dissimulate, impersonate, pass oneself off, pretend (to be)

mass n 1 = **piece**, block, chunk, hunk, lump 2 = **lot**, bunch, collection, heap, load, pile, quantity, stack 3 = **size**, bulk, greatness, magnitude ◆ adj 4 = **large–scale**, extensive, general, indiscriminate, wholesale, widespread ◆ v 6 = **gather**, accumulate, assemble, collect, congregate, rally, swarm, throng

massacre n 1 = **slaughter**, annihilation, blood bath, butchery, carnage,

extermination, holocaust, murder ◆ v 2 = **slaughter**, butcher, cut to pieces, exterminate, kill, mow down, murder, wipe out

massage n 1 = **rub–down**, manipulation ◆ v 2 = **rub down**, knead, manipulate

master n 1 = **head**, boss (*inf*), chief, commander, controller, director, governor, lord, manager, ruler ≠ **subject** 2 = **expert**, ace (*inf*), doyen, fundi (*S Afr*), genius, maestro, past master, virtuoso, wizard ≠ **novice** 5 = **teacher**, guide, guru, instructor, tutor ≠ **student** ◆ adj 6 = **main**, chief, foremost, leading, predominant, prime, principal ≠ **minor** ◆ v 8 = **learn**, get the hang of (*inf*), grasp 9 = **overcome**, conquer, defeat, tame, triumph over,

match for. **matchless** *adj* unequalled.
matchmaker *n* person who schemes to
bring about a marriage. **matchmaking** *n,
adj*

match² *n* small stick with a tip which
ignites when scraped on a rough surface.
matchbox *n* **matchstick** *n* 1 wooden part
of a match. ◆ *adj* 2 (of drawn figures) thin
and straight. **matchwood** *n* small
splinters.

mate¹ ❶ *n* 1 *Informal* friend. 2 *Informal*
common British and Australian term of
address between males. 3 associate or
colleague, e.g. *running mate; team-mate*. 4
sexual partner of an animal. 5 officer in a
merchant ship. 6 tradesman's assistant. ◆
v 7 pair (animals) or (of animals) be paired
for reproduction.

mate² *n, v Chess* checkmate.

material ❶ *n* 1 substance of which a thing
is made. 2 cloth. 3 information on which a
piece of work may be based. ◆ *pl* 4 things
needed for an activity. ◆ *adj* 5 of matter or
substance. 6 not spiritual. 7 affecting
physical wellbeing. 8 relevant. **materially**
adv considerably. **materialism** *n* 1
excessive interest in or desire for money
and possessions. 2 belief that only the
material world exists. **materialist** *adj, n*
materialistic *adj* **materialize** *v* 1 actually
happen. 2 come into existence or view.
materialization *n*

maternal ❶ *adj* 1 of a mother. 2 related
through one's mother. **maternity** *n* 1

motherhood. ◆ *adj* 2 of or for pregnant
women.

mathematics *n* science of number,
quantity, shape, and space. **mathematical**
adj **mathematically** *adv* **mathematician** *n*

maths *n Informal* mathematics.

matinée [mat–in–nay] *n* afternoon
performance in a theatre or cinema.

matins *pl n* early morning service in
various Christian Churches.

matriarch [mate–ree–ark] *n* female head
of a tribe or family. **matriarchal** *adj*
matriarchy *n* society governed by a
female, in which descent is traced through
the female line.

matriculate *v* enrol or be enrolled in a
college or university. **matriculation** *n*

matrimony ❶ *n* marriage. **matrimonial**
adj

matrix [may–trix] *n, pl* matrices 1
substance or situation in which something
originates, takes form, or is enclosed. 2
mould for casting. 3 *Maths* rectangular
array of numbers or elements.

matron *n* 1 staid or dignified married
woman. 2 woman who supervises the
domestic or medical arrangements of an
institution. 3 former name for NURSING
OFFICER. **matronly** *adj*

matter ❶ *n* 1 substance of which
something is made. 2 event, situation, or
subject. 3 written material in general. 4
pus. ◆ *v* 5 be of importance. **what's the
matter?** what is wrong?

vanquish ≠ **yield to**
match¹ *n* 1 = **game**, bout, competition,
contest, head–to–head, test, trial
2 = **equal**, counterpart, peer, rival
3 = **marriage**, alliance, pairing, partnership
◆ *v* 4 = **correspond**, accord, agree, fit, go
with, harmonize, tally 5 = **rival**, compare,
compete, emulate, equal, measure up to
mate¹ *n* 1 *Inf* = **friend**, buddy (*inf*), chum
(*inf*), comrade, crony, pal (*inf*)
3 = **colleague**, associate, companion
6 = **assistant**, helper, subordinate ◆ *v*
7 = **pair**, breed, couple

material *n* 1 = **substance**, matter, stuff
2 = **cloth**, fabric 3 = **information**, data,
evidence, facts, notes ◆ *adj* 5 = **tangible**,
concrete, palpable, substantial
6 = **physical**, bodily, corporeal
8 = **relevant**, applicable, apposite,
apropos, germane, pertinent
maternal *adj* 1 = **motherly**
matrimony *n* = **marriage**, nuptials,
wedding ceremony, wedlock
matter *n* 1 = **substance**, material, stuff
2 = **situation**, affair, business, concern,
event, incident, proceeding, question,

mattress *n* large stuffed flat case, often with springs, used on or as a bed.

mature ❶ *adj* 1 fully developed or grown-up. 2 ripe. ♦ *v* 3 make or become mature. 4 (of a bill or bond) become due for payment. **maturity** *n* **maturation** *n* process of becoming mature.

maudlin ❶ *adj* foolishly or tearfully sentimental.

maul ❶ *v* 1 handle roughly. 2 beat or tear.

mausoleum [maw-so-**lee**-um] *n* stately tomb.

mauve *adj* pale purple.

maverick ❶ *n, adj* independent and unorthodox (person).

maw *n* animal's mouth, throat, or stomach.

mawkish ❶ *adj* foolishly sentimental. **mawkishness** *n*

maxim ❶ *n* general truth or principle.

maximum ❶ *adj, n, pl* **-mums, -ma** greatest possible (amount or number). **maximal** *adj* **maximize** *v* increase to a maximum.

may *v, past tense* **might** used as an auxiliary to express possibility, permission, opportunity, etc. **maybe** *adv* perhaps, possibly.

✓ **WORD TIP**

In very careful usage *may* is used in preference to *can* for asking permission. *Might* is used to express a more tentative request: *May/might I ask a favour?*.

May *n* 1 fifth month of the year. 2 (m–) same as HAWTHORN. **mayfly** *n* short-lived aquatic insect. **maypole** *n* pole set up for dancing round on the first day of May to celebrate spring.

Mayday *n* international radio distress signal.

mayhem ❶ *n* violent destruction or confusion.

mayonnaise *n* creamy sauce of egg yolks, oil, and vinegar.

mayor *n* head of a municipality. **mayoralty** *n* (term of) office of a mayor.

maze ❶ *n* 1 complex network of paths or lines designed to puzzle. 2 any confusing network or system.

MBE Member of the Order of the British Empire.

MD 1 Doctor of Medicine. 2 Maryland.

me *pron* objective form of I.

THESAURUS

---

subject, topic ♦ *v* 5 = **be important**, carry weight, count, make a difference, signify **what's the matter?** = **problem**, complication, difficulty, distress, trouble, worry

mature *adj* 1 = **grown-up**, adult, full-grown, fully fledged, of age ≠ **immature** 2 = **ripe**, mellow, ready, seasoned ♦ *v* 3 = **develop**, age, bloom, blossom, come of age, grow up, mellow, ripen

maudlin *adj* = **sentimental**, mawkish, overemotional, slushy (*inf*), soppy (*Brit inf*), tearful, weepy (*inf*)

maul *v* 1 = **ill-treat**, abuse, batter, manhandle, molest 2 = **tear**, claw, lacerate, mangle

① **maverick** *n* = **rebel**, dissenter, eccentric, heretic, iconoclast, individualist, nonconformist, protester, radical

≠ **traditionalist**

② **maverick** *adj* = **rebel**, dissenting, eccentric, heretical, iconoclastic, individualistic, nonconformist, radical

mawkish *adj* = **sentimental**, emotional, maudlin, schmaltzy (*sl*), slushy (*inf*), soppy (*Brit inf*)

maxim *n* = **saying**, adage, aphorism, axiom, dictum, motto, proverb, rule

① **maximum** *adj* = **greatest**, highest, most, paramount, supreme, topmost, utmost ≠ **lowest**

② **maximum** *n* = **top**, ceiling, height, peak, pinnacle, summit, upper limit, utmost, zenith ≠ **bottom**

mayhem *n* = **chaos**, commotion, confusion, destruction, disorder, fracas, havoc, trouble, violence

maze *n* 1 = **labyrinth** 2 = **web**, confusion,

✓ **WORD TIP**
The use of *it's me* in preference to *it's I* is accepted as quite standard.

mead *n* alcoholic drink made from honey.
meadow ❶ *n* piece of grassland.
meagre ❶ *adj* scanty or insufficient.
meal¹ *n* 1 occasion when food is served and eaten. 2 the food itself.
meal² *n* grain ground to powder. **mealy** *adj* **mealy–mouthed** *adj* not outspoken enough.
mean¹ ❶ *v* **meaning, meant** 1 intend to convey or express. 2 signify, denote, or portend. 3 intend. 4 have importance as specified. **meaning** *n* sense, significance. **meaningful** *adj* **meaningless** *adj*
mean² ❶ *adj* 1 miserly, ungenerous, or petty. 2 despicable or callous. 3 *Chiefly US informal* bad–tempered. **meanly** *adv*
mean³ ❶ *n* 1 middle point between two extremes. 2 average. ◆ *pl* 3 method by which something is done. 4 money. ◆ *adj* 5 intermediate in size or quantity. 6 average. **by all means** certainly. **by no means** in no way. **means test** inquiry into a person's means to decide on eligibility for financial aid.
meander ❶ [mee–and–er] *v* 1 follow a winding course. 2 wander aimlessly. ◆ *n* 3 winding course.
measles *n* infectious disease producing red spots. **measly** *adj Informal* meagre.
measure ❶ *n* 1 size or quantity. 2 graduated scale etc. for measuring size or quantity. 3 unit of size or quantity. 4 extent. 5 action taken. 6 law. ◆ *v* 7 determine the size or quantity of. 8 be (a specified amount) in size or quantity. **measurable** *adj* **measured** *adj* 1 slow and steady. 2 carefully considered. **measurement** *n* 1 measuring. 2 size. **measure up to** *v* fulfil (expectations or requirements).
meat ❶ *n* animal flesh as food. **meaty** *adj* 1 (tasting) of or like meat. 2 brawny. 3 full of significance or interest.
mechanic *n* person skilled in repairing or operating machinery. **mechanics** *n* scientific study of motion and force. **mechanical** *adj* 1 of or done by machines. 2 (of an action) without thought or feeling. **mechanically** *adv*
mechanism ❶ *n* 1 way a machine works. 2 piece of machinery. 3 process or technique, e.g. *defence mechanism*. **mechanize** *v* 1 equip with machinery. 2 make mechanical or automatic. **mechanization** *n*

——— THESAURUS ———

imbroglio, tangle
meadow *n* = **field**, grassland, lea (*poet*), pasture
meagre *adj* = **insubstantial**, inadequate, measly, paltry, poor, puny, scanty, slight, small
mean¹ *v* 1 = **express**, convey, imply, indicate 2 = **signify**, denote, represent, spell, stand for, symbolize 3 = **intend**, aim, aspire, design, desire, plan, set out, want, wish
mean² *adj* 1 = **miserly**, mercenary, niggardly, parsimonious, penny–pinching, stingy, tight–fisted, ungenerous
≠ **generous** 2 = **dishonourable**, callous, contemptible, despicable, hard–hearted, petty, shabby, shameful, sordid, vile

≠ **good**
mean³ *n* 1 = **middle**, balance, compromise, happy medium, midpoint ◆ *adj* 6 = **average**, norm, standard
meander *v* 1 = **wind**, snake, turn, zigzag 2 = **wander**, ramble, stroll ◆ *n* 3 = **curve**, bend, coil, loop, turn, twist, zigzag
measure *n* 1 = **quantity**, allotment, allowance, amount, portion, quota, ration, share 2 = **gauge**, metre, rule, scale, yardstick 5 = **action**, act, deed, expedient, manoeuvre, means, procedure, step 6 = **law**, act, bill, resolution, statute ◆ *v* 7 = **quantify**, assess, calculate, calibrate, compute, determine, evaluate, gauge, weigh

medal *n* piece of metal with an inscription etc., given as a reward or memento. **medallion** *n* 1 disc–shaped ornament worn on a chain round the neck. 2 large medal. **medallist** *n* winner of a medal.

meddle ⊕ *v* interfere annoyingly. **meddlesome** *adj*

media *n* 1 a plural of MEDIUM. 2 the mass media collectively.

> ✓ **WORD TIP**
> *Media* is a plural noun. There is an increasing tendency to use it also as a singular noun because of the ambiguous senses of *medium*.

median *adj, n* middle (point or line).

mediate ⊕ *v* intervene in a dispute to bring about agreement. **mediation** *n* **mediator** *n*

medic *n Informal* doctor or medical student.

medicine ⊕ *n* 1 substance used to treat disease. 2 science of preventing, diagnosing, or curing disease. **medicinal** [med–**diss**–in–al] *adj* having therapeutic properties. **medical** *adj* **medicine man** witch doctor.

medieval [med–ee–**eve**–al] *adj* of the Middle Ages.

mediocre ⊕ [mee–dee–**oak**–er] *adj* 1 average in quality. 2 second–rate. **mediocrity** [mee–dee–**ok**–rit–ee] *n*

meditate ⊕ *v* 1 reflect deeply, esp. on spiritual matters. 2 think about or plan. **meditation** *n* **meditative** *adj*

medium ⊕ *adj* 1 midway between extremes, average. ◆ *n, pl* –**dia**, –**diums** 2 middle state, degree, or condition. 3 intervening substance producing an effect. 4 means of communicating news or information to the public, such as radio or newspapers. 5 person who can supposedly communicate with the dead. 6 surroundings or environment. **medium wave** radio wave with a wavelength between 100 and 1000 metres.

medley ⊕ *n* 1 miscellaneous mixture. 2 musical sequence of different tunes.

meek ⊕ *adj* submissive or humble. **meekly** *adv* **meekness** *n*

meet ⊕ *v* **meeting, met** 1 come together (with). 2 come into contact (with). 3 be at the place of arrival of. 4 make the acquaintance of. 5 satisfy (a need etc.). 6 experience. ◆ *n* 7 sports meeting. 8

————————| THESAURUS |————————

meat *n* = **food**, flesh, tucker (*Aust & NZ inf*)

mechanism *n* 2 = **machine**, apparatus, appliance, contrivance, device, instrument, tool 3 = **process**, agency, means, method, methodology, operation, procedure, system, technique, way

meddle *v* = **interfere**, butt in, intervene, intrude, pry, tamper

mediate *v* = **intervene**, arbitrate, conciliate, intercede, reconcile, referee, step in (*inf*), umpire

medicine *n* 1 = **remedy**, cure, drug, medicament, medication, nostrum

mediocre *adj* = **average**, indifferent, middling, ordinary, passable, pedestrian, run–of–the–mill, so–so (*inf*), undistinguished 2 = **second–rate**, inferior

meditate *v* 1 = **reflect**, cogitate, consider, contemplate, deliberate, muse, ponder,

ruminate, think 2 = **plan**, have in mind, intend, purpose, scheme

medium *adj* 1 = **average**, fair, intermediate, mean, median, mediocre, middle, middling, midway ≠ **unique** ◆ *n* 2 = **middle**, average, centre, compromise, mean, midpoint 3 = **means**, agency, channel, instrument, mode, organ, vehicle, way 5 = **spiritualist**, channeller 6 = **environment**, atmosphere, conditions, milieu, setting, surroundings

medley *n* 1 = **mixture**, assortment, farrago, hotchpotch, jumble, *melange*, miscellany, mishmash, mixed bag (*inf*), potpourri

meek *adj* = **submissive**, acquiescent, compliant, deferential, docile, gentle, humble, mild, modest, timid, unassuming, unpretentious assembly of a hunt. **meeting** n 1 coming together. 2 assembly.

megabyte n Computers 2^{20} or 1 048 576 bytes.

megalith n great stone, esp. as part of a prehistoric monument. **megalithic** adj

megalomania n craving for or mental delusions of power. **megalomaniac** adj, n

megaphone n cone–shaped instrument used to amplify the voice.

megaton n explosive power equal to that of one million tons of TNT.

melancholy ❶ [**mel**–an–kol–lee] n 1 sadness or gloom. ◆ adj 2 sad or gloomy. **melancholia** [mel–an–**kole**–lee–a] n state of depression. **melancholic** adj, n

melanin n dark pigment found in the hair, skin, and eyes of humans and animals.

mêlée ❶ [**mel**–lay] n noisy confused fight or crowd.

mellifluous ❶ [mel–**lif**–flew–uss] adj (of sound) smooth and sweet.

mellow ❶ adj 1 soft, not harsh. 2 kind–hearted, esp. through maturity. 3 (of fruit) ripe. ◆ v 4 make or become mellow.

melodrama n 1 play full of extravagant action and emotion. 2 overdramatic behaviour or emotion. **melodramatic** adj

melody ❶ n, pl –dies 1 series of musical notes which make a tune. 2 sweet sound. **melodic** [mel–**lod**–ik] adj 1 of melody. 2 melodious. **melodious** [mel–**lode**–ee–uss] adj 1 pleasing to the ear. 2 tuneful.

melon n large round juicy fruit with a hard rind.

melt ❶ v 1 (cause to) become liquid by heat. 2 dissolve. 3 disappear. 4 blend (into). 5 soften through emotion. **meltdown** n (in a nuclear reactor) melting of the fuel rods, with the possible release of radiation.

member ❶ n 1 individual making up a body or society. 2 limb. **membership** n

membrane n thin flexible tissue in a plant or animal body. **membranous** adj

memento ❶ n, pl –tos, –toes thing serving to remind, souvenir.

memo n, pl memos short for MEMORANDUM.

memoir ❶ [**mem**–wahr] n 1 biography or historical account based on personal knowledge. ◆ pl 2 collection of these. 3 autobiography.

——— THESAURUS ———

meet v 1 = **gather**, assemble, collect, come together, congregate, convene, muster ≠ **scatter** 2 a = **encounter**, bump into, chance on, come across, confront, contact, happen on, run across, run into ≠ **miss** b = **converge**, come together, connect, cross, intersect, join, link up, touch ≠ **diverge** 5 = **fulfil**, answer, come up to, comply with, discharge, match, measure up to, satisfy ≠ **fail**

melancholy n 1 = **sadness**, dejection, depression, despondency, gloom, low spirits, misery, sorrow, unhappiness ≠ **delight** ◆ adj 2 = **sad**, depressed, despondent, dispirited, downhearted, gloomy, glum, miserable, mournful, sorrowful ≠ **happy**

mêlée n = **fight**, brawl, fracas, free–for–all (inf), rumpus, scrimmage, scuffle, set–to (inf), skirmish, tussle

mellifluous adj = **sweet**, dulcet, euphonious, honeyed, silvery, smooth, soft, soothing, sweet–sounding

mellow adj 1 = **soft**, delicate 3 = **ripe**, full–flavoured, mature, rich, sweet ≠ **green** ◆ v 4 = **mature**, develop, improve, ripen, season, soften, sweeten

melody n 1 = **tune**, air, music, song, strain, theme 2 = **tunefulness**, euphony, harmony, melodiousness, musicality

melt v 1, 2 = **dissolve**, fuse, liquefy, soften, thaw 3 = **disappear**, disperse, dissolve, evanesce, evaporate, fade, vanish 5 = **soften**, disarm, mollify, outspan (S Afr), relax

member n 1 = **representative**, associate, fellow 2 = **limb**, appendage, arm, extremity, leg, part

memento n = **souvenir**, keepsake, memorial, relic, remembrance, reminder, token, trophy

memoir n 1 = **account**, biography, essay,

memory ❶ *n, pl* **–ries** 1 ability to remember. 2 sum of things remembered. 3 particular recollection. 4 length of time one can remember. 5 commemoration. 6 part of a computer which stores information. **memorable** *adj* **memorize** *v* commit to memory. **memorial** *n* 1 something serving to commemorate a person or thing. ◆ *adj* 2 serving as a memorial.

men *n* plural of MAN.

menace ❶ *n* 1 threat. 2 *Informal* nuisance. ◆ *v* 3 threaten, endanger. **menacing** *adj*

menagerie [min–**naj**–er–ee] *n* collection of wild animals for exhibition.

mend ❶ *v* 1 repair or patch. 2 recover or heal. 3 make or become better. ◆ *n* 4 mended area. **on the mend** regaining health.

menial ❶ [**mean**–nee–al] *adj* 1 involving boring work of low status. ◆ *n* 2 domestic servant.

meningitis [men–in–**jite**–iss] *n* inflammation of the membranes of the brain.

menopause *n* time when a woman's menstrual cycle ceases. **menopausal** *adj*

menstruation *n* approximately monthly discharge of blood and cellular debris from the womb of a nonpregnant woman. **menstruate** *v* **menstrual** *adj*

mensuration *n* measuring, esp. in geometry.

mental ❶ *adj* 1 of, in, or done by the mind. 2 of or for mental illness. 3 *Informal* insane. **mentally** *adv* **mentality** *n* way of thinking.

menthol *n* organic compound found in peppermint, used medicinally.

mention ❶ *v* 1 refer to briefly. 2 acknowledge. ◆ *n* 3 brief reference to a person or thing. 4 acknowledgment.

mentor ❶ *n* adviser or guide.

menu ❶ *n* 1 list of dishes to be served, or from which to choose. 2 *Computers* list of options displayed on a screen.

mercantile ❶ *adj* of trade or traders.

mercenary ❶ *adj* 1 influenced by greed. 2 working merely for reward. ◆ *n, pl* **–aries** 3 hired soldier.

merchant ❶ *n* person engaged in trade, wholesale trader. **merchandise** *n*

——————{ THESAURUS }——————

journal, life, monograph, narrative, record

memory *n* 1 = **recall**, retention 3 = **recollection**, remembrance, reminiscence 5 = **commemoration**, honour, remembrance

menace *n* 1 = **threat**, intimidation, warning 2 *Inf* = **nuisance**, annoyance, pest, plague, troublemaker ◆ *v* 3 = **threaten**, bully, frighten, intimidate, loom, lour *or* lower, terrorize

mend *v* 1 = **repair**, darn, fix, patch, refit, renew, renovate, restore, retouch 2 = **heal**, convalesce, get better, recover, recuperate 3 = **improve**, ameliorate, amend, correct, emend, rectify, reform, revise ◆ *n* 4 = **repair**, darn, patch, stitch **on the mend** = **convalescent**, getting better, improving, recovering, recuperating

menial *adj* 1 = **unskilled**, boring, dull, humdrum, low–status, routine ≠ **high** ◆ *n* 2 = **servant**, attendant, dogsbody (*inf*),

drudge, flunky, lackey, skivvy (*chiefly Brit*), underling ≠ **lord**

mental *adj* 1 = **intellectual**, cerebral 3 *Inf* = **insane**, deranged, disturbed, mad, mentally ill, psychotic, unbalanced, unstable

mention *v* 1 = **refer to**, bring up, declare, disclose, divulge, intimate, point out, reveal, state, touch upon ◆ *n* 3 = **reference**, allusion, indication, observation, remark 4 = **acknowledgment**, citation, recognition, tribute

mentor *n* = **guide**, adviser, coach, counsellor, guru, instructor, teacher, tutor

menu *n* 1 = **bill of fare**, carte du jour, tariff (*chiefly Brit*)

mercantile *adj* = **commercial**, trading

mercenary *adj* 1 = **greedy**, acquisitive, avaricious, grasping, money–grubbing (*inf*), sordid, venal ≠ **liberal** ◆ *n* commodities. **merchant bank** bank dealing mainly with businesses and investment. **merchantman** n trading ship. **merchant navy** ships or crew engaged in a nation's commercial shipping.

mercury n Chem silvery liquid metal. **mercurial** adj lively, changeable.

mercy ❶ n, pl **–cies 1** compassionate treatment of an offender or enemy who is in one's power. **2** merciful act. **merciful** adj **1** compassionate. **2** giving relief. **merciless** adj

mere ❶ adj nothing more than, e.g. mere chance. **merely** adv

merge ❶ v combine or blend. **merger** n combination of business firms into one.

meridian n imaginary circle of the earth passing through both poles.

meringue [mer–rang] n **1** baked mixture of egg whites and sugar. **2** small cake of this.

merit ❶ n **1** excellence or worth. ◆ pl **2** admirable qualities. ◆ v **–iting, –ited 3** deserve. **meritorious** adj deserving praise.

meritocracy [mer–it–tok–rass–ee] n rule by people of superior talent or intellect.

mermaid n imaginary sea creature with the upper part of a woman and the lower part of a fish.

merry ❶ adj **–rier, –riest 1** cheerful or jolly. **2** Informal slightly drunk. **merrily** adv **merriment** n **merry–go–round** n roundabout. **merrymaking** n noisy, cheerful celebrations or fun.

mesh ❶ n **1** network or net. **2** (open space between) strands forming a network. ◆ v **3** (of gear teeth) engage.

mesmerize ❶ v **1** hold spellbound. **2** Obs hypnotize.

mess ❶ n **1** untidy or dirty confusion. **2** trouble or difficulty. **3** place where servicemen eat. **4** group of servicemen who regularly eat together. ◆ v **5** muddle or dirty. **6** (foll. by about) potter about. **7** (foll. by with) interfere with.

message ❶ n **1** communication sent. **2** meaning or moral. **messenger** n bearer of a message.

━━━━━━ THESAURUS ━━━━━━

3 = **hireling**, soldier of fortune

merchant n = **tradesman**, broker, dealer, purveyor, retailer, salesman, seller, shopkeeper, supplier, trader, trafficker, vendor, wholesaler

mercy n **1** = **compassion**, clemency, forbearance, forgiveness, grace, kindness, leniency, pity ≠ **cruelty 2** = **blessing**, boon, godsend

mere adj = **simple**, bare, common, nothing more than, plain, pure, sheer

merge v = **combine**, amalgamate, blend, coalesce, converge, fuse, join, meet, mingle, mix, unite ≠ **part**

merit n **1** = **worth**, advantage, asset, excellence, goodness, integrity, quality, strong point, talent, value, virtue ◆ v **3** = **deserve**, be entitled to, be worthy of, earn, have a right to, rate, warrant

merry adj **1** = **cheerful**, blithe, carefree, convivial, festive, happy, jolly, joyous ≠ **sad 2** Inf = **tipsy**, happy, mellow, squiffy (Brit inf), tiddly (sl, chiefly Brit)

mesh n **1** = **net**, netting, network, tracery, web ◆ v **3** = **engage**, combine, connect, coordinate, dovetail, harmonize, interlock, knit

mesmerize v **1** = **entrance**, captivate, enthral, fascinate, grip, hold spellbound, hypnotize

mess n **1** = **disorder**, chaos, clutter, confusion, disarray, disorganization, hotchpotch, jumble, litter, shambles, untidiness **2** = **difficulty**, deep water, dilemma, fix (inf), hole (inf), jam (inf), muddle, pickle (inf), plight, predicament, tight spot ◆ v **5** = **dirty**, clutter, disarrange, dishevel, muck up (Brit sl), muddle, pollute, scramble **6** (foll. by about) = **potter**, amuse oneself, dabble, fool (about or around), muck about (inf), play about or around, trifle **7** (foll. by with) = **interfere**, fiddle (inf), meddle, play, tamper, tinker

message n **1** = **communication**, bulletin, communiqué, dispatch, letter,

Messiah *n* 1 Jews' promised deliverer. 2 Christ. **Messianic** *adj*

met *v* past of MEET[1].

metabolism [met-**tab**-oh-liz-zum] *n* chemical processes of a living body. **metabolic** *adj* **metabolize** *v* produce or be produced by metabolism.

metal *n* 1 chemical element, such as iron or copper, that is malleable and capable of conducting heat and electricity. 2 **metallic** *adj* **metallurgy** *n* scientific study of the structure, properties, extraction, and refining of metals. **metallurgical** *adj* **metallurgist** *n*

metamorphosis ❶ [met–a–**more**–foss–is] *n, pl* –**phoses** [–foss–eez] change of form or character. **metamorphic** *adj* (of rocks) changed in texture or structure by heat and pressure. **metamorphose** *v* transform.

metaphor ❶ *n* figure of speech in which a term is applied to something it does not literally denote in order to imply a resemblance, e.g. *he is a lion in battle*. **metaphorical** *adj* **metaphorically** *adv*

mete ❶ *v* (usu. with *out*) deal out as punishment.

meteor *n* small fast–moving heavenly body, visible as a streak of incandescence if it enters the earth's atmosphere. **meteoric** [meet-ee-**or**-rik] *adj* 1 of a meteor. 2 brilliant and very rapid. **meteorite** *n* meteor that has fallen to earth.

meteorology *n* study of the earth's atmosphere, esp. for weather forecasting. **meteorological** *adj* **meteorologist** *n*

meter *n* 1 instrument for measuring and recording something, such as the consumption of gas or electricity. ◆ *v* 2 measure by meter.

methane *n* colourless inflammable gas.

method ❶ *n* 1 way or manner. 2 technique. 3 orderliness. **methodical** *adj* orderly. **methodically** *adv* **methodology** *n* particular method or procedure.

meths *n Informal* methylated spirits.

methylated spirits *n* alcohol with methanol added, used as a solvent and for heating.

meticulous ❶ *adj* very careful about details. **meticulously** *adv*

metre *n* 1 basic unit of length equal to about 1.094 yards (100 centimetres). 2 rhythm of poetry. **metric** *adj* of the decimal system of weights and measures based on the metre. **metrical** *adj* 1 of measurement. 2 of poetic metre. **metrication** *n* conversion to the metric system.

metronome *n* instrument which marks musical time by means of a ticking pendulum.

metropolis [mit-**trop**-oh-liss] *n* chief city of a country or region. **metropolitan** *adj* of a metropolis.

mettle ❶ *n* courage or spirit.

mew *n* 1 cry of a cat. ◆ *v* 2 utter this cry.

mews *n* yard or street orig. of stables, now often converted into houses.

mezzanine [**mez**-zan-een] *n* intermediate storey, esp. between the ground and first floor.

——————— THESAURUS ———————

memorandum, note, tidings, word
2 = point, idea, import, meaning, moral, purport, theme

metamorphosis *n* = **transformation**, alteration, change, conversion, mutation, transmutation

metaphor *n* = **figure of speech**, allegory, analogy, image, symbol, trope

mete *v* = **distribute**, administer, apportion, assign, deal, dispense, dole, portion

method *n* 1 = **manner**, approach, mode,

modus operandi, procedure, process, routine, style, system, way **2 = technique**
3 = orderliness, order, organization, pattern, planning, purpose, regularity, system

meticulous *adj* = **thorough**, exact, fastidious, fussy, painstaking, particular, precise, punctilious, scrupulous, strict

mettle *n* = **courage**, bravery, fortitude, gallantry, life, nerve, pluck, resolution, spirit, valour, vigour

mezzo–soprano [**met**-so-] *n* voice or singer between a soprano and contralto (also **mezzo**).

mg milligram(s).

MI Michigan.

miasma [mee-**azz**-ma] *n* unwholesome or foreboding atmosphere.

mica [**my**-ka] *n* glasslike mineral used as an electrical insulator.

microbe ⓣ *n* minute organism, esp. one causing disease. **microbial** *adj*

microchip *n* small wafer of silicon containing electronic circuits.

microcosm *n* 1 miniature representation of something.

microfiche [**my**-kroh-feesh] *n* microfilm in sheet form.

microfilm *n* miniaturized recording of books or documents on a roll of film.

microphone *n* instrument for amplifying or transmitting sounds.

microprocessor *n* integrated circuit acting as the central processing unit in a small computer.

microscope *n* instrument with lens(es) which produces a magnified image of a very small object. **microscopic** *adj* 1 too small to be seen except with a microscope. 2 very small. 3 of a microscope. **microscopically** *adv* **microscopy** *n* use of a microscope.

microwave *n* 1 electromagnetic wave with a wavelength of a few centimetres, used in radar and cooking. 2 microwave oven. ◆ *v* 3 cook in a microwave oven. **microwave oven** oven using microwaves to cook food quickly.

mid *adj* intermediate, middle. **midnight** *n* twelve o'clock at night. **midway** *adj, adv* halfway.

middle ⓣ *adj* 1 equidistant from two extremes. 2 medium, intermediate. ◆ *n* 3 middle point or part. **middle age** period of life between youth and old age. **middle–aged** *adj* **Middle Ages** period from about 1000 AD to the 15th century. **middle class** social class of business and professional people. **middle–class** *adj* **Middle East** area around the eastern Mediterranean up to and including Iran. **middleman** *n* trader who buys from the producer and sells to the consumer. **middle–of–the–road** *adj* 1 politically moderate. 2 (of music) generally popular. **middleweight** *n* boxer weighing up to 160lb (professional) or 75kg (amateur).

midge *n* small mosquito–like insect.

midget ⓣ *n* very small person or thing.

midriff *n* middle part of the body.

midst ⓣ *n* **in the midst of** 1 surrounded by. 2 at a point during.

midwife *n* trained person who assists at childbirth. **midwifery** *n*

mien [**mean**] *n Lit* person's bearing, demeanour, or appearance.

might¹ *v* past tense of MAY.

✓ **WORD TIP**
Both *might* and *may* can be used to express a tentative request: *Might/may I ask a favour?*

might² ⓣ *n* power or strength. **mighty** *adj* 1 powerful. 2 important. ◆ *adv* 3 *US & Aust informal* very. **mightily** *adv*

migraine [**mee**-grain] *n* severe headache, often with nausea and visual disturbances.

migrate ⓣ *v* 1 move from one place to settle in another. 2 (of animals) journey between different habitats at specific

───────── THESAURUS ─────────

microbe *n* = **microorganism**, bacillus, bacterium, bug (*inf*), germ, virus

middle *adj* 1 = **central**, halfway, intermediate, intervening, mean, median, mid 2 = **medium** ◆ *n* 3 = **centre**, focus, halfway point, heart, midpoint, midsection, midst

midget *n* = **dwarf**, pygmy *or* pigmy, shrimp (*inf*), Tom Thumb

midst *n* **in the midst of** 1 = **among**, amidst, in the middle of, in the thick of, surrounded by 2 = **during**

might² *n* = **power**, energy, force, strength, vigour **with might and main** = **forcefully**, seasons. **migration** n **migrant** n 1 person or animal that moves from one place to another. ◆ adj 2 moving from one place to another. **migratory** adj

mike n Informal microphone.

mild ❶ adj 1 not strongly flavoured. 2 gentle. 3 calm or temperate. **mildly** adv **mildness** n

mildew n destructive fungus on plants or things exposed to moisture.

mile n unit of length equal to 1760 yards or 1.609 kilometres. **mileage** n 1 distance travelled in miles. 2 miles travelled by a motor vehicle per gallon of petrol. 3 Informal usefulness of something. **mileometer** n device that records the number of miles a vehicle has travelled. **milestone** n 1 significant event. 2 stone marker showing the distance to a certain place.

milieu ❶ [meal–**yer**] n, pl milieux, milieus [meal–**yerz**] environment or surroundings.

militant ❶ adj aggressive or vigorous in support of a cause. **militancy** n

military ❶ adj 1 of or for soldiers, armies, or war. ◆ n 2 armed services. **militarism** n belief in the use of military force and methods. **militarized** adj

militate ❶ v (usu. with against or for) have a strong influence or effect.

> ✓ **WORD TIP**
> Do not confuse militate with mitigate 'make less severe'.

milk ❶ n 1 white fluid produced by female mammals to feed their young. 2 milk of cows, goats, etc., used by humans as food. 3 fluid in some plants. ◆ v 4 draw milk from. 5 exploit (a person or situation). **milky** adj **Milky Way** luminous band of stars stretching across the night sky. **milkman** n man who delivers milk to people's houses. 1 **milkshake** n frothy flavoured cold milk drink. **milksop** n feeble man. **milk teeth** first set of teeth in young children.

mill ❶ n 1 factory. 2 machine for grinding, processing, or rolling. ◆ v 3 grind, press, or process in or as if in a mill. 4 cut fine grooves across the edges of (coins). 5 move in a confused manner. **miller** n

millennium n, pl –nia, –niums 1 period of a thousand years. 2 future period of peace and happiness.

millet n a cereal grass.

milli– combining form denoting a thousandth part, e.g. millisecond.

milliner n maker or seller of women's hats. **millinery** n

million n one thousand thousands. **millionth** adj, n **millionaire** n person who owns at least a million pounds, dollars, etc.

millipede n small animal with a jointed body and many pairs of legs.

mime ❶ n 1 acting without the use of words. 2 performer who does this. ◆ v 3 act in mime.

mimic ❶ v –icking, –icked 1 imitate (a

─────┤ T H E S A U R U S ├─────

lustily, manfully, mightily, vigorously

migrate v 1 = **move**, emigrate, journey, roam, rove, travel, trek, voyage, wander

mild adj 1 = **bland**, smooth 2 = **gentle**, calm, docile, easy–going, equable, meek, peaceable, placid ≠ **strong** 3 = **temperate**, balmy, calm, moderate, tranquil, warm ≠ **cold**

milieu n = **surroundings**, background, element, environment, locale, location, scene, setting

militant adj = **aggressive**, active, assertive,

combative, vigorous

military adj 1 = **warlike**, armed, martial, soldierly ◆ n 2 = **armed forces**, army, forces, services

militate v militate against = **counteract**, be detrimental to, conflict with, counter, oppose, resist, tell against, weigh against

milk v 5 = **exploit**, extract, pump, take advantage of

mill n 1 = **factory**, foundry, plant, works 2 = **grinder**, crusher ◆ v 3 = **grind**, crush, grate, pound, powder 5 = **swarm**, crowd,

person or manner), esp. for satirical effect.
◆ *n* **2** person or animal that is good at
mimicking. **mimicry** *n*

mimosa *n* shrub with fluffy yellow flowers
and sensitive leaves.

minaret *n* tall slender tower of a mosque.

mince ● *v* **1** cut or grind into very small
pieces. **2** walk or speak in an affected
manner. **3** soften or moderate (one's
words). ◆ *n* **4** minced meat. **mincer** *n*
machine for mincing meat. **mincing** *adj*
affected in manner. **mincemeat** *n* sweet
mixture of dried fruit and spices. **mince
pie** pie containing mincemeat.

mind ● *n* **1** thinking faculties. **2** memory or
attention. **3** intention. **4** sanity. ◆ *v* **5** take
offence at. **6** pay attention to. **7** take care
of. **8** be cautious or careful about
(something). **minded** *adj* having an
inclination as specified, e.g. *politically
minded*. **minder** *n Informal* aide or
bodyguard. **mindful** *adj* **1** heedful. **2**
keeping aware. **mindless** *adj* **1** stupid. **2**
requiring no thought.

mine[1] *pron* belonging to me.

mine[2] ● *n* **1** deep hole for digging out
coal, ores, etc. **2** bomb placed under the
ground or in water. **3** profitable source. ◆
v **4** dig for minerals. **5** dig (minerals) from
a mine. **6** place explosive mines in or on.
miner *n* **minefield** *n* area of land or water
containing mines. **minesweeper** *n* ship for
clearing away mines.

mineral *n* **1** naturally occurring inorganic
substance, such as metal. ◆ *adj* **2** of,
containing, or like minerals. **mineralogy**
[min–er–**al**–a–jee] *n* study of minerals.
mineralogist *n* **mineral water** water
containing dissolved mineral salts or gases.

minestrone [min–ness–**strone**–ee] *n* soup
containing vegetables and pasta.

mingle ● *v* **1** mix or blend. **2** come into
association (with).

mini *n, adj* **1** (something) small or
miniature. **2** short (skirt).

miniature ● *n* **1** small portrait, model, or
copy. ◆ *adj* **2** small-scale. **miniaturist** *n*
miniaturize *v* make to a very small scale.

minim *n Music* note half the length of a
semibreve.

minimum ● *adj, n, pl* **–mums, –ma** least
possible (amount or number). **minimal** *adj*
minimum. **minimize** *v* **1** reduce to a
minimum. **2** belittle.

THESAURUS

throng

mime *v* **3** = **act out**, gesture, represent,
simulate

mimic *v* **1** = **imitate**, ape, caricature, do
(*inf*), impersonate, parody, take off (*inf*) ◆
n **2** = **imitator**, caricaturist, copycat (*inf*),
impersonator, impressionist

mince *v* **1** = **cut**, chop, crumble, grind,
hash **3** = **tone down**, moderate, soften,
spare, weaken

mind *n* **1** = **intelligence**, brain(s) (*inf*), grey
matter (*inf*), intellect, reason, sense,
understanding, wits **2** = **memory**,
recollection, remembrance **3** = **intention**,
desire, disposition, fancy, inclination,
leaning, notion, urge, wish **4** = **sanity**,
judgment, marbles (*inf*), mental balance,
rationality, reason, senses, wits ◆ *v*
5 = **take offence**, be affronted, be
bothered, care, disapprove, dislike, object,
resent **6** = **pay attention**, heed, listen to,
mark, note, obey, observe, pay heed to,
take heed **7** = **guard**, attend to, keep an
eye on, look after, take care of, tend,
watch **8** = **be careful**, be cautious, be on
(one's) guard, be wary, take care, watch
make up one's mind = **decide**, choose,
determine, resolve

mine[2] *n* **1** = **pit**, colliery, deposit,
excavation, shaft **3** = **source**, abundance,
fund, hoard, reserve, stock, store, supply,
treasury, wealth ◆ *v* **4, 5** = **dig up**, dig for,
excavate, extract, hew, quarry, unearth

mingle *v* **1** = **mix**, blend, combine,
intermingle, interweave, join, merge, unite
≠ **part 2** = **associate**, consort, fraternize,
hang about *or* around, hobnob, rub
shoulders (*inf*), socialize ≠ **avoid**

miniature *adj* **2** = **small**, diminutive, little,
minuscule, minute, scaled-down, tiny, toy

minion ⊕ *n* servile assistant.

minister ⊕ *n* 1 head of a government department. 2 diplomatic representative. 3 clergyman. ◆ *v* 4 (foll. by *to*) attend to the needs of. **ministerial** *adj* **ministration** *n* giving of help. **ministry** *n, pl* –**tries** 1 profession or duties of a clergyman. 2 ministers collectively. 3 government department.

mink *n* 1 stoatlike animal. 2 its highly valued fur.

minnow *n* small freshwater fish.

minor ⊕ *adj* 1 lesser. 2 *Music* (of a scale) having a semitone between the second and third notes. ◆ *n* 3 person regarded legally as a child. 4 *Music* minor scale. **minority** *n* 1 lesser number. 2 smaller party voting together. 3 group in a minority in any state.

minster *n* cathedral or large church.

minstrel ⊕ *n* medieval singer or musician.

mint¹ *n* 1 plant with aromatic leaves used for seasoning and flavouring. 2 sweet flavoured with this.

mint² ⊕ *n* 1 place where money is coined. ◆ *v* 2 make (coins).

minuet [min–new–**wet**] *n* 1 stately dance.

2 music for this.

minus *prep, adj* 1 indicating subtraction. ◆ *adj* 2 less than zero. ◆ *n* 3 sign (–) denoting subtraction or a number less than zero.

minuscule ⊕ [**min**–niss–skyool] *adj* very small.

minute¹ ⊕ [**min**–it] *n* 1 60th part of an hour or degree. 2 moment. ◆ *pl* 3 record of the proceedings of a meeting. ◆ *v* 4 record in the minutes.

minute² ⊕ [my–**newt**] *adj* 1 very small. 2 precise. **minutely** *adv* **minutiae** [my–**new**–shee–eye] *pl n* trifling or precise details.

minx ⊕ *n* bold or flirtatious girl.

miracle ⊕ *n* 1 wonderful supernatural event. 2 marvel. **miraculous** *adj* **miraculously** *adv*

mirage ⊕ [mir–**rahzh**] *n* optical illusion, esp. one caused by hot air.

mire ⊕ *n* 1 swampy ground. 2 mud.

mirror ⊕ *n* 1 coated glass surface for reflecting images. ◆ *v* 2 reflect in or as if in a mirror.

mirth ⊕ *n* laughter, merriment, or gaiety.

mis– *prefix* wrong(ly), bad(ly).

① **minimum** *adj* = **least**, least possible, lowest, minimal, slightest, smallest ≠ **most**
② **minimum** *n* = **least**, lowest, nadir

minion *n* = **follower**, flunky, hanger-on, henchman, hireling, lackey, underling, yes man

minister *n* 3 = **clergyman**, cleric, parson, pastor, preacher, priest, rector, vicar ◆ *v* 4 = **attend to**, administer, cater to, pander to, serve, take care of, tend

minor *adj* 1 = **small**, inconsequential, insignificant, lesser, petty, slight, trivial, unimportant ≠ **important**

minstrel *n* = **musician**, bard, singer, songstress, troubadour

mint² *v* 2 = **make**, cast, coin, produce, punch, stamp, strike

minuscule *adj* = **tiny**, diminutive, infinitesimal, little, microscopic, miniature, minute

minute¹ *n* 2 = **moment**, flash, instant, jiffy (*inf*), second, tick (*Brit inf*), trice ◆ *pl* 3 = **record**, memoranda, notes, proceedings, transactions, transcript

minute² *adj* 1 = **small**, diminutive, infinitesimal, little, microscopic, miniature, minuscule, tiny ≠ **huge** 2 = **precise**, close, critical, detailed, exact, exhaustive, meticulous, painstaking, punctilious ≠ **rough**

minx *n* = **flirt**, coquette, hussy

miracle *n* 2 = **wonder**, marvel, phenomenon, prodigy

mirage *n* = **illusion**, hallucination, optical illusion

mire *n* 1 = **swamp**, bog, marsh, morass, quagmire 2 = **mud**, dirt, muck, ooze, slime

mirror *n* 1 = **looking-glass**, glass, reflector ◆ *v* 2 = **reflect**, copy, echo, emulate, follow

misadventure ⊕ *n* unlucky chance.

misanthrope [miz–zan–thrope] *n* person who dislikes people in general. **misanthropic** [miz–zan–**throp**–ik] *adj* **misanthropy** [miz–**zan**–throp–ee] *n*

misapprehension ⊕ *n* misunderstanding.

misappropriate ⊕ *v* take and use (money) dishonestly. **misappropriation** *n*

miscellaneous ⊕ [miss–sell–**lane**–ee–uss] *adj* mixed or assorted. **miscellany** [miss–**sell**–a–nee] *n* mixed assortment.

mischief ⊕ *n* 1 annoying but not malicious behaviour. 2 inclination to tease. 3 harm. **mischievous** *adj* 1 full of mischief. 2 intended to cause harm.

misconception ⊕ *n* wrong idea or belief.

misconduct ⊕ *n* immoral or unethical behaviour.

miscreant ⊕ [**miss**–kree–ant] *n* wrongdoer.

misdemeanour ⊕ *n* minor wrongdoing.

miser ⊕ *n* person who hoards money and hates spending it. **miserly** *adj*

miserable ⊕ *adj* 1 very unhappy, wretched. 2 causing misery. 3 squalid. 4 mean. **misery** *n, pl* –eries 1 great unhappiness. 2 *Informal* complaining person.

misfire ⊕ *v* 1 (of a firearm or engine) fail to fire correctly. 2 (of a plan) fail to turn out as intended.

misfit ⊕ *n* person not suited to his or her social environment.

misfortune ⊕ *n* (piece of) bad luck.

misgiving ⊕ *n* feeling of fear or doubt.

misguided ⊕ *adj* mistaken or unwise.

mishap ⊕ *n* minor accident.

————————— THESAURUS —————————

mirth *n* = **merriment**, amusement, cheerfulness, fun, gaiety, glee, hilarity, jollity, joviality, laughter, revelry

misadventure *n* = **misfortune**, accident, bad luck, calamity, catastrophe, debacle, disaster, mishap, reverse, setback

misapprehension *n* = **misunderstanding**, delusion, error, fallacy, misconception, misinterpretation, mistake

misappropriate *v* = **steal**, embezzle, misspend, misuse, peculate, pocket

miscellaneous *adj* = **mixed**, assorted, diverse, jumbled, motley, sundry, varied, various

mischief *n* 1 = **misbehaviour**, impishness, monkey business (*inf*), naughtiness, shenanigans (*inf*), trouble, waywardness 3 = **harm**, damage, evil, hurt, injury, misfortune, trouble

misconception *n* = **delusion**, error, fallacy, misapprehension, misunderstanding

misconduct *n* = **immorality**, impropriety, malpractice, mismanagement, wrongdoing

miscreant *n* = **wrongdoer**, blackguard, criminal, rascal, reprobate, rogue,

scoundrel, sinner, vagabond, villain

misdemeanour *n* = **offence**, fault, infringement, misdeed, peccadillo, transgression

miser *n* = **hoarder**, cheapskate (*inf*), niggard, penny–pincher (*inf*), Scrooge, skinflint

miserable *adj* 1 = **unhappy**, dejected, depressed, despondent, disconsolate, forlorn, gloomy, sorrowful, woebegone, wretched 2 = **despicable**, deplorable, lamentable, shameful, sordid, sorry 3 = **squalid**, wretched

misfire *v* 2 = **fail**, fall through, go pear–shaped (*inf*), go wrong, miscarry

misfit *n* = **nonconformist**, eccentric, fish out of water (*inf*), oddball (*inf*), square peg (in a round hole) (*inf*)

misfortune *n* = **bad luck**, adversity, hard luck, ill luck, infelicity

misgiving *n* = **unease**, anxiety, apprehension, distrust, doubt, qualm, reservation, suspicion, trepidation, uncertainty, worry

misguided *adj* = **unwise**, deluded, erroneous, ill–advised, imprudent, injudicious, misplaced, mistaken, unwarranted

misjudge ⊕ v judge wrongly or unfairly.
misjudgment, misjudgement n

mislay ⊕ v lose (something) temporarily.

mislead ⊕ v give false or confusing
information to. **misleading** adj

mismanage v organize or run
(something) badly. **mismanagement** n

misnomer [miss–**no**–mer] n 1 incorrect or
unsuitable name. 2 use of this.

misogyny [miss–**oj**–in–ee] n hatred of
women. **misogynist** n

misprint ⊕ n printing error.

miss ⊕ v 1 fail to notice, hear, hit, reach,
find, or catch. 2 not be in time for. 3
notice or regret the absence of. 4 avoid. 5
(of an engine) misfire. ◆ n 6 fact or
instance of missing. **missing** adj lost or
absent.

Miss n title of a girl or unmarried woman.

missal n book containing the prayers and
rites of the Mass.

missile ⊕ n object or weapon thrown,
shot, or launched at a target.

mission ⊕ n 1 specific task or duty. 2
group of people sent on a mission. 3

building in which missionaries work. 4
S Afr long and difficult process. **missionary**
n, pl **–aries** person sent abroad to do
religious and social work.

missive ⊕ n letter.

mist ⊕ n 1 thin fog. 2 fine spray of liquid.
misty adj 1 full of mist. 2 dim or obscure.

mistake ⊕ n 1 error or blunder. ◆ v –
taking, –took, –taken 2 misunderstand. 3
confuse (a person or thing) with another.

mistletoe n evergreen plant with white
berries growing as a parasite on trees.

mistress ⊕ n 1 woman who has a
continuing sexual relationship with a
married man. 2 woman in control of
people or animals. 3 female teacher.

mistrust ⊕ v 1 have doubts or suspicions
about. ◆ n 2 lack of trust. **mistrustful** adj

misunderstand ⊕ v fail to understand
properly. **misunderstanding** n

misuse ⊕ n 1 incorrect, improper, or
careless use. ◆ v 2 use wrongly. 3 treat
badly.

mite n 1 very small spider–like animal. 2
very small thing or amount.

mishap n = **accident**, calamity,
misadventure, mischance, misfortune

misjudge v = **miscalculate**, overestimate,
overrate, underestimate, underrate

mislay v = **lose**, lose track of, misplace

mislead v = **deceive**, delude, fool,
hoodwink, misdirect, misguide, misinform,
take in (inf)

misprint n = **mistake**, corrigendum,
erratum, literal, typo (inf)

miss v 1 = **omit**, leave out, let go, overlook,
pass over, skip 3 = **long for**, pine for,
yearn for 4 = **avoid**, escape, evade ◆ n
6 = **mistake**, blunder, error, failure,
omission, oversight

missile n = **rocket**, projectile, weapon

mission n 1 = **task**, assignment,
commission, duty, errand, job, quest,
undertaking 2 = **vocation**

missive n = **letter**, communication,
dispatch, epistle, memorandum, message,
note, report

mist n 1 = **fog**, cloud, film, haze, smog,
spray, steam, vapour

mistake n 1 = **error**, blunder, erratum,
fault, faux pas, gaffe, howler (inf),
miscalculation, oversight, slip ◆ v
2 = **misunderstand**, misapprehend,
misconstrue, misinterpret, misjudge,
misread 3 = **confuse with**, mix up with,
take for

mistress n 1 = **lover**, concubine, girlfriend,
kept woman, paramour

mistrust v 1 = **doubt**, be wary of, distrust,
fear, suspect ◆ n 2 = **suspicion**, distrust,
doubt, misgiving, scepticism, uncertainty,
wariness

misunderstand v = **misinterpret**, be at
cross–purposes, get the wrong end of the
stick, misapprehend, misconstrue,
misjudge, misread, mistake

misuse n 1 = **waste**, abuse, desecration,
misapplication, squandering ◆ v
3 = **waste**, abuse, desecrate, misapply,

mitigate ⊕ *v* make less severe. **mitigation** *n*

✓ **WORD TIP**

Mitigate is often confused with *militate* 'have an influence on'.

---

mitre [**my**–ter] *n* 1 bishop's pointed headdress. 2 joint between two pieces of wood bevelled to meet at right angles. ♦ *v* 3 join with a mitre joint.

mitt *n* 1 short for MITTEN. 2 baseball catcher's glove.

mitten *n* glove with one section for the thumb and one for the four fingers together.

mix ⊕ *v* 1 combine or blend into one mass. 2 form (something) by mixing. 3 be sociable. ♦ *n* 4 mixture. **mixed** *adj* **mix up** *v* 1 confuse. 2 make into a mixture. **mixed up** *adj* **mix–up** *n* **mixer** *n* 1 **mixture** *n* 1 something mixed. 2 combination.

mm millimetre(s).

mnemonic [nim–**on**–ik] *n, adj* (something, such as a rhyme) intended to help the memory.

moan ⊕ *n* 1 low cry of pain. 2 *Informal* grumble. ♦ *v* 3 make or utter with a moan. 4 *Informal* grumble.

moat *n* deep wide ditch, esp. round a castle.

mob ⊕ *n* 1 disorderly crowd. 2 *Slang* gang. ♦ *v* **mobbing, mobbed** 3 surround in a mob to acclaim or attack.

mobile ⊕ *adj* 1 able to move. ♦ *n* 2 same as MOBILE PHONE. 3 hanging structure designed to move in air currents. **mobile phone** cordless phone powered by batteries. **mobility** *n*

mobilize ⊕ *v* 1 (of the armed services) prepare for active service. 2 organize for a purpose. **mobilization** *n*

moccasin *n* soft leather shoe.

mocha [**mock**–a] *n* 1 kind of strong dark coffee. 2 flavouring made from coffee and chocolate.

mock ⊕ *v* 1 make fun of. 2 mimic. ♦ *adj* 3 sham or imitation. **mocks** *pl n Informal* (in England and Wales) practice exams taken before public exams. **mockery** *n* 1 derision. 2 inadequate or worthless attempt. **mockingbird** *n* N American bird which imitates other birds' songs. **mock– up** *n* full–scale model for test or study.

mode ⊕ *n* 1 method or manner. 2 current fashion.

————————————————[THESAURUS]————————————

prostitute, squander

mitigate *v* = **ease**, extenuate, lessen, lighten, moderate, soften, subdue, temper

mix *v* 1, 2 = **combine**, blend, cross, fuse, intermingle, interweave, join, jumble, merge, mingle 3 = **socialize**, associate, consort, fraternize, hang out (*inf*), hobnob, mingle ♦ *n* 4 = **mixture**, alloy, amalgam, assortment, blend, combination, compound, fusion, medley

moan *n* 1 = **groan**, lament, sigh, sob, wail, whine 2 *Inf* = **grumble**, complaint, gripe (*inf*), grouch (*inf*), grouse, protest, whine ♦ *v* 3 = **groan**, lament, sigh, sob, whine 4 *Inf* = **grumble**, bleat, carp, complain, groan, grouse, whine, whinge (*inf*)

mob *n* 1 = **crowd**, drove, flock, horde, host, mass, multitude, pack, swarm, throng 2 *Sl* = **gang**, crew (*inf*), group, lot,

set ♦ *v* 3 = **surround**, crowd around, jostle, set upon, swarm around

mobile *adj* 1 = **movable**, itinerant, moving, peripatetic, portable, travelling, wandering

mobilize *v* 1 = **call to arms**, activate, call up, marshal 2 = **prepare**, get *or* make ready, organize, rally, ready

mock *v* 1 = **laugh at**, deride, jeer, make fun of, poke fun at, ridicule, scoff, scorn, sneer, taunt, tease ≠ **respect** 2 = **mimic**, ape, caricature, imitate, lampoon, parody, satirize, send up (*Brit inf*) ♦ *adj* 3 = **imitation**, artificial, dummy, fake, false, feigned, phoney *or* phony (*inf*), pretended, sham, spurious ≠ **real**

mode *n* 1 = **method**, form, manner, procedure, process, style, system, technique, way 2 = **fashion**, craze, look, rage, style, trend, vogue

model ⚫ n 1 (miniature) representation. 2
pattern. 3 person or thing worthy of
imitation. 4 person who poses for an artist
or photographer. 5 person who wears
clothes to display them to prospective
buyers. 6 v –elling, –elled 7 make a model
of. 8 mould. 9 display (clothing) as a
model.

modem [mode–em] n device for
connecting two computers by a telephone
line.

moderate ⚫ adj 1 not extreme. 2 self–
restrained. 3 average. ♦ n 4 person of
moderate views. ♦ v 5 make or become
less violent or extreme. **moderately** adv
moderation n **moderator** n 1
(Presbyterian Church) minister appointed
to preside over a Church court, general
assembly, etc. 2 person who presides over
a public or legislative assembly.

modern ⚫ adj 1 of present or recent times.
2 up–to–date. **modernity** n **modernism** n
(support of) modern tendencies, thoughts,
or styles. **modernist** adj, n **modernize** v
bring up to date. **modernization** n

modest ⚫ adj 1 not vain or boastful. 2 not
excessive. 3 not showy. 4 shy. **modestly**
adv **modesty** n

modicum ⚫ n small quantity.
modify ⚫ v –fying, –fied 1 change slightly.
2 tone down. 3 (of a word) qualify
(another word). **modifier** n word that
qualifies the sense of another.
modification n

modulate ⚫ v 1 vary in tone. 2 adjust. 3
change the key of (music). **modulation** n

module n self–contained unit, section, or
component with a specific function.

mogul ⚫ [moh–gl] n important or
powerful person.

mohair n 1 fine hair of the Angora goat. 2
yarn or fabric made from this.

moist ⚫ adj slightly wet. **moisten** v make
or become moist. **moisture** n liquid
diffused as vapour or condensed in drops.
moisturize v add moisture to (the skin
etc.).

molar n large back tooth used for grinding.

molasses n dark syrup, a by–product of
sugar refining.

mole[1] n small dark raised spot on the skin.

mole[2] n 1 small burrowing mammal. 2
Informal spy who has infiltrated and
become a trusted member of an
organization. **molehill** n small mound of
earth thrown up by a burrowing mole.

——————— THESAURUS ———————

model n 1 = **representation**, copy,
dummy, facsimile, image, imitation,
miniature, mock–up, replica 2 = **pattern**,
example, original, paradigm, prototype,
standard 3 = **ideal**, archetype, paragon
4 = **sitter**, poser, subject ♦ v 8 = **shape**,
carve, design, fashion, form, mould, sculpt
9 = **show off**, display, sport (*inf*), wear

moderate adj 1 = **middle–of–the–road**,
limited 2 = **restrained**, controlled, gentle,
mild, modest, reasonable, steady
≠ **extreme** 3 = **average**, fair, indifferent,
mediocre, middling, ordinary, passable,
so–so (*inf*), unexceptional ≠ **unusual** ♦ v
5 = **lessen**, control, curb, ease, modulate,
regulate, restrain, soften, subdue, temper,
tone down ≠ **increase**

modern adj 1 = **current**, contemporary,
present–day, recent 2 = **up–to–date**, fresh,

new, newfangled, novel ≠ **old**

modest adj 1, 4 = **shy**, bashful, coy,
demure, diffident, reserved, reticent,
retiring, self–effacing 2 = **moderate**, fair,
limited, middling, small
3 = **unpretentious**, ordinary,
unexceptional

modicum n = **little**, bit, crumb, drop,
fragment, scrap, shred, touch

modify v 1 = **change**, adapt, adjust, alter,
convert, reform, remodel, revise, rework
2 = **tone down**, ease, lessen, lower,
moderate, qualify, restrain, soften, temper

modulate v 1 = **vary** 2 = **adjust**, attune,
balance, regulate 3 = **tune**

mogul n = **tycoon**, baron, big hitter (*inf*),
big noise (*inf*), big shot (*inf*), heavy hitter
(*inf*), magnate, V.I.P.

moist adj = **damp**, clammy, dewy, humid,

make a mountain out of a molehill exaggerate an unimportant matter out of all proportion.

molecule ⊕ [**mol**–lik–kyool] *n* **1** simplest freely existing chemical unit, composed of two or more atoms. **2** very small particle. **molecular** [mol–**lek**–yew lar] *adj*

molest ⊕ *v* **1** interfere with sexually. **2** annoy or injure. **molestation** *n*

moll *n Slang* gangster's female accomplice.

mollify ⊕ *v* –**fying**, –**fied** pacify or soothe. **mollification** *n*

mollusc *n* soft–bodied, usu. hard–shelled, animal, such as a snail or oyster.

mollycoddle ⊕ *v* pamper.

molten *adj* liquefied or melted.

moment ⊕ *n* **1** short space of time. **2** (present) point in time. **momentary** *adj* lasting only a moment. **momentarily** *adv*

> ✓ **WORD TIP**
>
> Note that some American speakers use *momentarily* to mean 'soon' rather than 'for a moment'.

momentous ⊕ [moh–**men**–tuss] *adj* of great significance.

momentum ⊕ *n* **1** impetus of a moving body. **2** product of a body's mass and velocity.

monarch ⊕ *n* sovereign ruler of a state. **monarchical** *adj* **monarchist** *n* supporter of monarchy. **monarchy** *n* government by or a state ruled by a sovereign.

monastery ⊕ *n*, *pl* –**teries** residence of a community of monks. **monastic** *adj* **1** of monks, nuns, or monasteries. **2** simple and austere. **monasticism** *n*

Monday *n* second day of the week.

money ⊕ *n* medium of exchange, coins or banknotes. **moneyed**, **monied** *adj* rich.

mongoose *n*, *pl* –**gooses** stoatlike mammal of Asia and Africa that kills snakes.

mongrel ⊕ *n* **1** animal, esp. a dog, of mixed breed. **2** something arising from a variety of sources. ◆ *adj* **3** of mixed breed or origin.

monitor ⊕ *n* **1** person or device that checks, controls, warns, or keeps a record of something. **2** pupil assisting a teacher with duties. **3** television set used in a studio to check what is being transmitted. ◆ *v* **4** watch and check on.

monk ⊕ *n* member of an all–male religious community bound by vows. **monkish** *adj*

monkey ⊕ *n* **1** long–tailed primate. **2** mischievous child. ◆ *v* **3** (usu. foll. by

─── THESAURUS ───

soggy, wet

molecule *n* **2 = particle**, jot, speck

molest *v* **1 = abuse**, ill–treat, interfere with, maltreat **2 = annoy**, attack, badger, beset, bother, disturb, harass, harm, hurt, persecute, pester, plague, torment, worry

mollify *v* **= pacify**, appease, calm, conciliate, placate, quiet, soothe, sweeten

mollycoddle *v* **= pamper**, baby, cosset, indulge, spoil

moment *n* **1 = instant**, flash, jiffy (*inf*), second, split second, trice, twinkling **2 = time**, juncture, point, stage

momentous *adj* **= significant**, critical, crucial, fateful, historic, important, pivotal, vital, weighty

momentum *n* **1, 2 = impetus**, drive, energy, force, power, propulsion, push, strength, thrust

monarch *n* **= ruler**, emperor *or* empress, king, potentate, prince *or* princess, queen, sovereign

monastery *n* **= abbey**, cloister, convent, friary, nunnery, priory

money *n* **= cash**, capital, coin, currency, hard cash, legal tender, lolly (*Aust & NZ sl*), readies (*inf*), riches, silver, wealth

mongrel *n* **1 = crossbreed**, cross, half–breed **2 = hybrid** ◆ *adj* **3 = hybrid**, crossbred

monitor *n* **1 = watchdog**, guide, invigilator, supervisor **2 = prefect** (*Brit*) ◆ *v* **4 = check**, follow, keep an eye on, keep tabs on, keep track of, observe, survey, watch

monk *n* **= friar** (*loosely*), brother

about or *around*) meddle or fool. **monkey nut** peanut. **monkey puzzle** coniferous tree with sharp stiff leaves. **monkey wrench** wrench with adjustable jaws.

mono– *combining form* single, e.g. *monosyllable.*

monochrome *adj* 1 *Photog* black–and–white. 2 in only one colour.

monocle *n* eyeglass for one eye only.

monogamy *n* custom of being married to one person at a time.

monogram *n* design of combined letters, esp. a person's initials.

monograph *n* book or paper on a single subject.

monolith *n* large upright block of stone. **monolithic** *adj*

monologue ❶ *n* 1 long speech by one person. 2 dramatic piece for one performer.

monopoly *n* 1 (*pl* **–lies**) exclusive possession of or right to do something. 2 (**M–**) ® board game for four to six players who deal in 'property' as they move around the board. **monopolize** *v* have or take exclusive possession of.

monotone *n* unvaried pitch in speech or sound. **monotonous** *adj* tedious due to lack of variety. **monotony** *n*

monsoon *n* 1 seasonal wind of SE Asia. 2 rainy season accompanying this.

monster ❶ *n* 1 imaginary, usu. frightening, beast. 2 huge person, animal, or thing. 3 very wicked person. ◆ *adj* 4 huge. **monstrosity** *n* large ugly thing. **monstrous** *adj* 1 unnatural or ugly. 2

outrageous or shocking. 3 huge.

month *n* 1 one of the twelve divisions of the calendar year. 2 period of four weeks. **monthly** *adj* 1 happening or payable once a month. ◆ *adv* 2 once a month. ◆ *n* 3 monthly magazine.

monument ❶ *n* something, esp. a building or statue, that commemorates something. **monumental** *adj* 1 large, impressive, or lasting. 2 of or being a monument. 3 *Informal* extreme. **monumentally** *adv*

mooch *v Slang* loiter about aimlessly.

mood¹ ❶ *n* temporary (gloomy) state of mind. **moody** *adj* 1 sullen or gloomy. 2 changeable in mood. **moodily** *adv*

mood² *n Grammar* form of a verb indicating whether it expresses a fact, wish, supposition, or command.

moon ❶ *n* 1 natural satellite of the earth. 2 natural satellite of any planet. ◆ *v* 3 (foll. by *about* or *around*) be idle in a listless or dreamy way. **moonlight** *n* 1 light from the moon. ◆ *v* 2 *Informal* work at a secondary job, esp. illegally. **moonshine** *n* 1 illicitly distilled whisky. 2 nonsense. **moonstone** *n* translucent semiprecious stone. **moonstruck** *adj* slightly mad or odd.

moor¹ ❶ *n* tract of open uncultivated ground covered with grass and heather. **moorhen** *n* small black water bird.

moor² ❶ *v* secure (a ship) with ropes etc. **mooring** *n* 1 place for mooring a ship. ◆ *pl* 2 ropes etc. used in mooring a ship.

moose *n* large N American deer.

moot ❶ *adj* 1 debatable, e.g. *a moot point.*

———————| THESAURUS |———————

monkey *n* 1 = **simian**, primate 2 = **rascal**, devil, imp, rogue, scamp ◆ *v* 3 (usu. foll. by *about* or *around*) = **fool**, meddle, mess, play, tinker

monologue *n* 1 = **speech**, harangue, lecture, sermon 2 = **soliloquy**

monster *n* 1 = **freak**, monstrosity, mutant 2 = **giant**, colossus, mammoth, titan 3 = **brute**, beast, demon, devil, fiend, villain ◆ *adj* 4 = **huge**, colossal, enormous, gigantic, immense, mammoth, massive,

stupendous, tremendous

monument *n* = **memorial**, cairn, cenotaph, commemoration, gravestone, headstone, marker, mausoleum, shrine, tombstone

mood¹ *n* = **state of mind**, disposition, frame of mind, humour, spirit, temper

moon *n* 1, 2 = **satellite** ◆ *v* 3 = **idle**, daydream, languish, mope, waste time

moor¹ *n* = **moorland**, fell (*Brit*), heath

moor² *v* = **tie up**, anchor, berth, dock, lash,

♦ *v* **2** bring up for discussion.

mop ❶ *n* **1** long stick with twists of cotton or a sponge on the end, used for cleaning. **2** thick mass of hair. ♦ *v* **mopping, mopped 3** clean or soak up with or as if with a mop.

mope ❶ *v* be gloomy and apathetic.

moped *n* light motorized cycle.

moral ❶ *adj* **1** concerned with right and wrong conduct. **2** based on a sense of right and wrong. **3** (of support or a victory) psychological rather than practical. ♦ *n* **4** lesson to be obtained from a story or event. ♦ *pl* **5** principles of behaviour with respect to right and wrong. **morally** *adv* **moralist** *n* person with a strong sense of right and wrong. **morality** *n* **1** good moral conduct. **2** moral goodness or badness. **moralize** *v* make moral pronouncements.

morale ❶ [mor–**rahl**] *n* degree of confidence or hope of a person or group.

morass ❶ *n* **1** marsh. **2** mess.

moratorium ❶ *n, pl* **–ria, –riums** legally authorized ban or delay.

morbid ❶ *adj* **1** unduly interested in death or unpleasant events. **2** gruesome.

mordant ❶ *adj* **1** sarcastic or scathing. ♦ *n* **2** substance used to fix dyes.

more ❶ *adj* **1** greater in amount or degree. **2** comparative of MUCH or MANY. **3** additional or further. ♦ *adv* **4** to a greater extent. **5** in addition. ♦ *pron* **6** greater or additional amount or number. **moreover** *adv* in addition to what has already been said.

mores [**more**–rayz] *pl n* customs and conventions embodying the fundamental values of a community.

morgue ❶ *n* mortuary.

moribund ❶ *adj* without force or vitality.

morning ❶ *n* part of the day before noon.

moron ❶ *n* **1** *Informal* foolish or stupid person. **2** (formerly) person with a low intelligence quotient. **moronic** *adj*

morose ❶ [mor–**rohss**] *adj* sullen or moody.

morphine, morphia *n* drug extracted

━━━━━━ THESAURUS ━━━━━━

make fast, secure

moot *adj* **1** = **debatable**, arguable, contestable, controversial, disputable, doubtful, undecided, unresolved, unsettled ♦ *v* **2** = **bring up**, broach, propose, put forward, suggest

mop *n* **1** = **squeegee**, sponge, swab **2** = **mane**, shock, tangle, thatch ♦ *v* **3** = **clean up**, soak up, sponge, swab, wash, wipe

mope *v* = **brood**, fret, languish, moon, pine, pout, sulk

moral *adj* **1, 2** = **good**, decent, ethical, high–minded, honourable, just, noble, principled, right, virtuous ≠ **immoral** ♦ *n* **4** = **lesson**, meaning, message, point, significance

morale *n* = **confidence**, esprit de corps, heart, self–esteem, spirit

morass *n* **1** = **marsh**, bog, fen, quagmire, slough, swamp **2** = **mess**, confusion, mix–up, muddle, tangle

moratorium *n* = **postponement**, freeze, halt, standstill, suspension

morbid *adj* **1** = **unwholesome**, ghoulish, gloomy, melancholy, sick, sombre, unhealthy ≠ **happy 2** = **gruesome**, dreadful, ghastly, grisly, hideous, horrid, macabre

mordant *adj* **1** = **sarcastic**, biting, caustic, cutting, incisive, pungent, scathing, stinging, trenchant

more *adj* **1** = **extra**, added, additional, further, new, new–found, other, supplementary ♦ *adv* **4** = **to a greater extent**, better, further, longer

morgue *n* = **mortuary**

moribund *adj* = **declining**, on its last legs, stagnant, waning, weak

morning *n* = **dawn**, a.m., break of day, daybreak, forenoon, morn (*poet*), sunrise

moron *n* **1** *Inf* = **fool**, blockhead, cretin, dunce, dunderhead, halfwit, idiot, imbecile, oaf

morose *adj* = **sullen**, depressed, dour, gloomy, glum, ill–tempered, moody, sour, from opium, used as an anaesthetic and sedative.

morrow n *Poetic* next day.

Morse n former system of signalling in which letters of the alphabet are represented by combinations of short and long signals.

morsel ⊕ n small piece, esp. of food.

mortal ⊕ adj 1 subject to death. 2 causing death. ◆ n 3 human being. **mortally** adv **mortality** n 1 state of being mortal. 2 great loss of life. 3 death rate. **mortal sin** *RC Church* sin meriting damnation.

mortar n 1 small cannon with a short range. 2 mixture of lime, sand, and water for holding bricks and stones together. 3 bowl in which substances are pounded. **mortarboard** n square academic cap.

mortgage n 1 conditional pledging of property, esp. a house, as security for the repayment of a loan. 2 the loan itself. ◆ v 3 pledge (property) as security thus. **mortgagee** n creditor in a mortgage. **mortgagor** n debtor in a mortgage.

mortify ⊕ v –fying, –fied 1 humiliate. 2 subdue by self–denial. 3 (of flesh) become gangrenous. **mortification** n

mortuary ⊕ n, pl –aries building where corpses are kept before burial or cremation.

mosaic [mow–**zay**–ik] n design or decoration using small pieces of coloured stone or glass.

mosque n Muslim temple.

mosquito n, pl –toes, –tos blood–sucking flying insect.

moss n small flowerless plant growing in masses on moist surfaces. **mossy** adj

most n 1 greatest number or degree. ◆ adj 2 greatest in number or degree. 3 superlative of MUCH *or* MANY. ◆ adv 4 in the greatest degree. **mostly** adv for the most part, generally.

motel n roadside hotel for motorists.

moth n nocturnal insect like a butterfly. **mothball** n 1 small ball of camphor or naphthalene used to repel moths from stored clothes. ◆ v 2 store (something operational) for future use. 3 postpone (a project etc.). **moth–eaten** adj 1 decayed or scruffy. 2 eaten or damaged by moth larvae.

mother ⊕ n 1 female parent. 2 head of a female religious community. ◆ adj 3 native or inborn, e.g. *mother wit*. ◆ v 4 look after as a mother. **motherhood** n **motherly** adj **mother–in–law** n mother of one's husband or wife. **mother of pearl** iridescent lining of certain shells. **mother tongue** one's native language.

motif ⊕ n [moh–**teef**] n (recurring) theme or design.

motion ⊕ n 1 process, action, or way of moving. 2 proposal in a meeting. 3 evacuation of the bowels. ◆ v 4 direct (someone) by gesture. **motionless** adj not moving. **motion picture** cinema film.

motive ⊕ n 1 reason for a course of action.

sulky, surly, taciturn

morsel n = **piece**, bit, bite, crumb, mouthful, part, scrap, *soupçon*, taste, titbit

mortal adj 1 = **human**, ephemeral, impermanent, passing, temporal, transient, worldly 2 = **fatal**, deadly, death–dealing, destructive, killing, lethal, murderous, terminal ◆ n 3 = **human being**, being, earthling, human, individual, man, person, woman

mortify v 1 = **humiliate**, chagrin, chasten, crush, deflate, embarrass, humble, shame 2 = **discipline**, abase, chasten, control,

deny, subdue 3 *Of flesh* = **putrefy**, cark (*Aust & NZ sl*), deaden, die, fester

mortuary n = **morgue**, funeral parlour

mother n 1 = **parent**, dam, ma (*inf*), mater, mum (*Brit inf*), mummy (*Brit inf*) ◆ adj 3 = **native**, inborn, innate, natural ◆ v 4 = **nurture**, care for, cherish, nurse, protect, raise, rear, tend

motif n a = **theme**, concept, idea, leitmotif, subject b = **design**, decoration, ornament, shape

motion n 1 = **movement**, flow, locomotion, mobility, move, progress,

♦ adj 2 causing motion. **motivate** v give incentive to. **motivation** n

motley ❶ adj 1 miscellaneous. 2 multicoloured.

motocross n motorcycle race over a rough course.

motor n 1 engine, esp. of a vehicle. 2 machine that converts electrical energy into mechanical energy. 3 car. ♦ v 4 travel by car. **motorist** n driver of a car. **motorized** adj equipped with a motor or motor transport. **motorbike** n **motorcycle** n **motorcyclist** n **motorway** n main road for fast-moving traffic.

mottled ❶ adj marked with blotches.

motto ❶ n, pl –toes, –tos 1 saying expressing an ideal or rule of conduct. 2 verse or maxim in a paper cracker.

mould¹ ❶ n 1 hollow container in which metal etc. is cast. 2 shape, form, or pattern. 3 nature or character. ♦ v 4 shape. 5 influence or direct. **moulding** n moulded ornamental edging.

mould² ❶ n fungal growth caused by dampness. **mouldy** adj 1 stale or musty. 2 dull or boring.

mould³ ❶ n loose soil. **moulder** v decay

into dust.

moult v 1 shed feathers, hair, or skin to make way for new growth. ♦ n 2 process of moulting.

mound ❶ n 1 heap, esp. of earth or stones. 2 small hill.

mount ❶ v 1 climb or ascend. 2 get up on (a horse etc.). 3 increase or accumulate. 4 fix on a support or backing. 5 organize, e.g. *mount a campaign.* ♦ n 6 backing or support on which something is fixed. 7 horse for riding. 8 hill.

mountain ❶ n 1 hill of great size. 2 large heap. **mountainous** adj 1 full of mountains. 2 huge. **mountaineer** n person who climbs mountains. **mountaineering** n **mountain bike** bicycle with straight handlebars and heavy-duty tyres, for cycling over rough terrain.

mountebank n charlatan or fake.

mourn ❶ v feel or express sorrow for (a dead person or lost thing). **mourner** n **mournful** adj sad or dismal. **mournfully** adv **mourning** n 1 grieving. 2 conventional symbols of grief for death, such as the wearing of black.

mouse n, pl **mice** 1 small long-tailed

travel 2 = **proposal**, proposition, recommendation, submission, suggestion ♦ v 4 = **gesture**, beckon, direct, gesticulate, nod, signal, wave

motive n 1 = **reason**, ground(s), incentive, inducement, inspiration, object, purpose, rationale, stimulus

motley adj 1 = **miscellaneous**, assorted, disparate, heterogeneous, mixed, varied 2 = **multicoloured**, chequered, variegated

mottled adj = **blotchy**, dappled, flecked, piebald, speckled, spotted, stippled, streaked

motto n 1 = **saying**, adage, dictum, maxim, precept, proverb, rule, slogan, tag-line, watchword

mould¹ n 1 = **cast**, pattern, shape 2 = **design**, build, construction, fashion, form, format, kind, pattern, shape, style 3 = **nature**, calibre, character, kind,

quality, sort, stamp, type ♦ v 4 = **shape**, construct, create, fashion, forge, form, make, model, sculpt, work 5 = **influence**, affect, control, direct, form, make, shape

mould² n = **fungus**, blight, mildew

mould³ n = **soil**, dirt, earth, humus, loam

mound n 1 = **heap**, drift, pile, rick, stack 2 = **hill**, bank, dune, embankment, hillock, knoll, rise

mount v 1 = **ascend**, clamber up, climb, go up, scale ≠ **descend** 2 = **get (up) on**, bestride, climb onto, jump on ≠ **get off** 3 = **increase**, accumulate, build, escalate, grow, intensify, multiply, pile up, swell ≠ **reduce** ♦ n 6 = **backing**, base, frame, setting, stand, support 7 = **horse**, steed (*lit*)

mountain n 1 = **peak**, alp, berg (*S Afr*), fell (*Brit*), mount 2 = **heap**, abundance, mass, mound, pile, stack, ton rodent. 2 timid person. 3 *Computers* hand–held device for moving the cursor without keying. **mousy** *adj* 1 like a mouse, esp. in hair colour. 2 meek and shy.

mousse *n* 1 dish of flavoured cream whipped and set.

moustache *n* hair on the upper lip.

mouth ❶ *n* 1 opening in the head for eating and issuing sounds. 2 entrance. 3 point where a river enters the sea. 4 opening. ♦ *v* 5 form (words) with the lips without speaking. 6 speak or utter insincerely, esp. in public. **mouthful** *n* 1 amount of food or drink put into the mouth at any one time when eating or drinking. 2 **mouth organ** same as HARMONICA. **mouthpiece** *n* 1 part of a telephone into which a person speaks. 2 part of a wind instrument into which the player blows. 3 spokesperson.

move ❶ *v* 1 change in place or position. 2 change (one's house etc.). 3 take action. 4 stir the emotions of. 5 incite. 6 suggest (a proposal) formally. ♦ *n* 7 moving. 8 action towards some goal. **movable, moveable** *adj* **movement** *n* 1 action or process of moving. 2 group with a common aim. 3 division of a piece of music. 4 moving

parts of a machine.

mow ❶ *v* **mowing, mowed, mowed** or **mown** cut (grass or crops). **mower** *n* **mow down** *v* kill in large numbers.

MP 1 Member of Parliament. 2 Military Police(man).

mph miles per hour.

MT Montana.

much ❶ *adj* **more, most** 1 large amount or degree of. ♦ *n* 2 large amount or degree. ♦ *adv* **more, most** 3 to a great degree. 4 nearly.

muck ❶ *n* 1 dirt, filth. 2 manure. 3 **mucky** *adj*

mucus [**mew**–kuss] *n* slimy secretion of the mucous membranes. **mucous membrane** tissue lining body cavities or passages.

mud ❶ *n* wet soft earth. **muddy** *adj* **mudguard** *n* cover over a wheel to prevent mud or water being thrown up by it. **cosmetic paste to improve the complexion**

muddle ❶ *v* 1 (often foll. by *up*) confuse. 2 mix up. ♦ *n* 3 state of confusion.

muesli [**mewz**–lee] *n* mixture of grain, nuts, and dried fruit, eaten with milk.

muff[1] *n* tube–shaped covering to keep the hands warm.

————————— THESAURUS —————————

mourn *v* = **grieve**, bemoan, bewail, deplore, lament, rue, wail, weep

mouth *n* 1 = **maw**, gob (*sl, esp. Brit*), jaws 2 = **lips** 3 = **door**, entrance, gateway, inlet 5 = **opening**, aperture, orifice

move *v* 1 = **change**, advance, budge, go, proceed, progress, shift, stir, switch, transfer, transpose 2 = **relocate**, leave, migrate, pack one's bags (*inf*), quit, remove 3 = **drive**, activate, operate, propel, shift, start, turn 4 = **touch**, affect, excite, impress, inspire, rouse 5 = **prompt**, cause, incite, induce, influence, motivate, persuade 6 = **propose**, advocate, put forward, recommend, suggest, urge ♦ *n* 7 = **transfer**, relocation, removal, shift 8 = **action**, manoeuvre, measure, ploy, step, stratagem, stroke, turn

mow *v* = **cut**, crop, scythe, shear, trim

much *adj* 1 = **great**, abundant, a lot of, ample, considerable, copious, plenty of, sizable *or* sizeable, substantial ♦ *n* 2 = **a lot**, a good deal, a great deal, heaps (*inf*), loads (*inf*), lots (*inf*), plenty ≠ **little** ♦ *adv* 3 = **greatly**, a great deal, a lot, considerably, decidedly, exceedingly

muck *n* 1 = **dirt**, filth, gunge (*inf*), mire, mud, ooze, slime, sludge 2 = **manure**, dung, kak (*S Afr sl*), ordure

mud *n* = **dirt**, clay, mire, ooze, silt, slime, sludge

muddle *v* 1 = **confuse**, befuddle, bewilder, confound, daze, disorient, perplex, stupefy 2 = **jumble**, disarrange, disorder, disorganize, mess, mix up, scramble, spoil, tangle ♦ *n* 3 = **confusion**, chaos, disarray, disorder, disorganization, jumble, mess, mix–up, predicament, tangle

muff² v bungle (an action).

muffin n light round flat yeast cake.

muffle ● v wrap up for warmth or to deaden sound. **muffler** n scarf

mug¹ ● n large drinking cup.

mug² ● n 1 Slang face. 2 Slang gullible person. ♦ v **mugging, mugged** 3 Informal attack in order to rob. **mugger** n

mug³ ● v **mugging, mugged** (foll. by up) Informal study hard.

muggy ● adj **–gier, –giest** (of weather) damp and stifling.

mulberry n 1 tree whose leaves are used to feed silkworms. 2 purple fruit of this tree.

mulch n 1 mixture of wet straw, leaves, etc., used to protect the roots of plants. ♦ v 2 cover (land) with mulch.

mule n offspring of a horse and a donkey. **mulish** adj obstinate. **muleteer** n mule driver.

mull ● v think (over) or ponder. **mulled** adj (of wine or ale) flavoured with sugar and spices and served hot.

multi– combining form many, e.g. multicultural; multistorey.

multifarious ● [mull-tee-**fare**-ee-uss] adj having many various parts

multiple ● adj 1 having many parts. ♦ n 2 quantity which contains another an exact number of times. **multiply** v 1 increase in number, quantity, or degree. 2 add (a number) to itself a given number of times. 3 increase in number by reproduction.

multitude ● n 1 great number. 2 great crowd. **multitudinous** adj very numerous.

mum n Informal mother.

mumble v speak indistinctly, mutter.

mummy¹ n, pl **–mies** body embalmed and wrapped for burial in ancient Egypt. **mummified** adj (of a body) preserved as a mummy.

mummy² n, pl **–mies** child's word for MOTHER.

mumps n infectious disease with swelling in the glands of the neck.

munch ● v chew noisily and steadily.

mundane ● adj 1 everyday. 2 earthly.

municipal ● adj relating to a city or town. **municipality** n 1 city or town with local self–government. 2 governing body of this.

munificent ● [mew-**niff**-fiss-sent] adj very generous. **munificence** n

munted adj NZ slang 1 destroyed or ruined. 2 abnormal or peculiar.

mural n painting on a wall.

murder ● n 1 unlawful intentional killing of a human being. ♦ v 2 kill in this way. **murderer, murderess** n **murderous** adj

THESAURUS

muffle v a = **wrap up**, cloak, cover, envelop, shroud, swaddle, swathe b = **deaden**, muzzle, quieten, silence, soften, stifle, suppress

mug¹ n = **cup**, beaker, pot, tankard

mug² n 1 Sl = **face**, countenance, features, visage 2 Sl = **fool**, chump (inf), easy or soft touch (sl), simpleton, sucker (sl) ♦ v 3 Inf = **attack**, assault, beat up, rob, set about or upon

mug³ v (foll. by up) Inf = **study**, bone up on (inf), burn the midnight oil (inf), cram (inf), swot (Brit inf)

muggy adj = **humid**, clammy, close, moist, oppressive, sticky, stuffy, sultry

mull v = **ponder**, consider, contemplate, deliberate, meditate, reflect on, ruminate, think over, weigh

multifarious adj = **diverse**, different, legion, manifold, many, miscellaneous, multiple, numerous, sundry, varied

multiple adj 1 = **many**, manifold, multitudinous, numerous, several, sundry, various

multitude n 2 = **mass**, army, crowd, horde, host, mob, myriad, swarm, throng

munch v = **chew**, champ, chomp, crunch

mundane adj 1 = **ordinary**, banal, commonplace, day–to–day, everyday, humdrum, prosaic, routine, workaday ≠ **interesting** 2 = **earthly**, mortal, secular, temporal, terrestrial, worldly ≠ **heavenly**

municipal adj = **civic**, public, urban

murder n 1 = **killing**, assassination,

murk n thick darkness. **murky** adj dark or gloomy.

murmur ❶ v **–muring, –mured 1** speak or say in a quiet indistinct way. **2** complain. ◆ n **3** continuous low indistinct sound.

muscle ❶ n **1** tissue in the body which produces movement by contracting. **2** strength or power. **muscular** adj **1** with well–developed muscles. **2** of muscles. **muscular dystrophy** disease with wasting of the muscles. **muscle in** v Informal force one's way in.

muse ❶ v ponder quietly.

museum n building where natural, artistic, historical, or scientific objects are exhibited and preserved.

mush n **1** soft pulpy mass. **2** Informal cloying sentimentality. **mushy** adj

mushroom n **1** edible fungus with a stem and cap. ◆ v **2** grow rapidly.

music n **1** art form using a melodious and harmonious combination of notes. **2** written or printed form of this. **musical** adj **1** of or like music. **2** talented in or fond of music. **3** pleasant–sounding. ◆ n **4** play or film with songs and dancing. **musically** adv **musician** n **musicology** n scientific study of music. **musicologist** n **music hall** variety theatre.

musk n scent obtained from a gland of the musk deer or produced synthetically.

musky adj **muskrat** n **1** N American beaver–like rodent. **2** its fur.

musket n Hist long–barrelled gun. **musketeer** n

Muslim n **1** follower of the religion of Islam. ◆ adj **2** of or relating to Islam.

muslin n fine cotton fabric.

mussel n edible shellfish with a dark hinged shell.

must ❶ v **1** used as an auxiliary to express obligation, certainty, or resolution. ◆ n **2** essential or necessary thing.

mustang n wild horse of SW USA.

mustard n **1** paste made from the powdered seeds of a plant, used as a condiment. **2** the plant. **mustard gas** poisonous gas causing blistering burns and blindness.

muster ❶ v **1** assemble. ◆ n **2** assembly of military personnel.

musty ❶ adj **mustier, mustiest** smelling mouldy and stale. **mustiness** n

mute ❶ adj **1** silent. **2** unable to speak. ◆ n **3** person who is unable to speak. **4** Music device to soften the tone of an instrument. **muted** adj **1** (of sound or colour) softened. **2** (of a reaction) subdued. **mutely** adv

mutilate ❶ [mew–till–ate] v **1** deprive of a limb or other part. **2** damage (a book or text). **mutilation** n

mutiny ❶ [mew–tin–ee] n, pl **–nies 1**

bloodshed, butchery, carnage, homicide, manslaughter, massacre, slaying ◆ v **2 = kill**, assassinate, bump off (sl), butcher, eliminate (sl), massacre, slaughter, slay

murmur v **1 = mumble**, mutter, whisper **2 = grumble**, complain, moan (inf) ◆ n **3 = drone**, buzzing, humming, purr, whisper

muscle n **1 = tendon**, sinew **2 = strength**, brawn, clout (inf), forcefulness, might, power, stamina, weight **muscle in** ◆ v Inf **= impose oneself**, butt in, force one's way in

muse v **= ponder**, brood, cogitate, consider, contemplate, deliberate,

meditate, mull over, reflect, ruminate

must n **= necessity**, essential, fundamental, imperative, prerequisite, requirement, requisite, sine qua non

muster v **1 = assemble**, call together, convene, gather, marshal, mobilize, rally, summon ◆ n **2 = assembly**, collection, congregation, convention, gathering, meeting, rally, roundup

musty adj **= stale**, airless, dank, fusty, mildewed, mouldy, old, smelly, stuffy

mute adj **1, 2 = silent**, dumb, mum, speechless, unspoken, voiceless, wordless

mutilate v **1 = maim**, amputate, cut up, damage, disfigure, dismember, injure, lacerate, mangle **2 = distort**, adulterate, rebellion against authority, esp. by soldiers or sailors. ◆ v **–nying, –nied 2** commit mutiny. **mutineer** n **mutinous** adj

mutter ❶ v **1** utter or speak indistinctly. **2** grumble. ◆ n **3** muttered sound or grumble.

mutton n flesh of sheep, used as food.

mutual ❶ [mew–chew–al] adj **1** felt or expressed by each of two people about the other. **2** common to both or all. **mutually** adv

> ### ✓ WORD TIP
>
> The objection that something *mutual* has to do with two people only is outdated; nowadays *mutual* is equivalent to 'shared, in common'.

muzzle ❶ n **1** animal's mouth and nose. **2** cover for these to prevent biting. **3** open end of a gun. ◆ v **4** prevent from being heard or noticed. **5** put a muzzle on.

muzzy adj **–zier, –ziest 1** confused or muddled. **2** blurred or hazy.

my adj **1** of, belonging to, or associated with the speaker or writer (me). **2** used in various forms of address: *my lord*. ◆ interj **3** an exclamation of surprise or awe.

myall n an Australian acacia with hard scented wood.

myelin [**my**-ill-in] n a white tissue forming an insulating sheath around certain nerve fibres.

mynah n Asian bird which can mimic human speech.

myopia ❶ [my–**oh**–pee-a] n short-sightedness. **myopic** [my-**op**-ik] adj

myriad ❶ [**mir**–ree-ad] adj **1** innumerable. ◆ n **2** large indefinite number.

myrrh [**mur**] n aromatic gum used in perfume, incense, and medicine.

myrtle [**mur**-tl] n flowering evergreen shrub.

myself pron **1** emphatic or reflexive form of I or ME. **2** I or me in person as distinct from anyone else. **3** my usual self.

mystery ❶ n, pl **–teries 1** strange or inexplicable event or phenomenon. **2** obscure or secret thing. **3** story or film that arouses suspense. **mysterious** adj **mysteriously** adv

mystic ❶ n **1** person who seeks spiritual knowledge. ◆ adj **2** mystical. **mystical** adj having a spiritual or religious significance beyond human understanding.

mysticism n **1** belief in or experience of a reality beyond normal human understanding or experience. **2** the use of prayer and meditation in an attempt to achieve direct intuitive experience of the divine.

mystify ❶ v **–fying, –fied** bewilder or puzzle. **mystification** n

mystique ❶ [miss–**steek**] n aura of

———————— THESAURUS ————————

bowdlerize, censor, cut, damage, expurgate

mutiny n **1** = **rebellion**, disobedience, insubordination, insurrection, revolt, revolution, riot, uprising ◆ v **2** = **rebel**, disobey, resist, revolt, rise up

mutter v **2** = **grumble**, complain, grouse, mumble, murmur, rumble

mutual adj **1** = **reciprocal**, requited, returned **2** = **shared**, common, interchangeable, joint

muzzle n **1** = **jaws**, mouth, nose, snout **2** = **gag**, guard ◆ v **4** = **suppress**, censor, curb, gag, restrain, silence, stifle

myriad adj **1** = **innumerable**, countless, immeasurable, incalculable, multitudinous, untold ◆ n **2** = **multitude**, army, horde, host, swarm

mystery n **1** = **puzzle**, conundrum, enigma, problem, question, riddle, secret, teaser **2** = **secrecy**, ambiguity, ambiguousness, darkness, mystique, obscurity, uncertainty

mystic adj **2** = **supernatural**, inscrutable, metaphysical, mysterious, occult, otherworldly, paranormal, preternatural, transcendental

mystify v = **puzzle**, baffle, bewilder, confound, confuse, flummox, nonplus, perplex, stump mystery or power.

myth ❶ *n* 1 tale with supernatural characters, usu. of how the world and mankind began. 2 untrue idea or explanation. 3 imaginary person or object.

mythical, mythic *adj* **mythology** *n* 1 myths collectively. 2 study of myths. **mythological** *adj*

myxomatosis [mix–a–mat–**oh**–siss] *n* contagious fatal viral disease of rabbits.

———— THESAURUS ————

mystique *n* = **fascination**, awe, charisma, charm, glamour, magic, spell

myth *n* 1 = **legend**, allegory, fable, fairy story, fiction, folk tale, saga, story

2 = **illusion**, delusion, fancy, fantasy, figment, imagination, superstition, tall story

N n

nab v **nabbing, nabbed** *Informal* **1** arrest (someone). **2** catch (someone) in wrongdoing.

nadir ❶ n **1** point in the sky opposite the zenith. **2** lowest point.

naff ❶ *adj Slang* lacking quality or taste.

nag¹ ❶ v **nagging, nagged 1** scold or find fault constantly. **2** be a constant source of discomfort or worry to. ◆ n **3** person who nags. **nagging** *adj, n*

nag² ❶ n *Informal* old horse.

nail ❶ n **1** pointed piece of metal with a head, hit with a hammer to join two objects together. **2** hard covering of the upper tips of the fingers and toes. ◆ v **3** attach (something) with nails **4** *Informal* catch or arrest. **hit the nail on the head** say something exactly correct **small metal file** used to smooth or shape the finger or toe nails.

naive ❶ [nye–eev] *adj* **1** innocent and gullible. **2** simple and lacking sophistication. **naively** *adv* **naivety,**

naïveté [nye–eev–tee] n

naked ❶ *adj* **1** without clothes. **2** without any covering. **the naked eye** the eye unassisted by any optical instrument. **nakedness** n

name ❶ n **1** word by which a person or thing is known. **2** reputation, esp. a good one. ◆ v **3** give a name to. **4** refer to by name. **5** fix or specify insult someone by using rude words to describe him or her. **nameless** *adj* **1** without a name. **2** unspecified. **3** too horrible to be mentioned. **namely** *adv* that is to say. **namesake** n person with the same name as another.

nanny n, pl **–nies** woman whose job is looking after young children. **nanny goat** female goat.

nap¹ ❶ n **1** short sleep. ◆ v **napping, napped 2** have a short sleep.

nap² ❶ n raised fibres of velvet or similar cloth.

nape n back of the neck.

THESAURUS

nab v *Inf* **1 = apprehend**, arrest, capture, catch, collar (*inf*) **2 = catch**, apprehend, arrest, capture, collar (*inf*), grab, seize

nadir n **2 = bottom**, depths, lowest point, minimum, rock bottom

naff *adj Sl* = **bad**, duff (*Brit inf*), inferior, low–grade, poor, rubbishy, second–rate, shabby, shoddy, worthless

nag¹ v **1 = scold**, badger (*inf*), henpeck, upbraid **2 = worry**, annoy, harass, hassle, irritate, pester, plague ◆ n **3 = scold**, harpy, shrew, tartar, virago

nag² n *Inf* = **horse**, hack

nail v **3 = fasten**, attach, fix, hammer, join, pin, secure, tack

naive *adj* **1 = gullible**, callow, credulous, green, innocent, trusting, unsuspicious, wet behind the ears (*inf*)
2 = unsophisticated, artless, guileless, ingenuous, innocent, simple, unworldly

naked *adj* **1 = nude**, bare, exposed, starkers (*inf*), stripped, unclothed, undressed, without a stitch on (*inf*) ≠ **covered**

name n **1 = title**, appellation, denomination, designation, epithet, handle (*sl*), moniker (*sl*), nickname, sobriquet, term
2 = fame, distinction, eminence, esteem, honour, note, praise, renown, repute ◆ v
4 = call, baptize, christen, denominate, dub, entitle, label, style, term

napkin ❶ *n* piece of cloth or paper for wiping the mouth or protecting the clothes while eating.

nappy *n, pl* **-pies** piece of absorbent material fastened round a baby's lower torso to absorb urine and faeces.

narcissism ❶ *n* exceptional interest in or admiration for oneself. **narcissistic** *adj*

narcissus *n, pl* **-cissi** yellow, orange, or white flower related to the daffodil.

narcotic ❶ *n, adj* (of) a drug, such as morphine or opium, which produces numbness and drowsiness, used medicinally but addictive.

nark ❶ *Slang* ◆ *v* **1** annoy. ◆ *n* **2** informer or spy. **3** someone who complains in an irritating manner. **narky** *adj Slang* irritable or complaining.

narrate ❶ *v* **1** tell (a story). **2** speak the words accompanying and telling what is happening in a film or TV programme. **narration** *n* **narrator** *n* **narrative** *n* account, story.

narrow ❶ *adj* **1** small in breadth in comparison to length. **2** limited in range, extent, or outlook. **3** with little margin, e.g. *a narrow escape.* ◆ *v* **4** make or become narrow. **narrows** *pl n* narrow part of a strait, river, or current. **narrowly** *adv* **narrowness** *n* **narrow-minded** *adj* intolerant or bigoted.

nasal *adj* **1** of the nose. **2** (of a sound) pronounced with air passing through the nose. **nasally** *adv*

nasturtium *n* plant with yellow, red, or orange trumpet-shaped flowers.

nasty ❶ *adj* **-tier, -tiest 1** unpleasant. **2** (of an injury) dangerous or painful. **3** spiteful or unkind. **nastily** *adv* **nastiness** *n*

nation ❶ *n* people of one or more cultures or races organized as a single state. **national** *adj* **1** of or serving a national as a whole. **2** characteristic of a particular nation. **nationality** *n* fact of being a citizen of a particular nation.

native ❶ *adj* **1** relating to a place where a person was born. **2** born in a specified place. **3** (foll. by *to*) originating (in). **4** inborn. ◆ *n* **5** person born in a specified place. **6** indigenous animal or plant. **7** member of the original race of a country. **Native American** (person) descended from the original inhabitants of the American continent.

nap[1] *n* **1** = **sleep**, catnap, forty winks (*inf*), kip (*Brit sl*), rest, siesta ◆ *v* **2** = **sleep**, catnap, doze, drop off (*inf*), kip (*Brit sl*), nod off (*inf*), rest, snooze (*inf*)

nap[2] *n* = **weave**, down, fibre, grain, pile

napkin *n* = **serviette**, cloth

narcissism *n* = **egotism**, self-love, vanity

① **narcotic** *n* = **drug**, anaesthetic, analgesic, anodyne, opiate, painkiller, sedative, tranquillizer

② **narcotic** *adj* = **sedative**, analgesic, calming, hypnotic, painkilling, soporific

nark *Sl v* **1** = **annoy**, bother, exasperate, get on one's nerves (*inf*), irritate, nettle

narrate *v* **1** = **tell**, chronicle, describe, detail, recite, recount, relate, report

narrow *adj* **1** = **thin**, attenuated, fine, slender, slim, spare, tapering ≠ **wide** **2** = **insular**, dogmatic, illiberal, intolerant, narrow-minded, partial, prejudiced, small-minded **3** = **limited**, close, confined, constricted, contracted, meagre, restricted, tight ≠ **big** ◆ *v* **4** = **tighten**, constrict, limit, reduce

nasty *adj* **1** = **objectionable**, disagreeable, loathsome, obnoxious, offensive, unpleasant, vile ≠ **nice 2** = **painful**, bad, critical, dangerous, serious, severe **3** = **spiteful**, despicable, disagreeable, distasteful, malicious, mean, unpleasant, vicious, vile ≠ **kind**

nation *n* = **country**, people, race, realm, society, state, tribe

native *adj* **1, 2** = **local**, domestic, home, indigenous **3** (foll. by *to*) = **indigenous 4** = **inborn**, congenital, hereditary, inbred, ingrained, innate, instinctive, intrinsic, natural ◆ *n* **5** = **inhabitant**, citizen, countryman, dweller, national, resident **7** = **aborigine**

NATO North Atlantic Treaty Organization.

natter ❶ *Informal* ◆ *v* 1 talk idly or chatter. ◆ *n* 2 long idle chat.

natty ❶ *adj* –tier, –tiest *Informal* smart and spruce.

nature ❶ *n* 1 whole system of the existence, forces, and events of the physical world that are not controlled by human beings. 2 fundamental or essential qualities. 3 kind or sort. **natural** *adj* normal or to be expected.

naturism *n* nudism. **naturist** *n*

naughty ❶ *adj* –tier, –tiest 1 disobedient or mischievous. 2 mildly indecent. **naughtily** *adv* **naughtiness** *n*

nausea ❶ [naw–zee–a] *n* feeling of being about to vomit. **nauseate** *v* 1 make (someone) feel sick. 2 disgust. **nauseous** *adj* 1 as if about to vomit. 2 sickening.

nautical ❶ *adj* of the sea or ships. **nautical mile** 1852 metres (6076.12 feet).

nave *n* long central part of a church.

navel *n* hollow in the middle of the abdomen where the umbilical cord was attached.

navigate ❶ *v* 1 direct or plot the path or position of a ship, aircraft, or car. 2 travel over or through. **navigation** *n* **navigator** *n*

navigable *adj* 1 wide, deep, or safe enough to be sailed through. 2 able to be steered.

navvy ❶ *n, pl* –vies labourer employed on a road or building site.

navy ❶ *n, pl* –vies 1 branch of a country's armed services comprising warships with their crews and organization. 2 warships of a nation. ◆ *adj* 3 navy–blue. **naval** *adj* of or relating to a navy or ships. **navy–blue** *adj* very dark blue.

nay *interj Obs* no.

NB 1 New Brunswick. 2 note well.

NC North Carolina.

ND North Dakota.

near ❶ *prep, adv, adj* 1 indicating a place or time not far away. ◆ *adj* 2 almost the thing specified, e.g. *a near disaster*. ◆ *v* 3 draw close (to). **nearly** *adv* almost. **nearness** *n* **nearby** *adj* not far away. **nearside** *n* side of a vehicle that is nearer the kerb.

neat ❶ *adj* 1 tidy and clean. 2 smoothly or competently done. 3 undiluted. **neatly** *adv* **neatness** *n*

nebulous ❶ *adj* vague, indistinct.

━━━━━━ THESAURUS ━━━━━━

natter *Inf v* 1 = **gossip**, blether, chatter, gabble, jaw (*sl*), prattle, rabbit (on) (*Brit inf*), talk ◆ *n* 2 = **gossip**, chat, chinwag (*Brit inf*), chitchat, conversation, gab (*inf*), jaw (*sl*), prattle, talk

natty *Inf adj* = **smart**, dapper, elegant, fashionable, neat, snazzy (*inf*), spruce, stylish, trim

nature *n* 1 = **creation**, cosmos, earth, environment, universe, world 2 = **make-up**, character, complexion, constitution, essence 3 = **kind**, category, description, sort, species, style, type, variety

naughty *adj* 1 = **disobedient**, bad, impish, misbehaved, mischievous, refractory, wayward, wicked, worthless ≠ **good** 2 = **obscene**, improper, lewd, ribald, risqué, smutty, vulgar ≠ **proper**

nausea *n* = **sickness**, biliousness, queasiness, retching, squeamishness, vomiting

nautical *adj* = **maritime**, marine, naval

navigate *v* 1 = **sail**, drive, guide, handle, manoeuvre, pilot, steer ◆ *v* 2 = **voyage**

navvy *n* = **labourer**, worker, workman

navy *n* 2 = **fleet**, armada, flotilla

near *adj* 1 = **close**, adjacent, adjoining, nearby, neighbouring 2 = **forthcoming**, approaching, imminent, impending, in the offing, looming, nigh, upcoming ≠ **remote**

neat *adj* 1 = **tidy**, orderly, shipshape, smart, spick-and-span, spruce, systematic, trim ≠ **disorderly** 2 = **elegant**, adept, adroit, deft, dexterous, efficient, graceful, nimble, skilful, stylish ≠ **clumsy** 3 = **undiluted**, pure, straight, unmixed

nebulous *adj* = **vague**, confused, dim, hazy, imprecise, indefinite, indistinct, shadowy, uncertain, unclear

necessary ⊕ *adj* 1 needed to obtain the desired result, e.g. *the necessary skills.* 2 certain or unavoidable, e.g. *the necessary consequences.* **necessarily** *adv* **necessitate** *v* compel or require. **necessitous** *adj* very needy. **necessity** *n* 1 circumstances that inevitably require a certain result. 2 something needed.

neck *n* 1 part of the body joining the head to the shoulders. 2 part of a garment round the neck. 3 long narrow part of a bottle or violin. ♦ *v* 4 *Slang* kiss and cuddle. **neck and neck** absolutely level in a race or competition. **neckerchief** *n* piece of cloth worn tied round the neck. **necklace** *n* decorative piece of jewellery worn around the neck.

nectar *n* 1 sweet liquid collected from flowers by bees. 2 drink of the gods.

nectarine *n* smooth-skinned peach.

née [nay] *prep* indicating the maiden name of a married woman.

need ⊕ *v* 1 require or be in want of. ♦ *n* 2 condition of lacking something. 3 requirement or necessity. 4 poverty. **needs** *adv* (preceded by or foll. by *must*) necessarily. **needy** *adj* poor, in need of financial support. **needful** *adj* necessary or required.

needless *adj* unnecessary.

needle ⊕ *n* 1 thin pointed piece of metal with an eye through which thread is passed for sewing. 2 long pointed rod used in knitting. 3 pointed part of a hypodermic syringe. 4 small pointed part in a record player that touches the record and picks up the sound signals, stylus. 5 pointer on a measuring instrument or compass. 6 long narrow stiff leaf. ♦ *v* 7 *Informal* goad or provoke. **needlework** *n* sewing and embroidery.

ne'er-do-well ⊕ *n* useless or lazy person.

nefarious [nif-**fair**-ee-uss] *adj* wicked.

negate ⊕ *v* 1 invalidate. 2 deny the existence of. **negation** *n*

negative ⊕ *adj* 1 expressing a denial or refusal. 2 lacking positive qualities. 3 (of an electrical charge) having the same electrical charge as an electron. ♦ *n* 4 negative word or statement. 5 *Photog* image with a reversal of tones or colours from which positive prints are made.

neglect ⊕ *v* 1 take no care of. 2 fail (to do something) through carelessness. 3 disregard. ♦ *n* 4 neglecting or being neglected. **neglectful** *adj*

negligee [**neg**-lee-zhay] *n* woman's

——————{ THESAURUS }——————

necessary *adj* 1 = **needed**, compulsory, essential, imperative, indispensable, mandatory, obligatory, required, requisite, vital ≠ **unnecessary** 2 = **certain**, fated, inescapable, inevitable, inexorable, unavoidable ≠ **unnecessary**

need *v* 1 = **require**, call for, demand, entail, lack, miss, necessitate, want ♦ *n* 2 = **lack**, inadequacy, insufficiency, paucity, shortage 3 = **requirement**, demand, desideratum, essential, necessity, requisite 4 = **poverty**, deprivation, destitution, penury

needle *v* 7 *Inf* = **irritate**, annoy, get on one's nerves (*inf*), goad, harass, nag, pester, provoke, rile, taunt

ne'er-do-well *n* = **layabout**, black sheep, good-for-nothing, idler, loafer, loser, skiver (*Brit sl*), wastrel

nefarious *adj* = **wicked**, criminal, depraved, evil, foul, heinous, infernal, villainous

negate *v* 1 = **invalidate**, annul, cancel, countermand, neutralize, nullify, obviate, reverse, wipe out 2 = **deny**, contradict, disallow, disprove, gainsay (*arch or lit*), oppose, rebut, refute ≠ **maintain**

negative *adj* 1 = **contradictory**, contrary, denying, dissenting, opposing, refusing, rejecting, resisting ≠ **positive**
2 = **pessimistic**, cynical, gloomy, jaundiced, uncooperative, unenthusiastic, unwilling ≠ **positive** ♦ *n*
4 = **contradiction**, denial, refusal

neglect *v* 2 = **forget**, be remiss, evade, omit, pass over, shirk, skimp
3 = **disregard**, disdain, ignore, overlook, rebuff, scorn, slight, spurn ♦ *n*

lightweight usu. lace–trimmed dressing gown.

negligence ❶ n neglect or carelessness. **negligent** adj **negligently** adv

negotiate ❶ v 1 discuss in order to reach (an agreement). 2 succeed in passing round or over (a place or problem). **negotiation** n **negotiator** n **negotiable** adj

neigh n 1 loud high–pitched sound made by a horse. ♦ v 2 make this sound.

neighbour n person who lives or is situated near another. **neighbouring** adj situated nearby. **neighbourhood** n 1 district. 2 surroundings. 3 people of a district. **neighbourly** adj kind, friendly, and helpful.

neither adj, pron 1 not one nor the other. ♦ conj 2 not.

> ✓ **WORD TIP**
> When *neither* is followed by a plural noun it is acceptable to make the verb plural too: *Neither of these books are useful.*

nemesis ❶ [nem–miss–iss] n, pl –ses retribution or vengeance.

neologism [nee–ol–a–jiz–zum] n newly–coined word or an established word used in a new sense.

neon n Chem colourless odourless gaseous element used in illuminated signs and lights.

nephew n son of one's sister or brother.

nepotism ❶ [nep–a–tiz–zum] n favouritism in business shown to relatives and friends.

nerve ❶ n 1 cordlike bundle of fibres that conducts impulses between the brain and other parts of the body. 2 bravery and determination. 3 impudence. ♦ pl 4 anxiety or tension. **get on someone's nerves** irritate someone. **nerve oneself** prepare oneself (to do something difficult or unpleasant). **nervy** adj excitable or nervous. **nerve centre** place from which a system or organization is controlled. **nerve–racking** adj very distressing or harrowing.

nestle ❶ v 1 snuggle. 2 be in a sheltered position.

net¹ ❶ n 1 fabric of meshes of string, thread, or wire with many openings. 2 piece of net used to protect or hold things or to trap animals. ♦ v **netting**, **netted** 3 catch (a fish or animal) in a net. **netting** n material made of net. **netball** n team game in which a ball has to be thrown through a net hanging from a ring at the top of a pole.

net² ❶, **nett** adj 1 left after all deductions. 2 (of weight) excluding the wrapping or container. ♦ v **netting**, **netted** 3 yield or earn as a clear profit.

——————————| THESAURUS |——————————

4 = **negligence**, carelessness, dereliction, failure, laxity, oversight, slackness ≠ **care**

negligence n = **carelessness**, dereliction, disregard, inattention, indifference, laxity, neglect, slackness, thoughtlessness

negotiate v 1 = **deal**, arrange, bargain, conciliate, cut a deal, debate, discuss, mediate, transact, work out 2 = **get round**, clear, cross, get over, get past, pass, surmount

nemesis n = **retribution**, destiny, destruction, fate, vengeance

nepotism n = **favouritism**, bias, partiality, patronage, preferential treatment

nerve n 2 = **bravery**, bottle (Brit sl),

courage, daring, fearlessness, grit, guts (inf), pluck, resolution, will 3 Inf = **impudence**, audacity, boldness, brazenness, cheek (inf), impertinence, insolence, temerity **nerve oneself = brace oneself**, fortify oneself, gee oneself up, steel oneself

nestle v 1 = **snuggle**, cuddle, curl up, huddle, nuzzle

net¹ n 1 = **mesh**, lattice, netting, network, openwork, tracery, web ♦ v 3 = **catch**, bag, capture, enmesh, ensnare, entangle, trap

net², **nett** adj 1 = **take–home**, after taxes, clear, final ♦ v 3 = **earn**, accumulate, bring

nether ⊕ *adj* lower.
nethermost *adj* lowest.
nettle *n* plant with stinging hairs on the leaves. **nettled** *adj* irritated or annoyed.
network ⊕ *n* **1** system of intersecting lines, roads, etc. **2** interconnecting group or system. **3** (in broadcasting) group of stations that all transmit the same programmes simultaneously.
neural *adj* of a nerve or the nervous system.
neuralgia *n* severe pain along a nerve.
neurosis ⊕ *n, pl* **-ses** mental disorder producing hysteria, anxiety, depression, or obsessive behaviour. **neurotic** *adj* **1** emotionally unstable. **2** suffering from neurosis. ◆ *n* **3** neurotic person.
neuter ⊕ *adj* **1** belonging to a particular class of grammatical inflections in some languages. ◆ *v* **2** castrate (an animal).
neutral ⊕ *adj* **1** taking neither side in a war or dispute. **2** of or belonging to a neutral party or country. **3** (of a colour) not definite or striking. ◆ *n* **4** neutral person or nation. **5** neutral gear. **neutrality** *n* **neutralize** *v* make ineffective or neutral. **neutral gear** position of the controls of a gearbox that leaves the gears unconnected to the engine.
neutron *n* electrically neutral elementary particle of about the same mass as a proton.
never ⊕ *adv* at no time. **nevertheless** *adv* in spite of that.

✓ **WORD TIP**

Avoid the use of *never* with the past tense to mean *not*: I didn't see her (not I never saw her).

new ⊕ *adj* **1** not existing before. **2** recently acquired. **3** having lately come into some state. **4** additional. **5** (foll. by *to*) unfamiliar. ◆ *adv* **6** recently. **newness** *n* **New Age** late 1980s philosophy characterized by a belief in alternative medicine and spiritualism. **newborn** *adj* recently or just born. **newcomer** *n* recent arrival or participant. **newfangled** *adj* objectionably or unnecessarily modern. **newlyweds** *pl n* recently married couple. **new moon** moon when it appears as a crescent at the start of its cycle.
news ⊕ *n* **1** important or interesting new happenings. **2** information about such events reported in the mass media. **newsy** *adj* full of news. **newsagent** *n* shopkeeper who sells newspapers and magazines. **newsflash** *n* brief important news item, which interrupts a radio or television programme. **newsletter** *n* bulletin issued periodically to members of a group. **newspaper** *n* weekly or daily publication containing news. **newsprint** *n* inexpensive paper used for newspapers. **newsreader**, **newscaster** *n* person who reads the news on the television or radio. **newsreel** *n* short film giving news. **newsroom** *n* room

———————— THESAURUS ————————

in, clear, gain, make, realize, reap
nether *adj* = **lower**, below, beneath, bottom, inferior, under, underground
network *n* **1**, **2** = **system**, arrangement, complex, form, grid, labyrinth, lattice, maze, organization, plan, set of channels, structure, web
neurosis *n* = **obsession**, abnormality, affliction, derangement, instability, maladjustment, mental illness, phobia
neuter *v* **2** = **castrate**, doctor (*inf*), emasculate, fix (*inf*), geld, spay
neutral *adj* **1** = **unbiased**, even-handed,

impartial, nonaligned, nonpartisan, uncommitted, uninvolved, unprejudiced ≠ **active 3** = **indeterminate**, dull, indistinct, intermediate, undefined
never *adv* = **at no time**, not at all, on no account, under no circumstances ≠ **always**
new *adj* **1** = **modern**, contemporary, current, fresh, ground-breaking, latest, novel, original, recent, state-of-the-art, unfamiliar, up-to-date ≠ **old 3** = **changed**, altered, improved, modernized, redesigned, renewed, restored **4** = **extra**,

where news is received and prepared for publication or broadcasting. **newsworthy** *adj* sufficiently interesting to be reported as news.

newt *n* small amphibious creature with a long slender body and tail.

newton *n* unit of force.

next ❶ *adj, adv* 1 immediately following. 2 nearest. **next–of–kin** *n* closest relative.

NF Newfoundland.

NH New Hampshire.

NHS National Health Service.

nib *n* writing point of a pen.

nibble ❶ *v* 1 take little bites (of). ◆ *n* 2 little bite.

nice ❶ *adj* 1 pleasant. 2 kind. 3 good or satisfactory. 4 subtle, e.g. *a nice distinction.* **nicely** *adv* **niceness** *n*

> ✓ **WORD TIP**
> It is mistaken to suggest that the adjective *nice* should never be used, but, since it has been overused, it should be used sparingly.

niche ❶ [neesh] *n* 1 hollow area in a wall. 2 suitable position for a particular person.

nick ❶ *v* 1 make a small cut in. 2 *Slang* steal. 3 *Slang* arrest. ◆ *n* 4 small cut. 5

Slang prison or police station. **in good nick** *Informal* in good condition. **in the nick of time** just in time.

nickel *n* 1 *Chem* silvery–white metal often used in alloys. 2 US coin worth five cents.

nickname ❶ *n* 1 familiar name given to a person or place. ◆ *v* 2 call by a nickname.

nicotine *n* poisonous substance found in tobacco.

niece *n* daughter of one's sister or brother.

nifty ❶ *adj* **–tier, –tiest** *Informal* neat or smart.

niggard ❶ *n* stingy person. **niggardly** *adj*

niggle ❶ *v* 1 worry slightly. 2 continually find fault (with). ◆ *n* 3 small worry or doubt.

nigh *adv, prep Lit* near.

night ❶ *n* 1 time of darkness between sunset and sunrise. 2 evening. 3 period between going to bed and morning. 4 nightfall or dusk. 5 an evening designated for a specified activity, e.g. *parents' night.* ◆ *adj* 6 of, occurring, or working at night, e.g. *the night shift.* **nightly** *adj, adv* (happening) each night. **nightcap** *n* 1 drink taken just before bedtime. 2 soft cap formerly worn in bed. **nightclub** *n* establishment for dancing, music, etc., open late at night. **nightdress** *n* woman's

──────── THESAURUS ────────

added, more, new–found, supplementary

news *n* 1, 2 = **information**, bulletin, communiqué, exposé, gossip, hearsay, intelligence, latest (*inf*), report, revelation, rumour, story

① **next** *adj* 1 = **following**, consequent, ensuing, later, subsequent, succeeding 2 = **nearest**, adjacent, adjoining, closest, neighbouring

② **next** *adv* 1 = **afterwards**, following, later, subsequently, thereafter

nibble *v* 1 = **bite**, eat, gnaw, munch, nip, peck, pick at ◆ *n* 2 = **taste**, crumb, morsel, peck, soupçon, titbit

nice *adj* 1 = **pleasant**, agreeable, attractive, charming, delightful, good, pleasurable ≠ **awful** 2 = **kind**, courteous, friendly, likable *or* likeable, polite, well–mannered

≠ **mean** 3 = **neat**, dainty, fine, tidy, trim 4 = **subtle**, careful, delicate, fastidious, fine, meticulous, precise, strict

niche *n* 1 = **alcove**, corner, hollow, nook, opening, recess 2 = **position**, calling, pigeonhole (*inf*), place, slot (*inf*), vocation

nick *v* 1 = **cut**, chip, dent, mark, notch, scar, score, scratch, snick 2 *Sl* = **steal**, pilfer, pinch (*inf*), swipe (*sl*) ◆ *n* 4 = **cut**, chip, dent, mark, notch, scar, scratch

nickname *n* 1 = **pet name**, diminutive, epithet, label, sobriquet

nifty *adj Inf* = **neat**, attractive, chic, deft, pleasing, smart, stylish

niggard *n* = **miser**, cheapskate (*inf*), Scrooge, skinflint

niggle *v* 1 = **worry**, annoy, irritate, rankle 2 = **criticize**, carp, cavil, find fault, fuss

loose dress worn in bed. **nightfall** n
approach of darkness. **nightie** n Informal
nightdress. **nightingale** n small bird with a
musical song usu. heard at night. **nightjar**
n nocturnal bird with a harsh cry. **nightlife**
n entertainment and social activities
available at night in a town or city.
nightmare n 1 very bad dream. 2 very
unpleasant experience. **night school** place
where adults can attend educational
courses in the evenings. **nightshade** n
plant with bell–shaped flowers which are
often poisonous. **night–time** n time from
sunset to sunrise.

nil ❶ n nothing, zero.

nimble ❶ adj agile and quick. **nimbly** adv

nimbus n, pl **–bi, –buses** dark grey rain
cloud.

nincompoop ❶ n Informal stupid person.

nine adj, n one more than eight. **ninth** adj,
n (of) number nine in a series. **ninepins** n
game of skittles.

nip¹ ❶ v **nipping, nipped** 1 Informal hurry.
2 pinch or squeeze. 3 bite lightly. 4 (of the
cold) cause pain. ◆ n 5 pinch or light bite.
6 sharp coldness, e.g. *a nip in the air*.
nippy adj **–pier, –piest** 1 frosty or chilly. 2
Informal quick or nimble. **nipper** n Informal
small child.

nip² ❶ n small alcoholic drink.

nipple n projection in the centre of a
breast.

nit n 1 egg or larva of a louse. 2 Informal
short for NITWIT. **nit–picking** adj Informal
overconcerned with insignificant detail,
esp. to find fault. **nitwit** n Informal stupid
person.

nitrogen [**nite**–roj–jen] n Chem colourless
odourless gas that forms four fifths of the
air. **nitric, nitrous, nitrogenous** adj of or
containing nitrogen. **nitrate** n compound
of nitric acid, used as a fertilizer.
nitroglycerine, nitroglycerin n explosive
liquid.

NJ New Jersey.

NM New Mexico.

no ❶ interj 1 expresses denial,
disagreement, or refusal. ◆ adj 2 not any,
not a. ◆ adv 3 not at all. ◆ n, pl **noes, nos**
4 answer or vote of 'no'. 5 person who
answers or votes 'no'. **no–go area** district
barricaded off so that the police or army
can enter only by force. **no–man's–land** n
land between boundaries, esp. contested
land between two opposing forces. **no–
one, no one** pron nobody.

✔ **WORD TIP**

When *no–one* refers to 'people in
general' it may be followed by a plural:
No–one finished their drink.

---

no. number.

noble ❶ adj 1 showing or having high
moral qualities. 2 of the nobility. 3
impressive and magnificent. ◆ n 4
member of the nobility. **nobility** n 1
quality of being noble. 2 class of people
holding titles and high social rank. **nobly**
adv **nobleman, noblewoman** n

nobody ❶ pron 1 no person. ◆ n, pl
–bodies 2 person of no importance.

─────┤ THESAURUS ├─────

night n 1 = **darkness**, dark, night–time
3 = **night–time**

nil n = **nothing**, love, naught, none, zero

nimble adj = **agile**, brisk, deft, dexterous,
lively, quick, sprightly, spry, swift ≠ **heavy**

nincompoop n Inf = **idiot**, blockhead,
chump, fool, nitwit (inf), numbskull or
numskull, twit (inf, chiefly Brit)

nip¹ v 2 = **pinch**, squeeze, tweak 3 = **bite**

nip² n = **dram**, draught, drop, mouthful,
shot (inf), sip, snifter (inf)

no interj 1 = **never**, nay, not at all, no way
≠ **yes** ◆ n 4 = **refusal**, denial, negation,
rejection ≠ **acceptance**

noble adj 1 = **worthy**, generous,
honourable, magnanimous, upright,
virtuous ≠ **selfish** 2 = **aristocratic**, blue–
blooded, highborn, lordly, patrician, titled
≠ **base** 3 = **impressive**, dignified,
distinguished, grand, great, imposing,
lofty, splendid, stately ≠ **mean** ◆ n
4 = **lord**, aristocrat, nobleman, peer

✓ **WORD TIP**

Nobody is equivalent in its uses to *no-one*.

nocturnal ● *adj* 1 of the night. 2 active at night.

nod ● *v* **nodding, nodded** 1 lower and raise (one's head) briefly in agreement or greeting. 2 let one's head fall forward with sleep. ◆ *n* 3 act of nodding. **nod off** *v Informal* fall asleep.

node *n* 1 point on a plant stem from which leaves grow. 2 point at which a curve crosses itself.

nodule *n* 1 small knot or lump. 2 rounded mineral growth on the root of a plant.

noise ● *n* sound, usu. a loud or disturbing one. **noisy** *adj* 1 making a lot of noise. 2 full of noise. **noisily** *adv* **noiseless** *adj*

nomad ● *n* member of a tribe with no fixed dwelling place, wanderer. **nomadic** *adj*

nomenclature ● *n* system of names used in a particular subject.

nominal ● *adj* 1 in name only. 2 very small in comparison with real worth. **nominally** *adv*

nominate ● *v* 1 suggest as a candidate. 2 appoint to an office or position. **nomination** *n* **nominee** *n* candidate.

nominative *n* form of a noun indicating the subject of a verb.

non– *prefix* indicating: 1 negation, e.g. *nonexistent.* 2 refusal or failure, e.g. *noncooperation.* 3 exclusion from a specified class, e.g. *nonfiction.* 4 lack or absence, e.g. *nonevent.*

nonchalant ● *adj* casually unconcerned or indifferent. **nonchalantly** *adv* **nonchalance** *n*

noncommissioned officer *n* (in the armed forces) a subordinate officer, risen from the ranks.

noncommittal ● *adj* not committing oneself to any particular opinion.

nonconformist ● *n* 1 person who does not conform to generally accepted patterns of behaviour or thought. 2 (N–) member of a Protestant group separated from the Church of England.

nondescript ● *adj* lacking outstanding features.

none ● *pron* 1 not any. 2 no-one. **nonetheless** *adv* despite that, however.

✓ **WORD TIP**

Although *none* means 'not one', and can take a singular verb, it more often takes a plural: *None of them are mine*.

nonentity ● [non–**enn**–tit–tee] *n, pl* **–ties**

————————— THESAURUS —————————

nobody *pron* 1 = **no-one** ◆ *n* 2 = **nonentity**, cipher, lightweight (*inf*), menial ≠ **star**

nocturnal *adj* = **nightly**, night-time

nod *v* 1 = **acknowledge**, bow, gesture, indicate, signal 2 = **sleep**, doze, drowse, nap ◆ *n* 3 = **gesture**, acknowledgment, greeting, indication, sign, signal

noise *n* 1 = **sound**, clamour, commotion, din, hubbub, racket, row, uproar ≠ **silence**

nomad *n* = **wanderer**, drifter, itinerant, migrant, rambler, rover, vagabond

nomenclature *n* = **terminology**, classification, codification, phraseology, taxonomy, vocabulary

nominal *adj* 1 = **so-called**, formal,

ostensible, professed, puppet, purported, supposed, theoretical, titular 2 = **small**, inconsiderable, insignificant, minimal, symbolic, token, trifling, trivial

nominate *v* 1 = **suggest**, propose, recommend 2 = **name**, appoint, assign, choose, designate, elect, select

nonchalant *adj* = **casual**, blasé, calm, careless, indifferent, insouciant, laid-back (*inf*), offhand, unconcerned, unperturbed

noncommittal *adj* = **evasive**, cautious, circumspect, equivocal, guarded, neutral, politic, temporizing, tentative, vague, wary

nonconformist *n* 1 = **maverick**, dissenter, eccentric, heretic, iconoclast, individualist, insignificant person or thing.

nonevent ❶ *n* disappointing or insignificant occurrence.

nonflammable *adj* not easily set on fire.

nonpareil [non–par–**rail**] *n* person or thing that is unsurpassed.

nonplussed *adj* perplexed.

nonsense ❶ *n* **1** something that has or makes no sense. **2** absurd language. **3** foolish behaviour. **nonsensical** *adj*

non sequitur [**sek**–wit–tur] *n* statement with little or no relation to what preceded it.

nook ❶ *n* sheltered place.

noon ❶ *n* twelve o'clock midday. **noonday** *adj* happening at noon.

noose *n* loop in the end of a rope, tied with a slipknot.

nor *conj* and not.

norm ❶ *n* standard that is regarded as usual. **normal** *adj* usual, regular, or typical.

north ❶ *n* **1** direction towards the North Pole, opposite south. **2** area lying in or towards the north. ♦ *adj* **3** to or in the north. ♦ *adv* **5** in, to, or towards the north. **northerly** *adj* **northern** *adj* **northerner** *n* person from

the north of a country or area. **northward** *adj, adv* **northwards** *adv* **North Pole** northernmost point on the earth's axis.

nose ❶ *n* **1** organ of smell, used also in breathing. **2** front part of a vehicle. ♦ *v* **3** move forward slowly and carefully. **4** pry or snoop. **nose dive** sudden drop. **nosey, nosy** *adj Informal* prying or inquisitive. **nosiness** *n*

nosh *Slang* ♦ *n* **1** food. ♦ *v* **2** eat.

nostalgia ❶ *n* sentimental longing for the past. **nostalgic** *adj*

nostril *n* one of the two openings at the end of the nose.

not *adv* expressing negation, refusal, or denial.

notable ❶ *adj* **1** worthy of being noted, remarkable. ♦ *n* **2** person of distinction. **notably** *adv* **notability** *n*

notary *n, pl* **–ries** person authorized to witness the signing of legal documents.

notation ❶ *n* **1** representation of numbers or quantities in a system by a series of symbols. **2** set of such symbols.

notch ❶ *n* **1** V–shaped cut. **2** *Informal* step or level. ♦ *v* **3** make a notch in. **4** (foll. by *up*) score or achieve.

protester, radical, rebel ≠ **traditionalist**

nondescript *adj* = **ordinary**, commonplace, dull, featureless, run–of–the–mill, undistinguished, unexceptional, unremarkable

none *pron* = **not any**, nil, nobody, no–one, nothing, not one, zero

nonentity *n* = **nobody**, cipher, lightweight (*inf*), mediocrity, small fry

nonevent *n* = **flop** (*inf*), disappointment, dud (*inf*), failure, fiasco, washout

nonsense *n* 1, 2 = **rubbish**, balderdash, claptrap (*inf*), double Dutch (*Brit inf*), drivel, gibberish, hot air (*inf*), stupidity, tripe (*inf*), twaddle

nook *n* = **niche**, alcove, corner, cubbyhole, hide–out, opening, recess, retreat

noon *n* = **midday**, high noon, noonday, noontide, twelve noon

norm *n* = **standard**, average, benchmark,

criterion, par, pattern, rule, yardstick

north *adj* 3 = **northern**, Arctic, boreal, northerly, polar ♦ *adv* 5 = **northward(s)**, northerly

nose *n* 1 = **snout**, beak, bill, hooter (*sl*), proboscis ♦ *v* 3 = **ease forward**, nudge, nuzzle, push, shove 4 = **pry**, meddle, snoop (*inf*)

nostalgia *n* = **reminiscence**, homesickness, longing, pining, regretfulness, remembrance, wistfulness, yearning

notable *adj* 1 = **remarkable**, conspicuous, extraordinary, memorable, noteworthy, outstanding, rare, striking, uncommon, unusual ≠ **hidden** ♦ *n* 2 = **celebrity**, big name, dignitary, luminary, personage, V.I.P. ≠ **unknown**

notation *n* 2 = **signs**, characters, code, script, symbols, system

note ⓘ *n* **1** short letter. **2** brief comment or record. **3** banknote. **4** (symbol for) a musical sound. **5** hint or mood. ◆ *v* **6** notice, pay attention to. **7** record in writing. **8** remark upon. **noted** *adj* well–known. **notebook** *n* book for writing in. **noteworthy** *adj* worth noting, remarkable.

nothing ⓘ *pron* **1** not anything. **2** matter of no importance. **3** figure 0. ◆ *adv* **4** not at all. **nothingness** *n* **1** nonexistence. **2** insignificance.

✓ **WORD TIP**

Nothing is usually followed by a singular verb but, if it comes before a plural noun, this can sound odd: *Nothing but books was/were on the shelf.* A solution is to rephrase the sentence: *Only books were...*

---

notice ⓘ *n* **1** observation or attention. **2** sign giving warning or an announcement. **3** advance notification of intention to end a contract of employment. ◆ *v* **4** observe, become aware of. **5** point out or remark upon.

noticeable ⓘ *adj* easily seen or detected, appreciable.

notify ⓘ *v* –fying, –fied inform. **notification** *n* **notifiable** *adj* having to be reported to the authorities.

notion ⓘ *n* **1** idea or opinion. **2** whim.

notional ⓘ *adj* speculative, imaginary, or unreal.

notorious ⓘ *adj* well known for something bad. **notoriously** *adv* **notoriety** *n*

notwithstanding ⓘ *prep* in spite of.

nougat *n* chewy sweet containing nuts and fruit.

nought ⓘ *n* **1** figure 0. **2** nothing.

noun *n* word that refers to a person, place, or thing.

nourish ⓘ *v* **1** feed. **2** encourage or foster (an idea or feeling). **nourishment** *n* **nourishing** *adj* providing the food necessary for life and growth.

Nov. November.

novel[1] ⓘ *n* long fictitious story in book form. **novelist** *n* writer of novels.

novel[2] ⓘ *adj* fresh, new, or original. **novelty** *n* **1** newness. **2** something new or

---

THESAURUS

notch *n* **1** = **cut**, cleft, incision, indentation, mark, nick, score **2** *Inf* = **level**, degree, grade, step ◆ *v* **3** = **cut**, indent, mark, nick, score, scratch

note *n* **1, 2** = **message**, comment, communication, epistle, jotting, letter, memo, memorandum, minute, remark, reminder ◆ *v* **6** = **see**, notice, observe, perceive **7** = **mark**, denote, designate, indicate, record, register **8** = **mention**, remark

nothing *pron* **1** = **nothingness**, emptiness, nullity, void **3** = **nought**, nil, zero

notice *n* **1** = **interest**, cognizance, consideration, heed, note, observation, regard ≠ **neglect 2** = **announcement**, advice, communication, instruction, intimation, news, notification, order, warning ◆ *v* **5** = **observe**, detect, discern, distinguish, mark, note, perceive, see, spot ≠ **ignore**

noticeable *adj* = **obvious**, appreciable, clear, conspicuous, evident, manifest, perceptible, plain, striking

notify *v* = **inform**, advise, alert, announce, declare, make known, publish, tell, warn

notion *n* **1** = **idea**, belief, concept, impression, inkling, opinion, sentiment, view **2** = **whim**, caprice, desire, fancy, impulse, inclination, wish

notional *adj* = **speculative**, abstract, conceptual, hypothetical, imaginary, theoretical, unreal

notorious *adj* = **infamous**, dishonourable, disreputable, opprobrious, scandalous

notwithstanding *prep* = **despite**, in spite of

nought *n* **1** = **zero**, nil **2** = **nothing**, nil, zero

nourish *v* **1** = **feed**, nurse, nurture, supply, sustain, tend **2** = **encourage**, comfort, cultivate, foster, maintain, promote, unusual. 3 cheap toy or trinket.

November n eleventh month of the year.

novice ⓘ n 1 beginner. 2 person who has entered a religious order but has not yet taken vows.

now ⓘ adv 1 at or for the present time. 2 immediately. ♦ conj 3 seeing that, since. **now and again**, **then** occasionally. **nowadays** adv in these times.

nowhere adv not anywhere.

noxious ⓘ adj 1 poisonous or harmful. 2 extremely unpleasant.

nozzle n projecting spout through which fluid is discharged.

NS Nova Scotia.

NSW New South Wales.

nuance ⓘ [new–ahnss] n subtle difference in colour, meaning, or tone.

nub n point or gist (of a story etc.).

nubile ⓘ [new–bile] adj (of a young woman) 1 sexually attractive. 2 old enough to get married.

nucleus ⓘ n, pl –clei 1 centre, esp. of an atom or cell. 2 central thing around which others are grouped.

nude ⓘ adj 1 naked. ♦ n 2 naked figure in painting, sculpture, or photography.

nudity n **nudism** n practice of not wearing clothes. **nudist** n

nudge ⓘ v 1 push gently, esp. with the elbow. ♦ n 2 gentle push or touch.

nugget ⓘ n 1 small lump of gold in its natural state. 2 something small but valuable. ♦ v 3 NZ & S Afr polish footwear.

nuisance ⓘ n something or someone that causes annoyance or bother.

nuke Slang ♦ v 1 attack with nuclear weapons. ♦ n 2 nuclear weapon.

null ⓘ adj **null and void** not legally valid. **nullity** n **nullify** v 1 make ineffective. 2 cancel.

numb ⓘ adj 1 without feeling, as through cold, shock, or fear. ♦ v 2 make numb. **numbness** n **numbskull** n stupid person.

number ⓘ n 1 sum or quantity. 2 word or symbol used to express a sum or quantity, numeral. 3 numeral or string of numerals used to identify a person or thing. 4 one of a series, such as a copy of a magazine. 5 song or piece of music. 6 group of people. 7 Grammar classification of words depending on how many persons or things are referred to. ♦ v 8 count. 9 give a number to. 10 amount to. 11 include in

———————— THESAURUS ————————

support

novel¹ n = **story**, fiction, narrative, romance, tale

novel² adj = **new**, different, fresh, innovative, original, strange, uncommon, unfamiliar, unusual

novice n 1 = **beginner**, amateur, apprentice, learner, newcomer, probationer, pupil, trainee ≠ **teacher**

now adv 1 = **nowadays**, any more, at the moment 2 = **immediately**, at once, instantly, promptly, straightaway **now and again** or **then** = **occasionally**, from time to time, infrequently, intermittently, on and off, sometimes, sporadically

noxious adj 1 = **harmful**, deadly, destructive, foul, hurtful, injurious, poisonous, unhealthy, unwholesome

nuance n = **subtlety**, degree, distinction, gradation, nicety, refinement, shade, tinge

nubile adj 2 = **marriageable**, ripe (inf)

nucleus n = **centre**, basis, core, focus, heart, kernel, nub, pivot

nude adj 1 = **naked**, bare, disrobed, stark–naked, stripped, unclad, unclothed, undressed, without a stitch on (inf)

nudge v, n = **push**, bump, dig, elbow, jog, poke, prod, shove, touch

nugget n = **lump**, chunk, clump, hunk, mass, piece

nuisance n = **problem**, annoyance, bother, drag (inf), hassle (inf), inconvenience, irritation, pain in the neck, pest, trouble

null adj **null and void** = **invalid**, inoperative, useless, valueless, void, worthless

numb adj 1 = **unfeeling**, benumbed, dead, deadened, frozen, immobilized, insensitive, paralysed, torpid ≠ **feeling** ♦ v 2 = **deaden**, benumb, dull, freeze, a group. **numberless** *adj* too many to be counted. **number crunching** *Computers* large–scale processing of numerical data. **number one** *n Informal* 1 oneself. 2 bestselling pop record in any one week. **numberplate** *n* plate on a car showing the registration number.

numeral ❶ *n* word or symbol used to express a sum or quantity.

numskull *n* same as NUMBSKULL.

nun *n* female member of a religious order. **nunnery** *n* convent.

nuptial ❶ *adj* relating to marriage. **nuptials** *pl n* wedding.

nurse ❶ *n* 1 person employed to look after sick people, usu. in a hospital. 2 woman employed to look after children. ◆ *v* 3 look after (a sick person). 4 breast–feed (a baby). 5 try to cure (an ailment). 6 harbour or foster (a feeling). **nursing home** private hospital or home for old people. **nursing officer** administrative head of the nursing staff of a hospital.

nurture ❶ *n* 1 act or process of promoting the development of a child or young plant. ◆ *v* 2 promote or encourage the development of.

nut ❶ *n* 1 fruit consisting of a hard shell and a kernel. 2 small piece of metal that screws onto a bolt. 3 (also **nutcase**) *Slang* insane or eccentric person. 4 *Slang* head. **nutty** *adj* 1 containing or resembling nuts. 2 *Slang* insane or eccentric. **nutter** *n Slang* insane person. **nutcracker** *n* device for cracking the shells of nuts. **nuthatch** *n* small songbird. **nutmeg** *n* spice made from the seed of a tropical tree.

nutrient *n* substance that provides nourishment.

nutrition ❶ *n* 1 process of taking in and absorbing nutrients. 2 process of being nourished. **nutritional** *adj* **nutritious, nutritive** *adj* nourishing.

nuzzle ❶ *v* push or rub gently with the nose or snout.

NV Nevada.

NWT Northwest Territories.

NY New York.

nylon *n* 1 synthetic material used for clothing etc. ◆ *pl* 2 stockings made of nylon.

nymph ❶ *n* 1 mythical spirit of nature, represented as a beautiful young woman. 2 larva of certain insects, resembling the adult form.

nymphomaniac *n* woman with an abnormally intense sexual desire.

THESAURUS

immobilize, paralyse

number *n* 1 = **quantity**, aggregate, amount, collection ≠ **want** 2 = **numeral**, character, digit, figure, integer 4 = **issue**, copy, edition, imprint, printing 6 = **throng**, collection, crowd, horde, multitude ◆ *v* 8 = **calculate**, account, add, compute, count, enumerate, include, reckon, total ≠ **guess**

numeral *n* = **number**, digit, figure, integer

nuptial *adj* = **marital**, bridal, conjugal, connubial, matrimonial

nurse *v* 3 = **look after**, care for, minister to, tend, treat 4 = **breast–feed**, feed, nourish, nurture, suckle, wet–nurse 6 = **foster**, cherish, cultivate, encourage, harbour,

preserve, promote, succour, support

nurture *n* 1 = **development**, discipline, education, instruction, rearing, training, upbringing ◆ *v* 2 = **develop**, bring up, discipline, educate, instruct, rear, school, train ≠ **ignore**

nut *n* 3 (also **nutcase**) *Sl* = **madman**, crank (*inf*), lunatic, maniac, nutcase (*sl*), psycho (*sl*) 4 *Sl* = **head**, brain, mind, reason, senses

nutrition *n* 1, 2 = **food**, nourishment, nutriment, sustenance

nuzzle *v* = **snuggle**, burrow, cuddle, fondle, nestle, pet

nymph *n* 1 = **sylph**, dryad, naiad

O o

oaf ⊕ *n* stupid or clumsy person. **oafish** *adj*

oak *n* 1 deciduous forest tree. 2 its wood, used for furniture. **oak apple** brownish lump found on oak trees.

OAP old–age pensioner.

oar *n* pole with a broad blade, used for rowing a boat.

oasis *n, pl* **–ses** fertile area in a desert.

oat *n* 1 hard cereal grown as food. ◆ *pl* 2 grain of this cereal. **sow one's wild oats** have many sexual relationships when young. **oatmeal** 1 *adj* 2 pale brownish–cream.

oath ⊕ *n* 1 solemn promise, esp. to be truthful in court. 2 swearword.

obdurate ⊕ *adj* hardhearted or stubborn. **obduracy** *n*

OBE Officer of the Order of the British Empire.

obelisk ⊕ [**ob**–bill–isk] *n* four–sided stone column tapering to a pyramid at the top.

obese ⊕ [oh–**beess**] *adj* very fat. **obesity** *n*

obey ⊕ *v* carry out instructions or orders.

obituary *n, pl* **–aries** announcement of someone's death, esp. in a newspaper.

object¹ ⊕ *n* 1 physical thing. 2 focus of thoughts or action. 3 aim or purpose. 4 *Grammar* word that a verb or preposition affects. **no object** not a hindrance.

object² ⊕ *v* express disapproval. **objection** *n* **objectionable** *adj* unpleasant. **objector** *n*

objective ⊕ *n* 1 aim or purpose. ◆ *adj* 2 not biased. 3 existing in the real world outside the human mind. **objectively** *adv* **objectivity** *n*

oblige ⊕ *v* 1 compel (someone) morally or by law to do something. 2 do a favour for (someone). **obliging** *adj* ready to help other people. **obligated** *adj* obliged to do something. **obligation** *n* duty. **obligatory** *adj* required by a rule or law.

oblique ⊕ [oh–**bleak**] *adj* 1 slanting. 2

THESAURUS

oaf *n* = **dolt**, blockhead, clod, dunce, fool, goon, idiot, lout, moron, numbskull *or* numskull

oath *n* 1 = **promise**, affirmation, avowal, bond, pledge, vow, word 2 = **swearword**, blasphemy, curse, expletive, profanity

obdurate *adj* = **stubborn**, dogged, hard–hearted, immovable, implacable, inflexible, obstinate, pig–headed, unyielding

obelisk *n* = **column**, monolith, monument, needle, pillar, shaft

obese *adj* = **fat**, corpulent, gross, heavy, overweight, paunchy, plump, portly, rotund, stout, tubby

obey *v* = **carry out**, abide by, act upon, adhere to, comply, conform, follow, heed,

keep, observe ≠ **rebel**

object¹ *n* 1 = **thing**, article, body, entity, item, phenomenon 2 = **target**, focus, recipient, victim 3 = **purpose**, aim, design, end, goal, idea, intention, objective, point

object² *v* = **protest**, argue against, demur, draw the line (at something), expostulate, oppose, take exception ≠ **accept**

objective *n* 1 = **purpose**, aim, ambition, end, goal, intention, mark, object, target ◆ *adj* 2 = **unbiased**, detached, disinterested, dispassionate, even–handed, fair, impartial, impersonal, open–minded, unprejudiced ≠ **prejudiced**

oblige *v* 1 = **compel**, bind, constrain, force, impel, make, necessitate, require 2 = **do (someone) a favour** *or* **a kindness**,

indirect. ◆ n 3 the symbol (/). **obliquely**
adv **oblique angle** angle that is not a right
angle.

obliterate ❶ v wipe out, destroy.
obliteration n

oblong adj 1 having two long sides, two
short sides, and four right angles. ◆ n 2
oblong figure.

obnoxious ❶ adj offensive.

oboe n double–reeded woodwind
instrument. **oboist** n

obscene ❶ adj 1 portraying sex
offensively. 2 disgusting. **obscenity** n

obscure ❶ adj 1 not well known. 2 hard to
understand. 3 indistinct. ◆ v 4 make
(something) obscure. **obscurity** n

obsequious ❶ [ob–**seek**–wee–uss] adj
overattentive in order to gain favour.
obsequiousness n

observe ❶ v 1 see or notice. 2 watch
(someone or something) carefully. 3
remark. 4 act according to (a law or
custom). **observation** n 1 action or habit
of observing. 2 remark. **observer** n
observance n observing of a custom.
observant adj quick to notice things.
observatory n building equipped for
studying the weather and the stars.

obsess v preoccupy (someone)
compulsively. **obsessed** adj **obsessive** adj
obsession n

obsolete ❶ adj no longer in use.
obsolescent adj becoming obsolete.
obsolescence n

obstacle ❶ n something that makes
progress difficult.

obstetrics n branch of medicine
concerned with pregnancy and childbirth.
obstetric adj **obstetrician** n

obstinate ❶ adj 1 stubborn. 2 difficult to
remove or change. **obstinacy** n

obstreperous ❶ adj unruly, noisy.

accommodate, benefit, gratify, indulge,
please ≠ **trouble**

oblique adj 1 = **slanting**, angled, aslant,
sloping, tilted 2 = **indirect**, backhanded,
circuitous, implied, roundabout, sidelong
≠ **open**

obliterate v = **destroy**, annihilate, blot
out, efface, eradicate, erase, expunge,
extirpate, root out, wipe out ≠ **make**

obnoxious adj = **offensive**, disagreeable,
insufferable, loathsome, nasty, nauseating,
objectionable, odious, repulsive, revolting,
unpleasant

obscene adj 1 = **indecent**, dirty, filthy,
immoral, improper, lewd, offensive,
pornographic, salacious, scungy (Aust &
NZ inf) 2 = **disgusting**, atrocious, evil,
heinous, loathsome, outrageous, shocking,
sickening, vile, wicked ≠ **seemly**

obscure adj 1 = **little–known**, humble,
lowly, out–of–the–way, remote,
undistinguished, unheard–of, unknown
≠ **major** 2 = **vague**, ambiguous, arcane,
confusing, cryptic, enigmatic, esoteric,
mysterious, opaque, recondite, unclear
≠ **clear** 3 = **dark**, blurred, cloudy, dim,

faint, gloomy, indistinct, murky, shadowy
≠ **distinct** ◆ v 4 = **conceal**, cover, disguise,
hide, obfuscate, screen, veil ≠ **show**

obsequious adj = **sycophantic**, cringing,
deferential, fawning, flattering, grovelling,
ingratiating, servile, submissive, unctuous

observe v 1 = **see**, detect, discern,
discover, note, notice, perceive, spot,
witness 2 = **watch**, check, keep an eye on
(inf), keep track of, look at, monitor,
scrutinize, study, survey, view 3 = **remark**,
comment, mention, note, opine, say, state
4 = **carry out**, abide by, adhere to,
comply, conform to, follow, heed, honour,
keep, obey, respect ≠ **ignore**

obsolete adj = **out of date**, antiquated,
archaic, discarded, disused, extinct, old,
old–fashioned, outmoded, passé

obstacle n = **difficulty**, bar, barrier, block,
hindrance, hitch, hurdle, impediment,
obstruction, snag, stumbling block ≠ **help**

obstinate adj 1 = **stubborn**, determined,
dogged, inflexible, intractable,
intransigent, pig–headed, refractory, self–
willed, strong–minded, wilful

obstreperous adj = **unruly**, disorderly,

obstruct ⊕ v block with an obstacle. **obstruction** n **obstructive** adj

obtain ⊕ v 1 acquire intentionally. 2 be customary. **obtainable** adj

obtrude v push oneself or one's ideas on others. **obtrusion** n **obtrusive** adj unpleasantly noticeable.

obtuse ⊕ adj 1 mentally slow. 2 Maths (of an angle) between 90° and 180°. 3 not pointed. **obtuseness** n

obverse n 1 opposite way of looking at an idea. 2 main side of a coin or medal.

obviate ⊕ v make unnecessary.

obvious ⊕ adj easy to see or understand, evident. **obviously** adv

occasion ⊕ n 1 time at which a particular thing happens. 2 reason, e.g. no occasion for complaint. 3 special event. ♦ v 4 cause. **occasional** adj happening sometimes. **occasionally** adv

Occident n Lit the West. **Occidental** adj

occult ⊕ adj relating to the supernatural.

occupy ⊕ v –pying, –pied 1 live or work in (a building). 2 take up the attention of (someone). 3 take up (space or time). 4 take possession of (a place) by force.

occupant n **occupation** n profession. **occupier** n

occur ⊕ v –curring, –curred 1 happen. 2 exist. **occur to** come to the mind of. **occurrence** n 1 something that occurs. 2 fact of occurring.

✓ **WORD TIP**

Avoid the use of occur (or happen) for events that are planned. Compare An accident occurred with A wedding took place.

---

ocean n vast area of sea between continents. **oceanic** adj **oceanography** n scientific study of the oceans.

ochre [oak–er] adj, n brownish–yellow (earth).

o'clock adv used after a number to specify an hour.

Oct. October.

octagon n geometric figure with eight sides. **octagonal** adj

octane n hydrocarbon found in petrol.

octave n Music (interval between the first and) eighth note of a scale.

THESAURUS

---

loud, noisy, riotous, rowdy, turbulent, unmanageable, wild

obstruct v 1 = **block**, bar, barricade, choke, clog, close, cut off, shut off, stop, stop up

obtain v 1 = **get**, achieve, acquire, attain, earn, gain, land, procure, secure ≠ **lose** 2 = **exist**, be in force, be prevalent, be the case, hold, prevail

obtuse adj 1 = **stupid**, dense, dull, dumb (inf), slow, stolid, thick, uncomprehending

obviate v = **preclude**, avert, prevent, remove

obvious adj = **evident**, apparent, clear, conspicuous, distinct, indisputable, manifest, noticeable, plain, self–evident, undeniable, unmistakable

occasion n 1 = **time**, moment, occurrence, point, stage 2 = **reason**, call, cause, excuse, ground(s), justification, motive, prompting, provocation 3 = **event**, affair,

celebration, experience, happening, occurrence ♦ v 4 = **cause**, bring about, engender, generate, give rise to, induce, inspire, lead to, produce, prompt, provoke

occult adj = **supernatural**, arcane, esoteric, magical, mysterious, mystical

occupy v 1 = **live in**, dwell in, inhabit, own, possess, reside in ≠ **abandon** 2 = **take up**, divert, employ, engage, engross, involve, monopolize, preoccupy, tie up 3 = **fill**, cover, permeate, pervade, take up 4 = **invade**, capture, overrun, seize, take over ≠ **withdraw**

occur v 1 = **happen**, befall, come about, crop up (inf), take place, turn up (inf) 2 = **exist**, appear, be found, be present, develop, manifest itself, show itself **occur to** = **come to mind**, cross one's mind, dawn on, enter one's head, spring to mind, strike one, suggest itself

octet n 1 group of eight performers. 2 music for such a group.

October n tenth month of the year.

octopus n, pl **–puses** sea creature with a soft body and eight tentacles.

odd ❶ adj 1 unusual. 2 occasional. 3 not divisible by two. 4 not part of a set. **odds** pl n (ratio showing) the probability of something happening. **at odds** in conflict. **odds and ends** small miscellaneous items. **oddity** n odd person or thing. **oddments** pl n things left over.

ode n lyric poem, usu. addressed to a particular subject.

odium [oh–dee–um] n widespread dislike. **odious** adj offensive.

odour ❶ n particular smell. **odorous** adj **odourless** adj

odyssey ❶ [odd–iss–ee] n long eventful journey.

oesophagus [ee–soff–a–guss] n, pl **–gi** passage between the mouth and stomach.

of prep 1 belonging to. 2 consisting of. 3 connected with. 4 characteristic of.

✔ **WORD TIP**

When *of* means 'belonging to' an apostrophe can be used: *Bill's dog* (the dog of Bill).

---

off ❶ prep 1 away from. ◆ adv 2 away. ◆ adj 3 not operating. 4 cancelled. 5 (of food) gone bad. ◆ n 6 Cricket side of the field to which the batsman's feet point. **off colour** slightly ill. **off-line** adj (of a computer) not directly controlled by a central processor.

✔ **WORD TIP**

Avoid using of after off: *He got off the bus* (not *off of*). The use of *off* to mean *from* is very informal: *They brought milk from* (rather than *off*) *a farmer.*

---

offal n edible organs of an animal, such as liver or kidneys.

offend ❶ v 1 hurt the feelings of, insult. 2 commit a crime. **offender** n **offence** n 1 (cause of) hurt feelings or annoyance. 2 illegal act. **offensive** adj 1 disagreeable. 2 insulting. 3 aggressive. ◆ n 4 position or action of attack.

offer ❶ v 1 present (something) for acceptance or rejection. 2 provide. 3 be willing (to do something). 4 propose as payment. ◆ n 5 instance of offering something. **offering** n thing offered.

office ❶ n 1 room or building where people work at desks. 2 department of a commercial organization. 3 formal position of responsibility. 4 place where tickets or information can be obtained. **officer** n 1 person in authority in the armed services. 2 member of the police force. 3 person with special responsibility in an organization.

official ❶ adj 1 of a position of authority.

THESAURUS

odd adj 1 = **unusual**, bizarre, extraordinary, freakish, irregular, munted (NZ sl), peculiar, rare, remarkable, singular, strange 2 = **occasional**, casual, incidental, irregular, periodic, random, sundry, various ≠ **regular** 4 = **unmatched**, extra, leftover, lone, single, surplus, uneven, unpaired

odour n = **smell**, aroma, bouquet, essence, fragrance, perfume, redolence, scent, stench, stink

odyssey n = **journey**, crusade, pilgrimage, quest, trek, voyage

off adv 2 = **away**, apart, aside, elsewhere,

out ◆ adj 4 = **cancelled**, finished, gone, postponed, unavailable 5 = **bad**, mouldy, rancid, rotten, sour, turned

offend v 1 = **insult**, affront, annoy, displease, hurt (someone's) feelings, outrage, slight, snub, upset, wound ≠ **please**

offer v 1 = **propose**, advance, submit, suggest 2 = **provide**, afford, furnish, present ≠ **refuse** 3 = **volunteer**, come forward, offer one's services 4 = **proffer**, bid, tender ◆ n 5 = **suggestion**, proposition, submission

office n 3 = **post**, function, occupation,

2 approved or arranged by someone in authority. ◆ n 3 person who holds a position of authority. **officially** adv **officialdom** n officials collectively.

officiate ❶ v act in an official role.

officious ❶ adj interfering unnecessarily.

offside adj, adv Sport (positioned) illegally ahead of the ball.

often ❶ adv frequently, much of the time. **oft** adv Poetic often.

ogle ❶ v stare at (someone) lustfully.

ogre ❶ n 1 giant that eats human flesh. 2 monstrous or cruel person.

oh interj exclamation of surprise, pain, etc.

OH Ohio.

ohm n unit of electrical resistance.

oil ❶ n 1 viscous liquid, insoluble in water and usu. flammable. 2 same as PETROLEUM. 3 petroleum derivative, used as a fuel or lubricant. ◆ pl 4 oil–based paints used in art. ◆ v 5 lubricate (a machine) with oil. **oily** adj **oilskin** n (garment made from) waterproof material.

ointment ❶ n greasy substance used for healing skin or as a cosmetic.

OK Oklahoma.

O.K., okay Informal ◆ interj 1 expression of approval. ◆ v 2 approve (something). ◆ n 3 approval.

old ❶ adj 1 having lived or existed for a long time. 2 of a specified age, e.g. two years old. 3 former. **olden** adj old, e.g. in the olden days. **oldie** n Informal old but popular song or film. **old–fashioned** adj no longer commonly used or valued. **old guard** group of people in an organization who have traditional values. **old hat** boring because so familiar. **old master** European painter or painting from the period 1500-1800. **old school tie** system of mutual help between former pupils of public schools. **Old Testament** part of the Bible recording Hebrew history. **Old World** world as it was known before the discovery of the Americas.

olfactory adj relating to the sense of smell.

oligarchy [ol–lee–gark–ee] n, pl –chies 1 government by a small group of people. 2 state governed this way. **oligarchic, oligarchical** adj

olive n 1 small green or black fruit used as food or pressed for its oil. 2 tree on which this fruit grows. ◆ adj 3 greyish–green. **olive branch** peace offering.

ombudsman n official who investigates complaints against government organizations.

omelette n dish of eggs beaten and fried.

─────[THESAURUS]─────

place, responsibility, role, situation

official adj 2 = **authorized**, accredited, authentic, certified, legitimate, licensed, sanctioned ≠ **casual** ◆ n 3 = **officer**, agent, bureaucrat, executive, functionary, office bearer, representative

officiate v = **preside**, chair, conduct, manage, oversee, serve, superintend

officious adj = **interfering**, dictatorial, intrusive, meddlesome, obtrusive, overzealous, pushy (inf), self–important

often adv = **frequently**, generally, repeatedly, time and again

ogle v = **leer**, eye up (inf)

ogre n 1 = **giant** 2 = **monster**, bogeyman, bugbear, demon, devil, spectre

oil v 5 = **lubricate**, grease

ointment n = **lotion**, balm, cream,

embrocation, emollient, liniment, salve, unguent

O.K., okay Inf interj 1 = **all right**, agreed, approved, correct, fair, fine, fitting, in order, permitted, right, roger, suitable, very good, very well, ya (S Afr), yebo (S Afr inf), yes ◆ v 2 = **approve**, agree to, authorize, endorse, give the green light, pass, permit, ratify, rubber–stamp (inf), sanction ◆ n 3 = **approval**, agreement, assent, authorization, consent, go–ahead (inf), green light, permission, sanction, say–so (inf), seal of approval

old adj 1 = **aged**, ancient, antediluvian, antiquated, antique, decrepit, elderly, mature, senile, timeworn, venerable ≠ **young** 3 = **former**, earlier, erstwhile,

omen ⊙ *n* happening or object thought to foretell success or misfortune. **ominous** *adj* worrying, seeming to foretell misfortune.

omit ⊙ *v* omitting, omitted 1 leave out. 2 neglect (to do something). **omission** *n*

omnibus *n* 1 several books or TV or radio programmes made into one. 2 *Old-fashioned* bus.

omnipotent ⊙ *adj* having unlimited power. **omnipotence** *n*

omniscient ⊙ [om–**niss**–ee–ent] *adj* knowing everything. **omniscience** *n*

omnivorous [om–**niv**–vor–uss] *adj* eating food obtained from both animals and plants. **omnivore** *n* omnivorous animal.

on *prep* 1 indicating position above, attachment, closeness, etc., e.g. *lying on the ground; a puppet on a string; on the coast.* ◆ *adv* 2 in operation. 3 continuing. 4 forwards. ◆ *adj* 5 operating. 6 taking place. ◆ *n* 7 *Cricket* side of the field on which the batsman stands. **on line, online** *adj* 1 (of a computer) directly controlled by a central processor. 2 relating to the Internet, e.g. *online shopping.*

ON Ontario.

once ⊙ *adv* 1 on one occasion. 2 formerly. ◆ *conj* 3 as soon as. **at once 1** immediately. 2 simultaneously. **once–over** *n Informal* quick examination.

one *adj* 1 single, lone. ◆ *n* 2 number or figure 1. 3 single unit. ◆ *pron* 4 any person. **oneness** *n* unity. **oneself** *pron* reflexive form of ONE. **one–liner** *n* witty remark. **one–night stand** sexual encounter lasting one night. **one–sided** *adj* considering only one point of view. **one–way** *adj* allowing movement in one direction only.

> ✓ **WORD TIP**
> Avoid overuse of the pronoun *one* as a substitute for *I*. Many listeners find it affected. The pronouns *I* and *one* should not be mixed within the same group of sentences. Choose one of them and continue with it.

onerous ⊙ [**own**–er–uss] *adj* (of a task) difficult to carry out.

onion *n* strongly flavoured edible bulb.

onlooker ⊙ *n* person who watches without taking part.

only ⊙ *adj* 1 alone of its kind. ◆ *adv* 2 exclusively. 3 merely. 4 no more than. ◆ *conj* 5 but.

> ✓ **WORD TIP**
> The use of *only* to connect sentences is rather informal: *I would come only I'm busy.* In formal use *only* is placed directly before the words it modifies: *The club opens only on Thursdays* but in everyday use this becomes: *The club only opens on Thursdays.*

onset ⊙ *n* beginning.

onslaught ⊙ *n* violent attack.

——————| THESAURUS |——————

one–time, previous

omen *n* = **sign**, foreboding, indication, portent, premonition, presage, warning

omit *v* 1 = **leave out**, drop, eliminate, exclude, pass over, skip ≠ **include** 2 = **forget**, neglect, overlook

omnipotent *adj* = **almighty**, all–powerful, supreme

omniscient *adj* = **all–knowing**, all–wise

once *adv* 2 = **at one time**, formerly, long ago, once upon a time, previously **at once** 1 = **immediately**, directly, forthwith, instantly, now, right away, straight away, this (very) minute 2 = **simultaneously**, at the same time, together

onerous *adj* = **difficult**, burdensome, demanding, exacting, hard, heavy, laborious, oppressive, taxing

onlooker *n* = **observer**, bystander, eyewitness, looker–on, spectator, viewer, watcher, witness

only *adj* 1 = **sole**, exclusive, individual, lone, single, solitary, unique ◆ *adv* 3 = **merely**, barely, just, purely, simply

onset *n* = **beginning**, inception, outbreak, start ≠ **ending**

onto *prep* 1 to a position on. 2 aware of, e.g. *she's onto us.*

onus ⓣ [own–uss] *n, pl* **onuses** responsibility or burden.

onward ⓣ *adj* 1 directed or moving forward. ◆ *adv* 2 (also **onwards**) ahead, forward.

onyx *n* type of quartz with coloured layers.

ooze¹ ⓣ *v* 1 flow slowly. 2 overflow with (a quality). ◆ *n* 3 sluggish flow. **oozy** *adj*

ooze² ⓣ *n* soft mud at the bottom of a lake or river.

opal *n* iridescent precious stone. **opalescent** *adj* iridescent like an opal.

opaque ⓣ *adj* not able to be seen through, not transparent. **opacity** *n*

open ⓣ *adj* 1 not closed. 2 not covered. 3 unfolded. 4 ready for business. 5 free from obstruction, accessible. 6 unrestricted. 7 not finalized. 8 frank. ◆ *v* 9 (cause to) become open. 10 begin. ◆ *n* 11 *Sport* competition which all may enter. **in the open** outdoors. **openly** *adv* without concealment. **opening** *n* 1 opportunity. 3 hole. ◆ *adj* 4 first. **opencast mining** mining at the surface and not underground. **open day** day on which a school or college is open to the public. **open–handed** *adj* generous. **open house** hospitality to visitors at any time. **open**

letter letter to an individual that the writer makes public in a newspaper or magazine. **open–minded** *adj* receptive to new ideas. **open–plan** *adj* (of a house or office) having few interior walls. **open prison** prison with minimal security.

opera *n* drama in which the text is sung to an orchestral accompaniment. **operatic** *adj* **operetta** *n* light–hearted comic opera. **opera glasses** small binoculars used by theatre audiences.

ophthalmic *adj* relating to the eye. **ophthalmology** *n* study of the eye and its diseases. **ophthalmologist** *n*

opinion ⓣ *n* personal belief or judgment. **opinionated** *adj* having strong opinions. **opine** *v Old–fashioned* express an opinion. **opinion poll** see POLL.

opium *n* addictive narcotic drug made from poppy seeds.

opossum *n* small marsupial of America or Australia.

opponent ⓣ *n* person one is working against in a contest, battle, or argument.

opportunity ⓣ *n, pl* **–ties** 1 favourable time or condition. 2 good chance. **opportunity shop** *Aust & NZ* shop selling second–hand clothes, sometimes for charity (also **op–shop**).

oppose ⓣ *v* work against. **be opposed to**

————————|THESAURUS|————————

onslaught *n* = **attack**, assault, blitz, charge, offensive, onrush, onset

onus *n* = **burden**, liability, load, obligation, responsibility, task

onward *adv* 2 (also **onwards**) = **ahead**, beyond, forth, forward, in front, on

ooze¹ *v* 1 = **seep**, drain, dribble, drip, escape, filter, leak

ooze² *n* = **mud**, alluvium, mire, silt, slime, sludge

opaque *adj* = **cloudy**, dim, dull, filmy, hazy, impenetrable, murky ≠ **clear**

open *adj* 1 = **unclosed**, agape, ajar, gaping, uncovered, unfastened, unlocked, yawning ≠ **closed** 3 = **extended**, unfolded, unfurled ≠ **shut** 5 = **accessible**, available, free, public, unoccupied, vacant

6 = **unrestricted** 7 = **unresolved**, arguable, debatable, moot, undecided, unsettled 8 = **frank**, candid, guileless, honest, sincere, transparent ≠ **reserved** ◆ *v* 9 = **unfasten**, expand, spread (out), unblock, uncork, uncover, undo, unfold, unfurl, unlock, unroll, untie, unwrap ≠ **close** 10 = **start**, begin, commence, inaugurate, initiate, kick off (*inf*), launch, set in motion

opinion *n* = **belief**, assessment, feeling, idea, impression, judgment, point of view, sentiment, theory, view

opponent *n* = **adversary**, antagonist, challenger, competitor, contestant, enemy, foe, rival ≠ **friend**

opportunity *n* = **chance**, moment,

disagree with or disapprove of. **opposite**
adj situated on the other side. **opposition**
n 1 obstruction or hostility. 2 group
opposing another. 3 political party not in
power.

oppress ❶ *v* 1 control by cruelty or force.
2 depress. **oppression** *n* **oppressor** *n*
oppressive *adj* 1 tyrannical. 2 (of weather)
hot and humid.

opt ❶ *v* show a preference, choose.

optic *adj* relating to the eyes or sight.
optics *n* science of sight and light. **optical**
adj

optimism *n* tendency to take the most
hopeful view. **optimist** *n* **optimistic** *adj*
optimistically *adv*

optimum ❶ *n, pl* **-ma, -mums** 1 best
possible conditions. ◆ *adj* 2 most
favourable. **optimal** *adj* **optimize** *v* make
the most of.

option ❶ *n* 1 choice. 2 thing chosen. 3
right to buy or sell something at a
specified price within a given time.
optional *adj* possible but not compulsory.

optometrist *n* person qualified to
prescribe glasses. **optometry** *n*

opulent ❶ [op–pew–lent] *adj* having or
indicating wealth. **opulence** *n*

opus ❶ *n, pl* **opuses, opera** artistic
creation, esp. a musical work.

or *conj* used to join alternatives, e.g. *tea or
coffee.*

OR Oregon.

oracle ❶ *n* 1 shrine of an ancient god. 2
prophecy, often obscure, revealed at a
shrine. 3 person believed to make infallible
predictions. 4 **oracular** *adj*

oral ❶ *adj* 1 spoken. 2 (of a drug) to be
taken by mouth. ◆ *n* 3 spoken
examination. **orally** *adv*

orange *n* 1 reddish–yellow citrus fruit. ◆
adj 2 reddish–yellow.

orang–utan, orang–utang *n* large
reddish–brown ape with long arms.

orator ❶ [or–rat–tor] *n* skilful public
speaker. **oration** *n* formal speech.

oratory ❶ [or–rat–tree] *n* art of making
speeches. **oratorical** *adj*

orb ❶ *n* ceremonial decorated sphere with
a cross on top, carried by a monarch.

orbit ❶ *n* 1 curved path of a planet,
satellite, or spacecraft around another
body. 2 sphere of influence. ◆ *v* **orbiting,
orbited** 3 move in an orbit around. 4 put
(a satellite or spacecraft) into orbit. **orbital**
adj

THESAURUS

occasion, opening, scope, time

oppose *v* 1 = **fight**, block, combat,
counter, defy, resist, take issue with, take
on, thwart, withstand ≠ **back**

oppress *v* 1 = **subjugate**, abuse, maltreat,
persecute, subdue, suppress, wrong ≠ **free**
2 = **depress**, afflict, burden, dispirit,
harass, sadden, torment, vex

opt *v* = **choose**, decide (on), elect, go for,
plump for, prefer

optimum *adj* 2 = **ideal**, best, highest,
optimal, peak, perfect, superlative

option *n* 1 = **choice**, alternative,
preference, selection

opulent *adj* = **rich**, affluent, filthy rich,
flush (*inf*), lavish, luxurious, moneyed,
prosperous, sumptuous, wealthy,
well–heeled, well–off, well–to–do
≠ **poor**

opus *n* = **work**, brainchild, composition,
creation, *oeuvre*, piece, production

oracle *n* 2 = **prophecy**, divination,
prediction, prognostication, revelation
3 = **authority**, adviser, guru, mana (*NZ*),
mastermind, mentor, pundit, wizard

oral *adj* 1 = **spoken**, verbal, vocal

orator *n* = **public speaker**, declaimer,
lecturer, rhetorician, speaker

oratory *n* = **eloquence**, declamation,
elocution, grandiloquence, public
speaking, rhetoric, speech–making

orb *n* = **sphere**, ball, circle, globe, ring

orbit *n* 1 = **path**, circle, course, cycle,
revolution, rotation, trajectory 2 = **sphere
of influence**, ambit, compass, domain,
influence, range, reach, scope, sweep ◆ *v*
3 = **circle**, circumnavigate, encircle,
revolve around

orchard *n* area where fruit trees are grown.

orchestra *n* **1** large group of musicians, esp. playing a variety of instruments. **2** (also **orchestra pit**) area of a theatre in front of the stage, reserved for the musicians. **orchestral** *adj* **orchestrate** *v* **1** arrange (music) for orchestra. **2** organize (something) to produce a particular result. **orchestration** *n*

orchid *n* plant with flowers that have unusual lip-shaped petals.

ordain ❶ *v* **1** make (someone) a member of the clergy. **2** order or establish with authority.

ordeal ❶ *n* painful or difficult experience.

ordinal number *n* number showing a position in a series, e.g. *first; second.*

ordinance *n* official rule or order.

ordinary ❶ *adj* **1** usual or normal. **2** dull or commonplace. **ordinarily** *adv*

ordnance *n* weapons and military supplies. **Ordnance Survey** official organization making maps of Britain.

ore *n* (rock containing) a mineral which yields metal.

oregano [or-rig-**gah**-no] *n* sweet-smelling herb used in cooking.

organ ❶ *n* **1** part of an animal or plant that has a particular function, such as the heart or lungs. **2** musical keyboard instrument in which notes are produced by forcing air

through pipes. **3** means of conveying information, esp. a newspaper. **organist** *n* organ player.

organism ❶ *n* any living animal or plant.

organize ❶ *v* **1** make arrangements for. **2** arrange systematically. **organization** *n* **1** group of people working together. **2** act of organizing. **organizational** *adj* **organizer** *n*

orgasm *n* most intense point of sexual pleasure. **orgasmic** *adj*

orgy ❶ *n, pl* **-gies 1** party involving promiscuous sexual activity. **2** unrestrained indulgence, e.g. *an orgy of destruction.*

orient ❶ orientate *v* **1** position (oneself) according to one's surroundings. **2** position (a map) in relation to the points of the compass. **orientation** *n* **orienteering** *n* sport in which competitors hike over a course using a compass and map.

orifice ❶ [**or**-rif-fiss] *n* opening or hole.

origami [or-rig-**gah**-mee] *n* Japanese decorative art of paper folding.

origin ❶ *n* point from which something develops. **original** *adj* **1** first or earliest. **2** new, not copied or based on something else. **3** able to think up new ideas. ◆ *n* **4** first version, from which others are copied. **original sin** human imperfection and mortality as a result of Adam's

———— THESAURUS ————

ordain *v* **1** = **appoint**, anoint, consecrate, invest, nominate **2** = **order**, decree, demand, dictate, fix, lay down, legislate, prescribe, rule, will

ordeal *n* = **hardship**, agony, anguish, baptism of fire, nightmare, suffering, test, torture, trial, tribulation(s)

ordinary *adj* **1** = **usual**, common, conventional, everyday, normal, regular, routine, standard, stock, typical **2** = **commonplace**, banal, humble, humdrum, modest, mundane, plain, run-of-the-mill, unremarkable, workaday ≠ **special**

organ *n* **1** = **part**, element, structure, unit **3** = **medium**, forum, mouthpiece, vehicle,

voice

organism *n* **1** = **creature**, animal, being, body, entity

organize *v* **1** = **plan**, arrange, coordinate, marshal, put together, run, set up, take care of ≠ **upset 2** = **put in order**, arrange, classify, group, systematize ≠ **scramble**

orgy *n* **1** = **revel**, bacchanalia, carousal, debauch, revelry, Saturnalia **2** = **spree**, binge (*inf*), bout, excess, indulgence, overindulgence, splurge, surfeit

orient, orientate *v* **1** = **adjust**, acclimatize, adapt, align, familiarize **2** = **get one's bearings**

orifice *n* = **opening**, aperture, cleft, hole, mouth, pore, rent, vent

disobedience. **originality** n **originally** adv
originate v come or bring into existence.
origination n **originator** n
ornament ❶ n 1 decorative object. ◆ v 2
decorate. **ornamental** adj **ornamentation**
n
ornate ❶ adj highly decorated, elaborate.
ornithology n study of birds.
ornithological adj **ornithologist** n
orphan n child whose parents are dead.
orphanage n children's home for orphans.
orphaned adj having no living parents.
orthodox ❶ adj conforming to established
views. **orthodoxy** n **Orthodox Church**
dominant Christian Church in Eastern
Europe.
oscillate ❶ [oss–ill–late] v swing back and
forth. **oscillation** n **oscilloscope** [oss–**sill**–
oh–scope] n instrument that shows the
shape of a wave on a cathode–ray tube.
osmosis n 1 movement of a liquid
through a membrane from a lower to a
higher concentration. 2 process of subtle
influence. **osmotic** adj
osprey n large fish–eating bird of prey.
ossify ❶ v –fying, –fied 1 (cause to)
become bone, harden. 2 become
inflexible. **ossification** n
ostensible ❶ adj apparent, seeming.
ostensibly adv

ostentation ❶ n pretentious display.
ostentatious adj
osteopathy n medical treatment involving
manipulation of the joints. **osteopath** n
ostracize ❶ v exclude (a person) from a
group. **ostracism** n
ostrich n large African bird that runs fast
but cannot fly.
other ❶ adj 1 remaining in a group of
which one or some have been specified. 2
different from the ones specified or
understood. 3 additional. ◆ n 4 other
person or thing. **otherwise** conj 1 or else,
if not. ◆ adv 2 differently, in another way.
otherworldly adj concerned with spiritual
rather than practical matters.
otter n small brown freshwater mammal
that eats fish.
ouch interj exclamation of sudden pain.
ought v used to express: 1 obligation, e.g.
you ought to pay. 2 advisability, e.g. you
ought to diet. 3 probability, e.g. you ought
to know by then.

✓ **WORD TIP**

In standard English did and had are not
used with ought: ought not to (not
didn't/hadn't ought to).
---

ounce n unit of weight equal to one

origin n 1 = **root**, base, basis, derivation,
foundation, fount, fountainhead,
inception, launch, source, start, wellspring
2 = **beginning**, birth, creation, emergence,
genesis ≠ **end**
ornament n 1 = **decoration**, accessory,
bauble, garnish, flounce, frill, knick–knack,
trinket ◆ v 2 = **decorate**, adorn, beautify,
embellish, festoon, garnish, gild, grace,
prettify
ornate adj = **elaborate**, baroque, busy,
decorated, fancy, florid, fussy,
ornamented, overelaborate, rococo
orthodox adj = **established**, accepted,
approved, conventional, customary,
official, received, traditional, well–
established ≠ **original**

oscillate v = **swing**, move back and forth,
move to and fro, rock, seesaw, sway, veer,
vibrate, wave
ossify v 2 = **harden**, solidify, stiffen
ostensible adj = **apparent**, outward,
pretended, professed, purported, seeming,
so–called, superficial, supposed
ostentation n = **display**, affectation,
exhibitionism, flamboyance, flashiness,
flaunting, parade, pomp, pretentiousness,
show, showing off (inf)
ostracize v = **exclude**, banish, cast out,
cold–shoulder, exile, give (someone) the
cold shoulder, reject, send to Coventry,
shun
other adj 1 = **spare** 2 = **different**,
alternative, contrasting, dissimilar, distinct,

sixteenth of a pound (28.4 grams).

our *adj* belonging to us. **ours** *pron* thing(s) belonging to us. **ourselves** *pron* emphatic and reflexive form of WE *or* US.

oust ① *v* force (someone) out, expel.

out ① *adv, adj* **1** denoting movement or distance away from, a state of being used up or extinguished, public availability, etc., e.g. *oil was pouring out; turn the light out; her new book is out.* ◆ *v* **2** *Informal* name (a public figure) as being homosexual. **out of** at or to a point outside. **out–of–date** *adj* old–fashioned. **outer** *adj* on the outside. **outermost** *adj* furthest out. **outing** *n* leisure trip. **outward** *adj* **1** apparent. ◆ *adv* **2** (also **outwards**) away from somewhere. **outwardly** *adv*

outbreak ① *n* sudden occurrence (of something unpleasant).

outburst ① *n* sudden expression of emotion.

outcast ① *n* person rejected by a

particular group.

outcome ① *n* result.

outcry ① *n, pl* **–cries** vehement or widespread protest.

outdoors *adv* **1** in(to) the open air. ◆ *n* **2** the open air. **outdoor** *adj*

outfit ① *n* **1** matching set of clothes. **2** *Informal* group of people working together. **outfitter** *n* supplier of men's clothes.

outgoing ① *adj* **1** leaving. **2** sociable. **outgoings** *pl n* expenses.

outlandish ① *adj* extremely unconventional.

outlaw ① *n* **1** *Hist* criminal deprived of legal protection, bandit. ◆ *v* **2** make illegal. **3** *Hist* make (someone) an outlaw.

outlay ① *n* expenditure.

outline ① *n* **1** short general explanation. **2** line defining the shape of something. ◆ *v* **3** summarize. **4** show the general shape of.

outlook ① *n* **1** attitude. **2** probable

diverse, separate, unrelated, variant **3 = additional**, added, auxiliary, extra, fresh, further, increased, more, new, spare, supplementary

oust *v* **= expel**, depose, dislodge, displace, dispossess, eject, throw out, topple, turn out, unseat

out *adj* **1 a = away**, abroad, absent, elsewhere, gone, not at home, not here, not there, not present, on vacation, outside **b = extinguished**, at an end, dead, ended, exhausted, expired, finished, used up ≠ **burning**

outbreak *n* **= eruption**, burst, epidemic, explosion, flare–up, outburst, rash, upsurge

outburst *n* **= outpouring**, deluge, eruption, explosion, issue, paroxysm, spasm, storm, stream, surge

outcast *n* **= pariah**, castaway, exile, leper, *persona non grata*, refugee, vagabond, wretch

outcome *n* **= result**, conclusion, consequence, end, issue, payoff (*inf*), upshot

outcry *n* **= protest**, clamour, commotion, complaint, hue and cry, hullaballoo, outburst, uproar

outfit *n* **1 = costume**, clothes, ensemble, garb, get–up (*inf*), kit, suit **2** *Inf* **= group**, company, crew, organization, setup (*inf*), squad, team, unit

outgoing *adj* **1 = leaving**, departing, former, retiring, withdrawing ≠ **arriving 2 = sociable**, approachable, communicative, expansive, extrovert, friendly, gregarious, open, warm ≠ **cold**

outlandish *adj* **= strange**, bizarre, exotic, fantastic, far–out (*sl*), freakish, outré, preposterous, unheard–of, weird

outlaw *n* **1** *Hist* **= bandit**, brigand, desperado, fugitive, highwayman, marauder, outcast, robber ◆ *v* **2 = forbid**, ban, bar, disallow, exclude, prohibit, proscribe ≠ **support 3** *Hist* **= put a price on (someone's) head**

outlay *n* **= expenditure**, cost, expenses, investment, outgoings, spending

outline *n* **1 = summary**, recapitulation, résumé, rundown, synopsis, thumbnail outcome.

outlying ⊕ *adj* distant from the main area.

outmoded ⊕ *adj* no longer fashionable or accepted.

outpatient *n* patient who does not stay in hospital overnight.

outpost *n* outlying settlement.

output ⊕ *n* **1** amount produced. **2** power, voltage, or current delivered by an electrical circuit. **3** *Computers* data produced. ◆ *v* **4** *Computers* produce (data) at the end of a process.

outrage ⊕ *n* **1** great moral indignation. **2** gross violation of morality. ◆ *v* **3** offend morally. **outrageous** *adj* **1** shocking. **2** offensive.

outright ⊕ *adj, adv* **1** absolute(ly). **2** open(ly) and direct(ly).

outset ⊕ *n* beginning.

outside ⊕ *prep, adj, adv* **1** indicating movement to or position on the exterior. ◆ *adj* **2** unlikely, e.g. *an outside chance*. **3** coming from outside. ◆ *n* **4** external area or surface. **outsider** *n* **1** person outside a specific group. **2** contestant thought unlikely to win.

✓ WORD TIP

Outside is not followed by *of* in standard English.

---

outsize ⊕ outsized *adj* larger than normal.

outskirts ⊕ *pl n* outer areas, esp. of a town.

outspan *v S Afr* relax.

outspoken ⊕ *adj* **1** tending to say what one thinks. **2** said openly.

outstanding ⊕ *adj* **1** excellent. **2** still to be dealt with or paid.

---

sketch **2 = shape**, configuration, contour, delineation, figure, form, profile, silhouette ◆ *v* **3 = summarize**, adumbrate **4 = draft**, delineate, plan, rough out, sketch (in), trace

outlook *n* **1 = attitude**, angle, frame of mind, perspective, point of view, slant, standpoint, viewpoint **2 = prospect**, expectations, forecast, future

outlying *adj* **= remote**, distant, far-flung, out-of-the-way, peripheral, provincial

outmoded *adj* **= old-fashioned**, anachronistic, antiquated, archaic, obsolete, out-of-date, outworn, passé, unfashionable

output *n* **1 = production**, achievement, manufacture, productivity, yield

outrage *n* **1 = indignation**, anger, fury, hurt, resentment, shock, wrath **2 = violation**, abuse, affront, desecration, indignity, insult, offence, sacrilege, violence ◆ *v* **3 = offend**, affront, incense, infuriate, madden, scandalize, shock

① **outright** *adj* **1 = absolute**, complete, out-and-out, perfect, thorough, thoroughgoing, total, unconditional, unmitigated, unqualified **2 = direct**, definite, flat, straightforward, unequivocal, unqualified

② **outright** *adv* **1 = absolutely**, completely, straightforwardly, thoroughly, to the full **2 = openly**, overtly

outset *n* **= beginning**, commencement, inauguration, inception, kickoff (*inf*), onset, opening, start

outside *adj* **1 = external**, exterior, extraneous, outer, outward ≠ **inside 2** *As in* **an outside chance = remote**, distant, faint, marginal, slight, slim, small, unlikely ◆ *n* **4 = exterior**, facade, face, front, skin, surface, topside

outsize, outsized *adj* **= extra-large**, giant, gigantic, huge, jumbo (*inf*), mammoth, monster, oversized ≠ **baby**

outskirts *pl n* **= edge**, boundary, environs, periphery, suburbia, suburbs

outspoken *adj* **1 = forthright**, abrupt, blunt, explicit, frank, open, unceremonious **2 = plain-spoken**, unequivocal

outstanding *adj* **1 = excellent**, exceptional, great, important, impressive, special, superior, superlative ≠ **ordinary 2 = unpaid**, due, payable, pending,

outweigh ⊕ v be more important, significant, or influential than.

outwit ⊕ v -witting, -witted get the better of (someone) by cunning.

oval ⊕ adj 1 egg-shaped. ◆ n 2 anything that is oval in shape.

ovary n, pl -ries female egg-producing organ. **ovarian** adj

ovation ⊕ n enthusiastic round of applause.

oven n heated compartment or container for cooking or for drying or firing ceramics.

over prep, adv 1 indicating position on the top of, movement to the other side of, amount greater than, etc., e.g. a room over the garage; climbing over the fence; over fifty pounds. ◆ adj 2 finished. ◆ n 3 Cricket series of six balls bowled from one end. **overly** adv excessively.

over- prefix 1 too much, e.g. overeat. 2 above, e.g. overlord. 3 on top, e.g. overshoe.

overall ⊕ adj, adv 1 in total. ◆ n 2 coat-

shaped protective garment. ◆ pl 3 protective garment consisting of trousers with a jacket or bib and braces attached.

overbearing ⊕ adj unpleasantly forceful.

overboard adv from a boat into the water. **go overboard** go to extremes, esp. in enthusiasm.

overcast ⊕ adj (of the sky) covered by clouds.

overcome ⊕ v 1 gain control over after an effort. 2 (of an emotion) affect strongly.

overdose n 1 excessive dose of a drug. ◆ v 2 take an overdose.

overdraft n 1 overdrawing. 2 amount overdrawn.

overdrive n very high gear in a motor vehicle.

overgrown adj thickly covered with plants and weeds.

overhaul ⊕ v 1 examine and repair. ◆ n 2 examination and repair.

overhead ⊕ adv, adj above one's head. **overheads** pl n general cost of maintaining a business.

remaining, uncollected, unsettled

outweigh v 1 = **override**, cancel (out), compensate for, eclipse, prevail over, take precedence over, tip the scales

outwit v = **outsmart** (inf), cheat, dupe, get the better of, outfox, outmanoeuvre, outthink, put one over on (inf), swindle, take in (inf)

oval adj 1 = **elliptical**, egg-shaped, ovoid

ovation n = **applause**, acclaim, acclamation, big hand, cheers, clapping, plaudits, tribute

① **over** prep 1 a = **on top of**, above, on, upon b = **more than**, above, exceeding, in excess of

② **over** adv 1 a = **above**, aloft, on high, overhead b = **extra**, beyond, in addition, in excess, left over

③ **over** adj 2 = **finished**, bygone, closed, completed, concluded, done (with), ended, gone, past

① **overall** adj 1 = **total**, all-embracing, blanket, complete, comprehensive,

general, global, inclusive, overarching

② **overall** adv 1 = **in general**, on the whole

overbearing adj = **dictatorial**, arrogant, bossy (inf), domineering, haughty, high-handed, imperious, supercilious, superior

overcast adj = **cloudy**, dismal, dreary, dull, grey, leaden, louring or lowering, murky

① **overcome** v 1 = **surmount**, master, overpower, overwhelm, prevail, subdue, subjugate, triumph over 2 = **conquer**, beat, defeat, humble, lick (inf), overpower, quell, subdue, vanquish

② **overcome** adj 2 = **affected**, at a loss for words, bowled over (inf), overwhelmed, speechless, swept off one's feet

overhaul v 1 = **check**, do up (inf), examine, inspect, recondition, repair, restore, service ◆ n 2 = **checkup**, check, examination, going-over (inf), inspection, reconditioning, service

① **overhead** adv = **above**, aloft, in the

overland *adj, adv* by land.

overlap *v* 1 share part of the same space or period of time (as). ♦ *n* 2 area overlapping.

overlook ❶ *v* 1 fail to notice. 2 ignore. 3 look at from above.

overseas *adv, adj* to, of, or from a distant country.

overshadow ❶ *v* 1 reduce the significance of (a person or thing) by comparison. 2 sadden the atmosphere of.

oversight ❶ *n* mistake caused by not noticing something.

overt ❶ *adj* open, not hidden. **overtly** *adv*

overtake ❶ *v* move past (a vehicle or person) travelling in the same direction.

overthrow ❶ *v* 1 defeat and replace. ♦ *n* 2 downfall, destruction.

overtime *n, adv* (paid work done) in addition to one's normal working hours.

overtone ❶ *n* additional meaning.

overture ❶ *n* 1 *Music* orchestral introduction. ♦ *pl* 2 opening moves in a new relationship.

overwhelm ❶ *v* 1 overpower, esp. emotionally. 2 defeat by force. **overwhelming** *adj*

overwrought ❶ *adj* nervous and agitated.

owe ❶ *v* be obliged to pay (a sum of money) to (a person). **owing to** as a result of.

owl *n* night bird of prey. **owlish** *adj*

own ❶ *adj* 1 used to emphasize possession, e.g. *my own idea.* ♦ *v* 2 possess. 3 **owner** *n* **ownership** *n* **own up** *v* confess.

ox *n, pl* **oxen** castrated bull.

oxide *n* compound of oxygen and one other element. **oxidize** *v* combine chemically with oxygen, as in burning or rusting.

oxygen *n Chem* gaseous element essential to life and combustion. **oxygenate** *v* add

---

sky, on high, skyward, up above, upward ≠ **below**

② **overhead** *adj* = **aerial**, overhanging, upper

overlook *v* 1 = **miss**, disregard, forget, neglect, omit, pass ≠ **note** 2 = **ignore**, condone, disregard, excuse, forgive, make allowances for, pardon, turn a blind eye to, wink at 3 = **have a view of**, look over or out on

overshadow *v* 1 = **outshine**, dominate, dwarf, eclipse, leave or put in the shade, surpass, tower above 2 = **spoil**, blight, mar, put a damper on, ruin, temper

oversight *n* = **mistake**, blunder, carelessness, error, fault, lapse, neglect, omission, slip

overt *adj* = **open**, blatant, clear, evident, flagrant, manifest, observable, obvious, plain, public, unconcealed, undisguised

overtake *v* 1 = **pass**, catch up with, cut up (*inf*), get past, go by, go past, leave behind, leave standing (*inf*), outdistance, outdo, outstrip, overhaul

overthrow *v* 1 = **defeat**, bring down, conquer, depose, dethrone, oust,

overcome, overpower, topple, unseat, vanquish ≠ **support** ♦ *n* 2 = **downfall**, defeat, destruction, dethronement, fall, ousting, undoing, unseating ≠ **defence**

overtone *n* = **hint**, connotation, implication, innuendo, intimation, nuance, sense, suggestion, undercurrent

overture *n* 1 *Music* = **introduction**, opening, prelude ≠ **finale** ♦ *pl* 2 = **approach**, advance, appeal, conciliatory move, invitation, offer, proposal, proposition ≠ **withdrawal**

overwhelm *v* 1 = **overcome**, bowl over (*inf*), devastate, knock (someone) for six (*inf*), stagger, sweep (someone) off his or her feet, take (someone's) breath away 2 = **destroy**, crush, cut to pieces, massacre, overpower, overrun, rout

overwrought *adj* = **agitated**, distracted, excited, frantic, keyed up, on edge, overexcited, tense, uptight, wired (*sl*) ≠ **controlled**

owe *v* 1 = **be in debt**, be in arrears, be beholden (to), be overdrawn, be under an obligation (to), 2 = **be obligated** or **indebted**

oxygen to.
oyster *n* edible shellfish.
oz. ounce.
Oz *n Slang* Australia.

ozone *n* strong-smelling form of oxygen.
ozone layer layer of ozone in the upper atmosphere that filters out ultraviolet radiation.

————————[THESAURUS]————————

own *adj* **1** = **personal**, individual, particular, private ♦ *v* **2** = **possess**, be in possession of, enjoy, have, hold, keep, retain **own up** = **confess**, admit, come clean, tell the truth

P p

p penny *or* pence.

pace ❶ *n* **1** single step in walking. **2** length of a step. **3** rate of progress. ♦ *v* **4** walk up and down, esp. in anxiety. **5** (foll. by *out*) cross or measure with steps. **pacemaker** *n* **1** electronic device surgically implanted in a person with heart disease to regulate the heartbeat. **2** person who, by taking the lead early in a race, sets the pace for the rest of the competitors.

pacify ❶ *v* **-fying, -fied** soothe, calm. **pacification** *n*

pack ❶ *v* **1** put (clothes etc.) together in a suitcase or bag. **2** put (goods) into containers or parcels. **3** fill with people or things. ♦ *n* **4** bag carried on a person's or animal's back. **5** *Chiefly US* same as PACKET. **6** set of playing cards. **7** group of dogs or wolves that hunt together. **pack in** *Informal* stop doing. **pack off** *v* send away.

pact ❶ *n* formal agreement.

pad ❶ *n* **1** piece of soft material used for protection, support, absorption of liquid, etc. **2** number of sheets of paper fastened at the edge. **3** fleshy underpart of an animal's paw. **4** place for launching rockets. **5** *Slang* home. ♦ *v* **padding, padded 6** protect or fill with soft material. **7** walk with soft steps. **padding** *n* **1** soft material used to pad something. **2** unnecessary words put into a speech or written work to make it longer.

paddle¹ ❶ *n* **1** short oar with a broad blade at one or each end. ♦ *v* **2** move (a canoe etc.) with a paddle. **paddle steamer** ship propelled by paddle wheels.

paddle² ❶ *v* walk barefoot in shallow water.

paddock *n* small field or enclosure for horses.

paddy field *n* field where rice is grown (also **paddy**).

pademelon, paddymelon [pad–ee– mel–an] *n* small Australian wallaby.

padlock *n* detachable lock with a hinged hoop fastened over a ring on the object to be secured.

paediatrics *n* branch of medicine concerned with diseases of children. **paediatrician** *n*

THESAURUS

pace¹ *n* **1 = step**, gait, stride, tread, walk **3 = speed**, rate, tempo, velocity ♦ *v* **4 = stride**, march, patrol, pound **5** (foll. by *out*) **= measure**, count, mark out, step

pacify *v* **= calm**, allay, appease, assuage, mollify, placate, propitiate, soothe

pack *v* **1 = package**, bundle, load, store, stow **2, 3 = cram**, compress, crowd, fill, jam, press, ram, stuff ♦ *n* **4 = bundle**, back pack, burden, kitbag, knapsack, load, parcel, rucksack **5** *Chiefly US* **= packet**, package **pack in** ♦ *v Inf* **= stop**, cease, chuck (*inf*), give up *or* over, kick (*inf*) **pack off** ♦ *v* **= send away**, dismiss, send packing (*inf*)

pact *n* **= agreement**, alliance, bargain, covenant, deal, treaty, understanding

pad *n* **1 = cushion**, buffer, protection, stuffing, wad **2 = writing pad**, block, jotter **3 = paw**, foot, sole **5** *Sl* **= home**, apartment, flat, place ♦ *v* **6 = pack**, cushion, fill, protect, stuff **7 = sneak**, creep, go barefoot, steal

paddle¹ *n* **1 = oar**, scull ♦ *v* **2 = row**, propel, pull, scull

paddle² *v* **= wade**, slop, splash (about)

paedophile *n* person who is sexually attracted to children.

paella [pie–**ell**–a] *n* Spanish dish of rice, chicken, shellfish, and vegetables.

pagan ❶ *n, adj* (person) not belonging to one of the world's main religions.

page¹ ❶ *n* 1 (one side of) a sheet of paper forming a book etc. 2 screenful of information from a website or teletext service.

page² ❶ *n* 1 (also **pageboy**) small boy who attends a bride at her wedding. 2 *Hist* boy in training for knighthood. ◆ *v* 3 summon (someone) by bleeper or loudspeaker, in order to pass on a message.

pageant ❶ *n* parade or display of people in costume, usu. illustrating a scene from history. **pageantry** *n*

pagoda *n* pyramid–shaped Asian temple or tower.

pail *n* (contents of) a bucket.

pain ❶ *n* 1 physical or mental suffering. ◆ *pl* 2 trouble, effort. **on pain of** subject to the penalty of. **painful** *adj* **painfully** *adv* **painless** *adj* **painlessly** *adv* **painkiller** *n* drug that relieves pain.

paint ❶ *n* 1 coloured substance, spread on a surface with a brush or roller. ◆ *v* 2

colour or coat with paint. 3 use paint to make a picture of. **painter** *n* **painting** *n*

pair ❶ *n* 1 set of two things matched for use together. ◆ *v* 2 group or be grouped in twos.

✓ **WORD TIP**

Pair is followed by a singular verb if it refers to a unit: *A pair of shoes was on the floor*, and by a plural verb if it refers to two individuals: *That pair are good friends*.

---

pal ❶ *n Informal* friend.

palace *n* 1 residence of a king, bishop, etc. 2 large grand building.

palate ❶ *n* 1 roof of the mouth. 2 sense of taste.

palaver ❶ [pal–**lah**–ver] *n* time–wasting fuss.

pale¹ ❶ *adj* 1 light, whitish. 2 whitish in the face, esp. through illness or shock. ◆ *v* 3 become pale. **pale in, by comparison with** appear inferior when compared with.

pale² ❶ *n* wooden or metal post used in fences. **beyond the pale** outside the limits of social convention.

palette *n* artist's flat board for mixing

THESAURUS

① **pagan** *n* = **heathen**, idolater, infidel, polytheist

② **pagan** *adj* = **heathen**, idolatrous, infidel, polytheistic

page¹ *n* 1 = **folio**, leaf, sheet, side

page² *n* (also **pageboy**) 1 = **attendant**, pageboy 2 *Hist* = **squire** ◆ *v* 3 = **call**, send for, summon

pageant *n* = **show**, display, parade, procession, spectacle, tableau

pain *n* 1 a = **hurt**, ache, discomfort, irritation, pang, soreness, tenderness, throb, twinge b = **suffering**, agony, anguish, distress, heartache, misery, torment, torture ◆ *pl* 2 = **trouble**, bother, care, diligence, effort ◆ *v* 3 a = **hurt**, smart, sting, throb b = **distress**, agonize, cut to the quick, grieve, hurt, sadden, torment, torture

paint *n* 1 = **colouring**, colour, dye, pigment, stain, tint ◆ *v* 2 = **coat**, apply, colour, cover, daub 3 = **depict**, draw, picture, portray, represent, sketch

pair *n* 2 = **couple**, brace, duo, twins ◆ *v* 3 = **couple**, bracket, join, match (up), team, twin

pal *n Inf* = **friend**, buddy (*inf*), chum (*inf*), cobber (*Aust or old–fashioned NZ inf*), companion, comrade, crony, mate (*inf*)

palate *n* 2 = **taste**, appetite, stomach

palaver *n* = **fuss**, business (*inf*), carry–on (*inf, chiefly Brit*), pantomime (*inf, chiefly Brit*), performance (*inf*), rigmarole, song and dance (*Brit inf*), to–do

pale¹ *adj* 1 = **white**, ashen, bleached, colourless, faded, light 2 = **ashen**, pallid, pasty, wan, white ≠ **glowing** ◆ *v* 3 = **become pale**, blanch, go white, lose colours on.

palindrome n word or phrase that reads the same backwards as forwards.

paling n wooden or metal post used in fences.

pall¹ ❶ n 1 cloth spread over a coffin. 2 dark cloud (of smoke). 3 depressing oppressive atmosphere. **pallbearer** n person who helps to carry the coffin at a funeral.

pall² ❶ v become boring.

pallet n portable platform for storing and moving goods.

palliate v lessen the severity of (something) without curing it. **palliative** adj 1 giving temporary or partial relief. ◆ n 2 something, for example a drug, that palliates.

pallid ❶ adj pale, esp. because ill or weak. **pallor** n

palm¹ n inner surface of the hand. **palm off** v get rid of (an unwanted thing or person), esp. by deceit.

palm² n tropical tree with long pointed leaves growing out of the top of a straight trunk. **Palm Sunday** Sunday before Easter.

palomino n, pl **-nos** gold-coloured horse with a white mane and tail.

palpable ❶ adj 1 obvious, e.g. a palpable

hit. 2 so intense as to seem capable of being touched, e.g. the tension is almost palpable. **palpably** adv

palpitate ❶ v 1 (of the heart) beat rapidly. 2 flutter or tremble. **palpitation** n

palsy [**pawl**–zee] n paralysis. **palsied** adj affected with palsy.

paltry ❶ adj **-trier, -triest** insignificant.

pamper ❶ v treat (someone) with great indulgence, spoil.

pamphlet ❶ n thin paper–covered booklet. **pamphleteer** n writer of pamphlets.

pan¹ ❶ n 1 wide long–handled metal container used in cooking. 2 bowl of a toilet. ◆ v **panning, panned** 3 sift gravel from (a river) in a pan to search for gold. 4 Informal criticize harshly. **pan out** v result.

pan² ❶ v **panning, panned** (of a film camera) be moved slowly so as to cover a whole scene or follow a moving object.

pan– combining form all, e.g. pan–American.

panacea ❶ [pan–a–**see**–a] n remedy for all diseases or problems.

panache ❶ [pan–**ash**] n confident elegant style.

pancake n thin flat circle of fried batter.

pancreas [**pang**–kree–ass] n large gland

━━━━━━━━━━━━ THESAURUS ━━━━━━━━━━━━

colour, whiten

pale² n = **post**, paling, palisade, picket, slat, stake, upright **beyond the pale** = **unacceptable**, barbaric, forbidden, improper, inadmissible, indecent, irregular, not done, out of line, unseemly, unspeakable, unsuitable

pall¹ n 2 = **cloud**, mantle, shadow, shroud, veil 3 = **gloom**, check, damp, damper

pall² v = **become boring**, become dull, become tedious, cloy, jade, sicken, tire, weary

pallid adj = **pale**, anaemic, ashen, colourless, pasty, wan

palpable adj 1 = **obvious**, clear, conspicuous, evident, manifest, plain, unmistakable, visible

palpitate v = **beat**, flutter, pound, pulsate,

throb, tremble

paltry adj = **insignificant**, contemptible, despicable, inconsiderable, meagre, mean, measly, minor, miserable, petty, poor, puny, slight, small, trifling, trivial, unimportant, worthless ≠ **major**

pamper v = **spoil**, coddle, cosset, indulge, mollycoddle, pet

pamphlet n = **booklet**, brochure, circular, leaflet, tract

pan¹ n 1 = **pot**, container, saucepan ◆ v 3 = **sift out**, look for, search for 4 Inf = **criticize**, censure, knock (inf), slam (sl), tear into (inf)

pan² v = **move**, follow, sweep, track

panacea n = **cure–all**, nostrum, universal cure

panache n = **style**, dash, élan,

behind the stomach that produces insulin and helps digestion. **pancreatic** adj

panda n large black–and–white bearlike mammal from China.

pandemonium ⊕ n wild confusion, uproar.

pander n person who procures a sexual partner for someone. **pander to** v indulge (a person or his or her desires).

pane n sheet of glass in a window or door.

panegyric [pan–ee–**jire**–ik] n formal speech or piece of writing in praise of someone or something.

panel n 1 flat distinct section of a larger surface, for example in a door. 2 group of people as a team in a quiz etc. 3 list of jurors, doctors, etc. 4 board or surface containing switches and controls to operate equipment. ♦ v –**elling**, –**elled** 5 cover or decorate with panels. **panelling** n panels collectively, esp. on a wall. **panellist** n member of a panel.

pang ⊕ n sudden sharp feeling of pain or sadness.

panic ⊕ n 1 sudden overwhelming fear, often affecting a whole group of people. ♦ v –**icking**, –**icked** 2 feel or cause to feel panic. **panicky** adj **panic–stricken** adj

pannier n 1 bag fixed on the back of a cycle. 2 basket carried by a beast of burden.

panoply ⊕ n magnificent array.

panorama ⊕ n wide unbroken view of a scene. **panoramic** adj

pansy n, pl –**sies** 1 small garden flower with velvety purple, yellow, or white petals. 2 Offens effeminate or homosexual man.

pant ⊕ v breathe quickly and noisily after exertion.

pantechnicon n large van for furniture removals.

panther n leopard, esp. a black one.

pantomime n play based on a fairy tale, performed at Christmas time.

pantry n, pl –**tries** small room or cupboard for storing food.

pants ⊕ pl n 1 undergarment for the lower part of the body. 2 US, Canadian, Aust & NZ trousers.

pap n 1 soft food for babies or invalids. 2 worthless entertainment or information.

papacy [**pay**–pa–see] n, pl –**cies** position or term of office of a pope. **papal** adj of the pope.

paper ⊕ n 1 material made in sheets from wood pulp or other fibres. 2 printed sheet of this. 3 newspaper. 4 set of examination questions. 5 article or essay. ♦ v 7 cover (walls) with wallpaper. **paperback** n book with covers made of flexible card. **paperweight** n heavy decorative object placed on top of loose papers. **paperwork** n clerical work, such as writing reports and letters.

papier–mâché [**pap**–yay **mash**–ay] n material made from paper mixed with paste and moulded when moist.

paprika n mild powdered seasoning made from red peppers.

═══════ THESAURUS ═══════

flamboyance

pandemonium n = **uproar**, bedlam, chaos, confusion, din, hullabaloo, racket, rumpus, turmoil

pang n = **twinge**, ache, pain, prick, spasm, stab, sting

panic n 1 = **fear**, alarm, fright, hysteria, scare, terror ♦ v 2 = **go to pieces**, alarm, become hysterical, lose one's nerve, scare, unnerve

panoply n = **array**, attire, dress, garb, regalia, trappings

panorama n = **view**, prospect, vista

pant v = **puff**, blow, breathe, gasp, heave, wheeze

pants pl n 1 = **underpants**, boxer shorts, briefs, brookies (S Afr inf), drawers, knickers, panties 2 US, Canad, Aust & NZ = **trousers**, slacks

paper n 3 = **newspaper**, daily, gazette, journal 5 = **essay**, article, dissertation, report, treatise ♦ pl 6 = **documents**, archive, certificates, deeds, diaries, dossier, file, letters, records ♦ v 7 = **wallpaper**,

papyrus [pap–*ire*–uss] *n, pl* –**ri**, –**ruses 1** tall water plant. **2** (manuscript written on) a kind of paper made from this plant.

par ❶ *n* **1** usual or average condition, e.g. *feeling under par.* **2** *Golf* expected standard score. **3** face value of stocks and shares. **on a par with** equal to.

parable ❶ *n* story that illustrates a religious teaching.

parachute *n* **1** large fabric canopy that slows the descent of a person or object from an aircraft. ◆ *v* **2** land or drop by parachute. **parachutist** *n*

parade ❶ *n* **1** procession or march. **2** street or promenade. ◆ *v* **3** display or flaunt. **4** march in procession.

paradise ❶ *n* **1** heaven. **2** place or situation that is near-perfect.

paradox ❶ *n* statement that seems self–contradictory but may be true. **paradoxical** *adj* **paradoxically** *adv*

paraffin *n* liquid mixture distilled from petroleum and used as a fuel or solvent.

paragon ❶ *n* model of perfection.

paragraph ❶ *n* section of a piece of writing starting on a new line.

parakeet *n* small long-tailed parrot.

parallel ❶ *adj* **1** separated by an equal distance at every point. **2** exactly corresponding. ◆ *n* **3** line separated from another by an equal distance at every point. **4** thing with similar features to another. **5** line of latitude. ◆ *v* **6** correspond to.

paralysis ❶ *n* inability to move or feel, because of damage to the nervous system. **paralyse** *v* **1** affect with paralysis. **2** make temporarily unable to move or take action. **paralytic** *n, adj* (person) affected with paralysis.

paramedic *n* person working in support of the medical profession.

parameter ❶ [par–*am*–it–er] *n* limiting factor, boundary.

paramilitary *adj* organized on military lines.

paramount ❶ *adj* of the greatest importance.

paranoia *n* **1** mental illness causing delusions of grandeur or persecution. **2** *Informal* intense fear or suspicion. **paranoid, paranoiac** *adj, n*

parapet *n* low wall or railing along the edge of a balcony or roof.

paraphernalia ❶ *n* personal belongings or bits of equipment.

paraphrase ❶ *v* put (a statement or text) into other words.

hang

par *n* **1** = **average**, level, mean, norm, standard, usual

parable *n* = **lesson**, allegory, fable, moral tale, story

parade *n* **1** = **procession**, array, cavalcade, march, pageant ◆ *v* **3** = **flaunt**, display, exhibit, show off (*inf*) **4** = **march**, process

paradise *n* **1** = **heaven**, Elysian fields, Happy Valley (*Islam*), Promised Land **2** = **bliss**, delight, felicity, heaven, utopia

paradox *n* **2** = **contradiction**, anomaly, enigma, oddity, puzzle

paragon *n* = **model**, epitome, exemplar, ideal, nonpareil, pattern, quintessence

paragraph *n* = **section**, clause, item, part, passage, subdivision

parallel *adj* **1** = **equidistant**, alongside, side by side ≠ **divergent 2** = **matching**, analogous, corresponding, like, resembling, similar ◆ *n* **4** = **similarity**, analogy, comparison, likeness, resemblance ≠ **difference**

paralysis *n* = **immobility**, palsy

parameter *n* = **limit**, framework, limitation, restriction, specification

paramount *adj* = **principal**, cardinal, chief, first, foremost, main, primary, prime, supreme

paraphernalia *n* = **equipment**, apparatus, baggage, belongings, effects, gear, stuff, tackle, things, trappings

paraphrase *v* **1** = **reword**, express in other words *or* one's own words, interpret, put another way, put into other words, rehash, render, rephrase, restate

paraplegia [par–a–**pleej**–ya] *n* paralysis of the lower half of the body. **paraplegic** *adj, n*

parasite 🟥 *n* **1** animal or plant living in or on another. **2** person who lives at the expense of others. **parasitic** *adj*

parasol *v* umbrella–like sunshade.

paratroops *pl n* troops trained to be dropped by parachute into a battle area. **paratrooper** *n* member of the paratroops.

parboil *v* boil until partly cooked.

parcel 🟥 *n* **1** something wrapped up, package. ◆ *v* **–celling, –celled 2** (often foll. by *up*) wrap up.

parch 🟥 *v* **1** make very hot and dry. **2** make thirsty.

parchment *n* thick smooth writing material made from animal skin.

pardon 🟥 *v* **1** forgive, excuse. ◆ *n* **2** forgiveness. **3** official release from punishment for a crime. **pardonable** *adj*

pare 🟥 *v* **1** cut off the skin or top layer of. **2** (often foll. by *down*) reduce in size or amount. **paring** *n* piece pared off.

parent 🟥 *n* father or mother. **parental** *adj* **parenthood** *n* **parentage** *n* ancestry or family. **parenting** *n* activity of bringing up children.

parenthesis [par–**en**–thiss–iss] *n, pl* **–ses 1** word or sentence inserted into a passage,

marked off by brackets or dashes. ◆ *pl* **2** round brackets, ( ). **parenthetical** *adj*

pariah 🟥 [par–**rye**–a] *n* social outcast.

parish 🟥 *n* area that has its own church and clergyman. **parishioner** *n* inhabitant of a parish.

parity 🟥 *n* equality or equivalence.

park 🟥 *n* **1** area of open land for recreational use by the public. **2** area containing a number of related enterprises, e.g. *a business park*. **3** area of private land around a large country house. ◆ *v* **4** stop and leave (a vehicle) temporarily.

parka *n* long jacket with a quilted lining and a fur–trimmed hood.

parlance 🟥 *n* particular way of speaking, idiom.

parley *n* **1** meeting between leaders or representatives of opposing forces to discuss terms. ◆ *v* **2** have a parley.

parliament 🟥 *n* law–making assembly of a country. **parliamentary** *adj*

parlour 🟥 *n Old–fashioned* living room for receiving visitors.

parochial 🟥 *adj* **1** narrow in outlook. **2** of a parish. **parochialism** *n*

parody 🟥 *n, pl* **–dies 1** exaggerated and amusing imitation of someone else's style. ◆ *v* **–dying, –died 2** make a parody of.

——— THESAURUS ———

parasite *n* **2** = **sponger** (*inf*), bloodsucker (*inf*), hanger–on, leech, scrounger (*inf*)

parcel *n* **1** = **package**, bundle, pack ◆ *v* **2** (often foll. by *up*) = **wrap**, do up, pack, package, tie up

parch *v* **1** = **dry up**, dehydrate, desiccate, evaporate, shrivel, wither

pardon *v* **1** = **forgive**, absolve, acquit, excuse, exonerate, let off (*inf*), overlook ≠ **condemn** ◆ *n* **2** = **forgiveness**, absolution, exoneration ≠ **penalty** **3** = **acquittal**, amnesty

pare *v* **1** = **peel**, clip, cut, shave, skin, trim **2** (often foll. by *down*) = **cut back**, crop, cut, decrease, dock, reduce

parent *n* = **father** *or* **mother**, procreator, progenitor, sire

pariah *n* = **outcast**, exile, undesirable, untouchable

parish *n* = **community**, church, congregation, flock

parity *n* = **equality**, consistency, equivalence, uniformity, unity

park *n* **3** = **parkland**, estate, garden, grounds, woodland

parlance *n* = **language**, idiom, jargon, phraseology, speech, talk, tongue

parliament *n* = **assembly**, congress, convention, council, legislature, senate

parlour *n Old–fashioned* = **sitting room**, drawing room, front room, living room, lounge

parochial *adj* **1** = **provincial**, insular, limited, narrow, narrow–minded, petty,

parole n 1 early freeing of a prisoner on condition that he or she behaves well. ♦ v 2 put on parole. **on parole** (of a prisoner) released on condition that he or she behaves well.

paroxysm ❶ n 1 uncontrollable outburst of rage, delight, etc. 2 spasm or convulsion of coughing, pain, etc.

parquet [par-kay] n floor covering made of wooden blocks arranged in a geometric pattern. **parquetry** n

parrot ❶ n 1 tropical bird with a short hooked beak and an ability to imitate human speech. ♦ v –roting, –roted 2 repeat (someone else's words) without thinking.

parry ❶ v –rying, –ried 1 ward off (an attack). 2 cleverly avoid (an awkward question).

parsimony n extreme caution in spending money. **parsimonious** adj

parsley n herb used for seasoning and decorating food.

parsnip n long tapering cream–coloured root vegetable.

parson ❶ n parish priest in the Church of England. **parsonage** n parson's house.

part ❶ n 1 one of the pieces that make up a whole. 2 one of several equal divisions. 3 actor's role. 4 (often pl) region, area. 5 component of a vehicle or machine. ♦ v 6 divide or separate. 7 (of people) leave each other. **take someone's part** support someone in an argument etc. **take (something) in good part** respond to (teasing or criticism) with good humour. **parting** n 1 occasion when one person leaves another. 2 line of scalp between sections of hair combed in opposite directions. 3 dividing or separating. **partly** adv not completely. **part of speech** particular grammatical class of words, such as noun or verb. **part–time** adj occupying or working less than the full working week. **part with** v give away, hand over.

partake ❶ v –taking, –took, –taken 1 (foll. by of) take (food or drink). 2 (foll. by in) take part in.

partial ❶ adj 1 not complete. 2 prejudiced. **partial to** having a liking for. **partiality** n **partially** adv

participate ❶ v become actively involved. **participant** n **participation** n

participle n form of a verb used in compound tenses or as an adjective, e.g. worried; worrying.

particle ❶ n 1 extremely small piece or amount. 2 Physics minute piece of matter, such as a proton or electron.

————————— THESAURUS —————————

small–minded

parody n 1 = **takeoff** (inf), burlesque, caricature, satire, send–up (Brit inf), skit, spoof (inf) ♦ v 2 = **take off** (inf), burlesque, caricature, do a takeoff of (inf), satirize, send up (Brit inf)

paroxysm n 2 = **outburst**, attack, convulsion, fit, seizure, spasm

parrot v 2 = **repeat**, copy, echo, imitate, mimic

parry v 1 = **ward off**, block, deflect, rebuff, repel, repulse 2 = **evade**, avoid, dodge, sidestep

parson n = **clergyman**, churchman, cleric, minister, pastor, preacher, priest, vicar

part n 1 = **piece**, bit, fraction, fragment, portion, scrap, section, share ≠ **mass**

2 = **division**, branch, component, constituent, member, unit 3 = **role**, character, lines 4 (often pl) = **region**, area, district, neighbourhood, quarter, vicinity ♦ v 6 = **divide**, break, come apart, detach, rend, separate, sever, split, tear ≠ **unite** 7 = **leave**, depart, go, go away, separate, split up, withdraw ≠ **gather**

partake v 1 (foll. by of) = **consume**, eat, take 2 (foll. by in) = **participate in**, engage in, share in, take part in

partial adj 1 = **incomplete**, imperfect, uncompleted, unfinished ≠ **complete** 2 = **biased**, discriminatory, one–sided, partisan, prejudiced, unfair, unjust ≠ **objective**

participate v = **take part**, be involved in,

particular ⦿ *adj* 1 relating to one person or thing, not general. 2 exceptional or special. 3 very exact. 4 difficult to please, fastidious. ◆ *n* 5 item of information, detail. **particularly** *adv*

partisan ⦿ *n* 1 strong supporter of a party or group. 2 guerrilla, member of a resistance movement. ◆ *adj* 3 prejudiced or one-sided.

partition ⦿ *n* 1 screen or thin wall that divides a room. 2 division of a country into independent parts. ◆ *v* 3 divide with a partition.

partner ⦿ *n* 1 either member of a couple in a relationship or activity. 2 member of a business partnership. ◆ *v* 3 be the partner of. **partnership** *n* joint business venture between two or more people.

partridge *n* game bird of the grouse family.

party ⦿ *n, pl* **–ties** 1 social gathering for pleasure. 2 group of people travelling or working together. 3 group of people with a common political aim. 4 person or people forming one side in a lawsuit or dispute. **party line** 1 official view of a political party. 2 telephone line shared by two or more subscribers.

pass ⦿ *v* 1 go by, past, or through. 2 be successful in (a test or examination). 3 spend (time) or (of time) go by. 4 give, hand. 5 be inherited by. 6 *Sport* hit, kick, or throw (the ball) to another player. 7 (of a law–making body) agree to (a law). 8 exceed. 9 choose not to answer a question or not to take one's turn in a game. 10 come to an end. ◆ *n* 11 successful result in a test or examination. 12 *Sport* transfer of a ball. 13 narrow gap through mountains. 14 permit or licence. **make a pass at** *Informal* make sexual advances to. **passable** *adj* 1 (just) acceptable. 2 (of a road) capable of being travelled along. **passing** *adj* 1 brief or transitory. 2 cursory or casual. **pass away** *v* die. **pass out** *v* *Informal* faint. **pass up** *v* *Informal* fail to take advantage of (something).

passage ⦿ *n* 1 channel or opening providing a way through. 2 hall or corridor. 3 section of a book etc. 4 journey by sea. 5 right or freedom to pass. **passageway** *n* passage or corridor.

join in, partake, perform, share

particle *n* 1 = **bit**, grain, iota, jot, mite, piece, scrap, shred, speck

particular *adj* 1 = **specific**, distinct, exact, peculiar, precise, special ≠ **general** 2 = **special**, especial, exceptional, marked, notable, noteworthy, remarkable, singular, uncommon, unusual 4 = **fussy**, choosy (*inf*), demanding, fastidious, finicky, pernickety (*inf*), picky (*inf*) ≠ **easy** ◆ *n* 5 = **detail**, circumstance, fact, feature, item, specification

partisan *n* 1 = **supporter**, adherent, devotee, upholder ≠ **leader** 2 = **underground fighter**, guerrilla, resistance fighter ◆ *adj* 3 = **prejudiced**, biased, interested, one–sided, partial, sectarian ≠ **impartial**

partition *n* 1 = **screen**, barrier, wall 2 = **division**, segregation, separation ◆ *v* 3 = **separate**, divide, screen

partner *n* 1 = **spouse**, consort, husband *or* wife, mate, significant other (*US inf*) 2 = **associate**, colleague

party *n* 1 = **get–together** (*inf*), celebration, do (*inf*), festivity, function, gathering, reception, social gathering 2 = **group**, band, company, crew, gang, squad, team, unit 3 = **faction**, camp, clique, coterie, league, set, side

pass *v* 1 = **go by** *or* **past**, elapse, go, lapse, move, proceed, run ≠ **stop** 2 = **qualify**, do, get through, graduate, succeed ≠ **fail** 3 = **spend**, fill, occupy, while away 4 = **give**, convey, deliver, hand, send, transfer 7 = **approve**, accept, decree, enact, legislate, ordain, ratify ≠ **refuse** 8 = **exceed**, beat, go beyond, outdo, outstrip, overtake, surpass 10 = **end**, blow over, cease, go ◆ *n* 13 = **gap**, canyon, gorge, ravine, route 14 = **licence**, authorization, passport, permit, ticket,

passé ① [pas–say] *adj* out–of–date.

passenger ① *n* 1 person travelling in a vehicle driven by someone else. 2 member of a team who does not pull his or her weight.

passion ① *n* 1 intense sexual love. 2 any strong emotion. 3 great enthusiasm. 4 (P–) *Christianity* the suffering of Christ. **passionate** *adj*

passive ① *adj* 1 not playing an active part. 2 submissive and receptive to outside forces. 3 *Grammar* (of a verb) in a form indicating that the subject receives the action, e.g. *was jeered* in *he was jeered by the crowd.* **passivity** *n* **passive smoking** inhalation of smoke from others' cigarettes by a nonsmoker.

passport *n* official document granting permission to travel abroad.

password ① *n* secret word or phrase that ensures admission.

past ① *adj* 1 of the time before the present. 2 ended, gone by. 3 *Grammar* (of a verb tense) indicating that the action specified took place earlier. ◆ *n* 4 period of time before the present. 5 person's earlier life, esp. a disreputable period. 6 *Grammar* past tense. ◆ *adv* 7 by, along. ◆ *prep* 8

beyond. **past it** *Informal* unable to do the things one could do when younger. **past master** person with great talent or experience in a particular subject.

pasta *n* type of food, such as spaghetti, that is made in different shapes from flour and water.

paste ① *n* 1 moist soft mixture, such as toothpaste. 2 adhesive, esp. for paper. 3 pastry dough. 4 shiny glass used to make imitation jewellery. ◆ *v* 5 fasten with paste. **pasting** *n* *Informal* 1 heavy defeat. 2 strong criticism.

pastel ① *n* 1 coloured chalk crayon for drawing. 2 picture drawn in pastels. 3 pale delicate colour. ◆ *adj* 4 pale and delicate in colour.

pasteurize *v* sterilize by heating. **pasteurization** *n*

pastiche ① [pass–teesh] *n* work of art that mixes styles or copies the style of another artist.

pastille *n* small fruit–flavoured and sometimes medicated sweet.

pastime ① *n* activity that makes time pass pleasantly.

pastor ① *n* clergyman in charge of a congregation. **pastoral** *adj* 1 of or

————————— THESAURUS —————————

warrant

passage *n* 1 = **way**, alley, avenue, channel, course, path, road, route 2 = **corridor**, hall, lobby, vestibule 3 = **extract**, excerpt, piece, quotation, reading, section, text 4 = **journey**, crossing, trek, trip, voyage 5 = **safe–conduct**, freedom, permission, right

passé *adj* = **out–of–date**, dated, obsolete, old–fashioned, old hat, outdated, outmoded, unfashionable

passenger *n* 1 = **traveller**, fare, rider

passion *n* 1 = **love**, ardour, desire, infatuation, lust 2 = **emotion**, ardour, excitement, feeling, fervour, fire, heat, intensity, warmth, zeal ≠ **indifference** 3 = **mania**, bug (*inf*), craving, craze, enthusiasm, fascination, obsession

passive *adj* 1, 2 = **submissive**, compliant,

docile, inactive, quiescent, receptive ≠ **spirited**

password *n* = **signal**, key word, watchword

past *adj* 1 = **former**, ancient, bygone, early, olden, previous ≠ **coming** 2 = **over**, done, ended, finished, gone ◆ *n* 4 = **former times**, days gone by, long ago, olden days ≠ **now** 5 = **background**, history, life, past life ◆ *prep* 8 = **beyond**, across, by, over

paste *n* 2 = **adhesive**, cement, glue, gum ◆ *v* 6 = **stick**, cement, glue, gum

pastel *adj* 4 = **pale**, delicate, light, muted, soft

pastiche *n* = **medley**, blend, hotchpotch, *melange*, miscellany, mixture

pastime *n* = **activity**, amusement, diversion, entertainment, game, hobby, recreation depicting country life. 2 of a clergyman or his duties.

pastry n, pl **–ries 1** baking dough made of flour, fat, and water. **2** cake or pie.

pasture ❶ n grassy land for farm animals to graze on.

pasty¹ ❶ [pay–stee] adj **pastier, pastiest** (of a complexion) pale and unhealthy.

pasty² [pass–tee] n, pl **pasties** round of pastry folded over a savoury filling.

pat¹ ❶ v **patting, patted 1** tap lightly. ◆ n **2** gentle tap or stroke. **3** small shaped mass of butter etc.

pat² ❶ adj quick, ready, or glib. **off pat** learned thoroughly.

patch ❶ n **1** piece of material sewn on a garment. **2** small contrasting section. **3** plot of ground. **4** protective pad for the eye. ◆ v **5** mend with a patch. **patchy** adj of uneven quality or intensity. **patch up** v **1** repair clumsily. **2** make up (a quarrel). **patchwork** n needlework made of pieces of different materials sewn together.

pate n Old–fashioned head.

pâté [pat–ay] n spread of finely minced liver etc.

patent ❶ n **1** document giving the exclusive right to make or sell an invention. ◆ adj **2** open to public inspection, e.g. letters patent. **3** obvious. **4** protected by a patent. ◆ v **5** obtain a patent for. **patently** adv obviously. **patent leather** leather processed to give a hard glossy surface.

paternal ❶ adj **1** fatherly. **2** related through one's father. **paternity** n fact or state of being a father. **paternalism** n authority exercised in a way that limits individual responsibility. **paternalistic** adj

path ❶ n **1** surfaced walk or track. **2** course of action.

pathetic ❶ adj **1** causing feelings of pity or sadness. **2** distressingly inadequate. **pathetically** adv

pathology n scientific study of diseases. **pathological** adj **1** of pathology. **2** Informal compulsively motivated. **pathologist** n

pathos ❶ n power of arousing pity or sadness.

patient ❶ adj **1** enduring difficulties or delays calmly. ◆ n **2** person receiving medical treatment. **patience** n **1** quality of being patient. **2** card game for one.

patio n, pl **–tios** paved area adjoining a house.

patriarch n **1** male head of a family or tribe. **2** highest–ranking bishop in Orthodox Churches. **patriarchal** adj

———————| THESAURUS |———————

pastor n = **clergyman**, churchman, ecclesiastic, minister, parson, priest, rector, vicar

pasture n = **grassland**, grass, grazing, meadow

pasty¹ adj = **pale**, anaemic, pallid, sickly, wan

pat¹ v **1** = **stroke**, caress, fondle, pet, tap, touch ◆ n **2** = **stroke**, clap, tap

pat² adj = **glib**, automatic, easy, facile, ready, simplistic, slick, smooth **off pat** = **perfectly**, exactly, faultlessly, flawlessly, precisely

patch n **1** = **reinforcement**, piece of material **2** = **spot**, bit, scrap, shred, small piece **3** = **plot**, area, ground, land, tract ◆ v **5** = **mend**, cover, reinforce, repair, sew up

patent n **1** = **copyright**, licence ◆ adj **3** = **obvious**, apparent, clear, evident, glaring, manifest

paternal adj **1** = **fatherly**, concerned, protective, solicitous

path n **1** = **way**, footpath, road, track, trail **2** = **course**, direction, road, route, way

pathetic adj **1** = **sad**, affecting, distressing, gut–wrenching, heart–rending, moving, pitiable, plaintive, poignant, tender, touching ≠ **funny**

pathos n = **sadness**, pitifulness, plaintiveness, poignancy

patient adj **1** = **long–suffering**, calm, enduring, persevering, philosophical, resigned, stoical, submissive, uncomplaining ≠ **impatient** ◆ n **2** = **sick person**, case, invalid, sufferer

patriarchy *n, pl* **-chies** society in which men have most of the power.

patrician *n* 1 member of the nobility. ♦ *adj* 2 of noble birth.

patriot ❶ *n* person who loves his or her country and supports its interests. **patriotic** *adj* **patriotism** *n*

patrol ❶ *n* 1 regular circuit by a guard. 2 person or small group patrolling. 3 unit of Scouts or Guides. ♦ *v* **-trolling, -trolled** 4 go round on guard, or reconnoitring.

patron ❶ *n* 1 person who gives financial support to charities, artists, etc. 2 regular customer of a shop, pub, etc. **patronage** *n* support given by a patron. **patronize** *v* 1 treat in a condescending way. 2 be a patron of. **patron saint** saint regarded as the guardian of a country or group.

patter¹ ❶ *v* 1 make repeated soft tapping sounds. ♦ *n* 2 quick succession of taps.

patter² *n* glib rapid speech.

pattern ❶ *n* 1 arrangement of repeated parts or decorative designs. 2 regular way that something is done. 3 diagram or shape used as a guide to make something. **patterned** *adj* decorated with a pattern.

paunch ❶ *n* protruding belly.

pauper ❶ *n* very poor person.

pause ❶ *v* 1 stop for a time. ♦ *n* 2 stop or rest in speech or action.

pave ❶ *v* form (a surface) with stone or brick. **pavement** *n* paved path for pedestrians.

pavilion *n* 1 building on a playing field etc. 2 building for housing an exhibition etc.

paw ❶ *n* 1 animal's foot with claws and pads. ♦ *v* 2 scrape with the paw or hoof. 3 *Informal* touch in a rough or overfamiliar way.

pawn¹ ❶ *v* deposit (an article) as security for money borrowed. **in pawn** deposited as security with a pawnbroker. **pawnbroker** *n* lender of money on goods deposited.

pawn² ❶ *n* 1 chessman of the lowest value. 2 person manipulated by someone else.

pay ❶ *v* **paying, paid** 1 give money etc. in return for goods or services. 2 settle a debt or obligation. 3 compensate (for). 4 give. 5 be profitable to. ♦ *n* 6 wages or salary. **payment** *n* 1 act of paying. 2 money paid. **payable** *adj* due to be paid. **payee** *n* person to whom money is paid or due. **pay off** *v* 1 pay (debt) in full. 2 turn out successfully. **pay out** *v* 1 spend. 2 release (a rope) bit by bit.

PC 1 personal computer. 2 Police

————————————| THESAURUS |————————————

patriot *n* = **nationalist**, chauvinist, loyalist

patrol *n* 1 = **policing**, guarding, protecting, vigilance, watching 2 = **guard**, patrolman, sentinel, watch, watchman ♦ *v* 4 = **police**, guard, inspect, keep guard, keep watch, safeguard

patron *n* 1 = **supporter**, backer, benefactor, champion, friend, helper, philanthropist, sponsor 2 = **customer**, buyer, client, frequenter, habitué, shopper

patter¹ *v* 1 = **tap**, beat, pat, pitter-patter ♦ *n* 2 = **tapping**, pattering, pitter-patter

patter² *n* = **spiel** (*inf*), line, pitch

pattern *n* 1 = **design**, arrangement, decoration, device, figure, motif 2 = **order**, method, plan, sequence, system 3 = **plan**, design, diagram, guide, original, stencil, template

paunch *n* = **belly**, pot, potbelly, spare tyre (*Brit sl*)

pauper *n* = **down-and-out**, bankrupt, beggar, mendicant, poor person

pause *v* 1 = **stop briefly**, break, cease, delay, halt, have a breather (*inf*), interrupt, rest, take a break, wait ≠ **continue** ♦ *n* 2 = **stop**, break, breather (*inf*), cessation, gap, halt, interlude, intermission, interval, lull, respite, rest, stoppage ≠ **advancement**

pave *v* = **cover**, concrete, floor, surface, tile

paw *v* 3 *Inf* = **manhandle**, grab, handle roughly, maul, molest

pawn¹ *v* = **hock** (*inf, chiefly US*), deposit, mortgage, pledge

pawn² *n* 2 = **tool**, cat's-paw, instrument, plaything, puppet, stooge (*sl*)

Constable. 3 politically correct. 4 Privy
Councillor.

PE physical education Prince Edward Island.

pea n 1 climbing plant with seeds growing
in pods. 2 its seed, eaten as a vegetable.

peace ① n 1 calm, quietness. 2 absence of
anxiety. 3 freedom from war. 4 harmony
between people. **peaceable** adj inclined
towards peace. **peaceably** adv **peaceful**
adj **peacefully** adv

peach n 1 soft juicy fruit with a stone and a
downy skin. 2 Informal very pleasing
person or thing. ◆ adj 3 pinkish–orange.

peacock n large male bird with a brilliantly
coloured fanlike tail. **peahen** n fem

peak ① n 1 pointed top, esp. of a
mountain. 2 point of greatest
development etc. 3 projecting piece on
the front of a cap. ◆ v 4 form or reach a
peak. ◆ adj 5 of or at the point of greatest
demand. **peaked** adj **peaky** adj pale and
sickly.

peal ① n 1 long loud echoing sound, esp.
of bells or thunder. ◆ v 2 sound with a
peal or peals.

peanut n 1 pea–shaped nut that ripens
underground. ◆ pl 2 Informal trifling
amount of money.

pear n sweet juicy fruit with a narrow top

and rounded base.

pearl n hard round shiny object found
inside some oyster shells and used as a
jewel. **pearly** adj

peasant ① n farmer or farmworker of a
low social class. **peasantry** n peasants
collectively.

peat n decayed vegetable material found in
bogs, used as fertilizer or fuel.

pebble n small roundish stone. **pebbly** adj
pebble dash coating for exterior walls
consisting of small stones set in plaster.

peccadillo ① n, pl –**loes**, –**los** trivial
misdeed.

peck ① v 1 strike or pick up with the beak.
2 Informal kiss quickly. ◆ n 3 pecking
movement. **peckish** adj Informal slightly
hungry. **peck at** v nibble, eat reluctantly.

pectoral adj 1 of the chest or thorax. ◆ n 2
pectoral muscle or fin.

peculiar ① adj 1 strange. 2 distinct,
special. 3 belonging exclusively to.
peculiarity n, pl –**ties** 1 oddity,
eccentricity. 2 distinguishing trait.

pedal n 1 foot–operated lever used to
control a vehicle or machine, or to modify
the tone of a musical instrument. ◆ v
–**alling**, –**alled** 2 propel (a bicycle) by
using its pedals.

———————[THESAURUS]———————

pay v 1, 2 = **reimburse**, give, remit,
remunerate, requite, reward, settle
3 = **compensate**, recompense 4 = **give**,
bestow, extend, grant, hand out, present
5 = **be profitable**, benefit, be worthwhile,
make a return, make money, repay ◆ n
6 = **wages**, allowance, earnings, fee,
income, payment, recompense,
reimbursement, remuneration, reward,
salary, stipend

peace n 1 = **stillness**, calm, calmness,
hush, quiet, repose, rest, silence,
tranquillity 2 = **serenity**, calm, composure,
contentment, repose 3 = **truce**, armistice,
treaty ≠ **war** 4 = **harmony**, accord,
agreement, concord

peak n 1 = **point**, apex, brow, crest,
pinnacle, summit, tip, top 2 = **high point**,

acme, climax, crown, culmination, zenith
◆ v 4 = **culminate**, climax, come to a head

peal n 1 = **ring**, blast, chime, clang, clap,
crash, reverberation, roar, rumble ◆ v
2 = **ring**, chime, crash, resound, roar,
rumble

peasant n = **rustic**, countryman

peccadillo n = **misdeed**, error,
indiscretion, lapse, misdemeanour, slip

peck[1] v 1 = **pick**, dig, hit, jab, poke, prick,
strike, tap

peculiar adj 1 = **odd**, abnormal, bizarre,
curious, eccentric, extraordinary, freakish,
funny, munted (NZ sl), offbeat,
outlandish, outré, quaint, queer, singular,
strange, uncommon, unconventional,
unusual, weird ≠ **expected** 2 = **specific**,
characteristic, distinctive, particular,

pedant ❶ *n* person who is excessively concerned with details and rules, esp. in academic work. **pedantic** *adj* **pedantry** *n*

peddle ❶ *v* sell (goods) from door to door. **peddler** *n* person who sells illegal drugs.

pedestal ❶ *n* base supporting a column, statue, etc.

pedestrian ❶ *n* 1 person who walks. ♦ *adj* 2 dull, uninspiring. **pedestrian crossing** place marked where pedestrians may cross a road.

pedigree ❶ *n* register of ancestors, esp. of a purebred animal.

pedlar ❶ *n* person who sells goods from door to door.

peek ❶ *v, n* peep or glance.

peel ❶ *v* 1 remove the skin or rind of (a vegetable or fruit). 2 (of skin or a surface) come off in flakes. ♦ *n* 3 rind or skin.

peep¹ ❶ *v* 1 look slyly or quickly. ♦ *n* 2 peeping look. **Peeping Tom** man who furtively watches women undressing.

peep² ❶ *v* 1 make a small shrill noise. ♦ *n* 2 small shrill noise.

peer¹ ❶ *n* 1 (*fem* **peeress**) member of the nobility. 2 person of the same status, age, etc. **peerage** *n* 1 whole body of peers. 2 rank of a peer. **peerless** *adj* unequalled, unsurpassed. **peer group** group of people of similar age, status, etc.

peer² ❶ *v* look closely and intently.

peeved *adj Informal* annoyed.

peevish ❶ *adj* fretful or irritable.

peewit *n* same as LAPWING.

peg ❶ *n* 1 pin or clip for joining, fastening, marking, etc. 2 hook or knob for hanging things on. ♦ *v* **pegging, pegged** 3 fasten with pegs. 4 stabilize (prices). **off the peg** (of clothes) ready-to-wear, not tailor-made.

pejorative ❶ [pij–**jor**–a–tiv] *adj* (of words etc.) with an insulting or critical meaning.

pelican *n* large water bird with a pouch beneath its bill for storing fish. **pelican crossing** road crossing with pedestrian-operated traffic lights.

pellet *n* small ball of something.

pelmet *n* ornamental drapery or board, concealing a curtain rail.

pelt¹ ❶ *v* 1 throw missiles at. 2 run fast, rush. 3 rain heavily. **at full pelt** at top speed.

pelt² ❶ *n* skin of a fur-bearing animal.

pelvis *n* framework of bones at the base of

special, unique ≠ **general**

pedant *n* = **hairsplitter**, nit-picker (*inf*), quibbler

peddle *v* = **sell**, flog (*sl*), hawk, market, push (*inf*), trade

pedestal *n* = **support**, base, foot, mounting, plinth, stand

pedestrian *n* 1 = **walker**, foot-traveller ≠ **driver** ♦ *adj* 2 = **dull**, banal, boring, commonplace, humdrum, mediocre, mundane, ordinary, prosaic, run-of-the-mill, uninspired ≠ **interesting**

pedigree *n* = **lineage**, ancestry, blood, breed, descent, extraction, family, family tree, genealogy, line, race, stock

pedlar *n* = **seller**, door-to-door salesman, hawker, huckster, vendor

① **peek** *v* = **glance**, eyeball (*sl*), look, peep

② **peek** *n* = **glance**, glimpse, look, look-see (*sl*), peep

peel *v* 1 = **skin**, pare, strip off 2 = **flake off**, scale ♦ *n* 3 = **skin**, peeling, rind

peep¹ *v* 1 = **peek**, eyeball (*sl*), look, sneak a look, steal a look ♦ *n* 2 = **look**, glimpse, look-see (*sl*), peek

peep² *v* 1 = **tweet**, cheep, chirp, squeak ♦ *n* 2 = **tweet**, cheep, chirp, squeak

peer¹ *n* 1 = **noble**, aristocrat, lord, nobleman 2 = **equal**, compeer, fellow, like

peer² *v* = **squint**, gaze, inspect, peep, scan, snoop, spy

peevish *adj* = **irritable**, cantankerous, childish, churlish, cross, crotchety (*inf*), fractious, fretful, grumpy, petulant, querulous, snappy, sulky, sullen, surly

peg *v* 3 = **fasten**, attach, fix, join, secure

pejorative *adj* = **derogatory**, deprecatory, depreciatory, disparaging, negative, uncomplimentary, unpleasant

pelt¹ *v* 1 = **throw**, batter, bombard, cast,

the spine, to which the hips are attached.
pelvic adj

pen¹ ❶ n 1 instrument for writing in ink. ◆
v **penning, penned** 2 write or compose.
pen friend friend with whom a person
corresponds without meeting. **penknife** n
small knife with blade(s) that fold into the
handle. **pen name** name used by a writer
instead of his or her real name.

pen² ❶ n 1 small enclosure for domestic
animals. ◆ v **penning, penned** 2 put or
keep in a pen. **penned in** trapped or
confined.

penal ❶ [pee–nal] adj of or used in
punishment. **penalize** v 1 impose a
penalty on. 2 handicap, hinder. **penalty** n,
pl **–ties** 1 punishment for a crime or
offence. 2 Sport handicap or disadvantage
imposed for breaking a rule.

penance ❶ n voluntary self–punishment to
make amends for wrongdoing.

pence n a plural of PENNY.

penchant ❶ [pon–shon] n inclination or
liking.

pencil n thin cylindrical instrument
containing graphite, for writing or
drawing. ◆ v **–cilling, –cilled** 2 draw,
write, or mark with a pencil.

pendant n ornament worn on a chain
round the neck.

pending ❶ prep 1 while waiting for. ◆ adj

2 not yet decided or settled.

pendulous adj hanging, swinging.

penetrate ❶ v 1 find or force a way into
or through. 2 arrive at the meaning of.
penetrable adj capable of being
penetrated. **penetrating** adj 1 (of a sound)
loud and unpleasant. 2 quick to
understand. **penetration** n

penguin n flightless black–and–white
Antarctic sea bird.

penicillin n antibiotic drug effective
against a wide range of diseases and
infections.

peninsula n strip of land nearly
surrounded by water. **peninsular** adj

penis n organ of copulation and urination
in male mammals.

penitent ❶ adj 1 feeling sorry for having
done wrong. ◆ n 2 someone who is
penitent. **penitence** n **penitentiary** n, pl –
ries 1 US prison. ◆ adj 2 (also **penitential**)
relating to penance.

pennant ❶ n long narrow flag.

penny n, pl **pence, pennies** 1 British
bronze coin worth one hundredth of a
pound. 2 former British coin worth one
twelfth of a shilling. **penniless** adj very
poor.

pension¹ ❶ n regular payment to people
above a certain age, retired employees,
widows, etc. **pensionable** adj **pensioner** n

hurl, pepper, shower, sling, strike
2 = **rush**, belt (sl), charge, dash, hurry,
run fast, shoot, speed, tear 3 = **pour**,
bucket down (inf), rain cats and dogs (inf),
rain hard, teem

pelt² n = **coat**, fell, hide, skin

pen¹ n 2 = **write**, compose, draft, draw up,
jot down **pen name** = **pseudonym**, nom
de plume

pen² n 1 = **enclosure**, cage, coop, fold,
hutch, pound, sty ◆ v 2 = **enclose**, cage,
confine, coop up, fence in, hedge, shut up
or in

penal adj = **disciplinary**, corrective,
punitive

penance n = **atonement**, penalty,

reparation, sackcloth and ashes

penchant n = **liking**, bent, bias, fondness,
inclination, leaning, partiality, predilection,
proclivity, propensity, taste, tendency

pending adj 2 = **undecided**, awaiting,
imminent, impending, in the balance,
undetermined, unsettled

penetrate v 1 = **pierce**, bore, enter, go
through, prick, stab 2 = **grasp**,
comprehend, decipher, fathom, figure out
(inf), get to the bottom of, suss (out) (sl),
work out

penitent adj 1 = **repentant**, abject,
apologetic, conscience–stricken, contrite,
regretful, remorseful, sorry

pennant n = **flag**, banner, ensign, pennon,

person receiving a pension. **pension off** v force (someone) to retire from a job and pay him or her a pension.

pension² [pon–syon] n boarding house in Europe.

pensive ⊕ adj deeply thoughtful, often with a tinge of sadness.

pentagon n 1 geometric figure with five sides. 2 (P–) headquarters of the US military. **pentagonal** adj

penthouse n flat built on the roof or top floor of a building.

penultimate adj second last.

penury ⊕ n extreme poverty.

peony n, pl **–nies** garden plant with showy red, pink, or white flowers.

people ⊕ pl n 1 persons generally. 2 the community. 3 one's family. ◆ n 4 race or nation. ◆ v 5 provide with inhabitants.

pep n Informal high spirits, energy, or enthusiasm. **pep talk** Informal talk designed to increase confidence and enthusiasm. **pep up** v **pepping, pepped** stimulate, invigorate.

pepper ⊕ n 1 sharp hot condiment made from the fruit of an East Indian climbing plant. 2 colourful tropical fruit used as a vegetable, capsicum. ◆ v 3 season with pepper. 4 sprinkle, dot. 5 pelt with missiles. **peppery** adj 1 tasting of pepper. 2 irritable. **peppercorn** n dried berry of the pepper plant.

per prep for each. **as per** in accordance with.

perambulate v walk through or about (a place). **perambulator** n pram.

per annum adv Latin in each year.

per capita adj, adv Latin of or for each person.

perceive ⊕ v 1 become aware of (something) through the senses. 2 understand. **perception** n

percentage n proportion or rate per hundred. **per cent** in each hundred.

perch¹ ⊕ n 1 resting place for a bird. ◆ v 2 alight, rest, or place on or as if on a perch.

perch² n edible freshwater fish.

perchance adv Old–fashioned perhaps.

percolate v 1 pass or filter through small holes. 2 spread gradually. 3 make (coffee) or (of coffee) be made in a percolator. **percolator** n coffeepot in which boiling water is forced through a tube and filters down through coffee.

percussion ⊕ n striking of one thing against another. **percussion instrument** musical instrument played by being struck, such as drums or cymbals.

peremptory ⊕ adj authoritative, imperious.

perennial ⊕ adj 1 lasting through many years. ◆ n 2 plant lasting more than two years. **perennially** adv

perfect ⊕ adj 1 having all the essential

THESAURUS

streamer

pension¹ n = **allowance**, annuity, benefit, superannuation

pensive adj = **thoughtful**, contemplative, dreamy, meditative, musing, preoccupied, reflective, sad, serious, solemn, wistful

penury n = **poverty**, beggary, destitution, indigence, need, privation, want

people pl n 1 = **persons**, humanity, mankind, men and women, mortals 2 = **nation**, citizens, community, folk, inhabitants, population, public 3 = **family**, clan, race, tribe ◆ v 5 = **inhabit**, colonize, occupy, populate, settle

pepper n 1 = **seasoning**, flavour, spice ◆ v

4 = **sprinkle**, dot, fleck, spatter, speck 5 = **pelt**, bombard, shower

perceive v 1 = **see**, behold, discern, discover, espy, make out, note, notice, observe, recognize, spot 2 = **understand**, comprehend, gather, grasp, learn, realize, see, suss (out) (sl)

perch¹ n 1 = **resting place**, branch, pole, post ◆ v 2 = **sit**, alight, balance, land, rest, roost, settle

percussion n 1 = **impact**, blow, bump, clash, collision, crash, knock, smash, thump

peremptory adj = **imperious**, authoritative, bossy (inf), dictatorial, elements. 2 faultless. 3 correct, precise. 4 utter or absolute. 5 excellent ♦ v 6 improve. 7 make fully correct. **perfectly** adv **perfection** n state of being perfect. **perfectionist** n person who demands the highest standards of excellence. **perfectionism** n

perforate ⊕ v make holes in. **perforation** n

perform ⊕ v 1 carry out (an action). 2 act, sing, or present a play before an audience. 3 fulfil (a request etc.). **performance** n

perfume ⊕ n 1 liquid cosmetic worn for its pleasant smell. 2 fragrance. ♦ v 3 give a pleasant smell to. **perfumery** n perfumes in general.

perfunctory ⊕ adj done only as a matter of routine, superficial. **perfunctorily** adv

perhaps ⊕ adv possibly, maybe.

peril ⊕ n great danger. **perilous** adj

perimeter ⊕ [per-**rim**-it-er] n (length of) the outer edge of an area.

period ⊕ n 1 particular portion of time. 2 single occurrence of menstruation. 3 division of time at school etc. when a particular subject is taught. 4 US full stop.

♦ adj 5 (of furniture, dress, a play, etc.) dating from or in the style of an earlier time. **periodic** adj recurring at intervals. **periodic table** Chem chart of the elements, arranged to show their relationship to each other. **periodical** n 1 magazine issued at regular intervals. ♦ adj 2 periodic.

peripatetic [per-rip-a-**tet**-ik] adj travelling about from place to place.

periphery [per-**if**-er-ee] n, pl -**eries** 1 boundary or edge. 2 fringes of a field of activity. **peripheral** [per-**if**-er-al] adj 1 unimportant, not central. 2 of or on the periphery.

periscope n instrument used, esp. in submarines, to give a view of objects on a different level.

perish ⊕ v 1 be destroyed or die. 2 decay, rot. **perishable** adj liable to rot quickly. **perishing** adj Informal very cold.

perk ⊕ n Informal incidental benefit gained from a job, such as a company car.

perm n 1 long-lasting curly hairstyle produced by treating the hair with chemicals. ♦ v 2 give (hair) a perm.

permanent ⊕ adj lasting forever.

———————| THESAURUS |———————

dogmatic, domineering, overbearing

perennial adj 1 = **lasting**, abiding, constant, continual, enduring, incessant, persistent, recurrent

perfect adj 1 = **complete**, absolute, consummate, entire, finished, full, sheer, unmitigated, utter, whole 2 = **faultless**, flawless, immaculate, impeccable, pure, spotless, unblemished ≠ **flawed** 3 = **exact**, accurate, correct, faithful, precise, true, unerring 5 = **excellent**, ideal, splendid, sublime, superb, superlative, supreme ≠ **bad** ♦ v 6 = **improve**, develop, polish, refine ≠ **mar**

perforate v = **pierce**, bore, drill, penetrate, punch, puncture

perform v 1, 3 = **carry out**, accomplish, achieve, complete, discharge, do, execute, fulfil, pull off, work 2 = **present**, act, enact, play, produce, put on, represent, stage

perfume n 2 = **fragrance**, aroma, bouquet,

odour, scent, smell

perfunctory adj = **offhand**, cursory, heedless, indifferent, mechanical, routine, sketchy, superficial

perhaps adv = **maybe**, conceivably, feasibly, it may be, perchance (arch), possibly

peril n = **danger**, hazard, jeopardy, menace, risk, uncertainty ≠ **security**

perimeter n = **boundary**, ambit, border, bounds, circumference, confines, edge, limit, margin, periphery

period n 1 = **time**, interval, season, space, span, spell, stretch, term, while

perish v 1 a = **be destroyed**, cark (Aust & NZ sl), collapse, decline, disappear, fall, vanish b = **die**, be killed, expire, lose one's life, pass away 2 = **rot**, decay, decompose, disintegrate, moulder, waste

perk n Inf = **bonus**, benefit, extra, fringe benefit, perquisite, plus permanence n

permeate ❶ v pervade or pass through the whole of (something). **permeable** adj able to be permeated, esp. by liquid.

permit ❶ v –mitting, –mitted 1 give permission, allow. ◆ n 2 document giving permission to do something. **permission** n authorization to do something. **permissible** adj **permissive** adj (excessively) tolerant, esp. in sexual matters.

permutation n any of the ways a number of things can be arranged or combined.

pernicious ❶ adj 1 wicked. 2 extremely harmful, deadly.

pernickety ❶ adj Informal (excessively) fussy about details.

peroxide n 1 hydrogen peroxide used as a hair bleach. 2 oxide containing a high proportion of oxygen.

perpendicular ❶ adj 1 at right angles to a line or surface. 2 upright or vertical. ◆ n 3 line or plane at right angles to another.

perpetrate ❶ v commit or be responsible for (a wrongdoing). **perpetration** n **perpetrator** n

perpetual ❶ adj 1 lasting forever. 2 continually repeated. **perpetually** adv **perpetuate** v cause to continue or be remembered. **perpetuation** n in **perpetuity** forever.

perplex ❶ v puzzle, bewilder. **perplexity** n, pl –ties

persecute ❶ v 1 treat cruelly because of race, religion, etc. 2 subject to persistent harassment. **persecution** n **persecutor** n

persevere ❶ v keep making an effort despite difficulties. **perseverance** n

persist ❶ v 1 continue to be or happen, last. 2 continue in spite of obstacles or objections. **persistent** adj **persistently** adv **persistence** n

person ❶ n 1 human being. 2 body of a human being. 3 Grammar form of pronouns and verbs that shows if a person is speaking, spoken to, or spoken of. **personal** adj individual, private. **personality** n distinctive character. in **person** actually present.

THESAURUS

permanent adj = **lasting**, abiding, constant, enduring, eternal, everlasting, immutable, perpetual, persistent, stable, steadfast, unchanging ≠ **changing**

permeate v = **pervade**, charge, fill, imbue, impregnate, infiltrate, penetrate, saturate, spread through

permit v 1 = **allow**, authorize, consent, enable, entitle, give leave or permission, give the green light to, grant, let, license, sanction ≠ **ban** ◆ n 2 = **licence**, authorization, pass, passport, permission, warrant ≠ **ban**

pernicious adj 1 = **wicked**, bad, evil 2 = **deadly**, damaging, dangerous, destructive, detrimental, fatal, harmful, hurtful, malign, poisonous

pernickety adj Inf = **fussy**, exacting, fastidious, finicky, overprecise, particular, picky (inf) ≠ **slack**

perpendicular adj 1, 2 = **upright**, at right angles to, on end, plumb, straight, vertical

perpetrate v = **commit**, carry out, do, enact, execute, perform, wreak

perpetual adj 1 = **everlasting**, endless, eternal, infinite, lasting, never–ending, perennial, permanent, unchanging, unending ≠ **passing** 2 = **continual**, constant, continuous–endless, incessant, interminable, never–ending, persistent, recurrent, repeated ≠ **temporary**

perplex v = **puzzle**, baffle, bewilder, confound, confuse, mystify, stump

persecute v 1 = **victimize**, afflict, ill–treat, maltreat, oppress, pick on, torment, torture ≠ **back** 2 = **harass**, annoy, badger, bother, hassle (inf), pester, tease ≠ **let alone**

persevere v = **keep going**, carry on, continue, go on, hang on, persist, remain, stick at or to

persist v 1 = **continue**, carry on, keep up, last, linger, remain 2 = **persevere**, continue, insist, stand firm

> ### ✓ WORD TIP
> *Person* is generally used in the singular and *people* is used to indicate more than one. The plural *persons* is restricted to formal notices.

persona [per-**soh**-na] *n, pl* –**nae** [–nee] someone's personality as presented to others.

personify ❶ *v* –**fying**, –**fied 1** give human characteristics to. **2** be an example of, typify. **personification** *n*

personnel ❶ *n* people employed in an organization.

perspective ❶ *n* **1** view of the relative importance of situations or facts. **2** method of drawing that gives the effect of solidity and relative distances and sizes.

Perspex *n* ® transparent acrylic substitute for glass.

perspicacious ❶ *adj* having quick mental insight. **perspicacity** *n*

perspire ❶ *v* sweat. **perspiration** *n*

persuade ❶ *v* **1** make (someone) do something by argument, charm, etc. **2** convince. **persuasion** *n* **1** act of persuading. **2** way of thinking or belief. **persuasive** *adj*

pert ❶ *adj* saucy and cheeky.

pertain ❶ *v* belong or be relevant (to).

pertinacious *adj* very persistent and determined. **pertinacity** *n*

pertinent ❶ *adj* relevant. **pertinence** *n*

perturb ❶ *v* disturb greatly. **perturbation** *n*

peruse ❶ *v* read in a careful or leisurely manner. **perusal** *n*

pervade ❶ *v* spread right through (something). **pervasive** *adj*

pervert ❶ *v* **1** use or alter for a wrong purpose. **2** lead into abnormal (sexual) behaviour. ♦ *n* **3** person who practises sexual perversion. **perversion** *n* **1** sexual act or desire considered abnormal. **2** act of perverting.

peseta [pa–**say**–ta] *n* monetary unit of Spain.

pessimism ❶ *n* tendency to expect the worst in all things. **pessimist** *n* **pessimistic** *adj*

pest ❶ *n* **1** annoying person. **2** insect or

—————— THESAURUS ——————

person *n* **1** = **individual**, being, body, human, soul **in person** = **personally**, bodily, in the flesh, oneself

personify *v* **2** = **embody**, epitomize, exemplify, represent, symbolize, typify

personnel *n* = **employees**, helpers, human resources, people, staff, workers, workforce

perspective *n* **1** = **objectivity**, proportion, relation, relative importance, relativity

perspicacious *adj* = **perceptive**, acute, alert, astute, discerning, keen, percipient, sharp, shrewd

perspire *v* = **sweat**, exude, glow, pour with sweat, secrete, swelter

persuade *v* **1** = **talk into**, bring round (*inf*), coax, entice, impel, incite, induce, influence, sway, urge, win over ≠ **forbid** **2** = **convince**, cause to believe, satisfy

pert *adj* = **impudent**, bold, cheeky, forward, impertinent, insolent, sassy (*US inf*), saucy

pertain *v* = **relate**, apply, befit, belong, be relevant, concern, refer, regard

pertinent *adj* = **relevant**, applicable, apposite, appropriate, apt, fit, fitting, germane, material, proper, to the point

perturb *v* = **disturb**, agitate, bother, disconcert, faze, fluster, ruffle, trouble, unsettle, vex, worry

peruse *v* = **read**, browse, check, examine, eyeball (*sl*), inspect, scan, scrutinize, study

pervade *v* = **spread through**, charge, fill, imbue, infuse, penetrate, permeate, suffuse

pervert *v* **1** = **distort**, abuse, falsify, garble, misrepresent, misuse, twist, warp **2** = **corrupt**, debase, debauch, degrade, deprave, lead astray ♦ *n* **3** = **deviant**, degenerate, weirdo *or* weirdie (*inf*)

pessimism *n* = **gloominess**, dejection, depression, despair, despondency,

animal that damages crops. **pesticide** n
chemical for killing insect pests.

pester ① v annoy or nag continually.

pestilence ① n deadly epidemic disease.
pestilent adj 1 annoying, troublesome. 2
deadly. **pestilential** adj

pestle n club–shaped implement for
grinding things to powder in a mortar.

pet ① n 1 animal kept for pleasure and
companionship. 2 person favoured or
indulged. ◆ adj 3 particularly cherished. ◆
v **petting**, **petted** 4 treat as a pet. 5 pat or
stroke affectionately. 6 Informal kiss and
caress erotically.

petal n one of the brightly coloured outer
parts of a flower.

petite ① adj (of a woman) small and
dainty.

petition ① n 1 formal request, esp. one
signed by many people and presented to
parliament. ◆ v 2 present a petition to.
petitioner n

petrel n sea bird with a hooked bill and
tubular nostrils.

petrify ① v **-fying**, **-fied** 1 frighten
severely. 2 turn to stone. **petrification** n

petroleum n thick dark oil found
underground.

petticoat n woman's skirt–shaped
undergarment.

pettifogging adj excessively concerned
with unimportant detail.

petty ① adj **-tier**, **-tiest** 1 unimportant,
trivial. 2 small–minded. 3 on a small scale,
e.g. petty crime. **pettiness** n **petty cash**
cash kept by a firm to pay minor
expenses. **petty officer** noncommissioned
officer in the navy.

petulant ① adj childishly irritable or
peevish. **petulance** n **petulantly** adv

petunia n garden plant with funnel–
shaped flowers.

pew n 1 fixed benchlike seat in a church. 2
Informal chair, seat.

pewter n greyish metal made of tin and
lead.

phallus n, pl **-luses**, **-li** penis, esp. as a
symbol of reproductive power in primitive
rites. **phallic** adj

phantom ① n 1 ghost. 2 unreal vision.

Pharaoh [**fare**–oh] n title of the ancient
Egyptian kings.

pharmaceutical adj of pharmacy.

pharmacy n 1 preparation and dispensing
of drugs and medicines. 2 pharmacist's
shop.

──────── THESAURUS ────────

distrust, gloom, hopelessness, melancholy

pest n 1 = **nuisance**, annoyance, bane,
bother, drag (inf), irritation, pain (inf),
thorn in one's flesh, trial, vexation
2 = **infection**, blight, bug, epidemic,
pestilence, plague, scourge

pester v = **annoy**, badger, bedevil, be on
one's back (sl), bother, bug (inf), harass,
harry, hassle (inf), nag, plague, torment

pestilence n = **plague**, epidemic, visitation

pet n 2 = **favourite**, darling, idol, jewel,
treasure ◆ adj 4 = **favourite**, cherished,
dearest, dear to one's heart, favoured ◆ v
4 = **pamper**, baby, coddle, cosset,
mollycoddle, spoil 5 = **fondle**, caress, pat,
stroke 6 Inf = **cuddle**, canoodle (sl), kiss,
neck (inf), smooch (inf), snog (Brit sl)

petite adj = **small**, dainty, delicate, elfin,
little, slight

petition n 1 = **appeal**, entreaty, plea,
prayer, request, solicitation, suit,
supplication ◆ v 2 = **appeal**, adjure, ask,
beg, beseech, entreat, plead, pray, solicit,
supplicate

petrify v 1 = **terrify**, horrify, immobilize,
paralyse, stun, stupefy, transfix
2 = **fossilize**, calcify, harden, turn to stone

petty adj 1 = **trivial**, contemptible,
inconsiderable, insignificant, little, measly
(inf), negligible, paltry, slight, small,
trifling, unimportant ≠ **major** 2 = **small–
minded**, mean, mean–minded, shabby,
spiteful, ungenerous ≠ **liberal**

petulant adj = **sulky**, bad–tempered, huffy,
ill–humoured, moody, peevish, sullen

phantom n 1 = **spectre**, apparition, ghost,
phantasm, shade (lit), spirit, spook (inf),
wraith 2 = **illusion**, figment of the

phase ❶ *n* 1 any distinct or characteristic stage in a development or chain of events. ◆ *v* 2 arrange or carry out in stages or to coincide with something else. **phase in, out** *v* introduce *or* discontinue gradually.

PhD Doctor of Philosophy.

pheasant *n* game bird with bright plumage.

phenomenon ❶ *n, pl* **-ena** 1 anything appearing or observed. 2 remarkable person or thing. **phenomenal** *adj* extraordinary, outstanding. **phenomenally** *adv*

> ✓ **WORD TIP**
> Avoid using *phenomena* as a singular.

phial *n* small bottle for medicine etc.

philanthropy ❶ *n* practice of helping people less well-off than oneself. **philanthropic** *adj* **philanthropist** *n*

philately [fill-**lat**–a–lee] *n* stamp collecting. **philatelist** *n*

philistine ❶ *adj, n* boorishly uncultivated (person). **philistinism** *n*

philosophy ❶ *n, pl* **-phies** 1 study of the meaning of life, knowledge, thought, etc. 2 theory or set of ideas held by a particular philosopher. 3 person's outlook on life. **philosopher** *n* person who studies philosophy. **philosophical, philosophic** *adj* 1 of philosophy. 2 calm in the face of difficulties or disappointments. **philosophize** *v* discuss in a philosophical manner.

phlegm [**flem**] *n* thick yellowish substance formed in the nose and throat during a cold.

phobia ❶ *n* intense and unreasoning fear or dislike.

phoenix *n* legendary bird said to set fire to itself and rise anew from its ashes.

phone ❶ *n, v Informal* telephone. **phonecard** *n* card used to operate certain public telephones. **phone–in** *n* broadcast in which telephone comments or questions from the public are transmitted live.

phonetic *adj* 1 of speech sounds. 2 (of spelling) written as it is sounded. **phonetics** *n* science of speech sounds. **phonetically** *adv*

phoney ❶ **phony** *Informal* ◆ *adj* **phonier, phoniest** 1 not genuine. 2 insincere. ◆ *n, pl* **phoneys, phonies** 3 phoney person or thing.

imagination, hallucination, vision

phase *n* 1 = **stage**, chapter, development, juncture, period, point, position, step, time

phenomenon *n* 1 = **occurrence**, circumstance, episode, event, fact, happening, incident 2 = **wonder**, exception, marvel, miracle, prodigy, rarity, sensation

philanthropy *n* = **humanitarianism**, beneficence, benevolence, brotherly love, charitableness, charity, generosity, kind–heartedness

① **philistine** *adj* = **uncultured**, boorish, ignorant, lowbrow, tasteless, uncultivated, uneducated, unrefined

② **philistine** *n* = **boor**, barbarian, ignoramus, lout, lowbrow, vulgarian, yahoo

philosophy *n* 1 = **thought**, knowledge, logic, metaphysics, rationalism, reasoning, thinking, wisdom 2, 3 = **outlook**, beliefs, convictions, doctrine, ideology, principles, tenets, thinking, values, viewpoint, world view

phobia *n* = **terror**, aversion, detestation, dread, fear, hatred, horror, loathing, repulsion, revulsion, thing (*inf*)

① **phone** *n Inf* = **telephone**, blower (*inf*)

② **phone** *v Inf* = **call**, get on the blower (*inf*), give someone a call, give someone a ring (*inf, chiefly Brit*), give someone a tinkle (*Brit inf*), make a call, ring (up) (*inf, chiefly Brit*), telephone

phoney, phony *Inf adj* 1 = **fake**, bogus, counterfeit, ersatz, false, imitation, pseudo (*inf*), sham ≠ **real** ◆ *n* 3 = **fake**, counterfeit, forgery, fraud, impostor, pseud (*inf*), sham

phosphorus *n Chem* toxic flammable nonmetallic element which appears luminous in the dark. **phosphate** *n* 1 compound of phosphorus. 2 fertilizer containing phosphorus.

photo *n, pl* **photos** short for PHOTOGRAPH. **photo finish** finish of a race in which the contestants are so close that a photograph is needed to decide the result.

photocopy *n, pl* **-copies** 1 photographic reproduction. ◆ *v* **-copying, -copied** 2 make a photocopy of. **photocopier** *n*

photogenic *adj* always looking attractive in photographs.

photograph ❶ *n* 1 picture made by the chemical action of light on sensitive film. ◆ *v* 2 take a photograph of. **photographer** *n* **photographic** *adj* **photography** *n*

photosynthesis *n* process by which a green plant uses sunlight to build up carbohydrate reserves.

phrase ❶ *n* 1 group of words forming a unit of meaning, esp. within a sentence. 2 short effective expression. ◆ *v* 3 express in words. **phrasal verb** phrase consisting of a verb and an adverb or preposition, with a meaning different from the parts, such as *take in* meaning *deceive*.

phylum *n, pl* **-la** major taxonomic division of animals and plants that contains one or more classes.

physical ❶ *adj* 1 of the body, as contrasted with the mind or spirit. 2 of material things or nature.

physician ❶ *n* doctor of medicine.

physics *n* science of the properties of matter and energy. **physicist** *n*

physiognomy [fiz-ee-**on**-om-ee] *n* face.

physiology *n* science of the normal function of living things. **physiological** *adj* **physiologist** *n*

physiotherapy *n* treatment of disease or injury by physical means such as massage, rather than by drugs. **physiotherapist** *n*

physique ❶ *n* person's bodily build and muscular development.

pi *n Maths* ratio of the circumference of a circle to its diameter.

piano[1] *n, pl* **pianos** musical instrument with strings which are struck by hammers worked by a keyboard (also **pianoforte**). **pianist** *n* **Pianola** *n* ® mechanically played piano.

piano[2] *adv Music* quietly.

picador *n* mounted bullfighter with a lance.

piccalilli *n* pickle of vegetables in mustard sauce.

piccolo *n, pl* **-los** small flute.

pick[1] ❶ *v* 1 choose. 2 remove (flowers or fruit) from a plant. 3 take hold of and move with the fingers. 4 provoke (a fight etc.) deliberately. 5 open (a lock) by means other than a key. ◆ *n* 6 choice. 7 best part. **pick-me-up** *n Informal* stimulating drink, tonic. **pick on** *v* continually treat unfairly. **pick out** *v* recognize, distinguish. **pick up** *v* 1 raise, lift. 2 collect. 3 improve, get better. 4 become acquainted with for a sexual purpose. **pick-up** *n* 1 small truck. 2 casual acquaintance made for a sexual purpose. 3 device for conversion of vibrations into electrical signals, as in a record player.

pick[2] *n* tool with a curved iron crossbar and wooden shaft, for breaking up hard ground or rocks.

picket ❶ *n* 1 person or group standing

photograph *n* 1 = **picture**, photo (*inf*), print, shot, snap (*inf*), snapshot, transparency ◆ *v* 2 = **take a picture of**, film, record, shoot, snap (*inf*), take (someone's) picture

phrase *n* 1 = **expression**, group of words, idiom, remark, saying ◆ *v* 3 = **express**, put, put into words, say, voice, word

physical *adj* 1 = **bodily**, corporal, corporeal, earthly, fleshly, incarnate, mortal 2 = **material**, natural, palpable, real, solid, substantial, tangible

physician *n* = **doctor**, doc (*inf*), doctor of medicine, general practitioner, G.P., M.D., medic (*inf*), medical practitioner

physique *n* = **build**, body, constitution,

outside a workplace to deter would–be
workers during a strike. **2** sentry or sentries
posted to give warning of an attack. **3**
pointed stick used as part of a fence. ◆ *v* **4**
form a picket outside (a workplace).
picket line line of people acting as pickets.

pickle ❶ *n* **1** food preserved in vinegar or
salt water. **2** *Informal* awkward situation. ◆
v **3** preserve in vinegar or salt water.
pickled *adj Informal* drunk.

picnic ❶ *n* **1** informal meal out of doors. ◆
v **–nicking, –nicked 2** have a picnic.

picture ❶ *n* **1** drawing or painting. **2**
photograph. **3** mental image. **4** image on
a TV screen. ◆ *pl* **5** cinema. ◆ *v* **6** visualize,
imagine. **7** represent in a picture.
picturesque *adj* **1** (of a place or view)
pleasant to look at. **2** (of language)
forceful, vivid.

pidgin *n* language, not a mother tongue,
made up of elements of two or more
other languages.

pie *n* dish of meat, fruit, etc. baked in
pastry. **pie chart** circular diagram with
sectors representing quantities.

piebald ❶ *n, adj* (horse) with irregular
black–and–white markings.

piece ❶ *n* **1** separate bit or part. **2** instance,
e.g. *a piece of luck*. **3** example, specimen. **4**
literary or musical composition. **5** coin. **6**
small object used in draughts, chess, etc.
piece together *v* make or assemble bit by
bit.

pier ❶ *n* **1** platform on stilts sticking out
into the sea. **2** pillar, esp. one supporting a
bridge.

pierce ❶ *v* **1** make a hole in or through
with a sharp instrument. **2** make a way
through. **piercing** *adj* **1** (of a sound) shrill
and high–pitched.

piety ❶ *n, pl* **–ties** deep devotion to God
and religion.

pig ❶ *n* **1** animal kept and killed for pork,
ham, and bacon. **2** *Informal* greedy, dirty,
or rude person. **piggish, piggy** *adj* **1**
Informal dirty. **2** greedy. **3** stubborn.
piggery *n, pl* **–geries** place for keeping
and breeding pigs. **pig–headed** *adj*
obstinate.

pigeon *n* bird with a heavy body and short

——————— THESAURUS ———————

figure, form, frame, shape, structure
pick¹ *v* **1** = **select**, choose, decide upon,
elect, fix upon, hand–pick, opt for, settle
upon, single out ≠ **decline 2** = **gather**,
collect, harvest, pluck, pull **4** = **provoke**,
incite, instigate, start **5** = **open**, break into,
break open, crack, force ◆ *n* **6** = **choice**,
decision, option, preference, selection
7 = **the best**, elect, elite, the cream
picket *n* **1** = **protester**, demonstrator,
picketer **2** = **lookout**, guard, patrol,
sentinel, sentry, watch **3** = **stake**, pale,
paling, post, stanchion, upright ◆ *v*
4 = **blockade**, boycott, demonstrate
pickle *n* **2** *Inf* = **predicament**, bind (*inf*),
difficulty, dilemma, fix (*inf*), hot water
(*inf*), jam (*inf*), quandary, scrape (*inf*), tight
spot ◆ *v* **3** = **preserve**, marinade, steep
picnic *n* **1** = **excursion**, outdoor meal,
outing
picture *n* **1** = **representation**, drawing,
engraving, illustration, image, likeness,

painting, portrait, print, sketch
2 = **photograph** ◆ *pl* **5** = **flicks** (*sl*), movies
(*US inf*) ◆ *v* **6** = **imagine**, conceive of,
envision, see, visualize **7** = **represent**,
depict, draw, illustrate, paint, photograph,
show, sketch
piebald *adj* = **pied**, black and white,
brindled, dappled, flecked, mottled,
speckled, spotted
piece *n* **1** = **bit**, chunk, fragment, morsel,
part, portion, quantity, segment, slice
4 = **work**, article, composition, creation,
item, study, work of art
pier *n* **1** = **jetty**, landing place, promenade,
quay, wharf **2** = **pillar**, buttress, column,
pile, post, support, upright
pierce *v* **1** = **penetrate**, bore, drill, enter,
perforate, prick, puncture, spike, stab,
stick into
piety *n* = **holiness**, faith, godliness,
piousness, religion, reverence
pig *n* **1** = **hog**, boar, porker, sow, swine

legs, sometimes trained to carry messages.
pigeonhole *n* 1 compartment for papers
in a desk etc. ♦ *v* 2 classify. 3 put aside
and do nothing about. **pigeon-toed** *adj*
with the feet or toes turned inwards.

piggyback *n* 1 ride on someone's
shoulders. ♦ *adv* 2 carried on someone's
shoulders.

pigment ⊕ *n* colouring matter, paint or
dye. **pigmentation** *n*

pigtail *n* plait of hair hanging from the
back or either side of the head.

pike[1] *n* large predatory freshwater fish.

pike[2] *n Hist* long-handled spear.

pikelet *n Aust & NZ* small thick pancake.

piker *n Aust & NZ slang* shirker.

pilau, pilaf, pilaff *n* Middle Eastern dish
of meat, fish, or poultry boiled with rice,
spices, etc.

pilchard *n* small edible sea fish of the
herring family.

pile[1] ⊕ *n* 1 number of things lying on top
of each other. 2 *Informal* large amount. 3
large building. ♦ *v* 4 collect into a pile. 5
(foll. by *in* or *out*) move in a group. **pile-
up** *n Informal* traffic accident involving
several vehicles.

pile[2] ⊕ *n* beam driven into the ground,
esp. as a foundation for building.

pile[3] ⊕ *n* fibres of a carpet or a fabric, esp.
velvet, that stand up from the weave.

piles *pl n* swollen veins in the rectum,
haemorrhoids.

pilfer ⊕ *v* steal in small quantities.

pilgrim ⊕ *n* person who journeys to a holy
place. **pilgrimage** *n*

pill ⊕ *n* small ball of medicine swallowed
whole. **the pill** pill taken by a woman to
prevent pregnancy.

pillage ⊕ *v* 1 steal property by violence in
war. ♦ *n* 2 violent seizure of goods, esp. in
war.

pillar ⊕ *n* 1 upright post, usu. supporting a
roof. 2 strong supporter. **pillar box** red
pillar-shaped letter box in the street.

pillion *n* seat for a passenger behind the
rider of a motorcycle.

pillory ⊕ *n, pl* **-ries** 1 *Hist* frame with holes
for the head and hands in which an
offender was locked and exposed to
public abuse. ♦ *v* **-rying, -ried** 2 ridicule
publicly.

pillow *n* 1 stuffed cloth bag for supporting
the head in bed. ♦ *v* 2 rest as if on a
pillow. **pillowcase, pillowslip** *n* removable
cover for a pillow.

pilot ⊕ *n* 1 person qualified to fly an
aircraft or spacecraft. 2 person employed
to steer a ship entering or leaving a
harbour. ♦ *adj* 3 experimental and
preliminary. ♦ *v* 4 act as the pilot of. 5
guide, steer. **pilot light** small flame

———————————— THESAURUS ————————————

2 *Inf* = **slob** (*sl*), boor, brute, glutton,
swine

pigment *n* = **colour**, colouring, dye, paint,
stain, tincture, tint

pile[1] *n* 1 = **heap**, accumulation, berg (*S Afr*),
collection, hoard, mass, mound,
mountain, stack 2 *Inf* = **a lot**, great deal,
ocean, quantity, stacks 3 = **building**,
edifice, erection, structure ♦ *v* 4 = **collect**,
accumulate, amass, assemble, gather,
heap, hoard, stack 5 (foll. by *in* or *out*)
= **crowd**, crush, flock, flood, jam, pack,
rush, stream

pile[2] *n* = **foundation**, beam, column, pillar,
post, support, upright

pile[3] *n* = **nap**, down, fibre, fur, hair, plush

pilfer *v* = **steal**, appropriate, embezzle,
filch, knock off (*sl*), lift (*inf*), nick (*sl, chiefly
Brit*), pinch (*inf*), purloin, snaffle (*Brit inf*),
swipe (*sl*), take

pilgrim *n* = **traveller**, wanderer, wayfarer

pill *n* = **tablet**, capsule, pellet **the pill** = **oral
contraceptive**

pillage *v* 1 = **plunder**, despoil, loot,
maraud, raid, ransack, ravage, sack ♦ *n*
2 = **plunder**, marauding, robbery, sack,
spoliation

pillar *n* 1 = **support**, column, pier, post,
prop, shaft, stanchion, upright
2 = **supporter**, leader, leading light (*inf*),
mainstay, upholder

pillory *v* 2 = **ridicule**, brand, denounce,

lighting the main one in a gas appliance.

pimento n, pl **–tos** mild–tasting red pepper.

pimp n 1 man who gets customers for a prostitute in return for a share of his or her earnings. ◆ v 2 act as a pimp.

pimpernel n wild plant with small star–shaped flowers.

pimple ⏣ n small pus–filled spot on the skin. **pimply** adj

pin ⏣ n 1 short thin piece of stiff wire with a point and head, for fastening things. 2 wooden or metal peg or stake. ◆ v **pinning, pinned** 3 fasten with a pin. 4 seize and hold fast. **pin down** v 1 force (someone) to make a decision, take action, etc. 2 define clearly. **pin money** small amount earned to buy small luxuries. **pin–up** n picture of a sexually attractive person, esp. (partly) naked.

pinafore n 1 apron. 2 dress with a bib top.

pincers pl n 1 tool consisting of two hinged arms, for gripping. 2 claws of a lobster etc.

pinch ⏣ v 1 squeeze between finger and thumb. 2 cause pain by being too tight. 3 Informal steal. 4 Informal arrest. 5 act of pinching. 6 as much as can be taken up between the finger and thumb. **at a pinch** if absolutely necessary. **feel the pinch** have

to economize.

pine¹ n 1 evergreen coniferous tree. 2 its wood.

pine² ⏣ v 1 (foll. by for) feel great longing (for). 2 become thin and ill through grief etc.

pineapple n large tropical fruit with juicy yellow flesh and a hard skin.

pinion ⏣ n 1 bird's wing. ◆ v 2 immobilize (someone) by tying or holding his or her arms.

pink ⏣ n 1 pale reddish colour. 2 fragrant garden plant. ◆ adj 3 of the colour pink. ◆ v 4 (of an engine) make a metallic noise because not working properly, knock. **in the pink** in good health.

pinnacle ⏣ n 1 highest point of success etc. 2 mountain peak. 3 small slender spire.

pint n liquid measure, ⅛ gallon (.568 litre).

pioneer ⏣ n 1 explorer or early settler of a new country. 2 originator or developer of something new. ◆ v 3 be the pioneer or leader of.

pious ⏣ adj deeply religious, devout.

pip¹ n small seed in a fruit.

pip² n 1 high–pitched sound used as a time signal on radio. 2 Informal star on a junior army officer's shoulder showing rank.

pip³ n **give someone the pip** Brit, NZ & S

━━━━━━━ THESAURUS ━━━━━━━

stigmatize

pilot n 1 = **airman**, aviator, flyer
2 = **helmsman**, navigator, steersman ◆ adj
3 = **trial**, experimental, model, test ◆ v 4,
5 = **fly**, conduct, direct, drive, guide,
handle, navigate, operate, steer

pimple n = **spot**, boil, plook (Scot), pustule,
zit (sl)

pin v 3 = **fasten**, affix, attach, fix, join,
secure 4 = **hold fast**, fix, hold down,
immobilize, pinion

pinch v 1 = **squeeze**, compress, grasp, nip,
press 2 = **hurt**, cramp, crush, pain 3 Inf
= **steal**, filch, knock off (sl), lift (inf), nick
(sl, chiefly Brit), pilfer, purloin, snaffle (Brit
inf), swipe (sl) ◆ n 5 = **squeeze**, nip

pine² v 1 (foll. by for) = **long**, ache, crave,

desire, eat one's heart out over, hanker,
hunger for, thirst for, wish for, yearn for
2 = **waste**, decline, fade, languish, sicken

pinion v 2 = **immobilize**, bind, chain,
fasten, fetter, manacle, shackle, tie

pink adj 3 = **rosy**, flushed, reddish, rose,
roseate, salmon

pinnacle n 2 = **peak**, apex, crest, crown,
height, summit, top, vertex, zenith

pioneer n 1 = **settler**, colonist, explorer
2 = **founder**, developer, innovator, leader,
trailblazer ◆ v 3 = **develop**, create,
discover, establish, initiate, instigate,
institute, invent, originate, show the way,
start

pious adj = **religious**, devout, God–fearing,
godly, holy, reverent, righteous, saintly

Afr slang annoy.

pipe ❶ *n* 1 tube for conveying liquid or gas. 2 tube with a small bowl at the end for smoking tobacco. 3 tubular musical instrument. ◆ *pl* 4 bagpipes. ◆ *v* 5 play on a pipe. 6 utter in a shrill tone. 7 convey by pipe. 8 decorate with piping. **piper** *n* player on a pipe or bagpipes. **piping** *n* 1 system of pipes. 2 decoration of icing on a cake etc. 3 fancy edging on clothes etc. **pipe down** *v Informal* stop talking. **pipe dream** fanciful impossible plan. **pipeline** *n* 1 long pipe for transporting oil, water, etc. 2 means of communication. **in the pipeline** in preparation. **pipe up** *v* speak suddenly or shrilly.

piquant ❶ [**pee** kant] *adj* 1 having a pleasant spicy taste. 2 mentally stimulating. **piquancy** *n*

pique ❶ [**peek**] *n* 1 feeling of hurt pride, baffled curiosity, or resentment. ◆ *v* 2 hurt the pride of. 3 arouse (curiosity).

piranha *n* small fierce freshwater fish of tropical America.

pirate ❶ *n* 1 sea robber. 2 person who illegally publishes or sells work owned by someone else. 3 person or company that broadcasts illegally. ◆ *v* 4 sell or reproduce (artistic work etc.) illegally. **piracy** *n* **piratical** *adj*

pirouette *v, n* (make) a spinning turn balanced on the toes of one foot.

pistachio *n, pl* **–chios** edible nut of a Mediterranean tree.

piste [**peest**] *n* ski slope.

pistol *n* short-barrelled handgun.

piston *n* cylindrical part in an engine that slides to and fro in a cylinder.

pit ❶ *n* 1 deep hole in the ground. 2 coal mine. 3 dent or depression. 4 servicing and refuelling area on a motor-racing track. 5 same as ORCHESTRA PIT. ◆ *v* **pitting, pitted** 6 mark with small dents or scars. **pit one's wits against** compete against in a test or contest.

pitch¹ ❶ *v* 1 throw, hurl. 2 set up (a tent). 3 fall headlong. 4 (of a ship or plane) move with the front and back going up and down alternately. 5 set the level or tone of. ◆ *n* 6 area marked out for playing sport. 7 degree or angle of slope. 8 degree of highness or lowness of a (musical) sound. 9 place where a street or market trader regularly sells. 10 *Informal* persuasive sales talk. **pitch in** *v* join in enthusiastically. **pitch into** *v Informal* attack.

pitch² *n* dark sticky substance obtained from tar. **pitch-black, pitch-dark** *adj* very dark.

───── THESAURUS ─────

≠ irreverent

pipe *n* 1 = **tube**, conduit, duct, hose, line, main, passage, pipeline ◆ *v* 5 = **play**, sound 6 = **whistle**, cheep, peep, sing, warble 7 = **convey**, channel, conduct

piquant *adj* 1 = **spicy**, biting, pungent, savoury, sharp, tangy, tart, zesty ≠ **mild** 2 = **interesting**, lively, provocative, scintillating, sparkling, stimulating ≠ **boring**

pique *n* 1 = **resentment**, annoyance, displeasure, huff, hurt feelings, irritation, offence, umbrage, wounded pride ◆ *v* 2 = **displease**, affront, annoy, get (*inf*), irk, irritate, nettle, offend, rile, sting 3 = **arouse**, excite, rouse, spur, stimulate, stir, whet

pirate *n* 1 = **buccaneer**, corsair, freebooter, marauder, raider 2 = **plagiarist**, cribber (*inf*), infringer, plagiarizer ◆ *v* 4 = **copy**, appropriate, crib (*inf*), plagiarize, poach, reproduce, steal

pit *n* 1 = **hole**, abyss, cavity, chasm, crater, dent, depression, hollow ◆ *v* 6 = **scar**, dent, indent, mark, pockmark

pitch¹ *v* 1 = **throw**, cast, chuck (*inf*), fling, heave, hurl, lob (*inf*), sling, toss 2 = **set up**, erect, put up, raise, settle 3 = **fall**, dive, drop, topple, tumble 4 = **toss**, lurch, plunge, roll ◆ *n* 6 = **sports field**, field of play, ground, park (*US & Canad*) 7 = **slope**, angle, degree, dip, gradient, height, highest point, incline, level, point, summit, tilt 8 = **tone**, modulation, sound,

pitcher n large jug with a narrow neck.

pith ⊕ n 1 soft white lining of the rind of oranges etc. 2 essential part. 3 soft tissue in the stems of certain plants. **pithy** adj short and full of meaning.

pittance ⊕ n very small amount of money.

pituitary n, pl –taries gland at the base of the brain, that helps to control growth (also **pituitary gland**).

pity ⊕ n, pl **pities** 1 sympathy or sorrow for others' suffering. 2 regrettable fact. ♦ v **pitying, pitied** 3 feel pity for. **piteous, pitiable** adj arousing pity. **pitiful** adj 1 arousing pity. 2 woeful, contemptible. **pitifully** adv **pitiless** adj feeling no pity or mercy.

pivot ⊕ n 1 central shaft on which something turns. ♦ v 2 provide with or turn on a pivot. **pivotal** adj of crucial importance.

pixie ⊕ n (in folklore) fairy.

pizza n flat disc of dough covered with a wide variety of savoury toppings and baked.

pizzicato [pit–see–**kah**–toe] adj Music played by plucking the string of a violin etc. with the finger.

placard ⊕ n notice that is carried or displayed in public.

placate ⊕ v make (someone) stop feeling angry or upset. **placatory** adj

place ⊕ n 1 particular part of an area or space. 2 particular town, building, etc. 3 position or point reached. 4 seat or space. 5 duty or right. 6 position of employment. 7 usual position. ♦ v 8 put in a particular place. 9 identify, put in context. 10 make (an order, bet, etc.). **be placed** (of a competitor in a race) be among the first three. **take place** happen, occur.

placebo [plas–**see**–bo] n, pl –**bos**, –**boes** sugar pill etc. given to an unsuspecting patient instead of an active drug.

placenta [plass–**ent**–a] n, pl –**tas**, –**tae** organ formed in the womb during pregnancy, providing nutrients for the fetus. **placental** adj

placid ⊕ adj not easily excited or upset, calm. **placidity** n

plague ⊕ n 1 fast–spreading fatal disease. 2 Hist bubonic plague. 3 widespread infestation. ♦ v **plaguing, plagued** 4 trouble or annoy continually.

plaice n edible European flatfish.

———————— THESAURUS ————————

timbre 11 Inf = **sales talk**, patter, spiel (inf)

pith n 2 = **essence**, core, crux, gist, heart, kernel, nub, point, quintessence, salient point

pittance n = **peanuts** (sl), chicken feed (sl), drop, mite, slave wages, trifle

pity n 1 = **compassion**, charity, clemency, fellow feeling, forbearance, kindness, mercy, sympathy ≠ **anger** 2 = **shame**, bummer (sl), crying shame, misfortune, sin ♦ v 3 = **feel sorry for**, bleed for, feel for, grieve for, have compassion for, sympathize with, weep for

pivot n 1 = **axis**, axle, centre, fulcrum, heart, hinge, hub, kingpin, spindle, swivel ♦ v 2 = **turn**, revolve, rotate, spin, swivel, twirl

pixie n = **elf**, brownie, fairy, sprite

placard n = **notice**, advertisement, bill, poster

placate v = **calm**, appease, assuage, conciliate, humour, mollify, pacify, propitiate, soothe

place n 1 = **spot**, area, location, point, position, site, venue, whereabouts 3 = **position**, grade, rank, station, status 6 = **duty**, affair, charge, concern, function, prerogative, responsibility, right, role 7 = **job**, appointment, employment, position, post ♦ v 8 = **put**, deposit, install, lay, locate, position, rest, set, situate, stand, station, stick (inf) 9 = **identify**, know, put one's finger on, recognize, remember **take place** = **happen**, come about, go on, occur, transpire (inf)

placid adj = **calm**, collected, composed, equable, even–tempered, imperturbable, serene, tranquil, unexcitable, unruffled, untroubled ≠ **emotional**

plague n 1 = **disease**, epidemic, infection,

plaid n 1 long piece of tartan cloth worn as part of Highland dress. 2 tartan cloth or pattern.

plain ❶ adj 1 easy to see or understand. 2 expressed honestly and clearly. 3 without decoration or pattern. 4 not beautiful. 5 simple, ordinary. ♦ n 6 large stretch of level country. **plainly** adv **plainness** n **plain clothes** ordinary clothes, as opposed to uniform. **plain sailing** easy progress.

plaintiff n person who sues in a court of law.

plaintive ❶ adj sad, mournful. **plaintively** adv

plait [platt] n 1 intertwined length of hair. ♦ v 2 intertwine separate strands in a pattern.

plan ❶ n 1 way thought out to do or achieve something. 2 diagram showing the layout or design of something. ♦ v **planning, planned** 3 arrange beforehand. 4 make a diagram of. **planner** n

plane[1] ❶ n 1 an aircraft. 2 Maths flat surface. 3 level of attainment etc. ♦ adj 4 perfectly flat or level. ♦ v 5 glide or skim.

plane[2] n 1 tool for smoothing wood. ♦ v 2 smooth (wood) with a plane.

plane[3] n tree with broad leaves.

planet n large body in space that revolves round the sun or another star. **planetary** adj

planetarium n, pl **-iums, -ia** building where the movements of the stars, planets, etc. are shown by projecting lights on the inside of a dome.

plank n long flat piece of sawn timber.

plankton n minute animals and plants floating in the surface water of a sea or lake.

plant ❶ n 1 living organism that grows in the ground and has no power to move. 2 equipment or machinery used in industrial processes. 3 factory or other industrial premises. ♦ v 4 put in the ground to grow. 5 place firmly in position. 6 Informal put (a person) secretly in an organization to spy. 7 Informal hide (stolen goods etc.) on a person to make him or her seem guilty. **planter** n 1 owner of a plantation.

plantation n 1 estate for the cultivation of tea, tobacco, etc. 2 wood of cultivated trees.

——— THESAURUS ———

pestilence 3 = **affliction**, bane, blight, curse, evil, scourge, torment ♦ v 4 = **pester**, annoy, badger, bother, harass, harry, hassle (inf), tease, torment, torture, trouble, vex

plain adj 1 = **clear**, comprehensible, distinct, evident, manifest, obvious, overt, patent, unambiguous, understandable, unmistakable, visible ≠ **hidden** 2 = **straightforward**, blunt, candid, direct, downright, forthright, frank, honest, open, outspoken, upfront (inf) ≠ **indirect** 3 = **unadorned**, austere, bare, basic, severe, simple, Spartan, stark, unembellished, unfussy, unornamented ≠ **adorned** 4 = **ugly**, ill-favoured, no oil painting (inf), not beautiful, unattractive, unlovely, unprepossessing ≠ **beautiful** 5 = **ordinary**, common, commonplace, everyday, simple, unaffected, unpretentious ≠ **worldly** ♦ n 6 = **flatland**,

grassland, plateau, prairie, steppe, veld

plaintive adj = **sorrowful**, heart-rending, mournful, pathetic, piteous, pitiful, sad

plan n 1 = **scheme**, design, method, plot, programme, proposal, strategy, suggestion, system 2 = **diagram**, blueprint, chart, drawing, layout, map, representation, sketch ♦ v 3 = **devise**, arrange, contrive, design, draft, formulate, organize, outline, plot, scheme, think out

plane[1] n 1 = **aeroplane**, aircraft, jet 2 Maths = **flat surface**, level surface 3 = **level**, condition, degree, position ♦ adj 4 = **level**, even, flat, horizontal, regular, smooth ♦ v 5 = **skim**, glide, sail, skate

plant n 1 = **vegetable**, bush, flower, herb, shrub, weed 2 = **machinery**, apparatus, equipment, gear 3 = **factory**, foundry, mill, shop, works, yard ♦ v 4 = **sow**, put in the ground, scatter, seed, transplant 5 = **place**, establish, fix, found, insert, put,

plaque *n* 1 inscribed commemorative stone or metal plate. 2 filmy deposit on teeth that causes decay.

plasma *n* clear liquid part of blood.

plaster ❶ *n* 1 mixture of lime, sand, etc. for coating walls. 2 adhesive strip of material for dressing cuts etc. ◆ *v* 3 cover with plaster. 4 coat thickly. **plastered** *adj* Slang drunk. **plaster of Paris** white powder which dries to form a hard solid when mixed with water, used for sculptures and casts for broken limbs.

plastic ❶ *n* 1 synthetic material that can be moulded when soft but sets in a hard long–lasting shape. 2 credit cards etc. as opposed to cash. ◆ *adj* 3 made of plastic. 4 easily moulded, pliant. **plasticity** *n* ability to be moulded. **plastic surgery** repair or reconstruction of missing or malformed parts of the body.

Plasticine *n* ® soft coloured modelling material used esp. by children.

plate ❶ *n* 1 shallow dish for holding food. 2 flat thin sheet of metal, glass, etc. 3 thin coating of metal on another metal. 4 dishes or cutlery made of gold or silver. 5 illustration, usu. on fine quality paper, in a book. 6 *Informal* set of false teeth. ◆ *v* 7 cover with a thin coating of gold, silver, or other metal. **plateful** *n* **plate glass** glass in thin sheets, used for mirrors and windows.

plateau ❶ *n, pl* **–teaus, –teaux** 1 area of level high land. 2 stage when there is no change or development.

platform ❶ *n* 1 raised floor. 2 raised area in a station from which passengers board trains. 3 structure in the sea which holds machinery, stores, etc. for drilling an oil well. 4 programme of a political party.

platinum *n* Chem valuable silvery–white metal. **platinum blonde** woman with silvery–blonde hair.

platitude ❶ *n* remark that is true but not interesting or original. **platitudinous** *adj*

platonic *adj* friendly or affectionate but not sexual.

platoon ❶ *n* smaller unit within a company of soldiers.

platter ❶ *n* large dish.

platypus *n* Australian egg–laying amphibious mammal, with dense fur, webbed feet, and a ducklike bill (also **duck–billed platypus**).

plausible ❶ *adj* 1 apparently true or reasonable. 2 persuasive but insincere. **plausibly** *adv* **plausibility** *n*

play ❶ *v* 1 occupy oneself in (a game or recreation). 2 compete against in a game or sport. 3 behave carelessly. 4 act (a part) on the stage. 5 perform on (a musical instrument). 6 cause (a radio, record player, etc.) to give out sound. 7 move lightly or irregularly, flicker. ◆ *n* 8 story performed on stage or broadcast. 9

———————————— THESAURUS ————————————

set

plaster *n* 1 = **mortar**, gypsum, plaster of Paris, stucco 2 = **bandage**, adhesive plaster, dressing, Elastoplast, sticking plaster ◆ *v* 4 = **cover**, coat, daub, overlay, smear, spread

plastic *adj* 4 = **pliant**, ductile, flexible, mouldable, pliable, soft, supple ≠ **hard**

plate *n* 1 = **platter**, dish, trencher (*arch*) 2 = **layer**, panel, sheet, slab 5 = **illustration**, lithograph, print ◆ *v* 7 = **coat**, cover, gild, laminate, overlay

plateau *n* 1 = **upland**, highland, table, tableland 2 = **levelling off**, level, stability, stage

platform *n* 1 = **stage**, dais, podium, rostrum, stand 4 = **policy**, manifesto, objective(s), party line, principle, programme

platitude *n* = **cliché**, banality, commonplace, truism

platoon *n* = **squad**, company, group, outfit (*inf*), patrol, squadron, team

platter *n* = **plate**, dish, salver, tray, trencher (*arch*)

plausible *adj* 1 = **believable**, conceivable, credible, likely, persuasive, possible, probable, reasonable, tenable ≠ **impossible** 2 = **glib**, smooth, smooth–talking, smooth–tongued, specious activities children take part in for amusement. 10 playing of a game. 11 conduct, e.g. *fair play.* 12 (scope for) freedom of movement. **player** *n* playful *adj* lively. **play back** *v* listen to or watch (something recorded). **play down** *v* minimize the importance of. **playing card** one of a set of 52 cards used in card games. **playing field** extensive piece of ground for sport. **play-lunch** *n Aust & NZ* child's mid-morning snack at school. **play off** *v* set (two people) against each other for one's own ends. **play on** *v* exploit or encourage (someone's sympathy or weakness). **plaything** *n* 1 toy. 2 person regarded or treated as a toy. **play up** *v* 1 give prominence to. 2 cause trouble. **playwright** *n* author of plays.

plaza *n* open space or square.

plea **⊕** *n* 1 serious or urgent request, entreaty. 2 statement of a prisoner or defendant. 3 excuse.

please **⊕** *v* 1 give pleasure or satisfaction to. ♦ *adv* 2 polite word of request. **pleasant** *adj* pleasing, enjoyable. **please oneself** do as one likes. **pleased** *adj* **pleasing** *adj* **pleasure** *n* 1 feeling of happiness and satisfaction. 2 something that causes this.

pleat *n* 1 fold made by doubling material back on itself. ♦ *v* 2 arrange (material) in pleats.

plebeian [pleb-ee-an] *adj* 1 of the lower social classes. 2 vulgar or rough. ♦ *n* 3 (also **pleb**) member of the lower social classes.

plectrum *n, pl* **-trums, -tra** small implement for plucking the strings of a guitar etc.

pledge **⊕** *n* 1 solemn promise. 2 something valuable given as a guarantee that a promise will be kept or a debt paid. ♦ *v* 3 promise solemnly. 4 bind by or as if by a pledge.

plenary *adj* (of a meeting) attended by all members.

plenipotentiary *adj* 1 having full powers. ♦ *n, pl* **-aries** 2 diplomat or representative having full powers.

plenitude *n* completeness, abundance.

plenty **⊕** *n* 1 large amount or number. 2 quite enough. **plentiful** *adj* existing in large amounts or numbers. **plentifully** *adv*

plethora **⊕** *n* excess.

pleurisy *n* inflammation of the membrane covering the lungs.

pliable **⊕** *adj* 1 easily bent. 2 easily influenced. **pliability** *n*

THESAURUS

play *v* 1 = **amuse oneself**, entertain oneself, fool, have fun, revel, romp, sport, trifle 2 = **compete**, challenge, contend against, participate, take on, take part 4 = **act**, act the part of, perform, portray, represent ♦ *n* 8 = **drama**, comedy, dramatic piece, farce, pantomime, piece, show, stage show, tragedy 9 = **amusement**, diversion, entertainment, fun, game, pastime, recreation, sport 12 = **space**, elbowroom, latitude, leeway, margin, room, scope

plea *n* 1 = **appeal**, entreaty, intercession, petition, prayer, request, suit, supplication 3 = **excuse**, defence, explanation, justification

please *v* 1 = **delight**, amuse, entertain, gladden, gratify, humour, indulge, satisfy,

suit ≠ **anger**

pledge *n* 1 = **promise**, assurance, covenant, oath, undertaking, vow, warrant, word 2 = **guarantee**, bail, collateral, deposit, pawn, security, surety ♦ *v* 3 = **promise**, contract, engage, give one's oath, give one's word, swear, vow

plenty *n* 1 = **lots** (*inf*), abundance, enough, great deal, heap(s) (*inf*), masses, pile(s) (*inf*), plethora, quantity, stack(s)

plethora *n* = **excess**, glut, overabundance, profusion, superabundance, surfeit, surplus

pliable *adj* 1 = **flexible**, bendable, bendy, malleable, plastic, pliant, supple ≠ **stiff** 2 = **compliant**, adaptable, docile, easily led, impressionable, pliant, receptive, responsive, susceptible, tractable

pliers *pl n* tool with hinged arms and jaws for gripping.

plight¹ ❶ *n* difficult or dangerous situation.

plight² v plight one's troth *Old–fashioned* promise to marry.

plimsolls *pl n* rubber–soled canvas shoes.

plinth *n* slab forming the base of a statue, column, etc.

plod ❶ *v* **plodding, plodded 1** walk with slow heavy steps. **2** work slowly but determinedly. **plodder** *n*

plonk¹ *v* put (something) down heavily and carelessly.

plonk² *n Informal* cheap inferior wine.

plop *n* **1** sound of an object falling into water without a splash. ◆ *v* **plopping, plopped 2** make this sound.

plot¹ ❶ *n* **1** secret plan to do something illegal or wrong. **2** story of a film, novel, etc. ◆ *v* **plotting, plotted 3** plan secretly, conspire. **4** mark the position or course of (a ship or aircraft) on a map. **5** mark and join up (points on a graph).

plot² *n* small patch of land.

plough ❶ *n* **1** agricultural tool for turning over soil. ◆ *v* **2** turn over (earth) with a plough. **3** (usu with *through*) move or work through slowly and laboriously.

ploughman *n* **ploughshare** *n* blade of a plough.

plover *n* shore bird with a straight bill and long pointed wings.

ploy ❶ *n* manoeuvre designed to gain an advantage.

pluck ❶ *v* **1** pull or pick off. **2** pull out the feathers of (a bird for cooking). **3** sound the strings of (a guitar etc.) with the fingers or a plectrum. ◆ *n* **4** courage. **plucky** *adj* brave. **pluckily** *adv* **pluck up** *v* summon up (courage).

plug ❶ *n* **1** thing fitting into and filling a hole. **2** device connecting an appliance to an electricity supply. **3** *Informal* favourable mention of a product etc., to encourage people to buy it. ◆ *v* **plugging, plugged 4** block or seal (a hole or gap) with a plug. **5** *Informal* advertise (a product etc.) by constant repetition. **plug away** *v Informal* work steadily. **plug in** *v* connect (an electrical appliance) to a power source by pushing a plug into a socket.

plum ❶ *n* **1** oval usu. dark red fruit with a stone in the middle. ◆ *adj* **2** dark purplish–red. **3** very desirable.

plumb ❶ *v* **1** understand (something obscure). **2** test with a plumb line.

————————[THESAURUS]————————

≠ **stubborn**

plight¹ *n* = **difficulty**, condition, jam (*inf*), predicament, scrape (*inf*), situation, spot (*inf*), state, trouble

plod *v* **1** = **trudge**, clump, drag, lumber, tramp, tread **2** = **slog**, grind (*inf*), labour, persevere, plough through, plug away (*inf*), soldier on, toil

plot¹ *n* **1** = **plan**, cabal, conspiracy, intrigue, machination, scheme, stratagem **2** = **story**, action, narrative, outline, scenario, story line, subject, theme ◆ *v* **3** = **devise**, collude, conceive, concoct, conspire, contrive, cook up, design, hatch, intrigue, lay (*inf*), machinate, manoeuvre, plan, scheme **4** = **chart**, calculate, locate, map, mark, outline

plot² *n* = **patch**, allotment, area, ground, lot, parcel, tract

plough *v* **2** = **turn over**, cultivate, dig, till **3** (usu. with *through*) = **forge**, cut, drive, plunge, press, push, wade

ploy *n* = **tactic**, device, dodge, manoeuvre, move, ruse, scheme, stratagem, trick, wile

pluck *v* **1** = **pull out** *or* **off**, collect, draw, gather, harvest, pick **3** = **strum**, finger, pick, twang ◆ *n* **4** = **courage**, backbone, boldness, bottle (*Brit sl*), bravery, grit, guts (*inf*), nerve

plug *n* **1** = **stopper**, bung, cork, spigot **3** *Inf* = **mention**, advert (*Brit inf*), advertisement, hype, publicity, push ◆ *v* **4** = **seal**, block, bung, close, cork, fill, pack, stop, stopper, stop up, stuff **5** *Inf* = **mention**, advertise, build up, hype, promote, publicize, push **plug away** *Inf* = **slog**, grind (*inf*), labour, peg away, plod, toil

plum *adj* **3** = **choice**, best, first–class, prize

♦ *adv* 3 exactly. **plumb the depths of** experience the worst extremes of (an unpleasant quality or emotion). **plumber** *n* person who fits and repairs pipes and fixtures for water and drainage systems. **plumbing** *n* pipes and fixtures used in water and drainage systems. **plumb in** *v* connect (an appliance such as a washing machine) to a water supply. **plumb line** string with a weight at the end, used to test the depth of water or to test whether something is vertical.

plume ❶ *n* feather, esp. one worn as an ornament.

plummet ❶ *v* –meting, –meted plunge downward.

plump¹ ❶ *adj* moderately or attractively fat. **plump up** *v* make (a pillow) fuller or rounded.

plump² ❶ *v* sit or fall heavily and suddenly. **plump for** *v* choose.

plunder ❶ *v* 1 take by force, esp. in time of war. ♦ *n* 2 things plundered, spoils.

plunge ❶ *v* 1 put or throw forcibly or suddenly (into). 2 descend steeply. ♦ *n* 3 plunging, dive. **take the plunge** *Informal* embark on a risky enterprise. **plunger** *n* rubber suction cup used to clear blocked pipes. **plunge into** *v* become deeply involved in.

plural *adj* 1 of or consisting of more than one. ♦ *n* 2 word indicating more than one.

plus ❶ *prep, adj* 1 indicating addition. ♦ *adj* 2 more than zero. 3 positive. 4 advantageous. ♦ *n* 5 sign (+) denoting addition. 6 advantage.

✓ **WORD TIP**

Avoid using *plus* to mean 'additionally' except in very informal contexts.

---

plush ❶ *n* 1 fabric with long velvety pile. ♦ *adj* 2 (also **plushy**) luxurious.

ply¹ ❶ *v* **plying, plied** 1 work at (a job or trade). 2 use (a tool). 3 (of a ship) travel regularly along or between. **ply with** *v* supply with or subject to persistently.

ply² ❶ *n* thickness of wool, fabric, etc.

PM prime minister.

p.m. 1 after noon. 2 postmortem.

pneumatic *adj* worked by or inflated with wind or air.

pneumonia *n* inflammation of the lungs.

PO 1 postal order. 2 Post Office.

poach¹ ❶ *v* 1 catch (animals) illegally on someone else's land. 2 encroach on or steal something belonging to someone else. **poacher** *n*

poach² *v* simmer (food) gently in liquid.

THESAURUS

---

plumb *v* 1 = **delve**, explore, fathom, gauge, go into, penetrate, probe, unravel ♦ *adv* 1 = **exactly**, bang, precisely, slap, spot–on (*Brit inf*) **plumb line = weight**, lead, plumb bob, plummet

plume *n* = **feather**, crest, pinion, quill

plummet *v* = **plunge**, crash, descend, dive, drop down, fall, nose–dive, tumble

plump¹ *adj* = **chubby**, corpulent, dumpy, fat, podgy, roly–poly, rotund, round, stout, tubby

plump² *v* = **flop**, drop, dump, fall, sink, slump **plump for = choose**, back, come down in favour of, favour, opt for, side with, support

plunder *v* 1 = **loot**, pillage, raid, ransack, rifle, rob, sack, strip ♦ *n* 2 = **loot**, booty,

ill–gotten gains, pillage, prize, spoils, swag (*sl*)

plunge *v* 1 = **throw**, career, cast, charge, dash, hurtle, jump, pitch, rush, tear 2 = **descend**, dip, dive, drop, fall, nose–dive, plummet, sink, tumble ♦ *n* 3 = **dive**, descent, drop, fall, jump

plus *prep* 1 = **and**, added to, coupled with, with ♦ *n* 6 = **advantage**, asset, benefit, bonus, extra, gain, good point

plush *adj* 2 = **luxurious**, de luxe, lavish, luxury, opulent, rich, sumptuous

ply¹ *v* 1 = **work at**, carry on, exercise, follow, practise, pursue 2 = **use**, employ, handle, manipulate, wield

ply² *n* = **thickness**, fold, layer, leaf, sheet, strand

pocket ⊕ *n* 1 small bag sewn into clothing for carrying things. 2 pouchlike container, esp. for catching balls at the edge of a snooker table. 3 isolated or distinct group or area. ◆ *v* pocketing, pocketed 4 put into one's pocket. 5 take secretly or dishonestly. ◆ *adj* 6 small. out of pocket having made a loss. pocket money 1 small regular allowance given to children by parents. 2 money for small personal expenses.

pod ⊕ *n* long narrow seed case of peas, beans, etc.

podgy ⊕ *adj* podgier, podgiest short and fat.

podium ⊕ *n, pl* –diums, –dia small raised platform for a conductor or speaker.

poem ⊕ *n* imaginative piece of writing in rhythmic lines.

poep *n Aust & NZ slang* emission of gas from the anus.

poet ⊕ *n* writer of poems. poetry *n* 1 poems. 2 art of writing poems. 3 beautiful or pleasing quality.

poignant ⊕ *adj* sharply painful to the feelings. poignancy *n*

point ⊕ *n* 1 main idea in a discussion, argument, etc. 2 aim or purpose. 3 detail or item. 4 characteristic. 5 particular position, stage, or time. 6 dot indicating decimals. 7 full stop. 8 sharp end. 9

headland. 10 unit for recording a value or score. 11 one of the direction marks of a compass. 12 movable rail used to change a train to other rails. 13 electrical socket. ◆ *pl* 14 electrical contacts in the distributor of an engine. ◆ *v* 15 show the direction or position of something or draw attention to it by extending a finger or other pointed object towards it. 16 direct or face towards. 17 finish or repair the joints in brickwork with mortar. 18 (of a gun dog) show where game is by standing rigidly with the muzzle towards it. on the point of very shortly going to. pointed *adj* 1 having a sharp end. 2 (of a remark) obviously directed at a particular person. pointedly *adv* pointer *n* 1 helpful hint. 2 indicator on a measuring instrument. 3 breed of gun dog. pointless *adj* meaningless, irrelevant. point–blank *adj* 1 fired at a very close target. 2 (of a remark or question) direct, blunt. ◆ *adv* 3 directly or bluntly. point duty control of traffic by a policeman at a road junction. point of view way of considering something. point–to–point *n* horse race across open country.

poise ⊕ *n* calm dignified manner. poised *adj* 1 absolutely ready. 2 behaving with or showing poise.

poison ⊕ *n* 1 substance that kills or injures

poach¹ *v* 2 = **encroach**, appropriate, infringe, intrude, trespass

pocket *n* 2 = **pouch**, bag, compartment, receptacle, sack ◆ *v* 5 = **steal**, appropriate, filch, lift (*inf*), pilfer, purloin, take ◆ *adj* 6 = **small**, abridged, compact, concise, little, miniature, portable

pod *n* = **shell**, hull, husk, shuck

podgy *adj* = **tubby**, chubby, dumpy, fat, plump, roly–poly, rotund, stout

podium *n* = **platform**, dais, rostrum, stage

poem *n* = **verse**, lyric, ode, rhyme, song, sonnet

poet *n* = **bard**, lyricist, rhymer, versifier

poignant *adj* = **moving**, bitter, distressing, gut–wrenching, heart–rending, intense,

painful, pathetic, sad, touching

point *n* 1 = **essence**, crux, drift, gist, heart, import, meaning, nub, pith, question, subject, thrust 2 = **aim**, end, goal, intent, intention, motive, object, objective, purpose, reason 3 = **item**, aspect, detail, feature, particular 4 = **characteristic**, aspect, attribute, quality, respect, trait 5 = **place**, instant, juncture, location, moment, position, site, spot, stage, time, very minute 7 = **full stop**, dot, mark, period, stop 8 = **end**, apex, prong, sharp end, spike, spur, summit, tip, top 9 = **headland**, cape, head, promontory 10 = **unit**, score, tally ◆ *v* 15 = **indicate**, call attention to, denote, designate, direct,

when swallowed or absorbed. ◆ v 2 give
poison to. 3 have a harmful or evil effect
on, spoil. **poisoner** n **poisonous** adj
poison–pen letter malicious anonymous
letter.

poke ⊙ v 1 jab or prod with one's finger, a
stick, etc. 2 thrust forward or out. ◆ n 3
poking. **poky** adj small and cramped.

poker n card game in which players bet on
the hands dealt. **poker–faced** adj
expressionless.

pole¹ ⊙ n long rounded piece of wood etc.

pole² ⊙ n 1 point furthest north or south
on the earth's axis of rotation. 2 either of
the opposite ends of a magnet or electric
cell.

poleaxe v hit or stun with a heavy blow.

polecat n small animal of the weasel
family.

police ⊙ n 1 organized force in a state
which keeps law and order. ◆ v 2 control
or watch over with police or a similar
body. **policeman, policewoman** n
member of a police force.

policy¹ ⊙ n, pl **–cies** plan of action
adopted by a person, group, or state.

policy² n, pl **–cies** document containing an
insurance contract.

polio n disease affecting the spinal cord,
which often causes paralysis (also
poliomyelitis).

polish ⊙ v 1 make smooth and shiny by
rubbing. 2 make more nearly perfect. ◆ n
3 substance used for polishing. 4 pleasing
elegant style. **polished** adj 1
accomplished. 2 done or performed well
or professionally. **polish off** v finish
completely, dispose of.

polite ⊙ adj 1 showing consideration for
others in one's manners, speech, etc. 2
socially correct or refined. **politely** adv
politeness n

politics ⊙ n 1 winning and using of power
to govern society. 2 (study of) the art of
government. 3 person's beliefs about how
a country should be governed. **political**
adj of the state, government, or public
administration. **politically** adv **politically
correct** (of language) intended to avoid
any implied prejudice. **political prisoner**
person imprisoned because of his or her
political beliefs. **politician** n person
actively engaged in politics, esp. a
member of parliament.

polka n 1 lively 19th–century dance. 2
music for this. **polka dots** pattern of bold

———————————— THESAURUS ————————————

show, signify 16 = **aim**, direct, level, train

poise n = **composure**, aplomb, assurance,
calmness, cool (sl), dignity, presence,
sang–froid, self–possession

poison n 1 = **toxin**, bane, venom ◆ v
2 = **murder**, give (someone) poison, kill
3 = **corrupt**, contaminate, defile, deprave,
infect, pervert, pollute, subvert, taint,
undermine, warp

poke v 1 = **jab**, dig, nudge, prod, push,
shove, stab, stick, thrust ◆ n 3 = **jab**, dig,
nudge, prod, thrust

pole¹ n = **rod**, bar, mast, post, shaft, spar,
staff, stick

pole² n 1 = **extremity**, antipode, limit,
terminus

police n 1 = **the law** (inf), boys in blue (inf),
constabulary, fuzz (sl), police force, the
Old Bill (sl) ◆ v 2 = **control**, guard, patrol,

protect, regulate, watch

policy¹ n = **procedure**, action, approach,
code, course, custom, plan, practice, rule,
scheme

polish v 1 = **shine**, brighten, buff, burnish,
rub, smooth, wax 2 = **perfect**, brush up,
enhance, finish, improve, refine, touch up
◆ n 3 = **varnish**, wax 4 = **sheen**,
brightness, finish, glaze, gloss, lustre
5 = **style**, breeding, class (inf), elegance,
finesse, finish, grace, refinement

polite adj 1 = **mannerly**, civil, complaisant,
courteous, gracious, respectful, well–
behaved, well–mannered ≠ **insulting**
2 = **refined**, civilized, cultured, elegant,
genteel, polished, sophisticated, well–bred
≠ **unrefined**

politics n 2 = **statesmanship**, affairs of
state, civics, government, political science

spots on fabric.

poll ❶ *n* **1** (also **opinion poll**) questioning of a random sample of people to find out general opinion. **2** voting. **3** number of votes recorded. ◆ *v* **4** receive (votes). **5** question in an opinion poll. **pollster** *n* person who conducts opinion polls. **polling station** building where people vote in an election.

pollen *n* fine dust produced by flowers to fertilize other flowers. **pollinate** *v* fertilize with pollen. **pollen count** measure of the amount of pollen in the air, esp. as a warning to people with hay fever.

pollute ❶ *v* contaminate with something poisonous or harmful. **pollution** *n* **pollutant** *n* something that pollutes.

polo *n* game like hockey played by teams of players on horseback. **polo neck** sweater with tight turned-over collar.

poltergeist *n* spirit believed to move furniture and throw objects around.

polyester *n* synthetic material used to make plastics and textile fibres.

polygamy [pol-**ig**-a-mee] *n* practice of having more than one husband or wife at the same time. **polygamous** *adj* **polygamist** *n*

polygon *n* geometrical figure with three or more angles and sides. **polygonal** *adj*

polystyrene *n* synthetic material used esp. as white rigid foam for packing and insulation.

polythene *n* light plastic used for bags etc.

polyunsaturated *adj* of a group of fats that do not form cholesterol in the blood.

polyurethane *n* synthetic material used esp. in paints.

pom *n Aust & NZ slang* person from England (also **pommy**).

pomegranate *n* round tropical fruit with a thick rind containing many seeds in a red pulp.

pommel *n* **1** raised part on the front of a saddle. **2** knob at the top of a sword hilt.

pomp ❶ *n* stately display or ceremony.

pompom *n* decorative ball of tufted wool, silk, etc.

pompous ❶ *adj* foolishly serious and grand, self-important. **pomposity** *n*

pond ❶ *n* small area of still water.

ponder ❶ *v* think thoroughly or deeply (about).

ponderous ❶ *adj* **1** serious and dull. **2** heavy and unwieldy. **3** (of movement) slow and clumsy.

pong *v, n Informal* (give off) a strong unpleasant smell.

pontiff *n* the Pope. **pontificate** *v* **1** state one's opinions as if they were the only possible correct ones. ◆ *n* **2** period of office of a Pope.

pontoon¹ *n* floating platform supporting a temporary bridge.

pontoon² *n* gambling card game.

pony *n, pl* **ponies** small horse. **ponytail** *n* long hair tied in one bunch at the back of the head.

———————— THESAURUS ————————

poll *n* **1** (also **opinion poll**) = **canvass**, census, sampling, survey **2** = **vote**, ballot, count, voting **3** = **figures**, returns, tally ◆ *v* **4** = **tally**, register **5** = **question**, ballot, canvass, interview, sample, survey

pollute *v* = **contaminate**, dirty, foul, infect, poison, soil, spoil, stain, taint ≠ **clean**

pomp *n* **a** = **show**, display, grandiosity, ostentation **b** = **ceremony**, flourish, grandeur, magnificence, pageant, pageantry, splendour, state

pompous *adj* **a** = **grandiloquent**, boastful, bombastic, high-flown, inflated ≠ **direct b**

= **self-important**, arrogant, grandiose, ostentatious, pretentious, puffed up, showy ≠ **simple**

pond *n* = **pool**, duck pond, fish pond, millpond, small lake, tarn

ponder *v* = **think**, brood, cogitate, consider, contemplate, deliberate, meditate, mull over, muse, reflect, ruminate

ponderous *adj* **1** = **dull**, heavy, long-winded, pedantic, tedious **2** = **unwieldy**, bulky, cumbersome, heavy, huge, massive, weighty **3** = **clumsy**, awkward, heavy-

poodle n dog with curly hair often clipped fancifully.

pool¹ ❶ n **1** small body of still water. **2** puddle of spilt liquid. **3** swimming pool.

pool² ❶ n **1** shared fund or group of workers or resources. **2** game like snooker. ◆ pl **3** short for FOOTBALL POOLS. ◆ v **4** put in a common fund.

poop n raised part at the back of a sailing ship.

poor ❶ adj **1** having little money and few possessions. **2** less, smaller, or weaker than is needed or expected. **3** inferior. **4** unlucky, pitiable. **poorly** adv **1** in a poor manner. ◆ adj **2** not in good health.

pop¹ ❶ v **popping, popped 1** make or cause to make a small explosive sound. **2** *Informal* go, put, or come unexpectedly or suddenly. ◆ n **3** small explosive sound. **4** nonalcoholic fizzy drink. **popcorn** n grains of maize heated until they puff up and burst.

pop² n **1** music of general appeal, esp. to young people. ◆ adj **2** popular. **pop art** movement in modern art that uses the methods, styles, and themes of popular culture and mass media.

Pope n head of the Roman Catholic Church.

poplar n tall slender tree.

poplin n ribbed cotton material.

poppadom n thin round crisp Indian bread.

poppy n, pl **–pies** plant with a large red flower.

populace ❶ n the ordinary people.

popular ❶ adj **1** widely liked and admired. **2** of or for the public in general. **popularly** adv **popularity** n **popularize** v **1** make popular. **2** make (something technical or specialist) easily understood.

populate ❶ v **1** live in, inhabit. **2** fill with inhabitants. **population** n **1** all the people who live in a particular place. **2** the number of people living in a particular place. **populous** adj densely populated.

porcelain n **1** fine china. **2** objects made of it.

porch n covered approach to the entrance of a building.

porcupine n animal covered with long pointed quills.

pore ❶ n tiny opening in the skin or in the surface of a plant.

pork n pig meat. **porker** n pig raised for food.

THESAURUS

footed, lumbering ≠ **light**

pool¹ n **1** = **pond**, lake, mere, puddle, tarn **3** = **swimming pool**, swimming bath

pool² n **1 a** = **kitty**, bank, funds, jackpot, pot **b** = **syndicate**, collective, consortium, group, team, trust ◆ v **4** = **combine**, amalgamate, join forces, league, merge, put together, share

poor adj **1** = **impoverished**, broke (*inf*), destitute, down and out, hard up (*inf*), impecunious, indigent, needy, on the breadline, penniless, penurious, poverty–stricken, short, skint (*Brit sl*), stony–broke (*Brit sl*) ≠ **rich 2** = **meagre**, deficient, inadequate, incomplete, insufficient, lacking, measly, scant, scanty, skimpy ≠ **complete 3** = **inferior**, below par, low–grade, mediocre, no great shakes (*inf*), rotten (*inf*), rubbishy, second–rate,

substandard, unsatisfactory **4** = **unfortunate**, hapless, ill–fated, pitiable, unlucky, wretched ≠ **successful**

pop¹ v **1** = **burst**, bang, crack, explode, go off, snap ◆ n **3** = **bang**, burst, crack, explosion, noise, report

Pope n = **Holy Father**, Bishop of Rome, pontiff, Vicar of Christ

populace n = **people**, general public, hoi polloi, masses, mob, multitude

popular adj **1** = **well–liked**, accepted, approved, fashionable, favourite, in, in demand, in favour, liked, sought–after ≠ **hated 2** = **common**, conventional, current, general, prevailing, prevalent, universal ≠ **rare**

populate v **1** = **inhabit**, colonize, live in, occupy, settle

pore n = **opening**, hole, orifice, outlet

pornography ⊕ n writing, films, or pictures designed to be sexually exciting. **pornographer** n producer of pornography. **pornographic** adj

porpoise n fishlike sea mammal.

porridge n 1 breakfast food made of oatmeal cooked in water or milk. 2 Slang term in prison.

port¹ ⊕ n (town with) a harbour.

port² n left side of a ship or aircraft when facing the front of it.

port³ n strong sweet wine, usu. red.

port⁴ n 1 opening in the side of a ship. 2 porthole.

portable ⊕ adj easily carried. **portability** n

portcullis n grating suspended above a castle gateway, that can be lowered to block the entrance.

portend ⊕ v be a sign of.

porter¹ ⊕ n 1 man who carries luggage. 2 hospital worker who transfers patients between rooms etc.

porter² ⊕ n doorman or gatekeeper of a building.

portfolio n, pl –os 1 (flat case for carrying) examples of an artist's work. 2 area of responsibility of a government minister. 3 list of investments held by an investor.

portico n, pl –coes, –cos porch or covered walkway with columns supporting the roof.

portion ⊕ n 1 part or share. 2 helping of food for one person. 3 destiny or fate.

portly ⊕ adj –lier, –liest rather fat.

portmanteau n, pl –teaus, –teaux 1 Old–fashioned large suitcase that opens into two compartments. ♦ adj 2 combining aspects of different things.

portray ⊕ v describe or represent by artistic means, as in writing or film. **portrait** n picture of a person. **portrayal** n

pose ⊕ v 1 place in or take up a particular position to be photographed or drawn. 2 raise (a problem). 3 ask (a question). ♦ n 4 position while posing. 5 behaviour adopted for effect. **pose as** pretend to be. **poser** n 1 puzzling question. 2 poseur. **poseur** n person who behaves in an affected way to impress others.

posh ⊕ adj Informal 1 smart, luxurious. 2 affectedly upper–class.

position ⊕ n 1 place. 2 usual or expected place. 3 way in which something is placed or arranged. 4 attitude, point of view. 5

———— THESAURUS ————

pornography n = **obscenity**, dirt, filth, indecency, porn (inf), smut

port¹ n = **harbour**, anchorage, haven, seaport

portable adj = **light**, compact, convenient, easily carried, handy, manageable, movable

portend v = **foretell**, augur, betoken, bode, foreshadow, herald, indicate, predict, prognosticate, promise, warn of

porter¹ n 1 = **baggage attendant**, bearer, carrier

porter² n = **doorman**, caretaker, concierge, gatekeeper, janitor

portion n 1 a = **part**, bit, fragment, morsel, piece, scrap, section, segment b = **share**, allocation, allotment, allowance, lot, measure, quantity, quota, ration 2 = **helping**, piece, serving 3 = **destiny**, fate, fortune, lot, luck **portion out** ♦ v

= **divide**, allocate, allot, apportion, deal, distribute, dole out, share out

portly adj = **stout**, burly, corpulent, fat, fleshy, heavy, large, plump

portray v a = **represent**, depict, draw, figure, illustrate, paint, picture, sketch b = **describe**, characterize, depict, put in words c = **play**, act the part of, represent

pose v 1 = **position**, arrange yourself, model, sit, strike a pose ♦ n 4 = **posture**, attitude, bearing, position, stance 5 = **act**, affectation, air, facade, front, mannerism, masquerade, posturing, pretence, role **pose as** ♦ v = **impersonate**, masquerade as, pass oneself off as, pretend to be, profess to be

posh adj Inf 1 = **smart**, classy (sl), grand, luxurious, ritzy (sl), stylish, swanky (inf), swish (inf, chiefly Brit) 2 = **upper–class**, high–class, up–market social standing. 6 job. ♦ v 7 place.

positive ❶ *adj* 1 feeling no doubts, certain. 2 confident, hopeful. 3 helpful, providing encouragement. 4 absolute, downright. 5 *Maths* greater than zero. 6 (of an electrical charge) having a deficiency of electrons. **positively** *adv* **positive discrimination** provision of special opportunities for a disadvantaged group.

possess ❶ *v* 1 have as one's property. 2 (of a feeling, belief, etc.) have complete control of, dominate. **possessor** *n* **possession** *n* 1 state of possessing, ownership. ♦ *pl* 2 things a person possesses. **possessive** *adj* 1 wanting all the attention or love of another person. 2 (of a word) indicating the person or thing that something belongs to. **possessiveness** *n*

possible ❶ *adj* 1 able to exist, happen, or be done. 2 worthy of consideration. ♦ *n* 3 person or thing that might be suitable or chosen. **possibility** *n, pl* **-ties. possibly** *adv* perhaps, not necessarily.

possum *n* same as OPOSSUM. **play possum** pretend to be dead or asleep to deceive an opponent.

post¹ ❶ *n* 1 official system of delivering letters and parcels. 2 (single collection or delivery of) letters and parcels sent by this system. ♦ *v* 3 send by post. **keep someone posted** supply someone regularly with the latest information. **postage** *n* charge for sending a letter or parcel by post. **postal** *adj* **postal order** written money order sent by post and cashed at a post office by the person who receives it. **postbag** *n* 1 postman's bag. 2 post received by a magazine, famous person, etc. **postbox** *n* same as LETTER BOX (sense 2). **postcode** *n* system of letters and numbers used to aid the sorting of mail. **postie** *Aust, NZ & Scot informal* postman. **postman, postwoman** *n* person who collects and delivers post. **postmark** *n* official mark stamped on letters showing place and date of posting. **postmaster, postmistress** *n* official in charge of a post office. **post office** place where postal business is conducted. **post shop** *NZ* shop providing postal services.

post² ❶ *n* 1 length of wood, concrete, etc. fixed upright to support or mark something. ♦ *v* 2 put up (a notice) in a public place.

post³ ❶ *n* 1 job. 2 position to which someone, esp. a soldier, is assigned for duty. 3 military establishment. ♦ *v* 4 send (a person) to a new place to work. 5 put (a guard etc.) on duty.

post- *prefix* after, later than, e.g. *postwar*.

THESAURUS

position *n* 1 = **place**, area, bearings, locale, location, point, post, situation, spot, station, whereabouts 3 = **posture**, arrangement, attitude, pose, stance 4 = **attitude**, belief, opinion, outlook, point of view, slant, stance, view, viewpoint 5 = **status**, importance, place, prestige, rank, reputation, standing, station, stature 6 = **job**, duty, employment, occupation, office, place, post, role, situation ♦ *v* 7 = **place**, arrange, lay out, locate, put, set, stand

positive *adj* 1, 2 = **certain**, assured, confident, convinced, sure ≠ **uncertain** 3 = **helpful**, beneficial, constructive, practical, productive, progressive, useful ≠ **useless** 4 a = **definite**, absolute, categorical, certain, clear, conclusive, decisive, explicit, express, firm, real b = **absolute**, complete, consummate, downright, out-and-out, perfect, thorough, utter ≠ **uncertain**

possess *v* 1 = **have**, enjoy, hold, own 2 = **dominate**, control, seize, take over

possible *adj* 1 a = **conceivable**, credible, hypothetical, imaginable, likely, potential b = **likely**, hopeful, potential, probable, promising ≠ **impossible** c = **feasible**, attainable, doable, practicable, realizable, viable, workable ≠ **impossible**

post¹ *n* 1 = **mail**, collection, delivery, postal service ♦ *v* 3 = **send**, dispatch, mail,

posterior *n* **1** buttocks. ◆ *adj* **2** behind, at the back of.

posterity ⊕ *n* future generations, descendants.

posthaste *adv* with great speed.

posthumous [poss–tume–uss] *adj* **1** occurring after one's death. **2** **posthumously** *adv*

postmortem *n* medical examination of a body to establish the cause of death.

postpone ⊕ *v* put off to a later time. **postponement** *n*

postscript ⊕ *n* passage added at the end of a letter.

postulate ⊕ *v* assume to be true as the basis of an argument or theory.

posture ⊕ *n* **1** position or way in which someone stands, walks, etc. ◆ *v* **2** behave in an exaggerated way to get attention.

posy *n, pl* **–sies** small bunch of flowers.

pot¹ ⊕ *n* **1** round deep container. **2** teapot. ◆ *pl* **3** *Informal* a lot. ◆ *v* **potting, potted 4** plant in a pot. **5** *Snooker* hit (a ball) into a pocket. **potted** *adj* **1** grown in a pot. **2** (of meat or fish) cooked or preserved in a pot. **3** *Informal* abridged. **potbelly** *n* bulging belly. **potsherd** *n* broken fragment of pottery. **pot shot** shot taken without

aiming carefully. **potting shed** shed where plants are potted.

pot² *n Slang* cannabis.

potassium *n Chem* silvery metallic element.

potato *n, pl* **–toes** roundish starchy vegetable that grows underground.

potent ⊕ *adj* **1** having great power or influence. **2** (of a male) capable of having sexual intercourse. **potency** *n*

potentate *n* ruler or monarch.

potential ⊕ *adj* **1** possible but not yet actual. ◆ *n* **2** ability or talent not yet fully used. **3** *Electricity* level of electric pressure. **potentially** *adv* **potentiality** *n, pl* **–ties**

pothole *n* **1** hole in the surface of a road. **2** deep hole in a limestone area. **potholing** *n* sport of exploring underground caves. **potholer** *n*

potion ⊕ *n* dose of medicine or poison.

potpourri [po–poor–ee] *n* **1** fragrant mixture of dried flower petals. **2** assortment or medley.

potter¹ *n* person who makes pottery.

potter² ⊕ *v* be busy in a pleasant but aimless way.

potty¹ *adj* **–tier, –tiest** *Informal* crazy or silly.

——————— THESAURUS ———————

transmit **keep someone posted = notify**, advise, brief, fill in on (*inf*), inform, report to

post² *n* **1** = **support**, column, picket, pillar, pole, shaft, stake, upright ◆ *v* **2** = **put up**, affix, display, pin up

post³ *n* **1** = **job**, appointment, assignment, employment, office, place, position, situation **2** = **station**, beat, place, position ◆ *v* **4** = **station**, assign, place, position, put, situate

posterity *n* **a** = **future**, succeeding generations **b** = **descendants**, children, family, heirs, issue, offspring, progeny

postpone *v* = **put off**, adjourn, defer, delay, put back, put on the back burner (*inf*), shelve, suspend

postscript *n* = **P.S.**, addition, afterthought, supplement

postulate *v* = **presuppose**, assume, hypothesize, posit, propose, suppose, take for granted, theorize

posture *n* **1** = **bearing**, attitude, carriage, disposition, set, stance ◆ *v* **2** = **show off** (*inf*), affect, pose, put on airs

pot¹ *n* **1** = **container**, bowl, pan, vessel

potent *adj* = **powerful**, authoritative, commanding, dominant, dynamic, forceful, influential, mighty, strong, vigorous ≠ **ineffective**

potential *adj* **1** = **possible**, dormant, future, hidden, inherent, latent, likely, promising ◆ *n* **2** = **ability**, aptitude, capability, capacity, possibility, potentiality, power, wherewithal

potion *n* = **concoction**, brew, dose, draught, elixir, mixture, philtre

potter² *v* = **mess about**, dabble, footle

potty[2] *n, pl* **–ties** bowl used by a small child as a toilet.

pouch ● *n* **1** small bag. **2** baglike pocket of skin on an animal.

poultice [**pole**–tiss] *n* moist dressing, often heated, applied to inflamed skin.

poultry *n* domestic fowls.

pounce ● *v* **1** spring upon suddenly to attack or capture. ◆ *n* **2** pouncing.

pound[1] *n* **1** monetary unit of Britain and some other countries. **2** unit of weight equal to 0.454 kg.

pound[2] ● *v* **1** hit heavily and repeatedly. **2** crush to pieces or powder. **3** (of the heart) throb heavily. **4** run heavily.

pound[3] ● *n* enclosure for stray animals or officially removed vehicles.

pour ● *v* **1** flow or cause to flow out in a stream. **2** rain heavily. **3** come or go in large numbers.

pout ● *v* **1** thrust out one's lips, look sulky. ◆ *n* **2** pouting look.

poverty ● *n* **1** state of being without enough food or money. **2** lack of, scarcity.

powder ● *n* **1** substance in the form of tiny loose particles. **2** medicine or cosmetic in this form. ◆ *v* **3** apply powder to. **powdery** *adj*

power ● *n* **1** ability to do or act. **2** strength. **3** position of authority or control. **4** person or thing having authority. **5** *Maths* product from continuous multiplication of a number by itself. **6** *Physics* rate at which work is done. **7** electricity supply. **8** particular form of energy, e.g. *nuclear power*. **powered** *adj* having or operated by mechanical or electrical power. **powerful** *adj* **powerless** *adj* **power cut** temporary interruption in the supply of electricity. **power station** installation for generating and distributing electric power.

pp (in signing a document) for and on behalf of.

✓ **WORD TIP**

The original meaning of *pp* (Latin *per procurationem*) is 'by delegation to', so traditionally *pp* is written before the name of the typist to show that she or he has signed the letter on behalf of someone else. Nowadays the meaning has been overtaken by the sense of 'on behalf of' and *pp* is often written before the name of the person who composed the letter.

PQ Quebec.

(*inf*), tinker

pouch *n* **1** = **bag**, container, pocket, purse, sack

pounce *v* **1** = **spring**, attack, fall upon, jump, leap at, strike, swoop ◆ *n* **2** = **spring**, assault, attack, bound, jump, leap, swoop

pound[2] *v* **1** = **beat**, batter, belabour, clobber (*sl*), hammer, pummel, strike, thrash, thump **2** = **crush**, powder, pulverize **3** = **pulsate**, beat, palpitate, pulse, throb **4** = **stomp** (*inf*), march, thunder, tramp

pound[3] *n* = **enclosure**, compound, pen, yard

pour *v* **1** = **flow**, course, decant, emit, gush, let flow, run, rush, spew, spill, splash, spout, stream **2** = **rain**, bucket down (*inf*), pelt (down), teem **3** = **stream**, crowd, swarm, teem, throng

pout *v* **1** = **sulk**, glower, look petulant, pull a long face ◆ *n* **2** = **sullen look**, glower, long face

poverty *n* **1** = **pennilessness**, beggary, destitution, hardship, indigence, insolvency, need, penury, privation, want ≠ **comfort 2** = **scarcity**, dearth, deficiency, insufficiency, lack, paucity, shortage ≠ **abundance**

powder *n* **1** = **dust**, fine grains, loose particles, talc ◆ *v* **3** = **dust**, cover, dredge, scatter, sprinkle, strew

power *n* **1** = **ability**, capability, capacity, competence, competency, faculty, potential ≠ **inability 2** = **strength**, brawn, energy, force, forcefulness, intensity,

PR 1 proportional representation. **2** public relations.

practical ❶ *adj* **1** involving experience or actual use rather than theory. **2** sensible, useful, and effective. **3** good at making or doing things. **4** in effect though not in name. ♦ *n* **5** examination in which something has to be done or made. **practically** *adv* **practical joke** trick intended to make someone look foolish.

practise ❶ *v* **1** do repeatedly so as to gain skill. **2** take part in, follow (a religion etc.). **3** work at, e.g. *practise medicine.* **4** do habitually. **practice** *n* something done regularly or habitually.

> ✓ **WORD TIP**
> Note the *–ise* ending for the verb, with *–ice* for the noun (*practice*).

pragmatic ❶ *adj* concerned with practical consequences rather than theory. **pragmatism** *n* **pragmatist** *n*

prairie *n* large treeless area of grassland, esp. in N America and Canada.

praise ❶ *v* **1** express approval or admiration of (someone or something). **2** express honour and thanks to (one's God). ♦ *n* **3** something said or written to show approval or admiration. **sing someone's praises** praise someone highly. **praiseworthy** *adj*

pram *n* four-wheeled carriage for a baby, pushed by hand.

prance ❶ *v* walk with exaggerated bouncing steps.

prank ❶ *n* mischievous trick.

prattle ❶ *v* **1** chatter in a childish or foolish way. ♦ *n* **2** childish or foolish talk.

prawn *n* edible shellfish like a large shrimp.

pray ❶ *v* **1** say prayers. **2** ask earnestly, entreat. **prayer** *n* **1** thanks or appeal addressed to one's God. **2** set form of words used in praying. **3** earnest request.

pre– *prefix* before, beforehand, e.g. *prenatal; prerecorded; preshrunk.*

preach ❶ *v* **1** give a talk on a religious theme as part of a church service. **2** speak in support of (an idea, principle, etc.). **preacher** *n*

might, muscle, potency, vigour ≠ **weakness 3 = control**, ascendancy, authority, command, dominance, domination, dominion, influence, mana (*NZ*), mastery, prerogative, privilege, rule

practical *adj* **1 = functional**, applied, empirical, experimental, factual, pragmatic, realistic, utilitarian ≠ **unrealistic 2 = sensible**, doable, down-to-earth, feasible, matter-of-fact, mundane, ordinary, practicable, realistic, serviceable, useful, workable ≠ **impossible 3 = skilled**, accomplished, efficient, experienced, proficient ≠ **inexperienced**

practise *v* **1 = rehearse**, drill, exercise, go over, go through, prepare, repeat, study, train **2 = follow**, observe, perform **3 = work at**, carry on, engage in, pursue

pragmatic *adj* **= practical**, businesslike, down-to-earth, hard-headed, realistic, sensible, utilitarian

praise *v* **1 = approve**, acclaim, admire,

applaud, cheer, compliment, congratulate, eulogize, extol, honour, laud ≠ **criticize 2 = give thanks to**, adore, bless, exalt, glorify, worship ♦ *n* **3 a = approval**, acclaim, acclamation, approbation, commendation, compliment, congratulation, eulogy, plaudit, tribute ≠ **criticism b = thanks**, adoration, glory, homage, worship

prance *v* **= dance**, caper, cavort, frisk, gambol, parade, romp, show off (*inf*), skip, stalk, strut, swagger, swank (*inf*)

prank *n* **= trick**, escapade, jape, lark (*inf*), practical joke

prattle *v* **1 = chatter**, babble, blather, blether, gabble, jabber, rabbit (on) (*Brit inf*), waffle (*inf, chiefly Brit*), witter (*inf*)

pray *v* **1 = say one's prayers**, offer a prayer, recite the rosary **2 = beg**, adjure, ask, beseech, entreat, implore, petition, plead, request, solicit

preamble ⊕ *n* introductory part to something said or written.

precarious ⊕ *adj* insecure, unsafe, likely to fall or collapse.

precaution ⊕ *n* action taken in advance to prevent something bad happening. **precautionary** *adj*

precede ⊕ *v* go or be before. **precedence** [**press** ee-denss] *n* formal order of rank or position. **take precedence over** be more important than. **precedent** *n* previous case or occurrence regarded as an example to be followed.

precept ⊕ *n* rule of behaviour.

precinct ⊕ *n* 1 area in a town closed to traffic. 2 enclosed area round a building. 3 *US* administrative area of a city. ♦ *pl* 4 surrounding region.

precious ⊕ *adj* 1 of great value and importance. 2 loved and treasured. 3 (of behaviour) affected, unnatural. **precious**

metal gold, silver, or platinum. **precious stone** rare mineral, such as a ruby, valued as a gem.

precipice ⊕ *n* very steep cliff or rockface. **precipitous** *adj* sheer.

precipitate ⊕ *v* 1 cause to happen suddenly. 2 *Chem* cause to be deposited in solid form from a solution. 3 throw headlong. ♦ *adj* 4 done rashly or hastily. **precipitately** *adv* **precipitation** *n* rain, snow, etc.

précis ⊕ [**pray**-see] *n, pl* **précis** 1 short written summary of a longer piece. ♦ *v* 2 make a précis of.

precise ⊕ *adj* 1 exact, accurate in every detail. 2 strict in observing rules or standards. **precisely** *adv* **precision** *n*

preclude ⊕ *v* make impossible to happen.

precocious ⊕ *adj* having developed or matured early or too soon. **precocity** *n*

precursor ⊕ *n* something that precedes

— THESAURUS —

preach *v* 1 = **deliver a sermon**, address, evangelize 2 = **lecture**, advocate, exhort, moralize, sermonize

preamble *n* = **introduction**, foreword, opening statement or remarks, preface, prelude

precarious *adj* = **dangerous**, dodgy (*Brit, Aust & NZ inf*), hazardous, insecure, perilous, risky, shaky, shonky (*Aust & NZ inf*), tricky, unreliable, unsafe, unsure ≠ **safe**

precaution *n* = **safeguard**, care, caution, forethought, protection, safety measure, wariness

precede *v* = **go before**, antedate, come first, head, introduce, lead, preface

precept *n* = **rule**, canon, command, commandment, decree, instruction, law, order, principle, regulation, statute

precinct *n* 1 = **area**, district, quarter, section, sector, zone 2 = **enclosure**, confine, limit

precious *adj* 1 = **valuable**, costly, dear, expensive, fine, invaluable, priceless, prized ≠ **cheap** 2 = **loved**, adored, beloved, cherished, darling, dear, prized,

treasured 3 = **affected**, artificial, overnice, overrefined, twee (*Brit inf*)

precipice *n* = **cliff**, bluff, crag, height, rock face

precipitate *v* 1 = **quicken**, accelerate, advance, bring on, expedite, hasten, hurry, speed up, trigger 3 = **throw**, cast, fling, hurl, launch, let fly ♦ *adj* 4 = **hasty**, abrupt, breakneck, brief, headlong, heedless, impetuous, impulsive, precipitous, quick, rapid, rash, reckless, rushing, sudden, swift, unexpected, without warning

précis *n* 1 = **summary**, abridgment, outline, résumé, synopsis ♦ *v* 2 = **summarize**, abridge, outline, shorten, sum up

precise *adj* 1 = **exact**, absolute, accurate, correct, definite, explicit, express, particular, specific, strict ≠ **vague** 2 = **strict**, careful, exact, fastidious, finicky, formal, meticulous, particular, punctilious, rigid, scrupulous, stiff ≠ **relaxed**

preclude *v* = **prevent**, check, debar, exclude, forestall, inhibit, obviate, prohibit, rule out, stop

and is a signal of something else,
forerunner.

predatory ❶ [pred–a–tree] *adj* habitually
hunting and killing other animals for food.
predator *n* predatory animal.

predecessor ❶ *n* 1 person who precedes
another in an office or position. 2
ancestor.

predicament ❶ *n* embarrassing or difficult
situation.

predict ❶ *v* tell about in advance,
prophesy. **predictable** *adj* **prediction** *n*

predispose ❶ *v* 1 influence (someone) in
favour of something. 2 make (someone)
susceptible to something. **predisposition**
n

predominate ❶ *v* be the main or
controlling element. **predominance** *n*
predominant *adj*

pre–eminent ❶ *adj* excelling all others,
outstanding. **pre–eminence** *n*

pre–empt ❶ *v* prevent an action by doing
something which makes it pointless or
impossible. **pre–emptive** *adj*

preen ❶ *v* (of a bird) clean or trim
(feathers) with the beak. **preen oneself** 1
smarten oneself. 2 show self–satisfaction.

prefabricated *adj* (of a building)
manufactured in shaped sections for rapid
assembly on site.

preface ❶ [pref–iss] *n* 1 introduction to a
book. ♦ *v* 2 serve as an introduction to (a
book, speech, etc.).

prefect *n* 1 senior pupil in a school, with
limited power over others. 2 senior
administrative officer in some countries.
prefecture *n* office or area of authority of
a prefect.

prefer ❶ *v* **–ferring, –ferred** 1 like better. 2
Law bring (charges) before a court.
preferable *adj* more desirable. **preferably**
adv **preference** *n* **preferential** *adj* showing
preference. **preferment** *n* promotion or
advancement.

prefix *n* 1 letter or group of letters put at
the beginning of a word to make a new
word, such as *un–* in *unhappy.* ♦ *v* 2 put as
an introduction or prefix (to).

pregnant ❶ *adj* 1 carrying a fetus in the
womb. 2 full of meaning or significance,
e.g. *a pregnant pause.* **pregnancy** *n, pl* **–
cies**

prehistoric ❶ *adj* of the period before
written history begins. **prehistory** *n*

——— THESAURUS ———

precocious *adj* = **advanced**, ahead, bright,
developed, forward, quick, smart

precursor *n* a = **herald**, forerunner,
harbinger, vanguard b = **forerunner**,
antecedent, forebear, predecessor

predatory *adj* = **hunting**, carnivorous,
predacious, raptorial

predecessor *n* 1 = **previous job holder**,
antecedent, forerunner, precursor
2 = **ancestor**, antecedent, forebear,
forefather

predicament *n* = **fix** (*inf*), dilemma, hole
(*sl*), jam (*inf*), mess, pinch, plight,
quandary, scrape (*inf*), situation, spot (*inf*)

predict *v* = **foretell**, augur, divine, forecast,
portend, prophesy

predispose *v* 1 = **incline**, affect, bias,
dispose, influence, lead, prejudice, prompt

predominate *v* = **prevail**, be most
noticeable, carry weight, hold sway,

outweigh, overrule, overshadow

pre–eminent *adj* = **outstanding**, chief,
distinguished, excellent, foremost,
incomparable, matchless, predominant,
renowned, superior, supreme

pre–empt *v* = **anticipate**, appropriate,
assume, usurp

preen *v* = **clean**, plume **preen oneself**
1 = **smarten**, dress up, spruce up, titivate
2 = **pride oneself**, congratulate oneself

preface *n* 1 = **introduction**, foreword,
preamble, preliminary, prelude, prologue
♦ *v* 2 = **introduce**, begin, open, prefix

prefer *v* 1 = **like better**, be partial to,
choose, desire, fancy, favour, go for,
incline towards, opt for, pick

pregnant *adj* 1 = **expectant**, big *or* heavy
with child, expecting (*inf*), in the club (*Brit
sl*), with child 2 = **meaningful**, charged,
eloquent, expressive, loaded, pointed,

prejudice ❶ n 1 unreasonable or unfair dislike or preference. ◆ v 2 cause (someone) to have a prejudice. 3 harm, cause disadvantage to. **prejudicial** adj harmful, disadvantageous.

preliminary ❶ adj 1 happening before and in preparation, introductory. ◆ n, pl –**naries** 2 preliminary remark, contest, etc.

prelude ❶ n 1 introductory movement in music. 2 event preceding and introducing something else.

premature ❶ adj 1 happening or done before the normal or expected time. 2 (of a baby) born before the end of the normal period of pregnancy. **prematurely** adv

premeditated ❶ adj planned in advance. **premeditation** n

premier ❶ n 1 prime minister. ◆ adj 2 chief, leading. **premiership** n

première n first performance of a play, film, etc.

premise ❶ premiss n statement assumed to be true and used as the basis of reasoning.

premises ❶ pl n house or other building and its land.

premium ❶ n 1 additional sum of money, as on a wage or charge. 2 (regular) sum paid for insurance. **at a premium** in great demand because scarce.

premonition ❶ n feeling that something unpleasant is going to happen; foreboding. **premonitory** adj

preoccupy v –**pying**, –**pied** fill the thoughts or attention of (someone) to the exclusion of other things. **preoccupation** n

preordained adj decreed or determined in advance.

prepare ❶ v make or get ready. **prepared** adj 1 willing. 2 ready. **preparation** n 1 preparing. 2 something done in readiness for something else. 3 mixture prepared for use as a cosmetic, medicine, etc. **preparatory** [prip–**par**–a–tree] adj preparing for. **preparatory school** private school for children going on to public school.

preposition n word used before a noun or

───┤ THESAURUS ├───

significant, telling, weighty

prehistoric adj = **earliest**, early, primeval, primitive, primordial

prejudice n 1 a = **discrimination**, bigotry, chauvinism, injustice, intolerance, narrow–mindedness, unfairness b = **bias**, partiality, preconceived notion, preconception, prejudgment ◆ v 2 = **bias**, colour, distort, influence, poison, predispose, slant 3 = **harm**, damage, hinder, hurt, impair, injure, mar, spoil, undermine

preliminary adj 1 = **first**, initial, introductory, opening, pilot, prefatory, preparatory, prior, test, trial ◆ n 2 = **introduction**, beginning, opening, overture, preamble, preface, prelude, start

prelude n 1 = **overture** 2 = **introduction**, beginning, foreword, preamble, preface, prologue, start

premature adj 1 a = **hasty**, ill–timed, overhasty, previous (inf), rash, too soon, untimely b = **early**

premeditated adj = **planned**, calculated, conscious, considered, deliberate, intentional, wilful

premier n 1 = **head of government**, chancellor, chief minister, P.M., prime minister ◆ adj 2 = **chief**, first, foremost, head, highest, leading, main, primary, prime, principal

première n = **first night**, debut, opening

premise, premiss n = **assumption**, argument, assertion, hypothesis, postulation, presupposition, proposition, supposition

premises pl n = **building**, establishment, place, property, site

premium n 1 = **bonus**, bounty, fee, perk (Brit inf), perquisite, prize, reward **at a premium = in great demand**, hard to come by, in short supply, rare, scarce

premonition n = **feeling**, foreboding, hunch, idea, intuition, presentiment, suspicion

prepare v = **make** or **get ready**, adapt,

pronoun to show its relationship with other words, such as *by* in *go by bus*. **prepositional** *adj*

> ✓ **WORD TIP**
>
> The practice of ending a sentence with a preposition, as in: *Venice is a place I should like to go to*, was formerly regarded as incorrect, but is now acceptable and is the preferred form in many contexts.

prepossessing ❶ *adj* making a favourable impression, attractive.
preposterous ❶ *adj* utterly absurd.
prerequisite ❶ *n, adj* (something) required before something else is possible.
prerogative ❶ *n* special power or privilege.
prescribe ❶ *v* 1 recommend the use of (a medicine). 2 lay down as a rule.
prescription *n* written instructions from a doctor for the making up and use of a medicine. **prescriptive** *adj* laying down rules.
present[1] ❶ *adj* 1 being in a specified place. 2 existing or happening now. 3

Grammar (of a verb tense) indicating that the action specified is taking place now. ◆ *n* 4 present time or tense. **presence** *n* 1 fact of being in a specified place. 2 impressive dignified appearance. **presently** *adv* 1 soon. 2 *US & Scot* now.
present[2] ❶ *n* 1 something given to bring pleasure to another person. ◆ *v* 2 introduce formally or publicly. 3 introduce and compère (a TV or radio show). 4 cause, e.g. *present a difficulty*. 5 give, award. **presentation** *n* **presentable** *adj* attractive, neat, fit for people to see. **presenter** *n* person introducing a TV or radio show.
presentiment [priz–**zen**–tim–ent] *n* sense of something unpleasant about to happen.
preserve ❶ *v* 1 keep from being damaged, changed, or ended. 2 treat (food) to prevent it decaying. ◆ *n* 3 area of interest restricted to a particular person or group. 4 fruit preserved by cooking in sugar. **preservation** *n* **preservative** *n* chemical that prevents decay.
preside ❶ *v* be in charge, esp. of a meeting. **president** *n* 1 head of state in

adjust, arrange, practise, prime, train, warm up
prepossessing *adj* = **attractive**, appealing, charming, engaging, fetching, good–looking, handsome, likable *or* likeable, pleasing
preposterous *adj* = **ridiculous**, absurd, crazy, incredible, insane, laughable, ludicrous, nonsensical, out of the question, outrageous, unthinkable
① **prerequisite** *n* = **requirement**, condition, essential, must, necessity, precondition, qualification, requisite, *sine qua non*
② **prerequisite** *adj* = **required**, essential, indispensable, mandatory, necessary, obligatory, requisite, vital
prerogative *n* = **right**, advantage, due, exemption, immunity, liberty, privilege
prescribe *v* 2 = **order**, decree, dictate,

direct, lay down, ordain, recommend, rule, set, specify, stipulate
present[1] *adj* 1 = **here**, at hand, near, nearby, ready, there ≠ **absent** 2 = **current**, contemporary, existent, existing, immediate, present–day ◆ *n* 4 = **now**, here and now, the present moment, the time being, today
present[2] *n* 1 = **gift**, boon, donation, endowment, grant, gratuity, hand–out, offering, prezzie (*inf*) ◆ *v* 2 = **introduce**, acquaint with, make known 3 = **put on**, display, exhibit, give, show, stage 5 = **give**, award, bestow, confer, grant, hand out, hand over
preserve *v* 1 a = **protect**, care for, conserve, defend, keep, safeguard, save, shelter, shield ≠ **attack** b = **maintain**, continue, keep, keep up, perpetuate, sustain, uphold ≠ **end** ◆ *n* 3 = **area**,

countries without a king or queen. 2 head of a society, institution, etc.

press ❶ v 1 apply force or weight to. 2 squeeze. 3 smooth by applying pressure or heat. 4 urge insistently. 5 crowd, push. ◆ n 6 printing machine. **pressed for** short of, e.g. *pressed for time.* **the press** 1 news media collectively, esp. newspapers. 2 reporters, journalists. **pressing** adj urgent. **press box** room at a sports ground reserved for reporters. **press conference** interview for reporters given by a celebrity. **press release** official announcement or account of a news item supplied to the press. **press stud** fastener in which one part with a projecting knob snaps into a hole on another part.

pressure ❶ n 1 force produced by pressing. 2 urgent claims or demands. 3 *Physics* force applied to a surface per unit of area. **pressure cooker** airtight pot which cooks food quickly by steam under pressure. **pressure group** group that tries to influence policies, public opinion, etc.

prestige ❶ n high status or respect resulting from success or achievements.

prestigious adj

presto adv *Music* very quickly.

presume ❶ v 1 suppose to be the case. 2 dare (to). **presumably** adv one supposes (that). **presumption** n 1 bold insolent behaviour. 2 strong probability. **presumptuous** adj doing things one has no right or authority to do. **presumptive** adj assumed to be true or valid until the contrary is proved.

presuppose ❶ v need as a previous condition in order to be true. **presupposition** n

pretend ❶ v claim or give the appearance of (something untrue) to deceive or in play. **pretender** n person who makes a false or disputed claim to a position of power. **pretence** n behaviour intended to deceive, pretending. **pretentious** adj making (unjustified) claims to special merit or importance. **pretension** n

pretext ❶ n false reason given to hide the real one.

pretty ❶ adj –tier, –tiest 1 pleasing to look at. ◆ adv 2 fairly, moderately, e.g. *I'm pretty certain.* **prettily** adv **prettiness** n

---

THESAURUS

domain, field, realm, sphere

preside v = **run**, administer, chair, conduct, control, direct, govern, head, lead, manage, officiate

press v 1 = **compress**, crush, depress, force down, jam, mash, push, squeeze 2 = **hug**, clasp, crush, embrace, fold in one's arms, hold close, squeeze 3 = **smooth**, flatten, iron 4 = **urge**, beg, entreat, exhort, implore, petition, plead, pressurize 5 = **crowd**, flock, gather, herd, push, seethe, surge, swarm, throng **the press** 1 = **newspapers**, Fleet Street, fourth estate, news media, the papers 2 = **journalists**, columnists, correspondents, reporters

pressure n 1 = **force**, compressing, compression, crushing, squeezing, weight 2 a = **power**, coercion, compulsion, constraint, force, influence, mana (*NZ*), sway b = **stress**, burden, demands, hassle

(*inf*), heat, load, strain, urgency

prestige n = **status**, credit, distinction, eminence, fame, honour, importance, kudos, renown, reputation, standing

presume v 1 = **believe**, assume, conjecture, guess (*inf, chiefly US & Canad*), infer, postulate, suppose, surmise, take for granted, think 2 = **dare**, go so far, make so bold, take the liberty, venture

presuppose v = **presume**, assume, imply, posit, postulate, take as read, take for granted

pretend v a = **feign**, affect, allege, assume, fake, falsify, impersonate, profess, sham, simulate b = **make believe**, act, imagine, make up, suppose

pretext n = **guise**, cloak, cover, excuse, ploy, pretence, ruse, show

pretty adj 1 = **attractive**, beautiful, bonny, charming, comely, fair, good–looking, lekker (*S Afr sl*), lovely ≠ **unattractive** ◆

prevail ❶ v 1 gain mastery. 2 be generally established. **prevailing** adj 1 widespread. 2 predominant. **prevalence** n **prevalent** adj widespread, common.

prevaricate ❶ v avoid giving a direct or truthful answer. **prevarication** n

prevent ❶ v keep from happening or doing. **preventable** adj **prevention** n **preventive** adj, n

preview ❶ n advance showing of a film or exhibition before it is shown to the public.

previous ❶ adj coming or happening before. **previously** adv

prey ❶ n 1 animal hunted and killed for food by another animal. 2 victim. **bird of prey** bird that kills and eats other birds or animals. **prey on** v 1 hunt and kill for food. 2 worry, obsess.

price ❶ n 1 amount of money for which a thing is bought or sold. 2 unpleasant thing that must be endured to get something desirable. ◆ v 3 fix or ask the price of. **priceless** adj 1 very valuable. 2 Informal very funny. **pricey** adj **pricier**, **priciest** Informal expensive.

prick ❶ v 1 pierce lightly with a sharp

point. 2 cause to feel mental pain. 3 (of an animal) make (the ears) stand erect. ◆ n 4 sudden sharp pain caused by pricking. 5 mark made by pricking. 6 remorse. **prick up one's ears** listen intently.

pride ❶ n 1 feeling of pleasure and satisfaction when one has done well. 2 too high an opinion of oneself. 3 sense of dignity and self-respect. 4 something that causes one to feel pride. 5 group of lions. **pride of place** most important position. **pride oneself on** feel pride about.

priest ❶ n 1 (in the Christian church) a person who can administer the sacraments and preach. 2 (in some other religions) an official who performs religious ceremonies. **priestess** n fem **priesthood** n **priestly** adj

prig ❶ n self-righteous person who acts as if superior to others. **priggish** adj **priggishness** n

prim ❶ adj **primmer**, **primmest** formal, proper, and rather prudish.

primacy n, pl **-cies** 1 state of being first in rank, grade, etc. 2 office of an archbishop.

prima donna n 1 leading female opera singer. 2 Informal temperamental person.

————————| THESAURUS |————————

adv 2 = **fairly**, kind of (inf), moderately, quite, rather, reasonably, somewhat
prevail v 1 = **win**, be victorious, overcome, overrule, succeed, triumph 2 = **be widespread**, abound, be current, be prevalent, exist generally, predominate
prevaricate v = **evade**, beat about the bush, cavil, deceive, dodge, equivocate, flannel (Brit inf), hedge
prevent v = **stop**, avert, avoid, foil, forestall, frustrate, hamper, hinder, impede, inhibit, obstruct, obviate, preclude, thwart
preview n 1 = **sample**, advance showing, foretaste, sneak preview, taster, trailer
previous adj = **earlier**, erstwhile, foregoing, former, past, preceding, prior ≠ later
prey n 1 = **quarry**, game, kill 2 = **victim**, dupe, fall guy (inf), mug (Brit sl), target
price n 1 = **cost**, amount, charge, damage

(inf), estimate, expense, fee, figure, rate, value, worth 2 = **consequences**, cost, penalty, toll ◆ v 3 = **evaluate**, assess, cost, estimate, rate, value
prick v 1 = **pierce**, jab, lance, perforate, punch, puncture, stab ◆ n 5 = **puncture**, hole, perforation, pinhole, wound
pride n 1 = **satisfaction**, delight, gratification, joy, pleasure 2 = **conceit**, arrogance, egotism, hubris, self-importance, vanity ≠ modesty 3 = **self-respect**, dignity, honour, self-esteem, self-worth 4 = **gem**, jewel, pride and joy, treasure
priest n 1 = **clergyman**, cleric, curate, divine, ecclesiastic, father, minister, pastor, vicar
prig n = **goody-goody** (inf), prude, puritan, stuffed shirt (inf)
prim adj = **prudish**, demure, fastidious, fussy, priggish, prissy (inf), proper,

primary ⓞ *adj* 1 chief, most important. 2 being the first stage, elementary. **primarily** *adv* **primary colours** (in physics) red, green, and blue or (in art) red, yellow, and blue, from which all other colours can be produced by mixing. **primary school** school for children from five to eleven years.

primate¹ *n* member of an order of mammals including monkeys and humans.

primate² *n* archbishop.

prime ⓞ *adj* 1 main, most important. 2 of the highest quality. ◆ *n* 3 time when someone is at his or her best or most vigorous. ◆ *v* 4 give (someone) information in advance to prepare them for something. 5 prepare (a surface) for painting. 6 prepare (a gun, pump, etc.) for use. **primer** *n* special paint applied to bare wood etc. before the main paint. **Prime Minister** leader of a government. **prime number** number that can be divided exactly only by itself and one.

primeval ⓞ [prime-**ee**-val] *adj* of the earliest age of the world.

primitive ⓞ *adj* 1 of an early simple stage of development. 2 basic, crude.

primrose *n* pale yellow spring flower.

prince ⓞ *n* 1 male member of a royal family, esp. the son of the king or queen. 2 male ruler of a small country. **princely** *adj* 1 of or like a prince. 2 generous, lavish, or magnificent. **princess** *n* female member of a royal family, esp. the daughter of the king or queen.

principal ⓞ *adj* 1 main, most important. ◆ *n* 2 head of a school or college. 3 person taking a leading part in something. 4 sum of money lent on which interest is paid. **principally** *adv*

> ✔ **WORD TIP**
>
> Distinguish the spellings of *principal* and *principle*. These are different words but often confused.

---

principle ⓞ *n* 1 moral rule guiding behaviour. 2 general or basic truth. 3 scientific law concerning the working of something. **in principle** in theory but not always in practice. **on principle** because of one's beliefs.

> ✔ **WORD TIP**
>
> Distinguish the spellings of *principle* and *principal*. These are different words but often confused

---

print ⓞ *v* 1 reproduce (a newspaper, book,

━━━━━━━━━━━ THESAURUS ━━━━━━━━━━━

puritanical, strait-laced

primary *adj* 1 = **chief**, cardinal, first, greatest, highest, main, paramount, prime, principal ≠ **secondary** 2 = **elementary**, introductory, rudimentary, simple

prime *adj* 1 = **main**, chief, leading, predominant, pre-eminent, primary, principal 2 = **best**, choice, excellent, first-class, first-rate, highest, quality, select, top ◆ *n* 3 = **peak**, bloom, flower, height, heyday, zenith ◆ *v* 4 = **inform**, brief, clue in (*inf*), coach, fill in (*inf*), get ready, make ready, notify, prepare, tell, train

primeval *adj* = **earliest**, ancient, early, first, old, prehistoric, primal, primitive, primordial

primitive *adj* 1 = **early**, elementary, first, original, primary, primeval, primordial ≠ **advanced** 2 = **crude**, rough, rudimentary, simple, unrefined ≠ **elaborate**

prince *n* 2 = **ruler**, lord, monarch, sovereign

principal *adj* 1 = **main**, cardinal, chief, essential, first, foremost, key, leading, paramount, pre-eminent, primary, prime ≠ **minor** ◆ *n* 2 = **headmaster** or **headmistress**, dean, head (*inf*), head teacher, master or mistress, rector 3 = **star**, lead, leader 4 = **capital**, assets, money

principle *n* 1 = **morals**, conscience, integrity, probity, scruples, sense of honour 2 = **rule**, canon, criterion, etc.) in large quantities by mechanical or electronic means. 2 reproduce (text or pictures) by pressing ink onto paper etc. 3 write in letters that are not joined up. 4 stamp (fabric) with a design. 5 *Photog* produce (pictures) from negatives. ◆ *n* 6 printed words etc. 7 printed copy of a painting. 8 printed lettering. 9 photograph. 10 printed fabric. 11 mark left on a surface by something that has pressed against it. **out of print** no longer available from a publisher. **printer** *n* 1 person or company engaged in printing. 2 machine that prints. 3 **printing** *n* **printed circuit** electronic circuit with wiring printed on an insulating base. **print–out** *n* printed information from a computer.

prior¹ ❶ *adj* earlier. **prior to** before.

prior² ** *n* head monk in a priory. **prioress *n* deputy head nun in a convent. **priory** *n, pl* **–ries** place where certain orders of monks or nuns live.

prise *v* force open by levering.

prism *n* transparent block usu. with triangular ends and rectangular sides, used to disperse light into a spectrum or refract it in optical instruments. **prismatic** *adj* 1 of or shaped like a prism. 2 (of colour) as if produced by refraction through a prism, rainbow–like.

prison ❶ *n* building where criminals and accused people are held. **prisoner** *n* person held captive. **prisoner of war** serviceman captured by an enemy in wartime.

pristine ❶ *adj* clean, new, and unused.

private ❶ *adj* 1 for the use of one person or group only. 2 secret. 3 personal, unconnected with one's work. 4 owned or paid for by individuals rather than by the government. 5 quiet, not likely to be disturbed. ◆ *n* 6 soldier of the lowest rank. **privately** *adv* **privacy** *n*

privation *n* loss or lack of the necessities of life.

privet *n* bushy evergreen shrub used for hedges.

privilege ❶ *n* advantage or favour that only some people have. **privileged** *adj* enjoying a special right or immunity.

privy ❶ *adj* 1 sharing knowledge of something secret. ◆ *n, pl* **privies** 2 *Obs* toilet, esp. an outside one **private council of the British monarch.**

prize¹ ❶ *n* 1 reward given for success in a competition etc. ◆ *adj* 2 winning or likely to win a prize. **prizefighter** *n* boxer who fights for money. **prizefight** *n*

prize² ❶ *v* value highly.

pro¹ *adv, prep* in favour of. **pros and cons**

————————| THESAURUS |————————

doctrine, dogma, fundamental, law, maxim, precept, standard, truth in **principle = in theory**, ideally, theoretically

print *v* 1 = **publish** 2 = **imprint**, impress, issue, mark, stamp ◆ *n* 6 = **publication**, book, magazine, newspaper, newsprint, periodical, printed matter 7 = **reproduction**, copy 9 = **photograph**, photo (*inf*), picture

prior¹ *adj* = **earlier**, foregoing, former, preceding, pre–existing, previous **prior to = before**, earlier than, preceding, previous to

prison *n* = **jail**, clink (*sl*), confinement, cooler (*sl*), dungeon, jug (*sl*), lockup, nick (*Brit sl*), penitentiary (*US*), slammer (*sl*)

pristine *adj* = **new**, immaculate, pure,

uncorrupted, undefiled, unspoiled, unsullied, untouched, virginal

private *adj* 1 = **exclusive**, individual, intimate, own, personal, reserved, special ≠ **public** 2 = **secret**, clandestine, confidential, covert, hush–hush (*inf*), off the record, unofficial ≠ **public** 5 = **separate**, isolated, secluded, secret, sequestered, solitary, withdrawn ≠ **busy**

privilege *n* = **right**, advantage, claim, concession, due, entitlement, freedom, liberty, prerogative

privy *adj* 1 = **secret**, confidential, private ◆ *n* 2 *Obs* = **lavatory**, latrine, outside toilet

prize¹ *n* 1 = **reward**, accolade, award, haul, honour, jackpot, purse, stakes, trophy, winnings ◆ *adj* 2 = **champion**, award–

arguments for and against.

pro² *n, pl* **pros** *Informal* 1 professional. 2 prostitute.

pro– *prefix* 1 in favour of, e.g. *pro–Russian.* 2 instead of, e.g. *pronoun.*

probable ⊕ *adj* likely to happen or be true. **probably** *adv* **probability** *n, pl* **–ties**

probate *n* 1 process of proving the validity of a will. 2 certificate stating that a will is genuine.

probation ⊕ *n* 1 system of dealing with law–breakers, esp. juvenile ones, by placing them under supervision. 2 period when someone is assessed for suitability for a job etc. **probationer** *n* person on probation.

probe ⊕ *v* 1 search into or examine closely. ◆ *n* 2 surgical instrument used to examine a wound, cavity, etc.

probity *n* honesty, integrity.

problem ⊕ *n* 1 something difficult to deal with or solve. 2 question or puzzle set for solution. **problematic, problematical** *adj*

proceed ⊕ *v* 1 start or continue doing. 2 *Formal* walk, go. 3 start a legal action. 4 arise from. **proceeds** *pl n* money obtained

from an event or activity. **proceedings** *pl n* 1 organized or related series of events. 2 minutes of a meeting. 3 legal action. **procedure** *n* way of doing something, esp. the correct or usual one.

process ⊕ *n* 1 series of actions or changes. 2 method of doing or producing something. ◆ *v* 3 handle or prepare by a special method of manufacture. **processed** *adj* (of food) treated to prevent it decaying. **processor** *n*

proclaim ⊕ *v* declare publicly. **proclamation** *n*

procrastinate ⊕ *v* put off taking action, delay. **procrastination** *n*

procreate *v Formal* produce offspring. **procreation** *n*

procure ⊕ *v* 1 get, provide. 2 obtain (people) to act as prostitutes. **procurement** *n* **procurer** *n,* **procuress** *n* person who obtains people to act as prostitutes.

prod ⊕ *v* **prodding, prodded** 1 poke with something pointed. 2 goad (someone) to take action. ◆ *n* 3 prodding.

prodigal ⊕ *adj* recklessly extravagant,

winning, best, first–rate, outstanding, top, winning

prize² *v* = **value**, cherish, esteem, hold dear, treasure

probable *adj* = **likely**, apparent, credible, feasible, plausible, possible, presumable, reasonable

probation *n* 2 = **trial period**, apprenticeship, trial

probe *v* 1 a = **examine**, explore, go into, investigate, look into, scrutinize, search b = **explore**, feel around, poke, prod ◆ *n* 3 = **examination**, detection, exploration, inquiry, investigation, scrutiny, study

problem *n* 1 = **difficulty**, complication, dilemma, dispute, predicament, quandary, trouble 2 = **puzzle**, conundrum, enigma, poser, question, riddle

proceed *v* 1 = **go on**, carry on, continue, go ahead, move on, press on, progress ≠ **stop** 4 = **arise**, come, derive, emanate,

flow, issue, originate, result, spring, stem

process *n* 1 = **development**, advance, evolution, growth, movement, progress, progression 2 = **procedure**, action, course, manner, means, measure, method, operation, performance, practice, system ◆ *v* 3 = **handle**

proclaim *v* = **declare**, advertise, announce, circulate, herald, indicate, make known, profess, publish ≠ **conceal**

procrastinate *v* = **delay**, dally, drag one's feet (*inf*), gain time, play for time, postpone, put off, stall, temporize

procure *v* 1 = **obtain**, acquire, buy, come by, find, gain, get, pick up, purchase, score (*sl*), secure, win

prod *v* 1 = **poke**, dig, drive, jab, nudge, push, shove 2 = **prompt**, egg on, goad, impel, incite, motivate, move, rouse, spur, stimulate, urge ◆ *n* 3 a = **poke**, dig, jab, nudge, push, shove b = **prompt**, cue, wasteful.

prodigy ⊕ *n, pl* **-gies 1** person with some marvellous talent. **2** wonderful thing. **prodigious** *adj* **1** very large, immense. **2** wonderful.

produce ⊕ *v* **1** bring into existence. **2** present to view, show. **3** make, manufacture. **4** present on stage, film, or television. ◆ *n* **5** food grown for sale. **producer** *n* **1** person with control over the making of a film, record, etc. **2** person or company that produces something.

profane ⊕ *adj* **1** showing disrespect for religion or holy things. **2** (of language) coarse, blasphemous. ◆ *v* **3** treat (something sacred) irreverently, desecrate. **profanity** *n, pl* **-ties** profane talk or behaviour, blasphemy.

profess *v* **1** state or claim (something as true), sometimes falsely. **2** have as one's

belief or religion. **professed** *adj* supposed.

proffer *v* offer.

proficient ⊕ *adj* skilled, expert. **proficiency** *n*

profile ⊕ *n* **1** outline, esp. of the face, as seen from the side. **2** brief biographical sketch.

profit ⊕ *n* **1** money gained. **2** benefit obtained. ◆ *v* **3** gain or benefit. **profitable** *adj* making profit. **profitably** *adv* **profitability** *n* **profiteer** *n* person who makes excessive profits at the expense of the public. **profiteering** *n*

profligate ⊕ *adj* **1** recklessly extravagant. **2** shamelessly immoral. ◆ *n* **3** profligate person. **profligacy** *n*

profound ⊕ *adj* **1** showing or needing great knowledge. **2** strongly felt, intense. **profundity** *n, pl* **-ties**

profuse ⊕ *adj* plentiful. **profusion** *n*

reminder, signal, stimulus

prodigal *adj* = **extravagant**, excessive, immoderate, improvident, profligate, reckless, spendthrift, wasteful ≠ **economical**

prodigy *n* **1** = **genius**, mastermind, talent, whizz (*inf*), wizard **2** = **wonder**, marvel, miracle, phenomenon, sensation

produce *v* **1** = **bring forth**, bear, beget, breed, bring about, cause, deliver, effect, generate, give rise to **2** = **show**, advance, demonstrate, exhibit, offer, present **3** = **make**, compose, construct, create, develop, fabricate, invent, manufacture **4** = **present**, direct, do, exhibit, mount, put on, show, stage ◆ *n* **5** = **fruit and vegetables**, crop, greengrocery, harvest, product, yield

profane *adj* **1** = **sacrilegious**, disrespectful, godless, impious, impure, irreligious, irreverent, sinful, ungodly, wicked ≠ **clean** **2** = **crude**, blasphemous, coarse, filthy, foul, obscene, vulgar ◆ *v* **3** = **desecrate**, commit sacrilege, debase, defile, violate

profess *v* **1** = **state**, admit, affirm, announce, assert, avow, confess, declare, proclaim, vouch **b** = **claim**, allege, fake,

feign, make out, pretend, purport

proficient *adj* = **skilled**, able, accomplished, adept, capable, competent, efficient, expert, gifted, masterly, skilful

profile *n* **1** = **outline**, contour, drawing, figure, form, side view, silhouette, sketch **2** = **biography**, characterization, sketch, thumbnail sketch, vignette

profit *n* **1** = **earnings**, gain, proceeds, receipts, return, revenue, takings, yield ≠ **loss 2** = **benefit**, advancement, advantage, gain, good, use, value ≠ **cost** ◆ *v* **3 a** = **make money**, earn, gain **b** = **benefit**, be of advantage to, gain, help, improve, promote, serve

profligate *adj* **1** = **extravagant**, immoderate, improvident, prodigal, reckless, spendthrift, wasteful **2** = **depraved**, debauched, degenerate, dissolute, immoral, licentious, shameless, wanton, wicked, wild ≠ **principled** ◆ *n* **3 a** = **spendthrift**, squanderer, waster, wastrel **b** = **degenerate**, debauchee, libertine, rake, reprobate, roué

profound *adj* **1** = **wise**, abstruse, deep, learned, penetrating, philosophical, sagacious, sage ≠ **stupid 2** = **sincere**,

progeny ❶ [proj–in–ee] *n*, *pl* –nies children. **progenitor** [pro–**jen**–it–er] *n* ancestor.

prognosis ❶ *n*, *pl* –noses 1 doctor's forecast about the progress of an illness. 2 any forecast.

program *n* sequence of coded computer instructions.

programme ❶ *n* 1 planned series of events. 2 broadcast on radio or television. 3 list of items or performers in an entertainment.

progress ❶ *n* 1 improvement, development. 2 movement forward. ♦ *v* 3 become more advanced or skilful. 4 move forward. **in progress** taking place. **progression** *n* 1 progressing. **progressive** *adj* 1 favouring political or social reform. 2 happening gradually. **progressively** *adv*

prohibit ❶ *v* forbid or prevent from happening. **prohibition** *n* 1 act of forbidding. 2 ban on the sale or drinking of alcohol. **prohibitive** *adj* (of prices) too high to be affordable. **prohibitively** *adv*

✓ **WORD TIP**
The idiom is *prohibit* someone *from* doing something.

---

project ❶ *n* 1 planned scheme to do or examine something over a period. ♦ *v* 2 make a forecast based on known data. 3 make (a film or slide) appear on a screen. 4 communicate (an impression). 5 stick out beyond a surface or edge. **projector** *n* apparatus for projecting photographic images, films, or slides on a screen. **projection** *n*

proletariat ❶ [pro–lit–**air**–ee–at] *n* working class. **proletarian** *adj*, *n*

proliferate ❶ *v* grow or reproduce rapidly. **proliferation** *n*

prolific ❶ *adj* very productive.

prologue ❶ *n* introduction to a play or book.

prolong ❶ *v* make (something) last longer. **prolongation** *n*

promenade ❶ *n* 1 paved walkway along

————————[THESAURUS]————————

acute, deeply felt, extreme, great, heartfelt, intense, keen ≠ **shallow**

profuse *adj* = **plentiful**, abundant, ample, bountiful, copious, luxuriant, overflowing, prolific ≠ **inadequate**

progeny *n* = **children**, descendants, family, issue, lineage, offspring, race, stock, young

prognosis *n* 1 = **diagnosis** 2 = **forecast**, prediction, prognostication, projection

programme *n* 1 = **schedule**, agenda, curriculum, line–up, list, listing, order of events, plan, syllabus, timetable 2 = **show**, broadcast, performance, presentation, production

progress *n* 1 = **development**, advance, breakthrough, gain, growth, headway, improvement ≠ **decline** 2 = **movement**, advance, course, headway, passage ≠ **regression** ♦ *v* 3 = **develop**, advance, gain, grow, improve ≠ **regress** 4 = **move on**, advance, continue, go forward, make headway, proceed, travel ≠ **recede in progress** = **going on**, being done,

happening, occurring, proceeding, taking place, under way

prohibit *v* a = **forbid**, ban, debar, disallow, outlaw, proscribe, veto ≠ **allow** b = **prevent**, hamper, hinder, impede, restrict, stop ≠ **let**

project *n* 1 = **scheme**, activity, assignment, enterprise, job, occupation, plan, task, undertaking, venture, work ♦ *v* 2 = **forecast**, calculate, estimate, extrapolate, gauge, predict, reckon 5 = **stick out**, bulge, extend, jut, overhang, protrude, stand out

proletariat *n* = **working class**, commoners, hoi polloi, labouring classes, lower classes, plebs, proles (*offens*), the common people, the masses

proliferate *v* = **increase**, breed, expand, grow rapidly, multiply

prolific *adj* = **productive**, abundant, copious, fecund, fertile, fruitful, luxuriant, profuse ≠ **barren**

prologue *n* = **introduction**, foreword,

the seafront at a holiday resort. ◆ v, n 2 Old–fashioned (take) a leisurely walk.
prominent ❶ adj 1 very noticeable. 2 famous, widely known. **prominence** n
promiscuous ❶ adj having many casual sexual relationships. **promiscuity** n
promise ❶ v 1 say that one will definitely do or not do something. 2 show signs of, seem likely. ◆ n 3 undertaking to do or not to do something. 4 indication of future success. **promising** adj likely to succeed or turn out well.
promontory ❶ n, pl –ries point of high land jutting out into the sea.
promote ❶ v 1 help to make (something) happen or increase. 2 raise to a higher rank or position. 3 encourage the sale of by advertising. **promoter** n person who organizes or finances an event etc. **promotion** n **promotional** adj
prompt ❶ v 1 cause (an action). 2 remind (an actor or speaker) of words that he or

she has forgotten. ◆ adj 3 done without delay. ◆ adv 4 exactly, e.g. six o'clock prompt. **promptly** adv immediately, without delay. **promptness** n **prompter** n person offstage who prompts actors.
promulgate ❶ v 1 put (a law etc.) into effect by announcing it officially. 2 make widely known. **promulgation** n
prone ❶ adj 1 (foll. by to) likely to do or be affected by (something). 2 lying face downwards.
prong ❶ n one spike of a fork or similar instrument.
pronoun n word, such as she or it, used to replace a noun.
pronounce ❶ v 1 form the sounds of (words or letters), esp. clearly or in a particular way. 2 declare formally or officially. **pronounceable** adj **pronounced** adj very noticeable. **pronouncement** n formal announcement. **pronunciation** n way in which a word or language is

preamble, preface, prelude
prolong v = **lengthen**, continue, delay, drag out, draw out, extend, perpetuate, protract, spin out, stretch
promenade n 1 = **walkway**, esplanade, parade, prom ◆ v, n 2 Old–fashioned = **stroll**, saunter, walk
prominent adj 1 = **noticeable**, conspicuous, eye–catching, obtrusive, obvious, outstanding, pronounced ≠ **insignificant** 2 = **famous**, distinguished, eminent, foremost, important, leading, main, notable, renowned, top, well–known ≠ **minor**
promiscuous adj = **licentious**, abandoned, debauched, fast, immoral, libertine, loose, wanton, wild ≠ **moral**
promise v 1 = **guarantee**, assure, contract, give one's word, pledge, swear, take an oath, undertake, vow, warrant 2 = **seem likely**, augur, betoken, indicate, look like, show signs of, suggest ◆ n 3 = **guarantee**, assurance, bond, commitment, oath, pledge, undertaking, vow, word
4 = **potential**, ability, aptitude, capability,

capacity, talent
promontory n = **point**, cape, foreland, head, headland
promote v 1 = **help**, advance, aid, assist, back, boost, encourage, forward, foster, gee up, support ≠ **prevent** 2 = **raise**, elevate, exalt, upgrade ≠ **downgrade** 3 = **advertise**, hype, plug (inf), publicize, push, sell
prompt v 1 = **cause**, elicit, give rise to, occasion, provoke 2 = **remind**, assist, cue, help out ◆ adj 3 = **immediate**, early, instant, quick, rapid, speedy, swift, timely ≠ **late** ◆ adv 4 = **exactly**, on the dot, promptly, punctually, sharp
promulgate v 2 = **make known**, broadcast, circulate, communicate, disseminate, make public, proclaim, promote, publish, spread
prone adj 1 (foll. by to) = **liable**, apt, bent, disposed, given, inclined, likely, predisposed, subject, susceptible, tending ≠ **disinclined** 2 = **face down**, flat, horizontal, prostrate, recumbent ≠ **erect**
prong n = **point**, spike, tine

pronounced.

proof ❶ n 1 evidence that shows that
something is true or has happened. 2
copy of something printed, such as the
pages of a book, for checking before final
production. ◆ adj 3 able to withstand, e.g.
proof against criticism. 4 denoting the
strength of an alcoholic drink, e.g. *seventy
proof.* **proofread** v read and correct
(printer's proofs).

prop[1] ❶ v propping, propped 1 support
(something) so that it stays upright or in
place. ◆ n 2 pole, beam, etc. used as a
support.

prop[2] n movable object used on the set of
a film or play.

propaganda ❶ n (organized promotion
of) information to assist or damage the
cause of a government or movement.
propagandist n

propagate ❶ v 1 spread (information and
ideas). 2 reproduce, breed, or grow.
propagation n

propel ❶ v –pelling, –pelled cause to
move forward. **propellant** n 1 something
that provides or causes propulsion. 2 gas
used in an aerosol spray. **propeller** n
revolving shaft with blades for driving a
ship or aircraft. **propulsion** n 1 method by
which something is propelled. 2 act of
propelling or state of being propelled.

propensity ❶ n, pl –ties natural tendency.

proper ❶ adj 1 real or genuine. 2 suited to
a particular purpose. 4 correct in
behaviour. 5 excessively moral. 6 *Informal*
complete. **properly** adv

property ❶ n, pl –ties 1 something
owned. 2 possessions collectively. 3 land
or buildings owned by somebody. 4
quality or attribute.

prophet ❶ n 1 person supposedly chosen
by God to spread His word. 2 person who
predicts the future. **prophetic** adj
prophetically adv **prophecy** n, pl –cies 1
prediction. 2 message revealing God's will.
prophesy v –sying, –sied foretell.

proponent n person who argues in favour

━━━━━━━━━━━━━━━━━ THESAURUS ━━━━━━━━━━━━━━━━━

pronounce v 1 = **say**, accent, articulate,
enunciate, sound, speak 2 = **declare**,
affirm, announce, decree, deliver,
proclaim

proof n 1 = **evidence**, authentication,
confirmation, corroboration,
demonstration, substantiation, testimony,
verification ◆ adj 3 = **impervious**,
impenetrable, repellent, resistant, strong

prop[1] v 1 = **support**, bolster, brace,
buttress, hold up, stay, sustain, uphold ◆ n
2 = **support**, brace, buttress, mainstay,
stanchion, stay

propaganda n = **information**, advertising,
disinformation, hype, promotion, publicity

propagate v 1 = **spread**, broadcast,
circulate, disseminate, promote,

promulgate, publish, transmit ≠ **suppress**
2 = **reproduce**, beget, breed, engender,
generate, increase, multiply, procreate,
produce

propel v = **drive**, force, impel, launch,
push, send, shoot, shove, thrust ≠ **stop**

propensity n = **tendency**, bent,
inclination, liability, penchant,
predisposition, proclivity

proper adj 2, 3 = **suitable**, appropriate,
apt, becoming, befitting, fit, fitting, right
≠ **inappropriate** 4 = **correct**, accepted,
conventional, established, formal,
orthodox, precise, right 5 = **polite**, decent,
decorous, genteel, gentlemanly, ladylike,
mannerly, respectable, seemly

property n 2 = **possessions**, assets,

of something.

proportion ⊕ *n* 1 relative size or extent. 2 correct relation between connected parts. 3 part considered with respect to the whole. ♦ *pl* 4 dimensions or size. ♦ *v* 5 adjust in relative amount or size. **in proportion** 1 comparable in size, rate of increase, etc. 2 without exaggerating. **proportional, proportionate** *adj* being in proportion. **proportionally, proportionately** *adv*

propose ⊕ *v* 1 put forward for consideration. 2 nominate. 3 intend or plan (to do). 4 make an offer of marriage. **proposal** *n* **proposition** *n* 1 offer. 2 statement or assertion. 3 *Maths* theorem. 4 *Informal* thing to be dealt with. ♦ *v* 5 *Informal* ask (someone) to have sexual intercourse.

propound *v* put forward for consideration.

proprietor *n* owner of a business establishment. **proprietress** *n fem*

proprietary *adj* 1 made and distributed under a trade name. 2 denoting or suggesting ownership.

propriety ⊕ *n, pl* –**ties** correct conduct.

propulsion ⊕ *n* see PROPEL.

prosaic ⊕ [pro-**zay**-ik] *adj* lacking imagination, dull.

proscribe ⊕ *v* prohibit, outlaw. **proscription** *n* **proscriptive** *adj*

prose *n* ordinary speech or writing in contrast to poetry.

prosecute ⊕ *v* 1 bring a criminal charge against. 2 continue to do. **prosecution** *n* **prosecutor** *n*

prospect ⊕ *n* 1 something anticipated. 2 *Old-fashioned* view from a place. ♦ *pl* 3 probability of future success. ♦ *v* 4 explore, esp. for gold. **prospective** *adj* 1 future. 2 expected. **prospector** *n* **prospectus** *n* booklet giving details of a university, company, etc.

prosper ⊕ *v* be successful. **prosperity** *n* success and wealth. **prosperous** *adj*

———— THESAURUS ————

belongings, capital, effects, estate, goods, holdings, riches, wealth 3 = **land**, estate, freehold, holding, real estate 4 = **quality**, attribute, characteristic, feature, hallmark, trait

prophet *n* 2 = **soothsayer**, clairvoyant, diviner, forecaster, oracle, prophesier, seer, sibyl

proportion *n* 1 = **relative amount**, ratio, relationship 2 = **balance**, congruity, correspondence, harmony, symmetry 3 = **part**, amount, division, fraction, percentage, quota, segment, share ♦ *pl n* 4 = **dimensions**, capacity, expanse, extent, size, volume

propose *v* 1 = **put forward**, advance, present, submit, suggest 2 = **nominate**, name, present, recommend 3 = **intend**, aim, design, have in mind, mean, plan, scheme 4 = **offer marriage**, ask for someone's hand (in marriage), pop the question (*inf*)

propriety *n* = **decorum**, courtesy, decency, etiquette, good form, good manners,

manners, politeness, refinement, respectability, seemliness ≠ **indecency**

propulsion *n* = **drive**, impetus, impulse, propelling force, push, thrust

prosaic *adj* = **dull**, boring, everyday, humdrum, matter-of-fact, mundane, ordinary, pedestrian, routine, trite, unimaginative

proscribe *v* a = **prohibit**, ban, embargo, forbid, interdict ≠ **allow** b = **outlaw**, banish, deport, exclude, exile, expatriate, expel, ostracize

prosecute *v* 1 = **put on trial**, arraign, bring to trial, indict, litigate, sue, take to court, try

prospect *n* 1 = **expectation**, anticipation, future, hope, odds, outlook, probability, promise 2 *Old-fashioned* = **view**, landscape, outlook, scene, sight, spectacle, vista ♦ *pl n* 3 = **likelihood**, chance, possibility ♦ *v* 4 = **look for**, fossick (*Aust & NZ*), search for, seek

prosper *v* = **succeed**, advance, do well, flourish, get on, progress, thrive

prostate n gland in male mammals that surrounds the neck of the bladder

prostitute ⓘ n 1 person who offers sexual intercourse in return for payment. ◆ v 2 make a prostitute of. 3 offer (oneself or one's talents) for unworthy purposes. **prostitution** n

prostrate ⓘ adj 1 lying face downwards. 2 physically or emotionally exhausted. ◆ v 3 lie face downwards. 4 exhaust physically or emotionally. **prostration** n

protagonist ⓘ n 1 supporter of a cause. 2 leading character in a play or a story.

protect ⓘ v defend from trouble, harm, or loss. **protection** n **protectionism** n policy of protecting industries by taxing competing imports. **protectionist** n, adj **protective** adj 1 giving protection, e.g. protective clothing. 2 tending or wishing to protect someone. **protector** n 1 person or thing that protects. 2 regent. **protectorate** n 1 territory largely controlled by a stronger state. 2 (period of) rule of a regent.

protégé, (fem) **protégée** [**pro**–ti–zhay] n person who is protected and helped by another.

protein n any of a group of complex organic compounds that are essential for life.

protest ⓘ n 1 declaration or demonstration of objection. ◆ v 2 object, disagree. 3 assert formally. **protestation** n strong declaration.

Protestant n 1 follower of any of the Christian churches that split from the Roman Catholic Church in the sixteenth century. ◆ adj 2 of or relating to such a church. **Protestantism** n

protocol ⓘ n rules of behaviour for formal occasions.

proton n positively charged particle in the nucleus of an atom.

prototype ⓘ n original or model to be copied or developed.

protract v lengthen or extend. **protracted** adj **protractor** n instrument for measuring angles.

protrude ⓘ v stick out, project. **protrusion** n

protuberant adj swelling out, bulging. **protuberance** n

proud ⓘ adj 1 feeling pleasure and satisfaction. 2 feeling honoured. 3 thinking oneself superior to other people. 4 dignified. **proudly** adv

───── THESAURUS ─────

prostitute n 1 = **whore**, call girl, fallen woman, harlot, hooker (US sl), loose woman, pro (sl), scrubber (Brit & Aust sl), streetwalker, strumpet, tart (inf), trollop ◆ v 3 = **cheapen**, debase, degrade, demean, devalue, misapply, pervert, profane

prostrate adj 1 = **prone**, flat, horizontal 2 = **exhausted**, dejected, depressed, desolate, drained, inconsolable, overcome, spent, worn out ◆ v 4 = **exhaust**, drain, fatigue, sap, tire, wear out, weary

protagonist n 1 = **supporter**, advocate, champion, exponent 2 = **leading character**, central character, hero or heroine, principal

protect v = **keep safe**, defend, guard, look after, preserve, safeguard, save, screen, shelter, shield, stick up for (inf), support, watch over

protest n 1 = **objection**, complaint, dissent, outcry, protestation, remonstrance ◆ v 2 = **object**, complain, cry out, demonstrate, demur, disagree, disapprove, express disapproval, oppose, remonstrate 3 = **assert**, affirm, attest, avow, declare, insist, maintain, profess

protocol n = **code of behaviour**, conventions, customs, decorum, etiquette, manners, propriety

prototype n = **original**, example, first, model, pattern, standard, type

protrude v = **stick out**, bulge, come through, extend, jut, obtrude, project, stand out

proud adj 1 = **satisfied**, content, glad, gratified, pleased, well-pleased ≠ **discontented** 3 = **conceited**, arrogant, boastful, disdainful, haughty, imperious,

prove ⊕ v **proving, proved, proved** or **proven 1** establish the validity of. **2** demonstrate, test. **3** be found to be. **proven** adj known from experience to work.

proverb ⊕ n short saying that expresses a truth or gives a warning. **proverbial** adj

provide ⊕ v make available. **provider** n **provided that, providing** on condition that. **provide for** v **1** take precautions (against). **2** support financially.

> ✓ **WORD TIP**
> The usage is either *providing* on its own or *provided that* (not *providing that*).

province ⊕ n **1** area governed as a unit of a country or empire. **2** area of learning, activity, etc. ◆ pl **3** parts of a country outside the capital. **provincial** adj **1** of a province or the provinces. **2** unsophisticated and narrow–minded. ◆ n **3** unsophisticated person. **4** person from a province or the provinces. **provincialism** n

narrow–mindedness and lack of sophistication.

provision ⊕ n **1** act of supplying something. **2** something supplied. **3** Law condition incorporated in a document. ◆ pl **4** food. ◆ v **5** supply with food. **provisional** adj temporary or conditional. **provisionally** adv

proviso ⊕ [pro–**vize**–oh] n, pl **–sos, –soes** condition, stipulation.

provoke ⊕ v **1** deliberately anger. **2** cause (an adverse reaction). **provocation** n **provocative** adj

prow n bow of a vessel.

prowess ⊕ n **1** superior skill or ability. **2** bravery, fearlessness.

prowl ⊕ v **1** move stealthily around a place as if in search of prey or plunder. ◆ n **2** prowling. **prowler** n

proximity ⊕ n **1** nearness in space or time. **2** nearness or closeness in a series.

proxy ⊕ n, pl **proxies 1** person authorized to act on behalf of someone else. **2** authority to act on behalf of someone

————————————— THESAURUS —————————————

lordly, overbearing, self–satisfied, snobbish, supercilious ≠ **modest**

prove v **1** = **verify**, authenticate, confirm, demonstrate, determine, establish, justify, show, substantiate ≠ **rule out 2** = **test**, analyse, assay, check, examine, try **3** = **turn out**, come out, end up, result

proverb n = **saying**, adage, dictum, maxim, saw

provide v **1** = **supply**, add, afford, bring, cater, equip, furnish, give, impart, lend, outfit, present, produce, purvey, render, serve, stock up, yield ≠ **refuse provide for 1** = **take precautions**, anticipate, forearm, plan ahead, plan for, prepare for **2** = **support**, care for, keep, maintain, sustain, take care of

province n **1** = **region**, colony, department, district, division, domain, patch, section, zone **2** = **area**, business, capacity, concern, duty, field, function, line, responsibility, role, sphere

provision n **1** = **supplying**, catering,

equipping, furnishing, providing **3** Law = **condition**, clause, demand, proviso, requirement, rider, stipulation, term ◆ pl **4** = **food**, comestibles, eatables, edibles, fare, foodstuffs, rations, stores, supplies, tucker (Aust & NZ inf), victuals

proviso n = **condition**, clause, qualification, requirement, rider, stipulation

provoke v **1** = **anger**, aggravate (inf), annoy, enrage, hassle (inf), incense, infuriate, irk, irritate, madden, rile ≠ **calm 2** = **rouse**, bring about, cause, elicit, evoke, incite, induce, occasion, produce, promote, prompt, stir ≠ **ease**

prowess n **1** = **skill**, ability, accomplishment, adeptness, aptitude, excellence, expertise, genius, mastery, talent ≠ **inability 2** = **bravery**, courage, daring, fearlessness, heroism, mettle, valiance, valour ≠ **fear**

prowl v **1** = **move stealthily**, skulk, slink, sneak, stalk, steal else.

prude *n* person who is excessively modest, prim, or proper. **prudish** *adj* **prudery** *n*

prudent ⊕ *adj* cautious, discreet, and sensible. **prudence** *n* **prudential** *adj* Old–fashioned prudent.

prune¹ *n* dried plum.

prune² ⊕ *v* 1 cut off dead parts or excessive branches from (a tree or plant). 2 shorten, reduce.

pry ⊕ *v* prying, pried make an impertinent or uninvited inquiry into a private matter.

PS postscript.

psalm ⊕ *n* sacred song. **psalmist** *n* writer of psalms.

pseudo– ⊕ *combining form* false, pretending, or unauthentic, e.g. *pseudoclassical.*

pseudonym ⊕ *n* fictitious name adopted esp. by an author.

psychic ⊕ *adj* (also **psychical**) 1 having mental powers which cannot be explained by natural laws. 2 relating to the mind. ◆ *n* 3 person with psychic powers.

PTO please turn over.

pub ⊕ *n* building with a bar licensed to sell alcoholic drinks.

puberty ⊕ *n* beginning of sexual maturity.

pubertal *adj*

pubic *adj* of the lower abdomen, e.g. *pubic hair.*

public ⊕ *adj* 1 of or concerning the people as a whole. 2 for use by everyone. 3 well-known. 4 performed or made openly. ◆ *n* 5 the community, people in general. **publicly** *adv* **public house** pub. **public relations** promotion of a favourable opinion towards an organization among the public. **public school** private fee-paying school in Britain. **public–spirited** *adj* having or showing an active interest in the good of the community.

publicity ⊕ *n* 1 process or information used to arouse public attention. 2 public interest so aroused. **publicize** *v* advertise. **publicist** *n* person, esp. a press agent or journalist, who publicizes something.

publish ⊕ *v* 1 produce and issue (printed matter) for sale. 2 announce formally or in public. **publication** *n* **publisher** *n*

puck *n* small rubber disc used in ice hockey.

pucker ⊕ *v* 1 gather into wrinkles. ◆ *n* 2 wrinkle or crease.

pudding ⊕ *n* 1 dessert, esp. a cooked one

THESAURUS

proximity *n* = **nearness**, closeness

proxy *n* 1 = **representative**, agent, delegate, deputy, factor, substitute

prudent *adj* a = **careful**, canny, cautious, discerning, judicious, shrewd, vigilant, wary ≠ **rash** b = **discreet**, politic c = **sensible**, wise ≠ **irrational**

prune² *v* 1 = **cut**, clip, dock, shape, snip, trim 2 = **reduce**, shorten

pry *v* = **be inquisitive**, be nosy (*inf*), interfere, intrude, meddle, poke, snoop (*inf*)

psalm *n* = **hymn**, chant

pseudo– *combining form* = **false**, artificial, fake, imitation, mock, phoney *or* phony (*inf*), pretended, sham, spurious

pseudonym *n* = **false name**, alias, assumed name, incognito, nom de plume, pen name

psychic *adj* (also **psychical**)

1 = **supernatural**, mystic, occult
2 = **mental**, psychological, spiritual

pub *n* = **tavern**, bar, inn

puberty *n* = **adolescence**, pubescence, teens

public *adj* 1 = **general**, civic, common, national, popular, social, state, universal, widespread 2 = **open**, accessible, communal, unrestricted ≠ **private** 3 = **well–known**, important, prominent, respected 4 = **known**, acknowledged, obvious, open, overt, patent, plain ≠ **secret** ◆ *n* 5 = **people**, citizens, community, electorate, everyone, nation, populace, society

publicity *n* 1 = **advertising**, attention, boost, hype, plug (*inf*), press, promotion

publish *v* 1 = **put out**, issue, print, produce 2 = **announce**, advertise, broadcast, circulate, disclose, divulge, proclaim, served hot. **2** savoury dish with pastry or batter, e.g. *steak–and–kidney pudding.* **3** sausage–like mass of meat, e.g. *black pudding.*

puddle *n* small pool of water, esp. of rain.

puerile ❶ *adj* silly and childish.

puff ❶ *n* **1** (sound of) a short blast of breath, wind, etc. **2** act of inhaling cigarette smoke. ◆ *v* **3** blow or breathe in short quick draughts. **4** take draws at a (cigarette). **5** send out in small clouds. **6** swell. **out of puff** out of breath. **puffy** *adj* ball–shaped fungus.

puffin *n* black–and–white sea bird with a brightly–coloured beak.

pug *n* small snub–nosed dog.

pugnacious *adj* ready and eager to fight. **pugnacity** *n*

pull ❶ *v* **1** exert force on (an object) to move it towards the source of the force. **2** strain or stretch. **3** remove or extract. **4** attract. ◆ *n* **5** act of pulling. **6** force used in pulling. **7** act of taking in drink or smoke. **8** *Informal* power, influence. **pull in** *v* **1** (of a vehicle or driver) draw in to the side of the road or stop. **2** reach a destination. **3** attract in large numbers. **4** *Slang* arrest. **pull off** *v Informal* succeed in performing. **pull out** *v* **1** (of a vehicle or driver) move away from the side of the

road or move out to overtake. **2** (of a train) depart. **3** withdraw. **4** remove by pulling. **pull up** *v* **1** (of a vehicle or driver) stop. **2** remove by the roots. **3** reprimand.

pulley *n* wheel with a grooved rim in which a belt, chain, or piece of rope runs in order to lift weights by a downward pull.

pullover *n* sweater that is pulled on over the head.

pulmonary *adj* of the lungs.

pulp ❶ *n* **1** soft wet substance made from crushed or beaten matter. **2** flesh of a fruit. **3** poor–quality books and magazines. ◆ *v* **4** reduce to pulp.

pulpit *n* raised platform for a preacher.

pulse¹ ❶ *n* **1** regular beating of blood through the arteries at each heartbeat. **2** any regular beat or vibration. **pulsate** *v* throb, quiver. **pulsation** *n*

pulse² *n* edible seed of a pod–bearing plant such as a bean or pea.

pulverize ❶ *v* **1** reduce to fine pieces. **2** destroy completely. **pulverization** *n*

puma *n* large American wild cat with a greyish–brown coat.

pumice [**pumm–iss**] *n* light porous stone used for scouring.

pummel ❶ *v* **–melling, –melled** strike repeatedly with or as if with the fists.

——————| THESAURUS |——————

publicize, reveal, spread

pucker *v* **1** = **wrinkle**, contract, crease, draw together, gather, knit, purse, screw up, tighten ◆ *n* **2** = **wrinkle**, crease, fold

pudding *n* **1** = **dessert**, afters (*Brit inf*), pud (*inf*), sweet

puerile *adj* = **childish**, babyish, foolish, immature, juvenile, silly, trivial

puff *n* **1** = **blast**, breath, draught, gust, whiff **2** = **smoke**, drag (*sl*), pull ◆ *v* **3** = **blow**, breathe, exhale, gasp, gulp, pant, wheeze **4** = **smoke**, drag (*sl*), draw, inhale, pull at *or* on, suck **6** = **swell**, bloat, dilate, distend, expand, inflate

pull *v* **1** = **draw**, drag, haul, jerk, tow, trail, tug, yank ≠ **drive** **2** = **strain**, dislocate, rip, sprain, stretch, tear, wrench **3** = **extract**,

draw out, gather, pick, pluck, remove, take out, uproot ≠ **plant** **4** = **attract**, draw, entice, lure, magnetize ≠ **discourage** ◆ *n* **5** = **tug**, jerk, twitch, yank ≠ **push** **7** = **puff**, drag (*sl*), inhalation **8** *Inf* = **influence**, clout (*inf*), mana (*NZ*), muscle, power, weight

pulp *n* **1** = **paste**, mash, mush **2** = **flesh**, soft part ◆ *v* **4** = **crush**, mash, pulverize, squash

pulse¹ *n* **1** = **beat**, beating, pulsation, throb, throbbing **2** = **vibration**, rhythm

pulverize *v* **1** = **crush**, granulate, grind, mill, pound **2** = **defeat**, annihilate, crush, demolish, destroy, flatten, smash, wreck

pummel *v* = **beat**, batter, hammer, pound, punch, strike, thump

pump¹ ● n 1 machine used to force a liquid or gas to move in a particular direction. ◆ v 2 raise or drive with a pump. 3 supply in large amounts. 4 operate or work in the manner of a pump. 5 extract information from.

pump² n light flat-soled shoe.

pumpkin n large round fruit with an orange rind, soft flesh, and many seeds.

pun ● n 1 use of words to exploit double meanings for humorous effect. ◆ v **punning, punned** 2 make puns.

punch¹ ● v 1 strike at with a clenched fist. ◆ n 2 blow with a clenched fist. 3 Informal effectiveness or vigour. **punchy** adj **punchier, punchiest** forceful. **punch-drunk** adj dazed by or as if by repeated blows to the head. **punch line** line of a joke or funny story that gives it its point. **punch-up** n Informal fight or brawl.

punch² ● n 1 tool or machine for shaping, piercing, or engraving. ◆ v 2 pierce, cut, stamp, shape, or drive with a punch.

punch³ n drink made from a mixture of wine, spirits, fruit, sugar, and spices.

punctilious ● adj 1 paying great attention to correctness in etiquette. 2 careful about small details.

punctual ● adj arriving or taking place at the correct time. **punctuality** n **punctually**

adv

punctuate ● v 1 put punctuation marks in. 2 interrupt at frequent intervals. **punctuation** n (use of) marks such as commas, colons, etc. in writing, to assist in making the sense clear.

puncture ● n 1 small hole made by a sharp object, esp. in a tyre. ◆ v 2 pierce a hole in.

pundit n expert who speaks publicly on a subject.

pungent ● adj having a strong sharp bitter flavour. **pungency** n

punish ● v cause (someone) to suffer or undergo a penalty for some wrongdoing. **punishing** adj harsh or difficult. **punishment** n

punitive ● [pew-nit-tiv] adj relating to punishment.

punnet n small basket for fruit.

punter ● n 1 person who bets. 2 any member of the public.

puny ● adj –nier, –niest small and feeble.

pup n young of certain animals, such as dogs and seals.

pupa n, pl –pae, –pas insect at the stage of development between a larva and an adult.

pupil¹ ● n person who is taught by a teacher.

THESAURUS

pump v 2 = **drive**, force, inject, push 3 = **supply**, pour, send 5 = **interrogate**, cross-examine, probe, quiz

pun n 1 = **play on words**, double entendre, quip, witticism

punch¹ v 1 = **hit**, belt (inf), bop (inf), box, pummel, smash, sock (sl), strike, swipe (inf) ◆ n 2 = **blow**, bop (inf), hit, jab, sock (sl), swipe (inf), wallop (inf) 3 Inf = **effectiveness**, bite, drive, forcefulness, impact, verve, vigour

punch² v 2 = **pierce**, bore, cut, drill, perforate, prick, puncture, stamp

punctilious adj 1 = **formal**, proper 2 = **particular**, exact, finicky, fussy, meticulous, nice, precise, strict

punctual adj = **on time**, exact, on the dot,

precise, prompt, timely

punctuate v 2 = **interrupt**, break, intersperse, pepper, sprinkle

puncture n 1 a = **hole**, break, cut, damage, leak, nick, opening, slit b = **flat tyre**, flat ◆ v 2 = **pierce**, bore, cut, nick, penetrate, perforate, prick, rupture

pungent adj = **strong**, acrid, bitter, hot, peppery, piquant, sharp, sour, spicy, tart ≠ **weak**

punish v = **discipline**, castigate, chasten, chastise, correct, penalize, sentence

punitive adj = **retaliatory**, in reprisal, retaliative

punter n 1 = **gambler**, backer, better 2 = **person**, man in the street

puny adj = **feeble**, frail, little, sickly,

pupil² *n* round dark opening in the centre of the eye.

puppet ❶ *n* **1** small doll or figure moved by strings or by the operator's hand. **2** person or country controlled by another. **puppeteer** *n*

puppy *n, pl* **–pies** young dog.

purchase ❶ *v* **1** obtain by payment. ◆ *n* **2** thing that is bought. **3** act of buying. **4** leverage, grip. **purchaser** *n*

pure ❶ *adj* **1** unmixed, untainted. **2** innocent. **3** complete, e.g. *pure delight*. **4** concerned with theory only, e.g. *pure mathematics*. **purely** *adv* **purity** *n* **purify** *v* **–fying, –fied** make or become pure. **purification** *n* **purist** *n* person obsessed with strict obedience to the traditions of a subject.

purée [**pure**–ray] *n* **1** pulp of cooked food. ◆ *v* **–reeing, –reed 2** make into a purée.

purgatory *n* **1** place or state of temporary suffering. **2** (**P–**) RC Church place where souls of the dead undergo punishment for their sins before being admitted to Heaven.

purge ❶ *v* **1** rid (a thing or place) of (unwanted things or people). ◆ *n* **2** purging. **purgative** *n, adj* (medicine) designed to cause defecation.

purl *n* **1** stitch made by knitting a plain stitch backwards. ◆ *v* **2** knit in purl.

purloin ❶ *v* steal.

purple *adj, n* (of) a colour between red and blue.

purport ❶ *v* **1** claim (to be or do something). ◆ *n* **2** apparent meaning, significance.

purpose ❶ *n* **1** reason for which something is done or exists. **2** determination. **3** practical advantage or use, e.g. *use the time to good purpose*. **purposely** *adv* intentionally (also **on purpose**).

purr *v* **1** (of cats) make low vibrant sound, usu. when pleased. ◆ *n* **2** this sound.

purse ❶ *n* **1** small bag for money. **2** *Chiefly US* handbag. **3** financial resources. **4** prize money. ◆ *v* **5** draw (one's lips) together into a small round shape. **purser** *n* ship's officer who keeps the accounts.

————————— THESAURUS —————————

stunted, tiny, weak ≠ **strong**

pupil¹ *n* = **learner**, beginner, disciple, novice, schoolboy *or* schoolgirl, student ≠ **teacher**

puppet *n* **1** = **marionette**, doll **2** = **pawn**, cat's-paw, instrument, mouthpiece, stooge, tool

purchase *v* **1** = **buy**, acquire, come by, gain, get, obtain, pay for, pick up, score (*sl*) ≠ **sell** ◆ *n* **2** = **buy**, acquisition, asset, gain, investment, possession, property **4** = **grip**, foothold, hold, leverage, support

pure *adj* **1 a** = **unmixed**, authentic, flawless, genuine, natural, real, simple, straight, unalloyed ≠ **mixed b** = **clean**, germ-free, neat, sanitary, spotless, squeaky-clean, sterilized, uncontaminated, unpolluted, untainted, wholesome ≠ **dirty**
2 = **innocent**, blameless, chaste, impeccable, modest, squeaky-clean, uncorrupted, unsullied, virginal, virtuous ≠ **corrupt 3** = **complete**, absolute,

outright, sheer, thorough, unmitigated, unqualified, utter ≠ **qualified**

purge *v* **1** = **get rid of**, do away with, eradicate, expel, exterminate, remove, wipe out ◆ *n* **2** = **removal**, ejection, elimination, eradication, expulsion

purloin *v* = **steal**, appropriate, filch, nick (*sl, chiefly Brit*), pilfer, pinch (*inf*), swipe (*sl*), thieve

purport *v* **1** = **claim**, allege, assert, profess ◆ *n* **2** = **significance**, drift, gist, idea, implication, import, meaning

purpose *n* **1 a** = **aim**, ambition, desire, end, goal, hope, intention, object, plan, wish **b** = **reason**, aim, idea, intention, object, point **2** = **determination**, firmness, persistence, resolution, resolve, single-mindedness, tenacity, will

purse *n* **1** = **pouch**, money–bag, wallet **3** = **money**, exchequer, funds, lolly (*Aust & NZ inf*), means, resources, treasury, wealth ◆ *v* **5** = **pucker**, contract, pout, press

pursue ⊕ v 1 chase. 2 follow (a goal). 3 engage in. 4 continue to discuss or ask about (something). **pursuer** n **pursuit** n 1 pursuing. 2 occupation or pastime.

purvey ⊕ v supply (provisions). **purveyor** n

pus n yellowish matter produced by infected tissue.

push ⊕ v 1 move or try to move by steady force. 2 drive or spur (oneself or another person) to do something. 3 *Informal* sell (drugs) illegally. ♦ n 4 act of pushing. 5 special effort. **the push** *Slang* dismissal from a job or relationship. **pusher** n person who sells illegal drugs. **pushy** adj too assertive or ambitious. **pushchair** n folding chair on wheels for a baby.

puss, pussy n, pl **pusses, pussies** *Informal* cat.

pustule n pimple containing pus.

put ⊕ v **putting, put** 1 cause to be (in a position, state, or place). 2 express. 3 throw (the shot) in the shot put. ♦ n 4 throw in putting the shot. **put across** v express successfully. **put off** v 1 postpone. 2 disconcert. 3 repel. **put up** v 1 erect. 2 accommodate. 3 nominate. **put-upon** adj taken advantage of.

putrid ⊕ adj rotten and foul-smelling. **putrefy** v **-fying, -fied** rot and produce an offensive smell. **putrefaction** n **putrescent** adj rotting.

putt *Golf* ♦ n 1 stroke on the putting green to roll the ball into or near the hole. ♦ v 2 strike (the ball) in this way. **putter** n golf club for putting.

putty n paste used to fix glass into frames and fill cracks in woodwork.

puzzle ⊕ v 1 perplex and confuse or be perplexed or confused. ♦ n 2 problem that cannot be easily solved. 3 toy, game, or question that requires skill or ingenuity to solve. **puzzlement** n **puzzling** adj

PVC polyvinyl chloride: plastic material used in clothes etc.

pygmy adj very small. ♦ n, pl **-mies** very small person or thing.

pyjamas pl n loose-fitting trousers and top worn in bed.

pylon n steel tower-like structure supporting electrical cables.

pyramid n 1 solid figure with a flat base and triangular sides sloping upwards to a point. 2 building of this shape, esp. an ancient Egyptian one. **pyramidal** adj

pyre n pile of wood for burning a corpse on.

pyromania n uncontrollable urge to set things on fire. **pyromaniac** n

pyrotechnics n 1 art of making fireworks. 2 firework display. **pyrotechnic** adj

python n large nonpoisonous snake that crushes its prey.

| THESAURUS |

together, tighten

pursue v 1 = **follow**, chase, dog, hound, hunt, hunt down, run after, shadow, stalk, tail (*inf*), track ≠ **avoid** 2 = **try for**, aim for, desire, seek, strive for, work towards ≠ **eschew** 3 = **engage in**, carry on, conduct, perform, practise 4 = **continue**, carry on, keep on, maintain, persevere in, persist in, proceed

purvey v = **supply**, cater, deal in, furnish, provide, sell, trade in

push v 1 = **shove**, depress, drive, press, propel, ram, thrust ≠ **pull** 2 = **urge**, encourage, gee up, hurry, impel, incite, persuade, press, spur ≠ **discourage** ♦ n 4 = **shove**, butt, nudge, thrust ≠ **pull**

5 = **drive**, ambition, dynamism, energy, enterprise, go (*inf*), initiative, vigour, vitality **the push** *Sl* = **dismissal**, discharge, one's cards (*inf*), the boot (*sl*), the sack (*inf*)

put v 1 = **place**, deposit, lay, position, rest, set, settle, situate 3 = **express**, phrase, state, utter, word 4 = **throw**, cast, fling, heave, hurl, lob, pitch, toss

putrid adj = **rotten**, bad, decayed, decomposed, off, putrefied, rancid, rotting, spoiled

puzzle v 1 = **perplex**, baffle, bewilder, confound, confuse, mystify, stump ♦ n 2, 3 = **problem**, conundrum, enigma, mystery, paradox, poser, question, riddle

Q q

QC Queen's Counsel.

QLD Queensland.

quack¹ *v* **1** (of a duck) utter a harsh guttural sound. **2** make a noise like a duck. ◆ *n* **3** sound made by a duck.

quack² ⦵ *n* **1** unqualified person who claims medical knowledge. **2** *Informal* doctor.

quadrangle *n* **1** (also **quad**) rectangular courtyard with buildings on all four sides. **2** geometric figure consisting of four points connected by four lines.

quadrant *n* **1** quarter of a circle. **2** quarter of a circle's circumference. **3** instrument for measuring the altitude of the stars.

quadrilateral *adj* **1** having four sides. ◆ *n* **2** polygon with four sides.

quadruped [**kwod**–roo–ped] *n* any animal with four legs.

quadruple *v* **1** multiply by four. ◆ *adj* **2** four times as much or as many. **3** consisting of four parts.

quadruplet *n* one of four offspring born at one birth.

quaff ⦵ [**kwoff**] *v* drink heartily or in one draught.

quagmire ⦵ [**kwog**–mire] *n* soft wet area of land.

quail¹ *n* small game bird of the partridge family.

quail² ⦵ *v* shrink back with fear.

quaint ⦵ *adj* attractively unusual, esp. in an old–fashioned style.

quake ⦵ *v* **1** shake or tremble with or as if with fear. ◆ *n* **2** *Informal* earthquake.

qualify ⦵ *v* –**fying**, –**fied 1** provide or be provided with the abilities necessary for a task, office, or duty. **2** moderate or restrict (a statement). **qualified** *adj* **qualification** *n* **1** official record of achievement in a course or examination. **2** quality or skill needed for a particular activity. **3** condition that modifies or limits. **4** act of qualifying.

quality ⦵ *n, pl* –**ties 1** degree or standard of excellence. **2** distinguishing characteristic or attribute. **3** basic character or nature of something. ◆ *adj* **4** excellent or superior. **qualitative** *adj* of or relating to quality.

qualm ⦵ [**kwahm**] *n* **1** pang of conscience. **2** sudden sensation of

---

THESAURUS

quack² *n* **1** = **charlatan**, fake, fraud, humbug, impostor, mountebank, phoney or phony (*inf*)

quaff *v* = **drink**, down, gulp, imbibe, swallow, swig (*inf*)

quagmire *n* = **bog**, fen, marsh, mire, morass, quicksand, slough, swamp

quail² *v* = **shrink**, blanch, blench, cower, cringe, falter, flinch, have cold feet (*inf*), recoil, shudder

quaint *adj* = **old–fashioned**, antiquated, old–world, picturesque ≠ **new**

quake *v* **1** = **shake**, move, quiver, rock, shiver, shudder, tremble, vibrate

qualify *v* **1** = **certify**, empower, equip, fit, permit, prepare, ready, train ≠ **prevent 2** = **moderate**, diminish, ease, lessen, limit, reduce, regulate, restrain, restrict, soften, temper

quality *n* **1** = **excellence**, calibre, distinction, grade, merit, position, rank, standing, status **2** = **characteristic**, aspect, attribute, condition, feature, mark, property, trait **3** = **nature**, character, kind, misgiving.

quandary ❶ *n, pl* **–ries** difficult situation or dilemma.

quango *n, pl* **–gos** quasi–autonomous nongovernmental organization: any partly independent official body set up by a government.

quantify *v* **–fying, –fied** discover or express the quantity of. **quantifiable** *adj*

quantity ❶ *n, pl* **–ties 1** specified or definite amount or number. **2** aspect of anything that can be measured, weighed, or counted. **quantitative** *adj* of or relating to quantity. **quantity surveyor** person who estimates the cost of the materials and labour necessary for a construction job.

quarantine *n* **1** period of isolation of people or animals to prevent the spread of disease. ◆ *v* **2** isolate in or as if in quarantine.

quarrel ❶ *n* **1** angry disagreement. **2** cause of dispute. ◆ *v* **–relling, –relled 3** have a disagreement or dispute. **quarrelsome** *adj*

quarry¹ *n, pl* **–ries 1** place where stone is dug from the surface of the earth. ◆ *v* **–rying, –ried 2** extract (stone) from a quarry.

quarry² **❶** *n, pl* **–ries** person or animal that is being hunted.

quart *n* unit of liquid measure equal to two pints.

quarter ❶ *n* **1** one of four equal parts of something. **2** fourth part of a year. **3** *Informal* unit of weight equal to 4 ounces. **4** region or district of a town or city. **5** *US* 25–cent piece. **6** mercy or pity, as shown towards a defeated opponent. ◆ *pl* **7** lodgings. ◆ *v* **8** divide into four equal parts. **9** billet or be billeted in lodgings. **quarterly** *adj* **1** occurring, due, or issued at intervals of three months. ◆ *n* **2** magazine issued every three months. ◆ *adv* **3** once every three months. **quarterdeck** *n Naut* rear part of the upper deck of a ship. **quarterfinal** *n* round before the semifinal in a competition. **quartermaster** *n* military officer responsible for accommodation, food, and equipment.

quartet *n* **1** group of four performers. **2** music for such a group.

quartz *n* hard glossy mineral.

quash ❶ *v* **1** annul or make void. **2** subdue forcefully and completely.

quasi– ❶ [**kway**–zie] *combining form* almost but not really, e.g. *quasi–religious; a quasi–scholar.*

quaver ❶ *v* **1** (of a voice) quiver or tremble. ◆ *n* **2** *Music* note half the length of a crotchet. **3** tremulous sound or note.

THESAURUS

make, sort

qualm *n* **1 = compunction**, scruple, twinge *or* pang of conscience **2 = misgiving**, anxiety, apprehension, disquiet, doubt, hesitation, uneasiness

quandary *n* **= difficulty**, cleft stick, dilemma, impasse, plight, predicament, puzzle, strait

quantity *n* **1 = amount**, lot, number, part, sum, total **2 = size**, bulk, capacity, extent, length, magnitude, mass, measure, volume

quarrel *n* **1 = disagreement**, argument, brawl, breach, contention, controversy, dispute, dissension, feud, fight, row, squabble, tiff ≠ **agreement** ◆ *v* **3 = disagree**, argue, bicker, brawl, clash, differ, dispute, fall out (*inf*), fight, row,

squabble ≠ **agree**

quarry² *n* **= prey**, aim, game, goal, objective, prize, victim

quarter *n* **4 = district**, area, locality, neighbourhood, part, place, province, region, side, zone **6 = mercy**, clemency, compassion, forgiveness, leniency, pity ◆ *pl* **7 = lodgings**, abode, barracks, billet, chambers, dwelling, habitation, residence, rooms ◆ *v* **9 = accommodate**, billet, board, house, lodge, place, post, station

quash *v* **1 = annul**, cancel, invalidate, overrule, overthrow, rescind, reverse, revoke **2 = suppress**, beat, crush, overthrow, put down, quell, repress, squash, subdue

quasi– *combining form* **= pseudo–**, apparent, seeming, semi–, so–called,

quay [kee] *n* wharf built parallel to the shore.

queasy ❶ *adj* **–sier, –siest** 1 having the feeling that one is about to vomit. 2 feeling or causing uneasiness.

queen ❶ *n* 1 female sovereign who is the official ruler or head of state. 2 wife of a king. 3 woman, place, or thing considered to be the best of her or its kind. **queenly** *adj* **Queen's Counsel** barrister appointed Counsel to the Crown.

queer ❶ *adj* 1 not normal or usual. 2 faint, giddy, or queasy. 3 *Offens* homosexual. ◆ *n* 4 *Offens* homosexual. **queer someone's pitch** *Informal* spoil someone's chances of something.

✓ **WORD TIP**

Although the term *queer* meaning homosexual is still considered derogatory when used by non–homosexuals, it is now being used by homosexuals of themselves as a positive term: *queer politics, queer cinema.*

quell ❶ *v* 1 suppress. 2 overcome.

quench ❶ *v* 1 satisfy (one's thirst). 2 put out or extinguish.

querulous ❶ [kwer–yoo–luss] *adj* complaining or whining.

query ❶ *n, pl* **–ries** 1 question, esp. one raising doubt. 2 question mark. ◆ *v* **–rying, –ried** 3 express uncertainty, doubt, or an objection concerning (something).

quest ❶ *n* 1 long and difficult search. ◆ *v* 2 (foll. by *for* or *after*) go in search of.

question ❶ *n* 1 form of words addressed to a person in order to obtain an answer. 2 point at issue. 3 difficulty or uncertainty. ◆ *v* 4 put a question or questions to (a person). 5 express uncertainty about. **in question** under discussion. **out of the question** impossible. **questionable** *adj* of disputable value or authority.

questionnaire *n* set of questions on a form, used to collect information from people. **question mark** 1 punctuation mark (?) written at the end of questions. 2 a doubt or uncertainty.

questioning *adj* 1 proceeding from or

would–be

quaver *v* 1 = **tremble**, flicker, flutter, quake, quiver, shake, vibrate, waver ◆ *n* 3 = **trembling**, quiver, shake, tremble, tremor, vibration

queasy *adj* 1 = **sick**, bilious, green around the gills (*inf*), ill, nauseated, off colour, squeamish, upset 2 = **uneasy**, anxious, fidgety, ill at ease, restless, troubled, uncertain, worried

queen *n* 1 = **sovereign**, consort, monarch, ruler 3 = **ideal**, model, star

queer *adj* 1 = **strange**, abnormal, curious, droll, extraordinary, funny, munted (*NZ sl*), odd, peculiar, uncommon, unusual, weird ≠ **normal** 2 = **faint**, dizzy, giddy, light–headed, queasy

quell *v* 1, 2 = **suppress**, conquer, crush, defeat, overcome, overpower, put down, quash, subdue, vanquish

quench *v* 1 = **satisfy**, allay, appease, sate, satiate, slake 2 = **put out**, crush, douse,

extinguish, smother, stifle, suppress

querulous *adj* = **complaining**, captious, carping, critical, discontented, dissatisfied, fault–finding, grumbling, peevish, whining

query *n* 1 = **question**, doubt, inquiry, objection, problem, suspicion ◆ *v* 3 = **doubt**, challenge, disbelieve, dispute, distrust, mistrust, question, suspect

quest *n* 1 = **search**, adventure, crusade, enterprise, expedition, fossick (*Aust & NZ*), hunt, journey, mission

question *n* 2 = **issue**, motion, point, point at issue, proposal, proposition, subject, theme, topic 3 = **difficulty**, argument, contention, controversy, dispute, doubt, problem, query ◆ *v* 4 = **ask**, cross–examine, examine, inquire, interrogate, interview, probe, quiz 5 = **dispute**, challenge, disbelieve, doubt, mistrust, oppose, query, suspect **in question** = **under discussion**, at issue, in doubt, open to debate **out of the question**

characterised by doubt or uncertainty. **2** intellectually inquisitive: *a questioning mind.* ◆ *n* **3** interrogation.

queue ⊙ *n* **1** line of people or vehicles waiting for something. ◆ *v* **queuing** or **queueing, queued 2** (often foll. by *up*) form or remain in a line while waiting.

quibble ⊙ *v* **1** make trivial objections. ◆ *n* **2** trivial objection.

quiche [keesh] *n* savoury flan with an egg custard filling to which vegetables etc. are added.

quick ⊙ *adj* **1** speedy, fast. **2** lasting or taking a short time. **3** alert and responsive. **4** easily excited or aroused. ◆ *n* **5** area of sensitive flesh under a nail. ◆ *adv* **6** *Informal* in a rapid manner. **cut someone to the quick** hurt someone's feelings deeply. **quickly** *adv* **quicken** *v* **1** make or become faster. **2** make or become more lively. **quicksand** *n* deep mass of loose wet sand that sucks anything on top of it into it. **quicksilver** *n* mercury. **quickstep** *n* fast modern ballroom dance.

quiet ⊙ *adj* **1** with little noise. **2** calm or tranquil. **3** untroubled. ◆ *n* **4** quietness. ◆ *v* **5** make or become quiet. **on the quiet** without other people knowing, secretly. **quietly** *adv* **quietness** *n* **quieten** *v* (often foll. by *down*) make or become quiet.

quiff *n* tuft of hair brushed up above the forehead.

quill *n* **1** pen made from the feather of a bird's wing or tail. **2** stiff hollow spine of a hedgehog or porcupine.

quilt ⊙ *n* padded covering for a bed. **quilted** *adj* consisting of two layers of fabric with a layer of soft material between them.

quinine *n* bitter drug used as a tonic and formerly to treat malaria.

quintessence ⊙ *n* most perfect representation of a quality or state. **quintessential** *adj*

quintet *n* **1** group of five performers. **2** music for such a group.

quintuplet *n* one of five offspring born at one birth.

quip ⊙ *n* **1** witty saying. ◆ *v* **quipping, quipped 2** make a quip.

quirk ⊙ *n* **1** peculiarity of character. **2** unexpected twist or turn, e.g. *a quirk of fate.* **quirky** *adj*

quit ⊙ *v* **quitting, quit 1** stop (doing something). **2** give up (a job). **3** depart from. **quitter** *n* person who lacks perseverance. **quits** *adj Informal* on an equal footing.

———————— THESAURUS ————————

= **impossible**, inconceivable, unthinkable

queue *n* **1** = **line**, chain, file, sequence, series, string, train

quibble *v* **1** = **split hairs**, carp, cavil ◆ *n* **2** = **objection**, cavil, complaint, criticism, nicety, niggle

quick *adj* **1** = **fast**, brisk, express, fleet, hasty, rapid, speedy, swift ≠ **slow 2** = **brief**, cursory, hasty, hurried, perfunctory **3** = **intelligent**, acute, alert, astute, bright (*inf*), clever, perceptive, quick–witted, sharp, shrewd, smart **4** = **excitable**, irascible, irritable, passionate, testy, touchy

quiet *adj* **1** = **silent**, hushed, inaudible, low, noiseless, peaceful, soft, soundless ≠ **loud 2, 3** = **calm**, mild, peaceful, placid, restful, serene, smooth, tranquil ≠ **noisy**

4 = **undisturbed**, isolated, private, secluded, sequestered, unfrequented ◆ *n* **5** = **peace**, calmness, ease, quietness, repose, rest, serenity, silence, stillness, tranquillity

quilt *n* = **bedspread**, continental quilt, counterpane, coverlet, duvet, eiderdown

quintessence *n* = **essence**, distillation, soul, spirit

quip *n* **1** = **joke**, gibe, jest, pleasantry, retort, riposte, sally, wisecrack (*inf*), witticism

quirk *n* **1** = **peculiarity**, aberration, characteristic, eccentricity, foible, habit, idiosyncrasy, kink, mannerism, oddity, trait

quit *v* **1** = **stop**, abandon, cease, discontinue, drop, end, give up, halt ≠ **continue 2** = **resign**, abdicate, go, leave,

quite ⓘ *adv* **1** somewhat, e.g. *she's quite pretty.* **2** absolutely, e.g. *you're quite right.* **3** in actuality, truly. ♦ *interj* **4** expression of agreement.

> ✓ **WORD TIP**
> Note that because *quite* can mean 'extremely': *quite amazing;* or can express a reservation: *quite friendly,* it should be used carefully.

quiver¹ ⓘ *v* **1** shake with a tremulous movement. ♦ *n* **2** shaking or trembling.

quiver² *n* case for arrows.

quiz ⓘ *n, pl* **quizzes 1** entertainment in which the knowledge of the players is tested by a series of questions. ♦ *v* **quizzing, quizzed 2** investigate by close questioning. **quizzical** *adj* questioning and mocking. **quizzically** *adv*

quoit *n* **1** large ring used in the game of quoits. ♦ *pl* **2** game in which quoits are tossed at a stake in the ground in attempts to encircle it.

quorum *n* minimum number of people required to be present at a meeting before any transactions can take place. **quorate** *adj* having or being a quorum.

quota ⓘ *n* **1** share that is due from, due to, or allocated to a group or person. **2** prescribed number or quantity allowed, required, or admitted.

quote ⓘ *v* **1** repeat (words) exactly from (an earlier work, speech, or conversation). **2** state (a price) for goods or a job of work. ♦ *n* **3** *Informal* quotation. **quotable** *adj* **quotation** *n* **1** written or spoken passage repeated exactly in a later work, speech, or conversation. **2** act of quoting. **3** estimate of costs submitted by a contractor to a prospective client.

quotient *n* result of the division of one number or quantity by another.

———————— THESAURUS ————————

pull out, retire, step down (*inf*) **3** = **depart**, go, leave, pull out

quite *adv* **1** = **somewhat**, fairly, moderately, rather, reasonably, relatively **2** = **absolutely**, completely, entirely, fully, perfectly, totally, wholly **3** = **truly**, in fact, in reality, in truth, really

quiver¹ *v* **1** = **shake**, oscillate, quake, quaver, shiver, shudder, tremble, vibrate ♦

n **2** = **shake**, oscillation, shiver, shudder, tremble, tremor, vibration

quiz *n* **1** = **examination**, investigation, questioning, test ♦ *v* **2** = **question**, ask, examine, interrogate, investigate

quota *n* **1** = **share**, allowance, assignment, part, portion, ration, slice, whack (*inf*)

quote *v* **1** = **repeat**, cite, detail, instance, name, recall, recite, recollect, refer to

R r

R 1 Queen. **2** King. **3** River.

rabbi [**rab**–bye] *n*, *pl* **–bis** Jewish spiritual leader. **rabbinical** *adj*

rabbit *n* small burrowing mammal with long ears. **rabbit on** *v* **rabbiting, rabbited** *Informal* talk too much.

rabble ⊕ *n* disorderly crowd of noisy people.

rabid ⊕ *adj* **1** fanatical. **2** having rabies.

rabies [**ray**–beez] *n* usu. fatal viral disease transmitted by dogs and certain other animals.

raccoon *n* small N American mammal with a long striped tail.

race¹ ⊕ *n* **1** contest of speed. ◆ *pl* **2** meeting for horse racing. ◆ *v* **3** compete with in a race. **4** run swiftly. **5** (of an engine) run faster than normal. **racer** *n* **racecourse** *n* **racehorse** *n* **racetrack** *n*

race² ⊕ *n* group of people of common ancestry with distinguishing physical features, such as skin colour. **racial** *adj* **racism, racialism** *n* hostile attitude or behaviour to members of other races, based on a belief in the innate superiority of one's own race. **racist, racialist** *adj*, *n*

rack ⊕ *n* **1** framework for holding particular articles, such as coats or luggage. **2** straight bar with teeth on its edge, to work with a cogwheel. **3** *Hist* instrument of torture that stretched the victim's body. ◆ *v* **4** cause great suffering to. **rack one's brains** try very hard to remember.

racket¹ ⊕ *n* **1** noisy disturbance. **2** occupation by which money is made illegally.

racket², racquet *n* bat with strings stretched in an oval frame, used in tennis etc. **rackets** *n* ball game played in a paved walled court.

raconteur [rak–on–**tur**] *n* skilled storyteller.

racy ⊕ *adj* **racier, raciest 1** slightly shocking. **2** spirited or lively.

radar *n* device for tracking distant objects by bouncing high–frequency radio pulses off them.

radial *adj* **1** spreading out from a common central point. **2** of a radius. **3** (also **radial–ply**) (of a tyre) having flexible sides strengthened with radial cords.

radiate ⊕ *v* **1** spread out from a centre. **2** emit or be emitted as radiation. **radiator** *n* **1** arrangement of pipes containing hot water or steam to heat a room. **2** tubes containing water as cooling apparatus for

---

THESAURUS

rabble *n* = **mob**, canaille, crowd, herd, horde, swarm, throng

rabid *adj* **1** = **fanatical**, extreme, fervent, irrational, narrow–minded, zealous ≠ **moderate 2** = **mad**, hydrophobic

race¹ *n* **1, 2** = **contest**, chase, competition, dash, pursuit, rivalry ◆ *v* **3** = **compete**, contest, run **4** = **run**, career, dart, dash, fly, gallop, hurry, speed, tear, zoom

race² *n* = **people**, blood, folk, nation, stock, tribe, type

rack *n* **1** = **frame**, framework, stand, structure ◆ *v* **4** = **torture**, afflict, agonize, crucify, harrow, oppress, pain, torment

racket¹ *n* **1** = **noise**, clamour, din, disturbance, fuss, outcry, pandemonium, row **2** = **fraud**, scheme

racy *adj* **1** = **risqué**, bawdy, blue, naughty, near the knuckle (*inf*), smutty, suggestive **2** = **lively**, animated, energetic, a car engine.

radical ⊕ *adj* 1 fundamental. 2 thorough. 3 advocating fundamental change. ◆ *n* 4 person advocating fundamental (political) change. 5 number expressed as the root of another. **radically** *adv* **radicalism** *n*

radio *n, pl* **–dios** 1 use of electromagnetic waves for broadcasting, communication, etc. 2 device for receiving and amplifying radio signals. 3 sound broadcasting. ◆ *v* 4 transmit (a message) by radio.

radioactive *adj* emitting radiation as a result of nuclear decay. **radioactivity** *n*

radiography [ray–dee–**og**–ra–fee] *n* production of an image on a film or plate by radiation. **radiographer** *n*

radiology [ray–dee–**ol**–a–jee] *n* science of using x–rays in medicine. **radiologist** *n*

radiotherapy *n* treatment of disease, esp. cancer, by radiation. **radiotherapist** *n*

radish *n* small hot–flavoured root vegetable eaten raw in salads.

radium *n Chem* radioactive metallic element.

radius *n, pl* **radii, radiuses** 1 (length of) a straight line from the centre to the circumference of a circle. 2 outer of two bones in the forearm.

RAF Royal Air Force.

raffia *n* prepared palm fibre for weaving mats etc.

raffle ⊕ *n* 1 lottery with goods as prizes. ◆ *v* 2 offer as a prize in a raffle.

raft *n* floating platform of logs, planks, etc.

rafter *n* one of the main beams of a roof.

rag *n* 1 fragment of cloth. 2 *Informal* newspaper. ◆ *pl* 3 tattered clothing. **from rags to riches** from being extremely poor to being extremely wealthy. **ragged** [**rag**–gid] *adj* 1 dressed in shabby or torn clothes. 2 torn. 3 lacking smoothness. **ragbag** *n* confused assortment, jumble.

ragamuffin ⊕ *n* ragged dirty child.

rage ⊕ *n* 1 violent anger or passion. ◆ *v* 2 speak or act with fury. 3 proceed violently and without check. **all the rage** very popular.

raglan *adj* (of a sleeve) joined to a garment by diagonal seams from the neck to the underarm.

raid ⊕ *n* 1 sudden surprise attack or search. ◆ *v* 2 make a raid on. **raider** *n*

rail¹ *n* 1 horizontal bar, esp. as part of a fence or track. 2 railway. **go off the rails** start behaving eccentrically or improperly. **railing** *n* fence made of rails supported by posts. **railcard** *n* card which pensioners, young people, etc. can buy, entitling them to cheaper rail travel. **railroad** *n* 1 *US* railway. ◆ *v* 2 *Informal* force (a person) into an action with haste or by unfair means. **railway** *n* 1 track of iron rails on which trains run. 2 company operating a railway.

rail² *v* (foll. by *at* or *against*) complain bitterly or loudly. **raillery** *n* teasing or joking.

rain ⊕ *n* 1 water falling in drops from the clouds. ◆ *v* 2 fall or pour down as rain. 3 fall rapidly and in large quantities. **rainy** *adj* **rainbow** *n* arch of colours in the sky.

entertaining, exciting, sparkling, spirited

radiate *v* 1 = **spread out**, branch out, diverge, issue 2 = **emit**, diffuse, give off *or* out, pour, scatter, send out, shed, spread

radical *adj* 1 = **fundamental**, basic, deep–seated, innate, natural, profound ≠ **minor** 2 = **extreme**, complete, drastic, entire, severe, sweeping, thorough 3 = **revolutionary**, extremist, fanatical ◆ *n* 4 = **extremist**, fanatic, militant, revolutionary ≠ **conservative**

raffle *n* 1 = **draw**, lottery, sweep,

sweepstake

ragamuffin *n* = **urchin**, guttersnipe

rage *n* 1 = **fury**, anger, frenzy, ire, madness, passion, rampage, wrath ≠ **pleasure** ◆ *v* 3 = **be furious**, blow one's top, blow up (*inf*), fly off the handle (*inf*), fume, go ballistic (*sl, chiefly US*), go up the wall (*sl*), lose it (*inf*), lose one's temper, lose the plot (*inf*), seethe, storm ≠ **accept**

raid *n* 1 = **attack**, foray, incursion, inroad, invasion, sally, sortie ◆ *v* 2 = **attack**, assault, foray, invade, pillage, plunder, rainfall *n* amount of rain. rainforest *n* dense forest in the tropics.

raise **O** *v* 1 lift up. 2 set upright. 3 increase in amount or intensity. 4 collect or levy. 5 bring up (a family). 6 put forward for consideration. 7 build. 8 end, e.g. *raise a siege*.

raisin *n* dried grape.

rake¹ **O** *n* 1 tool with a long handle and a crosspiece with teeth, used for smoothing earth or gathering leaves, hay, etc. ◆ *v* 2 gather or smooth with a rake. 3 search (through). 4 sweep (with gunfire). rake it in *Informal* make a large amount of money. rake up *v* revive memories of (a forgotten unpleasant event).

rake² **O** *n* dissolute or immoral man.

rakish **O** *adj* dashing or jaunty.

rally **O** *n, pl* -lies 1 large gathering of people for a meeting. 2 marked recovery of strength. 3 *Tennis etc.* lively exchange of strokes. 4 car-driving competition on

public roads. ◆ *v* -lying, -lied 5 bring or come together after dispersal or for a common cause. 6 regain health or strength, revive.

ram **O** *n* 1 male sheep. 2 hydraulic machine. ◆ *v* ramming, rammed 3 strike against with force. 4 force or drive.

ramble **O** *v* 1 walk without a definite route. 2 talk incoherently. ◆ *n* 3 walk, esp. in the country. rambler *n* 1 person who rambles. 2 climbing rose.

ramp **O** *n* slope joining two level surfaces.

rampage **O** *v* dash about violently. on the rampage behaving violently or destructively.

rampant **O** *adj* 1 growing or spreading uncontrollably. 2 (of a heraldic beast) on its hind legs.

rampart **O** *n* mound or wall for defence.

ramshackle **O** *adj* tumbledown, rickety, or makeshift.

ran *v* past tense of RUN.

sack

rain *n* 1 = **rainfall**, cloudburst, deluge, downpour, drizzle, fall, precipitation, raindrops, showers ◆ *v* 2 = **pour**, bucket down (*inf*), come down in buckets (*inf*), drizzle, pelt (down), teem 3 = **fall**, deposit, drop, shower, sprinkle

raise *v* 1 = **lift**, elevate, heave, hoist, rear, uplift 3 = **increase**, advance, amplify, boost, enhance, enlarge, exaggerate, heighten, inflate, intensify, magnify, strengthen ≠ **drop** 4 = **collect**, assemble, form, gather, mass, obtain, rally, recruit 5 = **bring up**, develop, nurture, rear 6 = **put forward**, advance, broach, introduce, moot, suggest 7 = **build**, construct, erect, put up ≠ **level**

rake¹ *v* 2 = **gather**, collect, remove 3 = **search**, comb, scour, scrutinize

rake² *n* = **libertine**, debauchee, lecher, playboy, roué, swinger (*sl*)

rakish *adj* = **dashing**, dapper, debonair, devil-may-care, jaunty, natty (*inf*), raffish, smart

rally *n* 1 = **gathering**, assembly, congress,

convention, meeting 2 = **recovery**, improvement, recuperation, revival ≠ **collapse** ◆ *v* 5 = **reassemble**, regroup, reorganize, unite 6 = **recover**, get better, improve, recuperate, revive ≠ **deteriorate**

ram *v* 3 = **hit**, butt, crash, dash, drive, force, impact, smash 4 = **cram**, crowd, force, jam, stuff, thrust

ramble *v* 1 = **walk**, range, roam, rove, saunter, stray, stroll, wander 2 = **babble**, rabbit (on) (*Brit inf*), waffle (*inf, chiefly Brit*), witter on (*inf*) ◆ *n* 3 = **walk**, hike, roaming, roving, saunter, stroll, tour

ramp *n* 1 = **slope**, gradient, incline, rise

rampage *v* = **go berserk**, rage, run amok, run riot, storm ◆ *n* on the rampage = **berserk**, amok, out of control, raging, riotous, violent, wild

rampant *adj* 1 = **widespread**, prevalent, profuse, rife, spreading like wildfire, unchecked, uncontrolled, unrestrained 2 = **upright**, erect, rearing, standing

rampart *n* = **defence**, bastion, bulwark, fence, fortification, wall

ramshackle *adj* = **rickety**, crumbling,

ranch *n* large cattle farm in the American West. **rancher** *n*

rancid ● *adj* (of butter, bacon, etc.) stale and having an offensive smell. **rancidity** *n*

rancour ● *n* deep bitter hate. **rancorous** *adj*

random ● *adj* made or done by chance or without plan. **at random** haphazard(ly).

randy ● *adj* **randier, randiest** *Informal* sexually aroused.

rang *v* past tense of RING¹.

range ● *n* 1 limits of effectiveness or variation. 2 distance that a missile or plane can travel. 3 distance of a mark shot at. 4 whole set of related things. 5 chain of mountains. 6 place for shooting practice or rocket testing. 7 kitchen stove. ◆ *v* 8 vary between one point and another. 9 cover or extend over. 10 roam. **ranger** *n* official in charge of a nature reserve etc.

rank¹ ● *n* 1 relative place or position. 2 status. 3 social class. 4 row or line. ◆ *v* 5 have a specific rank or position. 6 arrange

in rows or lines. **rank and file** ordinary people or members. **the ranks** common soldiers.

rank² ● *adj* 1 complete or absolute, e.g. *rank favouritism.* 2 smelling offensively strong. 3 growing too thickly.

rankle ● *v* continue to cause resentment or bitterness.

ransack ● *v* 1 search thoroughly. 2 pillage, plunder.

ransom ● *n* money demanded in return for the release of someone who has been kidnapped.

rant ● *v* talk in a loud and excited way.

rap ● *v* **rapping, rapped** 1 hit with a sharp quick blow. 2 utter (a command) abruptly. 3 perform a rhythmic monologue with musical backing. ◆ *n* 4 quick sharp blow. 5 rhythmic monologue performed to music. **take the rap** *Slang* suffer punishment for something whether guilty or not. **rapper** *n*

rapacious ● *adj* greedy or grasping.

rape¹ ● *v* 1 force to submit to sexual

decrepit, derelict, flimsy, shaky, tumbledown, unsafe, unsteady

rancid *adj* = **rotten**, bad, fetid, foul, off, putrid, rank, sour, stale, strong–smelling, tainted

rancour *n* = **hatred**, animosity, bad blood, bitterness, hate, ill feeling, ill will

random *adj* = **chance**, accidental, adventitious, casual, fortuitous, haphazard, hit or miss, incidental ≠ **planned at random** = **haphazardly**, arbitrarily, by chance, randomly, unsystematically, willy–nilly

randy *adj Inf* = **lustful**, amorous, aroused, horny (*sl*), hot, lascivious, turned–on (*sl*)

range *n* 1 = **limits**, area, bounds, orbit, province, radius, reach, scope, sphere 4 = **series**, assortment, collection, gamut, lot, selection, variety ◆ *v* 8 = **vary** 9 = **extend**, reach, run, stretch 10 = **roam**, ramble, rove, traverse, wander

rank¹ *n* 1, 2 = **status**, caste, class, degree, division, grade, level, order, position, sort, type 3 = **class**, caste 4 = **row**, column, file,

group, line, range, series, tier ◆ *v* 6 = **arrange**, align, array, dispose, line up, order, sort **rank and file** = **general public**, majority, mass, masses

rank² *adj* 1 = **absolute**, arrant, blatant, complete, downright, flagrant, gross, sheer, thorough, total, utter 2 = **foul**, bad, disgusting, noisome, noxious, offensive, rancid, revolting, stinking 3 = **abundant**, dense, lush, luxuriant, profuse

rankle *v* = **annoy**, anger, gall, get on one's nerves (*inf*), irk, irritate, rile

ransack *v* 1 = **search**, comb, explore, go through, rummage, scour, turn inside out 2 = **plunder**, loot, pillage, raid, strip

ransom *n* 1 = **payment**, money, payoff, price

rant *v* = **shout**, cry, declaim, rave, roar, yell

rap *v* 1 = **hit**, crack, knock, strike, tap ◆ *n* 4 = **blow**, clout (*inf*), crack, knock, tap **take the rap** *Sl* = **rebuke**, blame, punishment, responsibility

rapacious *adj* = **greedy**, avaricious, grasping, insatiable, predatory, preying, intercourse. ◆ n 2 act of raping. 3 any violation or abuse. **rapist** n

rape² n plant with oil–yielding seeds, also used as fodder.

rapid ⊕ adj quick, swift. **rapids** pl n part of a river with a fast turbulent current. **rapidity** n

rapier [ray–pyer] n fine–bladed sword.

rapport ⊕ [rap–pore] n harmony or agreement.

rapt ⊕ adj engrossed or spellbound. **rapture** n ecstasy. **rapturous** adj

rare¹ ⊕ adj 1 uncommon. 2 infrequent. 3 of uncommonly high quality. 4 (of air at high altitudes) having low density, thin. **rarely** adv seldom. **rarity** n

rare² ⊕ adj (of meat) lightly cooked.

raring ⊕ adj **raring to** enthusiastic, willing, or ready to.

rascal ⊕ n 1 rogue. 2 naughty (young) person. **rascally** adj

rash¹ ⊕ adj hasty, reckless, or incautious. **rashly** adv

rash² n 1 eruption of spots or patches on the skin. 2 outbreak of (unpleasant) occurrences.

rasher n thin slice of bacon.

rasp n 1 harsh grating noise. 2 coarse file. ◆ v 3 speak in a grating voice. 4 make a scraping noise.

raspberry n 1 red juicy edible berry. 2 Informal spluttering noise made with the tongue and lips, to show contempt.

Rastafarian n, adj (member) of a religion originating in Jamaica and regarding Haile Selassie as God (also **Rasta**).

rat n 1 small rodent. 2 Informal contemptible person, esp. a deserter or informer. ◆ v **ratting, ratted** 3 Informal inform (on). 4 hunt rats.

ratchet n set of teeth on a bar or wheel allowing motion in one direction only.

rate¹ ⊕ n 1 degree of speed or progress. 2 proportion between two things. 3 charge. ◆ pl 4 local tax on business. 5 v 6 consider or value. 7 estimate the value of. **at any rate** in any case. **rateable** adj 1 able to be rated. 2 (of property) liable to payment of rates.

rate² ⊕ v scold or criticize severely.

rather ⊕ adv 1 to some extent. 2 more

voracious

rape¹ v 1 = **sexually assault**, abuse, force, outrage, ravish, violate ◆ n 2 = **sexual assault**, outrage, ravishment, violation 3 = **desecration**, abuse, defilement, violation

rapid adj = **quick**, brisk, express, fast, hasty, hurried, prompt, speedy, swift ≠ **gradual**

rapport n = **bond**, affinity, empathy, harmony, link, relationship, sympathy, tie, understanding

rapt adj = **spellbound**, absorbed, engrossed, enthralled, entranced, fascinated, gripped ≠ **bored**

rare¹ adj 1 = **uncommon**, few, infrequent, scarce, singular, sparse, strange, unusual ≠ **common** 2 = **infrequent**, few, uncommon, unusual 3 = **superb**, choice, excellent, fine, great, peerless, superlative

rare² adj = **underdone**, bloody, half–cooked, half–raw, undercooked

raring adj As in raring to = **eager**, desperate, enthusiastic, impatient, keen, longing, ready

rascal n 1 = **rogue**, blackguard, devil, good–for–nothing, ne'er–do–well, scoundrel, villain 2 = **imp**, scamp

rash¹ adj = **reckless**, careless, foolhardy, hasty, heedless, ill–advised, impetuous, imprudent, impulsive, incautious

rash² n 1 = **outbreak**, eruption 2 = **spate**, flood, outbreak, plague, series, wave

rate¹ n 1 = **speed**, pace, tempo, velocity 2 = **degree**, proportion, ratio, scale, standard 3 = **charge**, cost, fee, figure, price ◆ v 6 = **evaluate**, consider, count, estimate, grade, measure, rank, reckon, value 7 = **estimate**, class, consider, count, evaluate, value **at any rate** = **in any case**, anyhow, anyway, at all events

rate² v = **scold**, bawl out (inf), berate,

truly or appropriately. **3** more willingly.
ratify ❶ v **–fying, –fied** give formal
  approval to. **ratification** n
rating ❶ n **1** valuation or assessment. **2**
  classification. **3** noncommissioned sailor. ◆
  pl **4** size of the audience for a TV
  programme.
ratio ❶ n, pl **–tios** relationship between
  two numbers or amounts expressed as a
  proportion.
ration ❶ n **1** fixed allowance of food etc. ◆
  v **2** limit to a certain amount per person.
rational ❶ adj **1** reasonable, sensible. **2**
  capable of reasoning. **rationally** adv
  rationality n **rationale** [rash–a–**nahl**] n
  reason for an action or decision.
  rationalism n philosophy that regards
  reason as the only basis for beliefs or
  actions. **rationalist** n **rationalize** v **1** justify
  by plausible reasoning. **2** reorganize to
  improve efficiency or profitability.
  rationalization n
rattle ❶ v **1** give out a succession of short
  sharp sounds. **2** shake briskly causing
  sharp sounds. **3** Informal confuse or fluster.

◆ n **4** short sharp sound. **5** instrument for
  making such a sound. **6 rattlesnake** n
  poisonous snake with loose horny
  segments on the tail that make a rattling
  sound.
raucous ❶ adj hoarse or harsh.
raunchy ❶ adj **–chier, –chiest** Slang
  earthy, sexy.
ravage ❶ v cause extensive damage to.
  ravages pl n damaging effects.
rave ❶ v **1** talk wildly or with enthusiasm.
  ◆ n **2** Slang large–scale party with
  electronic dance music. **raving** adj **1**
  delirious. **2** Informal exceptional, e.g. a
  raving beauty.
raven n **1** black bird like a large crow. ◆ adj
  2 (of hair) shiny black.
ravenous ❶ adj very hungry.
ravine ❶ [rav–**veen**] n narrow steep–sided
  valley worn by a stream.
ravioli pl n small squares of pasta with a
  savoury filling.
ravish ❶ v **1** enrapture. **2** Lit rape.
  ravishing adj lovely or entrancing.
raw ❶ adj **1** uncooked. **2** not manufactured

——————| THESAURUS |——————

blame, carpet (inf), castigate, censure,
chew out (US & Canad inf), chide, criticize
severely, give a rocket (Brit & NZ inf), haul
over the coals (inf), read the riot act,
rebuke, reprimand, reprove, roast (inf),
rouse on (Aust), take to task, tear into (inf),
tear (someone) off a strip (inf), tell off (inf),
tongue–lash, upbraid
rather adv **1 = to some extent**, a little,
  fairly, moderately, quite, relatively,
  somewhat, to some degree
  3 = preferably, more readily, more
  willingly, sooner
ratify v **= approve**, affirm, authorize,
  confirm, endorse, establish, sanction,
  uphold
rating n **2 = position**, class, degree, grade,
  order, placing, rank, rate, status
ratio n **= proportion**, fraction, percentage,
  rate, relation
ration n **1 = allowance**, allotment, helping,
  measure, part, portion, quota, share ◆ v

2 = limit, budget, control, restrict
rational adj **1, 2 = sensible**, intelligent,
  logical, lucid, realistic, reasonable, sane,
  sound, wise **≠ irrational**
rattle v **1 = clatter**, bang, jangle **2 = shake**,
  bounce, jar, jolt, vibrate **3** Inf **= fluster**,
  disconcert, disturb, faze, perturb, shake,
  upset
raucous adj **= harsh**, grating, hoarse, loud,
  noisy, rough, strident
raunchy adj Sl **= sexy**, coarse, earthy, lusty,
  sexual, steamy (inf)
ravage v **= destroy**, demolish, despoil,
  devastate, lay waste, ransack, ruin, spoil
rave v **1** a **= rant**, babble, be delirious,
  rage, roar b **= enthuse**, be mad about
  (inf), be wild about (inf), gush, praise
ravenous adj **= starving**, famished, starved
  ≠ full
ravine n **= canyon**, defile, gorge, gulch
  (US), gully, pass
ravish v **1 = enchant**, captivate, charm,

or refined. 3 inexperienced. 4 chilly. **raw deal** unfair or dishonest treatment.
rawhide *n* untanned hide.
ray[1] ⊕ *n* 1 single line or narrow beam of light.
ray[2] *n* large sea fish with a flat body and a whiplike tail.
rayon *n* (fabric made of) a synthetic fibre.
raze ⊕ *v* destroy (buildings or a town) completely.
razor *n* sharp instrument for shaving.
razzle–dazzle, razzmatazz *n Slang* showy activity.
RC 1 Roman Catholic. 2 Red Cross.
re ⊕ *prep* with reference to, concerning.

✓ **WORD TIP**
In commercial correspondence the use of *re* is becoming less frequent in favour of *with reference to* or *about*.

RE religious education.
re– *prefix* again, e.g. *re-enter; retrial.*
reach ⊕ *v* 1 arrive at. 2 make a movement in order to grasp or touch. 3 succeed in touching. 4 make contact or communication with. 5 extend as far as. ◆ *n* 6 distance that one can reach. 7 range

of influence. ◆ *pl* 8 stretch of a river.
react ⊕ *v* 1 act in response (to). 2 (foll. by *against*) act in an opposing or contrary manner. **reaction** *n* 1 physical or emotional response to a stimulus. 2 any action resisting another. 3 opposition to change. 4 chemical or nuclear change, combination, or decomposition.
reactionary *n, adj* (person) opposed to change, esp. in politics. **reactive** *adj* chemically active. **reactor** *n* apparatus in which a nuclear reaction is maintained and controlled to produce nuclear energy.
read ⊕ *v* **reading, read** 1 look at and understand or take in (written or printed matter). 2 look at and say aloud. 3 interpret the significance or meaning of. 4 (of an instrument) register. 5 study. ◆ *n* 6 matter suitable for reading, e.g. *a good read.* **readable** *adj* 1 enjoyable to read. 2 legible. **reader** *n* 1 person who reads. 2 textbook. 3 senior university lecturer. **readership** *n* readers of a publication collectively. **reading** *n*
ready ⊕ *adj* **readier, readiest** 1 prepared for use or action. 2 willing, prompt. **readily** *adv* **readiness** *n* **ready–made** *adj* for immediate use by any customer.

——————— THESAURUS ———————

delight, enrapture, entrance, fascinate, spellbind 2 *Lit* = **rape**, abuse, force, sexually assault, violate
raw *adj* 1 = **uncooked**, fresh, natural ≠ **cooked** 2 = **unrefined**, basic, coarse, crude, natural, rough, unfinished, unprocessed ≠ **prepared** 3 = **inexperienced**, callow, green, immature, new ≠ **experienced** 4 = **chilly**, biting, bitter, cold, freezing, parky (*Brit inf*), piercing
ray[1] *n* 1 = **beam**, bar, flash, gleam, shaft
raze *v* = **destroy**, demolish, flatten, knock down, level, pull down, ruin
re[1] *prep* = **concerning**, about, apropos, regarding, with reference to, with regard to
reach *v* 1 = **arrive at**, attain, get to, make 3, 5 = **touch**, contact, extend to, grasp,

stretch to 4 = **contact**, communicate with, get hold of, get in touch with, get through to ◆ *n* 6 = **range**, distance, extension, extent, grasp, stretch 7 = **power**, capacity, influence, mana (*NZ*), scope
react *v* 1 = **respond**, answer, reply
read *v* 1 = **look at**, comprehend, construe, decipher, discover, interpret, peruse, pore over, scan, see, study, understand 4 = **register**, display, indicate, record, show 5 = **study**, pore over
ready *adj* 1 = **prepared**, accessible, arranged, available, convenient, fit, handy, near, organized, present, primed, ripe, set ≠ **unprepared** 2 = **willing**, agreeable, alert, bright, clever, disposed, eager, glad, happy, inclined, keen, prompt, prone, quick ≠ **reluctant**

real ○ *adj* 1 existing in fact. 2 actual. 3 genuine. **really** *adv* 1 very. 2 truly. ◆ *interj* 3 exclamation of dismay, doubt, or surprise. **reality** *n* state of things as they are. **real ale** beer allowed to ferment in the barrel. **real estate** property consisting of land and houses.

✓ **WORD TIP**
To intensify an adjective, use the adverb form *really*, not *real: He's really strong.*

realize ○ *v* 1 become aware or grasp the significance of. 2 achieve (a plan, hopes, etc.). 3 convert into money. **realization** *n*

realm ○ *n* 1 kingdom. 2 sphere of interest.

ream *n* 1 twenty quires of paper, generally 500 sheets. ◆ *pl* 2 *Informal* large quantity (of written matter).

reap ○ *v* 1 cut and gather (a harvest). 2 receive the result of a previous activity. **reaper** *n*

rear¹ ○ *n* 1 back part. 2 part of an army, procession, etc. behind the others. **bring up the rear** come last. **rearmost** *adj* **rear admiral** high-ranking naval officer.

rearguard *n* troops protecting the rear of an army.

rear² ○ *v* 1 care for and educate (children). 2 breed (animals). 3 (of a horse) rise on its hind feet.

reason ○ *n* 1 cause or motive. 2 faculty of rational thought. 3 sanity. ◆ *v* 4 think logically in forming conclusions. **reason with** persuade by logical argument into doing something. **reasonable** *adj* 1 sensible. 2 not excessive. 3 logical. **reasonably** *adv*

reassure ○ *v* restore confidence to. **reassurance** ○

rebate ○ *n* discount or refund.

rebel ○ *v* –belling, –belled 1 revolt against the ruling power. 2 reject accepted conventions. ◆ *n* 3 person who rebels. **rebellion** *n* 1 organized open resistance to authority. 2 rejection of conventions. **rebellious** *adj*

rebound ○ *v* 1 spring back. 2 misfire so as to hurt the perpetrator of a plan or deed. **on the rebound** *Informal* while recovering from rejection.

rebuff ○ *v* 1 reject or snub. ◆ *n* 2 blunt refusal, snub.

———————| THESAURUS |———————

real *adj* = **genuine**, actual, authentic, factual, rightful, sincere, true, unfeigned, valid

realize *v* 1 = **become aware of**, comprehend, get the message, grasp, take in, understand 2 = **achieve**, accomplish, carry out *or* through, complete, do, effect, fulfil, perform

realm *n* 1 = **kingdom**, country, domain, dominion, empire, land 2 = **field**, area, branch, department, province, sphere, territory, world

reap *v* 1 = **collect**, bring in, cut, garner, gather, harvest 2 = **get**, acquire, derive, gain, obtain

rear¹ *n* 1 = **back**, end, rearguard, stern, tail, tail end ≠ **front**

rear² *v* 1 = **bring up**, educate, foster, nurture, raise, train 2 = **breed** 3 = **rise**

reason *n* 1 = **cause**, aim, goal, grounds,

incentive, intention, motive, object, purpose 2 = **sense**, intellect, judgment, logic, understanding ≠ **emotion** 3 = **sanity**, mind, rationality, soundness ◆ *v* 4 = **deduce**, conclude, infer, make out, think, work out **reason with** = **persuade**, bring round (*inf*), prevail upon, talk into *or* out of, urge, win over

reassure *v* = **encourage**, comfort, gee up, hearten, put *or* set one's mind at rest, restore confidence to

rebate *n* = **refund**, allowance, bonus, deduction, discount, reduction

rebel *v* 1 = **revolt**, mutiny, resist, rise up 2 = **defy** ◆ *n* 3 = **revolutionary**, insurgent, revolutionist, secessionist

rebound *v* 1 = **bounce**, recoil, ricochet 2 = **misfire**, backfire, boomerang, recoil

rebuff *v* 1 = **reject**, cold-shoulder, cut, knock back (*sl*), refuse, repulse, slight,

rebuke ⊕ v **1** scold sternly. ◆ n **2** stern scolding.

rebut ⊕ v **–butting, –butted** prove that (a claim) is untrue. **rebuttal** n

recalcitrant adj wilfully disobedient. **recalcitrance** n

recall ⊕ v **1** recollect or remember. **2** order to return. **3** annul or cancel. ◆ n **4** ability to remember. **5** order to return.

recant ⊕ v withdraw (a statement or belief) publicly. **recantation** n

recap Informal ◆ v **–capping, –capped 1** recapitulate. ◆ n **2** recapitulation.

recapitulate ⊕ v state again briefly, repeat. **recapitulation** n

recede v **1** move to a more distant place. **2** (of the hair) stop growing at the front.

receipt ⊕ n **1** written acknowledgment of money or goods received. **2** receiving or being received.

receive ⊕ v **1** take, accept, or get. **2** experience. **3** greet (guests). **received** adj

generally accepted. **receiver** n **1** part of telephone that is held to the ear. **2** equipment in a telephone, radio, or television that converts electrical signals into sound. **3** person appointed by a court to manage the property of a bankrupt. **receivership** n state of being administered by a receiver.

recent ⊕ adj **1** having happened lately. **2** new. **recently** adv

receptacle ⊕ n object used to contain something.

reception ⊕ n **1** area for receiving guests, clients, etc. **2** formal party. **3** manner of receiving. **4** welcome. **5** (in broadcasting) quality of signals received. **receptionist** n person who receives guests, clients, etc.

receptive ⊕ adj willing to accept new ideas, suggestions, etc. **receptivity** n

recess ⊕ n **1** niche or alcove. **2** holiday between sessions of work. **3** secret hidden place.

recession ⊕ n period of economic

snub, spurn, turn down ≠ **encourage** ◆ n **2** = **rejection**, cold shoulder, kick in the teeth (sl), knock–back (sl), refusal, repulse, slap in the face (inf), slight, snub

rebuke v **1** = **scold**, admonish, castigate, censure, chide, dress down (inf), give a rocket (Brit & NZ inf), haul (someone) over the coals (inf), reprimand, reprove, rouse on (Aust), tear (someone) off a strip (inf), tell off (inf) ≠ **praise** ◆ n **2** = **scolding**, admonition, censure, dressing–down (inf), reprimand, row, telling–off (inf)

rebut v = **disprove**, confute, invalidate, negate, overturn, prove wrong, refute

recall v **1** = **recollect**, bring or call to mind, evoke, remember **3** = **annul**, cancel, countermand, repeal, retract, revoke, withdraw ◆ n **4** = **recollection**, memory, remembrance **5** = **repeal**, rescindment, retraction, withdrawal

recant v = **withdraw**, disclaim, forswear, renege, repudiate, retract, revoke, take back

recapitulate v = **restate**, outline, recap

(inf), recount, repeat, summarize

recede v **1** = **fall back**, abate, draw back, ebb, regress, retire, retreat, return, subside, withdraw

receipt n **1** = **sales slip**, counterfoil, proof of purchase **2** = **receiving**, acceptance, delivery, reception

receive v **1** = **get**, accept, acquire, be given, collect, obtain, pick up, take **2** = **experience**, bear, encounter, suffer, sustain, undergo **3** = **greet**, accommodate, admit, entertain, meet, welcome

recent adj **1** = **late 2** = **new**, current, fresh, modern, novel, present–day, up–to–date ≠ **old**

receptacle n = **container**, holder, repository

reception n **2** = **party**, function, soiree **3** = **response**, acknowledgment, greeting, reaction, treatment, welcome **4** = **welcome**, greeting

receptive adj = **open**, amenable, interested, open–minded, open to suggestions, susceptible, sympathetic difficulty when little is being bought or sold. **recessive** *adj* receding.

recipe ⊕ *n* 1 directions for cooking a dish. 2 method for achieving something.

recipient *n* person who receives something.

reciprocal ⊕ [ris–**sip**–pro–kl] *adj* 1 mutual. 2 given or done in return. **reciprocate** *v* 1 give or feel in return. 2 (of a machine part) move backwards and forwards. **reciprocation** *n* **reciprocity** *n*

recite ⊕ *v* repeat (a poem etc.) aloud to an audience. **recital** *n* 1 musical performance by a soloist or soloists. 2 act of reciting. **recitation** *n* recital, usu. from memory, of poetry or prose.

reckless ⊕ *adj* heedless of danger. **recklessly** *adv* **recklessness** *n*

reckon ⊕ *v* 1 consider or think. 2 make calculations, count. 3 expect. **reckoning** *n*

reclaim ⊕ *v* 1 regain possession of. 2 make fit for cultivation. **reclamation** *n*

recline ⊕ *v* rest in a leaning position. **reclining** *adj*

recluse ⊕ *n* person who avoids other people. **reclusive** *adj*

recognize ⊕ *v* 1 identify as (a person or thing) already known. 2 accept as true or existing. 3 treat as valid. 4 notice, show appreciation of. **recognition** *n* **recognizable** *adj*

recoil ⊕ *v* 1 jerk or spring back. 2 draw back in horror. 3 (of an action) go wrong so as to hurt the doer. ◆ *n* 4 backward jerk. 5 recoiling.

recollect ⊕ *v* call back to mind, remember. **recollection** *n*

recommend ⊕ *v* 1 advise or counsel. 2 praise or commend. 3 make acceptable. **recommendation** *n*

recompense ⊕ *v* 1 pay or reward. 2 compensate or make up for. ◆ *n* 3 compensation. 4 reward or remuneration.

reconcile ⊕ *v* 1 harmonize (conflicting

———————| T H E S A U R U S |———————

≠ **unreceptive**

recess *n* 1 = **alcove**, bay, corner, hollow, niche, nook 2 = **break**, holiday, intermission, interval, respite, rest, vacation

recession *n* = **depression**, decline, drop, slump

recipe *n* 1 = **directions**, ingredients, instructions 2 = **method**, formula, prescription, procedure, process, technique

reciprocal *adj* 1, 2 = **mutual**, alternate, complementary, correlative, corresponding, equivalent, exchanged, interchangeable

recite *v* 1 = **repeat**, declaim, deliver, narrate, perform, speak

reckless *adj* = **careless**, hasty, headlong, heedless, imprudent, mindless, precipitate, rash, thoughtless, wild

reckon *v* 1 = **consider**, account, assume, believe, count, deem, esteem, guess (*inf, chiefly US & Canad*), imagine, judge, rate, regard, suppose, think 2 = **count**, add up, calculate, compute, figure, number, tally,

total

reclaim *v* 1 = **regain**, recapture, recover, redeem, retrieve 3 = **salvage**

recline *v* = **lean**, lie (down), loll, lounge, repose, rest, sprawl

recluse *n* = **hermit**, anchoress, anchorite, monk, solitary

recognize *v* 1 = **identify**, know, notice, place, recall, recollect, remember, spot 2 = **acknowledge**, accept, admit, allow, concede, grant ≠ **forget** 4 = **appreciate**, notice, respect

recoil *v* 1 = **jerk back**, kick, react, rebound, spring back 2 = **draw back**, falter, quail, shrink 3 = **backfire**, boomerang, go pear–shaped (*inf*), misfire, rebound ◆ *n* 4 = **reaction**, backlash, kick, rebound, repercussion

recollect *v* = **remember**, place, recall, summon up

recommend *v* 1 = **advise**, advance, advocate, counsel, prescribe, propose, put forward, suggest ≠ **reject** 2 = **commend**, approve, endorse, praise

recompense *v* 1 = **reward**, pay,

beliefs etc.). 2 bring back into friendship. 3 accept or cause to accept (an unpleasant situation). **reconciliation** n

reconnoitre ❶ [rek-a-**noy**-ter] v make a reconnaissance of.

reconstitute v 1 reorganize. 2 restore (dried food) to its former state by adding water. **reconstitution** n

record ❶ n [**rek**-ord] 1 document or other thing that preserves information. 2 disc with indentations which a record player transforms into sound. 3 best recorded achievement. 4 known facts about a person's past. ◆ v [rik-**kord**] 5 put in writing. 6 preserve (sound, TV programmes, etc.) on plastic disc, magnetic tape, etc., for reproduction on a playback device. 7 show or register. **off the record** not for publication. **recorder** n 1 person or machine that records, esp. a video, cassette, or tape recorder. 2 type of flute, held vertically. 3 judge in certain courts. **recording** n **record player** instrument for reproducing sound on records.

recount ❶ v tell in detail.

recoup ❶ [rik-**koop**] v 1 regain or make good (a loss). 2 recompense or compensate.

recourse ❶ n source of help. **have recourse to** turn to a source of help or course of action.

recover ❶ v 1 become healthy again. 2 regain a former condition. 3 find again. 4 get back (a loss or expense). **recovery** n

recreation ❶ n agreeable or refreshing occupation, relaxation, or amusement. **recreational** adj

recrimination ❶ n mutual blame.

recruit ❶ v 1 enlist (new soldiers, members, etc.). ◆ n 2 newly enlisted soldier. 3 new member or supporter. **recruitment** n

rectangle n oblong four-sided figure with

remunerate 2 = **compensate**, make up for, pay for, reimburse, repay, requite, ress ◆ n 3 = **compensation**, amends, damages, payment, remuneration, reparation, repayment, requital, restitution 4 = **reward**, payment, return, wages

reconcile v 1 = **resolve**, adjust, compose, put to rights, rectify, settle, square 2 = **make peace between**, appease, conciliate, propitiate, reunite 3 = **accept**, put up with (inf), resign oneself, submit, yield

reconnoitre v = **inspect**, case (sl), explore, investigate, observe, scan, spy out, survey

record n 1 = **document**, account, chronicle, diary, entry, file, journal, log, register, report 2 = **disc**, album, LP, single, vinyl 4 = **background**, career, history, performance ◆ v 5 = **set down**, chronicle, document, enter, log, minute, note, register, take down, write down 6 = **make a recording of**, tape, tape-record, video, video-tape 7 = **register**, give evidence of, indicate, say, show **off the record = not for publication**, confidential, private, unofficial

recount v = **tell**, depict, describe, narrate, recite, relate, repeat, report

recoup v 1 = **regain**, recover, retrieve, win back 2 = **compensate**, make up for, refund, reimburse, repay, requite

recourse n = **option**, alternative, choice, expedient, remedy, resort, resource, way out

recover v 1 = **get better**, convalesce, get well, heal, improve, mend, rally, recuperate, revive ≠ **weaken** 2–4 = **regain**, get back, recapture, reclaim, redeem, repossess, restore, retrieve ≠ **lose**

recreation n = **pastime**, amusement, diversion, enjoyment, entertainment, fun, hobby, leisure activity, play, relaxation, sport

recrimination n = **bickering**, counterattack, mutual accusation, quarrel, squabbling

recruit v 1 = **enlist**, draft, enrol, levy, mobilize, muster, raise ◆ n 3 = **beginner**, apprentice, convert, helper, initiate, learner, novice, trainee

four right angles. **rectangular** adj
rectify ⊕ v –**fying**, –**fied** put right, correct.
  rectification n
rectitude ⊕ n moral correctness.
rector n 1 clergyman in charge of a parish.
  2 head of certain academic institutions.
  rectory n rector's house.
rectum n, pl –**tums**, –**ta** final section of the
  large intestine.
recumbent adj lying down.
recuperate ⊕ v recover from illness.
  recuperation n **recuperative** adj
recur v –**curring**, –**curred** happen again.
  recurrence n repetition. **recurrent** adj
recycle ⊕ v reprocess (used materials) for
  further use.
red ⊕ adj **redder**, **reddest** 1 of a colour
  varying from crimson to orange and seen
  in blood, fire, etc. 2 flushed in the face
  from anger, shame, etc. ♦ n 3 red colour.
  4 (R–) Informal communist. **in the red**
  Informal in debt. **see red** Informal be
  angry. **redness** n **redden** v make or
  become red. **reddish** adj **red–blooded** adj
  Informal vigorous or virile. **red carpet** very
  special welcome for an important guest.
  redcurrant n small round edible red berry.

1 **red–handed** adj Informal (caught) in the
  act of doing something wrong or illegal.
  red herring something which diverts
  attention from the main issue. **red–hot** adj
  1 glowing red. 2 extremely hot. 3 very
  keen danger signal. **red tape** excessive
  adherence to official rules.
redeem ⊕ v 1 make up for. 2 reinstate
  (oneself) in someone's good opinion. 3
  free from sin. 4 buy back. 5 pay off (a loan
  or debt). **redeemable** adj **redemption** n
  redemptive adj
redolent ⊕ adj 1 reminiscent (of). 2 smelling
  strongly (of).
redouble v increase, multiply, or intensify.
redoubtable ⊕ adj formidable.
redress ⊕ v 1 make amends for. ♦ n 1
  compensation or amends.
reduce ⊕ v 1 bring down, lower. 2 lessen,
  weaken. 3 bring by force or necessity to
  some state or action. 4 slim. 5 simplify. 6
  make (a sauce) more concentrated.
  reducible adj **reduction** n
redundant ⊕ adj 1 (of a worker) no longer
  needed. 2 superfluous. **redundancy** n
reed n 1 tall grass that grows in swamps
  and shallow water. 2 tall straight stem of

——————| THESAURUS |——————

rectify v 1 = **correct**, adjust, emend, fix,
  improve, redress, remedy, repair, right
rectitude n = **morality**, decency,
  goodness, honesty, honour, integrity,
  principle, probity, virtue ≠ **corruption**
recuperate v = **recover**, convalesce, get
  better, improve, mend
recur v = **happen again**, come again,
  persist, reappear, repeat, return, revert
recycle v = **reprocess**, reclaim, reuse,
  salvage, save
red adj 1 = **crimson**, carmine, cherry, coral,
  ruby, scarlet, vermilion 2 = **flushed**,
  blushing, embarrassed, florid, shamefaced
  in the red Inf = **in debt**, in arrears,
  insolvent, overdrawn **see red** Inf = **lose
  one's temper**, be or get pissed (off) (taboo
  sl), blow one's top, crack up (inf), fly off
  the handle (inf), go ballistic (sl, chiefly US),
  go mad (inf), lose it (inf)

redeem v 1 = **make up for**, atone for,
  compensate for, make amends for
  2 = **reinstate**, absolve, restore to favour
  3 = **save**, deliver, free 4 = **buy back**,
  reclaim, recover, regain, repurchase,
  retrieve
redoubtable adj = **formidable**, fearful,
  fearsome, mighty, powerful, strong
redress v 1 = **make amends for**,
  compensate for, make up for ♦ n
  2 = **amends**, atonement, compensation,
  payment, recompense, reparation
reduce v 1, 2 = **lessen**, abate, curtail, cut,
  cut down, decrease, diminish, lower,
  moderate, shorten, weaken ≠ **increase**
  3 = **degrade**, break, bring low,
  downgrade, humble ≠ **promote**
redundant adj 1 = **unemployed**, jobless,
  out of work 2 = **superfluous**, extra,
  inessential, supernumerary, surplus,

this plant. 3 *Music* vibrating cane or metal strip in certain wind instruments. **reedy** *adj* 1 harsh and thin in tone.

reef *n* 1 ridge of rock or coral near the surface of the sea. 2 vein of ore.

reek ❶ *v* 1 smell strongly. ♦ *n* 2 strong unpleasant smell. **reek of** give a strong suggestion of.

reel¹ *n* 1 cylindrical object on which film, tape, thread, or wire is wound. 2 winding apparatus, as of a fishing rod. 3 roll of film. **reel in** *v* draw in by means of a reel. **reel off** *v* recite or write fluently or quickly.

reel² ❶ *v* stagger, sway, or whirl.

reel³ *n* lively Scottish dance.

refectory *n, pl* **-tories** room for meals in a college etc.

refer ❶ *v* **-ferring, -ferred** (foll. by *to*) 1 allude (to). 2 be relevant (to). 3 send (to) for information. 4 submit (to) for decision. **referral** *n* **reference** *n* 1 act of referring. 2 citation or direction in a book. 3 written testimonial regarding character or capabilities. **with reference to** concerning.

✓ WORD TIP

Refer includes the sense 'back' in its meaning. Avoid using *refer back* unless the context involves sending papers back to a committee for further consideration.

---

referee ❶ *n* 1 umpire in sports, esp. football or boxing. 2 person willing to testify to someone's character etc. 3

arbitrator. ♦ *v* **-eeing, -eed** 4 act as referee of.

referendum ❶ *n, pl* **-dums, -da** direct vote of the electorate on an important question.

refill *v* 1 fill again. ♦ *n* 2 second or subsequent filling. 3 replacement supply of something in a permanent container.

refine ❶ *v* 1 purify. 2 improve. **refined** *adj* 1 cultured or polite. 2 purified. **refinement** *n* 1 improvement or elaboration. 2 fineness of taste or manners. 3 subtlety. **refinery** *n* place where sugar, oil, etc. is refined.

reflect ❶ *v* 1 throw back, esp. rays of light, heat, etc. 2 form an image of. 3 show. 4 consider at length. 5 bring credit or discredit upon. **reflection** *n* 1 act of reflecting. 2 return of rays of heat, light, etc. from a surface. 3 image of an object given back by a mirror etc. 4 conscious thought or meditation. 5 attribution of discredit or blame. **reflective** *adj* 1 quiet, contemplative. 2 capable of reflecting images. **reflector** *n* polished surface for reflecting light etc.

reflex *n* 1 involuntary response to a stimulus or situation. ♦ *adj* 2 (of a muscular action) involuntary. 3 reflected. 4 (of an angle) more than 180°. **reflexive** *adj Grammar* denoting a verb whose subject is the same as its object, e.g. *dress oneself*.

reform ❶ *n* 1 improvement. ♦ *v* 2 improve. 3 abandon evil practices.

———————{ THESAURUS }———————

unnecessary, unwanted ≠ **needed**

reek *v* 1 = **stink**, pong (*Brit inf*), smell ♦ *n* 2 = **stink**, fetor, odour, pong (*Brit inf*), smell, stench

reel² *v* = **stagger**, lurch, pitch, revolve, rock, roll, spin, sway, swirl, whirl

refer *v* (foll. by *to*) 1 = **allude**, bring up, cite, mention, speak of 2 = **relate**, apply, belong, be relevant to, concern, pertain 3 = **consult**, apply, go, look up, turn to 4 = **direct**, guide, point, send

referee *n* 1 = **umpire**, adjudicator, judge,

ref (*inf*) 3 = **arbitrator**, arbiter ♦ *v* 4 a = **umpire**, adjudicate, judge b = **arbitrate**, mediate

referendum *n* = **public vote**, plebiscite

refine *v* 1 = **purify**, clarify, distil, filter, process 2 = **improve**, hone, perfect, polish

reflect *v* 1 = **throw back**, echo, return 2 = **mirror**, reproduce 3 = **show**, demonstrate, display, indicate, manifest, reveal 4 = **consider**, cogitate, meditate, muse, ponder, ruminate, think, wonder reformer *n* reformation *n* **1** a reforming. **2** (R–) religious movement in 16th–century Europe that resulted in the establishment of the Protestant Churches. **reformatory** *n* (formerly) institution for reforming young offenders.

refract *v* change the course of (light etc.) passing from one medium to another. **refraction** *n* **refractive** *adj*

refractory *adj* **1** unmanageable or rebellious. **2** *Med* resistant to treatment. **3** resistant to heat.

refrain¹ ❶ *v* **refrain from** keep oneself from doing.

refrain² ❶ *n* frequently repeated part of a song.

refresh ❶ *v* **1** revive or reinvigorate, as through food, drink, or rest. **2** stimulate (the memory). **refresher** *n* **refreshing** *adj* **1** having a reviving effect. **2** pleasantly different or new. **refreshment** *n* something that refreshes, esp. food or drink.

refrigerate ❶ *v* cool or freeze in order to preserve. **refrigeration** *n* **refrigerator** *n* full name for FRIDGE.

refuge ❶ *n* (source of) shelter or protection. **refugee** *n* person who seeks refuge, esp. in a foreign country.

refund ❶ *v* **1** pay back. ◆ *n* **2** return of money. **3** amount returned.

refurbish ❶ *v* renovate and brighten up.

refuse¹ ❶ *v* decline, deny, or reject. **refusal** *n* denial of anything demanded or offered.

refuse² ❶ *n* rubbish or useless matter.

refute ❶ *v* disprove. **refutation** *n*

> ✓ **WORD TIP**
> *Refute* is not the same as *deny*. It means 'show evidence to disprove something', while *deny* means only 'say something is not true'.

regain ❶ *v* **1** get back or recover. **2** reach again.

regal ❶ *adj* of or like a king or queen. **regally** *adv* **regalia** *pl n* ceremonial emblems of royalty or high office.

regale ❶ *v* entertain (someone) with stories etc.

regard ❶ *v* **1** consider. **2** look at. **3** heed. ◆ *n* **4** respect or esteem. **5** attention. **6** look. ◆ *pl* **7** expression of goodwill. **as regards, regarding** in respect of, concerning. **regardless** *adj* **1** heedless. ◆ *adv* **2** in spite of everything.

—————————— THESAURUS ——————————

reform *n* **1** = **improvement**, amendment, betterment, rehabilitation ◆ *v* **2** = **improve**, amend, correct, mend, rectify, restore **3** = **mend one's ways**, clean up one's act (*inf*), go straight (*inf*), pull one's socks up (*Brit inf*), shape up (*inf*), turn over a new leaf

refrain¹ *v* = **stop**, abstain, avoid, cease, desist, forbear, leave off, renounce

refrain² **refrain from** *n* = **chorus**, melody, tune

refresh *v* **1** = **revive**, brace, enliven, freshen, invigorate, revitalize, stimulate **2** = **stimulate**, jog, prompt, renew

refrigerate *v* = **cool**, chill, freeze, keep cold

refuge *n* = **shelter**, asylum, haven, hide–out, protection, retreat, sanctuary

refund *v* **1** = **repay**, pay back, reimburse,

restore, return ◆ *n* **2**, **3** = **repayment**, reimbursement, return

refurbish *v* = **renovate**, clean up, do up (*inf*), mend, overhaul, repair, restore, revamp

refuse¹ *v* **1** = **reject**, decline, deny, say no, spurn, turn down, withhold ≠ **allow**

refuse² *n* = **rubbish**, garbage, junk (*inf*), litter, trash, waste

refute *v* = **disprove**, discredit, negate, overthrow, prove false, rebut

regain *v* **1** = **recover**, get back, recapture, recoup, retrieve, take back, win back **2** = **get back to**, reach again, return to

regal *adj* = **royal**, kingly or queenly, magnificent, majestic, noble, princely

regale *v* = **entertain**, amuse, delight, divert

regard *v* **1** = **consider**, believe, deem, esteem, judge, rate, see, suppose, think,

regatta n meeting for yacht or boat races.

regenerate 🟕 v 1 (cause to) undergo spiritual, moral, or physical renewal. 2 reproduce or re–create. **regeneration** n **regenerative** adj

regent n 1 ruler of a kingdom during the absence, childhood, or illness of its monarch. ◆ adj 2 ruling as a regent, e.g. prince regent. **regency** n status or period of office of a regent.

reggae n style of Jamaican popular music with a strong beat.

regime 🟕 [ray–**zheem**] n 1 system of government. 2 particular administration.

regiment n organized body of troops as a unit of the army. **regimental** adj **regimentation** n **regimented** adj very strictly controlled.

region 🟕 n 1 administrative division of a country. 2 area considered as a unit but with no definite boundaries. 3 part of the body. **regional** adj

register 🟕 n 1 (book containing) an official list or record of things. 2 range of a voice or instrument. ◆ v 3 enter in a register or set down in writing. 4 show or be shown

on a meter or the face. **registration** n **registration number** numbers and letters displayed on a vehicle to identify it. **registrar** n 1 keeper of official records. 2 senior hospital doctor, junior to a consultant. **register office, registry office** place where births, marriages, and deaths are recorded.

regress 🟕 v revert to a former worse condition. **regression** n 1 act of regressing. 2 Psychol use of an earlier (inappropriate) mode of behaviour. **regressive** adj

regret 🟕 v –gretting, –gretted 1 feel sorry about. 2 express apology or distress. ◆ n 3 feeling of repentance, guilt, or sorrow. **regretful** adj **regrettable** adj

regular 🟕 adj 1 normal, customary, or usual. 2 symmetrical or even. 3 done or occurring according to a rule. 4 periodical. 5 employed continuously in the armed forces. ◆ n 6 regular soldier. 7 Informal frequent customer. **regularity** n **regularize** v **regularly** adv

regulate 🟕 v 1 control, esp. by rules. 2 adjust slightly. **regulation** n 1 rule. 2

──────── THESAURUS ────────

view 2 = **look at**, behold, check out (inf), clock (Brit sl), eye, eyeball (US sl), gaze at, observe, scrutinize, view, watch 3 = **heed**, attend, listen to, mind, pay attention to, take notice of ◆ n 4 = **respect**, care, concern, consideration, esteem, thought 5 = **heed**, attention, interest, mind, notice 6 = **look**, gaze, glance, scrutiny, stare ◆ pl 7 = **good wishes**, best wishes, compliments, greetings, respects **as regards, regarding** = **concerning**, about, in or with regard to, on the subject of, pertaining to, re, relating to, respecting, with reference to

regenerate v 1 = **renew**, breathe new life into, invigorate, reawaken, reinvigorate, rejuvenate, restore, revive

regime n 1, 2 = **government**, leadership, management, reign, rule, system

region n 1 = **area**, district, locality, part, place, quarter, section, sector, territory,

tract, zone

register n 1 = **list**, archives, catalogue, chronicle, diary, file, log, record, roll, roster ◆ v 3 = **record**, catalogue, chronicle, enlist, enrol, enter, list, note 4 = **show**, display, exhibit, express, indicate, manifest, mark, reveal

regress v = **revert**, backslide, degenerate, deteriorate, fall away or off, go back, lapse, relapse, return

regret v 1 = **feel sorry about**, bewail, deplore, lament 2 = **grieve**, bemoan, miss, mourn, repent, rue ◆ n 3 = **sorrow**, bitterness, compunction, contrition, penitence, remorse, repentance, ruefulness

regular adj 1 = **normal**, common, customary, habitual, ordinary, routine, typical, usual ≠ **rare** 2 = **even**, balanced, flat, level, smooth, straight, symmetrical, uniform ≠ **irregular** 3 = **systematic**, consistent, constant, even, fixed, ordered, regulating. **regulator** *n* device that automatically controls pressure, temperature, etc.

regurgitate ⊕ *v* 1 vomit. 2 (of some birds and animals) bring back (partly digested food) into the mouth. 3 reproduce (ideas, facts, etc.) without understanding them. **regurgitation** *n*

rehabilitate ⊕ *v* 1 help (a person) to readjust to society after illness, imprisonment, etc. 2 restore to a former position or rank. 3 restore the good reputation of. **rehabilitation** *n*

rehash ⊕ *v* 1 rework or reuse. ♦ *n* 2 old ideas presented in a new form.

rehearse ⊕ *v* 1 practise (a play, concert, etc.). 2 repeat aloud. **rehearsal** *n*

reign ⊕ *n* 1 period of a sovereign's rule. ♦ *v* 2 rule (a country). 3 be supreme.

reimburse ⊕ *v* refund, pay back. **reimbursement** *n*

rein ⊕ *v* 1 check or manage with reins. 2 control or limit. **reins** *pl n* 1 narrow straps

attached to a bit to guide a horse. 2 means of control.

reincarnation *n* 1 rebirth of a soul in successive bodies. 2 one of a series of such transmigrations. **reincarnate** *v*

reindeer *n, pl* –**deer,** –**deers** deer of arctic regions with large branched antlers.

reinforce ⊕ *v* 1 strengthen with new support, material, or force. 2 strengthen with additional troops, ships, etc. **reinforcement** *n*

reinstate ⊕ *v* restore to a former position. **reinstatement** *n*

reiterate ⊕ *v* repeat again and again. **reiteration** *n*

reject ⊕ *v* 1 refuse to accept or believe. 2 rebuff (a person). 3 discard as useless. ♦ *n* 4 person or thing rejected as not up to standard. **rejection** *n*

rejig ⊕ *v* –**jigging,** –**jigged** 1 re–equip (a factory or plant). 2 rearrange.

rejoice ⊕ *v* feel or express great happiness.

rejoin ⊕ *v* reply. **rejoinder** *n* answer, retort.

———————— THESAURUS ————————

set, stated, steady, uniform ≠ **varied**

regulate *v* 1 = **control**, direct, govern, guide, handle, manage, rule, run, supervise 2 = **adjust**, balance, fit, moderate, modulate, tune

regurgitate *v* 1 = **vomit**, disgorge, puke (*sl*), sick up (*inf*), spew (out *or* up), throw up (*inf*)

rehabilitate *v* 1 = **reintegrate**, adjust 3 = **redeem**, clear, reform, restore, save

rehash *v* 1 = **rework**, refashion, rejig (*inf*), reuse, rewrite ♦ *n* 2 = **reworking**, new version, rearrangement, rewrite

rehearse *v* 1 = **practise**, drill, go over, prepare, run through, train 2 = **repeat**, recite

reign *n* 1 = **rule**, command, control, dominion, monarchy, power ♦ *v* 2 = **rule**, be in power, command, govern, influence 3 = **be supreme**, hold sway, predominate, prevail

reimburse *v* = **pay back**, compensate, recompense, refund, remunerate, repay, return

rein *v* 2 = **control**, check, curb, halt, hold back, limit, restrain, restrict ♦ *pl n* 3 = **control**, brake, bridle, check, curb, harness, hold, restraint

reinforce *v* 1 = **emphasize**, stress 2 = **support**, bolster, fortify, prop, strengthen, supplement, toughen

reinstate *v* = **restore**, recall, re–establish, replace, return

reiterate *v* = **repeat**, do again, restate, say again

reject *v* 1 = **deny**, decline, disallow, exclude, renounce, repudiate, veto ≠ **allow** 2 = **rebuff**, jilt, refuse, repulse, say no to, spurn, turn down ≠ **accept** 3 = **discard**, eliminate, jettison, scrap, throw away *or* out ≠ **accept** ♦ *n* 4 = **castoff**, discard, failure, second ≠ **prize**

rejig *v* 2 = **rearrange**, alter, juggle, manipulate, reorganize, tweak

rejoice *v* = **be glad**, be happy, be overjoyed, celebrate, exult, glory

rejoin *v* = **reply**, answer, respond, retort, riposte

rejuvenate ❶ v restore youth or vitality to. **rejuvenation** n

relapse ❶ v 1 fall back into bad habits, illness, etc. ◆ n 2 return of bad habits, illness, etc.

relate ❶ v 1 establish a relation between. 2 have reference or relation to. 3 have an understanding (of people or ideas) 4 tell (a story) or describe (an event). **related** adj

relation ❶ n 1 connection between things. 2 relative. 3 connection by blood or marriage. 4 act of relating (a story). ◆ pl 5 social or political dealings. 6 family. 7 **relationship** n 1 dealings and feelings between people or countries. 2 emotional or sexual affair. 3 connection between two things. 4 association by blood or marriage, kinship. **relative** adj true to a certain degree or extent.

relax ❶ v 1 make or become looser, less tense, or less rigid. 2 ease up from effort or attention, rest. 3 be less strict about. 4 become more friendly. **relaxing** adj

relaxation n

relay ❶ n 1 fresh set of people or animals relieving others. 2 Electricity device for making or breaking a local circuit. 3 broadcasting station receiving and retransmitting programmes. ◆ v –laying, –layed 4 pass on (a message). **relay race** race between teams in which each runner races part of the distance.

release ❶ v 1 set free. 2 let go or fall. 3 issue (a record, film, etc.) for sale or public showing. 4 emit heat, energy, etc. ◆ n 5 setting free. 6 statement to the press. 7 act of issuing for sale or publication. 8 newly issued film, record, etc.

relegate ❶ v 1 put in a less important position. 2 demote (a sports team) to a lower league. **relegation** n

relent ❶ v give up a harsh intention, become less severe. **relentless** adj 1 unremitting. 2 merciless.

relevant ❶ adj to do with the matter in hand. **relevance** n

— THESAURUS —

rejuvenate v = **revitalize**, breathe new life into, refresh, regenerate, renew, restore

relapse v 1 a = **lapse**, backslide, degenerate, fail, regress, revert, slip back b = **worsen**, deteriorate, fade, fail, sicken, sink, weaken ≠ **improve** ◆ n 2 a = **lapse**, backsliding, regression, retrogression b = **worsening**, deterioration, turn for the worse, weakening ≠ **improvement**

relate v 1 = **connect**, associate, correlate, couple, join, link 2 = **concern**, apply, be relevant to, have to do with, pertain, refer 4 = **tell**, describe, detail, narrate, recite, recount, report

relation n 1 = **connection**, bearing, bond, comparison, correlation, link 2 = **relative**, kin, kinsman or kinswoman 3 = **kinship**, affinity, kindred ◆ pl 5 = **dealings**, affairs, connections, contact, interaction, intercourse, relationship 6 = **family**, clan, kin, kindred, kinsfolk, kinsmen, relatives, tribe

relax v 1 = **lessen**, abate, ease, ebb, let up, loosen, lower, moderate, reduce, relieve, slacken, weaken ≠ **tighten** 2 = **be or feel at ease**, calm, chill out (sl, chiefly US), outspan (S Afr), rest, take it easy, unwind 3 = **lighten up** (sl), chill out (sl, chiefly US), take it easy

relay n 1 = **shift**, relief, turn ◆ v 4 = **pass on**, broadcast, carry, communicate, send, spread, transmit

release v 1 = **set free**, discharge, drop, extricate, free, liberate, loose, unbridle, undo, unfasten ≠ **keep** 3 = **issue**, circulate, distribute, launch, make known, make public, publish, put out ≠ **suppress** ◆ n 5 = **liberation**, deliverance, discharge, emancipation, freedom, liberty ≠ **detention** 6 = **proclamation** 7 = **issue**, publication

relegate v = **demote**, downgrade

relent v = **be merciful**, capitulate, change one's mind, come round, have pity, show mercy, soften, yield ≠ **remain firm**

relevant adj = **significant**, apposite, appropriate, apt, fitting, germane, pertinent, related, to the point

reliable ⊕ *adj* able to be trusted, dependable. **reliably** *adv* **reliability** *n*

relic ⊕ *n* 1 something that has survived from the past. 2 body or possession of a saint, regarded as holy. ♦ *pl* 3 remains or traces widow.

relief ⊕ *n* 1 gladness at the end or removal of pain, distress, etc. 2 release from monotony or duty. 3 money or food given to victims of disaster, poverty, etc. 4 freeing of a besieged city etc. 5 person who replaces another. 6 projection of a carved design from the surface. 7 any vivid effect resulting from contrast, e.g. *comic relief*. **relieve** *v* bring relief to. **relieve oneself** urinate or defecate. **relief map** map showing the shape and height of land by shading.

religion *n* system of belief in and worship of a supernatural power or god. **religious** *adj* 1 of religion. 2 pious or devout. 3 scrupulous or conscientious.

relinquish ⊕ *v* give up or abandon.

relish ⊕ *v* 1 enjoy, like very much. ♦ *n* 2 liking or enjoyment. 3 appetizing savoury food, such as pickle. 4 zestful quality or flavour.

relocate *v* move to a new place to live or work. **relocation** *n*

reluctant ⊕ *adj* unwilling or disinclined. **reluctance** *n*

rely ⊕ *v* **-lying, -lied** 1 depend (on). 2 trust. **reliable** *adj* able to be trusted.

remain ⊕ *v* 1 continue. 2 stay, be left behind. 3 be left (over). 4 be left to be done, said, etc. **remains** *pl n* 1 relics, esp. of ancient buildings. 2 dead body. **remainder** *n* 1 part which is left. 2 amount left over after subtraction or division. ♦ *v* 3 offer (copies of a poorly selling book) at reduced prices.

remand *v* send back into custody or put on bail before trial. **on remand** in custody or on bail before trial. **remand centre** place where accused people are detained awaiting trial.

remark ⊕ *v* 1 make a casual comment (on). 2 say. 3 observe or notice. ♦ *n* 4 observation or comment. **remarkable** *adj* 1 worthy of note or attention. 2 striking or unusual. **remarkably** *adv*

remedy ⊕ *n, pl* **-edies** 1 means of curing pain or disease. 2 means of solving a problem. ♦ *v* **-edying, -edied** 3 put right. **remedial** *adj* intended to correct a specific disability, handicap, etc.

reliable *adj* = **dependable**, faithful, safe, sound, staunch, sure, true, trustworthy ≠ **irresponsible**

relic *n* 1 = **remnant**, fragment, keepsake, memento, souvenir, trace, vestige

relief *n* 1 = **ease**, comfort, cure, deliverance, mitigation, release, remedy, solace 2 = **rest**, break, breather (*inf*), relaxation, respite 3 = **aid**, assistance, help, succour, support

relinquish *v* = **give up**, abandon, abdicate, cede, drop, forsake, leave, let go, renounce, surrender

relish *v* 1 = **enjoy**, delight in, fancy, like, revel in, savour ≠ **dislike** ♦ *n* 2 = **enjoyment**, fancy, fondness, gusto, liking, love, partiality, penchant, predilection, taste ≠ **dislike** 3 = **condiment**, sauce, seasoning

4 = **flavour**, piquancy, smack, spice, tang, taste, trace

reluctant *adj* = **unwilling**, disinclined, hesitant, loath, unenthusiastic

rely *v* 1 = **depend**, bank, bet, count ♦ *n* 2 = **trust**

remain *v* 1 = **continue**, abide, dwell, endure, go on, last, persist, stand, stay, survive ≠ **go** 2 = **stay behind**, be left, delay, linger, wait

remark *v* 1, 2 = **comment**, declare, mention, observe, pass comment, reflect, say, state 3 = **notice**, espy, make out, mark, note, observe, perceive, see ♦ *n* 4 = **comment**, observation, reflection, statement, utterance

remedy *n* 1 = **cure**, medicine, nostrum, treatment ♦ *v* 3 = **put right**, correct, fix, rectify

remember 🛈 v 1 retain in or recall to one's memory. 2 keep in mind. **remembrance** n 1 memory. 2 token or souvenir. 3 honouring the memory of a person or event.

remind 🛈 v 1 cause to remember. 2 put in mind (of). **reminder** n 1 something that recalls the past. 2 note to remind a person of something not done.

reminisce 🛈 v talk or write of past times, experiences, etc. **reminiscence** n 1 remembering. 2 thing recollected. ◆ pl 3 memoirs. **reminiscent** adj reminding or suggestive (of).

remiss 🛈 adj negligent or careless.

remit 🛈 v [rim–**mitt**] –mitting, –mitted 1 send (money) for goods, services, etc., esp. by post. 2 cancel (a punishment or debt). 3 refer (a decision) to a higher authority or later date. ◆ n [**ree**–mitt] 4 area of competence or authority. **remittance** n money sent as payment.

remnant 🛈 n 1 small piece, esp. of fabric, left over. 2 surviving trace.

remonstrate 🛈 v argue in protest.

remorse 🛈 n feeling of sorrow and regret for something one did. **remorseful** adj **remorseless** adj 1 pitiless. 2 persistent.

remote 🛈 adj 1 far away, distant. 2 aloof. 3 slight or faint. **remotely** adv **remote control** control of an apparatus from a distance by an electrical device.

remove 🛈 v 1 take away or off. 2 get rid of. 3 dismiss from office. ◆ n 4 degree of difference. **removable** adj **removal** n removing, esp. changing residence.

remunerate 🛈 v reward or pay. **remuneration** n **remunerative** adj

renaissance 🛈 n 1 revival or rebirth. 2 (R–) revival of learning in the 14th-16th centuries.

renal [**ree**–nal] adj of the kidneys.

rend 🛈 v rending, rent 1 tear or wrench apart. 2 (of a sound) break (the silence) violently.

render 🛈 v 1 cause to become. 2 give or provide (aid, a service, etc.). 3 submit or present (a bill). 4 portray or represent. 5 cover with plaster. 6 melt down (fat).

rendezvous 🛈 [**ron**–day–voo] n, pl –**vous**

———— THESAURUS ————

remember v 1 = **recall**, call to mind, commemorate, look back (on), recollect, reminisce, think back ≠ **forget** 2 = **bear in mind**, keep in mind

remind v = **call to mind**, jog one's memory, make (someone) remember, prompt

reminisce v = **recall**, hark back, look back, recollect, remember, think back

remiss adj = **careless**, forgetful, heedless, lax, neglectful, negligent, thoughtless

remit v 1 = **send**, dispatch, forward, mail, post, transmit 2 = **cancel**, halt, repeal, rescind, stop 3 = **postpone**, defer, delay, put off, shelve, suspend

remnant n = **remainder**, end, fragment, leftovers, remains, residue, rest, trace, vestige

remonstrate v = **protest**, argue, dispute, dissent, object, take issue

remorse n = **regret**, anguish, compunction, contrition, grief, guilt,

penitence, repentance, shame, sorrow

remote adj 1 = **distant**, far, inaccessible, in the middle of nowhere, isolated, out–of–the–way, secluded ≠ **near** 2 = **aloof**, abstracted, cold, detached, distant, reserved, standoffish, uncommunicative, withdrawn ≠ **interested** 3 = **slight**, doubtful, dubious, faint, outside, slender, slim, small, unlikely ≠ **good**

remove v 1, 2 = **take away** or **off** or **out**, abolish, delete, detach, displace, eject, eliminate, erase, excise, extract, get rid of, wipe from the face of the earth, withdraw ≠ **replace** 3 = **dismiss**, depose, dethrone, discharge, expel, oust, throw out ≠ **install**

remunerate v = **pay**, compensate, recompense, reimburse, repay, requite, reward

renaissance n 1 = **rebirth**, reappearance, reawakening, renewal, restoration, resurgence, revival

rend v 1 = **tear**, rip, rupture, separate,

1 appointment. 2 meeting place. ♦ v 3 meet as arranged.

rendition ❶ n 1 performance. 2 translation.

renegade ❶ n person who deserts a cause.

renege ❶ [rin–**nayg**] v go back (on a promise etc.).

renew ❶ v 1 begin again. 2 make valid again. 3 grow again. 4 restore to a former state. 5 replace (a worn part). 6 restate or reaffirm. **renewable** adj **renewal** n

renounce ❶ v 1 give up (a belief, habit, etc.) voluntarily. 2 give up (a title or claim) formally. **renunciation** n

renovate ❶ v restore to good condition. **renovation** n

renown ❶ n widespread good reputation. **renowned** adj famous.

rent¹ ❶ v 1 give or have use of in return for regular payments. ♦ n 2 regular payment for use of land, a building, machine, etc. **rental** n sum payable as rent.

rent² ❶ n 1 tear or fissure. ♦ v 2 past of REND.

reorganize v organize in a new and more efficient way. **reorganization** n

repair¹ ❶ v 1 restore to good condition, mend. ♦ n 2 act of repairing. 3 repaired part. 4 state or condition, e.g. in good repair. **reparation** n something done or given as compensation.

repair² ❶ v go (to).

repartee ❶ n 1 interchange of witty retorts. 2 witty retort.

repatriate v send (someone) back to his or her own country. **repatriation** n

repay ❶ v repaying, repaid 1 pay back, refund. 2 do something in return for, e.g. repay hospitality. **repayable** adj **repayment** n

repeal ❶ v 1 cancel (a law) officially.

———— THESAURUS ————

wrench

render v 1 = **make**, cause to become, leave 2 = **provide**, furnish, give, hand out, pay, present, submit, supply, tender 4 = **represent**, act, depict, do, give, perform, play, portray

rendezvous n 1 = **appointment**, assignation, date, engagement, meeting, tryst (arch) 2 = **meeting place**, gathering point, venue ♦ v 3 = **meet**, assemble, come together, gather, join up

rendition n 1 = **performance**, arrangement, interpretation, portrayal, presentation, reading, rendering, version 2 = **translation**, interpretation, reading, transcription, version

renegade n = **deserter**, apostate, defector, traitor, turncoat

renege v = **break one's word**, back out, break a promise, default, go back

renew v = **recommence**, continue, extend, recreate, reopen, repeat, resume 4 = **restore**, mend, modernize, overhaul, refit, refurbish, renovate, repair 5 = **replace**, refresh, replenish, restock 6 = **reaffirm**

renounce v = **give up**, abjure, deny, disown, forsake, forswear, quit, recant, relinquish, waive ≠ **claim**

renovate v = **restore**, do up (inf), modernize, overhaul, recondition, refit, refurbish, renew, repair

renown n = **fame**, distinction, eminence, note, reputation, repute

rent¹ v 1 = **hire**, charter, lease, let ♦ n 2 = **hire**, fee, lease, payment, rental

rent² n 1 = **tear**, gash, hole, opening, rip, slash, slit, split

repair¹ v 1 = **mend**, fix, heal, patch, patch up, renovate, restore ≠ **damage** ♦ n 2, 3 = **mend**, darn, overhaul, patch, restoration 4 = **condition**, form, shape (inf), state

repair² v = **go**, betake oneself, head for, leave for, move, remove, retire, set off for, withdraw

repartee n 1 = **wit**, badinage, banter, wittiness, wordplay 2 = **riposte**

repay v 1 = **pay back**, compensate, recompense, refund, reimburse, requite, return, square 2 = **reciprocate**, avenge, get even with (inf), get one's own back on

DICTIONARY

◆ *n* 2 act of repealing.

repeat ① *v* 1 say or do again. **2** happen again, recur. ◆ *n* 3 act or instance of repeating. **4** programme broadcast again. **repeatedly** *adv* **repetition** *n* act of repeating.

repel ① *v* –pelling, –pelled 1 be disgusting to. **2** drive back, ward off. **3** resist. **repellent** *adj* **1** distasteful. **2** resisting water etc. ◆ *n* 3 something that repels, esp. a chemical to repel insects.

repent ① *v* feel regret for (a deed or omission). **repentance** *n* **repentant** *adj*

repertoire ① *n* stock of plays, songs, etc. that a player or company can give.

repetition ① *n* 1 act of repeating. **2** thing repeated. **repetitive, repetitious** *adj* full of repetition.

replace ① *v* 1 substitute for. **2** put back. **replacement** *n*

replay *n* 1 (also **action replay**) immediate reshowing on TV of an incident in sport, esp. in slow motion. **2** second sports match, esp. one following an earlier draw. ◆ *v* 3 play (a match, recording, etc.) again.

replenish ① *v* fill up again, resupply. **replenishment** *n*

replete ① *adj* filled or gorged.

replica ① *n* exact copy. **replicate** *v* make or be a copy of.

reply ① *v* –plying, –plied 1 answer or respond. ◆ *n, pl* –**plies** 2 answer or response.

report ① *v* 1 give an account of. **2** make a report (on). **3** make a formal complaint about. **4** present oneself (to). **5** be responsible (to). ◆ *n* 6 account or statement. **7** rumour. **8** written statement of a child's progress at school. **9** bang. **reportedly** *adv* according to rumour. **reporter** *n* person who gathers news for a newspaper, TV, etc.

repose ① *n* 1 peace. **2** composure. **3** sleep. ◆ *v* 4 lie or lay at rest.

THESAURUS

(*inf*), hit back, retaliate, revenge

repeal *v* **1** = **abolish**, annul, cancel, invalidate, nullify, recall, reverse, revoke ≠ **pass** ◆ *n* **2** = **abolition**, annulment, cancellation, invalidation, rescindment ≠ **introduction**

repeat *v* **1** = **reiterate**, echo, replay, reproduce, rerun, restate, retell ◆ *n* **3** = **repetition**, echo, reiteration, replay, rerun

repel *v* **1** = **disgust**, gross out (*US sl*), nauseate, offend, revolt, sicken ≠ **attract** **2, 3** = **drive off**, fight, hold off, parry, rebuff, repulse, resist, ward off ≠ **submit to**

repent *v* = **regret**, be sorry, feel remorse, rue

repertoire *n* **1** = **range**, collection, list, repertory, stock, supply

repetition *n* = **repeating**, echo, recurrence, reiteration, renewal, replication, restatement, tautology

replace *v* **1** = **take the place of**, follow, oust, substitute, succeed, supersede, supplant, take over from **2** = **put back**, re–establish, reinstate, restore

replenish *v* = **refill**, fill, provide, reload, replace, restore, top up ≠ **empty**

replete *adj* = **filled**, crammed, full, full up, glutted, gorged, sated, stuffed ≠ **empty**

replica *n* = **duplicate**, carbon copy (*inf*), copy, facsimile, imitation, model, reproduction ≠ **original**

reply *v* **1** = **answer**, counter, reciprocate, rejoin, respond, retaliate, retort ◆ *n* **2** = **answer**, counter, counterattack, reaction, rejoinder, response, retaliation, retort

report *v* **1, 2** = **communicate**, broadcast, cover, describe, detail, inform of, narrate, pass on, recount, relate, state, tell **4** = **present oneself**, appear, arrive, come, turn up ◆ *n* **6** = **account**, communication, description, narrative, news, record, statement, word **7** = **rumour**, buzz, gossip, hearsay, talk **9** = **bang**, blast, boom, crack, detonation, discharge, explosion, noise, sound

repose¹ *n* **1** = **peace**, ease, quietness, relaxation, respite, rest, stillness, tranquillity **2** = **composure**, calmness,

repossess v (of a lender) take back property from a customer who is behind with payments. **repossession** n

reprehensible ⊕ adj open to criticism, unworthy.

represent ⊕ v 1 act as a delegate or substitute for. 2 stand for. 3 symbolize. 4 make out to be. 5 portray, as in art. **representation** n **representative** n 1 person chosen to stand for a group. 2 (travelling) salesperson. ◆ adj 3 typical.

repress ⊕ v 1 keep (feelings) in check. 2 restrict the freedom of. **repression** n **repressive** adj

reprieve ⊕ v 1 postpone the execution of (a condemned person). 2 give temporary relief to. ◆ n 3 (document granting) postponement or cancellation of a punishment. 4 temporary relief.

reprimand ⊕ v 1 blame (someone) officially for a fault. ◆ n 2 official blame.

reprisal ⊕ n retaliation.

reproach ⊕ n, v blame, rebuke. **reproachful** adj

reprobate adj, n depraved or disreputable (person).

reproduce ⊕ v 1 produce a copy of. 2 bring new individuals into existence. 3 re–create. **reproduction** n 1 process of reproducing. 2 facsimile, as of a painting etc. 3 quality of sound from an audio system. **reproductive** adj

reprove ⊕ v speak severely to (someone) about a fault. **reproof** n severe blaming of someone for a fault.

reptile n cold–blooded egg–laying vertebrate with horny scales or plates, such as a snake or tortoise. **reptilian** adj

republic n 1 form of government in which the people or their elected representatives possess the supreme power. 2 country in which a president is the head of state. 3 **Republican** n, adj 1 (member or supporter) of the Republican Party, the more conservative of the two main political parties in the US. 2 **Republicanism** n

repudiate ⊕ [rip–**pew**–dee–ate] v 1 reject

─────── THESAURUS ───────

poise, self–possession 3 = **sleep**, slumber ◆ v 4 = **rest**, lie, lie down, recline, rest upon

reprehensible adj = **blameworthy**, bad, culpable, disgraceful, objectionable, shameful, unworthy

represent v 1, 2 = **stand for**, act for, betoken, mean, serve as, speak for, symbolize 3 = **exemplify**, embody, epitomize, personify, symbolize, typify 5 = **depict**, denote, describe, illustrate, outline, picture, portray, show

repress v 1 = **control**, bottle up, check, curb, hold back, inhibit, restrain, stifle, suppress ≠ **release** 2 = **subdue**, quell, subjugate ≠ **free**

reprieve v 1 = **grant a stay of execution to**, let off the hook (sl), pardon 2 = **relieve**, abate, allay, alleviate, mitigate, palliate ◆ n 3 = **stay of execution**, amnesty, deferment, pardon, postponement, remission 4 = **relief**, alleviation, mitigation, palliation, respite

reprimand v 1 = **blame**, censure, dress

down (inf), haul over the coals (inf), rap over the knuckles, rebuke, rouse on (Aust), scold, tear (someone) off a strip (Brit inf) ≠ **praise** ◆ n 2 = **blame**, censure, dressing–down (inf), rebuke, reproach, reproof, talking–to (inf) ≠ **praise**

reprisal n = **retaliation**, retribution, revenge, vengeance

① **reproach** n = **blame**, censure, condemnation, disapproval, opprobrium, rebuke

② **reproach** v = **blame**, censure, condemn, criticize, lambast(e), read the riot act, rebuke, reprimand, rouse on (Aust), scold, upbraid

reproduce v 1 = **copy**, duplicate, echo, imitate, match, mirror, recreate, repeat, replicate 2 = **breed**, multiply, procreate, propagate, spawn

reprove v = **rebuke**, berate, blame, censure, condemn, read the riot act, reprimand, rouse on (Aust), scold, tear into (inf), tear (someone) off a strip (Brit inf),

the authority or validity of. **2** disown.
repugnant ⦿ *adj* offensive or distasteful.
repugnance *n*
repulse ⦿ *v* **1** be disgusting to. **2** drive (an army) back. **3** rebuff or reject. ◆ *n* **4** driving back. **5** rejection or rebuff.
repulsion *n* **1** distaste or aversion. **2** *Physics* force separating two objects. **repulsive** *adj* loathsome, disgusting.
reputation ⦿ *n* estimation in which a person is held.
request ⦿ *v* **1** ask. ◆ *n* **2** asking. **3** thing asked for.
require ⦿ *v* **1** want or need. **2** demand.
requirement *n* **1** essential condition. **2** specific need or want.

> ✓ **WORD TIP**
> *Require* suggests a demand imposed by some regulation. *Need* is usually something that comes from a person.

requisite ⦿ [rek–wizz–it] *adj* **1** necessary, essential. ◆ *n* **2** essential thing.
requisition ⦿ *v* **1** demand (supplies). ◆ *n* **2** formal demand, such as for materials or supplies.
require ⦿ *v* return to someone (the same treatment or feeling as received).
requital *n*
rerun *n* **1** film or programme that is broadcast again, repeat. **2** race that is run again. ◆ *v* **3** broadcast again.
rescind ⦿ *v* annul or repeal.
rescue ⦿ *v* –cuing, –cued **1** deliver from danger or trouble, save. ◆ *n* **2** rescuing.
rescuer *n*
research ⦿ *n* **1** systematic investigation to discover facts or collect information. ◆ *v* **2** carry out investigations. **researcher** *n*
resemble ❶ *v* be or look like.
resemblance *n*
resent ⦿ *v* feel indignant or bitter about.
resentful *adj* **resentment** *n*

tell off (*inf*)
repudiate *v* **1** = **reject**, deny, disavow, disclaim, renounce ≠ **disown 2** = **disown**
repugnant *adj* = **distasteful**, abhorrent, disgusting, loathsome, nauseating, offensive, repellent, revolting, sickening, vile ≠ **attractive**
repulse *v* **1** = **disgust**, nauseate, offend, put off, repel, revolt, sicken, turn one's stomach **2** = **drive back**, beat off, fight off, rebuff, repel, ward off **3** = **reject**, rebuff, refuse, snub, spurn, turn down
reputation *n* = **name**, character, esteem, estimation, renown, repute, standing, stature
request *v* **1** = **ask (for)**, appeal for, demand, desire, entreat, invite, seek, solicit ◆ *n* **2** = **asking**, appeal, call, demand, desire, entreaty, suit
require *v* **1** = **need**, crave, desire, lack, miss, want, wish **2** = **order**, ask, bid, call upon, command, compel, demand, exact, insist upon
requisite *adj* **1** = **necessary**, called for, essential, indispensable, needed, needful,

obligatory, required ◆ *n* **2** = **necessity**, condition, essential, must, need, prerequisite, requirement
requisition *v* **1** = **demand**, call for, request ◆ *n* **2** = **demand**, call, request, summons
requite *v* = **return**, get even, give in return, pay (someone) back in his *or* her own coin, reciprocate, repay, respond, retaliate
rescind *v* = **annul**, cancel, countermand, declare null and void, invalidate, repeal, set aside
rescue *v* **1** = **save**, deliver, get out, liberate, recover, redeem, release, salvage ≠ **abandon** ◆ *n* **2** = **liberation**, deliverance, recovery, redemption, release, salvage, salvation, saving
research *n* **1** = **investigation**, analysis, examination, exploration, probe, study ◆ *v* **2** = **investigate**, analyse, examine, explore, probe, study
resemble *v* = **be like**, bear a resemblance to, be similar to, look like, mirror, parallel
resent *v* = **be bitter about**, begrudge, be angry about, be pissed (off) about (*taboo sl*), grudge, object to, take exception to,

reserve ❶ v **1** set aside, keep for future use. **2** obtain by arranging beforehand, book. **3** retain. ◆ n **4** something, esp. money or troops, kept for emergencies. **5** area of land reserved for a particular purpose. **6** *Sport* substitute. **7** concealment of feelings or friendliness. **reservation** n **1** doubt. **2** exception or limitation. **3** seat, room, etc. that has been reserved. **reserved** adj **1** not showing one's feelings, lacking friendliness. **2** set aside for use by a particular person. **reservist** n member of a military reserve.

reservoir ❶ n **1** natural or artificial lake storing water for community supplies. **2** store or supply of something.

reshuffle n **1** reorganization. ◆ v **2** reorganize.

reside ❶ v dwell permanently. **residence** n home or house. **resident** n, adj **residential** adj **1** (of part of a town) consisting mainly of houses. **2** providing living accommodation.

residue ❶ n what is left, remainder. **residual** adj

resign ❶ v **1** give up office, a job, etc. **2** reconcile (oneself) to. **resigned** adj content to endure. **resignation** n **1** resigning. **2** passive endurance of difficulties.

resilient ❶ adj **1** (of a person) recovering quickly from a shock etc. **2** able to return to normal shape after stretching etc. **resilience** n

resin [**rezz**–in] n **1** sticky substance from plants, esp. pines. **2** similar synthetic substance. **resinous** adj

resist ❶ v **1** withstand or oppose. **2** refrain from despite temptation. **3** be proof against. **resistance** n **1** act of resisting. **2** capacity to withstand something. **3** *Electricity* opposition offered by a circuit to the passage of a current through it. **resistant** adj **resistible** adj **resistor** n component of an electrical circuit producing resistance.

resit v **1** take (an exam) again. ◆ n **2** exam that has to be taken again.

resolute ❶ adj firm in purpose. **resolutely** adv **resolution** n **1** firmness of conduct or character. **2** thing resolved upon. **3** decision of a court or vote of an assembly. **4** act of resolving.

resolve ❶ v **1** decide with an effort of will. **2** form (a resolution) by a vote. **3** separate the component parts of. **4** make clear, settle. **resolved** adj determined.

resonance ❶ n **1** echoing, esp. with a

———————— THESAURUS ————————

take offence at

reserve v **1** = **keep**, hoard, hold, put by, retain, save, set aside, stockpile, store **2** = **book**, engage, prearrange, secure ◆ n **4** = **store**, cache, fund, hoard, reservoir, savings, stock, supply **5** = **reservation**, park, preserve, sanctuary, tract **6** *Sport* = **substitute** **7** = **shyness**, constraint, reservation, restraint, reticence, secretiveness, silence, taciturnity

reservoir n **1** = **lake**, basin, pond, tank **2** = **store**, pool, reserves, source, stock, supply

reside v = **live**, abide, dwell, inhabit, lodge, stay ≠ **visit**

residue n **1** = **remainder**, dregs, excess, extra, leftovers, remains, remnant, rest, surplus

resign v **1** = **quit**, abdicate, give in one's notice, leave, step down (*inf*), vacate **2** = **accept**, acquiesce, give in, resign oneself, submit, succumb, yield **3** = **give up**, abandon, forgo, forsake, relinquish, renounce, surrender, yield

resilient adj **1** = **tough**, buoyant, hardy, irrepressible, strong ≠ **weak** **2** = **flexible**, elastic, plastic, pliable, rubbery, springy, supple ≠ **stiff**

resist v **1** = **oppose**, battle, combat, defy, hinder, stand up to ≠ **accept** **2** = **refrain from**, abstain from, avoid, forbear, forgo, keep from ≠ **enjoy** **3** = **withstand**, be proof against

resolute adj = **determined**, dogged, firm, fixed, immovable, inflexible, set, steadfast, strong–willed, tenacious, unshakable, deep sound. **2** sound produced in one object by sound waves coming from another object. **resonant** *adj* **resonate** *v*

resort ⊕ *v* **1** have recourse (to) for help etc. ♦ *n* **2** place for holidays. **3** recourse.

resound ⊕ [riz–**zownd**] *v* echo or ring with sound. **resounding** *adj* **1** echoing. **2** clear and emphatic.

resource ⊕ *n* **1** thing resorted to for support. **2** ingenuity. **3** means of achieving something. ♦ *pl* **4** sources of economic wealth. **5** stock that can be drawn on, funds. **resourceful** *adj* **resourcefulness** *n*

respect ⊕ *n* **1** consideration. **2** deference or esteem. **3** point or aspect. **4** reference or relation, e.g. *with respect to.* ♦ *v* **5** treat with esteem. **6** show consideration for. **respecter** *n* **respectful** *adj* **respecting** *prep* concerning.

respiration [ress–per–**ray**–shun] *n* breathing. **respirator** *n* apparatus worn over the mouth and breathed through as protection against dust, poison gas, etc.,

or to provide artificial respiration. **respiratory** *adj* **respire** *v* breathe.

respite ⊕ *n* **1** pause, interval of rest. **2** delay.

resplendent ⊕ *adj* **1** brilliant or splendid. **2** shining.

respond ⊕ *v* **1** answer. **2** act in answer to any stimulus. **3** react favourably. **respondent** *n Law* defendant. **response** *n* **1** answer. **2** reaction to a stimulus. **responsive** *adj* readily reacting to some influence. **responsiveness** *n*

responsible ⊕ *adj* **1** having control and authority. **2** reporting or accountable (to). **3** sensible and dependable. **4** involving responsibility. **responsibly** *adv* **responsibility** *n, pl* **–ties 1** state of being responsible. **2** person or thing for which one is responsible.

rest¹ ⊕ *n* **1** freedom from exertion etc. **2** repose. **3** pause, esp. in music. **4** object used for support. ♦ *v* **5** take a rest. **6** give a rest (to). **7** be supported. **8** place on a

unwavering

resolve *v* **1** = **decide**, agree, conclude, determine, fix, intend, purpose **3** = **break down**, analyse, reduce, separate **4** = **work out**, answer, clear up, crack, fathom ♦ *n* **5** = **determination**, firmness, resoluteness, resolution, steadfastness, willpower ≠ **indecision**

resort *v* **1** = **have recourse to**, employ, fall back on, turn to, use, utilize ♦ *n* **2** = **holiday centre**, haunt, retreat, spot, tourist centre **3** = **recourse**, reference

resound *v* **1, 2** = **echo**, re–echo, resonate, reverberate, ring

resource *n* **2** = **ingenuity**, ability, capability, cleverness, initiative, inventiveness **3** = **means**, course, device, expedient, resort ♦ *pl* **4** = **assets**, capital, holdings, lolly (*Aust & NZ sl*), money, riches, wealth **5** = **funds**, reserves, supplies

respect *n* **1** = **consideration 2** = **regard**, admiration, deference, esteem, estimation, honour, recognition ≠ **contempt** **3** = **particular**, aspect, characteristic,

detail, feature, matter, point, sense, way **4** *As in* **with respect to** = **relation**, bearing, connection, reference, regard ♦ *v* **5** = **think highly of**, admire, defer to, esteem, have a good *or* high opinion of, honour, look up to, value **6** = **abide by**, adhere to, comply with, follow, heed, honour, obey, observe, show consideration for ≠ **ignore**

respite *n* **1** = **pause**, break, breathing space, cessation, halt, interval, lull, recess, relaxation, relief, rest

resplendent *adj* = **brilliant**, bright, dazzling, glorious, radiant, shining, splendid

respond *v* **1** = **answer**, counter, reciprocate, rejoin, reply, retort, return ≠ **ignore 2** = **react**

responsible *adj* **1** = **in charge**, in authority, in control **2** = **accountable**, answerable, liable ≠ **unaccountable 3** = **sensible**, dependable, level–headed, rational, reliable, trustworthy ≠ **irresponsible**

support. **restful** adj **restless** adj

rest² ❶ n 1 what is left. 2 others. ◆ v 3 remain, continue to be.

restaurant ❶ n commercial establishment serving meals. **restaurateur** [rest-er-a-**tur**] n person who owns or runs a restaurant.

restitution ❶ n 1 giving back. 2 reparation or compensation.

restive ❶ adj restless or impatient.

restore ❶ v 1 return (a building, painting, etc.) to its original condition. 2 cause to recover health or spirits. 3 give back, return. 4 re-establish. **restoration** n **restorative** adj 1 restoring. ◆ n 2 food or medicine to strengthen etc. **restorer** n

restrain ❶ v 1 hold (someone) back from action. 2 control or restrict. **restraint** n 1 control, esp. self-control. 2 restraining. **restrained** adj not displaying emotion.

restrict ❶ v confine to certain limits. **restriction** n **restrictive** adj

result ❶ n 1 outcome or consequence. 2

score. 3 number obtained from a calculation. 4 exam mark or grade. ◆ v 5 (foll. by from) be the outcome or consequence (of). 6 (foll. by in) end (in). **resultant** adj

resume ❶ v 1 begin again. 2 occupy or take again. **resumption** n

resurgence ❶ n rising again to vigour. **resurgent** adj

resurrect ❶ v 1 restore to life. 2 use once more (something discarded etc.), revive. **resurrection** n 1 rising again (esp. from the dead). 2 revival.

resuscitate ❶ [ris-**suss**-it-tate] v restore to consciousness. **resuscitation** n

retail n 1 selling of goods individually or in small amounts to the public. ◆ adv 2 by retail. ◆ v 3 sell or be sold retail. 4 recount in detail. **retailer** n

retain ❶ v 1 keep in one's possession. 2 engage the services of. **retainer** n 1 fee to retain someone's services. 2 old-

———————— THESAURUS ————————

rest¹ n 1 = **inactivity** 2 = **relaxation**, leisure, repose 3 = **pause**, break, cessation, halt, interlude, intermission, interval, lull, respite, stop 4 = **support**, base, holder, prop, stand ◆ v 5 a = **relax**, be at ease, put one's feet up, sit down, take it easy ≠ **work** b = **stop**, break off, cease, halt, have a break, take a breather (inf) ≠ **work** 7 = **be supported**, lean, lie, recline, repose, sit 8 = **place**, lean, lie, prop, sit

rest² n 1 = **remainder**, balance, excess, remains, remnants, residue, surplus 2 = **others**

restaurant n = **café**, bistro, cafeteria, diner (chiefly US & Canad), tearoom

restitution n 1 = **return**, restoration 2 = **compensation**, amends, recompense, reparation, requital

restive adj = **restless**, edgy, fidgety, impatient, jumpy, nervous, on edge, wired (sl)

restore v 1 = **repair**, fix, mend, rebuild, recondition, reconstruct, refurbish, renew, renovate ≠ **wreck** 2 = **revive**, build up, refresh, revitalize, strengthen ≠ **weaken**

3 = **return**, bring back, give back, recover, reinstate, replace ≠ **abolish** 4 = **reinstate**, re-establish, reintroduce

restrain v 1, 2 = **hold back**, check, constrain, contain, control, curb, curtail, hamper, hinder, inhibit, restrict ≠ **help**

restrict v = **limit**, bound, confine, contain, hamper, handicap, inhibit, regulate, restrain

result n 1 = **consequence**, effect, end, end result, outcome, product, sequel, upshot ≠ **beginning** ◆ v 5 (foll. by from) = **arise**, appear, derive, develop, ensue, follow, happen, issue, spring 6 (foll. by in) = **end**, culminate

resume v 1 = **begin again**, carry on, continue, go on, proceed, reopen, restart ≠ **stop**

resurgence n = **revival**, rebirth, re-emergence, renaissance, resumption, resurrection, return

resurrect v 1 = **restore to life**, raise from the dead 2 = **revive**, bring back, reintroduce, renew

resuscitate v = **revive**, bring round,

established servant of a family.

retaliate ❶ v repay an injury or wrong in kind. **retaliation** n **retaliatory** adj

retard ❶ v delay or slow (progress or development). **retarded** adj underdeveloped, esp. mentally. **retardation** n

retch ❶ v try to vomit.

reticent ❶ adj uncommunicative, reserved. **reticence** n

retina n, pl –nas, –nae light–sensitive membrane at the back of the eye.

retinue ❶ n band of attendants.

retire ❶ v 1 (cause to) give up office or work, esp. through age. 2 go away or withdraw. 3 go to bed. **retired** adj having retired from work etc. **retirement** n **retiring** adj shy.

retort[1] ❶ v 1 reply quickly, wittily, or angrily. ◆ n 2 quick, witty, or angry reply.

retort[2] n glass container with a bent neck used for distilling.

retrace v go back over (a route etc.) again.

retract ❶ v 1 withdraw (a statement etc.).

2 draw in or back. **retractable, retractile** adj able to be retracted. **retraction** n

retreat ❶ v 1 move back from a position, withdraw. ◆ n 2 act of or military signal for retiring or withdrawal. 3 place to which anyone retires, refuge.

retrench v reduce expenditure, cut back. **retrenchment** n

retribution ❶ n punishment or vengeance for evil deeds.

retrieve ❶ v 1 fetch back again. 2 restore to a better state. 3 recover (information) from a computer. **retrieval** n **retriever** n dog trained to retrieve shot game.

retroactive adj effective from a date in the past.

retrograde ❶ adj tending towards an earlier worse condition.

retrospect n **in retrospect** when looking back on the past. **retrospective** adj 1 looking back in time. 2 applying from a date in the past. ◆ n 3 exhibition of an artist's life's work.

return ❶ v 1 go or come back. 2 give, put,

————————| THESAURUS |————————

resurrect, revitalize, save

retain v 1 = **keep**, maintain, preserve, reserve, save ≠ **lose** 2 = **hire**, commission, employ, engage, pay, reserve

retaliate v = **pay (someone) back**, get even with (inf), get one's own back (inf), hit back, reciprocate, strike back, take revenge

retard v = **slow down**, arrest, check, delay, handicap, hinder, hold back or up, impede, set back

retch v = **gag**, be sick, heave, puke (sl), regurgitate, spew, throw up (inf), vomit

reticent adj = **uncommunicative**, close–lipped, quiet, reserved, silent, taciturn, tight–lipped, unforthcoming

retinue n = **attendants**, aides, entourage, escort, followers, servants

retire v 1 = **stop working**, give up work 2 = **withdraw**, depart, exit, go away, leave 3 = **go to bed**, hit the hay (sl), hit the sack (sl), turn in (inf)

retort[1] v 1 = **reply**, answer, come back

with, counter, respond, return, riposte ◆ n 2 = **reply**, answer, comeback (inf), rejoinder, response, riposte

retract v 1 = **withdraw**, deny, disavow, disclaim, eat one's words, recant, renege, renounce, revoke, take back 2 = **draw in**, pull back, pull in, sheathe

retreat v 1 = **withdraw**, back away, back off, depart, draw back, fall back, go back, leave, pull back ≠ **advance** ◆ n 2 = **withdrawal**, departure, evacuation, flight, retirement 3 = **refuge**, haven, hideaway, sanctuary, seclusion, shelter

retribution n = **punishment**, justice, Nemesis, reckoning, reprisal, retaliation, revenge, vengeance

retrieve v = **get back**, recapture, recoup, recover, redeem, regain, restore, save, win back

retrograde adj 1 = **deteriorating**, backward, declining, degenerative, downward, regressive, retrogressive, worsening or send back. **3** reply. **4** elect. ◆ *n* **5** returning. **6** (thing) being returned. **7** profit. **8** official report, as of taxable income. **9** return ticket. **return ticket** ticket allowing a passenger to travel to a place and back.

reunion *n* meeting of people who have been apart. **reunite** *v* bring or come together again after a separation.

rev *Informal* ◆ *n* **1** revolution (of an engine). ◆ *v* **revving, revved 2** (foll. by *up*) increase the speed of revolution of (an engine).

Rev., Revd. Reverend.

revalue *v* adjust the exchange value of (a currency) upwards. **revaluation** *n*

revamp ⊕ *v* renovate or restore.

reveal ⊕ *v* **1** make known. **2** expose or show. **revelation** *n*

reveille [riv-**val**–ee] *n* morning bugle call to waken soldiers.

revel ⊕ *v* –**elling, –elled 1** take pleasure (in). **2** make merry. **reveller** *n* **revelry** *n*

festivity.

revenge ⊕ *n* **1** retaliation for wrong done. ◆ *v* **2** make retaliation for. **3** avenge (oneself or another). **revengeful** *adj*

revenue ⊕ *n* income, esp. of a state.

reverberate ⊕ *v* echo or resound. **reverberation** *n*

revere ⊕ *v* be in awe of and respect greatly. **reverence** *n* awe mingled with respect and esteem. **Reverend** *adj* title of respect for a clergyman. **reverent** *adj* showing reverence. **reverential** *adj* marked by reverence.

reverie ⊕ *n* absent–minded daydream.

reverse ⊕ *v* **1** turn upside down or the other way round. **2** change completely. **3** move (a vehicle) backwards. ◆ *n* **4** opposite. **5** back side. **6** change for the worse. **7** reverse gear. ◆ *adj* **8** opposite or contrary. **reversal** *n* **reversible** *adj* **reverse gear** mechanism enabling a vehicle to move backwards.

return *v* **1** = **come back**, go back, reappear, rebound, recur, retreat, revert, turn back ≠ **leave 2** = **put back**, re–establish, reinstate, replace, restore ≠ **leave 3** = **reply**, answer, respond, retort **4** = **elect**, choose, vote in ◆ *n* **7** = **profit**, gain, income, interest, proceeds, revenue, takings, yield ≠ **loss 8** = **statement**, account, form, list, report, summary

revamp *v* = **renovate**, do up (*inf*), overhaul, recondition, refurbish, restore

reveal *v* **1** = **make known**, announce, disclose, divulge, give away, impart, let out, let slip, make public, proclaim, tell ≠ **hide 2** = **show**, display, exhibit, manifest, uncover, unearth, unmask, unveil ≠ **conceal**

revel *v* **1** reve **in** = **enjoy**, delight in, indulge in, lap up, luxuriate in, relish, take pleasure in, thrive on **2** = **celebrate**, carouse, live it up (*inf*), make merry **revels** ◆ *pl n* = **merrymaking**, carousal, celebration, festivity, gala, party, rave, knees-up, spree

revenge *n* **1** = **retaliation**, an eye for an

eye, reprisal, retribution, vengeance ◆ *v* **2, 3** = **avenge**, get even, get one's own back for (*inf*), repay, retaliate, take revenge for

revenue *n* = **income**, gain, proceeds, profits, receipts, returns, takings, yield

reverberate *v* = **echo**, re–echo, resound, ring, vibrate

revere *v* = **be in awe of**, exalt, honour, look up to, respect, reverence, venerate, worship

reverie *n* = **daydream**, abstraction, brown study, woolgathering

reverse *v* **1** = **turn round**, invert, transpose, turn back, turn over, turn upside down, upend **2** = **change**, overthrow, overturn ≠ **carry out 3** = **go backwards**, back, back up, move backwards, retreat ≠ **advance** ◆ *n* **4** = **opposite**, contrary, converse, inverse **5** = **back**, other side, rear, underside, wrong side ≠ **front 6** = **misfortune**, adversity, affliction, blow, disappointment, failure, hardship, misadventure, mishap, reversal, setback ◆ *adj* **8** = **opposite**,

revert ❶ v 1 return to a former state. 2 come back to a subject. 3 (of property) return to its former owner. **reversion** n

review ❶ n 1 critical assessment of a book, concert, etc. 2 publication with critical articles. 3 general survey. 4 formal inspection. ◆ v 5 hold or write a review of. 6 examine, reconsider, or look back on. 7 inspect formally. **reviewer** n writer of reviews.

revile ❶ v be abusively scornful of.

revise ❶ v 1 change or alter. 2 restudy (work) in preparation for an examination. **revision** n

revive ❶ v bring or come back to life, vigour, use, etc. **revival** n 1 reviving or renewal. 2 movement seeking to restore religious faith. **revivalism** n **revivalist** n

revoke ❶ v cancel (a will, agreement, etc.). **revocation** n

revolt ❶ n 1 uprising against authority. ◆ v 2 rise in rebellion. 3 cause to feel disgust. **revolting** adj disgusting, horrible.

revolve ❶ v turn round, rotate. **revolve around** be centred on. **revolver** n repeating pistol.

revue n theatrical entertainment with topical sketches and songs.

revulsion ❶ n strong disgust.

reward ❶ n 1 something given in return for a service. 2 sum of money offered for finding a criminal or missing property. ◆ v 3 pay or give something to (someone) for a service, information, etc. **rewarding** adj giving personal satisfaction, worthwhile.

rewind v run (a tape or film) back to an earlier point in order to replay.

rewire v provide (a house, engine, etc.) with new wiring.

rhapsody n, pl **–dies** 1 freely structured emotional piece of music. 2 expression of ecstatic enthusiasm. **rhapsodic** adj **rhapsodize** v speak or write with extravagant enthusiasm.

rhesus [**ree**–suss] n small long–tailed monkey of S Asia. **rhesus factor, Rh factor** antigen commonly found in human blood.

rhetoric ❶ n 1 art of effective speaking or

THESAURUS

contrary, converse

revert v 1, 2 = **return**, come back, go back, resume

review n 1 = **critique**, commentary, criticism, evaluation, judgment, notice 2 = **magazine**, journal, periodical 3 = **survey**, analysis, examination, scrutiny, study 4 = **inspection**, march past, parade ◆ v 5 = **assess**, criticize, evaluate, judge, study 6 = **look back on**, examine, inspect, reassess, recall, recollect, reconsider, re–evaluate, re–examine, reflect on, remember, rethink, revise, think over

revile v = **malign**, abuse, bad–mouth (sl, chiefly US & Canad), denigrate, knock (inf), reproach, run down, slag (off) (sl), vilify

revise v 1 = **change**, alter, amend, correct, edit, emend, redo, review, rework, update 2 = **study**, cram (inf), go over, run through, swot up (Brit inf)

revive v = **revitalize**, awaken, bring round, come round, invigorate, reanimate,

recover, refresh, rekindle, renew, restore ≠ **exhaust**

revoke v = **cancel**, annul, countermand, disclaim, invalidate, negate, nullify, obviate, quash, repeal, rescind, retract, reverse, set aside, withdraw

revolt n 1 = **uprising**, insurgency, insurrection, mutiny, rebellion, revolution, rising ◆ v 2 = **rebel**, mutiny, resist, rise 3 = **disgust**, gross out (US sl), make one's flesh creep, nauseate, repel, repulse, sicken, turn one's stomach

revolve v = **go round**, circle, orbit, rotate, spin, turn, twist, wheel, whirl

revulsion n = **disgust**, abhorrence, detestation, loathing, repugnance, repulsion

reward n 1 = **payment**, bonus, bounty, compensation, premium, prize, recompense, repayment, return, wages ≠ **fine** ◆ v 3 = **compensate**, pay, recompense, remunerate, repay ≠ **penalize**

writing. 2 artificial or exaggerated language. **rhetorical** adj (of a question) not requiring an answer. **rhetorically** adv

rheumatism n painful inflammation of joints or muscles. **rheumatic** n, adj (person) affected by rheumatism. **rheumatoid** adj of or like rheumatism.

rhinoceros n, pl **–oses, –os** large thick–skinned animal with one or two horns on its nose.

rhododendron n evergreen flowering shrub.

rhombus n, pl **–buses, –bi** parallelogram with sides of equal length but no right angles, diamond–shaped figure. **rhomboid** n parallelogram with adjacent sides of unequal length.

rhubarb n garden plant of which the fleshy stalks are cooked as fruit.

rhyme ❶ n 1 sameness of the final sounds at the ends of lines of verse, or in words. 2 word identical in sound to another in its final sounds. 3 verse marked by rhyme. ◆ v 4 make a rhyme.

rhythm ❶ n 1 any regular movement or beat. 2 arrangement of the durations of and stress on the notes of a piece of music, usu. grouped into a regular pattern. 3 (in poetry) arrangement of words to form a regular pattern of stresses. **rhythmic, rhythmical** adj **rhythmically** adv **rhythm and blues** popular music, orig. Black American, influenced by the blues.

RI Rhode Island.

rib n 1 one of the curved bones forming the framework of the upper part of the body. 2 cut of meat including the rib(s). 3 curved supporting part, as in the hull of a boat. 4 raised series of rows in knitting. ◆ v **ribbing, ibbed** 5 provide or mark with ribs. 6 knit to form a rib pattern. **ribbed** adj **ribbing** n **ribcage** n bony structure of ribs enclosing the lungs.

ribald ❶ adj humorously or mockingly rude or obscene. **ribaldry** n

ribbon n 1 narrow band of fabric used for trimming, tying, etc. 2 any long strip, for example of inked tape in a typewriter.

rice n 1 cereal plant grown on wet ground in warm countries. 2 its seeds as food.

rich ❶ adj 1 owning a lot of money or property, wealthy. 2 abounding. 3 fertile. 4 (of food) containing much fat or sugar. 5 mellow. 6 amusing. **riches** pl n wealth. **richly** adv 1 elaborately. 2 fully. **richness** n

rick[1] n stack of hay etc.

rick[2] v, n sprain or wrench.

rickets n disease of children marked by softening of the bones, bow legs, etc., caused by vitamin D deficiency.

rickshaw n light two–wheeled man–drawn Asian vehicle.

ricochet [**rik**–osh–ay] v 1 (of a bullet) rebound from a solid surface. ◆ n 2 such a rebound.

rid ❶ v **ridding, rid** clear or relieve (of). **get rid of** free oneself of (something undesirable). **good riddance** relief at getting rid of something or someone.

——————| T H E S A U R U S |——————

rhetoric n 1 = **oratory**, eloquence 2 = **hyperbole**, bombast, grandiloquence, magniloquence, verbosity, wordiness

rhyme n 3 = **poetry**, ode, poem, song, verse ◆ v 4 = **sound like**, harmonize

rhythm n 1 = **beat**, accent, cadence, lilt, metre, pulse, swing, tempo, time

ribald adj = **coarse**, bawdy, blue, broad, earthy, naughty, near the knuckle (inf), obscene, racy, rude, smutty, vulgar

rich adj 1 = **wealthy**, affluent, loaded (sl), moneyed, prosperous, well–heeled (inf),

well–off, well–to–do ≠ **poor** 2 = **well–stocked**, full, productive, well–supplied ≠ **wanting** 3 = **fruitful**, abounding, abundant, ample, copious, fertile, lush, luxurious, plentiful, productive, prolific ≠ **barren** 4 = **full–bodied**, creamy, fatty, luscious, succulent, sweet, tasty ≠ **dull**

rid v = **free**, clear, deliver, disburden, disencumber, make free, purge, relieve, unburden **get rid of** = **dispose of**, dump, eject, eliminate, expel, remove, throw away or out

ridden v 1 past participle of RIDE. ♦ adj 2 afflicted or affected by the thing specified, e.g. *disease-ridden*.

riddle¹ ❶ n 1 question made puzzling to test one's ingenuity 2 puzzling person or thing.

riddle² ❶ v 1 pierce with many holes. ♦ n 2 coarse sieve for gravel etc. **riddled with** full of.

ride ❶ v **riding, rode, ridden** 1 sit on and control or propel (a horse, bicycle, etc.). 2 go on horseback or in a vehicle. 3 travel over. 4 be carried on or across. 5 lie at anchor. ♦ n 6 journey on a horse etc., or in a vehicle. 7 type of movement experienced in a vehicle. **rider** n 1 person who rides. 2 supplementary clause added to a document. **ride up** v (of a garment) move up from the proper position.

ridge n 1 long narrow hill. 2 long narrow raised part on a surface. 3 line where two sloping surfaces meet. 4 *Meteorol* elongated area of high pressure. **ridged** adj

ridiculous ❶ adj deserving to be laughed at, absurd. **ridicule** n 1 treatment of a person or thing as ridiculous. ♦ v 2 laugh at, make fun of.

rife ❶ adj widespread or common. **rife with** full of.

riff n *Jazz, rock* short repeated melodic figure.

riffraff ❶ n rabble, disreputable people.

rifle¹ n 1 firearm with a long barrel. ♦ v 2 cut spiral grooves inside the barrel of a gun.

rifle² ❶ v 1 search and rob. 2 steal.

rift ❶ n 1 break in friendly relations. 2 crack, split, or cleft.

rig ❶ v **rigging, rigged** 1 arrange in a dishonest way. 2 equip, esp. a ship. ♦ n 3 apparatus for drilling for oil and gas. 4 way a ship's masts and sails are arranged. 5 *Informal* outfit of clothes. **rigging** n ship's spars and ropes. **rig up** v set up or build temporarily.

right ❶ adj 1 just. 2 true or correct. 3 proper. 4 in a satisfactory condition. 5 of the side that faces east when the front is turned to the north. 6 of the outer side of a fabric. ♦ adv 7 properly. 8 straight or directly. 9 on or to the right side. ♦ n 10 claim, title, etc. allowed or due. 11 what is just or due. 12 (R–) conservative political party or group. ♦ v 13 bring or come back to a normal or correct state. 14 bring or come back to a vertical position. **in the right** morally or legally correct. **right away** immediately. **rightly** adv **rightful** adj **rightist** n, adj (person) on the political right. **right angle** angle of 90°. **right-handed** adj using or for the right hand. **right-hand man** person's most valuable assistant. **right of way** 1 right of one vehicle to go before another. 2 legal right to pass over someone's land.

──────── THESAURUS ────────

riddle¹ n 1, 2 = **puzzle**, conundrum, enigma, mystery, poser, problem

riddle² v 1 = **pierce**, honeycomb, pepper, perforate, puncture ♦ n 2 = **sieve**, filter, screen, strainer

ride v 1 = **control**, handle, manage 2 = **travel**, be carried, go, move ♦ n 6 = **journey**, drive, jaunt, lift, outing, trip

ridiculous adj = **laughable**, absurd, comical, farcical, funny, ludicrous, risible, silly, stupid

rife adj = **widespread**, common, frequent, general, prevalent, rampant, ubiquitous, universal

riffraff n = **rabble**, hoi polloi, ragtag and bobtail

rifle² v = **ransack**, burgle, go through, loot, pillage, plunder, rob, sack, strip

rift n 1 = **breach**, disagreement, division, falling out (*inf*), quarrel, separation, split 2 = **split**, break, cleft, crack, crevice, fault, fissure, flaw, gap, opening

rig v 1 = **fix** (*inf*), arrange, engineer, gerrymander, manipulate, tamper with 2 = **equip**, fit out, furnish, kit out, outfit, supply ♦ n 3 = **apparatus**, equipment, fittings, fixtures, gear, tackle 5 (also **rigout**) *Inf* = **outfit**, costume, dress, garb,

righteous ⬧ [**rye**–chuss] *adj* 1 upright, godly, or virtuous. 2 morally justified. **righteousness** *n*

rigid ⬧ *adj* 1 inflexible or strict. 2 unyielding or stiff. **rigidly** *adv* **rigidity** *n*

rigmarole ⬧ *n* 1 long complicated procedure.

rigor mortis *n* stiffening of the body after death.

rigour ⬧ *n* 1 harshness, severity, or strictness. 2 hardship. **rigorous** *adj* harsh, severe, or stern.

rile *v* anger or annoy.

rim ⬧ *n* 1 edge or border. 2 outer ring of a wheel.

rind ⬧ *n* tough outer coating of fruits, cheese, or bacon.

ring[1] ⬧ *v* **ringing, rang, rung** 1 give out a clear resonant sound, as a bell. 2 cause (a bell) to sound. 3 telephone. 4 resound. ◆ *n* 5 ringing. 6 telephone call. **ring off** *v* end a telephone call. **ring up** *v* telephone.

✓ **WORD TIP**
The simple past is *rang*: *He rang the bell*. Avoid the use of the past participle *rung* for the simple past.

---

ring[2] ⬧ *n* 1 circle of gold etc., esp. for a finger. 2 any circular band, coil, or rim. 3 circle of people. 4 enclosed area, esp. a circle for a circus or a roped–in square for boxing. 5 group operating (illegal) control of a market. ◆ *v* 6 put a ring round. 7 mark (a bird) with a ring. 8 kill (a tree) by cutting the bark round the trunk. **ringer** *n Slang* person or thing apparently identical to another (also **dead ringer**). **ringlet** *n* curly lock of hair. **ringleader** *n* instigator of a mutiny, riot, etc. **ring road** main road that bypasses a town (centre). **ringside** *n* row of seats nearest a boxing or circus ring. **ringworm** *n* fungal skin disease in circular patches.

——————— THESAURUS ———————

gear (*inf*), get–up (*inf*), togs

right *adj* 1 = **just**, equitable, ethical, fair, good, honest, lawful, moral, proper ≠ **evil** 2 = **correct**, accurate, exact, factual, genuine, precise, true, valid 3 = **proper**, appropriate, becoming, desirable, done, fit, fitting, seemly, suitable ≠ **wrong** ◆ *adv* 7 = **suitably**, appropriately, aptly, fittingly, properly ≠ **improperly** 8 = **straight**, directly, promptly, quickly, straightaway ≠ **slowly** ◆ *n* 10 = **prerogative**, authority, business, claim, due, freedom, liberty, licence, mana (*NZ*), permission, power, privilege 11 = **justice**, fairness, lawfulness, legality, righteousness, truth ◆ *v* 13 = **rectify**, correct, fix, put right, redress, settle, sort out, straighten **in the right** = **vindicated**, borne out, justified, right, with the law on your side **right away** = **immediately**, at once, directly, forthwith, instantly, now, pronto (*inf*), straightaway

righteous[1] *adj* = **virtuous**, ethical, fair, good, honest, honourable, just, moral, pure, upright ≠ **bad**

rigid *adj* 1 = **strict**, exact, fixed, inflexible, rigorous, set, stringent, unbending, uncompromising ≠ **soft** 2 = **stiff**, inflexible, unyielding ≠ **flexible**

rigmarole *n* 1 = **procedure**, bother, carry– on (*inf, chiefly Brit*), fuss, hassle (*inf*), nonsense, palaver, pantomime (*inf*), performance (*inf*) 2 = **twaddle**, gibberish

rigour *n* 1 = **strictness**, harshness, inflexibility, rigidity, sternness, stringency 2 = **hardship**, ordeal, privation, suffering, trial

rile *v* = **anger**, aggravate (*inf*), annoy, get or put one's back up, irk, irritate

rim *n* 1 = **edge**, border, brim, brink, lip, margin, verge

rind *n* = **skin**, crust, husk, outer layer, peel

ring[1] *v* 1, 2 = **chime**, clang, peal, reverberate, sound, toll 3 = **phone**, buzz (*inf, chiefly Brit*), call, telephone ◆ *n* 5 = **chime**, knell, peal 6 = **call**, buzz (*inf, chiefly Brit*), phone call

ring[2] *n* 1, 2 = **circle**, band, circuit, halo, hoop, loop, round 4 = **arena**, circus, enclosure, rink 5 = **gang**, association,

rink *n* 1 sheet of ice for skating or curling. 2 floor for roller-skating.

rinse ● *v* 1 remove soap from (washed clothes, hair, etc.) by applying clean water. 2 wash lightly. ◆ *n* 3 rinsing. 4 liquid to tint hair.

riot ● *n* 1 disorderly unruly disturbance. 2 loud revelry. 3 profusion. 4 *Slang* very amusing person or thing. ◆ *v* 5 take part in a riot. **read the riot act** reprimand severely. **run riot** 1 behave without restraint. 2 grow profusely. **riotous** *adj* 1 unrestrained. 2 unruly or rebellious.

rip ● *v* **ripping, ripped** 1 tear violently. 2 tear away. 3 *Informal* rush. ◆ *n* 4 split or tear. **let rip** act or speak without restraint. **ripcord** *n* cord pulled to open a parachute. **rip off** *v Slang* cheat by overcharging. **rip-off** *n Slang* cheat or swindle. **rip-roaring** *adj Informal* boisterous and exciting.

RIP rest in peace.

ripe ● *adj* 1 ready to be reaped, eaten, etc. 2 matured. 3 ready or suitable. **ripen** *v* 1 grow ripe. 2 mature.

riposte ● [rip-**posst**] *n* 1 verbal retort. 2 counterattack, esp. in fencing. ◆ *v* 3 make a riposte.

ripple *n* 1 slight wave or ruffling of a surface. 2 sound like ripples of water. ◆ *v* 3 flow or form into little waves (on). 4 (of sounds) rise and fall gently.

rise ● *v* **rising, rose, risen** 1 get up from a lying, sitting, or kneeling position. 2 move upwards. 3 (of the sun or moon) appear above the horizon. 4 reach a higher level. 5 (of an amount or price) increase. 6 rebel. 7 (of a court) adjourn. 8 *n* 9 rising. 10 upward slope. 11 increase, esp. of wages. **give rise to** cause. **riser** *n* 1 person who rises, esp. from bed. 2 vertical part of a step. **rising** *n* 1 revolt. ◆ *adj* 2 increasing in rank or maturity.

risk ● *n* 1 chance of disaster or loss. 2 person or thing considered as a potential hazard. ◆ *v* 3 act in spite of the possibility of (injury or loss). 4 expose to danger or loss. **risky** *adj* full of risk, dangerous.

risotto *n, pl* **-tos** dish of rice cooked in stock with vegetables, meat, etc.

risqué ● [risk-**ay**] *adj* bordering on indecency.

THESAURUS

band, cartel, circle, group, mob, syndicate ◆ *v* 6 = **encircle**, enclose, gird, girdle, surround

rinse *v* 1, 2 = **wash**, bathe, clean, cleanse, dip, splash ◆ *n* 3 = **wash**, bath, dip, splash

riot *n* 1 = **disturbance**, anarchy, confusion, disorder, lawlessness, strife, tumult, turbulence, turmoil, upheaval 2 = **merrymaking**, carousal, festivity, frolic, high jinks, revelry 3 = **display**, extravaganza, profusion, show, splash ◆ *v* 5 = **rampage**, go on the rampage **run riot** 1 = **rampage**, be out of control, break or cut loose, go wild 2 = **grow profusely**, spread like wildfire

rip *v* 1 = **tear**, burst, claw, cut, gash, lacerate, rend, slash, slit, split ◆ *n* 4 = **tear**, cut, gash, hole, laceration, rent, slash, slit, split

ripe *adj* 1, 2 = **mature**, mellow, ready, ripened, seasoned ≠ **green** 3 = **suitable**,

auspicious, favourable, ideal, opportune, right, timely ≠ **inappropriate**

riposte *n* 1 = **retort**, answer, comeback (*inf*), rejoinder, reply, response, sally ◆ *v* 3 = **retort**, answer, come back, reply, respond

rise *v* 1 = **get up**, arise, get to one's feet, stand up 3 = **go up**, ascend, climb ≠ **fall** 4 = **advance**, get on, progress, prosper 5 = **increase**, go up, grow, intensify, mount ≠ **drop** 6 = **rebel**, mutiny, revolt ◆ *n* 9 = **advancement**, climb, progress, promotion 10 = **upward slope**, ascent, elevation, incline 11 = **increase**, increment, pay increase, raise (*US*), upsurge, upswing, upturn ≠ **fall give rise to** = **cause**, bring about, effect, produce, result in

risk *n* 1 = **danger**, chance, gamble, hazard, jeopardy, peril, pitfall, possibility ◆ *v* 3, 4 = **dare**, chance, endanger, gamble,

rissole n cake of minced meat, coated with breadcrumbs and fried.

rite ⊕ n formal practice or custom, esp. religious.

rival ⊕ n 1 person or thing that competes with or equals another for favour, success, etc. ◆ adj 2 in the position of a rival. ◆ v – **valling, –valled** 3 (try to) equal. **rivalry** n keen competition.

river ⊕ n 1 large natural stream of water. 2 plentiful flow.

rivet [riv–vit] n 1 bolt for fastening metal plates, the end being put through holes and then beaten flat. ◆ v **riveting, riveted** 2 fasten with rivets. 3 cause to be fixed, as in fascination. **riveting** adj very interesting and exciting.

rivulet n small stream.

RN Royal Navy.

road ⊕ n 1 way prepared for passengers, vehicles, etc. 2 route in a town or city with houses along it. 3 way or course, e.g. the road to fame. **on the road** travelling. **roadie** n Informal person who transports and sets up equipment for a band. **roadblock** n barricade across a road to stop traffic for inspection etc. **road hog** Informal selfish aggressive driver. **roadhouse** n pub or restaurant on a country road. **roadside** n, adj **road test** test of a vehicle etc. in actual use.

roadway n the part of a road used by vehicles. **roadworks** pl n repairs to a road, esp. blocking part of the road.

roadworthy adj (of a vehicle) mechanically sound.

roam ⊕ v wander about.

roar ⊕ v 1 make or utter a loud deep hoarse sound like that of a lion. 2 shout (something) as in anger. 3 laugh loudly. ◆ n 4 such a sound. **a roaring trade** Informal brisk and profitable business.

roast v 1 cook by dry heat, as in an oven. 2 make or be very hot. ◆ n 3 roasted joint of meat. ◆ adj 4 roasted. **roasting** Informal ◆ adj 1 extremely hot. ◆ n 2 severe criticism or scolding.

rob ⊕ v **robbing, robbed** 1 steal from. 2 deprive. **robber** n **robbery** n

robe ⊕ n 1 long loose outer garment. ◆ v 2 put a robe on.

robin n small brown bird with a red breast.

robot ⊕ n 1 automated machine, esp. one performing functions in a human manner. 2 person of machine–like efficiency. 3 S Afr set of coloured lights at a junction to control the traffic flow. **robotic** adj **robotics** n science of designing and using robots.

robust ⊕ adj very strong and healthy. **robustness** n

rock¹ ⊕ n 1 hard mineral substance that

——————| T H E S A U R U S |——————

hazard, imperil, jeopardize, venture

risqué adj = **suggestive**, bawdy, blue, improper, indelicate, naughty, near the knuckle (inf), racy, ribald

rite n = **ceremony**, custom, observance, practice, procedure, ritual

rival n 1 = **opponent**, adversary, competitor, contender, contestant ≠ **friend** ◆ adj 2 = **competing**, conflicting, opposing ◆ v 3 = **compete**, be a match for, compare with, equal, match

river n 1 = **stream**, brook, burn (Scot), creek, tributary, waterway 2 = **flow**, flood, rush, spate, torrent

road n 1 = **way**, course, highway, lane, motorway, path, pathway, roadway,

route, track

roam v = **wander**, prowl, ramble, range, rove, stray, travel, walk

roar v 2 = **cry**, bawl, bellow, howl, shout, yell 3 = **guffaw**, hoot, laugh heartily, split one's sides (inf) ◆ n 4 = **cry**, bellow, hoot, howl, outcry, shout, yell

rob v 1 = **steal from**, burgle, cheat, con (inf), defraud, dispossess, do out of (inf), hold up, loot, mug (inf), pillage, plunder, raid 2 = **deprive**, do out of

robe n 1 = **gown**, costume, habit ◆ v 2 = **clothe**, dress, garb

robot n 1 = **machine**, android, automaton, mechanical man

robust adj 1, 2 = **strong**, fit, hale, hardy,

makes up part of the earth's crust, stone. 2 large rugged mass of stone. 3 hard sweet in sticks. **on the rocks 1** (of a marriage) about to end. 2 (of an alcoholic drink) served with ice. **rocky** *adj* having many rocks. **rockery** *n* mound of stones in a garden for rock plants. **rock bottom** lowest possible level.

rock² ⊕ *v* 1 (cause to) sway to and fro. ◆ *n* 2 (also **rock music**) style of pop music with a heavy beat. **rocky** *adj* shaky or unstable. **rock and roll, rock'n'roll** style of pop music blending rhythm and blues and country music. **rocking chair** chair allowing the sitter to rock backwards and forwards.

rocket *n* 1 self-propelling device powered by the burning of explosive contents (used as a firework, weapon, etc.). 2 vehicle propelled by a rocket engine, as a weapon or carrying a spacecraft. ◆ *v* **-eting, -eted** 3 move fast, esp. upwards, like a rocket.

rock melon *n Aust, NZ & US* type of melon with sweet orange flesh.

rod ⊕ *n* 1 slender straight bar, stick. 2 cane.

rodent *n* animal with teeth specialized for gnawing, such as a rat, mouse, or squirrel.

rodeo *n, pl* **-deos** display of skill by cowboys, such as bareback riding.

roe¹ *n* mass of eggs in a fish, sometimes eaten as food.

roe² *n* small species of deer.

rogue ⊕ *n* 1 dishonest or unprincipled person. 2 mischief-loving person. ◆ *adj* 3 (of a wild beast) having a savage temper and living apart from the herd. **roguish** *adj*

role ⊕ **rôle** *n* 1 task or function. 2 actor's part.

roll ⊕ *v* 1 move by turning over and over. 2 move or sweep along. 3 wind round. 4 undulate. 5 smooth out with a roller. 6 (of a ship or aircraft) turn from side to side about a line from nose to tail. ◆ *n* 7 act of rolling over or from side to side. 8 piece of paper etc. rolled up. 9 small round individually baked piece of bread. 10 list or register. 11 continuous sound, as of drums, thunder, etc. 12 swaying unsteady movement or gait. 13 **roll call** calling out of a list of names, as in a school or the army, to check who is present. **rolling pin** cylindrical roller for flattening pastry. **rolling stock** locomotives and coaches of a railway. **rolling stone** restless wandering person. **roll up** *v Informal* appear or arrive.

rollicking *adj* boisterously carefree.

roly-poly ⊕ *adj* round or plump.

ROM *Computers* read only memory.

Roman *adj* of Rome or the Roman Catholic Church. **Roman Catholic** (member) of that section of the Christian Church that acknowledges the supremacy of the Pope. **Roman numerals** the letters I, V, X, L, C, D, M, used to represent numbers. **roman**

──────── THESAURUS ────────

healthy, muscular, powerful, stout, strapping, sturdy, tough, vigorous ≠ **weak**

rock¹ *n* 2 = **stone**, boulder

rock² *v* 1 = **sway**, lurch, pitch, reel, roll, swing, toss

rod *n* = **stick**, bar, baton, cane, pole, shaft, staff, wand

rogue *n* 1 = **scoundrel**, blackguard, crook (*inf*), fraud, rascal, scally (*NW Eng dial*), villain 2 = **scamp**, devil, imp, monkey, rascal, tyke (*inf*)

role, rôle *n* 1 = **job**, capacity, duty, function, part, position, post, task 2 = **part**, character, portrayal,

representation

roll *v* 1 = **turn**, go round, revolve, rotate, spin, swivel, trundle, twirl, wheel, whirl 3 = **wind**, bind, enfold, envelop, furl, swathe, wrap 4 = **flow**, run, undulate 5 = **level**, even, flatten, press, smooth 6 = **toss**, lurch, reel, rock, sway, tumble ◆ *n* 10 = **turn**, cycle, reel, revolution, rotation, spin, twirl, wheel, whirl 13 = **register**, census, index, list, record 15 = **rumble**, boom, reverberation, roar, thunder

roly-poly *adj* = **plump**, buxom, chubby, fat, podgy, rounded, tubby type plain upright letters in printing.

romance ⓣ *n* **1** love affair. **2** mysterious or exciting quality. **3** novel or film dealing with love, esp. sentimentally. **4** story with scenes remote from ordinary life. **romantic** *adj*

Romany *n, pl* **–nies**, *adj* Gypsy.

romp ⓣ *v* **1** play wildly and joyfully. ◆ *n* **2** boisterous activity. **rompers** *pl n* child's overalls.

roof *n, pl* **roofs 1** outside upper covering of a building, car, etc. ◆ *v* **2** put a roof on.

rooibos *n S Afr* tea prepared from the dried leaves of an African plant.

rook *n* **1** bird of the crow family. ◆ *v* **2** *Old-fashioned slang* swindle. **rookery** *n, pl* **–eries** colony of rooks, penguins, or seals.

rookie *n Informal* new recruit.

room ⓣ *n* **1** enclosed area in a building. **2** unoccupied space. **3** scope or opportunity. ◆ *pl* **4** lodgings. **roomy** *adj* spacious.

roost *n* **1** perch for fowls. ◆ *v* **2** perch. **rooster** *n* domestic cock.

root[1] ⓣ *n* **1** part of a plant that grows down into the earth obtaining nourishment. **2** plant with an edible root, such as a carrot. **3** part of a tooth, hair, etc. below the skin. **4** source or origin. **5** form of a word from which other words and forms are derived. **6** *Maths* factor of a quantity which, when multiplied by itself the number of times indicated, gives the quantity. ◆ *pl* **7** person's sense of belonging. ◆ *v* **8** establish a root and start to grow. **rootless** *adj* having no sense of belonging. **root for** *v Informal* cheer on. **root out** *v* get rid of completely. **rootstock** *n* rhizome.

root[2] ⓣ , **rootle** *v* **1** dig or burrow. **2** *Informal* search vigorously but unsystematically.

rope ⓣ *n* thick cord. **know the ropes** be thoroughly familiar with an activity. **rope in** *v* persuade to join in.

rort *n Aust informal* dishonest scheme.

rosary *n, pl* **–saries 1** series of prayers. **2** string of beads for counting these prayers.

rose *n* **1** shrub or climbing plant with prickly stems and fragrant flowers. **2** flower of this plant. **3** perforated flat nozzle for a hose. **4** pink colour. ◆ *adj* **5** pink. **roseate** [roe–zee–ate] *adj* rose–coloured. **rose window** circular window with spokes branching from the centre. **rosewood** *n* fragrant wood used to make furniture.

rosé [roe–zay] *n* pink wine.

rosemary *n* **1** fragrant flowering shrub. **2** its leaves as a herb.

roster ⓣ *n* list of people and their turns of duty.

rostrum ⓣ *n, pl* **–trums**, **–tra** platform or stage.

rot ⓣ *v* **rotting**, **rotted 1** decompose or

romance *n* **1** = **love affair**, affair, amour, attachment, liaison, relationship **3** = **excitement**, charm, colour, fascination, glamour, mystery **3, 4** = **story**, fairy tale, fantasy, legend, love story, melodrama, tale

romp *v* **1** = **frolic**, caper, cavort, frisk, gambol, have fun, sport ◆ *n* **2** = **frolic**, caper, lark (*inf*) **romp home** = **win easily**, walk it (*inf*), win by a mile (*inf*), win hands down

room *n* **1** = **chamber**, apartment, office **2** = **space**, area, capacity, expanse, extent, leeway, margin, range, scope **3** = **opportunity**, chance, occasion, scope

root[1] *n* **1** = **stem**, rhizome, tuber **4** = **source**, base, bottom, cause, core, foundation, heart, nucleus, origin, seat, seed ◆ *pl* **7** = **sense of belonging**, heritage, origins ◆ *v* **8** = **become established**, anchor, establish, fasten, fix, ground, implant, moor, set, stick

root[2], **rootle** *v* **1** = **dig**, burrow, ferret

rope *n* = **cord**, cable, hawser, line, strand **know the ropes** = **be experienced**, be an old hand, be knowledgeable

roster *n* = **rota**, agenda, catalogue, list, register, roll, schedule, table

rostrum *n* = **stage**, dais, platform, podium, stand

decay. **2** slowly deteriorate physically or mentally. ◆ *n* **3** decay. **4** *Informal* nonsense. **rotten** *adj*

rota *n* list of people who take it in turn to do a particular task.

rotary ❶ *adj* **1** revolving. **2** operated by rotation.

rote *n* mechanical repetition. **by rote** by memory.

rotor *n* **1** revolving portion of a dynamo, motor, or turbine. **2** rotating device with long blades that provides thrust to lift a helicopter.

rotund ❶ [roe-**tund**] *adj* **1** round and plump. **2** sonorous. **rotundity** *n*

rouge *n* red cosmetic used to colour the cheeks.

rough ❶ *adj* **1** uneven or irregular. **2** not careful or gentle. **3** difficult or unpleasant. **4** approximate. **5** violent, stormy, or boisterous. **6** in preliminary form. **7** lacking refinement. ◆ *v* **8** make rough. ◆ *n* **9** rough state or area. **rough it** live without the usual comforts etc. **roughen** *v* **roughly** *adv* **roughness** *n* **roughage** *n* indigestible constituents of food which aid digestion. **rough–and–ready** *adj* hastily prepared but adequate. **rough–and–tumble** *n* playful

fight. **roughhouse** *n* *Slang* fight. **1** rough out *v* prepare (a sketch or report) in preliminary form.

roulette *n* gambling game played with a revolving wheel and a ball.

round ❶ *adj* **1** spherical, cylindrical, circular, or curved. **2** complete or whole, e.g. *round numbers.* ◆ *adv, prep* **3** indicating an encircling movement, presence on all sides, etc., e.g. *tied round the waist; books scattered round the room.* ◆ *v* **4** move round. ◆ *n* **5** round shape. **6** recurrent duties. **7** customary course, as of a milkman. **8** game (of golf). **9** stage in a competition. **10** one of several periods in a boxing match etc. **11** number of drinks bought at one time. **12** bullet or shell for a gun. **13** part song in which singers join at equal intervals. **14** circular movement. **15** set of sandwiches. **roundly** *adv* thoroughly. **rounders** *n* bat–and–ball team game. **round robin** petition signed with names in a circle to conceal the order. **round–the–clock** *adj* throughout the day and night **round trip** journey out and back again. **round up** *v* gather (people or animals) together. **roundup** *n*

rouse[1] ❶ *v* **1** wake up. **2** provoke or excite.

rot *v* **1** = **decay**, crumble, decompose, go bad, moulder, perish, putrefy, spoil **2** = **deteriorate**, decline, waste away ◆ *n* **3** = **decay**, blight, canker, corruption, decomposition, mould, putrefaction **3** *Inf* = **nonsense**, claptrap (*inf*), codswallop (*Brit sl*), drivel, garbage (*chiefly US*), hogwash, kak (*S Afr sl*), poppycock (*inf*), rubbish, trash, tripe (*inf*), twaddle

rotary *adj* = **revolving**, rotating, spinning, turning

rotund *adj* **1** = **plump**, chubby, corpulent, fat, fleshy, globular, podgy, portly, rounded, spherical, stout, tubby ≠ **thin**

rough *adj* **1** = **uneven**, broken, bumpy, craggy, irregular, jagged, rocky, stony ≠ **even 2** = **harsh**, cruel, hard, nasty, tough, unfeeling, unpleasant, violent ≠ **civil 3** = **unpleasant**, arduous, difficult,

hard, tough, uncomfortable ≠ **easy 4** = **approximate**, estimated, general, imprecise, inexact, sketchy, vague ≠ **exact 5** = **stormy**, agitated, choppy, inclement, squally, tempestuous, turbulent, wild **6** = **basic**, crude, imperfect, incomplete, rudimentary, sketchy, unfinished, unpolished, unrefined ≠ **finished 7** = **ungracious**, blunt, brusque, charlish, coarse, curt, impolite, inconsiderate, indelicate, rude, unceremonious, uncivil, uncouth, unmannerly

round *adj* **1** = **spherical**, circular, curved, cylindrical, globular, rotund, rounded ◆ *v* **4** = **go round**, bypass, circle, encircle, flank, skirt, turn ◆ *n* **5** = **sphere**, ball, band, circle, disc, globe, orb, ring **7** = **course**, beat, circuit, routine, schedule, series, tour **9** = **stage**, division,

rousing adj lively, vigorous.
rouse² [**rhymes with mouse**] v (foll. by on) Aust scold or rebuke.
rout ① n 1 overwhelming defeat. 2 disorderly retreat. ◆ v 3 defeat and put to flight.
route ① n 1 roads taken to reach a destination. 2 chosen way. **routemarch** n long military training march.
routine ① n 1 usual or regular method of procedure. 2 set sequence. ◆ adj 3 ordinary or regular.
rove ① v wander. **rover** n
row¹ ① [**rhymes with go**] n straight line of people or things. **in a row** in succession.
row² [**rhymes with go**] v 1 propel (a boat) by oars. ◆ n 2 spell of rowing. **rowing boat** boat propelled by oars.
row³ ① [**rhymes with now**] Informal ◆ n 1 dispute. 2 disturbance. 3 reprimand. ◆ v 4 quarrel noisily.
rowan n tree producing bright red berries, mountain ash.
rowdy ① adj –dier, –diest 1 disorderly, noisy, and rough. ◆ n, pl –dies 2 person like this.
rowlock [**rol**–luk] n device on a boat that

holds an oar in place.
royal ① adj 1 of, befitting, or supported by a king or queen. 2 splendid. ◆ n 3 Informal member of a royal family. **royally** adv **royalist** n supporter of monarchy. **royalty** n 1 royal people. 2 rank or power of a monarch. 3 (pl –ties) payment to an author, musician, inventor, etc. **royal blue** deep blue.
rpm revolutions per minute.
RSVP please reply.
rub ① v rubbing, rubbed 1 apply pressure and friction to (something) with a circular or backwards–forwards movement. 2 clean, polish, or dry by rubbing. 3 chafe or fray through rubbing. ◆ n 4 act of rubbing. **rub it in** emphasize an unpleasant fact. **rub out** v remove with a rubber.
rubber n 1 strong waterproof elastic material, orig. made from the dried sap of a tropical tree, now usu. synthetic. 2 piece of rubber used for erasing writing. ◆ adj 3 made of or producing rubber. **rubberize** v coat or treat with rubber. **rubbery** adj **rubberneck** v US stare with unthinking curiosity. **rubber plant** house plant with

─────── THESAURUS ───────

lap, level, period, session, turn
rouse¹ v 1 = **wake up**, awaken, call, rise, wake 2 = **excite**, agitate, anger, animate, incite, inflame, move, provoke, stimulate, stir
rout n 1 = **defeat**, beating, debacle, drubbing, overthrow, pasting (sl), thrashing ◆ v 3 = **defeat**, beat, conquer, crush, destroy, drub, overthrow, thrash, wipe the floor with (inf)
route n 2 = **way**, beat, circuit, course, direction, itinerary, journey, path, road
routine n 1 = **procedure**, custom, method, order, pattern, practice, programme ◆ adj 3 = **usual**, customary, everyday, habitual, normal, ordinary, standard, typical ≠ **different**
rove v = **wander**, drift, ramble, range, roam, stray, traipse (inf)
row¹ n = **line**, bank, column, file, range,

series, string **in a row** = **consecutively**, one after the other, successively
row³ Inf n 1 = **quarrel**, brawl, dispute, squabble, tiff, trouble 2 = **disturbance**, commotion, noise, racket, rumpus, tumult, uproar ◆ v 4 = **quarrel**, argue, dispute, fight, squabble, wrangle
rowdy adj 1 = **disorderly**, loud, noisy, rough, unruly, wild ≠ **mannerly** ◆ n 2 = **hooligan**, lout, ruffian, tearaway (Brit), yob or yobbo (Brit sl)
royal adj 1 = **regal**, imperial, kingly, princely, queenly, sovereign 2 = **splendid**, grand, impressive, magnificent, majestic, stately
rub v 1 = **stroke**, caress, massage 2 = **polish**, clean, scour, shine, wipe 3 = **chafe**, abrade, fray, grate, scrape ◆ v 4 = **massage**, caress, kneading, polish, shine, stroke, wipe

glossy leaves. **rubber stamp 1** device for imprinting the date, a name, etc. **2** automatic authorization.

rubbish ❶ n **1** waste matter. **2** anything worthless. **3** nonsense. **rubbishy** adj

rubble n fragments of broken stone, brick, etc.

rubella n same as GERMAN MEASLES.

ruby n, pl –bies **1** red precious gemstone. ◆ adj **2** deep red.

ruck¹ n **1** rough crowd of common people. **2** Rugby loose scrummage.

ruck² n, v wrinkle or crease.

rucksack n large pack carried on the back.

rudder n vertical hinged piece at the stern of a boat or at the rear of an aircraft, for steering.

ruddy ❶ adj –dier, –diest of a fresh healthy red colour.

rude ❶ adj **1** impolite or insulting. **2** coarse, vulgar, or obscene. **3** unexpected and unpleasant. **4** roughly made. **5** robust. **rudely** adv **rudeness** n

rudiments ❶ pl n simplest and most basic stages of a subject. **rudimentary** adj basic, elementary.

rue ❶ v **ruing, rued** feel regret for. **rueful** adj regretful or sorry. **ruefully** adv

ruff n **1** starched and frilled collar. **2** natural collar of feathers, fur, etc. on certain birds and animals.

ruffian ❶ n violent lawless person.

rug n **1** small carpet. **2** thick woollen blanket.

rugby n form of football played with an oval ball which may be handled by the players.

rugged ❶ [rug–gid] adj **1** rocky or steep. **2** uneven and jagged. **3** strong–featured. **4** tough and sturdy.

ruin ❶ v **1** destroy or spoil completely. **2** impoverish. ◆ n **3** destruction or decay. **4** loss of wealth, position, etc. **5** broken–down unused building. **ruination** n **1** act of ruining. **2** state of being ruined. **3** cause of ruin. **ruinous** adj **1** causing ruin. **2** more expensive than can be afforded. **ruinously** adv

rule ❶ n **1** statement of what is allowed, for example in a game or procedure. **2** what

rubbish n **1, 2** = **waste**, garbage (chiefly US), junk (inf), litter, lumber, refuse, scrap, trash **3** = **nonsense**, claptrap (inf), codswallop (Brit sl), garbage (chiefly US), hogwash, hot air (inf), kak (S Afr sl), rot, tommyrot, trash, tripe (inf), twaddle

ruddy adj **1** = **rosy**, blooming, fresh, glowing, healthy, radiant, red, reddish, rosy–cheeked ≠ **white**

rude adj **1** = **impolite**, abusive, cheeky, discourteous, disrespectful, ill–mannered, impertinent, impudent, insolent, insulting, uncivil, unmannerly ≠ **civil 2** = **vulgar**, boorish, brutish, coarse, graceless, loutish, oafish, rough, uncivilized, uncouth, uncultured ≠ **learned 3** = **unpleasant**, abrupt, harsh, sharp, startling, sudden **4** = **roughly–made**, artless, crude, inartistic, inelegant, makeshift, primitive, raw, rough, simple ≠ **finished**

rudiments pl n = **basics**, beginnings, elements, essentials, foundation,

fundamentals

rue v = **regret**, be sorry for, kick oneself for, lament, mourn, repent

ruffian n = **thug**, brute, bully, heavy (sl), hoodlum, hooligan, rough (inf), tough

rugged adj **1** = **rocky**, craggy **2** = **uneven**, broken, bumpy, craggy, difficult, irregular, jagged, ragged, rough ≠ **even 3** = **strong–featured**, rough–hewn, weather–beaten **4** = **tough**, brawny, burly, husky (inf), muscular, robust, strong, sturdy, well–built ≠ **soft**

ruin v **1** = **destroy**, blow (sl), botch, crush, damage, defeat, demolish, devastate, lay waste, make a mess of, mess up, screw up (inf), smash, spoil, wreck ≠ **preserve 2** = **bankrupt**, impoverish, pauperize ◆ n **3** = **disrepair**, decay, disintegration, ruination, wreckage **4 a** = **destruction**, breakdown, collapse, defeat, devastation, downfall, fall, undoing, wreck ≠ **success b** = **bankruptcy**, destitution, insolvency is usual. **3** government, authority, or control. **4** measuring device with a straight edge. ◆ v **5** govern. **6** be pre-eminent. **7** give a formal decision. **8** mark with straight line(s). **9** restrain. **as a rule** usually. **ruler** n **1** person who governs. **2** measuring device with a straight edge. **ruling** n formal decision. **rule of thumb** practical but imprecise approach. **rule out** v exclude.

rum n alcoholic drink distilled from sugar cane.

rumba n lively ballroom dance of Cuban origin.

rumble v **1** make a low continuous noise. **2** *Informal* discover the (disreputable) truth about. ◆ n **3** deep resonant sound.

ruminate ⊕ v **1** chew the cud. **2** ponder or meditate. **ruminant** adj, n cud-chewing (animal, such as a cow, sheep, or deer). **rumination** n quiet meditation and reflection. **ruminative** adj

rummage ⊕ v **1** search untidily and at length. ◆ n **2** untidy search through a collection of things.

rummy n card game in which players try to collect sets or sequences.

rumour ⊕ n **1** unproved statement. **2** gossip or common talk. **rumoured** adj suggested by rumour.

rump ⊕ n **1** buttocks. **2** rear of an animal.

rumple v make untidy, crumpled, or dishevelled.

rumpus ⊕ n, pl **-puses** noisy commotion.

run ⊕ v **running, ran, run 1** move with a more rapid gait than walking. **2** go quickly (across). **3** compete in a race, election, etc. **4** travel according to schedule. **5** function. **6** manage. **7** continue in a particular direction or for a specified period. **8** expose oneself to (a risk). **9** flow. **10** spread. **11** (of stitches) unravel. **12** (of a newspaper) publish (a story). **13** smuggle (goods, esp. arms). ◆ n **14** act or spell of running. **15** ride in a car. **16** unrestricted access. **17** continuous period. **18** sequence. **19** heavy demand. **20** series of unravelled stitches, ladder. **21** steep snow-covered course for skiing. **22** enclosure for domestic fowls. **23** score of one at cricket. **run away** v make one's escape, flee. **run down** v **1** be rude about. **2** reduce in number or size. **3** stop working. **rundown** n **run-down** adj exhausted. **1 run into** v meet. **run-of-the-mill** adj ordinary. **run out** v be completely used up. **run over** v knock down (a person) with a moving vehicle. **run up** v incur (a debt).

rune n any character of the earliest

——————| THESAURUS |——————

rule n **1** = **regulation**, axiom, canon, decree, direction, guideline, law, maxim, precept, principle, tenet **2** = **custom**, convention, habit, practice, procedure, routine, tradition **3** = **government**, authority, command, control, dominion, jurisdiction, mana (*NZ*), mastery, power, regime, reign ◆ v **5** = **govern**, be in authority, be in power, command, control, direct, reign **7** = **decree**, decide, judge, pronounce, settle **as a rule** = **usually**, generally, mainly, normally, on the whole, ordinarily

ruminate v **2** = **ponder**, cogitate, consider, contemplate, deliberate, mull over, muse, reflect, think, turn over in one's mind

rummage v **1** = **search**, delve, forage,

hunt, ransack, root

rumour n **2** = **story**, buzz, dirt (*US sl*), gossip, hearsay, news, report, talk, whisper, word

rump n = **buttocks**, backside (*inf*), bottom, bum (*Brit sl*), butt (*US & Canad inf*), hindquarters, posterior, rear, rear end, seat

rumpus n = **commotion**, disturbance, furore, fuss, hue and cry, noise, row, uproar

run v **1** = **race**, bolt, dash, gallop, hare (*Brit inf*), hurry, jog, leg it (*inf*), lope, rush, scurry, sprint ≠ **walk 2** = **move**, course, glide, go, pass, roll, skim **3** = **compete**, be a candidate, contend, put oneself up for, stand, take part **5** = **work**, function, go, operate, perform **6** = **manage**, administer,

Germanic alphabet. **runic** *adj*

rung *n* crossbar on a ladder.

runt *n* 1 smallest animal in a litter. 2 undersized person.

rupture ✪ *n* 1 breaking, breach. 2 hernia. ♦ *v* 3 break, burst, or sever.

rural ✪ *adj* in or of the countryside.

ruse ✪ [rooz] *n* stratagem or trick.

rush¹ ✪ *v* 1 move or do very quickly. 2 force (someone) to act hastily. 3 make a sudden attack upon (a person or place). ♦ *n* 4 sudden quick or violent movement. ♦ *pl* 5 first unedited prints of a scene for a film. ♦ *adj* 6 done with speed, hasty. **rush hour** period at the beginning and end of the working day, when many people are travelling to or from work.

rush² *n* marsh plant with a slender pithy stem.

rusk *n* hard brown crisp biscuit, used esp. for feeding babies.

russet *adj* 1 reddish–brown. ♦ *n* 2 apple with rough reddish–brown skin.

rust ✪ *n* 1 reddish–brown coating formed on iron etc. that has been exposed to moisture. 2 disease of plants which produces rust–coloured spots. ♦ *adj* 3 reddish–brown. ♦ *v* 4 become coated with rust. **rusty** *adj* 1 coated with rust. 2 of a rust colour. 3 out of practice.

rustic ✪ *adj* 1 of or resembling country people. 2 rural. 3 crude, awkward, or uncouth. 4 (of furniture) made of untrimmed branches. ♦ *n* 5 person from the country.

rustle¹ ✪ *v, n* (make) a low whispering sound.

rustle² *v US* steal (cattle). **rustler** *n US* cattle thief. **rustle up** *v* prepare at short notice.

rut ✪ *n* 1 furrow made by wheels. 2 dull settled habits or way of living.

ruthless ✪ *adj* pitiless, merciless. **ruthlessness** *n*

rye *n* 1 kind of grain used for fodder and bread. 2 *US* whiskey made from rye.

———————— THESAURUS ————————

be in charge of, control, direct, handle, head, lead, operate 7 = **continue**, extend, go, proceed, reach, stretch ≠ **stop** 9 = **flow**, discharge, go, gush, leak, pour, spill, spout, stream 10 = **melt**, dissolve, go soft, liquefy 12 = **publish**, display, feature, print 13 = **smuggle**, bootleg, traffic in ♦ *n* 14 = **race**, dash, gallop, jog, rush, sprint, spurt 15 = **ride**, drive, excursion, jaunt, outing, spin (*inf*), trip 18 = **sequence**, course, period, season, series, spell, stretch, string 22 = **enclosure**, coop, pen

rupture *n* 1 = **break**, breach, burst, crack, fissure, rent, split, tear ♦ *v* 3 = **break**, burst, crack, separate, sever, split, tear

rural *adj* = **rustic**, agricultural, country, pastoral, sylvan ≠ **urban**

ruse *n* = **trick**, device, dodge, hoax, manoeuvre, ploy, stratagem, subterfuge

rush¹ *v* 1 = **hurry**, bolt, career, dash, fly, hasten, race, run, shoot, speed, tear ≠ **wait** 2 = **push**, hurry, hustle, press 3 = **attack**, charge, storm ♦ *n* 4 a = **hurry**,

charge, dash, haste, race, scramble, stampede, surge b = **attack**, assault, charge, onslaught ♦ *adj* 6 = **hasty**, fast, hurried, quick, rapid, swift, urgent ≠ **slow**

rust *n* 1 = **corrosion**, oxidation 2 = **mildew**, blight, mould, must, rot ♦ *v* 4 = **corrode**, oxidize

rustic *adj* 1, 2 = **rural**, country, pastoral, sylvan ≠ **urban** 3 = **uncouth**, awkward, coarse, crude, rough ♦ *n* 5 = **yokel**, boor, bumpkin, clod, clodhopper (*inf*), hick (*inf*, chiefly US & Canad*), peasant ≠ **sophisticate**

① **rustle¹** *v* = **crackle**, crinkle, whisper

② **rustle¹** *n* = **crackle**, crinkling, rustling, whisper

rut *n* 1 = **groove**, furrow, indentation, track, trough, wheel mark 2 = **habit**, dead end, pattern, routine, system

ruthless *adj* = **merciless**, brutal, callous, cruel, harsh, heartless, pitiless, relentless, remorseless

S s

Sabbath *n* day of worship and rest: Saturday for Jews, Sunday for Christians. **sabbatical** *adj, n* (denoting) leave for study.

sabotage 🛈 *n* 1 intentional damage done to machinery, systems, etc. ◆ *v* 2 damage intentionally. **saboteur** *n* person who commits sabotage.

sabre *n* curved cavalry sword.

sac *n* pouchlike structure in an animal or plant.

saccharin *n* artificial sweetener. **saccharine** *adj* excessively sweet.

sachet *n* small envelope or bag containing a single portion.

sack¹ 🛈 *n* 1 large bag made of coarse material. 2 *Informal* dismissal. 3 *Slang* bed. ◆ *v* 4 *Informal* dismiss. **sacking** *n* rough woven material used for sacks. **sackcloth** *n* coarse fabric used for sacks, formerly worn as a penance.

sack² 🛈 *n* 1 plundering of a captured town. ◆ *v* 2 plunder (a captured town).

sacrament *n* ceremony of the Christian Church, esp. Communion. **sacramental** *adj*

sacred 🛈 *adj* 1 holy. 2 connected with religion. 3 set apart, reserved.

sacrifice 🛈 *n* 1 giving something up. 2 thing given up. 3 making of an offering to a god. 4 thing offered. ◆ *v* 5 offer as a sacrifice. 6 give (something) up. **sacrificial** *adj*

sacrilege 🛈 *n* misuse or desecration of something sacred. **sacrilegious** *adj*

sacristy *n, pl* **–ties** room in a church where sacred objects are kept.

sacrosanct 🛈 *adj* regarded as sacred, inviolable.

sad 🛈 *adj* **sadder, saddest** 1 sorrowful, unhappy. 2 deplorably bad. **sadden** *v* make sad. **sadly** *adv* **sadness** *n*

THESAURUS

sabotage *n* 1 = **damage**, destruction, disruption, subversion, wrecking ◆ *v* 2 = **damage**, destroy, disable, disrupt, incapacitate, subvert, vandalize, wreck

sack¹ *n* 2 *Inf* = **dismissal**, discharge, the axe (*inf*), the boot (*sl*), the push (*sl*) ◆ *v* 4 *Inf* = **dismiss**, axe (*inf*), discharge, fire (*inf*), give (someone) the push (*inf*) kick out (*inf*), kiss off (*slang*)

sack² *n* 1 = **plundering**, looting, pillage ◆ *v* 2 = **plunder**, loot, pillage, raid, rob, ruin, strip

sacred *adj* 1 = **holy**, blessed, divine, hallowed, revered, sanctified ≠ **worldly** 2 = **religious**, ecclesiastical, holy ≠ **unconsecrated** 3 = **inviolable**, hallowed,

holy, inalienable, protected, sacrosanct

sacrifice *n* 1 = **surrender**, loss, renunciation 3, 4 = **offering**, oblation ◆ *v* 5 = **offer**, immolate, offer up 6 = **give up**, forego, forfeit, let go, lose, say goodbye to, surrender

sacrilege *n* = **desecration**, blasphemy, heresy, impiety, irreverence, profanation, violation ≠ **respect**

sacrosanct *adj* = **inviolable**, hallowed, inviolate, sacred, sanctified, set apart, untouchable

sad *adj* 1 = **unhappy**, blue, dejected, depressed, doleful, down, low, low–spirited, melancholy, mournful, woebegone ≠ **happy** 2 = **deplorable**, bad,

saddle ● *n* 1 rider's seat on a horse or bicycle. 2 joint of meat. ◆ *v* 3 put a saddle on (a horse). 4 burden (with a responsibility). **saddler** *n* maker or seller of saddles

sadism [**say**-dizz-um] *n* gaining of (sexual) pleasure from inflicting pain. **sadist** *n* **sadistic** *adj* **sadistically** *adv*

safari *n, pl* –**ris** expedition to hunt or observe wild animals, esp. in Africa. **safari park** park where lions, elephants, etc. are kept uncaged so that people can see them from cars.

safe ● *adj* 1 secure, protected. 2 uninjured, out of danger. 3 not involving risk. ◆ *n* 4 strong lockable container. **safely** *adv* **safe–conduct** *n* permit allowing travel through a dangerous area. **safekeeping** *n* protection. **safety** *n*

saffron *n* 1 orange–coloured flavouring obtained from a crocus. ◆ *adj* 2 orange.

sag ● *v* **sagging, sagged** 1 sink in the middle. 2 tire. 3 (of clothes) hang loosely. ◆ *n* 4 droop.

saga ● [**sah**–ga] *n* 1 legend of Norse heroes. 2 any long story.

sage[1] *n* 1 very wise man. ◆ *adj* 2 *Lit* wise. **sagely** *adv*

sage[2] *n* aromatic herb with grey–green leaves.

sago *n* starchy cereal from the powdered pith of the sago palm tree.

said *v* past of SAY.

sail ● *n* 1 sheet of fabric stretched to catch the wind for propelling a sailing boat. 2 arm of a windmill. ◆ *v* 4 travel by water. 5 begin a voyage. 6 move smoothly. **sailor** *n* member of a ship's crew.

saint *n* 1 *Christianity* person venerated after death as specially holy. 2 exceptionally good person. **saintly** *adj* **saintliness** *n*

sake ● *n* 1 benefit. 2 purpose. **for the sake of** 1 for the purpose of. 2 to please or benefit (someone).

salad *n* dish of raw vegetables, eaten as a meal or part of a meal.

salami *n* highly spiced sausage.

salary *n, pl* –**ries** fixed regular payment, usu. monthly, to an employee.

sale ● *n* 1 exchange of goods for money. 2 selling of goods at unusually low prices. 3 auction. **saleable** *adj* fit or likely to be sold. **salesman, saleswoman, salesperson** *n* person who sells goods. **salesmanship** *n* skill in selling.

salient ● [**say**–lee–ent] *adj* 1 prominent, noticeable. ◆ *n* 2 *Mil* projecting part of a front line.

saline [**say**–line] *adj* containing salt. **salinity** *n*

saliva *n* liquid that forms in the mouth, spittle. **salivary** *adj* **salivate** *v* produce

——————————— THESAURUS ———————————

lamentable, sorry, wretched ≠ **good**

saddle *v* 4 = **burden**, encumber, load, lumber (*Brit inf*)

safe *adj* 1 = **secure**, impregnable, in safe hands, out of danger, out of harm's way, protected, safe and sound ≠ **threatened** 2 = **unharmed**, all right, intact, O.K. *or* okay (*inf*), undamaged, unhurt, unscathed 3 = **risk–free**, certain, impregnable, secure, sound ◆ *n* 4 = **strongbox**, coffer, deposit box, repository, safe–deposit box, vault

sag *v* 1 = **sink**, bag, dip, droop, fall, give way, hang loosely, slump 2 = **tire**, droop, flag, wane, weaken, wilt

saga *n* 2 = **tale**, epic, narrative, story, yarn

sage[1] *n* 1 = **wise man**, authority, elder, expert, guru, mahatma, man of learning, master, philosopher ◆ *adj* 2 *Lit* = **wise**, judicious, sagacious, sapient, sensible

sail *v* 5 = **embark**, set sail 6 = **glide**, drift, float, fly, skim, soar, sweep, wing

sake *n* 1 = **benefit**, account, behalf, good, interest, welfare 1 = **purpose**, aim, end, motive, objective, reason

salary *n* = **pay**, earnings, income, wage, wages

sale *n* 1 = **selling**, deal, disposal, marketing, transaction

salient *adj* 1 = **prominent**, conspicuous, important, noticeable, outstanding, pronounced, striking saliva.

sallow ⊕ *adj* of an unhealthy pale or yellowish colour.

sally *n, pl* –**lies 1** witty remark. **2** sudden brief attack by troops. ◆ *v* –**lying, –lied** (foll. by *forth*) **3** rush out. **4** go out.

salmon *n* **1** large fish with orange–pink flesh valued as food. ◆ *adj* **2** orange–pink.

salmonella *n, pl* –**lae** bacterium causing food poisoning.

salon *n* **1** commercial premises of a hairdresser, beautician, etc. **2** elegant reception room for guests.

saloon *n* **1** car with a fixed roof. **2** large public room, as on a ship. **3** *US* bar serving alcoholic drinks. **saloon bar** more expensive bar in a pub.

salt ⊕ *n* **1** white crystalline substance used to season food. **2** chemical compound of acid and metal. ◆ *v* **3** season or preserve with salt. **with a pinch of salt** allowing for exaggeration. **worth one's salt** efficient. **salty** *adj* **saltcellar** *n* small container for salt at table.

salubrious ⊕ *adj* favourable to health.

salutary ⊕ *adj* producing a beneficial result.

salute ⊕ *n* **1** motion of the arm as a formal military sign of respect. **2** firing of guns as a military greeting of honour. ◆ *v* **3** greet with a salute. **4** make a salute. **5** acknowledge with praise. **salutation** *n* greeting by words or actions.

salvation ⊕ *n* fact or state of being saved from harm or the consequences of sin.

salve ⊕ *n* **1** healing or soothing ointment. ◆ *v* **2** soothe or appease.

salver *n* (silver) tray on which something is presented.

salvo *n, pl* –**vos, –voes 1** simultaneous discharge of guns etc. **2** burst of applause or questions.

same ⊕ *adj* **1** identical, not different, unchanged. **2** just mentioned. **sameness** *n*

sample ⊕ *n* **1** part taken as representative of a whole. ◆ *v* **2** take and test a sample of. **sampler** *n* piece of embroidery showing the embroiderer's skill.

sanatorium *n, pl* –**riums, –ria 1** institution for invalids or convalescents. **2** room for sick pupils at a boarding school.

sanctify ⊕ *v* –**fying, –fied** make holy.

sanctimonious ⊕ *adj* pretending to be religious and virtuous.

sanction ⊕ *n* **1** permission, authorization. **2** coercive measure or penalty. ◆ *v* **3** allow, authorize.

———— THESAURUS ————

sallow *adj* = **wan**, anaemic, pale, pallid, pasty, sickly, unhealthy, yellowish

salt *n* **1** = **seasoning**, flavour, relish, savour, taste **with a pinch of salt** = **sceptically**, cynically, disbelievingly, suspiciously, with reservations

salubrious *adj* = **health–giving**, beneficial, good for one, healthy, wholesome

salutary *adj* = **beneficial**, advantageous, good for one, profitable, useful, valuable

salute *n* **1** = **salutation** ◆ *v* **3** = **greet**, acknowledge, address, hail, welcome **5** = **honour**, acknowledge, pay tribute *or* homage to, recognize

salvation *n* = **saving**, deliverance, escape, preservation, redemption, rescue ≠ **loss**

salve *n* **1** = **ointment**, balm, cream, lotion

same *adj* **1 a** = **identical**, alike, corresponding, duplicate, equal, twin ≠ **different b** = **unchanged**, changeless, consistent, constant, invariable, unaltered, unvarying ≠ **altered 2** = **aforementioned**, aforesaid

sample *n* **1** = **specimen**, example, instance, model, pattern ◆ *v* **2** = **test**, experience, inspect, taste, try

sanctify *v* = **consecrate**, cleanse, hallow

sanctimonious *adj* = **holier–than–thou**, hypocritical, pious, self–righteous, smug

sanction *n* **1** = **permission**, approval, authority, authorization, backing (*inf*), mana (*NZ*), O.K. *or* okay, stamp *or* seal of approval ≠ **ban 2** = **ban**, boycott, coercive measures, embargo, penalty ≠ **authority** ◆ *v* **3** = **permit**, allow, approve, authorize,

sand *n* **1** substance consisting of small grains of rock, esp. on a beach or in a desert. ◆ *pl* **2** stretches of sand forming a beach or desert. ◆ *v* **3** smooth with sandpaper. **sander** *n* power tool for smoothing surfaces. **sandy** *adj* **1** covered with sand. **2** (of hair) reddish-fair. **sandbag** *n* bag filled with sand, used as protection against gunfire or flood water. **sandpaper** *n* paper coated with sand for smoothing a surface. **sandpiper** *n* shore bird with a long bill and slender legs. **sandstone** *n* rock composed of sand.

sandal *n* light shoe consisting of a sole attached by straps.

sandwich *n* **1** two slices of bread with a layer of food between. ◆ *v* **2** insert between two other things. **sandwich board** pair of boards hung over a person's shoulders to display advertisements in front and behind.

sane ❶ *adj* **1** of sound mind. **2** sensible, rational. **sanity** *n*

sang *v* past tense of SING.

sanguine ❶ *adj* cheerful, optimistic.

sanitary ❶ *adj* promoting health by getting rid of dirt and germs. **sanitation** *n* sanitary measures, esp. drainage or sewerage.

sap¹ ❶ *n* **1** moisture that circulates in plants. **2** *Informal* gullible person.

sap² ❶ *v* **sapping, sapped 1** undermine. **2** weaken. **3** **sapper** *n* soldier in an engineering unit.

sapphire *n* **1** blue precious stone. ◆ *adj* **2** deep blue.

sarcasm ❶ *n* (use of) bitter or wounding ironic language. **sarcastic** *adj* **sarcastically** *adv*

sarcophagus *n, pl* **-gi, -guses** stone coffin.

sardine *n* small fish of the herring family, usu. preserved in tightly packed tins.

sardonic ❶ *adj* mocking or scornful. **sardonically** *adv*

sargasso *n* type of floating seaweed.

sari, saree *n* long piece of cloth draped around the body and over one shoulder, worn by Hindu women.

sarmie *n S Afr slang* sandwich.

sartorial *adj* of men's clothes or tailoring.

sash *n* decorative strip of cloth worn round the waist or over one shoulder.

Satan ❶ *n* the Devil. **satanic** *adj* **1** of Satan. **2** supremely evil. **Satanism** *n* worship of Satan.

satchel *n* bag, usu. with a shoulder strap, for carrying school books.

satellite *n* **1** man-made device orbiting in space. **2** heavenly body that orbits another. **3** country that is dependent on a more powerful one. ◆ *adj* **4** of or used in the transmission of television signals from a satellite to the home.

satin *n* silky fabric with a glossy surface on one side. **satiny** *adj* of or like satin.

satire ❶ *n* **1** use of ridicule to expose vice or folly. **2** poem or other work that does this. **satirical** *adj* **satirist** *n* **satirize** *v* ridicule by means of satire.

————— THESAURUS —————

endorse ≠ **refuse**

sane *adj* **1** = **of sound mind**, all there (*inf*), *compos mentis*, in one's right mind, mentally sound ≠ **mad 2** = **sensible**, balanced, judicious, level-headed, rational, reasonable, sound ≠ **foolish**

sanguine *adj* **1** = **cheerful**, buoyant, confident, hopeful, optimistic ≠ **down**

sanitary *adj* **2** = **hygienic**, clean, germ-free, healthy, wholesome

sap¹ *n* **1** = **vital fluid**, essence, lifeblood **2** *Inf* = **fool**, idiot, jerk (*sl, chiefly US & Canad*), ninny, simpleton, twit (*inf*), wally (*sl*)

sap² *v* **1** = **undermine 2** = **weaken**, deplete, drain, exhaust

sarcasm *n* = **irony**, bitterness, cynicism, derision, mockery, satire

sardonic *adj* = **mocking**, cynical, derisive, dry, ironical, sarcastic, sneering, wry

Satan *n* = **The Devil**, Beelzebub, Lord of the Flies, Lucifer, Mephistopheles, Old Nick (*inf*), Prince of Darkness, The Evil One

satire *n* **1** = **mockery**, irony, ridicule

satisfy ⓥ *v* –**fying,** –**fied 1** please, content. **2** provide amply for (a need or desire). **3** convince, persuade. **satisfaction** *n* **satisfactory** *adj*

satsuma *n* kind of small orange.

saturate ⓥ *v* **1** soak thoroughly. **2** cause to absorb the maximum amount of something. **saturation** *n*

Saturday *n* seventh day of the week.

saturnine ⓥ *adj* gloomy in temperament or appearance.

satyr *n* **1** woodland god, part man, part goat. **2** lustful man.

sauce *n* **1** liquid added to food to enhance flavour. **2** *Informal* impudence. **saucy** *adj* **1** impudent. **2** pert, jaunty. **saucily** *adv*

saucepan *n* cooking pot with a long handle.

saucer *n* small round dish put under a cup.

sauerkraut *n* shredded cabbage fermented in brine.

sauna *n* Finnish–style steam bath.

saunter ⓥ *v* **1** walk in a leisurely manner, stroll. ◆ *n* **2** leisurely walk.

sausage *n* minced meat in an edible tube–shaped skin. **sausage roll** skinless sausage covered in pastry.

sauté [so–tay] *v* –**téing** or –**téeing,** –**téed**

fry quickly in a little fat.

savage ⓥ *adj* **1** wild, untamed. **2** cruel and violent. **3** uncivilized, primitive. ◆ *n* **4** uncivilized person. ◆ *v* **5** attack ferociously. **savagely** *adv* **savagery** *n*

save ⓥ *v* **1** rescue or preserve from harm, protect. **2** keep for the future. **3** set aside (money). **4** *Sport* prevent the scoring of (a goal). ◆ *n* **5** *Sport* act of preventing a goal. **saver** *n* **saving** *n* **1** economy. ◆ *pl* **2** money put by for future use.

saviour ⓥ *n* **1** person who rescues another. **2** (S–) Christ.

savour ⓥ *v* **1** enjoy, relish. **2** (foll. by *of*) have a flavour or suggestion of. ◆ *n* **3** characteristic taste or odour. **4** slight but distinctive quality. **savoury** *adj* **1** salty or spicy. ◆ *n, pl* –**vouries 2** savoury dish served before or after a meal.

saw¹ *n* **1** cutting tool with a toothed metal blade. ◆ *v* **sawing, sawed, sawed** or **sawn 2** cut with a saw. **3** move (something) back and forth. **sawyer** *n* person who saws timber for a living. **sawdust** *n* fine wood fragments made in sawing. **sawmill** *n* mill where timber is sawn into planks.

saw² *v* past tense of SEE¹.

──────── THESAURUS ────────

2 = parody, burlesque, caricature, lampoon

satisfy *v* **1 = content,** assuage, gratify, indulge, pacify, pander to, please, quench, sate, slake ≠ **frustrate 2 = be sufficient,** answer, be enough, do, fulfil, meet, serve, suffice **3 = convince,** assure, persuade, reassure ≠ **dissuade**

saturate *v* **= soak,** drench, imbue, souse, steep, suffuse, waterlog, wet through

saturnine *adj* **= gloomy,** dour, glum, grave, morose, sombre

saunter *v* **1 = stroll,** amble, meander, mosey (*inf*), ramble, roam, wander ◆ *n* **2 = stroll,** airing, amble, ramble, turn, walk

savage *adj* **1 = wild,** feral, rough, rugged, uncultivated, undomesticated, untamed ≠ **tame 2 = cruel,** barbarous, bestial,

bloodthirsty, brutal, ferocious, fierce, harsh, ruthless, sadistic, vicious ≠ **kind 3 = primitive,** rude, uncivilized, unspoilt ≠ **civilized** ◆ *n* **4 = lout,** boor, yahoo, yob (*Brit sl*) ◆ *v* **5 = attack,** lacerate, mangle, maul

save *v* **1 a = rescue,** deliver, free, liberate, recover, redeem, salvage ≠ **risk b = protect,** conserve, guard, keep safe, look after, preserve, safeguard **2, 3 = keep,** collect, gather, hoard, hold, husband, lay by, put by, reserve, set aside, store

saviour *n* **1 = rescuer,** defender, deliverer, liberator, preserver, protector, redeemer

savour *v* **1 = enjoy,** appreciate, delight in, luxuriate in, relish, revel in **2** (foll. by *of*) **= suggest,** be suggestive of, show signs of, smack of ◆ *n* **3 = flavour,** piquancy, relish, smack, smell, tang, taste **4 = trace,**

saxophone *n* brass wind instrument with keys and a curved body. **saxophonist** *n*

say ⊕ *v* **saying, said 1** speak or utter. **2** express (an idea) in words. **3** give as one's opinion. **4** suppose as an example or possibility. ◆ *n* **5** right or chance to speak. **6** share in a decision. **saying** *n* maxim, proverb.

scab *n* **1** crust formed over a wound. **2** *Offens* blackleg. **scabby** *adj* **1** covered with scabs. **2** *Informal* despicable.

scabbard *n* sheath for a sword or dagger.

scaffold *n* **1** temporary platform for workmen. **2** gallows. **scaffolding** *n* (materials for building) scaffolds.

scald *v* **1** burn with hot liquid or steam. **2** sterilize with boiling water. **3** heat (liquid) almost to boiling point. ◆ *n* **4** injury by scalding.

scale¹ ⊕ *n* **1** one of the thin overlapping plates covering fishes and reptiles. **2** thin flake. **3** coating which forms in kettles etc. due to hard water. **4** tartar formed on the teeth. ◆ *v* **5** remove scales from. **6** come off in scales. **scaly** *adj*

scale² *n* (often *pl*) weighing instrument.

scale³ ⊕ *n* **1** graduated table or sequence of marks at regular intervals, used as a reference in making measurements. **2** ratio of size between a thing and a representation of it. **3** relative degree or extent. **4** fixed series of notes in music. ◆ *v* **5** climb. **scale up, down** *v* increase or decrease proportionately in size.

scallop *n* **1** edible shellfish with two fan shaped shells. **2** one of a series of small curves along an edge.

scalp *n* **1** skin and hair on top of the head. ◆ *v* **2** cut off the scalp of.

scalpel *n* small surgical knife.

scamp ⊕ *n* mischievous child.

scamper ⊕ *v* **1** run about hurriedly or in play. ◆ *n* **2** scampering.

scampi *pl n* large prawns.

scan ⊕ *v* **scanning, scanned 1** scrutinize carefully. **2** glance over quickly. **3** examine or search (an area) by passing a radar or sonar beam over it. **4** (of verse) conform to metrical rules. ◆ *n* **5** scanning. **scanner** *n* electronic device used for scanning. **scansion** *n* metrical scanning of verse.

scandal ⊕ *n* **1** disgraceful action or event. **2** malicious gossip. **scandalize** *v* shock by scandal. **scandalous** *adj*

scant ⊕ *adj* barely sufficient, meagre.

scapegoat ⊕ *n* person made to bear the blame for others.

scar ⊕ *n* **1** mark left by a healed wound. **2**

distinctive quality

say *v* **1** = **speak**, announce, express, mention, pronounce, remark, state, utter, voice **2** = **express**, communicate, convey, imply **3** = **declare**, affirm, assert, maintain **4** = **suppose**, assume, conjecture, estimate, guess, imagine, presume, surmise ◆ *n* **5** = **chance to speak**, voice, vote **6** = **influence**, authority, clout (*inf*), mana (*NZ*), power, weight

scale¹ *n* = **flake**, lamina, layer, plate

scale³ *n* **1** = **graduation**, gradation, hierarchy, ladder, progression, ranking, sequence, series, steps **2** = **ratio**, proportion **3** = **degree**, extent, range, reach, scope ◆ *v* **5** = **climb**, ascend, clamber, escalade, mount, surmount **scale up, down** = **adjust**, proportion, regulate

scamp *n* = **rascal**, devil, imp, monkey, rogue, scallywag (*inf*)

scamper *v* **1** = **run**, dart, dash, hasten, hurry, romp, scoot, scurry, scuttle

scan *v* **1** = **scrutinize**, check, check out (*inf*), examine, eye, eyeball (*sl*), investigate **2** = **glance over**, look through, run one's eye over, run over, skim **3** = **survey**, scour, search, sweep

scandal *n* **1** = **crime**, disgrace, discreditable behaviour, dishonourable behaviour, embarrassment, misconduct, offence, sin, skeleton in the cupboard, wrongdoing **2** = **gossip**, aspersion, dirt, rumours, slander, talk, tattle

scant *adj* = **meagre**, barely sufficient, little, minimal, sparse ≠ **full**

scapegoat *n* = **whipping boy**, fall guy (*inf*)

permanent emotional damage left by an
unpleasant experience. ♦ v **scarring,
scarred** 3 mark or become marked with a
scar.

scarce ❶ adj 1 insufficient to meet
demand. 2 not common, rarely found.
make oneself scarce Informal go away.
scarcely adv 1 hardly at all. 2 definitely or
probably not. **scarcity** n

✓ WORD TIP

As *scarcely* has a negative sense it is
followed by *ever* or *any* (not *never* or
no).

---

scare ❶ v 1 frighten or be frightened. ♦ n
2 fright, sudden panic. **scary** adj Informal
frightening. **scarecrow** n 1 figure dressed
in old clothes, set up to scare birds away
from crops. 2 raggedly dressed person.
scaremonger n person who spreads
alarming rumours.

scarf n, pl **scarves, scarfs** piece of material
worn round the neck, head, or shoulders.

scarlet adj, n brilliant red. **scarlet fever**
infectious fever with a scarlet rash.

scathing ❶ adj harshly critical.

scatter ❶ v 1 throw about in various
directions. 2 disperse. **scatterbrain** n
empty–headed person.

scavenge v search for (anything usable)

among discarded material. **scavenger** n 1
person who scavenges. 2 animal that feeds
on decaying matter.

scenario ❶ n, pl –rios 1 summary of the
plot of a play or film. 2 imagined
sequence of future events.

scene ❶ n 1 place of action of a real or
imaginary event. 2 subdivision of a play or
film in which the action is continuous. 3
view of a place. 4 display of emotion. 5
Informal specific activity or interest, e.g. the
fashion scene. **behind the scenes** 1
backstage. 2 in secret. **scenery** n 1 natural
features of a landscape. 2 painted
backcloths or screens used on stage to
represent the scene of action. **scenic** adj
picturesque.

scent ❶ n 1 pleasant smell. 2 smell left in
passing, by which an animal can be
traced. 3 series of clues. 4 perfume. ♦ v 5
detect by smell. 6 suspect. 7 fill with
fragrance.

sceptic ❶ [**skep**–tik] n person who
habitually doubts generally accepted
beliefs. **sceptical** adj **sceptically** adv
scepticism n

sceptre n ornamental rod symbolizing
royal power.

schedule ❶ n 1 plan of procedure for a
project. 2 list. 3 timetable. ♦ v 4 plan to
occur at a certain time.

THESAURUS

scar n 1 = **mark**, blemish, injury, wound ♦
v 3 = **mark**, damage, disfigure
scarce adj 1 = **in short supply**, few, few
and far between, infrequent, insufficient
≠ **sufficient** 2 = **rare**, uncommon
≠ **common**
scare v 1 = **frighten**, alarm, dismay,
intimidate, panic, shock, startle, terrify ♦ n
2 = **fright**, panic, shock, start, terror
scathing adj = **critical**, biting, caustic,
cutting, harsh, sarcastic, scornful,
trenchant, withering
scatter v 1 = **throw about**, diffuse,
disseminate, fling, shower, spread,
sprinkle, strew ≠ **collect** 2 = **disperse**,
disband, dispel, dissipate ≠ **assemble**

scenario n 1 = **story line**, outline, résumé,
summary, synopsis
scene n 1 = **site**, area, locality, location,
place, position, setting, spot 2 = **act**,
division, episode, part 3 = **view**,
landscape, panorama, prospect, vista
4 = **fuss**, carry-on (inf, chiefly Brit),
commotion, exhibition, performance,
row, tantrum, to–do 5 Inf = **world**,
arena, business, environment, preserve,
realm
scent n 1 = **aroma**, bouquet, odour, smell
2 = **trail**, spoor, track 4 = **fragrance**,
perfume ♦ v 5 = **detect**, discern, nose out,
sense, smell, sniff
sceptic n = **doubter**, cynic, disbeliever,

schematic *adj* presented as a plan or diagram.

scheme **❶** *n* 1 systematic plan. 2 secret plot. ◆ *v* 3 plan in an underhand manner. **scheming** *adj, n*

schism **❶** [**skizz**–um] *n* (group resulting from) division in an organization. **schismatic** *adj, n*

schizophrenia *n* 1 mental disorder involving deterioration of or confusion about the personality. 2 *Informal* contradictory behaviour or attitudes. **schizophrenic** *adj, n*

school¹ **❶** *n* 1 place where children are taught or instruction is given in a subject. 2 group of artists, thinkers, etc. with shared principles or methods. ◆ *v* 3 educate or train. **scholar** *n* 1 learned person. 2 student receiving a scholarship. 3 pupil.

school² *n* shoal of fish, whales, etc.

schooner *n* 1 sailing ship rigged fore–and–aft. 2 large glass.

science **❶** *n* systematic study and knowledge of natural or physical

phenomena. **scientific** *adj* 1 of science. 2 systematic. **scientifically** *adv* **scientist** *n* person who studies or practises a science. **science fiction** stories making imaginative use of scientific knowledge.

scimitar *n* curved oriental sword.

scintillating **❶** *adj* very lively and amusing.

scissors *pl n* cutting instrument with two crossed pivoted blades.

scoff¹ **❶** *v* express derision.

scoff² **❶** *v Informal* eat rapidly.

scold **❶** *v* 1 find fault with, reprimand. ◆ *n* 2 person who scolds.

scone *n* small plain cake baked in an oven or on a griddle.

scope **❶** *n* 1 opportunity for using abilities. 2 range of activity.

scorch **❶** *v* 1 burn on the surface. 2 parch or shrivel from heat. ◆ *n* 3 slight burn. **scorcher** *n Informal* very hot day.

score **❶** *n* 1 points gained in a game or competition. 2 twenty. 3 written version of a piece of music showing parts for each musician. 4 mark or cut. 5 grievance, e.g.

———————— THESAURUS ————————

doubting Thomas

schedule *n* 1 = **plan**, agenda 2 = **list**, calendar, catalogue, inventory 3 = **timetable**, programme ◆ *v* 4 = **plan**, appoint, arrange, book, organize, programme

scheme *n* 1 = **plan**, contrivance, design, device, idea, programme, project, proposal, scenario, strategy, system, tactics 2 = **plot**, conspiracy, intrigue, manoeuvre, ploy, ruse, stratagem, subterfuge ◆ *v* 3 = **plot**, collude, conspire, intrigue, machinate, manoeuvre

schism *n* = **division**, breach, break, rift, rupture, separation, split

school¹ *n* 1 = **academy**, college, faculty, institute, institution, seminary 2 = **group**, adherents, circle, denomination, devotees, disciples, faction, followers, set ◆ *v* 3 = **train**, coach, discipline, drill, educate, instruct, tutor

science *n* 2 = **discipline**, body of

knowledge, branch of knowledge 3 = **skill**, art, technique

scintillating *adj* = **brilliant**, animated, bright, dazzling, exciting, glittering, lively, sparkling, stimulating

scoff¹ *v* 1 = **scorn**, belittle, deride, despise, jeer, knock (*inf*), laugh at, mock, pooh–pooh, ridicule, sneer

scoff² *v Inf* = **gobble (up)**, bolt, devour, gorge oneself on, gulp down, guzzle, wolf

scold *v* 1 = **reprimand**, berate, castigate, censure, find fault with, give (someone) a dressing–down, lecture, rebuke, reproach, reprove, rouse on (*Aust*), tell off (*inf*), tick off (*inf*), upbraid ≠ **praise** ◆ *n* 2 = **nag**, shrew, termagant (*rare*)

scope *n* 1 = **opportunity**, freedom, latitude, liberty, room, space 2 = **range**, area, capacity, orbit, outlook, reach, span, sphere

scorch *v* 1 = **burn**, roast, sear, singe

settle old scores. ◆ *pl* 6 lots. ◆ *v* 7 gain (points) in a game. 8 keep a record of points. 9 mark or cut. 10 (foll. by *out*) cross out. 11 arrange music (for). 12 achieve a success.

scorn ⊕ *n* 1 open contempt. ◆ *v* 2 despise. 3 reject with contempt. **scornful** *adj*

scorpion *n* small lobster–shaped animal with a sting at the end of a jointed tail.

Scotch *n* whisky distilled in Scotland.

scotch *v* put an end to.

scot–free *adj* without harm or punishment.

scoundrel ⊕ *n Old–fashioned* cheat or deceiver.

scour¹ ⊕ *v* 1 clean or polish by rubbing with something rough. 2 clear or flush out. **scourer** *n* small rough nylon pad used for cleaning pots and pans.

scour² ⊕ *v* search thoroughly and energetically.

scourge ⊕ *n* 1 person or thing causing severe suffering. 2 whip. ◆ *v* 3 cause

severe suffering to. 4 whip.

scout ⊕ *n* 1 person sent out to reconnoitre. 2 (S–) member of the Scout Association, an organization for boys which aims to develop character and promotes outdoor activities. ◆ *v* 3 act as a scout. 4 reconnoitre.

scowl ⊕ *v, n* (have) an angry or sullen expression.

scrabble ⊕ *v* scrape at with the hands, feet, or claws.

scrag *n* thin end of a neck of mutton. **scraggy** *adj* thin, bony.

scram ⊕ *v* **scramming, scrammed** *Informal* go away quickly.

scramble ⊕ *v* 1 climb or crawl hastily or awkwardly. 2 struggle with others (for). 3 mix up. 4 cook (eggs beaten up with milk). 5 (of an aircraft or aircrew) take off hurriedly in an emergency. 6 make (transmitted speech) unintelligible by the use of an electronic device. ◆ *n* 7 scrambling. 8 rough climb. 9 disorderly

2 = **shrivel**, parch, wither

score *n* 1 = **points**, grade, mark, outcome, record, result, total 5 = **grievance**, axe to grind, bone of contention, dispute, grudge, injury, injustice, wrong ◆ *pl* 6 = **lots**, hundreds, masses, millions, multitudes, myriads, swarms ◆ *v* 7 = **gain**, achieve, chalk up (*inf*), make, notch up (*inf*), win 8 = **keep count**, count, record, register, tally 9 = **cut**, deface, gouge, graze, mark, scrape, scratch, slash 10 (foll. by *out*) = **cross out**, cancel out, delete, obliterate, strike out 11 = **arrange**, adapt, orchestrate, set

scorn *n* 1 = **contempt**, derision, disdain, disparagement, mockery, sarcasm ≠ **respect** ◆ *v* 2 = **despise**, be above, deride, disdain, scoff at 3 = **reject**, flout, slight, spurn ≠ **esteem**

scoundrel *n Old–fashioned* = **rogue**, bastard (*offens*), blackguard, good–for–nothing, heel (*sl*), miscreant, ne'er–do–well, rascal, reprobate, rotter (*sl, chiefly Brit*), scally (*NW Eng dial*), scamp, swine,

villain

scour¹ *v* 1 = **rub**, abrade, buff, clean, polish, scrub 2 = **wash**, cleanse

scour² *v* 1 = **search**, beat, comb, hunt, ransack

scourge *n* 1 = **affliction**, bane, curse, infliction, misfortune, pest, plague, terror, torment ≠ **benefit** 2 = **whip**, cat, lash, strap, switch, thong ◆ *v* 3 = **afflict**, curse, plague, terrorize, torment 4 = **whip**, beat, cane, flog, horsewhip, lash, thrash

scout *n* 1 = **vanguard**, advance guard, lookout, outrider, precursor, reconnoitrer ◆ *v* 3, 4 = **reconnoitre**, investigate, observe, probe, recce (*sl*), spy, survey, watch

① **scowl** *v* = **glower**, frown, lour *or* lower
② **scowl** *n* = **glower**, black look, dirty look, frown

scrabble *v* 1 = **scrape**, claw, scramble, scratch

scram *v Inf* = **go away**, abscond, beat it (*sl*), clear off (*inf*), get lost (*inf*), leave, make oneself scarce (*inf*), make tracks, struggle. **10** motorcycle race over rough ground.

scrap¹ ① ** n **1 small piece. **2** waste metal collected for reprocessing. ◆ pl **3** leftover food. ◆ v **scrapping, scrapped 4** discard as useless. **scrappy** adj fragmentary, disjointed. **scrapbook** n book with blank pages in which newspaper cuttings or pictures are stuck.

scrap² ① ** n, v **scrapping, scrapped Informal fight or quarrel.

scrape ① ** v **1 rub with something rough or sharp. **2** clean or smooth thus. **3** rub with a harsh noise. **4** economize. ◆ n **5** act or sound of scraping. **6** mark or wound caused by scraping. **7** Informal awkward situation. **scraper** n **scrape through** v succeed in or obtain with difficulty.

scratch ① ** v **1 mark or cut with claws, nails, or anything rough or sharp. **2** scrape (skin) with nails or claws to relieve itching. **3** withdraw from a race or competition. ◆ n **4** wound, mark, or sound made by scratching. ◆ adj **5** put together at short notice. **from scratch** from the very beginning. **up to scratch** up to standard. **scratchy** adj

scrawl ① ** v **1 write carelessly or hastily. ◆ n **2** scribbled writing.

scrawny ① ** adj **scrawnier, scrawniest thin and bony.

scream ① ** v **1 utter a piercing cry, esp. of fear or pain. **2** utter with a scream. ◆ n **3** shrill piercing cry. **4** Informal very funny person or thing.

**screech ① ** v, n (utter) a shrill cry.

screed n long tedious piece of writing.

screen ① ** n **1 surface of a television set, VDU, etc., on which an image is formed. **2** white surface on which films or slides are projected. **3** movable structure used to shelter, divide, or conceal something. ◆ v **4** shelter or conceal with or as if with a screen. **5** examine (a person or group) to determine suitability for a task or to detect the presence of disease or weapons. **6** show (a film). **the screen** cinema generally.

━━━━━ THESAURUS ━━━━━

scarper (Brit sl), vamoose (sl, chiefly US)

scramble v **1** = **struggle**, climb, crawl, scrabble, swarm **2** = **strive**, contend, jostle, push, run, rush, vie ◆ n **8** = **climb**, trek **9** = **struggle**, commotion, competition, confusion, mêlée, race, rush, tussle

scrap¹ n **1** = **piece**, bit, crumb, fragment, grain, morsel, part, particle, portion, sliver, snippet **2** = **waste**, junk, offcuts ◆ pl **3** = **leftovers**, bits, leavings, remains ◆ v **4** = **get rid of**, abandon, discard, ditch (sl), drop, jettison, throw away or out, write off ≠ **bring back**

① **scrap²** n Inf = **fight**, argument, battle, disagreement, dispute, quarrel, row, squabble, wrangle

② **scrap²** v Inf = **fight**, argue, row, squabble, wrangle

scrape v **1** = **rub**, bark, graze, scratch, scuff **2** = **scour**, clean, erase, remove, rub, skin **3** = **grate**, grind, rasp, scratch, squeak **4** = **scrimp**, pinch, save, skimp, stint

◆ n **7** Inf = **predicament**, awkward situation, difficulty, dilemma, fix (inf), mess, plight, tight spot **scrape through** ◆ v = **get by** (inf), have a close shave, just make it, just pass, struggle

scratch v **1** = **mark**, claw, cut, damage, etch, grate, graze, lacerate, score, scrape **3** = **withdraw**, pull out ◆ n **4** = **mark**, blemish, claw mark, gash, graze, laceration, scrape ◆ adj **5** = **improvised**, impromptu, rough-and-ready

up to scratch = **adequate**, acceptable, average, satisfactory, sufficient, up to standard

scrawl v, n **1** = **scribble**, doodle, squiggle

scrawny adj = **thin**, bony, gaunt, lean, scraggy, skin-and-bones (inf), skinny, undernourished

scream v **1, 2** = **cry**, bawl, screech, shriek, yell ◆ n **3** = **cry**, howl, screech, shriek, yell, yelp

screech v, n = **cry**, scream, shriek

screen n **3 a** = **cover**, awning, canopy,

screw 🔊 *n* 1 metal pin with a spiral ridge along its length, twisted into materials to fasten them together. 2 *Slang* prison guard. ♦ *v* 3 turn (a screw). 4 twist. 5 fasten with screw(s). 6 *Informal* extort. **screwdriver** *n* tool for turning screws. **screw up** *v* 1 *Informal* bungle. 2 distort.

scribble 🔊 *v* 1 write hastily or illegibly. 2 make meaningless or illegible marks. ♦ *n* 3 something scribbled.

scribe 🔊 *n* 1 person who copied manuscripts before the invention of printing. 2 *Bible* scholar of the Jewish Law.

scrimp 🔊 *v* be very economical.

script 🔊 *n* 1 text of a film, play, or TV programme. 2 particular system of writing, e.g. *Arabic script*. 3 handwriting.

scripture *n* sacred writings of a religion. **scriptural** *adj*

scroll *n* 1 roll of parchment or paper. 2 ornamental carving shaped like a scroll. ♦ *v* 3 move (text) up or down on a VDU screen.

scrotum *n, pl* –ta, –tums pouch of skin containing the testicles.

scrounge 🔊 *v Informal* get by cadging or begging. **scrounger** *n*

scrub¹ 🔊 *v* scrubbing, scrubbed 1 clean by rubbing, often with a hard brush and water. 2 *Informal* delete or cancel. ♦ *n* 3 scrubbing.

scrub² *n* 1 stunted trees. 2 area of land covered with scrub. **scrubby** *adj* 1 covered with scrub. 2 stunted. 3 *Informal* shabby.

scruff¹ *n* nape (of the neck).

scruff² *n Informal* untidy person. **scruffy** *adj* unkempt or shabby.

scrum, scrummage *n* 1 *Rugby* restarting of play in which opposing packs of forwards push against each other to gain possession of the ball. 2 disorderly struggle.

scruple 🔊 *n* 1 doubt produced by one's conscience or morals. ♦ *v* 2 have doubts on moral grounds. **scrupulous** *adj* 1 very conscientious. 2 very careful or precise.

scrutiny 🔊 *n, pl* –nies close examination. **scrutinize** *v* examine closely.

scuba diving *n* sport of swimming under water using cylinders containing compressed air attached to breathing apparatus.

scud *v* scudding, scudded move along swiftly.

scuff *v* 1 drag (the feet) while walking. 2 scrape (one's shoes) by doing so. ♦ *n* 3 mark caused by scuffing.

scuffle 🔊 *v* 1 fight in a disorderly manner. ♦ *n* 2 disorderly struggle. 3 scuffling sound.

—————— THESAURUS ——————

guard, mesh, net, shade, shelter, shield b = **partition**, room divider c = **cloak** ♦ *v* 4 a = **protect**, defend, guard, shelter, shield b = **cover**, cloak, conceal, hide, mask, shade, veil 5 = **vet**, evaluate, examine, filter, gauge, scan, sift, sort 6 = **broadcast**, present, put on, show

screw *v* 3 = **turn**, tighten 4 = **twist** 6 *Inf* = **extort**, extract, wrest, wring

scribble *v* 1 = **scrawl**, dash off, jot, write

scribe *n* 1 = **copyist**, amanuensis, writer

scrimp *v* = **economize**, be frugal, save, scrape, skimp, stint, tighten one's belt

script *n* 1 = **text**, book, copy, dialogue, libretto, lines, words 4 = **handwriting**, calligraphy, penmanship, writing

scrounge *v Inf* = **cadge**, beg, blag (*sl*),

bludge (*Aust & NZ*), bum (*inf*), freeload (*sl*), sponge (*inf*)

scrub¹ *v* 1 = **scour**, clean, cleanse, rub 2 *Inf* = **cancel**, abolish, call off, delete, drop, forget about, give up

scruple *n* 1 = **misgiving**, compunction, doubt, hesitation, qualm, reluctance, second thoughts, uneasiness ♦ *v* 2 = **have misgivings about**, demur, doubt, have qualms about, hesitate, think twice about

scrutiny *n* 1 = **examination**, analysis, exploration, inspection, investigation, perusal, search, study

scuffle *v* 1 = **fight**, clash, grapple, jostle, struggle, tussle ♦ *n* 2 = **fight**, brawl, commotion, disturbance, fray, scrimmage, skirmish, tussle

DICTIONARY

scull *n* **1** small oar. ◆ *v* **2** row (a boat) using sculls.

scullery *n, pl* **–leries** small room where washing–up and other kitchen work is done.

sculpture ❶ *n* **1** art of making figures or designs in wood, stone, etc. **2** product of this art. ◆ *v* **3** (also **sculpt**) represent in sculpture. **sculptor, sculptress** *n* **sculptural** *adj*

scum ❶ *n* **1** impure or waste matter on the surface of a liquid. **2** worthless people. **scummy** *adj*

scungy *adj* **–ier, –iest** *Aust & NZ informal* sordid or dirty.

scurrilous ❶ *adj* untrue and defamatory.

scurry ❶ *v* **–rying, –ried 1** move hastily. ◆ *n* **2** act or sound of scurrying.

scurvy *n* disease caused by lack of vitamin C.

scuttle¹ *n* fireside container for coal.

scuttle² ❶ *v* **1** run with short quick steps. ◆ *n* **2** hurried run.

scuttle³ *v* make a hole in (a ship) to sink it.

scythe *n* **1** long–handled tool with a curved blade for cutting grass. ◆ *v* **2** cut with a scythe.

SD South Dakota.

sea ❶ *n* **1** mass of salt water covering three quarters of the earth's surface. **2** particular area of this. **3** vast expanse. **at sea 1** in a ship on the ocean. **2** confused or bewildered. **sea anemone** sea animal with

suckers like petals. **seaboard** *n* coast.

seafaring *adj* working or travelling by sea.

seafood *n* edible saltwater fish or shellfish.

seagull *n* gull. **sea horse** small sea fish with a plated body and horselike head.

sea lion kind of large seal. **seaman** *n* sailor. **seasick** *adj* suffering from nausea caused by the motion of a ship.

seasickness *n* **sea urchin** sea animal with a round spiky shell. **seaweed** *n* plant growing in the sea. **seaworthy** *adj* (of a ship) in fit condition for a sea voyage.

seal¹ ❶ *n* **1** piece of wax, lead, etc. with a special design impressed upon it, attached to a letter or document as a mark of authentication. **2** device or material used to close an opening tightly. ◆ *v* **3** close with or as if with a seal. **4** make airtight or watertight. **5** affix a seal to or stamp with a seal. **6** decide (one's fate) irrevocably. **sealant** *n* any substance used for sealing. **seal off** *v* enclose or isolate (a place) completely.

seal² *n* amphibious mammal with flippers as limbs.

seam ❶ *n* **1** line where two edges are joined, as by stitching. **2** thin layer of coal or ore. ◆ *v* **3** mark with furrows or wrinkles. **seamless** *adj* **seamy** *adj* sordid.

seance [**say**–anss] *n* meeting at which spiritualists attempt to communicate with the dead.

sear ❶ *v* scorch, burn the surface of

THESAURUS

sculpture *v* **3** (also **sculpt**) = **sculpt**, carve, chisel, fashion, form, hew, model, mould, shape

scum *n* **1** = **impurities**, dross, film, froth **2** = **rabble**, dregs of society, riffraff, trash (*chiefly US & Canad*)

scurrilous *adj* = **slanderous**, abusive, defamatory, insulting, scandalous, vituperative

scurry *v* **1** = **hurry**, dart, dash, race, scamper, scoot, scuttle, sprint ≠ **wander** ◆ *n* **2** = **flurry**, scampering, whirl

scuttle² *v* **1** = **run**, bustle, hasten, hurry, rush, scamper, scoot, scurry

sea *n* **1** = **ocean**, main, the deep, the waves **3** = **expanse**, abundance, mass, multitude, plethora, profusion **at sea 2** = **bewildered**, baffled, confused, lost, mystified, puzzled

seal¹ *n* **1** = **authentication**, confirmation, imprimatur, insignia, ratification, stamp ◆ *v* **4** = **close**, bung, enclose, fasten, plug, shut, stop, stopper, stop up **5** = **authenticate**, confirm, ratify, stamp, validate **6** = **settle**, clinch, conclude, consummate, finalize **seal off** = **isolate**, put out of bounds, quarantine, segregate

seam *n* **1** = **joint**, closure **2** = **layer**, lode, stratum, vein

searing adj 1 (of pain) very sharp. 2 highly critical.

search ❶ v 1 examine closely in order to find something. ◆ n 2 searching.

searching adj keen or thorough.

searchlight n powerful light with a beam that can be shone in any direction.

season ❶ n 1 one of four divisions of the year, each of which has characteristic weather conditions. 2 period during which a thing happens or is plentiful. 3 fitting or proper time. ◆ v 4 flavour with salt, herbs, etc. 5 dry (timber) till ready for use.

seasonable adj 1 appropriate for the season. 2 timely or opportune. **seasonal** adj depending on or varying with the seasons. **seasoned** adj experienced. **seasoning** n salt, herbs, etc. added to food to enhance flavour. **season ticket** ticket for a series of journeys or events within a specified period.

seat ❶ n 1 thing designed or used for sitting on. 2 place to sit in a theatre, esp. one that requires a ticket. 3 buttocks. 4 country house. 5 membership of a legislative or administrative body. ◆ v 6 cause to sit. 7 provide seating for. **seat belt** belt worn in a car or aircraft to prevent a person being thrown forward in a crash.

secateurs pl n small pruning shears.

secede ❶ v withdraw formally from a

political alliance or federation. **secession** n

seclude v keep (a person) from contact with others. **secluded** adj private, sheltered. **seclusion** n

second¹ ❶ adj 1 coming directly after the first. 2 alternate, additional. 3 inferior. ◆ n 4 person or thing coming second. 5 attendant in a duel or boxing match. ◆ pl 6 inferior goods. ◆ v 7 express formal support for (a motion proposed in a meeting). **secondly** adv **second–best** adj next to the best. **second–class** adj 1 inferior. 2 cheaper, slower, or less comfortable than first–class. **second–hand** adj 1 bought after use by another. 2 not from an original source. **second nature** something so habitual that it seems part of one's character. **second–rate** adj not of the highest quality. **second sight** supposed ability to predict events. **second thoughts** revised opinion on a matter already considered. **second wind** renewed ability to continue effort.

second² ❶ n 1 sixtieth part of a minute of an angle or time. 2 moment.

second³ [si–kawnd] v transfer (a person) temporarily to another job. **secondment** n

secondary ❶ adj 1 of less importance. 2 coming after or derived from what is primary or first. 3 relating to the education of people between the ages of 11 and 18.

secret ❶ adj 1 kept from the knowledge of

sear v = **scorch**, burn, sizzle

search v 1, 2 = **look**, comb, examine, explore, fossick (Aust & NZ), hunt, inspect, investigate, ransack, scour, scrutinize ◆ n 3 = **look**, examination, exploration, hunt, inspection, investigation, pursuit, quest

season v 4 = **flavour**, enliven, enrich, infuse, imbue, lace, pep up, salt, spice

seat n 1 = **chair**, armchair, banquette, bench, easy chair, folding chair, high chair, pew, recliner, rocker, rocking chair, settle, stall, stool 5 = **membership**, chair, constituency, incumbency, place ◆ v 6 = **sit**, fix, install, locate, place, set, settle 7 = **hold**, accommodate, cater for,

contain, sit, take

secede v = **withdraw**, break with, leave, pull out, quit, resign, split from

second¹ adj 1 = **next**, following, subsequent, succeeding 2 = **additional**, alternative, extra, further, other 3 = **inferior**, lesser, lower, secondary, subordinate ◆ n 5 = **supporter**, assistant, backer, helper ◆ v 7 = **support**, approve, assist, back, endorse, go along with

second² n 2 = **moment**, flash, instant, jiffy (inf), minute, sec (inf), trice

secondary adj 1 = **subordinate**, inferior, lesser, lower, minor, unimportant ≠ **main** 2 = **resultant**, contingent, derived, indirect others. ◆ *n* 2 something kept secret. 3 mystery. 4 underlying explanation, e.g. *the secret of my success.* **in secret** without other people knowing. **secretly** *adv* **secrecy** *n* **secretive** *adj* Inclined to keep things secret. **secretiveness** *n*

secretary *n, pl* –**ries** 1 person who deals with correspondence and general clerical work. 2 (**S–**) head of a state department, e.g. *Home Secretary.* **secretarial** *adj*

secrete¹ ❶ *v* (of an organ, gland, etc.) produce and release (a substance). **secretion** *n* **secretory** [sek-**reet**-or-ee] *adj*

secrete² ❶ *v* hide or conceal.

sect ❶ *n* subdivision of a religious or political group, esp. one with extreme beliefs. **sectarian** *adj* 1 of a sect. 2 narrow-minded.

section ❶ *n* 1 part cut off. 2 part or subdivision of something. 3 distinct part of a country or community. 4 cutting. 5 drawing of something as if cut through. ◆ *v* 6 cut or divide into sections. **sectional** *adj*

sector ❶ *n* 1 part or subdivision. 2 part of a circle enclosed by two radii and the arc which they cut off.

secular ❶ *adj* 1 worldly, as opposed to sacred. 2 not connected with religion or the church.

secure ❶ *adj* 1 free from danger. 2 free from anxiety. 3 firmly fixed. 4 reliable. ◆ *v* 5 obtain. 6 make safe. 7 make firm. 8 guarantee payment of (a loan) by giving something as security. **securely** *adv* **security** *n, pl* –**ties** 1 precautions against theft, espionage, or other danger. 2 state of being secure. 3 certificate of ownership of a share, stock, or bond. 4 something given or pledged to guarantee payment of a loan.

sedate¹ ❶ *adj* 1 calm and dignified. 2 slow or unhurried. **sedately** *adv*

sedate² *v* give a sedative drug to. **sedation** *n* **sedative** *adj* having a soothing or calming effect. ◆ *n* 2 sedative drug.

sediment ❶ *n* 1 matter which settles to the bottom of a liquid. 2 material deposited by water, ice, or wind. **sedimentary** *adj*

sedition ❶ *n* speech or action encouraging rebellion against the government. **seditious** *adj*

seduce ❶ *v* 1 persuade into sexual intercourse. 2 tempt into wrongdoing. **seducer, seductress** *n* **seduction** *n* **seductive** *adj*

see¹ ❶ *v* **seeing, saw, seen** 1 perceive with

───── | THESAURUS | ─────

≠ **original**
secret *adj* 1 = **concealed**, close, confidential, disguised, furtive, hidden, undercover, underground, undisclosed, unknown, unrevealed ◆ *n* 2 = **enigma**, answer, code, formula, key 3 = **mystery**, paradox, problem, puzzle **in secret** = **secretly**, slyly, surreptitiously

secrete¹ *v* = **give off**, emanate, emit, exude

secrete² *v* = **hide**, cache, conceal, harbour, stash (*inf*), stow

sect *n* = **group**, camp, denomination, division, faction, party, schism

section *n* 1 = **slice** 2 = **part**, division, fraction, instalment, passage, piece, portion, segment 3 = **district**, area, region, sector, zone

sector *n* 1 = **part**, division

secular *adj* 1 = **worldly**, earthly, nonspiritual, temporal 2 = **lay**, civil

secure *adj* 1 = **safe**, immune, protected, unassailable ≠ **endangered** 2 = **sure**, assured, certain, confident, easy, reassured ≠ **uncertain** 3 = **fixed**, fast, fastened, firm, immovable, stable, steady ≠ **loose** ◆ *v* 5 = **obtain**, acquire, gain, get, procure, score (*sl*) ≠ **lose** 7 = **fasten**, attach, bolt, chain, fix, lock, make fast, tie up ≠ **loose**

sedate¹ *adj* 1 = **calm**, collected, composed, cool, dignified, serene, tranquil ≠ **wild** 2 = **unhurried**, deliberate, slow-moving

sediment *n* 1 = **dregs**, deposit, grounds, lees, residue

sedition *n* = **rabble-rousing**, agitation, incitement to riot, subversion the eyes or mind. **2** understand. **3** watch. **4** find out. **5** make sure (of something). **6** consider or decide. **7** have experience of. **8** meet or visit. **9** interview. **10** frequent the company of. **11** accompany. **seeing** *conj* in view of the fact that.

see² ❶ *n* diocese of a bishop.

seed ❶ *n* **1** mature fertilized grain of a plant. **2** such grains used for sowing. **3** origin. **4** *Obs* offspring. **5** *Sport* player ranked according to his or her ability. ◆ *v* **6** sow with seed. **7** remove seeds from. **8** arrange (the draw of a sports tournament) so that the outstanding competitors will not meet in the early rounds. **go**, **run to seed 1** (of plants) produce or shed seeds after flowering. **2** lose vigour or usefulness. **seedling** *n* young plant raised from a seed. **seedy** *adj* **1** shabby. **2** *Informal* unwell.

seek ❶ *v* **seeking**, **sought 1** try to find or obtain. **2** try (to do something).

seem ❶ *v* appear to be. **seeming** *adj* apparent but not real. **seemingly** *adv*

seep ❶ *v* trickle through slowly, ooze. **seepage** *n*

seesaw ❶ *n* **1** plank balanced in the middle so that two people seated on either side ride up and down alternately. ◆ *v* **2** move up and down.

seethe ❶ *v* **seething**, **seethed 1** be very agitated. **2** (of a liquid) boil or foam.

segment ❶ *n* **1** one of several sections into which something may be divided. ◆ *v* **2** divide into segments. **segmentation** *n*

segregate ❶ *v* set apart. **segregation** *n*

seize ❶ *v* **1** take hold of forcibly or quickly. **2** take immediate advantage of. **3** (usu. foll. by *up*) (of mechanical parts) stick tightly through overheating. **seizure** *n* **1** sudden violent attack of an illness. **2** seizing or being seized.

seldom ❶ *adv* not often, rarely.

select ❶ *v* **1** pick out or choose. ◆ *adj* **2**

——————— THESAURUS ———————

seduce *v* **1** = **corrupt**, debauch, deflower, deprave, dishonour **2** = **tempt**, beguile, deceive, entice, inveigle, lead astray, lure, mislead

see¹ *v* **1** = **perceive**, behold, catch sight of, discern, distinguish, espy, eyeball (*sl*), glimpse, look, make out, notice, sight, spot, witness **2** = **understand**, appreciate, comprehend, fathom, feel, follow, get, grasp, realize **3** = **observe 4** = **find out**, ascertain, determine, discover, learn **5** = **make sure**, ensure, guarantee, make certain, see to it **6** = **consider**, decide, deliberate, reflect, think over **8** = **visit**, receive **9** = **speak to**, confer with, consult, interview **10** = **go out with**, court, date (*inf*, *chiefly US*), go steady with (*inf*) **11** = **accompany**, escort, lead, show, usher, walk

see² *n* = **diocese**, bishopric

seed *n* **1**, **2** = **grain**, germ, kernel, pip, spore **3** = **origin**, beginning, germ, nucleus, source, start **4** *Obs* = **offspring**, children, descendants, issue, progeny **go**, **run to seed 2** = **decline**, decay,

degenerate, deteriorate, go downhill (*inf*), go to pot, let oneself go

seek *v* **1** = **look for**, be after, follow, hunt, pursue, search for **2** = **try**, aim, aspire to, attempt, endeavour, essay, have a go at (*inf*), strive

seem *v* **1** = **appear**, assume, give the impression, look

seep *v* = **ooze**, exude, leak, permeate, soak, trickle, well

seesaw *v* **2** = **alternate**, fluctuate, oscillate, swing

seethe *v* **1** = **be furious**, be livid, be pissed (off) (*taboo sl*), fume, go ballistic (*sl*, *chiefly US*), rage, see red (*inf*), simmer **2** = **boil**, bubble, fizz, foam, froth

segment *n* **1** = **section**, bit, division, part, piece, portion, slice, wedge

segregate *v* **1** = **set apart**, dissociate, isolate, separate **2** = **discriminate against**

seize *v* **1** = **grab**, catch up, clutch, grasp, grip, latch on to, lay hands on, snap up, snatch, take ≠ **let go**

seldom *adv* = **rarely**, hardly ever, infrequently, not often chosen in preference to others. **3** restricted to a particular group, exclusive. **selection** n **1** selecting. **2** things that have been selected. **3** range from which something may be selected. **selective** adj chosen or choosing carefully. **selectively** adv **selectivity** n **selector** n

self n, pl **selves 1** distinct individuality or identity of a person or thing. **2** one's basic nature. **3** one's own welfare or interests. **selfish** adj caring too much about oneself and not enough about others. **selfishly** adv **selfishness** n **selfless** adj unselfish.

self– prefix used with many main words to mean: **1** of oneself or itself. **2** by, to, in, due to, for, or from the self. **3** automatic(ally). **self–coloured** adj having only a single colour. **self–conscious** adj embarrassed at being the object of others' attention. **self–contained** adj **1** containing everything needed, complete. **2** (of a flat) having its own facilities. **self–evident** adj obvious without proof. **self–made** adj having achieved wealth or status by one's own efforts. **self–possessed** adj having control of one's emotions, calm. **self–righteous** adj thinking oneself more virtuous than others. **selfsame** adj the very same. **self–seeking** adj, n seeking to promote only one's own interests. **self–styled** adj using a title or name that one has taken without right. **self–sufficient** adj able to provide for oneself without help.

sell ⊕ v **selling, sold 1** exchange (something) for money. **2** stock, deal in. **3** (of goods) be sold. **4** (foll. by for) have a specified price. **5** Informal persuade (someone) to accept (something). ◆ n **6** manner of selling. **seller** n **sell out** v **1** dispose of (something) completely by selling. **2** Informal betray. **sellout** n **1** performance of a show etc. for which all the tickets are sold. **2** Informal betrayal.

Sellotape n **1** ® type of adhesive tape. ◆ v **2** stick with Sellotape.

semaphore n system of signalling by holding two flags in different positions to represent letters of the alphabet.

semblance ⊕ n outward or superficial appearance.

semen n sperm–carrying fluid produced by male animals.

semi– prefix used with many main words to mean: **1** half, e.g. semicircle. **2** partly or almost, e.g. semiprofessional.

semibreve n musical note four beats long.

semicolon n the punctuation mark (;).

semiconductor n substance with an electrical conductivity that increases with temperature.

semidetached adj (of a house) joined to another on one side.

semifinal n match or round before the final.

seminal ⊕ adj **1** original and influential. **2** capable of developing. **3** of semen or seed.

seminar n meeting of a group of students for discussion.

semiprecious adj (of gemstones) having less value than precious stones.

semolina n hard grains of wheat left after the milling of flour, used to make puddings and pasta.

send ⊕ v **sending, sent 1** cause (a person or thing) to go to or be taken or transmitted to a place. **2** bring into a specified state or condition. **3** sendoff n demonstration of good wishes at a person's departure. **send up** v Informal

———————————[THESAURUS]———————————

select v **1** = **choose**, opt for, pick, single out ≠ **reject** ◆ adj **2** = **choice**, excellent, first–class, hand–picked, special, superior, top–notch (inf) ≠ **cheap 3** = **exclusive**, cliquish, elite, privileged ≠ **indiscriminate**

sell v **1** = **trade**, barter, exchange **2** = **deal in**, handle, market, peddle, retail, stock,

trade in, traffic in ≠ **buy**

semblance n = **appearance**, aspect, facade, mask, pretence, resemblance, show, veneer

seminal adj **1** = **influential**, formative, ground–breaking, important, innovative, original

make fun of by imitating. **send–up** n
Informal imitation.
senile ⊕ adj mentally or physically weak
because of old age. **senility** n
senior ⊕ adj 1 superior in rank or standing.
2 older. 3 of or for older pupils. ♦ n 4
senior person. **seniority** n
sensation ⊕ n 1 ability to feel things
physically. 2 physical feeling. 3 general
feeling or awareness. 4 state of
excitement. 5 exciting person or thing.
sensational adj 1 causing intense shock,
anger, or excitement. 2 Informal very
good. **sensationalism** n deliberate use of
sensational language or subject matter.
sensationalist adj, n
sense ⊕ n 1 any of the faculties of
perception or feeling (sight, hearing,
touch, taste, or smell). 2 ability to
perceive. 3 feeling perceived through one
of the senses. 4 awareness. 5 (sometimes
pl) sound practical judgment or
intelligence. 6 specific meaning. ♦ v 7
perceive. **senseless** adj
sensible ⊕ adj 1 having or showing good

sense. 2 practical, e.g. sensible shoes. 3
(foll. by of) aware. **sensibly** adv **sensibility**
n ability to experience deep feelings.
sensitive ⊕ adj 1 easily hurt or offended. 2
responsive to external stimuli. 3 (of a
subject) liable to arouse controversy or
strong feelings. 4 (of an instrument)
responsive to slight changes. **sensitively**
adv **sensitivity** n **sensitize** v make
sensitive.
sensor n device that detects or measures
the presence of something, such as
radiation.
sensory adj of the senses or sensation.
sensual ⊕ adj 1 giving pleasure to the
body and senses rather than the mind. 2
having a strong liking for physical
pleasures. **sensually** adv **sensuality** n
sensuous ⊕ adj pleasing to the senses.
sentence ⊕ n 1 sequence of words
capable of standing alone as a statement,
question, or command. 2 punishment
passed on a criminal. ♦ v 3 pass sentence
on (a convicted person).
sentient ⊕ [**sen**–tee–ent] adj capable of

—————— THESAURUS ——————

send v 1 = **dispatch**, convey, direct,
forward, remit, transmit 2 (foll. by for)
= **summon**, call for, order, request
senile adj = **doddering**, decrepit, doting, in
one's dotage
senior lower adj 1 = **higher ranking**, superior
≠ **lower** 2 = **older**, elder, major (Brit)
≠ **younger**
sensation n 3 = **feeling**, awareness,
consciousness, impression, perception,
sense 4 = **excitement**, commotion, furore,
stir, thrill
sense n 1 = **faculty** 3 = **feeling**, sensation
4 = **feeling**, atmosphere, aura, awareness,
consciousness, impression, perception 5
(sometimes pl) = **intelligence**, brains (inf),
cleverness, common sense, judgment,
reason, sagacity, sanity, sharpness,
understanding, wisdom, wit(s) ≠ **stupidity**
6 = **meaning**, drift, gist, implication,
import, significance ♦ v 7 = **perceive**, be
aware of, discern, feel, get the impression,

pick up, realize, understand ≠ **miss**
sensible adj 1 = **wise**, canny, down–to–
earth, intelligent, judicious, prudent,
rational, realistic, sage, sane, shrewd,
sound ≠ **ignorant** 2 = **practical** 3 (foll. by
of) = **aware of**, conscious of, mindful of,
sensitive to
sensitive adj 1 = **easily hurt**, delicate,
easily offended, easily upset, tender, thin–
skinned, touchy ≠ **tough** 2 = **susceptible**,
easily affected, impressionable, responsive
4 = **precise**, acute, fine, keen, responsive
≠ **imprecise**
sensual adj 1 = **physical**, animal, bodily,
carnal, fleshly, luxurious, voluptuous
2 = **erotic**, lascivious, lecherous, lewd,
lustful, raunchy (sl), sexual
sensuous adj = **pleasurable**, gratifying,
hedonistic, sybaritic
sentence n 2 = **punishment**,
condemnation, decision, decree,
judgment, order, ruling, verdict ♦ v

feeling.

sentiment ① n 1 thought, opinion, or attitude. 2 feeling expressed in words. 3 exaggerated or mawkish emotion. **sentimental** adj excessively romantic or nostalgic. **sentimentality** n

sentinel ① n sentry.

sentry n, pl **–tries** soldier on watch.

separate ① v 1 act as a barrier between. 2 distinguish between. 3 divide up into parts. 4 (of a couple) stop living together. ◆ adj 5 not the same, different. 6 set apart. 7 not shared, individual. **separately** adv **separation** n 1 separating or being separated. 2 Law living apart of a married couple without divorce. **separable** adj **separatist** n person who advocates the separation of a group from an organization or country.

sepia adj, n reddish–brown (pigment).

Sept. September.

September n ninth month of the year.

septet n 1 group of seven performers. 2 music for such a group.

septic ① adj 1 (of a wound) infected. 2 of or caused by harmful bacteria. **septic tank** tank in which sewage is decomposed by the action of bacteria.

septicaemia [sep–tis–**see**–mee–a] n infection of the blood.

sepulchre ① [**sep**–pull–ker] n tomb or burial vault. **sepulchral** [sip–**pulk**–ral] adj

gloomy.

sequel ① n 1 novel, play, or film that continues the story of an earlier one. 2 consequence.

sequence ① n 1 arrangement of two or more things in successive order. 2 the successive order of two or more things. 3 section of a film showing a single uninterrupted episode. **sequential** adj

sequin n small ornamental metal disc on a garment.

seraph n, pl **–aphs**, **–aphim** member of the highest order of angels. **seraphic** adj

serenade n 1 music played or sung to a woman by a lover. ◆ v 2 sing or play a serenade to (someone).

serendipity n gift of making fortunate discoveries by accident.

serene ① adj calm, peaceful. **serenely** adv **serenity** n

serf n medieval farm labourer who could not leave the land he worked on. **serfdom** n

sergeant n 1 noncommissioned officer in the army. 2 police officer ranking between constable and inspector. **sergeant major** highest rank of noncommissioned officer in the army.

series ① n, pl **–ries** 1 group or succession of related things, usu. arranged in order. 2 set of radio or TV programmes about the same subject or characters.

THESAURUS

3 = **condemn**, doom, penalize

sentient adj = **feeling**, conscious, living, sensitive

sentiment n 1 = **opinion**, attitude, belief, feeling, idea, judgment, view

3 = **sentimentality**, emotionalism, mawkishness, romanticism

sentinel n = **guard**, lookout, sentry, watch, watchman

separate v 2 = **single out**, isolate, segregate 3 = **divide** come between, detach, disconnect, disentangle, disjoin, keep apart, move apart 4 = **part**, break up, disunite, diverge, divorce, estrange, part company, split up ≠ **join** ◆ adj

6 = **unconnected**, detached, disconnected, divided, divorced, isolated, unattached ≠ **united** 7 = **individual**, alone, apart, distinct, particular, single, solitary

septic adj 1 = **infected**, festering, poisoned, putrefying, putrid, suppurating

sepulchre n = **tomb**, burial place, grave, mausoleum, vault

sequel n 2 = **follow–up**, continuation, development 3 = **consequence**, conclusion, end, outcome, result, upshot

sequence n 1, 2 = **succession**, arrangement, chain, course, cycle, order, progression, series

serene adj 1 = **calm**, composed, peaceful,

serious � *adj* **1** giving cause for concern. **2** concerned with important matters. **3** not cheerful, grave. **4** sincere, not joking. **5** **seriously** *adv* **seriousness** *n*

sermon ⓐ *n* **1** speech on a religious or moral subject by a clergyman in a church service. **2** long moralizing speech. **sermonize** *v* make a long moralizing speech.

serpent *n* snake. **serpentine** *adj* twisting like a snake.

serrated *adj* having a notched or sawlike edge.

serum [seer–um] *n* **1** watery fluid left after blood has clotted. **2** this fluid from the blood of immunized animals used for inoculation or vaccination.

serve ⓐ *v* **1** work for (a person, community, or cause). **2** perform official duties. **3** attend to (customers). **4** provide with food or drink. **5** present (food or drink). **6** provide with a service. **7** be a member of the armed forces. **8** spend (time) in prison. **9** be useful or suitable. **10** *Tennis etc.* put (the ball) into play. **11** deliver (a legal document) to (a person). ♦ *n* **12** *Tennis etc.* act of serving the ball. **servant** *n* person employed to do household work for another.

service ⓐ *n* **1** serving. **2** system that provides something needed by the public. **3** department of public employment and its employees. **4** maintenance of goods provided by a dealer after sale. **5** availability for use. **6** overhaul of a machine or vehicle. **7** set of dishes etc. for serving a meal. **8** formal religious ceremony. **9** *Tennis etc.* act, manner, or right of serving the ball. ♦ *pl* **10** armed forces. ♦ *adj* **11** serving the public rather than producing goods, e.g. *service industry.* ♦ *v* **12** provide a service or services to. **13** overhaul (a machine or vehicle).

serviette *n* table napkin.

servile ⓐ *adj* **1** too eager to obey people, fawning. **2** suitable for a slave. **servility** *n*

servitude *n* bondage or slavery.

sesame [sess–am–ee] *n* plant cultivated for its seeds and oil, which are used in cooking.

session ⓐ *n* **1** period spent in an activity. **2** meeting of a court, parliament, or council. **3** series or period of such meetings. **4** academic term or year.

set¹ ⓐ *v* **setting, set 1** put in a specified position or state. **2** make ready. **3** make or become firm or rigid. **4** put (a broken bone) or (of a broken bone) be put into a normal position for healing. **5** adjust (a clock) to a particular position. **6** establish,

---

THESAURUS

---

tranquil, unruffled, untroubled

series *n* **1** = **sequence**, chain, course, order, progression, run, set, string, succession, train

serious *adj* **1** = **grave**, acute, critical, dangerous, severe **2** = **important**, crucial, fateful, grim, momentous, no laughing matter, pressing, significant, urgent, worrying ≠ **insignificant 3** = **solemn**, grave, humourless, sober, unsmiling ≠ **frivolous 4** = **sincere**, earnest, genuine, honest, in earnest

sermon *n* = **homily**, address

serve *v* **1** = **work for**, aid, assist, help **2** = **perform**, act, complete, discharge, do, fulfil **3** = **attend to**, minister to, wait on **4**, **6** = **provide**, supply **5** = **present**, deliver,

dish up, set out **9** = **be adequate**, answer the purpose, be acceptable, do, function as, satisfy, suffice, suit

service *n* **1** = **help**, assistance, avail, benefit, use, usefulness **3** = **work**, business, duty, employment, labour, office, yakka (*Aust & NZ inf*) **6** = **overhaul**, check, maintenance **8** = **ceremony**, observance, rite, worship ♦ *v* **13** = **overhaul**, check, fine tune, go over, maintain, tune (up)

servile *adj* **1** = **subservient**, abject, fawning, grovelling, obsequious, sycophantic, toadying

session *n* **1** = **period 2** = **meeting**, discussion, hearing, sitting **3** = **congress**, assembly, conference arrange. **7** prescribe, assign. **8** arrange (hair) while wet, so that it dries in position. **9** place (a jewel) in a setting. **10** put to music. **11** arrange (type) for printing. **12** (of the sun) go down. **13** (of plants) produce (fruit or seeds). **14** (of a gun dog) face game. ◆ *n* **15** setting or being set. **16** bearing or posture. **17** scenery used in a play or film. ◆ *adj* **18** fixed or established beforehand. **19** rigid or inflexible. **20** conventional or stereotyped. **21** determined (to do something). **22** ready. **set back** *v* **1** hinder. **2** cost. **setback** *n* anything that delays progress. **set off** *v* **1** embark on a journey. **2** cause to begin. **3** cause to explode. **4** act as a contrast to. **set square** flat right-angled triangular instrument used for drawing angles. **set to** *v* begin working. **set-to** *n* brief fight. **set up** *v* arrange or establish. **setup** *n* way in which anything is organized or arranged.

set² ❶ *n* **1** number of things or people grouped or belonging together. **2** *Maths* group of numbers or objects that satisfy a given condition or share a property. **3** television or radio receiver. **4** *Sport* group

of games in a match. **5** series of songs performed by a musician or group. **set theory** branch of mathematics concerned with the properties of sets.

sett, set *n* badger's burrow.

settee *n* couch.

setting ❶ *n* **1** background or surroundings. **2** time and place where a film, book, etc. is supposed to have taken place. **3** music written for the words of a text. **4** decorative metalwork in which a gem is set. **5** plates and cutlery for a single place at table. **6** position or level to which the controls of a machine can be adjusted.

settle ❶ *v* **1** arrange or put in order. **2** come to rest. **3** establish or become established as a resident. **4** colonize. **5** make quiet, calm, or stable. **6** pay (a bill). **7** dispose of, conclude. **8** bestow (property) legally. **9** end (a dispute). **settlement** *n* **1** act of settling. **2** place newly colonized. **3** subsidence (of a building). **4** property bestowed legally. **settler** *n* colonist. **settle down** *v* **1** make or become calm. **2** (foll. by *to*) concentrate on. **3** adopt a routine way of life. **settle for** *v* accept in spite of dissatisfaction.

set¹ *v* **1** = **put**, deposit, lay, locate, place, plant, position, rest, seat, situate, station, stick **2** = **prepare**, arrange, lay, make ready, spread **3** = **harden**, cake, congeal, crystallize, solidify, stiffen, thicken **6** = **arrange**, appoint, decide (upon), determine, establish, fix, fix up, resolve, schedule, settle, specify **7** = **assign**, allot, decree, impose, ordain, prescribe, specify **12** = **go down**, decline, dip, disappear, sink, subside, vanish ◆ *n* **16** = **position**, attitude, bearing, carriage, posture **17** = **scenery**, scene, setting, stage set ◆ *adj* **18** = **fixed**, agreed, appointed, arranged, decided, definite, established, prearranged, predetermined, scheduled, settled **19** = **inflexible**, hard and fast, immovable, rigid, stubborn ≠ **open** **20** = **conventional**, stereotyped, traditional, unspontaneous

set² *n* **1 a** = **series**, assortment, batch, collection, compendium **b** = **group**, band, circle, clique, company, coterie, crowd, faction, gang

setting *n* **1** = **surroundings**, backdrop, background, location, scene, scenery, set, site **2** = **context**

settle *v* **1** = **put in order**, adjust, order, regulate, straighten out, work out **2** = **land**, alight, come to rest, descend, light **3** = **move to**, dwell, inhabit, live, make one's home, put down roots, reside, set up home, take up residence **4** = **colonize**, people, pioneer, populate **5** = **calm**, lull, outspan (*S Afr*), pacify, quell, quiet, quieten, reassure, relax, relieve, soothe ≠ **trouble** **6** = **pay**, clear, discharge, square (up) **7** = **decide**, agree, confirm, determine, establish, fix **9** = **resolve**, clear up, decide, put an end

seven *adj, n* one more than six. **seventh** *adj, n* (of) number seven in a series. **seventeen** *adj, n* ten and seven. **seventeenth** *adj, n* **seventy** *adj, n* ten times seven. **seventieth** *adj, n*

sever ❶ *v* 1 cut through or off. 2 break off (a relationship). **severance** *n*

several ❶ *adj* 1 some, a few. 2 various, separate. **severally** *adv* separately.

severe ❶ *adj* 1 strict or harsh. 2 very intense or unpleasant. 3 strictly restrained in appearance. **severely** *adv* **severity** *n*

sew *v* **sewing, sewed, sewn** *or* **sewed** 1 join with thread repeatedly passed through with a needle. 2 make or fasten by sewing.

sewage *n* waste matter or excrement carried away in sewers. **sewer** *n* drain to remove waste water and sewage. **sewerage** *n* system of sewers.

sex ❶ *n* 1 state of being male or female. 2 male or female category. 3 sexual intercourse. 4 sexual feelings or behaviour. ◆ *v* 5 find out the sex of. **sexy** *adj* 1 sexually exciting or attractive. 2 *Informal* exciting or trendy. **sexism** *n* discrimination on the basis of a person's sex. **sexist** *adj, n* **sexual** *adj* **sexually** *adv*

sexuality *n* sexual intercourse sexual act in which the male's penis is inserted into the female's vagina.

sextet *n* 1 group of six performers. 2 music for such a group.

shabby ❶ *adj* **–bier, –biest** 1 worn or dilapidated in appearance. 2 mean or unworthy, e.g. *shabby treatment.* **shabbily** *adv* **shabbiness** *n*

shack ❶ *n* rough hut.

shackle ❶ *n* 1 one of a pair of metal rings joined by a chain, for securing a person's wrists or ankles. ◆ *v* 2 fasten with shackles.

shade ❶ *n* 1 relative darkness. 2 place sheltered from sun. 3 screen or cover used to protect from a direct source of light. 4 depth of colour. 5 slight amount. 6 *Lit* ghost. ◆ *pl* 7 *Slang* sunglasses. ◆ *v* 8 screen from light. 9 darken. 10 represent (darker areas) in drawing. 11 change slightly or by degrees. **shady** *adj* 1 situated in or giving shade. 2 of doubtful honesty or legality.

shadow ❶ *n* 1 dark shape cast on a surface when something stands between a light and the surface. 2 patch of shade. 3 slight trace. 4 threatening influence. 5 inseparable companion. ◆ *v* 6 cast a shadow over. 7 follow secretly. **shadowy**

——————— THESAURUS ———————

to, reconcile

sever *v* 1 = **cut**, cut in two, detach, disconnect, disjoin, divide, part, separate, split ≠ **unite** 2 = **discontinue**, break off, dissociate, put an end to, terminate ≠ **continue**

several *adj* 1 = **some**, many 2 = **various**, sundry 3 = **different**, diverse, manifold

severe *adj* 1 = **strict**, austere, cruel, drastic, hard, harsh, oppressive, rigid, unbending ≠ **easy** 2 = **intense**, acute, extreme, fierce 3 a = **grim**, forbidding, grave, serious, stern, tight–lipped, unsmiling ≠ **genial** b = **plain**, austere, classic, restrained, simple, Spartan, unadorned, unembellished, unfussy ≠ **fancy**

sex *n* 1, 2 = **gender** 3 = **(sexual) intercourse**, coition, coitus, copulation, fornication, lovemaking, sexual relations

shabby *adj* 1 = **tatty**, dilapidated, mean, ragged, run–down, scruffy, seedy, tattered, threadbare, worn ≠ **smart** 2 = **mean**, cheap, contemptible, despicable, dirty, dishonourable, low, rotten (*inf*), scurvy ≠ **fair**

shack *n* = **hut**, cabin, shanty

shackle *n* 1 = **fetter**, bond, chain, iron, leg–iron, manacle ◆ *v* 2 = **fetter**, bind, chain, manacle, put in irons

shade *n* 1 = **dimness**, dusk, gloom, gloominess, semidarkness, shadow 3 = **screen**, blind, canopy, cover, covering, curtain, shield, veil 4 = **hue**, colour, tinge, tint, tone 5 = **dash**, hint, suggestion, trace 6 *Lit* = **ghost**, apparition, phantom, spectre, spirit ◆ *v* 8 = **cover**, conceal, hide, obscure, protect, screen, shield, veil 9 = **darken**, cloud, dim, shadow *adj*

shaft ❶ *n* 1 long narrow straight handle of a tool or weapon. 2 ray of light. 3 revolving rod that transmits power in a machine. 4 vertical passageway, as for a lift or a mine. 5 one of the bars between which an animal is harnessed to a vehicle.

shag *n* 1 coarse shredded tobacco. 2 tangled hair or wool. ♦ *adj* 3 (of a carpet) having a long pile. **shaggy** *adj* 1 covered with rough hair or wool. 2 tousled, unkempt. **shaggy–dog story** long anecdote with a humorous twist at the end.

shake ❶ *v* shaking, shook, shaken 1 move quickly up and down or back and forth. 2 make unsteady. 3 tremble. 4 grasp (someone's hand) in greeting or agreement. 5 shock or upset. ♦ *n* 6 shaking. 7 vibration. 8 *Informal* short period of time. **shaky** *adj* 1 unsteady. 2 uncertain or questionable. **shakily** *adv*

shaker *n* container used to shake a powdered substance onto somthing.

shale *n* flaky sedimentary rock.

shall *v, past tense* should used as an auxiliary to make the future tense or to indicate intention, obligation, or inevitability.

✔ **WORD TIP**
The use of *shall* with *I* and *we* is a matter of preference, not rule. *Shall* is commonly used for questions in southern England but less often in the north and Scotland.

shallow ❶ *adj* 1 not deep. 2 lacking depth of character or intellect. **shallows** *pl n* area of shallow water.

sham ❶ *n* 1 thing or person that is not genuine. ♦ *adj* 2 not genuine. ♦ *v* **shamming, shammed** 3 fake, feign.

shamble *v* walk in a shuffling awkward way.

shambles ❶ *n* disorderly event or place.

shame ❶ *n* 1 painful emotion caused by awareness of having done something dishonourable or foolish. 2 capacity to feel shame. 3 cause of shame. 4 cause for regret. ♦ *v* 5 cause to feel shame. 6 disgrace. 7 compel by shame. **shameful** *adj* causing or deserving shame. **shamefully** *adv* **shameless** *adj* with no sense of shame.

shampoo *n* liquid soap for washing hair, carpets, or upholstery.

shamrock *n* clover leaf, esp. as the Irish

——— THESAURUS ———

shadow *n* 2 = **dimness**, cover, darkness, dusk, gloom, shade 3 = **trace**, hint, suggestion, suspicion 4 = **cloud**, blight, gloom, sadness ♦ *v* 6 = **shade**, darken, overhang, screen, shield 7 = **follow**, stalk, tail (*inf*), trail

shaft *n* 1 = **handle**, pole, rod, shank, stem 2 = **ray**, beam, gleam

shake *v* 1 = **wave**, brandish, flourish 2 = **jolt**, bump, jar, rock 3 = **tremble**, quake, quiver, shiver, totter, vibrate 5 = **upset**, distress, disturb, frighten, rattle (*inf*), shock, unnerve ♦ *n* 6 = **quaking**, agitation, convulsion, jerk, jolt, shiver, shudder, trembling 7 = **vibration**, tremor

shallow *adj* 1 = **superficial**, empty, slight, surface, trivial 2 = **unintelligent**, foolish, frivolous, ignorant, puerile, simple

sham *n* 1 = **phoney** *or* **phony** (*inf*), counterfeit, forgery, fraud, hoax, humbug, imitation, impostor, pretence ≠ **original** ♦ *adj* 2 = **false**, artificial, bogus, counterfeit, feigned, imitation, mock, phoney *or* phony (*inf*), pretended, simulated ≠ **real** ♦ *v* 3 = **fake**, affect, assume, feign, pretend, put on, simulate

shambles *n* 1 = **chaos**, confusion, disarray, disorder, havoc, madhouse, mess, muddle

shame *n* 1 = **embarrassment**, abashment, humiliation, ignominy, mortification ≠ **boldness** 3 = **disgrace**, blot, discredit, dishonour, disrepute, infamy, reproach, scandal, smear ≠ **credit** ♦ *v* 6 = **embarrass**, abash, disgrace, humble, humiliate, mortify ≠ **make proud** 7 = **dishonour**, blot, debase, defile, emblem.

shandy n, pl **–dies** drink made of beer and lemonade.

shanty¹ ❶ n, pl **–ties** shack or crude dwelling. **shantytown** n slum consisting of shanties.

shanty² n, pl **–ties** sailor's traditional song.

shape ❶ n 1 outward form of an object. 2 way in which something is organized. 3 pattern or mould. 4 condition or state. ◆ v 5 form or mould. 6 devise or develop. **shapeless** adj **shapely** adj having an attractive shape.

shard n broken piece of pottery or glass.

share ❶ n 1 part of something that belongs to or is contributed by a person. 2 one of the equal parts into which the capital stock of a public company is divided. ◆ v 3 give or take a share of (something). 4 join with others in doing or using (something). 5 divide and distribute. **shareholder** n

shark n 1 large usu. predatory sea fish. 2 person who cheats others.

sharp ❶ adj 1 having a keen cutting edge or fine point. 2 not gradual. 3 clearly defined. 4 mentally acute. 5 clever but underhand. 6 shrill. 7 bitter or sour in taste. 8 Music above the true pitch. ◆ adv 9 promptly. 10 Music too high in pitch. ◆ n 11 Music symbol raising a note one semitone above natural pitch. **sharply** adv

sharpness n **sharpen** v make or become sharp or sharper. **sharpener** n **sharpshooter** n marksman.

shatter ❶ v 1 break into pieces. 2 destroy completely. **shattered** adj Informal 1 completely exhausted. 2 badly upset.

shave ❶ v **shaving, shaved, shaved** or **shaven** 1 remove (hair) from (the face, head, or body) with a razor or shaver. 2 pare away. 3 touch lightly in passing. ◆ n 4 shaving. **close shave** Informal narrow escape. **shaver** n electric razor. **shavings** pl n parings.

shawl n piece of cloth worn over a woman's head or shoulders or wrapped around a baby.

she pron refers to: 1 female person or animal previously mentioned. 2 something regarded as female, such as a car, ship, or nation.

sheaf n, pl **sheaves** 1 bundle of papers. 2 tied bundle of reaped corn.

shear v **shearing, sheared, sheared** or **shorn** 1 clip hair or wool from. 2 cut through. **shears** pl n large scissors or a cutting tool shaped like these. **shearer** n

sheath n 1 close–fitting cover, esp. for a knife or sword. 2 condom. **sheathe** v put into a sheath.

shebeen n Irish, S Afr & Scot place where alcohol is sold illegally.

shed¹ ❶ n building used for storage or

degrade, smear, stain ≠ **credit**

shanty¹ n = **shack**, cabin, hut, shed

shape n 1 = **form**, build, contours, figure, lines, outline, profile, silhouette 2 = **configuration** 3 = **pattern**, frame, model, mould 4 = **condition**, fettle, health, state, trim ◆ v 5 = **form**, create, fashion, make, model, mould, produce 6 = **develop**, adapt, devise, frame, modify, plan

share n 1 = **part**, allotment, allowance, contribution, due, lot, portion, quota, ration, whack (inf) ◆ v 3 = **divide**, assign, distribute, split 4 = **partake**, participate, receive 5 = **go halves**, go fifty–fifty (inf)

sharp adj 1 = **keen**, acute, jagged, pointed, serrated, spiky ≠ **dull** 2 = **sudden**, abrupt, distinct, extreme, marked ≠ **slow** 3 = **clear**, crisp, distinct, well–defined ≠ **blurred** 4 = **quick–witted**, alert, astute, bright, clever, discerning, knowing, penetrating, perceptive, quick ≠ **slow** 5 = **cunning**, artful, crafty, dishonest, sly, unscrupulous, wily 7 = **sour**, acid, acrid, hot, piquant, pungent, tart ◆ adv 9 = **promptly**, exactly, on the dot, on time, precisely, punctually ≠ **roughly**

shatter v 1 = **smash**, break, burst, crack, crush, pulverize 2 = **destroy**, demolish, ruin, torpedo, wreck shelter or as a workshop.

shed² ⊕ *v* shedding, shed 1 pour forth (tears). 2 cast off (skin, hair, or leaves).

sheen ⊕ *n* glistening brightness on the surface of something.

sheep *n, pl* sheep ruminant animal bred for wool and meat. **sheepdog** *n* dog used for herding sheep. **sheepskin** *n* skin of a sheep with the fleece still on, used for clothing or rugs.

sheer ⊕ *adj* 1 absolute, complete, e.g. *sheer folly*. 2 perpendicular, steep. 3 (of material) so fine as to be transparent. ◆ *adv* 4 steeply.

sheet ⊕ *n* 1 large piece of cloth used as an inner bed cover. 2 broad thin piece of any material. 3 large expanse. **sheeting** *n* material from which sheets are made. **sheet lightning** lightning that appears to flash across a large part of the sky at once.

sheikh, sheik [shake] *n* Arab chief.

shelf *n, pl* shelves 1 board fixed horizontally for holding things. 2 ledge. **shelf life** time a packaged product will remain fresh.

shell ⊕ *n* 1 hard outer covering of an egg, nut, or certain animals. 2 external frame of something. 3 explosive projectile fired from a large gun. ◆ *v* 4 take the shell from. 5 fire at with artillery shells. **shellfish**

n sea-living animal, esp. one that can be eaten, with a shell. **shell out** *v Informal* pay out or hand over (money). **shell shock** nervous disorder caused by exposure to battle conditions.

shelter ⊕ *n* 1 structure providing protection from danger or the weather. 2 protection. ◆ *v* 3 give shelter to. 4 take shelter.

shelve ⊕ *v* 1 put aside or postpone. 2 provide with shelves. **shelving** *n* (material for) shelves.

shepherd ⊕ *n* 1 person who tends sheep. ◆ *v* 2 guide or watch over (people). **shepherdess** *n fem* **shepherd's pie** baked dish of mince covered with mashed potato.

sherbet *n* fruit-flavoured fizzy powder.

sheriff *n* 1 (in the US) chief law enforcement officer of a county. 2 (in England and Wales) chief executive officer of the Crown in a county. 3 (in Scotland) chief judge of a district.

sherry *n, pl* -ries pale or dark brown fortified wine.

shield ⊕ *n* 1 piece of armour carried on the arm to protect the body from blows or missiles. 2 anything that protects. 3 sports trophy in the shape of a shield. ◆ *v* 4 protect.

╾━━━━━┤ T H E S A U R U S ├━━━━━

shave *v* 1, 2 = **trim**, crop, pare, shear

shed¹ *n* = **hut**, outhouse, shack

shed² *v* 1 = **cast**, drop 2 = **spill**, emit, give, give out, radiate, scatter, shower 3 = **cast off**, discard, moult, slough

sheen *n* = **shine**, brightness, gleam, gloss, lustre, polish

sheer *adj* 1 = **total**, absolute, complete, downright, out-and-out, pure, unmitigated, utter ≠ **moderate** 2 = **steep**, abrupt, precipitous ≠ **gentle** 3 = **fine**, diaphanous, gauzy, gossamer, see-through, thin, transparent ≠ **heavy**

sheet *n* 2 = **coat**, film, lamina, layer, overlay, panel, plate, slab, stratum, surface, veneer 3 = **expanse**, area, blanket, covering, stretch, sweep

shell *n* 1 = **case**, husk, pod 2 = **frame**, framework, hull, structure ◆ *v* 5 = **bomb**, attack, blitz, bombard, strafe

shelter *n* 1 = **cover**, screen 2 = **protection**, asylum, defence, guard, haven, refuge, retreat, safety, sanctuary, security ◆ *v* 3 = **protect**, cover, defend, guard, harbour, hide, safeguard, shield ≠ **expose** 4 = **take shelter**, hide, seek refuge

shelve *v* 1 = **postpone**, defer, freeze, put aside, put on ice, put on the back burner (*inf*), suspend, take a rain check on (*US & Canad inf*)

shepherd *n* 1 = **herdsman**, drover, grazier, stockman ◆ *v* 2 = **guide**, conduct, herd, steer, usher

shield *n* 2 = **protection**, cover, defence,

shift ❶ v 1 move. 2 transfer (blame or responsibility). 3 remove or be removed. ◆ n 4 shifting. 5 group of workers who work during a specified period. 6 period of time during which they work. 7 loose–fitting straight underskirt or dress. **shiftless** adj lacking in ambition or initiative. **shifty** adj evasive or untrustworthy. **shiftiness** n

shilling n former British coin, replaced by the 5p piece.

shimmer ❶ v, n (shine with) a faint unsteady light.

shin n 1 front of the lower leg. ◆ v **shinning, shinned** 2 climb by using the hands or arms and legs.

shine ❶ v **shining, shone** 1 give out or reflect light. 2 aim (a light). 3 polish. 4 excel. ◆ n 5 brightness or lustre. **take a shine to** Informal take a liking to (someone). **shiny** adj

shingle n 1 wooden roof tile. ◆ v 2 cover (a roof) with shingles.

shingles n disease causing a rash of small blisters along a nerve.

ship ❶ n 1 large seagoing vessel. ◆ v **shipping, shipped** 2 send or transport by carrier, esp. a ship. 3 bring or go aboard a ship. **shipment** n 1 act of shipping cargo. 2 consignment of goods shipped. **shipping** n 1 freight transport business. 2 ships collectively. **shipshape** adj orderly or neat. **shipwreck** n 1 destruction of a ship through storm or collision. ◆ v 2 cause to undergo shipwreck. **shipyard** n place where ships are built.

shire n county.

shirk ❶ v avoid (duty or work). **shirker** n

shirt n garment for the upper part of the body.

shirty adj **–tier, –tiest** Slang bad–tempered or annoyed.

shiver¹ ❶ v 1 tremble, as from cold or fear. ◆ n 2 shivering.

shiver² ❶ v splinter into pieces.

shoal¹ n large number of fish swimming together.

shoal² n 1 stretch of shallow water. 2 sandbank.

shock¹ ❶ v 1 horrify, disgust, or astonish. ◆ n 2 sudden violent emotional disturbance. 3 sudden violent blow or impact. 4 something causing this. 5 state of bodily collapse caused by physical or mental shock. 6 pain and muscular spasm caused by an electric current passing through the body. **shocker** n **shocking** adj 1 causing horror, disgust, or astonishment. 2 Informal very bad.

shock² n bushy mass (of hair).

shoddy ❶ adj **–dier, –diest** made or done badly.

shoe n 1 outer covering for the foot,

guard, safeguard, screen, shelter ◆ v 4 = **protect**, cover, defend, guard, safeguard, screen, shelter

shift v 1 = **move**, budge, displace, move around, rearrange, relocate, reposition ◆ n 4 = **move**, displacement, rearrangement, shifting

① **shimmer** v = **gleam**, glisten, scintillate, twinkle

② **shimmer** n = **gleam**, iridescence

shine v 1 = **gleam**, beam, flash, glare, glisten, glitter, glow, radiate, sparkle, twinkle 3 = **polish**, brush, buff, burnish 4 = **be outstanding**, be conspicuous, excel, stand out ◆ n 5 = **brightness**, glare, gleam, gloss, light, lustre, polish, radiance, sheen, shimmer, sparkle

ship n 1 = **vessel**, boat, craft

shirk v = **dodge**, avoid, evade, get out of, skive (Brit sl), slack

shiver¹ v 1 = **tremble**, quake, quiver, shake, shudder ◆ n 2 = **trembling**, flutter, quiver, shudder, tremor

shiver² v 1 = **splinter**, break, crack, fragment, shatter, smash, smash to smithereens

shock v 1 a = **horrify**, appal, disgust, nauseate, revolt, scandalize, sicken b = **astound**, jolt, shake, stagger, stun, stupefy ◆ n 2 = **upset**, blow, bombshell, distress, disturbance, stupefaction, stupor, trauma, turn (inf) 3 = **impact**, blow, clash, ending below the ankle. **2** horseshoe. ◆ *v* **shoeing, shod 3** fit with a shoe or shoes. **shoehorn** *n* smooth curved implement inserted at the heel of a shoe to ease the foot into it. **shoestring** *n* **on a shoestring** using a very small amount of money.

shonky *adj* **–kier, –kiest** *Aust & NZ informal* unreliable or unsound.

shoo *interj* **1** go away! ◆ *v* **2** drive away as by saying 'shoo'.

shoot ❶ *v* **shooting, shot 1** hit, wound, or kill with a missile fired from a weapon. **2** fire (a missile from) a weapon. **3** hunt. **4** send out or move rapidly. **5** (of a plant) sprout. **6** photograph or film. **7** *Sport* take a shot at goal. ◆ *n* **8** new branch or sprout of a plant. **9** hunting expedition. **10** **shooting star** meteor.

shop ❶ *n* **1** place for sale of goods and services. **2** workshop. ◆ *v* **shopping, shopped 3** visit a shop or shops to buy goods. **4** *Slang* inform against (someone). **talk shop** discuss one's work, esp. on a social occasion. **1 shop around** *v* visit various shops to compare goods and prices. **shop floor 1** production area of a factory. **2** workers in a factory. **shoplifter** *n* person who steals from a shop. **shopsoiled** *adj* soiled or faded from being displayed in a shop. **shop steward** trade-union official elected to represent his or her fellow workers.

shore¹ ❶ *n* edge of a sea or lake.

shore² ❶ *v* (foll. by *up*) prop or support.

short ❶ *adj* **1** not long. **2** not tall. **3** not lasting long, brief. **4** deficient, e.g. *short of cash.* **5** abrupt, rude. **6** (of a drink) consisting chiefly of a spirit. **7** (of pastry) crumbly. ◆ *adv* **8** abruptly. ◆ *n* **9** drink of spirits. **10** short film. **11** *Informal* short circuit. ◆ *pl* **12** short trousers. **13 shortage** *n* deficiency. **shorten** *v* make or become shorter. **shortly** *adv* **1** soon. **2** rudely. **shortbread, shortcake** *n* crumbly biscuit made with butter. **short–change** *v* **1** give (someone) less than the correct amount of change. **2** *Slang* swindle. **short circuit** faulty or accidental connection in a circuit, which deflects current through a path of low resistance. **shortcoming** *n* failing or defect. **short cut** quicker route or method. **shortfall** *n* deficit. **shorthand** *n* system of rapid writing using symbols to represent words. **short–handed** *adj* not having enough workers. **short list** selected list of candidates for a job or prize, from which the final choice will be made. **short–list** *v* put on a short list. **short shrift** brief and unsympathetic treatment. **short–sighted** *adj* **1** unable to see distant things clearly. **2** lacking in foresight. **short wave** radio wave with a wavelength of less than 60 metres.

shot ❶ *n* **1** shooting. **2** small lead pellets used in a shotgun. **3** person with specified skill in shooting. **4** *Slang* attempt. **5** *Sport* act or instance of hitting, kicking, or throwing the ball. **6** photograph. **7**

——————| THESAURUS |——————

collision

shoddy *adj* = **inferior**, cheap, poor, rubbishy, second-rate, slipshod, tawdry, trashy

shoot *v* **1** = **hit**, blast (*sl*), bring down, kill, open fire, plug (*sl*) **2** = **fire**, discharge, emit, fling, hurl, launch, project, propel **4** = **speed**, bolt, charge, dart, dash, fly, hurtle, race, rush, streak, tear ◆ *n* **8** = **sprout**, branch, bud, offshoot, sprig

shop *n* **1** = **store**, boutique, emporium, hypermarket, supermarket

shore¹ *n* **1** = **beach**, coast, sands, seashore,

strand (*poet*)

shore² *v* **1** (foll. by *up*) = **support**, brace, buttress, hold, prop, reinforce, strengthen, underpin

short *adj* **1** = **concise**, brief, compressed, laconic, pithy, succinct, summary, terse ≠ **long 2** = **small**, diminutive, dumpy, little, petite, squat ≠ **tall 3** = **brief**, fleeting, momentary **4** = **lacking**, deficient, limited, low (on), scant, scarce, wanting ≠ **sufficient 5** = **abrupt**, brusque, curt, discourteous, impolite, sharp, terse, uncivil ◆ *adv* **8** = **abruptly**, suddenly, without

uninterrupted film sequence. **8** *Informal* injection. **9** *Informal* drink of spirits.
shotgun *n* gun for firing a charge of shot at short range. **shotgun wedding** wedding enforced because the bride is pregnant.
should *v* past tense of **shall** used as an auxiliary to make the subjunctive mood or to indicate obligation or possibility.
shoulder ❶ *n* **1** part of the body to which an arm, foreleg, or wing is attached. **2** cut of meat including the upper foreleg. **3** side of a road. ◆ *v* **5** bear (a burden or responsibility). **6** push with one's shoulder. **7** put on one's shoulder. **shoulder blade** large flat triangular bone at the shoulder.
shout ❶ *n* **1** loud cry. ◆ *v* **2** cry out loudly. **3** *Aust & NZ informal* treat (someone) to (something, such as a drink). **shout down** *v* silence (someone) by shouting.
shove ❶ *v* **1** push roughly. **2** *Informal* put. ◆ *n* **3** rough push. **shove off** *v Informal* go away.
shovel ❶ *n* **1** tool for lifting or moving loose material. ◆ *v* **-elling, -elled 2** lift or move as with a shovel.
show ❶ *v* **showing, showed, shown** *or* **showed 1** make, be, or become noticeable or visible. **2** exhibit or display. **3** indicate. **4** instruct by demonstration. **5** prove. **6** guide. **7** reveal or display (an emotion). ◆ *n* **8** public exhibition. **9**

theatrical or other entertainment. **10** mere display or pretence. **showy** *adj* **1** gaudy. **2** ostentatious. **showily** *adv* **show business** the entertainment industry. **showcase** *n* **1** situation in which something is displayed to best advantage. **2** glass case used to display objects. **showdown** *n* confrontation that settles a dispute.
showjumping *n* competitive sport of riding horses to demonstrate skill in jumping. **showman** *n* man skilled at presenting anything spectacularly. **showmanship** *n* **show off** *v* **1** exhibit to invite admiration. **2** *Informal* behave flamboyantly in order to attract attention. **show-off** *n Informal* person who shows off. **showpiece** *n* excellent specimen shown for display or as an example. **showroom** *n* room in which goods for sale are on display. **show up** *v* **1** reveal or be revealed clearly. **2** expose the faults or defects of. **3** *Informal* embarrass. **4** *Informal* arrive.
shower ❶ *n* **1** kind of bath in which a person stands while being sprayed with water. **2** wash in this. **3** short period of rain, hail, or snow. **4** sudden abundant fall of objects. ◆ *v* **5** wash in a shower. **6** bestow (things) or present (someone) with things liberally. **showery** *adj*
shrapnel *n* **1** artillery shell filled with pellets which scatter on explosion. **2**

————————————— THESAURUS —————————————

warning
shot *n* **1 = throw**, discharge, lob, pot shot **2 = pellet**, ball, bullet, lead, projectile, slug **3 = marksman**, shooter **4** *Sl* **= attempt**, effort, endeavour, go (*inf*), stab (*inf*), try, turn
shoulder *v* **5 = bear**, accept, assume, be responsible for, carry, take on **6 = push**, elbow, jostle, press, shove
shout *n* **1 = cry**, bellow, call, roar, scream, yell ◆ *v* **2 = cry (out)**, bawl, bellow, call (out), holler (*inf*), roar, scream, yell
shove *v* **1 = push**, drive, elbow, impel, jostle, press, propel, thrust
shovel *v* **2 = move**, dredge, heap, ladle,

load, scoop, toss
show *v* **1 = be visible**, appear ≠ **be invisible 2 = present**, display, exhibit ≠ **hide 3 = indicate**, demonstrate, display, manifest, register, reveal ≠ **refute 4 = instruct**, demonstrate, explain, teach **5 = prove**, clarify, demonstrate, elucidate, point out **6 = guide**, accompany, attend, conduct, escort, lead ◆ *n* **8 = exhibition**, array, display, fair, parade, sight, spectacle **9 = entertainment**, pageant, presentation, production **10 = pretence**, affectation, air, appearance, display, illusion, parade, pose
shower *n* **3, 4 = deluge**, barrage, stream, torrent, volley ◆ *v* **6 = inundate**, deluge,

fragments from this.

shred ❶ *n* **1** long narrow strip torn from something. **2** small amount. ◆ *v* **shredding, shredded** *or* **shred 3** tear to shreds.

shrew ❶ *n* **1** small mouselike animal. **2** bad-tempered nagging woman.

shrewd ❶ *adj* clever and perceptive.

shriek ❶ *n* **1** shrill cry. ◆ *v* **2** utter (with) a shriek.

shrill ❶ *adj* (of a sound) sharp and high-pitched. **shrillness** *n* **shrilly** *adv*

shrimp *n* **1** small edible shellfish. **2** *Informal* small person.

shrine *n* place of worship associated with a sacred person or object.

shrink ❶ *v* **shrinking, shrank** *or* **shrunk, shrunk** *or* **shrunken 1** become or make smaller. **2** recoil or withdraw. ◆ *n* **3** *Slang* psychiatrist. **shrinkage** *n* decrease in size, value, or weight.

shrivel ❶ *v* **-elling, -elled** shrink and wither.

shroud ❶ *n* **1** piece of cloth used to wrap a dead body. **2** anything which conceals. ◆ *v* **3** conceal.

shrub *n* woody plant smaller than a tree. **shrubbery** *n, pl* **-beries** area planted with shrubs

shrug *v* **shrugging, shrugged 1** raise and then drop (the shoulders) as a sign of indifference, ignorance, or doubt. ◆ *n* **2** shrugging. **shrug off** *v* dismiss as unimportant.

shudder ❶ *v* **1** shake or tremble violently, esp. with horror. ◆ *n* **2** shaking or trembling.

shuffle ❶ *v* **1** walk without lifting the feet. **2** jumble together. **3** rearrange. ◆ *n* **4** shuffling. **5** rearrangement.

shun ❶ *v* **shunning, shunned** avoid.

shunt *v* **1** move (objects or people) to a different position. **2** move (a train) from one track to another.

shut ❶ *v* **shutting, shut 1** bring together or fold, close. **2** prevent access to. **3** (of a shop etc.) stop operating for the day. **shutter** *n* **1** hinged doorlike cover for closing off a window. **2** device in a camera letting in the light required to expose a film. **shut down** *v* close or stop (a factory, machine, or business). **shutdown** *n*

shuttle ❶ *n* **1** vehicle going to and fro over a short distance. **2** instrument which passes the weft thread between the warp threads in weaving. ◆ *v* **3** travel by or as if by shuttle.

shuttlecock *n* small light cone with feathers stuck in one end, struck to and fro in badminton.

heap, lavish, pour, rain

shred *n* **1** = **strip**, bit, fragment, piece, scrap, sliver, tatter **2** = **particle**, atom, grain, iota, jot, scrap, trace

shrew *n* **2** = **nag**, harpy, harridan, scold, spitfire, vixen

shrewd *adj* = **clever**, astute, calculating, canny, crafty, cunning, intelligent, keen, perceptive, perspicacious, sharp, smart

shriek *v, n* = **cry**, scream, screech, squeal, yell

shrill *adj* **1** = **piercing**, high, penetrating, sharp ≠ **deep**

shrink *v* **1** = **decrease**, contract, diminish, dwindle, grow smaller, lessen, narrow, shorten ≠ **increase 2** = **recoil**, cower, cringe, draw back, flinch, quail

shrivel *v* = **wither**, dehydrate, desiccate, shrink, wilt, wizen

shroud *n* **1** = **winding sheet**, grave clothes **2** = **covering**, mantle, pall, screen, veil ◆ *v* **3** = **conceal**, blanket, cloak, cover, envelop, hide, screen, veil

shudder *v* **1** = **shiver**, convulse, quake, quiver, shake, tremble ◆ *n* **2** = **shiver**, quiver, spasm, tremor

shuffle *v* **1** = **scuffle**, drag, scrape, shamble **2** = **jumble**, disarrange, disorder, mix **3** = **rearrange**

shun *v* = **avoid**, keep away from, steer clear of

shut *v* **1** = **close**, fasten, seal, secure, slam ≠ **open**

shuttle *v* **3** = **go back and forth**, alternate,

shy¹ ❶ *adj* **1** not at ease in company. **2** timid. **3** (foll. by *of*) cautious or wary. ♦ *v* **shying, shied 4** start back in fear. **5** (foll. by *away from*) avoid (doing something) through fear or lack of confidence. **shyly** *adv* **shyness** *n*

shy² ❶ *v* **shying, shied 1** throw. ♦ *n, pl* **shies 2** throw.

sibilant *adj* hissing.

sibling *n* brother or sister.

sick ❶ *adj* **1** vomiting or likely to vomit. **2** physically or mentally unwell. **3** *Informal* amused by something sadistic or morbid. **4** (foll. by *of*) *Informal* disgusted (by) or weary (of). **sickness** *n* **sicken** *v* **1** make nauseated or disgusted. **2** become ill. **sickly** *adj* **1** unhealthy, weak. **2** causing revulsion or nausea. **sickbay** *n* place for sick people, such as that on a ship.

sickle *n* tool with a curved blade for cutting grass or grain.

side ❶ *n* **1** line or surface that borders anything. **2** either of two halves into which something can be divided. **3** either surface of a flat object. **4** area immediately next to a person or thing. **5** region. **6** aspect or part. **7** one of two opposing groups or teams. **8** line of descent through one parent. **9** *Slang* conceit. ♦ *adj* **10** at or on the side. **11** subordinate. **on the side 1** as an extra. **2** unofficially. **siding** *n* short

stretch of railway track on which trains or wagons are shunted from the main line. **sideboard** *n* piece of furniture for holding plates, cutlery, etc. in a dining room. **sideburns, sideboards** *pl n* man's side whiskers. **side effect** additional undesirable effect. **sidekick** *n* *Informal* close friend or associate. **sidelight** *n* either of two small lights on the front of a vehicle. **sideline** *n* **1** subsidiary interest or source of income. **2** *Sport* line marking the boundary of a playing area. **sidelong** *adj* **1** sideways. ♦ *adv* **2** obliquely. **side-saddle** *n* saddle designed to allow a woman rider to sit with both legs on the same side of the horse. **sidestep** *v* **1** dodge (an issue). **2** avoid by stepping sideways. **sidetrack** *v* divert from the main topic. **sidewalk** *n* *US* pavement. **sideways** *adv* **1** to or from the side. **2** obliquely. **side with** *v* support (one side in a dispute).

sidle ❶ *v* move in a furtive manner.

siege *n* surrounding and blockading of a place.

siesta ❶ *n* afternoon nap, taken in hot countries.

sieve ❶ [siv] *n* **1** utensil with mesh through which a substance is sifted or strained. ♦ *v* **2** sift or strain through a sieve.

sift ❶ *v* **1** remove the coarser particles from

————[T H E S A U R U S]————

commute, go to and fro

shy¹ *adj* **1, 2 = timid**, bashful, coy, diffident, retiring, self-conscious, self-effacing, shrinking ≠ **forward 3** (foll. by *of*) = **cautious of**, chary of, distrustful of, hesitant about, suspicious of, wary of ≠ **rash** ♦ *v* **5** (foll. by *away from*) = **recoil**, balk, draw back, flinch, start

shy² *v* **1 = throw**, cast, fling, hurl, pitch, sling, toss

sick *adj* **1 = nauseous**, ill, nauseated, queasy **2 = unwell**, ailing, crook (*Aust & NZ sl*), diseased, indisposed, poorly (*inf*), under the weather ≠ **well 3** *Inf* = **morbid**, black, ghoulish, macabre, sadistic **4** (foll. by *of*) *Inf* = **tired**, bored, fed up, jaded,

weary

side *n* **1 = border**, boundary, division, edge, limit, margin, perimeter, rim, sector, verge **3 = surface**, facet **6 = part**, aspect, face, flank, hand, view **7 = party**, camp, cause, faction, sect, team **9** *Sl* = **conceit**, airs, arrogance ♦ *adj* **11 = subordinate**, ancillary, incidental, lesser, marginal, minor, secondary, subsidiary ≠ **main side with** ♦ *v* = **support**, ally with, favour, go along with, take the part of

sidle *v* = **edge**, creep, inch, slink, sneak, steal

siesta *n* = **nap**, catnap, doze, forty winks (*inf*), sleep, snooze (*inf*)

sieve *n* **1 = strainer**, colander ♦ *v* **2 = sift**, a substance with a sieve. **2** examine (information or evidence) to select what is important.

sigh *n* **1** long audible breath expressing sadness, tiredness, relief, or longing. ◆ *v* **2** utter a sigh.

sight 🟑 *n* **1** ability to see. **2** instance of seeing. **3** range of vision. **4** thing seen. **5** *Informal* unsightly thing. **6** device for guiding the eye while using a gun or optical instrument. **7** thing worth seeing. **8** *Informal* a lot. ◆ *v* **9** catch sight of. **sightless** *adj* blind. **sight–read** *v* play or sing printed music without previous preparation. **sightseeing** *n* visiting places of interest. **sightseer** *n*

sign 🟑 *n* **1** indication of something not immediately or outwardly observable. **2** gesture, mark, or symbol conveying a meaning. **3** notice displayed to advertise, inform, or warn. **4** omen. ◆ *v* **5** write (one's name) on (a document or letter) to show its authenticity or one's agreement. **6** communicate using sign language. **7** make a sign or gesture. **sign language** system of communication by gestures, as used by deaf people (also **signing**). **sign on** *v* **1** register as unemployed. **2** sign a document committing oneself to a job, course, etc. **signpost** *n* post bearing a sign that shows the way.

signal 🟑 *n* **1** sign or gesture to convey information. **2** sequence of electrical impulses or radio waves transmitted or received. ◆ *adj* **3** *Formal* very important. ◆ *v* **–nalling, –nalled 4** convey (information) by signal. **signally** *adv* **signal box** building from which railway signals are operated. **signalman** *n* railwayman in charge of signals and points.

signatory *n, pl* **–ries** one of the parties who sign a document.

signature *n* **1** person's name written by himself or herself in signing something. **2** sign at the start of a piece of music to show the key or tempo. **signature tune** tune used to introduce a particular television or radio programme.

signet *n* small seal used to authenticate documents. **signet ring** finger ring bearing a signet.

significant 🟑 *adj* **1** important. **2** having or expressing a meaning. **significantly** *adv* **significance** *n*

signify 🟑 *v* **–fying, –fied 1** indicate or suggest. **2** be a symbol or sign for. **3** be important. **signification** *n*

silage [**sile**–ij] *n* fodder crop harvested while green and partially fermented in a silo.

THESAURUS

separate, strain

sift *v* **1** = **sieve**, filter, separate **2** = **examine**, analyse, go through, investigate, research, scrutinize, work over

sight *n* **1** = **vision**, eye, eyes, eyesight, seeing **3** = **view**, range of vision, visibility **4** = **spectacle**, display, exhibition, pageant, scene, show, vista **5** *Inf* = **eyesore**, mess, monstrosity ◆ *v* **9** = **spot**, behold, catch sight of, discern, distinguish, espy, glimpse, make out, observe, perceive, see

sign *n* **1** = **indication**, clue, evidence, gesture, hint, mark, proof, signal, symptom, token **2** = **symbol**, badge, device, emblem, logo, mark **3** = **notice**, board, placard, warning **4** = **omen**,

augury, auspice, foreboding, portent, warning ◆ *v* **5** = **autograph**, endorse, initial, inscribe **7** = **gesture**, beckon, gesticulate, indicate, signal

signal *n* **1** = **sign**, beacon, cue, gesture, indication, mark, token ◆ *v* **4** = **gesture**, beckon, gesticulate, indicate, motion, sign, wave

significant *adj* **1** = **important**, critical, material, momentous, noteworthy, serious, vital, weighty ≠ **insignificant** **2** = **meaningful**, eloquent, expressive, indicative, suggestive ≠ **meaningless**

signify *v* **1, 2** = **indicate**, be a sign of, betoken, connote, denote, imply, intimate, mean, portend, suggest **3** = **matter**, be important, carry weight,

silence ⊕ n 1 absence of noise or speech.
♦ v 2 make silent. 3 put a stop to. **silent**
adj **silently** adv **silencer** n device to reduce
the noise of an engine exhaust or gun.

silhouette ⊕ n 1 outline of a dark shape
seen against a light background. ♦ v 2
show in silhouette.

silica n hard glossy mineral found as quartz
and in sandstone. **silicosis** n lung disease
caused by inhaling silica dust.

silicon n Chem brittle nonmetallic element
widely used in chemistry and industry.
silicone n tough synthetic substance made
from silicon and used in lubricants, paints,
and resins. **silicon chip** tiny wafer of
silicon processed to form an integrated
circuit.

silk n 1 fibre made by the larva (**silkworm**)
of a certain moth. 2 thread or fabric made
from this. **silky, silken** adj

sill n ledge at the bottom of a window or
door.

silly ⊕ adj –lier, –liest foolish. **silliness** n

silo n, pl –los 1 pit or airtight tower for
storing silage. 2 underground structure in
which nuclear missiles are kept ready for
launching.

silt ⊕ n 1 mud deposited by moving water.
♦ v 2 (foll. by up) fill or be choked with
silt.

silver n 1 white precious metal. 2 coins or
articles made of silver. ♦ adj 3 made of or

of the colour of silver. 4 **silverbeet** n Aust
& NZ leafy green vegetable with white
stalks. **silverfish** n small wingless silver–
coloured insect. **silverside** n cut of beef
from below the rump and above the leg.
silver wedding twenty–fifth wedding
anniversary.

similar ⊕ adj alike but not identical.
similarity n **similarly** adv

✔ **WORD TIP**

Do not confuse *similar* and *same*.
Similar is 'alike but not identical'; *same*
means 'identical'.

simile [**sim**–ill–ee] n figure of speech
comparing one thing to another, using
'as' or 'like', e.g. as blind as a bat.

simmer ⊕ v 1 cook gently at just below
boiling point. 2 be in a state of suppressed
rage. **simmer down** v Informal calm down.

simper ⊕ v 1 smile in a silly or affected
way. 2 utter (something) with a simper. ♦
n 3 simpering smile.

simple ⊕ adj 1 easy to understand or do. 2
plain or unpretentious. 3 not combined or
complex. 4 sincere or frank. 5 feeble-
minded. **simply** adv **simplicity** n **simplify**
v make less complicated. **simplification** n
simplistic adj too simple or naive.
simpleton n foolish or half–witted person.

simulate ⊕ v 1 make a pretence of. 2

——————— THESAURUS ———————

count
silence n 1 = **quiet**, calm, hush, lull, peace,
stillness ♦ v 2 = **quieten**, deaden, gag,
muffle, quiet, stifle, still, suppress
≠ support 3 = **cut off**, cut short

silhouette n 1 = **outline**, form, profile,
shape ♦ v 3 = **outline**, define, delineate,
demarcate, etch, stand out

silly adj = **foolish**, absurd, asinine, daft,
fatuous, idiotic, inane, ridiculous,
senseless, stupid, unwise ≠ **wise**

silt n 1 = **sediment**, alluvium, deposit,
ooze, sludge ♦ v 2 (foll. by up) = **clog up**,
choke up, congest

similar adj = **alike**, analogous, close,

comparable, like, resembling

simmer v 2 = **fume**, be angry, be pissed
(off) (taboo sl), rage, seethe, smoulder

simper v 1 = **smile coyly**, smile affectedly,
smirk

simple adj 1 = **uncomplicated**, clear, easy,
intelligible, lucid, plain, straightforward,
understandable, uninvolved ≠ **involved**
2 = **plain**, classic, homely, humble,
modest, naked, natural, stark,
unembellished, unfussy, unpretentious,
unsophisticated ≠ **elaborate** 3 = **pure**,
elementary, unalloyed, uncombined,
unmixed 4 = **sincere**, artless, bald,
childlike, direct, frank, guileless, honest,

imitate the conditions of (a particular situation). **3** have the appearance of. **simulation** *n* **simulator** *n*

simultaneous ❶ *adj* occurring at the same time.

sin ❶ *n* **1** breaking of a religious or moral law. **2** offence against a principle or standard. ◆ *v* **sinning, sinned 3** commit a sin. **sinful** *adj* **1** guilty of sin. **2** being a sin. **sinfully** *adv* **sinner** *n*

since *prep* **1** during the period of time after. ◆ *conj* **2** from the time when. **3** for the reason that. ◆ *adv* **4** from that time.

> ### ✓ WORD TIP
> Avoid the use of *ago* with *since*. It is redundant: *It is ten years since he wrote his book* (not *ten years ago since*).

sincere ❶ *adj* without pretence or deceit. **sincerely** *adv* **sincerity** *n*

sine *n* (in trigonometry) ratio of the length of the opposite side to that of the hypotenuse in a right-angled triangle.

sinew *n* **1** tough fibrous tissue joining muscle to bone. **2** muscles or strength. **sinewy** *adj*

sing ❶ *v* **singing, sang, sung 1** make musical sounds with the voice. **2** perform (a song). **3** make a humming or whistling sound. **singer** *n* **singsong** *n* **1** informal singing session. ◆ *adj* **2** (of the voice) repeatedly rising and falling in pitch.

> ### ✓ WORD TIP
> The simple past of *sing* is *sang*: *He sang the chorus.* Avoid the use of the past participle *sung* for the simple past.

singe ❶ *v* **singeing, singed 1** burn the surface of. ◆ *n* **2** superficial burn.

single ❶ *adj* **1** one only. **2** distinct from others of the same kind. **3** unmarried. **4** designed for one user. **5** formed of only one part. **6** (of a ticket) valid for an outward journey only. ◆ *n* **7** single thing. **8** thing intended for one person. **9** record with one short song or tune on each side. **10** single ticket. ◆ *pl* **11** game between two players. ◆ *v* **12** (foll. by *out*) pick out from others. **singly** *adv* **single file** (of people or things) arranged in one line. **single-handed** *adj* without assistance. **single-minded** *adj* having one aim only.

singlet *n* sleeveless vest.

singular ❶ *adj* **1** (of a word or form) denoting one person or thing. **2** remarkable, unusual. ◆ *n* **3** singular form of a word. **singularity** *n* **singularly** *adv*

sinister ❶ *adj* threatening or suggesting

——————— THESAURUS ———————

ingenuous, innocent, naive, natural, plain, unaffected ≠ **worldly 5** = **feeble-minded**, dumb (*inf*), foolish, half-witted, moronic, slow, stupid

simulate *v* **1, 2** = **pretend**, act, affect, feign, put on, sham

simultaneous *adj* = **coinciding**, at the same time, coincident, concurrent, contemporaneous, synchronous

sin *n* **1, 2** = **wrongdoing**, crime, error, evil, guilt, iniquity, misdeed, offence, transgression ◆ *v* **3** = **transgress**, err, fall, go astray, lapse, offend

sincere *adj* = **honest**, candid, earnest, frank, genuine, guileless, heartfelt, real, serious, true, unaffected

sing *v* **1, 2** = **warble**, carol, chant, chirp, croon, pipe, trill, yodel **3** = **hum**, buzz, purr, whine

singe *v* **1** = **burn**, char, scorch, sear

single *adj* **1** = **one**, individual, lone, only, separate, sole, solitary **2** = **individual**, distinct, exclusive, separate, undivided, unshared **3** = **unmarried**, free, unattached, unwed **5** = **simple**, unblended, unmixed ◆ *v* **12** (foll. by *out*) = **pick**, choose, distinguish, fix on, pick on or out, select, separate, set apart

singular *adj* **1** = **single**, individual, separate, sole **2 a** = **remarkable**, eminent, exceptional, notable, noteworthy, outstanding ≠ **common b** = **unusual**, curious, eccentric, extraordinary, munted (*NZ sl*), odd, peculiar, queer, strange evil or harm.

sink ⊕ *v* **sinking, sank, sunk** *or* **sunken 1**
submerge (in liquid). **2** descend or cause
to descend. **3** decline in value or amount.
4 become weaker in health. **5** dig or drill
(a hole or shaft). **6** invest (money). **7** *Golf,
snooker* hit (a ball) into a hole or pocket. ◆
n **8** fixed basin with a water supply and
drainage pipe. **sinker** *n* weight for a
fishing line. **sink in** *v* penetrate the mind.

sinuous *adj* **1** curving. **2** lithe.

sinus [**sine**–uss] *n* hollow space in a bone,
esp. an air passage opening into the nose.

sip ⊕ *v* **sipping, sipped 1** drink in small
mouthfuls. ◆ *n* **2** amount sipped.

siphon *n* **1** bent tube which uses air
pressure to draw liquid from a container.
◆ *v* **2** draw off thus. **3** redirect (resources).

sir *n* **1** polite term of address for a man. **2**
(**S–**) title of a knight or baronet.

sire *n* **1** male parent of a horse or other
domestic animal. **2** respectful term of
address to a king. ◆ *v* **3** father.

siren *n* **1** device making a loud wailing
noise as a warning. **2** dangerously alluring
woman.

sirloin *n* prime cut of loin of beef.

sis *interj S Afr informal* exclamation of
disgust.

sissy ⊕ *adj, n, pl* **–sies** weak or cowardly
(person).

sister *n* **1** girl or woman with the same
parents as another person. **2** female
fellow–member of a group. **3** senior nurse.

4 nun. ◆ *adj* **5** closely related, similar.
sisterhood *n* **1** state of being a sister. **2**
group of women united by common aims
or beliefs. **sisterly** *adj* **sister–in–law** *n, pl*
sisters–in–law 1 sister of one's husband or
wife. **2** one's brother's wife.

sit ⊕ *v* **sitting, sat 1** rest one's body
upright on the buttocks. **2** cause to sit. **3**
perch. **4** be situated. **5** pose for a portrait.
6 occupy an official position. **7** (of an
official body) hold a session. **8** take (an
examination). **sitting room** room in a
house where people sit and relax. **sit–in** *n*
protest in which demonstrators occupy a
place and refuse to move.

sitar *n* Indian stringed musical instrument.

site ⊕ *n* **1** place where something is, was,
or is intended to be located. ◆ *v* **2** provide
with a site.

situate *v* place. **situation** *n* **1** state of
affairs. **2** location and surroundings. **3**
position of employment. **situation
comedy** radio or television series involving
the same characters in various situations.

six *adj, n* one more than five. **sixth** *adj, n*
(of) number six in a series. **sixteen** *adj, n*
six and ten. **sixteenth** *adj, n* **sixty** *adj, n* six
times ten. **sixtieth** *adj, n*

size¹ ⊕ *n* **1** dimensions, bigness. **2** one of a
series of standard measurements of goods.
◆ *v* **3** arrange according to size. **sizeable,
sizable** *adj* quite large. **size up** *v Informal*
assess.

size² *n* gluey substance used as a protective

———————| THESAURUS |———————

≠ **normal**

sinister *adj* = **threatening**, dire,
disquieting, evil, malign, menacing,
ominous

sink *v* **1** = **submerge**, founder, go under
2 = **descend**, dip, drop, fall, go down,
lower, plunge, subside ≠ **arise 3** = **fall**,
abate, collapse, drop, lapse, slip, subside
4 = **decline**, decay, decrease, deteriorate,
diminish, dwindle, fade, fail, flag, lessen,
weaken, worsen ≠ **rise 5** = **dig**, bore, drill,
drive, excavate

sip *v* **1** = **drink**, sample, sup, taste ◆ *n*

2 = **swallow**, drop, taste, thimbleful

① **sissy** *adj* b = **wimpish** *or* **wimpy** (*inf*),
cowardly, effeminate, feeble, namby–
pamby, soft (*inf*), unmanly, weak, wet (*Brit
inf*)

② **sissy** *n* a = **wimp** (*inf*), coward,
milksop, mummy's boy, namby–pamby,
softie (*inf*), weakling, wet (*Brit inf*)

sit *v* **1–4** = **rest**, perch, settle **6** = **officiate**,
preside **7** = **convene**, assemble, deliberate,
meet

site *n* **1** = **location**, place, plot, position,
setting, spot ◆ *v* **2** = **locate**, install, place,

coating.

sizzle ⊕ v make a hissing sound like frying fat.

skate[1] n 1 boot with a steel blade or sets of wheels attached to the sole for gliding over ice or a hard surface. ◆ v 2 glide on or as if on skates. **skateboard** n board mounted on small wheels for riding on while standing up. **skate over, round** v avoid discussing or dealing with (a matter) fully.

skate[2] n large marine flatfish.

skein n 1 yarn wound in a loose coil. 2 flock of geese in flight.

skeleton ⊕ n 1 framework of bones inside a person's or animal's body. 2 essential framework of a structure. ◆ adj 3 reduced to a minimum. **skeletal** adj **skeleton key** key which can open many different locks.

sketch ⊕ n 1 rough drawing. 2 brief description. 3 short humorous play. ◆ v 4 make a sketch (of). **sketchy** adj incomplete or inadequate.

skew v 1 make slanting or crooked. ◆ adj 2 slanting or crooked.

skewer n 1 pin to hold meat together during cooking. ◆ v 2 fasten with a skewer.

ski n 1 one of a pair of long runners fastened to boots for gliding over snow or water. ◆ v **skiing, skied** or **ski'd** 2 travel on skis. **skier** n

skid v **skidding, skidded** 1 (of a moving vehicle) slide sideways uncontrollably. ◆ n 2 skidding.

skill ⊕ n 1 special ability or expertise. 2 something requiring special training or expertise. **skilful** adj having or showing skill. **skilfully** adv **skilled** adj

skim ⊕ v **skimming, skimmed** 1 remove floating matter from the surface of (a liquid). 2 glide smoothly over. 3 read quickly. **skimmed, skim milk** milk from which the cream has been removed.

skimp ⊕ v not invest enough time, money, material, etc. **skimpy** adj scanty or insufficient.

skin ⊕ n 1 outer covering of the body. 2 complexion. 3 outer layer or covering. 4 film on a liquid. 5 animal skin used as a material or container. ◆ v **skinning, skinned** 6 remove the skin of. **skinless** adj **skinny** adj thin. **skin–deep** adj superficial. **skin diving** underwater swimming using flippers and light breathing apparatus. **skinflint** n miser. **skinhead** n youth with very short hair.

skint adj Slang having no money.

skip[1] ⊕ v **skipping, skipped** 1 leap lightly from one foot to the other. 2 jump over a rope as it is swung under one. 3 Informal pass over, omit. ◆ n 4 skipping.

skip[2] n large open container for builders' rubbish.

skipper n, v captain.

skirmish ⊕ n 1 brief or minor fight or argument. ◆ v 2 take part in a skirmish.

skirt ⊕ n 1 woman's garment hanging

position, set, situate

size[1] n 1 = **dimensions**, amount, bulk, extent, immensity, magnitude, mass, proportions, range, volume

sizzle v = **hiss**, crackle, frizzle, fry, spit

skeleton n 2 = **framework**, frame, outline, structure

sketch n 1 = **drawing**, delineation, design, draft, outline, plan ◆ v 4 = **draw**, delineate, depict, draft, outline, represent, rough out

skill n 1 = **expertise**, ability, art, cleverness, competence, craft, dexterity, facility,

knack, proficiency, skilfulness, talent, technique

skim v 1 = **separate**, cream 2 = **glide**, coast, float, fly, sail, soar 3 = **scan**, glance, run one's eye over

skimp v = **stint**, be mean with, be sparing with, cut corners, scamp, scrimp

skin n 3 = **coating**, casing, crust, film, husk, outside, peel, rind 5 = **hide**, fell, pelt ◆ v 6 = **peel**, flay, scrape

skip[1] v 1 = **hop**, bob, bounce, caper, dance, flit, frisk, gambol, prance, trip 3 Inf = **pass over**, eschew, give (something) a from the waist. **2** part of a dress or coat below the waist. **3** cut of beef from the flank. ◆ *v* **4** border. **5** go round. **6** avoid dealing with (an issue). **skirting board** narrow board round the bottom of an interior wall.

skit ⓣ *n* brief satirical sketch.

skite *v, n Aust & NZ* boast.

skittish ⓣ *adj* playful or lively.

skive ⓣ *v Informal* evade work or responsibility.

skivvy *n, pl* **–vies** female servant who does menial work.

skulduggery ⓣ *n Informal* trickery.

skulk ⓣ *v* **1** move stealthily. **2** lurk.

skull *n* bony framework of the head. **skullcap** *n* close–fitting brimless cap.

skunk *n* **1** small black–and–white N American mammal which emits a foul–smelling fluid when attacked. **2** *Slang* despicable person.

sky ⓣ *n, pl* **skies** upper atmosphere as seen from the earth. **skydiving** *n* sport of jumping from an aircraft and performing manoeuvres before opening one's parachute. **skylark** *n* lark that sings while soaring at a great height. **skylight** *n* window in a roof or ceiling. **skyscraper** *n*

very tall building.

slab ⓣ *n* broad flat piece.

slack ⓣ *adj* **1** not tight. **2** negligent. **3** not busy. ◆ *n* **4** slack part. ◆ *pl* **5** informal trousers. ◆ *v* **6** neglect one's work or duty. **slackness** *n* **slacken** *v* make or become slack. **slacker** *n*

slag ⓣ *n* **1** waste left after metal is smelted. ◆ *v* **slagging, slagged 2** (foll. by *off*) *Slang* criticize.

slake ⓣ *v* **1** satisfy (thirst or desire). **2** combine (quicklime) with water.

slalom *n* skiing or canoeing race over a winding course.

slam ⓣ *v* **slamming, slammed 1** shut, put down, or hit violently and noisily. **2** *Informal* criticize harshly. ◆ *n* **3** act or sound of slamming.

slang *n* very informal language. **slangy** *adj* **slanging match** abusive argument.

slant ⓣ *v* **1** lean at an angle, slope. **2** present (information) in a biased way. ◆ *n* **3** slope. **4** point of view, esp. a biased one. **slanting** *adj*

slap ⓣ *n* **1** blow with the open hand or a flat object. ◆ *v* **slapping, slapped 2** strike with the open hand or a flat object. **3** *Informal* place forcefully or carelessly.

miss, leave out, miss out, omit

skirmish *n* **1** = **fight**, battle, brush, clash, conflict, encounter, fracas, scrap (*inf*) ◆ *v* **2** = **fight**, clash, collide

skirt *v* **4** = **border**, edge, flank **5, 6** = **avoid**, circumvent, evade, steer clear of

skit *n* = **parody**, burlesque, sketch, spoof (*inf*), takeoff (*inf*)

skittish *adj* = **lively**, excitable, fidgety, highly strung, jumpy, nervous, restive, wired (*sl*)

skive *v Inf* = **slack**, idle, malinger, shirk, swing the lead

skulduggery *n Inf* = **trickery**, double–dealing, duplicity, machinations, underhandedness

skulk *v* **1** = **sneak**, creep, prowl, slink **2** = **lurk**, lie in wait, loiter

sky *n* **1** = **heavens**, firmament

slab *n* = **piece**, chunk, lump, portion, slice, wedge

slack *adj* **1** = **loose**, baggy, lax, limp, relaxed ≠ stretched **2** = **negligent**, lax, neglectful, remiss, slapdash, slipshod ≠ strict **3** = **inactive**, idle, lazy ◆ *n* **4** = **room**, excess, give (*inf*), leeway ◆ *v* **6** = **shirk**, dodge, evade, get out of, idle, shun, sidestep, skive (*Brit sl*)

slag *v* **3** (foll. by *off*) *Sl* = **criticize**, abuse, deride, insult, malign, mock, slander, slate

slake *v* **1** = **satisfy**, assuage, quench, sate

slam *v* **1 a** = **bang**, crash, smash **b** = **throw**, dash, fling, hurl

slant *v* **1** = **slope**, bend, bevel, cant, heel, incline, lean, list, tilt **2** = **bias**, angle, colour, distort, twist ◆ *n* **3** = **slope**, camber, gradient, incline, tilt **4** = **bias**, angle, emphasis, one–sidedness, point of

slapdash adj careless and hasty. **slap-happy** adj Informal cheerfully careless.

slapstick n boisterous knockabout comedy. **slap-up** adj (of a meal) large and luxurious.

slash ❶ v 1 cut with a sweeping stroke. 2 gash. 3 reduce drastically. ◆ n 4 sweeping stroke. 5 gash.

slat n narrow strip of wood or metal.

slate¹ n 1 rock which splits easily into thin layers. 2 piece of this for covering a roof or, formerly, for writing on. ◆ v 3 cover with slates. 4 US plan or arrange. ◆ adj 5 dark grey.

slate² ❶ v Informal criticize harshly. **slating** n

slaughter ❶ v 1 kill (animals) for food. 2 kill (people) savagely or indiscriminately ◆ n 3 slaughtering. **slaughterhouse** n place where animals are killed for food.

slave ❶ n 1 person owned by another for whom he or she has to work. 2 person dominated by another or by a habit. 3 drudge. ◆ v 4 work like a slave. **slavery** n 1 state or condition of being a slave. 2 practice of owning slaves. **slavish** adj 1 of or like a slave. 2 imitative. **slave-driver** n person who makes others work very hard.

slaver [slav-ver] v dribble saliva from the mouth.

slay ❶ v slaying, slew, slain kill.

sleazy ❶ adj -zier, -ziest run-down or sordid. **sleaze** n

sledge¹, sled n 1 carriage on runners for sliding on snow. 2 light wooden frame for sliding over snow. ◆ v 3 travel by sledge.

sledge², sledgehammer n heavy hammer with a long handle.

sleek ❶ adj glossy, smooth, and shiny.

sleep ❶ n 1 state of rest characterized by unconsciousness. 2 period of this. ◆ v sleeping, slept 3 be in or as if in a state of sleep. 4 have sleeping accommodation for (a specified number). **sleeper** n 1 railway car fitted for sleeping in. 2 beam supporting the rails of a railway. 3 ring worn in a pierced ear to stop the hole from closing up. 4 person who sleeps. **sleepy** adj **sleepily** adv **sleepiness** n **sleepless** adj **sleeping bag** padded bag for sleeping in. **sleepout** n NZ small building for sleeping in. **sleep with, together** v have sexual intercourse (with).

sleet n rain and snow or hail falling together.

sleeve n 1 part of a garment which covers the arm. 2 tubelike cover. 3 gramophone record cover. **up one's sleeve** secretly ready.

sleigh n, v sledge.

slender ❶ adj 1 slim. 2 small in amount.

sleuth ❶ [slooth] n detective.

---

view, prejudice

slap n 1 = **smack**, blow, cuff, spank, swipe ◆ v 2 = **smack**, clap, cuff, spank, swipe

slash v 1, 2 = **cut**, gash, hack, lacerate, rend, rip, score, slit 3 = **reduce**, cut, drop, lower ◆ n 5 = **cut**, gash, incision, laceration, rent, rip, slit

slate² v Inf = **criticize**, censure, rebuke, rouse on (Aust), scold, tear into (inf)

slaughter v 2 = **slay**, butcher, kill, massacre, murder ◆ n 3 = **slaying**, bloodshed, butchery, carnage, killing, massacre, murder

slave n 1 = **servant**, serf, vassal 3 = **drudge**, skivvy (chiefly Brit) ◆ v 4 = **toil**, drudge, slog

slay v = **kill**, butcher, massacre, mow down, murder, slaughter

sleazy adj = **sordid**, disreputable, low, run-down, scungy (Aust & NZ sl), seedy, squalid

sleek adj 1 = **glossy**, lustrous, shiny, smooth ≠ rough

sleep n 1, 2 = **slumber(s)**, doze, forty winks (inf), hibernation, nap, siesta, snooze (inf), zizz (Brit inf) ◆ v 3 = **slumber**, catnap, doze, drowse, hibernate, snooze (inf), take a nap

slender adj 1 = **slim**, lean, narrow, slight, willowy ≠ fat 2 = **meagre**, little, scant, scanty, small ≠ large

sleuth n = **detective**, private eye (inf),

slice ⓸ *n* 1 thin flat piece cut from something. 2 share. 3 kitchen tool with a broad flat blade. 4 *Sport* hitting of a ball so that it travels obliquely. ◆ *v* 5 cut into slices. 6 *Sport* hit (a ball) with a slice.

slick *adj* 1 persuasive and glib. 2 skilfully devised or carried out. 3 well–made and attractive, but superficial. ◆ *n* 4 patch of oil on water. ◆ *v* 5 make smooth or sleek.

slide ⓸ *v* **sliding, slid** 1 slip smoothly along (a surface). 2 pass unobtrusively. ◆ *n* 3 sliding. 4 piece of glass holding an object to be viewed under a microscope. 5 photographic transparency. 6 surface or structure for sliding on or down. 7 ornamental hair clip. **slide rule** mathematical instrument formerly used for rapid calculations. **sliding scale** variable scale according to which things such as wages alter in response to changes in other factors.

slight ⓸ *adj* 1 small in quantity or extent. 2 not important. 3 slim and delicate. ◆ *v, n* 4 snub. **slightly** *adv*

slim ⓸ *adj* **slimmer, slimmest** 1 not heavy or stout, thin. 2 slight. ◆ *v* **slimming, slimmed** 3 make or become slim by diet and exercise. **slimmer** *n*

slime *n* unpleasant thick slippery substance. **slimy** *adj* 1 of, like, or covered with slime. 2 ingratiating.

sling ⓸ *n* 1 bandage hung from the neck to support an injured hand or arm. 2 rope or strap for lifting something. 3 strap with a string at each end for throwing a stone. ◆ *v* **slinging, slung** 4 throw. 5 carry, hang, or throw with or as if with a sling. **slingback** *n* shoe with a strap that goes around the back of the heel.

slink ⓸ *v* **slinking, slunk** move furtively or guiltily. **slinky** *adj* (of clothes) figure–hugging.

slip¹ ⓸ *v* **slipping, slipped** 1 lose balance by sliding. 2 move smoothly, easily, or quietly. 3 place quickly or stealthily. 4 (foll. by *on* or *off*) put on or take off easily or quickly. 5 pass out of (the mind). 6 become worse. 7 dislocate (a bone). ◆ *n* 8 slipping. 9 mistake. 10 petticoat. 11 *Cricket* fielding position behind and to the offside of the wicketkeeper. **give someone the slip** escape from someone. **slippy** *adj Informal* slippery. **slipknot** *n* knot tied so that it will slip along the rope round which it is made. **slip–on** *adj* (of a garment or shoe) made to be put on easily. **slipped disc** painful condition in which one of the discs connecting the bones of the spine becomes displaced. **slip road** narrow road giving access to a motorway. **slipshod** *adj* (of an action) careless. **slipstream** *n* stream of air forced backwards by a fast–moving object. **slip up** *v* make a mistake. **slipway** *n* launching slope on which ships are built or repaired.

slip² ⓸ *n* 1 small piece (of paper). 2 cutting from a plant. 3 slender person.

slipper *n* light shoe for indoor wear.

(private) investigator

slice *n* 1, 2 = **piece**, cut, helping, portion, segment, share, sliver, wedge ◆ *v* 5, 6 = **cut**, carve, divide, sever

slick *adj* 1 = **glib**, plausible, polished, smooth, specious 2 = **skilful**, adroit, deft, dexterous, polished, professional ≠ **amateur** ◆ *v* 5 = **smooth**, plaster down, sleek

slide *v* 1 = **slip**, coast, glide, skim, slither

slight *adj* 2 = **small**, feeble, insignificant, meagre, measly, minor, paltry, scanty, trifling, trivial, unimportant ≠ **great**

3 = **slim**, delicate, feeble, fragile, lightly–built, small, spare ≠ **solid** ◆ *v, n* 4 = **snub**, affront, disdain, ignore, insult, rebuff, scorn, slap in the face (*inf*) ≠ **praise**

slim *adj* 1 = **slender**, lean, narrow, slight, svelte, thin, trim ≠ **wide** 2 = **slight**, faint, poor, remote, slender ≠ **good** ◆ *v* 3 = **lose weight**, diet, reduce ≠ **put on weight**

sling *v* 4 = **throw**, cast, chuck (*inf*), fling, heave, hurl, lob (*inf*), shy, toss 5 = **hang**, dangle, suspend

slink *v* = **creep**, prowl, skulk, slip, sneak, steal

slippery ① adj 1 so smooth or wet as to cause slipping or be difficult to hold. 2 (of a person) untrustworthy.

slit ① n 1 long narrow cut or opening. ◆ v **slitting, slit** 2 make a long straight cut in.

slither ① v slide unsteadily.

sliver ① [sliv-ver] n small thin piece.

slob ① n Informal lazy and untidy person.

slobber ① v dribble or drool. **slobbery** adj

slog ① v **slogging, slogged** 1 work hard and steadily. 2 make one's way with difficulty. 3 hit hard. ◆ n 4 long and exhausting work or walk.

slogan ① n catchword or phrase used in politics or advertising.

slop ① v **slopping, slopped** 1 splash or spill. ◆ n 2 spilt liquid. 3 liquid food. ◆ pl 4 liquid refuse and waste food used to feed animals. **sloppy** adj 1 careless or untidy. 2 gushingly sentimental.

slope ① v 1 slant. ◆ n 2 sloping surface. 3 degree of inclination. ◆ pl 4 hills. **slope off** v Informal go furtively.

slot ① n 1 narrow opening for inserting something. 2 Informal place in a series or scheme. ◆ v **slotting, slotted** 3 make a slot or slots in. 4 fit into a slot. **slot machine** automatic machine worked by placing a coin in a slot.

sloth ① [rhymes with **both**] n 1 slow-moving animal of tropical America. 2 laziness. **slothful** adj lazy or idle.

slouch ① v 1 sit, stand, or move with a drooping posture. ◆ n 2 drooping posture. **be no slouch** Informal be very good or talented.

slovenly ① adj 1 dirty or untidy. 2 careless.

slow ① adj 1 taking a longer time than is usual or expected. 2 not fast. 3 (of a clock or watch) showing a time earlier than the correct one. 4 stupid. ◆ v 5 reduce the speed (of). **slowly** adv **slowness** n **slowcoach** n Informal person who moves or works slowly.

THESAURUS

slip¹ v 1 = **fall**, skid 2 = **slide**, glide, skate, slither 3 = **sneak**, conceal, creep, hide, steal ◆ n 9 = **mistake**, blunder, error, failure, fault, lapse, omission, oversight **give someone the slip** = **escape from**, dodge, elude, evade, get away from, lose (someone) **slip up** ◆ v = **make a mistake**, blunder, err, miscalculate

slip² n 1 = **strip**, piece, sliver 2 = **cutting**, offshoot, runner, scion, shoot, sprig, sprout

slippery adj 1 = **smooth**, glassy, greasy, icy, slippy (inf), unsafe 2 = **untrustworthy**, crafty, cunning, devious, dishonest, evasive, shifty, tricky

slit n 1 = **cut**, gash, incision, opening, rent, split, tear ◆ v 2 = **cut (open)**, gash, knife, lance, pierce, rip, slash

slither v = **slide**, glide, slink, slip, snake, undulate

sliver n = **shred**, fragment, paring, shaving, splinter

slob n Inf = **layabout**, couch potato (sl), good-for-nothing, idler, loafer, lounger

slobber v = **drool**, dribble, drivel, salivate, slaver

slog v 1 = **work**, labour, plod, plough through, slave, toil 2 = **trudge**, tramp, trek 3 = **hit**, punch, slug, sock (sl), strike, thump, wallop (inf) ◆ n 4 a = **labour**, effort, exertion, struggle b = **trudge**, hike, tramp, trek

slogan n = **catch phrase**, catchword, motto, tag-line

slop v 1 = **spill**, overflow, slosh (inf), splash

slope v 1 = **slant**, drop away, fall, incline, lean, rise, tilt ◆ n 2 = **incline**, ramp, rise, slant, tilt 3 = **inclination**, gradient **slope off** ◆ v Inf = **slink away**, creep away, slip away

slot n 1 = **opening**, aperture, groove, hole, slit, vent 2 Inf = **place**, opening, position, space, time, vacancy ◆ v 4 = **fit in**, fit, insert

sloth n 2 = **laziness**, idleness, inactivity, inertia, slackness, sluggishness, torpor

slouch v 1 = **slump**, droop, loll, stoop

slovenly adj 1 = **untidy**, disorderly 2 = **careless**, negligent, slack, slapdash, slipshod, sloppy (inf) ≠ **careful**

sludge ⊕ *n* 1 thick mud. 2 sewage.

slug[1] *n* land snail with no shell. **sluggish** *adj* slow–moving, lacking energy. **sluggishly** *adv* **sluggishness** *n* **sluggard** *n* lazy person.

slug[2] *n* 1 bullet. 2 *Informal* mouthful of an alcoholic drink.

slug[3] *v* **slugging, slugged** 1 hit hard. ◆ *n* 2 heavy blow.

sluice *n* 1 channel carrying off water. 2 sliding gate used to control the flow of water in this. 3 water controlled by a sluice. ◆ *v* 4 pour a stream of water over or through.

slum *n* 1 squalid overcrowded house or area. ◆ *v* **slumming, slummed** 2 temporarily and deliberately experience poorer places or conditions than usual.

slumber ⊕ *v, n Lit* sleep.

slump ⊕ *v* 1 (of prices or demand) decline suddenly. 2 sink or fall heavily. ◆ *n* 3 sudden decline in prices or demand. 4 time of substantial unemployment.

slur ⊕ *v* **slurring, slurred** 1 pronounce or utter (words) indistinctly. 2 *Music* sing or play (notes) smoothly without a break. ◆ *n* 3 slurring of words. 4 remark intended to discredit someone. 5 *Music* slurring of notes. 6 curved line indicating notes to be slurred.

slurp *Informal* ◆ *v* 1 eat or drink noisily. ◆ *n* 2 slurping sound.

slurry *n, pl* **–ries** muddy liquid mixture.

slush *n* 1 watery muddy substance. 2 sloppy sentimental talk or writing. **slushy** *adj* **slush fund** fund for financing bribery or corruption.

slut ⊕ *n Offens* dirty or immoral woman. **sluttish** *adj*

sly ⊕ *adj* **slyer, slyest** *or* **slier, sliest** 1 crafty. 2 secretive and cunning. 3 roguish. **on the sly** secretly. **slyly** *adv* **slyness** *n*

smack[1] ⊕ *v* 1 slap sharply. 2 open and close (the lips) loudly in enjoyment or anticipation. ◆ *n* 3 sharp slap. 4 loud kiss. 5 slapping sound. ◆ *adv* 6 *Informal* squarely or directly, e.g. *smack in the middle*. **smacker** *n Slang* 1 loud kiss. 2 pound note or dollar bill.

smack[2] *n* 1 slight flavour or trace. 2 *Slang* heroin. ◆ *v* 3 have a slight flavour or trace (of).

small ⊕ *adj* 1 not large in size, number, or amount. 2 unimportant. 3 mean or petty. ◆ *n* 4 narrow part of the lower back. ◆ *pl* 5 *Informal* underwear. **smallness** *n*

slow *adj* 1 = **late**, backward, behind, delayed, lingering, long–drawn–out, prolonged, protracted, tardy 2 = **unhurried**, dawdling, gradual, lackadaisical, laggard, lazy, leisurely, ponderous, sluggish 4 = **stupid**, braindead (*inf*), dense, dim, dozy (*Brit inf*), dull–witted, obtuse, retarded, thick ≠ **quick** ◆ *v* 5 = **reduce speed**, brake, decelerate, handicap, hold up, retard, slacken (off) ≠ **accelerate**

sludge *n* 1 = **sediment**, mire, muck, mud, ooze, residue, silt, slime

slum *n* 1 = **hovel**, ghetto

slumber *v Lit* = **sleep**, doze, drowse, nap, snooze (*inf*), zizz (*Brit inf*)

slump *v* 1 = **fall**, collapse, crash, plunge, sink, slip ≠ **increase** 2 = **sag**, droop, hunch, loll, slouch ◆ *n* 3 = **fall**, collapse, crash, decline, downturn, drop, reverse, trough ≠ **increase** 4 = **recession**, depression

slur *n* 4 = **insult**, affront, aspersion, calumny, innuendo, insinuation, smear, stain

slut *n Offens* = **tart**, scrubber (*Brit & Aust sl*), slag (*Brit sl*), slapper (*Brit sl*), trollop

sly *adj* 1, 2 = **cunning**, artful, clever, crafty, devious, scheming, secret, shifty, stealthy, subtle, underhand, wily ≠ **open** 3 = **roguish**, arch, impish, knowing, mischievous **on the sly** = **secretly**, covertly, on the quiet, privately, surreptitiously

smack[1] *v* 1 = **slap**, clap, cuff, hit, spank, strike, swipe ◆ *n* 3 = **slap**, blow, swipe ◆ *adv* 6 *Inf* = **directly**, exactly, precisely, right, slap (*inf*), squarely, straight

smallholding n small area of farming land.
small hours hours just after midnight.
small-minded adj intolerant, petty.
smallpox n contagious disease with blisters that leave scars. **small talk** light social conversation. **small-time** adj insignificant or minor.

smart ❶ adj 1 well-kept and neat. 2 astute. 3 witty. 4 fashionable. 5 brisk. ◆ v 6 feel or cause stinging pain. ◆ n 7 stinging pain. **smart aleck** Informal irritatingly clever person. **smart card** plastic card used for storing and processing computer data. **smarten** v make or become smart.

smash ❶ v 1 break violently and noisily. 2 throw (against) violently. 3 collide forcefully. 4 destroy. ◆ n 5 act or sound of smashing. 6 violent collision of vehicles. 7 Informal popular success. 8 Sport powerful overhead shot. **smasher** n Informal attractive person or thing. **smashing** adj Informal excellent.

smattering ❶ n slight knowledge.

smear ❶ v 1 spread with a greasy or sticky substance. 2 rub so as to produce a dirty mark or smudge. 3 slander. ◆ n 4 dirty mark or smudge. 5 slander. 6 Med sample of a secretion smeared on to a slide for examination under a microscope.

smell ❶ v smelling, smelt or smelled 1 perceive (a scent or odour) by means of the nose. 2 have or give off a smell. 3 have

an unpleasant smell. 4 detect by instinct. ◆ n 5 ability to perceive odours by the nose. 6 odour or scent. 7 smelling. **smelly** adj having a nasty smell. **smelling salts** preparation of ammonia used to revive a person who feels faint.

smelt v extract (a metal) from (an ore) by heating. **smelter** n

smile n 1 turning up of the corners of the mouth to show pleasure, amusement, or friendliness. ◆ v 2 give a smile. **smile on, upon** v regard favourably.

smirk ❶ n 1 smug smile. ◆ v 2 give a smirk.

smite v smiting, smote, smitten 1 Old-fashioned strike hard. 2 affect severely.

smith n worker in metal. **smithy** n blacksmith's workshop.

smithereens pl n shattered fragments.

smock n 1 loose overall. 2 woman's loose blouselike garment. ◆ v 3 gather (material) by sewing in a honeycomb pattern. **smocking** n

smog n mixture of smoke and fog.

smoke n 1 cloudy mass that rises from something burning. 2 act of smoking tobacco. ◆ v 3 give off smoke. 4 inhale and expel smoke of (a cigar, cigarette, or pipe). 5 do this habitually. 6 cure (meat, fish, or cheese) by treating with smoke. **smokeless** adj **smoker** n **smoky** adj **smoke screen** something said or done to

———— THESAURUS ————

small adj 1 = **little**, diminutive, mini, miniature, minute, petite, pygmy or pigmy, teeny, teeny-weeny, tiny, undersized, wee ≠ **great** 2 = **unimportant**, insignificant, minor, negligible, paltry, petty, trifling, trivial ≠ **major** 3 = **petty**, base, mean, narrow

smart adj 1 = **neat**, spruce, trim 2 = **astute**, acute, bright, canny, clever, ingenious, intelligent, keen, shrewd ≠ **thick** 3 = **sharp**, quick 4 = **chic**, elegant, natty (inf), snappy, stylish ≠ **scruffy** 5 = **brisk**, lively, quick, vigorous ◆ v 6 = **sting**, burn, hurt ◆ n 7 = **sting**, pain, soreness

smash v 1 = **break**, crush, demolish,

pulverize, shatter 3 = **collide**, crash 4 = **destroy**, lay waste, ruin, trash (sl), wreck ◆ n 5 = **destruction**, collapse, downfall, failure, ruin 6 = **collision**, accident, crash

smattering n = **modicum**, bit, rudiments

smear v 1 = **spread over**, bedaub, coat, cover, daub, rub on 2 = **dirty**, smudge, soil, stain, sully 3 = **slander**, besmirch, blacken, malign ◆ n 4 = **smudge**, blot, blotch, daub, splotch, streak 5 = **slander**, calumny, defamation, libel

smell v 1 = **sniff**, scent 3 = **stink**, pong (Brit inf), reek ◆ n 7 = **odour**, aroma, bouquet, fragrance, perfume, scent hide the truth.

smooth ⓣ *adj* 1 even in surface, texture, or consistency. 2 without obstructions or difficulties. 3 charming and polite but possibly insincere. 4 free from jolts. 5 not harsh in taste. ◆ *v* 6 make smooth. 7 calm. **smoothly** *adv*

smother ⓣ *v* 1 suffocate or stifle. 2 suppress. 3 cover thickly.

smoulder ⓣ *v* 1 burn slowly with smoke but no flame. 2 (of feelings) exist in a suppressed state.

smudge ⓣ *v* 1 make or become smeared or soiled. ◆ *n* 2 dirty mark. 3 blurred form. **smudgy** *adj*

smug ⓣ *adj* smugger, smuggest self-satisfied.

smuggle *v* 1 import or export (goods) secretly and illegally. 2 take somewhere secretly. **smuggler** *n*

smut *n* 1 obscene jokes, pictures, etc. 2 speck of soot or dark mark left by soot. **smutty** *adj*

snack ⓣ *n* light quick meal. **snack bar** place where snacks are sold.

snag ⓣ *n* 1 difficulty or disadvantage. 2 sharp projecting point. 3 hole in fabric caused by a sharp object. ◆ *v* snagging, snagged 4 catch or tear on a point.

snail *n* slow-moving mollusc with a spiral

shell. **snail's pace** very slow speed.

snake *n* 1 long thin scaly limbless reptile. ◆ *v* 2 move in a winding course like a snake. **snaky** *adj* twisted or winding.

snap ⓣ *v* snapping, snapped 1 break suddenly. 2 (cause to) make a sharp cracking sound. 3 move suddenly. 4 bite (at) suddenly. 5 speak sharply and angrily. 6 take a snapshot of. ◆ *n* 7 act or sound of snapping. 8 *Informal* snapshot. 9 sudden brief spell of cold weather. 11 card game in which the word 'snap' is called when two similar cards are put down. ◆ *adj* 12 made on the spur of the moment. **snappy** *adj* 1 (also **snappish**) irritable. 2 *Slang* quick. 3 *Slang* smart and fashionable. **snapshot** *n* informal photograph. **snap up** *v* take eagerly and quickly.

snare ⓣ *n* 1 trap with a noose. ◆ *v* 2 catch in or as if in a snare.

snarl[1] *v* 1 (of an animal) growl with bared teeth. 2 speak or utter fiercely. ◆ *n* 3 act or sound of snarling.

snarl[2] ⓣ *n* 1 tangled mess. ◆ *v* 2 make tangled. **snarl-up** *n Informal* confused situation such as a traffic jam.

snatch ⓣ *v* 1 seize or try to seize suddenly. 2 take (food, rest, etc.) hurriedly. ◆ *n* 3 snatching. 4 fragment.

sneak ⓣ *v* 1 move furtively. 2 bring, take,

smirk *n* 1 = **smug look**, simper

smooth *adj* 1 = **even**, flat, flush, horizontal, level, plane ≠ **rough** 2 = **easy**, effortless, well-ordered 3 = **suave**, facile, glib, persuasive, slick, smarmy (*Brit inf*), unctuous, urbane 4 = **flowing**, regular, rhythmic, steady, uniform 5 = **mellow**, agreeable, mild, pleasant ◆ *v* 6 = **flatten**, iron, level, plane, press 7 = **ease**, appease, assuage, calm, mitigate, mollify, soften, soothe ≠ **aggravate**

smother *v* 1 a = **suffocate**, choke, strangle b = **extinguish**, snuff, stifle 3 = **suppress**, conceal, hide, muffle, repress, stifle

smoulder *v* 2 = **seethe**, boil, fume, rage, simmer

smudge *v* 1 = **smear**, daub, dirty, mark,

smirch ◆ *n* 2 = **smear**, blemish, blot

smug *adj* = **self-satisfied**, complacent, conceited, superior

snack *n* = **light meal**, bite, refreshment(s)

snag *n* 1 = **difficulty**, catch, complication, disadvantage, downside, drawback, hitch, obstacle, problem ◆ *v* 4 = **catch**, rip, tear

snap *v* 1 = **break**, crack, separate 2 = **crackle**, click, pop 4 = **bite at**, bite, nip, snatch 5 = **speak sharply**, bark, jump down (someone's) throat (*inf*), lash out at ◆ *n* 7 = **crackle**, pop ◆ *adj* 12 = **instant**, immediate, spur-of-the-moment, sudden

snare *n* 1 = **trap**, gin, net, noose, wire ◆ *v* 2 = **trap**, catch, entrap, net, seize, wire

snarl[2] *v* 2 = **tangle**, entangle, entwine, muddle, ravel or put furtively. **3** *Informal* tell tales. ◆ *n* **4** cowardly or underhand person. **sneaking** *adj* **1** slight but persistent. **2** secret. **sneaky** *adj*

sneer ❶ *n* **1** contemptuous expression or remark. ◆ *v* **2** show contempt by a sneer.

sneeze *v* **1** expel air from the nose suddenly, involuntarily, and noisily. ◆ *n* **2** act or sound of sneezing.

snide ❶ *adj* critical in an unfair and nasty way.

sniff ❶ *v* **1** inhale through the nose in short audible breaths. **2** smell by sniffing. ◆ *n* **3** act or sound of sniffing. **sniffle** *v* **1** sniff repeatedly, as when suffering from a cold. ◆ *n* **2** slight cold. **sniff at** *v* express contempt for.

snigger ❶ *n* **1** sly disrespectful laugh, esp. one partly stifled. ◆ *v* **2** utter a snigger.

snip ❶ *v* **snipping, snipped 1** cut in small quick strokes with scissors or shears. ◆ *n* **2** *Informal* bargain. **3** act or sound of snipping. **snippet** *n* small piece.

snipe ❶ *n* **1** wading bird with a long straight bill. ◆ *v* **2** (foll. by *at*) shoot at (a person) from cover. **3** make critical remarks about. **sniper** *n*

snivel ❶ *v* **-elling, -elled** cry in a whining way.

snob ❶ *n* **1** person who judges others by social rank. **2** person who feels smugly superior in his or her tastes or interests.

snobbery *n* **snobbish** *adj*

snooker *n* **1** game played on a billiard table. ◆ *v* **2** leave (a snooker opponent) in a position such that another ball blocks the target ball. **3** *Informal* put (someone) in a position where he or she can do nothing.

snoop ❶ *Informal* ◆ *v* **1** pry. ◆ *n* **2** snooping.

snooty *adj* **snootier, snootiest** *Informal* haughty.

snooze ❶ *Informal* ◆ *v* **1** take a brief light sleep. ◆ *n* **2** brief light sleep.

snore *v* **1** make snorting sounds while sleeping. ◆ *n* **2** sound of snoring.

snorkel *n* **1** tube allowing a swimmer to breathe while face down on the surface of the water. ◆ *v* **-kelling, -kelled 2** swim using a snorkel.

snort *v* **1** exhale noisily through the nostrils. **2** express contempt or anger by snorting. ◆ *n* **3** act or sound of snorting.

snout *n* animal's projecting nose and jaws.

snow *n* **1** frozen vapour falling from the sky in flakes. **2** *Slang* cocaine. ◆ *v* **3** fall as or like snow. **be snowed under** be overwhelmed, esp. with paperwork. **snowy** *adj* **snowball** *n* **1** snow pressed into a ball for throwing. ◆ *v* **2** increase rapidly. **snowdrift** *n* bank of deep snow. **snowdrop** *n* small white bell-shaped spring flower. **snowflake** *n* single crystal

---

THESAURUS

snatch *v* **1** = **seize**, clutch, grab, grasp, grip **2** = **grab** ◆ *n* **4** = **bit**, fragment, part, piece, snippet

sneak *v* **1** = **slink**, lurk, pad, skulk, slip, steal **2** = **slip**, smuggle, spirit **3** *Inf* = **inform on**, grass on (*Brit sl*), shop (*sl, chiefly Brit*), tell on (*inf*), tell tales ◆ *n* **4** = **informer**, telltale

sneer *n* **1** = **scorn**, derision, gibe, jeer, mockery, ridicule ◆ *v* **2** = **scorn**, deride, disdain, jeer, laugh, mock, ridicule

snide *adj* = **nasty**, cynical, disparaging, hurtful, ill-natured, malicious, sarcastic, scornful, sneering, spiteful

sniff *v* **1, 2** = **inhale**, breathe, smell

snigger *n, v* = **laugh**, giggle, snicker, titter

snip *v* **1** = **cut**, clip, crop, dock, shave, trim ◆ *n* **2** *Inf* = **bargain**, giveaway, good buy, steal (*inf*) **4** = **bit**, clipping, fragment, piece, scrap, shred

snipe *v* **3** = **criticize**, carp, denigrate, disparage, jeer, knock (*inf*), put down

snivel *v* **1** = **whine**, cry, grizzle (*inf, chiefly Brit*), moan, whimper, whinge (*inf*) **2** = **sniffle**

snob *n* = **elitist**, highbrow, prig

snoop *Inf v* **1** = **pry**, interfere, poke one's nose in (*inf*), spy

snooze *Inf v* **1** = **doze**, catnap, nap, take forty winks (*inf*) ◆ *n* **2** = **doze**, catnap, of snow. **snowman** n figure shaped out of snow. **snowplough** n vehicle for clearing away snow. **snowshoes** pl n racket–shaped shoes for travelling on snow.

snub ❶ v snubbing, snubbed 1 insult deliberately. ◆ n 2 deliberate insult. ◆ adj 3 (of a nose) short and blunt. **snub–nosed** adj

snuff¹ n powdered tobacco for sniffing up the nostrils.

snuff² v extinguish (a candle). **snuff it** Informal die.

snuffle v breathe noisily or with difficulty.

snug ❶ adj snugger, snuggest 1 warm and comfortable. 2 comfortably close–fitting. ◆ n 3 small room in a pub. **snugly** adv

snuggle ❶ v nestle into a person or thing for warmth or from affection.

so adv 1 to such an extent. 2 in such a manner. 3 very. 4 also. 5 thereupon. ◆ conj 6 in order that. 7 with the result that. 8 therefore. ◆ interj 9 exclamation of surprise, triumph, or realization. **so–and–so** n 1 Informal person whose name is not specified. 2 unpleasant person or thing. **so–called** adj called (in the speaker's opinion, wrongly) by that name. **so long** goodbye. **so that** in order that.

soak ❶ v 1 make wet. 2 put or lie in liquid so as to become thoroughly wet. 3 (of liquid) penetrate. ◆ n 4 soaking. 5 Slang drunkard. **soaking** n, adj **soak up** v

absorb.

soap n 1 compound of alkali and fat, used with water as a cleaning agent. 2 Informal soap opera. ◆ v 3 apply soap to. **soapy** adj **soap opera** radio or television serial dealing with domestic themes.

soar ❶ v 1 rise or fly upwards. 2 increase suddenly.

sob ❶ v sobbing, sobbed 1 weep with convulsive gasps. 2 utter with sobs. ◆ n 3 act or sound of sobbing. **sob story** tale of personal distress told to arouse sympathy.

sober ❶ adj 1 not drunk. 2 serious. 3 (of colours) plain and dull. ◆ v 4 make or become sober. **sobriety** n state of being sober.

soccer n football played by two teams of eleven kicking a spherical ball.

sociable ❶ adj 1 friendly or companionable. 2 (of an occasion) providing companionship. **sociability** n **sociably** adv

social ❶ adj 1 living in a community. 2 of society or its organization. 3 sociable. ◆ n 4 informal gathering. **socially** adv **socialize** v meet others socially. **socialite** n member of fashionable society. **social security** state provision for the unemployed, aged, or sick. **social work** work which involves helping people with serious financial or family problems.

socialism n political system which advocates public ownership of industries,

——————| T H E S A U R U S |——————

forty winks (inf), nap, siesta

snub v 1 = **insult**, cold–shoulder, cut (inf), humiliate, put down, rebuff, slight ◆ n 2 = **insult**, affront, put–down, slap in the face

snug adj 1 = **cosy**, comfortable, comfy (inf), warm

snuggle v = **nestle**, cuddle, nuzzle

soak v 1, 2 = **wet**, bathe, damp, drench, immerse, moisten, saturate, souse, steep, suffuse, waterlog 3 = **penetrate**, permeate, seep **soak up** = **absorb**, assimilate

soar v 1 = **ascend**, fly, mount, rise, wing ≠ **fall** 2 = **rise**, climb, escalate, rocket,

shoot up

sob v 1 = **cry**, howl, shed tears, weep

sober adj 2 = **serious**, composed, cool, grave, level–headed, rational, reasonable, sedate, solemn, staid, steady ≠ **unrealistic** 3 = **plain**, drab, drab, quiet, sombre, subdued ≠ **bright**

sociable adj 1 = **friendly**, affable, companionable, convivial, cordial, genial, gregarious, outgoing, social, warm

social adj 2 = **communal**, collective, common, community, general, group, public ◆ n 4 = **get–together** (inf), resources, and transport. **socialist** n, adj

society ❶ n, pl **-ties** 1 human beings considered as a group. 2 organized community. 3 structure and institutions of such a community. 4 organized group with common aims and interests. 5 upper class or fashionable people collectively. 6 companionship.

sociology n study of human societies. **sociological** adj **sociologist** n

sock[1] n cloth covering for the foot.

sock[2] Slang ◆ v 1 hit hard. ◆ n 2 hard blow.

socket n hole or recess into which something fits.

sod n (piece of) turf.

soda n 1 compound of sodium. 2 soda water. **soda water** fizzy drink made from water charged with carbon dioxide.

sodden ❶ adj soaked.

sodium n Chem silvery-white metallic element. **sodium bicarbonate** white soluble compound used in baking powder.

sodomy n anal intercourse.

sofa ❶ n couch.

soft ❶ adj 1 not hard, rough, or harsh. 2 (of a breeze or climate) mild. 3 (too) lenient. 4 easily influenced or imposed upon. 5 feeble or silly. 6 not robust. 7 (of drugs) not liable to cause addiction. 8 Informal easy. 9 (of water) containing few

mineral salts. **softly** adv **soften** v make or become soft or softer. **soft drink** nonalcoholic drink. **soft furnishings** curtains, rugs, lampshades, and furniture covers. **soft option** easiest alternative. **soft-pedal** v deliberately avoid emphasizing something. **soft-soap** v Informal flatter. **software** n computer programs. **softwood** n wood of a coniferous tree.

soggy ❶ adj **-gier, -giest** 1 soaked. 2 moist and heavy. **sogginess** n

soil[1] ❶ n 1 top layer of earth. 2 country or territory.

soil[2] ❶ v 1 make or become dirty. 2 disgrace.

solace ❶ [sol-iss] n, v comfort in distress.

solar adj 1 of the sun. 2 using the energy of the sun. **solar plexus** 1 network of nerves at the pit of the stomach. 2 this part of the stomach. **solar system** the sun and the heavenly bodies that go round it.

solarium n, pl **-lariums, -laria** place with beds and ultraviolet lights used for acquiring an artificial suntan.

solder n 1 soft alloy used to join two metal surfaces. ◆ v 2 join with solder.

soldier ❶ n 1 member of an army. ◆ v 2 serve in an army. **soldierly** adj **soldier on** v persist doggedly.

sole[1] ❶ adj 1 one and only. 2 not shared,

gathering, party

society n 1 = **civilization**, humanity, mankind, people, the community, the public 4 = **organization**, association, circle, club, fellowship, group, guild, institute, league, order, union 5 = **upper classes**, beau monde, elite, gentry, high society 6 = **companionship**, company, fellowship, friendship

sodden adj 1 = **soaked**, drenched, saturated, soggy, sopping, waterlogged

sofa n = **couch**, chaise longue, divan, settee

soft adj 1 = **pliable**, bendable, elastic, flexible, gelatinous, malleable, mouldable, plastic, pulpy, spongy, squashy, supple, yielding ≠ **hard** 2 = **mild**, balmy,

temperate 3 = **lenient**, easy-going, indulgent, lax, overindulgent, permissive, spineless ≠ **strict** 6 = **out of condition**, effeminate, flabby, flaccid, limp, weak 8 Inf = **easy**, comfortable, cushy (inf), undemanding

soggy adj = **sodden**, dripping, moist, saturated, soaked, sopping, waterlogged

soil[1] n 1 = **earth**, clay, dirt, dust, ground 2 = **land**, country

soil[2] v 1, 2 = **dirty**, befoul, besmirch, defile, foul, pollute, spot, stain, sully, tarnish ≠ **clean**

① **solace** n = **comfort**, consolation, relief

② **solace** v = **comfort**, console

soldier n 1 = **fighter**, man-at-arms,

exclusive. **solely** adv 1 only, completely. 2 alone.

sole² n 1 underside of the foot. 2 underside of a shoe. ◆ v 3 provide (a shoe) with a sole.

sole³ n small edible flatfish.

solemn ⊕ adj 1 serious, deeply sincere. 2 formal. **solemnity** n **solemnize** v 1 celebrate or perform (a ceremony). 2 make solemn.

solicit v **–iting, –ited** 1 request. 2 (of a prostitute) offer (a person) sex for money. **solicitation** n

solid ⊕ adj 1 (of a substance) keeping its shape. 2 not liquid or gas. 3 not hollow. 4 of the same substance throughout. 5 strong or substantial. 6 sound or reliable. 7 having three dimensions. ◆ n 8 three–dimensional shape. 9 solid substance. **solidify** v make or become solid or firm. **solidity** n

soliloquy n, pl **–quies** speech made by a person while alone, esp. in a play.

solitary ⊕ adj 1 alone, single. 2 (of a place) lonely. **solitude** n state of being alone.

solo n, pl **–los** 1 music for one performer. 2 any act done without assistance. ◆ adj 3 done alone. ◆ adv 4 by oneself, alone. **soloist** n

solstice n either the shortest (in winter) or longest (in summer) day of the year.

solve ⊕ v find the answer to (a problem). **solvable** adj

sombre ⊕ adj dark, gloomy.

sombrero n, pl **–ros** wide–brimmed

Mexican hat.

some adj 1 unknown or unspecified. 2 unknown or unspecified quantity or number of. 3 considerable number or amount of. 4 Informal remarkable. ◆ pron 5 certain unknown or unspecified people or things. 6 unknown or unspecified number or quantity. **somebody** pron 1 some person. ◆ n 2 important person. **somehow** adv in some unspecified way. **someone** pron somebody. **something** pron 1 unknown or unspecified thing or amount. 2 impressive or important thing. **sometime** adv 1 at some unspecified time. ◆ adj 2 former. **sometimes** adv from time to time, now and then. **somewhat** adv to some extent, rather. **somewhere** adv in, to, or at some unspecified or unknown place.

✓ WORD TIP

Somebody and *someone* are singular and in formal usage are followed by a singular verb or pronoun. Informal usage favours the use of the plural *they* to avoid the use of the clumsy *he or she*: If I annoy somebody, *they* (rather than *he or she*) will take it out on me.

---

somersault n 1 leap or roll in which the trunk and legs are turned over the head. ◆ v 2 perform a somersault.

son n male offspring. **son–in–law** n, pl **sons–in–law** daughter's husband.

sonar n device for detecting underwater objects by the reflection of sound waves.

serviceman, squaddie or squaddy (*Brit sl*), trooper, warrior

sole¹ adj 1 = **only**, individual, one, single, solitary 2 = **alone**, exclusive

solemn adj 1 = **serious**, earnest, grave, sedate, sober, staid ≠ **bright** 2 = **formal**, ceremonial, dignified, grand, grave, momentous, stately ≠ **informal**

solid adj 1 = **firm**, compact, concrete, dense, hard ≠ **unsubstantial** 5 = **strong**, stable, sturdy, substantial, unshakable

≠ **unstable** 6 = **reliable**, dependable, genuine, good, pure, real, sound, trusty, upright, upstanding, worthy ≠ **unreliable**

solitary adj 1 = **single**, alone, lone, sole 2 = **isolated**, hidden, lonely, out–of–the–way, remote, unfrequented ≠ **public**

solve v = **answer**, clear up, crack, decipher, disentangle, get to the bottom of, resolve, suss (out) (*sl*), unravel, work out

sombre adj = **gloomy**, dark, dim, dismal, doleful, drab, dull, grave, joyless,

sonata *n* piece of music in several movements for one instrument with or without piano.

song ❶ *n* 1 music for the voice. 2 tuneful sound made by certain birds. 3 singing. **for a song** very cheaply. **songster, songstress** *n* singer. **songbird** *n* any bird with a musical call.

sonic *adj* of or producing sound.

sonnet *n* fourteen-line poem with a fixed rhyme scheme.

sonorous *adj* (of sound) deep or resonant.

soon ❶ *adv* in a short time. **sooner** *adv* rather, e.g. *I'd sooner go alone.* **sooner or later** eventually.

soot *n* black powder formed by the incomplete burning of an organic substance. **sooty** *adj*

soothe ❶ *v* 1 make calm. 2 relieve (pain etc.).

soothsayer *n* seer or prophet.

sop *n* 1 concession to pacify someone. ◆ *v* **sopping, sopped** 2 mop up or absorb (liquid). **sopping** *adj* completely soaked. **soppy** *adj Informal* oversentimental.

sophistry *n* clever but invalid argument.

soporific ❶ *adj* 1 causing sleep. ◆ *n* 2 drug that causes sleep.

soprano *n, pl* **-pranos** 1 (singer with) the highest female or boy's voice. 2 highest pitched of a family of instruments.

sorbet *n* flavoured water ice.

sorcerer ❶ *n* magician. **sorceress** *n fem* **sorcery** *n* witchcraft or magic.

sordid ❶ *adj* 1 dirty, squalid. 2 base, vile. 3 selfish and grasping.

sore ❶ *adj* 1 painful. 2 causing annoyance. 3 resentful. 4 (of need) urgent. ◆ *n* 5 painful area on the body. ◆ *adv* 6 *Obs* greatly. **sorely** *adv* greatly. **soreness** *n*

sorrow ❶ *n* 1 grief or sadness. 2 cause of sorrow. ◆ *v* 3 grieve. **sorrowful** *adj* **sorrowfully** *adv*

sorry ❶ *adj* **-rier, -riest** 1 feeling pity or regret. 2 pitiful or wretched.

sort ❶ *n* 1 group all sharing certain qualities or characteristics. 2 *Informal* type of character. ◆ *v* 3 arrange according to kind. 4 mend or fix. **out of sorts** slightly unwell or bad-tempered.

THESAURUS

lugubrious, mournful, sad, sober ≠ **happy**

song *n* 1 = **ballad**, air, anthem, carol, chant, chorus, ditty, hymn, number, psalm, tune

soon *adv* = **before long**, in the near future, shortly

soothe *v* 1 = **calm**, allay, appease, hush, lull, mollify, pacify, quiet, still ≠ **worry** 2 = **relieve**, alleviate, assuage, ease ≠ **irritate**

soporific *adj* 1 = **sleep-inducing**, sedative, somnolent, tranquillizing ◆ *n* 2 = **sedative**, narcotic, opiate, tranquillizer

sorcerer, sorceress *n* = **magician**, enchanter, necromancer, warlock, witch, wizard

sordid *adj* 1 = **dirty**, filthy, foul, mean, scungy (*Aust & NZ sl*), seedy, sleazy, squalid, unclean 2 = **base**, debauched, degenerate, low, shabby, shameful, vicious, vile 3 = **mercenary**, avaricious, covetous, grasping, selfish

sore *adj* 1 = **painful**, angry, burning, inflamed, irritated, raw, sensitive, smarting, tender 2 = **annoying**, severe, sharp, troublesome 3 = **annoyed**, aggrieved, angry, cross, hurt, irked, irritated, pained, pissed (*taboo sl*), pissed (off) (*taboo sl*), resentful, stung, upset 4 = **urgent**, acute, critical, desperate, dire, extreme, pressing

sorrow *n* 1 = **grief**, anguish, distress, heartache, heartbreak, misery, mourning, regret, sadness, unhappiness, woe ≠ **joy** 2 = **affliction**, hardship, misfortune, trial, tribulation, trouble, woe ≠ **good fortune** ◆ *v* 3 = **grieve**, agonize, bemoan, be sad, bewail, lament, mourn ≠ **celebrate**

sorry *adj* 1 = **regretful**, apologetic, conscience-stricken, contrite, penitent, remorseful, repentant, shamefaced ≠ **unrepentant** 2 = **wretched**, mean, miserable, pathetic, pitiful, poor, sad 3 = **deplorable**

> ✅ **WORD TIP**
> Note the singular/plural usage: *this* (or *that*) *sort of thing; these* (or *those*) *sorts of thing.* In the second, plural example you can also say *these sorts of things.*

sortie *n* 1 relatively short return trip. 2 operational flight made by military aircraft.

SOS *n* 1 international code signal of distress. 2 call for help.

so–so *adj Informal* mediocre.

soufflé [**soo–**flay] *n* light fluffy dish made with beaten egg whites and other ingredients.

soul ❶ *n* 1 spiritual and immortal part of a human being. 2 essential part or fundamental nature. 3 deep and sincere feelings. 4 person regarded as typifying some quality. 5 person. 6 type of Black music combining blues, pop, and gospel. **soulful** *adj* full of emotion. **soulless** *adj* 1 lacking human qualities, mechanical. 2 (of a person) lacking sensitivity.

sound¹ ❶ *n* 1 something heard, noise. ◆ *v* 2 make or cause to make a sound. 3 seem to be as specified. 4 pronounce. **soundproof** *adj* 1 not penetrable by sound. ◆ *v* 2 make soundproof. **soundtrack** *n* recorded sound

accompaniment to a film.

sound² ❶ *adj* 1 in good condition. 2 firm, substantial. 3 financially reliable. 4 showing good judgment. 5 ethically correct. 6 (of sleep) deep. 7 thorough. **soundly** *adv*

sound³ ❶ *v* 1 find the depth of (water etc.). 2 examine (the body) by tapping or with a stethoscope. 3 ascertain the views of. **sounding board** person or group used to test a new idea.

sound⁴ ❶ *n* channel or strait.

soup *n* liquid food made from meat, vegetables, etc. **soupy** *adj* **soup kitchen** place where food and drink is served to needy people. **souped–up** *adj* (of an engine) adjusted so as to be more powerful than normal.

sour ❶ *adj* 1 sharp–tasting. 2 (of milk) gone bad. 3 (of a person's temperament) sullen. ◆ *v* 4 make or become sour.

source ❶ *n* 1 origin or starting point. 2 person, book, etc. providing information. 3 spring where a river or stream begins.

south *n* 1 direction towards the South Pole, opposite north. 2 area lying in or towards the south. ◆ *adj* 3 to or in the south. 4 (of a wind) from the south. ◆ *adv* 5 in, to, or towards the south. **southerly** *adj* **southern** *adj* **southerner** *n* person

THESAURUS

sort *n* 1 = **kind**, brand, category, class, ilk, make, nature, order, quality, style, type, variety ◆ *v* 3 = **arrange**, categorize, classify, divide, grade, group, order, put in order, rank

soul *n* 1 = **spirit**, essence, life, vital force 2 = **essence**, embodiment, epitome, personification, quintessence, type 5 = **person**, being, body, creature, individual, man or woman

sound¹ *n* 1 = **noise**, din, report, reverberation, tone ◆ *v* 2 = **resound**, echo, reverberate 3 = **seem**, appear, look 4 = **pronounce**, announce, articulate, declare, express, utter

sound² *adj* 1 = **perfect**, fit, healthy, intact, solid, unhurt, unimpaired, uninjured,

whole ≠ **weak** 4 = **sensible**, correct, logical, proper, prudent, rational, reasonable, right, trustworthy, valid, well–founded, wise ≠ **irresponsible** 6 = **deep**, unbroken, undisturbed, untroubled ≠ **broken**

sound³ *v* 1 = **fathom**, plumb, probe

sound⁴ *n* = **channel**, arm of the sea, fjord, inlet, passage, strait, voe

sour *adj* 1 = **sharp**, acetic, acid, bitter, pungent, tart ≠ **sweet** 2 = **gone off**, curdled, gone bad, turned ≠ **fresh** 3 = **ill–natured**, acrimonious, disagreeable, embittered, ill–tempered, peevish, tart, ungenerous, waspish ≠ **pleasant**

source *n* 1 = **origin**, author, beginning, cause, derivation, fount, originator

from the south of a country or area.
southward *adj, adv* **southwards** *adv*
southpaw *n Informal* left–handed person,
esp. a boxer. **South Pole** southernmost
point on the earth's axis.
souvenir ❶ *n* keepsake, memento.
sou'wester *n* seaman's waterproof hat
covering the head and back of the neck.
sovereign ❶ *n* 1 king or queen. 2 former
British gold coin worth one pound. ◆ *adj* 3
(of a state) independent. 4 supreme in
rank or authority. 5 excellent. **sovereignty**
n
sow¹ ❶ *n* [rhymes with **know**] *v* **sowing,
sowed, sown** *or* **sowed** 1 scatter or plant
(seed) in or on (the ground). 2 implant or
introduce.
sow² [rhymes with **cow**] *n* female adult
pig.
soya *n* plant whose edible bean (**soya
bean**) is used for food and as a source of
oil. **soy sauce** sauce made from fermented
soya beans, used in Chinese and Japanese
cookery.
spa *n* resort with a mineral–water spring.
space ❶ *n* 1 unlimited expanse in which all
objects exist and move. 2 interval. 3 blank
portion. 4 unoccupied area. 5 the universe
beyond the earth's atmosphere. ◆ *v* 6
place at intervals. **spacecraft, spaceship** *n*
vehicle for travel beyond the earth's
atmosphere. **space shuttle** manned
reusable vehicle for repeated space flights.

spacious ❶ *adj* having a large capacity or
area.
spade¹ *n* tool for digging. **spadework** *n*
hard preparatory work.
spade² *n* playing card of the suit marked
with black leaf–shaped symbols.
spaghetti *n* pasta in the form of long
strings.
span ❶ *n* 1 space between two points. 2
complete extent. 3 distance from thumb
to little finger of the expanded hand. ◆ *v*
spanning, spanned 4 stretch or extend
across.
spangle *n* 1 small shiny metallic ornament.
◆ *v* 2 decorate with spangles.
spaniel *n* dog with long ears and silky hair.
spank *v* 1 slap with the open hand, on
the buttocks or legs. ◆ *n* 2 such a slap.
spanking *n*
spanner *n* tool for gripping and turning a
nut or bolt.
spar¹ *n* pole used as a ship's mast, boom,
or yard.
spar² ❶ *v* **sparring, sparred** 1 box or fight
using light blows for practice. 2 argue
(with someone).
spare ❶ *adj* 1 extra. 2 in reserve. 3 (of a
person) thin. ◆ *n* 4 duplicate kept in case
of damage or loss. ◆ *v* 5 refrain from
punishing or harming. 6 protect
(someone) from (something unpleasant).
7 afford to give. **to spare** in addition to
what is needed. **sparing** *adj* economical

2 = **informant**, authority
souvenir *n* = **keepsake**, memento,
reminder
sovereign *n* 1 = **monarch**, chief, emperor
or empress, king *or* queen, potentate,
prince *or* princess, ruler ◆ *adj*
4 = **supreme**, absolute, imperial, kingly *or*
queenly, principal, royal, ruling
5 = **excellent**, effectual, efficacious,
efficient
sow¹ *v* 1 = **scatter**, plant, seed 2 = **implant**
space *n* 1 = **expanse**, extent 2 = **interval**,
capacity, duration, elbowroom, leeway,
margin, period, play, room, scope, span,

time, while 3 = **gap**, blank, distance,
interval, omission
spacious *adj* = **roomy**, ample, broad,
capacious, commodious, expansive,
extensive, huge, large, sizable *or* sizeable
span *n* 1 = **period**, duration, spell, term
2 = **extent**, amount, distance, length,
reach, spread, stretch ◆ *v* 4 = **extend
across**, bridge, cover, cross, link, traverse
spank *v* 1 = **smack**, cuff, slap
spar² *v* 2 = **argue**, bicker, row, scrap (*inf*),
squabble, wrangle
spare *adj* 1 = **extra**, additional, free,
leftover, odd, over, superfluous, surplus,

spark ⚐ *n* 1 fiery particle thrown out from a fire or caused by friction. 2 flash of light produced by an electrical discharge. 3 trace or hint (of a particular quality). ◆ *v* 4 give off sparks. 5 initiate. **sparkie** *n NZ informal* electrician.

sparkle ⚐ *v* 1 glitter with many points of light. 2 be vivacious or witty. ◆ *n* 3 sparkling points of light. 4 vivacity or wit. **sparkler** *n* hand-held firework that emits sparks. **sparkling** *adj* (of wine or mineral water) slightly fizzy.

sparrow *n* small brownish bird. **sparrowhawk** *n* small hawk.

sparse ⚐ *adj* thinly scattered. **sparsely** *adv* **sparseness** *n*

spartan *adj* strict and austere.

spasm ⚐ *n* 1 involuntary muscular contraction. 2 sudden burst of activity or feeling. **spasmodic** *adj* occurring in spasms. **spasmodically** *adv*

spastic *n* 1 person with cerebral palsy. ◆ *adj* 2 suffering from cerebral palsy. 3 affected by spasms.

spate ⚐ *n* 1 large number of things happening within a period of time. 2 sudden outpouring or flood.

spatial *adj* of or in space.

spatter *v* 1 scatter or be scattered in drops over (something). ◆ *n* 2 spattering sound. 3 something spattered.

spatula *n* utensil with a broad flat blade for spreading or stirring.

spawn *n* 1 jelly-like mass of eggs of fish, frogs, or molluscs. ◆ *v* 2 (of fish, frogs, or molluscs) lay eggs. 3 generate.

spay *v* remove the ovaries from (a female animal).

speak ⚐ *v* **speaking, spoke, spoken** 1 say words, talk. 2 communicate or express in words. 3 give a speech or lecture. 4 know how to talk in (a specified language). **speaker** *n* 1 person who speaks, esp. at a formal occasion. 2 loudspeaker. 3 (S–) official chairman of a body.

spear *n* 1 weapon consisting of a long shaft with a sharp point. ◆ *v* 2 pierce with or as if with a spear. **spearhead** *v* 1 lead (an attack or campaign). ◆ *n* 2 leading force in an attack or campaign.

spearmint *n* type of mint.

special ⚐ *adj* 1 distinguished from others of its kind. 2 for a specific purpose. 3 exceptional. 4 particular. **specially** *adv* **specialist** *n* expert in a particular activity or subject. **speciality** *n* 1 special interest or skill. 2 product specialized in. **specialize** *v* be a specialist. **specialization** *n*

species ⚐ *n, pl* **-cies** group of plants or animals that are related closely enough to interbreed naturally.

specific ⚐ *adj* 1 particular, definite. ◆ *n*

———————————— THESAURUS ————————————

unoccupied, unused, unwanted ≠ **needed** 3 = **thin**, gaunt, lean, meagre, wiry ≠ **heavy** ◆ *v* 5 = **have mercy on**, be merciful to, go easy on (*inf*), leave, let off (*inf*), pardon, save from ≠ **condemn** 7 = **afford**, do without, give, grant, let (someone) have, manage without, part with

spark *n* 1 = **flicker**, flare, flash, gleam, glint 3 = **trace**, atom, hint, jot, scrap, vestige ◆ *v* 5 = **start**, inspire, precipitate, provoke, set off, stimulate, trigger (off)

sparkle *v* 1 = **glitter**, dance, flash, gleam, glint, glisten, scintillate, shimmer, shine, twinkle ◆ *n* 3 = **glitter**, brilliance, flash, flicker, gleam, glint, twinkle 4 = **vivacity**,

dash, élan, life, liveliness, spirit, vitality

sparse *adj* = **scattered**, few and far between, meagre, scanty, scarce

spasm *n* 1 = **convulsion**, contraction, paroxysm, twitch 2 = **burst**, eruption, fit, frenzy, outburst, seizure

spate *n* 2 = **flood**, deluge, flow, outpouring, rush, torrent

speak *v* 1, 2 = **talk**, articulate, converse, express, pronounce, say, state, tell, utter 3 = **lecture**, address, declaim, discourse, hold forth

special *adj* 1, 2, 4 = **specific**, appropriate, distinctive, individual, particular, precise ≠ **general** 3 = **exceptional**, extraordinary, important, memorable, significant,

drug used to treat a particular disease. ◆ *pl*
3 particular details. **specifically** *adv*
specification *n* detailed description of
something to be made or done. **specify** *v*
refer to or state specifically.

specimen ❶ *n* 1 individual or part
typifying a whole. 2 sample of blood etc.
taken for analysis.

specious [**spee**–shuss] *adj* apparently true,
but actually false.

speck ❶ *n* small spot or particle. **speckle** *n*
1 small spot. ◆ *v* 2 mark with speckles.

spectacle ❶ *n* 1 strange, interesting, or
ridiculous sight. 2 impressive public show.
◆ *pl* 3 pair of glasses for correcting faulty
vision. **spectacular** *adj* 1 impressive. ◆ *n* 2
spectacular public show. **spectacularly**
adv

spectre ❶ *n* 1 ghost. 2 menacing mental
image. **spectral** *adj*

spectrum *n, pl* –tra 1 range of different
colours, radio waves, etc. in order of their
wavelengths. 2 entire range of anything.
spectroscope *n* instrument for producing
or examining spectra.

speculate ❶ *v* 1 guess, conjecture. 2 buy
property, shares, etc. in the hope of selling
them at a profit. **speculation** *n*

speculative *adj* **speculator** *n*
speech ❶ *n* 1 act, power, or manner of
speaking. 2 talk given to an audience. 3
language or dialect. **speechify** *v* make
speeches, esp. boringly. **speechless** *adj*
unable to speak because of great emotion.

speed ❶ *n* 1 swiftness. 2 rate at which
something moves or acts. 3 *Slang*
amphetamine. ◆ *v* **speeding, sped** or
speeded 4 go quickly. 5 drive faster than
the legal limit. **speedy** *adj* 1 prompt. 2
rapid. **speedily** *adv* **speedboat** *n* light fast
motorboat. **speedometer** *n* instrument to
show the speed of a vehicle. **speed up** *v*
accelerate. **speedway** *n* track for
motorcycle racing. **speedwell** *n* plant with
small blue flowers.

spell¹ ❶ *v* **spelling, spelt** or **spelled** 1 give
in correct order the letters that form (a
word). 2 (of letters) make up (a word). 3
indicate. **spelling** *n* 1 way a word is spelt.
2 person's ability to spell. **spell out** *v* make
explicit.

spell² ❶ *n* 1 formula of words supposed to
have magic power. 2 effect of a spell. 3
fascination. **spellbound** *adj* entranced.

spell³ ❶ *n* period of time of weather or
activity.

uncommon, unique, unusual ≠ **common**
species *n* = **kind**, breed, category, class,
group, sort, type, variety
specific *adj* 1 = **particular**, characteristic,
distinguishing, special ≠ **general**
specimen *n* 1 = **example**, exemplification,
instance, model, pattern, representative,
sample, type 2 = **sample**
speck *n* = **particle**, atom, bit, blemish, dot,
fleck, grain, iota, jot, mark, mite, mote,
shred, speckle, spot, stain
spectacle *n* 1 = **sight**, curiosity, marvel,
phenomenon, scene, wonder 2 = **show**,
display, event, exhibition, extravaganza,
pageant, performance
spectre *n* 1 = **ghost**, apparition, phantom,
spirit, vision, wraith
speculate *v* 1 = **conjecture**, consider,
guess, hypothesize, suppose, surmise,

theorize, wonder 2 = **gamble**, hazard, risk,
venture
speech *n* 1 = **communication**,
conversation, dialogue, discussion, talk
3 = **talk**, address, discourse, homily,
lecture, oration, spiel (*inf*) 4 = **language**,
articulation, dialect, diction, enunciation,
idiom, jargon, parlance, tongue
speed *n* 1 = **swiftness**, haste, hurry, pace,
quickness, rapidity, rush, velocity
≠ **slowness** ◆ *v* 5 = **race**, career, gallop,
hasten, hurry, make haste, rush, tear,
zoom ≠ **creep**
spell¹ *v* 3 = **indicate**, augur, imply, mean,
point to, portend, signify
spell² *n* 1 = **incantation**, charm 2,
3 = **enchantment**, allure, bewitchment,
fascination, glamour, magic
spell³ *n* = **period**, bout, course, interval,

spend ① *v* spending, spent 1 pay out (money). 2 use or pass (time). 3 use up completely. **spendthrift** *n* person who spends money wastefully.

sperm *n* sperms or sperm 1 male reproductive cell. 2 semen. **spermicide** *n* substance that kills sperm.

spew ① *v* 1 vomit. 2 send out in a stream.

sphere ① *n* 1 perfectly round solid object. 2 field of activity. **spherical** *adj*

spice ① *n* 1 aromatic substance used as flavouring. 2 something that adds zest or interest. ◆ *v* 3 flavour with spices. **spicy** *adj* 1 flavoured with spices. 2 *Informal* slightly scandalous.

spick–and–span *adj* neat and clean.

spider *n* small eight–legged creature which spins a web to catch insects for food. **spidery** *adj*

spike ① *n* 1 sharp point. 2 sharp pointed metal object. ◆ *pl* 3 sports shoes with spikes for greater grip. ◆ *v* 4 put spikes on. 5 pierce or fasten with a spike. 6 add alcohol to (a drink). **spike someone's guns** thwart someone. **spiky** *adj*

spill ① *v* spilling, spilt or spilled 1 pour from or as if from a container. 2 come out of a place. 3 shed (blood). ◆ *n* 4 fall. 5 amount spilt. **spill the beans** *Informal* give away a secret. **spillage** *n*

spin ① *v* spinning, spun 1 revolve or cause to revolve rapidly. 2 draw out and twist (fibres) into thread. ◆ *n* 3 revolving

motion. 4 continuous spiral descent of an aircraft. 5 *Informal* short drive for pleasure. **spin a yarn** tell an improbable story. **spinner** *n* **spin–dry** *v* dry (clothes) in a spin–dryer. **spin–dryer** *n* machine in which washed clothes are spun in a perforated drum to remove excess water. **spin–off** *n* incidental benefit. **spin out** *v* prolong.

spinach *n* dark green leafy vegetable.

spindle *n* 1 rotating rod that acts as an axle. 2 weighted rod rotated for spinning thread by hand. **spindly** *adj* long, slender, and frail.

spine ① *n* 1 backbone. 2 edge of a book on which the title is printed. 3 sharp point on an animal or plant. **spinal** *adj* of the spine. **spineless** *adj* lacking courage. **spiny** *adj* covered with spines.

spinster *n* unmarried woman.

spiral ① *n* 1 continuous curve formed by a point winding about a central axis at an ever–increasing distance from it. 2 steadily accelerating increase or decrease. ◆ *v* –ralling, –ralled 3 move in a spiral. 4 increase or decrease with steady acceleration. ◆ *adj* 5 having the form of a spiral.

spire *n* pointed part of a steeple.

spirit¹ ① *n* 1 nonphysical aspect of a person concerned with profound thoughts. 2 nonphysical part of a person believed to live on after death. 3 prevailing feeling. 4 mood or attitude. 5

──────── THESAURUS ────────

season, stretch, term, time

spend *v* 1 = **pay out**, disburse, expend, fork out (*sl*) ≠ **save** 2 = **pass**, fill, occupy, while away 3 = **use up**, consume, dissipate, drain, empty, exhaust, run through, squander, waste ≠ **keep**

spew *v* 1 = **vomit**, disgorge, puke (*sl*), regurgitate, throw up (*inf*)

sphere *n* 1 = **ball**, circle, globe, globule, orb 2 = **field**, capacity, department, domain, function, patch, province, realm, scope, territory, turf (*US sl*)

spice *n* 1 = **seasoning**, relish, savour 2 = **excitement**, colour, pep, piquancy,

zest, zing (*inf*)

spike¹ *n* 1 = **point**, barb, prong, spine ◆ *v* 5 = **impale**, spear, spit, stick

spill *v* 1 = **pour**, discharge, disgorge, overflow, slop over ◆ *n* 4 = **fall**, tumble

spin *v* 1 = **revolve**, gyrate, pirouette, reel, rotate, turn, twirl, whirl ◆ *n* 3 = **revolution**, gyration, roll, whirl 5 *Inf* = **drive**, joy ride (*inf*), ride

spine *n* 1 = **backbone**, spinal column, vertebrae, vertebral column 3 = **barb**, needle, quill, ray, spike, spur

spiral *n* 1 = **coil**, corkscrew, helix, whorl ◆ *adj* 5 = **coiled**, helical, whorled, winding temperament or disposition. **6** liveliness. **7** courage. **8** essential meaning as opposed to literal interpretation. **9** ghost. ◆ *pl* **10** emotional state. ◆ *v* **-iting, -ited 11** carry away mysteriously. **spirited** *adj* **1** lively. **2** characterized by the mood specified, e.g. *low spirited.*

spirit² *n* liquid obtained by distillation. **spirit level** glass tube containing a bubble in liquid, used to check whether a surface is level.

spit¹ ❶ *v* **spitting, spat 1** eject (saliva or food) from the mouth. **2** throw out particles explosively. **3** rain slightly. **4** utter (words) in a violent manner. ◆ *n* **5** saliva. **spitting image** *Informal* person who looks very like another. **spittle** *n* fluid produced in the mouth, saliva. **spittoon** *n* bowl to spit into.

spit² *n* **1** sharp rod on which meat is skewered for roasting. **2** long strip of land projecting into the sea.

spite ❶ *n* **1** deliberate nastiness. ◆ *v* **2** annoy or hurt from spite. **in spite of** in defiance of. **spiteful** *adj* **spitefully** *adv*

splash ❶ *v* **1** scatter liquid on (something). **2** scatter (liquid) or (of liquid) be scattered in drops. **3** print (a story or photograph)

prominently in a newspaper. ◆ *n* **4** splashing sound. **5** patch (of colour or light). **6** extravagant display. **7** small amount of liquid added to a drink. **splash out** *v Informal* spend extravagantly.

splatter *v, n* splash.

splay *v* spread out, with ends spreading in different directions.

spleen *n* **1** abdominal organ which filters bacteria from the blood. **2** bad temper. **splenetic** *adj* spiteful or irritable.

splendid ❶ *adj* **1** excellent. **2** brilliant in appearance. **splendour** *n*

splice *v* join by interweaving or overlapping ends. **get spliced** *Slang* get married.

splint *n* rigid support for a broken bone.

splinter ❶ *n* **1** thin sharp piece broken off, esp. from wood. ◆ *v* **2** break into fragments. **splinter group** group that has broken away from an organization.

split ❶ *v* **splitting, split 1** break into separate pieces. **2** separate. **3** share. ◆ *n* **4** crack or division caused by splitting. ◆ *pl* **5** act of sitting with the legs outstretched in opposite directions. **6** split second very short period of time.

splutter *v* **1** utter with spitting or choking

———————{ THESAURUS }———————

spirit¹ *n* **2 = life force**, life, soul, vital spark **3 = feeling**, atmosphere, gist, tenor, tone **4, 5 = temperament**, attitude, character, disposition, outlook, temper **6 = liveliness**, animation, brio, energy, enthusiasm, fire, force, life, mettle, vigour, zest **7 = courage**, backbone, gameness, grit, guts (*inf*), spunk (*inf*) **8 = Intention**, essence, meaning, purport, purpose, sense, substance **9 = ghost**, apparition, phantom, spectre ◆ *pl* **10 = mood**, feelings, frame of mind, morale ◆ *v* **11 = remove**, abduct, abstract, carry away, purloin, seize, steal, whisk away

spit¹ *v* **1 = eject**, expectorate, splutter **2 = throw out** ◆ *n* **5 = saliva**, dribble, drool, slaver, spittle

spite *n* **1 = malice**, animosity, hatred, ill will, malevolence, spitefulness, spleen,

venom ≠ **kindness** ◆ *v* **2 = annoy**, harm, hurt, injure, vex ≠ **help in spite of = despite**, (even) though, notwithstanding, regardless of

splash *v* **1, 2 = scatter**, shower, slop, spatter, spray, sprinkle, wet **3 = publicize**, broadcast, tout, trumpet ◆ *n* **5 = dash**, burst, spatter, spattering, touch **6 = display**, effect, impact, sensation, stir

splendid *adj* **1 = excellent**, cracking (*Brit inf*), fantastic (*inf*), first-class, glorious, great (*inf*), marvellous, wonderful ≠ **poor 2 = magnificent**, costly, gorgeous, grand, impressive, lavish, luxurious, ornate, resplendent, rich, sumptuous, superb ≠ **drab**

splinter *n* **1 = sliver**, chip, flake, fragment ◆ *v* **2 = shatter**, disintegrate, fracture, split

split *v* **1 = break**, burst, come apart, come

sounds. 2 make hissing spitting sounds. ♦
n 3 spluttering.

spoil ⊕ *v* **spoiling, spoilt** *or* **spoiled** 1
damage. 2 harm the character of (a child)
by giving it all it wants. 3 rot, go bad.
spoils *pl n* booty. **spoiling for** eager for.
spoilsport *n* person who spoils the
enjoyment of others.

spoke² *n* bar joining the hub of a wheel to
the rim.

spokesman, spokeswoman,
spokesperson *n* person chosen to speak
on behalf of a group.

sponge *n* 1 sea animal with a porous
absorbent skeleton. 2 skeleton of a
sponge, or a substance like it, used for
cleaning. 3 type of light cake. ♦ *v* 4 wipe
with a sponge. 5 live at the expense of
others. **sponger** *n Slang* person who
sponges on others. **spongy** *adj*

sponsor ⊕ *n* 1 person who promotes
something. 2 person who agrees to give
money to a charity on completion of a
specified activity by another. 3 godparent.
♦ *v* 4 act as a sponsor for. **sponsorship** *n*

spontaneous ⊕ *adj* 1 not planned or
arranged. 2 occurring through natural
processes without outside influence.
spontaneity *n*

spoof ⊕ *n* mildly satirical parody.

spook ⊕ *n Informal* ghost. **spooky** *adj*

spool *n* cylinder round which something
can be wound.

spoon *n* 1 shallow bowl attached to a
handle for eating, stirring, or serving food.
♦ *v* 2 lift with a spoon. **spoonful** *n*
spoon–feed *v* 1 feed with a spoon. 2 give
(someone) too much help.

sporadic ⊕ *adj* intermittent, scattered.
sporadically *adv*

spore *n* minute reproductive body of some
plants.

sporran *n* pouch worn in front of a kilt.

sport ⊕ *n* 1 activity for pleasure,
competition, or exercise. 2 such activities
collectively. 3 enjoyment. 4 playful joking.
5 person who reacts cheerfully. ♦ *v* 6 wear
proudly. **sporting** *adj* 1 of sport. 2
behaving in a fair and decent way.
sporting chance reasonable chance of
success. **sporty** *adj* **sportive** *adj* playful.
sports car fast low–built car, usu. open–
topped. **sports jacket** man's casual jacket.
sportsman, sportswoman *n* 1 person
who plays sports. 2 person who plays fair
and is good–humoured when losing.
sportsmanship *n*

spot ⊕ *n* 1 small mark on a surface. 2
pimple. 3 location. 4 *Informal* small
quantity. 5 *Informal* awkward situation. ♦ *v*
spotting, spotted 6 notice. 7 mark with
spots. 8 watch for and take note of. **on**

undone, crack, give way, open, rend, rip
2 = **separate**, branch, cleave, disband,
disunite, diverge, fork, part 3 = **share out**,
allocate, allot, apportion, distribute,
divide, halve, partition ♦ *n* 7 = **crack**,
breach, division, fissure, gap, rent, rip,
separation, slit, tear

spoil *v* 1 = **ruin**, damage, destroy, disfigure,
harm, impair, injure, mar, mess up, trash
(*sl*), wreck ≠ **save** 2 = **overindulge**,
coddle, cosset, indulge, mollycoddle,
pamper ≠ **deprive** 3 = **go bad**, addle,
curdle, decay, decompose, go off (*Brit inf*),
rot, turn

sponsor *n* 1 = **backer**, patron, promoter ♦
v 4 = **back**, finance, fund, patronize,

promote, subsidize

spontaneous *adj* 1 = **unplanned**,
impromptu, impulsive, instinctive, natural,
unprompted, voluntary, willing ≠ **planned**

spoof *n Inf* 1 = **parody**, burlesque,
caricature, mockery, satire, send–up (*Brit
inf*), take–off (*inf*)

spooky *adj* = **eerie**, chilling, creepy (*inf*),
frightening, scary (*inf*), spine-chilling,
uncanny, unearthly, weird

sporadic *adj* = **intermittent**, irregular,
occasional, scattered, spasmodic

sport *n* 1, 2 = **game**, amusement,
diversion, exercise, pastime, play,
recreation 4 = **fun**, badinage, banter, jest,
joking, teasing ♦ *v* 6 = **wear**, display,

the spot 1 at the place in question. 2 immediately. 3 in an awkward predicament. spotless adj absolutely clean. spotty adj with spots. spot check random examination. spotlight n 1 powerful light illuminating a small area. 2 centre of attention. spot-on adj Informal absolutely accurate.

spouse ❶ n husband or wife.

spout ❶ v 1 pour out in a stream or jet. 2 Slang utter (a stream of words) lengthily. ♦ n 3 projecting tube or lip for pouring liquids. 4 stream or jet of liquid.

sprain v 1 injure (a joint) by a sudden twist. ♦ n 2 such an injury.

sprat n small sea fish.

sprawl ❶ v 1 lie or sit with the limbs spread out. 2 spread out in a straggling manner. ♦ n 3 part of a city that has spread untidily over a large area.

spray¹ ❶ n 1 (device for producing) fine drops of liquid. ♦ v 2 scatter in fine drops. 3 cover with a spray.

spray² ❶ n 1 branch with buds, leaves, flowers, or berries. 2 ornament like this.

spread ❶ v spreading, spread 1 open out or be displayed to the fullest extent. 2

extend over a larger expanse. 3 apply as a coating. 4 send or be sent in all directions. ♦ n 5 spreading. 6 extent. 7 Informal large meal. 8 soft food which can be spread. spread-eagled adj with arms and legs outstretched. spreadsheet n computer program for manipulating figures.

spree ❶ n session of overindulgence, usu. in drinking or spending money.

sprig n 1 twig or shoot.

sprightly ❶ adj –lier, –liest lively and brisk. sprightliness n

spring ❶ v springing, sprang or sprung, sprung 1 move suddenly upwards or forwards in a single motion, jump. 2 develop unexpectedly. 3 originate (from). 4 Informal arrange the escape of (someone) from prison. ♦ n 5 season between winter and summer. 6 jump. 7 coil which can be compressed, stretched, or bent and returns to its original shape when released. 8 natural pool forming the source of a stream. 9 elasticity. springy adj elastic. springboard n flexible board used to gain height or momentum in diving or gymnastics. spring-clean v clean (a house) thoroughly.

exhibit, show off

spot n 1 = mark, blemish, blot, blotch, scar, smudge, speck, speckle, stain 2 = pimple, pustule, zit (sl) 3 = place, location, point, position, scene, site 5 Inf = predicament, difficulty, hot water (inf), mess, plight, quandary, tight spot, trouble ♦ v 6 = see, catch sight of, detect, discern, espy, make out, observe, recognize, sight 7 = mark, dirty, fleck, mottle, smirch, soil, spatter, speckle, splodge, splotch, stain

spouse n = partner, consort, husband or wife, mate, significant other (US inf)

spout v 1 = stream, discharge, gush, shoot, spray, spurt, surge

sprawl v 1 = loll, flop, lounge, slouch, slump 2 = spread, ramble, straggle, trail

spray¹ n 1 = aerosol, atomizer, sprinkler 2 = droplets, drizzle, fine mist ♦ v 3 = scatter, diffuse, shower, sprinkle

spray² n 1 = sprig, branch 2 = corsage, floral arrangement

spread v 1 = open (out), broaden, dilate, expand, extend, sprawl, stretch, unfold, unroll, widen 4 = circulate, broadcast, disseminate, make known, propagate ≠ repress ♦ n 5 = increase, advance, development, dispersal, dissemination, expansion, proliferation 6 = extent, span, stretch, sweep

spree n = binge (inf), bacchanalia, bender (inf), carousal, fling, orgy, revel

sprightly adj = lively, active, agile, brisk, energetic, nimble, spirited, spry, vivacious

spring v 1 = jump, bounce, bound, leap, vault 2 = appear, develop, mushroom, shoot up 3 = originate, arise, come, derive, descend, issue, proceed, start, stem ♦ n 6 = jump, bound, leap, vault 9 = elasticity, bounce, buoyancy,

springbok _n_ S African antelope.

sprinkle ⊕ _v_ scatter (liquid or powder) in tiny drops or particles over (something). **sprinkler** _n_ **sprinkling** _n_ small quantity or number.

sprint ⊕ _n_ 1 short race run at top speed. 2 fast run. ◆ _v_ 3 run a short distance at top speed. **sprinter** _n_

sprite ⊕ _n_ elf.

sprocket _n_ wheel with teeth on the rim, that drives or is driven by a chain.

sprout ⊕ _v_ 1 put forth shoots. 2 begin to grow or develop. ◆ _n_ 3 shoot. 4 short for BRUSSELS SPROUT.

spruce[1] _n_ kind of fir.

spruce[2] ⊕ _adj_ neat and smart. **spruce up** _v_ make neat and smart.

spry ⊕ _adj_ **spryer**, **spryest** _or_ **sprier**, **spriest** active or nimble.

spur ⊕ _n_ 1 stimulus or incentive. 2 spiked wheel on the heel of a rider's boot used to urge on a horse. 3 projection. ◆ _v_ **spurring**, **spurred** 4 urge on, incite (someone). **on the spur of the moment** on impulse.

spurious ⊕ _adj_ not genuine.

spurn ⊕ _v_ reject with scorn.

spurt ⊕ _v_ 1 gush or cause to gush out in a jet. ◆ _n_ 2 short sudden burst of activity or speed. 3 sudden gush.

spy ⊕ _n_, _pl_ **spies** 1 person employed to obtain secret information. 2 person who secretly watches others. ◆ _v_ **spying**, **spied** 3 act as a spy. 4 catch sight of.

squabble ⊕ _v_, _n_ (engage in) a petty or noisy quarrel.

squad ⊕ _n_ small group of people working or training together.

squalid ⊕ _adj_ 1 dirty and unpleasant. 2 morally sordid. **squalor** _n_ disgusting dirt and filth.

squall[1] _n_ sudden strong wind.

squall[2] _v_ 1 cry noisily, yell. ◆ _n_ 2 harsh cry.

squander ⊕ _v_ waste (money or resources).

square ⊕ _n_ 1 geometric figure with four equal sides and four right angles. 2 open area in a town in this shape. 3 product of a number multiplied by itself. ◆ _adj_ 4 square in shape. 5 denoting a measure of area. 6 straight or level. 7 fair and honest. 8 with all accounts or debts settled. ◆ _v_ 9 multiply (a number) by itself. 10 make square. 11 be or cause to be consistent. ◆ _adv_ 12 squarely, directly. **squarely** _adv_ 1 in

—————— THESAURUS ——————

flexibility, resilience

sprinkle _v_ 1 = **scatter**, dredge, dust, pepper, powder, shower, spray, strew

sprint _v_ 3 = **race**, dart, dash, hare (_Brit inf_), shoot, tear

sprout _v_ 1, 2 = **grow**, bud, develop, shoot, spring

spruce[2] _adj_ = **smart**, dapper, natty (_inf_), neat, trim, well-groomed, well turned out

spry _adj_ = **active**, agile, nimble, sprightly, supple

spur _n_ 1 = **stimulus**, impetus, impulse, incentive, incitement, inducement, motive 2 = **goad**, prick ◆ _v_ 4 = **incite**, animate, drive, goad, impel, prick, prod, prompt, stimulate, urge on **the spur of the moment** = **on impulse**, impromptu, impulsively, on the spot, without planning

spurious _adj_ = **false**, artificial, bogus, fake, phoney _or_ phony (_inf_), pretended, sham,

specious, unauthentic

spurn _v_ = **reject**, despise, disdain, rebuff, repulse, scorn, slight, snub

spurt _v_ 1 = **gush**, burst, erupt, shoot, squirt, surge ◆ _n_ 2 = **burst**, fit, rush, spate, surge

spy _n_ 1 = **undercover agent**, mole, nark (_Brit, Aust & NZ sl_) ◆ _v_ 4 = **catch sight of**, espy, glimpse, notice, observe, spot

① **squabble** _v_ = **quarrel**, argue, bicker, dispute, fight, row, wrangle

② **squabble** _n_ = **quarrel**, argument, disagreement, dispute, fight, row, tiff

squad _n_ = **team**, band, company, crew, force, gang, group, troop

squalid _adj_ = **dirty**, filthy, scungy (_Aust & NZ sl_), seedy, sleazy, slummy, sordid, unclean ≠ **clean**

squander _v_ = **waste**, blow (_sl_), expend, fritter away, misspend, misuse, spend a direct way. **2** in an honest and frank manner. **square meal** substantial meal. **square root** number of which a given number is the square. **square up to** v prepare to confront (a person or problem).

squash¹ 𝕋 v **1** crush flat. **2** suppress. **3** push into a confined space. **4** humiliate with a crushing retort. ◆ n **5** sweet fruit drink diluted with water. **6** crowd of people in a confined space.

squash² n marrow–like vegetable.

squat v **squatting, squatted 1** crouch with the knees bent and the weight on the feet. **2** occupy unused premises to which one has no legal right. ◆ n **3** place where squatters live. ◆ adj **4** short and broad. **squatter** n illegal occupier of unused premises.

squawk 𝕋 n **1** loud harsh cry. ◆ v **2** utter a squawk.

squeak 𝕋 n **1** short shrill cry or sound. ◆ v **2** make or utter a squeak. **squeaky** adj

squeal 𝕋 n **1** long shrill cry or sound. ◆ v **2** make or utter a squeal. **3** Slang inform on someone to the police.

squeamish 𝕋 adj easily sickened or shocked.

squeeze 𝕋 v **1** grip or press firmly. **2** crush or press to extract liquid. **3** push into a confined space. **4** hug. **5** obtain

(something) by force or great effort. ◆ n **6** squeezing. **7** amount extracted by squeezing. **8** hug. **9** crush of people in a confined space. **10** restriction on borrowing.

squelch v **1** make a wet sucking sound, as by walking through mud. ◆ n **2** squelching sound.

squid n sea creature with a long soft body and ten tentacles.

squiggle n wavy line.

squint 𝕋 v **1** have eyes which face in different directions. **2** glance sideways. ◆ n **3** squinting condition of the eye. **4** Informal glance. ◆ adj **5** crooked.

squire n **1** country gentleman, usu. the main landowner in a community. **2** Hist knight's apprentice.

squirm 𝕋 v **1** wriggle, writhe. **2** feel embarrassed. ◆ n **3** wriggling movement.

squirrel n small bushy–tailed tree–living animal.

squirt v **1** force (a liquid) or (of a liquid) be forced out of a narrow opening. **2** squirt liquid at. ◆ n **3** jet of liquid. **4** Informal small or insignificant person.

st. stone (weight).

stab 𝕋 v **stabbing, stabbed 1** pierce with something pointed. **2** jab (at). ◆ n **3** stabbing. **4** sudden unpleasant sensation. **5** Informal attempt.

THESAURUS

square adj **7** = **honest**, above board, ethical, fair, genuine, kosher (inf), on the level (inf), straight ◆ v **11** = **match**, agree, correspond, fit, reconcile, tally

squash¹ v **1** = **crush**, compress, distort, flatten, mash, press, pulp, smash **2** = **suppress**, annihilate, crush, humiliate, quell, silence

squawk v **2** = **cry**, cackle, crow, hoot, screech, yelp

squeak v **2** = **peep**, pipe, squeal

squeal n **1** = **scream**, screech, shriek, wail, yell ◆ v **2** = **scream**, screech, shriek, wail, yell

squeamish adj = **fastidious**, delicate, nauseous, prudish, queasy, sick, strait–

laced ≠ **tough**

squeeze v **1** = **press**, clutch, compress, crush, grip, pinch, squash, wring **3** = **cram**, crowd, force, jam, pack, press, ram, stuff **4** = **hug**, clasp, cuddle, embrace, enfold **5** = **extort**, milk, pressurize, wrest ◆ n **8** = **hug**, clasp, embrace **9** = **crush**, congestion, crowd, jam, press, squash

squint adj **5** = **crooked**, askew, aslant, awry, cockeyed, skew–whiff (inf)

squirm v **1** = **wriggle**, twist, writhe

stab v **1** = **pierce**, impale, jab, knife, spear, stick, thrust, transfix, wound ◆ n **3** = **wound**, gash, incision, jab, puncture, thrust **4** = **twinge**, ache, pang, prick **5** Inf

stabilize v make or become stable. **stabilization** n **stabilizer** n device for stabilizing a child's bicycle, an aircraft, or a ship.

stable¹ n 1 building in which horses are kept. 2 establishment that breeds and trains racehorses. 3 establishment that manages or trains several entertainers or athletes. ◆ v 4 put or keep (a horse) in a stable.

stable² ⓣ adj 1 firmly fixed or established. 2 firm in character. 3 Science not subject to decay or decomposition. **stability** n

staccato [stak-**ah**-toe] adj, adv 1 Music with the notes sharply separated. ◆ adj 2 consisting of short abrupt sounds.

stack ⓣ n 1 ordered pile. 2 large amount. 3 chimney. ◆ v 4 pile in a stack. 5 control (aircraft waiting to land) so that they fly at different altitudes.

stadium n, pl –diums, –dia sports arena with tiered seats for spectators.

staff ⓣ n 1 people employed in an organization. 2 stick used as a weapon, support, etc. ◆ v 3 supply with personnel. **staff nurse** qualified nurse of the rank below a sister.

stag n adult male deer. **stag night, party** party for men only.

stage ⓣ n 1 step or period of development. 2 platform in a theatre where actors perform. 3 portion of a journey. ◆ v 4 put (a play) on stage. 5 organize and carry out (an event). **the stage** theatre as a profession. **stagecoach** n large horse–drawn vehicle formerly used to carry passengers and mail. **stage fright** nervousness felt by a person about to face an audience. **stage whisper** loud whisper intended to be heard by an audience.

stagger ⓣ v 1 walk unsteadily. 2 astound. 3 set apart to avoid congestion. ◆ n 4 staggering.

staid ⓣ adj sedate, serious, and rather dull.

stain ⓣ v 1 discolour, mark. 2 colour with a penetrating pigment. ◆ n 3 discolouration or mark. 4 moral blemish or slur. 5 penetrating liquid used to colour things. **stainless** adj **stainless steel** steel alloy that does not rust.

stairs pl n flight of steps between floors, usu. indoors. **staircase, stairway** n flight of stairs with a handrail or banisters.

stake¹ ⓣ n 1 pointed stick or post driven into the ground as a support or marker. ◆ v 2 support or mark out with stakes. **stake a claim** to claim a right to. **stake out** v Slang (of police) keep (a place) under surveillance.

stake² ⓣ n 1 money wagered. 2 interest, usu. financial, held in something. ◆ pl 3 prize in a race or contest. ◆ v 4 wager, risk. 5 support financially. **at stake** being

─────── THESAURUS ───────

= **attempt**, endeavour, go, try

stable² adj 1 = **firm**, constant, established, fast, fixed, immovable, lasting, permanent, secure, sound, strong ≠ **uncertain** 2 = **steady**, reliable, staunch, steadfast, sure ≠ **unstable**

stack n 1, 2 = **pile**, berg (S Afr), heap, load, mass, mound, mountain ◆ v 4 = **pile**, accumulate, amass, assemble, heap up, load

staff n 1 = **workers**, employees, personnel, team, workforce 2 = **stick**, cane, crook, pole, rod, sceptre, stave, wand

stage n 1 = **step**, division, juncture, lap, leg, level, period, phase, point

stagger v 1 = **totter**, lurch, reel, sway, wobble 2 = **astound**, amaze, astonish, confound, overwhelm, shake, shock, stun, stupefy 3 = **alternate**, overlap, step

staid adj = **sedate**, calm, composed, grave, serious, sober, solemn, steady

stain v 1 = **mark**, blemish, blot, dirty, discolour, smirch, soil, spot, tinge 2 = **dye**, colour, tint ◆ n 3 = **mark**, blemish, blot, discoloration, smirch, spot 4 = **stigma**, disgrace, dishonour, shame, slur 5 = **dye**, colour, tint

stake¹ n 1 = **pole**, pale, paling, palisade, picket, post, stick

stake² n 1 = **bet**, ante, pledge, wager

stalactite *n* lime deposit hanging from the roof of a cave.

stalagmite *n* lime deposit sticking up from the floor of a cave.

stale ❶ *adj* 1 not fresh. 2 lacking energy or ideas through overwork or monotony. 3 uninteresting from overuse.

stalk[1] *n* plant's stem.

stalk[2] ❶ *v* 1 follow or approach stealthily. 2 pursue persistently and, sometimes, attack (a person with whom one is obsessed). 3 walk in a stiff or haughty manner. **stalking-horse** *n* pretext.

stall[1] *n* 1 small stand for the display and sale of goods. 2 compartment in a stable. 3 small room or compartment. ♦ *pl* 4 ground-floor seats in a theatre or cinema. 5 row of seats in a church for the choir or clergy. ♦ *v* 6 stop (a motor vehicle or engine) or (of a motor vehicle or engine) stop accidentally.

stall[2] ❶ *v* employ delaying tactics.

stallion *n* uncastrated male horse.

stalwart ❶ [stawl–wart] *adj* 1 strong and sturdy. 2 dependable. ♦ *n* 3 stalwart person.

stamina ❶ *n* enduring energy and strength.

stammer ❶ *v* 1 speak or say with involuntary pauses or repetition of syllables. ♦ *n* 2 tendency to stammer.

stamp ❶ *n* 1 (also **postage stamp**) piece of gummed paper stuck to an envelope or parcel to show that the postage has been paid. 2 act of stamping. 3 instrument for stamping a pattern or mark. 4 pattern or mark stamped. 5 characteristic feature. ♦ *v* 6 bring (one's foot) down forcefully. 7 walk with heavy footsteps. 8 characterize. 9 impress (a pattern or mark) on. 10 stick a postage stamp on. **stamping ground** favourite meeting place. **stamp out** *v* suppress by force.

stampede ❶ *n* 1 sudden rush of frightened animals or of a crowd. ♦ *v* 2 (cause to) take part in a stampede.

stance ❶ *n* 1 attitude. 2 manner of standing.

stanch ❶ [stahnch] *v* same as STAUNCH[2].

stanchion *n* upright bar used as a support.

stand ❶ *v* **standing, stood** 1 be in, rise to, or place in an upright position. 2 be situated. 3 be in a specified state or position. 4 remain unchanged or valid. 5 tolerate. 6 offer oneself as a candidate. 7 *Informal* treat to. ♦ *n* 8 stall for the sale of goods. 9 structure for spectators at a sports ground. 10 firmly held opinion. 11 *US & Aust* witness box. 12 rack or piece of furniture on which things may be placed. **standing** *adj* 1 permanent, lasting. ♦ *n* 2 reputation or status. 3 duration. 4 **stand for** *v* 1 represent or mean. 2 *Informal* tolerate. **stand in** *v* act as a substitute. **stand-in** *n* substitute. **standoffish** *adj* reserved or haughty. 1 **stand up for** *v*

---

2 = **interest**, concern, investment, involvement, share ♦ *v* 4 = **bet**, chance, gamble, hazard, risk, venture, wager

stale *adj* 1 = **old**, decayed, dry, flat, fusty, hard, musty, sour ≠ **fresh** 2,

3 = **unoriginal**, banal, hackneyed, overused, stereotyped, threadbare, trite, worn–out ≠ **new**

stalk[2] *v* 1, 2 = **pursue**, follow, haunt, hunt, shadow, track

stall[2] *v* = **play for time**, hedge, temporize

stalwart *adj* 1 = **strong**, stout, strapping, sturdy ≠ **feeble** 2 = **loyal**, dependable, reliable, staunch

stamina *n* = **staying power**, endurance, energy, force, power, resilience, strength

stammer *v* 1 = **stutter**, falter, hesitate, pause, stumble

stamp *n* 3 = **imprint**, brand, earmark, hallmark, mark, signature ♦ *v* 6 = **trample**, crush 8 = **identify**, brand, categorize, label, mark, reveal, show to 9 = **imprint**, impress, mark, print

stampede *n* 1 = **rush**, charge, flight, rout

stance *n* 1 = **attitude**, position, stand, standpoint, viewpoint 2 = **posture**, bearing, carriage, deportment

stanch see STAUNCH[2]

support or defend.

standard ❶ n 1 level of quality. 2 example against which others are judged or measured. 3 moral principle. 4 distinctive flag. 5 upright pole. ◆ adj 6 usual, regular, or average. 7 of recognized authority. 8 accepted as correct. **standardize** v cause to conform to a standard. **standardization** n

standpipe n tap attached to a water main to provide a public water supply.

standpoint ❶ n point of view.

standstill n complete halt.

stanza n verse of a poem.

staple n 1 U–shaped piece of metal used to fasten papers or secure things. ◆ v 2 fasten with staples. **stapler** n small device for fastening papers together.

star ❶ n 1 hot gaseous mass in space, visible in the night sky as a point of light. 2 star–shaped mark used to indicate excellence. 3 asterisk. 4 celebrity in the entertainment or sports world. ◆ pl 5 astrological forecast, horoscope. ◆ v **starring, starred** 6 feature or be featured as a star. 7 mark with a star or stars. ◆ adj 8 leading, famous. **stardom** n status of a star in the entertainment or sports world. **starry** adj full of or like stars. **starry–eyed**

adj full of naive optimism. **starfish** n star–shaped sea creature.

starboard n 1 right–hand side of a ship, when facing forward. ◆ adj 2 of or on this side.

starch n 1 carbohydrate forming the main food element in bread, potatoes, etc., and used mixed with water for stiffening fabric. ◆ v 2 stiffen (fabric) with starch. **starchy** adj 1 containing starch. 2 stiff and formal.

stare ❶ v 1 look or gaze fixedly (at). ◆ n 2 fixed gaze.

stark ❶ adj 1 harsh, unpleasant, and plain. 2 desolate, bare. 3 absolute. ◆ adv 4 completely.

starling n songbird with glossy black speckled feathers.

start ❶ v 1 take the first step, begin. 2 set or be set in motion. 3 make a sudden involuntary movement from fright. 4 establish or set up. ◆ n 5 first part of something. 6 place or time of starting. 7 advantage or lead in a competitive activity. 8 sudden movement made from fright. **starter** n 1 first course of a meal. 2 device for starting a car's engine. 3 person who signals the start of a race.

startle ❶ v slightly surprise or frighten.

———————— THESAURUS ————————

stand v 1 a = **be upright**, be erect, be vertical, rise b = **put**, mount, place, position, set 4 = **exist**, be valid, continue, hold, obtain, prevail, remain 5 = **tolerate**, abide, allow, bear, brook, countenance, endure, handle, put up with (inf), stomach, take ◆ n 8 = **stall**, booth, table 10 = **position**, attitude, determination, opinion, stance 12 = **support**, base, bracket, dais, platform, rack, stage, tripod

standard n 1 = **level**, gauge, grade, measure 2 = **criterion**, average, benchmark, example, guideline, model, norm, yardstick 3 = **principles**, ethics, ideals, morals 4 = **flag**, banner, ensign ◆ adj 6 = **usual**, average, basic, customary, normal, orthodox, regular, typical ≠ **strange** 7, 8 = **accepted**, approved,

authoritative, definitive, established, official, recognized ≠ **unofficial**

standpoint n = **point of view**, angle, position, stance, viewpoint

star n 1 = **heavenly body** 4 = **celebrity**, big name, luminary, main attraction, megastar (inf), name ◆ adj 8 = **leading**, brilliant, celebrated, major, prominent, well–known

stare v 1 = **gaze**, eyeball (sl), gape, gawk, gawp (Brit sl), goggle, look, watch

stark adj 1, 2 = **harsh**, austere, bare, barren, bleak, grim, hard, plain, severe 3 = **absolute**, blunt, downright, out–and–out, pure, sheer, unmitigated, utter ◆ adv 4 = **absolutely**, altogether, completely, entirely, quite, utterly, wholly

start v 1 = **begin**, appear, arise, commence, embark upon, issue, make a beginning,

starve *v* **1** die or suffer or cause to die or suffer from hunger. **2** deprive of something needed. **starvation** *n*

stash *Informal* ♦ *v* **1** store in a secret place. ♦ *n* **2** secret store.

state ⊕ *n* **1** condition of a person or thing. **2** sovereign political power or its territory. **3** (**S–**) the government. **4** *Informal* excited or agitated condition. **5** pomp. ♦ *adj* **6** of or concerning the State. **7** involving ceremony. ♦ *v* **8** express in words. **stately** *adj* dignified or grand. **statehouse** *n NZ* publicly–owned house rented to a low–income tenant. **statement** *n* **1** something stated. **2** printed financial account. **stateroom** *n* **1** private cabin on a ship. **2** large room in a palace, used for ceremonial occasions. **statesman**, **stateswoman** *n* experienced and respected political leader. **statesmanship** *n*

static ⊕ *adj* **1** stationary or inactive. **2** (of a force) acting but producing no movement. ♦ *n* **3** crackling sound or speckled picture caused by interference in radio or television reception. **4** (also **static electricity**) electric sparks produced by friction.

station ⊕ *n* **1** place where trains stop for passengers. **2** headquarters or local offices of the police or a fire brigade. **3** building with special equipment for a particular purpose, e.g. *power station*. **4** television or radio channel. **5** position in society. ♦ *v* **6** assign (someone) to a particular place. **station wagon** *US & Aust* estate car.

statue *n* large sculpture of a human or animal figure. **statuary** *n* statues collectively. **statuesque** *adj* (of a woman) tall and well–proportioned. **statuette** *n* small statue.

stature ⊕ *n* **1** person's height. **2** reputation of a person or their achievements.

status ⊕ *n* **1** social position. **2** prestige. **3** person's legal standing. **status quo** existing state of affairs.

statute *n* written law. **statutory** *adj* required or authorized by law.

staunch¹ ⊕ *adj* loyal, firm.

staunch² ⊕ , **stanch** *v* stop (a flow of blood).

stave *n* **1** one of the strips of wood forming a barrel. **2** *Music* same as STAFF².

originate, set about, take the first step ≠ **stop 2** = **set in motion**, activate, get going, initiate, instigate, kick–start, open, originate, trigger ≠ **end 3** = **jump**, flinch, jerk, recoil, shy **4** = **establish**, begin, create, found, inaugurate, initiate, institute, launch, pioneer, set up ≠ **stop** ♦ *n* **5**, **6** = **beginning**, birth, dawn, foundation, inception, initiation, onset, opening, outset **7** = **advantage**, edge, head start, lead **8** = **jump**, convulsion, spasm

startle *v* = **surprise**, frighten, make (someone) jump, scare, shock

state *n* **1** = **condition**, attitude, circumstances, equation, frame of mind, humour, mood, position, predicament, shape, situation, spirits **2** = **country**, commonwealth, federation, kingdom, land, nation, republic, territory

5 = **ceremony**, display, glory, grandeur, majesty, pomp, splendour, style ♦ *v* **8** = **express**, affirm, articulate, assert, declare, expound, present, say, specify, utter, voice

static *adj* **1** = **stationary**, fixed, immobile, motionless, still, unmoving

station *n* **2** = **headquarters**, base, depot **5** = **position**, post, rank, situation, standing, status ♦ *v* **6** = **assign**, establish, install, locate, post, set

stature *n* **2** = **importance**, consequence, eminence, prestige, prominence, rank, standing

status *n* **1**, **2** = **position**, condition, consequence, eminence, grade, prestige, rank, standing

staunch¹ *adj* = **loyal**, faithful, firm, sound, stalwart, steadfast, true, trusty

staunch², **stanch** *v* = **stop**, check, dam,

stave in v staving, stove burst a hole in.
stave off v staving, staved ward off.
stay¹ ❶ v 1 remain in a place or condition.
2 reside temporarily. 3 endure. ◆ n 4
period of staying in a place. 5
postponement. **staying power** stamina.
stay² ❶ n 1 prop or buttress. ◆ pl 2 corset.
stead n **in someone's stead** in someone's
place. **stand someone in good stead** be
useful to someone.
steady ❶ adj **steadier, steadiest** 1 not
shaky or wavering. 2 regular or
continuous. 3 sensible and dependable. ◆
v **steadying, steadied** 4 make steady. ◆
adv 5 in a steady manner. **steadily** adv
steadiness n
steak n 1 thick slice of meat, esp. beef. 2
slice of fish.
steal ❶ v **stealing, stole, stolen** 1 take
unlawfully or without permission. 2 move
stealthily.
stealth ❶ n secret or underhand
behaviour. **stealthy** adj **stealthily** adv
steam n 1 vapour into which water
changes when boiled. 2 power, energy, or
speed. ◆ v 3 give off steam. 4 (of a
vehicle) move by steam power. 5 cook or
treat with steam. **steamer** n 1 steam–
propelled ship. 2 container used to cook
food in steam. 3 **steam engine** engine

worked by steam. **steamroller** n 1 steam–
powered vehicle with heavy rollers, used
to level road surfaces. ◆ v 2 use
overpowering force to make (someone)
do what one wants.
steed n Lit horse.
steel n 1 hard malleable alloy of iron and
carbon. 2 steel rod used for sharpening
knives. 3 hardness of character or attitude.
◆ v 4 prepare (oneself) for something
unpleasant. **steely** adj
steep¹ ❶ adj 1 sloping sharply. 2 Informal
(of a price) unreasonably high.
steep² ❶ v soak or be soaked in liquid.
steeped in filled with.
steeple n church tower with a spire.
steeplejack n person who repairs steeples
and chimneys.
steer¹ ❶ v 1 direct the course of (a vehicle
or ship). 2 direct (one's course). **steerage**
n cheapest accommodation on a
passenger ship.
steer² n castrated male ox.
stellar adj of stars.
stem¹ ❶ n 1 long thin central part of a
plant. 2 long slender part, as of a
wineglass. 3 part of a word to which
inflections are added. ◆ v **stemming,
stemmed** 4 **stem from** originate from.
stem² ❶ v **stemming, stemmed** stop (the

———————————— THESAURUS ————————————

halt, stay, stem
stay¹ v 1 = **remain**, abide, continue, halt,
linger, loiter, pause, stop, tarry, wait ≠ **go**
◆ n 4 = **visit**, holiday, sojourn, stop,
stopover 5 = **postponement**, deferment,
delay, halt, stopping, suspension
stay² n 1 = **support**, brace, buttress, prop,
reinforcement, shoring, stanchion
steady adj 1 = **firm**, fixed, safe, secure,
stable ≠ **unstable** 2 = **continuous**,
ceaseless, consistent, constant, incessant,
nonstop, persistent, regular, unbroken,
uninterrupted ≠ **occasional**
3 = **dependable**, balanced, calm, equable,
level–headed, reliable, sensible, sober
≠ **unpredictable** ◆ v 4 = **stabilize**, brace,
secure, support ≠ **shake**

steal v 1 = **take**, appropriate, embezzle,
filch, lift (inf), misappropriate, nick (sl,
chiefly Brit), pilfer, pinch (inf), purloin,
thieve 2 = **sneak**, creep, slink, slip, tiptoe
stealth n = **secrecy**, furtiveness, slyness,
sneakiness, stealthiness, surreptitiousness,
unobtrusiveness
steep¹ adj 1 = **sheer**, abrupt, precipitous
≠ **gentle** 2 Inf = **high**, exorbitant,
extortionate, extreme, overpriced,
unreasonable ≠ **fair**
steep² v = **soak**, drench, immerse,
marinate (Cookery), moisten, souse,
submerge **steeped in = saturated**, filled
with, imbued, infused, permeated,
pervaded, suffused
steer¹ v 1 = **drive**, control, direct, guide,

flow of something).

stench *n* foul smell.

stencil *n* 1 thin sheet with cut–out pattern through which ink or paint passes to form the pattern on the surface below. 2 pattern made thus. ◆ *v* **–cilling, –cilled** 3 make (a pattern) with a stencil.

step *v* **stepping, stepped** 1 move and set down the foot, as when walking. 2 walk a short distance. ◆ *n* 3 stepping. 4 distance covered by a step. 5 sound made by stepping. 6 foot movement in a dance. 7 one of a sequence of actions taken in order to achieve a goal. 8 degree in a series or scale. 9 flat surface for placing the foot on when going up or down. ◆ *pl* 10 stepladder. **step in** *v* intervene. **stepladder** *n* folding portable ladder with supporting frame. **stepping stone** 1 one of a series of stones for stepping on in crossing a stream. 2 means of progress towards a goal. **step up** *v* increase (something) by stages.

stereophonic *adj* using two separate loudspeakers to give the effect of naturally distributed sound.

stereotype *n* 1 standardized idea of a type of person or thing. ◆ *v* 2 form a stereotype of.

sterile *adj* 1 free from germs. 2 unable to produce offspring or seeds. 3 lacking inspiration or vitality. **sterility** *n* **sterilize** *v* make sterile. **sterilization** *n*

sterling *n* 1 British money system. ◆ *adj* 2 genuine and reliable.

stern¹ *adj* severe, strict.

stern² *n* rear part of a ship.

sternum *n, pl* **–na, –nums** same as BREASTBONE.

steroid *n* organic compound containing a carbon ring system, such as many hormones.

stethoscope *n* medical instrument for listening to sounds made inside the body.

stew *n* 1 food cooked slowly in a closed pot. 2 *Informal* troubled or worried state. ◆ *v* 3 cook slowly in a closed pot.

steward *n* 1 person who looks after passengers on a ship or aircraft. 2 official who helps at a public event such as a race. 3 person who administers another's property. **stewardess** *n fem*

stick¹ *n* 1 long thin piece of wood. 2 such a piece of wood shaped for a special purpose, e.g. *hockey stick*. 3 something like a stick, e.g. *stick of celery*. 4 *Slang* verbal abuse, criticism. **the sticks** *Informal* remote country area. **stick insect** tropical insect resembling a twig.

stick² *v* **sticking, stuck** 1 push (a pointed object) into (something). 2 fasten or be fastened by or as if by pins or glue. 3 (foll. by *out*) extend beyond something else, protrude. 4 *Informal* put. 5 jam. 6 come to a standstill. 7 remain for a long time. 8 *Slang* tolerate, abide. **sticker** *n* adhesive label or sign. **sticky** *adj* 1 covered with an adhesive substance. 2 *Informal* difficult, unpleasant. 3 (of weather) warm and humid. **stick around** *v Informal* remain

---

handle, pilot

stem¹ *n* 1 = **stalk**, axis, branch, shoot, trunk ◆ *v* 4 stem from = **originate from**, arise from, be caused by, derive from

stem² *v* = **stop**, check, curb, dam, hold back, staunch

stench *n* = **stink**, foul smell, pong (*Brit inf*), reek, whiff (*Brit sl*)

step *v* 1 = **walk**, move, pace, tread ◆ *n* 3 = **footstep**, footfall, footprint, pace, print, stride, track 7 = **action**, act, deed, expedient, means, measure, move

8 = **degree**, level, rank

stereotype *n* 1 = **formula**, pattern ◆ *v* 3 = **categorize**, pigeonhole, standardize, typecast

sterile *adj* 1 = **germ–free**, aseptic, disinfected, sterilized ≠ **dirty** 2 = **barren**, bare, dry, empty, fruitless, unfruitful, unproductive ≠ **productive**

sterling *adj* 2 = **excellent**, fine, genuine, sound, superlative, true

stern¹ *adj* = **severe**, austere, forbidding, grim, hard, harsh, inflexible, rigid, serious, in a place. **stick-in-the-mud** *n* person who does not like anything new. **stick-up** *n Slang* robbery at gunpoint. **stick up for** *v Informal* support or defend.

stickleback *n* small fish with sharp spines on its back.

stickler ❶ *n* person who insists on something, e.g. *stickler for detail*.

stiff ❶ *adj* 1 not easily bent or moved. 2 severe, e.g. *stiff punishment*. 3 unrelaxed or awkward. 4 firm in consistency. 5 strong, e.g. *a stiff drink.* ◆ *n* 6 *Slang* corpse. **stiffly** *adv* **stiffness** *n* **stiffen** *v* make or become stiff. **stiff-necked** *adj* haughtily stubborn.

stifle ❶ *v* 1 suppress. 2 suffocate.

stigma ❶ *n, pl* **-mas, -mata** 1 mark of social disgrace. 2 part of a plant that receives pollen. **stigmata** *pl n* marks resembling the wounds of the crucified Christ. **stigmatize** *v* mark as being shameful.

stile *n* set of steps allowing people to climb a fence.

still[1] ❶ *adv* 1 now or in the future as before. 2 up to this or that time. 3 even or

yet, e.g. *still more insults.* 4 quietly or without movement. 5 motionless. 6 silent and calm, undisturbed. 7 (of a drink) not fizzy. ◆ *n* 8 photograph from a film scene. ◆ *v* 9 make still. **stillness** *n* **stillborn** *adj* born dead. **still life** painting of inanimate objects.

still[2] *n* apparatus for distilling alcoholic drinks.

stimulus ❶ *n, pl* **-li** something that rouses a person or thing to activity. **stimulant** *n* something, such as a drug, that acts as a stimulus. **stimulate** *v* act as a stimulus (on). **stimulation** *n*

sting ❶ *v* **stinging, stung** 1 (of certain animals or plants) wound by injecting with poison. 2 feel or cause to feel sharp physical or mental pain. 3 *Slang* cheat (someone) by overcharging. ◆ *n* 4 wound or pain caused by or as if by stinging. 5 mental pain. 6 sharp pointed organ of certain animals or plants by which poison can be injected.

stingy ❶ *adj* **-gier, -giest** mean or miserly. **stinginess** *n*

———————— THESAURUS ————————

strict ≠ **warm**

stick[1] *n* 1, 2 = **cane**, baton, crook, pole, rod, staff, twig 4 *Sl* = **abuse**, criticism, flak (*inf*)

stick[2] *v* 1 = **poke**, dig, jab, penetrate, pierce, prod, puncture, spear, stab, thrust, transfix 2 = **fasten**, adhere, affix, attach, bind, bond, cling, fix, glue, hold, join, paste, weld 3 (foll. by *out*) = **protrude**, bulge, extend, jut, obtrude, poke, project, show 4 *Inf* = **put**, deposit, lay, place, set 7 = **stay**, linger, persist, remain 8 *Sl* = **tolerate**, abide, stand, stomach, take

stickler *n* = **fanatic**, fusspot (*Brit inf*), perfectionist, purist

stiff *adj* 1 = **inflexible**, firm, hard, inelastic, rigid, solid, taut, tense, tight, unbending, unyielding ≠ **flexible** 2 = **severe**, drastic, extreme, hard, harsh, heavy, strict 3 = **awkward**, clumsy, constrained, forced, formal, graceless, inelegant, jerky (*inf*), stilted, ungainly, ungraceful

unnatural, unrelaxed ≠ **easy**

stifle *v* 1 = **suppress**, check, hush, repress, restrain, silence, smother, stop 2 = **choke** 3 = **suffocate**, asphyxiate, choke, smother, strangle

stigma *n* 1 = **disgrace**, dishonour, shame, slur, smirch, stain

still[1] *adj* 5 = **motionless**, calm, peaceful, restful, serene, stationary, tranquil, undisturbed ≠ **moving** 6 = **silent**, hushed, quiet ≠ **noisy** ◆ *v* 9 = **quieten**, allay, calm, hush, lull, pacify, quiet, settle, silence, soothe

stimulus *n* = **incentive**, encouragement, fillip, geeing-up, goad, impetus, incitement, inducement, shot in the arm (*inf*), spur

sting *v* 2 = **hurt**, burn, pain, smart, tingle, wound 3 *Sl* = **cheat**, defraud, do (*sl*), fleece, overcharge, rip off (*sl*), swindle

stingy *adj* = **mean**, miserly, niggardly, parsimonious, penny-pinching (*inf*),

stink ⊕ *n* 1 strong unpleasant smell. 2 *Slang* unpleasant fuss. ◆ *v* **stinking, stank** or **stunk, stunk** 3 give off a strong unpleasant smell. 4 *Slang* be very unpleasant.

stint ⊕ *v* 1 (foll. by *on*) be miserly with (something). ◆ *n* 2 allotted amount of work.

stipulate ⊕ *v* specify as a condition of an agreement. **stipulation** *n*

stir ⊕ *v* **stirring, stirred** 1 mix up (a liquid) by moving a spoon etc. around in it. 2 move. 3 excite or stimulate (a person) emotionally. ◆ *n* 4 a stirring. 5 strong reaction, usu. of excitement.

stirrup *n* metal loop attached to a saddle for supporting a rider's foot.

stitch *n* 1 link made by drawing thread through material with a needle. 2 loop of yarn formed round a needle or hook in knitting or crochet. 3 sharp pain in the side. ◆ *v* 4 sew. **in stitches** *Informal* laughing uncontrollably. **not a stitch** *Informal* no clothes at all.

stoat *n* small mammal of the weasel family, with brown fur that turns white in winter.

stock ⊕ *n* 1 total amount of goods available for sale in a shop. 2 supply stored for future use. 3 financial shares in, or capital of, a company. 4 livestock. 5 lineage. 6 handle of a rifle. 7 liquid produced by boiling meat, fish, bones, or vegetables. 8 fragrant flowering plant. 9 standing or status. ◆ *pl* 10 *Hist* instrument of punishment consisting of a wooden frame with holes into which the hands and feet of the victim were locked. ◆ *adj* 11 kept in stock, standard. 12 hackneyed. ◆ *v* 13 keep for sale or future use. 14 supply (a farm) with livestock or (a lake etc.) with fish. **stockist** *n* dealer who stocks a particular product. **stocky** *adj* (of a person) broad and sturdy. **stockbroker** *n* person who buys and sells stocks and shares for customers. **stock car** car modified for a form of racing in which the cars often collide. **stock exchange, market** institution for the buying and selling of shares. **stockpile** *v* 1 store a large quantity of (something) for future use. ◆ *n* 2 accumulated store. **stock-still** *adj* motionless. **stocktaking** *n* counting and valuing of the goods in a shop.

stockade *n* enclosure or barrier made of stakes.

stocking *n* close-fitting covering for the foot and leg.

stodgy ⊕ *adj* **stodgier, stodgiest** 1 (of food) heavy and starchy. 2 (of a person) serious and boring. **stodge** *n* heavy starchy food.

stoep [stoop] *n S Afr* verandah.

tightfisted, ungenerous

stink *n* 1 = **stench**, fetor, foul smell, pong (*Brit inf*) ◆ *v* 3 = **reek**, pong (*Brit inf*)

stint *v* 1 (foll. by *on*) = **be mean**, be frugal, be sparing, hold back, skimp on ◆ *n* 2 = **share**, period, quota, shift, spell, stretch, term, time, turn

stipulate *v* = **specify**, agree, contract, covenant, insist upon, require, settle

stir *v* 1 = **mix**, agitate, beat, shake 3 = **stimulate**, arouse, awaken, excite, incite, move, provoke, rouse, spur ≠ **curb** ◆ *n* 5 = **commotion**, activity, bustle, disorder, disturbance, excitement, flurry, fuss

stock *n* 1 = **goods**, array, choice, commodities, merchandise, range, selection, variety, wares 2 = **supply**, fund, hoard, reserve, stockpile, store 3 = **property**, assets, capital, funds, investment 4 = **livestock**, beasts, cattle, domestic animals ◆ *adj* 11 = **standard**, conventional, customary, ordinary, regular, routine, usual 12 = **hackneyed**, banal, overused, trite ◆ *v* 13 = **sell**, deal in, handle, keep, supply, trade in 14 = **provide with**, equip, fit out, furnish, supply

stodgy *adj* 1 = **heavy**, filling, leaden, starchy ≠ **light** 2 = **dull**, boring, fuddy-duddy (*inf*), heavy going, staid, stuffy, tedious, unexciting ≠ **interesting**

stoic ⊕ [**stow**–ik] *n* **1** person who suffers hardship without showing his or her feelings. ◆ *adj* **2** (also **stoical**) suffering hardship without showing one's feelings. **stoically** *adv* **stoicism** [**stow**–iss–izz–um] *n*

stoke *v* feed and tend (a fire or furnace). **stoker** *n*

stole *n* long scarf or shawl.

stolid ⊕ *adj* showing little emotion or interest.

stomach ⊕ *n* **1** organ in the body which digests food. **2** front of the body around the waist. **3** desire or inclination. ◆ *v* **4** put up with.

stomp *v Informal* tread heavily.

stone *n* **1** material of which rocks are made. **2** piece of this. **3** gem. **4** hard central part of a fruit. **5** unit of weight equal to 14 pounds or 6.350 kilograms. **6** hard deposit formed in the kidney or bladder. ◆ *v* **7** throw stones at. **8** remove stones from (a fruit). **stoned** *adj Slang* under the influence of alcohol or drugs. **stony** *adj* **1** of or like stone. **2** unfeeling or hard. **stony–broke** *adj Slang* completely penniless. **stonily** *adv* **stone–deaf** *adj* completely deaf. **stonewall** *v* obstruct or hinder discussion. **stoneware** *n* hard kind of pottery fired at a very high temperature.

stooge *n* **1** actor who feeds lines to a comedian or acts as the butt of his jokes. **2** *Slang* person taken advantage of by a superior.

stool *n* **1** chair without arms or back. **2** piece of excrement.

stoop ⊕ *v* **1** bend (the body) forward and downward. **2** carry oneself habitually in this way. **3** degrade oneself. ◆ *n* **4** stooping posture.

stop ⊕ *v* **stopping, stopped** **1** cease or cause to cease from doing (something). **2** bring to or come to a halt. **3** prevent or restrain. **4** withhold. **5** block or plug. **6** stay or rest. ◆ *n* **7** stopping or being stopped. **8** place where something stops. **9** full stop. **10** knob on an organ that is pulled out to allow a set of pipes to sound. **stoppage** *n* **stopper** *n* plug for closing a bottle etc. **stopcock** *n* valve to control or stop the flow of fluid in a pipe. **stopgap** *n* temporary substitute. **stopover** *n* short break in a journey. **stop press** news item put into a newspaper after printing has been started. **stopwatch** *n* watch which can be stopped instantly for exact timing of a sporting event.

store ⊕ *v* **1** collect and keep (things) for future use. **2** put (furniture etc.) in a warehouse for safekeeping. **3** stock (goods). **4** *Computers* enter or retain (data). ◆ *n* **5** shop. **6** supply kept for future use. **7** storage place, such as a warehouse. ◆ *pl* **8** stock of provisions. **in store** about to happen. **set great store by** value greatly. **storage** *n* **1** storing. **2** space for storing.

storey *n* floor or level of a building.

————————— THESAURUS —————————

stoic *adj* **2** (also **stoical**) = **resigned**, dispassionate, impassive, long–suffering, philosophic, phlegmatic, stolid

stolid *adj* = **apathetic**, dull, lumpish, unemotional, wooden

stomach *n* **2** = **belly**, abdomen, gut (*inf*), pot, tummy (*inf*) **3** = **inclination**, appetite, desire, relish, taste ◆ *v* **4** = **bear**, abide, endure, swallow, take, tolerate

stoop *v* **1** = **bend**, bow, crouch, duck, hunch, lean **3** = **lower oneself by**, descend to, resort to, sink to ◆ *n* **4** = **slouch**, bad posture

stop *v* **1, 2** = **halt**, cease, conclude, cut short, desist, discontinue, end, finish, pause, put an end to, quit, refrain, shut down, terminate ≠ **start** **3** = **prevent**, arrest, forestall, hinder, hold back, impede, repress, restrain ≠ **further** **5** = **plug**, block, obstruct, seal, staunch, stem **6** = **stay**, lodge, rest ◆ *n* **7** = **end**, cessation, finish, halt, standstill **8** = **station**, depot, terminus

store *v* **1, 2** = **put by**, deposit, garner, hoard, keep, put aside, reserve, save, stockpile ◆ *n* **5** = **shop**, market, mart,

stork n large wading bird.

storm ❶ n 1 violent weather with wind, rain, or snow. 2 strongly expressed reaction. ◆ v 3 attack or capture (a place) suddenly. 4 shout angrily. 5 rush violently or angrily. **stormy** adj 1 characterized by storms. 2 involving violent emotions.

story ❶ n, pl –ries 1 description of a series of events told or written for entertainment. 2 plot of a book or film. 3 news report. 4 Informal lie.

stout ❶ adj 1 fat. 2 thick and strong. 3 brave and resolute. ◆ n 4 strong dark beer. **stoutly** adv

stove n apparatus for cooking or heating.

stow ❶ v pack or store. **stowaway** n person who hides on a ship or aircraft in order to travel free. **stow away** v hide as a stowaway.

straddle v have one leg or part on each side of (something).

straggle v go or spread in a rambling or irregular way. **straggler** n **straggly** adj

straight ❶ adj 1 not curved or crooked. 2 level or upright. 3 orderly. 4 honest or frank. 5 in continuous succession. 6 (of spirits) undiluted. 7 Theatre serious. 8 Slang heterosexual. 9 Slang conventional. ◆ adv 10 in a straight line. 11 immediately. 12 in a level or upright position. ◆ n 13 straight part, esp. of a racetrack. **go straight** Informal reform after being a criminal. **straighten** v **straightaway** adv immediately. **straight face** serious facial expression concealing a desire to laugh. **straightforward** adj 1 honest, frank. 2 (of a task) easy.

strain¹ ❶ v 1 cause (something) to be used or tested beyond its limits. 2 make an intense effort. 3 injure by overexertion. 4 sieve. ◆ n 5 tension or tiredness. 6 force exerted by straining. 7 injury from overexertion. 8 great demand on strength or resources. 9 melody or theme. **strained** adj 1 not natural, forced. 2 not relaxed, tense. **strainer** n sieve.

strain² ❶ n 1 breed or race. 2 trace or streak.

——————— THESAURUS ———————

outlet 6 = **supply**, accumulation, cache, fund, hoard, quantity, reserve, stock, stockpile 7 = **repository**, depository, storeroom, warehouse

storm n 1 = **tempest**, blizzard, gale, hurricane, squall 2 = **outburst**, agitation, commotion, disturbance, furore, outbreak, outcry, row, rumpus, strife, tumult, turmoil ◆ v 3 = **attack**, assail, assault, charge, rush 4 = **rage**, bluster, rant, rave, thunder 5 = **rush**, flounce, fly, stamp

story n 1 = **tale**, account, anecdote, history, legend, narrative, romance, yarn 3 = **report**, article, feature, news, news item, scoop

stout adj 1 = **fat**, big, bulky, burly, corpulent, fleshy, heavy, overweight, plump, portly, rotund, tubby ≠ **lean** 2 = **strong**, able–bodied, brawny, muscular, robust, stalwart, strapping, sturdy ≠ **frail** 3 = **brave**, bold, courageous, fearless, gallant, intrepid, plucky, resolute, valiant ≠ **fearful**

stow v = **pack**, bundle, load, put away, stash (inf), store

straight adj 1 = **direct**, near, short 2 a = **level**, aligned, even, horizontal, right, smooth, square, true b = **upright**, erect, plumb, vertical 3 = **orderly**, arranged, in order, neat, organized, shipshape, tidy 4 a = **honest**, above board, fair, honourable, just, law–abiding, reliable, respectable, trustworthy, upright b = **frank**, blunt, bold, candid, forthright, honest, outright, plain, straightforward ≠ **vague** 5 = **successive**, consecutive, continuous, nonstop, running, solid ≠ **interrupted** 6 = **undiluted**, neat, pure, unadulterated, unmixed 9 Sl = **conventional**, bourgeois, conservative ◆ adv 11 = **directly**, at once, immediately, instantly

strain¹ v 2 = **strive**, bend over backwards (inf), endeavour, give it one's best shot (inf), go for it (inf), knock oneself out (inf), labour, struggle ≠ **rest** 3 = **overexert**, injure, overtax, overwork, pull, sprain, tax,

strait ⊕ n 1 narrow channel connecting two areas of sea. ◆ pl 2 position of acute difficulty. **straitjacket** n strong jacket with long sleeves used to bind the arms of a violent person. **strait–laced, straight–laced** adj prudish or puritanical.

strand¹ v 1 run aground. 2 leave in difficulties. ◆ n 3 Poetic shore.

strand² ⊕ n single thread of string, wire, etc.

strange ⊕ adj 1 odd or unusual. 2 not familiar. 3 inexperienced (in) or unaccustomed (to). **strangely** adv **strangeness** n **stranger** n person who is not known or is new to a place or experience.

strangle ⊕ v 1 kill by squeezing the throat. 2 prevent the development of. **strangler** n **strangulation** n strangling. **stranglehold** n 1 strangling grip in wrestling. 2 powerful control.

strap ⊕ n 1 strip of flexible material for lifting, fastening, or holding in place. ◆ v **strapping, strapped** fasten with a strap or straps. **strapping** adj tall and sturdy.

strategy ⊕ n, pl **–gies** 1 overall plan. 2 art of planning in war. **strategic** [strat–**ee**–jik] adj 1 advantageous. 2 (of weapons) aimed at an enemy's homeland. **strategically** adv

strategist n

stratosphere n atmospheric layer between about 15 and 50 kilometres above the earth.

stratum [**strah**–tum] n, pl **strata** 1 layer, esp. of rock. 2 social class. **stratification** n

straw n 1 dried stalks of grain. 2 single stalk of straw. 3 long thin tube used to suck up liquid into the mouth. **straw poll** unofficial poll taken to determine general opinion.

stray ⊕ v 1 wander. 2 digress. 3 deviate from certain moral standards. ◆ adj 4 having strayed. 5 scattered, random. ◆ n 6 stray animal.

streak ⊕ n 1 long band of contrasting colour or substance. 2 quality or characteristic. 3 short stretch (of good or bad luck). ◆ v 4 mark with streaks. 5 move rapidly. 6 Informal run naked in public. **streaker** n **streaky** adj

stream ⊕ n 1 small river. 2 steady flow, as of liquid, speech, or people. 3 schoolchildren grouped together because of similar ability. ◆ v 4 flow steadily. 5 move in unbroken succession. 6 float in the air. 7 group (pupils) in streams. **streamer** n 1 strip of coloured paper that unrolls when tossed. 2 long narrow flag.

——————| THESAURUS |——————

tear, twist, wrench 4 = **sieve**, filter, purify, sift ◆ n 5 = **stress**, anxiety, burden, pressure, tension 6 = **exertion**, effort, force, struggle ≠ **ease** 7 = **injury**, pull, sprain, wrench

strain² n 1 = **breed**, ancestry, blood, descent, extraction, family, lineage, race 2 = **trace**, streak, suggestion, tendency

strait n 1 = **channel**, narrows, sound ◆ pl 2 = **difficulty**, dilemma, distress, embarrassment, extremity, hardship, plight, predicament

strand² n 1 = **filament**, fibre, string, thread

strange adj 1 = **odd**, abnormal, bizarre, curious, extraordinary, munted (NZ sl), peculiar, queer, uncommon, weird, wonderful ≠ **usual** 2 = **unfamiliar**, alien, exotic, foreign, new, novel, unknown,

untried ≠ **familiar**

strangle v 1 = **throttle**, asphyxiate, choke, strangulate 2 = **suppress**, inhibit, repress, stifle

strap n 1 = **belt**, thong, tie ◆ v 2 = **fasten**, bind, buckle, lash, secure, tie

strategy n 1 = **plan**, approach, policy, procedure, scheme

stray v 1 = **wander**, drift, err, go astray 2 = **digress**, deviate, diverge, get off the point ◆ adj 4 = **lost**, abandoned, homeless, roaming, vagrant 5 = **random**, accidental, chance

streak n 1 = **band**, layer, line, slash, strip, stripe, stroke, vein 2 = **trace**, dash, element, strain, touch, vein ◆ v 5 = **speed**, dart, flash, fly, hurtle, sprint, tear, whizz (inf), zoom

street ❶ *n* public road, usu. lined with buildings. **streetcar** *n US* tram. **streetwise** *adj* knowing how to survive in big cities.

strength ❶ *n* 1 quality of being strong. 2 quality or ability considered an advantage. 3 degree of intensity. 4 total number of people in a group. **on the strength of** on the basis of. **strengthen** *v*

strenuous ❶ *adj* requiring great energy or effort.

stress ❶ *n* 1 tension or strain. 2 emphasis. 3 stronger sound in saying a word or syllable. 4 *Physics* force producing strain. ◆ *v* 5 emphasize. 6 put stress on (a word or syllable). **stressed–out** *adj Informal* suffering from tension.

stretch ❶ *v* 1 extend or be extended. 2 be able to be stretched. 3 extend the limbs or body. 4 strain (resources or abilities) to the utmost. ◆ *n* 5 stretching. 6 continuous expanse. 7 period. 8 *Informal* term of imprisonment. **stretchy** *adj* **stretcher** *n* frame covered with canvas, on which an injured person is carried.

strew *v* **strewing, strewed, strewed** or **strewn** scatter (things) over a surface.

stricken *adj* seriously affected by disease,

grief, pain, etc.

stricture *n* severe criticism.

stride *v* **striding, strode, stridden** 1 walk with long steps. ◆ *n* 2 long step. 3 regular pace. ◆ *pl* 4 progress.

strident ❶ *adj* loud and harsh. **stridently** *adv* **stridency** *n*

strife ❶ *n* conflict, quarrelling.

strike ❶ *v* **striking, struck** 1 cease work as a protest. 2 hit. 3 attack suddenly. 4 ignite (a match) by friction. 5 (of a clock) indicate (a time) by sounding a bell. 6 enter the mind of. 7 afflict. 8 discover (gold, oil, etc.). 9 agree (a bargain). 10 take up (a posture). 11 make (a coin) by stamping it. ◆ *n* 12 stoppage of work as a protest. 13 striking. **strike camp** dismantle and pack up tents. **strike home** have the desired effect. **striker** *n* 1 striking worker. 2 attacking footballer. **striking** *adj* 1 impressive. 2 noteworthy. **strike off, out** *v* cross out. **strike up** *v* 1 begin (a conversation or friendship). 2 begin to play music.

string ❶ *n* 1 thin cord used for tying. 2 set of objects threaded on a string. 3 series of things or events. 4 stretched wire or cord

———— THESAURUS ————

stream *n* 1 = **river**, bayou, beck, brook, burn (*Scot*), rivulet, tributary 2 = **flow**, course, current, drift, run, rush, surge, tide, torrent ◆ *v* 4, 5 = **flow**, cascade, flood, gush, issue, pour, run, spill, spout

street *n* = **road**, avenue, lane, roadway, row, terrace

strength *n* 1 = **might**, brawn, courage, fortitude, muscle, robustness, stamina, sturdiness, toughness ≠ **weakness** 2 = **strong point**, advantage, asset ≠ **failing** 3 = **power**, effectiveness, efficacy, force, intensity, potency, vigour ≠ **feebleness**

strenuous *adj* = **demanding**, arduous, hard, laborious, taxing, tough, uphill ≠ **easy**

stress *n* 1 = **strain**, anxiety, burden, pressure, tension, trauma, worry 2 = **emphasis**, force, significance, weight

3 = **accent**, accentuation, beat, emphasis ◆ *v* 5 = **emphasize**, accentuate, dwell on, underline

stretch *v* 1 = **extend**, cover, put forth, reach, spread, unroll 2 = **distend**, draw out, elongate, expand, strain, tighten 4 = **strain** ◆ *n* 6 = **expanse**, area, distance, extent, spread, tract 7 = **period**, space, spell, stint, term, time

strident *adj* = **harsh**, discordant, grating, jarring, rasping, raucous, screeching, shrill ≠ **soft**

strife *n* = **conflict**, battle, clash, discord, dissension, friction, quarrel

strike *v* 1 = **walk out**, down tools, mutiny, revolt 2 = **hit**, beat, clobber (*sl*), clout (*inf*), cuff, hammer, knock, punch, slap, smack, swipe, thump, wallop (*inf*) 3 = **attack**, assail, assault, deal a blow to, devastate, hit 6 = **occur to**, come to, dawn on a musical instrument that produces sound when vibrated. ◆ *pl* 5 restrictions or conditions. 6 section of an orchestra consisting of stringed instruments. ◆ *v* **stringing, strung** 7 provide with a string or strings. 8 thread on a string. **pull strings** use one's influence. **stringed** *adj* (of a musical instrument) having strings that are plucked or played with a bow. **stringy** *adj* 1 like string. 2 (of meat) fibrous. **string along** *v* 1 deceive over a period of time. **string up** *v Informal* kill by hanging.

stringent ❶ [strin–jent] *adj* strictly controlled or enforced. **stringency** *n*

strip[1] ❶ *v* **stripping, stripped** 1 take (the covering or clothes) off. 2 take a title or possession away from (someone). 3 remove (paint) from (a surface). 4 dismantle (an engine). ◆ *n* 5 act of stripping. **stripper** *n* person who performs a striptease. **striptease** *n* entertainment in which a performer undresses to music.

strip[2] ❶ *n* 1 long narrow piece. 2 clothes a football team plays in. **strip cartoon** sequence of drawings telling a story.

stripe *n* 1 long narrow band of contrasting colour or substance. 2 chevron on a uniform to indicate rank. **striped, stripy, stripey** *adj*

strive ❶ *v* **striving, strove, striven** make a great effort.

stroke ❶ *v* 1 touch or caress lightly with the hand. ◆ *n* 2 light touch or caress with the hand. 3 rupture of a blood vessel in the brain. 4 blow. 5 action or occurrence of the kind specified, e.g. *a stroke of luck.* 6 chime of a clock. 7 mark made by a pen or paintbrush. 8 style or method of swimming.

stroll ❶ *v* 1 walk in a leisurely manner. ◆ *n* 2 leisurely walk.

strong ❶ *adj* 1 having physical power. 2 not easily broken. 3 great in degree or intensity. 4 having moral force. 5 having a specified number, e.g. *twenty strong.* **strongly** *adv* **stronghold** *n* 1 area of predominance of a particular belief. 2 fortress. **strongroom** *n* room designed for the safekeeping of valuables.

stroppy *adj* **–pier, –piest** *Slang* angry or awkward.

structure ❶ *n* 1 complex construction. 2 manner or basis of construction or organization. ◆ *v* 3 give a structure to. **structural** *adj* **structuralism** *n* approach to literature, social sciences, etc., which sees changes in the subject as caused and organized by a hidden set of universal rules. **structuralist** *n, adj*

━━━━ THESAURUS ━━━━

on *or* upon, hit, register (*inf*)
string *n* 1 = **cord**, fibre, twine 3 = **series**, chain, file, line, procession, row, sequence, succession
stringent *adj* = **strict**, inflexible, rigid, rigorous, severe, tight, tough
strip[1] *v* 1 = **undress**, disrobe, unclothe 2 = **divest**, rob
strip[2] *n* 1 = **piece**, band, belt, fillet, ribbon, shred
strive *v* = **try**, attempt, bend over backwards (*inf*), break one's neck (*inf*), do one's best, give it one's best shot (*inf*), go all out (*inf*), knock oneself out (*inf*), labour, make an all–out effort (*inf*), struggle, toil
stroke *v* 1 = **caress**, fondle, pet, rub ◆ *n* 3 = **apoplexy**, attack, collapse, fit, seizure

4 = **blow**, hit, knock, pat, rap, swipe, thump
stroll *v* 1 = **walk**, amble, promenade, ramble, saunter ◆ *n* 2 = **walk**, breath of air, constitutional, excursion, promenade, ramble, turn
strong *adj* 1 = **powerful**, athletic, brawny, burly, hardy, lusty, muscular, robust, strapping, sturdy, tough ≠ **weak** 2 = **durable**, hard–wearing, heavy–duty, sturdy, substantial, well–built ≠ **fragile** 3 = **intense**, acute, deep, fervent, fervid, fierce, firm, keen, vehement, violent, zealous 4 = **persuasive**, compelling, convincing, effective, potent, sound, telling, weighty, well–founded
structure *n* 1 = **building**, construction,

struggle ❶ v 1 work, strive, or make one's way with difficulty. 2 move about violently in an attempt to get free. 3 fight (with someone). ◆ n 4 striving. 5 fight.

strum v strumming, strummed play (a guitar or banjo) by sweeping the thumb or a plectrum across the strings.

strut ❶ v strutting, strutted 1 walk pompously, swagger. ◆ n 2 bar supporting a structure.

strychnine [strik-neen] n very poisonous drug used in small quantities as a stimulant.

stub ❶ n 1 short piece left after use. 2 counterfoil of a cheque or ticket. ◆ v stubbing, stubbed 3 strike (the toe) painfully against an object. 4 put out (a cigarette) by pressing the end against a surface. **stubby** adj short and broad.

stubble n 1 short stalks of grain left in a field after reaping. 2 short growth of hair on the chin of a man who has not shaved recently. **stubbly** adj

stubborn ❶ adj 1 refusing to agree or give in. 2 difficult to deal with. **stubbornly** adv **stubbornness** n

stucco n plaster used for coating or decorating walls.

stud¹ ❶ n 1 small piece of metal attached to a surface for decoration. 2 disc-like removable fastener for clothes. 3 one of several small round objects fixed to the sole of a football boot to give better grip. ◆ v studding, studded 4 set with studs.

**stud² ** n 1 male animal, esp. a stallion, kept for breeding. 2 (also stud farm) place where horses are bred. 3 Slang virile or sexually active man.

studio ❶ n, pl -dios 1 workroom of an artist or photographer. 2 room or building in which television or radio programmes, records, or films are made.

study ❶ v studying, studied 1 be engaged in learning (a subject). 2 investigate by observation and research. 3 scrutinize. ◆ n, pl studies 4 act or process of studying. 5 room for studying in. 6 book or paper produced as a result of study. 7 sketch done as practice or preparation. 8 musical composition designed to improve playing technique. **student** n person who studies a subject, esp. at university. **studied** adj carefully practised or planned. **studious** adj 1 fond of study. 2 careful and deliberate. **studiously** adv

stuff ❶ n 1 substance or material. 2 collection of unnamed things. ◆ v 3 pack, cram, or fill completely. 4 fill (food) with a

---

edifice, erection 2 = **arrangement**, configuration, construction, design, form, formation, make-up, organization ◆ v 3 = **arrange**, assemble, build up, design, organize, shape

struggle v 1 = **strive**, exert oneself, give it one's best shot (inf), go all out (inf), knock oneself out (inf), labour, make an all-out effort (inf), strain, toil, work 3 = **fight**, battle, compete, contend, grapple, wrestle ◆ n 4 = **effort**, exertion, labour, pains, scramble, toil, work, yakka (Aust & NZ inf) 5 = **fight**, battle, brush, clash, combat, conflict, contest, tussle

strut v 1 = **swagger**, parade, peacock, prance

stub n 1 = **butt**, dog-end (inf), end, remnant, stump, tail, tail end

2 = **counterfoil**

stubborn adj = **obstinate**, dogged, headstrong, inflexible, intractable, obdurate, pig-headed, recalcitrant, tenacious, unyielding ≠ **yielding**

stud¹ v 4 = **ornament**, dot, spangle, spot

studio n 1 = **workshop**, atelier

study v 1 = **learn**, cram (inf), mug up (Brit sl), read up, swot (up) (Brit inf) 2 = **contemplate**, consider, examine, go into, ponder, pore over, read 3 = **examine**, analyse, investigate, look into, research, scrutinize, survey ◆ n 4 a = **learning**, application, lessons, reading, research, school work, swotting (Brit inf) b = **examination**, analysis, consideration, contemplation, inquiry, inspection, investigation, review, scrutiny, survey seasoned mixture. **5** fill (an animal's skin) with material to restore the shape of the live animal. **stuffing** *n* **1** seasoned mixture with which food is stuffed. **2** padding.

stumble ⚊ *v* **1** trip and nearly fall. **2** walk in an unsure way. **3** make frequent mistakes in speech. ♦ *n* **4** stumbling. **stumble across** *v* discover accidentally. **stumbling block** obstacle or difficulty.

stump ⚊ *n* **1** base of a tree left when the main trunk has been cut away. **2** part of a thing left after a larger part has been removed. **3** *Cricket* one of the three upright sticks forming the wicket. ♦ *v* **4** baffle. **5** *Cricket* dismiss (a batsman) by breaking his wicket with the ball. **6** walk with heavy steps. **stumpy** *adj* short and thick. **stump up** *v Informal* give (the money required).

stun ⚊ *v* **1 stunning, stunned 1** shock or overwhelm. **2** knock senseless. **stunning** *adj* very attractive or impressive.

stunt[1] *v* prevent or impede the growth of.

stunt[2] ⚊ *n* **1** acrobatic or dangerous action. **2** anything spectacular done to gain publicity.

stupefy ⚊ *v* –fying, –fied **1** make insensitive or lethargic. **2** astound. **stupefaction** *n*

stupendous ⚊ *adj* very large or impressive.

stupid ⚊ *adj* **1** lacking intelligence. **2** silly. **3** in a stupor. **stupidity** *n* **stupidly** *adv*

stupor ⚊ *n* dazed or unconscious state.

sturdy ⚊ *adj* –dier, –diest **1** healthy and robust. **2** strongly built. **sturdily** *adv*

sturgeon *n* fish from which caviar is obtained.

stutter ⚊ *v* **1** speak with repetition of initial consonants. ♦ *n* **2** tendency to stutter.

sty *n, pl* **sties** pen for pigs.

stye, sty *n, pl* **styes, sties** inflammation at the base of an eyelash.

style ⚊ *n* **1** shape or design. **2** manner of writing, speaking, or doing something. **3** elegance, refinement. **4** prevailing fashion. ♦ *v* **5** shape or design. **6** name or call. **stylish** *adj* smart, elegant, and fashionable. **stylist** *n* **1** hairdresser. **2** person who writes or performs with great attention to style. **stylistic** *adj* of literary or

stuff *n* **1 = substance**, essence, matter **2 = things**, belongings, bits and pieces, effects, equipment, gear, kit, objects, paraphernalia, possessions, tackle **5 = material**, cloth, fabric, raw material, textile

stumble *v* **1 = trip**, fall, falter, lurch, reel, slip, stagger **stumble across = discover**, chance upon, come across, find, locate, turn up, uncover, unearth

stump *v* **4 = baffle**, bewilder, confuse, flummox, mystify, nonplus, perplex, puzzle

stun *v* **1 = overcome**, astonish, astound, bewilder, confound, confuse, overpower, shock, stagger, stupefy **2 = knock out**, daze

stunt[2] *n* **= feat**, act, deed, exploit, trick

stupefy *v* **2 = astound**, amaze, daze, dumbfound, shock, stagger, stun

stupendous *adj* **a = wonderful**, amazing,

astounding, breathtaking, jaw–dropping, marvellous, overwhelming, sensational (*inf*), staggering, superb ≠ **average b = huge**, colossal, enormous, gigantic, mega (*sl*), vast ≠ **tiny**

stupid *adj* **1 = unintelligent**, brainless, dense, dim, half–witted, moronic, obtuse, simple, simple–minded, slow, slow–witted, thick ≠ **bright 2 = silly**, asinine, daft (*inf*), foolish, idiotic, imbecilic, inane, nonsensical, pointless, rash, senseless, unintelligent ≠ **wise 3 = dazed**, groggy, insensate, semiconscious, stunned, stupefied

stupor *n* **= daze**, coma, insensibility, stupefaction, unconsciousness

sturdy *adj* **1 = robust**, athletic, brawny, hardy, lusty, muscular, powerful ≠ **weak 2 = substantial**, durable, solid, well–built, well–made ≠ **frail**

stutter *v* **1 = stammer**, falter, hesitate,

artistic style. **stylize** v cause to conform to an established stylistic form.

stylus n needle–like device on a record player that rests in the groove of the record and picks up the sound signals.

suave 🛈 [swahv] adj smooth and sophisticated in manner.

sub n 1 subeditor. 2 submarine. 3 subscription. 4 substitute. 5 Informal advance payment of wages or salary. ◆ v **subbing, subbed** 6 act as a substitute. 7 grant advance payment to.

subconscious 🛈 adj 1 happening or existing without one's awareness. ◆ n 2 Psychoanalysis that part of the mind of which one is not aware but which can influence one's behaviour.

subdivide v divide (a part of something) into smaller parts. **subdivision** n

subdue 🛈 v –duing, –dued 1 overcome. 2 make less intense.

subject 🛈 n 1 person or thing being dealt with or studied. 2 Grammar word or phrase that represents the person or thing performing the action of the verb in a sentence. 3 person under the rule of a monarch or government. ◆ adj 4 being under the rule of a monarch or

government. ◆ v (foll. by to) 5 cause to undergo. **subject to 1** liable to. 2 conditional upon. **subjection** n **subjective** adj based on personal feelings or prejudices. **subjectively** adv

subjugate 🛈 v bring (a group of people) under one's control. **subjugation** n

sublet v –letting, –let rent out (property rented from someone else).

sublime 🛈 adj 1 of high moral, intellectual, or spiritual value. 2 unparalleled, supreme. ◆ v 3 Chem change from a solid to a vapour without first melting. **sublimely** adv

subliminal adj relating to mental processes of which the individual is not aware.

submarine n 1 vessel which can operate below the surface of the sea. ◆ adj 2 below the surface of the sea.

submerge 🛈 v put or go below the surface of water or other liquid. **submersion** n

subordinate 🛈 adj 1 of lesser rank or importance. ◆ n 2 subordinate person or thing. ◆ v 3 make or treat as subordinate. **subordination** n

subscribe 🛈 v 1 pay (a subscription). 2

———————— THESAURUS ————————

stumble

style n 1 = **design**, cut, form, manner 2 = **manner**, approach, method, mode, technique, way 3 = **elegance**, affluence, chic, comfort, ease, élan, flair, grandeur, luxury, panache, polish, smartness, sophistication, taste 4 = **fashion**, mode, rage, trend, vogue ◆ v 5 = **design**, adapt, arrange, cut, fashion, shape, tailor 6 = **call**, designate, dub, entitle, label, name, term

suave adj = **smooth**, charming, courteous, debonair, polite, sophisticated, urbane

subconscious adj 1 = **hidden**, inner, intuitive, latent, repressed, subliminal ≠ **knowing**

subdue v 1 = **overcome**, break, conquer, control, crush, defeat, master, overpower, quell, tame, vanquish 2 = **moderate**, mellow, quieten down, soften, suppress,

tone down ≠ **provoke**

subject n 1 = **topic**, affair, business, issue, matter, object, point, question, substance, theme 3 = **citizen**, national, subordinate ◆ adj 4 = **subordinate**, dependent, inferior, obedient, satellite ◆ v (foll. by to) 5 = **put through**, expose, lay open, submit, treat **subject to 1** = **liable to**, prone to 2 = **conditional on**, contingent on, dependent on

subjugate v = **conquer**, enslave, master, overcome, overpower, quell, subdue, suppress, vanquish

sublime adj 1 = **noble**, elevated, exalted, glorious, grand, great, high, lofty ≠ **ordinary**

submerge v 1 = **immerse**, deluge, dip, duck, engulf, flood, inundate, overflow, overwhelm, plunge, sink, swamp

give support or approval (to). **subscriber** *n*
subscription *n* 1 payment for issues of a
publication over a period. 2 money
contributed to a charity etc. 3
membership fees paid to a society.
subsequent ❶ *adj* occurring after,
succeeding.
subservient ❶ *adj* submissive, servile.
subservience *n*
subside ❶ *v* 1 become less intense. 2 sink
to a lower level. **subsidence** *n* act or
process of subsiding.
subsidiary ❶ *adj* 1 of lesser importance. ◆
n, pl **–aries** 2 subsidiary person or thing.
subsidize ❶ *v* help financially. **subsidy** *n*,
pl **–dies** financial aid.
subsist *v* manage to live. **subsistence** *n*
substance ❶ *n* 1 physical composition of
something. 2 solid, powder, liquid, or
paste. 3 essential meaning of something. 4
solid or meaningful quality. 5 wealth.
substantial *adj* 1 of considerable size or
value. 2 (of food or a meal) sufficient and
nourishing. 3 solid or strong. 4 real.
substantially *adv* **substantiate** *v* support
(a story) with evidence. **substantiation** *n*
substantive *n* 1 noun. ◆ *adj* 2 of or being

the essential element of a thing.
substitute ❶ *v* 1 take the place of or put
in place of another. ◆ *n* 2 person or thing
taking the place of (another). **substitution**
n
subsume *v* include (an idea, case, etc.)
under a larger classification or group.
subterfuge ❶ *n* trick used to achieve an
objective.
subterranean *adj* underground.
subtitle *n* 1 secondary title of a book. ◆ *pl*
2 printed translation at the bottom of the
picture in a film with foreign dialogue. ◆ *v*
3 provide with a subtitle or subtitles.
subtle ❶ *adj* 1 not immediately obvious. 2
having or requiring ingenuity. **subtly** *adv*
subtlety *n*
subtract ❶ *v* take (one number or
quantity) from another. **subtraction** *n*
suburb *n* residential area on the outskirts
of a city. **suburban** *adj* 1 of or inhabiting a
suburb. 2 narrow or unadventurous in
outlook. **suburbia** *n* suburbs and their
inhabitants.
subvert ❶ *v* overthrow the authority of.
subversion *n* **subversive** *adj, n*
subway *n* 1 passage under a road or

——— THESAURUS ———

subordinate *adj* 1 = **lesser**, dependent,
inferior, junior, lower, minor, secondary,
subject ≠ **senior** ◆ *n* 2 = **inferior**, aide,
assistant, attendant, junior, second
≠ **head**
subscribe *v* 1 = **contribute**, donate, give
2 = **support**, advocate, endorse
subsequent *adj* = **following**, after,
ensuing, later, succeeding, successive
subservient *adj* = **servile**, abject,
deferential, obsequious, slavish,
submissive, sycophantic ≠ **bossy**
subside *v* 1 = **decrease**, abate, diminish,
ease, ebb, lessen, quieten, slacken, wane
≠ **rise** 2 = **collapse**, cave in, drop, lower,
settle, sink
subsidiary *adj* 1 = **lesser**, ancillary,
auxiliary, minor, secondary, subordinate,
supplementary ≠ **leading**
subsidize *v* = **fund**, finance, promote,

sponsor, support
substance *n* 1 = **material**, body, element,
fabric, stuff 3 = **meaning**, essence, gist,
import, main point, significance
4 = **reality**, actuality, concreteness
5 = **wealth**, affluence, assets, estate,
means, property, resources, riches
substitute *v* 1 = **replace**, change,
exchange, interchange, swap, switch ◆ *n*
2 = **replacement**, agent, deputy, locum,
proxy, reserve, sub, surrogate
subterfuge *n* = **trick**, deception, dodge,
manoeuvre, ploy, ruse, stratagem
subtle *adj* 1 = **faint**, delicate, implied,
slight, understated ≠ **blatant** 2 = **crafty**,
artful, cunning, devious, ingenious,
shrewd, sly, wily ≠ **straightforward**
subtract *v* = **take away**, deduct, diminish,
remove, take from, take off
subvert *v* = **overturn**, sabotage,

railway. 2 underground railway.

succeed ❶ *v* 1 accomplish an aim. 2 turn out satisfactorily. 3 come next in order after (something). 4 take over a position from (someone). **success** *n* 1 achievement of something attempted. 2 attainment of wealth, fame, or position. 3 successful person or thing. **successful** *adj* having success. **successfully** *adv* **succession** *n* 1 series of people or things following one another in order. 2 act or right by which one person succeeds another in a position. **successive** *adj* consecutive. **successively** *adv* **successor** *n* person who succeeds someone in a position.

succinct ❶ *adj* brief and clear.

succour ❶ *v*, *n* help in distress.

succulent ❶ *adj* 1 juicy and delicious. 2 (of a plant) having thick fleshy leaves. ◆ *n* 3 succulent plant. **succulence** *n*

succumb ❶ *v* 1 (foll. by *to*) give way (to something overpowering). 2 die of (an illness).

such *adj* 1 of the kind specified. 2 so great, so much. ◆ *pron* 3 such things. **such-and-such** *adj* specific, but not known or named. **suchlike** *pron* such or similar things.

suck *v* 1 draw (liquid or air) into the mouth. 2 take (something) into the mouth and moisten, dissolve, or roll it around with the tongue. 3 (foll. by *in*) draw in by irresistible force. ◆ *n* 4 sucking. **sucker** *n* 1

Slang person who is easily deceived or swindled. 2 organ or device which adheres by suction. 3 shoot coming from a plant's root or the base of its main stem. **suck up to** *v* *Informal* flatter (someone) for one's own profit.

suckle *v* feed at the breast. **suckling** *n* unweaned baby or young animal.

suction *n* 1 sucking. 2 force produced by drawing air out of a space to make a vacuum that will suck in a substance from another space.

sudden ❶ *adj* done or occurring quickly and unexpectedly. **all of a sudden** quickly and unexpectedly. **suddenly** *adv* **suddenness** *n*

suds *pl n* froth of soap and water, lather.

sue ❶ *v* suing, sued start legal proceedings against.

suede *n* leather with a velvety finish on one side.

suet *n* hard fat obtained from sheep and cattle, used in cooking.

suffer ❶ *v* 1 undergo or be subjected to. 2 tolerate. **sufferer** *n* **suffering** *n* **sufferance** *n* **on sufferance** tolerated with reluctance.

suffice ❶ [suf-**fice**] *v* be enough for a purpose. **sufficiency** *n* adequate amount. **sufficient** *adj* enough, adequate. **sufficiently** *adv*

suffix *n* letter or letters added to the end of a word to form another word.

suffocate ❶ *v* 1 kill or be killed by

undermine

succeed *v* 1, 2 = **make it** (*inf*), be successful, crack it (*inf*), do well, flourish, make good, make the grade (*inf*), prosper, thrive, triumph, work ≠ **fail** 3 = **follow**, come next, ensue, result ≠ **precede** 4 = **take over**, accede, assume the office of, come into, come into possession of, inherit

succinct *adj* = **brief**, compact, concise, laconic, pithy, terse

① **succour** *v* = **help**, aid, assist

② **succour** *n* = **help**, aid, assistance

succulent *adj* 1 = **juicy**, luscious, lush,

moist

succumb *v* 1 (foll. by *to*) = **surrender**, capitulate, cave in (*inf*), give in, submit, yield ≠ **beat** 2 = **die**, cark (*Aust & NZ sl*), fall

sudden *adj* = **quick**, abrupt, hasty, hurried, rapid, rash, swift, unexpected

sue *v* = **take (someone) to court**, charge, indict, prosecute, summon

suffer *v* 1 = **undergo**, bear, endure, experience, go through, sustain 2 = **tolerate**, put up with (*inf*)

suffice *v* = **be enough**, be adequate, be sufficient, do, meet requirements, serve

0

0

off

deprivation of oxygen. 2 feel uncomfortable from heat and lack of air. **suffocation** n

suffrage n right to vote in public elections. **suffragette** n (in Britain in the early 20th century) a woman who campaigned militantly for the right to vote.

suffuse v spread through or over (something). **suffusion** n

sugar n 1 sweet crystalline carbohydrate found in many plants and used to sweeten food and drinks. ◆ v 2 sweeten or cover with sugar. **sugary** adj **sugar beet** beet grown for the sugar obtained from its roots. **sugar cane** tropical grass grown for the sugar obtained from its canes.

suggest ❶ v 1 put forward (an idea) for consideration. 2 bring to mind by the association of ideas. 3 give a hint of. **suggestible** adj easily influenced. **suggestion** n 1 thing suggested. 2 hint or indication. **suggestive** adj 1 suggesting something indecent. 2 conveying a hint (of). **suggestively** adv

suicide n 1 killing oneself intentionally. 2 person who kills himself intentionally. 3 self–inflicted ruin of one's own prospects or interests. **suicidal** adj liable to commit suicide. **suicidally** adv

suit ❶ n 1 set of clothes designed to be worn together. 2 outfit worn for a specific purpose. 3 one of the four sets into which a pack of cards is divided. 4 lawsuit. ◆ v 5 be appropriate for. 6 be acceptable to.

suitable adj appropriate or proper. **suitably** adv **suitability** n **suitcase** n portable travelling case for clothing.

suite ❶ n 1 set of connected rooms in a hotel. 2 matching set of furniture. 3 set of musical pieces in the same key.

suitor ❶ n Old–fashioned man who is courting a woman.

sulk v 1 be silent and sullen because of resentment or bad temper. ◆ n 2 resentful or sullen mood. **sulky** adj **sulkily** adv

sullen ❶ adj unwilling to talk or be sociable. **sullenness** n

sully ❶ v –lying, –lied 1 ruin (someone's reputation). 2 make dirty.

sulphur n Chem pale yellow nonmetallic element. **sulphuric, sulphurous** adj of or containing sulphur.

sultan n sovereign of a Muslim country. **sultana** n 1 kind of raisin. 2 sultan's wife, mother, or daughter. **sultanate** n territory of a sultan.

sultry ❶ adj –trier, –triest 1 (of weather or climate) hot and humid. 2 passionate, sensual.

sum ❶ n 1 result of addition, total. 2 problem in arithmetic. 3 quantity of money. **sum total** complete or final total. **sum up** v **summing, summed** 1 summarize. 2 form a quick opinion of.

summary ❶ n, pl –ries 1 brief account giving the main points of something. ◆ adj 2 done quickly, without formalities. **summarily** adv **summarize** v make or be a

————— THESAURUS —————

suffocate v 1 = **choke**, asphyxiate, smother, stifle 2 = **stifle**, choke

suggest v 1 = **recommend**, advise, advocate, prescribe, propose 2 = **bring to mind**, evoke 3 = **hint**, imply, indicate, intimate

suit n 2 = **outfit**, clothing, costume, dress, ensemble, habit 4 = **lawsuit**, action, case, cause, proceeding, prosecution, trial ◆ v 5 = **befit**, agree, become, go with, harmonize, match, tally 6 = **be acceptable to**, do, gratify, please, satisfy

suite n 1 = **rooms**, apartment

suitor n Old–fashioned = **admirer**, beau, young man

sullen adj = **morose**, cross, dour, glowering, moody, sour, sulky, surly, unsociable

sully v 1 = **dishonour**, besmirch, disgrace, ruin, smirch 2 = **defile**, stain, tarnish

sultry adj 1 = **humid**, close, hot, muggy, oppressive, sticky, stifling ≠ **fresh** 2 = **seductive**, provocative, sensual, sexy (inf)

sum n 1 = **total**, aggregate, amount, tally, whole

summary of (something). **summation** n 1 summary. 2 adding up.

summer n warmest season of the year, between spring and autumn. **summery** adj **summerhouse** n small building in a garden. **summertime** n period or season of summer.

summit ⊕ n 1 top of a mountain or hill. 2 highest point. 3 conference between heads of state.

summon ⊕ v 1 order (someone) to come. 2 call upon (someone) to do something. 4 gather (one's courage, strength, etc.). **summons** n 1 command summoning someone. 2 order requiring someone to appear in court. ◆ v 3 order (someone) to appear in court.

sumo n Japanese style of wrestling.

sumptuous ⊕ adj lavish, magnificent.

sun n 1 star around which the earth and other planets revolve. 2 any star around which planets revolve. 3 heat and light from the sun. ◆ v **sunning, sunned** 4 expose (oneself) to the sun's rays. **sunless** adj **sunny** adj 1 full of or exposed to sunlight. 2 cheerful. **sunbathe** v lie in the sunshine in order to get a suntan. **sunbeam** n ray of sun. **sunburn** n painful reddening of the skin caused by overexposure to the sun. **sunburnt, sunburned** adj **sundial** n device showing the time by means of a pointer that casts a shadow on a marked dial. **sundown** n sunset. **sunflower** n tall plant with large golden flowers. **sunrise** n 1 daily appearance of the sun above the horizon. 2 time of this. **sunset** n 1 daily

disappearance of the sun below the horizon. 2 time of this. **sunshine** n light and warmth from the sun. **sunspot** n 1 dark patch appearing temporarily on the sun's surface. 2 Aust small area of skin damage caused by exposure to the sun. **sunstroke** n illness caused by prolonged exposure to intensely hot sunlight. **suntan** n browning of the skin caused by exposure to the sun.

sundae n ice cream topped with fruit etc.

Sunday n first day of the week and the Christian day of worship. **Sunday school** school for teaching children about Christianity.

sundry ⊕ adj several, various. **sundries** pl n several things of various sorts. **all and sundry** everybody.

sup v **supping, supped** 1 take (liquid) by sips. ◆ n 2 sip.

super ⊕ adj Informal excellent.

super– prefix used with many main words to mean: 1 above or over, e.g. superimpose. 2 outstanding, e.g. superstar. 3 of greater size or extent, e.g. supermarket.

superannuation n 1 regular payment by an employee into a pension fund. 2 pension paid from this.

superb ⊕ adj excellent, impressive, or splendid. **superbly** adv

supercilious ⊕ adj showing arrogant pride or scorn.

superficial ⊕ adj 1 not careful or thorough. 2 (of a person) without depth of character, shallow. 3 of or on the surface. **superficially** adv **superficiality** n

——————— THESAURUS ———————

summary n 1 = **synopsis**, abridgment, outline, précis, résumé, review, rundown

summit n 1, 2 = **peak**, acme, apex, head, height, pinnacle, top, zenith ≠ **base**

summon v 1 = **send for**, bid, call, invite 4 = **gather**, draw on, muster

sumptuous adj = **luxurious**, gorgeous, grand, lavish, opulent, splendid, superb

sundry adj = **various**, assorted, different, miscellaneous, several, some

super adj Inf = **excellent**, cracking (Brit inf), glorious, magnificent, marvellous, outstanding, sensational (inf), smashing (inf), superb, terrific (inf), wonderful

superb adj = **splendid**, excellent, exquisite, fine, first–rate, grand, magnificent, marvellous, superior, superlative, world–class ≠ **bad**

supercilious adj = **scornful**, arrogant, contemptuous, disdainful, haughty, lofty,

superfluous ❶ [soo–**per**–flew–uss] *adj* more than is needed. **superfluity** *n*

superhuman ❶ *adj* beyond normal human ability or experience.

superimpose *v* place (something) on or over something else.

superintend *v* supervise (a person or activity). **superintendent** *n* 1 senior police officer. 2 supervisor.

superior ❶ *adj* 1 greater in quality, quantity, or merit. 2 higher in position or rank. 3 believing oneself to be better than others. ◆ *n* 4 person of greater rank or status. **superiority** *n*

superlative ❶ [soo–**per**–lat–iv] *adj* 1 of outstanding quality. 2 *Grammar* denoting the form of an adjective or adverb indicating *most*. ◆ *n* 3 *Grammar* superlative form of a word.

supermarket *n* large self–service store selling food and household goods.

supernatural ❶ *adj* of or relating to things beyond the laws of nature. **the supernatural** supernatural forces, occurrences, and beings collectively.

supernumerary *adj* 1 exceeding the required or regular number. ◆ *n, pl* –**ries** 2 supernumerary person or thing.

superpower *n* extremely powerful nation.

supersede ❶ *v* replace, supplant.

supersonic *adj* of or travelling at a speed greater than the speed of sound.

superstition *n* 1 belief in omens, ghosts, etc. 2 idea or practice based on this. **superstitious** *adj*

superstructure *n* 1 structure erected on something else. 2 part of a ship above the main deck.

supervise ❶ *v* watch over to direct or check. **supervision** *n* **supervisor** *n* **supervisory** *adj*

supine *adj* lying flat on one's back.

supper *n* light evening meal.

supplant ❶ *v* take the place of, oust.

supple ❶ *adj* 1 (of a person) moving and bending easily and gracefully. 2 bending easily without damage. **suppleness** *n*

supplement ❶ *n* 1 thing added to complete something or make up for a lack. 2 magazine inserted into a newspaper. 3 section added to a publication to supply further information. ◆ *v* 4 provide or be a supplement to (something). **supplementary** *adj*

———— THESAURUS ————

snooty (*inf*), stuck–up (*inf*)

superficial *adj* 1 = **hasty**, casual, cursory, desultory, hurried, perfunctory, sketchy, slapdash ≠ **comprehensive** 2 = **shallow**, empty–headed, frivolous, silly, trivial ≠ **serious** 3 = **surface**, exterior, external, on the surface, slight

superfluous *adj* = **excess**, extra, left over, redundant, remaining, spare, supernumerary, surplus

superhuman *adj* = **heroic**, paranormal, phenomenal, prodigious, supernatural

superior *adj* 1 a = **better**, grander, greater, higher, surpassing, unrivalled ≠ **worse** b = **first–class**, choice, de luxe, excellent, exceptional, exclusive, first–rate ≠ **average** 3 = **supercilious**, condescending, disdainful, haughty, lofty, lordly, patronizing, pretentious, snobbish ◆ *n* 4 = **boss** (*inf*), chief, director, manager,

principal, senior, supervisor ≠ **subordinate**

superlative *adj* 1 = **supreme**, excellent, outstanding, unparalleled, unrivalled, unsurpassed

supernatural *adj* = **paranormal**, ghostly, miraculous, mystic, occult, psychic, spectral, uncanny, unearthly

supersede *v* = **replace**, displace, oust, supplant, take the place of, usurp

supervise *v* = **oversee**, control, direct, handle, look after, manage, run, superintend

supplant *v* = **replace**, displace, oust, supersede, take the place of

supple *adj* 1 = **flexible**, limber, lissom(e), lithe ≠ **stiff** 2 = **pliant**, pliable ≠ **firm**

supplement *n* 1 = **addition**, add–on, extra 2 = **pull–out**, insert 3 = **appendix**, postscript ◆ *v* 4 = **add**, augment, extend, reinforce

supply ❶ v **-plying, -plied 1** provide with something required. ◆ n, pl **-plies 2** supplying. **3** amount available. **4** Economics willingness and ability to provide goods and services. ◆ pl **5** food or equipment. **supplier** n

support ❶ v **1** bear the weight of. **2** provide the necessities of life for. **3** give practical or emotional help to. **4** take an active interest in (a sports team, political principle, etc.). **5** help to prove (a theory etc.). **6** speak in favour of. ◆ n **7** supporting. **8** means of support. **supporter** n person who supports a team, principle, etc. **supportive** adj

suppose ❶ v **1** presume to be true. **2** consider as a proposal for the sake of discussion. **supposed** adj presumed to be true without proof, doubtful. **supposed to 1** expected or required to, e.g. you were supposed to phone me. **2** permitted to, e.g. we're not supposed to swim here. **supposedly** adv **supposition** n **1** supposing. **2** something supposed.

suppress ❶ v **1** put an end to. **2** prevent publication of (information). **3** restrain (an emotion or response). **suppression** n

suppurate v (of a wound etc.) produce pus.

supreme ❶ adj highest in authority, rank, or degree. **supremely** adv extremely. **supremacy** n **1** supreme power. **2** state of being supreme. **supremo** n Informal person in overall authority.

surcharge n additional charge.

sure ❶ adj **1** free from uncertainty or doubt. **2** reliable. **3** inevitable. ◆ adv, interj **4** Informal certainly. **surely** adv it must be true that. **sure-footed** adj unlikely to slip or stumble.

surf n **1** foam caused by waves breaking on the shore. ◆ v **2** take part in surfing. **3** **surfing** n sport of riding towards the shore on a surfboard on the crest of a wave. **surfer** n **surfboard** n long smooth board used in surfing.

surface ❶ n **1** outside or top of an object. **2** material covering the surface of an object. **3** superficial appearance. ◆ v **4** rise to the surface. **5** put a surface on.

supply v **1 = provide**, contribute, endow, equip, furnish, give, grant, produce, stock, yield ◆ n **3 = store**, cache, fund, hoard, quantity, reserve, source, stock ◆ pl **5 = provisions**, equipment, food, materials, necessities, rations, stores, tucker (Aust & NZ inf)

support v **1 = bear**, brace, buttress, carry, hold, prop, reinforce, sustain **2 = provide for**, finance, fund, keep, look after, maintain, sustain ≠ **live off 3 = help**, aid, assist, back, champion, defend, second, side with **5 = bear out**, confirm, corroborate, substantiate, verify ≠ **deny** ◆ n **7 = help**, aid, assistance, backing, encouragement, loyalty **8 = prop**, brace, foundation, pillar, post ≠ **antagonist**

suppose v **1 = presume**, assume, conjecture, expect, guess (inf, chiefly US & Canad), imagine, think **2 = imagine**, conjecture, consider, hypothesize, postulate, pretend

suppress v **1 = stop**, check, conquer, crush, overpower, put an end to, quash, quell, subdue **3 = restrain**, conceal, contain, curb, hold in or back, repress, silence, smother, stifle

supreme adj **= highest**, chief, foremost, greatest, head, leading, paramount, pre-eminent, prime, principal, top, ultimate ≠ **lowest**

sure adj **1 = certain**, assured, confident, convinced, decided, definite, positive ≠ **uncertain 2 = reliable**, accurate, dependable, foolproof, infallible, undeniable, undoubted, unerring, unfailing ≠ **unreliable 3 = inevitable**, assured, bound, guaranteed, inescapable ≠ **unsure**

surface n **1 = outside**, exterior, face, side, top **2 = covering**, veneer **3 = veneer** ◆ v **5 = appear**, arise, come to light, come up, crop up (inf), emerge, materialize, transpire

surfeit ⊕ *n* excessive amount.

surge ⊕ *n* 1 sudden powerful increase. 2 strong rolling movement, esp. of the sea. ◆ *v* 3 increase suddenly. 4 move forward strongly.

surgeon *n* doctor who specializes in surgery. **surgery** *n* 1 treatment in which the patient's body is cut open in order to treat the affected part. 2 (*pl* –**geries**) place where, or time when, a doctor, dentist, MP, etc. can be consulted. **surgical** *adj* **surgically** *adv*

surly ⊕ *adj* –**lier**, –**liest** ill–tempered and rude. **surliness** *n*

surmise ⊕ *v*, *n* guess, conjecture.

surmount *v* 1 overcome (a problem). 2 be on top of (something). **surmountable** *adj*

surname *n* family name.

surpass ⊕ *v* be greater than or superior to.

surplus ⊕ *n* amount left over in excess of what is required.

surprise ⊕ *n* 1 unexpected event. 2 amazement and wonder. ◆ *v* 3 cause to feel amazement or wonder. 4 come upon, attack, or catch suddenly and unexpectedly.

surrealism *n* movement in art and literature involving the combination of incongruous images, as in a dream. **surreal** *adj* bizarre. **surrealist** *n, adj* **surrealistic** *adj*

surrender ⊕ *v* 1 give oneself up. 2 give (something) up to another. 3 yield (to a temptation or influence). ◆ *n* 4 surrendering.

surreptitious ⊕ *adj* done secretly or stealthily.

surrogate ⊕ *n* substitute. **surrogate mother** woman who gives birth to a child on behalf of a couple who cannot have children.

surround ⊕ *v* 1 be, come, or place all around (a person or thing). ◆ *n* 2 border or edging. **surroundings** *pl n* area or environment around a person, place, or thing.

surveillance ⊕ *n* close observation.

survey ⊕ *v* 1 view or consider in a general way. 2 make a map of (an area). 3 inspect (a building) to assess its condition and value. 4 find out the incomes, opinions, etc. of (a group of people). ◆ *n* 5 surveying. 6 report produced by a survey.

surfeit *n* = **excess**, glut, plethora, superfluity

surge *n* 1 = **rush**, flood, flow, gush, outpouring 2 = **wave**, billow, roller, swell ◆ *v* 3 = **rush**, gush, rise 4 = **roll**, heave

surly *adj* = **ill–tempered**, churlish, cross, grouchy (*inf*), morose, sulky, sullen, uncivil, ungracious

① **surmise** *v* = **guess**, conjecture, imagine, presume, speculate, suppose

② **surmise** *n* = **guess**, assumption, conjecture, presumption, speculation, supposition

surpass *v* = **outdo**, beat, eclipse, exceed, excel, outshine, outstrip, transcend

surplus *n* 1 = **excess**, balance, remainder, residue, surfeit ◆ *adj* 2 = **extra**, excess, odd, remaining, spare, superfluous ≠ **insufficient**

surprise *n* 1 = **shock**, bombshell, eye– opener (*inf*), jolt, revelation 2 = **amazement**, astonishment, incredulity, wonder ◆ *v* 4 = **amaze**, astonish, stagger, stun, take aback 5 = **catch unawares** *or* **off–guard**, discover, spring upon, startle

surrender *v* 1 = **give in**, capitulate, cave in (*inf*), give way, submit, succumb, yield ≠ **resist** 2 = **give up**, abandon, cede, concede, part with, relinquish, renounce, waive, yield 3 = **yield**, give in ◆ *n* 4 = **submission**, capitulation, cave–in (*inf*), relinquishment, renunciation, resignation

surreptitious *adj* = **secret**, covert, furtive, sly, stealthy, underhand

surrogate *n* = **substitute**, proxy, representative, stand–in

surround *v* 1 = **enclose**, encircle, encompass, envelop, hem in, ring

surveillance *n* = **observation**, inspection,

surveyor n

survive ⊕ v 1 continue to live or exist after (a difficult experience). 2 live after the death of (another). **survival** n 1 condition of having survived. 2 **survivor** n

susceptible ≠ adj liable to be influenced or affected by. **susceptibility** n

suspect ⊕ v 1 believe (someone) to be guilty without having any proof. 2 think (something) to be false or questionable. 3 believe (something) to be the case. ◆ adj 4 not to be trusted. ◆ n 5 person who is suspected.

suspend ⊕ v 1 hang from a high place. 2 cause to remain floating or hanging. 3 cause to cease temporarily. 4 remove (someone) temporarily from a job or team. **suspenders** pl n 1 straps for holding up stockings. 2 US braces

suspense ⊕ n state of uncertainty while awaiting news, an event, etc.

suspicion ⊕ n 1 feeling of not trusting a person or thing. 2 belief that something is true without definite proof. 3 slight trace. **suspicious** adj feeling or causing suspicion.

sustain ⊕ v 1 maintain or prolong. 2 keep up the vitality or strength of. 3 suffer (an injury or loss). 4 support. **sustenance** n food.

svelte adj attractively or gracefully slim.

swab n 1 small piece of cotton wool used to apply medication, clean a wound, etc. ◆ v swabbing, swabbed 2 clean (a wound) with a swab. 3 clean (the deck of a ship) with a mop.

swag n Slang stolen property. **swagman** n Aust tramp who carries his belongings in a bundle on his back.

swagger ⊕ v 1 walk or behave arrogantly. ◆ n 2 arrogant walk or manner.

swallow[1] ⊕ v 1 cause to pass down one's throat. 2 make a gulping movement in the throat, as when nervous. 3 Informal believe (something) gullibly. 4 refrain from showing (a feeling). 5 engulf or absorb. ◆ n 6 swallowing. 7 amount swallowed.

swallow[2] n small migratory bird with long pointed wings and a forked tail.

swamp ⊕ n 1 watery area of land, bog. ◆ v 2 cause (a boat) to fill with water and sink. 3 overwhelm. **swampy** adj

scrutiny, supervision, watch

survey v 1 = **look over**, contemplate, examine, inspect, observe, scrutinize, view 2 = **plot**, measure, plan, size up 3 = **estimate**, appraise, assess ◆ n 5 = **examination**, inspection, scrutiny 6 = **study**, report, review

survive v = **remain alive**, endure, last, live on, outlast, outlive

susceptible adj = **liable**, disposed, given, impressionable, inclined, prone, receptive, responsive, sensitive, subject, suggestible, vulnerable ≠ **unresponsive**

suspect v 1 = **believe**, consider, feel, guess, speculate, suppose ≠ **be certain** 2 = **distrust**, doubt, mistrust ≠ **trust** ◆ adj 4 = **dubious**, doubtful, iffy (inf), questionable ≠ **innocent**

suspend v 1 = **hang**, attach, dangle 3 = **postpone**, cease, cut short, defer, discontinue, interrupt, put off, shelve

≠ **continue**

suspense n = **uncertainty**, anxiety, apprehension, doubt, expectation, insecurity, irresolution, tension

suspicion n 1 = **distrust**, doubt, dubiety, misgiving, mistrust, qualm, scepticism, wariness 2 = **idea**, guess, hunch, impression, notion 3 = **trace**, hint, shade, soupçon, streak, suggestion, tinge, touch

sustain v 1 = **maintain**, continue, keep up, prolong, protract 2 = **keep alive**, aid, assist, help, nourish 3 = **suffer**, bear, endure, experience, feel, undergo, withstand 4 = **support**, bear, uphold

swagger v 1 = **show off** (inf), boast, brag, parade, skite (Aust & NZ)

swallow[1] v 1 = **gulp**, consume, devour, drink, eat, swig (inf)

swamp n 1 = **bog**, fen, marsh, mire, morass, quagmire, slough ◆ v 2 = **flood**, capsize, engulf, inundate, sink, submerge

swan n 1 large usu. white water bird with a long graceful neck. ◆ v **swanning, swanned** 2 Informal wander about idly. **swan song** person's last performance before retirement or death.

swap ❶ v **swapping, swapped** 1 exchange (something) for something else. ◆ n 2 exchange.

swarm¹ ❶ n 1 large group of bees or other insects. 2 large crowd. ◆ v 3 move in a swarm. 4 (of a place) be crowded or overrun.

swarm² v (foll. by up) climb (a ladder or rope) by gripping with the hands and feet.

swarthy ❶ adj **–thier, –thiest** dark–complexioned.

swastika n symbol in the shape of a cross with the arms bent at right angles, used as the emblem of Nazi Germany.

swat v **swatting, swatted** 1 hit sharply. ◆ n 2 sharp blow.

swathe ❶ v 1 wrap in bandages or layers of cloth. ◆ n 2 long strip of cloth wrapped around something. 3 (also **swath**) the width of one sweep of a scythe or mower.

sway ❶ v 1 swing to and fro or from side to side. 2 waver or cause to waver in opinion. ◆ n 3 power or influence. 4 swaying motion.

swear ❶ v **swearing, swore, sworn** 1 use obscene or blasphemous language. 2 state or promise on oath. 3 state earnestly. **swear by** v have complete confidence in.

swear in v cause to take an oath.

swearword n word considered obscene or blasphemous.

sweat ❶ n 1 salty liquid given off through the pores of the skin. 2 Slang drudgery or hard labour. ◆ v 3 have sweat coming through the pores. 4 be anxious. **sweaty** adj **sweatshirt** n long–sleeved cotton jersey. **sweatshop** n place where employees work long hours in poor conditions for low pay.

sweater n (woollen) garment for the upper part of the body.

swede n 1 kind of turnip.

sweep ❶ v **sweeping, swept** 1 remove dirt from (a floor) with a broom. 2 move smoothly and quickly. 3 spread rapidly. 4 move majestically. 5 carry away suddenly or forcefully. 6 stretch in a long wide curve. ◆ n 7 sweeping. 8 sweeping motion. 9 wide expanse. 10 sweepstake. 11 chimney sweep. **sweeping** adj 1 wide–ranging. 2 indiscriminate. **sweepstake** n lottery in which the stakes of the participants make up the prize.

sweet ❶ adj 1 tasting of or like sugar. 2 kind and charming. 3 agreeable to the senses or mind. 4 (of wine) with a high sugar content. ◆ n 5 shaped piece of food consisting mainly of sugar. 6 dessert. **sweetly** adv **sweetness** n **sweeten** v **sweetener** n 1 sweetening agent that does not contain sugar. 2 Slang bribe. 3

──────── ┤ T H E S A U R U S ├────────

3 = **overwhelm**, engulf, flood, inundate, overload, submerge

swap v 1 = **exchange**, barter, interchange, switch, trade

swarm¹ n 2 = **multitude**, army, crowd, flock, herd, horde, host, mass, throng ◆ v 3 = **crowd**, flock, mass, stream, throng 4 = **teem**, abound, bristle, crawl

swarthy adj = **dark–skinned**, black, brown, dark, dark–complexioned, dusky

swathe v 1 = **wrap**, bundle up, cloak, drape, envelop, shroud

sway v 1 = **bend**, lean, rock, roll, swing 2 = **influence**, affect, guide, induce,

persuade ◆ n 3 = **power**, authority, clout (inf), control, influence, mana (NZ)

swear v 1 = **curse**, be foul-mouthed, blaspheme 2 = **vow**, attest, promise, testify 3 = **declare**, affirm, assert

sweat n 1 = **perspiration** 2 Sl = **labour**, chore, drudgery, toil 3 Inf = **worry**, agitation, anxiety, distress, panic, strain ◆ v 3 = **perspire**, glow 4 = **worry**, agonize, fret, suffer, torture oneself

sweep v 1 = **clear**, brush, clean, remove 2 = **sail**, fly, glide, pass, skim, tear, zoom ◆ n 8 = **stroke**, move, swing 9 = **extent**, range, scope, stretch

sweetbread *n* animal's pancreas used as food. **sweet corn** type of maize with sweet yellow kernels, eaten as a vegetable. **sweetheart** *n* lover. **sweetmeat** *n Old–fashioned* sweet delicacy such as a small cake. **sweet pea** climbing plant with bright fragrant flowers. **sweet-talk** *v Informal* coax or flatter. **sweet tooth** strong liking for sweet foods.

swell ❶ *v* **swelling, swelled, swollen** or **swelled** 1 expand or increase. 2 (of a sound) become gradually louder. ◆ *n* 3 swelling or being swollen. 4 movement of waves in the sea. 5 *Old–fashioned slang* fashionable person. ◆ *adj* 6 *US slang* excellent or fine. **swelling** *n* enlargement of part of the body, caused by injury or infection.

swerve ❶ *v* 1 turn aside from a course sharply or suddenly. ◆ *n* 2 swerving.

swift ❶ *adj* 1 moving or able to move quickly. ◆ *n* 2 fast–flying bird with pointed wings. **swiftly** *adv* **swiftness** *n*

swig *n* 1 large mouthful of drink. ◆ *v* **swigging, swigged** 2 drink in large mouthfuls.

swill *v* 1 drink greedily. 2 rinse (something) in large amounts of water. ◆ *n* 3 sloppy mixture containing waste food, fed to pigs. 4 deep drink.

swim *v* **swimming, swam, swum** 1 move along in water by movements of the limbs. 2 be covered or flooded with liquid. 3 reel, e.g. *her head was swimming*. ◆ *n* 4 act or period of swimming. **swimmer** *n* **swimmingly** *adv* successfully and effortlessly. **swimming pool** (building containing) an artificial pond for swimming in.

swindle ❶ *v* 1 cheat (someone) out of money. ◆ *n* 2 instance of swindling. **swindler** *n*

swine *n* 1 contemptible person. 2 pig.

swing ❶ *v* **swinging, swung** 1 move to and fro, sway. 2 move in a curve. 3 (of an opinion or mood) change sharply. 4 hit out with a sweeping motion. 5 *Slang* be hanged. ◆ *n* 6 swinging. 7 suspended seat on which a child can swing to and fro. 8 sudden or extreme change.

swingeing ❶ **[swin-jing]** *adj* punishing, severe.

swipe ❶ *v* 1 strike (at) with a sweeping blow. 2 *Slang* steal. 3 pass (a credit card) through a machine which electronically reads information stored in the card. ◆ *n* 4 hard blow.

swirl ❶ *v* 1 turn with a whirling motion. ◆ *n* 2 whirling motion. 3 twisting shape.

swish *v* 1 move with a whistling or hissing

━━━━━━━━━━ THESAURUS ━━━━━━━━━━

sweet *adj* 1 = **sugary**, cloying, icky (*inf*), saccharine ≠ **sour** 2 = **charming**, appealing, engaging, kind, likable *or* likeable, lovable, winning ≠ **nasty** 3 = **fragrant**, agreeable, aromatic, clean, fresh, pure ≠ **rank** ◆ *n* 5 = **confectionery**, bonbon, candy (*US*), lolly (*Aust & NZ inf*) 6 = **dessert**, afters (*Brit inf*), last course, pud, pudding, sweet course

swell *v* 1 = **expand**, balloon, bloat, bulge, dilate, distend, enlarge, grow, increase, rise ≠ **fall** 2 = **increase**, heighten, intensify, mount, surge ≠ **contract** ◆ *n* 4 = **wave**, billow, surge

swerve *v* 1 = **veer**, bend, deflect, deviate, diverge, stray, swing, turn, turn aside

swift *adj* 1, 2 = **quick**, fast, hurried, prompt, rapid, speedy ≠ **slow**

swindle *v* 1 = **cheat**, con, defraud, do (*sl*), fleece, rip (someone) off (*sl*), skin (*sl*), sting (*inf*), trick ◆ *n* 2 = **fraud**, con trick (*inf*), deception, fiddle (*Brit inf*), racket, rip-off (*sl*), scam (*sl*)

swing *v* 1 = **sway**, oscillate, rock, veer, wave 2 = **curve** 5 *Sl* = **hang** ◆ *n* 6 = **swaying**, oscillation

swingeing *adj* = **severe**, drastic, excessive, harsh, heavy, punishing, stringent

swipe *v* 1 = **hit**, lash out at, slap, strike, wallop (*inf*) 2 *Sl* = **steal**, appropriate, filch, lift (*sl*), nick (*sl, chiefly Brit*), pinch (*inf*), purloin ◆ *n* 4 = **blow**, clout (*inf*), cuff, slap, smack, thump, wallop (*inf*)

swirl *v* 1 = **whirl**, churn, eddy, spin, twist

sound. ◆ n 2 whistling or hissing sound. ◆ adj 3 *Informal* fashionable, smart.

switch ❶ n 1 device for opening and closing an electric circuit. 2 abrupt change. 3 exchange or swap. 4 flexible rod or twig. ◆ v 5 change abruptly. 6 exchange or swap. **switchback** n road or railway with many sharp hills or bends. **switchboard** n installation in a telephone exchange or office where telephone calls are connected. **switch on, off** v turn (a device) on or off by means of a switch.

swivel ❶ v -elling, -elled 1 turn on a central point. ◆ n 2 coupling device that allows an attached object to turn freely.

swoop ❶ v 1 sweep down or pounce on suddenly. ◆ n 2 swooping.

sword n weapon with a long sharp blade. **swordfish** n large fish with a very long upper jaw. **swordsman** n person skilled in the use of a sword.

sworn v 1 past participle of SWEAR. ◆ adj 2 bound as if by an oath.

swot ❶ *Informal* ◆ v swotting, swotted 1 study hard. ◆ n 2 person who studies hard.

sycamore n tree with five-pointed leaves and two-winged fruits.

sycophant ❶ n person who uses flattery to win favour from people with power or influence. **sycophantic** adj **sycophancy** n

syllable n part of a word pronounced as a unit. **syllabic** adj

syllabus ❶ n, pl -buses, -bi list of subjects for a course of study.

✓ **WORD TIP**
The usual plural is *syllabuses*.

syllogism n form of logical reasoning consisting of two premises and a conclusion.

symbol ❶ n sign or thing that stands for something else. **symbolic** adj **symbolically** adv **symbolism** n 1 representation of something by symbols. 2 movement in art and literature using symbols to express abstract and mystical ideas. **symbolist** n, adj **symbolize** v 1 be a symbol of. 2 represent with a symbol.

symmetry ❶ n state of having two halves that are mirror images of each other. **symmetrical** adj **symmetrically** adv

sympathy ❶ n, pl -thies 1 compassion for someone's pain or distress. 2 agreement with someone's feelings or interests. **sympathetic** adj 1 feeling or showing sympathy. 2 likeable or appealing. **sympathetically** adv **sympathize** v feel or express sympathy. **sympathizer** n

symphony n, pl -nies composition for orchestra, with several movements. **symphonic** adj

symposium n, pl -siums, -sia conference for discussion of a particular topic.

symptom ❶ n 1 sign indicating the presence of an illness. 2 sign that something is wrong. **symptomatic** adj

synagogue n Jewish place of worship and religious instruction.

——————| THESAURUS |——————

switch n 2 = **change**, reversal, shift
3 = **exchange**, substitution, swap ◆ v
5 = **change**, deflect, deviate, divert, shift
6 = **exchange**, substitute, swap
swivel v 1 = **turn**, pivot, revolve, rotate, spin
swoop v 1 = **pounce**, descend, dive, rush, stoop, sweep ◆ n 2 = **pounce**, descent, drop, lunge, plunge, rush, stoop, sweep
swot v *Inf* 1 = **study**, cram (*inf*), mug up (*Brit sl*), revise
sycophant n = **crawler**, bootlicker (*inf*),

fawner, flatterer, toady, yes man
syllabus n = **course of study**, curriculum
symbol n = **sign**, badge, emblem, figure, image, logo, mark, representation, token
symmetry n = **balance**, evenness, order, proportion, regularity
sympathy n 1 = **compassion**, commiseration, pity, understanding ≠ **indifference** 2 = **affinity**, agreement, fellow feeling, rapport ≠ **opposition**
symptom n 2 = **sign**, expression, indication, mark, token, warning

synchromesh adj (of a gearbox) having a device that synchronizes the speeds of gears before they engage.

synchronize v 1 (of two or more people) perform (an action) at the same time. 2 set (watches) to show the same time. 3 match (the soundtrack and action of a film) precisely. **synchronization** n **synchronous** adj happening or existing at the same time.

syncopate v Music stress the weak beats in (a rhythm) instead of the strong ones. **syncopation** n

syndicate n 1 group of people or firms undertaking a joint business project. 2 agency that sells material to several newspapers. ♦ v 3 publish (material) in several newspapers. 4 form a syndicate. **syndication** n

syndrome n 1 combination of symptoms indicating a particular disease. 2 set of characteristics indicating a particular problem.

synod n church council.

synonym n word with the same meaning as another. **synonymous** adj

synopsis ❶ n, pl –ses summary or outline.

syntax n Grammar way in which words are arranged to form phrases and sentences. **syntactic** adj

synthesis n, pl –ses 1 combination of objects or ideas into a whole. 2 artificial production of a substance. **synthesize** v produce by synthesis. **synthesizer** n electronic musical instrument producing a range of sounds. **synthetic** adj 1 (of a substance) made artificially. 2 not genuine, insincere. **synthetically** adv

syphilis n serious sexually transmitted disease.

syringe n 1 device for withdrawing or injecting fluids, consisting of a hollow cylinder, a piston, and a hollow needle. ♦ v 2 wash out or inject with a syringe.

syrup n 1 solution of sugar in water. 2 thick sweet liquid. **syrupy** adj

system ❶ n 1 method or set of methods. 2 scheme of classification or arrangement. 3 network or assembly of parts that form a whole. **systematic** adj **systematically** adv **systemic** adj affecting the entire animal or body.

———————— THESAURUS ————————

synopsis n = **summary**, abridgement, abstract, digest, outline, précis, review, rundown

system n 1 = **method**, practice, procedure, routine, technique 3 = **arrangement**, classification, organization, scheme, structure

T t

ta *interj Informal* thank you.

tab *n* small flap or projecting label. **keep tabs on** *Informal* watch closely.

Tabasco *n* ® very hot red pepper sauce.

tabby *n, pl* **–bies**, *adj* (cat) with dark stripes on a lighter background.

table ❶ *n* **1** piece of furniture with a flat top supported by legs. **2** arrangement of information in columns. ◆ *v* **3** submit (a motion) for discussion by a meeting. **4** *US* suspend discussion of (a proposal).
tablespoon *n* large spoon for serving food. **table tennis** game like tennis played on a table with small bats and a light ball.

tableau ❶ [**tab**–loh] *n, pl* **–leaux** silent motionless group arranged to represent some scene.

tablet *n* **1** pill of compressed medicinal substance. **2** inscribed slab of stone etc.

tabloid *n* small–sized newspaper with many photographs and a concise, usu. sensational style.

taboo ❶ *n, pl* **–boos 1** prohibition resulting

from religious or social conventions. ◆ *adj* **2** forbidden by a taboo.

tacit ❶ [**tass**–it] *adj* implied but not spoken.

taciturn ❶ [**tass**–it–turn] *adj* habitually uncommunicative. **taciturnity** *n*

tack¹ ❶ *n* **1** short nail with a large head. **2** long loose stitch. ◆ *v* **3** fasten with tacks. **4** stitch with tacks. **tack on** *v* append.

tack² ❶ *n* **1** course of a ship sailing obliquely into the wind. **2** course of action. ◆ *v* **3** sail into the wind on a zigzag course.

tack³ *n* riding harness for horses.

tackies, takkies *pl n, sing* **tacky** *S Afr informal* tennis shoes or plimsolls.

tackle ❶ *v* **1** deal with (a task). **2** confront (an opponent). **3** *Sport* attempt to get the ball from (an opposing player). ◆ *n* **4** *Sport* act of tackling an opposing player. **5** equipment for a particular activity. **6** set of ropes and pulleys for lifting heavy weights.

tacky¹ ❶ *adj* **tackier, tackiest** slightly

THESAURUS

table *n* **1** = **counter**, bench, board, stand **2** = **list**, catalogue, chart, diagram, record, register, roll, schedule, tabulation ◆ *v* **3** = **submit**, enter, move, propose, put forward, suggest

tableau *n* = **picture**, representation, scene, spectacle

taboo *n* **1** = **prohibition**, anathema, ban, interdict, proscription, restriction ◆ *adj* **2** = **forbidden**, anathema, banned, outlawed, prohibited, proscribed, unacceptable, unmentionable ≠ **allowed**

tacit *adj* = **implied**, implicit, inferred, undeclared, understood, unexpressed, unspoken, unstated

taciturn *adj* = **uncommunicative**, quiet, reserved, reticent, silent, tight–lipped, unforthcoming, withdrawn

tack¹ *n* **1** = **nail**, drawing pin, pin ◆ *v* **3** = **fasten**, affix, attach, fix, nail, pin **4** = **stitch**, baste, sew **tack on** = **append**, add, attach, tag

tack² *n* **2** = **course**, approach, direction, heading, line, method, path, plan, procedure, way

tackle *v* **1** = **deal with**, attempt, come *or* get to grips with, embark upon, get stuck into (*inf*), have a go *or* stab at (*inf*), set about, undertake **2** = **confront**, challenge, grab, grasp, halt, intercept, seize, stop ◆ *n* sticky.

tacky² 🟊 *adj* **tackier, tackiest 1** *Informal* vulgar and tasteless. **2** shabby.

tact 🟊 *n* skill in avoiding giving offence. **tactful** *adj* **tactless** *adj*

tactics *n* art of directing military forces in battle. **tactic** *n* method or plan to achieve an end. **tactical** *adj* **tactician** *n*

tactile *adj* of or having the sense of touch.

tadpole *n* limbless tailed larva of a frog or toad.

taffeta *n* shiny silk or rayon fabric.

tag¹ 🟊 *n* **1** label bearing information. **2** pointed end of a cord or lace. **3** quotation. ◆ *v* **tagging, tagged 4** attach a tag to. **tag along** *v* accompany someone, esp. if uninvited.

tag² *n* **1** children's game where the person being chased becomes the chaser upon being touched. ◆ *v* **tagging, tagged 2** touch and catch in this game.

tail 🟊 *n* **1** rear part of an animal's body, usu. forming a flexible appendage. **2** rear or last part or parts of something. **3** *Informal* person employed to follow and spy on another. ◆ *pl* **4** *Informal* tail coat. ◆ *adj* **5** at the rear. ◆ *v* **6** *Informal* follow (someone) secretly. **turn tail** run away.

tailless *adj* **tails** *adv* with the side of a coin uppermost that does not have a portrait of a head on it. **tailback** *n* queue of traffic stretching back from an obstruction. **tailboard** *n* removable or hinged rear

board on a lorry etc. **tail coat** man's coat with a long back split into two below the waist. **tail off, away** *v* diminish gradually. **tailspin** *n* uncontrolled spinning dive of an aircraft. **tailwind** *n* wind coming from the rear.

tailor 🟊 *n* **1** person who makes men's clothes. ◆ *v* **2** adapt to suit a purpose. **tailor–made** *adj* **1** made by a tailor. **2** perfect for a purpose.

taint 🟊 *v* **1** spoil with a small amount of decay, contamination, or other bad quality. ◆ *n* **2** something that taints.

take 🟊 *v* **taking, took, taken 1** remove from a place. **2** carry or accompany. **3** use. **4** get possession of, esp. dishonestly. **5** capture. **6** require (time, resources, or ability). **7** assume. **8** accept. **9** write down. **10** subtract or deduct. ◆ *n* **11** one of a series of recordings from which the best will be used. **take place** happen. **taking** *adj* charming. **takings** *pl n* money received by a shop. **take after** *v* look or behave like (a parent etc.). **take away** *v* remove or subtract. **takeaway** *n* **1** shop or restaurant selling meals for eating elsewhere. **2** meal bought at a takeaway. **take in** *v* **1** understand. **2** deceive or swindle. **3** make (clothing) smaller. **take off** *v* **1** (of an aircraft) leave the ground. **2** *Informal* depart. **3** *Informal* parody. **takeoff** *n* **takeover** *n* act of taking control of a company by buying a large number of its

4 *Sport* = **challenge**, block **5** = **equipment**, accoutrements, apparatus, gear, paraphernalia, tools, trappings

tacky¹ *adj* = **sticky**, adhesive, gluey, gummy, wet

tacky² *adj* **1** *Inf* = **vulgar**, cheap, naff (*Brit sl*), sleazy, tasteless **2** = **shabby**, seedy, shoddy, tatty

tact *n* = **diplomacy**, consideration, delicacy, discretion, sensitivity, thoughtfulness, understanding

tag¹ *n* **1** = **label**, flap, identification, mark, marker, note, slip, tab, ticket ◆ *v* **4** = **label**, mark **tag along** = **accompany**, attend,

follow, shadow, tail (*inf*), trail

tail *n* **1, 2** = **extremity**, appendage, end, rear end, tailpiece ◆ *v* **6** *Inf* = **follow**, shadow, stalk, track, trail **turn tail** = **run away**, cut and run, flee, retreat, run off, take to one's heels

tailor *n* **1** = **outfitter**, clothier, costumier, couturier, dressmaker, seamstress ◆ *v* **2** = **style**, alter **3** = **adapt**, adjust, customize, fashion, modify, mould, shape

taint *v* **1** = **spoil**, blemish, contaminate, corrupt, damage, defile, pollute, ruin, stain, sully, tarnish ≠ **clean** ◆ *n* **2** = **stain**, black mark, blemish, blot, defect, demerit, shares. **take up** v 1 occupy or fill (space or time). 2 adopt the study or activity of. 3 shorten (a garment). 4 accept (an offer).

talc n 1 talcum powder. 2 soft mineral of magnesium silicate. **talcum powder** powder, usu. scented, used to dry or perfume the body.

tale ⊕ n 1 story. 2 malicious piece of gossip.

talent ⊕ n 1 natural ability. 2 ancient unit of weight or money. **talented** adj

talisman ⊕ n, pl **-mans** object believed to have magic power. **talismanic** adj

talk ⊕ v 1 express ideas or feelings by means of speech. 2 utter. 3 discuss, e.g. let's talk business. 4 reveal information. 5 (be able to) speak in a specified language. ◆ n 6 speech or lecture. **talker** n **talkative** adj fond of talking. **talk back** v answer impudently. **talkback** n NZ broadcast in

which telephone comments or questions from the public are transmitted live. **talking-to** n Informal telling-off.

tall ⊕ adj 1 higher than average. 2 of a specified height. **tall order** difficult task. **tall story** unlikely and probably untrue tale.

tally ⊕ v -lying, -lied 1 (of two things) correspond. ◆ n, pl -lies 2 record of a debt or score.

talon n bird's hooked claw.

tambourine n percussion instrument like a small drum with jingling metal discs attached.

tame ⊕ adj 1 (of animals) brought under human control. 2 (of animals) not afraid of people. 3 meek or submissive. 4 uninteresting. ◆ v 5 make tame. **tamely** adv **tamer** n

tamper ⊕ v (foll. by with) interfere.

fault, flaw, spot

take v 2 = **carry**, accompany, bear, bring, conduct, convey, convoy, escort, ferry, fetch, guide, haul, lead, transport, usher ≠ **send** 4 = **obtain**, acquire, appropriate, catch, get, grasp, grip, misappropriate, pinch (inf), pocket, purloin, secure, seize, steal ≠ **give** 5 = **capture**, seize ≠ **free** 6 = **require**, call for, demand, necessitate, need 7 = **assume**, believe, consider, perceive, presume, regard, understand 8 = **accept**, accommodate, contain, have room for, hold 10 = **subtract**, deduct, eliminate, remove

tale n 1 = **story**, account, anecdote, fable, legend, narrative, saga, yarn (inf)

talent n 1 = **ability**, aptitude, capacity, flair, genius, gift, knack

talisman n = **charm**, amulet, fetish, lucky charm, mascot

talk v 1, 2 = **speak**, chat, chatter, communicate, converse, gossip, natter, utter 3 = **discuss**, confabulate, confer, negotiate, parley 4 = **inform**, blab, give the game away, grass (Brit sl), let the cat out of the bag, tell all ◆ n 6 = **speech**, address, discourse, disquisition, lecture,

oration, sermon

tall adj 1 = **high**, big, elevated, giant, lanky, lofty, soaring, towering ≠ **small tall order** = **difficult**, demanding, hard, unreasonable, well-nigh impossible **tall story** = **implausible**, absurd, cock-and-bull (inf), exaggerated, far-fetched, incredible, preposterous, unbelievable ≠ **true**

tally v 1 = **agree**, accord, coincide, concur, conform, correspond, fit, harmonize, match, square ≠ **conflict** ◆ n 2 = **record**, count, mark, reckoning, running total, score, total

tame adj 1 = **broken**, amenable, disciplined, docile, gentle, obedient, tractable ≠ **wild** 2 = **domesticated** 3 = **submissive**, compliant, docile, manageable, meek, obedient, subdued, unresisting ≠ **aggressive** 4 = **unexciting**, bland, boring, dull, humdrum, insipid, uninspiring, uninteresting, vapid ≠ **interesting** ◆ v 5 a = **domesticate**, house-train, train b = **subdue**, break in, master ≠ **arouse**

tamper v (foll. by with) = **interfere with**, alter, fiddle with (inf), fool about with (inf),

tampon n absorbent plug of cotton wool inserted into the vagina during menstruation.

tan n 1 brown coloration of the skin from exposure to sunlight. ◆ v **tanning, tanned** 2 (of skin) go brown from exposure to sunlight. 3 convert (a hide) into leather. ◆ adj 4 yellowish–brown. **tannery** n place where hides are tanned.

tandem n bicycle for two riders, one behind the other. **in tandem** together.

tandoori adj (of food) cooked in an Indian clay oven.

tang n 1 strong taste or smell. 2 trace or hint. **tangy** adj

tangent n 1 line that touches a curve without intersecting it. 2 (in trigonometry) ratio of the length of the opposite side to that of the adjacent side of a right–angled triangle. **go off at a tangent** suddenly take a completely different line of thought or action. **tangential** adj 1 of superficial relevance only. 2 of a tangent.

tangerine n small orange–like fruit of an Asian citrus tree.

tangible ❶ adj 1 able to be touched. 2 clear and definite. **tangibly** adv

tangle ❶ n 1 confused mass or situation. ◆ v 2 twist together in a tangle. 3 (often foll. by with) come into conflict.

tango n, pl **–gos** 1 S American dance. ◆ v 2 dance a tango.

tank n 1 container for liquids or gases. 2 armoured fighting vehicle moving on tracks. **tanker** n ship or lorry for carrying liquid in bulk.

tankard n large beer–mug, often with a hinged lid.

Tannoy n ® type of public–address system.

tantalize ❶ v torment by showing but withholding something desired. **tantalizing** adj

tantamount ❶ adj **tantamount to** equivalent in effect to.

tantrum ❶ n childish outburst of temper.

tap¹ ❶ v **tapping, tapped** 1 knock lightly and usu. repeatedly. ◆ n 2 light knock. **tap dancing** style of dancing in which the feet beat out an elaborate rhythm.

tap² ❶ n 1 valve to control the flow of liquid from a pipe or cask. ◆ v **tapping, tapped** 2 listen in on (a telephone call) secretly by making an illegal connection. 3 draw off with or as if with a tap. **on tap 1** Informal readily available. 2 (of beer etc.) drawn from a cask.

tape ❶ n 1 narrow long strip of material. 2 (recording made on) a cassette containing magnetic tape. 3 string stretched across a race track to mark the finish. ◆ v 4 record on magnetic tape. 5 bind or fasten with tape. **tape measure** tape marked off in centimetres or inches for measuring. **tape recorder** device for recording and reproducing sound on magnetic tape.

━━━━━━━━━━━━━ THESAURUS ━━━━━━━━━━━━━

meddle with, mess about with, tinker with

tangible adj 1 = **palpable**, actual, concrete, material, real 2 = **definite**, perceptible, positive

tangle n 1 a = **knot**, coil, entanglement, jungle, twist, web b = **confusion**, complication, entanglement, fix (inf), imbroglio, jam, mess, mix–up ◆ v 2 = **twist**, coil, entangle, interweave, knot, mat, mesh, ravel ≠ **unravel** 3 (often foll. by with) = **come into conflict with**, come up against, contend with, contest, cross swords with, dispute with, lock horns with

tantalize v = **torment**, frustrate, lead on, taunt, tease, torture

tantamount adj **tantamount to** = **equivalent to**, commensurate with, equal to, synonymous with

tantrum n = **outburst**, fit, flare–up, hysterics, temper

tap¹ v 1 = **knock**, beat, drum, pat, rap, strike, touch ◆ n 2 = **knock**, pat, rap, touch

tap² n 1 = **valve**, stopcock ◆ v 2 = **listen in on**, bug (inf), eavesdrop on 4 = **draw off**, bleed, drain, siphon off **on tap 1** Inf = **available**, at hand, in reserve, on hand, ready 2 = **on draught**

tapeworm n long flat parasitic worm living in the intestines of vertebrates.

taper ❶ v 1 become narrower towards one end. ◆ n 2 long thin candle. 3 **taper off** v become gradually less.

tapestry n, pl **–tries** fabric decorated with coloured woven designs.

tapioca n beadlike starch made from cassava root, used in puddings.

tar n 1 thick black liquid distilled from coal etc. ◆ v **tarring, tarred** 2 coat with tar.

tarantula n large hairy spider with a poisonous bite.

tardy adj **tardier, tardiest** slow or late. **tardily** adv **tardiness** n

target ❶ n 1 object or person a missile is aimed at. 2 goal or objective. 3 object of criticism. ◆ v **–geting, –geted** 4 aim or direct.

tariff ❶ n 1 tax levied on imports. 2 list of fixed prices.

Tarmac n 1 ® mixture of tar, bitumen, and crushed stones used for roads etc. 2 (t–) airport runway.

tarn n small mountain lake.

tarnish ❶ v 1 make or become stained or less bright. 2 damage or taint. ◆ n 3 discoloration or blemish.

tarot [**tarr**–oh] n special pack of cards used mainly in fortune–telling. **tarot card** card in a tarot pack.

tarpaulin n (sheet of) heavy waterproof fabric.

tarragon n aromatic herb.

tarry v **–rying, –ried** Old–fashioned 1 linger or delay. 2 stay briefly.

tart¹ ❶ n pie or flan with a sweet filling.

tart² ❶ adj sharp or bitter. **tartly** adv **tartness** n

tartan n 1 design of straight lines crossing at right angles, esp. one associated with a Scottish clan. 2 cloth with such a pattern.

tartar n 1 hard deposit on the teeth. 2 deposit formed during the fermentation of wine.

task ❶ n (difficult or unpleasant) piece of work to be done. **take to task** criticize or scold. **task force** (military) group formed to carry out a specific task. **taskmaster** n person who enforces hard work.

tassel n decorative fringed knot of threads.

taste ❶ n 1 sense by which the flavour of a substance is distinguished in the mouth. 2 distinctive flavour. 3 small amount tasted. 4 brief experience of something. 5 liking. 6 ability to appreciate what is beautiful or excellent. ◆ v 7 distinguish the taste of (a substance). 8 take a small amount of (something) into the mouth. 9 have a specific taste. 10 experience briefly. **tasteful** adj having or showing good taste. **tasteless** adj 1 bland or insipid. 2 showing bad taste. **tastelessly** adv **tasty** adj pleasantly flavoured. **taste bud** small organ on the tongue which perceives flavours.

┤ THESAURUS ├

tape n 1 = **strip**, band, ribbon ◆ v 4 = **record**, tape–record, video 5 = **bind**, seal, secure, stick, wrap

taper v 1 = **narrow**, come to a point, thin ≠ **widen taper off** = **decrease**, die away, dwindle, fade, lessen, reduce, subside, wane, wind down

target n 2 = **goal**, aim, ambition, end, intention, mark, object, objective 3 = **victim**, butt, scapegoat

tariff n 1 = **tax**, duty, excise, levy, toll 2 = **price list**, menu, schedule

tarnish v 1 = **stain**, blemish, blot, darken, discolour 2 = **damage**, blacken, smirch,

sully, taint ≠ **enhance** ◆ n 3 = **stain**, blemish, blot, discoloration, spot, taint

tart¹ n = **pie**, pastry, tartlet

tart² adj = **sharp**, acid, bitter, piquant, pungent, sour, tangy, vinegary ≠ **sweet**

task n = **job**, assignment, chore, duty, enterprise, exercise, mission, undertaking **take to task** = **criticize**, blame, censure, rebuke, reprimand, reproach, reprove, rouse on (Aust), scold, tell off (inf), upbraid

taste n 2 = **flavour**, relish, savour, smack, tang ≠ **blandness** 3 = **bit**, bite, dash, morsel, mouthful, sample, soupçon, spoonful, titbit 5 = **liking**, appetite, fancy,

tattered *adj* ragged or torn. **in tatters** in ragged pieces.

tattle *v*, *n* gossip or chatter.

tattoo[1] *n* 1 pattern made on the body by pricking the skin and staining it with indelible inks. ◆ *v* **–tooing, –tooed** 2 make such a pattern on the skin. **tattooist** *n*

tattoo[2] *n* 1 military display or pageant. 2 drumming or tapping.

tatty ❶ *adj* **–tier, –tiest** shabby or worn out.

taunt ❶ *v* 1 tease with jeers. ◆ *n* 2 jeering remark.

taupe *adj* brownish–grey.

taut ❶ *adj* 1 drawn tight. 2 showing nervous strain. **tauten** *v* make or become taut.

tavern ❶ *n Old–fashioned* pub.

tawdry ❶ *adj* **–drier, –driest** cheap, showy, and of poor quality.

tawny *adj* **–nier, –niest** yellowish–brown.

tax ❶ *n* 1 compulsory payment levied by a government on income, property, etc. to raise revenue. ◆ *v* 2 levy a tax on. 3 make heavy demands on. **taxable** *adj* **taxation** *n* levying of taxes. **taxpayer** *n* **tax return** statement of personal income for tax purposes.

taxi *n* 1 (also **taxicab**) car with a driver that may be hired to take people to any specified destination. ◆ *v* **taxiing, taxied** 2 (of an aircraft) run along the ground before taking off or after landing. **taxi rank** place where taxis wait to be hired.

taxidermy *n* art of stuffing and mounting animal skins to give them a lifelike appearance. **taxidermist** *n*

TB tuberculosis.

tea *n* 1 drink made from infusing the dried leaves of an Asian bush in boiling water. 2 leaves used to make this drink. 3 main evening meal. 4 light afternoon meal of tea, cakes, etc. 5 drink like tea, made from other plants. **tea bag** small porous bag of tea leaves. **tea cosy** covering for a teapot to keep the tea warm. **teapot** *n* container with a lid, spout, and handle for making and serving tea. **teaspoon** *n* small spoon for stirring tea. **tea towel, tea cloth** towel for drying dishes.

teach ❶ *v* **teaching, taught** 1 tell or show (someone) how to do something. 2 give lessons in (a subject). 3 cause to learn or understand. **teacher** *n* **teaching** *n*

teak *n* very hard wood of an E Indian tree.

team ❶ *n* 1 group of people forming one side in a game. 2 group of people or animals working together. **teamster** *n US* lorry driver. **team up** *v* make or join a team. **teamwork** *n* cooperative work by a

fondness, inclination, partiality, penchant, predilection, preference ≠ **dislike**
6 = refinement, appreciation, discernment, discrimination, elegance, judgment, sophistication, style ≠ **tackiness** ◆ *v* **7 = distinguish**, differentiate, discern, perceive ≠ **fail to discern 8 = sample**, savour, sip, test, try **9 = have a flavour of**, savour of, smack of **10 = experience**, encounter, know, meet with, partake of, undergo ≠ **miss**

tatty *adj* **= shabby**, bedraggled, dilapidated, down at heel, neglected, ragged, run–down, scruffy, threadbare, worn

taunt *v* **1 = jeer**, deride, insult, mock, provoke, ridicule, tease, torment ◆ *n*

2 = jeer, derision, dig, gibe, insult, provocation, ridicule, sarcasm, teasing

taut *adj* **1 = tight**, flexed, rigid, strained, stressed, stretched, tense ≠ **relaxed**

tavern *n Old–fashioned* **= inn**, alehouse (*arch*), bar, hostelry, pub (*inf, chiefly Brit*), public house

tawdry *adj* **= vulgar**, cheap, gaudy, gimcrack, naff (*Brit sl*), tacky (*inf*), tasteless, tatty

tax *n* **1 = charge**, duty, excise, levy, tariff, tithe, toll ◆ *v* **2 = charge**, assess, rate **3 = strain**, burden, exhaust, load, stretch, test, try, weaken, weary

teach *v* **= instruct**, coach, drill, educate, enlighten, guide, inform, show, train, tutor team.

tear¹ ⊕ , **teardrop** n drop of fluid appearing in and falling from the eye. **in tears** weeping. **tearful** adj weeping or about to weep. **tear gas** gas that stings the eyes and causes temporary blindness. **tear–jerker** n Informal excessively sentimental film or book.

tear² ⊕ v **tearing, tore, torn** 1 rip a hole in. 2 rip apart. 3 rush. ♦ n 4 hole or split. **tearaway** n wild or unruly person.

tease ⊕ v 1 make fun of (someone) in a provoking or playful way. ♦ n 2 person who teases. **teasing** adj, n **tease out** v remove tangles from (hair etc.) by combing.

teat n 1 nipple of a breast or udder. 2 rubber nipple of a feeding bottle.

technical ⊕ adj 1 of or specializing in industrial, practical, or mechanical arts and applied sciences. 2 skilled in technical subjects. 3 relating to a particular field. 4 according to the letter of the law. 5 showing technique, e.g. technical brilliance. **technicality** n petty point based on a strict application of rules. **technician** n person skilled in a particular technical field. **technical college** higher educational institution with courses in art and technical subjects. **technique** n 1 method or skill used for a particular task. 2 technical proficiency.

Technicolor n ® system of colour photography used for the cinema.

technology n 1 application of practical or mechanical sciences to industry or commerce. 2 scientific methods used in a particular field. **technological** adj **technologist** n

tedious ⊕ adj causing fatigue or boredom. **tedium** n monotony.

tee n 1 small peg from which a golf ball can be played at the start of each hole. 2 area of a golf course from which the first stroke of a hole is made. **tee off** v make the first stroke of a hole in golf.

teem¹ v be full of.

teem² v rain heavily.

teens pl n period of being a teenager.

teeter ⊕ v wobble or move unsteadily.

teeth n plural of TOOTH.

teethe v (of a baby) grow his or her first teeth. **teething troubles** problems during the early stages of something.

teetotal adj drinking no alcohol. **teetotaller** n

Teflon n ® substance used for nonstick coatings on saucepans etc.

telecommunications n communications using telephone, radio, television, etc.

telegram n formerly, a message sent by telegraph.

telegraph n 1 formerly, a system for sending messages over a distance along a cable. ♦ v 2 communicate by telegraph. **telegraphist** n **telegraphy** n

telepathy ⊕ n direct communication between minds. **telepathic** adj **telepathically** adv

telephone ⊕ n 1 device for transmitting

━━━━━━ THESAURUS ━━━━━━

team n 1 = **side**, line–up, squad 2 = **group**, band, body, bunch, company, gang, set **team up** = **join**, band together, cooperate, couple, get together, link, unite, work together

tear¹ n in tears = **weeping**, blubbering, crying, distressed, sobbing

tear² v 1 = **rip**, rend, rupture, scratch, shred, split 2 = **pull apart**, claw, lacerate, mangle, mutilate 3 = **rush**, bolt, charge, dash, fly, hurry, race, run, speed, sprint, zoom ♦ n 4 = **hole**, laceration, rent, rip,

rupture, scratch, split

tease v 1 = **mock**, goad, provoke, pull someone's leg (inf), taunt, torment

technical adj 1, 2 = **scientific**, hi-tech or high–tech, skilled, specialist, specialized, technological

tedious adj = **boring**, drab, dreary, dull, humdrum, irksome, laborious, mind–numbing, monotonous, tiresome, wearisome

teeter v = **wobble**, rock, seesaw, stagger, sway, totter, waver

sound over a distance along wires. ◆ v 2
call or talk to (a person) by telephone.
telephony n **telephonic** adj **telephonist** n
person operating a telephone
switchboard.

teleprinter n apparatus like a typewriter
for sending and receiving typed messages
by wire.

telescope ❶ n 1 optical instrument for
magnifying distant objects. ◆ v 2 shorten.
telescopic adj

television ❶ n 1 system of producing a
moving image and accompanying sound
on a distant screen. 2 device for receiving
broadcast signals and converting them
into sound and pictures. 3 content of
television programmes. **televise** v
broadcast on television.

telex n 1 international communication
service using teleprinters. 2 message sent
by telex. ◆ v 3 transmit by telex.

tell ❶ v **telling, told** 1 make known in
words. 2 order or instruct. 3 give an
account of. 4 discern or distinguish. 5
have an effect. 6 Informal reveal secrets.

teller n 1 narrator. 2 bank cashier. 3
person who counts votes. **telling** adj
having a marked effect. **tell off** v
reprimand. **telling–off** n **telltale** n 1
person who reveals secrets. ◆ adj 2
revealing.

telly n, pl **–lies** Informal television.

temerity ❶ [tim–**merr**–it–tee] n boldness
or audacity.

temp Informal ◆ n 1 temporary employee,
esp. a secretary. ◆ v 2 work as a temp.

temper ❶ n 1 outburst of anger. 2
tendency to become angry. 3 calm mental
condition, e.g. I lost my temper. 4 frame of
mind. ◆ v 5 make less extreme. 6
strengthen or toughen (metal).

temperament ❶ n person's character or
disposition. **temperamental** adj 1 having
changeable moods. 2 Informal erratic and
unreliable. **temperamentally** adv

temperate ❶ adj 1 (of climate) not
extreme. 2 self–restrained or moderate.
temperance n 1 moderation. 2 abstinence
from alcohol.

temperature n 1 degree of heat or cold. 2

telepathy n = **mind–reading**, sixth sense
telephone n 1 = **phone**, dog and bone
(sl), handset, line, mobile (phone) ◆ v
2 = **call**, dial, phone, ring (chiefly Brit)
telescope n 1 = **glass**, spyglass ◆ v
2 = **shorten**, abbreviate, abridge,
compress, condense, contract, shrink
≠ extend
television n 2 = **TV**, small screen (inf), telly
(Brit inf), the box (Brit inf), the tube (sl)
tell v 1 = **inform**, announce, communicate,
disclose, divulge, express, make known,
notify, proclaim, reveal, state 2 = **instruct**,
bid, call upon, command, direct, order,
require, summon 3 = **describe**, chronicle,
depict, narrate, portray, recount, relate,
report 4 = **distinguish**, differentiate,
discern, discriminate, identify 5 = **have** or
take effect, carry weight, count, make its
presence felt, register, take its toll, weigh
temerity n = **audacity**, boldness, cheek,
chutzpah (US & Canad inf), effrontery,

front, impudence, nerve (inf), rashness,
recklessness
temper n 1 = **rage**, bad mood, fury,
passion, tantrum 2 = **irritability**, hot–
headedness, irascibility, passion,
petulance, resentment, surliness
≠ goodwill 3 = **self–control**, calmness,
composure, cool (sl), equanimity ≠ anger
4 = **frame of mind**, constitution,
disposition, humour, mind, mood, nature,
temperament ◆ v 5 = **moderate**, assuage,
lessen, mitigate, mollify, restrain, soften,
soothe, tone down ≠ intensify
6 = **strengthen**, anneal, harden, toughen
≠ soften
temperament n a = **nature**, bent,
character, constitution, disposition,
humour, make–up, outlook, personality,
temper b = **excitability**, anger, hot–
headedness, moodiness, petulance,
volatility
temperate adj 1 = **mild**, calm, cool, fair,

Informal abnormally high body temperature.

tempest ❶ *n* violent storm. **tempestuous** *adj* violent or stormy.

template *n* pattern used to cut out shapes accurately.

temple[1] ❶ *n* building for worship.

temple[2] *n* region on either side of the forehead.

tempo *n, pl* **–pi, –pos** 1 rate or pace. 2 speed of a piece of music.

temporal *adj* 1 of time. 2 worldly rather than spiritual.

temporary ❶ *adj* lasting only for a short time. **temporarily** *adv*

tempt ❶ *v* entice (a person) to do something wrong. **tempt fate** take foolish or unnecessary risks. **tempter, temptress** *n* **temptation** *n* 1 tempting. 2 tempting thing. **tempting** *adj* attractive or inviting.

ten *adj, n* one more than nine. **tenth** *adj, n* (of) number ten in a series.

tenable ❶ *adj* able to be upheld or maintained.

tenacious ❶ *adj* 1 holding fast. 2 stubborn. **tenacity** *n*

tenant ❶ *n* person who rents land or a building. **tenancy** *n*

tench *n, pl* **tench** freshwater game fish of the carp family.

tend[1] ❶ *v* 1 be inclined. 2 go in the direction of. **tendency** *n* inclination to act in a certain way. **tendentious** *adj* biased, not impartial.

tend[2] ❶ *v* take care of.

tender[1] ❶ *adj* 1 not tough. 2 gentle and affectionate. 3 vulnerable or sensitive. **tenderly** *adv* **tenderness** *n* **tenderize** *v* soften (meat) by pounding or treatment with a special substance. **tenderizer** *n* **tenderloin** *n* tender cut of pork from between the sirloin and the ribs.

tender[2] ❶ *v* 1 offer. 2 make a formal offer to supply goods or services at a stated cost. ◆ *n* 3 such an offer. **legal tender** currency that must, by law, be accepted as payment.

tendon *n* strong tissue attaching a muscle to a bone.

tendril *n* slender stem by which a climbing plant clings.

tenement *n* building divided into several

——————[THESAURUS]——————

gentle, moderate, pleasant ≠ **severe**
2 = **moderate**, calm, composed, dispassionate, even–tempered, mild, reasonable, self–controlled, self–restrained, sensible ≠ **wild**

tempest *n* = **storm**, cyclone, gale, hurricane, squall, tornado, typhoon ≠ **peace**

temple[1] *n* = **shrine**, church, sanctuary

temporary *adj* = **impermanent**, brief, ephemeral, fleeting, interim, momentary, provisional, short–lived, transitory ≠ **permanent**

tempt *v* 1 = **entice**, coax, invite, lead on, lure, seduce, tantalize ≠ **discourage**

tenable *adj* = **sound**, arguable, believable, defensible, justifiable, plausible, rational, reasonable, viable

tenacious *adj* 1 = **firm**, clinging, forceful, immovable, iron, strong, tight, unshakable
2 = **stubborn**, adamant, determined,

dogged, obdurate, obstinate, persistent, resolute, steadfast, unswerving, unyielding ≠ **wavering**

tenant *n* = **leaseholder**, inhabitant, lessee, occupant, occupier, renter, resident

tend[1] *v* 1 = **be inclined**, be apt, be liable, gravitate, have a tendency, incline, lean
2 = **go**, aim, bear, head, lead, make for, move, point

tend[2] *v* = **take care of**, attend, cultivate, keep, look after, maintain, manage, nurture, watch over ≠ **ignore**

tender[1] *adj* 2 = **gentle**, affectionate, caring, compassionate, considerate, kind, loving, sympathetic, tenderhearted, warm–hearted ≠ **hard** 3 = **sensitive**, bruised, inflamed, painful, raw, sore, vulnerable

tender[2] *v* 1 = **offer**, give, hand in, present, proffer, propose, put forward, submit, volunteer ◆ *n* 3 = **offer**, bid, estimate, proposal, submission flats.

tenet [ten–nit] *n* doctrine or belief.

tennis *n* game in which players use rackets to hit a ball back and forth over a net.

tenor *n* 1 (singer with) the second highest male voice. 2 general meaning. ◆ *adj* 3 (of a voice or instrument) between alto and baritone.

tenpin bowling *n* game in which players try to knock over ten skittles by rolling a ball at them.

tense[1] ⊕ *adj* 1 emotionally strained. 2 stretched tight. ◆ *v* 3 make or become tense. **tension** *n* 1 hostility or suspense. 2 emotional strain. 3 degree of stretching.

tense[2] *n Grammar* form of a verb showing the time of action.

tent *n* portable canvas shelter.

tentacle *n* flexible organ of many invertebrates, used for grasping, feeding, etc.

tentative ⊕ *adj* 1 provisional or experimental. 2 cautious or hesitant. **tentatively** *adv*

tenterhooks *pl n* **on tenterhooks** in anxious suspense.

tenuous ⊕ *adj* slight or flimsy.

tenure *n* (period of) the holding of an office or position.

tepee [tee–pee] *n* cone–shaped tent, formerly used by Native Americans.

tepid ⊕ *adj* 1 slightly warm. 2 half-hearted.

tequila *n* Mexican alcoholic drink.

term ⊕ *n* 1 word or expression. 2 fixed period. 3 period of the year when a school etc. is open or a lawcourt holds sessions. ◆ *pl* 4 conditions. 5 mutual relationship. ◆ *v* 6 name or designate.

terminal ⊕ *adj* 1 (of an illness) ending in death. 2 at or being an end. ◆ *n* 3 place where people or vehicles begin or end a journey. 4 point where current enters or leaves an electrical device. 5 keyboard and VDU having input and output links with a computer. **terminally** *adv*

terminate ⊕ *v* bring or come to an end. **termination** *n*

terminology ⊕ *n* technical terms relating to a subject.

terminus ⊕ *n*, *pl* –**ni**, –**nuses** railway or bus station at the end of a line.

termite *n* white antlike insect that destroys timber.

tern *n* gull–like sea bird with a forked tail and pointed wings.

terrace *n* 1 row of houses built as one block. 2 paved area next to a building. 3 level tier cut out of a hill. ◆ *pl* 4 (also

tense[1] *adj* 1 = **nervous**, anxious, apprehensive, edgy, jumpy, keyed up, on edge, on tenterhooks, strained, uptight (*inf*), wired (*sl*) ≠ **collected** 2 = **tight**, rigid, strained, stretched, taut ≠ **relaxed** ◆ *v* 3 = **tighten**, brace, flex, strain, stretch ≠ **relax**

tentative *adj* 1 = **unconfirmed**, conjectural, experimental, indefinite, provisional, speculative, unsettled ≠ **final** 2 = **hesitant**, cautious, diffident, doubtful, faltering, timid, uncertain, undecided, unsure ≠ **confident**

tenuous *adj* = **slight**, doubtful, dubious, flimsy, insubstantial, nebulous, shaky, sketchy, weak ≠ **strong**

tepid *adj* 1 = **lukewarm**, warmish 2 = **half-hearted**, apathetic, cool, indifferent,

lukewarm, unenthusiastic ≠ **keen**

term *n* 1 = **word**, expression, name, phrase, title 2 = **period**, duration, interval, season, span, spell, time, while ◆ *v* 6 = **call**, designate, dub, entitle, label, name, style

terminal *adj* 1 = **fatal**, deadly, incurable, killing, lethal, mortal 2 = **final**, concluding, extreme, last, ultimate, utmost ≠ **first** ◆ *n* 3 = **terminus**, depot, end of the line, station

terminate *v* = **end**, abort, cease, close, complete, conclude, discontinue, finish, stop ≠ **start**

terminology *n* = **language**, jargon, nomenclature, phraseology, terms, vocabulary

terminus *n* = **end of the line**, depot,

terracing) tiered area in a stadium where spectators stand. ◆ v 5 form into or provide with a terrace.

terracotta adj, n 1 (made of) brownish–red unglazed pottery. ◆ adj 2 brownish–red.

terrain ⊕ n area of ground, esp. with reference to its physical character.

terrapin n small turtle–like reptile.

terrestrial ⊕ adj 1 of the earth. 2 of or living on land.

terrible ⊕ adj 1 very serious. 2 Informal very bad. 3 causing fear. **terribly** adv

terrier n any of various breeds of small active dog.

terrific ⊕ adj 1 great or intense. 2 Informal excellent.

terrify ⊕ v –fying, –fied fill with fear. **terrified** adj **terrifying** adj

territory ⊕ n, pl –ries 1 district. 2 area under the control of a particular government. 3 area inhabited and defended by an animal. 4 area of knowledge. **territorial** adj **Territorial Army** reserve army.

terror ⊕ n 1 great fear. 2 terrifying person or thing. 3 Informal troublesome person or thing. **terrorism** n use of violence and intimidation to achieve political ends.

terrorist n, adj **terrorize** v force or oppress by fear or violence.

terse ⊕ adj 1 neat and concise. 2 curt. **tersely** adv

tertiary [**tur**–shar–ee] adj third in degree, order, etc.

Terylene n ® synthetic polyester yarn or fabric.

test ⊕ v 1 try out to ascertain the worth, capability, or endurance of. 2 carry out an examination on. ◆ n 3 critical examination. 4 Test match. **testing** adj **test case** lawsuit that establishes a precedent. **Test match** one of a series of international cricket or rugby matches. **test tube** narrow round–bottomed glass tube used in scientific experiments. **test–tube baby** baby conceived outside the mother's body.

testament ⊕ n 1 proof or tribute. 2 Law will. 3 (T–) one of the two main divisions of the Bible.

testate adj having left a valid will. **testacy** n **testator** [test–**tay**–tor], (fem) **testatrix** [test–**tay**–triks] n maker of a will.

testicle n either of the two male reproductive glands.

testify ⊕ v –fying, –fied give evidence under oath. **testify to** be evidence of.

————— THESAURUS —————

garage, last stop, station

terrain n = **ground**, country, going, land, landscape, topography

terrestrial adj 1 = **earthly**, global, worldly

terrible adj 1 = **serious**, dangerous, desperate, extreme, severe ≠ **mild** 2 Inf = **bad**, abysmal, awful, dire, dreadful, poor, rotten (inf) ≠ **great** 3 = **fearful**, dreadful, frightful, horrendous, horrible, horrifying, monstrous, shocking, terrifying

terrific adj 1 = **great**, enormous, fearful, gigantic, huge, intense, tremendous ≠ **moderate** 2 Inf = **excellent**, amazing, brilliant, fantastic (inf), magnificent, marvellous, outstanding, sensational (inf), stupendous, superb, wonderful ≠ **bad**

terrify v = **frighten**, alarm, appal, horrify, make one's hair stand on end, scare,

shock, terrorize

territory n 1 = **district**, area, country, domain, land, patch, province, region, zone

terror n 1 = **fear**, alarm, anxiety, dread, fright, horror, panic, shock 2 = **scourge**, bogeyman, bugbear, devil, fiend, monster

terse adj 1 = **concise**, brief, condensed, laconic, monosyllabic, pithy, short, succinct ≠ **lengthy** 2 = **curt**, abrupt, brusque, short, snappy ≠ **polite**

test v 1 = **try out**, experiment, put to the test 2 = **check**, analyse, assess, examine, investigate, research ◆ n 3 = **examination**, acid test, analysis, assessment, check, evaluation, investigation, research, trial

testament n 1 = **proof**, demonstration, evidence, testimony, tribute, witness 2 Law

testimony ⊕ *n, pl* **-nies 1** declaration of truth or fact. **2** evidence given under oath. **testimonial** *n* **1** recommendation of the worth of a person or thing. **2** tribute for services or achievement.

> ✓ **WORD TIP**
>
> A *testimonial* is an open letter of recommendation about someone. A *reference* is a confidential report that is not read by the person who is the subject.

testy *adj* **-tier, -tiest** irritable or touchy. **testily** *adv* **testiness** *n*

tetanus *n* acute infectious disease producing muscular spasms and convulsions.

tête-à-tête *n, pl* **-têtes, -tête** private conversation.

tether ⊕ *n* **1** rope or chain for tying an animal to a spot. ◆ *v* **2** tie up with rope. **at the end of one's tether** at the limit of one's endurance.

tetrahedron [tet-ra **heed**-ron] *n, pl* **-drons, -dra** solid figure with four faces.

text ⊕ *n* **1** main body of a book as distinct from illustrations etc. **2** passage of the Bible as the subject of a sermon. **3** novel or play studied for a course. **textual** *adj*
textbook *n* **1** standard book on a particular subject. ◆ *adj* **2** perfect, e.g. *a textbook landing*.

textile *n* fabric or cloth, esp. woven.

texture ⊕ *n* structure, feel, or consistency. **textured** *adj* **textural** *adj*

than *conj, prep* used to introduce the second element of a comparison.

thank ⊕ *v* **1** express gratitude to. **2** hold responsible. **thanks** *pl n* **1** words of gratitude. ◆ *interj* **2** (also **thank you**) polite expression of gratitude. **thanks to** because of. **thankful** *adj* grateful. **thankless** *adj* unrewarding or unappreciated.

> ✓ **WORD TIP**
>
> When *thank you* is used to express gratitude it should be written as two words: *Thank you for the gift*. When it is used as an adjective, use a hyphen: *a thank-you note*.

that *adj, pron* **1** used to refer to something already mentioned or familiar, or further away. ◆ *conj* **2** used to introduce a clause. ◆ *pron* **3** used to introduce a relative clause.

> ✓ **WORD TIP**
>
> The relative pronoun *that* may often be used interchangeably with *which* in defining clauses: *the coat that/which you bought*. Some people, however, prefer to reserve *which* for the type of clause (called nondefining) that contains explanations and amplifications and is divided by a comma from the rest of the sentence; *he found the book, which was a start*.

thatch *n* **1** roofing material of reeds or straw. ◆ *v* **2** roof (a house) with reeds or straw.

thaw ⊕ *v* **1** make or become unfrozen. **2**

———— THESAURUS ————

= **will**, last wishes

testify *v* = **bear witness**, affirm, assert, attest, certify, corroborate, state, swear, vouch ≠ **dispute**

testimony *n* **1** = **proof**, corroboration, demonstration, evidence, indication, manifestation, support, verification **2** = **evidence**, affidavit, deposition, statement, submission

tether *n* **1** = **rope**, chain, fetter, halter,
lead, leash ◆ *v* **2** = **tie**, bind, chain, fasten, fetter, secure **at the end of one's tether** = **exasperated**, at one's wits' end, exhausted

text *n* **1** = **contents**, body **2** = **words**, wording

texture *n* = **feel**, consistency, grain, structure, surface, tissue

thank *v* **1** = **say thank you**, show one's appreciation become more relaxed or friendly. ♦ n 3 thawing. 4 weather causing snow or ice to melt.

the adj the definite article, used before a noun.

theatre n 1 place where plays etc. are performed. 2 hospital operating room. 3 drama and acting in general. **theatrical** adj 1 of the theatre. 2 exaggerated or affected. **theatricals** pl n (amateur) dramatic performances. **theatrically** adv **theatricality** n

thee pron Obs objective form of THOU.

theft ① n act or an instance of stealing.

their adj of or associated with them. **theirs** pron (thing or person) belonging to them.

> ✓ **WORD TIP**
>
> Be careful not to confuse *their* with *there*. *Their* is used for possession: *their new baby*. *There* indicates place and has a similar '-ere' spelling pattern to *here* and *where*.

them pron refers to people or things other than the speaker or those addressed. **themselves** pron emphatic and reflexive form of THEY or THEM.

> ✓ **WORD TIP**
>
> *Them* may be used after a singular to avoid the clumsy *him or her*: *If you see a person looking lost, help them.*

theme ① n 1 main idea or subject being discussed. 2 recurring melodic figure in music. **thematic** adj **theme park** leisure area in which all the activities and displays are based on a single theme.

then adv 1 at that time. 2 after that. 3 that being so.

thence adv 1 from that place or time. 2 therefore.

theology n, pl –gies study of religions and religious beliefs. **theologian** n **theological** adj **theologically** adv

theorem n proposition that can be proved by reasoning.

theory ① n, pl –ries 1 set of ideas to explain something. 2 abstract knowledge or reasoning. 3 idea or opinion. **in theory** in an ideal or hypothetical situation. **theoretical** adj based on theory rather than practice or fact. **theoretically** adv **theorist** n **theorize** v form theories, speculate.

therapy ① n, pl –pies curing treatment. **therapist** n **therapeutic** [ther–rap–**pew**–tik] adj curing. **therapeutics** n art of curing.

there adv 1 in or to that place. 2 in that respect. **thereby** adv by that means. **therefore** adv consequently, that being so. **thereupon** adv immediately after that.

> ✓ **WORD TIP**
>
> Be careful not to confuse *there* with *their*. *There* indicates place and has a similar '-ere' spelling pattern to *here* and *where*. *Their* indicates possession: *their new baby*.

therm n unit of measurement of heat. **thermal** adj 1 of heat. 2 hot or warm. 3 (of clothing) retaining heat. ♦ n 4 rising current of warm air.

thermodynamics n scientific study of the relationship between heat and other forms of energy.

thermometer n instrument for measuring temperature.

Thermos n ℞ vacuum flask.

| T H E S A U R U S |

thaw v 1 = **melt**, defrost, dissolve, liquefy, soften, unfreeze, warm

theft n = **stealing**, embezzlement, fraud, larceny, pilfering, purloining, robbery, thieving

theme n 1 = **subject**, idea, keynote, subject matter, topic 2, 3 = **motif**, leitmotif

theory n 3 = **hypothesis**, assumption, conjecture, presumption, speculation, supposition, surmise, thesis ≠ fact

therapy n = **remedy**, cure, healing, treatment

thermostat *n* device for automatically regulating temperature. **thermostatic** *adj* **thermostatically** *adv*

thesaurus [thiss–**sore**–uss] *n, pl* **–ruses** book containing lists of synonyms and related words.

these *adj, pron* plural of THIS.

thesis **❶** *n, pl* **theses** 1 written work submitted for a degree. 2 opinion supported by reasoned argument.

thespian *n* 1 actor or actress. ◆ *adj* 2 of the theatre.

they *pron* refers to: 1 people or things other than the speaker or people addressed. 2 people in general. 3 *Informal* he or she.

> ✔ **WORD TIP**
> *They* may be used after a singular to
> avoid the clumsy *he or she: If a person is
> born gloomy, they cannot help it.*

thick **❶** *adj* 1 of great or specified extent from one side to the other. 2 having a dense consistency. 3 *Informal* stupid or insensitive. 4 *Informal* friendly. **a bit thick** *Informal* unfair or unreasonable. **the thick** busiest or most intense part. **thick with**

full of. **thicken** *v* make or become thick or thicker. **thickness** *n* 1 state of being thick. 2 dimension through an object. 3 layer. **thickset** *adj* 1 stocky in build.

thicket **❶** *n* dense growth of small trees.

thief **❶** *n, pl* **thieves** person who steals. **thieve** *v* steal. **thieving** *adj*

thigh *n* upper part of the human leg.

thimble *n* cap protecting the end of the finger when sewing.

thin **❶** *adj* **thinner, thinnest** 1 not thick. 2 slim or lean. 3 sparse or meagre. 4 of low density. 5 poor or unconvincing. ◆ *v* **thinning, thinned** 6 make or become thin. **thinness** *n*

thing **❶** *n* 1 material object. 2 object, fact, or idea considered as a separate entity. 3 *Informal* obsession. ◆ *pl* 4 possessions, clothes, etc.

think **❶** *v* **thinking, thought** 1 consider, judge, or believe. 2 make use of the mind. 3 be considerate enough or remember to do something. **thinker** *n* **thinking** *adj, n* **think–tank** *n* group of experts studying specific problems. **think up** *v* invent or devise.

third *adj* 1 of number three in a series. 2

——————————— THESAURUS ———————————

thesis *n* 1 = **dissertation**, essay, monograph, paper, treatise 2 = **proposition**, contention, hypothesis, idea, opinion, proposal, theory, view

thick *adj* 1 = **wide**, broad, bulky, fat, solid, substantial ≠ **thin** 2 = **dense**, close, compact, concentrated, condensed, heavy, impenetrable, opaque ≠ **clear** 3 *Inf* = **stupid**, brainless, dense, dopey (*inf*), moronic, obtuse, slow, thickheaded ≠ **bright** 4 *Inf* = **friendly**, close, devoted, familiar, inseparable, intimate, pally (*inf*) ≠ **distant** **a bit thick** *Inf* = **unreasonable**, unfair, unjust

thicket *n* = **wood**, brake, coppice, copse, covert, grove

thief *n* = **robber**, burglar, embezzler, housebreaker, pickpocket, pilferer, plunderer, shoplifter, stealer

thin *adj* 1 = **narrow**, attenuated, fine

≠ **thick** 2 = **slim**, bony, emaciated, lean, scrawny, skeletal, skinny, slender, slight, spare, spindly ≠ **heavy** 3 = **meagre**, deficient, scanty, scarce, scattered, skimpy, sparse, wispy 4 = **fine**, delicate, diaphanous, filmy, flimsy, gossamer, sheer, unsubstantial 5 = **unconvincing**, feeble, flimsy, inadequate, lame, poor, superficial, weak ≠ **strong**

thing *n* 1, 2 = **object**, article, being, body, entity, something, substance ◆ *n* 3 *Inf* = **obsession**, bee in one's bonnet, fetish, fixation, hang-up (*inf*), mania, phobia, preoccupation ◆ *pl n* 4 = **possessions**, belongings, clobber (*Brit sl*), effects, equipment, gear, luggage, stuff

think *v* 1 = **believe**, consider, deem, estimate, imagine, judge, reckon, regard, suppose 2 = **ponder**, cerebrate, cogitate, contemplate, deliberate, meditate, muse,

rated or graded below the second level. ◆
n 3 one of three equal parts. **third degree**
violent interrogation. **third party** (applying
to) a person involved by chance or only
incidentally in legal proceedings, an
accident, etc.

thirst ⊕ n 1 desire to drink. 2 craving or
yearning. ◆ v 3 feel thirst. **thirsty** adj
thirstily adv

thirteen adj, n three plus ten. **thirteenth**
adj, n

thirty adj, n three times ten. **thirtieth** adj, n

this adj, pron 1 used to refer to a thing or
person nearby, just mentioned, or about
to be mentioned. ◆ adj 2 used to refer to
the present time, e.g. this morning.

thistle n prickly plant with dense flower
heads.

thither adv Obs to or towards that place.

thong n thin strip of leather etc.

thorax n, pl **thoraxes, thoraces** part of the
body between the neck and the abdomen.
thoracic adj

thorn ⊕ n 1 prickle on a plant. 2 bush with
thorns. **thorn in one's side, flesh** source
of irritation. **thorny** adj

thorough ⊕ adj 1 complete. 2 careful or
methodical. **thoroughly** adv

thoroughness n **thoroughbred** n, adj
(animal) of pure breed. **thoroughfare** n
way through from one place to another.

those adj, pron plural of THAT.

thou pron Obs singular form of YOU.

though ⊕ conj 1 despite the fact that. ◆
adv 2 nevertheless.

thought ⊕ v 1 past of THINK. ◆ n 2
thinking. 3 concept or idea. 4 ideas typical
of a time or place. 5 consideration. 6
intention or expectation. **thoughtful** adj 1
considerate. 2 showing careful thought. 3
pensive or reflective. **thoughtless** adj
inconsiderate.

thousand adj, n 1 ten hundred. 2 large but
unspecified number. **thousandth** adj, n
(of) number one thousand in a series.

thrash ⊕ v 1 beat, esp. with a stick or
whip. 2 defeat soundly. 3 move about
wildly. 4 thresh. **thrashing** n severe
beating. **thrash out** v solve by thorough
argument.

thread ⊕ n 1 fine strand or yarn. 2
unifying theme. 3 spiral ridge on a screw,
nut, or bolt. ◆ v 4 pass thread through. 5
pick (one's way etc.). **threadbare** adj 1 (of
fabric) with the nap worn off. 2
hackneyed. 3 shabby.

———————[THESAURUS]———————

obsess, reason, reflect, ruminate

thirst n 1 = **thirstiness**, drought, dryness
2 = **craving**, appetite, desire, hankering,
keenness, longing, passion, yearning
≠ **dislike**

thorn n 1 = **prickle**, barb, spike, spine

thorough adj 1 = **complete**, absolute,
out–and–out, outright, perfect, total,
unmitigated, unqualified, utter ≠ **partial**
2 = **careful**, assiduous, conscientious,
efficient, exhaustive, full, in–depth,
intensive, meticulous, painstaking
≠ **cursory**

though conj 1 = **although**, even if, even
though, notwithstanding, while ◆ adv
2 = **nevertheless**, for all that, however,
nonetheless, notwithstanding, still, yet

thought n 2 = **thinking**, cogitation,
consideration, deliberation, meditation,

musing, reflection, rumination 3 = **idea**,
concept, judgment, notion, opinion, view
5 = **consideration**, attention, heed,
regard, scrutiny, study 6 a = **intention**,
aim, design, idea, notion, object, plan,
purpose b = **expectation**, anticipation,
aspiration, hope, prospect

thrash v 1 = **beat**, belt (inf), cane, flog,
give (someone) a (good) hiding (inf),
scourge, spank, whip 2 = **defeat**, beat,
crush, drub, rout, run rings around (inf),
slaughter (inf), trounce, wipe the floor
with (inf) 3 = **thresh**, flail, jerk, toss and
turn, writhe

thread n 1 = **strand**, fibre, filament, line,
string, yarn 2 = **theme**, direction, drift,
plot, story line, train of thought ◆ v
4 = **string** 5 = **pass**, ease, pick (one's way),
squeeze through

threat ❶ *n* **1** declaration of intent to harm. **2** dangerous person or thing. **threaten** *v* **1** make or be a threat to. **2** be a menacing indication of.

three *adj, n* one more than two. **threesome** *n* group of three. **three-dimensional, 3-D** *adj* having three dimensions.

thresh *v* beat (wheat etc.) to separate the grain from the husks and straw. **thresh about** move about wildly.

threshold ❶ *n* **1** bar forming the bottom of a doorway. **2** entrance. **3** starting point. **4** point at which something begins to take effect.

thrice *adv Lit* three times.

thrift ❶ *n* **1** wisdom and caution with money. **2** low growing plant with pink flowers. **thrifty** *adj*

thrill ❶ *n* **1** sudden feeling of excitement. ◆ *v* **2** (cause to) feel a thrill. **thrilling** *adj*

thrive ❶ *v* **thriving, thrived** *or* **throve, thrived** *or* **thriven 1** flourish or prosper. **2** grow well.

throat *n* **1** passage from the mouth and nose to the stomach and lungs. **2** front of the neck. **throaty** *adj* (of the voice) hoarse.

throb ❶ *v* **throbbing, throbbed 1** pulsate repeatedly. **2** vibrate rhythmically. ◆ *n* **3** throbbing.

throes *pl n* violent pangs or pains. **in the throes of** struggling to cope with.

thrombosis *n, pl* **-ses** forming of a clot in a blood vessel or the heart.

throne *n* **1** ceremonial seat of a monarch or bishop. **2** sovereign power.

throng ❶ *n, v* crowd.

throttle ❶ *n* **1** device controlling the amount of fuel entering an engine. ◆ *v* **2** strangle.

through ❶ *prep* **1** from end to end or side to side of. **2** because of. **3** during. ◆ *adj* **4** finished. **5** (of transport) going directly to a place. **through and through** completely. **throughout** *prep, adv* in every part (of). **throughput** *n* amount of material processed.

throw ❶ *v* **throwing, threw, thrown 1** hurl through the air. **2** move or put suddenly or carelessly. **3** bring into a specified state, esp. suddenly. **4** move (a switch, lever, etc.). **5** shape (pottery) on a wheel. **6** give (a party). **7** *Informal* baffle or disconcert. **8** direct (a look, light, etc.). **9** project (the voice) so that it seems to come from elsewhere. ◆ *n* **10** throwing. **11** distance thrown. **throwaway** *adj* **1** done or said casually. **2** designed to be

threat *n* **1** = **menace**, threatening remark **2** = **warning**, foreboding, foreshadowing, omen, portent, presage, writing on the wall **3** = **danger**, hazard, menace, peril, risk

threshold *n* **2** = **entrance**, door, doorstep, doorway **3** = **start**, beginning, brink, dawn, inception, opening, outset, verge ≠ **end 4** = **minimum**, lower limit

thrift *n* **1** = **economy**, carefulness, frugality, parsimony, prudence, saving, thriftiness

thrill *n* **1** = **pleasure**, buzz (*sl*), kick (*inf*), stimulation, tingle, titillation ≠ **boredom** ◆ *v* **2** = **excite**, arouse, electrify, move, stimulate, stir, titillate

thrive *v* **1** = **prosper**, boom, develop, do well, flourish, get on, increase, succeed **2** = **grow**

throb *v* **1** = **pulsate**, beat, palpitate, pound, pulse, thump **2** = **vibrate** ◆ *n* **3** = **pulse**, beat, palpitation, pounding, pulsating, thump, thumping, vibration

① **throng** *n* = **crowd**, crush, horde, host, mass, mob, multitude, pack, swarm

② **throng** *v* = **crowd**, congregate, converge, flock, mill around, pack, swarm around ≠ **separate**

throttle *v* **2** = **strangle**, choke, garrotte, strangulate

through *prep* **1** = **from one side to the other of**, between, by, past **2** = **because of**, by means of, by way of, using, via **3** = **during**, in, throughout ◆ *adj* **4** = **completed**, done, ended, finished **through and through** = **completely**, altogether, entirely, fully, thoroughly,

discarded after use. **throwback** *n* person
or thing that reverts to an earlier type.
throw up *v* vomit.

thrush *n* brown songbird.

thrust ❶ *v* **thrusting, thrust 1** push
forcefully. ◆ *n* **2** forceful stab. **3** force or
power. **4** intellectual or emotional drive.

thud ❶ *n* **1** dull heavy sound. ◆ *v*
thudding, thudded 2 make such a sound.

thug ❶ *n* violent man, esp. a criminal.
thuggery *n* **thuggish** *adj*

thumb *n* **1** short thick finger set apart from
the others. ◆ *v* **2** touch or handle with the
thumb. **3** signal with the thumb for a lift
in a vehicle. **thumb through** flick through
(a book or magazine).

thump ❶ *n* **1** (sound of) a dull heavy blow.
◆ *v* **2** strike heavily.

thunder ❶ *n* **1** loud noise accompanying
lightning. ◆ *v* **2** rumble with thunder. **3**
shout. **4** move fast, heavily, and noisily.
thunderous *adj* **thundery** *adj* **thunderbolt**
n **1** lightning flash. **2** something sudden
and unexpected. **thunderclap** *n* peal of
thunder. **thunderstruck** *adj* amazed.

Thursday *n* fifth day of the week.

thus ❶ *adv* **1** therefore. **2** in this way.

thwart ❶ *v* **1** foil or frustrate. ◆ *n* **2** seat

across a boat.

thy *adj Obs* of or associated with you
(thou). **thyself** *pron Obs* emphatic form of
THOU.

thyme [time] *n* aromatic herb.

tiara *n* semicircular jewelled headdress.

tibia *n, pl* **tibiae, tibias** inner bone of the
lower leg. **tibial** *adj*

tic *n* spasmodic muscular twitch.

tick¹ ❶ *n* **1** mark (✓) used to check off or
indicate the correctness of something. **2**
recurrent tapping sound, as of a clock. **3**
Informal moment. ◆ *v* **4** mark with a tick. **5**
make a ticking sound. **tick off** *v* **1** mark
with a tick. **2** reprimand. **tick over** *v* **1** (of
an engine) idle. **2** function smoothly.
ticktack *n* bookmakers' sign language.

tick² *n* tiny bloodsucking parasitic animal.

ticket ❶ *n* **1** card or paper entitling the
holder to admission, travel, etc. **2** label,
esp. showing price. **3** official notification
of a parking or traffic offence. **4** declared
policy of a political party. ◆ *v* **–eting,**
–eted 5 attach or issue a ticket to.

tickle *v* **1** touch or stroke (a person) to
produce laughter. **2** itch or tingle. **3** please
or amuse. ◆ *n* **4** tickling. **ticklish** *adj* **1**
sensitive to tickling. **2** requiring care or

totally, utterly, wholly

throw *v* **1, 2** = **hurl**, cast, chuck (*inf*), fling,
launch, lob (*inf*), pitch, send, sling, toss
7 *Inf* = **confuse**, astonish, baffle, confound,
disconcert, dumbfound, faze ◆ *n*
10 = **toss**, fling, heave, lob (*inf*), pitch,
sling

thrust *v* **1** = **push**, drive, force, jam,
plunge, propel, ram, shove ◆ *n* **2** = **push**,
drive, lunge, poke, prod, shove, stab
3 = **momentum**, impetus

thud *n, v* **1, 2** = **thump**, crash, knock,
smack

thug *n* = **ruffian**, bruiser (*inf*), bully boy,
gangster, heavy (*sl*), hooligan, tough

thump *n* **1** a = **thud**, bang, clunk, crash,
thwack b = **blow**, clout (*inf*), knock,
punch, rap, smack, swipe, wallop (*inf*),
whack ◆ *v* **2** = **strike**, beat, clobber (*sl*),

clout (*inf*), hit, knock, pound, punch,
smack, swipe, wallop (*inf*), whack

thunder *n* **2** = **rumble**, boom, crash,
explosion ◆ *v* **3** = **rumble**, boom, crash,
peal, resound, reverberate, roar **4** = **shout**,
bark, bellow, roar, yell

thus *adv* **1** = **therefore**, accordingly,
consequently, ergo, for this reason, hence,
on that account, so, then **2** = **in this way**,
as follows, like this, so

thwart *v* **1** = **frustrate**, foil, hinder,
obstruct, outwit, prevent, snooker, stymie

tick¹ *n* **1** = **mark**, dash, stroke **2** = **tapping**,
clicking, ticktock **3** *Inf* = **moment**, flash,
instant, minute, second, split second,
trice, twinkling ◆ *v* **4** = **mark**, check off,
indicate **5** = **tap**, click, ticktock

ticket *n* **1** = **voucher**, card, certificate,
coupon, pass, slip, token **2** = **label**, card,

tact.

tiddlywinks *n* game in which players try to flip small plastic discs into a cup.

tide 🟊 *n* 1 rise and fall of the sea caused by the gravitational pull of the sun and moon. 2 current caused by this 3 widespread feeling or tendency. **tidal** *adj* **tidal wave** large destructive wave. **tide over** *v* help (someone) temporarily.

tidings *pl n* news.

tidy 🟊 *adj* –dier, –diest 1 neat and orderly. 2 *Informal* considerable. ♦ *v* –dying, –died 3 put in order. **tidily** *adv* **tidiness** *n*

tie 🟊 *v* tying, tied 1 fasten or be fastened with string, rope, etc. 2 make (a knot or bow) in (something). 3 restrict or limit. 4 score the same as another competitor. ♦ *n* 5 long narrow piece of material worn knotted round the neck. 6 bond or fastening. 7 drawn game or contest. **tied** *adj* 1 (of a cottage etc.) rented to the tenant only as long as he or she is employed by the owner.

tier 🟊 *n* one of a set of rows placed one above and behind the other.

tiff *n* petty quarrel.

tiger *n* large yellow–and–black striped Asian cat. **tigress** *n* 1 female tiger. 2 *Informal* fierce woman.

tight 🟊 *adj* 1 stretched or drawn taut. 2 closely fitting. 3 secure or firm. 4 cramped. 5 *Informal* not generous. 6 (of a match or game) very close. 7 *Informal* drunk. **tights** *pl n* one–piece clinging garment covering the body from the waist to the feet. **tighten** *v* make or become tight or tighter. 1 **tightrope** *n* rope stretched taut on which acrobats perform.

tile *n* 1 flat piece of ceramic, plastic, etc. used to cover a roof, floor, or wall. ♦ *v* 2 cover with tiles. **tiling** *n* tiles collectively.

till¹ *conj, prep* until.

till² 🟊 *v* cultivate (land).

till³ *n* drawer for money, usu. in a cash register.

tiller *n* lever to move a rudder of a boat.

tilt 🟊 *v* 1 slant at an angle. 2 *Hist* compete against in a jousting contest. ♦ *n* 3 slope. 4 *Hist* jousting contest. 5 attempt. **at full tilt** at full speed or force.

timber 🟊 *n* 1 wood as a building material. 2 trees collectively. 3 wooden beam in the frame of a house, boat, etc.

timbre 🟊 [**tam**–bra] *n* distinctive quality of

---

docket, marker, slip, sticker, tab, tag

tide *n* 2 = **current**, ebb, flow, stream, tideway, undertow 3 = **tendency**, direction, drift, movement, trend

tidy *adj* 1 = **neat**, clean, methodical, orderly, shipshape, spruce, well–kept, well–ordered 2 *Inf* = **considerable**, ample, generous, goodly, handsome, healthy, large, sizable *or* sizeable, substantial ≠ **little** ♦ *v* 3 = **neaten**, clean, groom, order, spruce up, straighten ≠ **mess up**

tie *v* 1 = **fasten**, attach, bind, connect, join, knot, link, secure, tether ≠ **loose** 3 = **restrict**, bind, confine, hamper, hinder, limit, restrain ≠ **free** 4 = **draw**, equal, match ♦ *n* 6 a = **bond**, affiliation, allegiance, commitment, connection, liaison, relationship b = **fastening**, bond, cord, fetter, knot, ligature, link 7 = **draw**, dead heat, deadlock, stalemate

tier *n* = **row**, bank, layer, level, line, rank, storey, stratum

tight *adj* 1 = **taut**, rigid, stretched ≠ **relaxed** 2 = **close–fitting**, close 3 = **secure**, fast, firm, fixed 4 = **cramped**, constricted, narrow, snug ≠ **loose** 5 *Inf* = **miserly**, grasping, mean, niggardly, parsimonious, stingy, tightfisted ≠ **generous** 6 = **close**, even, evenly–balanced, well–matched 7 *Inf* = **drunk**, inebriated, intoxicated, paralytic (*inf*), plastered (*sl*), tipsy, under the influence (*inf*) ≠ **sober**

till² *v* = **cultivate**, dig, plough, work

till³ *n* = **cash register**, cash box

tilt *v* 1 = **slant**, heel, incline, lean, list, slope, tip ♦ *n* 3 = **slope**, angle, inclination, incline, list, pitch, slant 4 *Hist* = **joust**, combat, duel, fight, lists, tournament (**at**) **full tilt** = **full speed**, for dear life, headlong sound of a voice or instrument.

time ⊙ n **1** past, present, and future as a continuous whole. **2** specific point in time. **3** unspecified interval. **4** instance or occasion. **5** period with specific features. **6** musical tempo. **7** *Slang* imprisonment. ♦ v **8** note the time taken by. **9** choose a time for. **timeless** *adj* **1** unaffected by time. **2** eternal. **timely** *adj* at the appropriate time. **time–honoured** *adj* sanctioned by custom. **time–lag** n period between cause and effect. **timepiece** n watch or clock. **timeserver** n person who changes his or her views to gain support or favour. **time sharing 1** system of part ownership of a holiday property for a specified period each year. **2 timetable** n plan showing the times when something takes place, the departure and arrival times of trains or buses, etc.

timid ⊙ *adj* **1** easily frightened. **2** shy, not bold. **timidity** n **timorous** *adj* timid.

timpani [**tim**–pan–ee] *pl* n set of kettledrums. **timpanist** n

tin n **1** soft metallic element. **2** (airtight) metal container. **tinned** *adj* (of food) preserved by being sealed in a tin. **tinny** *adj* (of sound) thin and metallic. **tinpot** *adj Informal* worthless or unimportant.

tinder n dry easily–burning material used to start a fire. **tinderbox** n

tinge ⊙ n **1** slight tint. **2** trace. ♦ v **tingeing, tinged 3** give a slight tint or trace to.

tingle ⊙ v, n (feel) a prickling or stinging sensation.

tinker ⊙ n **1** travelling mender of pots and pans. **2** *Scot & Irish* Gypsy. ♦ v **3** fiddle with (an engine etc.) in an attempt to repair it.

tinkle v **1** ring with a high tinny sound like a small bell. ♦ n **2** this sound or action.

tinsel n **1** decorative metallic strips or threads.

tint ⊙ n **1** (pale) shade of a colour. **2** dye for the hair. ♦ v **3** give a tint to.

tiny ⊙ *adj* **tinier, tiniest** very small.

tip¹ ⊙ n **1** narrow or pointed end of anything. **2** small piece forming an end. ♦ v **tipping, tipped 3** put a tip on.

tip² ⊙ n **1** money given in return for service. **2** helpful hint or warning. **3** piece of inside information. ♦ v **tipping, tipped 4** give a tip to. **tipster** n person who sells tips about races.

tip³ ⊙ v **tipping, tipped 1** tilt or overturn. **2** dump (rubbish). ♦ n **3** rubbish dump.

tipple ⊙ v **1** drink alcohol habitually, esp.

timber n **1** = **wood**, boards, logs, planks **2** = **trees**, forest **3** = **beams**

timbre n = **tone**, colour, resonance, ring

time n **3** = **period**, duration, interval, season, space, span, spell, stretch, term **4** = **occasion**, instance, juncture, point, stage **6** = **tempo**, beat, measure, rhythm ♦ v **9** = **schedule**, set

timid *adj* **1** = **fearful**, apprehensive, faint–hearted, shrinking, timorous **2** = **shy**, bashful, coy, diffident

tinge n **1** = **tint**, colour, shade **2** = **bit**, dash, drop, smattering, sprinkling, suggestion, touch, trace ♦ v **3** = **tint**, colour, imbue, suffuse

① **tingle** v = **prickle**, have goose pimples, itch, sting, tickle

② **tingle** n = **quiver**, goose pimples, itch,

pins and needles (*inf*), prickling, shiver, thrill

tinker v **3** = **meddle**, dabble, fiddle (*inf*), mess about, play, potter

tint n **1** = **shade**, colour, hue, tone **2** = **dye**, rinse, tincture, tinge, wash ♦ v **3** = **dye**, colour

tiny *adj* = **small**, diminutive, infinitesimal, little, microscopic, miniature, minute, negligible, petite, slight

tip¹ n **1** = **end**, extremity, head, peak, pinnacle, point, summit, top ♦ v **3** = **cap**, crown, finish, surmount, top

tip² n **1** = **gratuity**, gift **2** = **hint**, pointer, suggestion ♦ v **4** a = **reward**, remunerate **b** = **advise**, suggest

tip³ v **1** = **tilt**, incline, lean, list, slant **2** = **dump**, empty, pour out, unload ♦ n in small quantities. ◆ n 2 alcoholic drink. **tippler** n

tipsy adj **–sier, –siest** slightly drunk.

tiptoe v **–toeing, –toed** walk quietly with the heels off the ground.

tiptop adj of the highest quality or condition.

tirade ❶ n long angry speech.

tire ❶ v 1 reduce the energy of, as by exertion. 2 weary or bore. **tired** adj 1 exhausted. 2 hackneyed or stale. **tiring** adj **tireless** adj energetic and determined. **tiresome** adj boring and irritating.

tissue n 1 substance of an animal body or plant. 2 piece of thin soft paper used as a handkerchief etc. 3 interwoven series.

tit n any of various small songbirds.

titanic adj huge or very important.

titanium n Chem strong light metallic element used to make alloys.

titbit ❶ n 1 tasty piece of food. 2 pleasing scrap of scandal.

tithe n 1 esp. formerly, one tenth of one's income or produce paid to the church as a tax.

titillate ❶ v excite or stimulate pleasurably. **titillating** adj **titillation** n

title ❶ n 1 name of a book, film, etc. 2 name signifying rank or position. 3 formal designation, such as Mrs. 4 Sport championship. 5 Law legal right of possession. **titled** adj aristocratic.

titter ❶ v 1 laugh in a suppressed way. ◆ n 2 suppressed laugh.

titular adj 1 in name only. 2 of a title.

TNT n trinitrotoluene, a powerful explosive.

to prep 1 indicating movement towards, equality or comparison, etc., e.g. walking to school; forty miles to the gallon. 2 used to mark the indirect object or infinitive of a verb. ◆ adv 3 to a closed position, e.g. pull the door to. **to and fro** back and forth.

toad n animal like a large frog.

toast[1] ❶ n 1 sliced bread browned by heat. ◆ v 2 brown (bread) by heat. 3 warm or be warmed. **toaster** n electrical device for toasting bread.

toast[2] ❶ n 1 tribute or proposal of health or success marked by people raising glasses and drinking together. 2 person or thing so honoured. ◆ v 3 drink a toast to.

tobacco n, pl **–cos, –coes** plant with large leaves dried for smoking. **tobacconist** n person or shop selling tobacco, cigarettes, etc.

toboggan n 1 narrow sledge for sliding over snow. ◆ v **–ganing, –ganed** 2 ride a toboggan.

today n 1 this day. 2 the present age. ◆ adv 3 on this day. 4 nowadays.

toddle v walk with short unsteady steps. **toddler** n child beginning to walk.

to-do n, pl **–dos** fuss or commotion.

toe n 1 digit of the foot. 2 part of a shoe or sock covering the toes. ◆ v **toeing, toed** 3 touch or kick with the toe. 4 **toe the line** conform.

toffee n chewy sweet made of boiled sugar.

toga [**toe**–ga] n garment worn by citizens

THESAURUS

3 = **dump**, refuse heap, rubbish heap

tipple v 1 = **drink**, imbibe, indulge (inf), quaff, swig, tope ◆ n 2 = **alcohol**, booze (inf), drink, liquor

tirade n = **outburst**, diatribe, fulmination, harangue, invective, lecture

tire v 1 = **exhaust**, drain, fatigue, wear out, weary ≠ **restore** 2 = **bore**, exasperate, irk, irritate, weary

titbit n 1 = **delicacy**, dainty, morsel, snack, treat

titillate v = **excite**, arouse, interest,

stimulate, tantalize, tease, thrill

title n 1 = **name**, designation, handle (sl), term 4 Sport = **championship**, crown 5 Law = **ownership**, claim, entitlement, prerogative, privilege, right

titter v 1 = **snigger**, chortle (inf), chuckle, giggle, laugh

toast[1] v 2 = **brown**, grill, roast 3 = **warm**, heat

toast[2] n 1 = **tribute**, compliment, health, pledge, salutation, salute 2 = **favourite**, darling, hero or heroine ◆ v 3 = **drink to**, of ancient Rome.

together ⓥ *adv* 1 in company. 2 simultaneously. ♦ *adj* 3 *Informal* organized.

> ✓ **WORD TIP**
> Two nouns linked by *together with* do not make a plural subject so the following verb must be singular: *Jones, together with his partner, has had great success.*

toggle *n* 1 small bar–shaped button inserted through a loop for fastening. 2 switch used to turn a machine or computer function on or off.

toil ⓥ *n* 1 hard work. ♦ *v* 2 work hard. 3 progress with difficulty.

toilet ⓥ *n* 1 (room with) a bowl connected to a drain for receiving and disposing of urine and faeces. 2 washing and dressing. **toiletry** *n, pl* –**ries** object or cosmetic used to clean or groom oneself. **toilet water** light perfume.

token ⓥ *n* 1 sign or symbol. 2 voucher exchangeable for goods of a specified value. 3 disc used as money in a slot machine. ♦ *adj* 4 nominal or slight. **tokenism** *n* policy of making only a token

effort, esp. to comply with a law.

tolerate ⓥ *v* 1 allow to exist or happen. 2 endure patiently. **tolerable** *adj* 1 bearable. 2 *Informal* quite good. **tolerably** *adv* **tolerance** *n* 1 acceptance of other people's rights to their own opinions or actions. 2 ability to endure something. **tolerant** *adj* **toleration** *n*

toll¹ ⓥ *v* 1 ring (a bell) slowly and regularly, esp. to announce a death. ♦ *n* 2 tolling.

toll² ⓥ *n* 1 charge for the use of a bridge or road. 2 total loss or damage from a disaster.

tom *n* male cat.

tomahawk *n* fighting axe of the Native Americans.

tomato *n, pl* –**toes** red fruit used in salads and as a vegetable.

tomb ⓥ *n* 1 grave. 2 monument over a grave. **tombstone** *n* gravestone.

tombola *n* lottery with tickets drawn from a revolving drum.

tomboy *n* girl who acts or dresses like a boy.

tome *n* large heavy book.

tomfoolery ⓥ *n* foolish behaviour.

tomorrow *adv, n* 1 (on) the day after today. 2 (in) the future.

drink (to) the health of, salute

together *adv* 1 = **collectively**, as one, hand in glove, in concert, in unison, jointly, mutually, shoulder to shoulder, side by side ≠ **individually** 2 = **at the same time**, at one fell swoop, concurrently, contemporaneously, simultaneously ♦ *adj* 3 *Inf* = **self-possessed**, composed, well–adjusted, well–balanced

toil *n* 1 = **hard work**, application, drudgery, effort, elbow grease (*inf*), exertion, graft (*inf*), slog, sweat ≠ **inertia** ♦ *v* 2 = **labour**, drudge, graft (*inf*), slave, slog, strive, struggle, sweat (*inf*), work, work one's fingers to the bone

toilet *n* 1 = **lavatory**, bathroom, convenience, gents *or* ladies (*Brit inf*), ladies' room, latrine, loo (*Brit inf*), privy,

urinal, water closet, W.C.

token *n* 1 = **symbol**, badge, expression, indication, mark, note, representation, sign ♦ *adj* 4 = **nominal**, hollow, minimal, perfunctory, superficial, symbolic

tolerate *v* 1 = **allow**, accept, brook, condone, permit, put up with (*inf*), take ≠ **ban** 2 = **endure**, put up with (*inf*), stand, stomach, take

toll¹ *v* 1 = **ring**, chime, clang, knell, peal, sound, strike ♦ *n* 2 = **ringing**, chime, clang, knell, peal

toll² *n* 1 = **charge**, duty, fee, levy, payment, tariff, tax 2 = **damage**, cost, loss, penalty

tomb *n* = **grave**, catacomb, crypt, mausoleum, sarcophagus, sepulchre, vault

tomfoolery *n* = **foolishness**, buffoonery, clowning, fooling around (*inf*), horseplay, shenanigans (*inf*), silliness, skylarking (*inf*)

tom–tom n drum beaten with the hands.

ton n unit of weight equal to 2240 pounds or 1016 kilograms (**long ton**) or, in the US, 2000 pounds or 907 kilograms (**short ton**). **tonnage** n weight capacity of a ship.

tone ❶ n 1 sound with reference to its pitch, volume, etc. 2 *US* musical note. 3 *Music* (also **whole tone**) interval of two semitones. 4 quality of a sound or colour. 5 general character. 6 healthy bodily condition. ◆ v 7 harmonize (with). 8 give tone to. **tonal** adj *Music* written in a key. **tonality** n **toneless** adj **tone–deaf** adj unable to perceive subtle differences in pitch. **tone down** v make or become more moderate.

tongs pl n large pincers for grasping and lifting.

tongue ❶ n 1 muscular organ in the mouth, used in speaking and tasting. 2 language. 3 animal tongue as food. 4 thin projecting strip. 5 flap of leather on a shoe.

tonic ❶ n 1 medicine to improve body tone. ◆ adj 2 invigorating.

tonight adv, n (in or during) the night or evening of this day.

tonne [tunn] n unit of weight equal to 1000 kilograms.

tonsil n small gland in the throat. **tonsillectomy** n surgical removal of the tonsils. **tonsillitis** n inflammation of the tonsils.

tonsure n 1 shaving of all or the top of the head as a religious or monastic practice. 2 shaved part of the head. **tonsured** adj

too ❶ adv 1 also, as well. 2 to excess. 3 extremely.

tool ❶ n 1 implement used by hand. 2 person used by another to perform unpleasant or dishonourable tasks.

toot n 1 short hooting sound. ◆ v 2 (cause to) make such a sound.

tooth n, pl **teeth** 1 bonelike projection in the jaws of most vertebrates for biting and chewing. 2 toothlike prong or point. **sweet tooth** strong liking for sweet food. **toothless** adj **toothpaste** n paste used to clean the teeth. **toothpick** n small stick for removing scraps of food from between the teeth.

top¹ ❶ n 1 highest point or part. 2 lid or cap. 3 highest rank. 4 garment for the upper part of the body. ◆ adj 5 at or of the top. ◆ v **topping, topped** 6 form a top on. 7 be at the top of. 8 exceed or surpass. **topping** n sauce or garnish for food. **topless** adj (of a costume or woman) with no covering for the breasts. **topmost** adj highest or best. **top brass** most important officers or leaders. **top hat** man's tall cylindrical hat. **top–heavy** adj unstable through being overloaded at the top. **top–notch** adj excellent, first-class. **topsoil** n surface layer of soil.

top² n toy which spins on a pointed base.

───── THESAURUS ─────

≠ **seriousness**

tone n 1 = **pitch**, inflection, intonation, modulation, timbre 4 = **colour**, hue, shade, tinge, tint 5 = **character**, air, attitude, feel, manner, mood, spirit, style, temper ◆ v 7 = **harmonize**, blend, go well with, match, suit

tongue n 2 = **language**, dialect, parlance, speech

tonic n 2 = **stimulant**, boost, fillip, pick–me–up (inf), restorative, shot in the arm (inf)

too adv 1 = **also**, as well, besides, further, in addition, likewise, moreover, to boot 2,

3 = **excessively**, extremely, immoderately, inordinately, overly, unduly, unreasonably, very

tool n 1 = **implement**, appliance, contraption, contrivance, device, gadget, instrument, machine, utensil 2 = **puppet**, cat's–paw, hireling, lackey, minion, pawn, stooge (sl)

top¹ n 1 = **peak**, apex, crest, crown, culmination, head, height, pinnacle, summit, zenith ≠ **base** 2 = **lid**, cap, cover, stopper 3 = **first place**, head, lead ◆ adj 5 = **leading**, best, chief, elite, finest, first, foremost, head, highest, pre–eminent,

topaz [**toe**–pazz] *n* semiprecious stone in various colours.

topiary [**tope**–yar–ee] *n* art of trimming trees and bushes into decorative shapes.

topic ⊕ *n* subject of a conversation, book, etc. **topical** *adj* relating to current events. **topicality** *n*

topography *n, pl* –**phies** (science of describing) the surface features of a place. **topographical** *adj*

topple ⊕ *v* 1 (cause to) fall over. 2 overthrow (a government etc.).

topsy–turvy ⊕ *adj* 1 upside down. 2 in confusion.

tor *n* high rocky hill.

torch *n* 1 small portable battery–powered lamp. 2 wooden shaft dipped in wax and set alight. ◆ *v* 3 *Informal* deliberately set (a building) on fire.

toreador [**torr**–ee–a–dor] *n* bullfighter.

torment ⊕ *v* 1 cause (someone) great suffering. 2 tease cruelly. ◆ *n* 3 great suffering. 4 source of suffering. **tormentor** *n*

tornado ⊕ *n, pl* –**dos**, –**does** violent whirlwind.

torpedo *n, pl* –**does** 1 self–propelled underwater missile. ◆ *v* –**doing**, –**doed** 2

attack or destroy with or as if with torpedoes.

torpid *adj* sluggish and inactive. **torpor** *n* torpid state.

torrent ⊕ *n* 1 rushing stream. 2 rapid flow of questions, abuse, etc. **torrential** *adj* (of rain) very heavy.

torrid ⊕ *adj* 1 very hot and dry. 2 highly emotional.

torsion *n* twisting of a part by equal forces being applied at both ends but in opposite directions.

torso *n, pl* –**sos** 1 trunk of the human body. 2 statue of a nude human trunk.

tortilla *n* thin Mexican pancake.

tortoise *n* slow–moving land reptile with a dome–shaped shell. **tortoiseshell** *n* 1 mottled brown shell of a turtle, used for making ornaments. ◆ *adj* 2 having brown, orange, and black markings.

tortuous ⊕ *adj* 1 winding or twisting. 2 not straightforward.

torture ⊕ *v* 1 cause (someone) severe pain or mental anguish. ◆ *n* 2 severe physical or mental pain. 3 torturing. **torturer** *n*

Tory *n, pl* **Tories** 1 member of the Conservative Party in Great Britain or Canada. ◆ *adj* 2 of Tories.

————— THESAURUS —————

principal, uppermost ≠ **worst** ◆ *v* 6 = **cover**, cap, crown, finish, garnish 7 = **lead**, be first, head 8 = **surpass**, beat, better, eclipse, exceed, excel, outstrip, transcend ≠ **fall short of**

topic *n* = **subject**, issue, matter, point, question, subject matter, theme

topple *v* 1 = **fall over**, collapse, fall, keel over, overbalance, overturn, totter, tumble 2 = **overthrow**, bring down, bring low, oust, overturn, unseat

topsy–turvy *adj* 1 = **upside–down** 2 = **disorganized**, chaotic, confused, disorderly, inside–out, jumbled, messy, mixed–up

torment *v* 1 = **torture**, crucify, distress, rack ≠ **soothe** 2 = **tease**, annoy, bother, harass, hassle (*inf*), irritate, nag, pester, vex ◆ *n* 3 = **suffering**, agony, anguish,

distress, hell, misery, pain, torture ≠ **joy**

tornado *n* = **whirlwind**, cyclone, gale, hurricane, squall, storm, tempest, typhoon

torrent *n* 1 = **stream**, cascade, deluge, downpour, flood, flow, rush, spate, tide

torrid *adj* 1 = **arid**, dried, parched, scorched 2 = **passionate**, ardent, fervent, intense, steamy (*inf*)

tortuous *adj* 1 = **winding**, circuitous, convoluted, indirect, mazy, meandering, serpentine, sinuous, twisting 2 = **complicated**, ambiguous, convoluted, devious, indirect, involved, roundabout, tricky ≠ **direct**

torture *v* 1 = **torment**, afflict, crucify, distress, persecute, put on the rack, rack ≠ **comfort** ◆ *n* 2 = **agony**, anguish, distress, pain, persecution, suffering, torment ≠ **delight**

toss ● v 1 throw lightly. 2 fling or be flung about. 3 coat (food) by gentle stirring or mixing. 4 (of a horse) throw (its rider). 5 throw up (a coin) to decide between alternatives by guessing which side will land uppermost. ◆ n 6 tossing. **toss up** v toss a coin. **toss–up** n even chance or risk.

tot¹ ● n 1 small child. 2 small drink of spirits.

tot² ● v totting, totted. tot up add (numbers) together.

total ● n 1 whole, esp. a sum of parts. ◆ adj 2 complete. 3 of or being a total. ◆ v –talling, –talled 4 amount to. 5 add up. **totally** adv **totality** n

totalitarian ● adj of a dictatorial one–party government. **totalitarianism** n

totem n tribal badge or emblem. **totem pole** post carved or painted with totems by Native Americans.

totter ● v 1 move unsteadily. 2 be about to fall.

toucan n tropical American bird with a large bill.

touch ● v 1 come into contact with. 2 tap,

feel, or stroke. 3 affect. 4 move emotionally. 5 eat or drink. 6 equal or match. 7 Slang ask for money. ◆ n 8 sense by which an object's qualities are perceived when they come into contact with part of the body. 9 gentle tap, push, or caress. 10 small amount. 11 characteristic style. 12 detail. **touch and go** risky or critical. **touched** adj 1 emotionally moved. 2 slightly mad. **touching** adj emotionally moving. **touchy** adj easily offended. **touch down** v (of an aircraft) land. **touchline** n side line of the pitch in some games. **touch on** v refer to in passing. **touch–type** v type without looking at the keyboard.

touché [too–shay] interj acknowledgment of the striking home of a remark or witty reply.

tough ● adj 1 strong or resilient. 2 difficult to chew or cut. 3 firm and determined. 4 rough and violent. 5 difficult. 6 Informal unlucky or unfair. ◆ n 7 Informal rough violent person. **toughness** n **toughen** v make or become tough or tougher.

THESAURUS

toss v 1 = **throw**, cast, fling, flip, hurl, launch, lob (inf), pitch, sling 2 = **thrash**, rock, roll, shake, wriggle, writhe ◆ n 7 = **throw**, lob (inf), pitch

tot¹ n 1 = **infant**, baby, child, mite, toddler 2 = **measure**, dram, finger, nip, shot (inf), slug, snifter (inf)

tot² v **tot up** = **add up**, calculate, count up, reckon, tally, total

total n 1 = **whole**, aggregate, entirety, full amount, sum, totality ≠ part ◆ adj 2, 3 = **complete**, absolute, comprehensive, entire, full, gross, overarching, thoroughgoing, undivided, utter, whole ≠ part ◆ v 4 = **amount to**, come to, mount up to, reach 5 = **add up**, reckon, tot up ≠ deduct

totalitarian adj = **dictatorial**, authoritarian, despotic, oppressive, tyrannous, undemocratic

totter v 1 = **falter** 2 = **stagger**, lurch, reel, stumble, sway, wobble

touch v 1 = **come into contact**, abut, adjoin, be in contact, border, contact, graze, impinge upon, meet 2 = **handle**, brush, caress, contact, feel, finger, fondle, stroke, tap 3 = **affect**, impress, influence, inspire 4 = **move**, disturb, stir 5 = **consume**, drink, eat, partake of 6 = **match**, compare with, equal, hold a candle to (inf), parallel, rival ◆ n 8 = **feeling**, handling, physical contact 9 = **contact**, brush, caress, stroke 10 = **bit**, dash, drop, jot, small amount, smattering, soupçon, spot, trace 11 = **style**, manner, method, technique, trademark, way **touch on** = **refer to**, allude to, bring in, cover, deal with, mention, speak of

tough adj 1 = **resilient**, durable, hard, inflexible, leathery, resistant, rugged, solid, strong, sturdy ≠ delicate 3 = **firm**, hard, hardy, resolute, seasoned, stern, stout, strapping, strong, sturdy, unbending,

toupee [too–pay] *n* small wig.

tour ⊕ *n* **1** journey visiting places of interest along the way. **2** trip to perform or play in different places. ♦ *v* **3** make a tour (of). **tourism** *n* tourist travel as an industry. **tourist** *n* person travelling for pleasure. **touristy** *adj Informal, often derogatory* full of tourists or tourist attractions.

tourmaline *n* crystalline mineral.

tournament ⊕ *n* **1** sporting competition with several stages to decide the overall winner. **2** *Hist* contest between knights on horseback.

tourniquet [tour–nick–kay] *n* something twisted round a limb to stop bleeding.

tousled *adj* ruffled and untidy.

tout [rhymes with **shout**] *v* **1** seek business in a persistent manner. **2** recommend (a person or thing). ♦ *n* **3** person who sells tickets for a popular event at inflated prices.

tow ⊕ *v* **1** drag, esp. by means of a rope. ♦ *n* **2** towing. **in tow** following closely behind. **on tow** being towed. **towbar** *n* metal bar on a car for towing vehicles. **towpath** *n* path beside a canal or river, originally for horses towing boats. **towrope** *n* rope or cable used for towing a vehicle or vessel.

towards ⊕ toward *prep* **1** in the direction of. **2** with regard to. **3** as a contribution to.

✅ **WORD TIP**

Towards is usual. The form *toward* is chiefly American.

---

towel *n* cloth for drying things. **towelling** *n* material used for making towels.

tower ⊕ *n* tall structure, often forming part of a larger building. **tower of strength** person who supports or comforts. **tower over** *v* be taller than.

town *n* **1** group of buildings larger than a village. **2** central part of this. **3** people of a town. **township** *n* **1** small town. **2** (in S Africa) urban settlement of Black or Coloured people.

toxic ⊕ *adj* **1** poisonous. **2** caused by poison. **toxicity** *n* **toxicology** *n* study of poisons. **toxin** *n* poison of bacterial origin.

toy ⊕ *n* **1** something designed to be played with. ♦ *adj* **2** (of a dog) of a variety much smaller than is normal for that breed. **toy with** *v* play or fiddle with.

toy–toy *S Afr* ♦ *n* **1** dance of political protest. ♦ *v* **2** perform this dance.

trace ⊕ *v* **1** track down and find. **2** follow the course of. **3** copy exactly by drawing on a thin sheet of transparent paper set on top of the original. ♦ *n* **4** track left by something. **5** minute quantity. **6** indication. **traceable** *adj* **tracery** *n* pattern of interlacing lines. **tracing** *n* traced copy. **trace element** chemical element occurring

---

THESAURUS

vigorous **4** = **rough**, hard–bitten, merciless, pugnacious, ruthless, violent ≠ **soft 5** = **difficult**, arduous, exacting, hard, laborious, strenuous, troublesome, uphill **6** *Inf* = **unlucky**, lamentable, regrettable, unfortunate ♦ *n* **7** *Inf* = **ruffian**, bruiser (*inf*), bully, hooligan, roughneck (*sl*), thug

tour *n* **1** = **journey**, excursion, expedition, jaunt, outing, trip ♦ *v* **3** = **visit**, explore, go round, journey, sightsee, travel through

tournament *n* **1** = **competition**, contest, event, meeting, series

tow *v* **1** = **drag**, draw, haul, lug, pull, tug, yank

towards *prep* **1** = **in the direction of**, en route for, for, on the way to, to **2** = **regarding**, about, concerning, for, with regard to, with respect to

tower *n* = **column**, belfry, obelisk, pillar, skyscraper, steeple, turret

toxic *adj* **1** = **poisonous**, deadly, harmful, lethal, noxious, pernicious, pestilential, septic

toy *n* **1** = **plaything**, doll, game **toy with** ♦ *v* = **play**, amuse oneself with, dally with, fool (about *or* around) with, trifle in very small amounts in soil etc.

trachea [track-**kee**–a] *n, pl* **tracheae** windpipe. **tracheotomy** [track–ee–**ot**–a–mee] *n* surgical incision into the trachea.

track ❶ *n* **1** rough road or path. **2** mark or trail left by the passage of anything. **3** railway line. **4** course for racing. **5** separate section on a record, tape, or CD. **6** course of action or thought. **7** endless band round the wheels of a tank, bulldozer, etc. ♦ *v* **8** follow the trail or path of. **track down** *v* hunt for and find. **track event** athletic sport held on a running track. **track record** past accomplishments of a person or organization. **tracksuit** *n* warm loose–fitting suit worn by athletes etc., esp. during training.

tract¹ ❶ *n* **1** wide area. **2** *Anat* system of organs with a particular function.

tract² ❶ *n* pamphlet, esp. a religious one.

traction ❶ *n* **1** pulling, esp. by engine power. **2** *Med* application of a steady pull on an injured limb by weights and pulleys. **3** grip of the wheels of a vehicle on the ground. **traction engine** old–fashioned steam–powered vehicle for pulling heavy loads.

tractor *n* motor vehicle with large rear wheels for pulling farm machinery.

trade ❶ *n* **1** buying, selling, or exchange of goods. **2** person's job or craft. **3** (people engaged in) a particular industry or business. ♦ *v* **4** buy and sell. **5** exchange. **6** engage in trade. **trader** *n* **trading** *n* **trade–in** *n* used article given in part payment for a new one. **trademark** *n* (legally registered) name or symbol used by a firm to distinguish its goods. **trade–off** *n* exchange made as a compromise. **tradesman** *n* **1** skilled worker. **2** shopkeeper. **trade union** society of workers formed to protect their interests. **trade wind** wind blowing steadily towards the equator.

tradition ❶ *n* **1** body of beliefs, customs, etc. handed down from generation to generation. **2** custom or practice of long standing. **traditional** *adj*

traffic ❶ *n* **1** vehicles coming and going on a road. **2** (illicit) trade. ♦ *v* **–ficking, –ficked 3** trade, usu. illicitly. **trafficker** *n* **traffic lights** set of coloured lights at a junction to control the traffic flow. **traffic warden** person employed to control the movement and parking of traffic.

tragedy ❶ *n, pl* **–dies 1** shocking or sad event. **2** serious play, film, etc. in which the hero is destroyed by a personal failing

—————— THESAURUS ——————

trace *v* **1 = find**, detect, discover, ferret out, hunt down, track, unearth **2 = outline**, draw, sketch **3 = copy** ♦ *n* **4 = track**, footmark, footprint, footstep, path, spoor, trail **5 = bit**, drop, hint, shadow, suggestion, suspicion, tinge, touch, whiff **6 = remnant**, evidence, indication, mark, record, sign, survival, vestige

track *n* **1 = path**, course, line, orbit, pathway, road, trajectory, way **2 = trail**, footmark, footprint, footstep, mark, path, spoor, trace, wake **3 = line**, permanent way, rails ♦ *v* **8 = follow**, chase, hunt down, pursue, shadow, stalk, tail (*inf*), trace, trail

tract¹ *n* **1 = area**, district, expanse, extent, plot, region, stretch, territory

tract² *n* **= treatise**, booklet, dissertation,

essay, homily, monograph, pamphlet

traction *n* **1 = pulling**, pull **3 = grip**, friction, purchase, resistance

trade *n* **1 = commerce**, barter, business, dealing, exchange, traffic, transactions, truck **2 = job**, business, craft, employment, line of work, métier, occupation, profession ♦ *v* **4 = deal**, bargain, cut a deal, do business, have dealings, peddle, traffic, transact, truck **5 = exchange**, barter, swap, switch

tradition *n* **2 = lore**, folklore **3 = custom**, convention, habit, institution, ritual

traffic *n* **1 = transport**, freight, transportation, vehicles **2 = trade**, business, commerce, dealings, exchange, peddling, truck ♦ *v* **3 = trade**, bargain, cut a deal, deal, do business, exchange, have in adverse circumstances. **tragedian** [traj–jee–dee–an], **tragedienne** [traj–jee–dee–enn] *n* person who acts in or writes tragedies. **tragic** *adj* of or like a tragedy. **tragically** *adv* **tragicomedy** *n* play with both tragic and comic elements.

trail **①** *n* 1 path, track, or road. 2 tracks left by a person, animal, or object. ◆ *v* 3 drag along the ground. 4 lag behind. 5 follow the tracks of. **trailer** *n* 1 vehicle designed to be towed by another vehicle. 2 extract from a film or programme used to advertise it.

train **①** *v* 1 instruct in a skill. 2 learn the skills needed to do a particular job or activity. 3 prepare for a sports event etc. 4 aim (a gun etc.). 5 cause (an animal) to perform or (a plant) to grow in a particular way. ◆ *n* 6 line of railway coaches or wagons drawn by an engine. 7 sequence or series. 8 long trailing back section of a dress. **trainer** *n* 1 person who trains an athlete or sportsman. 2 sports shoe. **trainee** *n* person being trained.

traipse **①** *v Informal* walk wearily.

trait **①** *n* characteristic feature.

traitor **①** *n* person guilty of treason or

treachery. **traitorous** *adj*

trajectory **①** *n, pl* **–ries** line of flight, esp. of a projectile.

tram *n* public transport vehicle powered by an overhead wire and running on rails laid in the road. **tramlines** *pl n* track for trams.

tramp **①** *v* 1 travel on foot, hike. 2 walk heavily. ◆ *n* 3 homeless person who travels on foot. 4 hike. 5 sound of tramping. 6 cargo ship available for hire. 7 *US & Aust slang* promiscuous woman.

trample **①** *v* tread on and crush.

trampoline *n* 1 tough canvas sheet attached to a frame by springs, used by acrobats etc. ◆ *v* 2 bounce on a trampoline.

trance **①** *n* unconscious or dazed state.

tranche *n* portion of something large, esp. a sum of money.

tranquil **①** *adj* calm and quiet. **tranquilly** *adv* **tranquillity** *n* **tranquillize** *v* make calm. **tranquillizer** *n* drug which reduces anxiety or tension.

trans– *prefix* across, through, or beyond.

transact *v* conduct or negotiate (a business deal). **transaction** *n* business deal transacted.

dealings, peddle

tragedy *n* 1 = **disaster**, adversity, calamity, catastrophe, misfortune ≠ **success**

trail *n* 1 = **path**, footpath, road, route, track, way 2 = **tracks**, footprints, marks, path, scent, spoor, trace, wake ◆ *v* 3 = **drag**, dangle, draw, haul, pull, tow 4 = **lag**, dawdle, follow, hang back, linger, loiter, straggle, traipse (*inf*) 5 = **follow**, chase, hunt, pursue, shadow, stalk, tail (*inf*), trace, track

train *v* 1 = **instruct**, coach, drill, educate, guide, prepare, school, teach, tutor 3 = **exercise**, prepare, work out 4 = **aim**, direct, focus, level, point ◆ *n* 7 = **sequence**, chain, progression, series, set, string, succession

traipse *v Inf* = **trudge**, drag oneself, slouch, trail, tramp

trait *n* = **characteristic**, attribute, feature,

idiosyncrasy, mannerism, peculiarity, quality, quirk

traitor *n* = **betrayer**, apostate, back–stabber, defector, deserter, Judas, quisling, rebel, renegade, turncoat

trajectory *n* = **path**, course, flight path, line, route, track

tramp *v* 1 = **hike**, march, ramble, roam, rove, slog, trek, walk 2 = **trudge**, plod, stump, toil, traipse (*inf*) ◆ *n* 3 = **vagrant**, derelict, down–and–out, drifter 4 = **hike**, march, ramble, slog, trek 5 = **tread**, footfall, footstep

trample *v* = **crush**, flatten, run over, squash, stamp, tread, walk over

trance *n* = **daze**, abstraction, dream, rapture, reverie, stupor, unconsciousness

tranquil *adj* = **calm**, peaceful, placid, quiet, restful, sedate, serene, still, undisturbed ≠ **troubled**

transcend ⊕ v 1 rise above. 2 be superior to. **transcendence** n **transcendent** adj
transcendental adj 1 based on intuition rather than experience. 2 supernatural or mystical. **transcendentalism** n

transcribe ⊕ v 1 write down (something said). 2 record for a later broadcast. 3 arrange (music) for a different instrument. **transcript** n copy.

transfer ⊕ v –ferring, –ferred 1 move or send from one person or place to another. ♦ n 2 transferring. 3 design which can be transferred from one surface to another. **transferable** adj **transference** n transferring.

transfigure v change in appearance. **transfiguration** n

transfix ⊕ v 1 astound or stun. 2 pierce through.

transform ⊕ v change the shape or character of. **transformation** n **transformer** n device for changing the voltage of an alternating current.

transgress ⊕ v break (a moral law). **transgression** n **transgressor** n

transient ⊕ adj lasting only for a short time. **transience** n

transistor n 1 semiconducting device used to amplify electric currents. 2 portable radio using transistors.

transit ⊕ n movement from one place to another. **transition** n change from one state to another. **transitional** adj **transitive** adj Grammar (of a verb) requiring a direct object. **transitory** adj not lasting long.

translate ⊕ v turn from one language into another. **translation** n **translator** n

translucent adj letting light pass through, but not transparent. **translucency, translucence** n

transmit ⊕ v –mitting, –mitted 1 pass (something) from one person or place to another. 2 send out (signals) by radio waves. 3 broadcast (a radio or television programme). **transmission** n 1 transmitting. 2 shafts and gears through which power passes from a vehicle's engine to its wheels. **transmittable** adj **transmitter** n

transmute v change the form or nature of. **transmutation** n

transparent ⊕ adj 1 able to be seen through, clear. 2 easily understood or recognized. **transparency** n 1 transparent quality. 2 colour photograph on transparent film that can be viewed by means of a projector.

——————— THESAURUS ———————

transcend v 1 = **rise above** 2 = **surpass**, eclipse, exceed, excel, go beyond, outdo, outstrip

transcribe v 1 = **write out**, copy out, reproduce, take down, transfer

transfer v 1 = **move**, change, convey, hand over, pass on, relocate, shift, transplant, transport, transpose ♦ n 2 = **move**, change, handover, relocation, shift, transference, translation, transmission, transposition

transfix v 1 = **stun**, engross, fascinate, hold, hypnotize, mesmerize, paralyse ≠ **bore** 2 = **pierce**, impale, puncture, run through, skewer, spear

transform v = **change**, alter, convert, remodel, revolutionize, transmute

transgress v = **break**, break the law, contravene, disobey, exceed, go beyond, infringe, offend, overstep, sin, trespass, violate

transient adj = **brief**, ephemeral, fleeting, impermanent, momentary, passing, short-lived, temporary, transitory

transit n = **movement**, carriage, conveyance, crossing, passage, transfer, transport, transportation

translate v = **interpret**, construe, convert, decipher, decode, paraphrase, render

transmit v 1 = **pass on**, bear, carry, convey, disseminate, hand on, impart, send, spread, transfer 3 = **broadcast**, disseminate, radio, relay, send out

transparent adj 1 = **clear**, crystalline, diaphanous, limpid, lucid, see-through, sheer, translucent ≠ **thick** 2 = **obvious**,

transpire ❶ v 1 become known. 2 *Informal* happen. 3 give off water vapour through pores. **transpiration** n

✅ **WORD TIP**

Transpire is so often used for 'happen' or 'occur' that the objection that it should be used only for 'become known' is no longer valid.

transplant ❶ v 1 transfer (an organ or tissue) surgically from one part or body to another. 2 remove and transfer (a plant) to another place. ◆ n 3 surgical transplanting. 4 thing transplanted. **transplantation** n

transport ❶ v 1 convey from one place to another. 2 *Hist* exile (a criminal) to a penal colony. 3 enrapture. ◆ n 4 business or system of transporting. 5 vehicle used in transport. 6 ecstasy or rapture. **transportation** n **transporter** n large goods vehicle.

transpose ❶ v 1 interchange two things. 2 put (music) into a different key. **transposition** n

transverse adj crossing from side to side.

transvestite n person who seeks sexual pleasure by wearing the clothes of the opposite sex. **transvestism** n

trap ❶ n 1 device for catching animals. 2 plan for tricking or catching a person. 3 bend in a pipe containing liquid to prevent the escape of gas. 4 stall in which greyhounds are enclosed before a race. 5 two–wheeled carriage. 6 *Slang* mouth. ◆ v **trapping, trapped** 7 catch. 8 trick. **trapper** n person who traps animals for their fur. **trapdoor** n door in floor or roof.

trapeze n horizontal bar suspended from two ropes, used by circus acrobats.

trapezium n, pl **–ziums, –zia** quadrilateral with two parallel sides of unequal length. **trapezoid** [trap–piz–zoid] n 1 quadrilateral with no sides parallel. 2 *Chiefly US* trapezium.

trappings ❶ pl n accessories that symbolize an office or position.

trash ❶ n 1 anything worthless. 2 *US* rubbish. **trashy** adj

trauma ❶ [traw–ma] n 1 emotional shock. 2 injury or wound. **traumatic** adj **traumatize** v

travail n *Lit* labour or toil.

travel ❶ v **–elling, –elled** 1 go from one place to another, through an area, or for a

evident, explicit, manifest, patent, plain, recognizable, unambiguous, undisguised ≠ **hidden**

transpire v 1 = **become known**, come out, come to light, emerge 2 *Inf* = **happen**, arise, befall, chance, come about, occur, take place

transplant v 2 = **transfer**, displace, relocate, remove, resettle, shift, uproot

transport v 1 = **convey**, bear, bring, carry, haul, move, take, transfer 2 *Hist* = **exile**, banish, deport 3 = **enrapture**, captivate, delight, enchant, entrance, move, ravish ◆ n 4 = **vehicle**, conveyance, transportation 5 = **transference**, conveyance, shipment, transportation 6 = **ecstasy**, bliss, delight, enchantment, euphoria, heaven, rapture, ravishment

transpose v 1 = **interchange**, alter,

change, exchange, move, reorder, shift, substitute, swap, switch, transfer

trap n 1 = **snare**, ambush, gin, net, noose, pitfall 2 = **trick**, ambush, deception, ruse, stratagem, subterfuge, wile ◆ v 7 = **catch**, corner, enmesh, ensnare, entrap, snare, take 8 = **trick**, ambush, beguile, deceive, dupe, ensnare, inveigle

trappings pl n = **accessories**, accoutrements, equipment, finery, furnishings, gear, panoply, paraphernalia, things, trimmings

trash n 1 = **nonsense**, drivel, hogwash, kak (*S Afr sl*), moonshine, poppycock (*inf*), rot, rubbish, tripe (*inf*), twaddle ≠ **reason** 2 *US* = **litter**, dross, garbage, junk (*inf*), refuse, rubbish, waste

trauma n 1 = **shock**, anguish, ordeal, pain, suffering, torture 2 = **injury**, agony, specified distance. ◆ n 2 travelling, esp. as a tourist. ◆ pl 3 (account of) travelling. **traveller** n **travelogue** n film or talk about someone's travels.

traverse ⊕ v move over or back and forth over.

travesty ⊕ n, pl **-ties** 1 grotesque imitation or mockery.

trawl n 1 net dragged at deep levels behind a fishing boat. ◆ v 2 fish with such a net. **trawler** n trawling boat.

tray n 1 flat board, usu. with a rim, for carrying things. 2 open receptacle for office correspondence.

treachery ⊕ n, pl **-eries** wilful betrayal. **treacherous** adj 1 disloyal. 2 unreliable or dangerous.

treacle n thick dark syrup produced when sugar is refined. **treacly** adj

tread ⊕ v **treading, trod, trodden** or **trod** 1 set one's foot on. 2 crush by walking on. ◆ n 3 way of walking or dancing. 4 upper surface of a step. 5 part of a tyre or shoe that touches the ground. **treadmill** n 1 Hist cylinder turned by treading on steps projecting from it. 2 dreary routine.

treadle [tred-dl] n lever worked by the foot to turn a wheel.

treason ⊕ n 1 betrayal of one's sovereign or country. 2 treachery or disloyalty. **treasonable** adj

treasure ⊕ n 1 collection of wealth, esp. gold or jewels. 2 valued person or thing. ◆ v 3 prize or cherish. **treasurer** n official in charge of funds. **treasury** n 1 storage place for treasure. 2 (T–) government department in charge of finance. **treasure–trove** n treasure found with no evidence of ownership.

treat ⊕ v 1 deal with or regard in a certain manner. 2 give medical treatment to. 3 subject to a chemical or industrial process. 4 provide (someone) with (something) as a treat. ◆ n 5 pleasure, entertainment, etc. given or paid for by someone else. **treatment** n 1 medical care. 2 way of treating a person or thing.

treatise ⊕ [treat–izz] n formal piece of writing on a particular subject.

treaty ⊕ n, pl **-ties** signed contract between states.

treble adj 1 triple. 2 Music high–pitched. ◆

THESAURUS

damage, hurt, wound

travel v 1 = **go**, journey, move, progress, roam, tour, trek, voyage, wander ◆ pl n 3 = **journey**, excursion, expedition, globetrotting, tour, trip, voyage, wandering

traverse v = **cross**, go over, span, travel over

travesty n 1 = **mockery**, burlesque, caricature, distortion, lampoon, parody, perversion ◆ v 2 = **mock**, burlesque, caricature, lampoon, make a mockery of, parody, ridicule

treachery n = **betrayal**, disloyalty, double–dealing, duplicity, faithlessness, infidelity, perfidy, treason

tread v 1 = **step**, hike, march, pace, stamp, stride, walk 2 = **crush underfoot**, squash, trample ◆ n 3 = **step**, footfall, footstep, gait, pace, stride, walk

treason n = **disloyalty**, duplicity, lese–

majesty, mutiny, perfidy, sedition, traitorousness, treachery

treasure n 1 = **riches**, cash, fortune, gold, jewels, money, valuables, wealth 2 = **darling**, apple of one's eye, gem, jewel, nonpareil, paragon, pride and joy ◆ v 3 = **prize**, adore, cherish, esteem, hold dear, idolize, love, revere, value

treat v 1 = **behave towards**, act towards, consider, deal with, handle, look upon, manage, regard, use 2 = **take care of**, attend to, care for, nurse 4 = **provide**, entertain, lay on, regale, stand (inf) ◆ n 5 a = **pleasure**, delight, enjoyment, fun, joy, satisfaction, surprise, thrill b = **entertainment**, banquet, celebration, feast, gift, party, refreshment

treatise n = **paper**, dissertation, essay, monograph, pamphlet, study, thesis, tract, work

treaty n = **agreement**, alliance, compact,

n 3 (singer with or part for) a soprano voice. ◆ v 4 increase three times. **trebly** adv

tree n large perennial plant with a woody trunk. **treeless** adj **tree surgery** repair of damaged trees.

trek ⊕ n 1 long difficult journey, esp. on foot. 2 S Afr migration by ox wagon. ◆ v **trekking, trekked** 3 make such a journey.

trellis n framework of horizontal and vertical strips of wood.

tremble ⊕ v 1 shake or quiver. 2 feel fear or anxiety. ◆ n 3 trembling. **trembling** adj

tremendous ⊕ adj 1 huge. 2 Informal great in quality or amount.

tremor ⊕ n 1 involuntary shaking. 2 minor earthquake.

tremulous adj trembling, as from fear or excitement.

trench ⊕ n long narrow ditch, esp. one used as a shelter in war. **trench coat** double-breasted waterproof coat.

trenchant adj 1 incisive. 2 effective.

trend ⊕ n 1 general tendency or direction. 2 fashion. **trendy** adj, n Informal consciously fashionable (person). **trendiness** n

trepidation ⊕ n fear or anxiety.

trespass ⊕ v 1 go onto another's property without permission. ◆ n 2 trespassing. 3 Old-fashioned sin or wrongdoing. **trespasser** n **trespass on** v take unfair advantage of (someone's friendship, patience, etc.).

trestle n board fixed on pairs of spreading legs, used as a support.

trevally n, pl -lies Aust & NZ any of various food and game fishes.

trews pl n close-fitting tartan trousers.

tri- combining form three.

trial ⊕ n 1 Law investigation of a case before a judge. 2 trying or testing. 3 thing or person straining endurance or patience. ◆ pl 4 sporting competition for individuals.

triangle n 1 geometric figure with three sides. 2 triangular percussion instrument. 3 situation involving three people. **triangular** adj

tribe ⊕ n group of clans or families believed to have a common ancestor. **tribal** adj **tribalism** n loyalty to a tribe.

tribulation n great distress.

tribunal ⊕ n 1 board appointed to inquire into a specific matter. 2 lawcourt.

—————— THESAURUS ——————

concordat, contract, entente, pact

trek n 1 = **journey**, expedition, hike, march, odyssey, safari, slog, tramp ◆ v 3 = **journey**, hike, march, slog, traipse (inf), tramp, trudge

tremble v 1 = **shake**, quake, quiver, shiver, shudder, totter, vibrate, wobble ◆ n 3 = **shake**, quake, quiver, shiver, shudder, tremor, vibration, wobble

tremendous adj 1 = **huge**, colossal, enormous, formidable, gigantic, great, immense, stupendous, terrific ≠ **little** 2 Inf = **excellent**, amazing, brilliant, exceptional, extraordinary, fantastic (inf), great, marvellous, sensational (inf), wonderful ≠ **average**

tremor n 1 = **shake**, quaking, quaver, quiver, shiver, trembling, wobble 2 = **earthquake**, quake (inf), shock

trench n = **ditch**, channel, drain,

excavation, furrow, gutter, trough

trend n 1 = **tendency**, bias, current, direction, drift, flow, inclination, leaning 2 = **fashion**, craze, fad (inf), mode, rage, style, thing, vogue

trepidation n = **anxiety**, alarm, apprehension, consternation, disquiet, dread, fear, nervousness, uneasiness, worry

trespass v 1 = **intrude**, encroach, infringe, invade, obtrude ◆ n 2 = **intrusion**, encroachment, infringement, invasion, unlawful entry

trial n 1 Law = **hearing**, litigation, tribunal 2 = **test**, audition, dry run (inf), experiment, probation, test-run 3 = **hardship**, adversity, affliction, distress, ordeal, suffering, tribulation, trouble

tribe n = **race**, clan, family, people

tribunal n 2 = **hearing**, court, trial

tributary n, pl **-taries** 1 stream or river flowing into a larger one. ◆ adj 2 (of a stream or river) flowing into a larger one.

tribute ❶ n 1 sign of respect or admiration. 2 tax paid by one state to another.

trice n in a trice instantly.

trick ❶ n 1 deceitful or cunning action or plan. 2 joke or prank. 3 feat of skill or cunning. 4 mannerism. 5 cards played in one round. ◆ v 6 cheat or deceive. **trickery** n **trickster** n **tricky** adj 1 difficult, needing careful handling. 2 crafty.

trickle ❶ v 1 (cause to) flow in a thin stream or drops. 2 move gradually. ◆ n 3 gradual flow.

tricolour [**trick**–kol–lor] n three–coloured striped flag.

tricycle n three–wheeled cycle.

trident n three–pronged spear.

trifle ❶ n 1 insignificant thing or amount. 2 dessert of sponge cake, fruit, custard, and cream. **trifling** adj insignificant. **trifle with** v toy with.

trigger ❶ n 1 small lever releasing a catch on a gun or machine. 2 action that sets off a course of events. ◆ v 3 (usu. foll. by off) set (an action or process) in motion.

trigger–happy adj too quick to use guns.

trigonometry n branch of mathematics dealing with relations of the sides and angles of triangles.

trilby n, pl **-bies** man's soft felt hat.

trill n 1 Music rapid alternation between two notes. 2 shrill warbling sound made by some birds. ◆ v 3 play or sing a trill.

trillion n 1 one million million, 10^{12}. 2 Brit (formerly) one million million million, 10^{18}.

✓ WORD TIP

A trillion is what British speakers used to call 'a billion'.

---

trilogy n, pl **-gies** series of three related books, plays, etc.

trim ❶ adj **trimmer, trimmest** 1 neat and smart. 2 slender. ◆ v **trimming, trimmed** 3 cut or prune into good shape. 4 decorate with lace, ribbons, etc. 5 adjust the balance of (a ship or aircraft) by shifting the cargo etc. ◆ n 6 decoration. 7 upholstery and decorative facings in a car. 8 trim state. 9 haircut that neatens the existing style. **trimming** n 1 decoration. ◆ pl 2 usual accompaniments.

trinitrotoluene n full name for TNT.

THESAURUS

tribute n 1 = **accolade**, commendation, compliment, eulogy, panegyric, recognition, testimonial ≠ **blame** 2 = **tax**, charge, homage, payment, ransom

trick n 1 = **deception**, fraud, hoax, manoeuvre, ploy, ruse, stratagem, subterfuge, swindle, trap, wile 2 = **joke**, antic, jape, leg–pull (Brit inf), practical joke, prank, stunt 3 = **secret**, hang (inf), knack, know–how (inf), skill, technique 4 = **mannerism**, characteristic, foible, habit, idiosyncrasy, peculiarity, practice, quirk, trait ◆ v 6 = **deceive**, cheat, con (inf), dupe, fool, hoodwink, kid (inf), mislead, swindle, take in (inf), trap

trickle v 1 = **dribble**, drip, drop, exude, ooze, run, seep, stream ◆ n 3 = **dribble**, drip, seepage

trifle n 1 = **knick–knack**, bagatelle, bauble, plaything, toy **trifle with** ◆ v = **toy with**, dally with, mess about, play with

trigger v 3 = **set off**, activate, cause, generate, produce, prompt, provoke, spark off, start ≠ **stop**

trim adj 1 = **neat**, dapper, natty (inf), shipshape, smart, spruce, tidy, well-groomed ≠ **disorderly** 2 = **slender**, fit, shapely, sleek, slim, streamlined, svelte, willowy ◆ v 3 = **cut**, clip, crop, even up, pare, prune, shave, tidy 4 = **decorate**, adorn, array, beautify, deck out, dress, embellish, ornament ◆ n 6 = **decoration**, adornment, border, edging, embellishment, frill, ornamentation, piping, trimming 8 = **condition**, fettle, fitness, health, shape (inf), state, wellness 9 = **cut**, clipping, crop, shave, tidying up

trinity n, pl **–ties 1** group of three. **2** (T–) Christianity union of three persons, Father, Son, and Holy Spirit, in one God.

trinket ⊕ n small or worthless ornament or piece of jewellery.

trio ⊕ n, pl **trios 1** group of three. **2** piece of music for three performers.

trip ⊕ n **1** journey to a place and back, esp. for pleasure. **2** stumble. **3** Informal hallucinogenic drug experience. **4** switch on a mechanism. ♦ v **tripping, tripped 5** (cause to) stumble. **6** (often foll. by up) catch (someone) in a mistake. **7** move or tread lightly. **8** Informal experience the hallucinogenic effects of a drug. **tripper** n tourist.

tripe n **1** stomach of a cow used as food. **2** Informal nonsense.

triple ⊕ adj **1** having three parts. **2** three times as great or as many. ♦ v **3** increase three times. **triplet** n one of three babies born at one birth. **triple jump** athletic event in which competitors make a hop, a step, and a jump as a continuous movement.

triplicate adj triple. **in triplicate** in three copies.

tripod [**tripe**–pod] n three–legged stand, stool, etc.

trite ⊕ adj (of a remark or idea) commonplace and unoriginal.

triumph ⊕ n **1** (happiness caused by)

victory or success. ♦ v **2** be victorious or successful. **3** rejoice over a victory. **triumphal** adj celebrating a triumph. **triumphant** adj feeling or showing triumph.

troll n giant or dwarf in Scandinavian folklore.

trolley n **1** small wheeled table for food and drink. **2** wheeled cart for moving goods.

trollop n promiscuous or slovenly woman.

trombone n brass musical instrument with a sliding tube. **trombonist** n

troop ⊕ n **1** large group. **2** artillery or cavalry unit. **3** Scout company. ♦ pl **4** soldiers. ♦ v **5** move in a crowd. **trooper** n cavalry soldier.

trophy ⊕ n, pl **–phies 1** cup, shield, etc. given as a prize. **2** memento of success.

tropic n **1** either of two lines of latitude at 23½°N (**tropic of Cancer**) or 23½°S (**tropic of Capricorn**). ♦ pl **2** part of the earth's surface between these lines. **tropical** adj **1** of or in the tropics. **2** (of climate) very hot.

trot ⊕ v **trotting, trotted 1** (of a horse) move at a medium pace, lifting the feet in diagonal pairs. **2** (of a person) move at a steady brisk pace. ♦ n **3** trotting. **trotter** n pig's foot. **trot out** v repeat (old ideas etc.) without fresh thought.

troubadour [**troo**–bad–oor] n medieval

——————— | THESAURUS | ———————

trinket n = **ornament**, bagatelle, bauble, knick–knack, toy, trifle

trio n **1** = **threesome**, triad, trilogy, trinity, triumvirate

trip n **1** = **journey**, errand, excursion, expedition, foray, jaunt, outing, run, tour, voyage **2** = **stumble**, fall, misstep, slip ♦ v **5** = **stumble**, fall, lose one's footing, misstep, slip, tumble **6** = **catch out**, trap **7** = **skip**, dance, gambol, hop

triple adj = **threefold**, three–way, tripartite ♦ v **4** = **treble**, increase threefold

trite adj = **unoriginal**, banal, clichéd, commonplace, hackneyed, stale, stereotyped, threadbare, tired

triumph n **1 a** = **joy**, elation, exultation, happiness, jubilation, pride, rejoicing **b** = **success**, accomplishment, achievement, attainment, conquest, coup, feat, victory ≠ **defeat** ♦ v **2** = **succeed**, overcome, prevail, prosper, vanquish, win ≠ **lose 3** = **rejoice**, celebrate, crow, exult, gloat, glory, revel

troop n **1** = **group**, band, body, crowd, horde, multitude, team, unit **2** = **company**, squad ♦ pl **4** = **soldiers**, armed forces, army, men, servicemen, soldiery ♦ v **5** = **flock**, march, stream, swarm, throng, traipse (inf)

trophy n **1** = **prize**, award, booty, cup

travelling poet and singer.

trouble ❶ *n* **1** (cause of) distress or anxiety. **2** disease or malfunctioning. **3** state of disorder or unrest. **4** care or effort. ♦ *v* **5** (cause to) worry. **6** exert oneself. **7** cause inconvenience to. **troubled** *adj* **troublesome** *adj* **troubleshooter** *n* person employed to locate and deal with faults or problems.

trough ❶ [troff] *n* **1** long open container, esp. for animals' food or water. **2** narrow channel between two waves or ridges. **3** *Meteorol* area of low pressure.

trounce ❶ *v* defeat utterly.

troupe ❶ [troop] *n* company of performers. **trouper** *n*

trousers *pl n* two-legged outer garment with legs reaching usu. to the ankles. **trouser** *adj* of trousers.

trousseau [troo–so] *n, pl* **–seaux, –seaus** bride's collection of clothing etc. for her marriage.

trout *n* game fish related to the salmon.

trowel *n* hand tool with a wide blade for spreading mortar, lifting plants, etc.

truant ❶ *n* pupil who stays away from school without permission. **play truant** stay away from school without permission. **truancy** *n*

truce ❶ *n* temporary agreement to stop fighting.

truck[1] *n* **1** railway goods wagon. **2** lorry. **trucker** *n Chiefly US* lorry driver.

truck[2] *n* **have no truck with** refuse to be involved with.

truculent [truck–yew–lent] *adj* aggressively defiant. **truculence** *n*

trudge ❶ *v* walk heavily or wearily. ♦ *n* **2** long tiring walk.

true ❶ *adj* **truer, truest 1** in accordance with facts. **2** genuine. **3** faithful. **4** exact. **truly** *adv* **truism** *n* self-evident truth. **truth** *n* **1** state of being true. **2** something true. **truthful** *adj* **1** honest. **2** exact.

truffle *n* **1** edible underground fungus. **2** sweet flavoured with chocolate.

trump *n, adj* **1** (card) of the suit outranking the others. ♦ *v* **2** play a trump card on (another card). ♦ *pl n* **3** suit outranking the others. **turn up trumps** achieve an

---

THESAURUS

2 = **memento**, laurels, souvenir, spoils

trot *v* **1, 2** = **run**, canter, jog, lope, scamper ♦ *n* **3** = **run**, canter, jog, lope

trouble *n* **1** = **distress**, anxiety, disquiet, grief, misfortune, pain, sorrow, torment, woe, worry ≠ **pleasure 2** = **ailment**, complaint, defect, disease, disorder, failure, illness, malfunction **3** = **disorder**, agitation, bother (*inf*), commotion, discord, disturbance, strife, tumult, unrest ≠ **peace 4** = **effort**, care, exertion, inconvenience, labour, pains, thought, work ≠ **facility** ♦ *v* **5** = **bother**, disconcert, distress, disturb, pain, perturb, plague, sadden, upset, worry ≠ **please 6** = **take pains**, exert oneself, make an effort, take the time ≠ **avoid 7** = **inconvenience**, bother, burden, disturb, impose upon, incommode, put out ≠ **relieve**

trough *n* **1** = **manger**, water trough **2** = **channel**, canal, depression, ditch, duct, furrow, gully, gutter, trench

trounce *v* = **defeat utterly**, beat, crush, drub, give a hiding (*inf*), hammer (*inf*), rout, slaughter (*inf*), thrash, wipe the floor with (*inf*)

troupe *n* = **company**, band, cast

truant *n* = **absentee**, malingerer, piker (*Aust & NZ sl*), runaway, shirker, skiver (*Brit sl*)

truce *n* = **ceasefire**, armistice, cessation, let-up (*inf*), lull, moratorium, peace, respite

trudge *v* **1** = **plod**, lumber, slog, stump, traipse (*inf*), tramp, trek ♦ *n* **2** = **tramp**, hike, march, slog, traipse (*inf*), trek

true *adj* **1** = **correct**, accurate, factual, precise, right, truthful, veracious ≠ **false 2** = **genuine**, authentic, real **3** = **faithful**, dedicated, devoted, dutiful, loyal, reliable, staunch, steady, trustworthy ≠ **untrue 4** = **exact**, accurate, on target, perfect, precise, spot-on (*Brit inf*), unerring ≠ **incorrect**

unexpected success. **trumped up** invented or concocted.

trumpet ❶ v valved brass instrument with a flared tube. ◆ v **–peting, –peted** 2 proclaim loudly. 3 (of an elephant) cry loudly. **trumpeter** n

truncate ❶ v cut short.

truncheon n small club carried by a policeman.

trundle v move heavily on wheels.

trunk ❶ n 1 main stem of a tree. 2 large case or box for clothes etc. 3 person's body excluding the head and limbs. 4 elephant's long nose. 5 US car boot. ◆ pl 6 man's swimming shorts. **trunk call** long-distance telephone call. **trunk road** main road.

truss ❶ v 1 tie or bind up. ◆ n 2 device for holding a hernia in place. 3 framework supporting a roof, bridge, etc.

trust ❶ v 1 believe in and rely on. 2 consign to someone's care. 3 expect or hope. ◆ n 4 confidence in the truth, reliability, etc. of a person or thing. 5 obligation arising from responsibility. 6 arrangement in which one person administers property, money, etc. on another's behalf. 7 property held for another. 8 Brit self–governing hospital or group of hospitals within the National Health Service. 9 group of companies joined to control a market. **trustee** n person holding property on another's behalf. **trustful, trusting** adj inclined to trust others. **trustworthy** adj reliable or

honest. **trusty** adj faithful or reliable.

try ❶ v **trying, tried** 1 make an effort or attempt. 2 test or sample. 3 put strain on, e.g. he tries my patience. 4 investigate (a case). 5 examine (a person) in a lawcourt. ◆ n, pl **tries** 6 attempt or effort. 7 Rugby score gained by touching the ball down over the opponent's goal line. **try it on** Informal try to deceive or fool someone. **trying** adj Informal difficult or annoying.

✓ **WORD TIP**

The idiom *try to* can be used at any time. The alternative *try and* is less formal and often signals a 'dare': *Just try and stop me!*.

---

tryst n arrangement to meet.

T–shirt n short–sleeved casual shirt or top.

tub n 1 open, usu. round container. 2 bath. **tubby** adj (of a person) short and fat.

tuba [**tube**–a] n valved low–pitched brass instrument.

tube n 1 hollow cylinder. 2 flexible cylinder with a cap to hold pastes. **the tube** underground railway, esp. the one in London. **tubing** n 1 length of tube. 2 system of tubes. **tubular** [**tube**–yew–lar] adj of or shaped like a tube.

tuber [**tube**–er] n fleshy underground root of a plant such as a potato. **tuberous** adj

tuberculosis [tube–berk–yew–**lohss**–iss] n infectious disease causing tubercles, esp. in the lungs. **tubercular** adj **tuberculin** n extract from a bacillus used to test for

---

truncate v = **shorten**, abbreviate, curtail, cut short, dock, lop, pare, prune, trim

trunk n 1 = **stem**, bole, stalk 2 = **chest**, box, case, casket, coffer, crate 3 = **body**, torso

truss v 1 = **tie**, bind, fasten, make fast, secure, strap, tether ◆ n 2 = **support**, bandage 3 = **joist**, beam, brace, buttress, prop, stanchion, stay, strut, support

trust v 1 = **believe in**, bank on, count on, depend on, have faith in, rely upon ≠ **doubt** 2 = **entrust**, assign, commit,

confide, consign, delegate, give 3 = **expect**, assume, hope, presume, suppose, surmise ◆ n 4 = **confidence**, assurance, belief, certainty, conviction, credence, credit, expectation, faith, reliance

try v 1 = **attempt**, aim, endeavour, have a go, make an effort, seek, strive, struggle 2 = **test**, appraise, check out, evaluate, examine, investigate, put to the test, sample, taste ◆ n 6 = **attempt**, crack (inf), effort, go (inf), shot (inf), stab (inf), whack tuberculosis.

tuck ❶ v 1 push or fold into a small space. 2 stitch in folds. ◆ n 3 stitched fold. 4 *Informal* food. **tuck away** v eat (a large amount of food).

tucker n *Aust & NZ informal* food.

Tuesday n third day of the week.

tuft ❶ n bunch of feathers, grass, hair, etc. held or growing together at the base.

tug ❶ v **tugging, tugged** 1 pull hard. ◆ n 2 hard pull. 3 (also **tugboat**) small ship used to tow other vessels. **tug of war** contest in which two teams pull against one another on a rope.

tuition ❶ n instruction, esp. received individually or in a small group.

tulip n plant with bright cup-shaped flowers.

tumble ❶ v 1 (cause to) fall, esp. awkwardly or violently. 2 roll or twist, esp. in play. 3 rumple. ◆ n 4 fall. 5 somersault. **tumbler** n 1 stemless drinking glass. 2 acrobat. 3 spring catch in a lock. **tumbledown** adj dilapidated. **tumble dryer, drier** machine that dries laundry by rotating it in warm air. **tumble to** v *Informal* realize, understand.

tummy n, pl **-mies** *Informal* stomach.

tumour ❶ [tew-mer] n abnormal growth in or on the body.

tumult ❶ n uproar or commotion. **tumultuous** [tew-**mull**-tew-uss] adj

tuna n large marine food fish.

tundra n vast treeless Arctic region with permanently frozen subsoil.

tune ❶ n 1 (pleasing) sequence of musical notes. 2 correct musical pitch, e.g. *she sang out of tune.* ◆ v 3 adjust (a musical instrument) so that it is in tune. 4 adjust (a machine) to obtain the desired performance. **tuneful** adj **tunefully** adv **tuneless** adj **tuner** n **tune in** v adjust (a radio or television) to receive (a station or programme).

tungsten n *Chem* greyish-white metal.

tunic n 1 close-fitting jacket forming part of some uniforms. 2 loose knee-length garment.

tunnel ❶ n 1 underground passage. ◆ v **-nelling, -nelled** 2 make a tunnel (through).

turban n Muslim, Hindu, or Sikh man's head covering, made by winding cloth round the head.

turbine n machine or generator driven by gas, water, etc. turning blades.

turbot n large European edible flatfish.

tureen n serving dish for soup.

turf ❶ n, pl **turfs, turves** 1 short thick even grass. 2 square of this with roots and soil attached. ◆ v 3 cover with turf. **the turf** 1 racecourse. 2 horse racing. **turf accountant** bookmaker. **turf out** v *Informal* throw out.

turgid [tur-jid] adj 1 (of language) pompous. 2 swollen and thick.

── THESAURUS ──

(*inf*)

tuck v 1 = **push**, fold, gather, insert ◆ n 3 = **fold**, gather, pleat 4 *Inf* = **food**, grub (*sl*), nosh (*sl*)

tuft n = **clump**, bunch, cluster, collection, knot, tussock

tug v 1 = **pull**, jerk, wrench, yank ◆ n 2 = **pull**, jerk, yank

tuition n = **training**, education, instruction, lessons, schooling, teaching, tutelage, tutoring

tumble v 1 = **fall**, drop, flop, plummet, stumble, topple ◆ n 4 = **fall**, drop, plunge, spill, stumble, trip

tumour n = **growth**, cancer, carcinoma (*Path*), lump, sarcoma (*Med*), swelling

tumult n = **commotion**, clamour, din, hubbub, pandemonium, riot, row, turmoil, upheaval, uproar ≠ **peace**

tune n 1 = **melody**, air, song, strain, theme 2 = **concord**, consonance, euphony, harmony, pitch ◆ v 3 = **adjust**, adapt, attune, harmonize, pitch, regulate

tunnel n 1 = **passage**, burrow, channel, hole, passageway, shaft, subway, underpass ◆ v 2 = **dig**, burrow, excavate, mine, scoop out

turf n 1, 2 = **grass**, sod, sward **the turf**

turkey *n* large bird bred for food.

Turkish *adj* 1 of Turkey, its people, or their language. ◆ *n* 2 Turkish language. **Turkish bath** steam bath. **Turkish delight** jelly–like sweet coated with icing sugar.

turmoil ⓣ *n* agitation or confusion.

turn ⓣ *v* 1 change the position or direction (of). 2 move around an axis, rotate. 3 (usu. foll. by *into*) change in nature or character. 4 reach or pass in age, time, etc., e.g. *she has just turned twenty.* 5 shape on a lathe. 6 become sour. ◆ *n* 7 turning. 8 opportunity to do something as part of an agreed succession. 9 direction or drift. 10 period or spell. 11 short theatrical performance. **good, bad turn** helpful *or* unhelpful act. **turning** *n* road or path leading off a main route. **turncoat** *n* person who deserts one party or cause to join another. **turn down** *v* 1 reduce the volume or brightness (of). 2 refuse or reject. **turn in** *v* 1 go to bed. 2 hand in. **turning point** moment when a decisive change occurs. **turn off** *v* stop (something) working by using a knob etc. **turn on** *v* 1 start (something) working by using a knob etc. 2 become aggressive towards. 3 *Informal* excite, esp. sexually. **turnout** *n* number of people appearing at a gathering. **turnover** *n* 1 total sales made by a business over a certain period. 2 small pastry. 3 rate at which staff leave and are replaced. **turnpike** *n* road where a toll is collected at barriers. **turnstile** *n* revolving gate for admitting one person at a time. **turntable** *n* revolving platform. **turn up** *v* 1 arrive or appear. 2 find or be found. 3 increase the volume or brightness (of). **turn–up** *n* 1 turned–up fold at the bottom of a trouser leg. 2 *Informal* unexpected event.

turnip *n* root vegetable with orange or white flesh.

turpentine *n* (oil made from) the resin of certain trees. **turps** *n* turpentine oil.

turquoise *adj* 1 blue–green. ◆ *n* 2 blue–green precious stone.

turret *n* 1 small tower. 2 revolving gun tower on a warship or tank.

turtle *n* sea tortoise. **turn turtle** capsize. **turtledove** *n* small wild dove. **turtleneck** *n* (sweater with) a round high close–fitting neck.

tusk *n* long pointed tooth of an elephant, walrus, etc.

tussle ⓣ *n*, *v* fight or scuffle.

tutor ⓣ *n* 1 person teaching individuals or small groups. ◆ *v* 2 act as a tutor to. **tutorial** *n* period of instruction with a tutor.

tutu *n* short stiff skirt worn by ballerinas.

tuxedo *n*, *pl* **–dos** *US & Aust* dinner jacket.

TV television.

twang *n* 1 sharp ringing sound. 2 nasal speech. ◆ *v* 3 (cause to) make a twang.

tweak ⓣ *v* 1 pinch or twist sharply. ◆ *n* 2 tweaking.

twee *adj Informal* too sentimental, sweet, or

———— THESAURUS ————

2 = **horse–racing**, racing, the flat

turmoil *n* = **confusion**, agitation, chaos, commotion, disarray, disorder, tumult, upheaval

turn *v* 1 = **change course**, move, shift, swerve, switch, veer, wheel 2 = **rotate**, circle, go round, gyrate, pivot, revolve, roll, spin, twist, whirl 3 (usu. foll. by *into*) = **change into**, alter, convert, mould, mutate into, remodel, shape, transform into 5 = **shape**, fashion, frame, make, mould 6 = **go bad**, curdle, go off (*Brit inf*), sour, spoil, taint ◆ *n* 7 = **rotation**, circle, cycle, gyration, revolution, spin, twist, whirl 8 = **opportunity**, chance, crack (*inf*), go, stint, time, try 9 = **direction**, drift, heading, tendency, trend

① **tussle** *n* = **fight**, battle, brawl, conflict, contest, scrap (*inf*), scuffle, struggle

② **tussle** *v* = **fight**, battle, grapple, scrap (*inf*), scuffle, struggle, vie, wrestle

tutor *n* 1 = **teacher**, coach, educator, guardian, guide, guru, instructor, lecturer, mentor ◆ *v* 2 = **teach**, coach, drill, educate, guide, instruct, school, train

tweak *v*, *n* 1, 2 = **twist**, jerk, pinch, pull,

pretty.

tweed n 1 thick woollen cloth. ◆ pl 2 suit of tweed. **tweedy** adj

tweet n, v chirp. **tweeter** n loudspeaker reproducing high–frequency sounds.

tweezers pl n small pincer–like tool.

twelve adj, n two more than ten. **twelfth** adj, n (of) number twelve in a series.

twenty adj, n two times ten. **twentieth** adj, n

twerp n Informal silly person.

twice adv two times.

twiddle v fiddle or twirl in an idle way. **twiddle one's thumbs** be bored, have nothing to do.

twig ❶ n small branch or shoot.

twilight ❶ n soft dim light just after sunset.

twill n fabric woven to produce parallel ridges.

twin ❶ n 1 one of a pair, esp. of two children born at one birth. ◆ v **twinning, twinned** 2 pair or be paired.

twine n 1 string or cord. ◆ v 2 twist or coil round.

twinge ❶ n sudden sharp pain or emotional pang.

twinkle ❶ v 1 shine brightly but intermittently. ◆ n 2 flickering brightness.

twirl ❶ v 1 turn or spin around quickly. 2 twist or wind, esp. idly.

twist ❶ v 1 turn out of the natural position. 2 distort or pervert. 3 wind or twine. ◆ n 4 twisting. 5 twisted thing. 6 unexpected development in the plot of a film, book, etc. 7 bend or curve. 8 distortion. **twisted** adj (of a person) cruel or perverted.

twit[1] v **twitting, twitted** poke fun at (someone).

twit[2] ❶ n Informal foolish person.

twitch ❶ v 1 move spasmodically. 2 pull sharply. ◆ n 3 nervous muscular spasm. 4 sharp pull.

twitter v 1 (of birds) utter chirping sounds. ◆ n 2 act or sound of twittering.

two adj, n one more than one. **two–edged** adj (of a remark) having both a favourable and an unfavourable interpretation. **two–faced** adj deceitful, hypocritical. **two–time** v Informal deceive (a lover) by having an affair with someone else.

TX Texas.

tycoon ❶ n powerful wealthy businessman.

type ❶ n 1 class or category. 2 Informal

—————— THESAURUS ——————

squeeze

twig n = **branch**, shoot, spray, sprig, stick

twilight n 1 = **dusk**, dimness, evening, gloaming (Scot or poet), gloom, half–light, sundown, sunset ≠ **morning**

twin n 1 = **double**, clone, counterpart, duplicate, fellow, likeness, lookalike, match, mate ◆ v 2 = **pair**, couple, join, link, match, yoke

twine n 1 = **string**, cord, yarn ◆ v 2 = **coil**, bend, curl, encircle, loop, spiral, twist, wind

twinge n = **pain**, pang, prick, spasm, stab, stitch

twinkle v 1 = **sparkle**, blink, flash, flicker, gleam, glint, glisten, glitter, shimmer, shine ◆ n 2 = **sparkle**, flash, flicker, gleam, glimmer, shimmer, spark

twirl v 1 = **turn**, pirouette, pivot, revolve, rotate, spin, wheel, whirl 2 = **twist**, wind

twist v 1 = **screw**, curl, spin, swivel, wrap, wring ≠ **untwist** 2 = **distort**, contort, screw up ≠ **straighten** 3 = **wind**, coil ◆ n 4 = **wind**, coil, curl, spin, swivel 6 = **development**, change, revelation, slant, surprise, turn, variation 7 = **curve**, arc, bend, meander, turn, undulation, zigzag 8 = **distortion**, defect, deformation, flaw, imperfection, kink, warp

twit[2] n Inf = **fool**, ass, chump (inf), halfwit, idiot, nincompoop, numbskull or numskull, prat (sl), twerp or twirp (inf)

twitch v 1 = **jerk**, flutter, jump, squirm 2 = **pull**, pluck, tug, yank ◆ n 3 = **jerk**, flutter, jump, spasm, tic

tycoon n = **magnate**, baron, capitalist, fat cat (sl, chiefly US), financier, industrialist, mogul, plutocrat person, esp. of a specified kind. **3** block with a raised character used for printing. **4** printed text. ◆ v **5** print with a typewriter or word processor. **6** typify. **7** classify. **typist** n person who types with a typewriter or word processor. **typecast** v continually cast (an actor or actress) in similar roles. **typewriter** n machine which prints a character when the appropriate key is pressed.

typhoid fever n acute infectious feverish disease.

typhoon ❶ n violent tropical storm.

typhus n infectious feverish disease.

typical ❶ adj true to type, characteristic. **typically** adv **typify** v **–fying, –fied** be typical of.

typography n art or style of printing. **typographical** adj **typographer** n

tyrant ❶ n **1** oppressive or cruel ruler. **2** person who exercises authority oppressively. **tyrannical** adj like a tyrant, oppressive. **tyrannize** v exert power (over) oppressively or cruelly. **tyrannous** adj **tyranny** n tyrannical rule.

tyre n rubber ring, usu. inflated, over the rim of a vehicle's wheel to grip the road.

──────┤ T H E S A U R U S ├──────

type n **1** = **kind**, category, class, genre, group, order, sort, species, style, variety

typhoon n = **storm**, cyclone, squall, tempest, tornado

typical adj = **characteristic**, archetypal, average, model, normal, orthodox, representative, standard, stock, usual ≠ **unique**

tyrant n = **dictator**, absolutist, authoritarian, autocrat, bully, despot, martinet, oppressor, slave–driver

U u

ubiquitous ❶ [yew-**bik**-wit-uss] *adj* being or seeming to be everywhere at once. **ubiquity** *n*

udder *n* large baglike milk-producing gland of cows, sheep, or goats.

UFO unidentified flying object.

ugly ❶ *adj* **uglier, ugliest 1** of unpleasant appearance. **2** ominous or menacing. **ugliness** *n*

ukulele, ukelele [yew-kal-**lay**-lee] *n* small guitar with four strings.

ulcer ❶ *n* open sore on the surface of the skin or mucous membrane. **ulceration** *n* **ulcerous** *adj* of, like, or characterized by ulcers.

ulterior ❶ *adj* (of an aim, reason, etc.) concealed or hidden.

ultimate ❶ *adj* **1** final in a series or process. **2** highest or supreme. **ultimately** *adv*

ultra– *prefix* **1** beyond a specified extent, range, or limit, e.g. *ultrasonic.* **2** extremely, e.g. *ultramodern.*

ultraviolet *adj, n* (of) light beyond the limit of visibility at the violet end of the spectrum.

umbrage *n* **take umbrage** feel offended or upset.

umbrella *n* **1** portable device used for protection against rain, consisting of a folding frame covered in material attached to a central rod. **2** single organization, idea, etc. that contains or covers many different organizations, ideas, etc.

umpire ❶ *n* **1** official who rules on the playing of a game. ◆ *v* **2** act as umpire in (a game).

umpteen *adj Informal* very many. **umpteenth** *n, adj*

un– *prefix* **1** not, e.g. *unidentified.* **2** denoting reversal of an action, e.g. *untie.* **3** denoting removal from, e.g. *unthrone.*

unaccountable ❶ *adj* **1** unable to be explained. **2** (foll. by *to*) not answerable to. **unaccountably** *adv*

unanimous ❶ [yew-**nan**-im-uss] *adj* **1** in complete agreement. **2** agreed by all. **unanimity** *n*

unassuming ❶ *adj* modest or unpretentious.

THESAURUS

ubiquitous *adj* = **everywhere**, ever-present, omnipresent, pervasive, universal

ugly *adj* **1** = **unattractive**, distasteful, homely (*chiefly US*), horrid, ill-favoured, plain, unlovely, unpleasant, unprepossessing, unsightly ≠ **pretty** **2** = **ominous**, baleful, dangerous, menacing, sinister ≠ **friendly**

ulcer *n* = **sore**, abscess, boil, gumboil, peptic ulcer, pustule

ulterior *adj* = **hidden**, concealed, covert, secret, undisclosed

ultimate *adj* **1** = **final**, end, last

2 = **supreme**, extreme, greatest, highest, paramount, superlative, utmost

umpire *n* **1** = **referee**, arbiter, arbitrator, judge ◆ *v* **2** = **referee**, adjudicate, arbitrate, judge

unaccountable *adj* **1** = **inexplicable**, baffling, mysterious, odd, puzzling, unexplainable, unfathomable ≠ **understandable 2** (foll. by *to*) = **not answerable to**, exempt, not responsible to

unanimous *adj* **1** = **agreed**, common, concerted, harmonious, in agreement,

unaware ⓘ *adj* not aware or conscious.
unawares *adv* **1** by surprise, e.g. *caught unawares*. **2** without knowing.

> ✓ **WORD TIP**
> Note the difference between the adjective *unaware*, usually followed by *of* or *that*, and the adverb *unawares*.

unbending ⓘ *adj* rigid or inflexible.
uncanny ⓘ *adj* weird or mysterious.
uncannily *adv*
unceremonious *adj* **1** relaxed and informal. **2** abrupt or rude.
uncertain ⓘ *adj* **1** not able to be accurately known or predicted. **2** not able to be depended upon. **3** changeable.
uncertainty *n*
uncle *n* **1** brother of one's father or mother. **2** husband of one's aunt.
unconscious ⓘ *adj* **1** lacking normal awareness through the senses. **2** not aware of one's actions or behaviour. ◆ *n* **3** part of the mind containing instincts and ideas that exist without one's awareness.
unconsciously *adv* **unconsciousness** *n*
uncouth ⓘ *adj* lacking in good manners, refinement, or grace.

unction *n* act of anointing with oil in sacramental ceremonies.
under ⓘ *prep, adv* **1** indicating movement to or position beneath the underside or base. ◆ *prep* **2** less than. **3** subject to.
under– *prefix* **1** below, e.g. *underground*. **2** insufficient or insufficiently, e.g. *underrate*.
underarm *adj* **1** *Sport* denoting a style of throwing, bowling, or serving in which the hand is swung below shoulder level. ◆ *adv* **2** *Sport* in an underarm style.
undercarriage *n* **1** landing gear of an aircraft. **2** framework supporting the body of a vehicle.
undercurrent ⓘ *n* **1** current that is not apparent at the surface. **2** underlying opinion or emotion.
undercut *v* charge less than (a competitor) to obtain trade.
underdog ⓘ *n* person or team in a weak or underprivileged position.
undergo ⓘ *v* experience, endure, or sustain.
undergraduate *n* person studying in a university for a first degree.
underground ⓘ *adj* **1** occurring, situated, used, or going below ground level. **2** secret. ◆ *n* **3** electric passenger railway

——————— THESAURUS ———————

like–minded, united ≠ **split**
unassuming *adj* = **modest**, humble, quiet, reserved, retiring, self-effacing, unassertive, unobtrusive, unpretentious
unaware *adj* = **ignorant**, not in the loop (*inf*), oblivious, unconscious, uninformed, unknowing
unbending *adj* = **inflexible**, firm, intractable, resolute, rigid, severe, strict, stubborn, tough, uncompromising
uncanny *adj* = **weird**, mysterious, strange, supernatural, unearthly, unnatural
uncertain *adj* **1** = **unpredictable**, doubtful, indefinite, questionable, risky, speculative ≠ **decided 2** = **unsure**, dubious, hazy, irresolute, unclear, unconfirmed, undecided, vague ≠ **sure**
unconscious *adj* **1** = **senseless**, insensible, knocked out, out, out cold, stunned

≠ **conscious 2** a = **unintentional**, accidental, inadvertent, unwitting ≠ **planned** b = **unaware**, ignorant, oblivious, unknowing ≠ **aware**
uncouth *adj* = **coarse**, barbaric, boorish, crude, graceless, ill-mannered, loutish, oafish, rough, rude, vulgar
① **under** *prep* **1** = **below**, beneath, underneath **3** = **subject to**, governed by, secondary to, subordinate to
② **under** *adv* **1** = **below**, beneath, down, lower ≠ **over**
undercurrent *n* **1** = **undertow**, riptide **2** = **undertone**, atmosphere, feeling, hint, overtone, sense, suggestion, tendency, tinge, vibes (*sl*)
underdog *n* = **weaker party**, little fellow (*inf*), outsider
undergo *v* = **experience**, bear, endure, go

operated in underground tunnels. **4** movement dedicated to overthrowing a government or occupation forces.

undergrowth ❶ *n* small trees and bushes growing beneath taller trees in a wood or forest.

underhand ❶ *adj* sly, deceitful, and secretive.

underlie *v* **1** lie or be placed under. **2** be the foundation, cause, or basis of. **underlying** *adj* fundamental or basic.

underline ❶ *v* **1** draw a line under. **2** state forcibly, emphasize.

underling *n* subordinate.

undermine ❶ *v* **1** weaken gradually.

underneath *prep, adv* **1** under or beneath. ◆ *adj, n* **2** lower (part or surface).

underpants *pl n* man's undergarment for the lower part of the body.

underpass *n* section of a road that passes under another road or a railway line.

underpin *v* give strength or support to.

understand ❶ *v* **1** know and comprehend the nature or meaning of. **2** realize or grasp (something). **3** assume, infer, or believe. **understandable** *adj* **understandably** *adv* **understanding** *n* **1** ability to learn, judge, or make decisions.

2 personal interpretation of a subject. **3** mutual agreement, usu. an informal or private one. ◆ *adj* **4** kind and sympathetic.

understudy ❶ *n* **1** actor who studies a part in order to be able to replace the usual actor if necessary. ◆ *v* **2** act as an understudy for.

undertake ❶ *v* **1** agree or commit oneself to (something) or to do (something). **2** promise. **undertaking** *n* **1** task or enterprise. **2** agreement to do something.

undertone ❶ *n* **1** quiet tone of voice. **2** underlying quality or feeling.

underwear ❶ *n* clothing worn under the outer garments and next to the skin.

underworld ❶ *n* **1** criminals and their associates. **2** *Greek & Roman myth* regions below the earth's surface regarded as the abode of the dead.

underwrite ❶ *v* **1** accept financial responsibility for (a commercial project). **2** sign and issue (an insurance policy), thus accepting liability. **underwriter** *n*

undo ❶ *v* **1** open, unwrap. **2** reverse the effects of. **3** cause the downfall of. **undone** *adj* **undoing** *n* cause of someone's downfall.

undulate *v* move in waves. **undulation** *n*

——————— THESAURUS ———————

through, stand, suffer, sustain

underground *adj* **1** = **subterranean**, buried, covered **2** = **secret**, clandestine, covert, hidden ◆ *n* **3** = **the tube** (*Brit*), the metro, the subway **4** = **the Resistance**, partisans

undergrowth *n* = **scrub**, bracken, briars, brush, underbrush

underhand *adj* = **sly**, crafty, deceitful, devious, dishonest, furtive, secret, sneaky, stealthy

underline *v* **1** = **underscore**, mark **2** = **emphasize**, accentuate, highlight, stress ≠ **play down**

undermine *v* **1** = **weaken**, disable, sabotage, sap, subvert ≠ **promote**

understand *v* **2** = **comprehend**, conceive, fathom, follow, get, grasp, perceive, realize, see, take in **3** = **believe**, assume,

gather, presume, suppose, think

understudy *n* **1** = **stand-in**, replacement, reserve, substitute

undertake *v* **1** = **agree**, bargain, contract, engage **2** = **promise**, guarantee, pledge

undertone *n* **1** = **murmur**, whisper **2** = **undercurrent**, hint, suggestion, tinge, touch, trace

underwear *n* = **underclothes**, lingerie, undergarments, underthings, undies (*inf*)

underworld *n* **1** = **criminals**, gangland (*inf*), gangsters, organized crime **2** *Greek & Roman myth* = **nether world**, Hades, nether regions

underwrite *v* **1** = **finance**, back, fund, guarantee, insure, sponsor, subsidize **2** = **sign**, endorse, initial

undo *v* **1** = **open**, disentangle, loose, unbutton, unfasten, untie **2** = **reverse**,

unearth ❶ v 1 reveal or discover by searching. 2 dig up out of the earth.

uneasy ❶ adj 1 (of a person) anxious or apprehensive. 2 (of a condition) precarious or uncomfortable. **uneasily** adv **uneasiness** n **unease** n 1 feeling of anxiety. 2 state of dissatisfaction.

unemployed ❶ adj out of work. **unemployment** n

unexceptionable adj beyond criticism or objection.

unfold ❶ v 1 open or spread out from a folded state. 2 reveal or be revealed.

ungainly ❶ adj –lier, –liest lacking grace when moving.

uni– combining form of, consisting of, or having only one, e.g. unicellular.

unicorn n imaginary horselike creature with one horn growing from its forehead.

uniform ❶ n 1 special identifying set of clothes for the members of an organization, such as soldiers. ◆ adj 2 regular and even throughout, unvarying. 3 alike or like. **uniformly** adv **uniformity** n

unify ❶ v –fying, –fied make or become one. **unification** n

unilateral adj made or done by only one person or group. **unilaterally** adv

union ❶ n 1 uniting or being united. 2 short for TRADE UNION. 3 association or confederation of individuals or groups for a common purpose. **unionist** n member or supporter of a trade union. **unionize** v organize (workers) into a trade union. **unionization** n

unique ❶ [yoo–**neek**] adj 1 being the only one of a particular type. 2 without equal or like. **uniquely** adv

---

> ✓ **WORD TIP**
>
> Because of its meaning, avoid using *unique* with modifiers like *very* and *rather*.

---

unison ❶ n 1 complete agreement. 2 *Music* singing or playing of the same notes together at the same time.

unit ❶ n 1 single undivided entity or whole. 2 group or individual regarded as a basic element of a larger whole. 3 fixed quantity etc., used as a standard of measurement. 4 piece of furniture designed to be fitted with other similar pieces. **unit trust** investment trust that issues units for public sale and invests the money in many different businesses.

——————— THESAURUS ———————

annul, cancel, invalidate, neutralize, offset 3 = **ruin**, defeat, destroy, overturn, quash, shatter, subvert, undermine, upset, wreck

unearth v 1 = **discover**, expose, find, reveal, uncover 2 = **dig up**, dredge up, excavate, exhume

uneasy adj 1 = **anxious**, disturbed, edgy, nervous, on edge, perturbed, troubled, uncomfortable, worried ≠ **relaxed** 2 = **precarious**, awkward, insecure, shaky, strained, tense, uncomfortable

unemployed adj 1 = **out of work**, idle, jobless, laid off, redundant

unfold v 1 = **open**, expand, spread out, undo, unfurl, unravel, unroll, unwrap 2 = **reveal**, disclose, divulge, make known, present, show, uncover

ungainly adj = **awkward**, clumsy, inelegant, lumbering, ungraceful

uniform n 1 = **outfit**, costume, dress, garb, habit, livery, regalia, suit ◆ adj 2 = **unvarying**, consistent, constant, even, regular, smooth, unchanging ≠ **varying** 3 = **alike**, equal, like, same, similar

unify v = **unite**, amalgamate, combine, confederate, consolidate, join, merge

union n 1 = **uniting**, accord, agreement, amalgamation, blend, combination, concord, conjunction, fusion, harmony, joining, mixture, unanimity, unison, unity 3 = **alliance**, association, coalition, confederacy, federation, league

unique adj 1 = **single**, lone, only, solitary 2 = **unparalleled**, matchless, unequalled, unmatched, without equal

unison n 1 = **agreement**, accord, concert, concord, harmony, unity

unit n 1 = **item**, entity, whole 2 = **part**,

unite ❶ *v* 1 make or become an integrated whole. 2 (cause to) enter into an association or alliance.

universe ❶ *n* 1 whole of all existing matter, energy, and space. 2 the world.

universal *adj* 1 of or typical of the whole of mankind or of nature. 2 existing everywhere. **universally** *adv* **universality** *n*

university *n*, *pl* –ties institution of higher education with the authority to award degrees.

unkempt ❶ *adj* 1 (of the hair) not combed. 2 slovenly or untidy.

unless *conj* except under the circumstances that.

unlike ❶ *adj* 1 dissimilar or different. ◆ *prep* 2 not like or typical of.

unravel *v* –elling, –elled 1 reduce (something knitted or woven) to separate strands. 2 become unravelled. 3 explain or solve.

unrest ❶ *n* rebellious state of discontent.

unruly ❶ *adj* –lier, –liest difficult to control or organize.

unsavoury ❶ *adj* distasteful or objectionable.

unscathed ❶ *adj* not harmed or injured.

unsightly ❶ *adj* unpleasant to look at.

unthinkable ❶ *adj* out of the question, inconceivable.

until *conj* 1 up to the time that. ◆ *prep* 2 in or throughout the period before. **not until** not before (a time or event).

unto *prep Old-fashioned* to.

untoward ❶ *adj* causing misfortune or annoyance.

unwieldy ❶ *adj* too heavy, large, or awkward to be easily handled.

unwind ❶ *v* 1 relax after a busy or tense time. 2 slacken, undo, or unravel.

unwitting ❶ *adj* 1 not intentional. 2 not knowing or conscious. **unwittingly** *adv*

component, constituent, element, member, section, segment 3 = **measure**, measurement, quantity

unite *v* 1 = **join**, amalgamate, blend, combine, couple, fuse, link, merge, unify ≠ **part** 2 = **cooperate**, ally, band, collaborate, join forces, pool ≠ **separate**

universe *n* 1 = **cosmos**, creation, macrocosm, nature

unkempt *adj* 1 = **uncombed**, shaggy, tousled 2 = **untidy**, dishevelled, disordered, messy, scruffy, slovenly, ungroomed ≠ **neat**

unlike *adj* 1 = **different**, dissimilar, distinct, diverse, not alike, opposite, unequal ≠ **similar to**

unravel *v* 1 = **undo**, disentangle, free, separate, untangle, unwind 3 = **solve**, explain, figure out (*inf*), resolve, work out

unrest *n* = **discontent**, agitation, discord, dissension, protest, rebellion, sedition, strife ≠ **peace**

unruly *adj* = **uncontrollable**, disobedient, mutinous, rebellious, wayward, wild, wilful

unsavoury *adj* = **distasteful**, nasty, nauseating, obnoxious, offensive, repellent, repulsive, revolting, sickening, unpleasant

unscathed *adj* = **unharmed**, safe, unhurt, uninjured, unmarked, whole

unsightly *adj* = **ugly**, disagreeable, hideous, horrid, repulsive, unattractive

unthinkable *adj* a = **impossible**, absurd, out of the question, unreasonable b = **inconceivable**, implausible, incredible, unimaginable

untoward *adj* a = **unfavourable**, adverse, inauspicious, inopportune, unlucky b = **troublesome**, annoying, awkward, inconvenient, irritating, unfortunate

unwieldy *adj* a = **bulky**, clumsy, hefty, massive, ponderous b = **awkward**, cumbersome, inconvenient, unmanageable

unwind *v* 1 = **relax**, loosen up, take it easy, wind down 2 = **unravel**, slacken, uncoil, undo, unroll, untwine, untwist

unwitting *adj* 1 = **unintentional**, accidental, chance, inadvertent, involuntary, unplanned ≠ **intended** 2 = **unknowing**, ignorant, innocent, unaware, unconscious, unsuspecting

up *prep, adv* **1** indicating movement to or position at a higher place. ◆ *adv* **2** indicating readiness, intensity or completeness, etc., e.g. *warm up; drink up.* ◆ *adj* **3** of a high or higher position. **4** out of bed. ◆ *v* **upping, upped 5** increase or raise. **up against** having to cope with. **up and** *Informal* do something suddenly, e.g. *he upped and left.* **ups and downs** alternating periods of good and bad luck. **1 what's up?** *Informal* what is wrong? **upward** *adj* **1** directed or moving towards a higher place or level. ◆ *adv* **2** (also **upwards**) from a lower to a higher place, level, or condition.

upbringing ● *n* education of a person during the formative years.

update ● *v* bring up to date.

upfront *adj* **1** open and frank. ◆ *adv, adj* **2** (of money) paid out at the beginning of a business arrangement.

upgrade ● *v* promote (a person or job) to a higher rank.

upheaval ● *n* strong, sudden, or violent disturbance.

uphold ● *v* **1** maintain or defend against opposition. **2** give moral support to.

upholster *v* fit (a chair or sofa) with padding, springs, and covering. **upholsterer** *n* **upholstery** *n* soft covering on a chair or sofa.

upkeep ● *n* act, process, or cost of keeping something in good repair.

upon *prep* **1** on. **2** up and on.

upper ● *adj* **1** higher or highest in physical position, wealth, rank, or status. ◆ *n* **2** part of a shoe above the sole. **uppermost** *adj* **1** highest in position, power, or importance. ◆ *adv* **2** in or into the highest place or position. **upper class** highest social class. **upper–class** *adj* **upper crust** *Informal* upper class. **upper hand** position of control.

upright ● *adj* **1** vertical or erect. **2** honest or just. ◆ *adv* **3** vertically or in an erect position. ◆ *n* **4** vertical support, such as a post.

uprising ● *n* rebellion or revolt.

uproar ● *n* disturbance characterized by loud noise and confusion. **uproarious** *adj* **1** very funny. **2** (of laughter) loud and boisterous.

uproot ● *v* **1** pull up by or as if by the roots. **2** displace (a person or people) from their native or usual surroundings.

upset ● *adj* **1** emotionally or physically disturbed or distressed. ◆ *v* **2** tip over. **3** disturb the normal state or stability of. **4** disturb mentally or emotionally. **5** make physically ill. ◆ *n* **6** unexpected defeat or reversal. **7** disturbance or disorder of the emotions, mind, or body. **upsetting** *adj*

———————— THESAURUS ————————

≠ **knowing**
upbringing *n* = **education**, breeding, raising, rearing, training
update *v* = **bring up to date**, amend, modernize, renew, revise
upgrade *v* = **promote**, advance, better, elevate, enhance, improve, raise ≠ **degrade**
upheaval *n* = **disturbance**, disorder, disruption, revolution, turmoil
uphold *v* **1** = **defend**, maintain, sustain **2** = **support**, advocate, aid, back, champion, endorse, promote
upkeep *n* **a** = **maintenance**, keep, repair, running, subsistence **b** = **running costs**, expenditure, expenses, overheads

upper *adj* **1 a** = **higher**, high, loftier, top, topmost ≠ **lower b** = **superior**, eminent, greater, important ≠ **lower**
upright *adj* **1** = **vertical**, erect, perpendicular, straight ≠ **flat 2** = **honest**, conscientious, ethical, good, honourable, just, principled, righteous, virtuous ≠ **corrupt**
uprising *n* = **rebellion**, disturbance, insurgence, insurrection, mutiny, revolt, revolution, rising
uproar *n* = **commotion**, din, furore, mayhem, noise, outcry, pandemonium, racket, riot, turmoil
uproot *v* **1** = **pull up**, dig up, rip up, root out, weed out **2** = **displace**, exile

upshot ❶ *n* final result or conclusion.

upside down ❶ *adj* 1 turned over completely. 2 *Informal* confused or jumbled. ♦ *adv* 3 in an inverted fashion. 4 in a chaotic manner.

upsurge *n* rapid rise or swell.

upstage *adj* 1 at the back half of the stage. ♦ *v* 2 *Informal* draw attention to oneself from (someone else).

upstart ❶ *n* person who has risen suddenly to a position of power and behaves arrogantly.

uptight ❶ *adj Informal* nervously tense, irritable, or angry.

uranium *n Chem* radioactive silvery–white metallic element, used chiefly as a source of nuclear energy.

urban ❶ *adj* of or living in a city or town. **urbanize** *v* make (a rural area) more industrialized and urban. **urbanization** *n*

urbane ❶ *adj* characterized by courtesy, elegance, and sophistication. **urbanity** *n*

urchin ❶ *n* mischievous child.

urge ❶ *n* 1 strong impulse, inner drive, or yearning. ♦ *v* 2 plead with or press (a person to do something). 3 advocate earnestly. 4 force or drive onwards. **urgent** *adj* needing attention at once.

urine *n* pale yellow fluid excreted by the kidneys to the bladder and passed as waste from the body. **urinary** *adj* **urinate** *v* discharge urine. **urination** *n* **urinal** *n* sanitary fitting used by men for urination.

urn *n* 1 vase used as a container for the ashes of the dead. 2 large metal container with a tap, used for making and holding tea or coffee.

us *pron* objective case of WE.

use ❶ *v* 1 put into service or action. 2 take advantage of, exploit. 3 consume or expend. ♦ *n* 4 using or being used. 5 ability or permission to use. 6 usefulness or advantage. 7 purpose for which something is used. **user** *n* **user–friendly** *adj* easy to familiarize oneself with, understand, and use. **usable** *adj* able to be used. **usage** *n* 1 regular or constant use. 2 way in which a word is used in a language. **use–by date** *Aust, NZ, S Afr &* *US* date on packaged food after which it should not be sold. **used** *adj* second–hand. **used to** *adj* 1 accustomed to. ♦ *v* 2 used as an auxiliary to express past habitual or accustomed actions, e.g. *I used to live there.* **useful** *adj* **usefully** *adv* **usefulness** *n* **useless** *adj*

    THESAURUS

upset *adj* 1 a = **distressed**, agitated, bothered, dismayed, disturbed, grieved, hurt, put out, troubled, worried b = **sick**, ill, queasy ♦ *v* 2 = **tip over**, capsize, knock over, overturn, spill 3 = **mess up**, change, disorder, disorganize, disturb, spoil 4 = **distress**, agitate, bother, disconcert, disturb, faze, fluster, grieve, perturb, ruffle, trouble ♦ *n* 6 = **reversal**, defeat, shake–up (*inf*) 7 a = **distress**, agitation, bother, disturbance, shock, trouble, worry b = **illness**, bug (*inf*), complaint, disorder, malady, sickness

upshot *n* = **result**, culmination, end, end result, finale, outcome, sequel

upside down *adj* 1 = **inverted**, overturned, upturned 2 *Inf* = **confused**, chaotic, disordered, higgledy–piggledy (*inf*), muddled, topsy–turvy

upstart *n* = **social climber**, arriviste, *nouveau riche*, parvenu

uptight *adj Inf* = **tense**, anxious, edgy, on edge, uneasy, wired (*sl*)

urban *adj* = **civic**, city, dorp (*S Afr*), metropolitan, municipal, town

urbane *adj* = **sophisticated**, cultivated, cultured, debonair, polished, refined, smooth, suave, well–bred

urchin *n* = **ragamuffin**, brat, gamin, waif

urge *n* 1 = **impulse**, compulsion, desire, drive, itch, longing, thirst, wish, yearning ≠ **reluctance** ♦ *v* 2 = **beg**, beseech, entreat, exhort, implore, plead 3 = **advocate**, advise, counsel, recommend, support ≠ **discourage** 4 = **drive**, compel, encourage, force, gee up, goad, impel, incite, induce, press, push, spur

✓ **WORD TIP**
In the negative there are two common combinations: *didn't use to* and *used not to*. The abbreviated form is *usedn't to*.

usher ❶ n 1 official who shows people to their seats, as in a church. ◆ v 2 conduct or escort. **usherette** n female assistant in a cinema who shows people to their seats.

usual ❶ adj of the most normal, frequent, or regular type. **usually** adv most often, in most cases.

usurp ❶ [yewz–**zurp**] v seize (a position or power) without authority. **usurper** n

utensil n tool or container for practical use.

uterus [**yew**–ter–russ] n womb. **uterine** adj

utility ❶ n 1 usefulness. 2 (pl –ties) public service, such as electricity. ◆ adj 3 designed for use rather than beauty.
utility truck Aust & NZ small truck with an open body and low sides.

utmost ❶ adj, n (of) the greatest possible degree or amount.

Utopia ❶ [yew–**tope**–ee–a] n any real or imaginary society, place, or state considered to be perfect or ideal.

utter¹ ❶ v express (something) in sounds or words. **utterance** n 1 something uttered. 2 act or power of uttering.

utter² ❶ adj total or absolute. **utterly** adv

——————————| T H E S A U R U S |——————————

use v 1 = **employ**, apply, exercise, exert, operate, practise, utilize, work 2 = **take advantage of**, exploit, manipulate 3 = **consume**, exhaust, expend, run through, spend ◆ n 4 = **usage**, application, employment, exercise, handling, operation, practice, service 6 = **good**, advantage, avail, benefit, help, point, profit, service, usefulness, value 7 = **purpose**, end, object, reason
usher n 1 = **attendant**, doorkeeper, doorman, escort, guide ◆ v 2 = **escort**, conduct, direct, guide, lead
usual adj = **normal**, common, customary, everyday, general, habitual, ordinary, regular, routine, standard, typical
usurp v = **seize**, appropriate, assume,

commandeer, take, take over, wrest
utility n 1 = **usefulness**, benefit, convenience, efficacy, practicality, serviceableness
① **utmost** adj a = **greatest**, chief, highest, maximum, paramount, pre–eminent, supreme b = **farthest**, extreme, final, last
② **utmost** n b = **greatest**, best, hardest, highest
Utopia n = **paradise**, bliss, Eden, Garden of Eden, heaven, Shangri–la
utter¹ v = **express**, articulate, pronounce, say, speak, voice
utter² adj = **absolute**, complete, downright, outright, sheer, thorough, total, unmitigated

V v

VA Virginia.

vacant ❶ *adj* 1 (of a toilet, room, etc.) unoccupied. 2 without interest or understanding. **vacancy** *n, pl* **–cies** 1 unfilled job. 2 unoccupied room in a guesthouse. 3 state of being unoccupied.

vacate ❶ *v* 1 cause (something) to be empty by leaving. 2 give up (a job or position). **vacation** *n* 1 time when universities and law courts are closed. 2 *Chiefly US* holiday.

vaccinate *v* inject with a vaccine. **vaccination** *n* **vaccine** *n* substance designed to cause a mild form of a disease to make a person immune to the disease itself.

vacillate [**vass**–ill–late] *v* keep changing one's mind or opinions. **vacillation** *n*

vacuous ❶ *adj* not expressing intelligent thought. **vacuity** *n*

vacuum ❶ *n, pl* **vacuums, vacua** 1 empty space from which all or most air or gas has been removed. ♦ *v* 2 clean with a vacuum cleaner. **vacuum cleaner** electrical appliance which sucks up dust and dirt from carpets and upholstery. **vacuum flask** double–walled flask with a vacuum between the walls that keeps drinks hot or cold. **vacuum–packed** *adj* contained in packaging from which the air has been removed.

vagabond ❶ *n* person with no fixed home, esp. a beggar.

vagina [vaj–**jine**–a] *n* (in female mammals) passage from the womb to the external genitals. **vaginal** *adj*

vagrant ❶ [**vaig**–rant] *n* 1 person with no settled home. ♦ *adj* 2 wandering. **vagrancy** *n*

vague ❶ *adj* 1 not clearly explained. 2 unable to be seen or heard clearly. 3 absent–minded. **vaguely** *adv*

vain ❶ *adj* 1 excessively proud, esp. of one's appearance. 2 bound to fail, futile. **in vain** unsuccessfully.

vale *n Lit* valley.

valentine *n* (person to whom one sends) a romantic card on Saint Valentine's Day.

THESAURUS

vacant *adj* 1 = **unoccupied**, available, empty, free, idle, unfilled, untenanted, void ≠ **taken** 2 = **blank**, absent–minded, abstracted, dreamy, idle, inane, vacuous, vague ≠ **lively**

vacate *v* 1 = **leave**, evacuate, quit

vacuous *adj* = **unintelligent**, blank, inane, stupid, uncomprehending, vacant

vacuum *n* 1 = **emptiness**, gap, nothingness, space, vacuity, void

vagabond *n* = **vagrant**, beggar, down–and–out, itinerant, rover, tramp

vagrant *n* 1 = **tramp**, drifter, hobo (*US*), itinerant, rolling stone, wanderer ♦ *adj* 2 = **itinerant**, nomadic, roaming, rootless, roving, unsettled, vagabond ≠ **settled**

vague *adj* 1 = **unclear**, hazy, imprecise, indefinite, loose, uncertain, unspecified, woolly ≠ **clear** 3 = **indistinct**, hazy, ill–defined, indeterminate, nebulous, unclear ≠ **distinct**

vain *adj* 1 = **proud**, arrogant, conceited, egotistical, narcissistic, self–important, swaggering ≠ **modest** 2 = **futile**, abortive, fruitless, idle, pointless, senseless, unavailing, unprofitable, useless, worthless ≠ **successful** **in vain** = **to no avail**, fruitless(ly), ineffectual(ly),

14th February.

valet n man's personal male servant.

valiant 𝕠 adj brave or courageous.

valid 𝕠 adj 1 soundly reasoned. 2 having legal force. **validate** v make valid. **validation** n **validity** n

Valium n ® drug used as a tranquilliser.

valley 𝕠 n low area between hills, often with a river running through it.

valour 𝕠 n Lit bravery.

value 𝕠 n 1 importance, usefulness. 2 monetary worth. ◆ pl 3 moral principles. ◆ v valuing, valued 4 assess the worth or desirability of. 5 have a high regard for. **valuable** adj having great worth. **valuables** pl n valuable personal property. **valuation** n assessment of worth. **valueless** adj **valuer** n **value–added tax** Brit see VAT. **value judgment** opinion based on personal belief.

valve n 1 device to control the movement of fluid through a pipe. 2 Anat flap in a part of the body allowing blood to flow in one direction only. 3 Physics tube containing a vacuum, allowing current to flow from a cathode to an anode.

vampire n (in folklore) corpse that rises at

night to drink the blood of the living. **vampire bat** tropical bat that feeds on blood.

van[1] n 1 motor vehicle for transporting goods. 2 Brit & Aust railway carriage for goods, luggage, or mail.

van[2] n short for VANGUARD.

vandal 𝕠 n person who deliberately damages property. **vandalism** n **vandalize** v

vane n flat blade on a rotary device such as a weathercock or propeller.

vanguard 𝕠 n 1 unit of soldiers leading an army. 2 most advanced group or position in a movement or activity.

vanilla n seed pod of a tropical climbing orchid, used for flavouring.

vanish 𝕠 v 1 disappear suddenly or mysteriously. 2 cease to exist.

vanity 𝕠 n, pl –ties (display of) excessive pride.

vanquish 𝕠 v Lit defeat (someone) utterly.

vantage n **vantage point** position that gives one an overall view.

vapid 𝕠 adj lacking character, dull.

vapour 𝕠 n 1 moisture suspended in air as steam or mist. 2 gaseous form of

———————— THESAURUS ————————

unsuccessful(ly), useless(ly), vain(ly)

valiant adj = **brave**, bold, courageous, fearless, gallant, heroic, intrepid, lion–hearted

valid adj 1 = **sound**, cogent, convincing, good, logical, telling, well–founded, well–grounded ≠ **weak** 2 = **legal**, authentic, bona fide, genuine, lawful, legitimate, official ≠ **illegal**

valley n = **hollow**, dale, dell, depression, glen, vale

valour n Lit = **bravery**, boldness, courage, fearlessness, gallantry, heroism, intrepidity, spirit

value n 1 = **importance**, advantage, benefit, desirability, merit, profit, usefulness, utility, worth ≠ **insignificance** 2 = **cost**, market price, rate ◆ pl 3 = **principles**, ethics, (moral) standards ◆ v 4 = **evaluate**, appraise, assess, estimate,

price, rate, set at 5 = **regard highly**, appreciate, cherish, esteem, hold dear, prize, respect, treasure ≠ **underestimate**

vandal n = **hooligan**, delinquent, rowdy, yob or yobbo (Brit sl)

vanguard n 2 = **forefront**, cutting edge, forerunners, front line, leaders, spearhead, trailblazers, trendsetters, van

vanish v = **disappear**, dissolve, evanesce, evaporate, fade (away), melt (away) ≠ **appear**

vanity n = **pride**, arrogance, conceit, conceitedness, egotism, narcissism ≠ **modesty**

vanquish v Lit = **defeat**, beat, conquer, crush, master, overcome, overpower, triumph over

vapid adj = **dull**, bland, boring, flat, insipid, tame, uninspiring, uninteresting, weak, wishy–washy (inf) something that is liquid or solid at room temperature. **vaporize** v **vaporizer** n **vaporous** adj

variable ⊕ adj 1 not always the same, changeable. ◆ n 2 Maths expression with a range of values. **variability** n

variegated adj having patches or streaks of different colours. **variegation** n

variety ⊕ n, pl -ties 1 state of being diverse or various. 2 different things of the same kind. 3 particular sort or kind. 4 light entertainment composed of unrelated acts.

various ⊕ adj of several kinds. **variously** adv

varnish ⊕ n 1 solution of oil and resin, put on a surface to make it hard and glossy. ◆ v 2 apply varnish to.

vary ⊕ v **varying, varied** 1 change. 2 cause differences in. **varied** adj

vase n ornamental jar, esp. for flowers.

Vaseline n ® thick oily cream made from petroleum, used in skin care.

vast ⊕ adj extremely large. **vastly** adv **vastness** n

vat n large container for liquids.

VAT Brit value–added tax: tax on the difference between the cost of materials and the selling price.

vault[1] ⊕ n 1 secure room for storing valuables. 2 underground burial chamber.

vault[2] ⊕ v 1 jump over (something) by resting one's hand(s) on it. ◆ n 2 such a jump.

veal n calf meat.

vector n 1 Maths quantity that has size and direction, such as force. 2 animal, usu. an insect, that carries disease.

veer ⊕ v change direction suddenly.

vegan [**vee**–gan] n 1 person who eats no meat, fish, eggs, or dairy products. ◆ adj 2 suitable for a vegan. **veganism** n

vegetable n 1 edible plant. 2 Informal severely brain–damaged person. ◆ adj 3 of or like plants or vegetables.

vegetarian n 1 person who eats no meat or fish. ◆ adj 2 suitable for a vegetarian. **vegetarianism** n

vegetate ⊕ v live a dull boring life with no mental stimulation.

vehement ⊕ adj expressing strong feelings. **vehemence** n **vehemently** adv

vehicle ⊕ n 1 machine, esp. with an engine and wheels, for carrying people or objects. 2 something used to achieve a particular purpose or as a means of expression. **vehicular** adj

veil ⊕ n 1 piece of thin cloth covering the

——————————— THESAURUS ———————————

vapour n 1 = **mist**, exhalation, fog, haze, steam

variable adj 1 = **changeable**, flexible, fluctuating, inconstant, mutable, shifting, temperamental, uneven, unstable, unsteady

variety n 1 = **diversity**, change, difference, discrepancy, diversification, multifariousness, variation ≠ **similarity** 2 = **range**, array, assortment, collection, cross section, medley, miscellany, mixture 3 = **type**, brand, breed, category, class, kind, sort, species, strain

various adj = **different**, assorted, disparate, distinct, diverse, miscellaneous, several, sundry, varied ≠ **same**

varnish n, v 1, 2 = **lacquer**, glaze, gloss, polish

vary v 1 = **change**, alter, fluctuate 2 = **alternate**

vast adj = **huge**, boundless, colossal, enormous, gigantic, great, immense, massive, monumental, wide

vault[1] n 1 = **strongroom**, depository, repository 2 = **crypt**, catacomb, cellar, charnel house, mausoleum, tomb, undercroft

vault[2] v 1 = **jump**, bound, clear, hurdle, leap, spring

veer v = **change direction**, change course, sheer, shift, swerve, turn

vegetate v = **stagnate**, deteriorate, go to seed, idle, languish, loaf ≠ **grow**

vehement adj = **strong**, ardent, emphatic, fervent, fierce, forceful, impassioned, intense, passionate, powerful

head or face. 2 something that masks the
truth, e.g. *a veil of secrecy*. ◆ 3 cover with
or as if with a veil. **take the veil** become a
nun. **veiled** *adj* disguised.

vein ❶ *n* 1 tube that takes blood to the
heart. 2 line in a leaf or an insect's wing. 3
layer of ore or mineral in rock. 4 streak in
marble, wood, or cheese. 5 feature of
someone's writing or speech, e.g. *a vein of
humour*. 6 mood or style, e.g. *in a lighter
vein*.

Velcro *n* ® fastening consisting of one
piece of fabric with tiny hooked threads
and another with a coarse surface that
sticks to it.

velocity ❶ *n, pl* –**ties** speed of movement
in a given direction.

velvet *n* fabric with a thick soft pile.
velvety *adj* soft and smooth. **velveteen** *n*
cotton velvet.

vend *v* sell. **vendor** *n* vending machine
machine that dispenses goods when coins
are inserted.

vendetta ❶ *n* prolonged quarrel between
families, esp. one involving revenge
killings.

veneer ❶ *n* 1 thin layer of wood etc.
covering a cheaper material. 2 superficial
appearance, e.g. *a veneer of sophistication*.

venerable ❶ *adj* worthy of deep respect.

venerate *v* hold (a person) in deep
respect. **veneration** *n*

vengeance ❶ *n* revenge. **vengeful** *adj*
wanting revenge.

venison *n* deer meat.

venom ❶ *n* 1 malice or spite. 2 poison
produced by snakes etc. **venomous** *adj*

vent ❶ *n* 1 outlet releasing fumes or fluid.
◆ *v* 2 express (an emotion) freely. **give
vent to** release (an emotion) in an
outburst.

ventilate *v* 1 let fresh air into. 2 discuss
(ideas or feelings) openly. **ventilation** *n*
ventilator *n*

ventricle *n Anat* one of the four cavities of
the heart or brain.

ventriloquist *n* entertainer who can speak
without moving his or her lips, so that a
voice seems to come from elsewhere.
ventriloquism *n*

venture ❶ *n* 1 risky undertaking, esp. in
business. ◆ *v* 2 do something risky. 3 dare
to express (an opinion). 4 go to an
unknown place. **venturesome** *adj* daring.

venue *n* place where an organized
gathering is held.

veracious *adj* habitually truthful. **veracity**
n

verandah, veranda *n* open porch
attached to a house.

vehicle *n* 1 = **transport**, conveyance,
transportation 2 = **medium**, apparatus,
channel, means, mechanism, organ

veil *n* 1 = **cover**, blind, cloak, curtain,
disguise, film, mask, screen, shroud ◆ *v*
3 = **cover**, cloak, conceal, disguise, hide,
mask, obscure, screen, shield ≠ **reveal**

vein *n* 1 = **blood vessel** 3 = **seam**, lode,
stratum 4 = **streak**, stripe 6 = **mood**,
mode, note, style, temper, tenor, tone

velocity *n* = **speed**, pace, quickness,
rapidity, swiftness

vendetta *n* 2 = **feud**, bad blood, quarrel

veneer *n* 1 = **layer**, finish, gloss 2 = **mask**,
appearance, facade, front, guise, pretence,
semblance, show

venerable *adj* = **respected**, august,

esteemed, honoured, revered, sage, wise,
worshipped

vengeance *n* = **revenge**, reprisal, requital,
retaliation, retribution ≠ **pardon**

venom *n* 1 = **malice**, acrimony, bitterness,
hate, rancour, spite, spleen, virulence
≠ **love** 2 = **poison**, bane, toxin

vent *n* 1 = **outlet**, aperture, duct, opening,
orifice ◆ *v* 2 = **express**, air, discharge,
emit, give vent to, pour out, release, utter,
voice ≠ **repress**

venture *n* 1 = **undertaking**, adventure,
endeavour, enterprise, gamble, hazard,
project, risk ◆ *v* 2 = **risk**, chance, hazard,
speculate, stake, wager 3 = **dare**, hazard,
make bold, presume, take the liberty,
volunteer 4 = **go**, embark on, plunge into,

verb n word that expresses the idea of action, happening, or being. **verbal** adj **1** spoken. **2** of a verb. **verbally** adv **verbalize** v express (something) in words

verbose ❼ [verb–**bohss**] adj speaking at tedious length. **verbosity** n

verdant ❼ adj Lit covered in green vegetation.

verdict ❼ n **1** decision of a jury. **2** opinion formed after examining the facts.

verge ❼ n grass border along a road. **on the verge of** having almost reached (a point or condition). **verge on** v be near to (a condition).

verger n C of E church caretaker.

verify ❼ v **–ifying, –ified** check the truth or accuracy of. **verifiable** adj **verification** n

veritable adj rightly called, without exaggeration, e.g. a veritable feast. **veritably** adv

vermilion adj orange–red.

vermin pl n animals, esp. insects and rodents, that spread disease or cause damage. **verminous** adj

vernacular ❼ [ver–**nak**–yew–lar] n most widely spoken language of a particular people or place.

verruca [ver–**roo**–ka] n wart, usu. on the foot.

versatile ❼ adj having many skills or uses.

versatility n

verse n **1** group of lines forming part of a song or poem. **2** poetry as distinct from prose. **3** subdivision of a chapter of the Bible. **versed in** knowledgeable about. **versify** v write in verse. **versification** n

version ❼ n **1** form of something, such as a piece of writing, with some differences from other forms. **2** account of an incident from a particular point of view.

versus prep **1** in opposition to or in contrast with. **2** Sport, Law against.

vertebra n, pl **vertebrae** one of the bones that form the spine. **vertebral** adj **vertebrate** n, adj (animal) having a spine.

vertical ❼ adj **1** straight up and down. ◆ n **2** vertical direction.

vertigo ❼ n dizziness, usu. when looking down from a high place. **vertiginous** adj

verve ❼ n enthusiasm or liveliness.

very adv **1** more than usually, extremely. ◆ adj **2** absolute, exact, e.g. the very top; the very man.

vespers pl n RC Church (service of) evening prayer.

vessel ❼ n **1** ship. **2** Lit container, esp. for liquids. **3** Biol tubular structure in animals and plants that carries body fluids, such as blood or sap.

vest ❼ n **1** undergarment worn on the top

——————— THESAURUS ———————

set out

verbose adj = **long–winded**, circumlocutory, diffuse, periphrastic, prolix, tautological, windy, wordy

verdant adj Lit = **green**, flourishing, fresh, grassy, leafy, lush

verdict n = **decision**, adjudication, conclusion, finding, judgment, opinion, sentence

verge n = **border**, boundary, brim, brink, edge, limit, margin, threshold **verge on** ◆ v = **come near to**, approach, border

verify v = **check**, authenticate, bear out, confirm, corroborate, prove, substantiate, support, validate ≠ **deny**

vernacular n **1** = **dialect**, idiom, parlance, patois, speech

versatile adj = **adaptable**, adjustable, all purpose, all–round, flexible, multifaceted, resourceful, variable ≠ **limited**

version n **1 a** = **form**, design, model, style, variant **1 b** = **adaptation**, portrayal, rendering **2** = **account**, interpretation

vertical adj **1** = **upright**, erect, on end, perpendicular

vertigo n = **dizziness**, giddiness, light–headedness

verve n = **enthusiasm**, animation, energy, gusto, liveliness, sparkle, spirit, vitality

very adv **1** = **extremely**, acutely, decidedly, deeply, exceedingly, greatly, highly, profoundly, really, uncommonly, unusually ◆ adj **2** = **exact**, precise, selfsame

vessel n **1** = **ship**, boat, craft **2** Lit

half of the body. **2** *US & Aust* waistcoat. ♦
v **3** (foll. by *in* or *with*) give (authority) to
(someone). **vested interest** interest
someone has in a matter because he or
she might benefit from it.

vestibule ⊕ *n* small entrance hall.

vestige ⊕ [**vest**–ij] *n* small amount or
trace. **vestigial** *adj*

vestry *n, pl* **–tries** room in a church used as
an office by the priest or minister.

vet ⊕ *n* **1** short for VETERINARY SURGEON. ♦ *v*
vetting, vetted 2 check the suitability of.

veteran ⊕ *n* **1** person with much
experience in a particular activity, esp.
military service. ♦ *adj* **2** long–serving.

veterinary *adj* concerning animal health.
veterinary surgeon medical specialist who
treats sick animals.

veto ⊕ *n, pl* **–toes 1** official power to
cancel a proposal. ♦ *v* **–toing, –toed 2**
enforce a veto against.

vex ⊕ *v* frustrate, annoy. **vexation** *n* **1**
something annoying. **2** being annoyed.
vexatious *adj* **vexed question** much
debated subject.

VHF very high frequency: radio frequency
band between 30 and 300 MHz.

VI Vancouver Island.

via *prep* by way of.

viable ⊕ *adj* **1** able to be put into practice.
2 *Biol* able to live and grow independently.
viability *n*

viaduct *n* bridge over a valley.

vibrate ⊕ *v* **1** move back and forth rapidly.
2 (cause to) resonate. **vibration** *n* **vibrator**
n device that produces vibratory motion,
used for massage or as a sex aid.

VIC Victoria (Australian state).

vicar *n* C of E clergyman in charge of a
parish. **vicarage** *n* vicar's house.

vicarious ⊕ [vick–**air**–ee–uss] *adj* **1** felt
indirectly by imagining what another
person experiences. **2** delegated.
vicariously *adv*

vice[1] ⊕ *n* **1** immoral or evil habit or action.
2 habit regarded as a weakness in
someone's character. **3** criminal
immorality, esp. involving sex.

vice[2] *n* tool with a pair of jaws for holding
an object while working on it.

vice[3] *adj* serving in place of.

viceroy *n* governor of a colony who
represents the monarch.

vice versa ⊕ [**vie**–see **ver**–sa] *adv Latin*
conversely, the other way round.

vicinity ⊕ [viss–**in**–it–ee] *n* surrounding

THESAURUS

= **container**, pot, receptacle, utensil

vest *v* **3** (foll. by *in* or *with*) = **place in**,
bestow upon, confer on, consign to,
endow with, entrust with, invest with,
settle on

vestibule *n* = **hall**, anteroom, foyer, lobby,
porch, portico

vestige *n* = **trace**, glimmer, indication,
remnant, scrap, suspicion

vet *v* **2** = **check**, appraise, examine,
investigate, review, scrutinize

veteran *n* **1** = **old hand**, old stager, past
master, warhorse (*inf*) ≠ **novice** ♦ *adj*
2 = **long–serving**, battle–scarred, old,
seasoned

veto *n* **1** = **ban**, boycott, embargo,
interdict, prohibition ≠ **approval** ♦ *v*
2 = **ban**, boycott, disallow, forbid,
prohibit, reject, rule out, turn down

≠ **pass**

vex *v* = **annoy**, bother, distress, exasperate,
irritate, plague, trouble, upset, worry

viable *adj* **1** = **workable**, applicable,
feasible, operable, practicable, usable

vibrate *v* **1** = **shake**, fluctuate, judder (*inf*),
oscillate, pulsate, quiver, sway, throb,
tremble **2** = **reverberate**

vicarious *adj* **1** = **indirect**, at one remove,
substituted, surrogate **2** = **delegated**,
deputed

vice[1] *n* **1** = **wickedness**, corruption,
depravity, evil, immorality, iniquity, sin,
turpitude ≠ **virtue 2** = **fault**, blemish,
defect, failing, imperfection, shortcoming,
weakness

vice versa *adv Latin* = **conversely**,
contrariwise, in reverse, the other way
round

area.

vicious ❶ *adj* cruel and violent. **vicious circle, cycle** situation in which an attempt to resolve one problem creates new problems that recreate the original one.

victim ❶ *n* person or thing harmed or killed. **victimize** *v* 1 punish unfairly. 2 discriminate against. **victimization** *n*

victor ❶ *n* person who has defeated an opponent, esp. in war or in sport. **victorious** *adj* **victory** *n* winning of a battle or contest.

video *n, pl* **–os** 1 short for VIDEO CASSETTE (RECORDER). ♦ *v* **videoing, videoed** 2 record (a TV programme or event) on video. ♦ *adj* 3 relating to or used in producing television images.

vie ❶ *v* **vying, vied** compete (with someone).

view ❶ *n* 1 opinion or belief. 2 everything that can be seen from a given place. 3 picture of this. ♦ *v* 4 think of (something) in a particular way. 5 **in view of** taking into consideration. **on view** exhibited to the public. **viewer** *n* 1 person who watches television. 2 hand-held device for looking at photographic slides. **viewfinder** *n* window on a camera showing what will appear in a photograph.

vigil [**vij**–ill] *n* night–time period of staying awake to look after a sick person, pray, etc. **vigilant** *adj* watchful in case of danger. **vigilance** *n*

vigilante [vij–ill–**ant**–ee] *n* person, esp. as one of a group, who takes it upon himself or herself to enforce the law.

vignette [vin–**yet**] *n* 1 concise description of the typical features of something. 2 small decorative illustration in a book.

vigour ❶ *n* physical or mental energy. **vigorous** *adj* **vigorously** *adv*

vile ❶ *adj* 1 very wicked. 2 disgusting. **vilely** *adv* **vileness** *n*

vilify ❶ *v* **–ifying, –ified** attack the character of. **vilification** *n*

villa *n* 1 large house with gardens. 2 holiday home, usu. in the Mediterranean.

village *n* 1 small group of houses in a country area. 2 rural community. **villager** *n*

villain ❶ *n* 1 wicked person. 2 main wicked character in a play. **villainous** *adj* **villainy** *n*

vindicate ❶ *v* 1 clear (someone) of guilt. 2 provide justification for. **vindication** *n*

vindictive ❶ *adj* maliciously seeking revenge. **vindictiveness** *n* **vindictively** *adv*

vine *n* climbing plant, esp. one producing

THESAURUS

vicinity *n* = **neighbourhood**, area, district, environs, locality, neck of the woods (*inf*), proximity

vicious *adj* a = **malicious**, cruel, mean, spiteful, venomous, vindictive b = **savage**, barbarous, cruel, ferocious, violent ≠ **kind**

victim *n* 1 = **casualty**, fatality, sufferer ≠ **survivor** 2 = **sacrifice**, martyr, scapegoat

victor *n* = **winner**, champion, conqueror, prizewinner, vanquisher

vie *v* = **compete**, contend, strive, struggle

view *n* 1 = **opinion**, attitude, belief, conviction, feeling, point of view, sentiment 2 = **impression** 3 = **scene**, landscape, outlook, panorama, perspective, picture, prospect, spectacle, vista ♦ *v* 5 = **regard**, consider, deem, look on

vigour *n* = **energy**, animation, dynamism, forcefulness, gusto, liveliness, power, spirit, strength, verve, vitality

vile *adj* 1 = **wicked**, corrupt, degenerate, depraved, evil, nefarious, perverted ≠ **pure** 2 = **disgusting**, foul, horrid, nasty, nauseating, offensive, repugnant, repulsive, revolting, sickening ≠ **lovely**

vilify *v* = **malign**, abuse, berate, denigrate, disparage, revile, slander, smear

villain *n* 1 = **evildoer**, blackguard, criminal, miscreant, reprobate, rogue, scoundrel, wretch ≠ **hero** 2 = **antihero**, baddy (*inf*)

vindicate *v* 1 = **clear**, absolve, acquit, exculpate, exonerate, rehabilitate ≠ **accuse** 2 = **justify**, defend, excuse

vindictive *adj* = **vengeful**, implacable, malicious, resentful, revengeful, spiteful,

grapes. **vineyard** [**vinn**–yard] n plantation
of grape vines, esp. for making wine.

vinegar n acid liquid made from wine,
beer, or cider. **vinegary** adj

vintage ❶ n 1 wine from a particular
harvest of grapes. ◆ adj 2 best and most
typical.

vinyl [**vine**–ill] n type of plastic, used in
mock leather and records.

viola [vee–**oh**–la] n stringed instrument
lower in pitch than a violin.

violate ❶ v 1 break (a law or agreement).
2 disturb (someone's privacy). 3 treat (a
sacred place) disrespectfully. 4 rape.
violation n **violator** n

violence ❶ n 1 use of physical force, usu.
intended to cause injury or destruction. 2
great force or strength in action, feeling,
or expression. **violent** adj **violently** adv

violet n 1 plant with bluish–purple flowers.
◆ adj 2 bluish–purple.

violin n small four–stringed musical
instrument played with a bow. **violinist** n

VIP ❶ very important person.

viper n poisonous snake.

viral adj of or caused by a virus.

virgin ❶ n 1 person, esp. a woman, who
has not had sexual intercourse. ◆ adj 2 not
having had sexual intercourse. 3 not yet
exploited or explored. **virginal** adj 1 like a

virgin. ◆ n 2 early keyboard instrument like
a small harpsichord. **virginity** n

virile ❶ adj having the traditional male
characteristics of physical strength and a
high sex drive. **virility** n

virtue ❶ n 1 moral goodness. 2 positive
moral quality. 3 merit. **by virtue of** by
reason of. **virtuous** adj morally good.

virtuoso ❶ n, pl –sos, –si person with
impressive esp. musical skill. **virtuosity** n

virulent ❶ [**vir**–yew–lent] adj 1 very
infectious. 2 violently harmful.

virus n 1 microorganism that causes
disease in humans, animals, and plants. 2
Computers program that propagates itself,
via disks and electronic networks, to cause
disruption.

visa n permission to enter a country,
granted by its government and shown by
a stamp on one's passport.

visage [**viz**–zij] n Lit face.

vis-à-vis [veez–ah–**vee**] prep in relation to,
regarding.

viscount [**vie**–count] n British nobleman
ranking between an earl and a baron.

viscous ❶ adj thick and sticky. **viscosity** n

visible ❶ adj 1 able to be seen. 2 able to
be perceived by the mind. **visibly** adv
visibility n range or clarity of vision.

vision ❶ n 1 ability to see. 2 mental image

——————| THESAURUS |——————

unforgiving, unrelenting

vintage adj 2 = **best**, choice, classic, prime,
select, superior

violate v 1 = **break**, contravene, disobey,
disregard, infringe, transgress ≠ **respect**
2 = **encroach upon** 3 = **desecrate**, abuse,
befoul, defile, dishonour, pollute, profane
≠ **honour** 4 = **rape**, abuse, assault,
debauch, ravish

violence n 1 = **force**, bloodshed, brutality,
cruelty, ferocity, fighting, savagery,
terrorism 2 = **intensity**, abandon, fervour,
force, severity, vehemence

VIP n = **celebrity**, big hitter (*inf*), big name,
heavy hitter (*inf*), luminary, personality,
somebody, star

virgin n 1 = **maiden** (*arch*), girl ◆ adj

2 = **pure**, chaste, immaculate,
uncorrupted, undefiled, vestal, virginal
≠ **corrupted**

virile adj = **manly**, lusty, macho, manlike,
masculine, red–blooded, strong, vigorous

virtue n 1, 2 = **goodness**, incorruptibility,
integrity, morality, probity, rectitude,
righteousness, uprightness, worth ≠ **vice**
3 = **merit**, advantage, asset, attribute,
credit, good point, plus (*inf*), strength
≠ **failing**

virtuoso n = **master**, artist, genius,
maestro, magician

virulent adj 2 = **deadly**, lethal, pernicious,
poisonous, toxic, venomous ≠ **harmless**

viscous adj = **thick**, gelatinous, sticky,
syrupy

of something. **3** foresight. **4** hallucination. **visionary** *adj* **1** showing foresight. **2** idealistic but impractical. ◆ *n* **3** visionary person.

visit ❶ *v* –iting, –ited **1** go or come to see. **2** stay temporarily with. **3** (foll. by *upon*) *Lit* afflict. ◆ *n* **4** instance of visiting. **5** official call. **visitor** *n* **visitation** *n* **1** formal visit or inspection. **2** catastrophe seen as divine punishment.

visor [**vize**–or] *n* **1** transparent part of a helmet that pulls down over the face. **2** eyeshade, esp. in a car. **3** peak on a cap.

vista ❶ *n* (beautiful) extensive view.

visual ❶ *adj* **1** done by or used in seeing. **2** designed to be looked at. **visualize** *v* form a mental image of. **visualization** *n* **visual display unit** device with a screen for displaying data held in a computer.

vital ❶ *adj* **1** essential or highly important. **2** lively. **3** necessary to maintain life. **vitals** *pl n* bodily organs necessary to maintain life. **vitally** *adv* **vitality** *n* physical or mental energy. **vital statistics 1** statistics of births, deaths, and marriages. **2** *Informal* woman's bust, waist, and hip measurements.

vitamin *n* one of a group of substances that are essential in the diet for specific body processes.

viva *Interj* long live (a person or thing).

vivacious ❶ *adj* full of energy and enthusiasm. **vivacity** *n*

vivid ❶ *adj* **1** very bright. **2** conveying images that are true to life. **vividly** *adv* **vividness** *n*

vivisection *n* performing surgical experiments on living animals. **vivisectionist** *n*

vixen *n* **1** female fox. **2** *Informal* spiteful woman.

vizor *n* same as VISOR.

vocabulary ❶ *n, pl* –aries **1** all the words that a person knows. **2** all the words in a language. **3** specialist terms used in a given subject. **4** list of words in another language with their translation.

vocal ❶ *adj* **1** relating to the voice. **2** outspoken. **vocals** *pl n* singing part of a piece of pop music. **vocally** *adv* **vocalist** *n* singer. **vocalize** *v* express with or use the voice. **vocalization** *n* **vocal cords** membranes in the larynx that vibrate to produce sound.

THESAURUS

visible *adj* **1 = apparent**, clear, discernible, evident, in view, manifest, observable, perceptible, unconcealed

vision *n* **1 = sight**, eyesight, perception, seeing, view **2 = image**, concept, conception, daydream, dream, fantasy, idea, ideal **3 = foresight**, discernment, farsightedness, imagination, insight, intuition, penetration, prescience **4 = hallucination**, apparition, chimera, delusion, illusion, mirage, revelation

visit *v* **1 = call on**, drop in on (*inf*), look (someone) up, stop by **2 = stay with** ◆ *n* **4 = call**, sojourn, stay, stop

vista *n* **= view**, panorama, perspective, prospect

visual *adj* **1 = optical**, ocular, optic **2 = observable**, discernible, perceptible, visible ≠ **invisible**

vital *adj* **1 = essential**, basic, fundamental,

imperative, indispensable, necessary, requisite ≠ **unnecessary 2 = lively**, animated, dynamic, energetic, spirited, vibrant, vigorous, vivacious, zestful ≠ **lethargic 3 = important**, critical, crucial, decisive, key, life–or–death, significant, urgent

vivacious *adj* **= lively**, bubbling, ebullient, high–spirited, sparkling, spirited, sprightly, upbeat (*inf*), vital

vivid *adj* **1 = bright**, brilliant, clear, colourful, glowing, intense, rich ≠ **dull 2 = clear**, dramatic, graphic, lifelike, memorable, powerful, realistic, stirring, telling, true to life ≠ **vague**

vocabulary *n* **2 = words**, dictionary, glossary, language, lexicon

vocal *adj* **1 = spoken**, oral, said, uttered, voiced **2 = outspoken**, articulate, eloquent, expressive, forthright, frank,

vocation ❶ *n* 1 profession or trade. 2 occupation that someone feels called to. **vocational** *adj* directed towards a particular profession or trade.

vociferous ❶ *adj* shouting, noisy.

vodka *n* (Russian) spirit distilled from potatoes or grain.

vogue ❶ *n* 1 popular style. 2 period of popularity.

voice ❶ *n* 1 (quality of) sound made when speaking or singing. 2 expression of opinion by a person or group. 3 property of verbs that makes them active or passive. ◆ *v* 4 express verbally. **voiceless** *adj* **voice-over** *n* film commentary spoken by someone off-camera.

void ❶ *adj* 1 not legally binding. 2 empty. ◆ *n* 3 empty space. ◆ *v* 4 make invalid. 5 empty.

vol. volume.

volatile ❶ *adj* 1 liable to sudden change, esp. in behaviour. 2 evaporating quickly. **volatility** *n*

volcano *n, pl* **-noes, -nos** mountain with a vent through which lava is ejected. **volcanic** *adj*

vole *n* small rodent.

volition ❶ *n* ability to decide things for oneself. **of one's own volition** through one's own choice.

volley ❶ *n* 1 simultaneous discharge of ammunition. 2 burst of questions or critical comments. 3 *Sport* stroke or kick at a moving ball before it hits the ground. ◆ *v* 4 discharge (ammunition) in a volley. 5 hit or kick (a ball) in a volley. **volleyball** *n* team game where a ball is hit with the hands over a high net.

volt *n* unit of electric potential. **voltage** *n* electric potential difference expressed in volts. **voltmeter** *n* instrument for measuring voltage.

voluble ❶ *adj* talking easily and at length. **volubility** *n* **volubly** *adv*

volume ❶ *n* 1 size of the space occupied by something. 2 amount. 3 loudness of sound. 4 book, esp. one of a series. **voluminous** *adj* 1 (of clothes) large and roomy. 2 (of writings) extensive.

voluntary ❶ *adj* 1 done by choice. 2 done or maintained without payment. 3 (of muscles) controlled by the will. ◆ *n, pl* **-taries** 4 organ solo in a church service. **voluntarily** *adv*

THESAURUS

plain-spoken, strident, vociferous ≠ **reserved**

vocation *n* 1 = **profession**, career, job, pursuit, trade 2 = **calling**, mission

vociferous *adj* = **noisy**, clamorous, loud, outspoken, strident, uproarious, vehement, vocal

vogue *n* 1 = **fashion**, craze, custom, mode, style, trend, way **in vogue** = **popular**, accepted, current, in favour, in use, prevalent

voice *n* 1 = **sound**, articulation, tone, utterance 2 = **say**, view, vote, will, wish ◆ *v* 4 = **express**, air, articulate, declare, enunciate, utter

void *adj* 1 = **invalid**, ineffective, inoperative, null and void, useless, vain, worthless 2 = **empty**, bare, free, tenantless, unfilled, unoccupied, vacant ◆ *n* 3 = **emptiness**, blankness, gap, lack, space, vacuity,

vacuum ◆ *v* 4 = **invalidate**, cancel, nullify, rescind 5 = **empty**, drain, evacuate

volatile *adj* 1 a = **changeable**, erratic, explosive, inconstant, unsettled, unstable, unsteady, up and down (*inf*), variable ≠ **stable** b = **temperamental**, fickle, mercurial ≠ **calm**

volition *n* = **free will**, choice, choosing, discretion, preference, will

volley *n* 1 = **barrage**, blast, bombardment, burst, cannonade, fusillade, hail, salvo, shower

voluble *adj* = **talkative**, articulate, fluent, forthcoming, glib, loquacious

volume *n* 1 = **capacity**, compass, dimensions 2 = **amount**, aggregate, body, bulk, mass, quantity, total 4 = **book**, publication, title, tome, treatise

voluntary *adj* 1 = **unforced**, optional, spontaneous, willing ≠ **forced**

voluptuous ⊕ *adj* **1** (of a woman) sexually alluring through fullness of figure. **2** sensually pleasurable. **voluptuary** *n* person devoted to sensual pleasures.

vomit *v* –iting, –ited **1** eject (the contents of the stomach) through the mouth. ◆ *n* **2** matter vomited.

voodoo *n* religion involving ancestor worship and witchcraft, practised by Black people in the West Indies, esp. in Haiti.

voracious ⊕ *adj* **1** craving great quantities of food. **2** insatiably eager. **voracity** *n*

vortex ⊕ *n, pl* –texes, –tices whirlpool.

vote ⊕ *n* **1** choice made by a participant in a shared decision, esp. in electing a candidate. **2** right to this choice. **3** total number of votes cast. **4** collective voting power of a given group, e.g. *the Black vote.* ◆ *v* **5** make a choice by a vote. **6** authorize (something) by vote. **voter** *n*

vouch *v* **vouch for 1** give one's personal assurance about. **2** provide evidence for.

vow ⊕ *n* **1** solemn and binding promise. ◆ *pl* **2** formal promises made when marrying or entering a religious order. ◆ *v* **3** promise solemnly.

vowel *n* **1** speech sound made without obstructing the flow of breath. **2** letter representing this.

voyage ⊕ *n* **1** long journey by sea or in space. ◆ *v* **2** make a voyage. **voyager** *n*

VT Vermont.

vulcanize *v* strengthen (rubber) by treating it with sulphur. **vulcanization** *n*

vulgar ⊕ *adj* showing lack of good taste, decency, or refinement. **vulgarity** *n* **vulgarian** *n* vulgar (rich) person. **vulgarism** *n* coarse word or phrase. **vulgar fraction** simple fraction.

vulnerable ⊕ *adj* **1** liable to be physically or emotionally hurt. **2** exposed to attack. **vulnerability** *n*

vulture *n* large bird that feeds on the flesh of dead animals.

THESAURUS

2 = discretionary, free
voluptuous *adj* **1 = buxom**, ample, curvaceous (*inf*), enticing, seductive, shapely **2 = sensual**, epicurean, hedonistic, licentious, luxurious, self–indulgent, sybaritic ≠ **Spartan**
vomit *v* **1 = be sick**, disgorge, emit, heave, regurgitate, retch, spew out *or* up, throw up (*inf*)
voracious *adj* **1 = gluttonous**, greedy, hungry, insatiable, omnivorous, ravenous **2 = avid**, hungry, insatiable, rapacious, uncontrolled, unquenchable ≠ **moderate**
vortex *n* **1 = whirlpool**, eddy, maelstrom
vote *n* **1 = poll**, ballot, franchise, plebiscite,

referendum, show of hands ◆ *v* **5 = cast one's vote**, elect, opt
vow *n* **1 = promise**, oath, pledge ◆ *v* **3 = promise**, affirm, pledge, swear
voyage *n* **1 = journey**, crossing, cruise, passage, trip
vulgar *adj* **1 = crude**, coarse, common, impolite, indecent, ribald, risqué, rude, tasteless, uncouth, unrefined
vulnerable *adj* **1 = susceptible**, sensitive, tender, thin–skinned, weak ≠ **immune** **2 = exposed**, accessible, assailable, defenceless, unprotected, wide open ≠ **guarded**

W w

WA 1 Washington. 2 Western Australia.

wacky *adj* **wackier, wackiest** *Informal*
eccentric or funny.

wad ❶ *n* 1 small mass of soft material. 2
roll or bundle, esp. of banknotes. **wadding**
n soft material used for padding or
stuffing.

waddle ❶ *v* 1 walk with short swaying
steps. ◆ *n* 2 swaying walk.

wade ❶ *v* 1 walk with difficulty through
water or mud. 2 proceed with difficulty.
wader *n* 1 long–legged water bird. ◆ *pl* 2
angler's long waterproof boots.

wafer *n* 1 thin crisp biscuit. 2 thin disc of
unleavened bread used at Communion. 3
thin slice.

waffle[1] ❶ *Informal* ◆ *v* 1 speak or write in a
vague wordy way. ◆ *n* 2 vague wordy talk
or writing.

waffle[2] *n* square crisp pancake with a
gridlike pattern.

waft ❶ *v* 1 drift or carry gently through the
air. ◆ *n* 2 something wafted.

wag ❶ *v* **wagging, wagged** 1 move rapidly
from side to side. ◆ *n* 2 wagging
movement. 3 *Old–fashioned* humorous
witty person.

wage ❶ *n* 1 (often pl) payment for work
done, esp. when paid weekly. ◆ *v* 2
engage in (an activity).

wager ❶ *n, v* bet on the outcome of
something.

waggle ❶ *v* move with a rapid shaking or
wobbling motion.

wagon, waggon *n* 1 four–wheeled
vehicle for heavy loads. 2 railway freight
truck.

waif ❶ *n* young person who is, or seems,
homeless or neglected.

wail ❶ *v* 1 cry out in pain or misery. ◆ *n* 2
mournful cry.

waist *n* 1 part of the body between the

THESAURUS

wad *n* 1 = **mass**, hunk 2 = **roll**, bundle

waddle *v* 1 = **shuffle**, sway, toddle, totter,
wobble

wade *v* 1 = **walk through**, ford, paddle,
splash 2 = **plough through**, drudge at,
labour at, peg away at, toil at, work one's
way through

waffle[1] *v* 1 *Inf* = **prattle**, blather, jabber,
prate, rabbit (on) (*Brit inf*), witter on (*inf*) ◆
n 2 = **verbosity**, padding, prolixity,
verbiage, wordiness

waft *v* 1 = **carry**, bear, convey, drift, float,
transport

wag *v* 1 = **wave**, bob, nod, quiver, shake,
stir, vibrate, waggle, wiggle ◆ *n* 2 = **wave**,
bob, nod, quiver, shake, vibration,
waggle, wiggle 3 *Old–fashioned* = **joker**,

card (*inf*), clown, comedian, comic,
humorist, jester, wit

wage *n* 1 (often pl) = **payment**, allowance,
emolument, fee, pay, recompense,
remuneration, reward, stipend ◆ *v*
2 = **engage in**, carry on, conduct, practise,
proceed with, prosecute, pursue,
undertake

① **wager** *n* = **bet**, flutter (*Brit inf*), gamble,
punt (*chiefly Brit*)

② **wager** *v* = **bet**, chance, gamble, lay,
risk, speculate, stake, venture

waggle *v* = **wag**, flutter, oscillate, shake,
wave, wiggle, wobble

waif *n* = **stray**, foundling, orphan

wail *v* 1 = **cry**, bawl, grieve, howl, lament,
weep, yowl ◆ *n* 2 = **cry**, complaint, howl,

ribs and hips. **2** narrow middle part.
waistband *n* band of material sewn on to the waist of a garment to strengthen it.
waistcoat *n* sleeveless garment which buttons up the front, usu. worn over a shirt and under a jacket. **waistline** *n* (size of) the waist of a person or garment.
wait �go *v* **1** remain inactive in expectation (of something). **2** be ready (for something). **3** delay or be delayed. **4** serve in a restaurant etc. ◆ *n* **5** act or period of waiting. **waiter** *n* man who serves in a restaurant etc. **waitress** *n fem*
waive ⓖ *v* refrain from enforcing (a law, right, etc.). **waiver** *n* (written statement of) this act.
wake¹ ⓖ *v* **waking, woke, woken 1** rouse from sleep or inactivity. ◆ *n* **2** vigil beside a corpse the night before the funeral. **waken** *v* wake. **wakeful** *adj*
wake² ⓖ *n* track left by a moving ship. **in the wake of** following, often as a result.
walk ⓖ *v* **1** move on foot with at least one foot always on the ground. **2** pass through or over on foot. **3** escort or accompany on foot. ◆ *n* **4** act or instance of walking. **5** distance walked. **6** manner of walking. **7** place or route for walking. **walk of life** social position or profession. **walker** *n*

walkabout *n* informal walk among the public by royalty etc. **walkie-talkie** *n* portable radio transmitter and receiver. **walking stick** stick used as a support when walking. **walk into** *v* meet with unwittingly. **Walkman** *n* ® small portable cassette player with headphones. **walkout** *n* **1** strike. **2** act of leaving as a protest. **walkover** *n* easy victory.
wall ⓖ *n* **1** structure of brick, stone, etc. used to enclose, divide, or support. **2** something having the function or effect of a wall. ◆ *v* **3** enclose or seal with a wall or walls. **wallflower** *n* **1** fragrant garden plant. **2** (at a dance) woman who remains seated because she has no partner. **wallpaper** *n* decorative paper to cover interior walls.
wallaby *n, pl* **-bies** marsupial like a small kangaroo.
wallet ⓖ *n* small folding case for paper money, documents, etc.
wallop ⓖ *Informal* ◆ *v* **-loping, -loped 1** hit hard. ◆ *n* **2** hard blow. **walloping** *Informal* ◆ *n* **1** thrashing. ◆ *adj* **2** large or great.
wallow ⓖ *v* **1** revel in an emotion. **2** roll in liquid or mud. ◆ *n* **3** act or instance of wallowing.

lament, moan, weeping, yowl
wait *v* **1** = **remain**, hang fire, hold back, linger, pause, rest, stay, tarry ≠ **go** ◆ *n* **3** = **delay**, halt, hold-up, interval, pause, rest, stay
waive *v* = **set aside**, abandon, dispense with, forgo, give up, relinquish, remit, renounce ≠ **claim**
wake¹ *v* **1** a = **awaken**, arise, awake, bestir, come to, get up, rouse, stir ≠ **sleep** b = **activate**, animate, arouse, excite, fire, galvanize, kindle, provoke, stimulate, stir up ◆ *n* **2** = **vigil**, deathwatch, funeral, watch
wake² *n* = **slipstream**, aftermath, backwash, path, track, trail, train, wash, waves
walk *v* **1, 2** = **go**, amble, hike, march,

move, pace, step, stride, stroll **3** = **escort**, accompany, convoy, take ◆ *n* **4** = **stroll**, hike, march, promenade, ramble, saunter, trek, trudge **6** = **gait**, carriage, step **7** = **path**, alley, avenue, esplanade, footpath, lane, promenade, trail **walk of life** = **profession**, calling, career, field, line, trade, vocation
wall *n* **1** = **partition**, enclosure, screen **2** = **barrier**, fence, hedge, impediment, obstacle, obstruction
wallet *n* = **holder**, case, pouch, purse
wallop *Inf v* **1** = **hit**, batter, beat, clobber (*sl*), pound, pummel, strike, swipe, thrash, thump, whack ◆ *n* **2** = **blow**, bash, punch, slug, smack, swipe, thump, thwack, whack
wallow *v* **1** = **revel**, bask, delight, glory, luxuriate, relish, take pleasure ≠ **avoid**

walnut *n* **1** edible nut with a wrinkled shell. **2** tree it grows on. **3** its wood, used for making furniture.

walrus *n, pl* **–ruses, –rus** large sea mammal with long tusks.

waltz *n* **1** ballroom dance. **2** music for this. ◆ *v* **3** dance a waltz. **4** *Informal* move in a relaxed confident way.

wan ❶ [rhymes with **swan**] *adj* **wanner, wannest** pale and sickly looking.

wand ❶ *n* thin rod, esp. one used in performing magic tricks.

wander ❶ *v* **1** move about without a definite destination or aim. **2** go astray, deviate. ◆ *n* **3** act or instance of wandering. **wanderer** *n* **wanderlust** *n* great desire to travel.

wane ❶ *v* **1** decrease gradually in size or strength. **2** (of the moon) decrease in size. **on the wane** decreasing in size, strength, or power.

wangle ❶ *v* *Informal* get by devious methods.

want ❶ *v* **1** need or long for. **2** desire or wish. ◆ *n* **3** act or instance of wanting. **4** thing wanted. **5** lack or absence. **6** state of being in need, poverty. **wanted** *adj* sought by the police. **wanting** *adj* **1** lacking. **2** not good enough.

wanton ❶ *adj* **1** without motive, provocation, or justification. **2** *Old–fashioned* (of a woman) sexually unrestrained or immodest.

war ❶ *n* **1** fighting between nations. **2** conflict or contest. ◆ *adj* **3** of, like, or caused by war. ◆ *v* **warring, warred 4** conduct a war. **warring** *adj* **warlike** *adj* **1** of or relating to war. **2** hostile and eager to have a war. **3** **warfare** *n* fighting or hostilities. **warhead** *n* explosive front part of a missile. **warmonger** *n* person who encourages war. **warship** *n* ship designed and equipped for naval combat.

warble ❶ *v* sing in a trilling voice. **warbler** *n* any of various small songbirds.

ward ❶ *n* **1** room in a hospital for patients needing a similar kind of care. **2** electoral division of a town. **3** child under the care of a guardian or court. **warder** *n* prison officer. **wardress** *n fem* **ward off** *v* avert or repel. **wardroom** *n* officers' quarters on a warship.

THESAURUS

2 = **roll about**, splash around

wan *adj* = **pale**, anaemic, ashen, pallid, pasty, sickly, washed out, white

wand *n* = **stick**, baton, rod

wander *v* **1** = **roam**, drift, meander, ramble, range, rove, stray, stroll
2 = **deviate**, depart, digress, diverge, err, go astray, swerve, veer ◆ *n* **3** = **excursion**, cruise, meander, ramble

wane *v* **1** = **decline**, decrease, diminish, dwindle, ebb, fade, fail, lessen, subside, taper off, weaken ≠ **rise on the wane** = **declining**, dwindling, ebbing, fading, obsolescent, on the decline, tapering off, weakening

wangle *v Inf* = **contrive**, arrange, engineer, fiddle (*inf*), fix (*inf*), manipulate, manoeuvre, pull off

want *v* **1** = **need**, call for, demand, lack, miss, require **2** = **desire**, covet, crave, hanker after, hope for, hunger for, long for, thirst for, wish, yearn for ≠ **have** ◆ *n* **3** = **wish**, appetite, craving, desire, longing, need, requirement, yearning **5** = **lack**, absence, dearth, deficiency, famine, insufficiency, paucity, scarcity, shortage ≠ **plenty 6** = **poverty**, destitution, neediness, penury, privation ≠ **ease**

wanton *adj* **1** = **unprovoked**, arbitrary, gratuitous, groundless, motiveless, needless, senseless, uncalled-for, unjustifiable, wilful ≠ **justified 3** *Old–fashioned* = **promiscuous**, dissipated, dissolute, immoral, lecherous, libidinous, loose, lustful, shameless, unchaste ≠ **prudish**

war *n* **1, 2** = **fighting**, battle, combat, conflict, enmity, hostilities, struggle, warfare ≠ **peace** ◆ *v* **4** = **fight**, battle, campaign against, clash, combat, take up arms, wage war ≠ **co–operate**

warble *v* = **sing**, chirp, trill, twitter

warden ❶ *n* 1 person in charge of a building and its occupants. 2 official responsible for the enforcement of regulations.

wardrobe ❶ *n* 1 cupboard for hanging clothes in. 2 person's collection of clothes. 3 costumes of a theatrical company.

ware *n* 1 articles of a specified type or material, e.g. *silverware.* ◆ *pl* 2 goods for sale. **warehouse** *n* building for storing goods prior to sale or distribution.

warm ❶ *adj* 1 moderately hot. 2 providing warmth. 3 (of a colour) predominantly yellow or red. 4 affectionate. 5 enthusiastic. ◆ *v* 6 make or become warm. **warmth** *n* 1 mild heat. 2 cordiality. 3 intensity of emotion. 4 **warm up** *v* 1 make or become warmer. 2 do preliminary exercises before a race or more strenuous exercise. 3 make or become more lively. **warm–up** *n*

warn ❶ *v* 1 make aware of possible danger or harm. 2 caution or scold. 3 inform (someone) in advance. **warning** *n* 1 something that warns. 2 scolding or caution. **warn off** *v* advise (someone) not to become involved with.

warp ❶ *v* 1 twist out of shape. 2 pervert. ◆ *n* 3 state of being warped. 4 lengthwise threads on a loom.

warrant ❶ *n* 1 (document giving) official authorization. ◆ *v* 2 make necessary. 3 guarantee. **warranty** *n, pl* –ties (document giving) a guarantee. **warrant officer** officer in certain armed services with a rank between a commissioned and noncommissioned officer.

warren *n* 1 series of burrows in which rabbits live. 2 overcrowded building or part of a town.

warrigal *Aust* ◆ *n* 1 dingo. ◆ *adj* 2 wild.

warrior ❶ *n* person who fights in a war.

wart *n* small hard growth on the skin. **wart hog** kind of African wild pig.

wary ❶ [ware–ree] *adj* warier, wariest watchful or cautious. **warily** *adv* **wariness** *n*

was *v* first and third person singular past tense of BE.

wash ❶ *v* 1 clean (oneself, clothes, etc.) with water and usu. soap. 2 be washable. 3 flow or sweep over or against. 4 *Informal* be believable or acceptable, e.g. *that excuse won't wash.* ◆ *n* 5 act or process of washing. 6 clothes washed at one time. 7 thin coat of paint. 8 disturbance in the water after a ship has passed by. **washable** *adj* **washer** *n* ring put under a nut or bolt or in a tap as a seal. **washing** *n* clothes to be washed. **washing–up** *n* (washing of) dishes and cutlery needing to be cleaned after a meal. **washout** *n*

THESAURUS

ward *n* 1 = **room**, apartment, cubicle 2 = **district**, area, division, precinct, quarter, zone 3 = **dependant**, charge, minor

warden *n* 1 = **keeper**, administrator, caretaker, curator, custodian, guardian, ranger, superintendent

wardrobe *n* 1 = **clothes cupboard**, closet 2 = **clothes**, apparel, attire

warm *adj* 1 = **heated**, balmy, lukewarm, pleasant, sunny, tepid, thermal ≠ **cool** 4 = **affectionate**, amorous, cordial, friendly, hospitable, kindly, loving, tender ≠ **cold** ◆ *v* 6 = **heat**, heat up, melt, thaw, warm up

warn *v* 1 = **alert**, tip off 2 = **caution**

3 = **forewarn**, advise, apprise, give notice, inform, make (someone) aware, notify

warp *v* 1 = **twist**, bend, contort, deform, distort ◆ *n* 3 = **twist**, bend, contortion, distortion, kink

warrant *n* 1 = **authorization**, authority, licence, mana (*NZ*), permission, permit, sanction ◆ *v* 2 = **call for**, demand, deserve, excuse, justify, license, necessitate, permit, require, sanction 3 = **guarantee**, affirm, attest, certify, declare, pledge, vouch for

warrior *n* = **soldier**, combatant, fighter, gladiator, man–at–arms

wary *adj* = **cautious**, alert, careful, chary, circumspect, distrustful, guarded, suspicious, vigilant, watchful ≠ **rash**

Informal complete failure. **1 wash up** *v* wash dishes and cutlery after a meal.

wasp *n* stinging insect with a slender black–and–yellow striped body. **waspish** *adj* bad–tempered.

waste ⊕ *v* **1** use pointlessly or thoughtlessly. **2** fail to take advantage of. ◆ *n* **3** act of wasting or state of being wasted. **4** anything wasted. **5** rubbish. ◆ *pl* **6** desert. ◆ *adj* **7** rejected as worthless or surplus to requirements. **8** not cultivated or inhabited. **waste away** (cause to) decline in health or strength. **wastage** *n* **1** loss by wear or waste. **2** reduction in size of a workforce by not filling vacancies. **wasteful** *adj* extravagant. **waster, wastrel** *n* layabout.

watch ⊕ *v* **1** look at closely. **2** guard or supervise. ◆ *n* **3** portable timepiece for the wrist or pocket. **4** (period of) watching. **5** sailor's spell of duty. **watchable** *adj* **watcher** *n* **watchful** *adj* vigilant or alert. **watchdog** *n* **1** dog kept to guard property. **2** person or group guarding against inefficiency or illegality. **watchman** *n* man employed to guard a building or property. **watchword** *n* word or phrase that sums up the attitude of a particular group.

water ⊕ *n* **1** clear colourless tasteless liquid that falls as rain and forms rivers etc. **2** body of water, such as a sea or lake. **3** level of the tide. **4** urine. ◆ *v* **5** put water on or into. **6** (of the eyes) fill with tears. **7** (of the mouth) salivate. **watery** *adj* **water closet** *Old–fashioned* (room containing) a toilet flushed by water. **watercolour** *n* **1** paint thinned with water. **2** painting done in this. **watercress** *n* edible plant growing in clear ponds and streams. **water down** *v* dilute, make less strong. **waterfall** *n* place where the waters of a river drop vertically. **waterfront** *n* part of a town alongside a body of water. **1 water lily** water plant with large floating leaves. **watermark** *n* faint translucent design in a sheet of paper. **watermelon** *n* melon with green skin and red flesh. **water polo** team game played by swimmers with a ball. **waterproof** *adj* **1** not letting water through. ◆ *n* **2** waterproof garment. ◆ *v* **3** make waterproof. **watershed** *n* **1** important period or factor serving as a dividing line. **2** line separating two river systems. **water–skiing** *n* sport of riding over water on skis towed by a speedboat. **watertight** *adj* **1** not letting water through. **2** with no loopholes or weak points.

watt [wott] *n* unit of power. **wattage** *n* electrical power expressed in watts.

wave ⊕ *v* **1** move the hand to and fro as a

wash *v* **1** = **clean**, bathe, cleanse, launder, rinse, scrub **3** = **sweep away**, bear away, carry off, move **4** *Inf* = **be plausible**, bear scrutiny, be convincing, carry weight, hold up, hold water, stand up, stick ◆ *n* **5** = **cleaning**, cleansing, laundering, rinse, scrub **7** = **coat**, coating, film, layer, overlay **8** = **swell**, surge, wave

waste *v* **1** = **squander**, blow (*sl*), dissipate, fritter away, lavish, misuse, throw away ≠ **save** ◆ *n* **3** = **squandering**, dissipation, extravagance, frittering away, misuse, prodigality, wastefulness ≠ **saving** **5** = **rubbish**, debris, dross, garbage, leftovers, litter, refuse, scrap, trash ◆ *pl* **6** = **desert**, wasteland, wilderness ◆ *adj*

7 = **unwanted**, leftover, superfluous, supernumerary, unused, useless, worthless ≠ **needed 8** = **uncultivated**, bare, barren, desolate, empty, uninhabited, unproductive, wild ≠ **developed waste away** = **decline**, atrophy, crumble, decay, dwindle, fade, wane, wear out, wither

watch *v* **1** = **look at**, contemplate, eye, eyeball (*sl*), observe, regard, see, view **2, 4** = **guard**, keep, look after, mind, protect, superintend, take care of, tend ◆ *n* **5** = **wristwatch**, chronometer, timepiece **6** = **lookout**, observation, surveillance, vigil

water *n* **1** = **liquid**, H_2O ◆ *v* **5** = **moisten**, dampen, douse, drench, hose, irrigate, soak, spray greeting or signal. **2** move or flap to and fro. ◆ *n* **3** moving ridge on water. **4** curve(s) in the hair. **5** prolonged spell of something. **6** gesture of waving. **7** vibration carrying energy through a medium. **wavy** *adj* **wavelength** *n* distance between the same points of two successive waves.

waver ⊕ *v* **1** hesitate or be irresolute. **2** be or become unsteady. **waverer** *n*

wax¹ *n* **1** solid shiny fatty or oily substance used for sealing, making candles, etc. **2** similar substance made by bees. **3** waxy secretion of the ear. ◆ *v* **4** coat or polish with wax. **waxen** *adj* made of or like wax. **waxy** *adj* **waxwork** *n* **1** lifelike wax model of a (famous) person. ◆ *pl* **2** place exhibiting these.

wax² ⊕ *v* **1** increase in size or strength. **2** (of the moon) get gradually larger.

way ⊕ *n* **1** manner or method. **2** characteristic manner. **3** route or direction. **4** track or path. **5** distance. **6** room for movement or activity, e.g. *you're in the way.* **7** passage or journey. **8** *Informal* state or condition. **wayfarer** *n* traveller. **waylay** *v* lie in wait for and accost or attack. **wayside** *adj, n* (situated by) the side of a road.

WC water closet.

we *pron* (used as the subject of a verb) **1** the speaker or writer and one or more others. **2** people in general. **3** formal word for 'I' used by editors and monarchs.

weak ⊕ *adj* **1** lacking strength. **2** liable to give way. **3** unconvincing. **4** lacking flavour. **weaken** *v* make or become weak. **weakling** *n* feeble person or animal. **weakly** *adv* **1** feebly. **2** weakness *n* **1** being weak. **2** failing. **3** self-indulgent liking.

weal *n* raised mark left on the skin by a blow.

wealth ⊕ *n* **1** state of being rich. **2** large amount of money and valuables. **3** great amount or number. **wealthy** *adj*

wean *v* **1** accustom (a baby or young mammal) to food other than mother's milk. **2** coax (someone) away from former habits.

weapon *n* **1** object used in fighting. **2** anything used to get the better of an opponent. **weaponry** *n* weapons collectively.

wear ⊕ *v* **wearing, wore, worn 1** have on the body as clothing or ornament. **2** show as one's expression. **3** (cause to) deteriorate by constant use or action. **4** endure constant use. ◆ *n* **6** clothes suitable for a particular time or purpose, e.g. *beach*

THESAURUS

wave *v* **1** = **signal**, gesticulate, gesture, sign **2** = **flap**, brandish, flourish, flutter, oscillate, shake, stir, swing, wag ◆ *n* **3** = **ripple**, billow, breaker, ridge, roller, swell, undulation **5** = **outbreak**, flood, rash, rush, stream, surge, upsurge

waver *v* **1** = **hesitate**, dither, falter, fluctuate, hum and haw, seesaw, vacillate ≠ **resolve 2** = **tremble**, flicker, quiver, shake, totter, wobble

wax² *v* **1** = **increase**, develop, enlarge, expand, grow, magnify, swell ≠ **contract**

way *n* **1** = **method**, fashion, manner, means, mode, procedure, process, system, technique **2** = **style**, custom, habit, manner, nature, personality, practice,

wont **3** = **route**, channel, course, direction **4** = **track**, path, pathway, road, trail **5** = **distance**, length, stretch **7** = **journey**, approach, march, passage

weak *adj* **1** = **feeble**, debilitated, effete, fragile, frail, infirm, puny, sickly, unsteady ≠ **strong 2** = **unsafe**, defenceless, exposed, helpless, unguarded, unprotected, vulnerable **3** = **unconvincing**, feeble, flimsy, hollow, lame, pathetic, unsatisfactory ≠ **powerful 4** = **tasteless**, diluted, insipid, runny, thin, watery ≠ **potent**

wealth *n* **2** = **riches**, affluence, capital, fortune, lolly (*Aust & NZ sl*), money, opulence, prosperity ≠ **poverty 3** = **plenty**, abundance, copiousness, cornucopia, *wear.* **7** damage caused by use. **wearer** *n* **wear off** *v* gradually decrease in intensity. **wear on** *v* (of time) pass slowly.

weary ❶ *adj* **–rier, –riest 1** tired or exhausted. **2** tiring. ◆ *v* **–rying, –ried 3** make or become weary. **wearily** *adv* **weariness** *n* **wearisome** *adj* tedious.

weasel *n* small carnivorous mammal with a long body and short legs.

weather ❶ *n* **1** day–to–day atmospheric conditions of a place. ◆ *v* **2** (cause to) be affected by the weather. **3** come safely through. **under the weather** *Informal* slightly ill. **weather–beaten** *adj* worn, damaged, or (of skin) tanned by exposure to the weather. **weathercock,** **weathervane** *n* device that revolves to show the direction of the wind.

weave ❶ *v* **weaving, wove** or **weaved, woven** or **weaved 1** make (fabric) by interlacing (yarn) on a loom. **2** compose (a story). **3** move from side to side while going forwards. **weaver** *n*

web ❶ *n* **1** net spun by a spider. **2** anything intricate or complex, e.g. *web of deceit.* **3** skin between the toes of a duck, frog, etc. **the Web** short for WORLD WIDE WEB. **webbed** *adj* **webbing** *n* strong fabric woven in strips. **webcam** *n* camera that

transmits images over the Internet. **webcast** *n* broadcast of an event over the Internet. **website** *n* group of connected pages on the World Wide Web.

wed ❶ *v* **wedding, wedded** or **wed 1** marry. **2** unite closely. **3 wedding** *n* act or ceremony of marriage. **wedlock** *n* marriage.

wedge ❶ *n* **1** piece of material thick at one end and thin at the other. ◆ *v* **2** fasten or split with a wedge. **3** squeeze into a narrow space.

Wednesday *n* fourth day of the week.

wee *adj* small.

weed *n* **1** plant growing where undesired. **2** *Informal* thin ineffectual person. ◆ *v* **3** clear of weeds. **weedy** *adj Informal* (of a person) thin and weak. **weed out** *v* remove or eliminate (what is unwanted).

week *n* **1** period of seven days, esp. one beginning on a Sunday. **2** hours or days of work in a week. **weekly** *adj, adv* **1** happening, done, etc. once a week. ◆ *n, pl* **–lies 2** newspaper or magazine published once a week. **weekday** *n* any day of the week except Saturday or Sunday. **weekend** *n* Saturday and Sunday.

weep ❶ *v* **weeping, wept 1** shed tears. **2** ooze liquid. **weepy** *adj* liable to cry.

weigh ❶ *v* **1** have a specified weight. **2**

fullness, profusion, richness

wear *v* **1 = be dressed in**, don, have on, put on, sport (*inf*) **2 = show**, display, exhibit **3 = deteriorate**, abrade, corrode, erode, fray, grind, rub ◆ *n* **6 = clothes**, apparel, attire, costume, dress, garb, garments, gear (*inf*), things **7 = damage**, abrasion, attrition, corrosion, deterioration, erosion, wear and tear ≠ **repair**

weary *adj* **1 = tired**, done in (*inf*), drained, drowsy, exhausted, fatigued, flagging, jaded, sleepy, worn out ≠ **fresh 2 = tiring**, arduous, laborious, tiresome, wearisome ≠ **exciting** ◆ *v* **3 = tire**, drain, enervate, fatigue, sap, take it out of (*inf*), tax, tire out, wear out

weather *n* **1 = climate**, conditions ◆ *v* **3 = withstand**, brave, come through, endure, overcome, resist, ride out, stand, survive ≠ **yield to**

weave *v* **1 = knit**, braid, entwine, interlace, intertwine, plait **2 = create**, build, construct, contrive, fabricate, make up, put together, spin **3 = zigzag**, crisscross, wind

web *n* **1 = spider's web**, cobweb **2 = network**, lattice, tangle

wed *v* **1 = marry**, get married, take the plunge (*inf*), tie the knot (*inf*) ≠ **divorce 2 = unite**, ally, blend, combine, interweave, join, link, merge ≠ **disunite**

wedge *n* **1 = block**, chunk, lump ◆ *v* **3 = squeeze**, cram, crowd, force, jam,

measure the weight of. **3** consider
carefully. **4** be influential. **5** be
burdensome. **weigh anchor** raise a ship's
anchor or (of a ship) have its anchor
raised. **weighbridge** *n* machine for
weighing vehicles by means of a metal
plate set into the road.

weir *n* river dam.

weird 🛈 *adj* **1** strange or bizarre. **2**
unearthly or eerie.

welcome 🛈 *v* **-coming, -comed 1** greet
with pleasure. **2** receive gladly. ◆ *n* **3**
kindly greeting. ◆ *adj* **4** received gladly. **5**
freely permitted.

weld 🛈 *v* **1** join (pieces of metal or plastic)
by softening with heat. **2** unite closely. ◆ *n*
3 welded joint. **welder** *n*

welfare 🛈 *n* **1** wellbeing. **2** help given to
people in need. **welfare state** system in
which the government takes responsibility
for the wellbeing of its citizens.

well¹ 🛈 *adv* **better, best 1** satisfactorily. **2**
skilfully. **3** completely. **4** prosperously. **5**
suitably. **6** intimately. **7** favourably. **8**
considerably. **9** very likely. ◆ *adj* **10** in

good health. **11** satisfactory. ◆ *interj* **12**
exclamation of surprise, interrogation, etc.

well² 🛈 *n* **1** hole sunk into the earth to
reach water, oil, or gas. **2** deep open shaft.
◆ *v* **3** flow upwards or outwards.

wellies *pl n Informal* wellingtons.

wellingtons *pl n* high waterproof rubber
boots.

welter *n* jumbled mass.

wench *n Facetious* young woman.

wend *v* go or travel.

went *v* past tense of GO.

were *v* **1** form of the past tense of **be** used
after *we, you, they,* or a plural noun. **2**
subjunctive of BE.

werewolf *n* (in folklore) person who can
turn into a wolf.

west *n* **1** (direction towards) the part of the
horizon where the sun sets. **2** region lying
in this direction. **3** (W–) western Europe
and the US. ◆ *adj* **4** to or in the west. **5** (of
a wind) from the west. ◆ *adv* **6** in, to, or
towards the west. **westerly** *adj* **western**
adj **1** of or in the west. ◆ *n* **2** film or story
about cowboys in the western US.

───── THESAURUS ─────

lodge, pack, ram, stuff, thrust

weep *v* **1** = **cry**, blubber, lament, mourn,
shed tears, snivel, sob, whimper

weigh *v* **1** = **have a weight of**, tip the
scales at (*inf*) **3** = **consider**, contemplate,
deliberate upon, evaluate, examine,
meditate upon, ponder, reflect upon,
think over **4** = **matter**, carry weight, count

weird *adj* **1** = **strange**, bizarre, freakish,
odd, queer, unnatural ≠ **natural 2** = **eerie**,
creepy (*inf*), mysterious, spooky (*inf*)

welcome *v* **1** = **greet**, embrace, hail, meet
≠ **refuse 2** = **receive** ◆ *n* **3** = **greeting**,
acceptance, hospitality, reception,
salutation ≠ **slight** ◆ *adj* **4** = **acceptable**,
agreeable, appreciated, delightful,
desirable, gratifying, pleasant, refreshing
≠ **unacceptable 5** = **free**, under no
obligation

weld *v* **1** = **solder**, fuse **2** = **unite**, bind,
bond, connect, join, link

welfare *n* **1** = **wellbeing**, advantage,

benefit, good, happiness, health, interest,
prosperity

well¹ *adv* **1** = **satisfactorily**, agreeably,
nicely, pleasantly, smoothly, splendidly,
successfully ≠ **wrongly 2** = **skilfully**, ably,
adeptly, adequately, admirably, correctly,
efficiently, expertly, proficiently, properly
≠ **badly 3** = **fully**, thoroughly
4 = **prosperously**, comfortably
5 = **suitably**, fairly, fittingly, justly,
properly, rightly **6** = **intimately**, deeply,
profoundly ≠ **somewhat 7** = **favourably**,
approvingly, glowingly, highly, kindly,
warmly **8** = **considerably**, abundantly,
amply, fully, greatly, heartily, highly,
substantially, thoroughly, very much ◆ *adj*
10 = **healthy**, fit, in fine fettle, sound
11 = **satisfactory**, agreeable, fine,
pleasing, proper, right

well² *n* **1, 2** = **hole**, bore, pit, shaft ◆ *v*
3 = **flow**, gush, jet, pour, spout, spring,
spurt, surge

westernize v adapt to the customs and culture of the West. **westward** adj, adv **westwards** adv

wet 🔊 adj **wetter, wettest** 1 covered or soaked with water or another liquid. 2 not yet dry. 3 rainy. 4 Informal (of a person) feeble or foolish. ◆ n 5 moisture or rain. 6 Informal feeble or foolish person. ◆ v **wetting, wet** or **wetted** 7 make wet. **wet blanket** Informal person who has a depressing effect on others. **wetland** n area of marshy land. **wet nurse** woman employed to breast–feed another's child. **wet suit** close–fitting rubber suit worn by divers etc.

whack 🔊 v 1 strike with a resounding blow. ◆ n 2 such a blow. 3 Informal share. 4 Informal attempt. **whacked** adj exhausted. **whacking** adj Informal huge.

wharf 🔊 n, pl **wharves, wharfs** platform at a harbour for loading and unloading ships. **wharfie** n Aust person employed to load and unload ships.

what pron 1 which thing. 2 that which. 3 request for a statement to be repeated. ◆ interj 4 exclamation of anger, surprise, etc. ◆ adv 5 in which way, how much, e.g. what do you care? what for? why? **whatever** pron 1 everything or anything that. 2 no matter what. **whatnot** n Informal similar unspecified things. **whatsoever** adj at all.

wheat n 1 grain used in making flour, bread, and pasta. 2 plant producing this.

wheaten adj **wheatmeal** adj, n (made with) brown, but not wholemeal, flour.

wheedle 🔊 v coax or cajole.

wheel 🔊 n 1 disc that revolves on an axle. 2 pivoting movement. ◆ v 3 push or pull (something with wheels). 4 turn as if on an axis. 5 turn round suddenly. **wheeling and dealing** use of shrewd and sometimes unscrupulous methods to achieve success. **wheeler–dealer** n **wheelbarrow** n shallow box for carrying loads, with a wheel at the front and two handles. **wheelbase** n distance between a vehicle's front and back axles. **wheelchair** n chair mounted on wheels for use by people who cannot walk.

wheeze 🔊 v 1 breathe with a hoarse whistling noise. ◆ n 2 wheezing sound. 3 Informal trick or plan. **wheezy** adj

whelk n edible snail–like shellfish.

when adv 1 at what time? ◆ conj 2 at the time that. 3 although. 4 considering the fact that. ◆ pron 5 at which time. **whenever** adv, conj at whatever time.

✓ **WORD TIP**

Some people dislike the use of when in definitions: famine is when food runs low, but it is very common in informal usage. More formally, write ...a situation/condition in which....

---

where adv 1 in, at, or to what place? ◆

wet adj 1 = **damp**, dank, moist, saturated, soaking, sodden, soggy, sopping, waterlogged, watery ≠ **dry** 3 = **rainy**, drizzling, pouring, raining, showery, teeming ≠ **sunny** 4 Inf = **feeble**, effete, ineffectual, namby–pamby, soft, spineless, timorous, weak, weedy (inf) ◆ n 5 = **moisture**, condensation, damp, dampness, drizzle, humidity, liquid, rain, water, wetness 6 Inf = **weakling**, drip (inf), weed (inf), wimp (inf) ◆ v 7 = **moisten**, dampen, douse, irrigate, saturate, soak, spray, water

whack v 1 = **strike**, bang, belt (inf), clobber (sl), hit, smack, swipe, thrash, thump, thwack, wallop (inf) ◆ n 2 = **blow**, bang, belt (inf), hit, smack, stroke, swipe, thump, thwack, wallop (inf) 3 Inf = **share**, bit, cut (inf), part, portion, quota 4 Inf = **attempt**, bash (inf), crack (inf), go (inf), shot (inf), stab (inf), try, turn

wharf n = **dock**, jetty, landing stage, pier, quay

wheedle v = **coax**, cajole, entice, inveigle, persuade

wheel n 2 = **circle**, gyration, pivot,

pron 2 in, at, or to which place. ♦ *conj* 3 in the place at which. **whereabouts** *n* 1 present position. ♦ *adv* 2 at what place. **whereas** *conj* but on the other hand. **whereby** *pron* by which. **wherefore** *Obs* ♦ *adv* 1 why. ♦ *conj* 2 consequently. **whereupon** *conj* at which point. **wherever** *conj, adv* at whatever place. **wherewithal** *n* necessary funds, resources, etc.

✓ **WORD TIP**

Where includes the ideas *to* and *at* so avoid the use of these prepositions: *where was it?* (not *where was it at?*).

---

whet ❶ *v* **whetting, whetted** sharpen (a tool). **whet someone's appetite** increase someone's desire. **whetstone** *n* stone for sharpening tools.

whether *conj* used to introduce an indirect question or a clause expressing doubt or choice.

whey [way] *n* watery liquid that separates from the curd when milk is clotted.

which *adj, pron* 1 used to request or refer to a choice from different possibilities. ♦ *pron* 2 used to refer to a thing already mentioned. **whichever** *adj, pron* 1 any out of several. 2 no matter which.

whiff ❶ *n* 1 puff of air or odour. 2 trace or hint.

while *conj* 1 at the same time that. 2

whereas. ♦ *n* 3 period of time. **whilst** *conj* while. **while away** *v* pass (time) idly but pleasantly.

whim ❶ *n* sudden fancy. **whimsy** *n* 1 capricious idea. 2 light or fanciful humour. **whimsical** *adj* unusual, playful, and fanciful.

whimper ❶ *v* 1 cry in a soft whining way. ♦ *n* 2 soft plaintive whine.

whine ❶ *n* 1 high-pitched plaintive cry. 2 peevish complaint. ♦ *v* 3 make such a sound. **whining** *n, adj*

whinge ❶ *Informal* ♦ *v* 1 complain. ♦ *n* 2 complaint.

whinny *v* **-nying, -nied** 1 neigh softly. ♦ *n, pl* **-nies** 2 soft neigh.

whip ❶ *n* 1 cord attached to a handle, used for beating animals or people. 2 politician responsible for organizing and disciplining fellow party members. 3 call made on members of Parliament to attend for important votes. 4 dessert made from beaten cream or egg whites. ♦ *v* **whipping, whipped** 5 strike with a whip, strap, or cane. 6 *Informal* pull, remove, or move quickly. 7 beat (esp. eggs or cream) to a froth. 8 rouse into a particular condition. 9 *Informal* steal. **whiplash injury** neck injury caused by a sudden jerk to the head, as in a car crash. **whip-round** *n Informal* collection of money.

whippet *n* racing dog like a small

THESAURUS

revolution, rotation, spin, turn ♦ *v* 4, 5 = **turn**, gyrate, pirouette, revolve, rotate, spin, swing, swivel, twirl, whirl

wheeze *v* 1 = **gasp**, cough, hiss, rasp, whistle ♦ *n* 2 = **gasp**, cough, hiss, rasp, whistle 3 *Inf* = **trick**, idea, plan, ploy, ruse, scheme, stunt

whet *v* 1 = **sharpen**, hone ≠ **depress whet someone's appetite** = **stimulate**, arouse, awaken, enhance, excite, kindle, quicken, rouse, stir

whiff *n* 1 = **smell**, aroma, hint, odour, scent, sniff

whim *n* = **impulse**, caprice, fancy, notion, urge

whimper *v* 1 = **cry**, moan, snivel, sob, weep, whine, whinge (*inf*) ♦ *n* 2 = **sob**, moan, snivel, whine

whine *n* 1 = **cry**, moan, sob, wail, whimper 2 = **complaint**, gripe (*inf*), grouch (*inf*), grouse, grumble, moan, whinge (*inf*) ♦ *v* 3 = **cry**, moan, sniffle, snivel, sob, wail, whimper

whinge *Inf v* 1 = **complain**, bleat, carp, gripe (*inf*), grouse, grumble, moan ♦ *n* 2 = **complaint**, gripe (*inf*), grouch, grouse, grumble, moan, whine

whip *n* 1 = **lash**, birch, cane, cat-o'-nine-tails, crop, scourge ♦ *v* 5 = **lash**, beat, birch, cane, flagellate, flog, scourge, greyhound.

whirl ❶ v 1 spin or revolve. 2 be dizzy or confused. ♦ n 3 whirling movement. 4 bustling activity. 5 confusion or giddiness. **whirlpool** n strong circular current of water. **whirlwind** n 1 column of air whirling violently upwards in a spiral. ♦ adj 2 much quicker than normal.

whirr, whir n 1 prolonged soft buzz. ♦ v **whirring, whirred** 2 (cause to) make a whirr.

whisk ❶ v 1 move or remove quickly. 2 beat (esp. eggs or cream) to a froth. ♦ n 3 egg-beating utensil.

whisker n 1 any of the long stiff hairs on the face of a cat or other mammal. ♦ pl 2 hair growing on a man's face. **by a whisker** Informal only just.

whisky n, pl –**kies** spirit distilled from fermented cereals. **whiskey** n, pl –**keys** Irish or American whisky.

whisper ❶ v 1 speak softly, without vibration of the vocal cords. 2 rustle. ♦ n 3 soft voice. 4 Informal rumour. 5 rustling sound.

whist n card game in which one pair of players tries to win more tricks than another pair.

whistle v 1 produce a shrill sound, esp. by forcing the breath through pursed lips. 2 signal by a whistle. ♦ n 3 whistling sound. 4 instrument blown to make a whistling sound. **blow the whistle on** Informal inform on or put a stop to.

white ❶ adj 1 of the colour of snow. 2 pale. 3 light in colour. 4 (of coffee) served with milk. ♦ n 5 colour of snow. 6 clear fluid round the yolk of an egg. 7 white part, esp. of the eyeball. 8 (W–) member of the race of people with light-coloured skin. **whiten** v make or become white or whiter. **whitish** adj **white-collar** adj denoting professional and clerical workers. **white elephant** useless or unwanted possession. **white flag** signal of surrender or truce. **white goods** large household appliances such as cookers and fridges. **white-hot** adj very hot. **white lie** minor unimportant lie.

whither adv Obs to what place.

whittle ❶ v cut or carve (wood) with a knife. **whittle down, away** v reduce or wear away gradually.

whizz, whiz v **whizzing, whizzed** 1 make a loud buzzing sound. 2 Informal move quickly. ♦ n, pl **whizzes** 3 loud buzzing sound. 4 Informal person skilful at something. **whizz kid, whiz kid** Informal person who is outstandingly able for his or her age.

who pron 1 which person. 2 used to refer to a person or people already mentioned. **whoever** pron 1 any person who. 2 no matter who.

whodunnit, whodunit [hoo-**dun**-nit] n Informal detective story, play, or film.

whole ❶ adj 1 containing all the elements or parts. 2 uninjured or undamaged. ♦ n 3 complete thing or system. **on the whole** taking everything into consideration.

———————— THESAURUS ————————

spank, strap, thrash 6 Inf = **dash**, dart, dive, fly, rush, shoot, tear, whisk 7 = **whisk**, beat 8 = **incite**, agitate, drive, foment, goad, spur, stir, work up

whirl v 1 = **spin**, pirouette, revolve, roll, rotate, swirl, turn, twirl, twist 2 = **feel dizzy**, reel, spin ♦ n 3 = **revolution**, pirouette, roll, rotation, spin, swirl, turn, twirl, twist 4 = **bustle**, flurry, merry-go-round, round, series, succession 5 = **confusion**, daze, dither, giddiness, spin

whisk v 1 = **flick**, brush, sweep, whip 2 = **beat**, fluff up, mix vigorously, stir vigorously, whip ♦ n 3 = **beater**

whisper v 1 = **murmur**, breathe ≠ shout 2 = **rustle**, hiss, sigh, swish ♦ n 3 = **murmur**, undertone 4 Inf = **rumour**, gossip, innuendo, insinuation, report 5 = **rustle**, hiss, sigh, swish

white adj 2 = **pale**, ashen, pallid, pasty, wan

whittle v = **carve**, cut, hew, pare, shape, shave, trim

wholly *adv* wholefood *n* food that has been processed as little as possible.
wholehearted *adj* sincere or enthusiastic.
wholemeal *adj* 1 (of flour) made from the whole wheat grain. 2 made from wholemeal flour. whole number number that does not contain a fraction.

whom *pron* objective form of WHO.

whoop *v*, *n* shout or cry to express excitement.

whooping cough *n* infectious disease marked by convulsive coughing and noisy breathing.

whopper ❶ *n Informal* 1 anything unusually large. 2 huge lie. whopping *adj*

whore ❶ [hore] *n* prostitute.

whose *pron* of whom or of which.

why *adv* 1 for what reason. ◆ *pron* 2 because of which.

wick *n* cord through a lamp or candle which carries fuel to the flame.

wicked ❶ *adj* 1 morally bad. 2 mischievous. wickedness *n*

wicker *adj* made of woven cane. wickerwork *n*

wicket *n* 1 set of three cricket stumps and two bails. 2 ground between the two wickets on a cricket pitch.

wide ❶ *adj* 1 large from side to side. 2 having a specified width. 3 spacious or extensive. 4 far from the target. 5 opened fully. ◆ *adv* 6 to the full extent. 7 over an extensive area. 8 far from the target.
widely *adv* widen *v* make or become wider. 1 widespread *adj* affecting a wide area or a large number of people.

widow *n* woman whose husband is dead and who has not remarried. widowed *adj* widowhood *n* widower *n* man whose wife is dead and who has not remarried.

wield ❶ *v* 1 hold and use (a weapon). 2 have and use (power).

wife ❶ *n*, *pl* wives woman to whom a man is married.

wig *n* artificial head of hair.

wiggle ❶ *v* 1 move jerkily from side to side. ◆ *n* 2 wiggling movement.

wild ❶ *adj* 1 (of animals) not tamed or domesticated. 2 (of plants) not cultivated. 3 not civilized. 4 lacking restraint or control. 5 violent or stormy. 6 *Informal* excited. 7 *Informal* furious. 8 random. wilds *pl n* desolate or uninhabited place. wild-goose chase search that has little chance of success.

wildebeest *n* gnu.

THESAURUS

whole *adj* 1 = complete, entire, full, total, unabridged, uncut, undivided ≠ cut 2 = undamaged, in one piece, intact, unbroken, unharmed, unscathed, untouched ≠ broken ◆ *n* 3 = totality, ensemble, entirety ≠ part on the whole = all in all, all things considered, by and large

whopper *n Inf* 1 = giant, colossus, crackerjack (*inf*), jumbo (*inf*), leviathan, mammoth, monster 2 = big lie, fabrication, falsehood, tall story (*inf*), untruth

whore *n* = prostitute, call girl, streetwalker, tart (*inf*)

wicked *adj* 1 = bad, corrupt, depraved, devilish, evil, fiendish, immoral, sinful, vicious, villainous ≠ good 2 = mischievous, impish, incorrigible, naughty, rascally, roguish ≠ obedient

wide *adj* 1 = broad, expansive, extensive, far-reaching, immense, large, overarching, sweeping, vast ≠ narrow 3 = spacious, baggy, capacious, commodious, full, loose, roomy ≠ tight 4 = distant, off course, off target, remote 5 = expanded, dilated, distended, outspread, outstretched ≠ closed ◆ *adv* 6 = fully, completely ≠ partly 8 = off target, astray, off course, off the mark, out

wield *v* 1 = brandish, employ, flourish, handle, manage, manipulate, ply, swing, use 2 = exert, exercise, have, maintain, possess

wife *n* = spouse, better half (*hum*), bride, mate, partner

wiggle *v*, *n* 1, 2 = jerk, jiggle, shake, shimmy, squirm, twitch, wag, waggle,

wilderness ⊕ *n* uninhabited uncultivated region.

wildfire *n* spread like wildfire spread quickly and uncontrollably.

wilful ⊕ *adj* 1 headstrong or obstinate. 2 intentional. **wilfully** *adv*

will[1] *v, past* **would** used as an auxiliary to form the future tense or to indicate intention, ability, or expectation.

☑ **WORD TIP**

Will is normal for discussing the future. The use of *shall* with *I* and *we* is a matter of preference, not of rule. *Shall* is commonly used for questions in Southern England but less often in the North and Scotland.

---

will[2] ⊕ *n* 1 strong determination. 2 desire or wish. 3 directions written for disposal of one's property after death. ◆ *v* 4 use one's will in an attempt to do (something). 5 wish or desire. 6 leave (property) by a will. **willing** *adj* 1 ready or inclined (to do something). 2 keen and obliging. **willingly** *adv* **willingness** *n* **willpower** *n* ability to control oneself and one's actions.

will–o'–the–wisp *n* 1 elusive person or thing. 2 pale light sometimes seen over marshes at night.

willow *n* 1 tree with thin flexible branches. 2 its wood, used for making cricket bats. **willowy** *adj* slender and graceful.

willy–nilly *adv* whether desired or not.

wilt ⊕ *v* (cause to) become limp or lose strength.

wimp ⊕ *n Informal* feeble ineffectual person.

wimple *n* garment framing the face, worn by medieval women and now by nuns.

win ⊕ *v* **winning, won** 1 come first in (a competition, fight, etc.). 2 gain (a prize) in a competition. 3 get by effort. ◆ *n* 4 victory, esp. in a game. **winner** *n* **winning** *adj* 1 gaining victory. 2 charming. **winnings** *pl n* sum won, esp. in gambling. **win over** *v* gain the support or consent of (someone).

wince ⊕ *v* 1 draw back, as if in pain. ◆ *n* 2 wincing.

winch *n* 1 machine for lifting or hauling

---

writhe

wild *adj* 1 = **untamed**, feral, ferocious, fierce, savage, unbroken, undomesticated ≠ **broken** 2 = **uncultivated**, natural ≠ **planted** 3 = **uncivilized**, barbaric, barbarous, brutish, ferocious, fierce, primitive, savage 4 = **uncontrolled**, disorderly, riotous, rowdy, turbulent, undisciplined, unmanageable, unrestrained, unruly, wayward ≠ **controlled** 5 = **stormy**, blustery, choppy, raging, rough, tempestuous, violent 6 *Inf* = **excited**, crazy (*inf*), enthusiastic, hysterical, raving ◆ *pl n* **wilds** = **wilderness**, back of beyond (*inf*), desert, middle of nowhere (*inf*), wasteland

wilderness *n* 1 = **desert**, jungle, wasteland, wilds

wilful *adj* 1 = **obstinate**, determined, headstrong, inflexible, intransigent, obdurate, perverse, pig–headed, stubborn, uncompromising ≠ **yielding** 2 = **intentional**, conscious, deliberate, intended, purposeful, voluntary ≠ **unconscious**

will[2] *n* 1 = **determination**, purpose, resolution, resolve, willpower 2 = **wish**, desire, fancy, inclination, mind, preference, volition 3 = **testament**, last wishes ◆ *v* 5 = **wish**, desire, prefer, see fit, want 6 = **bequeath**, confer, give, leave, pass on, transfer

wilt *v* a = **droop**, sag, shrivel, wither b = **weaken**, fade, flag, languish, wane

wimp *n Inf* = **weakling**, coward, drip (*inf*), mouse, sissy, softy *or* softie

win *v* 1 = **triumph**, come first, conquer, overcome, prevail, succeed, sweep the board ≠ **lose** 3 = **gain**, achieve, acquire, attain, earn, get, land, obtain, procure, secure ≠ **lose** ◆ *n* 4 = **victory**, conquest, success, triumph ≠ **loss**

using a cable wound round a drum. ◆ v 2 lift or haul using a winch.

wind[1] ❶ n 1 current of air. 2 hint or suggestion. 3 breath. 4 flatulence. 5 idle talk. ◆ v 6 render short of breath. **windy** adj **windward** adj, n (of or in) the direction from which the wind is blowing. **windfall** n 1 unexpected good luck. 2 fallen fruit. **wind instrument** musical instrument played by blowing. **windmill** n machine for grinding or pumping driven by sails turned by the wind. **windpipe** n tube linking the throat and the lungs. **windscreen** n front window of a motor vehicle. **windscreen wiper** device that wipes rain etc. from a windscreen. **windsock** n cloth cone on a mast at an airfield to indicate wind direction. **windsurfing** n sport of riding on water using a surfboard propelled and steered by a sail.

wind[2] ❶ v **winding, wound** 1 coil or wrap around. 2 tighten the spring of (a clock or watch). 3 move in a twisting course. **wind up** v 1 bring to or reach an end. 2 tighten the spring of (a clock or watch). 3 Informal make tense or agitated. 4 Slang tease.

window n 1 opening in a wall to let in light or air. 2 glass pane or panes fitted in such an opening. 3 display area behind the window of a shop. 4 area on a computer screen that can be manipulated separately from the rest of the display area. 5 period of unbooked time in a diary or schedule. **window–dressing** n 1 arrangement of goods in a shop window. 2 attempt to make something more attractive than it really is. **window–shopping** n looking at goods in shop windows without intending to buy.

wine n 1 alcoholic drink made from fermented grapes. 2 similar drink made from other fruits. **wine and dine** entertain or be entertained with fine food and drink.

wing ❶ n 1 one of the limbs or organs of a bird, insect, or bat that are used for flying. 2 one of the winglike supporting parts of an aircraft. 3 projecting side part of a building. 4 faction of a political party. 5 part of a car body surrounding the wheels. 6 Sport (player on) either side of the pitch. ◆ pl 7 sides of a stage. ◆ v 8 fly. 9 wound slightly in the wing or arm. **winged** adj **winger** n Sport player positioned on a wing.

wink ❶ v 1 close and open (an eye) quickly as a signal. 2 twinkle. ◆ n 3 winking. 4 smallest amount of sleep.

winkle n shellfish with a spiral shell. **winkle out** v Informal extract or prise out.

winsome adj charming or winning.

winter n 1 coldest season. ◆ v 2 spend the winter. **wintry** adj 1 of or like winter. 2 cold or unfriendly. **winter sports** open–air sports held on snow or ice.

wipe ❶ v 1 clean or dry by rubbing. 2 erase (a tape). ◆ n 3 wiping. **wipe out** v destroy completely.

wire n 1 thin flexible strand of metal. 2 length of this used to carry electric current. 3 Obs telegram. ◆ v 4 equip with wires. **wiring** n system of wires. **wiry** adj 1 lean and tough. 2 like wire. **wire–haired** adj (of a dog) having a stiff wiry coat.

THESAURUS

wince v 1 = **flinch**, blench, cower, cringe, draw back, quail, recoil, shrink, start ◆ n 2 = **flinch**, cringe, start

wind[1] n 1 = **air**, blast, breeze, draught, gust, zephyr 2 = **hint**, inkling, notice, report, rumour, suggestion, warning, whisper 3 = **breath**, puff, respiration 4 = **flatulence**, gas 5 = **talk**, babble, bluster, boasting, hot air

wind[2] v 1 = **coil**, curl, encircle, loop, reel,

roll, spiral, twist 3 = **meander**, bend, curve, ramble, snake, turn, twist, zigzag

wing n 4 = **faction**, arm, branch, group, section ◆ v 8 = **fly**, glide, soar 9 = **wound**, clip, hit

wink v 1 = **blink**, bat, flutter 2 = **twinkle**, flash, gleam, glimmer, sparkle ◆ n 3 = **blink**, flutter

wipe v 1 = **clean**, brush, mop, rub, sponge, swab 2 = **erase**, remove ◆ n 3 = **rub**, brush

wise ❶ *adj* having intelligence and knowledge. **wisely** *adv* **wiseacre** *n* person who wishes to seem wise.

wish ❶ *v* 1 want or desire. 2 feel or express a hope about someone's wellbeing, success, etc. ◆ *n* 3 expression of a desire. 4 thing desired. **wishful** *adj* too optimistic. **wishbone** *n* V–shaped bone above the breastbone of a fowl.

wishy–washy *adj Informal* insipid or bland.

wisp *n* 1 light delicate streak. 2 twisted bundle or tuft. **wispy** *adj*

wistful ❶ *adj* sadly longing. **wistfully** *adv*

wit ❶ *n* 1 ability to use words or ideas in a clever and amusing way. 2 person with this ability. 3 (sometimes *pl*) practical intelligence. **witless** *adj* foolish.

witch ❶ *n* 1 person, usu. female, who practises (black) magic. 2 ugly or wicked woman. **witchcraft** *n* use of magic. **witch doctor** (in certain societies) a man appearing to cure or cause injury or disease by magic. **witch–hunt** *n* campaign against people with unpopular views.

with *prep* indicating presence alongside, possession, means of performance, characteristic manner, etc., e.g. *walking with his dog; a man with two cars; hit with a hammer; playing with skill*. **within** *prep, adv* in or inside. **without** *prep* not accompanied by, using, or having.

withdraw ❶ *v* –drawing, –drew, –drawn take or move out or away. **withdrawal** *n* **withdrawn** *adj* unsociable.

wither ❶ *v* wilt or dry up. **withering** *adj* (of a look or remark) scornful.

withhold ❶ *v* –holding, –held refrain from giving.

withstand ❶ *v* –standing, –stood oppose or resist successfully.

witness ❶ *n* 1 person who has seen something happen. 2 person giving evidence in court. 3 evidence or testimony. ◆ *v* 4 see at first hand. 5 sign (a document) to certify that it is genuine.

wizard ❶ *n* 1 magician. 2 person with outstanding skill in a particular field. **wizardry** *n*

wizened ❶ [**wiz**–zend] *adj* shrivelled or wrinkled.

wobble ❶ *v* 1 move unsteadily. 2 shake. ◆

—————— THESAURUS ——————

wise *adj* = **sensible**, clever, discerning, enlightened, erudite, intelligent, judicious, perceptive, prudent, sage ≠ **stupid**

wish *v* 1 = **want**, aspire, crave, desire, hanker, hope, long, yearn ◆ *n* 3 = **desire**, aspiration, hope, intention, urge, want, whim, will ≠ **dislike**

wistful *adj* = **melancholy**, contemplative, dreamy, longing, meditative, pensive, reflective, thoughtful

wit *n* 1 = **humour**, badinage, banter, drollery, jocularity, raillery, repartee, wordplay ≠ **gravity** 2 = **humorist**, card (*inf*), comedian, joker, wag 3 (sometimes *pl*) = **cleverness**, acumen, brains, common sense, ingenuity, intellect, sense, wisdom ≠ **ignorance**

witch *n* = **enchantress**, crone, hag, magician, sorceress

withdraw *v* = **remove**, draw back, extract, pull out, take away, take off ≠ **go on**

wither *v* 1 = **wilt**, decline, perish, shrivel ≠ **develop** 2 = **fade**, decay, disintegrate, waste

withhold *v* = **keep back**, conceal, hide, hold back, refuse, reserve, retain, suppress ≠ **give**

withstand *v* = **resist**, bear, cope with, endure, hold off, oppose, stand up to, suffer, tolerate

witness *n* 1 = **observer**, beholder, bystander, eyewitness, looker–on, onlooker, spectator, viewer, watcher 2 = **testifier**, corroborator ◆ *v* 4 = **see**, note, notice, observe, perceive, view, watch 5 = **sign**, countersign, endorse

wizard *n* 1 = **magician**, conjuror, magus, necromancer, occultist, shaman, sorcerer, warlock, witch

wizened *adj* = **wrinkled**, dried up, gnarled, lined, shrivelled, shrunken, withered

DICTIONARY

n **3** wobbling movement or sound. **wobbly** *adj*

woe ❶ *n* grief. **woeful** *adj* **1** extremely sad. **2** pitiful. **woefully** *adv* **woebegone** *adj* looking miserable.

wok *n* bowl–shaped Chinese cooking pan, used for stir–frying.

wolf *n, pl* **wolves 1** wild predatory canine mammal. ♦ *v* **2** eat ravenously. **cry wolf** raise a false alarm. **wolf whistle** whistle by a man indicating that he thinks a woman is attractive.

wolverine *n* carnivorous mammal of Arctic regions.

woman ❶ *n, pl* **women 1** adult human female. **2** women collectively. **womanhood** *n* **womanish** *adj* effeminate. **womanly** *adj* having qualities traditionally associated with a woman. **womanizing** *n* practice of indulging in casual affairs with women. **womanizer** *n*

womb *n* hollow organ in female mammals where babies are conceived and develop.

wombat *n* small heavily–built burrowing Australian marsupial.

won *v* past of WIN.

wonder ❶ *v* **1** be curious about. **2** be amazed. ♦ *n* **3** wonderful thing. **4** emotion caused by an amazing or unusual thing. ♦ *adj* **5** spectacularly successful, e.g. *a wonder drug*. **wonderful** *adj* **1** very fine. **2** remarkable. **wonderfully** *adv* **wonderment** *n* **wondrous** *adj* Old–fashioned wonderful.

wont [rhymes with **don't**] *adj* **1** accustomed. ♦ *n* **2** custom.

woo ❶ *v* **1** try to persuade. **2** Old–fashioned try to gain the love of.

wood ❶ *n* **1** substance trees are made of, used in carpentry and as fuel. **2** area where trees grow. **3** long–shafted golf club, usu. with wooden head. **wooded** *adj* covered with trees. **wooden** *adj* **1** made of wood. **2** without expression. **woody** *adj* **woodbine** *n* honeysuckle. **woodcock** *n* game bird. **woodcut** *n* (print made from) an engraved block of wood. **woodland** *n* forest. **woodlouse** *n* small insect–like creature with many legs. **woodpecker** *n* bird which searches tree trunks for insects. **woodwind** *adj, n* (of) a type of wind instrument made of wood. **1 woodworm** *n* insect larva that bores into wood.

woof *n* barking noise made by a dog. **woofer** *n* loudspeaker reproducing low–frequency sounds.

wool ❶ *n* **1** soft hair of sheep, goats, etc. **2** yarn spun from this. **woollen** *adj* **woolly** *adj* **1** of or like wool. **2** vague or muddled. ♦ *n* **3** knitted woollen garment. **woolgathering** *n* daydreaming.

wop–wops *pl n* NZ informal remote rural areas.

word ❶ *n* **1** smallest single meaningful unit of speech or writing. **2** chat or discussion. **3** brief remark. **4** message. **5** promise. **6** command. ♦ *v* **7** express in words. **wordy** *adj* using too many words. **wording** *n* choice and arrangement of words. **word processor** keyboard, microprocessor, and VDU for electronic organization and storage of text. **word processing**

THESAURUS

wobble *v* **1** = **sway**, rock, teeter, totter **2** = **shake**, tremble ♦ *n* **3** = **unsteadiness**, shake, tremble, tremor

woe *n* = **grief**, agony, anguish, distress, gloom, misery, sadness, sorrow, unhappiness, wretchedness ≠ **pleasure**

woman *n* **1** = **lady**, female, girl

wonder *v* **1** = **think**, conjecture, meditate, ponder, puzzle, query, question, speculate **2** = **be amazed**, be astonished, gape, marvel, stare ♦ *n* **3** = **phenomenon**, curiosity, marvel, miracle, prodigy, rarity, sight, spectacle **4** = **amazement**, admiration, astonishment, awe, bewilderment, fascination, surprise, wonderment

woo *v* **1** = **court**, cultivate, pursue

wood *n* **1** = **timber**, planks **3** = **woodland**, coppice, copse, forest, grove, thicket

wool *n* **1** = **fleece**, hair **2** = **yarn**

word *n* **1** = **term**, expression, name **2** = **chat**, confab (*inf*), consultation,

wore *v* past tense of WEAR.

work ❶ *n* **1** physical or mental effort directed to making or doing something. **2** paid employment. **3** duty or task. **4** something made or done. ◆ *pl* **5** factory. **6** total of a writer's or artist's achievements. **7** *Informal* full treatment. **8** mechanism of a machine. ◆ *adj* **9** of or for work. ◆ *v* **10** (cause to) do work. **11** be employed. **12** (cause to) operate. **13** (of a plan etc.) be successful. **14** cultivate (land). **15** manipulate, shape, or process. **16** (cause to) reach a specified condition. **work–to–rule** *n* protest in which workers keep strictly to all regulations to reduce the rate of work. **workable** *adj* **worker** *n* **workaholic** *n* person obsessed with work. **workhorse** *n* person or thing that does a lot of dull or routine work. **workhouse** *n Hist* institution where the poor were given food and lodgings in return for work. **working class** social class consisting of wage earners, esp. manual workers. **working–class** *adj* **working party** committee investigating a specific problem. **workman** *n* manual worker. **workmanship** *n* skill with which an object is made. **workshop** *n* **1** room or building for a manufacturing process. **2** worktop *n* surface in a kitchen, used for food preparation.

world ❶ *n* **1** the planet earth. **2** mankind. **3** society of a particular area or period. **4** sphere of existence. ◆ *adj* **5** of the whole world. **worldly** *adj* **1** not spiritual. **2** concerned with material things. **3** wise in the ways of the world. **world–weary** *adj* no longer finding pleasure in life. **World Wide Web** global network of linked computer files.

worm *n* **1** small limbless invertebrate animal. **2** *Informal* wretched or spineless person. **3** shaft with a spiral thread forming part of a gear system. ◆ *pl* **4** illness caused by parasitic worms in the intestines. ◆ *v* **5** rid of worms. **worm one's way 1** crawl. **2** insinuate (oneself). **wormy** *adj* **wormcast** *n* coil of earth excreted by a burrowing worm. **worm–eaten** *adj* eaten into by worms. **worm out** *v* extract (information) craftily.

worn ❶ *v* past participle of WEAR.

worry ❶ *v* –rying, –ried **1** (cause to) be anxious or uneasy. **2** annoy or bother. **3** (of a dog) chase and try to bite (sheep etc.). ◆ *n, pl* –ries **4** (cause of) anxiety or concern. **worried** *adj* **worrying** *adj, n*

worse *adj, adv* comparative of BAD *or* BADLY.

———————— THESAURUS ————————

discussion, talk, tête-à-tête **3 = remark**, comment, utterance **4 = message**, communiqué, dispatch, information, intelligence, news, notice, report **5 = promise**, assurance, guarantee, oath, pledge, vow **6 = command**, bidding, decree, mandate, order ◆ *v* **7 = express**, couch, phrase, put, say, state, utter

work *n* **1 = effort**, drudgery, elbow grease (*facetious*), exertion, industry, labour, sweat, toil ≠ **rest** **2 = employment**, business, duty, job, livelihood, occupation, profession, trade ≠ **play** **3 = task**, assignment, chore, commission, duty, job, stint, undertaking **4 = creation**, achievement, composition, handiwork, opus, piece, production ◆ *v* **10 = labour**, drudge, exert oneself, peg away, slave,

slog (away), sweat, toil ≠ **play** **11 = be employed**, be in work **12 = operate**, control, drive, handle, manage, manipulate, move, run, use **14 = cultivate**, dig, farm, till **15 = manipulate**, fashion, form, knead, mould, shape

world *n* **1 = earth**, globe **2 = mankind**, everybody, everyone, humanity, humankind, man, the public **4 = sphere**, area, domain, environment, field, realm

worn *adj* = **ragged**, frayed, shabby, tattered, tatty, the worse for wear, threadbare

worry *v* **1 = be anxious**, agonize, brood, fret, obsess **2 = trouble**, annoy, bother, disturb, perturb, pester, unsettle, upset, vex ≠ **comfort** ◆ *n* **4 a = problem**, bother, care, hassle (*inf*), trouble **b = anxiety**,

worst *adj, adv* **1** superlative of BAD or BADLY. ◆ *n* **2** worst thing. **worsen** *v* make or grow worse.

worship ⊕ *v* –**shipping,** –**shipped 1** show religious devotion to. **2** love and admire. ◆ *n* **3** act or instance of worshipping. **4** (W–) title for a mayor or magistrate. **worshipper** *n* **worshipful** *adj* worshipping.

worsted [**wooss**–tid] *n* type of woollen yarn or fabric.

worth ⊕ *prep* **1** having a value of. **2** meriting or justifying. ◆ *n* **3** value or price. **4** excellence. **5** amount to be had for a given sum. **worthless** *adj* **worthy** *adj* **1** deserving admiration or respect. ◆ *n* **2** *Informal* notable person. **worthily** *adv* **worthiness** *n* **worthwhile** *adj* worth the time or effort involved.

would *v* used as an auxiliary to express a request, describe a habitual past action, or form the past tense or subjunctive mood of WILL¹. **would–be** *adj* wishing or pretending to be.

wound¹ ⊕ *n* **1** injury caused by violence. **2** injury to the feelings. ◆ *v* **3** inflict a wound on.

wound² *v* past of WIND².

wove *v* a past tense of WEAVE. **woven** *v* a past participle of WEAVE.

wow *interj* **1** exclamation of astonishment.

◆ *n* **2** *Informal* astonishing person or thing.

wowser *n Aust & NZ slang* **1** puritanical person. **2** teetotaller.

wraith *n* ghost.

wrangle ⊕ *v* **1** argue noisily. ◆ *n* **2** noisy argument.

wrap ⊕ *v* **wrapping, wrapped 1** fold (something) round (a person or thing) so as to cover. ◆ *n* **2** garment wrapped round the shoulders. **wrapper** *n* cover for a product. **wrapping** *n* material used to wrap. **wrap up** *v* **1** fold paper round. **2** put warm clothes on. **3** *Informal* finish or settle (a matter).

wrath ⊕ [roth] *n* intense anger. **wrathful** *adj*

wreak *v* **wreak havoc** cause chaos. **wreak vengeance on** take revenge on.

wreath ⊕ *n* twisted ring or band of flowers or leaves used as a memorial or tribute. **wreathed** *adj* surrounded or encircled.

wreck ⊕ *v* **1** destroy. ◆ *n* **2** remains of something that has been destroyed or badly damaged, esp. a ship. **3** person in very poor condition. **wrecker** *n* **wreckage** *n* wrecked remains.

wren *n* small brown songbird.

wrench ⊕ *v* **1** twist or pull violently. **2** sprain (a joint). ◆ *n* **3** violent twist or pull.

——————— THESAURUS ———————

apprehension, concern, fear, misgiving, trepidation, trouble, unease

worship *v* **1** = **praise**, adore, exalt, glorify, honour, pray to, revere, venerate ≠ **mock** **2** = **love**, adore, idolize, put on a pedestal ≠ **despise** ◆ *n* **3** = **praise**, adoration, adulation, devotion, glory, honour, regard, respect, reverence

worth *n* **3** = **value**, cost, price, rate, valuation ≠ **worthlessness** **4** = **importance**, excellence, goodness, merit, quality, usefulness, value, worthiness ≠ **wretchedness**

wound¹ *n* **1** = **injury**, cut, gash, hurt, laceration, lesion, trauma (*Path*) **2** = **insult**, offence, slight ◆ *v* **3 a** = **injure**, cut, gash, hurt, lacerate, pierce, wing **b** = **offend**,

annoy, cut (someone) to the quick, hurt, mortify, sting

wrangle *v* **1** = **argue**, bicker, contend, disagree, dispute, fight, quarrel, row, squabble ◆ *n* **2** = **argument**, altercation, bickering, dispute, quarrel, row, squabble, tiff

wrap *v* **1** = **cover**, bind, bundle up, encase, enclose, enfold, pack, package, shroud, swathe ≠ **open** ◆ *n* **2** = **cloak**, cape, mantle, shawl, stole

wrath *n* = **anger**, displeasure, fury, indignation, ire, rage, resentment, temper

wreath *n* = **garland**, band, chaplet, crown, festoon, ring

wreck *v* **1** = **destroy**, break, demolish, devastate, ruin, shatter, smash, spoil

4 sprain. 5 difficult or painful parting. 6 adjustable spanner.

wrest ❶ v 1 twist violently. 2 take by force.

wrestle ❶ v 1 fight, esp. as a sport, by grappling with and trying to throw down an opponent. 2 struggle hard with. **wrestler** n **wrestling** n

wretch ❶ n 1 despicable person. 2 pitiful person. **wretched** [retch–id] adj 1 miserable or unhappy. 2 worthless.

wriggle ❶ v 1 move with a twisting action. 2 manoeuvre oneself by devious means. ◆ n 3 wriggling movement.

wring ❶ v wringing, wrung 1 twist, esp. to squeeze liquid out of. 2 clasp and twist (the hands). 3 obtain by forceful means.

wrinkle ❶ n 1 slight crease, esp. one in the skin due to age. ◆ v 2 make or become slightly creased. **wrinkly** adj

wrist n joint between the hand and the arm. **wristwatch** n watch worn on the wrist.

writ ❶ n written legal command.

write ❶ v writing, wrote, written 1 mark

paper etc. with symbols or words. 2 set down in words. 3 communicate by letter. 4 be the author or composer of. **writing** n **writer** n 1 author. 2 person who has written something specified. **write-off** n Informal something damaged beyond repair. **write-up** n published account of something.

writhe ❶ v twist or squirm in or as if in pain.

wrong ❶ adj 1 incorrect or mistaken. 2 immoral or bad. 3 not intended or suitable. 4 not working properly. ◆ adv 5 in a wrong manner. ◆ n 6 something immoral or unjust. ◆ v 7 treat unjustly. 8 malign. **wrongly** adv **wrongful** adj **wrongdoing** n immoral or illegal behaviour. **wrongdoer** n

wrote v past tense of WRITE.

wrought [rawt] v 1 Lit past of WORK. ◆ adj 2 (of metals) shaped by hammering or beating. **wrought iron** pure form of iron used for decorative work.

wrung v past of WRING.

———— THESAURUS ————

≠ **build** ◆ n 2 = **shipwreck**, hulk

wrench v 1 = **twist**, force, jerk, pull, rip, tear, tug, yank 2 = **sprain**, rick, strain ◆ n 3 = **twist**, jerk, pull, tug, yank 4 = **sprain**, strain, twist 5 = **blow**, pang, shock, upheaval 6 = **spanner**, adjustable spanner

wrest v 2 = **seize**, extract, force, take, win, wrench

wrestle v = **fight**, battle, combat, grapple, scuffle, struggle, tussle

wretch n 1 = **scoundrel**, good-for-nothing, miscreant, rascal, rogue, swine, worm

wriggle v 1 = **crawl**, jerk, jiggle, slink, snake, squirm, turn, twist, waggle, wiggle, worm, writhe, zigzag 2 = **manoeuvre**, dodge, extricate oneself ◆ n 3 = **twist**, jerk, jiggle, squirm, turn, waggle, wiggle

wring v 1 = **twist**, squeeze 3 = **force**, extract, screw

wrinkle n 1 = **crease**, corrugation, crinkle, crow's-foot, crumple, fold, furrow, line ◆ v

2 = **crease**, corrugate, crumple, fold, furrow, gather, pucker, rumple ≠ **level**

writ n = **summons**, court order, decree, document

write v 1, 2 = **record**, draft, draw up, inscribe, jot down, pen, scribble, set down

writhe v = **squirm**, jerk, struggle, thrash, thresh, toss, twist, wiggle, wriggle

wrong adj 1 = **incorrect**, erroneous, fallacious, false, inaccurate, mistaken, untrue, wide of the mark 2 = **bad**, criminal, dishonest, evil, illegal, immoral, sinful, unjust, unlawful, wicked, wrongful ≠ **just** 3 = **inappropriate**, incongruous, incorrect, unacceptable, unbecoming, undesirable, unseemly, unsuitable ≠ **correct** 4 = **defective**, amiss, askew, awry, faulty ◆ adv 5 = **incorrectly**, badly, erroneously, inaccurately, mistakenly, wrongly ≠ **correctly** ◆ n 6 = **offence**, crime, error, injury, injustice, misdeed, sin, transgression ◆ v 7 = **mistreat**, cheat, oppress, take advantage of 8 = **malign**,

wry ❶ *adj* **wrier, wriest** *or* **wryer, wryest 1** drily humorous. **2** (of a facial expression) contorted. **wryly** *adv*

WV West Virginia.
WY Wyoming.

─────── THESAURUS ───────

abuse, dishonour, harm, hurt
wrongdoer = offender, criminal, culprit, delinquent, evildoer, lawbreaker, miscreant, sinner, transgressor, villain
wrongful = improper, illegal, illicit,

inappropriate, unethical, unjust, unlawful
wry *adj* **1 = ironic**, droll, dry, mocking, sarcastic, sardonic **2 = contorted**, crooked, twisted, uneven ≠ **even**

X x Y y Z z

X 1 indicating an error, a choice, or a kiss. 2 indicating an unknown, unspecified, or variable factor, number, person, or thing. 3 the Roman numeral for ten.

xenophobia [zen–oh–**fobe**–ee–a] *n* fear or hatred of people from other countries.

Xerox [**zeer**–ox] *n* 1 ® machine for copying printed material. 2 ® copy made by a Xerox machine. ♦ *v* 3 copy (a document) using such a machine.

Xmas ❶ [**eks**–mass] *n Informal* Christmas.

X–ray, x–ray *n* 1 stream of radiation that can pass through some solid materials. 2 picture made by sending X–rays through someone's body to examine internal organs. ♦ *v* 3 photograph, treat, or examine using X–rays.

xylophone [**zile**–oh–fone] *n* musical instrument made of a row of wooden bars played with hammers.

ya *interj S Afr* yes.

yacht [**yott**] *n* large boat with sails or an engine, used for racing or pleasure cruising. **yachting** *n* **yachtsman, yachtswoman** *n*

yak *n* Tibetan ox with long shaggy hair.

yakka *n Aust & NZ informal* work.

yam *n* tropical root vegetable.

yank ❶ *v* 1 pull or jerk suddenly. ♦ *n* 2 sudden pull or jerk.

yap *v* **yapping, yapped** 1 bark with a high–pitched sound. 2 *Informal* talk continuously. ♦ *n* 3 high–pitched bark.

yard[1] *n* unit of length equal to 36 inches or about 91.4 centimetres. **yardstick** *n* standard against which to judge other people or things.

yard[2] *n* enclosed area, usu. next to a building and often used for a particular purpose, e.g. *builder's yard*.

yarn ❶ *n* 1 thread used for knitting or making cloth. 2 *Informal* long involved story.

yawn *v* 1 open the mouth wide and take in air deeply, often when sleepy or bored. 2 (of an opening) be large and wide. ♦ *n* 3 act of yawning. **yawning** *adj*

ye [**yee**] *pron Obs* you.

year *n* 1 time taken for the earth to make one revolution around the sun, about 365 days. 2 twelve months from January 1 to December 31. 3 **yearly** *adj, adv* (happening) every year or once a year. **yearling** *n* animal between one and two years old.

yearn ❶ *v* want (something) very much. **yearning** *n, adj*

yeast *n* fungus used to make bread rise and to ferment alcoholic drinks.

yebo *interj S Afr informal* yes.

yell ❶ *v* 1 shout or scream in a loud or piercing way. ♦ *n* 2 loud cry of pain, anger, or fear.

yellow *n* 1 the colour of gold, a lemon,

THESAURUS

Xmas *n Inf* = **Christmas**, Noel, Yule (*arch*)

yank *v, n* = **pull**, hitch, jerk, snatch, tug, wrench

yarn *n* 1 = **thread**, fibre 2 *Inf* = **story**, anecdote, cock–and–bull story (*inf*), fable, tale, tall story, urban legend, urban myth

yearn *v* 1 = **long**, ache, covet, crave, desire, hanker, hunger, itch

yell *v* 1 = **scream**, bawl, holler (*inf*), howl, screech, shout, shriek, squeal ≠ **whisper** ♦ *n* 2 = **scream**, cry, howl, screech, shriek, whoop etc. ◆ adj **2** of this colour. **3** Informal cowardly. ◆ v **4** make or become yellow. **yellow fever** serious infectious tropical disease.

yelp ⊕ v, n (give) a short sudden cry.

yen ⊕ n Informal longing or desire.

yeoman [**yo**–man] n, pl –men Hist farmer owning and farming his own land.

yes interj **1** expresses consent, agreement, or approval. **2** used to answer when one is addressed. **yes man** person who always agrees with their superior.

yesterday adv, n **1** (on) the day before today. **2** (in) the recent past.

yet ⊕ conj **1** nevertheless, still. ◆ adv **2** up until then or now. **3** still. **4** now.

yeti n same as ABOMINABLE SNOWMAN.

yew n evergreen tree with needle–like leaves and red berries.

yield ⊕ v **1** produce or bear. **2** give up control of, surrender. **3** give in. ◆ n **4** amount produced. **yielding** adj **1** submissive. **2** soft or flexible.

yob ⊕ **yobbo** n Slang bad–mannered aggressive youth.

yodel v –delling, –delled sing with abrupt changes between a normal and a falsetto voice.

yoga n Hindu method of exercise and discipline aiming at spiritual, mental, and physical wellbeing. **yogi** n person who practises yoga.

yogurt, yoghurt n slightly sour custard–

like food made from milk that has had bacteria added to it, often sweetened and flavoured with fruit.

yoke n **1** wooden bar put across the necks of two animals to hold them together. **2** frame fitting over a person's shoulders for carrying buckets. **3** Lit oppressive force, e.g. the yoke of the tyrant. **4** fitted part of a garment to which a fuller part is attached. ◆ v **5** put a yoke on. **6** unite or link.

yokel ⊕ n Offens person who lives in the country and is usu. simple and old–fashioned.

yolk n yellow part of an egg that provides food for the developing embryo.

Yorkshire pudding n baked batter made from flour, milk, and eggs.

you pron refers to: **1** the person or people addressed. **2** an unspecified person or people in general.

young ⊕ adj **1** in an early stage of life or growth. ◆ pl n **2** young people in general. **3** offspring, esp. young animals. **youngster** n young person.

your adj **1** of, belonging to, or associated with you. **2** of, belonging to, or associated with an unspecified person or people in general. **yours** pron something belonging to you. **yourself** pron

youth ⊕ n **1** time of being young. **2** boy or young man. **3** young people as a group. **youthful** adj **youth club** club that provides leisure activities for young people. **youth**

yelp v = **cry**, yap, yowl

yen n Inf = **longing**, ache, craving, desire, hankering, hunger, itch, passion, thirst, yearning

yet conj **1** = **nevertheless**, however, notwithstanding, still ◆ adv **2** = **so far**, as yet, thus far, until now, up to now **3** = **still**, besides, in addition, into the bargain, to boot **4** = **now**, just now, right now, so soon

yield v **1** = **produce**, bear, bring forth, earn, generate, give, net, provide, return, supply ≠ **use 2**, **3** = **surrender**, bow, capitulate, cave in (inf), give in, relinquish, resign,

submit, succumb ≠ **keep** ◆ n **6** = **profit**, crop, earnings, harvest, income, output, produce, return, revenue, takings ≠ **loss**

yob, yobbo n Inf = **thug**, hooligan, lout, roughneck (sl), ruffian

yokel n Offens = **peasant**, (country) bumpkin, countryman, hick (inf, chiefly US & Canad), hillbilly, rustic

young adj **1** = **immature**, adolescent, callow, early, fledgling, green, infant, junior, juvenile, little, new, recent, undeveloped, youthful ≠ **adult** ◆ pl n **3** = **offspring**, babies, brood, family, issue, litter, progeny ≠ **parents**

hostel inexpensive lodging place for young people travelling cheaply.

YT Yukon Territory.

Yule *n Lit* Christmas (season).

yuppie *n* 1 young highly–paid professional person, esp. one who has a fashionable way of life. ◆ *adj* 2 typical of or reflecting the values of yuppies.

zany ❶ [**zane**–ee] *adj* zanier, zaniest comical in an endearing way.

zap *v* zapping, zapped 1 *Slang* kill (by shooting). 2 change TV channels rapidly by remote control.

zeal ❶ *n* great enthusiasm or eagerness. **zealot** [**zel**–lot] *n* fanatic or extreme enthusiast. **zealous** [**zel**–luss] *adj* extremely eager or enthusiastic.

zebra *n* black–and–white striped African animal of the horse family. **zebra crossing** pedestrian crossing marked by black and white stripes on the road.

Zen *n* Japanese form of Buddhism that concentrates on learning through meditation and intuition.

zenith ❶ *n* 1 highest point of success or power. 2 point in the sky directly above an observer.

zephyr [**zef**–fer] *n* soft gentle breeze.

zero ❶ *n, pl* –ros, –roes 1 (symbol representing) the number 0. 2 point on a scale of measurement from which the graduations commence. 3 lowest point.

nothing, nil. ◆ *adj* 5 having no measurable quantity or size. **zero in on** *v* 1 aim at. 2 *Informal* concentrate on.

zest ❶ *n* 1 enjoyment or excitement. 2 interest, flavour, or charm. 3 peel of an orange or lemon.

zigzag *n* 1 line or course having sharp turns in alternating directions. ◆ *v* – zagging, –zagged 2 move in a zigzag. ◆ *adj* 3 formed in or proceeding in a zigzag.

zilch *n Slang* nothing.

zinc *n Chem* bluish–white metallic element used in alloys and to coat metal.

zing ❶ *n Informal* quality in something that makes it lively or interesting.

Zionism *n* movement to found and support a Jewish homeland in Israel. **Zionist** *n, adj*

zip ❶ *n* 1 fastener with two rows of teeth that are closed or opened by a small clip pulled between them. 2 *Informal* energy, vigour. ◆ *v* zipping, zipped 3 fasten with a zip. 4 move with a sharp whizzing sound.

zircon *n* mineral used as a gemstone and in industry.

zirconium *n Chem* greyish-white metallic element that is resistant to corrosion.

zither *n* musical instrument consisting of strings stretched over a flat box and plucked to produce musical notes.

zodiac *n* imaginary belt in the sky within which the sun, moon, and planets appear

————— THESAURUS —————

youth *n* 1 = **immaturity**, adolescence, boyhood *or* girlhood, girlhood, salad days ≠ **age** 3 = **boy**, adolescent, kid (*inf*), lad, stripling, teenager, young man, youngster

zany *adj* = **comical**, clownish, crazy, eccentric, goofy (*inf*), madcap, wacky (*sl*)

zeal *n* = **enthusiasm**, ardour, eagerness, fanaticism, fervour, gusto, keenness, passion, spirit, verve, zest

zealot *n* = **fanatic**, bigot, enthusiast, extremist, militant

zealous *adj* = **enthusiastic**, ablaze, afire, ardent, burning, devoted, eager, fanatical, fervent, impassioned, keen, passionate, rabid, spirited

zenith *n* 1 = **height**, acme, apex, apogee, climax, crest, high point, peak, pinnacle, summit, top

zero *n* 1 = **nothing**, nil, nought 2 = **nought** 3 = **bottom**, nadir, rock bottom 4 = **nil**, nothing

zest *n* 1 = **enjoyment**, appetite, gusto, keenness, relish, zeal ≠ **loathing** 2 = **flavour**, charm, interest, piquancy, pungency, relish, spice, tang, taste

zing *n inf* = **vitality**, animation, brio, clash, energy, go (*inf*), life, liveliness, pep, spirit, vigour, zest, zip

zip *n* 2 *Inf* = **energy**, drive, gusto, liveliness, verve, vigour, zest ≠ **apathy**

to move, divided into twelve equal areas, called signs of the zodiac, each named after a constellation.

zombie, zombi *n* **1** person who appears to be lifeless, apathetic, or totally lacking in independent judgment. **2** corpse brought back to life by witchcraft.

zone ❶ *n* **1** area with particular features or properties. **2** one of the divisions of the earth's surface according to temperature. ◆ *v* **3** divide into zones. **zonal** *adj*

zoo *n, pl* **zoos** place where live animals are kept for show.

zoology *n* study of animals. **zoologist** *n* **zoological** *adj* **zoological garden** zoo.

zoom ❶ *v* **1** move or rise very rapidly. **2** make or move with a buzzing or humming sound. **zoom lens** lens that can make the details of a picture larger or smaller while keeping the picture in focus.

zucchini [zoo–**keen**–ee] *n, pl* **–ni, –nis** *US & Aust* courgette.

zygote *n* fertilized egg cell.

zone *n* **1** = **area**, belt, district, region, section, sector, sphere

zoom *v* **1** = **speed**, dash, flash, fly, hurtle, pelt, rush, shoot, whizz (*inf*)

Good Writing Guide

Contents

Supplements

1 Introduction

The purpose of this part of the dictionary is to help you to use the rest of the dictionary more effectively. A dictionary tells you things like what words mean, how they are pronounced and where they come from. Sometimes the dictionary gives examples of how a word is used in a sentence, but it cannot tell you how to fit words into larger contexts like conversations, diaries, letters and reports. To do this you need to be aware of the usage of the word (there Is some help in this dictionary on this), its connotations, level of formality and of larger grammatical structures. This all sounds very daunting but it is something every one of us does every day with only the occasional slip-up.

✦ *Grammar, style and appropriateness*

People often feel self-conscious about how they use language and worry about making grammatical errors in their speech or writing. The good news is that for native English speakers it is almost impossible to make a 'mistake' in grammar since grammar is based on the way in which native speakers produce their language. It is however possible to use language inappropriately.

Except when we are talking to ourselves there is always an audience for the language we produce and good style consists in making sure that we use the right language for the right audience. The area where most people feel uncomfortable is in formal situations and this guide will therefore focus on formal English, but it should be remembered that appropriateness works in all aspects of our language use: it is just as inappropriate to send out printed invitations for a drink down the pub as it is to address the queen as 'Your Maj'.

2 Formal, informal and other types of language

Formal language is used in formal settings and it usually closely
follows the rules of standard English.

✦ *Standard English*

Here is how a recent government document defines standard English:

Standard English is the variety of English used in public
communication, particularly in writing. It is the form taught
in schools and used by educated speakers. It is not limited to
a particular region and can be spoken with any accent.

There are differences in vocabulary and grammar between
standard English and other varieties. For example, *we were
robbed* and *look at those trees* are standard English; *we was
robbed* and *look at them trees* are non-standard.

To communicate effectively in a range of situations – written
and oral – it is necessary to be able to use standard English,
and to recognize when it is appropriate to use it in preference to any other variety.

Note that standard British English is not the only standard
variety; other English-speaking countries, such as the United
States and Australia, have their own standard forms.

(National Literacy Strategy Glossary – DfEE)

Even the government agrees that standard English is only a *variety* of
English and that it might be appropriate *not* to use it in some situations. However, standard English is the variety with the most social
prestige and it is the one that people are most worried about getting
right.

When you begin any piece of writing you need to be aware of the expectations of your audience. Would they expect you to be informal and friendly, slangy and colloquial, or formal and correct? This dictionary can help you to some extent with these choices. Some words and expressions, for instance, only ever occur in formal contexts and are marked as such in the word's entry. Others may be labelled *informal*, *slang* or *taboo*.

✦ *Formal language*

Formal language is speech or writing which most closely adheres to Standard English. It is used most often in serious situations, for instance in job applications or official reports. Its purpose is to make meaning as clear as possible. Formal language can be found in things like television news reports, speeches in debates, legal documents, encyclopedia entries and application forms.

Generally, formal English:

- ❏ aims at an unknown audience
- ❏ tries to be clear and explicit
- ❏ tends to contain more sentences in the passive voice
- ❏ avoids contractions such as *can't*
- ❏ makes full use of specialist terms
- ❏ avoids colloquialism and slang
- ❏ avoids constructions that have been criticized as poor grammar, such as double negatives, split infinitives and hanging participles

✦ *Formal usage and strict usage*

In this dictionary you will often find references to *strict usage*. The guidelines provided in such entries represent English on its very best behaviour and often involve rules that would be taken note of only by very pedantic people. The trouble is that when you are writing a job application you just don't know how pedantic your prospective employers are likely to be.

✦ *Informal language*

When a word or phrase is labelled as informal in the dictionary this simply means that it is not suitable for formal use. The meaning of informal changes with the context of your speech or writing. For instance, an informal interview would be relaxed and chatty in tone but it would seem very serious compared to an informal conversation between friends. Similarly, an informal newspaper article would be much more highly structured than an informal note to the milkman.

Informal language is usually friendly in tone and more tolerant of non-standard words or expressions. There are many levels of informal language but in general it:

> ❏ is personal rather than impersonal
> ❏ is addressed to a known or familiar audience
> ❏ uses contractions such as *it's* or *can't*
> ❏ uses more comment clauses such as *I think* or *unfortunately*
> ❏ uses active rather than passive verbs
> ❏ often addresses the reader as *you*
> ❏ makes some use of colloquial language

Colloquial language is the type used in conversation. It is informally structured and often includes slang, dialect terms and contracted forms of words.

✦ *Dialect*

Standard English is a dialect of English. There are many others, both within and beyond the British Isles, such as Yorkshire dialect, Estuary English, American English and Jamaican English. People often confuse dialect with accent and assume that because someone is speaking with a regional accent they must be using a dialect. This is not the case. Dialects have their own grammatical rules and vocabulary whereas accent is concerned only with pronunciation. Dialect forms were seen as sub-standard English in the past but nowadays the only objection to them is that they might make communication difficult outside the area in which the dialect is used.

✦ *Jargon*

In this dictionary you will often find certain words marked with specialist subject labels such as *medicine* or *computers*. If these words are used in a medical or computing context they do not present a problem but if they are used outside their specialist fields they are referred to as jargon. Jargon has two uses: it helps people in the same group or profession to identify each other and exclude others and it makes the user seem knowledgeable to outsiders. Jargon is acceptable in informal contexts, particularly when a known audience is being addressed, but it is considered impolite and possibly confusing to use it when addressing an unknown audience. Some groups make up a jargon deliberately to exclude others, for instance Cockney rhyming slang was originally a thieves' jargon designed to confuse the law enforcement agents.

✦ Slang

Slang is usually deliberately non-standard English. Slang is often restricted in its use to a particular group of people or to a particular place. Like jargon it helps groups of people to identify with each other and to exclude outsiders. For this reason slang frequently changes when it becomes too widely known. Many slang terms are inventive and colourful but their use tends to be short-lived. Some slang terms from the past are now part of standard English, though usually at the informal end of usage, for instance *wicked* in the sense of good, or *hassle* meaning problems or vexation.

✦ Taboo words

Taboo words are frowned upon in formal use. Most are sexual in nature or to do with the body or bodily functions. Taboo words are common in informal speech and can be extremely versatile in how they are applied. Words labelled *taboo* in this dictionary are likely to give offence to some readers and are generally best avoided unless the intention is to shock or to give a flavour of spoken English.

✦ Usage notes

You will also find usage notes attached to some entries. These vary in their purpose; some are to alert you to possible confusions between words such as *militate* and *mitigate*, others refer to how the entry word combines with others, for example in the notes on *otherwise*, and some describe how the word in question is used in particular contexts, as in the note on *very*.

You should be aware that these notes reflect current usage. The meanings of words are not fixed and change over time. If you look at the note on *doubt* you will see that its use with *whether* and *if* has changed relatively recently. The meanings of some words are clearly still in dispute as you will see if you look at the note on *disinterested*. *Disinterested* used to mean 'unbiased' but today many writers use it to mean 'uninterested' or 'bored'. If the distinction between 'disinterested' and 'uninterested' continues to be ignored by the majority of writers then it will cease to exist and the two words will be completely interchangeable. Usage is also an issue when you find a word labelled *old-fashioned*. These words or the senses marked as old-fashioned have gone out of current use. You might well read them in a nineteenth-century novel, for instance, but unless you wish to sound like a nineteenth-century novel you will probably not write them.

✦ Clichés

One final type of language that is frequently criticized is the **cliché**. A dictionary cannot really help with identifying clichés as they consist of phrases rather than words. A cliché is an expression which has been overused to the point that it has either lost its original meaning or is irritating to large numbers of people. Clichés become overused because they express a common situation or because they are fashionable. 'All's fair in love and war' is an example of the former type and 'at the end of the day' of the latter.

Clichés are effective in speech because they give users time to think as they repeat the set phrase but it is a good idea to avoid them in writing where this excuse does not apply.

3 What do dictionary definitions mean?

People use dictionaries for a number of reasons, such as:

- ❏ to find out the meaning of a word
- ❏ to check its spelling
- ❏ to find out a word's origin
- ❏ to settle arguments about words
- ❏ to explore how a word is used

All of these reasons are perfectly valid, and there are many more, but it is perhaps worth considering what we are doing when we consult a dictionary to find out the meaning of a word.

Some people assume that the meaning of a word is fixed and that dictionaries are simply records of these meanings. If this were the case you could use the same dictionary throughout your life, perhaps adding an occasional supplement to cope with new words every few years. Unfortunately this is not how words work. All words in current use are subject to change. Consider the word *text* for instance. Two hundred years ago most people would have thought that it meant a short passage from the Bible. Fifty years ago students would have used it to mean their textbooks. For most of the word's history it was only used as a noun, but today it is frequently used as a verb meaning 'to send a text message on a mobile phone.' People who send such messages have become known as *texters* and the mobile phone meaning of text is probably the one that comes first to most people's minds. So does the word *text* really mean a short passage from the Bible or a mobile phone message? The answer is of course that *text* means both, plus several other things as well. When we use the word we can usually work out which of its meanings we wish to apply, as in the sentence:

I texted him a text from my RE textbook.

Old fashioned lexicographers, writers of dictionaries, thought that they could 'fix' the meaning of words by getting as many of them as possible in between the covers of their books. In such dictionaries the primary or 'original' meaning was always listed first irrespective of whether that was the meaning that the word had for most people.

Modern lexicographers use large databases or 'corpora' that contain millions of words – The Bank of English on which this dictionary is based contains over 450 million words. Modern lexicographers are thus able to look at very large samples of how a particular word is really used and decide on its most common meaning.

You can see an example of this if you look up the word *decimate*. Some people say that *decimate* 'really' means to reduce by a tenth because it refers to the practice of Roman armies killing every tenth man in a rebellious unit. However, most people use *decimate* to mean to destroy or kill a large proportion and you will therefore find that this is the meaning given in this dictionary.

Just as word meanings change over time so too does word usage. Many usage changes go unnoticed whereas others are the subject of much public discussion. In recent years, for instance, there has been a great deal of debate about 'politically correct' language. This has caused careful writers and speakers to drop expressions that identify the sex of the person referred to. Thus *chairman* and *chairwoman* have been replaced by the gender-neutral *chair*, and *firemen* and *-women* have become *firefighters*. There have even been changes in what is grammatically acceptable so that a sentence such as

> Any passenger with special dietary requirements should make their wishes known to a steward.

is now acceptable.

Their should in theory refer to more than one person but it is acceptable in this sentence because it avoids the clumsy sounding 'his or her'.

Old-fashioned lexicographers and grammarians tended to be *prescriptive*; that is they had no problem telling their readers what words 'really' meant and how they ought to be used. Modern lexicographers and grammarians tend to be *descriptive*; they go to a great deal of trouble to find out what words mean most of the time and how they are actually used.

11

The influence of the past has not disappeared completely, however, and careful writers in formal contexts need to be aware of some of the rules that were once rigorously enforced by grammarians and lexicographers. Perhaps the most famous rule from the past is the one which states that you should not split infinitives. Infinitives are verbs in the form *to run* or *to go*. Grammarians who thought that English grammar should reflect Latin grammar noticed that infinitives were never split in Latin (this is because the infinitive form in Latin is one word) and therefore they should not be split in English. English speakers and writers had been happily slipping words in between the *to* and the verb for hundreds of years before this rule was invented, and in many sentences it makes better sense to split the infinitive, but the practice is still condemned by some people.

Whether you split an infinitive or not will often depend on the emphasis you wish to give to a sentence. For instance,

> I want you to quickly sort through those files

splits the infinitive but places stress on *quickly*

> I want you to sort quickly through those files

gives more stress to the sorting process.

Another old-fashioned rule states that you should not end sentences with a preposition like *at, with, on* or *up*. This rule also derives from English grammarians who were more interested in Latin and it has often been criticized, most famously by Sir Winston Churchill who said

> This is the sort of nonsense up with which I will not put.

These rules as well as some others are now generally recognized as at best silly and at worst prejudiced. In informal contexts they can safely be ignored, but in very formal contexts there is still some likelihood that someone in your audience will consider your disregard for these rules to be ignorance rather than confidence in your own written style and voice.

✦ Are you shamed by your mistakes in English?

The heading for this section is based on an advertisement that appears regularly in many newspapers. The advertisers obviously hope you are ashamed of your English so that you will buy their product but shame is an important concept in language use.

When we speak we usually make lots of 'mistakes'. We start sentences and don't finish them, we start a sentence with one idea and finish it off with a different one, we hesitate, we utter meaningless phrases, we get interrupted, we lose the thread of our conversation, and there are many other things which might hinder the flow of conversation. Amazingly, very few of these factors actually harm understanding. We are so focused on meaning and intention that we simply don't notice or edit out the noise of our mistakes.

Writing is much less forgiving. Whatever we say can be inspected any number of times and analysed for errors of meaning, vocabulary, organization and style. Also writing can circulate beyond people we can see face to face and is often read by total strangers.

As if all of this wasn't bad enough writing is governed by a set of rules that are not always intuitive and many of which were developed hundreds of years ago. It is easy for those who know the rules of writing to put down those who don't and many people avoid writing simply to avoid such situations.

Becoming a good writer takes practice, both in reading and writing. You need to read to gain experience of how others have expressed themselves and you need to write to improve your existing techniques and experiment with new and different ones. Remember that there are very many different types of writing and although you might not want to write a novel you can become an expert in any kind of writing given time.

4 Beginning to write

The best writing is tailored to match the needs, interests and expectations of its audience. You can find excellence in a witty one-liner or in a multi-volume encyclopedia but all writers begin with the same set of questions.

- ❏ Who is my audience?
- ❏ What am I trying to say?
- ❏ What form am I writing in?

The answers to these questions determine everything from the kind of words and expressions you might choose to the actual look of your writing on the page.

✦ *Audience*

All writing has an audience even if, as in the case of diaries, it is only your future self. When you think about your audience you need to think about whether it is:

- ❏ known or unknown
- ❏ specific or general
- ❏ expecting to be entertained, informed, persuaded, or instructed

The less you know personally about your audience the more careful you have to be about your language. If your audience is the selection panel for a job then you will need to be very formal in your use of language and precise about the information you give. If you are writing a letter to a friend you can be as free as you like in your choice of language and expression. If you are writing up a science experiment your audience will expect certain kinds of information in a particular format and so on.

Writing is a form of communication at a distance and in assessing your audience it is a good idea to remove that distance. What would you say to the person you are writing for? Would you be on your best behaviour or would you be relaxed? Would you behave conventionally or would you take risks in what you might say?

It is when you are on your best behaviour that you need to take most care with what you write.

✦ *Purpose*

The purpose of your writing will also have an effect on which words you choose and the rules you apply to them. If you are writing a story designed to entertain you can choose from a whole variety of styles or invent your own. If you are writing an informative report on the implementation of your company's IT policy you will use a formal style and numerous technical terms.

✦ *Format*

The look of your words on the page will be determined by the format you choose. A novel will consist of blocks of text, while an advertisement will probably have very little text but might include images. Some formats, like tax assessments, require formal careful writing, while others can be informal like a note to the window cleaner.

The most important thing you need to achieve is a match between these three elements.

terms of tone and style or it might, as in an academic essay, be a clear statement of what is to be examined. As with conversation your aim is to get on well with your audience; you don't want to bore or confuse them.

✦ *The middle*

The middle section of any piece of writing contains its main points. These need to be clearly and logically arranged so that readers can easily and efficiently make sense of what you write.

Different writing formats have different conventions for helping readers to find their way around. Novels use chapters, articles have headings and subheadings and diaries are organized by date. You can also help your reader by including sequencing words and by making use of *topic sentences* at the beginnings of paragraphs.

✦ *The end*

The final section of your writing is likely to have a strong effect on the impression it leaves on your readers. Again, it is helpful to think of your writing as a social encounter. After a pleasant evening some guests leave abruptly whilst others seem to find it impossible to say goodbye. You should aim to conclude your writing cleanly but not too suddenly or rudely. A good ending should recall the main points of your writing and give readers some sense of resolution.

5 Organizing your writing

You organize your writing at every level. Arranging the letters of each word is called spelling, putting the words together into sentences is called syntax, which is an aspect of grammar. Beyond this you need to plan how your sentences will fit into paragraphs and how the paragraphs will make up a whole text.

✦ *Planning*

Apart from the briefest of notes most writing benefits from planning. If you are about to embark on a report you need to review the information you wish to convey, how it is linked together and the best order in which to present it. If you are writing a letter of complaint you might jot down notes of the relevant facts, dates and times and the actions you wish to be taken.

Plans can be anything from a brief list to a complex spider diagram showing relationships and connections but their purpose is always the same: to help you to present your information in a clear and logical order.

Once you have given some consideration to the overall content of your writing you need to think about the specifics. These will vary according to the format you are using but roughly speaking every kind of writing has a beginning, a middle, and an end.

✦ *The beginning*

You should think of the beginning of most pieces of writing as a sort of shop window. Shop windows tell you what is on offer inside and they are designed to grab the attention of passers-by.

Newspaper reports, for instance, start off with their main points in the first paragraph because journalists know that unless readers are instantly engaged they will move on to another article. In contrast, a friendly letter might begin with some general news and chat before going on to the main news in order to avoid seeming rude and abrupt.

A good start to a piece of writing engages the reader and gives him or her some idea of what is to come. This 'preview' might only be in

6 Paragraphs and other navigational devices

Unbroken blocks of writing are difficult to navigate and so long texts are split into paragraphs. You should always start a new paragraph when you introduce a new topic or idea but you can start them for other reasons as well.

✦ *Topic sentences*

You should try to use topic sentences for two main reasons. Firstly, they announce the theme of a paragraph and make your writing easier to understand. Secondly, they provide your readers with 'signposts' that help them to find their way around your writing. You can see this for yourself by reading through the first sentences of a piece of writing. The topic sentences act as a kind of summary of what is going on.

A well-structured paragraph, then, tells the reader what its main idea is, and then develops the idea by providing illustrations of examples. You can see how this works below.

You should try to use topic sentences for two main reasons.	◄ Topic sentence – States the theme. You should use topic sentences.
Firstly, they announce the theme of a paragraph and make your writing easier to understand.	◄ Development of theme – reason for using topic sentences
Secondly, they provide your readers with 'signposts' that help them find their way around your writing.	◄ Further development – second reason for using topic sentences
You can see this yourself by reading through the first sentences of a piece of writing.	◄ Illustration of use of topic sentences to back up initial statement
The topic sentences act as a kind of summary of what is going on.	◄ Sentence summing up the paragraph

✦ Other reasons for starting a new paragraph

Paragraphs form the blocks of sense in a piece of writing. If you have to interrupt your own reading you tend to read on until you finish the paragraph rather than the sentence or page that you are on. This is because you want to complete the idea or action that is being dealt with at that point. In your writing, therefore, you can use paragraphs to control your reader's attention span. This means that you should think about varying the lengths of your paragraphs.

Using plenty of short paragraphs generally makes your writing easy to read but it can be distracting and leave the reader uninvolved as none of your ideas are explored in any depth. Using mostly long paragraphs makes your writing look serious and gives you the opportunity to develop your ideas but too many long paragraphs can be off-putting for some readers.

Using a very short paragraph after a series of long ones makes it stand out.

New paragraphs are necessary when you are using direct speech. The rule 'new speaker, new line' is a very sensible one as it helps your readers to work out who is speaking without the aid of too many intrusive 'said Jane' clauses.

If you have planned your writing carefully you tend to find that the main headings of your plan become your topic sentences. Sometimes you start a new paragraph to move on to what might be a subheading in your plan.

Because a paragraph deals with the same topic you need to be careful not to overuse your key term as this can grate on your readers. Remember that you can use a pronoun to replace it, or you can use synonyms.

✦ Further navigational aids

Most writing involves some kind of sequence. It is helpful to your readers if you give them some idea of where they are by using sequencing terms such as:

Two days previously	*Firstly*	*As a consequence*
The next attempt	*Later*	*In response*
Because	*Suddenly*	*At six o'clock*

Words and phrases of this type help to show the connections between the different parts of your writing as well as the order of events.

Layout devices are frequently used in non-fiction writing but even stories use things like chapter headings.

Newspapers in headlines shock!

Usually the size of the type in a headline indicates the importance of the story. Headline writers also try to make them interesting and attention-grabbing.

✦ *Subheadings*
Longer newspaper articles also use subheadings to mark different stages in the story and to maintain readers' attention by piquing their curiosity.

✦ *Headings and subheadings*
Headings and subheadings are used in other non-fiction texts such as reports and textbooks. Their purpose is to mark out the different parts of the text so that readers can find relevant pieces of the text as quickly as possible.

In some documents headings are preceded by letters or numbers. The way these are used varies but one common system uses the following conventions:

❑ capital letters mark the most important headings
❑ numbers are used to mark the next level
❑ lower case letters refer to minor sections
❑ roman numerals indicate subsections

Thus paragraph *A.2.b.(iv)* represents a very minor subsection.

Within sections of a document you might wish to emphasize a number of points. If they are in some kind of sequence or in order of importance they might be numbered, or if the order is not important bullet points can be used. Bullet points:

❑ draw attention to specific points
❑ stand out on the page
❑ are easy for readers to grasp at a glance

> Sometimes boxes are used to draw attention to a particular piece of text. The text might be a summary of a particular section or it might provide additional background information.

All of these devices draw the reader's attention to particular sections of a text. There are also devices that can be used to create emphasis within sentences. These include capital letters, bold and italic type, and underlining. These devices should be employed sparingly as over-use can be a distraction.

CAPITAL LETTERS are the written equivalent of shouting. They can also be used to represent a loud noise.

Italic type is often used to mark the titles of books, films, or plays. It is also used to show the stress a speaker would place on a word as in 'It was *so* hot'.

Bold type is more emphatic than plain text. Particularly important parts of documents may be in bold or a single word might be picked out to make sure people notice it:

Candidates should **not** bring their books into the exam.

Underlining does the job of italic or bold type in handwriting. It is seldom used nowadays in printed texts.

White space is the term used to describe the parts of a page which contain no writing or illustrations. In terms of the visual impact of a document white space can be very powerful. If there is too little white space documents seem cramped and poorly laid out. A small amount of text surrounded by a great deal of space stands out and suggests that the text is important in some way.

✦ *More to writing than writing*

Modern word processors and desktop-publishing packages allow a great deal of control over how writing appears on the page. As with all aspects of writing the ideal to aim for is clarity. You can experiment with founts and any number of layout devices but it is important to ask yourself, "Is this document easy to read and easy to follow?"

If you are producing a document by hand, presentation is also important. Neat and legible handwriting is the first priority and you can help yourself to achieve this by producing more than one draft of anything but the briefest of notes. White space can be deployed effectively in handwritten documents to produce a neat and uncluttered appearance.

7 Sentences

Sentences are the basic building blocks of any piece of writing. They should contain complete ideas or actions and therefore should make sense on their own. Grammarians have identified three types of sentences:

> simple, compound, and complex.

✦ Simple sentences
Simple sentences must have a subject and a verb.
e.g. The bus arrived on time.

✦ Compound sentences
Compound sentences consist of simple sentences joined by conjunctions such as *and* or *but*.
e.g. The bus arrived on time but I still missed it.

✦ Complex sentences
Complex sentences contain a main clause and at least one other clause that is related to it. The two clauses are joined by conjunctions such as *although, because* and *in order to*.
e.g. The bus arrived on time although I had expected it to be late.

But wait! There is one other type of sentence which makes sense but which lacks some features of a full sentence. These are sometimes called *minor sentences* and most frequently lack a subject for their verbs. For instance *No smoking* or *Listen!*

You might think that to accomplish a complex writing task like a report you would need mostly complex sentences but a recent study of writing in exams showed that the best candidates used the greatest number of simple sentences and that weaker candidates tended to overuse compound sentences.

Simple sentences have the advantage of clarity, but if you overuse them your writing does not flow in a natural manner.

Compound sentences help the flow of ideas but if they consist of just a train of undeveloped actions they come across as rather flat and uninteresting, like a boring speaker who just goes on and on and doesn't know when to stop.

Complex sentences show the relationships between different actions or ideas and are particularly useful in explanation and analysis. However, they can be difficult to follow as readers have to hold a number of ideas in their heads at the same time. You should avoid using too many complex sentences at once.

Generally, good writing will have a combination of all the different types of sentences.

✦ *Active and passive sentences*
An active sentence is one in which the subject and verb are present. For instance

> The cat ate the cream.

It is possible to remove the subject of this sentence (the cat) by placing its object (the cream) first:

> The cream was eaten.

This sentence is said to be in the passive voice.

Passive sentences are useful if you are interested in what happened but not in who performed the action. Typically, passive constructions are used in scientific and technical contexts where the thing done is the focus of attention rather than the doer.

Passive sentences are also useful if the identity of the person performing an action is not known, as in

> My watch was stolen.

It is sometimes politer to use a passive construction than an active one. Think of the difference between

> My watch was stolen.

and

> You stole my watch.

It is possible to identify the doer in a passive construction. You could say

> The cream was eaten by the cat.

but this is a clumsy and rather indirect way of expressing a simple idea. Many people (and grammar checkers in word processors) complain about passive constructions because they are unnecessarily wordy and because they allow people to duck responsibility. For example the sentence

> Your tax demand was wrongly calculated.

makes the mistake seem almost natural whereas

> We wrongly calculated your tax demand.

takes responsibility for the mistake.

Active sentences have the advantage of clarity and force since they give more information about an event than a passive equivalent. If you have a choice between an active and passive construction it is almost always better and clearer to use the active one.

✦ Sentence order

Simple sentences often begin with their subject which is then followed by the verb and any further information. This is a good practice as it ensures clarity but there is still room for variation. For instance, here is a simple sentence starting with its subject which is then followed by the verb:

> Harry bought the dog on Tuesday.

If you wish to emphasize when the dog was bought you can write

> On Tuesday Harry bought the dog.

You can even use a passive construction (but see above) if you want to place the emphasis on the dog.

> The dog was bought by Harry on Tuesday.

There is room for even more variation in compound sentences. For instance:

> Shelley left the club reluctantly but Reshad stayed on.
> Reluctantly Shelley left the club but Reshad stayed on.
> Reshad stayed on but Shelley reluctantly left the club.

The order in which you present information is not fixed and you should always give some thought to which piece of information you wish to make most noticeable by placing it first in your sentence.

In complex sentences the main clause containing the subject of the sentence usually comes first, as in:

> We had a really good time in France although we only went for a week.

You can alter this by putting the second part of the sentence first

> Although we only went for a week we had a really good time in France.

As complex sentences don't make sense until you reach the main verb this arrangement creates a form of suspense.

In any piece of writing you should aim for variety in the order of your sentences both to maintain your readers' interest and to be as precise as possible in the emphasis you give to your information.

✦ Sentence rhythms
Just as it is important to vary the lengths of your paragraphs you should also think about the lengths of your sentences and the effect that they might have.

Short sentences have impact. They are easy to understand. Using too many short sentences creates a choppy, abrupt style. Longer sentences create a sense of flow and continuity so that your readers can get involved in your meaning but on the other hand they can become confusing if they go on for too long.

Your choice of sentence length can be affected by what you are talking about. If you are describing a continuous process, for instance, you might want to make the description fit into a number of longer sentences. If you want to make details stand out you might put each one into a separate sentence.

As with paragraphs, contrast is a useful tool. A long sentence will stand out amongst a series of short ones and a single short sentence after a number of long ones is a very effective way of arresting your readers' attention.

8 Spelling

Spelling is probably the aspect of writing that causes the most trouble and anxiety. This is because there is a mismatch between the number of sounds we use to speak English – about forty-four – and the number of letters we use to spell it. This is further complicated by the fact that we do not always use the same letters or the same combination of letters to represent the same sounds.

The good news is that only about five hundred words in all the millions of words in English have really irregular spellings. The bad news is that these irregular spellings occur in some of the commonest words. It has been estimated that about 3% of words in everyday use are so irregular that they simply have to be learned by heart whilst the rest follow some sort of rule or pattern.

The first thing to remember about spelling is that it is a writing skill which can only be improved by writing. When we read we do not need to look at all the letters in a word to understand it but we do have to get every single letter in its correct place if we wish our writing to be understood.

✦ *General strategies*

The most effective way of learning to spell unfamiliar words is the Look, Cover, Write, Check method. This simply involves the following steps:

❏ *Look* at the word, carefully studying every letter
❏ *Cover* the word
❏ *Write* it down
❏ *Check* what you have written against the correct spelling

Repeat this process until the two spellings match.

The more times you write a word correctly the better, as this gives you a 'feel' for the word. (You notice this when you write down several possible spellings to see which one seems right.) The old teaching strategy of making you write out your spelling corrections five times was a good one for this reason.

If you write on a regular basis, jot down in a notebook words you have difficulty spelling and then gradually work through them using the Look, Cover, Write, Check method.

Collect or make up mnemonics for words you have difficulty with. For example:

environment	– there is **iron** in the env**iron**ment
friend	– the end of fri**end** is **end**
fulfil	– knock the *l* out of ful*l* and fil*l*
necessary	– it is necessary to have one **c**ollar and two **s**ocks
stationery	– **e**nvelopes are station**e**ry

You can use mnemonics to help with pairs of words that sound alike, such as *council* and *counsel*, *accept* and *except*, or *principal* and *principle*.

Think of other words that are similar which you can spell. For instance, knowing how to spell:

> *finite* will help you with *definite* and *definitely*
> *liberate* will help you with *deliberate* and *deliberately*

Mental mispronunciation can be useful with words that have silent letters. You say *subtle* as if it was pronounced *suttle* – but there is nothing to stop you pronouncing it in your head as it is spelt.

If you go to the trouble of looking a word up in a dictionary make sure that you write it down and use Look, Cover, Write, Check.

Many word processors spellcheck as you type. Make a mental note of the words that you mistype and practise them later. You also need to remember that word processors cannot recognize words that are correctly spelt but wrongly used. You therefore need to be particularly vigilant about commonly confused words like *there* and *their* or *your* and *you're*.

✦ Some useful spelling rules
The following rules give useful examples and illustrate some basic principles of spelling. The first few rules, for instance, are all to do with the role of vowels. It would seem that English spelling has evolved to

avoid too many vowels together and that consonants act as buffers to prevent them interacting with each other.

✦ *Adding endings to words ending with a silent E*

A final silent *E* is dropped when a suffix beginning with a vowel is added:

> *abbreviate + ion* → *abbreviat + ion = abbreviation*
> *appreciate + ive* → *appreciat + ive = appreciative*
> *desire + able* → *desir + able = desirable*
> *guide + ance* → *guid + ance = guidance*
> *hope + ing* → *hop + ing = hoping*

In the above examples the *E* is interacting with the previous vowel and it can be replaced but when the *E* is attached to a consonant like *C* or *G* it cannot be removed.

> *change + able = changeable*
> *courage + ous = courageous*
> *notice + able = noticeable*

The *–CE* or *–GE* in the above examples are soft sounds which would be lost without the *E*.

✦ *Doubling letters*

In the following set of patterns we see the buffering effect of consonants. They are doubled to keep two vowels in close proximity from affecting each other.

When a suffix beginning with a vowel is added to a word which ends in a single vowel plus a consonant, the consonant is doubled if the stress is on the end of the word:

> *begin + ing* → *beginn + ing = beginning*
> *commit + ed* → *committ + ed = committed*
> *handicap + ing* → *handicapp + ing = handicapping*
> *kidnap + ed* → *kidnapp + ed = kidnapped*

When a suffix beginning with a vowel is added to a word which ends in a single vowel plus **L**, the **L** is always doubled:

> appal + ing   →   appall + ing = appalling
> cancel + ation   →   cancell + ation = cancellation

When an ending beginning with **E**, **I**, or **Y** is added to a word which ends in **C**, a **K** is also added to the **C** to keep its hard sound – this is the equivalent of doubling the **C**:

> picnic + ing   →   picnick + ing = picnicking
> panic + y   →   panick + y = panicky

✦ Adding endings to words ending in –OUR

The principle here is the avoidance of too many vowels together. When the endings **–OUS** and **–ARY** are added to a word which ends in **–OUR**, the **U** of the **–OUR** is dropped:

> glamour + ous   →   glamor + ous = glamorous
> honour + ary   →   honor + ary = honorary
> humour + ous   →   humor + ous = humorous

✦ Adding endings to words ending in –Y

When an ending is added to a word which ends in a consonant plus **Y**, the **Y** changes to **I**:

> apply + ance   →   appli + ance = appliance
> beauty + ful   →   beauti + ful = beautiful
> happy + ness   →   happi + ness = happiness

If the suffix already begins with an **I** the avoidance of the 'too many vowels together' rule comes into play:

> supply + ing   →   supply + ing = supplying

✦ Forming plurals

Most plurals are formed by adding an **S** to the end of the word. However a number of spelling problems occur with the rather slippery 'semi-vowel' **Y**.

The plural of a word which ends in a consonant plus **Y** is made by changing the **Y** to **I** and adding **–ES**:

> *jelly* → *jelli + es = jellies*
> *memory* → *memori + es = memories*

The plural of a word which ends in a vowel plus **Y** is made by adding **S** as part of the 'not too many vowels' principle:

> *journey + s = journeys*
> *kidney + s = kidneys*

The plurals of words ending in **S**, **X**, **Z**, **–SH**, or **–CH** are formed by adding **–ES**:

> *bus + es = buses*
> *focus + es = focuses*

The plural of a word which ends in **–EAU** may be made by adding **S** or **X**:
> *gateau + s = gateaus*   *gateau + x = gateaux*

✦ Words beginning AL–
We spell *all* on its own with two **L**s, but when this sound is added at the beginning of a word to make a new word, it is spelt with one **L**:

> *al + ready = already*
> *al + though = although*
> *al + together = altogether*

✦ Words ending in –FUL
The principle which applies for *all* at the beginning of words applies to *full* at the ends. Here the suffix **–FUL** is always spelt with one **L**:

> *beautiful*   *colourful*   *grateful*

✦ Words ending in –OUS
The 'uss' sound at the end of an adjective is almost always spelt **–OUS**:

> *anonymous*   *anxious*   *atrocious*
> *conscientious* *humorous*

✦ Words ending in –IZE and –ISE

In Britain both **–IZE** and **–ISE** are acceptable. In American English **–IZE** is the preferred ending for many verbs.

> *emphasize* or *emphasise*
> *specialize* or *specialise*

Some words are always spelt with **–ISE**. In these words there is usually no stand-alone form of the word without the ending.

advise	*chastise*	*despise*	*devise*
revise	*supervise*	*surprise*	*televise*

A few words are spelt **–YSE**:

> *analyse*   *breathalyse*

✦ The I before E rule

This rule is well known and often criticized because there are so many exceptions to it. The rule works quite well however if you remember the second part about the sound.

I comes before ***E*** when they make the sound "ee"...:

> *achieve*   *believe*   *field*   *hygiene*

... except after **C**:

> *conceive*   *deceive*   *receipt*

✦ Some commonly confused words

There are three possible spellings of the sound at the beginning of this sentence. How do you know which one to choose? From a spelling point of view it is not a good idea to discuss the three spellings together but rather to look at the groups to which the words belong. Thus you should try to remember that

> *here, there,* and *where*

are all to do with place...

> *they're, we're,* and *you're*

all contain an abbreviated form of *are*. You can test whether you have got the right spelling in these cases by saying the words in full.

> *They're they go*

might just about seem plausible but

> *They are they go*

is definitely nonsense.

This just leaves *their* and *your* which are both possessive adjectives to do with belonging.

✦ *Its and it's*

The confusion between these two terms arises because one of them is a possessive pronoun (*its*) and the other one (*it's*) has an apostrophe which is frequently used to mark possession. In fact *it's* is an abbreviated form of *it is* or *it has*. Again a simple test will tell you which one is appropriate.

> *The dog finished it's dinner*

looks acceptable but if you mentally spell out the abbreviation you get

> *The dog finished it is dinner*

which is a sentence that not even the dog could make sense of.

9 Grammar

In the past people would worry about using 'correct' grammar whereas today it is much more useful to think about using appropriate grammar and to communicate clearly. The decisions you make about how you express yourself will depend partly on the degree of formality you are adopting and partly on your desire to express yourself clearly.

The advice below therefore concerns highly formal language and grammatical barriers to communication.

Highly formal rules

We have already looked at how some of the 'rules' of grammar developed (see page 11) but however wrong-headed some of the rules below appear it is worthwhile knowing about them if you wish to avoid any criticism of your grammar.

✦ Ending with a preposition

Avoid ending sentences with prepositions unless the sentence would otherwise sound awkward. For example, *He is a man for whom I have great respect* is preferred to *He is a man I have great respect for*.

✦ Split infinitives

Both parts of an infinitive should be together where possible. For example, *I asked her to call occasionally* is preferable to *I asked her to occasionally call*.

✦ Shall and will

This rule has almost disappeared but in the past, *shall* was used with *I* and *we*, and *will* with *you, he, she, it* and *they* to express intention. Nowadays either is acceptable, although *shall* is less common than *will*.

✦ Double negatives

The double negative rule represents the triumph of mathematics over language. In speech it is natural to throw as many negative terms as possible into a statement for emphasis, but in writing the fact that one negative cancels out the other is more noticeable. A sentence like

> *There isn't no food in the fridge*

has the force of two negatives in speech but in writing we notice that it actually means that there *is* food in the fridge.

The *I don't know nothing* kind of double negative should be avoided in writing but you can use the *not un-*sort as in:

> *The room was not uncomfortable*
> *He is a not unreliable witness*

Communication difficulties

✦ *Care with pronouns*
A common source of confusion is a pronoun that could refer to two different nouns. For example, in the sentence

> *Mr White has given the job to Robert because he knows what has to be done*

it is unclear whether *he* refers to Mr White or to Robert. In such cases you should reword the sentence to make your meaning clear:

> *Mr White has given the job to Robert, who knows what has to be done.*

✦ *Dangling participles*
Dangling participles often occur when a sentence begins with the *–ing* or *–ed* form of a word. The writer assumes that the subject of the sentence is understood but this is not always clear to the reader. To take an example from Shakespeare, the sentence

> *Sleeping in the garden, a serpent stung me*

seems to say that the serpent was asleep when it did its stinging. Confusion can be avoided by introducing a subject to the first part of the sentence, for instance

> *As I was sleeping in the garden, a serpent stung me.*

✦ Misplaced modifiers

Words like *almost, only, nearly, scarcely, hardly, just,* and *even* can modify the word or phrase next to them. If the sentence in which they occur is not written carefully it can be unclear as to which word or phrase they apply. In the sentence

> *I can deliver two packages only on Saturday*

it is unclear whether *only* refers to the number of packages or the day of delivery. Rephrase the sentence to make your meaning clear:

> *Saturday is the only day on which I can deliver two packages.*
> *I can only deliver two packages on Saturday.*

✦ Making comparisons

The endings *–er* and *–est* can be added to most shorter adjectives to change the meaning:

> *My bed is hard; your bed is harder; hers is the hardest.*

Most long adjectives and most adverbs use *more* and *most* (or *less* and *least*) instead of *–er* and *–est*:

> *My house is beautiful; your house is more beautiful;*
> *his is the most beautiful.*

You should not combine these two ways of comparing things – avoid phrases such as *more faster*.

In formal English you should also avoid using comparisons with adjectives such as *empty, dead, unique,* and *perfect*.

Some readers get particularly annoyed about *unique*, pointing out that the word means 'singular' and there can be no degrees of uniqueness; something is either unique or not unique. Although phrases such as *very unique* and *quite unique* are common in spoken English they should be avoided in writing.

✦ *Agreement between subject and verb*

If the person doing the action – the *subject* of the sentence – is singular, use a singular verb; if the subject is plural, use a plural verb:

> *Michael plays the violin; the girls play cellos.*

The subject and verb should agree no matter how many words come between them:

> *Michael, who used to play recorder in the school orchestra, now plays the violin.*

If two or more subjects are joined by *and*, use a plural verb:

> *A notebook and pen are all I need.*

Collective nouns such as *family* or *team* usually take a singular verb, even though they refer to more than one thing. The exception to this is if you wish to focus on the members of a group rather than the group itself:

> *The committee is discussing the matter*

refers to the action of the whole committee but

> *The committee are discussing the matter amongst themselves*

places greater emphasis on the members of the committee.

Words like *anyone, each, everyone, neither,* and *nobody* take a singular verb.

✦ *Complete sentences*

Except for minor sentences and special, usually literary, effects you should ensure that all your sentences contain a subject, and a verb.

You should avoid joining two clauses with a comma if each can stand as a sentence in its own right. Join them with a semicolon, or by using a conjunction:
> *Our team won easily; it had a better coach.*
> *Our team won easily because it had a better coach.*

✦ *Using the correct form of irregular verbs*
Many irregular verbs use different forms for the past tense and the past participle. The past tense stands on its own (for example *rang*), whereas the past participle is used along with other verbs (for example *has rung*):

> *The bell rang at midday.*
> *The bell has rung twice already.*

Many people find *lie, lay* and *laid* confusing. *Lays* as in

> *He often lays on his bed all day.*

is a non-standard English form and should be avoided in formal writing. The standard English form is *lies*.

✦ *Past and passed*
The confusion between these two words comes from their sound but if you remember that *passed* is a verb form you should be able to distinguish them. The rule is that *passed* can stand on its own as in the sentence

> *The car passed dangerously close.*

whereas *past* always needs a verb to go with it. For instance

> *We walked past the incident without noticing anything.*

✦ *I and me*
I and *me* tend to cause confusion when in combination with other nouns or pronouns. Politeness dictates that you should mention others before yourself in sentences like

> *My friends and I play golf every weekend.*

However, in spoken English *me* is often used in such circumstances:

> *My friends and me play golf every weekend.*
or even

> *Me and my friends play golf every weekend.*

The problem is easily solved if you remove the extra factor. If you take out any mention of the friends, the errors in the second two examples would be immediately apparent. No one above the age of three would write

> *Me play golf every weekend*

The second problem with *I* and *me* arises from what is known as hyper-correction. No doubt remembering that you shouldn't say *my friends and me,* some speakers overuse the *and I* construction and say things like

> *This trophy was awarded to my friends and I*

Again, if the friends are removed the correct version of the above sentence is clear:

> *This trophy was awarded to me*

In grammatical terms *I* is used as the subject of a sentence whereas *me* is used as the object.

✦ *Who and whom*
Whom is rarely used in spoken English as it sounds rather formal. In writing you need to remember to use *who* when referring to the subject of the verb and *whom* when referring to the object of the verb or after a preposition.

> *This is the woman who saw me at the station.*
> *This is the woman whom I saw at the station.*
> *To whom does this document refer?*

10 Punctuation

Punctuation involves using symbols other than the letters of the
alphabet to give information about intonation and meaning.
Punctuation marks are used within words, clauses and sentences.
Some have a grammatical function, others show such things as missing letters or where a pause in breathing is intended.

✦ Full stops (.)

Full stops mark the end of sentences. They tell the reader to pause for
a few moments in his or her reading. You cannot omit full stops unless
they are replaced by either a question mark or an exclamation mark.

> *The cattle moved slowly down the lane.*
> *Martin disappeared.*

Full stops are also used with some abbreviations:

> *e.g.   a.m.   i.e.*

Full stops also apply to minor sentences.

> *Good morning.*
> *No smoking.*

✦ Commas (,)

Commas indicate a short pause in a sentence and separate words,
phrases, or clauses. They are not as obligatory in sentences as full
stops, exclamation marks, or question marks and their position is often
a matter of style or choice.

Commas can be used to separate items in a list. Usually the items in
the list are the same part of speech and they can consist of words,
phrases or clauses.

> *Red, blue, yellow and gold*
> *Running, jumping and standing still*
> *Planets, stars, nebulas or galaxies*

And or *or* is usually used before the last item in a list.

Commas also separate items in a string of adjectives before a noun.

>*Her long, neatly combed, red hair.*
>*The pointless, stupid, squalid war.*

A final *and* is not required in such lists.

Commas are often used to mark a relative clause, that is, extra information that is not necessary for a full understanding of the sentence.

>*The car, which had only recently been painted, was now a complete wreck.*

They are not used if the information is essential

>*The car which I painted was better than this one.*

Commas generally mark off comments inserted into sentences, such as *therefore, however* and *moreover*

>*The cost of the lost luggage was not, however, recoverable.*

Commas are used to attach extra information to either the beginning or end of a sentence

>*The weather had improved, as far as I could tell.*
>*In the long run, we will all be dead.*

Commas normally introduce direct speech. When there are no question marks or exclamation marks, a comma replaces the full stop at the end of a sentence in direct speech

>*"I'll be with you in a minute," he said.*
>*He asked, "Can I go now?"*

Commas can also be used to separate items for clarity

>*Inside, the house was a complete mess*

✦ Colons (:)

The colon marks a stronger pause in a sentence than a semicolon, and is particularly used to introduce lists, explanations or, sometimes, quotations. You do not need to use a capital letter after a colon.

> *The three cardinal virtues are: faith, hope and charity.*
> *I'm sorry I didn't turn up: I got lost.*
> *Shakespeare's* Twelfth Night *begins: If music be the food of love, play on.*

✦ Semicolons (;)

Semicolons indicate a short pause in a sentence, between a comma and a colon in length. They are used to link statements:

> *I sent a bunch of flowers; it was the least I could do.*

Semicolons are also used to separate items in a list when commas might be confusing.

> *In the car were: Joseph, my friend; Max, my cousin; Ralph the dog; and finally, me.*

✦ Question marks (?)

Question marks are used to indicate that a sentence is a question. Some questions are shown by the order of words in a sentence. Other questions are in the form of statements but they are made into questions by the addition of a question mark.

> *Are you going out tonight?*
> *Hamed will be coming, won't he?*
> *Cara is late?*

Question marks are not used after indirect questions or polite requests.

> *Dani asked if there was any toast.*
> *Could you please send an invoice.*

✦ Exclamation marks (!)

An exclamation mark is used to show the way a sentence should be pronounced. They must be used in imperatives or sentences giving orders.

43

Stop!
Be quiet!
Look out!

When an exclamation mark is added to a statement it changes the tone of the statement.

It was cold.   *It was cold!* (stronger)
They were very silly.   *They were very silly!* (less serious)
I am going to my room. *I am going to my room!* (angry)

✦ Apostrophes (')

Apostrophes are used to show either a missing letter or possession. An apostrophe and an S are added to a singular noun to show possession.

Ian's bike.
The bird's wing.

If the noun is plural and does not end in S then an apostrophe and an S is added.

The men's coats.
The sheep's wool.

If the noun is plural and ends in S an apostrophe only is added after the S.

The bees' knees.
The girls' books.

Some names ending in S can end in simply an apostrophe or can add an extra S:

Dickens' novels or *Dickens's novels*
Keats' poetry or *Keats's poetry*

Strictly speaking, numbers such as *the 1900's* are plurals but they are often written with an apostrophe.

Almost any first name or surname followed by an S should have an apostrophe but this is often missed out by sign writers and logo designers on modern shops.

> *Woolworth's* is usually written *Woolworths.*
> *Boot's* is usually written *Boots.*

✦ Dashes or hyphens (-)

A hyphen or dash is a general-purpose mark that can be used in the place of commas, semicolons and brackets. In sentences it represents a short pause. It is frequently used in less formal writing.

> *I left my coat – the new one – on the train.*
> *Sara made a new appointment at the dentist's – she had missed the last one.*
> *Don't forget to include an e-mail address – if you have one – and a daytime telephone number.*

In some books, dashes are used as substitutes for inverted commas.

> *– Well, sir, he began…*
> *– I foresee, Mr Deasy said, that you will not remain here very long at this work. You were not born to be a teacher, I think. Perhaps I am wrong.*
> *– A learner rather, Stephen said.*   *Ulysses* James Joyce

Hyphens are also used to join words.

> *user-friendly*   *light-headed*   *soft-headed*

When a word combination has been in use for a long time the hyphen is frequently dropped.

> *software*   *lighthouse*

✦ Inverted commas or speech marks (" ") (' ')

Inverted commas or speech marks are used to show the beginning and end of direct speech, titles or quotations.

> *"Curiouser and curiouser," said Alice.*
> *Martha asked, "Which way now?"*
> *Charles Dickens wrote 'Our Mutual Friend.'*

> *The words 'To be or not to be' begin one of the most famous speeches in 'Hamlet'.*

Single inverted commas (') are often used for quotations and titles whilst double inverted commas (") are more frequently used to enclose speech. Quotation marks are also used to show that a word or phrase is being used in an unusual way – often ironically – or that the word itself is the subject of discussion.

> *Braille allows a blind person to 'see' with his fingers.*
> *He said he 'found' the money.*
> *What rhymes with 'orange'?*

✦ Brackets ( ) [ ]

Brackets are used to mark off part of a sentence. Usually the part of the sentence inside the brackets is additional information and is not essential to a complete understanding of the sentence.

> *Three students (Mark, Anne and Steve) gained top marks.*
> *NATO (The North Atlantic Treaty Organization) is a major military alliance.*
> *Proust (in my opinion) is overrated.*

Brackets can often be replaced by commas. Square brackets are used to enclose remarks and explanations which were not part of an original quotation but which have been added to make the sense clearer.

> *He said, "Two thousand [pounds] will be enough".*

✦ Ellipsis (…)

Ellipsis is a series of three dots that shows that part of a statement has been omitted or that the statement has been broken off abruptly.

> *The report showed: 'high level of radiation…inadequate decontamination procedures and…poor management'.*

Ellipsis is also used to show pauses or hesitation

> *Is that…er…my coffee?*

✦ Numbers

In formal writing it is usual to write out numbers in words rather than to use numerals.

You may use numerals instead of words when the number would be too long to show in words (as a rule of thumb, more than two words).

two million   *2 567 683*

Use numerals for dates, addresses, and numbers in references.

> *We lived at 16 Cypress Avenue until 1985.*
> *See chapter 7, pages 85–93.*

Use a hyphen when writing numbers from 21–99 in words, if the number consists of two words.

twenty-one   *thirty-first*

Numbers between 1000 and 9999 should be written without spaces or commas between the numerals. For numbers above 9999 a space should be left between each set of three figures. Also, there should be a space between each set of three figures after a decimal point.

4567   *123 456 789*   *3.141 592*

11 Electronic communication

✦ *E-mails*

As more and more people gain access, at home or at work, to the Internet, more and more e-mail communication takes place. E-mails are used almost exclusively for internal communication in offices, and for many people they have replaced letters as a means of keeping in touch with family and friends. Most e-mails are written very quickly and are the equivalent of informal notes. They are not without rules however.

E-mails sent person to person can be very informal in tone as the audience is known. However, 'posts' to newsgroups can be read by hundreds of people and therefore require a little more care and fore-thought. The rules of polite behaviour for e-mail conversation are known as 'netiquette' and are comparable to etiquette in social inter-action. Not keeping to these rules can cause misunderstanding or annoyance. Many of the rules relate to sharing a 'public' message space and the need to keep messages short because, in many instances, it costs money to be connected to the Internet.

Some rules of netiquette are:

- ❑ Do not write in capital letters. This is like shouting in speech and is considered impolite.
- ❑ Do not use the usual opening and closing conventions for print letters (e.g. *To whom it may concern*, or *Yours sincerely*).
- ❑ Use asterisks (*) before and after a word if you want to emphasize it.
- ❑ Be careful about using irony or sarcasm. Readers can't see facial expressions or hear the tone of voice and so state-ments intended as jokes can be taken seriously.
- ❑ Jokes can be shown by using a 'smiley' or 'emoticon' such as :-). On the other hand do not use too many of these.
- ❑ Avoid 'flames'. A flame is an angry response to a message. Exchanges of flames, or 'flame wars' can be very annoying to other readers on a list or newsgroup.
- ❑ Always include the subject of a message in the subject line.
- ❑ Messages should be relatively short and to the point.
- ❑ Do not forward other people's e-mail messages without the author's permission.

❑ Include the parts of the original message being responded to in new e-mails or posts to newsgroups.
❑ Think carefully about who you include in the 'cc' box. You do not want to fill up other people's mailboxes with irrelevant e-mails.

✦ Smileys

Smileys or emoticons are often used to indicate tone. These symbols are read with the head tilted on the left shoulder.
The basic smiley is:

   :-)

This means 'I'm happy to hear from you', and is sometimes used after a sarcastic or joking statement.

Tongue-in-cheek remarks might use a winking 'smiley'.

   ;-)

There are many others; see under **Text messaging** for a fuller list.

✦ Net abbreviations

Net abbreviations have developed over the years to shorten messages, avoid repetitive phrases, and to speed up typing. Some of the more common ones are:

BTW	By the way
FAQ	Frequently asked questions
FWIW	For what it's worth
FYI	For your information
FUA	Frequently used acronyms
IAE	In any event
IMO	In my opinion
IMCO	In my considered opinion
IMHO	In my humble opinion
IOW	In other words
NRN	No reply necessary

OTOH	On the other hand
ROFL	Rolling on floor laughing
RSN	Real soon now [often used ironically]
SITD	Still in the dark
TIA	Thanks in advance (also AtDhVaAnNkCsE)
TIC	Tongue in cheek
TLA	Three letter acronym

✦ Text messaging

Text messaging is a recent development in the use of mobile phones. Text messages are cheaper to send than voice messages and they can be composed and read in places where voice messages might not be appropriate, such as classrooms or nightclubs.

The problem with text messaging is that most mobile phones do not have keyboards and so senders of messages have to key through the letters attached to the numeric keypad. This can be very tedious and so text messages tend to be short and use a large number of abbreviations and spelling short cuts. As with e-mail, emoticons are also used.

Some of the commoner symbols and abbreviations are listed below. As you will see, many of them reflect the concerns of the younger people that tend to use text messaging most.

Emoticons

o:-)	Angel
:-o zz zz ZZ	Bored or tired
:-E	Bucktoothed vampire
})i({	Butterfly
;/	Confused
>:-)	Devil

8)	Frog
:-%	Get lost!
:-)	Happy
:-s	I'm not making sense
B-)	I'm wearing glasses
8(:-)	Mickey Mouse
:-p	Naughty
=^)	Open-minded
:@)	Pig
:-(	Sad
:-O	Shouting
:o	Surprised
:-@!	Swearing
;&	Tongue-tied
@:-)	Wearing a turban
:-"	Whistling

Abbreviations

1CE	once
2DAY	today
2MOR	tomorrow
2NITE	tonight

ASAP	as soon as possible
B	be
BCNU	be seeing you
BRB	be right back
BTDT	been there done that
BTW	by the way
C	see
CID	consider it done
COZ	because
CU	see you
DA	the
EZ	easy
F2T	free to talk
FOTFLOL	falling on the floor, laughing out loud
GAL	get a life
GR8	great
GTG	got to go
H8	hate
K	okay
L8	late
L8ER	later
LOL	laughing out loud or loads of love
LV	love
M8	mate
MMFU	my mate fancies you
NE	any
NE1	anyone
NETHNG	anything
NO1	no one
NP	no problem
OIC	oh, I see
OMG	oh, my God
PLS	please
PPL	people
R	are
RTFM	read the flippin' manual

RU	are you
RUOK	are you okay
SOZ	sorry
STFU	shut up
SUM1	someone
THANQ	thank you
THX	thanks
TMB	text me back
TTYL	talk to you later
TXT BAC	text back
TYVM	thank you very much
U	you
W/O	without
WAN2	want to
WBS	write back soon
WIV	with
WKND	weekend
WUD?	what you doing?
XLNT	excellent
Y	why
YR	your
YYSSW	yeah yeah sure sure whatever

As with all forms of communication the aim of text messaging is to make yourself understood. The shortcuts and strange spellings are convenient but should be avoided if you are not sure that your recipient is familiar with them.

12 Avoiding offensive language

When you are writing for an unknown audience you need to be particularly careful not to give offence to other groups within society. Broadly speaking, this means being aware of the issues that certain groups have identified and taking the time and trouble not to reinforce stereotypes or promote negative attitudes to those groups. Everyone needs to take care not to use terms which may cause offence.

✦ Sexism

You can avoid most sexism in your writing if you do not assume that masculinity is the norm and if you eliminate gender-specific terms.

Many aspects of English assume a male norm such as referring to *mankind* or *manning* a task. These terms can be replaced with words like *humanity* or *staffing* but it is much harder to replace more basic terms like gender-specific pronouns. Unfortunately English lacks singular gender neutral terms and has to fall back on constructions such as *s/he, he* or *she, her/him* and so on. Some people find these constructions inelegant but there are ways round them.

❏ Use plurals – this allows you to use gender neutral terms like *they, their* and *them*
❏ In longer documents alternate between male and female pronouns in different paragraphs
❏ Use female pronouns as the norm
❏ Declare which policy you are using and why

Gender-specific terms like *poetess, manageress,* and *authoress* can be replaced by neutral terms such as *poet, manager,* and *author,* and words ending in *–man,* such as *chairman,* can be replaced with words which carry no gender associations, such as *president.*

✦ Racism

It is illegal to publish language that is abusive to members of another race. The words that can be used when you want to make an unbiased reference to people belonging to a minority culture within a society undergo frequent changes of use. Currently, *Black* is the acceptable term for referring to people of West Indian or African origin, while

Asian is the acceptable term for referring to people of Asian origin.
Beware of colloquial terms describing a person of a particular race,
such as *Jock*, as these are likely to cause offence.

Avoid words that reinforce negative stereotypes about supposed
national characteristics. The use of *Irish* to mean 'illogical', or *Jewish* to
mean 'miserly', is likely to cause offence.

✦ Disability

Do not refer to groups of people as *the blind, the deaf,* etc., as this
describes people solely in terms of their disability. Use the phrases
blind people, deaf people, etc., instead.

Do not misuse terms which properly describe medical conditions. For
example, the term *schizophrenic* denotes a medical condition, and
may cause offence if it is used informally to mean 'contradictory'.

The word *spastic* is now considered offensive. You should not say that
someone is a spastic but that he or she has cerebral palsy.

The word *mongol* is no longer acceptable for referring to someone
affected by Down's syndrome.

Avoid the term *deaf-and-dumb*. Use the term *deaf-mute* or *deaf without-
out speech* instead.

✦ Sexuality

The term *gay* is acceptable as a means of referring to homosexuals.
Although this word can refer to male and female homosexuals, the
phrase *gay and lesbian* is often used to refer to male and female
homosexuals as a group.

The term *queer* is still considered derogatory when used by non-
homosexuals, but it is now being used by homosexuals of themselves
as a positive term, as in the phrases *queer politics* and *queer cinema*.

✦ Political correctness

To avoid causing offence, some writers have attempted to establish
politically correct language. This language is designed to avoid prejudice of any kind. However, sometimes it can seem unnatural and even
ridiculous when taken to extremes. If you think carefully about the
words you use and the feelings of your readers, you should manage to
avoid causing offence while preserving a clear, natural style.

Writing Letters

Letters can range from extremely informal notes to friends to highly formal letters to do with job applications, finance or the law. A letter to a friend actually needs little more than the date at the top so that the recipient knows when it is written, but it is polite to include your address as well so that there are no obstacles to a reply. A more formal letter is set out opposite.

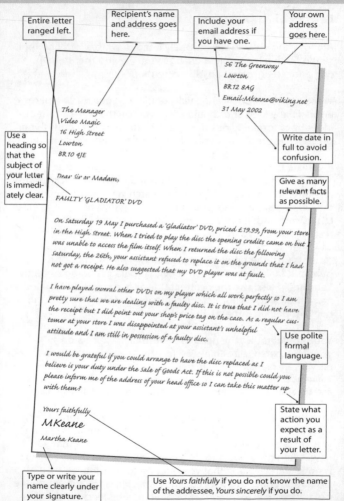

Entire letter ranged left.

Recipient's name and address goes here.

Include your email address if you have one.

Your own address goes here.

56 The Greenway
Lowton
BR12 8AG
Email:Mkeane@viking.net
31 May 2002

The Manager
Video Magic
16 High Street
Lowton
BR10 4JE

Use a heading so that the subject of your letter is immediately clear.

Write date in full to avoid confusion.

Dear Sir or Madam,

FAULTY 'GLADIATOR' DVD

Give as many relevant facts as possible.

On Saturday 19 May I purchased a 'Gladiator' DVD, priced £19.99, from your store in the High Street. When I tried to play the disc the opening credits came on but I was unable to access the film itself. When I returned the disc the following Saturday, the 26th, your assistant refused to replace it on the grounds that I had not got a receipt. He also suggested that my DVD player was at fault.

I have played several other DVDs on my player which all work perfectly so I am pretty sure that we are dealing with a faulty disc. It is true that I did not have the receipt but I did point out your shop's price tag on the case. As a regular customer at your store I was disappointed at your assistant's unhelpful attitude and I am still in possession of a faulty disc.

Use polite formal language.

I would be grateful if you could arrange to have the disc replaced as I believe is your duty under the Sale of Goods Act. If this is not possible could you please inform me of the address of your head office so I can take this matter up with them?

State what action you expect as a result of your letter.

Yours faithfully
MKeane
Martha Keane

Type or write your name clearly under your signature.

Use *Yours faithfully* if you do not know the name of the addressee, *Yours sincerely* if you do.

Letters of Application

Along with a CV you will probably need to write a letter of application. Such a letter might change your life and therefore it demands the greatest possible attention.

A good letter of application will contain no spelling or typing errors of any kind and should always err on the side of caution in terms of formality of language. You simply don't know if your prospective employer has a thing about split infinitives or not.

If you are basing your application on a newspaper advertisement you should gather all the information you can from there and attempt to do some further research via the Internet or through personal connections. If the company you are applying to has sent you information read this thoroughly and try to respond to it in your letter.

Address it to the person in charge of the employment procedure and make sure that you spell that person's name correctly. You should also use their correct title as it appears on any documentation. Begin your letter *Dear Professor Fforde* if this is the relevant person rather than *Dear Sir*....

You should not let the need to be formal in expression stifle your own personality. Employers look for interesting, interested people who are prepared to state their commitment and enthusiasm. Remember that the prime task of the letter is to get you an interview and that this will not happen if you come across as dull or pedantic.

In the introduction of your letter attempt to make some specific comments about the job and about the company with whom you are seeking employment. This will demonstrate that you have taken the trouble to do some research and that your letter is not a standard one that you print off for any job.
Do not be afraid to use occupation-specific language as you are usually being assessed in terms of your knowledge and experi-

ence. On the other hand do not be tempted to use jargon simply to impress your prospective employers.

In the main part of your letter you should relate whatever you write to the job criteria you have been given. When there are large numbers of applications for a job, many are rejected simply because they have not fulfilled all the relevant criteria. You should aim to sound confident and knowledgeable in this section.

If it is appropriate, draw your reader's attention to sections of your CV and explain how your previous experience relates to your new job. Also don't forget the human side of things, and comment on your ability to work with or motivate others.

Remember to use topic sentences. These will help selectors to find their way around your letter easily both at this stage and at the interview.

It is a good idea to finish with some consideration of how your appointment might specifically benefit your employer.

Curricula Vitae

A curriculum vitae or CV will often be the first thing that a prospective employer will see from you. It is important, therefore, to make your CV as clear as possible. You should ensure that it is printed on good quality paper and that it is as free from errors as possible.

Keep your CV short and to the point – employers see a great deal – try not to exceed two pages.

Your personal details will be used to contact you – check phone numbers and your e-mail address carefully.

Curriculum Vitae – David Jones

PERSONAL DETAILS

Name: David Jones

Date of Birth: 6 November 1976   **Nationality:**   British

Address: 11 Glebe Road
Brixton
London
SW2 3JD

Telephone: Home – 0208 673 8488
Work – 0208 988 4821
Fax: 0208 989 4803
E-mail: djones24@viking.net

You can also give this information in reverse order so that the most relevant qualifications come first.

EDUCATION

1988 – 1995	Carrisbrook High School, Basingstoke, Herts.
1993	**GCSEs:** English, English Literature, Maths, Physics, Chemistry, History, Geography, French
1995	**A–Levels:** French (A), History (A), Psychology (B).
1995 – 1998	University of Kent at Canterbury. BA Hons (Class I) Media Studies

PROFESSIONAL EXPERIENCE

1998 – 2000	Fortune Magazine	Canterbury
	Journalist and Film Reviewer.	
2000 – 2002	Cherish Magazine	Bath
	Journalist, editor Arts and Reviews. Established new reviewing policy and restyled features sections.	
2002 – Present	Here and Now	London
	Arts features editor. Young journalist of the year award 2002. Responsible for five in-house journalists and large pool of freelance talent.	

State key achievements in each job as well as names, dates and places of employment.

OTHER SKILLS
Clean driving licence, shorthand, QuarkXpress, fluent French

Make sure the skills you mention are related to the employment you are seeking.

INTERESTS
Photography, film, theatre, squash and tennis
I play the guitar and am learning to play the saxophone

Your interests should give some clue to the type of person you are.

The first CV is quite traditional, but in a competitive job market you might wish to try something a little more complex and visually appealing such as the CV opposite. This one prioritizes information in a way that will be relevant to prospective employers.

There are many other ways of designing and presenting a CV but the two most important factors in good ones are relevance of information and clarity of presentation. It is probably best to avoid the temptation to include too many 'features', such as boxes and borders.

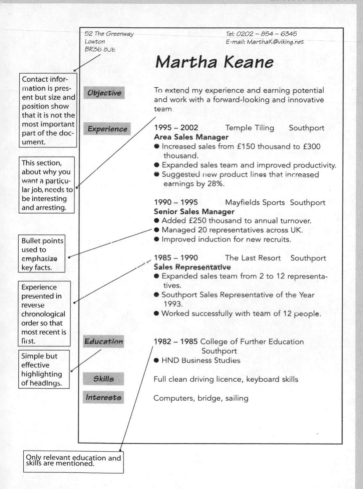

52 The Greenway
Lowton
BR36 8JE

Tel: 0202 – 854 – 6345
E-mail: MarthaK@viking.net

Martha Keane

Contact information is present but size and position show that it is not the most important part of the document.

Objective

To extend my experience and earning potential and work with a forward-looking and innovative team.

This section, about why you want a particular job, needs to be interesting and arresting.

Experience

1995 – 2002   Temple Tiling   Southport
Area Sales Manager
- Increased sales from £150 thousand to £300 thousand.
- Expanded sales team and improved productivity.
- Suggested new product lines that increased earnings by 28%.

1990 – 1995   Mayfields Sports Southport
Senior Sales Manager
- Added £250 thousand to annual turnover.
- Managed 20 representatives across UK.
- Improved induction for new recruits.

Bullet points used to emphasize key facts.

1985 – 1990   The Last Resort   Southport
Sales Representative
- Expanded sales team from 2 to 12 representatives.
- Southport Sales Representative of the Year 1993.
- Worked successfully with team of 12 people.

Experience presented in reverse chronological order so that most recent is first.

Simple but effective highlighting of headings.

Education

1982 – 1985 College of Further Education
              Southport
- HND Business Studies

Skills

Full clean driving licence, keyboard skills

Interests

Computers, bridge, sailing

Only relevant education and skills are mentioned.

63